International Marketing

10e

International Marketing

Michael R. Czinkota
Georgetown University

Ilkka A. Ronkainen
Georgetown University

SOUTH-WESTERN
CENGAGE Learning

Australia • Brazil • Japan • Korea • Mexico • Singapore • Spain • United Kingdom • United States

SOUTH-WESTERN
CENGAGE Learning

International Marketing, Tenth Edition
Michael R. Czinkota and Ilkka A. Ronkainen

Senior Vice President, LRS/Acquisitions & Solutions Planning: Jack W. Calhoun

Editorial Director, Business & Economics: Erin Joyner

Executive Editor: Mike Roche

Developmental Editor: Sarah Blasco

Editorial Assistant: Megan Fischer

Marketing Manager: Gretchen Swann

Media Editor: John Rich

Manufacturing Planner: Ron Montgomery

Marketing Communications Manager: Jim Overly

Art and Cover Direction, Production Management, and Composition: PreMediaGlobal

Rights Acquisition Director: Audrey Pettengill

Rights Acquisitions Specialist (Image): Deanna Ettinger

Rights Acquisitions Specialist (Text): Audrey Pettengill

Cover Image: © LOOK Die Bildagentur der Fotografen GmbH/Alamy

Library of Congress Control Number: 2012939204

ISBN-13: 978-1-133-62751-7

ISBN-10: 1-133-62751-X

South-Western
5191 Natorp Boulevard
Mason, OH 45040
USA

Cengage Learning is a leading provider of customized learning solutions with office locations around the globe, including Singapore, the United Kingdom, Australia, Mexico, Brazil, and Japan. Locate your local office at: **www.cengage.com/global**

Cengage Learning products are represented in Canada by Nelson Education, Ltd.

For your course and learning solutions, visit **www.cengage.com**

Purchase any of our products at your local college store or at our preferred online store **www.cengagebrain.com**

Printed at CLDPC, USA, 07-18

To Ilona and Margaret Victoria—MRC
To Susan, Sanna, and Alex—IAR

PREFACE

Thank you for reading our book! Practicing international marketing and writing a text on the subject have much in common. The focus is on delighting the customer; it is a lot of work; the competition is tough; and it's fun to succeed. It is therefore with great pleasure that we present the tenth edition of *International Marketing* to you.

In the rapidly changing world of business, only a small portion of textbooks ever see a second edition, much less a tenth one. Publishers change, markets move in new directions, competitors emerge, and authors adjust their commitments to new life situations. So we are very pleased to have served the international marketing market for 30 years now, which, of course, is largely a sign of the continued faith and confidence of our colleagues in our work. Thank you for allowing us to shape the field and have a major impact on what people know about international marketing.

Over the years, we have always made key improvements in our new editions, but never before have our revisions resulted in so much of a new text. There has been unprecedented change in the field of international marketing. When domestic economic activities decrease, then international marketing decreases as well, only much more so. Austerity brings changes in production and consumption patterns and introduces new dimensions into the decision-making process. The role of governments is growing by leaps and bounds, making them key entities to dictate the direction and strength of international marketing activities. There is a rising tendency to restrict imports and encourage exports in order to keep home industries safe and gradually reduce global imbalances.

In dire economic times, international marketers are key agents of social change, who provide insight and knowledge that helps society understand the trade-offs and consequences of actions and thus make good decisions. The business field is looked upon expectantly by nations and their governments, who frantically search for ways for their economies to emerge from slow growth conditions. International marketing increasingly is the key option that can deliver major increases in economic activity.

The challenge is great. Nations around the world attempt to stabilize and revitalize their economies. Typically, each nation's emphasis rests with domestic issues. But any international intervention of one nation is likely to rapidly affect other countries and may trigger economic and policy responses. Protectionism, once introduced, can quickly become contagious and catch fire around the world. The rationale for the prevalence of a market economy is not automatically understood any more. Key tenets of the marketing discipline, such as risk, profit, competition, and ownership, are being redefined and reassessed.

International marketers develop the knowledge and talents that serve to disentangle the competing priorities confronting individuals, companies, and governments. They explain and justify the principle that nations must be able and willing to buy each other's goods if world economies are to blossom. Marketers show how competition and consumer choice are crucial to the achievement of a higher plateau of well-being. They demonstrate that a rising tide can lift all boats, but only if the boat and the sails are in good condition and the crew is prepared and well trained.

Through their field-specific knowledge and their understanding of the effects of culture and emotions, and by sitting at the table and contributing their insights, international marketers can make major strides in ensuring a better world. When there is some disagreement and some sparring, we ask you to apply to international marketers the advice rendered by the great scholar Ludwig von Wittgenstein: "A philosopher who is not taking part in discussions is like a boxer who never goes into the ring."

But international marketing is not an uncontroversial discipline. There is a large historic burden carried by the field of marketing. For many years, marketers, particularly in the international arena, have primarily focused on selling more, and also tried to provide an increase in customer satisfaction. However, very little effort has focused on the societal impact of certain marketing strategies, on the long-term repercussions on consumers (e.g., obesity due to overconsumption of fast food), and on the literal chain of consumption with which individuals have been restricted, inhibited, and burdened. Drip marketing is just one example of such a predatory practice. Also called "vampire marketing," the practice consists of charging consumers more and more money as they get deeper into product usage. For example, once you are in a hotel room, the minibar late at night becomes your only ability to assuage hunger—at a very high price. As a result of all these practices, we have developed and present in this volume the concept of "curative marketing," which identifies malpractices of the past, avoids them in the future, and makes major efforts to cure the negative effects of the past transgressions. At various places in the book, we highlight the capability of curative marketing to "do better."

There have of course also been key changes since data and information have increasingly pervaded our society. By taking measurements and comparing outcomes in the context of change, there is much to be learned for the marketing discipline. However, just like for most things in life: moderation is crucial. By looking for numbers only, there appears to be a trend by some towards forgetting that international marketing is a social science applied across borders. In spite of growing quantification, international marketing remains a discipline linked most deeply with people, their emotions, and their behavior. Therefore, even a researcher with a white lab coat, who may prefer to work with numbers only, must pay major attention to individual human interaction in order to propel the discipline forward and achieve societal benefit. While important to marketing and business overall, this issue is particularly relevant in international marketing, where variations in contexts, cultures, and behaviors bring out the importance of direct interaction and individual awareness. We must understand the people who contribute to decisions and consider their contextual constraints if we wish to truly improve the performance of the international marketing discipline. Our book takes this guideline as its mission for its descriptions, its analyses, and its approach to the future.

Doing so grows in importance as the focus on international marketing is rising. In academia we see great increases in student enrollment—perhaps they want to stock up on knowledge and capabilities during bad times in order to be ready for the good ones. Companies and governments need to do the same. In times of slack resources, one can explore new market opportunities, customs, and customers. When economic conditions get better, one can convert that capability into market results and receive a payoff from all the prior research and preparation. International marketing is a vital economic stimulus. Our focus and presentation of all these issues makes this tenth edition of *International Marketing* the best one yet!

We reflect many new dimensions, emotions, and boundaries that affect the discipline. Here are the key features that make this book stand out:

- We paint a broader picture of the implications of adapting or rejecting a market orientation. In doing so, we introduce the concept of curative marketing, which highlights ethical and sustainability issues, discusses the shortcomings encountered in corporate transparency and executive veracity, and develops new alternative explanations and approaches.
- We provide substantial data analysis and thorough support. For example, we discuss all economic regions, offering comparative benchmarks not only from the economically advanced world but also from China, Australia, Kenya, and Brazil.
- We cover the full spectrum of international marketing, from start-up operations to the formation of virtual alliances. We offer a thorough discussion of the operations of multinational corporations, and also present a specific focus on the activities of small- and medium-sized firms, which are increasingly major players in the international market and will be the employers of many students.
- We provide a hands-on analysis of the growing interaction between government and business. We have served in government positions and advised international marketers. As governments take on an expanding role in business, our policy orientation greatly enhances the managerial relevance of this book.
- We cover both the theory and the application of international marketing. Based on our personal research record and business experience, we can offer research insights from around the globe and show how corporations are adjusting to the marketplace realities of today. In this way we enhance the presentation of our material by closely linking concepts with parables, analogies, and similes so that the meaning becomes more obvious to the reader and is better recalled.
- We acknowledge and give clear examples of how the world has changed in an era of terrorism, hostility, and distrust. We look at the marketing repercussions of these changes on people management, sourcing policies, cargo security, inventory management, and port utilization. However, we also draw on our work with corporations to find new forms of collaboration and network building without compromising safety or security. We reflect the use of social media in reaching out to customers, suppliers, and even competitors in order to achieve greater satisfaction and more progress for society.
- We address the concerns of emerging and developing markets throughout the text. We present the issue of underserved markets, with a population of 5 billion, and also explore and suggest how these people and countries need to become greater participants in international marketing efforts.
- Our analysis and presentation is made from a truly global perspective. By addressing, confronting, and examining the existence of different environments, expectations, and market conditions, we highlight the need for awareness, sensitivity, and adaptation.
- We integrate the impact of the Internet on the international marketer. We discuss the revolutionary changes in communication between firms and their customers and suppliers, and present the latest consequences for international market research and market entry.

Personal Support

Most important, we personally stand behind our product and we will work hard to delight you. Should you have any questions or comments on this book, you can contact us, talk to us, and receive feedback from us.

Michael R. Czinkota
(202) 687-4204
czinkotm@georgetown.edu

Ilkka A. Ronkainen
(202) 687-3788
ronkaii@georgetown.edu

ORGANIZATION

The text is designed primarily for the advanced undergraduate student with prior exposure to the marketing field. Because of its in-depth coverage, it also presents an excellent challenge for graduate instruction and executive education.

The text is divided into four parts. We open with the examination of the international marketing environment, where we examine economic and cultural contexts, shifts bought about by globalization, and key international institutions, regulations, and legal issues. We then examine how to find global customers by first analyzing the global consumer in detail, followed by strategic planning, the juxtaposition of people and markets, market entry activities, and the necessary organization for international marketing. Our third part concentrates on the global marketing mix by presenting the core international adjustments and expansions that have to be built on top of purely domestic considerations. We conclude with a section on leadership in global marketing, where we present the impact of social networks and communications, analyze the meaning of responsibility and sustainability, and highlight new directions and challenges.

KEY FEATURES

This tenth edition reflects the highly dynamic nature of international marketing. We offer a perspective on the shift in the role of market forces and the impact of this revolution on international marketers in terms of outreach, research, and competition. Our *International Marketplace* vignettes reflect state-of-the-art corporate practices. To make it easier for the reader to follow up on information obtained through the book, we have included links to the websites of companies, data sources, governments, international organizations, and monitors of international marketing issues.

Our focus on the physical environment and geography is strong. Updated maps provide context in terms of social and economic data. An appendix directly addresses the relationship between geography and international marketing. New text components, marketplaces, and several cases specifically focus on the environment and the opportunities, challenges, and ambiguities that it poses to international marketers.

We also have increased our emphasis on international institutions and their role for the international marketer. The World Bank, the World Trade Organization, the International Monetary Fund, and the United Nations are covered along with the public debate surrounding these institutions.

We broaden our highlights of emerging markets by systematically addressing the bottom of the income pyramid. Our revised strategy section is now linked directly with organization, implementation, and research concerns. We have recast the chapter on market entry and expansion to include a wider variety of ways in which firms go global. All of these strategies are now integrated into one chapter, organized around our model of the internationalization process.

Our appendix on international employment opportunities helps students prepare for the implementation steps they have yet to take.

INNOVATIVE LEARNING TOOLS

Contemporary Realism

Each chapter offers current examples of real-world business situations in *The International Marketplace* boxes. Also new is a Challenge Us section at the end of each chapter that details complex issues and asks the student questions for discussion. These features allow the reader to develop an appreciation for and an understanding of the linkage between theory and practice. These materials focus on real marketing situations, including the environment and sustainability, and help students absorb the presented materials. The instructor can highlight the boxes to exemplify theory or use them as mini cases for class discussion.

Research Emphasis

A special effort has been made to provide current research information and data from around the world. Chapter notes are augmented by lists of relevant recommended readings incorporating the latest research findings. In addition, a wide variety of sources and organizations that provide international information are offered in the text. These materials enable the instructor and the student to go beyond the text when desired.

Internet Focus

The Internet affects all of international marketing. We highlight how the way of reaching customers and suppliers has changed given the new technology. We explain the enhanced ability of firms to position themselves internationally in competition with other larger players. We offer insights into the electronic marketing research process and present details of how companies cope with new market realities. Whenever appropriate, we direct readers to Internet resources that can be useful in obtaining up-to-date information. Each chapter also provides several Internet questions in order to offer training opportunities that make use of the Internet.

GEOGRAPHY

This edition contains several maps covering the social, economic, and political features of the world. In addition, several chapters have maps particularly designed for this book, which integrate the materials discussed in the text and reflect a truly global perspective. These maps enable the instructor to visually demonstrate concepts such as socioeconomic variables or exposure to terrorism. An appendix dealing specifically with the impact of geography on international marketing is part of Chapter 1.

CASES

Following each part of the text are a variety of cases. Most of our cases are either new or updated especially for this edition. These cases present students with real business situations and cover international marketing conditions from around the world. All cases address the activities of actual or former companies and cover a broad geographic spectrum. In addition, videos available online further help to enliven classroom activity. Challenging questions accompany each case, permitting in-depth discussion of the materials covered in the chapters. Additional cases and case updates are also posted on the companion site linked to this book so that readers can always reach out to the most current material.

ANCILLARY PACKAGE

Instructor's Resource CD

Key instructor ancillaries (Instructor's Manual, Test Bank, ExamView, and PowerPoint slides) are provided on CD, giving instructors the ultimate tool for customizing lectures and presentations.

Instructor's Manual

Available on the Instructor's Resource CD (IRCD) and the password-protected instructor's resource website, the text is accompanied by an in-depth *Instructor's Manual* devised to provide major assistance to the professor. The material in the manual includes a chapter outline and summary of key points, teaching suggestions for the chapter content, a list of key terms and definitions, and answers for the end-of-chapter discussion questions and Internet exercises. Also supplied is a detailed case-chapter matrix that delineates which cases are most appropriate for each area of the international marketing field. In addition, case discussion questions are answered in detail.

Test Bank

Available on the IRCD and the password-protected instructor's resource website, the revised and updated Test Bank includes a variety of multiple-choice, true/false, and short-answer questions, which emphasize the important concepts presented in each chapter. The Test Bank questions vary in levels of difficulty and meet a full range of tagging requirements so that instructors can tailor their testing to meet their specific needs.

ExamView® Test Bank

Available on the IRCD, ExamView contains all of the questions in the Test Bank. This electronic program consists of easy-to-use test creation software. Instructors can add or edit questions, instructions, and answers and select questions (randomly or numerically), thereby creating their own test.

PowerPoint® Presentation Slides

Available on the IRCD and the password-protected instructor's resource website, the PowerPoint lecture presentation enables instructors to customize their own multimedia classroom presentations. The slides include lecture outlines and summaries of key points as well as select figures and tables from the text. Material is organized by chapter and can be modified or expanded for individual classroom use.

Videos

A video package has been prepared to correspond with the key concepts taught in the text. These video cases are available on a DVD or the password-protected instructor's resource website and feature companies such as BP and Doc Martens. Professors can present the videos in class or use these video cases to simply illustrate a key point.

CourseMate

CourseMate online resources provide a full complement of study aids in a very user friendly interface. Materials included are additional cases, written specifically for this textbook, flashcards, student PPT slides, and chapter and media quizzes.

ACKNOWLEDGMENTS

We are deeply grateful to professors, friends, and our reading public in general. Most instrumental were Gary Knight, Charles Skuba, and Susan Ronkainen, who have helped us all in major ways. Their work was crucial in refining the text, providing additional research, and further discussion of societal dimensions. Thank you very much!

We are grateful to all the professors, students, and professionals using this book. Your interest demonstrates the need for more knowledge about international marketing. As our market, you are telling us that our product adds value to your lives. As a result, you add value to ours. Thank you! We thank the many reviewers for their constructive and imaginative comments and criticisms, which were instrumental in making this edition even better. They are:

Jo Ann L. Asquith
St. Cloud State University

Thomas Belich
University of Minnesota

John Besaw, Ph.D.
University of Washington–Tacoma

Andrew J. Czaplewski
University of Colorado at Colorado Springs

Yara DeAndrade
Webster University

Matt Elbeck
Troy University

Ken Fairweather
LeTourneau University

Thomas F. List
Saginaw Valley State University

Drew Martin
University of Hawaii at Hilo

Paul Myer
University of Maine

Frank Novakowski
Davenport University

Tagi Sagafi-nejad
Texas A&M International University

Milena Simic
Missouri Valley College

Kevin E. Voss
Oklahoma State University

A. N. M. Waheeduzzaman
Texas A&M University–Corpus Christi

Theodore O. Wallin
Whitman School of Management

Wendel Weaver
Oklahoma Wesleyan University

Mark D. Woodhull, Ph.D.
Schreiner University

We remain indebted to the reviewers and survey respondents of earlier editions of this text:

Sanjeev Agarwal
Iowa State University

Zafar Ahmed
Texas A&M–Commerce

Lyn S. Amine
St. Louis University

Jessica M. Bailey
The American University

Subir Bandyopadhyay
Indiana University Northwest

Warren Bilkey
University of Wisconsin

Katharine A. Bohley Hubbard
University of Indianapolis

S. Tamer Cavusgil
Georgia State University

Samit Chakravorti
Florida International University

Shih-Fen Chen
Kansas State University

Alex Christofides
Ohio State University

Farok J. Contractor
Rutgers University

Robert Dahlstrom
University of Kentucky

Paul Dowling
University of Utah

Carl E. Dresden
Coastal Carolina University

John Dyer
University of Miami

Luiz Felipe
IBMEC Business School (Rio de Janeiro, Brazil)

Dr. John P. Fraderich
Southern Illinois University–Carbondale

Roberto Friedmann
University of Georgia

Shenzhao Fu
University of San Francisco

Jim Gentry
University of Nebraska

Donna Goehle
Michigan State University

Needlima Gogumala
Kansas State University

Peter J. Gordon
Southeast Missouri State University

Paul Groke
Northern Illinois University

Andrew Gross
Cleveland State University

John Hadjimarcou
University of Texas at El Paso

Hari Hariharan
DePaul University

Braxton Hinchey
University of Lowell

Carol Howard
Oklahoma City University

Basil Janavaras
Mankato State University

Denise Johnson
University of Louisville

Sudhir Kale
Arizona State University

Ceyhan Kilic
DePaul University

Hertha Krotkoff
Towson State University

Kathleen La Francis
Central Michigan University

Ann L. Langlois
Palm Beach Atlantic University

Trina Larsen
Drexel University

Edmond Lausier
University of Southern California

Bertil Liander
University of Massachusetts

Mushtaq Luqmani
Western Michigan University

Isabel Maignan
Florida State University

James Maskulka
Lehigh University

James McCullouch
Washington State University

Fred Miller
Murray State University

Joseph Miller
Indiana University

Mark Mitchell
University of South Carolina–Spartanburg

Tomasz Mroczkowski
American University

Amit Mukherjee
Auburn University

Henry Munn
California State University, Northridge

Cheryl Nakata
University of Illinois–Chicago

Jacob Naor
University of Maine–Orono

Urban Ozanne
Florida State University

Tony Peloso
Queensland University of Technology (Australia)

Ilsa Penaloza
University of Connecticut

Zahir A. Quraeshi
Western Michigan University

John Ryans
Kent State University

F. J. Sarknas
Duquesne University

Regina P. Schlee
Seattle Pacific University

Matthew Sim
Temesek Business School (Singapore)

James Spiers
Arizona State University

Odile J. Streed
Concordia College

Janda Swinder
Kansas State University

Ray Taylor
Villanova University

Tyzoon T. Tyebjee
Santa Clara University

Robert Underwood
Virginia Polytechnic Institute and State University

Robert Weigand
University of Illinois at Chicago

John Wilkinson
University of South Australia

Sumas Wongsunopparat
University of Wisconsin–Milwaukee

Nittaya Wongtada
Thunderbird

Van R. Wood
Texas Tech University

William Louden
Austin Community College

Mike Harvey
Dominican University

Many thanks to all the colleagues and students who have helped us sharpen our thinking by cheerfully providing challenging comments and questions. In particular, we thank Bernard LaLonde, Ohio State University; Tamer Cavusgil, Georgia State University; and James Wills, University of Hawaii.

Many colleagues, friends, and business associates graciously gave their time and knowledge to clarify concepts; provide us with ideas, comments, and suggestions; and deepen our understanding of issues. Without the direct links to business and policy that you have provided, this book could not offer its refreshing realism. In particular, we are grateful to secretaries Malcolm Baldridge, C. William Verity, Clayton Yeutter, and William Brock for the opportunity to gain international business policy experience and to William Morris, Paul Freedenberg, and J. Michael Farrell for enabling its implementation. We thank William Casselman of Stairs Dillenbeck Kelly Merle and Finley, Robert Conkling, Lew Cramer of the Utah World Trade Center, Mark Dowd of IBM, David Danjczek, Greg Foster, Craig O'Connor, Veikko Jääskeläinen, Reijo Luostarinen, and Hannu Seristö of Aalto University. A special tip of the hat goes to Thomas Czinkota for all his inspiring thoughts and comments. Thank you very much. We thank the colleagues who have generously written new cases to contribute to this new edition of our book. They are Agnes Gifty Adjei-Sam, head of the Ghana Export Trade Information Center; Professor Aurelia Lefaix-Durand, HEC, Montreal; Professor James H. Sood, American University; Erik Pöntiskoski, Ph.D. candidate at Aalto University; Eric Johnson, Deloitte Consulting; Professor Nittaya Wongtada of the National Institute of Development Administration in Thailand; Professor Juan Carlos Schiappa, Pietra of the Universidad Ricardo Palma in Peru, and Professor Thomas Cooke of Georgetown University. Thank you so much for your intellectual help and stimulation.

Valuable research assistance was provided by our elite student research team. They made important and substantive contributions to this book. They pursued research information with tenacity and relentlessness; they organized and analyzed research materials, prepared drafts of vignettes and cases, and reinforced everyone on the fourth floor of the Hariri Building with their can-do spirit. They are Ireene Leoncio, Sophia Berhie, Mariele Marki, Elizabeth Garbitelli, Diana Garza, Wilbert Hidalgo, Nishtha Jain, Julian Mendoza, Brian Moran, Rafael Rivas, Mengyang Tian, Doria Xu, and Jim Ang, all of Georgetown University.

A very special word of thanks to the people at Cengage. Mike Roche has the vision. Sarah Blasco supported the lengthy process of writing a text with her input and feedback.

Foremost, we are grateful to our families, who have truly participated in our labors. Only the patience, understanding, and love of Ilona and Margaret Victoria Czinkota and Susan, Sanna, and Alex Ronkainen enabled us to have the energy, stamina, and inspiration to write this book.

Michael R. Czinkota
Ilkka A. Ronkainen
Washington, DC
July 1, 2012

ABOUT THE AUTHORS

MICHAEL R. CZINKOTA presents international marketing and business issues at the Graduate School and the Robert Emmett McDonough School of Business at Georgetown University and is the chaired professor emeritus for international marketing at the University of Birmingham in the United Kingdom. He has held professorial appointments at universities in Asia, Australia, Europe, and the Americas.

Dr. Czinkota served in the U.S. government as deputy assistant secretary of commerce. He also served as head of the U.S. delegation to the OECD Industry Committee in Paris and as senior advisor for Export Controls.

His background includes 10 years of private-sector business experience as a partner in a fur-trading firm and in an advertising agency. His research has been supported by the U.S. government, the National Science Foundation, the Organization of American States, and the American Management Association. He was listed as one of the three most published contributors to international business research in the world by the *Journal of International Business Studies* and has written several books, including *As I Was Saying: Observations on International Business and Trade Policy, Exports, Education, and the Future (Businessexpertpress, 2012)*. Dr. Czinkota was chairman of the National Center for Export-Import Studies, served on the Global Advisory Board of the American Marketing Association, the Global Council of the American Management Association, and the Board of Governors of the Academy of Marketing Science. He is on the editorial boards of *Journal of Academy of Marketing Science*, *Journal of International Marketing*, and *Asian Journal of Marketing*. He is an editorial contributor to the *Washington Times*, the *Korea Times*, and the *Handelsblatt* in Germany.

For his work in international business and trade policy, he was named a distinguished fellow of the Academy of Marketing Science, a fellow of the Chartered Institute of Marketing, and a fellow of the Royal Society of Arts in the United Kingdom. He has been awarded honorary degrees from the Universidad Pontificia Madre y Maestra in the Dominican Republic and the Universidad del Pacifico in Lima, Peru. In 2012, the Universidad Ricardo Palma's School of Global Marketing and Business was named after Dr. Czinkota

He serves on several corporate boards and has worked with corporations such as AT&T, IBM, GE, Nestlé, and US WEST. He advises the Executive Office of the President of the United States, the United Nations, and the World Trade Organization. Dr. Czinkota has often testified before the U.S. Congress.

Dr. Czinkota was born and raised in Germany and educated in Austria, Scotland, Spain, and the United States. He studied law and business administration at the University of Erlangen–Nürnberg and was awarded a two-year Fulbright scholarship. He holds an MBA in international business and a Ph.D. in logistics from The Ohio State University.

ILKKA A. RONKAINEN is a member of the faculty of marketing and international business at the School of Business at Georgetown University. From 1981 to 1986 he served as associate director and from 1986 to 1987 as chairman of the National Center for Export-Import Studies. Currently, he directs Georgetown University's Hong Kong Program.

Dr. Ronkainen serves as docent of international marketing at the Helsinki School of Economics (HSE). He was visiting professor at HSE during the 1997–1998 and 1991–1992 academic years and continues to teach in its Executive MBA, International MBA, and International BBA programs. He is currently the chair holder at the Saastamoinen Foundation Professorship in International Marketing.

Dr. Ronkainen holds a Ph.D. and a master's degree from the University of South Carolina as well as an M.S. (economics) degree from the Helsinki School of Economics.

Dr. Ronkainen has published extensively in academic journals and the trade press. He is a coauthor of a number of international business and marketing texts, including *Best Practices in International Marketing and Mastering Global Markets* (Thomson). He serves on the review boards of the *Journal of Business Research*, *International Marketing Review*, and *Journal of Travel Research* and has reviewed for the *Journal of International Marketing* and the *Journal of International Business Studies*. He served as the North American coordinator for the European Marketing Academy, 1984–1990. He was a member of the board of the Washington International Trade Association from 1981 to 1986 and started the association's newsletter, *Trade Trends*.

Dr. Ronkainen has served as a consultant to a wide range of U.S. and international institutions. He has worked with entities such as IBM, the Rand Organization, and the Organization of American States. He maintains close relations with a number of Finnish companies and their internationalization and educational efforts.

BRIEF CONTENTS

CONTENTS

15 Global Distribution and Logistics 496

PART ONE

The International Marketing Environment

Part One introduces the international trade framework and environment. It highlights the need for international marketing activities and explores recent developments in world trade and global markets, including an overview of regional and international trade agreements. These chapters are largely devoted to macroenvironmental forces that firms and managers must be aware of when marketing internationally. In order to be successful, the marketer must adapt to the international environment and must be able to resolve conflicts stemming from differences in cultural, economic, political, and legal factors.

CHAPTER 1

Global Environmental Drivers

LEARNING OBJECTIVES

By the time you complete this chapter, you will be able to:

- Understand the rationale behind international marketing.
- Appreciate the linkages between international marketing and international trade.
- See the benefits and challenges to which international marketing exposes consumers, suppliers, competitors, and countries.

THE INTERNATIONAL MARKETPLACE 1.1

Global Trends Impose New Strategic Marketing Requirements

International marketing experts agree that global business trends are even more important to marketing strategy than they were only a few years ago. Keeping on top of global trends with a focus on long-term profitable growth and competitive advantage will be vital to success. A look at the business plans of top global marketers confirms the importance of emerging markets as drivers of significant growth. For example, population increases and urbanization in large emerging markets are reshaping international marketing strategy. With an eye to the needs of global consumers, Coca-Cola, Danone, and Nestlé increasingly market nutrition rather than just food.

We expect a greater emphasis on the markets provided by second-tier cities, which are large cities not yet in the political or economic spotlight, particularly in China, India, Brazil, and Russia. In China, for example, many cities beyond Beijing, Shanghai, and Guangzhou have millions of increasingly affluent consumers yet are unfamiliar to most Western marketers. Firms will need to expand their distribution and market-entry strategies to these large population centers, thus creating new regional hubs. There must also be collaboration with the public sector to encourage infrastructural investments in these regions.

Smaller firms can also benefit from the globalization of markets by seeking opportunity in niche markets, especially those neglected or abandoned by the large players. As large corporations seek economies of scale and category dominance through billion-dollar global brands, smaller players may discover important customer needs that have been left underserved. Valuable smaller brands may be jettisoned by the giants. For example, P&G has divested great brands like Pringles, Folgers, and Jif. Of course, smaller players will need to seek efficiencies through strategic alliances and other joint efforts to compete globally. They will also be heavily dependent on industry and government efforts to establish open markets and global technology standards.

Nations, countries, regions, and cities will also pursue niche strategies as they further specialize in the development of industry clusters. Firms will open subsidiaries, R&D centers, and representative offices in order to take advantage of proximity to customers, suppliers, new channels, research providers, and competitors. Governments will seek advantage through clusters and place greater emphasis on the special educational needs of the workforce in those industrial centers.

With more dynamic growth coming from emerging markets, the more developed economies seem destined for slower growth patterns. Inevitably, those who do not participate in economic expansion will become frustrated and seek relief through government remedies. Government has again become, and will remain, an important factor in international marketing. The dangers of an insular focus lurk. Changing times will require strong leadership from the public sector and corporations to avoid the easy, but wrong, answer of protectionism.

SOURCE: Michael R. Czinkota and Charles J. Skuba, "International Business Not as Usual," *Marketing Management*, Summer 2010.

You are about to begin an exciting, important, and necessary task: the exploration of international marketing. International marketing is exciting because it combines the science and the art of business with many other disciplines. Economics, anthropology, cultural studies, geography, history, languages, jurisprudence, statistics, demographics, and many other fields combine to help you explore the global market. Different business environments will stimulate your intellectual curiosity, which will enable you to absorb and understand new phenomena. International marketing has been compared by many who have been active in the field to the task of mountain climbing: challenging, arduous, and exhilarating.

International marketing is important because the world has become globalized. Increasingly, we all are living up to the claim of the Greek philosopher Socrates, who stated, "I am a citizen, not of Athens or Greece, but of the world." International marketing takes place all around us every day, has a major effect on our lives, and offers new opportunities and challenges. After reading through this book and observing international marketing phenomena, you will see what happens, understand what happens, and, at some time in the future, perhaps even make it happen. All of this is much better than to stand by and wonder what happened.

International marketing is necessary because, from a national standpoint, economic isolationism has become impossible. Failure to participate in the global marketplace assures a nation of declining economic capability and its citizens of a decrease in their standard of living. Successful international marketing, however, holds the promise of an improved quality of life, a better society, and more efficient business transactions. *The International Marketplace 1.1* not only highlights how global market forces and marketers need to adjust to a changing environment but also clarifies how market forces and marketers are the critical catalysts between individuals, businesses, and society.

This chapter is designed to increase your awareness of what international marketing is about. It describes current levels of world trade activities, projects future developments, and discusses the repercussions on countries, institutions, and individuals worldwide. Both the opportunities and the threats that spring from the global marketplace are highlighted, and the need for an international "marketing" approach on the part of individuals and institutions is emphasized.

While international marketing often offers more choices and lower prices to consumers, it also opens up markets to competition, which in many instances has been unexpected and is difficult to cope with. As a result, international marketing activities do not favor everyone to the same degree. Just like Janus, the two-faced god of the Romans, international marketing can bring benefits and opportunity to some, while delivering drawbacks and problems to others. International marketers, as well as consumers of international products and services, need to understand how to make globalization work for them as well as to think about how to ensure that these benefits are afforded to a wide variety of people and countries. Therefore, both as an opportunity and a challenge, international marketing is of vital concern to countries, companies, and individuals.

This chapter concludes with an explanation of the major organizational thrust of this book, which differentiates in each functional chapter between the beginning internationalist and the global corporation. This theme ties the book together by taking into account the concerns, capabilities, and goals of firms that will differ widely based on their level of international expertise, resources, and involvement. The approach to international marketing taken here will therefore permit you to understand the entire range of international activities and allow you easily to transfer your acquired knowledge into practice.

INTERNATIONAL MARKETING DEFINED

In brief, **international marketing** consists of the activity, institutions, and processes across national borders that create, communicate, deliver, and exchange offerings that have value for stakeholders and society. International marketing has forms ranging from export–import trade to licensing, joint ventures, wholly owned subsidiaries, turnkey operations, and management contracts.

As this definition indicates, international marketing very much retains the basic marketing tenets of *value* and *exchange*. There is also the focus on stakeholders and society whose present positions are to be improved. The fact that a transaction takes place across national borders highlights the difference between domestic and international marketing. The international marketer is subject to a new set of macroenvironmental factors, to different constraints, and to quite frequent conflicts resulting from different laws, cultures, and societies. The basic principles of marketing still apply, but their applications, complexity, and intensity may vary substantially. It is in the international marketing field where one can observe most closely the role of marketing as a key agent of societal change and as a key instrument for the development of socially responsive business strategy. When we look, for example, at the emerging market economies of China and Russia, we can see the many new challenges confronting international marketing. How does the marketing concept fit into these societies? How can marketing contribute to economic development and the improvement of society? How should distribution systems be organized? How should the price mechanism work? Similarly, in the areas of social responsibility and ethics, the international marketer is faced with a multicultural environment of differing expectations and often inconsistent legal systems when it comes to monitoring environmental pollution, maintaining safe working conditions, copying technology or trademarks, or paying bribes.[1] In addition, the long-term repercussions of marketing actions need to be understood and evaluated in terms of their societal impact, using not just today's criteria but considering also the long-term perspective of future affected parties.

These are just a few of the issues that the international marketer needs to address. The capability to master these challenges successfully affords a company the potential for new opportunities and high rewards. *The International Marketplace 1.2* shows how General Electric (GE) leverages its leadership in environmental business areas to seek new ideas and communicate its international marketing strategy.

THE INTERNATIONAL MARKETPLACE — ENVIRONMENT & SUSTAINABILITY — **1.2**

Environment and Sustainability: A Global Challenge for Ideas

Environmental concerns have become a global phenomenon, and marketers see opportunity. Clean energy, water stewardship, and sustainable manufacturing practices have become high priorities for global marketers as customers and governments worldwide have increased their expectations for corporate environmental performance.

Some corporations have chosen not only to implement sustainability programs but also to align their business strategies with the global movement towards sustainability. One such company is GE, which has included its "ecomagination" program as part of its global marketing campaign of "imagination at work." In the first of two phases of GE's Ecomagination Challenge, a "Powering the Grid" challenge was conducted in 2010 to invite ideas on how to build the next-generation power grid. Beth Comstock, GE's chief marketing officer, commented about the first phase: "We ended up with about 4,000 submissions from 150 different countries. We awarded $55 million to over 20 different great ideas."

In the second phase of its Ecomagination Challenge, GE launched a $200 million "Powering Your Home" challenge in 2011 to seek new business ideas. GE invited technologists and entrepreneurs worldwide to submit ideas on how to improve household energy efficiency and to harness wind, solar, hydro, and biomass power. The 856 entrants to the challenge had the opportunity to win cash prizes and to partner with GE to develop their ideas with capital backing from leading venture capital firms. Regarding the second phase, Comstock said: "What we're hoping is that the world's great inventors can come up with more of these kind of ideas that we can fund, that we can maybe bring to market, that we can license." With its Ecomagination Challenge, GE focuses its search for product innovation on global customer needs and highlights it with a global public relations program.

© Sean Blake/Gallo Images/Getty Images

Korea Smart Green City Jeju display model.

SOURCES: "GE and Partners Seek Best Ideas for Eco Home of the Future in Next Phase of $200 Million 'Ecomagination Challenge,'" GE press release, www.genewscenter.com/Press-Releases/GE-and-Partners-Seek-Best-Ideas-for-Eco-Home-of-the-Future-in-Next-Phase-of-200-Million-ecomagination-Challenge-2db8.aspx; and Adam Aston, "What GE Has in Store for Round 2 of the Ecomagination Challenge," GreenBiz.com, www.greenbiz.com/blog/2011/01/28/what-ge-has-store-round-2-ecomagination-challenge.

The emphasis on stakeholders and society at large indicates the need for the marketer to look beyond narrow self-interest and to understand that there are many parties touched by marketing. Willing or unwilling, they all participate in the outcome of the marketing effort, and their interests must be considered.

International marketing also focuses on the need to create, communicate, and deliver value internationally. These dimensions indicate that marketing internationally is an activity that needs to be pursued, often aggressively. Those who do not participate in the transactions are still exposed to international marketing and subject to its changing influences. The international marketer is part of the exchange and recognizes the constantly changing nature of transactions. This need for adjustment, for comprehending change, and, in spite of it all, for successfully delivering value highlights the fact that international marketing is as much art as science.

To achieve success in the art of international marketing, it is necessary to be firmly grounded in its scientific aspects. Only then will individual consumers, policymakers, and business executives be able to incorporate international marketing considerations into their thinking and planning. Only then will they be able to consider international issues and repercussions and make decisions based on answers to questions such as the following:

- Where are my current and potential customers?
- Does my need-to-have market have borders?
- Does international activity increase risk?
- What marketing adjustments are or will be necessary?
- What threats from global competition should I expect?
- How do innovation and entrepreneurship change the global marketplace?
- What are my strategic global alternatives?

If all these issues are integrated into each decision made by individuals and by firms, international markets can become a source of growth, profit, needs satisfaction, and quality of life that would not have existed for them had they limited themselves to domestic activities. The purpose of this book is to aid in this decision process.

THE IMPORTANCE OF WORLD TRADE

World trade has assumed an importance heretofore unknown to the global community. In past centuries, trade was conducted internationally, but never before did it have the broad and simultaneous impact on nations, firms, and individuals that it has today. Within the last decade, world trade in merchandise has expanded from $6.2 trillion in 2000 to over $15.2 trillion in 2010. World trade in services has expanded from $1.5 trillion to $3.6 trillion in the same period of time. That represents a growth of 140 percent for trade in both merchandise and services![2] Even with the severe recession that affected much of the world's economy in 2008 and 2009, world trade strongly rebounded in 2010. Such economic growth is exceptional, particularly because, as Exhibit 1.1 shows, global growth of trade has typically outperformed the growth of domestic economies in the past few decades. Many countries and firms have found it highly desirable to become major participants in international marketing.

The Iron Curtain has disintegrated and newly emerging economies have liberalized their economic systems, bringing billions of new consumers into the global economic system and offering a vast array of new marketing opportunities—albeit amid uncertainty. Firms invest on a global scale, with the result that entire industries shift their locations. International specialization and cross-sourcing have made production much more efficient. New technologies have changed the way we do business, allowing us to both supply and receive products from across the world by using the Internet. As a result, consumers, union leaders, policymakers, and sometimes even the firms themselves are finding it increasingly

EXHIBIT 1.1 Volume of World Merchandise Exports, 1990–2011

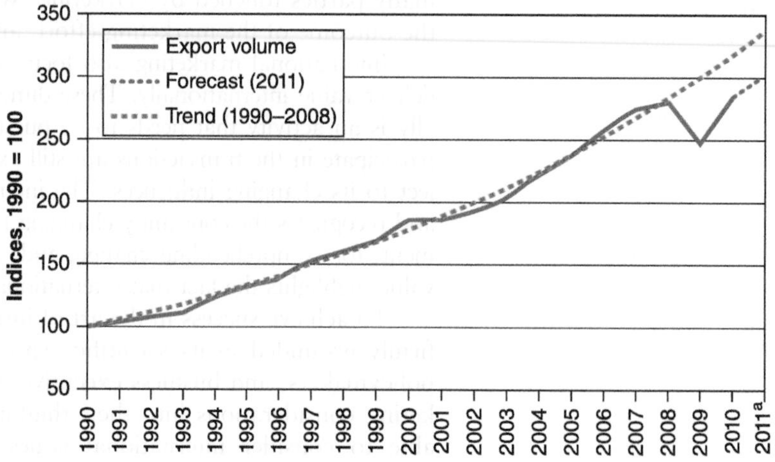

[a]Figures for 2011 are projections.

SOURCE: WTO Secretariat, www.wto.org/english/news_e/pres11_e/pr628_e.htm.

difficult to define where a particular product has been made. There are trading blocs such as the European Union in Europe, NAFTA in North America, MERCOSUR in Latin America, and ASEAN in Asia. These blocs encourage trade relations among their members, but, through their rules and standards, they also affect the trade and investment flows of nonmember countries.

Individuals and firms have come to recognize that they are competing not only domestically but also globally. World trade has given rise to global linkages of markets, technology, and living standards that were previously unknown and unanticipated. At the same time, it has deeply affected domestic policymaking and has often resulted in the emergence of totally new opportunities as well as threats to firms and individuals. *The International Marketplace 1.3* provides an example.

Global Linkages

World trade has forged a network of **global linkages** that bind us all—countries, institutions, and individuals—much more closely than ever before. These linkages were first widely recognized during the worldwide oil crisis of 1970, but they continue to increase, as was demonstrated dramatically in the financial crisis that was triggered in 2007. Now, a drought in Brazil and its effect on coffee production and prices is felt around the world. U.S. subsidies for ethanol production from corn affect prices for other agricultural crops and livestock in the far reaches of the world. European and American business executives learned how to pronounce *Eyjafjallajokull* in 2010 as plumes of ash from that Icelandic volcano closed airports and stranded air travelers in many European cities. They received another Icelandic language lesson in 2011 when the Grimsvotn volcano erupted, although to lesser aviation effect. Grimsvotn caused

Ash plume from Eyjafjallajokull Volcano.

THE INTERNATIONAL MARKETPLACE 1.3

New Sources for Outsourcing

Since the 1980s, corporations in developed nations have been sending entire business functions and management roles to developing countries. Companies have been outsourcing by using efficient call centers for information technology and technical and software support. Multinational companies cut costs while developing countries benefit from an upsurge in jobs and income. Outsourcing of business processes (BPO), information technology (ITO), and infrastructure management services allow firms to remain focused on their core business capabilities but access innovative best practices and technologies in noncore areas by delegating to outsourcing specialists.

During the financial crisis of 2008 and 2009, there was significant concern that the global outsourcing business would suffer. A 2011 report by the International Association of Outsourcing Professionals (IAOP) indicates that those concerns appear to have been misplaced. The IAOP reported that 2010 commercial outsourcing revenues exceeded $93 billion, a 24 percent increase from the previous year, despite political pressures on corporations in developed countries where unemployment continued at high rates.

However, the shape and geography of the sourcing industry continues to evolve. In its 2011 survey of the world's offshore outsourcing market, Morrison & Foerster reported that outsourcing to China is increasing relative to India and was "boosted by the Chinese government's announcement of generous tax incentives to outsourcing service providers in China's most important cities." The survey showed that outsourcing to China was principally in the area of information technology but that there was growth as well in areas such as R&D and film animation.

The annual *A.T. Kearney Global Services Location Index 2011* found that Asian countries were the top locations for offshoring of services, with India, China, Malaysia, Indonesia, Thailand, Vietnam, and the Philippines ranked among the top 10 locations. "India, with its first-mover advantage and deep skill base, still maintains the lion's share of the IT services market" and "is the all-around stand-out, able to provide manpower for any type of offshoring activity." A.T. Kearney reported that "China has begun offering specialized skills not only in English, but also Korean, Japanese, and Chinese" and that China's "most attractive areas are high-end analytics and advanced IT, where it is an alternative to Russia and Eastern Europe, and BPO, where it can be competitive with India."

SOURCES: "The 2011 Global Outsourcing 100," International Association of Outsourcing Professionals and *Fortune* magazine, May 23, 2011; "Global Sourcing Trends in 2011," Morrison & Foerster Global Sourcing Group, January 2011; and "Offshoring Opportunities amid Economic Turbulence: A.T. Kearney Global Services Location Index™, 2011," A.T. Kearney, www.atkearney.com/index.php/Publications/offshoring-opportunities-amid-economic-turbulence-the-at-kearney-global-services-location-index-gsli-2011.html.

President Obama to cut short his visit to Ireland to avoid potential flight problems. The March 2011 earthquake and tsunami off the northeastern coast of Japan caused massive casualties and destroyed or damaged much of the regional Japanese port and highway infrastructure. This also caused a series of disasters at the Fukushima Daiichi nuclear plant that led to a level 7 "major accident" on the International Nuclear and Radiological Event Scale. This resulted in worldwide disruptions in manufacturing and trade with automotive plant closures or production cutbacks in Japan, the United States, Europe, and other parts of the world. The "just-in-time" supply chains of the automotive, semiconductor, smartphone, digital camera, and personal computer industries were immediately jeopardized around the world. The financial crisis of 2008 demonstrated how these linkages have caused shortcoming in funds, credits, and loans that affect the entire global economy. Even countries that considered themselves as distanced and independent from any particular economic event in far-away countries found, to their unexpected chagrin, that their firms, budgets, and plans were deeply affected.

These linkages have also become more intense on an individual level. Communication has built new international bridges, be it through music or international programs transmitted by CNN, BBC, Al Arabiya, Al Jazeera, and social media. All this has encouraged similar activities around the world—where many of us wear jeans, dance to the same music on our iPods, and eat kebabs, curry, and sushi. Transportation linkages let individuals from different countries see and meet each other with unprecedented ease. Common cultural pressures result in similar social phenomena and behavior—for example, more dual-income families are emerging around the world, which leads to more frequent, but also more stressful, shopping.[3]

World trade is also bringing about a global reorientation of corporate processes, which opens up entirely new horizons. Never before has it been so easy to gather, manipulate, analyze, and disseminate information—but never before has the pressure been so great to do so. Ongoing global technological innovation in marketing has direct effects on the efficiency and effectiveness of all business activities. Products can be produced more quickly, obtained less expensively from sources around the world, distributed at lower cost, and customized to meet diverse clients' needs. As an example, only a decade ago, it would have been thought impossible for a firm to produce parts for a car in more than one country, assemble the car in yet another country, and sell it in still other nations. Today, such global investment strategies, coupled with production and distribution sharing, are becoming a matter of routine. Of course, these changes increase the level of global competition, which in turn increases the challenge of staying in a leadership position.

Advances in technology also allow firms to separate their activities by content and context. Firms can operate in a "market space" rather than a marketplace[4] by keeping the content while changing the context of a transaction. For example, a newspaper can be distributed online globally rather than house-to-house on paper, thereby allowing outreach to entirely new customer groups.

The level of global investment is at an unprecedented high. The shifts in financial flows have had major effects. They have resulted in the buildup of international debt by governments, affected the international value of currencies, provided foreign capital for firms, and triggered major foreign direct-investment activities. Societies can grow concerned about these shifts. For example, in the United States, the PATRIOT Act defines critical infrastructure as systems and assets so vital that any breakdown in them "would have a debilitating impact on security, national economic security, national public health, or safety." A national strategy was developed for the protection of critical infrastructure in 11 sectors: agriculture and food, water, public health, emergency services, defense industrial bases, telecommunications, energy, transportation, banking and finance, chemical industry and hazardous material, and postal services and shipping. The "key assets" identified are national monuments and icons, nuclear power plants, dams, government facilities, and commercial key assets.[5] The fact that there is increasing foreign investment in such key assets indicates that nations, firms, and people grow more and more dependent on one another.

This interdependence, however, is not stable. On almost a daily basis, realignments taking place on both micro and macro levels make past trade orientations at least partially obsolete. For example, for the first 200 years of its history, the United States looked to Europe for markets and sources of supply. Today, U.S. two-way trade with Asia far outpaces U.S. trade with Europe. The participants in international marketing also are changing their roles. For example, the International Monetary Fund (IMF) was founded in 1944 to help restructure impoverished economies. More recently, however, the fund has been assisting nations that used to be categorized as "wealthy," such as Iceland, and member states of the European Union, such as Greece and Ireland. It appears to become increasingly difficult to differentiate between "rich" and "poor." For example, based on its foreign currency reserves of $3.2 trillion, China easily qualifies for the upper echelons of the wealthy countries.[6] However, the nation's GDP per capita would still let it be classified as a developing nation.

Not only is the environment changing, but the pace of change is accelerating as well. Atari's Pong was first introduced in the early 1980s; today, action games and movies are made with computerized humans. The first office computers emerged in the mid-1980s; today, tablet computers have become commonplace. E-mail was introduced to a mass market only in the 1990s; today, many college students hardly ever send personal notes using a stamp and envelope and are more likely to communicate with each other via texting than e-mail.[7]

These changes and the speed with which they come about significantly affect countries, corporations, and individuals. One change is the role participants play. For example, the United States accounted for nearly 25 percent of world merchandise exports in the 1950s, but by 2010 this share had declined by two-thirds. Also, the way countries participate in world trade is shifting. As Exhibit 1.2 shows, while the United States and developed nations have grown their exports more slowly, since 2008 many developing economies have realized dramatic gains in exports. Of course, one needs to consider the base from which this growth has taken place. Here the European Union, China, and the United States are the consistent leaders. Also, in the past two decades, the role of primary commodities in international trade has dropped precipitously, while the importance of manufactured goods and services has increased. Most important, the growth in the overall volume and value of both merchandise and services trade has had a major impact on firms, countries, and individuals.

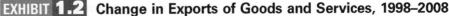

EXHIBIT 1.2 Change in Exports of Goods and Services, 1998–2008

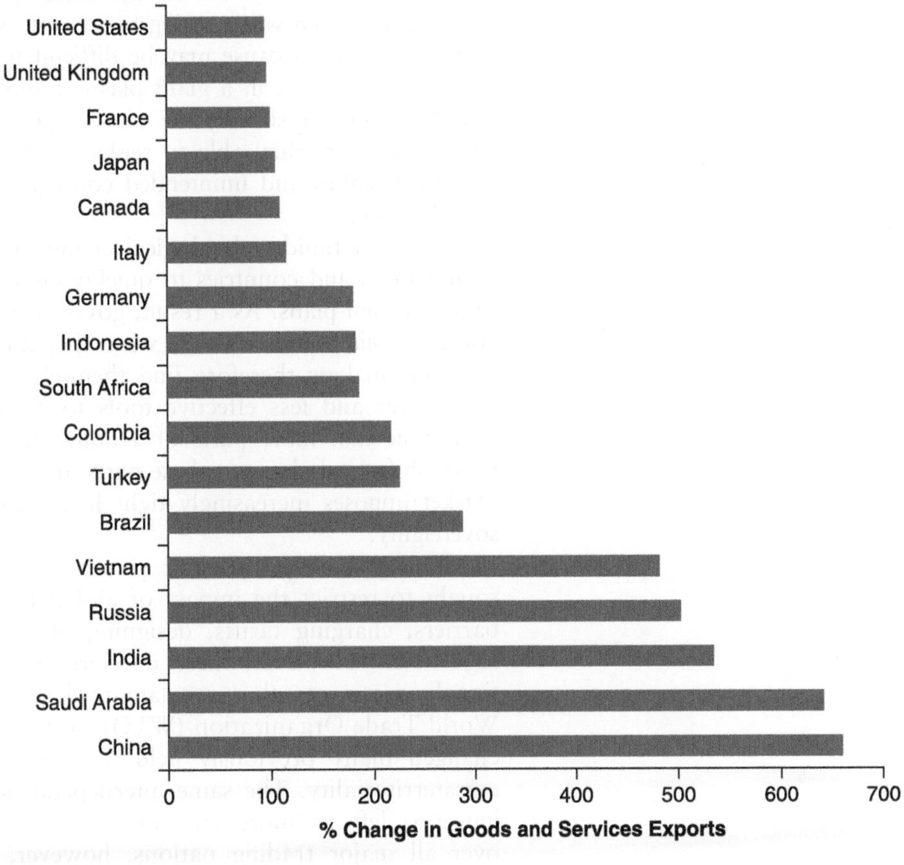

SOURCE: 2011 National Export Strategy, U.S. Trade Promotion Coordinating Committee, June 2011.

Domestic Policy Repercussions

The effects of closer global linkages on the economics of countries have been dramatic. Policymakers have increasingly come to recognize that it is very difficult to isolate domestic economic activity from international market events. Decisions that once were clearly in the domestic purview have now become subject to revision by influences from abroad, and domestic policy measures are often canceled out or counteracted by the activities of global market forces.

A lowering of interest rates domestically may make consumers happy or may be politically wise, but it quickly becomes unsustainable if it results in a major outflow of funds to countries that offer higher interest rates. In 2010 and 2011, a U.S. monetary policy of "quantitative easing," intended to stimulate the domestic economy, brought complaints from Latin American countries because of the escalation effect on their currencies. Agricultural and farm policies, which historically have been strictly domestic issues, are suddenly thrust into the international realm. Any policy consideration must now be seen in light of international repercussions due to influences from global trade and investment.

To some extent, the economic world as we knew it has been turned upside down. For example, trade flows traditionally have been used to determine currency flows and therefore the level of the exchange rate. In the more recent past, **currency flows** took on a life of their own. Independent of trade, they set exchange rates, which are the values of currencies relative to each other. These **exchange rates** in turn have now begun to determine the level of trade. Governments that wish to counteract these developments with monetary policies find that currency flows outnumber trade flows by 100 to 1. Also, private-sector financial flows vastly exceed the financial flows that can be marshaled by governments, even when acting in concert. Major economic change can be swift and harsh, and its cause may be difficult to identify. An analogy might consist of persons traveling in a giant plastic bubble filled with vital air. Suddenly the bubble begins to shrink, the air escapes, but the passengers don't find the rupture, nor are they able to replenish the air sufficiently. Rash reaction may lead to mistakes and unintended consequences, but no reaction will lead to a hard landing.

Constant rapid technological change and vast advances in communication permit firms and countries to quickly emulate innovation and counteract carefully designed plans. As a result, governments are often powerless to implement effective policy measures even when they know what to do.

Policymakers therefore find themselves with increasing responsibilities yet with fewer and less effective tools to carry out these responsibilities. At the same time that more parts of a domestic economy are vulnerable to international shifts and changes, these parts are becoming less controllable. The global market imposes increasingly tight limits on national economic regulation and sovereignty.

To regain some of their power to influence events, policymakers have sought to restrict the impact of global trade and financial flows by erecting barriers, charging tariffs, designing quotas, and implementing other import regulations. However, these measures too have been restrained by international agreements that regulate trade restrictions, particularly through the World Trade Organization (WTO) (www.wto.org). Global trade has therefore changed many previously held notions about nation-state sovereignty and extraterritoriality. The same interdependence that has made us more affluent has also left us more vulnerable. Because this vulnerability is spread out over all major trading nations, however, some have credited international marketing with being a pillar of international peace. Clearly, closer economic relations can result in many positive effects. At the same time, however, interdependence brings with it risks, such as dislocations of people and economic resources and a decrease in a nation's capability to do things its own way. Given the ease—and sometimes the desirability—of blaming a foreign rather than a domestic culprit for economic failure, it may well also be a key task for the international marketer to stimulate societal acceptance of the long-term benefits of interdependence.

OPPORTUNITIES AND CHALLENGES IN INTERNATIONAL MARKETING

To prosper in a world of abrupt changes and discontinuities, of newly emerging forces and dangers, and of unforeseen influences from abroad, firms need to prepare themselves and develop active responses. New strategies need to be envisioned, new plans need to be made, and the way of doing business needs to be changed. The way to obtain and retain leadership, economically, politically, or morally, is—as the examples of Rome, Constantinople, and London have amply demonstrated—not through passivity but rather through a continuous, alert adaptation to the changing world environment. To help a country remain a player in the world economy, governments, firms, and individuals need to respond aggressively with innovation, process improvements, and creativity.[8]

The growth of global business activities offers increased opportunities. International activities can be crucial to a firm's survival and growth. By transferring knowledge around the globe, an international firm can build and strengthen its competitive position. Firms that heavily depend on long production runs can expand their activities far beyond their domestic markets and benefit from reaching many more customers. Market saturation can be avoided by lengthening or rejuvenating product life cycles in other countries. Production sites once were inflexible, but now plants can be shifted from one country to another, and suppliers can be found on every continent. Cooperative agreements can be formed that enable all parties to bring their major strengths to the table and emerge with better products, services, and ideas than they could produce on their own. In addition, research has found that multinational corporations face a lower risk of insolvency and pay higher wages than do domestic companies.[9] For example, in the United States, jobs supported by goods exports pay 13 to 16 percent above the average wage.[10] At the same time, international marketing enables consumers all over the world to find greater varieties of products at lower prices and to improve their lifestyles and comfort.[11]

International opportunities require careful exploration. What is needed is an awareness of global developments, an understanding of their meaning, and a development of capabilities to adjust to change. Firms must adapt to the international market if they are to be successful.

One key facet of the marketing concept is adaptation to the environment, particularly the market. Even though many executives understand the need for such an adaptation in their domestic market, they often believe that international customers are just like the ones the firm deals with at home. It is here that many firms commit grave mistakes that lead to inefficiency, lack of consumer acceptance, and sometimes even corporate failure. As *The International Marketplace 1.4* explains, there are quite substantial differences in this world between consumer groups.

Firms increasingly understand that many of the key difficulties encountered in doing business internationally are marketing problems. Judging by corporate needs, a background in international marketing is highly desirable for business students seeking employment, not only for today but also for long-term career plans.

THE INTERNATIONAL MARKETPLACE 1.4

Emerging Consumers Bring a Smile to Coca-Cola and Consumer Goods Companies

Historically, the leading consumer goods companies of the world have focused the bulk of their marketing efforts on the most developed countries, where economic wealth and disposable income were concentrated and infrastructure allowed for them to efficiently reach consumers. Return on marketing investment was greatest in the United States, Western Europe, and Japan. However, as a result of economic liberalization and the embrace of Western capitalism by the largest emerging and developing economies, firms are taking a new look at where to find new customers.

The Coca-Cola Company "refreshes" consumers in over 200 countries. In its Vision 2020 statement, the firm summarized the dynamics of the changing global marketplace in relation to its market opportunity: "By 2020, we believe the world will experience significant social and economic shifts, from a population increase of more than 800 million people to nearly 900 million people moving into urban areas and more than 1 billion people joining the middle class. These trends indicate there will be more people with more disposable income who potentially will tap into refreshment and convenience." That must bring a smile to Coca-Cola executives and those of other companies as well.

Firms are increasingly turning their attention east and south, where much of this change is occurring. Philips, the Amsterdam-based global health and well-being company, has stated its objective to generate at least 40 percent of its global sales in emerging markets by 2015, using the rationale that "as the number of middle-class households in these markets grows, we expect demand for our products will increase as people have more money to spend on feeling and staying healthy."

Procter & Gamble (P&G), which sells its brands to consumers in more than 180 countries, has similar ambitions and has simplified the expression of its strategy for growth: "touching and improving the lives of more consumers in more parts of the world, more completely." As a part of this strategy, P&G's CEO, Robert McDonald, stated that in 2010 "we reached an additional 200 million consumers, bringing the total served to 4.2 billion—on track toward our goal of reaching 5 billion consumers by fiscal 2015. Average per capita spending on P&G products increased in 70% of our top countries, up from 60% in fiscal 2009. And, global household penetration—the percentage of households using at least one P&G product—increased nearly two percentage points, to 61%."

These companies are not ignoring their traditional markets either. As Coca-Cola's 2020 Vision states: "Over the next 10 years and beyond, the United States will have some of the world's most attractive demographics for our business. By 2020, the United States will add about 31 million people, and its teen population will also be around 31 million. Only India and China will have larger teen populations."

© Doug Kanter/Bloomberg via Getty Images

Coca-Cola employees at one of three new bottling plants in China.

SOURCES: Dan Sewell, "P&G plans for Asian Growth," Associated Press, *The Journal Gazette*, April 17, 2011, www.journalgazette.net /article/20110417/BIZ/304179953/1031/BIZ; Robert A. McDonald, "Letter to Shareholders," P&G 2010 Annual Report; and The Coca Cola Company, 2009 Annual Report.

Many firms do not participate in the global market. Often, managers believe that international marketing should only be carried out by large multinational corporations. It is true that there are some very large players from many countries active in the world market. But smaller firms are major players, too. For example, 50 percent of German exports are created by firms with 19 or fewer employees, while 97.6 percent of U.S. exporters are small- and medium-sized enterprises.[12] Increasingly we find smaller firms, particularly in the computer and telecommunications industries, that are born global because they achieve a worldwide presence within a very short time.[13]

Those firms and industries that are not participating in the world market have to recognize that in today's trade environment isolation has become impossible. Willing or unwilling, firms are becoming participants in global business affairs. Even if not by choice, most firms and individuals are affected directly or indirectly by economic and political developments that occur in the international marketplace. Those firms that refuse to participate are relegated to reacting to the global marketplace and therefore are unprepared for harsh competition from abroad.

Some industries have recognized the need for international adjustments. Farmers understand the need for high productivity in light of stiff international competition. Computer makers and firms in other technologically advanced industries have learned to forge global relationships to stay in the race. Firms in the steel, textile, and leather sectors have shifted production, and perhaps even adjusted their core business, in response to overwhelming onslaughts from abroad. Other industries in some countries have been caught unaware and have been unable to adjust. The result is the extinction of firms or entire industries, such as VCRs in the United States and coal mining and steel smelting in other countries.

THE GOALS OF THIS BOOK

This book aims to make you a better, more successful participant in the international marketplace by providing information about how international markets work, how a changing context affects the marketing functions, and by eventually helping you to translate knowledge into successful business transactions. By learning about both theory and practice, you can obtain a good conceptual understanding of the field of international marketing as well as become firmly grounded in the realities of the global marketplace. Therefore, this book approaches international marketing in the way the manager of a firm does, reflecting different levels of international involvement and the importance of business–government relations.

Firms differ widely in their international activities and needs, depending on their level of experience, resources, and capabilities. For the firm that is just beginning to enter the global market, the level of knowledge about international complexities is low, the demand on time is high, expectations about success are uncertain, and the international environment is often inflexible. Conversely, for a multinational firm that is globally oriented and employs thousands of people on each continent, much more leeway exists in terms of resource availability, experience, and information. In addition, the multinational firm has the option of responding creatively to the environment by shifting resources or even shaping the environment itself. For example, the heads of large corporations have access to government ministers to plead their case for a change in policy, an alternative that is rarely afforded to smaller firms.

To become a large international corporation, a firm usually has to start out small. Similarly, to direct far-flung global operations, managers first have to learn the basic issues and their cultural, economic, financial, political, and legal dimensions.

For each component of the marketing mix, the book discusses in detail the beginning internationalization of the firm. Some basic, yet essential, issues

International Trade as a Percentage of Gross Domestic Product

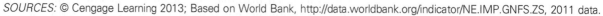

SOURCES: © Cengage Learning 2013; Based on World Bank, http://data.worldbank.org/indicator/NE.IMP.GNFS.ZS, 2011 data.

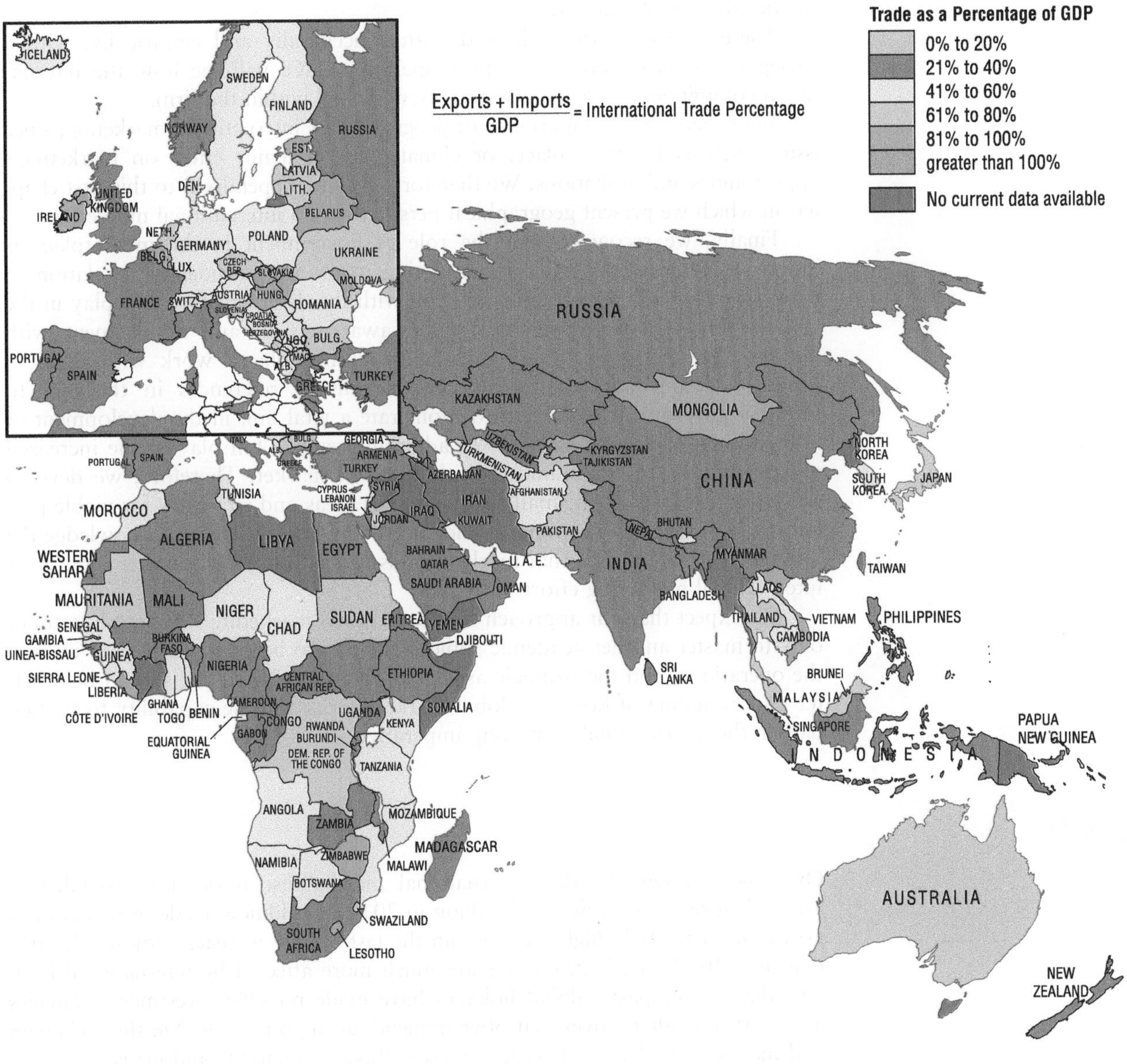
Trade as a Percentage of GDP
0% to 20%
21% to 40%
41% to 60%
61% to 80%
81% to 100%
greater than 100%
No current data available
Exports + Imports / GDP = International Trade Percentage
ICELAND
SWEDEN
FINLAND
NORWAY
RUSSIA
EST.
LATVIA
LITH.
DEN.
UNITED KINGDOM
IRELAND
BELARUS
NETH.
GERMANY
POLAND
BELG.
LUX.
CZECH REP.
SLOVAKIA
UKRAINE
MOLDOVA
FRANCE
SWITZ.
AUSTRIA
HUNG.
ROMANIA
SLOVENIA
CROATIA
BOSNIA HERZEGOVINA
YUGO.
BULG.
MAC.
ALB.
PORTUGAL
SPAIN
ITALY
GREECE
TURKEY
RUSSIA
KAZAKHSTAN
MONGOLIA
GEORGIA
ARMENIA
AZERBAIJAN
UZBEKISTAN
TURKMENISTAN
KYRGYZSTAN
TAJIKISTAN
NORTH KOREA
SOUTH KOREA
JAPAN
CHINA
TUNISIA
MOROCCO
CYPRUS
LEBANON
ISRAEL
SYRIA
IRAQ
IRAN
AFGHANISTAN
JORDAN
KUWAIT
PAKISTAN
BHUTAN
NEPAL
ALGERIA
LIBYA
EGYPT
BAHRAIN
QATAR
U. A. E.
INDIA
MYANMAR
TAIWAN
WESTERN SAHARA
SAUDI ARABIA
OMAN
BANGLADESH
LAOS
MAURITANIA
MALI
NIGER
SUDAN
ERITREA
YEMEN
THAILAND
VIETNAM
PHILIPPINES
SENEGAL
GAMBIA
GUINEA-BISSAU
GUINEA
CHAD
DJIBOUTI
CAMBODIA
BURKINA FASO
SIERRA LEONE
LIBERIA
NIGERIA
ETHIOPIA
CENTRAL AFRICAN REP.
SRI LANKA
BRUNEI
MALAYSIA
GHANA
TOGO
BENIN
CAMEROON
CÔTE D'IVOIRE
UGANDA
SOMALIA
SINGAPORE
PAPUA NEW GUINEA
CONGO
GABON
RWANDA
BURUNDI
KENYA
EQUATORIAL GUINEA
DEM. REP. OF THE CONGO
TANZANIA
INDONESIA
ANGOLA
ZAMBIA
MOZAMBIQUE
MADAGASCAR
NAMIBIA
ZIMBABWE
MALAWI
BOTSWANA
AUSTRALIA
SWAZILAND
SOUTH AFRICA
LESOTHO
NEW ZEALAND

addressed are: What is the difference between domestic and international marketing? Does the applicability of marketing principles change when they are transferred to the global environment? How do marketers find out whether there is a market for a product abroad without spending a fortune in time and money on research? How can the firm promote its products in foreign markets? How do marketers find and evaluate a foreign distributor, and how do they make sure that their firm gets paid? How can marketers minimize government red tape, yet take advantage of any governmental programs that are of use to them? How much do governments allow or restrict the ability of marketers to implement the variable elements of the marketing mix? (See Appendix A: A Brief Review of Marketing.)

These questions are addressed both conceptually and empirically, with a strong focus on export and import operations. We will see how the international commitment is developed and strengthened within the firm.

We believe in the importance of geography for international marketing, since issues such as location, place, or climate have a major effect on marketing's opportunities and limitations. We therefore have an Appendix B to this first chapter, in which we present geographical perspectives on international marketing.

Finally, we recognize that the role of government in the marketplace is increasing dramatically. All the marketing issues are considered in relation to national policies so as to familiarize you with the divergent forces at play in the global market. Governments' increased awareness of and involvement with international marketing require managers to be able to work with them in order to attain marketing goals. The continued references in the text to business–government interaction demonstrate a vital link in the development of international marketing strategy. In addition, we give full play to the increased ability of firms to communicate with a global market. Therefore, we develop and offer, for firms both small and large, our ideas and strategies for viable participation in electronic commerce and social networks. We also acknowledge the difference between firms that market goods versus those that market services as international marketing efforts vary.

We expect that our approach to international marketing will permit you not only to master another academic subject but also to become well versed in both the operational and the strategic aspects of the field. The result should be a better understanding of how the global market works and the capability to participate in the international marketing imperative.

SUMMARY

Over the last few decades, international merchandise trade has expanded at astounding rates to reach \$16.3 trillion in 2011. In addition, trade in services has grown at particularly high rates within the last decade to reach almost \$3.7 trillion in 2010. As a result, nations are much more affected by international business than in the past. Global linkages have made possible investment strategies and marketing alternatives that offer tremendous opportunities. Yet these changes and the speed of change also can represent threats to nations and firms.

On the policy front, decision makers have come to realize that it is very difficult to isolate domestic economic activity from international market events. Factors such as currency exchange rates, financial flows, and foreign economic actions increasingly render the policymaker powerless to implement a domestic agenda. International interdependence, which has contributed to greater affluence, has also increased our vulnerability.

Both firms and individuals are greatly affected by international trade. Whether willing or not, they are participating in global business affairs. Entire industries have been threatened in their survival as a result of international trade flows and have either adjusted to new market realities or left the market. Some individuals have lost their workplace and experienced reduced salaries. At the same time, global business changes have increased the opportunities available. Firms can now reach many more customers, product life cycles have been lengthened, sourcing policies have become variable, new jobs have been created, and consumers all over the world can find greater varieties of products at lower prices.

To benefit from the opportunities and deal with the adversities of international trade, business needs to adopt the international marketing concept. The new set of macroenvironmental factors has to be understood and responded to in order to let international markets become a source of growth, profit, and needs satisfaction.

KEY TERMS

international marketing
global linkage
currency flows
exchange rate

QUESTIONS FOR DISCUSSION

1. What effect did the financial crisis and recession have upon world trade in 2011?
2. Do increased global linkages mean increased risk or more reward?
3. What impact does international marketing have on firms and consumers? Is it beneficial to all concerned?
4. Can you think of examples of international marketing contributing to world peace?
5. Describe some opportunities and challenges in international marketing created by new advances in information technology and social media.

INTERNET EXERCISES

1. Using World Trade Organization data (www.wto.org), identify the following: (1) world trade volume of merchandise goods and services for the preceding year and (2) projections for world trade volume of merchandise goods and services in the current year. Which category (goods or services) is growing faster?
2. Consult the resources available on the World Economic Forum (www.weforum.org/issues/global-risks), the Eurasia Group (www.eurasiagroup.net), and other websites. Identify three of the top global risks that international marketing firms should consider in their work abroad.

CHALLENGE US

Who Is Responsible for a Sustainable Environment?

All of us want a clean and sustainable environment. The disagreements tend to emerge when the issue of payment arises. Therefore, we should discuss who should spend the money for the environment.

For Discussion

1. Is it the rich countries that have exploited their own nations and many oppressed colonies for centuries? Or is it the emerging nations who have yet to have a chance to grow rich on the destruction of forests, land, and seas?
2. Are global sanctions and embargoes a fair method of enforcement, say, of the prevention of hunting elephants for their tusks, or does that deprive poor villagers of their only means of support?

RECOMMENDED READINGS

Bernstein, William J. *A Splendid Exchange: How Trade Shaped the World.* New York: Atlantic Monthly Press, 2009.

Friedman, Thomas and Michael Mandelbaum. *That Used to Be Us: How America Fell Behind in the World It Invented and How We Can Come Back.* New York: Farrar, Strauss, Giroux, 2012.

Griswold, Daniel T. *Mad about Trade: Why Main Street America Should Embrace Globalization.* Washington, DC: Cato Institute, 2009.

Hufbauer, Gary Clyde, and Kati Suominen. *Globalization at Risk: Challenges to Finance and Trade.* New Haven, CT: Yale University Press, 2010.

Rodrick, Dani. *The Globalization Paradox: Democracy and the Future of the World Economy.* New York: W. W. Norton & Company, 2011.

Sinclair, John. *Advertising, the Media, and Globalization: A World in Motion.* Routledge, 2012.

Stiglitz, Joseph E. *Freefall: America, Free Markets, and the Sinking of the World Economy.* W. W. Norton & Company, 2011.

ENDNOTES

1. Robert W. Armstrong and Jill Sweeney, "Industrial Type, Culture, Mode of Entry, and Perceptions of International Marketing Ethics Problems: A Cross-Culture Comparison," *Journal of Business Ethics* 13, no. 10: 775–85.
2. World Trade Organization, "Statistics Database," http://stat.wto.org/Home/WSDBHome.aspx?Language=E, accessed December 14, 2011.
3. Eugene H. Fram and Riad Ajami, "Globalization of Markets and Shopping Stress: Cross-Country Comparisons," *Business Horizons*, January–February 1994, 17–23.
4. John J. Sviokla and Jeffrey F. Rayport, "Mapping the Marketspace: Information Technology and the New Marketing Environment," *Harvard Business School Bulletin* 71 (June 1995): 45–51.
5. E. Kaplan and L. Teslik, "Foreign Ownership of U.S. Infrastructure," Council on Foreign Relations, www.cfr.org/business-and-foreign-policy/foreign-ownership-us-infrastructure/p10092, updated February 13, 2007.
6. *Financial Times*, July 12, 2011.
7. Michael R. Czinkota and Sarah McCue, *The STAT-USA Companion to International Business* (Washington, DC: U.S. Department of Commerce, Economics and Statistics Administration, 2001), 16.
8. Peter R. Dickson and Michael R. Czinkota, "How the U.S. Can Be Number One Again: Resurrecting the Industrial Policy Debate," *The Columbia Journal of World Business* 31, no. 3 (Fall 1996): 76–87.
9. Howard Lewis III and J. David Richardson, *Why Global Commitment Really Matters* (Washington, DC: Institute for International Economics, 2001).
10. World Trade Organization, www.wto.org, accessed December 14, 2011.
11. Michael R. Czinkota, "Freedom and International Marketing: Janis Joplin's Candidacy as Patron of the Field," *Thunderbird International Business Review* 47, no. 1 (January–February 2005): 1–13.
12. "Small & Medium-Sized Exporting Companies: Statistical Overview," 2011, Data.gov, http://explore.data.gov/Foreign-Commerce-and-Aid/Small-Medium-Sized-Exporting-Companies-Statistical/62te-ypp5, accessed December 14, 2011; and U.S. International Trade Administration, "Export Fact Sheet," May 11, 2011.
13. Michael Kutschker, "Internationalisierung der Wirtschaft," in *Perspektiven der Internationalen Wirtschaft* (Wiesbaden, Germany: Gabler GmbH, 1999), 22.

APPENDIX A

A Brief Review of Marketing

This appendix provides a summary of the basic concepts in marketing for the reader who wishes to review them before applying them to international marketing. The American Marketing Association defines **marketing** as "the activity, set of institutions, and processes for creating, communicating, delivering, and exchanging offerings that have value for customers, clients, partners, and society at large."[1]

It is useful to focus on the definition's components to fully understand its meaning. Marketing as an *activity* indicates the proactive nature of the discipline, with a specific thrust that gives direction to its user. *Sets of institutions and processes* highlights that there are inside and outside participants in the marketing effort and that the activity goes beyond a single transaction. *Creating, communicating, and delivering* emphasizes that the marketing discipline takes leadership in its activities from beginning to end and that the art and the practical implementation dimensions of the discipline are crucial in their simultaneity. The fact that there are an "exchange" and "offerings" involved is a crucial dimension setting marketing apart from other disciplines and other forms of resource acquisition. Each party gives up something of value and receives something of equal (or even perceived higher) value. It is important to recognize the powerful effect of the "offering," which highlights the voluntary nature of the exchange and signifies the existence of freedom of choice. Carrying out the exchange is then designed to achieve satisfaction with the transaction.

Value for customers, clients, partners, and society at large presents the core focus of marketing. Physicians have as their overriding principle the Hippocratic oath, "Do no harm." Marketers should consider any action through the prism of "Are my stakeholders better off?" There is both a dyadic and plurilateral (many-sided) aspect to marketing. Is it an individual interaction between, say, the firm and its customers? Of course it is, but there are also the relationships among the customers themselves and the consequences of the marketing effort for other parties, such as suppliers, distributors, investors, or family members, who can play the role of both clients and partners. All of these form part of a network that is defined by the interactions and relationships between its members and that creates the society in which we live.

Because marketers will be major influencers on this relationship, they need to take into account the repercussions that their actions are likely to have on these linkages. *Relationships* are key as they are indicative of the fact that actions build upon each other and are instrumental in forging bonds and inflaming disagreements. The marketer therefore cannot see any product or effort as an isolated event. Rather, it has to be understood as a component of an entire series of steps that define the bridge between entities. Using this perspective, marketing has a very broad mission. The discipline is not narrowly confined to relationships that emerge when money is exchanged for goods. Rather, marketing has its application just as well when there is performance of a service (say, coaching Little League or fund-raising for a charity) in exchange for obtaining a good feeling and a sense of fulfillment.

The fact that marketing develops and adds value is critical. Marketing needs to be seen, after all, in the context of a planned and purposeful activity. It seeks a definite, favorable outcome for the participants of the marketing pursuit. Again, it is important to recognize that this benefit need not be seen strictly in terms of mammon. Rather, the organization itself is the one that defines what it determines to be beneficial. Therefore, there is ample room for both macro benefits, such as "more positive images of our country," as well as micro benefits, such as "increased desire to participate in project," in addition to the business benefits customarily seen to be in the purview of organizations. As a result, marketing finds a full range of applicability in not-for-profit areas, such as medicine, the arts, or government areas typically wrongfully excluded from the need for marketing. The various stakeholders are also indicative of this breadth of marketing in that it gives recognition to others who have an interest in either the process or the outcome of marketing activities.

As you can see, this definition packs a lot of punch and lets marketing make a major contribution to the welfare of individuals and organizations. Nevertheless, based on our view of marketing, we will expand this definition on several dimensions. First, we believe that the terms *create*, *deliver*, and *value* overemphasize transactions as one-time events. Therefore, we add the terms *maintain* and *value stream* to highlight the long-term nature of marketing that encourages customers to continue to come back. We also believe that, as the scope of marketing is broadened, societal goals need to be added to individuals and organizations, properly reflecting the overarching reach and responsibility of marketing as a social change agent that responds to and develops social concerns about the environment, technology, and ethics. Equally important is the need to specifically broaden our marketing understanding beyond national borders. Today, sourcing and supply linkages exist around the globe, competition emerges from all corners of the earth, and marketing opportunities evolve worldwide. As a result, many crucial dimensions of marketing need to be reevaluated and adapted in a global context.

Based on these considerations, our expanded definition of marketing is "an organizational function and a set of processes for creating, communicating, delivering, and maintaining value streams to consumers and for managing customer relationships in ways that benefit the organization, its stakeholders, and society in the context of a global environment."[2]

The concepts of satisfaction and exchange are at the core of marketing. For an exchange to take place, two or more parties must come together in person, through the mail, or through technology, and they must communicate and deliver things of perceived value. Potential customers should be perceived as information seekers who evaluate marketers' efforts in terms of their own drives and needs. When the offering is consistent with their needs, they tend to choose the product; if it is not, they choose other alternatives. A key task of the marketer is to recognize the ever-changing nature of needs and wants. Increasingly, the goal of marketing has been expanded from sensing, serving, and satisfying individual customers to taking into consideration the long-term interests of society.

Marketing is not limited to business entities but involves governmental and nonbusiness units as well. Marketing techniques are applied not only to goods but also to ideas (for example, a "Made in Japan" campaign) and to services (for example, international advertising agencies). The term *business marketing* is used for activities directed at other businesses, governmental entities, and various types of institutions. Business marketing accounts for well over 50 percent of all marketing activities.

STRATEGIC MARKETING

The marketing manager's task is to plan and execute programs that will ensure a long-term competitive advantage for the company. This task has two integral parts: (1) the determining of specific target markets and (2) marketing management, which consists of developing and operationalizing marketing mix elements to best satisfy the needs of individual target markets.

Target Market Selection

Characteristics of intended target markets are of critical importance to the marketer. These characteristics can be summarized by eight Os: occupants, objects, occasions, objectives, outlets, organization, operations, and opposition.[3]

Occupants are targets of the marketing effort. The marketer must determine which customers to approach and also define them along numerous dimensions, such as demographics (age, sex, and nationality, for example), geography (country or region), psychographics (attitudes, interests, and opinions), or product-related variables (usage rate and brand loyalty, for example). Included in this analysis must be the major influences on the occupants during their buying processes.

Objects are what is being bought at present to satisfy a particular need. Included in this concept are physical objects, services, ideas, organizations, places, and persons.

Occasions are moments when members of the target market buy the product or service. This characteristic is important to the marketer because a product's consumption may be tied to a particular time period—for example, imported beer and a festival.

Objectives are the motivations behind the purchase or adoption of the marketed concept. A computer manufacturer markets not hardware but solutions to problems. Additionally, many customers look for hidden value in the product they purchase, which may be expressed, for example, through national origin of the product or through brand name.

Outlets are places where customers expect to be able to procure a product or to be exposed to messages about it. Outlets include not only the entities themselves but also spots within a particular place. Although aseptic packaging made it possible to shelve milk outside the refrigerated area in supermarkets, customers' acceptance of the arrangement was not automatic: the product was not where it was supposed to be. In the area of services, outlet involves (1) making a particular service available and communicating its availability and (2) selecting the particular types of facilitators (such as brokers) who bring the parties together.

Organization describes how the buying or acceptance of a (new) idea takes place. Organization expands the analysis beyond the individual consumer to the decision-making unit (DMU). The DMU varies in terms of its size and its nature from relatively small and informal groups like a family to large groups (more than 10 people) to formal buying committees. Compare, for example, the differences between a family buying a new home-entertainment center and the governing board at a university deciding which architectural firm to use. In either case, to develop proper products and services, the marketer should know as much as possible about the decision-making processes and the roles of various individuals.

Operations represent the behavior of the organization buying products and services. Increasingly, industrial organizations are concentrating their purchases with fewer suppliers and making longer-term commitments. Supermarkets may make available only the leading brands in a product category, thereby complicating the marketer's attempts to place new products in these outlets.

Opposition refers to the competition to be faced in the marketplace. The nature of competition will vary from direct product-type competition to competition from other products that satisfy the same need. For example, Prince tennis rackets face a threat not only from other racket manufacturers but also from any company that provides a product or service for leisure-time use. Competitive situations will vary from one market and from one segment to the next. Gillette is number one in the U.S. market for disposable razors, with Bic a distant runner-up; however, elsewhere, particularly in Europe, the roles are reversed. In the long term, threats may come from outside the industry in which the marketer operates. As an example, digital watches originated in the electronics industry rather than the watch industry.

Analyzing Kotler's eight Os, and keeping in mind other uncontrollable factors in the environment (cultural, political, legal, technological, societal, and economic), the marketer must select the markets to which efforts will be targeted. In the short term, the marketer has to adjust to these environmental forces; in the long term, they can be manipulated to some extent by judicious marketing activity. Consumerism, one of the major forces shaping marketing activities, is concerned with protecting the consumer whenever an exchange relationship exists with any type of organization. Manifestations of the impact of consumerism on marketing exist in labeling, product specifications, promotional campaigns, recycling expectations, and demands for environmentally friendly products.

Because every marketer operates in a corporate environment of scarcity and comparative strengths, the target market decision is a crucial one. In some cases, the marketer may select only one segment of the market (for example, motorcycles of 1,000+ cc) or multiple segments (for example, all types of motorcycles), or the firm may opt for a very broad approach to the market (for example, any two-wheeled conveyance, with or without an engine, with or without a cover, usable for one or more passengers).

Marketing Management

The marketing manager, having analyzed the characteristics of the target market(s), is in a position to specify the mix of marketing variables that will best serve each target market. The variables the marketing manager controls are known as the elements of the marketing mix, or the four Ps: product, price, place, and promotion.[4] Each consists of a submix of variables, and policy decisions must be made on each.

Product policy is concerned with all the elements that make up the good, service, or idea that is offered by the marketer. Included are all possible tangible characteristics (such as the core product and packaging) and intangible characteristics (such as branding and warranties). Many products are a combination of a concrete product and the accompanying service; for example, in buying an Otis elevator, the purchaser buys not only the product but an extensive service contract as well.

Pricing policy determines the cost of the product to the customer—a point somewhere between the floor created by the costs to the firm and the ceiling created by the strength of demand. An important consideration of pricing policy is pricing within the channel of distribution; margins to be made by the middlemen who assist in the marketing effort must be taken into account. Discounts to middlemen include functional, quantity, seasonal, and cash discounts as well as promotional allowances. An important point to remember is that price is the only revenue-generating element of the marketing mix.

Distribution policy covers the place variable of the marketing mix and has two components: channel management and logistics management. Channel management is concerned with the entire process of setting up and operating the contractual organization, consisting of various types of middlemen (such as wholesalers, agents, retailers, and facilitators). Logistics management is focused on providing product availability at appropriate times and places in the marketing channel.[5] Place is the most long term of all the marketing mix elements; it is the most difficult to change in the short term.

Communications policy uses promotion tools to interact with customers, middlemen, and the public at large. The communications element consists of these tools: advertising, sales promotion, personal selling, and publicity. Because the purpose of all communications is to persuade, this is the most visible and sensitive of the marketing mix elements.

Blending the various elements into a coherent program requires trade-offs based on the type of product or service being offered (for example, detergents versus fighter aircraft), the stage of the product's life cycle (a new product versus one that is being revived), and resources available for the marketing effort (money and personnel) as well as the type of customer at whom the marketing efforts are directed.

THE MARKETING PROCESS

The actual process of marketing consists of four stages: analysis, planning, implementation, and control.

Analysis begins with collecting data on the eight Os and using various quantitative and qualitative techniques of marketing research. Data sources will vary from secondary to primary, internal to external (to the company), and informal to formal. The data are used to determine company opportunities by screening a plethora of environmental opportunities. The company opportunities must then be checked against the company's resources to judge their viability. The key criterion is competitive advantage.

Planning refers to the blueprint generated to react to and exploit the opportunities in the marketplace. The planning stage involves both long-term strategies and short-term tactics. A marketing plan developed for a particular market includes a situation analysis, objectives and goals to be met, strategies and tactics, and cost and profit estimates. Included in the activity is the formation of a new organizational structure or adjustments in the existing one to prepare for the execution of the plan.

Implementation is the actual carrying out of the planned activity. If the plans drawn reflect market conditions, and if they are based on realistic assessments of the company's fit into the market, the implementation process will be a success. Plans must take into account unforeseeable changes within the company and environmental forces and allow for corresponding changes to occur in implementing the plans.

For this reason, concurrently with implementation, **control** mechanisms must be put into effect. The marketplace is ever dynamic and requires the monitoring of environmental forces, competitors, channel participants, and customer receptiveness. Short-term control tools include annual plan control (such as comparing actual sales to quota), profitability control, and efficiency control. Long-term control is achieved through comprehensive or functional audits to make sure that marketing not only is doing things right but is doing the right things. The results of the control effort provide valuable input for subsequent planning efforts.

These marketing basics do not vary regardless of the type of market one is planning to enter or to continue operating within. They have been called the "technical universals" of marketing.[6] The different environments in which the marketing manager must operate will give varying emphases to the variables and will cause the values of the variables to change.

KEY TERMS

marketing	place	planning
product	promotion	implementation
price	analysis	control

ENDNOTES

1. American Marketing Association, "Definition of Marketing," www.marketingpower.com/Pages/default.aspx, accessed December 19, 2011.
2. Michael R. Czinkota and Massaki Kotabe, *Marketing Management*, 3rd ed. (Cincinnati: Atomic Dog Publishing, 2005), 4–5.
3. Philip Kotler presents the eight Os in the eighth edition of *Marketing Management: Analysis, Planning, and Control* (Englewood Cliffs, NJ: Prentice Hall, 1994), 174–75.
4. The four Ps were popularized originally by E. Jerome McCarthy. See William Perreault, Jr., Joseph Cannon, and E. Jerome McCarthy, *Basic Marketing*, 17th ed. (Burr Ridge, IL: Irwin/McGraw-Hill, 2009).
5. Bert Rosenbloom, *Marketing View*, 7th ed., custom (Mason, OH: Thomson Business & Professional Publishing, 2005).
6. Robert Bartels, "Are Domestic and International Marketing Dissimilar?" *Journal of Marketing* 36 (July 1968): 56–61.

APPENDIX B

Geographical Perspectives on International Marketing

The globalization of business has made geography indispensable for the study of international marketing. Without significant attention to the study of geography, critical ideas and information about the world in which business occurs will be missing.

Just as the study of business has changed significantly in recent decades, so has the study of geography. Once considered by many to be simply a descriptive inventory that filled in blank spots on maps, geography has emerged as an analytical approach that uses scientific methods to answer important questions.

Geography focuses on answering "Where?" questions. Where are things located? What is their distribution across the surface of the earth? An old aphorism holds, "If you can map it, it's geography." That statement is true because we use maps to gather, store, analyze, and present information that answers "Where?" questions. Identifying where things are located is only the first phase of geographic inquiry. Once locations have been determined, "Why?" and "How?" questions can be asked. Why are things located where they are? How do different things relate to one another at a specific place? How do different places relate to each other? How have geographic patterns and relationships changed over time? These are the questions that take geography beyond mere description and make it a powerful approach for analyzing and explaining geographical aspects of a wide range of different kinds of problems faced by those engaged in international marketing.

Geography answers questions related to the location of different kinds of economic activity and the transactions that flow across national boundaries. It provides insights into the natural and human factors that influence patterns of production and consumption in different parts of the world. It explains why patterns of trade and exchange evolve over time. And because a geographic perspective emphasizes the analysis of processes that result in different geographic patterns, it provides a means for assessing how patterns might change in the future.

Geography has a rich tradition. Classical Greeks, medieval Arabs, Enlightenment European explorers, and contemporary scholars in the United States and elsewhere have organized geographic knowledge in many different ways. In recent decades, however, geography has become more familiar and more relevant to many people because emphasis has been placed on five fundamental themes as ways to structure geographic questions and to provide answers for those questions. Those themes are (1) location, (2) place, (3) interaction, (4) movement, and (5) region. The five themes are neither exclusive nor exhaustive. They complement other disciplinary approaches for organizing information, some of which are better suited to addressing specific kinds of questions. Other questions require insights related to two or more of the themes. Experience has shown, however, that the five themes provide a powerful means for introducing students to the geographic perspective. As a result, they provide the structure for this discussion.

LOCATION

For decades, people engaged in real estate development have said that the value of a place is a product of three factors: location, location, and location. This statement also reflects the importance of location for international marketing. Learning the location and characteristics of

NOTE: This appendix was contributed by Thomas J. Baerwald. Dr. Baerwald is a senior science advisor and geography program director at the National Science Foundation in Arlington, Virginia. He is coauthor of *Prentice Hall World Geography* (2010)—a best-selling geography textbook.

other places has always been important to those interested in conducting business outside their local areas. The drive to learn about different areas, especially their resources and potential as markets, has stimulated geographic exploration throughout history. Explorations of the Mediterranean by the Phoenicians, Marco Polo's journey to China, and voyages undertaken by Christopher Columbus, Vasco da Gama, Henry Hudson, and James Cook not only improved general knowledge of the world but also expanded business opportunities.

Assessing the role of location requires more than simply determining specific locations where certain activities take place. Latitude and longitude often are used to fix the exact location of features on the earth's surface, but to simply describe a place's coordinates provides relatively little information about that place. Of much greater significance is its location relative to other features. The city of Singapore, for example, is between 1 and 2 degrees north latitude and is just west of 104 degrees east longitude. Other locational characteristics are far more important if you want to understand why Singapore has emerged as such an important locale for international business. Singapore is at the southern tip of the Malay Peninsula near the eastern end of the Strait of Malacca, a critical shipping route connecting the Indian Ocean with the South China Sea. For almost 150 years, this location made Singapore an important center for trade in the British Empire. After it attained independence in 1965, Singapore's leaders diversified its economy and complemented trade in its bustling port with numerous manufacturing plants that export products to nations around the world. Singapore quickly became one of the world's leading manufacturers of disk drives and other electronic components, using its pivotal location on global air routes to quickly ship these lightweight, high-value goods around the world. The same locational advantages have spurred its rise in recent decades as a business and financial-services center for eastern Asia.

An understanding of the way location influences business therefore is critical for the international marketing executive. Without clear knowledge of an enterprise's location relative to its suppliers, to its market, and to its competitors, an executive operates like the captain of a fogbound vessel that has lost all navigational instruments and is heading for dangerous shoals.

PLACE

In addition to its location, each place has a diverse set of characteristics. Although many of those characteristics are present in other places, the ensemble makes each place unique. The characteristics of places—both natural and human—profoundly influence the ways that business executives in different places participate in international economic transactions.

Natural Features

Many of the characteristics of a place relate to its natural attributes. Geologic characteristics can be especially important, as the presence of critical minerals or energy resources may make a place a world-renowned supplier of valuable products. Gold and diamonds help make South Africa's economy the most prosperous on that continent. Rich deposits of iron ore in southern parts of the Amazon Basin have made Brazil the world's leading exporter of that commodity, while Chile remains a preeminent exporter of copper. Coal deposits provided the foundation for massive industrial development in the eastern United States, in the Rhine River Basin of Europe, in western Russia, and in northeastern China. Because of abundant pools of petroleum beneath desert sands, standards of living in Saudi Arabia and nearby nations have risen rapidly to be among the highest in the world.

The geology of a place also shapes its terrain. People traditionally have clustered in lower, flatter areas because valleys and plains have permitted the agricultural development necessary to feed the local population

A Chilean mine extracting copper; one of the preeminent exporters of copper.

and to generate surpluses that can be traded. Hilly and mountainous areas may support some people, but their population densities are invariably lower. Terrain also plays a critical role in focusing and inhibiting the movement of people and goods. Business leaders throughout the centuries have capitalized on this fact. Just as feudal masters sought control of mountain passes in order to collect tolls and other duties from traders who traversed an area, modern executives maintain stores and offer services near bridges and at other points where terrain slows down travel.

The terrain of a place is related to its hydrology. Rivers, lakes, and other bodies of water influence the kinds of economic activities that occur in a place. In general, abundant supplies of water boost economic development because water is necessary for the sustenance of people and for both agricultural and industrial production. Locations like Los Angeles and Saudi Arabia have prospered despite having little local water because other features offer advantages that more than exceed the additional costs incurred in delivering water supplies from elsewhere. While sufficient water must be available to meet local needs, overabundance of water may pose serious problems, such as in Bangladesh, where development has been inhibited by frequent flooding.

The character of a place's water bodies also is important. Smooth-flowing streams and placid lakes can stimulate transportation within a place and connect it more easily with other places, while waterfalls and rapids can prevent navigation on streams. The rapid drop in elevation of such streams may boost their potential for hydroelectric power generation, however, thereby stimulating development of industries requiring considerable amounts of electricity. Large plants producing aluminum, for example, are found in the Tennessee and Columbia river valleys of the United States and in Quebec and British Columbia in Canada. These plants refine materials that originally were extracted elsewhere, especially bauxite and alumina from Caribbean nations like Jamaica and the Dominican Republic. Although the transport costs incurred in delivery of these materials to the plants is high, those costs are more than offset by the presence of abundant and inexpensive electricity.

Climate is another natural feature that has a profound impact on the economic activity within a place. Many activities are directly affected by climate. Locales blessed with pleasant climates have become popular recreational havens, attracting tourists whose spending fuels the local economy. Florida, the Côte d'Azur of France, the Crimean Peninsula of Ukraine, and the "Gold Coast" of northeastern Australia are just a few examples of popular tourist destinations whose primary attribute is a salubrious climate. Agricultural production is also influenced by climate. The average daily and evening temperatures, the amount and timing of precipitation, the timing of frosts and freezing weather, and the variability of weather from one year to the next all influence the kinds of crops grown in an area. Plants producing bananas and sugar cane flourish in moist tropical areas while cooler climates are more conducive for crops such as wheat and potatoes. Climate influences other industries as well. The aircraft manufacturing industry in the United States developed largely in warmer, drier areas, where conditions for test flights were more beneficial throughout the year. In a similar way, major rocket-launching facilities have been placed in locations where climatic conditions are most favorable. As a result, the primary launch site of the European Space Agency is not in Europe at all but rather in the South American territory of French Guiana. Climate also affects the length of the work day and the length of economic seasons. For example, in some regions of the world, the construction industry can build only during a few months of the year because permafrost makes construction prohibitively expensive the rest of the year. Construction demand can be spurred by climate-related disasters, however, as occurred following massive devastation along the central Gulf Coast in the southern United States.

Variations in soils have a profound impact on agricultural production. The world's great grain-exporting regions, including the central United States, the prairie provinces of Canada, the "Fertile Triangle" stretching from central Ukraine through southern Russia into northern Kazakhstan, and the Pampas of northern Argentina, all have been blessed with mineral-rich soils made even more fertile by humus from natural grasslands that once dominated the landscape. Soils are less fertile in much of the Amazon Basin of Brazil and in central Africa, where heavy rains leave few nutrients in upper layers of the soil. As a result, few commercial crops are grown.

The interplay between climate and soils is especially evident in the production of wines. Hundreds of varieties of grapes have been bred in order to take advantage of the different physical characteristics of various places. The wines fermented from these grapes are shipped around the world to consumers, who differentiate among various wines based not only on the grapes but also on the places where they were grown and the conditions during which they matured.

Human Features

The physical features of a place provide natural resources and influence the types of economic activities in which people engage, but its human characteristics also are critical. The population of a place is important because farm production may require intensive labor to be successful, as is true in rice-growing areas of eastern Asia. The skills and qualifications of the population also play a role in determining how a place fits into global economic affairs. Although blessed with few mineral resources and a terrain and climate that limit agricultural production, the Swiss have emphasized high levels of education and training in order to maintain a labor force that manufactures sophisticated products for export around the world. In recent decades, Japan and smaller nations such as South Korea and Taiwan have increased the productivity of their workers to become major industrial exporters.

As people live in a place, they modify it, creating a **built environment** that can be as important as or more important than the natural environment in economic terms. The most pronounced areas of human activity and their associated structures are in cities. In nations around the world, cities grew dramatically during the twentieth century. Much of the growth of cities has resulted from the migration of people from rural areas. This influx of new residents broadens the labor pool and creates vast new demand for goods and services. As urban populations have grown, residences and other facilities have replaced rural land uses. Executives seeking to conduct business in foreign cities need to be aware that the geographic patterns found in their home cities are not evident in many other nations. For example, in the United States, wealthier residents generally have moved out of cities, and as they established their residences, stores and services followed. Residential patterns in the major cities of Latin America and other developing nations tend to be reversed, with the wealthy remaining close to the city center while poorer residents are consigned to the outskirts of town. A store-location strategy that is successful in the United States therefore may fail miserably if transferred directly to another nation without knowledge of the different geographic patterns of that nation's cities.

INTERACTION

The international marketing professional seeking to take advantage of opportunities present in different places learns not to view each place separately. The way a place functions depends on the presence and form of certain characteristics as well as the interactions among them. Fortuitous combinations of features can spur a region's economic development. The presence of high-grade supplies of iron ore, coal, and limestone powered the growth of Germany's Ruhr Valley as one of Europe's foremost steel-producing regions, just as the proximity of the fertile Pampas and the deep channel of the Rio de la Plata combined to make Buenos Aires the leading economic center in southern South America.

Interactions among different features change over time within a place, and as they do, so do that place's character and economic activities. Human activities can have profound impacts on natural features. The courses of rivers and streams are altered as dams are erected and meanders are straightened. Soil fertility can be improved through fertilization. Vegetation is transformed, with naturally growing plants replaced by crops and other varieties that require careful management.

Many human modifications have been successful. For centuries, the Dutch have constructed dikes and drainage systems, slowly creating polders—land that once was covered by the North Sea but that now is used for agricultural production. But other human activities have had disastrous impacts on natural features. A large area in Ukraine and Belarus was rendered uninhabitable by radioactive materials leaked from the Chernobyl reactor in 1986. In countless other places around the globe, improper disposal of wastes has seriously harmed land and water resources. In some places, damage can be repaired, as has happened in rivers and lakes of the United States following the passage of measures to curb water pollution in the latter third of the twentieth century, but in other locales restoration may be impossible. At times, human activity can have counterproductive results for unforeseen reasons. In large parts of Bangladesh and the West Bengal state of India, arsenic concentrations in drinking water drawn from wells is far above acceptable levels, and increasing numbers of residents are exhibiting signs of arsenic poisoning. Ironically, the wells were drilled to provide a supposedly safer alternative to the highly polluted surface water on which residents previously relied.

Growing concerns about environmental quality have led many people in more economically advanced nations to call for changes in economic systems that harm the natural environment. Concerted efforts are under way, for example, to halt the destruction of forests in the Amazon Basin, thereby preserving the vast array of different plant and animal species in the region and saving vegetation that can help moderate the world's climate. Cooperative ventures have been established to promote selective harvesting of nuts, hardwoods, and other products taken from natural forests. Furthermore, an increasing number of restaurants and grocers are refusing to purchase beef raised on pastures that are established by clearing forests.

Market mechanisms have also been developed to try to facilitate environmentally friendly practices. Emissions trading has emerged as an administrative approach that can be instituted by a central unit to limit the overall level of pollution that is released in the area under that administrative unit's authority. The administrative unit can be a local government, state, nation, or even a set of nations. Based on historical patterns and other factors, maximum emission levels are established for subunits in the area. If some subunits expect to exceed the upper limits established for them, they can purchase credits from other subunits whose emissions are below their limits. This system provides incentives for subunits that have higher emissions levels to reduce their pollution in order to reduce costs, while other subunits may seek to reduce their emissions even more in order to reap income from the sale of additional credits. The system has been implemented across a range of geographic scales. The state of Illinois established an emissions reduction market system in the Chicago area in 2000 through which more than 100 major polluters trade credits in order to reduce the emission of volatile organic compounds. Starting in 2003, nine northeastern states in the United States sought to collectively limit carbon dioxide emissions. The European Union's 27 member nations instituted a greenhouse gas emission trading scheme in 2005 to limit overall emissions across Europe. Emissions trading is envisioned as a way to help the world's nations stabilize atmospheric greenhouse gas concentrations in accordance with the terms of the Kyoto Protocol, which was signed in 1997. This protocol called for reductions in the emission of carbon dioxide and five other greenhouse gases. The U.S. Senate in 1997 and U.S. administrations since 2001 objected to the Kyoto Protocol because it did not seek to limit emissions from all industrializing nations. Opponents of the Kyoto Protocol argue that this places an unfairly heavy economic burden on the United States, which emits about one-quarter of the world's greenhouse gases.

As with so many other geographical relationships, the nature of human–environmental interaction changes over time. With technological advances, people have been able to modify and adapt to natural features in increasingly sophisticated ways. The development of air conditioning has permitted people to function more effectively in torrid tropical environments, thereby enabling the populations of cities such as Houston, Rio de Janeiro, and Jakarta to multiply many times over in recent decades. Owners of winter resorts now can generate snow artificially to ensure favorable conditions for skiers. Advanced irrigation systems now permit crops to be grown in places such as the southwestern United States, northern Africa, and Israel. The use of new technologies may cause serious problems over the long run, however. Extensive irrigation in large parts of the U.S. Great Plains has seriously depleted groundwater supplies. In central Asia, the diversion of river water to irrigate cotton fields in Kazakhstan and Uzbekistan has reduced the size of the Aral Sea by more than one-half since 1960. In future years, business leaders may need to factor into their decisions the additional costs associated with the restoration of environmental quality after they have finished using a place's resources.

Other business leaders may have to deal with issues associated with the social, ecological, and ethical dimensions associated with genetically modified foods and organisms. These products are created by combining genes from different organisms in order to achieve certain desirable qualities. Researchers found that between 1996 and 2010, production of genetically altered crops increased by 87-fold. Other crops have been engineered to have greater nutritional value. The rapid growth in genetic modification of crops has led to concerns regarding potential introduction of new allergens, the unintended transfer of genes through cross-pollination, and potentially adverse impacts on other organisms. As a result, some nations have prohibited their own farmers from producing genetically modified crops as well as the importation of such products grown elsewhere. The need for accurate labeling of products so that consumers know what kinds of products they are buying will be an issue that international marketers will need to address in the future.

MOVEMENT

Whereas the theme of interaction encourages consideration of different characteristics within a place, movement provides a structure for considering how different places relate to each other. International marketing exists because movement permits the transportation of people and goods and communication of information and ideas among different places. No matter how much people in one place want something found elsewhere, they cannot have it unless transportation systems permit the good to be brought to them or allow them to move to the location of the good.

The location and character of transportation and communication systems long have had powerful influences on the economic standing of places. Especially significant have been places on which transportation routes have focused. Many ports evolved to be prosperous cities because they channeled the movement of goods and people between ocean and inland waterways. New York became the largest city in North America because its harbor provided sheltered anchorage for ships crossing the Atlantic and the Hudson River provided access leading into the interior of the continent. In eastern Asia, Hong Kong grew under similar circumstances as British traders used its splendid harbor as an exchange point for goods moving in and out of southern China.

Businesses also have succeeded at well-situated places along overland routes. The fabled oasis of Timbuktu has been an important trading center for centuries because it had one of the few dependable sources of water in the Sahara. Chicago's ascendancy as the premier city of the U.S. heartland came when its early leaders engineered its selection as the termination point for a dozen railroad lines converging from all directions. Not only did much of the rail traffic moving through the region have to pass through Chicago, but passengers and freight passing through the city had to be transferred from one line to another. This process generated numerous jobs and added considerably to the wealth of many businesses in the city.

In addition to the business associated directly with the movement of people and goods, other forms of economic activity have become concentrated at critical points in the transportation network. Places where transfers from one mode of transportation to another were required often were chosen as sites for manufacturing activities. Buffalo, New York, was the most active flour-milling center in the United States for much of the twentieth century because it was the point where Great

Lakes freighters carrying wheat from the northern Great Plains and Canadian prairies were unloaded. Rather than simply transfer the wheat into rail cars for shipment to the large urban markets of the northeastern United States, millers transformed the wheat into flour in Buffalo, thereby reducing the additional handling of the commodity.

Global patterns of resource refining also demonstrate the wisdom of careful selection of sites with respect to transportation systems. Some of the world's largest oil refineries are located at places like Bahrain and Houston, where pipelines bring oil to points where it is processed and loaded onto ships in the form of gasoline or other distillates for transport to other locales. Massive refinery complexes also have been built in the Tokyo and Nagoya areas of Japan and near Rotterdam in the Netherlands to process crude oil brought by giant tankers from the Middle East and other oil-exporting regions. For similar reasons, the largest new steel mills in the United States are near Baltimore and Philadelphia, where iron ore shipped from Canada and Brazil is processed. Some of the most active aluminum works in Europe are beside Norwegian fjords, where abundant local hydroelectric power is used to process imported alumina.

Favorable location along transportation lines is beneficial for a place. Conversely, an absence of good transportation severely limits the potential for firms to succeed in a specific place. Transportation patterns change over time, however, and so does their impact on places. Some places maintain themselves because their business leaders use their size and economic power to become critical nodes in newly evolving transportation networks. New York's experience provides a good example of this process. New York became the United States' foremost business center in the early nineteenth century because it was ideally situated for water transportation. As railroad networks evolved later in that century, they sought New York connections in order to serve its massive market. During the twentieth century, a complex web of roadways and major airports reinforced New York's supremacy in the eastern United States. In similar ways, London, Moscow, and Tokyo reasserted themselves as transportation hubs for their nations through successive advances in transport technology.

Failure to adapt to changing transportation patterns can have harmful impacts on a place. During the middle of the nineteenth century, business leaders in St. Louis discouraged railroad construction, seeking instead to maintain the supremacy of river transportation. Only after it became clear that railroads were the mode of preference did St. Louis officials seek to develop rail connections for the city, but by then it was too late; Chicago had ascended to a dominant position in the region. For about 30 years during the middle part of the twentieth century, airports at Gander (Newfoundland, Canada) and Shannon (Ireland) became important refueling points for transatlantic flights. The development of planes that could travel nonstop for much longer distances returned those places to sleepy oblivion.

Continuing advances in transportation technology have effectively "shrunk" the world. Just a few centuries ago, travel across an ocean took harrowing months. As late as 1873, readers marveled when Jules Verne wrote of a hectic journey around the world in 80 days. Today's travelers can fly around the globe in less than 80 hours, and the speed and dependability of modern modes of transport have transformed the ways in which business is conducted. Modern manufacturers have transformed the notion of relationships among suppliers, manufacturers, and markets. Automobile manufacturers, for example, once maintained large stockpiles of parts in assembly plants that were located near the parts plants or close to the places where the cars would be sold. Contemporary auto assembly plants now are built in places where labor costs and worker productivity are favorable and where governments have offered attractive inducements. They keep relatively few parts on hand, calling on suppliers for rapid delivery of parts as they are needed when orders for new cars are received. This "just-in-time" system of production leaves manufacturers subject to disruptions caused by work stoppages at supply plants and

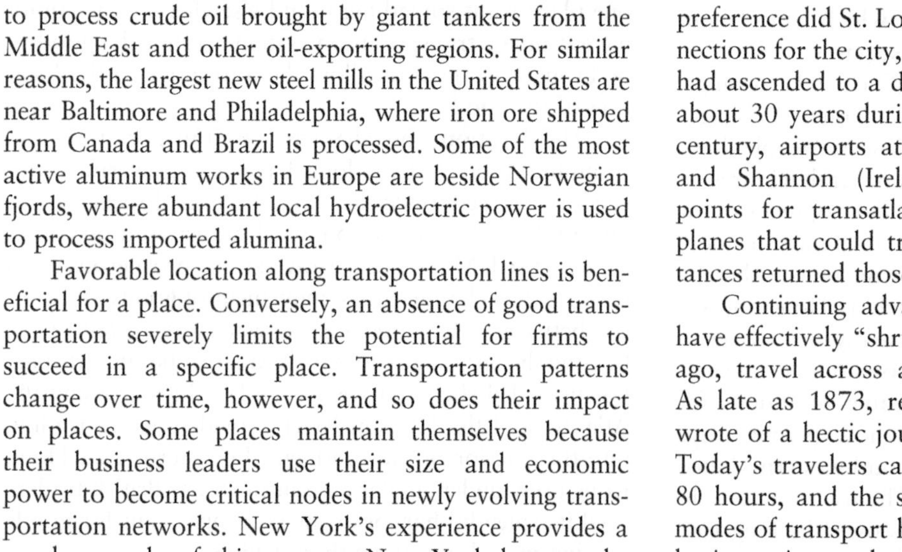

Location is important for key resources, like oil refinery plants.

to weather-related delays in the transportation system, but losses associated with these infrequent events are more than offset by reduced operating costs under normal conditions.

The role of advanced technology and its effect on international marketing are even more apparent with respect to advances in communications systems. Sophisticated forms of telecommunication that began more than 170 years ago with the telegraph have advanced through the telephone to facsimile transmissions and e-mail networks. As a result, distance has practically ceased to be a consideration with respect to the transmission of information. Whereas information once moved only as rapidly as the person carrying the paper on which the information was written, data and ideas now can be sent instantaneously almost anywhere in the world.

These communication advances have had a staggering impact on the way that international marketing is conducted. They have fostered the growth of multinational corporations, which operate in diverse sites around the globe while maintaining effective links with headquarters and regional control centers. International financial operations also have been transformed because of communication advances. Money and stock markets in New York, London, Tokyo, and Frankfurt now are connected by computer systems that process transactions around the clock. As much as any other factor, the increasing mobility of money has enabled modern business executives to engage in activities around the world.

REGION

In addition to considering places by themselves or how they relate to other places, regions provide alternative ways to organize groups of places in more meaningful ways. A region is a set of places that share certain characteristics. Many regions are defined by characteristics that all of the places in the group have in common. When economic characteristics are used, the delimited regions include places with similar kinds of economic activity. Agricultural regions include areas where certain farm products dominate. Corn is grown throughout the "Corn Belt" of the central United States, for example, although many farmers in the region also plant soybeans and many raise hogs. Regions where intensive industrial production is a prominent part of local economic activity include the manufacturing belts of the northeastern United States, southern Canada, northwestern Europe, and southern Japan.

Regions can also be defined by patterns of movement. Transportation or communication linkages among places may draw them together into configurations that differentiate them from other locales. Studies by economic geographers of the locational tendencies of modern high-technology industries have identified complex networks of firms that provide products and services to each other. Because of their linkages, these firms cluster together into well-defined regions. The "Silicon Valley" of northern California, the "Western Crescent" on the outskirts of London, and the "Technopolis" of the Tokyo region all are distinguished as much by connections among firms as by the economic landscapes they have established.

Economic aspects of movement may help define functional regions by establishing areas where certain types of economic activity are more profitable than others. In the early nineteenth century, German landowner Johann Heinrich von Thünen demonstrated how different costs for transporting various agricultural goods to market helped to define regions where certain forms of farming would occur. Although theoretically simple, patterns predicted by von Thünen can still be found in the world today. Goods such as vegetables and dairy products that require more intensive production and are more expensive to ship are produced closer to markets, while less demanding goods and commodities that can be transported at lower costs come from more remote production areas. Advances in transportation have dramatically altered such regional patterns. Once, a New York City native enjoyed fresh vegetables and fruits only in the summer and early autumn when New Jersey, upstate New York, and New England producers brought their goods to market. Today, New Yorkers buy fresh produce year-round, with new shipments flown in daily from Florida, California, Chile, Columbia, and even more remote locations during the colder months.

Governments have a strong impact on the conduct of business, and the formal borders of government jurisdictions often coincide with the functional boundaries of economic regions. The divisive character of these lines on the map has been altered in many parts of the world in recent decades. The formation of common markets and free trade areas in Western Europe, North America, and other parts of the world has dramatically changed the patterns and flows of economic activity, and similar kinds of formal restructuring of relationships among nations likely will continue into the next century. As a result, business analysts increasingly need to consider regions that cross international boundaries.

KEY TERMS

geologic characteristic
terrain
hydrology
climate
soil
population
built environment
Kyoto Protocol

CHAPTER 2

International Trade Frameworks and Policy

LEARNING OBJECTIVES

By the time you complete this chapter, you will be able to:

- Understand how trade has influenced human history.
- Comprehend the role of international institutions.
- Appreciate how governments influence and manage trade.

THE INTERNATIONAL MARKETPLACE 2.1

A Trade Negotiator's Glossary: What They Said and What They Really Meant

"An ambitious proposal"
(It is unlikely to get any support.)

"An innovative proposal"
(This one really is out of the trees.)

"This paper is unbalanced."
(It does not contain any of our views.)

"This proposal strikes a good balance."
(Our interests are completely safeguarded.)

"I should like to make some brief comments."
(You have time for a cup of coffee.)

"We will be making detailed comments at a later stage."
(Expect that your posting will be over before you hear from us.)

"This paper contains some interesting features."
(I am going to give you some face-saving reasons why it should be withdrawn.)

"The paper will provide useful background to our discussions."
(I haven't read it.)

"We need transparency in the process."
(I am worried that I won't be included in the back-room negotiations.)

"English is not my mother tongue."
(I am about to give you a lecture on a fine point of syntax.)

"The delegate of ... spoke eloquently on this subject."
(I haven't the faintest idea what he or she means.)

"A comprehensive paper"
(It's over two pages in length and seems to have an awful lot of headings.)

SOURCE: Anonymous.

The international environment is changing rapidly. Firms, individuals, and policymakers are affected by these changes. These changes not only offer new opportunities but also represent new challenges. Although major economic and security shifts will have a profound impact on the world, coping with them successfully through imagination, investment, and perseverance can produce a new, better world order and an improved quality of life.

This chapter begins by highlighting the importance of trade to humankind. Selected historical developments that were triggered or influenced by international trade are delineated. Subsequently, more recent trade developments are presented, together with the international institutions that have emerged to regulate and facilitate trade. As *The International Marketplace 2.1* shows, the attempts by nations to negotiate trade terms and regulate international trade can be tedious and bureaucracy-ridden.

The chapter will analyze and discuss the country positions in the world trade environment and explain the impact of trade. Various efforts undertaken by governments to manage trade by restricting or promoting exports, imports, technology transfer, and investments will be described. Finally, the chapter will present a strategic outlook for future developments in trade relations.

THE HISTORICAL DIMENSION

Many peoples throughout history have gained preeminence in the world through their trade activities. Among them were the Etruscans, Phoenicians, Egyptians, Chinese, Spaniards, and Portuguese. To underscore the role of trade, we will take a closer look at some selected examples.

One of the major world powers in ancient history was the Roman Empire. Its impact on thought, knowledge, and development can still be felt today. Even while expanding their territories through armed conflicts, the Romans placed primary emphasis on encouraging international business activities. The principal approaches used to implement this emphasis were the **Pax Romana**, or the Roman Peace, and the common coinage. The Pax Romana ensured that merchants were able to travel safely on roads that were built, maintained, and protected by the Roman legions and their affiliated troops. The common coinage, in turn, ensured that business transactions could be carried out easily throughout the empire. In addition, Rome developed a systematic law, central market locations through the founding of cities, and an excellent communication system that resembled an early version of the Pony Express; all of these measures contributed to the functioning of the international marketplace and to the reduction of business uncertainty. As a result, economic well-being within the empire rose sharply compared to the outside.

Soon, city-nations and tribes that were not part of the empire wanted to share in the benefits of belonging. They joined the empire as allies and agreed to pay tribute and taxes. Or, more distant eastern kingdoms would indulge Roman tastes for spices and luxury items through trading relationships. Indirect Roman trade networks extended across the Red Sea, the Arabian Gulf, and the Indian Ocean and through Arab and Indian merchants.[1] Thus, the immense growth of the Roman Empire occurred through the linkages of business rather than through the marching of its legions and warfare alone. Of course, the Romans had to engage in substantial efforts to facilitate business in order to make it worthwhile for others to belong. For example, when pirates threatened the seaways, Rome, under Pompeius, sent out a large fleet to subdue them. The cost of international distribution, and therefore the cost of international marketing, was substantially reduced because fewer goods were lost to pirates. As a result, goods could be made available at lower prices, which, in turn, translated into larger demand. Of course, only few things are new under the sun. As you can see in *The International Marketplace 2.2*, even today, pirates still threaten the seaways.

THE INTERNATIONAL MARKETPLACE 2.2

The Modern-Day Pirate

More than two millennia ago Pompeius, the Roman general and consul, needed to equip a fleet to subdue pirates that disrupted the shipping of goods. He did battle, hanged the enemy survivors, and thus disposed of the problem. In 2011, large-scale piracy has returned, with a major effect on shipping costs and practices. The International Maritime Organization (IMO) reported that significant numbers of pirate attacks had occurred in 2010 in East Africa, the Indian Ocean, the Arabian Sea, and the South China Sea as well as in West Africa, South America, and the Caribbean.

For 2010, the IMO reported that 1,027 ships' crew members were reported to have been taken hostage and 57 ships hijacked. The most attacks occurred in the Gulf of Aden, making it the most dangerous water to cross. The Gulf of Aden connects the Indian Ocean to the Red Sea, establishing it as a vital pathway for 22,000 ships per year. Over 4 percent of the world's oil supply is transported across the gulf. Somali pirates have changed how business is conducted there.

These pirates are equipped with some of the best weaponry and transportation, using speedboats with ladders, grappling hooks, grenades, and assault rifles. Despite the fact that 30 countries have sent resources to patrol the Gulf of Aden and the waters off the coast of Somalia, the pirates are very active and successful. Somali pirates received an estimated $238 million in ransom money in 2010 from individuals, corporations, or nations. Considering that most Somalis have little means for other income, piracy is an attractive business.

These Somali pirates are able to escape the most powerful navies in the world due to their weapons and their intimate knowledge of the environment. Companies simply pay the ransom money in order to avoid harm to their cargo and crew members. The use of alternate shipping routes would be extremely expensive. It would require that ships go around the Cape of Good Hope of South Africa, a route that is thousands of miles longer. According to Noel Choong, head of the International Maritime Bureau's piracy reporting center, running a ship costs $20,000 to $30,000 a day. However, progress is being made. In 2011, through the counterpiracy efforts of joint naval operations such as NATO's Operation Ocean Shield, naval warships have achieved growing success in preventing hijackings and freeing hostages. But until countries can fully secure the waters of the Gulf of Aden, and as long as ransom costs remain below the cost of rerouting ships, Somali pirates will continue to reap their profits.

U.S. Navy photo of a suspected pirate skiff being destroyed by missiles.

SOURCES: John Lyman, "Piracy in the Gulf of Aden: A Focused Approach," *Journal of Foreign Relations*, April 19, 2011; NATO, Operation Ocean Shield, www.manw.nato.int/page_operation_ocean_shield.aspx; "World's Navies Scramble to Curb Upturn in Piracy," *Washington Post*, September 11, 2008; "100 Hostages Held by Somali Pirates," *Washington Post*, September 27, 2008; and Operation Ocean Shield, Wikipedia, http://en.wikipedia.org/wiki/Operation_Ocean_Shield.

The fact that international business was one of the primary factors holding the Roman Empire together can also be seen in its decay. When "barbaric" tribes overran the empire, it was not mainly through war and prolonged battles that Rome lost ground. The outside tribes were actually attacking an empire that was already substantially weakened because it could no longer offer the benefits of affiliation. Former allies no longer saw any advantage in being associated with the Romans and willingly cooperated with the invaders rather than face prolonged battles.

In a similar fashion, one could interpret the evolution of European feudalism to be a function of trade and marketing. Because farmers were frequently deprived of their harvests as a result of incursions by other (foreign) tribes or even individuals, they decided to band together and provide for their own protection. By delivering a certain portion of their "earnings" to a protector, they could be assured of retaining most of their gains. Although this system initially worked quite well in reducing the cost of production and the cost of marketing, it did ultimately result in the emergence of the feudal system, which, perhaps, was not what the initiators had intended it to be.

Interestingly, the feudal system encouraged the development of a closed-state economy that was inwardly focused and ultimately conceived for self-sufficiency and security. However, medieval commerce still thrived and developed through export trade. In Italy, the Low Countries, and the German Hanse towns, the impetus for commerce was provided by East–West trade. Among the greatest international businesses in this period were the spice merchants who supplied highly priced spices to meet the seemingly insatiable demands of the medieval European palate and medical self-help prescriptions of the time. The spice trade brought pepper and cinnamon from India and Sri Lanka and nutmeg, mace, and cloves from the then-mysterious Spice Islands, the Moluccas in today's Indonesia, through Muslim merchants in Alexandria and Baghdad to Venetian traders in the Mediterranean.[2] Profits from the spice trade through the Middle East created the wealth of Venice and other Mediterranean ports. Europe also imported rice, oranges, dyes, cotton, and silk. Western European merchants in turn exported timber, arms, and woolen clothing in exchange for these luxury goods. A remaining legacy of this trade is found in the many English and French words of Arabic origin, such as *divan*, *bazaar*, *artichoke*, *orange*, *jar*, and *tariff*.[3]

The importance of trade has not always persisted, however. For example, in 1896, the Empress Dowager Tz'u-hsi, in order to finance the renovation of the summer palace, impounded government funds that had been designated for Chinese shipping and its navy. As a result, China's participation in world trade almost came to a halt. In the subsequent decades, China operated in almost total isolation, without any transfer of knowledge from the outside, without major inflow of goods, and without the innovation and productivity increases that result from exposure to international trade.

The effect of turning away from international trade was highlighted during the 1930s. The Smoot-Hawley Act raised duties to reduce the volume of imports into the United States in the hopes that this would restore domestic employment. The result, however, was an increase of duties and other barriers to imports by most other trading nations as well. These measures were contributing factors in the subsequent worldwide depression and the collapse of the world financial system, which in turn set the scene for World War II.

International marketing and international trade have also long been seen as valuable tools for foreign policy purposes. The use of economic coercion—for example, by nations or groups of nations—can be traced back as far as the time of the Greek city-states and the Peloponnesian War or, in more recent times, to the Napoleonic wars. Combatants used blockades to achieve their goal of "bringing about commercial ruin and shortage of food by dislocating trade."[4] Similarly, during the Civil War in the United States, the North consistently pursued a strategy of denying international trade opportunities to the South and thus deprived it of export revenue needed to import necessary products. In the 1990s, the Iraqi invasion of Kuwait resulted in a trade embargo of Iraq by the United Nations with the goal of reversing the aggression. Following government suppression of civil protests in Uzbekistan, the European Union imposed a series of sanctions against the country. These included travel bans for top Uzbek officials and a ban on the sale or transfer to Uzbekistan of arms, military equipment, or any other equipment that might be used for internal repression.[5] Although such deprivations of trade do not often bring about policy change, they can have a profound impact on the standard of living of a nation's citizens.

Global Division

After 1945, the world was sharply split ideologically into West and East, a division that had major implications for trade relations. The Soviet Union, as the leader of the Eastern bloc, developed the Council for Mutual Economic Assistance (CMEA or COMECON), which focused on developing strong linkages among the members of the Soviet bloc and discouraged relations with the West. The United States, in turn, was the leading proponent of creating a "Pax Americana," or American peace, for the Western world, driven by the belief that international trade was a key to worldwide prosperity. Many months of international negotiations in London, Geneva, and Lake Success (New York) culminated on March 24, 1948, in Havana, Cuba, with the signing of the charter for an International Trade Organization (ITO).

This charter, a series of agreements among 53 countries, was designed to cover international commercial policies, domestic business practices, commodity agreements, employment and reconstruction, economic development and international investment, and a constitution for a new United Nations agency to administer the whole. In addition, a General Agreement on Tariffs and Trade (GATT) was initiated, with the purpose of reducing tariffs among countries, and international institutions such as the World Bank and the International Monetary Fund were created.

Even though the ITO incorporated many farsighted notions, most nations refused to ratify it, fearing its power, its bureaucratic size, and its threat to national sovereignty. As a result, the most forward-looking approach to international trade never came about. However, other organizations conceived at the time are still in existence and have made major contributions toward improving international trade.

TRANSNATIONAL INSTITUTIONS AFFECTING WORLD TRADE

World Trade Organization

The World Trade Organization (WTO) has its origins in the GATT, to which it became the successor organization in January of 1995. In order to better understand the emergence of the WTO, a brief review of the GATT is appropriate. GATT has been called "a remarkable success story of a postwar international organization that was never intended to become one."[6] It began in 1947 as a set of rules for nondiscrimination, transparent procedures, and settlement of disputes in international trade. One of the most important tools is the most-favored nation (MFN) clause, which calls for each member country of the GATT to grant every other member country the most favorable treatment it accords to any other country with respect to imports and exports. In effect, MFN is the equal opportunity clause of international trade. Over time, the GATT evolved into an institution that sponsored successive rounds of international trade negotiations with a key focus on a reduction of prevailing high tariffs.

Early in its existence, the GATT achieved the liberalization of trade in 50,000 products, amounting to two-thirds of the value of the trade among its participants. In subsequent years, special GATT negotiations such as the Kennedy Round and the Tokyo Round further reduced trade barriers and developed improved dispute-settlement mechanisms, better provisions dealing with subsidies, and a more explicit definition of rules for import controls.

In spite of, or perhaps because of, these impressive gains, GATT became less effective over time. Duties had already been drastically reduced—for example, the average U.S. tariff rate fell from 26 percent in 1946 to an average of 1.3 percent by 2010.[7] Further reductions are therefore unlikely to have a major impact on world trade. Most imports either enter the United States duty free or are subject to low tariffs. The highest tariffs apply mainly to imports of dairy products and tobacco and beverage products, as well as clothing, sugars and confectionary. In these industries, tariffs tend to increase with the degree of processing.[8]

Many nations developed new tools for managing and distorting trade flows, nontariff tools that were not covered under GATT rules. Examples are "voluntary agreements" to restrain trade, bilateral or multilateral special trade agreements such as the multifiber accord that restricted trade in textiles and apparel, and other nontariff barriers. Also, the GATT, which was founded by 24 like-minded governments, was designed to operate by consensus. As membership grew, this consensus rule often led to a stalemate of many GATT activities.

After many years of often contentious negotiations, the Uruguay Round accord was finally ratified in January of 1995. As part of this ratification, a new institution, the World Trade Organization, was created, which now is the umbrella organization responsible for overseeing the implementation of all the multilateral agreements negotiated in the Uruguay Round and those that will be negotiated in the future.[9] The GATT has ceased to exist as a separate institution and has become part of the WTO, which also is responsible for the General Agreement on Trade in Services (GATS), Agreements on Trade-Related Aspects of Intellectual Property Rights (TRIPS), and Trade-Related Investment Measures (TRIMS) and administers a broad variety of international trade and investment accords. As of August 2011, the WTO had 153 members, with Vanuatu, Samoa, and Russia awaiting membership, as can be seen in *The International Marketplace 2.3*.

The creation of the WTO has greatly broadened the scope of international trade agreements. Many of the areas left uncovered by the GATT, such as services and agriculture, are now addressed at least to some degree by international rules, speedier dispute-settlement procedures have been developed, and the decision-making process has been streamlined. Even though the WTO will attempt to continue to make decisions based on consensus, provisions are now made for decisions to be made by majority vote if such consensus cannot be achieved.

The WTO makes major contributions to improve trade and investment flows around the world. However, a successful WTO may well infringe on the sovereignty of nations. For example, more streamlined dispute settlements mean that decisions are made more quickly and that nations in violation of international trade rules are confronted more often. Negative WTO decisions affecting large trading nations are likely to be received with resentment. Some governments intend to broaden the mandate of the WTO to also deal with social causes and issues such as labor laws, competition, and emigration freedoms. As many nations fear that social causes can be used to devise new rules of protectionism against their exports, the addition of such issues may become a key reason for divisiveness and dissent within the WTO.[10] Outside groups such as nongovernmental organizations and special interest alliances believe that international trade and the WTO represent a threat to their causes.

THE INTERNATIONAL MARKETPLACE 2.3

The WTO's Missing Member

Membership in the WTO is now considered a requirement for any market economy. In 2011, the WTO was set to expand to 155 member nations with the planned accession of Vanuatu and Samoa. While international trade, particularly in tourism and coconut derivatives, is vital to the economies of these two countries, their prospective membership in the WTO is not attracting much international attention compared to the next country in line for membership—Russia.

Russia, the 11th largest economy in the world with 2011 GDP approaching $1.5 trillion, is the most important country in the world that had not yet joined the WTO by 2011. After 17 years of negotiation, Russia's membership is being viewed as likely in the near future. Russia has essentially agreed to consolidate the tariff cuts it has agreed to in multiple bilateral negotiations with some 50 nations and to harmonize its laws related to market access with WTO requirements.

Russian accession had been subject to a number of obstacles with WTO members, including the European Union, the United States, and Georgia among others. In 2010, Russia and the EU reached agreements that set the terms for resolving key issues, including pricing policies for lumber exports, railway fees, and aircraft flyover rights in Siberia. With the United States, several thorny issues remained. These included U.S. concerns over human rights and Russia's commitment to the rule of law, as well as trade issues such as investment restrictions, intellectual property rights protection, and food safety standards. Russia expects the U.S. Congress to revoke the Jackson-Vanik amendment, which imposed tariffs and trade penalties on Russia in 1975 to penalize the country for its restrictive emigration policies, long since removed.

Perhaps the biggest obstacle to Russian accession is its neighbor country Georgia. Since the two nations fought a war in 2008, Russian troops still occupy the Georgian territories of Abkhazia and South Ossetia and Russia imposes its own customs administration in these areas. Since any one WTO member state can veto a new membership, Georgia is in a position of power. This situation shows that there are always unintended consequences to war.

Russia's bid to join the WTO.

SOURCES: CIA World Factbook, www.cia.gov/library/publications/the-world-factbook; World Trade Organization, www.wto.org/english/thewto_e/acc_e/a1_russie_e.htm; Jennifer M. Freedman, "Russia Moves Closer to WTO Membership with EU Deal," *Bloomberg Businessweek*, December 7, 2010; Josh Rogin, "Foreign Policy," *The Cable*, October 29, 2010; and Doug Palmer, "Obama Wants Russia Trade Vote before WTO Deal: Trade Official," Reuters, June 22, 2011.

In 2001, a new round of international trade negotiations was initiated. Because the agreement to do so was reached in the city of Doha (Qatar), the negotiations are now called the "Doha Round." The aim was to further hasten implementation of liberalization, particularly to help impoverished and developing nations. In addition, the goal was to expand the role of the WTO to encompass more of the trade activities in which there were insufficient rules for their definition and structure. This was due to either purposeful exclusion of governments in earlier negotiations or new technology changing the global marketplace. Examples include trade in agricultural goods, antidumping regulations, and electronic commerce.

The negotiations have been largely marked by disagreement between developed and developing economies. The most divisive issues continue to be agricultural tariffs and subsidies in the EU and the United States, and tariffs on merchandise goods in developing countries. While there were many attempts at compromise, the parties continue to struggle to find a path forward for agreement. After 11 years of ongoing meetings, concessions, and dissent, the negotiations still are not set to conclude.[11]

Unless trade advocates and the WTO are supported by their member governments and other outside stakeholders in trade issues, there is unlikely to be major progress on further liberalization of trade and investment. It will therefore be important to have the WTO focus on its core mission, which is the facilitation of international trade and investment, while ensuring that an effective forum exists to afford a hearing and subsequent achievements for concerns surrounding the core.

International Monetary Fund

The International Monetary Fund (IMF), conceived in 1944 at Bretton Woods in New Hampshire, was designed to provide stability for the international monetary framework. It obtained funding from its members, who subscribed to a quota based on expected trade patterns and paid 25 percent of the quota in gold or dollars and the rest in their local currencies. These funds were to be used to provide countries with protection against temporary fluctuations in the value of their currency. Therefore, it was the original goal of the IMF to provide for fixed exchange rates between countries.

The perhaps not so unintended result of using the U.S. dollar as the main world currency was a glut of dollar supplies in the 1960s. This forced the United States to abandon the gold standard and devalue the dollar and resulted in flexible or floating exchange rates in 1971. However, even though this major change occurred, the IMF as an institution has clearly contributed toward providing international liquidity and toward facilitating international trade.

Over time, the IMF system has experienced substantial pressures. In the 1980s, some of this pressure was triggered by the substantial debts incurred by less-developed countries as a result of overextended development credits and changes in the cost of energy. In the 1990s, major additional pressure resulted from the financial requirements of the former socialist countries searching for funds to improve their economies. Twelve former Soviet republics joined the IMF. Major currency fluctuations among old customers have also stretched the resources of the IMF.

In 2005, the IMF agreed to write off $3.3 billion of debt owed to it by virtually all of the world's 20 poorest nations.[12] In 2008, the IMF needed to take on entirely new activities designed to stabilize the global financial system and to develop a global economic stimulus. In light of the worldwide slowdown of economies and the financial crisis, the IMF needed to go beyond its traditional customers of emerging markets and developing economies. Even already accomplished market economies, such as Iceland, Ireland, and Greece, required financial help. In order to ensure that a local stimulus would not be suffocated by global restrictions, the IMF worked to ensure simultaneous expansions in economies. The overall goal of new short-term lending facilities changed to rapid establishment of liquidity and the development of new trust in order to extinguish the crisis of confidence.[13] In her opening press conference in her role as the new managing director of the IMF in 2011, Christine Lagarde identified the two most pressing issues for the IMF. First were the sovereign debt issues facing euro-zone countries and others. The second area of concern was the issue of massive capital flows to emerging economies as investors were seeking higher rates of return than were available in the developed economies.[14]

As a result of all these global financial needs, the future role of the IMF may be very different. If the institution can mobilize its members to provide the financial means for an active role, its past accomplishments may pale in view of the new opportunities and requirements. At the same time, however, the new orientation will also require a rethinking of the rules under which the IMF operates. For example, it is quite unclear whether stringent economic rules and performance measures are equally applicable to all countries seeking IMF assistance. New economic conditions that have not been experienced to date may require different types of approaches. Also, perhaps the link between economic and political stability will magnify but also change the mission of the IMF.

World Bank

The World Bank's official name is the International Bank for Reconstruction and Development. It was formed in 1944 to aid countries suffering from the destruction of war. After completing this process most successfully, it has since taken on the task of aiding world development. With new nations emerging from the colonial fold of the world powers of the early twentieth century, the bank has made major efforts to assist fledgling economies to participate in a modern economic trade framework. More recently, the bank has begun to participate actively with the IMF to resolve the debt problems of the developing world and to bring a market economy to the former members of the Eastern bloc.

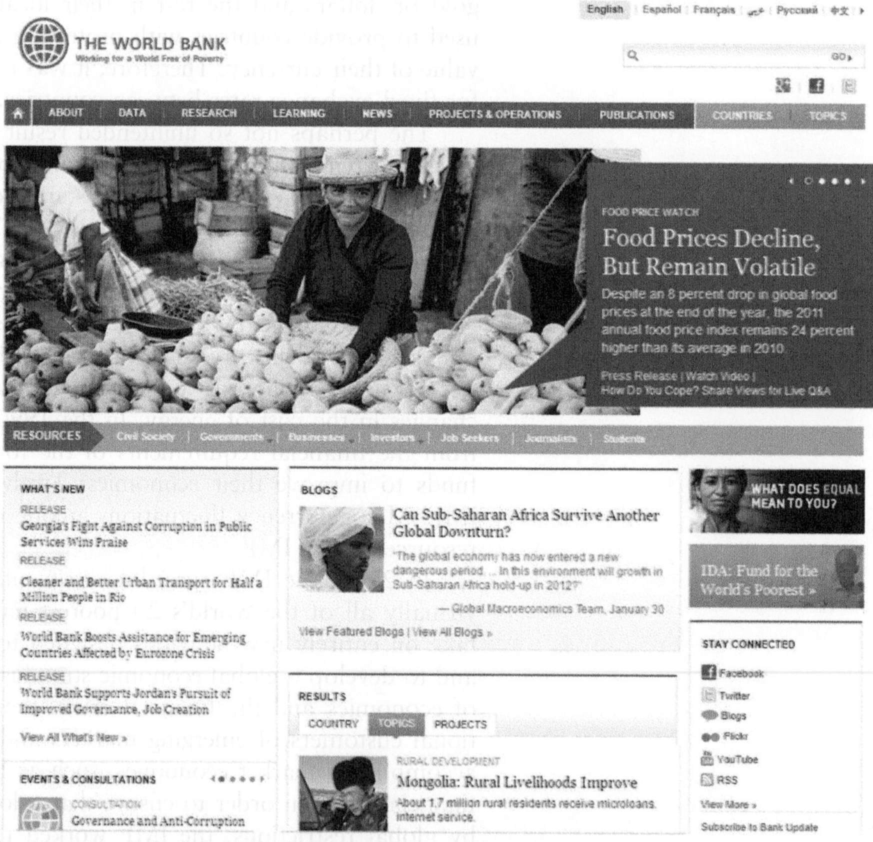

© The World Bank

One key task of the World Bank is to reduce world poverty.

Major debates surround the effectiveness of the bank's expenditures. In the 1970s and 1980s, funds were invested into infrastructure projects in developing countries based on the expectation that such investment would rapidly propel the economies of these nations forward. However, in retrospect, it appears that many of these funds were squandered by corrupt regimes and that many large projects have turned into white elephants—producing little in terms of economic progress. In addition, some projects have had major negative side effects for the recipient nations. For example, the highway through the rainforest in Brazil has mainly resulted in the migration of people to the area and is upsetting a very fragile ecological balance.

The World Bank tries now to reorient its outlook, focusing more on capacity building and the development of human capital through investments into education and health. Key performance criteria are now the sustainability of growth and development, addressing higher commodity prices, agricultural assistance in times of higher food prices, opening world trade to all countries, and greater participation of rising economic powers and developing nations in the bank's governance.[15] As it approaches its major challenge of reducing global poverty, the World Bank "delivers technical, financial and other assistance to those most in need and where it can have the greatest impact and promote growth: to the poorest countries, fragile states, and the Arab World; to middle-income countries; to solving global public goods issues; and to delivering knowledge and learning services."[16]

Regional Institutions

The WTO, IMF, and World Bank operate on a global level. Regional changes have also taken place based on the notion that trade between countries needs to be encouraged. Of particular importance was the formation of **economic blocs** that integrated the economic and political activities of nations.

The concept of regional integration was used more than 170 years ago when Germany developed the Zollverein to remove internal customs barriers. Its modern-day development began in 1952 with the establishment of the European Coal and Steel Community, which was designed to create a common market among six countries in coal, steel, and iron. Gradually, these nations developed a customs union and created common external tariffs. The ultimate goal envisioned was the completely free movement of capital, services, and people across national borders and the joint development of common international policies. Over time, the goals have been largely attained. The European Union (EU) now represents a formidable market size internally and market power externally, and the well-being of all EU members has increased substantially since the bloc's formation.

Similar market agreements have been formed by other groups of nations. Examples are the North American Free Trade Agreement (NAFTA), the MERCOSUR in Latin America, and the Gulf Cooperation Council (GCC). These unions were formed for different reasons and operate with different degrees of cohesiveness as appropriate for the specific environment. They focus on issues such as forming a customs union, a common market, an economic union, or a political union.

Simultaneous with these economic bloc formations, the private sector has begun to develop international trade institutions of its own. Particularly when governments are not quick enough to address major issues of concern to global marketers, business has taken the lead by providing a forum for the discussion of such issues. One example is the Transatlantic Business Dialogue (TBD), which is a nongovernmental organization composed of business leaders from Europe and the United States. Recognizing the inefficiency of competing and often contradictory standards and lengthy testing procedures, this group is working to achieve mutual recognition agreements on an industry basis. The executives of leading international firms that participate in this organization attempt to simplify global marketing by searching for ways to align international standards and regulations.

The activities of all these institutions demonstrate that the joining of forces internationally permits better, more successful international marketing activities, results in an improved standard of living, and provides an effective counterbalance to large economic blocs. Just as in politics, trade has refuted the old postulate of "the strong is most powerful alone." Nations have come to recognize that trade activities are of substantial importance to their economic well-being. Over the long term, the export activities of a nation are the key to the inflow of imports and therefore to the provision of choice, competition, and new insights. In the medium and long run, the balance of payments has to be maintained. In the short run, "an external deficit can be financed by drawing down previously accumulated assets or by accumulating debts to other countries. In time, however, an adjustment process must set in to eliminate the deficit."[17]

The urgency of the adjustment will vary according to the country in question. Some countries find it very hard to obtain acceptance for an increasing number of IOUs. Others, like the United States, can run deficits of trillions of dollars and are still a preferred borrower because of political stability, perceived economic security, and the worldwide use of the U.S. dollar as a reserve and business reference currency. Such temporary advantages can change, of course. Before the rise of the dollar, the British pound was the reserve currency of choice for many years.

TRADE POSITIONS COMPARED

Over the years, international trade positions have changed substantially when measured in terms of world market share. For example, in the 1950s, U.S. exports composed 25 percent of total world exports. Since then, this share has declined precipitously. It is not that U.S. exports have actually dropped during that time. The history of the U.S. success in world market share began with the fact that the U.S. economy was not destroyed by the war. Because other countries had little to export and a great need for imports, the U.S. export position was powerful. Over time, however, as other trade partners entered the picture and aggressively obtained a larger world market share for themselves, U.S. export growth was not able to keep pace with total world export growth. Exhibit 2.1 shows the world share of exports and imports of various trading countries and regions. Notable is the degree to which U.S. imports exceed exports.

Another important development is the rise of China's trade position. In just one decade, China increased its trade in merchandise more than four times. China now runs a trade surplus with the world's three major economic centers: the United States, the European Union, and Japan. China also replaced Mexico as the U.S. second most important trading partner and is now the third largest market for U.S. exports.[18]

Exhibit 2.2 highlights the dramatic rise of China. In 1990, China's share of world exports was approximately 2 percent, but by 2010, China's share exceeded 10 percent. In 2010, China was the number one trading partner of six of the G20 nations and the number two partner of five other G20 countries.[19]

A Diagnosis of the U.S. Trade Position

The developments just enumerated foster the question: why did these shifts occur? We should not attribute changes in U.S. trade performance merely to temporary factors such as the value of the dollar, the subsidization of exports from abroad, or the price of oil. We need to search further to determine the root causes for the decline in U.S. international competitiveness.

EXHIBIT 2.1 Merchandise Exports and Imports as a Percentage of World Trade, 2008–2011

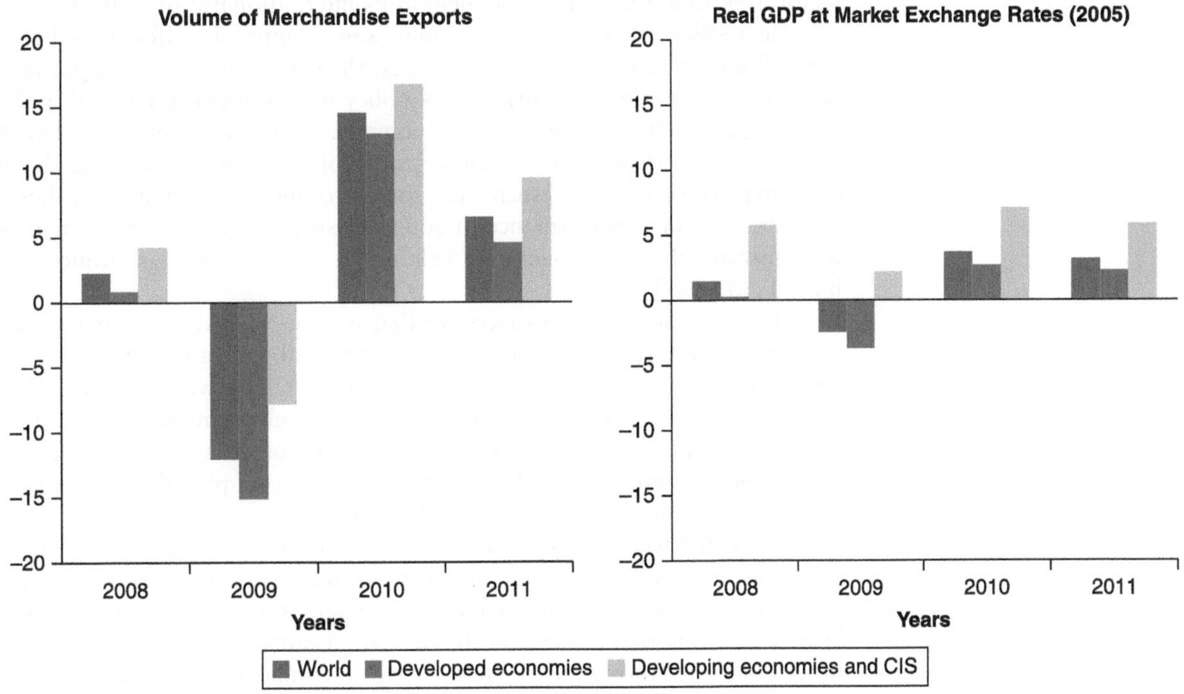

SOURCE: World Trade Organization, Country Trade Profiles, www.wto.org.

EXHIBIT 2.2 The China Factor

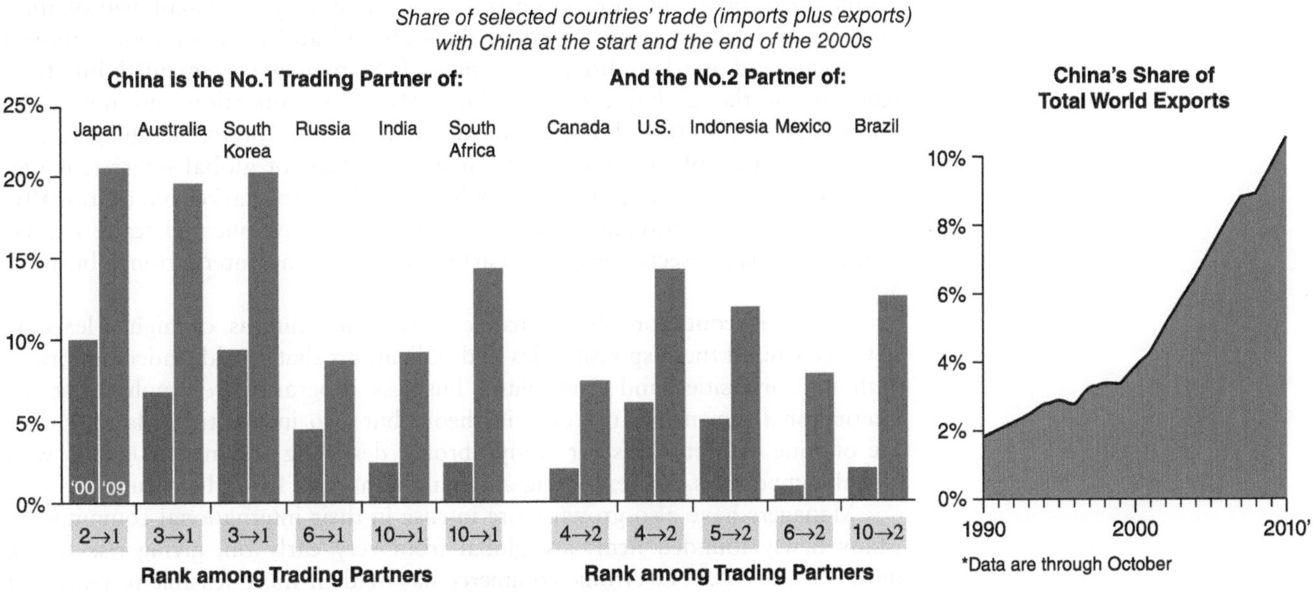

SOURCE: International Monetary Fund Direction of Trade Statistics via Karim Foda at Brookings Institution.

Since World War II, it has been ingrained in the minds of American policymakers that the United States is the leading country in world power and world trade. Together with this opinion came the feeling that the United States should assist other countries with their trade performance because without American help they would never be able to play a meaningful role in the world economy.

At the same time, there was admiration for "Yankee ingenuity"—the idea that U.S. firms were the most aggressive in the world. Therefore, the U.S. private sector appeared not to need any help in its international trade efforts.

The result of this overall philosophy was a continuing effort to aid countries abroad in their economic development. At the same time, no particular attention was paid to U.S. domestic firms. This policy was well conceived and well intentioned and resulted in spectacular successes. Books written in the late 1940s describe the overwhelming economic power of the United States and the apparently impossible task of resurrecting foreign economies. Comparing those texts with the economic performance of countries such as Japan and Germany today demonstrates that the policies of helping to stimulate foreign economies were indeed crowned by success.

These policies were so successful that no one wished to tamper with them. The United States continued to encourage trade abroad and not to aid domestic firms throughout the 1990s. Although the policies were well conceived, the environment to which they were applied was changing. In the 1950s and early 1960s, the United States successfully encouraged other nations again to become full partners in world trade. However, U.S. firms were placed at a distinct disadvantage when these policies continued for too long.

U.S. firms were assured that "because of its size and the diversity of its resources, the American economy can satisfy consumer wants and national needs with a minimum of reliance on foreign trade."[20] The availability of a large U.S. domestic market and the relative distance to foreign markets resulted in U.S. manufacturers simply not feeling a compelling need to seek business beyond national borders. Subsequently, the perception emerged within the private sector that exporting and international marketing were too risky, complicated, and not worth it.

This perception also resulted in increasing gaps in international marketing knowledge between managers in the United States and those abroad. Whereas business executives in most countries were forced, by the small size of their markets, to look very quickly to markets abroad and to learn about cultural sensitivity and market differences, most U.S. managers remained blissfully ignorant of the global economy. Similarly, U.S. education did not make knowledge about the global business environment, foreign languages, and cultures an area of major priority. Given such lack of global interest, inadequacy of information, ignorance of where and how to market internationally, unfamiliarity with foreign market conditions, and complicated trade regulations, the private sector became fearful of conducting international business activities.

However, conditions have changed. Most institutions of higher learning have recognized the responsibilities and obligations that world leadership brings with it. Universities and particularly business programs are emphasizing the international dimension, not only in theory but also in practice. Many schools are offering opportunities for study abroad, designing summer programs with global components, and expecting a global orientation from their students.

Managers have also grown more intense in their international commitment. Many newly founded firms are global from very early on, giving rise to the term **born global**.[21] Electronic commerce has made it more feasible to reach out to the global business community, whether the firm be large or small. The U.S. Department of State offers training in business–government relations to new ambassadors and instructs them to pay close attention to the needs of the U.S. business community.

In effect, the interest given to international markets as both an opportunity for finding customers and sources of supply is growing. As a result, the need for international marketing expertise can be expected to rise substantially as well.

THE IMPACT OF TRADE AND INVESTMENT

The Effect of Trade

Exports are important, in a macroeconomic sense, in terms of balancing the trade account. Exports are special because they can affect currency values and the fiscal and monetary policies of governments, shape public perception of competitiveness, and determine the level of imports a country can afford. The steady erosion of the U.S. share of total world exports has had more than purely optical repercussions. It has also resulted in a merchandise **trade deficit**, which has been continuous since 1975. By 1987, the United States posted a then-record trade deficit with imports of products exceeding exports by more than $171 billion. Due to increases in exports, the merchandise trade deficit declined in the following years, only to climb again to record heights in 2010 by reaching $635 billion.[22] Detailed updates of U.S. trade statistics can be seen at the U.S. International Trade Administration website (www.trade.gov). Such large trade deficits are unsustainable in the longer run.[23]

These trade deficits have a major impact on the United States and its citizens. They indicate that a country, in its international activities, is consuming more than it is producing. One key way to reduce trade deficits is to increase exports. Such an approach is highly beneficial for various reasons.

Exports can be instrumental in creating jobs. For example, in the United States, export-related employment is 39.5 percent in the domestic computer and electronics industry and 34 percent in the leather industry.[24] One billion dollars worth of exports supported, in 2001, on average the creation of 11,500 jobs.[25] By 2011 this number of jobs created had declined to 5,000 per billion of exports, largely due to greater efficiency and automation.[26]

Equally important, through exporting firms can achieve **economies of scale**. By broadening its market reach and serving customers abroad, a firm can produce more and do so more efficiently. As a result, the firm may achieve lower costs and higher profits both at home and abroad. Through exporting, the firm also benefits from market diversification. It can take advantage of different growth rates in different markets and gain stability by not being overly dependent on any particular market. Exporting also lets the firm learn from the competition, makes it sensitive to different demand structures and cultural dimensions, and proves its ability to survive in a less-familiar environment in spite of higher transaction costs. All these lessons can make the firm a stronger competitor at home.[27]

On the import side, firms become exposed to new competition, which may offer new approaches, better processes, or better products and services. In order to maintain their market share, firms are forced to compete more effectively by improving their own products and activities. Consumers in turn receive more choices when it comes to their selection. The competitive pressures exerted by imports also work to keep quality high and prices low.

The Effect of International Investment

International marketing activities consist not only of trade but also of a spectrum of involvement, much of which results in international direct investment activities. Such investment activities can be crucial to a firm's success in new and growing markets.

For decades, the United States was the leading foreign direct investor in the world. U.S. multinationals and subsidiaries sprouted everywhere. Today, however, international firms from many countries increasingly invest around the world.

Foreign direct investment is extensive in many U.S. industries. Almost one of every seven U.S. manufacturing employees works for a **foreign affiliate**, a U.S. firm in which at least 10 percent is owned by foreign entities. However, the foreign ownership is not equally distributed across all industries. Foreign direct investment tends to be concentrated in specific sectors where the foreign investors believe they are able to contribute the best and benefit the most from their investment.

Overall, foreign affiliates account for more than 5.6 million jobs in the United States.[28] Between 2003 and February 2011, over 7,500 new "greenfield" investment projects, which are entirely new projects, were announced or opened.[29] As a result of foreign investment, some individuals and policymakers may grow concerned about dependency on foreign owners, even though firm proof for the validity of such concern has been difficult to establish.

To some extent, these foreign direct investments substitute for trade activities. As a result, firms operating only in the domestic market may be surprised by the onslaught of foreign competition and, unprepared to respond quickly, may lose their domestic market share. However, the substitution for trade is far from complete. In many instances, foreign affiliates themselves are major participants in trade. They may import raw materials or components and export some of their output.

Even though theory suggests an open investment policy that welcomes foreign corporations, some degree of uneasiness exists about the rapid growth of such investment. Therefore, many countries review major incoming investment projects as to their effect and desirability. For example, in the United States, the government review is done by an interagency committee called the Committee for Foreign Investments in the United States (CFIUS). This committee primarily scrutinizes foreign investment activities from the standpoint of their impact on U.S. national security, and occasionally denies them. CFIUS denied clearance to Chinese telecom equipment manufacturer Huawei in 2011 for its planned acquisition of U.S. defense supplier 3Leaf Systems, leading to a complaint by Chinese officials about unfair treatment.[30] In another example, in 2010, Canadian officials blocked the acquisition of PotashCorp by the Australian firm BHP Billiton on the grounds of national interest.

While restrictions may serve national security or policy goals, they also impose a cost on society. Domestic industries may be preserved, but only at great peril to the free flow of capital and at substantial cost to consumers. A restriction of investments may permit more domestic control over industries, yet it also denies access to foreign capital and often innovation. This in turn can result in a tightening up of credit markets, higher interest rates, and a decrease in willingness to adapt to changing world market conditions.

POLICY RESPONSES TO TRADE PROBLEMS

The word *policy* implies that there is a coordinated set of continuous activities in the legislative and executive branches of government to attempt to deal with U.S. international trade. Unfortunately, such concerted efforts only rarely come about. Policy responses have consisted mainly of political ad hoc reactions, which over the years have changed from deep regret to protectionism. Whereas in the last century most lawmakers and administration officials simply regretted the lack of U.S. performance in international markets, more recently industry pressures have forced increased action.

Restrictions of Imports

In light of persistent trade deficits, growing foreign direct investment, and the tendency by some firms and industries to seek legislative redress for failures in the marketplace, the U.S. Congress has increasingly been willing to provide the president with more powers to restrict trade. Many resolutions have also been passed and legislation enacted admonishing the president to pay closer attention to trade. However, most of these admonitions provided only for an increasing threat against foreign importers, not for better conditions for U.S. exporters. The power of the executive to improve international trade opportunities for U.S.

firms through international negotiations and a relaxation of rules, regulations, and laws has become increasingly restricted over time.

A tendency has also existed to disregard the achievements of past international negotiations. For example, in Congress an amendment was attached to protectionistic legislation, stipulating that U.S. international trade legislation should not take effect if it is not in conformity with internationally negotiated rules. The amendment was voted down by an overwhelming majority, demonstrating a legislative lack of concern for such international trade agreements. There has also been a tendency to seek short-term political favors domestically in lieu of long-term international solutions. Trade legislation has become increasingly oriented to specific trading partners and specific industries. The United States often attempts to transfer its own trade laws abroad, in areas such as antitrust or export controls, resulting in bilateral conflicts. During international trade negotiations, U.S. expectations regarding production costs, social structure, and cultural patterns are often expected to be adopted in full abroad.

Yet in spite of all these developments, the United States is still one of the strongest advocates of free trade, to which its large volume of imports and ongoing trade deficit attest. Although this advocacy is shared, at least officially, by nations around the world, governments have become very creative in designing and implementing trade barriers, examples of which are listed in Exhibit 2.3.

One typical method consists of "voluntary" import restraints that are applied selectively against trading partners. Such measures have been used mainly in areas such as textiles, automobiles, and steel. Voluntary restrictions—which are, of course, implemented with the assistance of severe threats against trading partners—are intended to aid domestic industries to reorganize, restructure, and recapture their trade prominence of years past. They fail to take into account that importers may not have caused the economic decline of the domestic industry.

The steel industry provides a good example. World steel production capacity and supply clearly exceed world demand. This is the result both of overly ambitious industrial development projects motivated by nationalistic aspirations and of technological innovation. However, a closer look at the steel industries of developed nations shows that demand for steel has also been reduced. In the automobile industry, for example, fewer automobiles are being produced, and they are being produced differently than 10 years ago. Automobiles are more compact, lighter, and much more fuel efficient as a result of changing consumer preferences, government regulation, and higher oil prices. The weight of automobiles has been reduced by up to 40 percent from the 1970s.[31] Accordingly, less steel is needed for its production. In addition, many components formerly made of steel are now being replaced by components made from other materials such as plastic. If imports of steel were to be totally eliminated, the steel industries would still not regain the sales lost from a substantial change in the automotive industry.

If countries do not use the subtle mechanism of voluntary agreements, they often resort to old-fashioned tariffs. For example, Japanese heavy motorcycles imported into the United States were assessed a duty of 49.4 percent. This regulation kept the last U.S. producer of motorcycles, the Harley-Davidson Company, in business. Even though these tariffs have since been removed—and one year early at that—one can rightfully question whether the cost imposed on U.S. consumers who preferred foreign products during the four years of tariff imposition was justified. Even though average tariffs have been substantially reduced, their specific application can still have a major effect on trade flows.

A third major method by which trade has been restricted is through nontariff barriers. Compared with tariffs or even subsidies, which are visible and at least force products to compete for market acceptance on dimensions other than

The Global Environment: A Source of Conflict between Developed and Less-Developed Nations

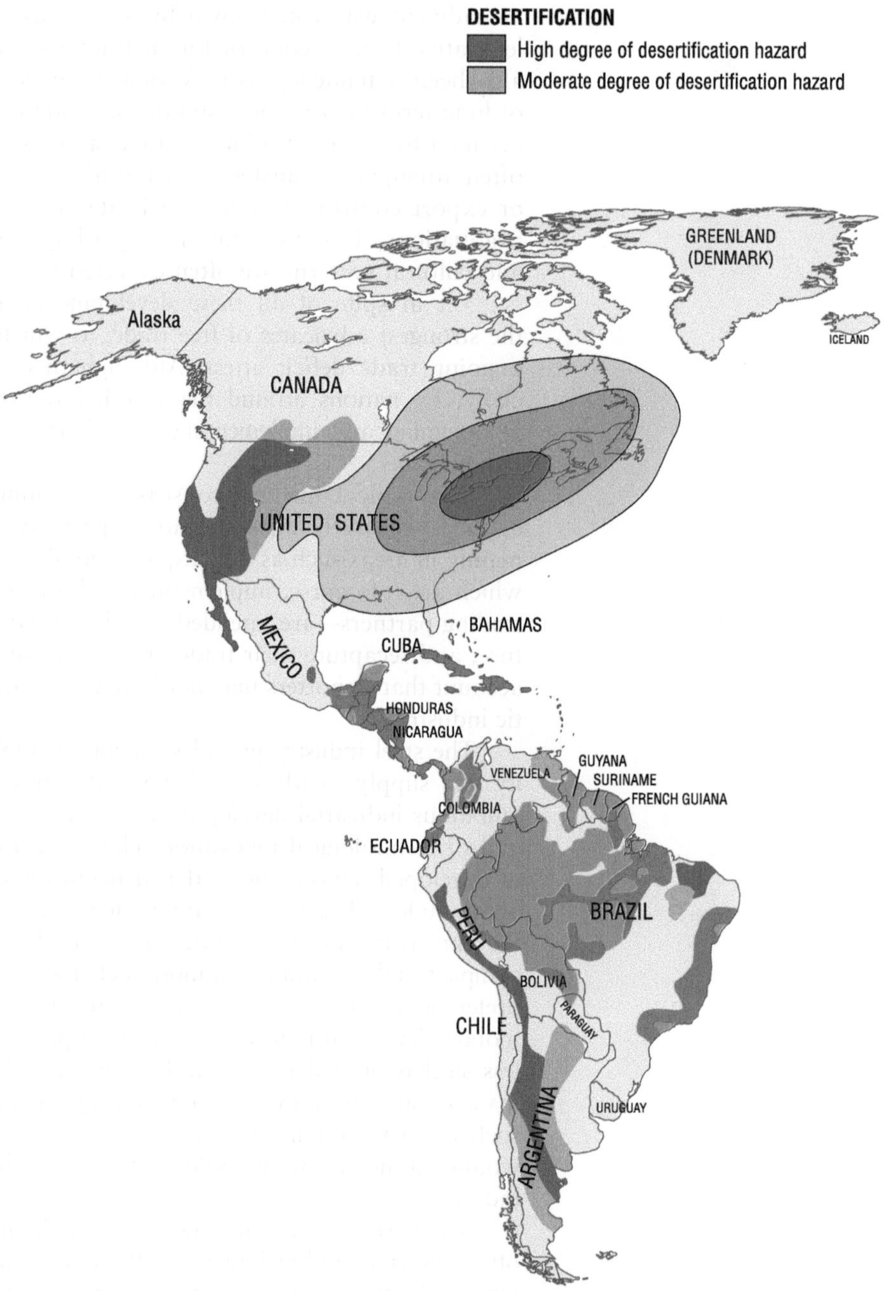

SOURCES: © Cengage Learning 2013; Based on *Environment Atlas*.

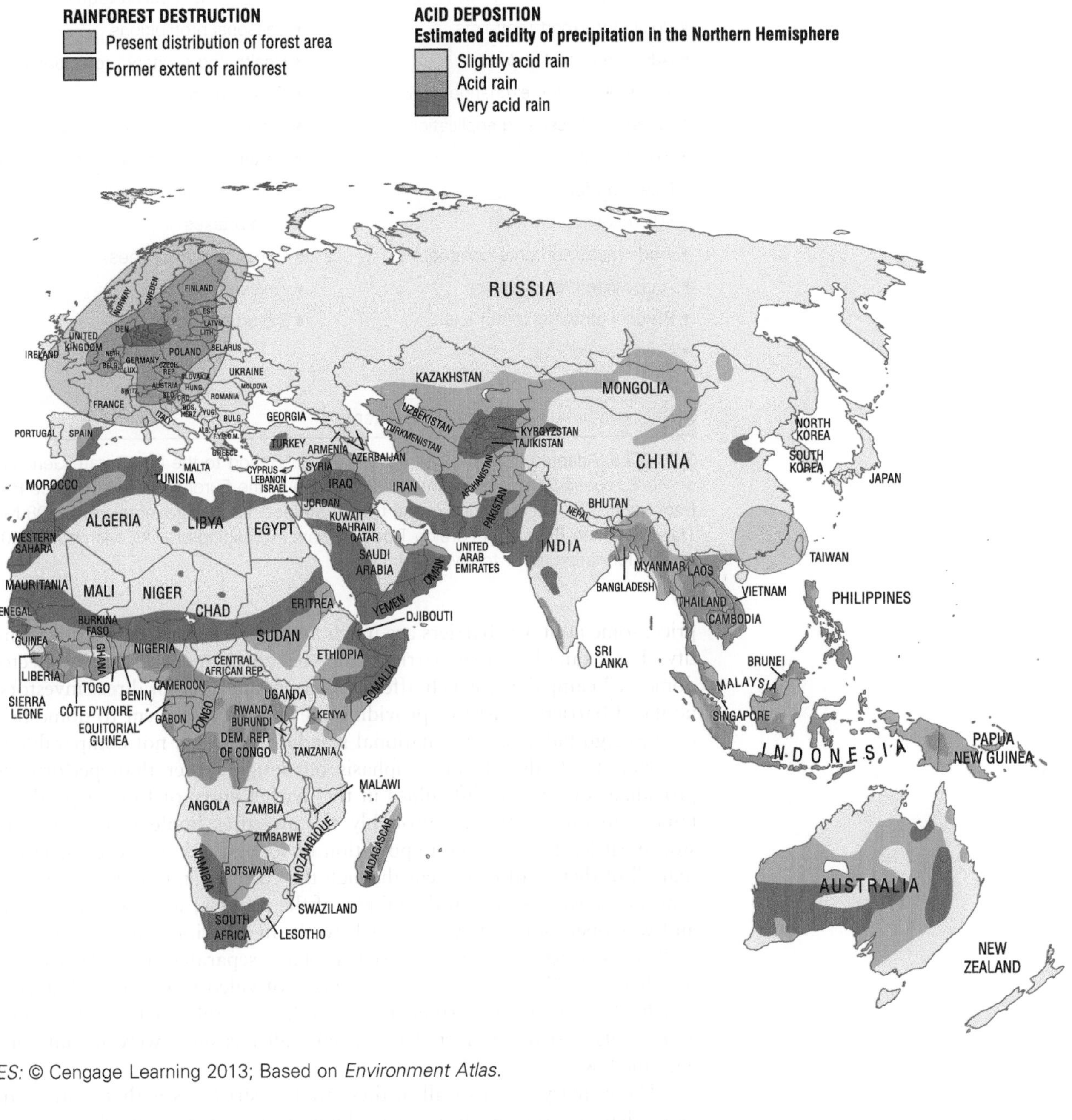

SOURCES: © Cengage Learning 2013; Based on *Environment Atlas.*

EXHIBIT 2.3 Trade Barriers

There are literally hundreds of ways to build a barrier.
The following list provides just a few of the trade barriers that exporters face.

• Special import authorization	• Country quotas
• Restrictions on data processing	• Testing and labeling requirements
• Voluntary export restraints	• Seasonal prohibitions
• Advance import deposits	• Health and sanitary prohibitions
• Taxes on foreign exchange deals	• Certification
• Preferential licensing applications	• Foreign exchange licensing
• Excise duties	• Barter and countertrade requirements
• Licensing fees	• Customs surcharges
• Discretionary licensing	• Stamp taxes
• Trade restriction on e-commerce	• Consular invoice fees
• Anticompetitive practices	• Taxes on transport
• Burdensome marketing rules	• Export subsidies
• Green barriers	
• Discriminatory tax measures	
• Failure to protect copyrights and patents	

SOURCES: Adapted from Crowell and Mooring, "Report to the Directorate General Trade of the European Commission, Interim Evaluation of the European Union's Trade Barrier Regulation," 2005; and Office of the United States Trade Representative, "2008 National Trade Estimate Report on Foreign Trade Barriers," Washington, DC, March 28, 2008. For more information, refer to www.ustr.gov.

price, some nontariff barriers are much more difficult to detect, prove, and quantify. For example, these barriers may be government or private-sector "buy domestic" campaigns, which affect importers and foreign direct investors. Other nontariff barriers consist of providing preferential treatment to domestic bidders over foreign bidders, using national standards that are not comparable to international standards, placing emphasis on design rather than performance, and providing for general difficulties in the market entry of foreign products. Most famous in this regard are probably the measures implemented by France. To stop or at least reduce the importation of foreign video recorders, France ruled that all of them had to be sent through the customs station at Poitiers. This customs house was located in the middle of the country, was woefully understaffed, and was open only a few days each week. In addition, the few customs agents at Poitiers insisted on opening each package separately in order to inspect the merchandise. Within a few weeks, imports of video recorders in France came to a halt. The French government, however, was able to point to international agreements and to the fact that officially all measures were in full compliance with the law.

The primary result of all of these trade restrictions is that many actions are taken that are contrary to what we know is good for the world and its citizens. Industries are preserved, but only at great peril to the world trade framework and at substantial cost to consumers. The direct costs of these actions are hidden and do not evoke much public complaint because they are spread out over a multitude of individuals. Yet these costs are real and burdensome and directly affect the standard of living of individuals and the competitiveness of firms. For example, if agricultural subsidies and tariffs were eliminated in the Doha Round of trade negotiations, the gains to the world economy by 2015 have been estimated to be $287 billion annually! These gains do not necessarily mean that prices would decrease. The elimination of artificial distortions would increase the prices for some agricultural goods. For example, projections show that cotton prices would increase by 21 percent, but the increase would primarily benefit the countries of sub-Saharan Africa, currently one of the poorest regions in the world.[32]

Export Promotion Efforts

Many countries provide export promotion assistance to their firms. Key reasons for such assistance are the national need to earn foreign currency, the encouragement of domestic employment, and the increase in domestic economic activity. Many forms of export promotion can be seen as government distortion of trade because government support simply results in a subsidization of profitability or reduction of risk. Yet there are instances where such intervention may be justified. Government support can be appropriate if it annuls unfair foreign practices, increases market transparency and therefore contributes to the better functioning of markets,[33] or helps overcome, in the interest of long-term national competitiveness, the short-term orientation of firms.[34]

The U.S. Department of Commerce provides companies with an impressive array of data on foreign trade and marketing developments. Its Commercial Service provides a link with U.S. businesses in terms of information flow and market assistance. Efforts are made to coordinate the activities of diverse federal agencies. As a result of these efforts, a national network of export assistance centers has been created, capable of providing one-stop shops for exporters in search of export counseling and financial assistance. In addition, an official interagency advocacy network was created that helps U.S. companies win overseas contracts for large government purchases abroad. A variety of agencies now collaborate in order to continue to improve services to U.S. exporters.

In terms of comparative efforts, however, U.S. export promotion activities still lag far behind the support provided by other major industrial nations. Many countries also provide substantial levels of private-sector support, which exists to a much lesser degree in the United States. Even more importantly, of the total U.S. export promotion expenditures, the largest portion (almost 50 percent) continues to go to the agricultural sector, and relatively few funds are devoted to export counseling and market research for manufacturing and service firms. However, it also needs to be considered that WTO regulations sharply restrict the ability of governments to promote their manufacturing exports—though the opportunity for the promotion of service exports is substantially less regulated.

A new focus has come about in the area of export financing. Policymakers have increasingly recognized that U.S. business may be placed at a disadvantage if it cannot meet the subsidized financing rates of foreign suppliers. The Export-Import Bank of the United States, charged with the mission of aggressively meeting foreign export-financing conditions, has in recent years even resorted to offering **mixed aid credits**. These take the form of loans composed partially of commercial interest rates and partially of highly subsidized developmental-aid interest rates. The bank has also launched a major effort to reach out to smaller-sized businesses and assist in their export success.

Tax legislation that inhibited the employment of Americans by U.S. firms abroad has also been altered to be more favorable to U.S. firms. In the past, U.S. nationals living abroad were, with some minor exclusion, fully subject to U.S. federal taxation. Because the cost of living abroad can often be quite high—rent for a small apartment can approach the range of $4,000 or more per month—this tax structure often imposed a significant burden on U.S. firms and citizens, and companies frequently were not able to send U.S. employees abroad. However, as the result of a tax code revision that allows a substantial amount of income (up to $85,700 in 2007) to remain tax-free,[35] more Americans can now be posted abroad. In their work they may specify the use of U.S. products and thus enhance the competitive opportunities of U.S. firms.

One other export-promotion development was the passage of the Export Trading Company Act of 1982. Intended to be the U.S. response to Japanese *sogoshoshas*, or international trading firms, this legislation permits firms to work together to form **export consortia**. The basic idea was to provide the foreign buyer with a one-stop shopping center in which a group of U.S. firms could offer a variety of complementary and competitive products. By exempting U.S. firms from current antitrust statutes, and by permitting banks to cooperate in the formation of these ventures through direct capital participation and the financing of trading activities, the government hoped that more firms could participate in the international marketplace. Although this legislation was originally hailed as a masterstroke and a key measure in turning around the decline in U.S. competitiveness abroad, it has not attracted a large number of successful firms. It appears that the legislation may not have provided sufficient incentive for banks, export service firms, or exporters to participate. Banks simply may find domestic profit margins to be more attractive and safe; export service firms may be too small; and exporters themselves may be too independent to participate in such consortia.

A STRATEGIC OUTLOOK FOR TRADE AND INVESTMENT POLICIES

All countries have international trade and investment policies. The importance and visibility of these policies have grown dramatically as international trade and investment flows have become more relevant to the well-being of most countries. Given the growing links among countries, it will be increasingly difficult to consider domestic policy without looking at international repercussions.

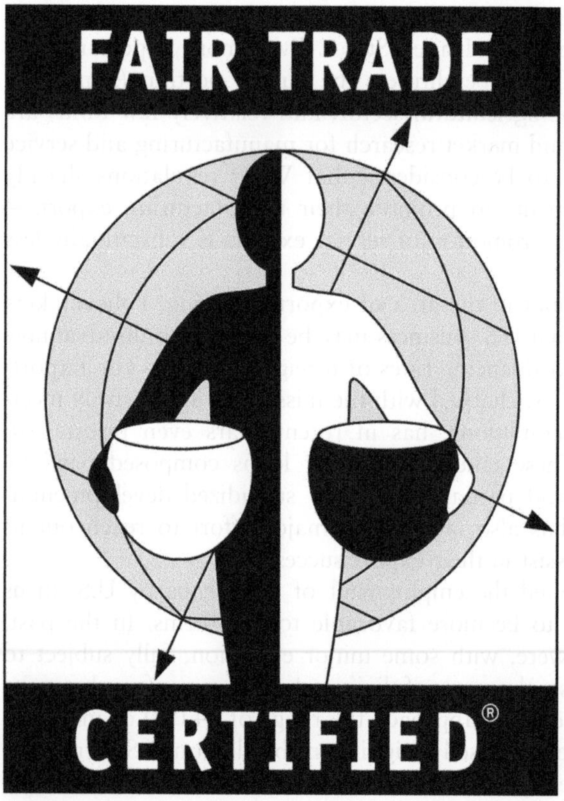

© AP Images/PRNewsFoto/Green & Black's

This Fair Trade Certified mark designates an item as in accordance with the Fair Trade Act.

A U.S. Perspective

The U.S. need is for a positive trade policy rather than reactive, ad hoc responses to specific situations. **Protectionistic legislation** can be helpful, provided it is not enacted. Proposals in Congress, for example, can be quite useful as bargaining chips in international negotiations. If passed and signed into law, however, protectionistic legislation can result in the destruction of the international trade and investment framework. For example, the U.S. House of Representatives passed the Currency Reform for Fair Trade Act in 2010 to authorize the U.S. Department of Commerce to impose countervailing duties to address the subsidization of exports by any foreign country through an artificially undervalued currency. This bill was specifically aimed at China. The U.S. Senate has delayed bringing this bill to a vote through 2011, perhaps because it provides useful leverage for the United States in trade negotiations with China.

It has been suggested that a variety of regulatory agencies could become involved in administering U.S. trade policy. Although such agencies could be useful from the standpoint of addressing narrowly defined grievances, they carry the danger that commercial policy will be determined by a new chorus of discordant voices. Shifting the power of setting trade and investment policy from the executive branch to agencies or even states could give the term *new federalism* a quite unexpected meaning and might cause progress at the international negotiation level to grind to a halt. No U.S. negotiator can expect to retain the goodwill of foreign counterparts if he or she cannot place issues on the table that can be negotiated without constantly having to check back with various authorities.

Continuing large U.S. trade deficits have brought much disenchantment with past trade policies. Disappointment with past trade negotiations is mainly the result of overblown expectations. Too often, the public has mistakenly expected successful trade negotiations to affect the domestic economy in a major way, even though the issue addressed or resolved was only of minor economic importance. Yet cumulatively and over time, the decrease in international tariffs and nontariff barriers has dramatically affected the economic well-being of consumers.

U.S. trade policy does need to change. Rather than treating trade policy as a strictly "foreign" phenomenon, it must be recognized that domestic economic performance mainly determines global competitiveness. Therefore, trade policy must become more domestically oriented at the same time that domestic policy must become more international in vision. Such a new approach should pursue at least five key goals. First, the nation must improve the quality and amount of information government and business share to facilitate competitiveness. Second, policy must encourage collaboration among companies in such areas as goods and process technologies. Third, U.S. industry collectively must overcome its export reluctance and its short-term financial orientation. Fourth, the United States must invest in its people, providing education and training suited to the competitive challenges of the twenty-first century. Finally, the executive branch must be given authority by Congress to negotiate international agreements with a reasonable certainty that the negotiation outcome will not be subject to minute amendments. Therefore, renewal of **trade promotion authority (TPA)**, which retains Congress' right to accept or reject trade treaties and agreements but reduces the amendment procedures, is quite important. Such authority is instrumental for new, large-scale trade accords such as the Doha Round or the Trans Pacific Partnership to succeed. However, TPA expired on July 1, 2007, and the Obama administration had not asked for its renewal as of 2012.

It will also be necessary to achieve a new perspective on government–business relations. In previous decades, government and business stayed at arm's length, and it was seen as inappropriate to involve the government in private-sector activities. Now, however, closer government–business collaboration is seen as one key to enhanced competitiveness. More mutual listening to each other and joint consideration of the long-term domestic and international repercussions of policy actions and business strategy can indeed pay off. Perhaps it will make both business and government more responsive to each other's needs. At least it will reduce the failures that can result from a lack of collaboration and insufficient understanding of linkages.

An International Perspective

From an international perspective, trade and investment negotiations must continue. In doing so, trade and investment policy can take either a multilateral or bilateral approach. **Bilateral negotiations** are carried out mainly between two nations, while **multilateral negotiations** are carried out among a number of nations. The approach can also be broad, covering a wide variety of goods, services, or investments, or it can be narrow in that it focuses on specific problems.

In order to address narrowly defined trade issues, bilateral negotiations and a specific approach seem quite appealing. Very specific problems can be discussed and resolved expediently. However, to be successful on a global scale, negotiations need to produce winners. Narrowly based bilateral negotiations require that there be, for each issue, a clearly identified winner and loser. Therefore, such negotiations have less chance for long-term success because no one wants to be the loser. This points toward multilateral negotiations on a broad scale, where concessions can be traded off among countries, and which make it possible for all participants to emerge and declare themselves as winners. The difficulty lies in devising enough incentives to bring the appropriate and desirable partners to the bargaining table. One area that would benefit greatly from multilateral negotiations is the regulation of e-commerce and the Internet as described in *The International Marketplace 2.4* (for more on e-commerce, see Chapter 9).

Policymakers must be willing to trade off short-term achievements for long-term goals. All too often, measures that would be beneficial in the long term are

THE INTERNATIONAL MARKETPLACE 2.4

The Trade Reality of E-Commerce

The Internet presents an opportunity for businesses and individuals to collaborate and communicate faster and cheaper than ever before. However, the new technology also poses challenges to modern policymakers, businesses, and consumers. As more information is stored online and more people purchase with their computers, security is becoming a major problem. Hackers have been able to use security holes in websites and databases to steal information, including credit card and social security numbers. They have also attacked personal, corporate, and government computers connected to the Internet by exploiting weaknesses in operating systems and browser security. With the globalization of technology, hacking becomes much more than a simple break-in and entry. Who has the legal jurisdiction in these cases? Is it the country in which the computer that was hacked into is located? The country from which the hacker is attacking? Or the country in which the company is based? Many nations have yet to develop laws regarding Internet crimes, and the existing laws vary greatly between nations.

In the past, consumers were able to buy foreign products through distributors and retailers in their home country. Today, they can skip intermediaries entirely and buy the product directly from the manufacturer over the Internet. But what happens if a consumer buys a product from a relatively little-known company and the product is defective or the consumer is hurt by the product? Many countries have fairly extensive consumer protection laws, but many do not. Can the consumer sue based on the laws of his or her country, or on the laws of the country where the company is headquartered? Given the differences in legal theories and damage awards, should corporations be concerned about lawsuits from every country in the world?

One issue of particular importance to international e-commerce is data privacy. The United States works together with the European Union through a bilateral mechanism, the U.S.–EU Safe Harbor Framework, which allows U.S. companies to meet the more stringent requirements of the EU's Directive on Data Privacy through a self-certification process. In 2009, the U.S. Department of Commerce hosted the Safe Harbor Conference in Washington, with the 2011–2012 conference expected to be hosted in Europe. The United States also has ongoing bilateral discussions with Switzerland, Japan, India, and its free trade agreement partners on data privacy.

One landmark for e-commerce was the Internet portal Yahoo! case. Some French web surfers chose to sell Nazi artifacts. The Ligue International Contre le Racism et 1-Antisemitisme and the Union of French Jewish Students took legal action in order to stop Yahoo! from selling these artifacts. They were able to sue under French laws that prohibited any type of incitation or promotion of Nazi memorabilia.

Some critics of e-commerce have suggested that it be regulated by the World Trade Organization. In 2005, the WTO actually did take action in regard to the international online gambling industry. Nonetheless, as of 2011, the WTO has not made much progress in e-commerce regulation. Dispute settlements are left up to national courts. The technology is difficult to keep up with, and there is a lack of government constituents. As e-commerce becomes more popular, however, some steps to protect people's security and privacy will be needed.

SOURCES: Global Reach, www.guava.co.uk, accessed February 15, 2012; International Association for Computer Information Systems, www.iacis.org, accessed February 15, 2012; "E-commerce is 'business channel of the future,'" September 25, 2008, http://networking.onestopclick.com/technology_news/e-commerce-is-'business-channel-of-the-future'_18796870.htm; and U.S. Department of Commerce, "2009 Electronic Commerce Industry Assessment," http://web.ita.doc.gov, accessed July 14, 2011.

sacrificed to short-term expediency to avoid temporary pain and the resulting political cost. Given the increasing links among nations and their economies, however, such adjustments are inevitable. In the recent past, trade and investment volume continued to grow for everyone. Conflicts were minimized and adjustment possibilities were increased manifold. In times of increasing competition and resource scarcity, however, conflicts are likely to increase significantly. Thoughtful economic coordination will therefore be required among the leading trading nations. Such coordination will result to some degree in the loss of national sovereignty.

New mechanisms to evaluate restraint measures will also need to be designed. The beneficiaries of trade and investment interference are usually clearly defined and have much to gain, whereas the losers are much less visible, which will make coalition building a key issue. The total cost of policy measures affecting trade and investment flows must be assessed, must be communicated, and must be taken into consideration before such measures are implemented.

The affected parties need to be concerned and join forces. The voices of retailers, consumers, wholesalers, and manufacturers all need to be heard. However, the different groups promoting government intervention or subsidies also will need to clearly demonstrate what they will deliver in exchange for government action. A specific performance plan will then need to be developed in order to ensure the continued wise use of resources. Such steps will place government action and corporate expectations in a context that is transparent and acceptable to consumers.

SUMMARY

International trade has often played a major role in world history. The rise and fall of the Roman Empire and the emergence of feudalism can be attributed to trade. Since 1945, the Western nations have made concerted efforts to improve the trade environment and expand trade activities. In order for them to do so, various multinational organizations, such as the WTO, the IMF, and the World Bank, were founded. In addition, several economic blocs such as the EU, NAFTA, and MERCOSUR were formed. Many of these organizations have been very successful in their mission, yet new realities of the trade environment demand new types of action.

Recall from Chapter 1 that the last few decades have been marked by tremendous growth in world trade. In addition, there have been significant changes in the trade positions of many countries. For example, the U.S. share of world exports has declined precipitously from 25 percent in the 1950s, while China's share in world trade has risen substantially in the last few years alone. Furthermore, foreign direct investment has come to play an important role in the world economy.

The WTO is the key forum for trade disputes and negotiations. However, there are growing tensions between developed and developing countries, particularly in the sphere of agriculture.

Despite calls for trade liberalization, some policymakers intend to enhance trade performance by threatening the world with increasing protectionism. The danger of such a policy lies in the fact that world trade would shrink and standards of living would decline. Protectionism cannot, in the long run, prevent adjustment or increase productivity and competitiveness. It is therefore important to improve the capability of firms to compete internationally, to provide an international trade framework that facilitates international marketing activities, but also to keep in mind the displacement consequences of trade, which may require adjustment preparations.

KEY TERMS

Pax Romana
economic bloc
born global
trade deficit
economies of scale
foreign direct investment
foreign affiliate
nontariff barrier
mixed aid credit
export consortia
protectionistic legislation
trade promotion authority (TPA)
bilateral negotiation
multilateral negotiation

QUESTIONS FOR DISCUSSION

1. Why is international trade important to a nation?
2. How did the GATT lead to the creation of the WTO?
3. Provide examples of multilateral versus bilateral trade agreements.
4. What is the current status of the Doha Round of multilateral trade negotiations? Is the agreement moving forward?
5. How do consumer preferences for different products affect a country's trade position?
6. What are the different roles of the WTO, the IMF, and the World Bank?
7. Should countries restrict foreign direct investment in their domestic industries?

INTERNET EXERCISES

1. What are the five major branches of the World Bank, and what are their missions? (Use information from the World Bank at **www.worldbank.org**.)
2. For the latest year, what are the five leading country exporters of world merchandise? What are the five leading country exporters of commercial services? (Use data from the World Trade Organization at **www.wto.org**.)
3. What countries are negotiating to join the Trans Pacific Partnership (TPP)? What countries may be interested in joining this group? (Use information from the U.S. Trade Representative at **www.ustr.gov** and the international trade agencies of other TPP negotiating countries.)

CHALLENGE US

The Pirate Effect

Pirates drive up the cost of cargo and the prices of shipments. Some believe that shippers should simply take the "long route" to gain distance from pirates. Others argue that proper arming of the crew will lead to brief battles with the pirates losing and the cargo being safe.

Who is right?

For Discussion

1. Why is piracy a problem for ocean commerce?
2. Who is right? Should shippers take the long route or should shippers prepare for battles?
3. What should shipping companies do to protect their crews and cargo?

RECOMMENDED READINGS

Aaronson, S., and J. Zimmerman, *Trade Imbalance: The Struggle to Reconcile Human Rights Concerns in Trade Policy Making*. Cambridge University Press, 2008.

Bernstein, William J. *A Splendid Exchange: How Trade Shaped the World*. New York: Grove Press, 2009.

Brown, Chad. *Self-Enforcing Trade: Developing Countries and WTO Dispute Settlement*. Washington, DC: Brookings Institution, 2010.

Chanda, Nayan. *Bound Together: How Traders, Preachers, Adventurers, and Warriors Shaped Globalization*. New Haven, CT: Yale University Press, 2009.

Finger, Michael J. *Institutions and Trade Policy*. Northampton, MA: Edward Elgar, 2002.

Razeen, Sally. *New Frontiers in Free Trade: Globalization's Future and Asia's Rising Role*. Washington, DC: Cato Institute, 2008.

Ryan, Damian, and Calvin Jones. *Understanding Digital Marketing: Marketing Strategies for Engaging the Digital Generation*, 2nd ed. London: Kogan Page, 2012.

ENDNOTES

1. Nayan Chanda, *Bound Together* (New Haven, CT: Yale University Press, 2009).
2. William J. Bernstein, *A Splendid Exchange: How Trade Shaped the World* (New York: Grove Press, 2009), 110–11.
3. Henri Pirenne, *Economic and Social History of Medieval Europe* (New York: Harcourt, Brace, and World, 1933), 142–46.
4. Margaret P. Doxey, *Economic Sanctions and International Enforcement* (New York: Oxford University Press, 1980), 10.
5. Russian News and Information Agency, http://en.rian.ru, accessed December 7, 2011.
6. Thomas R. Graham, "Global Trade: War and Peace," *Foreign Policy* (Spring 1983): 124–37.
7. World Trade Organization, www.wto.org, accessed December 7, 2011.
8. "WTO Trade Policy Review of the United States 2010 WTO Secretariat Summary," press release, www.wto.org/english/tratop_e/tpr_e/tp_rep_e.htm, accessed December 7, 2011.
9. *Business Guide to Uruguay Round* (Geneva, Switzerland: International Trade Centre and Commonwealth Secretariat, 1995).
10. Michael R. Czinkota, "The World Trade Organization—Perspectives and Prospects," *Journal of International Marketing* 3, no. 1 (1995): 85–92.
11. World Trade Organization, www.wto.org, accessed December 7, 2011.
12. "IMF Backs Poverty Debt Write-Off," BBC News, December 21, 2005, http://news.bbc.co.uk/2/hi/business/4550778.stm.
13. "IMF to Launch New Facility for Emerging Markets Hit by Crisis," International Monetary Fund, Washington, DC, October 29, 2008.
14. International Monetary Fund, transcript of July 6, 2011 press conference, www.imf.org, accessed December 7, 2011.
15. World Bank, *Global Monitoring Report* (Washington, DC: World Bank, 2008).
16. World Bank, www.worldbank.org, accessed December 7, 2011.
17. Mordechai E. Kreinin, *International Economics: A Policy Approach*, 5th ed. (New York: Harcourt Brace Jovanovich, 1987), 12.
18. T. Lum and Dick Nanto, *China's Trade with the United States and the World*, CRS Report to Congress, January 4, 2007.
19. World Trade Data, WTO, Geneva 2011.
20. Krenin, *International Economics*, 6.
21. Gary Knight and S. Tamer Cavusgil, "Innovation, Organizational Capabilities, and the Born Global Firm," *Journal of International Business Studies* 35, no. 2 (2004): 124–41.
22. International Trade Administration, www.trade.gov.
23. Catherine L. Mann, *Is the U.S. Trade Deficit Sustainable?* September 1999, www.iie.com.
24. *U.S. Jobs Supported by Exports of Goods and Services* (Washington, DC: U.S. Department of Commerce, 2002).
25. Office of Industry and Trade Information, *Total Jobs Related to Manufacturing Employment* (Washington, DC: U.S. Department of Commerce, 2002).
26. Discussion with Commerce Department Analysts, Washington, DC, 2012.
27. Michael R. Czinkota, "A National Export Development Strategy for New and Growing Businesses," remarks delivered to the National Economic Council, Washington, DC, August 6, 1993.
28. Invest in America, www.investamerica.gov/home/iia_main_001154.asp, accessed July 12, 2011.
29. Ibid.
30. Troutman Sanders, www.troutmansanders.com, accessed July 12, 2011.
31. European Commission, "Success for Low-Weight Auto Parts Project," http://ec.europa.eu/research/transport/news/items/success_for_low_weight_auto_parts_project_en.htm, accessed December 9, 2011.
32. Kym Anderson, Will Martin, and Dominique van der Mensbrugghe, *Distortions to World Trade: Impacts on Agricultural Markets and Farm Incomes* (Washington, DC: World Bank, 2005).
33. Michael R. Czinkota, "The Export Promotion Rationale," *Marketing Management*, January 2012.
34. Masaaki Kotabe and Michael R. Czinkota, "State Government Promotion of Manufacturing Exports: A Gap Analysis," *Journal of International Business Studies*, Winter 1992, 637–58.
35. *Publication 54, Tax Guide for US Citizens and Resident Aliens Abroad* (Washington, DC: Internal Revenue Service, 2012).

CHAPTER 3

The Role of Culture

LEARNING OBJECTIVES

By the time you complete this chapter, you will be able to:

- Define and demonstrate the effect of culture's various dimensions on business.
- Examine ways in which cultural knowledge can be acquired and individuals and organizations prepared for cross-cultural interaction.
- Illustrate ways in which cultural risk poses a challenge to the effective conduct of business communications and transactions.
- Suggest ways in which businesses act as change agents in the diverse cultural environments in which they operate.
- Evaluate the ways in which training programs assist international managers to develop the international business skills of their employees.
- Analyze the strategies corporations can take to work with cultural differences in order to expand their businesses internationally.

THE INTERNATIONAL MARKETPLACE 3.1

IMAX Broadens Presence

With 583 theatres around the world and close to 300 theater systems in backlog as of September 30, 2011, IMAX is in 48 countries and continues to roll out its global theater network. Several economic factors have contributed to the global rise of IMAX, including the flattening of the global economy, the increase of GDP per capita, and the rise of consumer discretionary spending. Going to see movies in IMAX, which is considered a luxury experience in many countries, has now become more attainable for the average moviegoer.

For IMAX, the catalysts for this growth are the global demand for film product and the rapid expansion of theatrical screens. From 2006 to 2010, the international box office grew by 30 percent. Although worldwide screens have remained constant at just under 150,000 over the past five years, digital screens have increased dramatically. In 2010, the number of digital screens globally increased by 122 percent; growth was generally consistent across all regions with each region more than doubling its screen count. The rollout of digital screens provides economies of scale in theater development as well as a more robust exhibition infrastructure for the IMAX footprint.

Outside the United States, the next biggest IMAX presence is China. As of September 30, 2011, IMAX has 49 theaters open in mainland China. By 2016, the company expects to have 300 theaters operating in China. In order to better manage the burgeoning theater network, the creation of a subsidiary, IMAX China, was established. The rapid deployment of IMAX theaters in China offers a window into China's evolving attitude toward the film business, which government leaders have identified in recent years as an economic and cultural growth priority. China is racing to build more modern theaters to entertain an expanding, cinema-loving middle class. The country is also ramping up local film production, partly as a way to spread its culture across the globe. China currently has about 6,000 movie screens, up from roughly 1,500 three years ago. The Chinese government has said it expects 20,000 screens to be operating by 2015 and 40,000 by 2040, bringing it on par with movie exhibition in North America.

The rollout of IMAX theaters in China is good news for Hollywood studios, which fervently want to expand in China but face a government-enforced quota; only 20 non-Chinese films may be shown in local theaters each year. China has a strong record of approving Hollywood films that IMAX wants to show. IMAX, which has become one of the entertainment industry's fasting growing companies, has a strong brand in China because its premium theaters, which often play films in 3D, offer an affordable luxury to the ardent Chinese moviegoers. When IMAX showed *Avatar* in 2010, Chinese customers waited up to six hours for tickets that cost approximately $16 each.

Looking ahead, one of the most significant initiatives going forward for IMAX in China is to increase the number of Chinese-produced films that IMAX screens per year. In 2010, the first local-language digital media remastering (DMR) film, *Aftershock: The IMAX Experience*, was released in China with major critical and commercial success. IMAX expects to see that number grow dramatically in the near future as China's film industry further develops.

After China, Russia is the second biggest international market for IMAX with 17 screens open (21 including Kazakhstan and the Ukraine) as of September 30, 2011. The territory, which expects to have 50 IMAX theaters by 2014, is currently experiencing a box-office boom. Box-office ticket sales in Russia have grown from $3 million a year in 1993 to more than $1 billion in 2010. IMAX theaters are generating twice as much revenue there, about $3 million per screen annually, than in North America. Part of the reason IMAX has been so successful in Russia is that cinemagoers there respond extremely well to the visually thrilling blockbusters (especially 3D films) that IMAX presents. Of the top ten films of 2010 in Russia, eight were 3D movies. That year, 3D films raked in 33 percent of the total box office. This figure places Russia as the second biggest consumer of 3D theatrical content on a percentage basis in the world. Several of the 3D titles in 2010 were not top performers in the United States or other international territories. This suggests that many Russian moviegoers are driven more by presentation and spectacle rather than narrative quality.

In a reflection of a cultural identity shaped by years of oligarchic rule, the IMAX theater presence in Russia is one that exemplifies the high societal value placed on luxury goods in Russia. IMAX theaters are in the top malls and multiplexes in the country, thereby experiencing a positive brand association in the eyes of the consumer. Although Russia is still to some extent a class-based society, even those who are not billionaire oil industrialists can pay up to $25 to see *Pirates of the Caribbean: On Stranger Tides: The IMAX Experience* and feel like a tycoon. While IMAX represents the highest-quality theatrical presentation in the Russian market, the company is launching its first Sapphire theater in Moscow to offer an even more exclusive and luxurious experience.

With only three theaters in the country as of September 30, 2011, IMAX does not have a large presence in India. However, the subcontinent represents one of the biggest future growth prospects for the company. On March 30, 2011, IMAX and PVR Cinemas, India's leading cinema brand and operator of the country's top-performing multiplexes, announced an agreement to install theater systems in four key locations throughout India. India has a vibrant moviegoing culture, and it is one of the most important and largely untapped film industry growth markets. In 2009, 677 feature films were produced in the United States and Canada. Compare that to the 1,288 Indian films produced, and immediately one can see that India is a country that takes its movies seriously. Bollywood films often outperform Hollywood films at the Indian box office and typically feature over-the-top musical numbers in their stories. In 2010, there were 2,705,939,000 theater admissions in India. To put that in perspective, the

Photo courtesy IMAX Corporation

One of IMAX's worldwide locations.

United States and Canada combined had 1,341,790,000 admissions. Although admissions were more than double the U.S. and Canada totals, gross box office receipts were only 15 percent of the combined U.S.–Canada total. However, GDP per capita is quickly on the rise in India, which should translate into an increase in discretionary spending, supporting a further IMAX expansion into the region.

SOURCE: IMAX.

The ever-increasing level of world trade, opening of markets, enhanced purchasing power of customers, and intensifying competition all have allowed and even forced marketers to expand their operations. The challenge for the marketing manager is to handle the differences in values and attitudes, and subsequent behavioral patterns that govern human interaction, on two levels: first as they relate to customer behavior, and second as they affect the implementation of marketing programs within individual markets and across markets.

For years, marketers have been heralding the arrival of the global customer, an individual or entity that would both think and purchase alike the world or region over.[1] These universal needs could then be translated into marketing programs that would exploit these similarities. However, if this approach were based on the premise of standardization, a critical and fatal mistake would be made. First, a wide variety of metrics shows that just 10 to 25 percent of activity is truly global. Second, overseas success is very much a function of cultural adaptability: patience, flexibility, and tolerance for others' beliefs. For example, foreign studios say they face an opaque approval process for getting their films into China. In 2011, the Chinese government allowed only 54 foreign films into the country, and U.S. studios were able to share a percentage of box-office revenue on just 21. An understanding of differences allows marketers to determine when adaptation may be necessary and when commonalities allow for regional or global approaches, as seen in *The International Marketplace 3.1*.[2]

To take advantage of global markets or global segments, marketers are required to have or attain a thorough understanding of what drives customer behavior in different markets and to detect the extent to which similarities exist or can be achieved through marketing efforts. For instance, as appliance makers such as Whirlpool study the habits and preferences of consumers in different countries, they develop specialized appliances (e.g., grinders for coffee and spices) and features (e.g., a fifth burner for ranges). Interestingly, as cooking habits have extended to include food from other cultures—from pizza to pot roast to tortillas—the new features have found new adopters. For example, non-Latinos want griddle cook tops for pancakes as well as fajitas.[3]

In expanding their presence, marketers will acquire not only new customers but new partners as well. These essential partners, whose efforts are necessary for market development and penetration, include agents, distributors, other facilitating agents (such as advertising agencies and law firms), and, in many cases, the government. Expansion will also mean new employees or strategic alliance partners whose motivations will either make or break marketing programs. Thus understanding the hot buttons and turnoffs of these groups becomes critical. For example, unlike in other countries, about 80 percent of Häagen-Dazs revenue in China comes from shops. That is because grocery stores typically stop carrying most ice cream during winter, when demand wanes. Freezer space in Chinese homes is also limited, and refrigeration in stores is not up to Häagen-Dazs's chilly standards—so much so that the company has installed 5,000 of its own freezers, at $15,000 apiece, in grocery stores around the country.[4]

Therefore, cultural competence must be recognized as a key management skill. Cultural incompetence, or inflexibility, can easily jeopardize millions of dollars through wasted negotiations; lost purchases, sales, and contracts; and poor customer relations. Furthermore, the internal efficiency of a multinational corporation may be weakened if managers and workers are not "on the same wavelength."

The intent of this chapter is to analyze the concept of culture and its various elements and then to provide suggestions for not only meeting the cultural challenge but also making it a base for obtaining and maintaining a competitive advantage.

CULTURE DEFINED

Culture gives an individual an anchoring point—an identity—as well as codes of conduct. Of the 164 definitions of *culture* analyzed by Alfred Kroeber and Clyde Kluckhohn, some conceive of culture as separating humans from nonhumans, some define it as communicable knowledge, and some see it as the sum of historical achievements produced by humanity's social life.[5] All the definitions have common elements: Culture is learned, shared, and transmitted from one generation to the next. Culture is primarily passed on by parents to their children but also by social organizations, special-interest groups, the government, the schools, and religious institutions. Common ways of thinking and behaving that are developed are then reinforced through social pressure. Geert Hofstede calls this the "collective programming of the mind."[6] Culture is also multidimensional, consisting of a number of common elements that are interdependent. Changes occurring in one of the dimensions will affect the others as well.

For the purposes of this text, **culture** is defined as an integrated system of learned behavior patterns that are distinguishing characteristics of the members of any given society. It includes everything that a group thinks, says, does, and makes—its customs, language, material artifacts, and shared systems of attitudes and feelings. The definition therefore encompasses a wide variety of elements from the materialistic to the spiritual. Culture is inherently conservative, resisting change and fostering continuity. Every person is encultured into a particular culture, learning the "right way" of doing things. Problems may arise when a person encultured in one culture has to adjust to another one. The process of **acculturation**—adjusting and adapting to a specific culture other than one's own—is one of the keys to success in international operations.

© Jon Feingersh/Blend Images/Jupiterimages

The international marketer must recognize and understand all the varying cultures in this world.

Edward T. Hall, who has made some of the most valuable studies on the effects of culture on business, makes a distinction between high- and low-context cultures.[7] In high-context cultures, such as Japan and Saudi Arabia, context is at least as important as what is actually said. The speaker and the listener rely on a common understanding of the context. In low-context cultures, however, most of the information is contained explicitly in the words. North American cultures engage in low-context communications. Unless we are aware of this basic difference, messages and intentions can easily be misunderstood. If performance appraisals of marketing personnel are to be centrally guided or conducted in a multinational corporation, those involved must be acutely aware of cultural nuances. One of the interesting differences is that the U.S. system emphasizes the individual's development, whereas the Japanese system focuses on the group within which the individual works. In the United States, criticism is more direct and is recorded formally, whereas in Japan it is more subtle and verbal. What is not being said can carry more meaning than what is said.

Few cultures today are as homogeneous as those of Japan and Saudi Arabia. Elsewhere, intracultural differences based on nationality, religion, race, or geographic areas have resulted in the emergence of distinct subcultures. The international manager's task is to distinguish relevant cross-cultural and intracultural differences and then to isolate potential opportunities and problems. For example, IKEA's research in the United States found that Latin families wanted bigger dining-room tables to accommodate bigger families.[8] On the other hand, borrowing and interaction between national cultures may lead to narrowing gaps between cultures. Here the international business entity will act as a change agent by introducing new products or ideas and practices (as can be seen in *The International Marketplace* 3.2). Although this may consist of no more than shifting consumption from one product brand to another, it may lead to massive social change in the manner of consumption, the type of products consumed, and social organization.

In some cases, the international marketer may be accused of cultural imperialism, especially if the changes brought about are dramatic or if culture-specific adaptations are not made in the marketing approach. There is a growing fear among many countries that globalization is bringing a surge of foreign products across their borders that will threaten their cultural heritage. In 2005, the United Nations Educational, Scientific, and Cultural Organization passed the Convention on the Protection and Promotion of Diversity of Cultural Expressions, which declares the right of countries to "maintain, adopt, and implement policies and measures that they deem appropriate for the protection and promotion of music, art, language, and ideas as well as cultural activities, goods and services."[9] Some countries, such as Brazil, Canada, France, and Indonesia, protect their cultural industries through restrictive rules and subsidies. France's measures include, for example, *prix unique du livre*, a limitation on the percent of discount on books (to support small publishing houses and help maintain small bookstores); quotas on non-French movies on French national TV channels and mandatory financing of films by TV channels (as a provision in their license) as well as for French music on radio channels; and *avance sur recettes* or *fonds de soutien*, a state financial advance on all French films.[10] Such subsidies have allowed the French to make 200 films a year, twice as many as the United Kingdom. Similar measures have been taken to protect geographic indications; for example, signs on goods that have a specific geographic origin and possess qualities or a reputation due to that place of origin. Some countries have started taking measures to protect their traditions in areas such as medicine, in which the concern is biopiracy of natural remedies (e.g., in Africa).[11]

THE INTERNATIONAL MARKETPLACE 3.2

From Hollywood to Bollywood

India is an appealing target for hit-making entertainers such as Britney Spears, 50 Cent, Akon, and Enrique Iglesias. In fact, Lady Gaga has just tapped the New York–based Desi Hits to expand her brand to the Bollywood-crazed India market. She is only the latest U.S. entertainer who has turned to Desi Hits to crack the Indian market with a new hybrid pop sound. People who like music also like certain clothing, phones, and shoes, and India, with 700 million people under the age of 30, is an attractive market for most entertainers. Desi Hits' cofounder says that India's mass-music industry is driven by the film industry so most of their hits are from mainstream movies. Artists, therefore, need to understand Bollywood to penetrate the pop culture in India. Desi Hits' goal, however, is to reach a global audience.

Desi Hits' website attracts 1.5 million youth and young adult visitors a month. Their aim is to make South Asian culture more widely dispersed and understood, as well as to offer a platform for South Asian artists to promote themselves globally. Ms. Acharia-Bath, her husband Ranj Bath, and Arun Sandhu, three British Indians, founded Desi Hits (*desi* is Hindi for everything from the Indian subcontinent) with the concept of bicultural remixing or fusing the Western world with the South Asian artistic platform.

Desi Hits remixed Lady Gaga's "Born This Way" hit single with two sets of Bollywood producers. The videos are available through YouTube and DesiHits.com. Photo shoots, celebrity gossip interviews, and promotions are also available on the website of Desi Hits, which straddles Hollywood skinny jeans and their Eastern cousin, a traditional Indian scarf in the waistband. The biggest dilemma for the artists is how South Asian they want to appear versus how Western they want to be.

Desi Hits' top five songs as of fall 2011 are:

1. Lady Gaga, "Born This Way (Salim & Sulaimain Mix)"
2. Sukshinder Shinda, "Samne"
3. Britney Spears, "Till The World Ends (Culture Shock Mix)"
4. Foji, "Pumbeeri"
5. Chris Brown ft. Busta Rhymes, "Look at Me Now"

© photosindia/Getty Images

SOURCES: Lee Hawkins, "Lady Gaga Romances India," *Wall Street Journal*, June 2, 2011, B9; Sharin Bhatti, "Lady Gaga over Bollywood," *Hindustan Times*, April 1, 2011; Megha Bahree, "Dance Floor Diplomats," Forbes.com, August 9, 2010, 1–2; Lisa Tsering, "Universal Ties Up with Desi Hits to Create Music Label," *India-West*, July 20, 2010, C10; Joseph Plambeck, "A New Label's Mission: Indian Music," nytimes.com, July 19, 2010; and Desi Hits, www.desihits.com.

Even if a particular country is dominant in a cultural sector, such as the United States in movies and television programming, the commonly suggested solution of protectionism may not work. Although the European Union has a rule that 40 percent of its programming has to be domestic, anyone wanting a U.S. program can choose an appropriate channel or rent a video. Quotas will also result in behavior not intended by regulators. U.S. programming tends to be scheduled during prime time, while the 60 percent of domestic programming may wind up being shown during less attractive times. Furthermore, quotas may also lead to local productions designed to satisfy official mandates and capture subsidies that accompany them. Recently, a question has been raised over whether movies produced by foreign-owned companies would be eligible for government subsidies.

Popular culture is not only a U.S. bastion. Given the ethnic diversity in the United States (as in many other country markets), programming from around the world is made readily available. Many of the greatest successes among cultural products in the last five years in the United States have been imports; for instance, in television programming, *The X Factor* and *Pop Idol* are a British concept, as is the best-seller in children's literature, the Harry Potter series. In cartoons, *Pokémon* hails from Japan. Global marketers and media have made it possible for national and regional artists to break into worldwide markets. Beatriz Luengo, one of Europe's most renowned talents, is about to unveil her first album globally, so the U.S. and Latin American publics will have the chance to enjoy the songwriter's prowess.[12]

THE ELEMENTS OF CULTURE

The study of culture has led to generalizations that may apply to all cultures. Such characteristics are called **cultural universals**, which are manifestations of the total way of life of any group of people. These include such elements as bodily adornments, courtship, etiquette, family gestures, joking, mealtimes, music, personal names, status differentiation, and trade.[13] These activities occur across cultures, but their manifestation may be unique in a particular society, bringing about cultural diversity. Common denominators can indeed be found, but the ways in which they are actually accomplished may vary dramatically. Even when a segment may be perceived to be similar across borders, such as in the case of teenagers and the affluent, cultural differences make marketers' jobs challenging. For example, distinguishing China's wealthy consumers from their foreign counterparts is their youth: some 80 percent are under 45 years of age, compared with 30 percent in the United States and 19 percent in Japan.[14]

Observation of the major denominators summarized in Exhibit 3.1 suggests that the elements are both material (such as tools) and abstract (such as attitudes). The sensitivity and adaptation to these elements by an international firm depends on the firm's level of involvement in the market—for example, licensing versus direct investment—and the product or service marketed. Naturally, some products and services or management practices require very little adjustment, whereas others have to be adapted dramatically.

EXHIBIT 3.1 Elements of Culture

Language • Verbal • Nonverbal	Manners and customs Material elements Aesthetics
Religion	Education
Values and attitudes	Social institutions

SOURCE: © Cengage Learning 2013.

Language

The world's languages may have all descended from a single ancestral tongue spoken by early African humans between 50,000 and 70,000 years ago.[15] A total of 6,912 known living languages exist in the world, with 311 being spoken in the United States, 297 in Mexico, 13 in Finland, and 241 in China.[16] The European Union has 23 official languages for its bureaucracy. Interestingly, a total of 96 percent of the world's languages are spoken by just 4 percent of the world's population. Language has been described as the mirror of culture. Language itself is multidimensional by nature. This is true not only of the spoken word but also of what can be called the nonverbal language of international business. Messages are conveyed by the words used, by the way the words are spoken (e.g., tone of voice), and by nonverbal means such as gestures, body position, and eye contact. In addition, with the global use of new technologies such as video cameras on PCs, short message service (SMS), and miniblogging sites such as Twitter, research must be conducted on how those tools affect virtual cross-cultural communication and what impact non-face-to-face body language can have.

Very often, mastery of the language is required before a person is acculturated to a culture other than his or her own. Language mastery must go beyond technical competency because every language has words and phrases that can be readily understood only in context. Such phrases are carriers of culture; they represent special ways a culture has developed to view some aspect of human existence.

Language capability serves four distinct roles in international marketing:[17]

1. Language aids in information gathering and evaluation efforts. Rather than rely completely on the opinions of others, the manager is able to see and hear personally what is going on. People are far more comfortable speaking their own language, and this should be treated as an advantage. The best intelligence on a market is gathered by becoming part of the market rather than observing it from the outside. For example, local managers of a multinational corporation should be the firm's primary source of political information to assess potential risk.
2. Language provides access to local society. Although English may be widely spoken and may even be the official company language, speaking the local language may make a dramatic difference. For example, firms that translate promotional materials and information are seen as being serious about doing business in the country.
3. Language capability is increasingly important in company communications, whether within the corporate family or with channel members. Imagine the difficulties encountered by a country manager who must communicate with employees through an interpreter.
4. Language provides more than the ability to communicate. It extends beyond mechanics to the interpretation of contexts. Realize that in several cultures, "yes" will not mean "I agree" but rather only signals "I hear what you're saying," so it does not convey consent.

The manager's command of the national language(s) in a market must be greater than simple word recognition. Consider, for example, how dramatically different English terms can be when used in Australia, the United Kingdom, or the United States. In negotiations, for U.S. delegates "tabling a proposal" means that they want to delay a decision, whereas their British counterparts understand the expression to mean that immediate action is to be taken. If the British promise something "by the end of the day," this does not mean within 24 hours but rather when they have completed the job. Additionally, they may say that negotiations "bombed," meaning that they were a success; to a U.S. manager, this could convey exactly the opposite message. Similar challenges occur with other languages and markets. Swedish is spoken as a mother tongue by 6 percent of the population in Finland, where it has idioms that are not well understood by Swedes. Goodyear has identified five different terms for the word *tires* in the Spanish-speaking Americas: *cauchos* in Venezuela, *cubiertas* in Argentina, *gomas* in Puerto Rico, *neumaticos* in Chile, and *llantas* in most of the other countries in the region.

An advertising campaign presented by Electrolux highlights the difficulties in transferring advertising campaigns between markets. Electrolux's theme in marketing its vacuum cleaners, "Nothing Sucks Like an Electrolux," is interpreted literally in the United Kingdom, but in the United States, the slang implications would interfere with the intended message. The danger exists of translingual homonyms; an innocent word may have a strong resemblance to another word not used in polite company in another country. For example, global elevator maker Kone wanted to ensure correct pronunciation of its name and added an accent (Koné) to its name in French-speaking countries to avoid controversy. Other features of language have to be considered as well. In an LG ad, adaptation into Arabic was carried out without considering that Arabic reads from right to left. As a result, the creative concept in this execution was destroyed.

The role of language extends beyond that of a communications medium. Linguistic diversity often is an indicator of other types of diversity. In Quebec, the French language has always been a major consideration of most francophone governments because it is one of the clear manifestations of the identity of the province that separates it from the English-speaking provinces. The Charter of the French Language states that the rights of the francophone collectivity are, among others, the right of consumers to be informed and served in French. The Bay, a major Quebec retailer, spends $8 million annually on its translation operations. It even changed its name to La Baie in appropriate areas. Similarly, in trying to battle English as the lingua franca, the French government has tried to ban the use of any foreign term or expression wherever an officially approved French equivalent exists (e.g., *mercatique*, not *un brainstorming*).[18] This applies also to websites that bear the *.fr* designation; they have to be in the French language. Similarly, the Hong Kong government is promoting the use of Cantonese, rather than English, as the language of commerce.

Despite the fact that English is encountered daily by those on the Internet, the *e* in e-business does not translate into "English." Companies that tend to do the best job at web globalization are those that strive to treat customers in all markets equally. Instead of viewing themselves as *domestic* companies with *foreign* customers, they view themselves as *global* companies with *local* customers. This way of thinking permeates the design, functionality, and content of the websites, ensuring that a web user in South Korea has the same experience as a web user in Florida. For example, in 2011, Hotels.com, which is owned by Expedia, was ranked as the best global travel website. It supports over 35 languages in addition to English. Hotels.com meets not only language needs but also branding and design requirements. Each of the international Hotels.com sites has the same core design.[19]

Starting in late 2007, Internet users have been able to use addresses in 11 languages that do not use the Roman alphabet. Russians, for example, are able to type in web addresses entirely in Cyrillic characters instead of having to revert to English.[20] These are 2 billion people on the Internet, and the top languages by number of users are English, Chinese, Spanish, Japanese, Portuguese, German, Arabic, French, Russian, and Korean.[21]

Dealing with the language problem invariably requires the use of local assistance. A good local advertising agency and a good local market research firm can prevent many problems. When translation is required, as when communicating with suppliers or customers, care should be taken in selecting the translator or translation software. One of the simplest methods of control is

South Korea

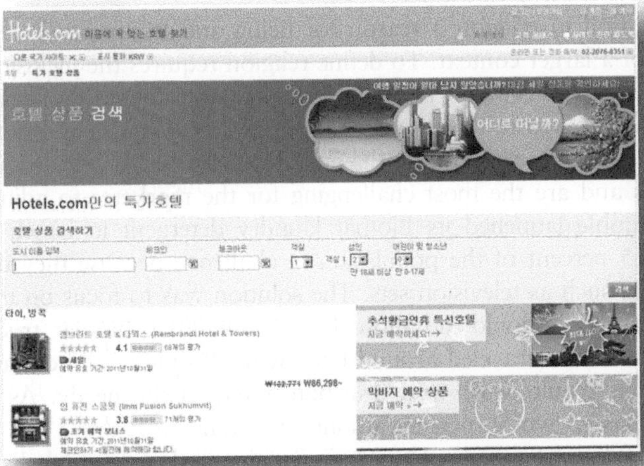

Greece

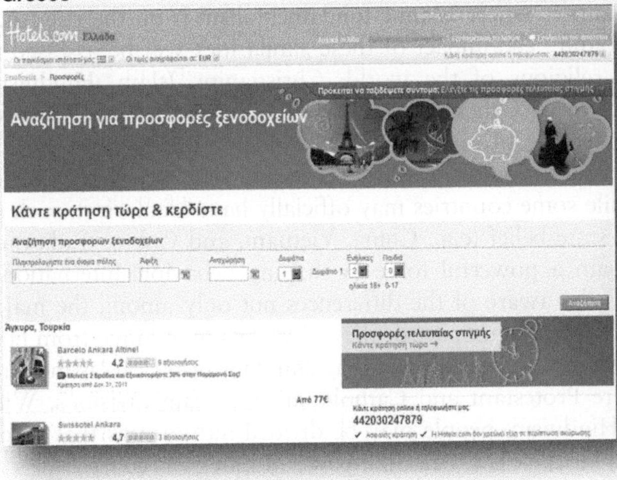

Courtesy of Hotels.com

Hotels.com's websites meet country language and design requirements.

back-translation—the translating of a foreign-language version back to the original language by a different person from the one who made the first translation. This approach may help to detect only omissions and blunders, however. To assess the quality of the translation, a complete evaluation with testing of the message's impact is necessary. In essence this means that international marketers should never translate words but emotion, which then in turn may well lead to the use of completely different words.

Nonverbal Language

Managers must analyze and become fluent in a diversity of culturally derived behavioral displays.[22] Five key topics—time, space, material possessions, friendship patterns, and business agreements—offer a starting point from which managers can begin to acquire the understanding necessary to do business in foreign countries. In many parts of the world, time is flexible and not seen as a limited commodity; people come late to appointments or may not come at all. In Hong Kong, for example, it is futile to set exact meeting times because getting from one place to another may take minutes or hours depending on the traffic. Showing indignation or impatience at such behavior would astonish an Arab, Latin American, or Asian.

In some countries, extended social acquaintance and the establishment of appropriate personal rapport are essential to conducting business. The feeling is that one should know one's business partner on a personal level before transactions can occur. Therefore, rushing straight to business will not be rewarded because deals are made not only on the basis of the best product or price but also on the entity or person deemed most trustworthy. Contracts may be bound on handshakes, not lengthy and complex agreements—a fact that makes some, especially Western, businesspeople uneasy.

Individuals vary in the amount of space they want separating them from others. Arabs and Latin Americans like to stand close to people they are talking with. If a U.S. executive, who may not be comfortable at such close range, backs away from an Arab, this might incorrectly be taken as a negative reaction.

International body language must be included in the nonverbal language of international business. For example, a U.S. manager may, after successful completion of negotiations, impulsively give a finger-and-thumb OK sign. In southern France, the manager will have indicated that the sale is worthless, and in Japan that a little bribe has been asked for; the gesture is grossly insulting to Brazilians. An interesting exercise is to compare and contrast the conversation styles of different nationalities. Northern Europeans are quite reserved in using their hands and maintain a good amount of personal space, whereas Southern Europeans involve their bodies to a far greater degree in making a point.

Misunderstanding nonverbal cues can undermine international negotiations. While Chinese negotiators usually lean back and make frequent eye contact while projecting negativity, Western negotiators usually avert their gaze.[23]

Religion

In most cultures, people find in religion a reason for being and legitimacy in the belief that they are part of a larger context. To define religion requires the inclusion of the supernatural and the existence of a higher power. Religion defines the ideals for life, which in turn are reflected in the values and attitudes of societies and individuals. Such values and attitudes shape the behavior and practices of institutions and members of cultures and are the most challenging for the marketer to adjust to. When Procter & Gamble launched its Biomat laundry detergent in Israel, it found Orthodox Jews (15 percent of the population) a challenge because they do not own traditional media such as television sets. The solution was to focus on the segment's core belief that they should aid those less fortunate. A Biomat truck equipped with washing machines traveled around key towns. People would donate their clothing, and Biomat would wash and distribute them to the needy. As a result, the brand's share has grown 50 percent among the segment.[24]

Religion provides the basis for transcultural similarities under shared beliefs and behavior. The impact will vary depending on the strength of the dominant religious tenets. While religion's impact may be quite indirect in Protestant Northern Europe, its impact in countries where Islamic fundamentalism is on the rise (such as Algeria) may be profound. The impact of these similarities will be assessed in terms of the dominant religions of the world: Christianity, Islam, Hinduism, Buddhism, and Confucianism. Other religions may have smaller numbers of followers, such as Judaism with 14 million followers around the world, but their impact is still significant due to the many centuries during which they have influenced world history. While some countries may officially have secularism, such as Marxism-Leninism, as a state belief (e.g., China, Vietnam, and Cuba), traditional religious beliefs still remain a powerful force in shaping behavior. International marketing managers must be aware of the differences not only among the major religions but also within them. The impact of these divisions may range from hostility, as in Sri Lanka, to barely perceptible but long-standing suspicion, as in many European countries where Protestant and Catholic are the main divisions. With some religions, such as Hinduism, people may be divided into groups that determine their status and to a large extent their ability to consume.

Christianity has the largest following among world religions, with more than 2 billion people.[25] While there are many significant groups within Christianity, the major ones are Catholicism and Protestantism. A prominent difference between the two is their attitude toward making money. While Catholicism has questioned it, the Protestant ethic has emphasized the importance of work and the accumulation of wealth for the glory of God. At the same time, frugality is stressed, and the residual accumulation of wealth from hard work has formed the basis for investment. It has been proposed that this is the basis for the development of capitalism in the Western world and for the rise of predominantly Protestant countries to world economic leadership in the twentieth century.

Major holidays are often tied to religion. Holidays will be observed differently from one culture to another, and the same holiday may have different connotations. Christian cultures observe Christmas and exchange gifts on either December 24 or 25, with the exception of the Dutch, who exchange gifts on St. Nicholas Day, December 6. Tandy Corporation (now RadioShack Corporation), in its first year in the Netherlands, targeted its major Christmas promotion for the third week of December with less than satisfactory results. The international marketing manager must see to it that local holidays, such as Mexico's *Dìa de los Muertos* (November 1 and 2), are taken into account in the scheduling of events ranging from fact-finding missions to marketing programs.

Islam, which reaches from the west coast of Africa to the Philippines and across a wide band that includes Tanzania, central Asia, western China, India, and Malaysia, has more than 1.2 billion followers. Islam is also a significant minority religion in many parts of the world, including Europe. It plays a

Prevailing World Religions

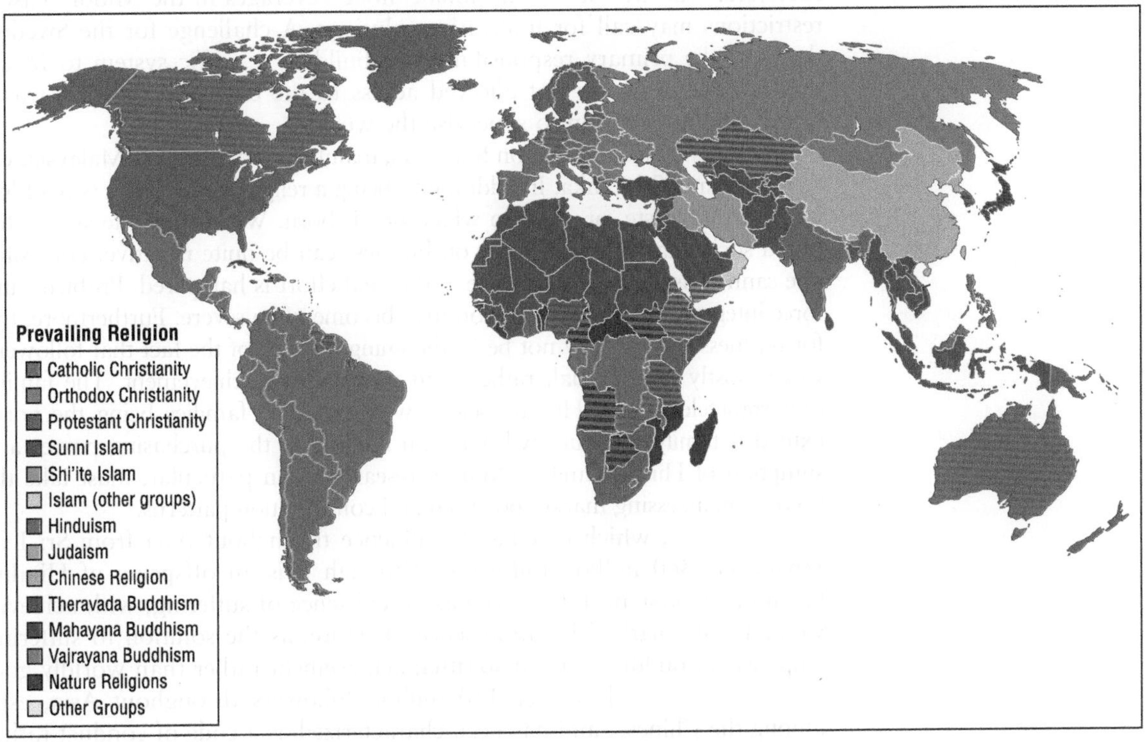

SOURCES: © Cengage Learning 2013; http://en.wikipedia.org/wiki/List_of_religious_populations.

pervasive role in the life of its followers, referred to as Muslims, through the *shari'ah* (law of Islam). This is most obvious in the five stated daily periods of prayer, fasting during the holy month of Ramadan, and the pilgrimage to Mecca, Islam's holy city. While Islam is supportive of entrepreneurship, it nevertheless strongly discourages acts that may be interpreted as exploitation. Islam also lacks discrimination except for those outside the religion. Some have argued that Islam's basic fatalism (that is, nothing happens without the will of Allah) and traditionalism have deterred economic development in countries observing the religion.

One of the important segments in the financial sector is Islamic banking. Given that Islam considers interest payments usury, bankers and Muslim scholars have worked to create interest-free banking that relies on lease agreements, mutual funds, and other methods to avoid paying interest. Banks and other financial companies have been successful in creating numerous Islamic finance instruments that have been judged as satisfying the Koran's concept of a just transaction. The market for Islamic finance has been growing at a rate of 15 percent annually and is becoming a competitive arena for Islamic banks and funds as well as global financial players. Currently, there are over 250 Islamic financial institutions managing funds of over $200 billion.[26]

The role of women in business is tied to religion, especially in the Middle East, where women are not able to function as they would in the West. The effects of this are numerous; for example, a firm may be limited in its use of female managers or personnel in these areas, and women's roles as consumers and influencers in the consumption process may be different. Except for food purchases, men make the final purchase decisions. Access to women in Islamic countries may only be possible through the use of female sales personnel, direct marketing, and women's specialty shops.[27]

Religion affects the marketing of products and service delivery. When beef or poultry is exported to an Islamic country, the animal must be killed in the *halal* method and certified appropriately. Recognition of religious restrictions on products (e.g., alcoholic beverages) can reveal opportunities, as evidenced by successful launches of several nonalcoholic beverages in the Middle East. Other restrictions may call for innovative solutions. A challenge for the Swedish firm that had the primary responsibility for building a traffic system to Mecca was that non-Muslims are not allowed access to the city. The solution was to use closed-circuit television to supervise the work.

Hinduism has 860 million followers, mainly in India, Nepal, Malaysia, Guyana, Suriname, and Sri Lanka. In addition to being a religion, it is also a way of life predicated on the caste, or class, to which one is born. While the caste system has produced social stability, its impact on business can be quite negative. For example, if one cannot rise above one's caste, individual effort is hampered. Problems in workforce integration and coordination may become quite severe. Furthermore, the drive for business success may not be forthcoming because of the fact that followers place value mostly on spiritual, rather than materialistic, achievement. The family is an important element in Hindu society, with extended families being the norm. The extended family structure will have an impact on the purchasing power and consumption of Hindu families. Market researchers, in particular, must take this into account in assessing market potential and consumption patterns.

Buddhism, which extends its influence throughout Asia from Sri Lanka to Japan, has 360 million followers. Although it is an offspring of Hinduism, it has no caste system. Life is seen as an existence of suffering, with achieving nirvana, a state marked by an absence of desire, as the solution to suffering. The emphasis in Buddhism is on spiritual achievement rather than worldly goods.

Confucianism has over 150 million followers throughout Asia, especially among the Chinese, and has been characterized as a code of conduct rather than a religion. However, its teachings that stress loyalty and relationships have been broadly adopted. Loyalty to central authority and placing the good of a group before that of the individual may explain the economic success of Japan, South Korea, Singapore, and the Republic of China. These factors also have led to cultural misunderstandings: in Western societies there has been a perception that the subordination of the individual to the common good has resulted in the sacrifice of human rights. The emphasis on relationships is very evident when developing business ties in Asia. The preparatory stage may take years before the needed level of understanding is reached and actual business transactions can take place.

Values and Attitudes

Values are shared beliefs or group norms that have been internalized by individuals.[28] Attitudes are evaluations of alternatives based on these values. The Japanese culture raises an almost invisible—yet often unscalable—wall against all *gaijin*, foreigners. Many middle-aged bureaucrats and company officials, for example, feel that buying foreign products is unpatriotic. The resistance therefore is not so much against foreign products as it is against those who produce and market them. As a result, foreign-based corporations have had difficulty in hiring university graduates or midcareer personnel because of bias against foreign employers. Dealing in China and with the Chinese, the international marketing manager will have to realize that marketing has more to do with cooperation than competition. The Chinese believe that one should build the relationship first, and if that is successful, transactions will follow. The relationship, or *guanxi*, is a set of exchanges of favors to establish trust.[29]

The more rooted values and attitudes are in central beliefs (such as religion), the more cautiously the international marketing manager has to move. Attitude toward change is basically positive in industrialized countries, whereas in more tradition-bound societies change is viewed with great suspicion, especially when it comes from a foreign entity.

To counter the perceived influence of Mattel's Barbie and Ken dolls on Iranian values, a government agency affiliated with Iran's Ministry of Education is marketing its own Dara and Sara dolls. The new products, a brother and sister, are modeled on Iranian school book characters. Sara is dressed in a white headscarf covering black or brown curls. A popular outfit is a full-length, flower-dotted chador, which covers the doll from head to toe. One toy seller explained that playing with Mattel's golden-haired, skimpily dressed Barbie may lead girls to grow up into women who reject Iranian values.[30]

Cultural attitudes are not always a deterrent to foreign business practices or foreign goods. Japanese youth, for instance, display extremely positive attitudes toward Western goods, from popular music to Nike sneakers to Louis Vuitton haute couture to Starbucks lattes. Even in Japan's faltering economy, global brands are able to charge premium prices if they are able to tap into cultural attitudes that revere imported goods. Similarly, attitudes of U.S. youth toward Japanese "cool" have increased the popularity of authentic Japanese "manga" comics and animated cartoons. Pokémon cards and the popular cooking show *Iron Chef* are examples of Japanese products that caught on in the United States almost as quickly as in Japan.[31]

In Asia, price is a crucial part of customization. Levi Strauss recently announced that it would let customers in India pay in three monthly installments for jeans costing more than $33. A pilot version of the program in Bangalore showed the company that consumers who took advantage of this option spent an average of 50 percent more. Introducing this adaptation enabled Levi Strauss to preserve the status of its jeans as an upmarket, aspirational product while bringing them within reach of millions of less affluent young consumers.[32] Retailers and consumer product companies are learning that fast supply chains for some categories assure fresher products and a quicker response to trends in everything from fashion to consumer electronics.

Manners and Customs

Changes occurring in manners and customs must be carefully monitored, especially in cases that seem to indicate narrowing of cultural differences between peoples. Phenomena such as McDonald's and Coke have met with success around the world, but this does not mean that the world is becoming Westernized. Modernization and Westernization are not at all the same, as can be seen in Saudi Arabia, for example. Both views are superficially right, and both miss the most significant uniformity generated by globalization: *in our ways of thinking and living*. Globalization cannot be rejected because it represents a transformation that we ourselves have brought about—and which has already transformed us—also called cultural convergence.

Understanding manners and customs is especially important in negotiations because interpretations based on one's own frame of reference may lead to an incorrect conclusion. To negotiate effectively abroad, one needs to read correctly all types of communication. U.S. executives often interpret inaction and silence as a negative sign, so Japanese executives tend to expect their U.S. counterparts to lower prices or sweeten the deal if they just say as little as possible. Even a simple agreement may take days to negotiate in the Middle East because the Arab party may want to talk about unrelated issues or do something else for a while. The abrasive style of Russian negotiators, and their usual last-minute change requests, may cause astonishment and concern on the part of ill-prepared negotiators. And consider the reaction of a U.S. businessperson if a Finnish counterpart were to propose the continuing of negotiations in the sauna. Preparation is needed not only in the business sense but in a cultural sense as well. Some of the potential areas in which marketers may not be prepared include (1) insufficient understanding of different ways of thinking; (2) insufficient attention to the necessity of saving face; (3) insufficient knowledge and appreciation of the host country—its history, culture, government, and image of foreigners; (4) insufficient recognition of the decision-making process and the role of personal relations and personalities; and (5) insufficient allocation of time for negotiations.[33]

EXHIBIT 3.2 When to Give Gifts and What to Give

China	Germany	India	Japan	Mexico	Saudi Arabia	Russia
Chinese New Year (January or February)	Christmas/ New Year	Hindu Diwali festival (October or November)	Oseibo (January 1)	Christmas/ New Year	Id al-Fitr (December or January)	Christmas/ New Year
✓ Liqueur, fine pens, solar calculators, kitchen gadgets, stamps, cigarette lighters	✓ Quality pens, tasteful office items, imported liquor, fine chocolates	✓ Chocolates, sweets, Dutch wooden shoes or clogs, Swiss knives, French perfume, framed photographs	✓ Company gifts or something represents your culture, good alcohol or name-brand items	✓ Items with your company's logo, wine or Scotch	✓ Handmade carpet, traditional perfume	✓ Chocolates, dessert items, good wine or other alcohol (something other than vodka)
✗ Scissors, knives, straw sandals, clocks, handkerchiefs, four of any item	✗ Red roses are for lovers, lilies are used in funerals, beer	✗ Leather items, snake images	✗ Gifts that come in sets of four or nine	✗ Silver items	✗ Gold jewelry or silk garments	✗ Pencils, pens, lighters, cheap wine or vodka, notebooks

SOURCE: www.executiveplanet.com/index.php, accessed August 22, 2011.

One instance when preparation and sensitivity are called for is in the area of gift giving. Exhibit 3.2 provides examples of what to give and when. An ideal gift is one that represents the giver's own culture while being sensitive to the recipient's. For example, a Finn may give a Suunto compass to a Saudi business partner (to help him determine the direction for daily prayers). Giving gifts that are easily available in that country (e.g., chocolates to a Swiss) is not advisable. Some gifts are not suitable: clocks or other timepieces are symbols of death in China, while handkerchiefs symbolize tears in Latin America and Korea. Gifts are an important part of relationship management during visits and a way of recognizing partners during holidays. Care should be taken with the way the gift is wrapped; for example, it should be in appropriately colored paper. If delivered in person, the actual giving has to be executed correctly; in China, this is done by extending the gift to the recipient using both hands.[34] It should be noted, however, that many companies in the United States have policies that do not allow the giving and receiving of gifts.

Managers must be concerned with differences in the ways products are used. The international manager must ask, "What are we selling?" "What are the use benefits we should be providing?" and "Who or what are we competing against?" Campbell Soup has targeted China as one of the markets with the strongest growth potentials for soup. However, homemade soups account for 99 percent of the consumption. With this in mind, Campbell's prices have been kept at an attractive level, and the product is promoted on convenience. Care should be taken not to assume cross-border similarities even if many of the indicators converge. For example, a jam producer noted that the Brazilian market seemed to hold significant potential because per capita jelly and jam consumption was one-tenth that of Argentina, clearly a difference not justified by obvious factors. However, Argentines consume jam at tea time, a custom that does not exist in Brazil. Furthermore, Argentina's climate and soil favor growing wheat, leading it to consume three times the amount of bread Brazil does.[35]

Approaches that might be rarely taken in the United States or Europe could be recommended in other regions; for example, Conrad Hotels (the international arm of Hilton) experienced low initial occupancy rates at its Hong Kong facility until the firm brought in a *feng shui* practitioner. These traditional consultants are foretellers of future events and the unknown through occult means and are used extensively by Hong Kong businesses, especially for advising about where to locate offices and how to position office equipment.[36] In Conrad's case, the suggestion was to move a piece of sculpture outside of the hotel's lobby because one of the characters in the statue looked like it was trying to run out of the hotel.

Meticulous research plays a major role in avoiding these types of problems. Concept tests determine the potential acceptance and proper understanding of a proposed new product. **Focus groups**, each consisting of 8 to 12 consumers representative of the proposed target audience, can be interviewed and their responses used to check for disasters and to fine-tune research findings. The most sensitive types of products, such as consumer packaged goods, require consumer usage and attitude studies as well as retail distribution studies and audits to analyze the movement of the product to retailers and eventually to households. H.J. Heinz Co. uses focus groups to determine what consumers want in ketchup in the way of taste and image. U.S. consumers prefer a relatively sweet ketchup, while Europeans go for a spicier variety. In Central Europe and Sweden, Heinz sells a hot ketchup in addition to the classic variety.

In addition to changes in the product, the company may need to promote new usage situations. For example, in Greece this may mean running advertisements showing how ketchup can be poured on pasta, eggs, and cuts of meat. While some markets consider Heinz's U.S. origin a plus, there are others where it has to be played down. In Northern Europe, where ketchup is served as an accompaniment to traditional meatballs and fishballs, Heinz deliberately avoids reminding consumers of its heritage. Their messages tend to be health related. A new European innovation center is opening in December 2012, and the building will be an inspiring location where consumers, clients, researchers, and marketing people come together to work at the latest Heinz innovations.[37] **In-depth studies** are also used to study consumer needs across markets. Intel, for example, has a team of 10 ethnographers traveling the world to find out how to redesign existing products or to come up with new ones to fit different cultures and demographic groups.

The adjustment to cultural variables in the marketplace may have to be long term and accomplished through trial and error. For example, U.S. retailers have found that Japanese consumers are baffled by the warehouse-like atmosphere of the U.S-style retail outlets. When Office Depot reduced the size of its Tokyo store by a third and crammed the merchandise closer together, sales remained at the same level as before.[38]

Material Elements

Material culture results from technology and is directly related to the way a society organizes its economic activity. It is manifested in the availability and adequacy of the basic economic, social, financial, and marketing **infrastructures**. The basic economic infrastructure consists of transportation, energy, and communications systems. Social infrastructure refers to housing, health, and educational systems. Financial and marketing infrastructures provide the facilitating agencies for the international firm's operation in a given market in terms of, for example, banks and research firms. In some parts of the world, the international firm may have to be an integral partner in developing the various infrastructures before it can operate, whereas in others it may greatly benefit from their high level of sophistication.

While infrastructure is often a good indicator of potential demand, goods sometimes discover unexpectedly rich markets due to the informal economy at work in developing nations. In Kenya, for example, where most of the country's 41 million people live on less than $2 to $20 dollar a day, more than 22 million people have signed up for mobile phone service.[39] Leapfrogging older technologies, mobile phones are especially attractive to Kenya's thousands of small-business entrepreneurs—market stall owners, taxi drivers, and even hustlers who sell on the sidewalks. For most, income goes unreported, creating an invisible wealth on the streets. Mobile phones outnumber fixed lines in Kenya as well as in Uganda, Venezuela, Cambodia, South Korea, and Chile. This development is attractive for marketers as well, given the expense of laying land lines.

Future ability to purchase things by waving our phones and ultimately replacing our wallets with them is a hot topic among tech enthusiasts at the moment, but it is going to be a few years before the technology is widespread enough to be used by a majority of consumers.[40] Eighty-five percent of point-of-sale (POS) terminals will support near-field communications (NFC) for mobile payments by 2016. "M-payments" have taken off in Japan and Korea but failed to reach estimated potential within the European Union and the United States. Reasons for this can be found in the lack of readiness in existing technology, unwillingness of the various stakeholders (banks, credit card issuers, handset makers, and telecommunication companies) to collaborate, as well as cultural variables in terms of existing usage patterns and perceptions of risk and relative advantage of a new technology. In markets where mobile diffusion is high (such as the Nordic countries) or in countries where cash still accounts for a majority of retail transactions (e.g., Germany and Central Europe), chances may be better. In Central Europe, for example, merchants may be eager to switch to cashless systems at the expense of handling currency. At the same time, all of the stakeholders need to demonstrate to mobile phone users that m-payments are much more attractive than other familiar payment schemes. The bundle of convenience items (safe, secure, available, fast, transparent) needs to be packaged and sold to target groups.[41] Visa announced that it will launch a next-generation digital wallet service. The platform will allow consumers to create a digitized version of their actual wallet in which they load all their cards, whether Visa or not. Even merchant loyalty cards will be supported. Visa teamed up with Samsung in order to bring NFC-enabled mobile payments to the London 2012 Olympics. With any NFC-capable phone, mobile users will be able to pay for purchases using only their phone at over 60,000 locations in London. Banks are also ramping up for the mobile payments revolution.

Again, however, the advent of new technologies must be culturally calibrated, as seen in *The International Marketplace 3.3*.

Aesthetics

Each culture makes a clear statement concerning good taste as expressed in the arts and in the particular symbolism of colors, form, and music. What is and what is not acceptable may vary dramatically even in otherwise highly similar markets. Sex in advertising is an example. In an apparent attempt to preserve the purity of Japanese womanhood, Japanese advertisers frequently turn to blonde, blue-eyed foreign models to make the point. In introducing the shower soap Fa from the European market to the Middle East, Africa, Asia Pacific region, and Latin America, Henkel also extended its European advertising campaign to the new market. The main difference was to have the young woman in the waves don a bathing suit rather than be naked, as in the German original.

Color is often used as a mechanism for brand identification, feature reinforcement, and differentiation. In international markets, colors have more symbolic value than in domestic markets. Black, for instance, is considered the color of mourning in the United States and Europe, whereas white has the same symbolic value in China, India, and most of the Far East. LG, interested in entering the Indian market, heavily invested in local R&D and staffed its operations with thousands of top-notch Indian designers and engineers in their Bangalore product innovation center. LG entered the Indian marketplace with brighter-color refrigerators and smaller freezers, big family washing machines, and one-touch "Indian menu"–function microwaves.[42]

International firms have to take into consideration local tastes and concerns in designing their facilities. They may have a general policy of uniformity in building or office space design, but local tastes may often warrant modifications. Respecting local cultural traditions may also generate goodwill toward

THE INTERNATIONAL MARKETPLACE 3.3

Global SEM: A Story in Three Acts

International search engine marketing (SEM) can be difficult on any given day with multiple languages and locations and complicated cultural subtones. The goal is to achieve consistent branding across cultures while crafting communications that are meaningful for web surfers in each micromarket. Finding the right skilled language service provider with the cultural and linguistic expertise to guide you through the process can make the path smoother.

Before You Localize Your Website ...

First, pick the right domain extension for each new locale. Search engines have traditionally given preference to sites with local top-level domain name extensions such as .fi, .cn, .de, .uk, and .au. The Internet Corporation for Assigned Names and Numbers (ICANN) policy enables top-level domain and URL creation in any language or script, not just ASCII (English keyboard norms). The key to this experience is to find the best language vendor partner and to obtain a local IP address, as international search bots have a proven local bias. Check out your competition's website, source code, pay-per-click campaigns, and landing pages. Examine what needs to be translated from your home site to save time and money.

As You Localize Your Site ...

Now you need to work closely with your language partner to adapt the site to best target markets with SEO (search engine optimization) keywords. Keyword creation and seeding is challenging in the domestic market but can be both an art and science when you cross cultures and borders. Your language partner will create an ontology list of keywords with different options and rank them, providing you with their recommendations for the highest performance. Once you have decided on the keywords and phrases, seed them throughout your foreign-language websites from titles, headings, and URLs, to descriptions and image and video tags.

After You Localize Your Site ...

Always incorporate references to local events and holidays in your ads for the biggest impact. An in-country expert will be able to help develop your holiday promotion editorial calendar. Holidays worldwide, such as Mother's Day, do not always coincide across countries. Carefully choose your website's "positive" keywords with native-speaker instincts and an emphasis on local bias, but also be aware of the "negative" keywords in any campaign. Everything from your copy to visuals to functionality must be culturally appropriate and consistent with your ads, incorporating your keywords. This ensures international web browsers can easily follow the trail to your website.

Finally, promote your site through social media channels and with link building. An in-country expert can work with you to select and concentrate on the most popular social media sites. With some careful planning, research, and the right language partner, you will be well on your way to joining the ranks of today's star international marketers.

SOURCES: Michael Kris, "Global SEM: A Story in Three Acts," *Marketing News*, September 30, 2011; and Acclaro, www.acclaro.com.

the international marketer. For example, McDonald's painstakingly renovated a seventeenth-century building for its third outlet in Moscow. History may also play a role. The Shanghai World Financial Center (developed largely by the Japanese Mori Building Corporation) became the second tallest structure in China at 492 meters (1,641 feet). The most distinctive feature in the design of the building is an opening at the peak (the functional reason of which is to allow airflow). The opening originally was meant to be a circular moon gate, but the intended design met with opposition from the Chinese, who saw it resembling the rising sun design of the Japanese flag. It was replaced by a trapezoidal hole featuring an observation deck on the 100th floor.

Education

Education, either formal or informal, plays a major role in the passing on and sharing of culture. Educational levels of a culture can be assessed using literacy rates and enrollment in secondary or higher education, information available

The Shanghai World Financial Center is the second tallest structure in China.

from secondary data sources. International firms also need to know about the qualitative aspects of education, namely, varying emphases on particular skills and the overall level of the education provided. Japan and the Republic of Korea, for example, emphasize the sciences, especially engineering, to a greater degree than do Western countries.

Educational levels will have an impact on various business functions. Training programs for a production facility will have to take the educational backgrounds of trainees into account. For example, a high level of illiteracy will suggest the use of visual aids rather than printed manuals. Local recruiting for sales jobs will be affected by the availability of suitably trained personnel. In some cases, international firms routinely send locally recruited personnel to headquarters for training.

The international marketing manager may also have to be prepared to fight obstacles in recruiting a suitable sales force or support personnel. For example, highly skilled Chinese professionals preferred working for Western multinationals by 41 percent in 2007. Attracting talent in emerging markets has always been a challenge for Western multinationals, but historically they did enjoy an advantage. However, with Western firms and their brands taking a significant financial hit, reducing hiring, cutting expenses, and laying off employees, there has been shrinkage in Chinese professionals seeking these jobs in 2011. International marketing managers are finding that these highly skilled candidates prefer to stay domestic, potentially optimizing their immediate and long-term career development opportunities in one of the world's fastest-growing economies.[43]

Social Institutions

Social institutions affect the ways in which people relate to each other. The family unit, which in Western industrialized countries consists of parents and children, in a number of cultures is extended to include grandparents and other relatives. This will have an impact on consumption patterns and must be taken into account, for example, when conducting market research.

The concept of kinship, or blood relations between individuals, is defined in a very broad way in societies such as those in sub-Saharan Africa. Family relations and a strong obligation to family are important factors to be considered in human resource management in those regions. Understanding tribal politics in countries such as Nigeria may help the manager avoid unnecessary complications in executing business transactions.

The division of a particular population into classes is termed **social stratification**. Stratification ranges from the situation in Northern Europe, where most people are members of the middle class, to highly stratified societies such as India, in which the higher strata control most of the buying power and decision-making positions.

An important part of the socialization process of consumers worldwide is **reference groups**. These groups provide the values and attitudes that become influential in shaping behavior. Primary reference groups include the family, coworkers, and other intimate groupings, whereas secondary groups are social organizations in which less-continuous interaction takes place, such as professional associations and trade organizations. Besides socialization, reference groups develop an individual's concept of self, which manifests itself, for example, through the use of products. Reference groups also provide a baseline for compliance with group norms through either conforming to or avoiding certain behaviors.

Social organization also determines the roles of managers and subordinates and the way they relate to one another. In some cultures, managers and subordinates are separated explicitly and implicitly by various boundaries ranging from social class differences to separate office facilities. In others, cooperation is elicited through equality. For example, Nissan USA has no reserved parking spaces and no private dining rooms, everyone wears the same type of white coveralls, and the president sits in the same room with a hundred other white-collar workers. The fitting of an organizational culture for internal marketing purposes to the larger context of a national culture has to be executed with care. Changes that are too dramatic may cause disruption of productivity or, at the minimum, suspicion.

Sources of Cultural Knowledge

The concept of cultural knowledge is broad and multifaceted. **Cultural knowledge** can be defined by the way it is acquired. Objective or **factual information** is obtained from others through communication, research, and education. **Experiential knowledge**, on the other hand, can be acquired only by being involved in a culture other than one's own. A summary of the types of knowledge needed by the international manager is provided in Exhibit 3.3. Both factual and experiential information can be general or country specific. In fact, the more a manager becomes involved in the international arena, the more he or she is able to develop a metaknowledge, that is, ground rules that apply to a great extent whether in Kuala Lumpur, Malaysia, or Asunción, Paraguay. Market-specific knowledge does not necessarily travel well; the general variables on which the information is based do.

In a survey on how to acquire international expertise, managers ranked eight factors in terms of their importance, as shown in Exhibit 3.4. These managers emphasized the experiential acquisition of knowledge. Written materials were indicated to play an important but supplementary role, very often providing general or country-specific information before operational decisions must be made. Interestingly, many of today's international managers have precareer experience in government, the Peace Corps, the armed forces, or missionary service. Although the survey emphasized travel, a one-time trip to London with a stay at a large hotel and scheduled sight-seeing tours does not contribute to cultural knowledge in a significant way. Travel that involves meetings with company personnel, intermediaries, facilitating agents, customers, and government officials, on the other hand, does contribute.

However, from the corporate point of view, the development of a global capability requires experience acquisition in more involved ways. This translates into foreign assignments and networking across borders, for example through

EXHIBIT 3.3 Types of International Information

	Type of Information	
Source of Information	**General**	**Country-Specific**
Objective	Examples: • Impact of GDP • Regional integration	Examples: • Tariff barriers • Government regulations
Experiential	Example: • Corporate adjustment to internationalization	Examples: • Product acceptance • Program appropriateness

SOURCE: © Cengage Learning 2013.

EXHIBIT 3.4 Managers' Ranking of Factors Involved in Acquiring International Expertise

Factor	Considered Critical	Considered Important	Not Important
1. Assignments overseas	84%	16%	0%
2. Business travel	57	38	5
3. Training programs	43	49	8
4. Nonbusiness travel	9	66	25
5. Reading	30	58	12
6. Graduate courses	24	65	11
7. Precareer activities	14	55	31
8. Undergraduate courses	6	38	57

SOURCE: Data collected by authors from 115 executives, by questionnaire, April 2011.

the use of multicountry, multicultural teams to develop strategies and programs. At Nestlé, for example, managers shuffle around a region (such as Asia or Latin America) at four- to five-year intervals and may have tours at headquarters for two to three years between such assignments. This allows these managers to pick up ideas and tools to be used in markets where they have not been used or where they have not been necessary up to now. In Thailand, where supermarkets are revolutionizing consumer-goods marketing, techniques perfected elsewhere in the Nestlé system are being put to effective use. These experiences will then in turn be used to develop newly emerging markets in the same region, such as Vietnam.

Various sources and methods are available to the manager for extending his or her knowledge of specific cultures. Most of these sources deal with factual information that provides a necessary basis for market studies. Beyond the normal business literature and its anecdotal information, country-specific studies are published by governments, private companies, and universities. The U.S. Department of Commerce's (www.commerce.gov) *Country Commercial Guides* cover 133 countries, while the Economist Intelligence Unit's (www.eiu.com) *Country Reports* cover 180 countries. *Culturegrams* (www.culture-grams.com), which detail the customs of peoples of 187 countries, are published by the Center for International and Area Studies at Brigham Young University. Many facilitating agencies—such as advertising agencies, banks, consulting firms, and transportation companies—provide background information on the markets they serve for their clients. These range from AIRINC's (www.air-inc.com) international reports on site selections and cost of living for 125 countries and the Hong Kong and Shanghai Banking Corporation's (www.hsbc.com) "Business Profile" series (Dubai, Hong Kong, Singapore, South Africa, UK), to *World Trade* magazine's (http://worldtrademag.com) "Put Your Best Foot Forward" series, which covers Europe, Asia, Canada and Mexico, and Russia.

Many of the marketer's facilitators are equipped for advising the marketer on the cultural dimensions of their efforts. Their task is integrating culture as an ingredient of success in the program. See Exhibit 3.5 for an example of such a service provider.

International business success requires not only comprehensive fact finding and preparation but also an ability to understand and fully appreciate the nuances of different cultural traits and patterns. Gaining this interpretive knowledge requires "getting one's feet wet" over a sufficient length of time. Over the long run, culture can become a factor in the firm's overall success.

EXHIBIT 3.5 An Example of Culture Consulting

UNLOCK THE BUYING POWER
OF ASIAN AMERICAN CUSTOMERS.

SOURCE: © interTrend Communications, Inc.

CULTURAL ANALYSIS

The key variable of the model is to try to understand and explain differences among cultures and subsequently in cross-cultural behavior, the marketer must function within these three constructs: (1) the cultural lifestyle of individuals in terms of how deeply held their traditional beliefs and attitudes are, and also which elements of culture are dominant; (2) change agents (such as international marketers and their practices) and strategic opinion leaders (e.g., social elites); and (3) communication about the innovation from commercial sources, neutral sources (such as government), and social sources (such as friends and relatives).

It has been argued that differences in cultural lifestyle can be accounted for by five major dimensions of culture.[44] These dimensions consist of (1) individualism–collectivism (e.g., "I" consciousness versus "we" consciousness), (2) power distance (e.g., level of equality in a society), (3) uncertainty avoidance (e.g., need for formal rules and regulations), (4) gender-role orientation (e.g., attitudes toward achievement, roles of men and women), and (5) long-term versus short-term orientation (e.g., virtues oriented toward future rewards). Exhibit 3.6 presents a summary of 12 countries' positions along these dimensions. All the high-scoring

EXHIBIT 3.6 Culture Dimension Scores for 12 Countries (0 = Low; 100 = High)

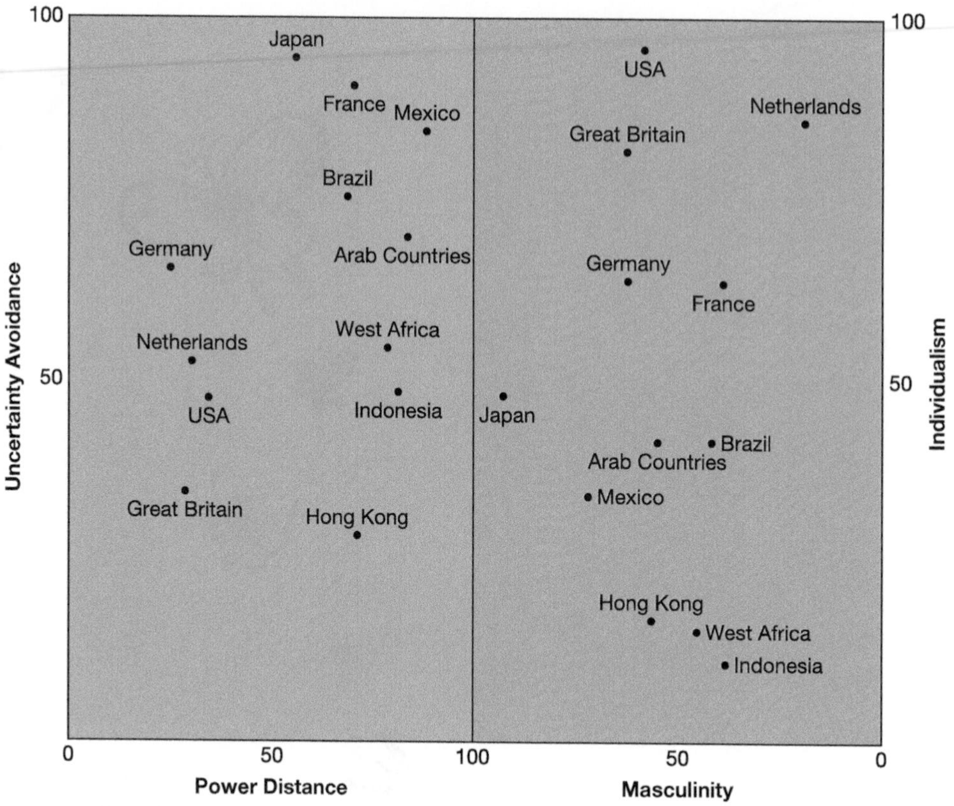

SOURCE: Data for the figure derived from Geert Hofstede, "Management Scientists Are Human," *Management Science* 40, no. 1 (1994): 4–13.

countries on the fifth dimension (not shown in the exhibit) are Asian (e.g., China, Hong Kong, Taiwan, Japan, and South Korea), while most Western countries (such as the United States and Britain) have low scores. Some have argued that this cultural dimension may explain the Japanese marketing success based on market-share (rather than short-term profit) motivation in market development.[45]

The Global Leadership and Organizational Behavior Effectiveness Research Project (GLOBE) is an international group of social scientists and management scholars who study cross-cultural leadership. GLOBE has focused on universals and culture-based differences in perceived effectiveness of leadership attributes by asking middle managers whether certain leader characteristics and behaviors would help or hinder a person in becoming an outstanding leader.[46]

Knowledge of similarities along these dimensions allows us to cluster countries and regions and establish regional and national marketing programs. An example is provided in Exhibit 3.7, in which the global wireless communication market is segmented along cultural lines for the development of programs. Research has shown that the take-off point for new products (i.e., when initial sales turn into mass-market sales) is six years on average in Europe. However, in Northern Europe, new products take off almost twice as fast as they do in Southern Europe. Culturally, consumers in cluster 5 are far more open to new ideas and products, and this has remained at the forefront of technological innovation and adoption. Cluster 3, consisting of south-central Europe, Latin America, and several Asian countries, represents the youngest technology market and displays the highest level of uncertainty avoidance. It should, therefore, be targeted with risk-reducing marketing programs such as extended warranties and return privileges. It is important to position the product as a continuous innovation that does not require radical changes in consumption patterns.[47]

EXHIBIT 3.7 Culture-Based Segmentation

	Cultural Characteristics				
	Power Distance	**Uncertainty Avoidance**	**Individualism**	**Masculinity**	**Illustrative Marketing Implications**
Cluster 1: Argentina, Italy, Belgium, Japan, Brazil, Poland, France, Spain, Germany, Turkey, Greece, United Arab Emirates	Medium	Strong	Medium	High	Early to medium technology adopters (with Japan increasingly acting as an outlier/innovator); appeal to consumer's status power position; reduce perceived risk in product purchase and use; emphasize product functionality.
Cluster 2: Australia, Austria, United States, Ireland, Israel, Switzerland, United Kingdom	Small	Medium	High	High	Early technology adopters; preference for "high-performance" products; use "successful-achiever" theme in advertising; desire for novelty, variety, and pleasure; fairly risk averse.
Cluster 3: Chile, Colombia, Costa Rica, El Salvador, Ecuador, Estonia, Iran, Korea, Latvia, Lithuania, Pakistan, Panama, Peru, Portugal, Romania, Slovenia, Thailand, Taiwan, Venezuela	High	Strong	Low	Medium-low	Late technology adopters; highly risk averse, partly due to lower discretionary income levels; emphasize product practicality, durability, and functionality.
Cluster 4: China, Hong Kong, Singapore	High	Low	Low	Medium	Medium to late technology adopters; however, rapid dissemination through imitation, once adopted; "status-symbol"–themed advertising.
Cluster 5: Denmark, Finland, Netherlands, Norway, Sweden	Small	Low	High	Low	Innovators and early technology adopters; relatively weak resistance to new products; strong consumer desire for novelty and variety.

SOURCE: Reprinted from *Journal of Business Research*, 58 (1), Sanna Sundqvist, Lauri Frank, and Kaisu Puumalainen, "The Effects of Country Characteristics, Cultural Similarity and Adoption Timing on the Diffusion of Wireless Communications," 107–110, © 2005, reprinted with permission from Elsevier.

Understanding the implications of the dimensions helps the marketer prepare for encounters. When negotiating in Germany, one can expect a counterpart who is not only thorough, systematic, very well prepared, but also rather dogmatic and therefore lacking in flexibility and compromise; great emphasis is placed on efficiency. In Mexico, however, the counterpart may prefer to address problems on a personal and private basis rather than on a business level. This means more emphasis on socializing and conveying one's humanity, sincerity, loyalty, and friendship. Also, the differences in pace and business practices of the region have to be accepted. Boeing found in its annual study on world aviation safety that countries with both low individualism and substantial power distances had accident rates 2.6 times greater than at the other end of the scale. These findings will naturally have an impact on training and service operations of airlines.

Communication about the innovation takes place through the physical product itself (samples) or through a new policy in the company. If a new practice, such as quality circles or pan-regional planning, is in question, results may be communicated in reports or through word of mouth by the participating employees. Communication content depends on the following factors: the product's or policy's relative advantage over existing alternatives; compatibility with established behavioral patterns; complexity, or the degree to which the product or process is perceived as difficult to understand and use; trialability, or the degree to which the product or process may be experimented with and not incur major risk; and observability, which is the extent to which the consequences of the innovation are visible.

Before the product or policy is evaluated, information about it will be compared with existing beliefs about the circumstances surrounding the situation.

Distortion will occur as a result of selective attention, exposure, and retention. As examples, anything foreign may be seen in a negative light, another multinational company's efforts may have failed, or the government may implicitly discourage the proposed activity. Additional information may then be sought from any of the input sources or from opinion leaders in the market.

Adoption tendency refers to the likelihood that the product or process will be accepted. Individualism has a significant positive relationship and uncertainty avoidance a negative relationship with acceptance and diffusion rates of new products.[48] Similar findings have been reached on the penetration of e-commerce in different markets.[49] If an innovation clears the hurdles, it may be adopted and slowly diffused into the entire market. An international manager has two basic choices: adapt company offerings and methods to those in the market or try to change market conditions to fit company programs.

In Japan, a number of Western companies have run into obstructions in the Japanese distribution system, where great value is placed on established relationships; everything is done on the basis of favoring the familiar and fearing the unfamiliar. In most cases, this problem is solved by joint venturing with a major Japanese entity that has established contacts. On occasion, when the company's approach is compatible with the central beliefs of a culture, the company may be able to change existing customs rather than adjust to them. Initially, Procter & Gamble's traditional hard-selling style in television commercials jolted most Japanese viewers accustomed to more subtle approaches. Now the ads are being imitated by Japanese competitors. The emphasis in Japan is still on who speaks rather than on what is spoken. That is why, for example, Japan is a market where Procter & Gamble's company name is presented, as well as the brand name of the product, in the marketing communication for a brand rather than using only the product's brand name, which is customary in the U.S. and European markets.

Any analysis is incomplete without the basic recognition of cultural differences. Adjusting to differences requires putting one's own cultural values aside. Most international business problems are rooted in a self-reference criterion—the unconscious reference to one's own cultural values. However, recognizing and admitting this are often quite difficult. The following analytical approach is recommended to reduce the influence of one's own cultural values:

1. Define the problem or goal in terms of domestic cultural traits, habits, or norms.
2. Define the problem or goal in terms of foreign cultural traits, habits, or norms. Make no value judgments.
3. Isolate the self-reference criterion influence in the problem and examine it carefully to see how it complicates the problem.
4. Redefine the problem without the self-reference criterion influence and solve for the optimal goal situation.

This approach can be applied to product introduction. If Kellogg Co. wants to introduce breakfast cereals into markets where breakfast is traditionally not eaten or where consumers drink very little milk, managers must consider very carefully how to instill this new habit. The traits, habits, and norms of breakfast are quite different in the United States, France, and Brazil, and they have to be outlined before the product can be introduced. In France, Kellogg's commercials are aimed as much at providing nutrition lessons as they are at promoting the product. In Brazil, the company advertised on a soap opera to gain entry into the market because Brazilians often emulate the characters of these television shows.

Analytical procedures require constant monitoring of changes caused by outside events as well as the changes caused by the business entity itself. Controlling ethnocentrism—the belief that one's own culture is superior to others—can be achieved only by acknowledging it and properly adjusting to its possible effects in managerial decision making. The international manager needs to be prepared and able to put that preparedness to effective use.

THE TRAINING CHALLENGE

International managers face a dilemma in terms of international and intercultural competence. The lack of adequate foreign language and international business skills has resulted in lost contracts, weak negotiations, and ineffectual management. The race is on among nations to create knowledge-fueled innovation economies. In Singapore, Germany, China, Brazil, Korea, and other countries around the world, educational improvement is viewed as a critical part of that mission. Nations and states are therefore working hard to benchmark their educational systems to establish a solid foundation for economic development in the twenty-first century. Some are finding innovative ways to measure their students' progress internationally. Others are examining high-performing and fast-improving nations to learn about best practices that they then adapt or adopt to improve their own systems.[50]

The increase in overall international activity of firms has increased the need for cultural sensitivity training at all levels of the organization. Today's training must take into consideration not only outsiders to the firm but interaction within the corporate family as well. However inconsequential the degree of interaction may seem, it can still cause problems if proper understanding is lacking. Consider, for example, the date 11/12/12 on a message; a European will interpret this as the 11th of December, but in the United States it is the 12th of November.

Some companies try to avoid the training problem by hiring only nationals or well-traveled executives for their international operations. This makes sense for the management of overseas operations but will not solve the training need, especially if transfers to a culture unfamiliar to the manager are likely. International experience may not necessarily transfer from one market to another.

To foster cultural sensitivity and acceptance of new ways of doing things within the organization, management must institute internal education programs. Samsung, for instance, has several shorter-term assignments to try to allow people to gain global experience earlier in their careers. For longer-term assignments, they have available a "region expert" program for assistant managers, who take a one-year foreign assignment to do regional research, business analysis, and networking. Samsung also offers a "field expert" program, which lasts six months to one year and allows selected employees to experience working in an overseas branch and living in a foreign culture. Finally, to give high-performing foreign employees more global experience, Samsung offers a two-year opportunity to work in South Korea, giving employees the chance to observe the business style at headquarters and have the Korean culture experience.[51]

The objective of formal training programs is to foster the four critical characteristics of preparedness, sensitivity, patience, and flexibility in managers and other personnel. These programs vary dramatically in terms of their rigor, involvement, and, of course, cost. A summary of these programs is provided in Exhibit 3.8.

Environmental briefings and cultural orientation programs are types of **area studies** programs. These programs provide factual preparation for a manager to operate in, or work with people from, a particular country. Area studies should be a basic prerequisite for other types of training programs. Alone, they serve little practical purpose because they do not really get the manager's feet wet; in other words, action learning is the key.[52] Other, more involved programs contribute the context in which to put facts so that they can be properly understood.

The **cultural assimilator** is a program in which trainees must respond to scenarios of specific situations in a particular country. These programs have been developed for the Arab countries, Thailand, Central America, and Greece. The results of the trainees' assimilator experience are evaluated by a panel of judges. This type of program has been used in particular in cases of transfers abroad on short notice.

When more time is available, managers can be trained extensively in language. This may be required if an exotic language is involved. **Sensitivity training**

EXHIBIT 3.8 Cross-Cultural Training Methods

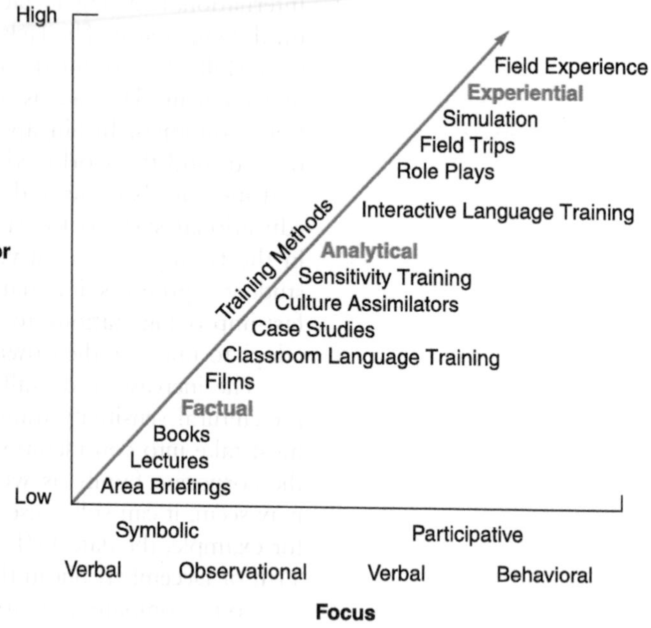

SOURCE: J. Stewart Black and Mark Mendenhall, "A Practical but Theory-Based Framework for Selecting Cross-Cultural Training Methods," in *International Human Resources Management*, eds. Mark Mendenhall and Gary Oddou. Copyright © 1991, p. 188. Reprinted by permission of the authors.

focuses on enhancing a manager's flexibility in situations that are quite different from those at home. The approach is based on the assumption that understanding and accepting oneself is critical to understanding a person from another culture. While most of the methods discussed are best delivered in face-to-face settings, web-based training is becoming more popular, as seen in *The International Marketplace 3.4*.

Finally, training may involve **field experience**, which exposes a manager to a different cultural environment for a limited amount of time. Although the expense of placing and maintaining an expatriate is high (and therefore the cost of failure is high), field experience is rarely used in training. One field experience technique that has been suggested when the training process needs to be rigorous is the host-family surrogate. This technique places a trainee (and possibly his or her family) in a domestically located family of the nationality to which they are assigned.

Regardless of the degree of training, preparation, and positive personal characteristics, a manager will always remain foreign. A manager should never rely on his or her own judgment when local managers can be consulted. In many instances, a manager should have an interpreter present at negotiations, especially if the manager is not completely bilingual. Overconfidence in one's language capabilities can create problems.

MAKING CULTURE WORK FOR MARKETING SUCCESS

Culture should not be viewed as a challenge but rather as an opportunity that can be exploited. This requires, as has been shown in this chapter, an understanding of culture differences and their fundamental determinants. Differences can quite easily be dismissed as indicators of inferiority or viewed as approaches to be changed; however, the opposite may actually be the case. Best practice knows no one particular origin, nor should it acknowledge boundaries. The

THE INTERNATIONAL MARKETPLACE 3.4

Cultural Awareness Online

Managers heading abroad to negotiate a deal, operations relocating to a foreign environment, or multicultural teams working within large organizations are just some of the scenarios that benefit from cross-cultural training. Skimping on training in this area can be potentially hazardous. For example, those unprepared for high levels of etiquette and ceremony risk offending valuable clients. Employees who move to Hong Kong are often responsible for working with multiple countries and therefore require the know-how to work in a variety of cultural settings.

However, it is nearly impossible to cover such complex cross-cultural training in one- or two-day training periods. Furthermore, such training costs in excess of $1,000 per person per day. Therefore, many organizations are adding online training following the face-to-face classroom training in order to gain continuous and additional training. Many of the programs use the following elements:

- *Detailed scenarios.* Training materials feature realistic business situations and events tied to elements in the learner's background. More than a briefing, sessions become a guided, narrated experience full of custom-created learning opportunities.
- *Gradual delivery.* The ability to control the flow of information to the participant supports the learning process. Not only is training flexible enough to fit into a busy schedule but it effectively mimics the real-life flow of data that informs decision making.
- *Support.* Participants have instant access to detailed materials at any time of day and from any location. They can check their perceptions against training materials or complete tailor-made exercises, reinforcing learning. They can also seek feedback on key issues.
- *Online discussions.* Sessions can be simulcast to hundreds of participants around the world. Participants benefit from pooled learning experience, which mimics real-life decision making.

Argonaut, a cultural learning system that aims to enable international teams to work efficiently together, was conceptualized by Coghill and Beery International, UK. A user can take the entire course—choosing the relevant culture from the base of 54 cultures—and finish it in about 15 hours. Naturally, nobody would do it over that period; normally it would take about a month with breaks.

Expanding on this, power distance refers to the relative standing of an employee with his or her boss in different cultures. In Sweden, for example, power distance is about 30 compared to India's 95. (In India, strict obedience is found at the upper levels.) This would imply that a Swedish employee coming to India for the first time might be considered rude toward his or her employer, whereas the reverse situation might find the Swedish employer put in a distinctly uncomfortable position if he or she finds the new Indian employee giving a lot more respect than is normal.

In addition, the software also allows the user to perform a corporate culture audit or interdepartmental audit—it has feedback options, tutorials, articles, and discussions. As a result, it aims at enhancing relations overall and not just at cross-cultural efficiency.

SOURCES: Ross Bentley, "It Pays to Be a Cross-Cultural Vulture," *Personnel Today*, January 23, 2007, 8; Abhinav Ramnarayan, "Connect with Culture," *Business Line*, October 16, 2006, 8; and Jessica Caplan, "Innovations in Intercultural Training," *China Staff*, November 2004, 1.

following rules serve as summary of how culture and its appreciation may serve as tool to secure success.

Embrace Local Culture

Many corporate credos include a promise to be the best possible corporate citizens in every community they operate in. For the past 10 years, the Walt Disney Company has made it a priority to build its international business in television, movies, retail, and theme parks with the goal of half of their profits to come from overseas. Disney's theme park in Hong Kong, which opened in 2005, suffered a 30 percent drop in attendance in its second year, largely due to not appealing to mainland Chinese audiences. The first big opportunity to reverse the trend was a stroke of astrological fortune: the year 2008 was the Year of the Rat, allowing Disney to proclaim it the "Year of the Mouse." The Disneyland Chinese New Year campaign featured a logo with the mouse ears added on the top. Inside the park, dumplings and turnip cakes were featured on the menus. The parade down Main Street USA was joined by the "Rhythm of Life Procession," featuring a dragon dance and puppets of birds, flowers, and fish set to traditional Chinese music. At Disneyland Hong Kong, the feng shui master rotated the front gate, repositioned cash registers, and ordered boulders set in key locations to ensure the park's prosperity.[53]

Build Relationships

Each country market has its own unique set of constituents who need to be identified and nurtured. Establishing and nurturing local ties at the various stages of the market-development cycle develops relationships that can be invaluable in expansion and countering political risk. The Hong Kong government has faced heavy public criticism for investing about HK$13.35 billion in land, equity, and debt for the construction of the Disney parks, while Disney only committed HK$3.5 billion. Hong Kong Disneyland, the smallest of Disney parks, has been criticized for having too few rides and attractions. Disney has said that the expansion will focus on "universally understood" stories, adding that many of the new attractions will be unique to the Hong Kong park. One new themed area, Grizzly Trail, is set in an American frontier gold-mining town and features a roller coaster patterned after a runaway mine train. Another, Mystic Point, emphasizes supernatural and mysterious forces. The third, Toy Story Land, is based on the film series by Pixar animation studio.

Hong Kong Disneyland's long-awaited expansion comes as Disney moves forward with its plans to build a theme park in Shanghai province. The Hong Kong government and Disney have said they believe the proposed Shanghai development will further complement the Hong Kong park. Disney will be operating the theme park, which broke ground in April 2011 and is expected to take five years to complete.[54]

Employ Locals in Order to Gain Cultural Knowledge

Disney undertook major efforts to give its Hong Kong park a more Chinese character. Research was conducted in the homes of Chinese consumers, who were asked about their knowledge of the Disney brand and their lifestyles. As a

Performers dressed as Disney characters dance on stage during a groundbreaking ceremony of the world's sixth Disney amusement park in Shanghai on April 8, 2011.

result, for example, Disneyland ads now feature only one child (Chinese government rules limit most couples to just one child), two parents, and two grandparents (many households are extended ones) sharing branded Disney activities such as watching a movie or giving a plush version of the mouse as a gift.

Help Employees Understand You

Employing locals will give a marketer a valuable asset in market development (i.e., acculturation). However, these employees also need their own process of adjustment (i.e., "corporatization") in order to be effective. Disney has given more power to local managers to develop completely local approaches, to adapt U.S. franchises and make local versions of them, or to build interest in U.S. shows such as *Hannah Montana* and *Kim Possible*. It is also important to help employees understand the firm better. Chinese executives and staff benefit from visits to Burbank, California, and interaction with Disney executives from around the world to combine Disney and Chinese values.

Adapt Products and Processes to Local Markets

Nowhere is commitment to local markets as evident as in product offerings. The gods of wealth, longevity, and happiness have been added to the Hong Kong Disneyland gang. To support the marketing efforts of the theme park, Disney has expanded its TV, online, and film businesses in China. *The Secret of the Magic Gourd* was the first-ever movie made just for Chinese audiences. The movie also meant a departure from Disney's obsession with going it alone in that it joined local experts (including the state-run China Film Group) to produce the culturally customized product.

Coordinate by Region

The same processes are being replicated in the other emerging markets targeted by Disney. Local versions of *High School Musical* for India, Latin America, and Russia are part of Disney's $100 million investment in movies outside of the United States by 2010. *High School Musical*'s cast for the Indian version was chosen in an *American Idol*–style competition. To create interest, Disney aired a dubbed version of the American movie and launched "My School Rocks," a dance competition featuring *High School Musical* songs. A CD of the movie soundtrack with Hindi lyrics and Indian instruments has been successful due to the low cost at retail. The goal of this cross-pollination is to come up with regional programs and "Asianize" or even globalize a product more quickly. Joint endeavors build cross-border "esprit de corps," especially when managers may have their own markets' interest primarily at heart.

SUMMARY

Culture is one of the most challenging elements of the international marketplace. This system of learned behavior patterns characteristic of the members of a given society is constantly shaped by a set of dynamic variables: language, religion, values and attitudes, manners and customs, aesthetics, technology, education, and social institutions. An international manager seeking to cope with this system needs both factual and interpretive knowledge of the culture. To some extent, the factual knowledge can be learned; the interpretation comes only through experience.

The most complicated problems in dealing with the cultural environment stem from the fact that we cannot learn culture—we have to live it. Two schools of thought exist in the business world on how to deal with cultural diversity. One is that business is business the world around, following the model of Nokia and the iPhone. In some cases, globalization is a fact of life; however, cultural differences are still far from converging.

The other school proposes that companies must tailor business approaches to individual cultures. Setting up policies and procedures in each country has been compared to an organ transplant; the critical question centers on acceptance or rejection. The major challenge to the international manager is to make sure that rejection is not a result of cultural myopia or even blindness.

The internationally successful companies all share an important quality: patience. They have not rushed into situations but rather built their operations carefully by following the most basic business principles. These principles are to know your challenger, know your audience, and know your customer.

KEY TERMS

culture
acculturation
high-context culture
low-context culture
change agent
cultural imperialism
cultural universals
back-translation
Christianity
Islam
Hinduism
Buddhism
Confucianism
cultural convergence
focus group
in-depth study
infrastructure
social stratification
reference group
cultural knowledge
factual information
experiential knowledge
interpretive knowledge
self-reference criterion
ethnocentrism
area studies
cultural assimilator
sensitivity training
field experience

QUESTIONS FOR DISCUSSION

1. Culture risk is just as important as commercial or political risk in the international marketing arena. Why?
2. You are on your first business visit to one of the South Asian countries. You feel confident about your ability to speak the language (you studied the language in school and have taken a refresher course), and you decide to use it. During introductions, you want to break the ice by insisting that everyone call you by your first name. Speculate as to the reaction.
3. Gifts should always be chosen with great care. An ideal gift is one that represents the giver's own culture while being sensitive to the recipient's. For example, a Finn may give a Suunto compass to a Saudi business partner (to help him determine the direction for daily prayers). Some gifts are not suitable: clocks or other timepieces are symbols of death in China, while handkerchiefs symbolize tears in Latin America and Korea. What can a company do to culture-sensitize its staff?
4. What can be learned about a culture from reading and attending to factual materials?
5. Using a range of training tools, from case studies to web-based activities and exercises, programs cover such topics as intercultural adaptation, recognizing differences in communication styles, negotiation strategies, and practical information aspects of business and daily life. Is that too much?
6. Jack Daniel's whiskey uses its core American values of authenticity, masculinity, and fraternalism successfully in other English-speaking countries like the United Kingdom, Australia, and South Africa. How can they interpret the values of the brand to be more approachable in a culture like China? (For example, which is very status-oriented in terms of the middle class.)

INTERNET EXERCISES

1. Many companies, such as Intercultural Group, provide cross-cultural consulting, coaching, and training. Using the company's website (www.interculturalgroup.com), assess the different ways such consultants can play an important role in mastering cultural competency.
2. The company recently said on its blog that over 60 percent of Twitter users are based outside the United States, and it now provides its interface in French, German, Italian, Spanish, and Japanese (with more languages likely to follow). Twitter said that introducing different language versions dramatically increased the number of users signing up from countries speaking those languages—and just as people search predominantly in their own language, they tweet in it too. Why? (The International Search Summit, www.internationalsearchsummit.com, is an event series dedicated to international and multilingual search and social media marketing.)

CHALLENGE US

France versus Internet

As the Internet continues to evolve, new uses for digital communication tools like Facebook, MySpace, Twitter, Badoo, Skyrock, and YouTube continue to increase beyond expectations, creating large global communities acting in concert for social, environmental, and even political change. Although a direct affront to authoritarian governments, this explosion of international online communities raises questions for nations like France and its policies to protect its own unique culture from outside invasion. Yet, as part of a trend toward globalization, scores of participating citizens are transcending France's cultural borders to join these powerful online communities and in turn are bypassing established policies concerning the free flow of information, isolation, and protectionism.

Cultural convergence theorists would see a potential fusion of cultures here that does not bode well for cultural protectionists, especially since the American culture would be predominant. American-centered Google and Microsoft sites are the most visited in France. Google's YouTube was the top-ranked video site in France, with 25 million people watching 2.3 billion videos online—in spite of concerns by French government officials who claim these particular sites have the strongest potential for American dominance and imperialism. Recent polls indicate that a majority of today's youth—often referred to as "digital natives" who grew up with laptops and wireless Internet connections—are creating and consuming online content on an international scale.

For Discussion

1. Should nations like France protect their unique culture and still participate in the new global technological innovations?
2. To what extent will cultural convergence take place?

SOURCES: Hazel G. Warlaumont, "Social Networks and Globalization: Facebook, YouTube and the Impact of Online Communities on France's Protectionist Policies," *French Politics* (July 2010): 204–214; and "The 2010 Europe Digital Year in Review," ComScore, February 24, 2011, www.comscore.com/Press_Events/Presentations_Whitepapers/2011/2010_Europe_Digital_Year_in_Review.

RECOMMENDED READINGS

Axtell, Roger E. *Essential Do's and Taboos: The Complete Guide to International Business and Leisure Travel.* Hoboken, NJ: Wiley, 2007.

Brett, Jeanne M. *Negotiating Globally: How to Negotiate Deals, Resolve Disputes, and Make Decisions across Cultural Boundaries.* San Francisco, CA: Jossey-Bass, 2007.

Carté, Penny, and Chris J. Fox. *Bridging the Culture Gap: A Practical Guide to International Business Communication.* London, England: Kogan Page, 2008.

Cellich, Claude, and Subhash C. Jain. *Global Business Negotiations: A Practical Guide.* Mason, OH: Thomson/South-Western, 2003.

Hofstede, Geert H., Gert Jan Hofstede, and Michael Minkov. *Cultures and Organizations: Software of the Mind: Intercultural Cooperation and Its Importance for Survival.* New York: McGraw-Hill, 2010.

Lewis, Richard D. *When Cultures Collide: Leading across Cultures.* Boston, MA: Nicholas Brealey, 2005.

Matsumoto, David Ricky. *Cross-cultural Research Methods in Psychology.* Cambridge, MA: Cambridge University Press, 2010.

Trompenaars, Alfons, and Charles Hampden-Turner. *Riding the Waves of Innovation: Harness the Power of Global Culture to Drive Creativity and Growth.* New York: McGraw-Hill, 2010.

Yunker, John. *The Art of the Global Gateway: Strategies for Successful Multilingual Navigation.* Ashland, OR: Byte Level Books, 2010.

ENDNOTES

1. Pankaj Ghemawat, "Remapping Your Strategic Mind-set," *McKinsey Quarterly*, no. 3 (2011): 56–67.
2. Ben Fritz and John Horn, "Reel China: U.S. Film Producers Are Engaging the Chinese,"*Los Angeles Times*, August 24, 2011, E2.
3. "Melting Pots," *Washington Post*, January 6, 2006, H1, H4.
4. David A. Kaplan, "General Mills' Global Sweet Spot," *Fortune*, May 23, 2011, 194–201.
5. Alfred Kroeber and Clyde Kluckhohn, *Culture: A Critical Review of Concepts and Definitions* (New York: Random House, 1985), 11.
6. Geert Hofstede, Gert Jan Hofstede, and Michael Minkov, *Cultures and Organizations: Software of the Mind* (New York: McGraw-Hill, 2010).
7. Edward T. Hall, "Context and Meaning," in *Intercultural Communication: A Reader*, ed. L. A. Samovar and R. E. Porter (Belmont, CA: Wadsworth, 2000), 34–43.
8. Kerry Capell, "How a Swedish Retailer Became a Global Cult Brand," *Businessweek*, November 14, 2005, 96–106.
9. "U.N. Body Endorses Cultural Protection," *Washington Post*, October 21, 2005, A14.
10. French Movies, www.understandfrance.org/France/FrenchMovies.html.
11. Oduor Ong'wen, "Biopiracy, the Intellectual Property Regime and Livelihoods in Africa," *The Monitor*, October 25, 2010, 4.
12. Sony Music Latin, www.sonymusiclatin.com.

13. James Peoples and Garrick Bailey, *Humanity: An Introduction to Cultural Anthropology* (New York: Wadsworth Publishing, 2011).
14. Yuval Atsmon, Vinay Dixit, and Cathy Wu, "Tapping China's Luxury-Goods Market," *McKinsey Quarterly*, no. 2 (2011): 32–33.
15. Quentin D. Atkinson, "Phonemic Diversity Supports a Serial Founder Effect Model of Language Expansion from Africa," *Science*, April 2011, 346–49.
16. Ethnologue, www.ethnologue.com.
17. David A. Ricks, *Blunders in International Business* (Malden, MA: Wiley-Blackwell, 2006), Ch. 1.
18. "We Are Tous Québécois," *The Economist*, January 8, 2005, 39.
19. "Secrets of Well-Traveled Web Sites," Lionbridge, 2011, http://en-us.lionbridge.com/uploadedFiles/Lionbridge/~Files/Landing_Pages/Travel-Hospitality-Global-Websites.pdf.
20. "Russian Government Wants to Introduce Cyrillic Version of the Internet," Reuters, January 4, 2008.
21. "Internet World Users by Language," Internet World Stats, www.internetworldstats.com/stats7.htm.
22. Mark L. Knapp and Judith A. Hall, *Nonverbal Communication in Human Interaction* (Florence, KY: Wadsworth, 2009), Ch. 1; and Edward T. Hall, "The Silent Language of Overseas Business," *Harvard Business Review* 38 (May–June 1960): 87–96.
23. Zhalech Semnami-Azad and Wendi L. Adair, "Reading the Body Language in International Negotiations," *Strategy+Business*, September 16, 2011.
24. "Anywhere, Anytime," *Wall Street Journal*, November 21, 2005, R6.
25. *World Almanac and the Book of Facts 2011*, FACTS (New York, NY: Infobase Publishing, 2010), 717.
26. Carla Power, "Faith in the Market," *Foreign Policy* (January/February 2009): 70–75; and "Profit versus the Prophet: Islamic Law has Transformed Some Muslims into Creative Bankers," *Los Angeles Times*, February 10, 2008, M11.
27. "Out from Under," *Marketing News*, July 21, 2003, 1, 9.
28. Frank Kardes, Maria Cronley, and Thomas Cline, *Consumer Behavior* (Mason, OH: South-Western College 2010), 10.
29. Flora F. Gu, Kineta Hung, and David K. Tse, "When Does GuanxiMatter? Issues of Capitalization and Its Dark Sides," *Journal of Marketing* (July 2008): 12–28.
30. Charlotte Bailey, "Muslim 'Barbie and Ken' Dolls Created by Iranian Government," *The Telegraph*, September 24, 2008, 24.
31. Amelia Newcomb, "Japan Cracking US Pop Culture Hegemony," *Christian Science Monitor*, December 15, 2008; and Douglas McGray, "Japan's Gross National Cool," *Foreign Policy* (May/June 2002): 44.
32. Zac Bissonnette, "Levi's Selling Jeans on Installment in India," *DailyFinance.com*, August 24, 2009.
33. "About Us," Sergey Frank International, www.sergey-frank.com.
34. "Religious seasonal days of celebration and holy days," www.religioustolerance.org/main_day.htm; and "Holidays and Observances," www.yahoo.com/society_and_culture/holidays_and_observances.
35. James A.Gingrich, "Five Rules for Winning Emerging Market Consumers," *Strategy+Business* (second quarter, 1999): 68–76.
36. Ole Bruun, *An Introduction to Feng Shui* (Cambridge, England: Cambridge University Press, 2008).
37. Heinz - Innovation, www.heinz.com/our-food/innovation.aspx.
38. "U.S. Superstores Find Japanese Are a Hard Sell," *Wall Street Journal*, February 14, 2000, B1, B4.
39. "List of mobile network operators of the Middle East and Africa - Kenya," www.answers.com/topic/list-of-mobile-network-operators-of-the-middle-east-and-africa#Kenya, 2010 data.
40. John Paul Titlow, Wireless Mobile Payments to Reach 85% of POS Terminals by 2016," ReadWriteWeb, August 15, 2011, www.readwriteweb.com/archives/wireless_mobile_payments_to_reach_85_of_pos_termin.php.
41. "Global M-Payment Report Update—2009," in *Arthur D. Little's M-payment Surging Ahead* (Boston, MA: Arthur D. Little, 2009).
42. Todd Guild, "Think Regionally, Act Locally: Four Steps to Reaching the Asian Consumer," *McKinsey Quarterly*, no. 4 (2009): 245–253.
43. Conrad Schmidt, "The Battle for China's Talent," *Harvard Business Review*, March 2011, 25–27.
44. Geert H. Hofstede, Gert Jan Hofstede, and Michael Minkov, *Cultures and Organizations: Software of the Mind: Intercultural Cooperation and Its Importance for Survival* (New York: McGraw-Hill, 2010), 12.
45. Harry Triandis, "The Made Dimensions of Culture," *Academy of Management Executive* 18 (2004): 88–93.
46. Rosalie Tung and Alain Verbeke, "Beyond Hofstede and GLOBE: Improving the Quality of Cross-cultural Research," *Journal of International Business Studies* 41 (2010): 1259–1274; and Mansour Javidan and Robert House, "Leadership and Cultures around the World: Findings from GLOBE: An Introduction to the Special Issue," *Journal of World Business* 37, no. 1 (2002): 1–2.
47. Sanna Sundqvist, Lauri Frank, and Kaisu Puumalainen, "The Effects of Country Characteristics, Cultural Similarity and Adoption Timing on the Diffusion of Wireless Communications," *Journal Business Research* 58, no. 1 (2005): 107–110.
48. Sengun Yeniyurt and Janell Townsend, "Does Culture Explain Acceptance of New Products in a Country? An Empirical Investigation," *International Marketing Review* 20, no. 4 (2003): 377–397.
49. Izak Benbasat, David Gefen, and Paul Pavlou, "Is E-Commerce Boundary-less? Effects of Individualism–Collectivism and Uncertainty Avoidance on Internet Shopping," *Journal of International Business Studies* 35, no. 6 (2004): 545–560.
50. UNESCO, www.unesco.org/new/en/unesco.
51. Siegfried Russwurm, Luis Hernández, Susan Chambers, and Keumyong Chung, "Developing Your Global Know-How," *Harvard Business Review*, March 2011, 89–98; and "Special Interest Group Operations," www.samsung.com.
52. Maureen Lewis, "Why Cross-Cultural Training Simulations Work," *Journal of European Industrial Training* 29, no. 7 (2005): 593–598.
53. "The Feng Shui Kingdom," *New York Times*, April 25, 2005, A14.
54. "World News: Chinese Village Hopes for a Disney Windfall," *Wall Street Journal*, August 24, 2009, A8.

CHAPTER 4

The Economic Environment

LEARNING OBJECTIVES

By the time you complete this chapter, you will be able to:

- Understand population, infrastructure, geographic features, and involvement.
- Suggest corporate responses to advancing economic integration.
- Survey the vast opportunities for trade offered by emerging markets.
- Illustrate growth in developing countries by encouraging potential.
- Suggest corporate responses to advancing economic integration.

THE INTERNATIONAL **MARKETPLACE** 4.1

Global Middle-Class Market

Multinational corporations are transforming themselves by repositioning and rethinking their goods and services to tap into and capture the new global middle-class market. This worldwide economic phenomenon encompasses a huge customer base. In 2011, it included about 400 million people in the mature middle class of the United States, Europe, and Japan but also another 300 to 500 million people in emerging economies' middle class. The World Bank defines the middle class as people who are above the median poverty line of their own countries. This may make them poor by European and U.S. standards but gives them purchasing power to become consumers of manufactured goods and services. This new global middle class is particularly evident in Brazil, China, India, Indonesia, Mexico, Nigeria, Turkey, Vietnam, and other countries with relatively large working populations and rapid economic growth rates.

The middle classes of these emerging economies each have their own unique demand profile. They are all recovering from the global recession with increasingly urbanized lifestyles, and their numbers are expanding at very high rates. They have the buying power, needs, and desires of the middle class, seeking products that have some premium features and quality but at a lower price point. Each geographic market wants to buy products that fulfill local needs and desires. Companies identify which product attributes these new consumers want to add value.

All industrializing countries follow an evolutionary path of economic change, starting with a nascent economy (emerging from subsistence, with a large youth population) to finally emerge as a mature economy with relatively flat growth and a large mature population. The in-between stage, a stage of urbanization and economic momentum, is critical. During the momentum phase, there is a large young population with high economic growth rates.

Three types of corporate players are jockeying for position in these markets. First, *local upstarts* have traditionally provided low-priced goods for the bottom-of-the-pyramid consumers in their home markets. These companies are now trying to provide a better quality of product and service with increased brand status. *Global aspirant* companies have already developed products for their domestic middle markets and are now seeking to parlay their existing capabilities to serve the external global middle class. *Multinational incumbents* are mature global companies intent on adapting their existing product lines to capture these new, emerging global middle markets.

Look no further than the Chinese automobile sector to see all three types of competitors. Chery Automobile Company, Wall Motor Company, and

© Feng Li/Staff/Getty Images

A new Buick car at the Shanghai International Automobile Industry Exhibition.

Geely Automobile were local upstarts in China. Geely purchased Volvo in 2010 and immediately raised production plans. Global aspirants in China include South Korea's Hyundai Motor Company, which achieved success with a redesigned Elantra model. Multinational incumbents seeking to carve out shares in China's middle markets have included GM, with its Chevrolet Spark and Buick Excelle, and Volkswagen with its Polo and Golf models. All the multinationals pursue this market through joint ventures with Chinese partners.

SOURCES: Edward Tse, Bill Russo, and Ronald Haddock, "Competing for the Global Middle Class," *Strategy+Business*, Autumn 2011; George Stalk and David Michael, "What the West Doesn't Get about China," *Harvard Business Review*, June 2011, 25–27; and David Court and Laxman Narasimham, "Capturing the World's Emerging Middle Class," *McKinsey Quarterly*, July 2010.

The assessment of a foreign market environment should start with the evaluation of economic variables relating to the size and nature of the market. Because of the large number of worthwhile alternatives, initial screening of markets should be done efficiently yet effectively enough, with a wide array of economic criteria, to establish a preliminary estimate of market potential. One of the most basic characterizations of the world economy is provided in Exhibit 4.1, which incorporates many of the economic variables pertinent to marketers.

The **Group of Five** (the United States, Britain, France, Germany, and Japan) consists of the major industrialized countries of the world. This group is sometimes expanded to the **Group of Seven** (by adding Italy and Canada) and the **Group of Ten** (by adding Sweden, the Netherlands, and Belgium). It may also be expanded to encompass the members of the Organization for Economic Cooperation and Development, or OECD (which consists of 30 countries: Western Europe, the United States, Australia, Canada, Czech Republic, Hungary, Japan, Mexico, New Zealand, Poland, Slovakia, South Korea, and Turkey). The **Group of Twenty** (the Group of Seven plus Argentina, Australia, Brazil, China, India, Indonesia, Mexico, Russia, Saudi Arabia, South Africa, South Korea, and Turkey, as well as the European Union) has been prominent in dealing with the current economic crisis.

Important among the middle-income developing countries are the newly industrialized countries (NICs), which include Singapore, Taiwan, Korea, Hong Kong, Brazil, and Mexico (some propose adding Malaysia and the Philippines to the list as well), as discussed in *The International Marketplace 4.1*. Some of these NICs will earn a new acronym, RIC (rapidly industrializing country). Over the past 30 years, Singapore has served as a hub providing critical financial and managerial services to the Southeast Asian markets. Singapore

EXHIBIT 4.1 Top World Economies (GDP in million dollars)

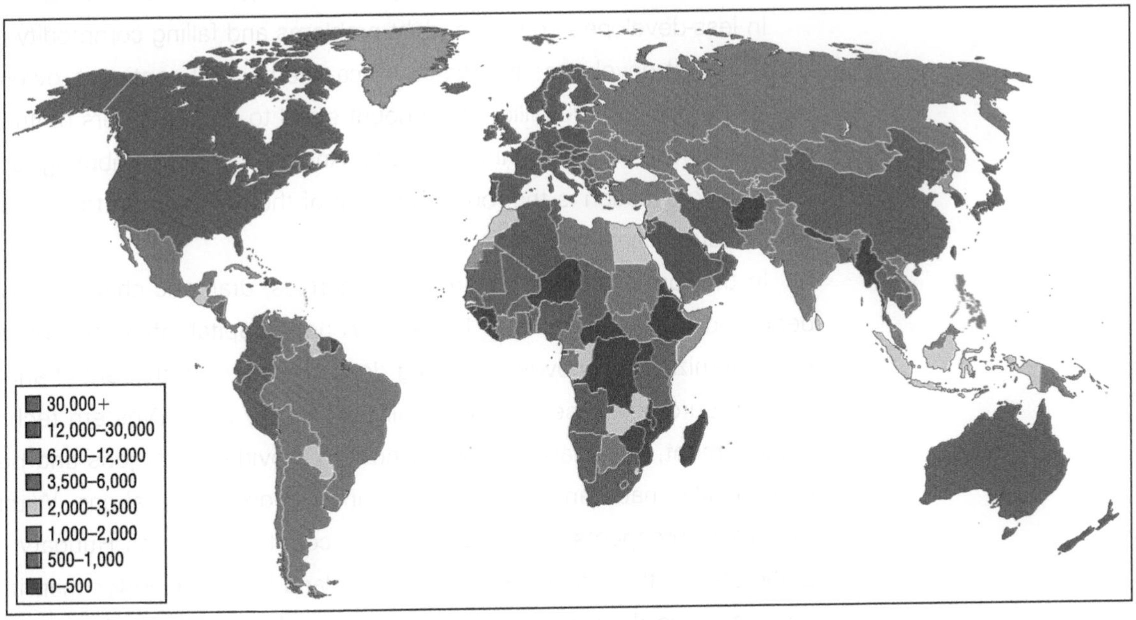

SOURCES: © Cengage Learning 2013; http://en.wikipedia.org/wiki/List_of_countries_by_GDP_%28nominal%29_per_capita.

has successfully attracted foreign investment, mostly regional corporate headquarters and knowledge-intensive industries, and has served as one of the main gateways for Asian trade. Its exports have reached well over 220 percent of GDP.[1]

The major oil-exporting countries, in particular the 11 members of the Organization of Petroleum Exporting Countries (OPEC: Algeria, Angola, Ecuador, Islamic Republic of Iran, Iraq, Kuwait, Libya, Nigeria, Qatar, Saudi Arabia, the United Arab Emirates, and Venezuela) and countries such as Russia, are dependent on the price of oil for their world market participation. A relatively high dollar price per barrel (as high as $140 in 2008) works very much in these countries' favor, while lower prices (as low as $40 in 2009) cause significant economic hardship.[2]

Many of the emerging economies will depend on the success of their industrialization efforts in the years to come, even in the case of resource-rich countries that may find commodity prices being driven down by human-made substitutes. This applies especially to the BRIC (Brazil, Russia, India, China) group. China has become the world's largest exporter of textiles since beginning to increase production in the 1980s. Despite an image of hopeless poverty, India has nearly 300 million middle-class consumers, more than Germany. These countries, which constitute the majority of the world's population, may also provide the biggest potential market opportunity for marketers in the twenty-first century.[3] Even if they lack the scale of the BRICs, 11 countries (also known as the "Next 11") could rival the Group of

Seven in time. These include Bangladesh, Egypt, Indonesia, Iran, Korea, Mexico, Nigeria, Pakistan, the Philippines, Turkey, and Vietnam.[4]

In less-developed countries, debt problems and falling commodity prices make market development difficult. Africa, the poorest continent, owes the rest of the world $200 billion, an amount equal to three-quarters of its GDP and nearly four times its annual exports. Another factor contributing to the challenging situation is that only 1 percent of the world's private investment goes to sub-Saharan Africa.[5]

In the former centrally planned economies, dramatic changes have been under way for the last 15 years. A hefty capital inflow has been key to modernizing the newly emerging democracies of both Central and Eastern Europe. These countries will desperately need Western technology, management, and marketing know-how to provide better jobs and put more locally made and imported consumer goods in the shops. Within the group, prospects vary: the future for countries such as Hungary, the Baltic states, the Czech Republic, and Poland looks far better than it does for Russia, as they reap the benefits of membership in the European Union.

Classifications of markets will vary by originator and intended use. Marketers will combine economic variables to fit their planning purposes by using those that relate directly to the product and/or service the company markets, such as the market's ability to buy. For example, a company marketing electrical products (from power generators to appliances) may take into account both general country considerations—such as population, GNP, geography, manufacturing as a percentage of national product, infrastructure, and per capita income—and narrower, industry-specific considerations of interest to the company and its marketing efforts, such as extent of use of the product, total imports, and Asia, EU, and NAFTA shares of these imports.

The discussion that follows summarizes a set of criteria that helps identify foreign markets and screen the most opportune ones for future entry or change of entry mode. The variables discussed are those on which information is readily available from secondary sources such as international organizations, individual governments, and private organizations or associations.

World Bank and United Nations publications and individual countries' *Statistical Abstracts* provide the starting point for market investigations. The more developed the market, the more data are available. Data are available on past developments as well as on projections of broader categories such as population and income. Euromonitor International market research focuses on industry, country, company, and consumer lifestyle research. Euromonitor analyzes companies and markets in more than 200 categories across 80 countries.

MARKET CHARACTERISTICS

The main dimensions of a market can be captured by considering variables such as those relating to the population and its various characteristics, infrastructure, and social development.

Population

The total world population exceeded seven billion people in 2011 and is expected to close in on eight billion by 2025.[6] The number of people in a particular market provides one of the most basic indicators of market size and is in itself indicative of the potential demand for certain staple items that have universal appeal and are generally affordable. As indicated by the data in Exhibit 4.2, population is not evenly divided among the major regions of the world; Asia holds over 60 percent the world's population.

These population figures can be analyzed in terms of marketing implications by noting that the inclusion of 27 countries will bring the population of the EU up to half a billion people. The greatest population densities are also to be

EXHIBIT 4.2 World Population: Present and the Shape of Things to Come

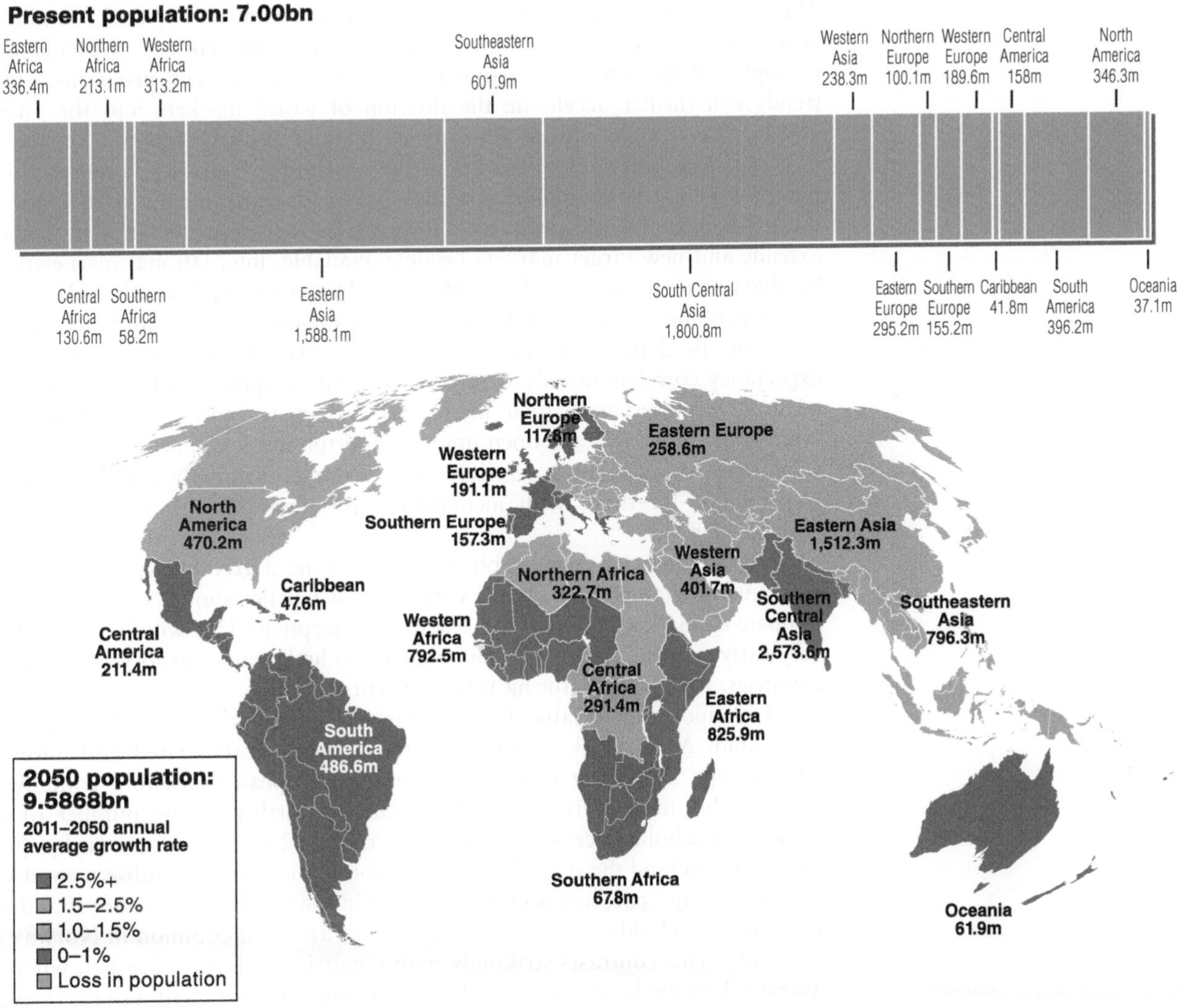

SOURCES: © Cengage Learning 2013; Based on *Population Reference Bureau*, 2011.

found in Europe, providing the global marketer with a strategically located center of operation and ready access to the major markets of the world. The two largest entities in Asia—China and India—constitute nearly 70 percent of Asia's population. The United States, which has a population 10 times the size of Canada, continues to provide Canadian marketers with a large and geographically close target market.

Population figures themselves must be broken down into meaningful categories in order for the marketer to take better advantage of them. Because market entry decisions may lie in the future, it is worthwhile to analyze population projections in the areas of interest and focus on their possible implications. Exhibit 4.2 includes United Nations projections that point to a population explosion, but mainly in the developing countries. Northern Europe will show nearly zero population growth for the next 30 years, whereas the population of Africa will triple. Even in the low- or zero-growth markets, the news is not necessarily bad for the international marketer. Those in the 25 to 45 age group, whose numbers are increasing, are among the most affluent consumers of all, having formed family units and started to consume household goods in large quantities as they reach the peak of their personal earnings potential. Early in this century, they are expected to start spending more on leisure goods and health care and related services.[7]

To influence population growth patterns, governments will have to undertake, with the help of private enterprise, quite different social marketing tasks. These will range from promoting and providing incentives for larger families (in Scandinavia, for example) to increased family planning efforts (in Thailand, for example). Regardless of the outcome of such government programs, current trends will further accelerate the division of world markets into the "haves" and the "have-nots." More adjustment capability will be required on the part of companies that want to market in the developing countries because of lower purchasing power of individuals and increasing government participation in the marketing of basic products. However, as the life expectancy in a market extends and new target markets become available, international marketers may be able to extend their products' life cycles by marketing them abroad.

Depending on the marketer's interest, population figures can be classified to show specific characteristics of their respective markets. Age distribution and life expectancy correlate heavily with the level of development of the market. Industrialized countries, with their increasing median age and a large share of the population above 65, will open unique opportunities for international marketers with new products and services. For example, Kimberly-Clark markets its Depend line for those with incontinence problems in Australia, Europe, and North America.

Interpretation of demographics requires some degree of experiential knowledge. As an example, which age categories of females should be included in an estimate of market potential for a new contraceptive? This would vary from the very early teens in the developing countries to higher age categories in developed countries, where the maturing process occurs later.

An important variable for the international marketer is the size of the household. A **household** includes all the persons, both related and unrelated, who occupy a housing unit.[8] The average European household contains 2.5 people. This number is expected to decrease further as the number of one-person households increases from 30 percent in 2000 to 36 percent by 2015.[9] One factor behind the overall growth in households, and the subsequent decline in their average size, has been the increase in the numbers of divorced and sole-survivor households. One-person households are most common in Norway and Germany. This contrasts strikingly with countries such as Colombia, where the average household size is six. With economic development usually bringing about more but smaller households, international marketers of food products, appliances, and household goods have to adjust to varying patterns of demand;

for example, they may offer single-serving portions of frozen foods and smaller appliances.

The increased urbanization of many markets has distinctly changed consumption patterns. Urban populations as a percentage of the total vary from a low of 9 percent in Bhutan to a high of 100 percent in Monaco. The degree of urbanization often dictates the nature of the marketing task the company faces, not only in terms of distribution but also in terms of market potential and buying habits. Urban areas provide larger groups of consumers who may be more receptive to marketing efforts because of their exposure to other consumers (the demonstration effect) and to communication media. In markets where urbanization is recent and taking place rapidly, the marketer faces additional responsibility as a change agent, especially when incomes may be low and the conditions for the proper use of the products may not be adequate. This is especially true in countries where rapid industrialization is taking place, such as Greece, Spain, and Portugal.

When using international data sources, the international marketer must recognize that definitions of a construct may vary among the many secondary sources. The concept of **urbanization**, for example, has different meanings depending on where one operates. In the United States, an urban area is defined as a place of 2,500 or more inhabitants; in Sweden, it is a built-up area with at least 200 inhabitants with no more than 200 meters between houses; in Mauritius, it is a town with proclaimed legal limits. Comparability, therefore, is concerned with the ends and not the means (or the definition).

Income

Markets require not only people but also purchasing power, which is a function of income, prices, savings, and credit availability. World markets can be divided into four tiers of consumers based on broad measures of income, as shown in Exhibit 4.3. Tier 1 consists of 100 million consumers from around the world. Typically, this means consumers in developed markets, such as the OECD, but it also includes the rich elites in developing markets. Tier 2 consists of the lower-income segments in developed markets, while Tier 3 includes the rising middle-class consumers in emerging markets. Tiers 4 and 5 are home to the consumer in developing markets.

EXHIBIT 4.3 World Economic Pyramid

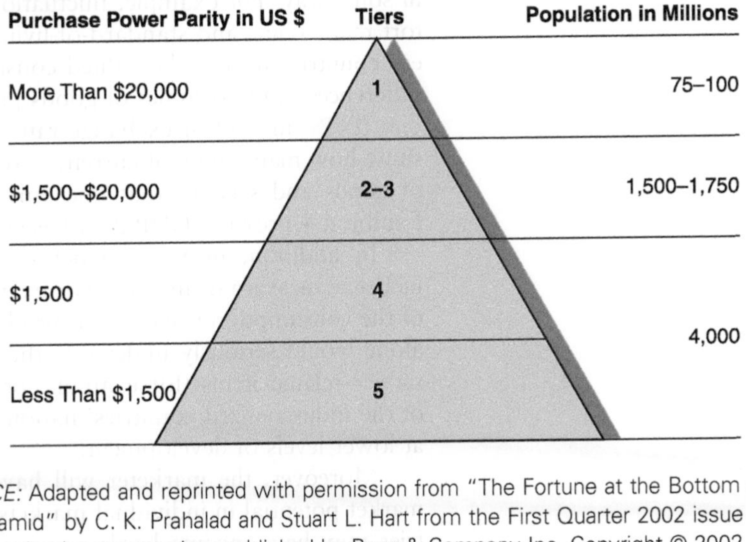

SOURCE: Adapted and reprinted with permission from "The Fortune at the Bottom of the Pyramid" by C. K. Prahalad and Stuart L. Hart from the First Quarter 2002 issue of *strategy+business* magazine, published by Booz & Company Inc. Copyright © 2002. All rights reserved. www.strategy-business.com.

Apart from basic staple items, for which population figures provide an estimate, income is most indicative of the market potential for most consumer and industrial products and services. For the marketer to make use of information on the gross domestic products of various nations, further knowledge is needed on distribution of income. Per capita GDP is often used as a primary indicator for evaluating purchasing power. This figure shows great variation between countries, as indicated by Qatar's $179,000 and Burundi's $192. The wide use of GDP figures can be explained by their easy availability, but they should nevertheless be used with caution. In industrialized countries, the richest 10 percent of the population consume 20 percent of all goods and services, whereas the respective figure for a developing country may be as high as 50 percent.[10] In some markets, income distribution produces wide gaps between population groups. The more developed the economy, the more income distribution tends to converge toward the middle class.

The international marketer can use the following classification as a planning guide:

1. *Very low family incomes.* Subsistence economies tend to be characterized by rural populations in which consumption relies on personal output or barter. Some urban centers may provide markets. Example: Cameroon.
2. *Very low and very high family incomes.* Some countries exhibit strongly bimodal income distributions. The majority of the population may live barely above the subsistence level, but there is a strong market in urban centers and a growing middle class. The affluent are truly affluent and consume accordingly. Examples: India, Mexico.
3. *Low, medium, and high family incomes.* Industrialization produces an emerging middle class with increasing disposable income. The very low and very high income classes tend to remain for traditional reasons of social class barriers. Example: Portugal.
4. *Mostly medium family incomes.* The advanced industrial nations tend to develop institutions and policies that reduce extremes in income distribution, resulting in a large and comfortable middle class able to purchase a wide array of both domestic and imported products and services. Example: Denmark.

Although the national income figures provide a general indication of a market's potential, they suffer from various distortions. Figures available from secondary sources are often in U.S. dollars. The per capita income figures may not be a true reflection of purchasing power if the currencies involved are distorted in some way. For example, fluctuations in the value of the U.S. dollar may distort real-income and standard-of-living figures. The goods and services in different countries have to be valued consistently if the differences are to reflect real differences in the volumes of goods produced. The use of purchasing power parities (PPPs) instead of exchange rates is intended to achieve this objective. PPPs show how many units of currency are needed in one country to buy the amount of goods and services that one unit of currency will buy in another country. Exhibit 4.4 provides GDP data based on PPPs for selected countries.

In addition, using a monetary measure may not be a proper and all-inclusive measure of income. For example, in developing economies where most of the consumption is either self-produced or bartered, reliance on financial data alone would seriously understate the standard of living. Further, several of the service-related items (for example, protective services and travel), characteristic of the industrialized countries' national income figures, do not exist for markets at lower levels of development.

Moreover, the marketer will have to take into consideration variations in market potential in individual markets. Major urban centers in developing countries may have income levels comparable to those in more developed markets, while rural areas may not have incomes needed to buy imported goods.

EXHIBIT 4.4 Gross Domestic Product per Capita Adjusted to Purchasing Power (Parities for Selected Countries, 2010)

Highest			Lowest		
1.	Qatar	179,000	225.	Zimbabwe	500
3.	Luxembourg	82,600	217.	Afghanistan	900
7.	Norway	54,600	199.	Kenya	1,600
11.	United States	47,200	196.	Bangladesh	1,700
13.	Hong Kong	45,900	168.	Uzbekistan	3,100
17.	Switzerland	42,600	167.	Vietnam	3,100
18.	Australia	41,000	164.	Philippines	3,500
22.	Canada	39,400	163.	India	3,500
27.	Ireland	37,300	157.	Indonesia	4,200
32.	Taiwan	35,700	152.	Bolivia	4,800
33.	Germany	35,700	142.	Bhutan	5,500
34.	Finland	35,400	138.	Egypt	6,200
37.	United Kingdom	34,800	126.	China	7,600
38.	Japan	34,000	103.	Brazil	10,800
42.	European Union	32,700	99.	World	11,200

SOURCE: CIA Factbook, available at www.cia.gov/cia/publications/factbook.

In general, income figures are useful in the initial screening of markets. However, in product-specific cases, income may not play a major role, and startling scenarios may emerge. Some products, such as autos and television sets in China, are in demand regardless of their high price in relation to wages because of their high prestige value.

Some products are in demand because of their foreign origin. As an example, European luxury jewelry has lucrative markets in countries where per capita income figures may be low but there are wealthy consumers who are able and willing to buy them. For example, India will witness a tenfold jump in jewelry sales from $3 billion at present to $30 billion by 2015. People in the segment "Globals" earn more than $36,000 a year, are well educated, travel overseas, are aspirational, are aware of brands, value quality and convenience, and have tastes shaped by what is happening not just in India but abroad as well. In India, 43 percent of the wealthy households are in Delhi and Mumbai. And the top eight Indian cities, which include Pune, Hyderabad, Chennai, Bangalore, Ludhiana, and Kolkata, make up 60 percent of wealthy households. Notably, wealth is more concentrated in India than it is in China.[11]

© Graham Crouch/Bloomberg via Getty Images

The storefronts of Gucci Group NV and LVMH Moet Hennessy Louis Vuitton SA stand at the DLF Emporio shopping mall in New Delhi, India.

Consumption Patterns

Depending on the sophistication of a country's data collection systems, economic data on consumption patterns can be obtained and analyzed. The share of income spent on necessities will provide an indication of the market's development level as well as an approximation of how much money the consumer has left for other purchases. Engel's laws provide some generalizations about consumers' spending patterns and are useful generalizations when precise data are not available. They state that as a family's income increases, the percentage

EXHIBIT 4.5 Consumer Spending by Category as Percentage of Total, 2010

Countries	Food and Nonalcoholic Beverages	Clothing and Footwear	Household Goods and Services	Housing	Leisure and Education	Transport and Communications	Hotels/ Catering
Argentina	20.2	7.2	6.6	15.2	10.0	16.5	7.3
Australia	10.7	3.2	4.9	21.1	14.7	13.2	6.8
Brazil	24.8	3.2	5.0	14.7	10.6	18.8	2.6
Canada	9.8	4.0	8.3	24.1	10.8	16.5	6.8
China	22.3	7.5	4.7	14.8	10.1	11.3	8.4
Colombia	18.8	6.0	4.2	16.1	9.7	16.2	11.7
Eastern Europe*	26.1	7.1	6.1	16.5	8.7	16.9	3.9
Western Europe**	12.8	5.3	6.0	22.7	10.1	16.1	8.8
India	27.7	6.4	3.9	14.5	3.7	19.9	2.9
Indonesia	32.1	3.1	5.3	13.8	3.5	8.6	13.7
Japan	14.8	3.4	3.7	23.8	13.1	14.7	7.5
Mexico	22.7	2.2	4.7	22.9	7.6	20.7	4.1
Nigeria	39.7	7.2	4.1	19.0	6.1	9.6	1.3
Singapore	7.5	2.5	6.1	20.3	12.4	17.1	9.1
South Korea	15.0	4.1	3.9	17.3	13.6	16.5	7.3
Thailand	25.0	6.2	5.0	7.0	8.1	20.8	7.0
United States	6.8	3.5	4.2	19.1	11.7	12.0	6.2
Russia	29.0	9.2	7.5	11.7	9.2	20.0	3.0
Finland	12.5	4.6	5.3	25.2	12.5	14.1	6.6
Germany	11.0	5.3	6.6	24.4	10.3	16.3	5.7
Spain	13.1	4.5	4.7	17.4	11.1	14.8	19.6
United Kingdom	9.7	5.5	5.0	22.3	12.6	17.7	10.0

*Eastern Europe includes Albania, Belarus, Bosnia-Herzegovina, Bulgaria, Croatia, Czech Republic, Estonia, Georgia, Hungary, Latvia, Lithuania, Macedonia, Moldova, Montenegro, Poland, Romania, Russia, Serbia, Slovakia, Slovenia, and Ukraine.

**Western Europe includes Austria, Belgium, Cyprus, Denmark, Finland, France, Germany, Greece, Iceland, Ireland, Italy, Liechtenstein, Luxembourg, Malta, Monaco, Netherlands, Norway, Portugal, Spain, Sweden, Switzerland, Turkey, and the United Kingdom.

SOURCE: Compiled from Global Market Information Database.

spent on food will decrease, the percentage spent on housing and household operations will be roughly constant, and the amount saved or spent on other purchases will increase. Private expenditure comparisons reveal that the percentage spent on food in 2010 varied from 6.8 percent in the United States to 32.1 percent in Indonesia (see Exhibit 4.5).

In Western Europe, expenditures on clothing typically account for 5 to 9 percent of all spending, but in poorer countries the proportion may be lower. In some low-wage areas, a significant proportion of clothing is homemade or locally made at low cost, making comparisons not entirely accurate. Eastern European households spend an inordinate proportion of their incomes on foodstuffs but quite a low proportion on housing. The remaining, less absolutely central areas of consumption (household goods, leisure, and transportation) are most vulnerable to short-term cancellation or postponement and thus serve as indicators for the strength of confidence in the market in general.

In large markets, such as Brazil, China, India, and the United States, marketers need to exercise care in not assuming uniformity across regions. In China, for example, marked differences exist between geographic markets and between consumers in urban and rural markets. Nearly 60 percent of PCs sold find customers in the economically developed east, north, and south, especially in the big coastal cities. In the submarket of servers, the share is even higher at 65 percent. Urban consumers spend 2.5 times more on food and 10 times more on entertainment than their rural counterparts. This does not mean that inland urban markets and rural areas are without opportunity. Massive investments by the central and provincial governments have linked these areas to the coastal ports and export/import markets by multilane highways in an attempt to close some of the income gaps between regions in China.[12] Similarly, Brazil's northeast is an emerging market within an emerging market, a poverty-stricken but fast-growing region of 53 million people sometimes called the "China of Brazil." In Nielsen's study of the northeast market, regional brands accounted for almost 80 percent of total sales in 12 categories, including 87 percent of bottled water and 68 percent of coffee sales.[13]

Data on product saturation or diffusion—information on the percentage of households in a market that own a particular product—allow a further evaluation of market potential. Exhibit 4.6 presents the percentage of households that own certain appliances and indicates that saturation levels in the markets for which the data exist are quite high. This does not necessarily indicate lack of market potential; replacement markets or the demand for auxiliary products may offer attractive opportunities to the international marketer. Low rates of diffusion should be approached cautiously because they can signal a market opportunity or a lack thereof resulting from low income levels, use of a substitute product, or lack of acceptance.

General consumption figures are valuable, but they must be viewed with caution because they may conceal critical product-form differences; for example, appliances in Asian and European households tend to be smaller than their U.S. counterparts. Information about existing product usage can nevertheless provide indirect help to international marketers. People will depend on a far wider range of devices to keep them connected to friends, colleagues, and others around the clock. It is hard to predict exactly what shape and form all of these gadgets will take, but there are going to be plenty of them. In places such as Africa, cheap smartphones could well turn out to be people's primary computing devices.[14]

Another problem for marketers in general is **inflation**; varying inflation rates complicate this problem in international markets. Many of the industrialized countries, such as the United States, Germany, and Japan, have recently been

EXHIBIT 4.6 Percentage of Households Owning Selected Appliances

	USA	Brazil	China	India	Japan	Mexico	Saudi Arabia	Singapore	South Africa	South Korea	Vietnam
Passenger car	88.3	35.9	3.9	3.6	85.5	43.8	92.5	40.3	26.1	67.9	1.1
CD player	61.1	17.9	2.6	1.5	69.5	8.9	34.4	54.9	6.3	22.6	1.5
Dishwasher	63.1	7.1	0.3	0.5	26.9	8.6	18.5	18.4	12.1	7.0	1.0
Freezer	36.0	15.7	4.3	11.6	38.6	15.8	73.4	35.0	23.6	33.2	11.4
Microwave oven	96.2	35.0	29.0	16.2	97.5	28.2	30.5	64.1	41.7	92.4	17.1
Personal computer	80.5	35.5	31.8	6.3	86.5	28.0	51.1	81.9	22.1	81.7	15.7
Refrigerator	99.9	93.0	60.1	17.9	98.7	84.9	98.3	99.1	65.7	99.7	35.7
Telephone	94.8	46.0	81.2	19.0	95.2	62.6	84.0	99.9	16.6	94.6	50.1
Color TV set	99.0	95.6	96.5	33.8	99.6	95.3	98.0	99.4	67.7	96.6	89.7
Tumble dryer	84.8	2.5	2.2	1.4	25.2	5.2	41.3	19.2	3.1	3.2	1.2
Vacuum cleaner	98.5	34.6	28.2	31.6	98.8	33.5	96.1	67.7	44.9	86.4	30.7
Washing machine	85.8	43.0	71.4	21.1	99.5	66.7	96.5	96.6	27.0	98.7	17.7

SOURCE: Compiled from *International Marketing Data and Statistics 2011* (London: Euromonitor, 2011), table 15.12.

EXHIBIT 4.7 Consumer Price Index for Selected Countries

Country	2001	2004	2007	2010
Argentina	−1.1	4.4	8.8	10.78
Australia	4.4	2.3	2.3	2.8
Bangladesh	2.0	9.2	9.1	8.1
Brazil	6.8	6.6	3.6	5.0
Canada	2.5	1.9	2.1	1.8
China (PRC, excluding Hong Kong)	0.7	3.9	4.8	3.3
Ecuador	37.7	2.7	2.3	3.6
Egypt	2.3	11.3	9.3	11.3
France	1.6	2.1	1.5	1.5
Ghana	32.9	12.6	10.7	10.7
India	3.7	3.8	6.4	12.0
Japan	−0.8	0.0	0.1	−0.7
Mexico	6.4	4.7	4.0	4.2
Romania	34.5	11.9	4.8	6.1
South Africa	5.7	1.4	7.1	4.3
South Korea	4.1	3.6	2.5	2.9
Turkey	54.4	10.6	8.8	8.6
United States	2.8	2.7	2.9	1.6
United Kingdom	1.8	3.0	4.3	4.6
Venezuela	12.5	21.7	18.7	29.1

SOURCE: Compiled data from *International Financial Statistics* (Washington, DC: International Monetary Fund, various editions), www.imf.org.

able to keep inflation rates at single-digit levels, while some have suffered from chronic inflation (see Exhibit 4.7). Inflation affects the ability of both industrial customers and consumers to buy and also introduces uncertainty into both the marketer's planning process and consumers' buying habits. In high-inflation markets, the marketer may have to make changes in the product (more economical without compromising quality), promotion (more rational), and distribution (more customer involvement) to meet customer needs and maintain demand. In response to rapidly escalating prices, a government will often invoke price controls. The setting of maximum prices for products may cause the international marketer to face unacceptable profit situations, future investments may not be made, and production may even have to be stopped.

Infrastructure

The availability and quality of an infrastructure is critically important in evaluating marketing operations abroad. Each international marketer will rely heavily on services provided by the local market for transportation, communication, and energy as well as on organizations participating in the facilitating functions of marketing: marketing communications, distributing, information, and financing. Indicators such as steel consumption, cement production, and electricity production relate to the overall industrialization of the market and can be used effectively by suppliers of industrial products and services. As an example, energy consumption per capita may serve as an indicator of market potential for electrical markets, provided evenness of distribution exists over the market. Yet the marketer must make sure that the energy is affordable and compatible (in terms of current and voltage) with the products to be marketed.

The existence and expansion of basic infrastructure has contributed significantly to increased agricultural output in Asia and Latin America. The Philippines has allocated 5 percent of agricultural development funds to rural electrification programs. On a similar level, basic roads are essential to moving agricultural products. In many parts of Africa, farmers are more than a day's walk from the nearest road. As a result, measures to improve production without commensurate improvements in transportation and communications are of little use because the crops cannot reach the market. In addition, the lack of infrastructure cuts the farmers off from new technology, inputs, and ideas.

Transportation networks by land, rail, waterway, or air are essential for physical distribution. An analysis of rail traffic by freight tons per kilometer offers a possible way to begin an investigation of transportation capabilities; however, these figures may not always indicate the true state of the system. Since late 2008, when China enacted a fiscal stimulus program to avert the contagion effects of a global economic slowdown, the country has embarked on a building binge, including new highways, high-speed rail lines, bridges, municipal subway systems, terminal buildings, and nearly a hundred new airports. A new rail line cut travel time between Beijing and Shanghai to just five hours. The world's longest bridge over water opened in 2011 in the city of Qingdao, spanning 26 miles across the Jiaozhou Bay. China is on track to soon surpass the United States in the number of highway miles built. China now has about 46,000 miles of expressways—a close second to the United States—with plans to build that out to 112,500 miles by 2030.[15] Communication is as important as transportation. The ability of a firm to communicate with entities both outside and within the market can be estimated by using indicators of the communications infrastructure: telephones, computers, broadcast media, and print media in use. Wireless technology is changing the world landscape in communications in many ways. ABI Research estimates more than five billion mobile subscriptions were active worldwide in 2011. It expects mobile subscriptions to reach 6.4 billion by 2015, of which 169 million will be subscribed to 4G technologies.[16]

Developed, emerging, and developing markets will require different adjustments by marketers. As several markets have achieved greater than 100 percent penetration, handset vendors and network operators have to provide new features such as cameras, MP3 music, and mobile TV. New growth will come from markets such as China, India, Eastern Europe, Latin America, and Africa. By the end of 2011, China had 952 million subscribers and India's growth reached 865 million. Brazil's telecom regulator announced in 2011 that there were now more mobile phones in use in the country than there were people. The number of active mobile subscriptions in Africa crossed the half-billion mark to reach 506 million in 2011. Africa accounted for 10 percent of the world's mobile subscriptions and was one of the world's fastest-growing regions.[17]

The diffusion of Internet technology into core business processes and into the lifestyles of consumers has been rapid, especially in industrialized countries. The number of Internet hosts (computers through which users connect to the network) has increased to 2,095 million by 2011, up from 56.2 million in 1999.[18] The total number of people using the Internet is difficult to estimate (see Exhibit 4.8). There are naturally significant differences within regions as well; for example, within the European Union, the Nordic countries have penetration rates of 85.2 percent, while new members, such as Romania, are at less than 30 percent.[19] Given the changes expected in the first years of the twenty-first century, all the estimates indicating explosive growth may be low. The number of users will start evening out around the globe, with new technologies assisting. Computers priced at less than $500 or even $200 will boost global computer ownership and subsequent online activity. Developments in television, cable, phone, and wireless technologies not only will make the market broader but will also allow for more services to be delivered more efficiently.

EXHIBIT 4.8 World Internet Usage and Population Statistics, 2011

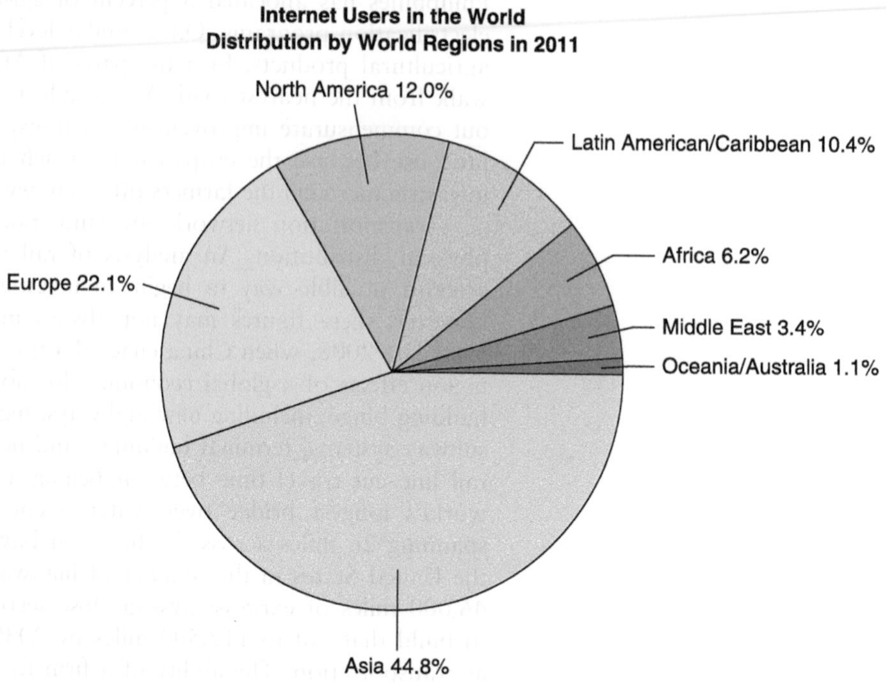

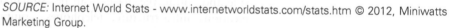

SOURCE: Internet World Stats - www.internetworldstats.com/stats.htm © 2012, Miniwatts Marketing Group.

For example, with the third-generation mobile communications technology, systems had a 100-fold increase in data transfer, allowing the viewing of videos on mobile phones. Worldwide service revenues generated by Long-Term Evolution (LTE) mobile networks are forecast to grow quickly once networks are launched, reaching $100 billion by 2014. These revenues will be driven by laptops, smartphones, and other devices.[20]

Data on the availability of commercial (marketing-related) infrastructure are often not readily available. Data on which to base an assessment may be provided by government sources, such as overseas business reports; by trade associations, such as the Business Equipment Manufacturers' Association or the American Chambers of Commerce; and by trade publications, such as *Advertising Age*. The more extensive the firm's international involvement, the more it can rely on its existing support network of banks, advertising agencies, and distributors to assess new markets.

Impact of the Economic Environment on Social Development

Many of the characteristics discussed are important beyond numbers. Economic success comes with a price tag. All the social traumas that were once believed to be endemic only to the West are now hitting other parts of the world as well. Many countries, including the nations of Southeast Asia, were able to achieve double-digit growth for decades while paying scant attention to problems that are now demanding treatment: infrastructure limits, labor shortages, demands for greater political freedom, environmental destruction, urban congestion, and even the spread of drug addiction.[21]

Because of the close relationship between economic and social development, many of the figures can be used as social indicators as well. Consider the following factors and their significance: share of urban population, life expectancy, number of physicians per capita, literacy rate, percentage of income received by the richest 5 percent of the population, and percentage of the population with access to electricity. In addition to these factors, several other variables can be used as cultural indicators: number of public libraries, registered borrowings, book titles published, and number of daily newspapers. The **Physical Quality of Life Index (PQLI)** is a composite measure of the level of welfare in a country. It has three components: life expectancy, infant mortality, and adult literacy rates.[22] The three components of the PQLI are among the few social indicators available to provide a comparison of progress through time in all of the countries of the world.

Differences in the degree of urbanization of target markets in less-developed countries influence international marketers' product strategies. If products are targeted only to urban areas, products will need minimal adjustments, mainly to qualify them for market entry. However, when targeting national markets, firms may need to make extensive adaptations to match more closely the expectations and the narrower consumption experiences of the rural population.

In terms of infrastructure, improved access in rural areas brings with it an expansion of nonfarm enterprises such as shops, repair, and services. It may also include changes in customs, attitudes, and values. As an example, in 2008, the World Bank launched the Adolescent Girls Initiative (AGI) to promote the transition of adolescent girls and young women from school to productive employment and economic empowerment in the countries of Afghanistan, Jordan, Laos, Rwanda, South Sudan, Haiti, and Yemen. The initiative teaches business development, technical and vocational training, and high-demand skill training. A girl's education, health, and wealth can have a positive impact on both her family's livelihood and the whole community.[23]

As societies attain a certain level of wealth, income becomes less of a factor in people's level of contentment. Emotional well-being may be determined by the quality of social relationships, enjoyment at work, job stability, and overall conditions in the country (such as democratic institutions). Countries like

International Groupings

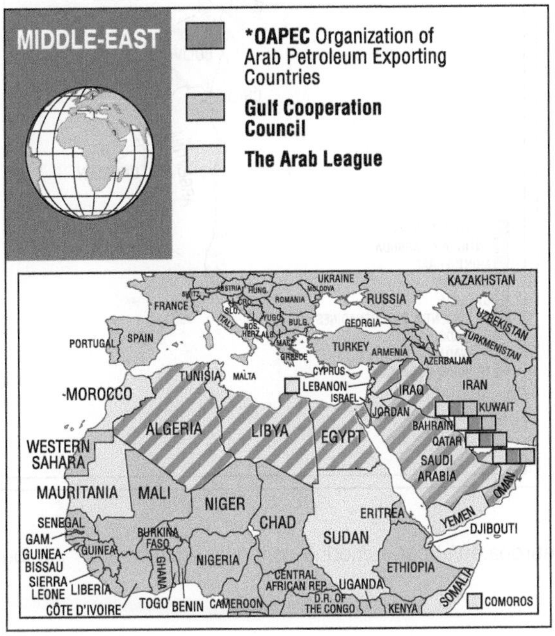

PACIFIC BASIN
AFTA ASEAN (Association of South East Asian Nations) Free Trade Area
MYANMAR
LAOS
THAILAND
CAMBODIA
VIETNAM
PHILIPPINES
BRUNEI
MALAYSIA
SINGAPORE
INDONESIA
PAPUA NEW GUINEA

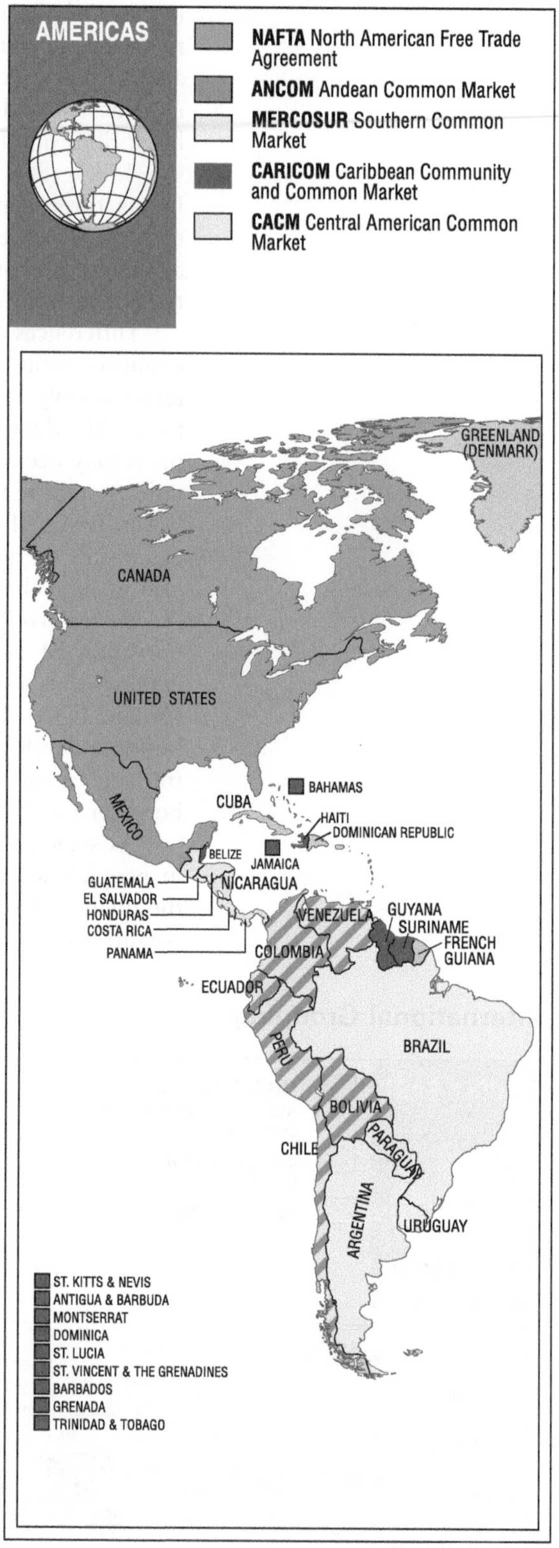
AMERICAS
NAFTA North American Free Trade Agreement
ANCOM Andean Common Market
MERCOSUR Southern Common Market
CARICOM Caribbean Community and Common Market
CACM Central American Common Market
GREENLAND (DENMARK)
CANADA
UNITED STATES
MEXICO
CUBA
BAHAMAS
HAITI
DOMINICAN REPUBLIC
BELIZE
JAMAICA
GUATEMALA
EL SALVADOR
HONDURAS
COSTA RICA
PANAMA
NICARAGUA
VENEZUELA
GUYANA
SURINAME
FRENCH GUIANA
COLOMBIA
ECUADOR
PERU
BRAZIL
BOLIVIA
PARAGUAY
CHILE
ARGENTINA
URUGUAY
ST. KITTS & NEVIS
ANTIGUA & BARBUDA
MONTSERRAT
DOMINICA
ST. LUCIA
ST. VINCENT & THE GRENADINES
BARBADOS
GRENADA
TRINIDAD & TOBAGO

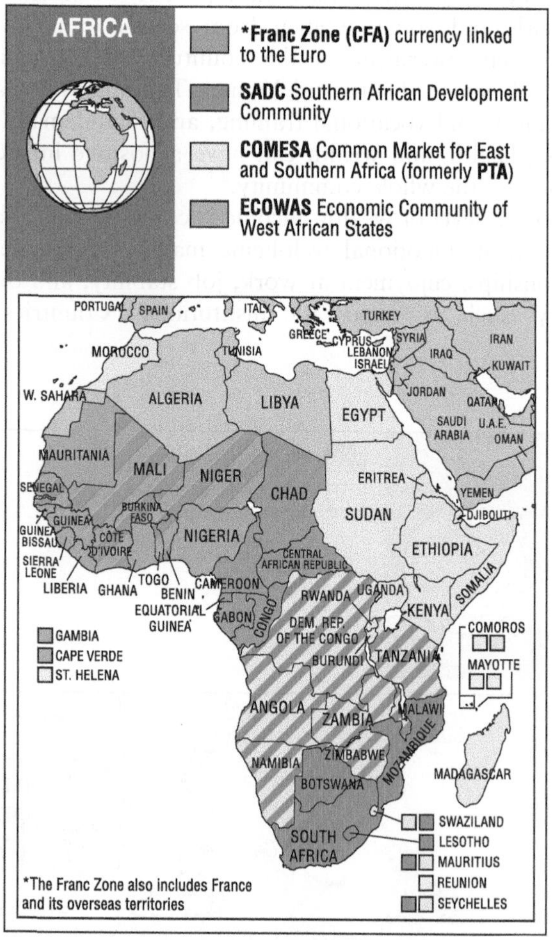
AFRICA
*Franc Zone (CFA) currency linked to the Euro
SADC Southern African Development Community
COMESA Common Market for East and Southern Africa (formerly PTA)
ECOWAS Economic Community of West African States
PORTUGAL
SPAIN
ITALY
TURKEY
GREECE
CYPRUS
SYRIA
LEBANON
ISRAEL
IRAQ
IRAN
KUWAIT
MOROCCO
TUNISIA
JORDAN
W. SAHARA
ALGERIA
LIBYA
EGYPT
QATAR
SAUDI ARABIA
U.A.E.
OMAN
MAURITANIA
MALI
NIGER
CHAD
ERITREA
YEMEN
SENEGAL
BURKINA FASO
SUDAN
DJIBOUTI
GUINEA
GUINEA BISSAU
CÔTE D'IVOIRE
NIGERIA
ETHIOPIA
SIERRA LEONE
CENTRAL AFRICAN REPUBLIC
LIBERIA
GHANA
TOGO
BENIN
CAMEROON
EQUATORIAL GUINEA
GABON
CONGO
RWANDA
UGANDA
SOMALIA
KENYA
DEM. REP. OF THE CONGO
BURUNDI
TANZANIA
COMOROS
MAYOTTE
GAMBIA
CAPE VERDE
ST. HELENA
ANGOLA
ZAMBIA
MALAWI
NAMIBIA
ZIMBABWE
MOZAMBIQUE
BOTSWANA
MADAGASCAR
SOUTH AFRICA
SWAZILAND
LESOTHO
MAURITIUS
REUNION
SEYCHELLES
*The Franc Zone also includes France and its overseas territories

SOURCES: © Cengage Learning 2013; Based on European Union, http://europa.eu/about-eu/countries/index_en.htm; and "Afrabet Soup," *Economist*, February 8, 2001, p. 77.

Denmark and Finland score high on a national well-being index, while Haiti and Togo are among the lowest.[24]

The presence of multinational corporations, which by their very nature are change agents, will accelerate social change. If government control is weak, the multinational corporation bears the social responsibility for its actions. In some cases, governments restrict the freedom of multinational corporations if their actions may affect the environment. As an example, the Indonesian government places construction restrictions (such as building height) on hotels in Bali to avoid the overcrowding and ecological problems incurred in Hawaii when that state vigorously developed its tourism sector.

REGIONAL ECONOMIC INTEGRATION

Economic integration has been one of the main economic developments affecting world markets since World War II. Countries have wanted to engage in economic cooperation to use their respective resources more effectively and to provide larger markets for member-country producers. Some integration efforts have had quite ambitious goals, such as political integration; some have failed as the result of perceptions of unequal benefits from the arrangement or a political parting of ways. Exhibit 4.9, a summary of the major forms of economic cooperation in regional markets, shows the varying degrees of formality with which integration can take place. These economic integration efforts are dividing the world into trading blocs. Of the 32 groupings in existence, some have superstructures of nation-states (such as the European Union); some (such as ASEAN Free Trade Area) are multinational agreements that are currently more political than economic. Some are not trading blocs per se but work to further them. Blocs are joining bigger blocs as in the case of the Asia Pacific Economic Cooperation, which brings partners together from multiple continents (including NAFTA and individual countries such as Australia, China, Japan, and Russia). The United States, Canada, Japan, and Mexico have expressed interest in joining 12 countries (also including Australia, Brunei, Chile, Malaysia, New Zealand, Peru, Singapore, and Vietnam) in discussing a free-trade pact.

EXHIBIT 4.9 Forms of Economic Integration in Regional Markets

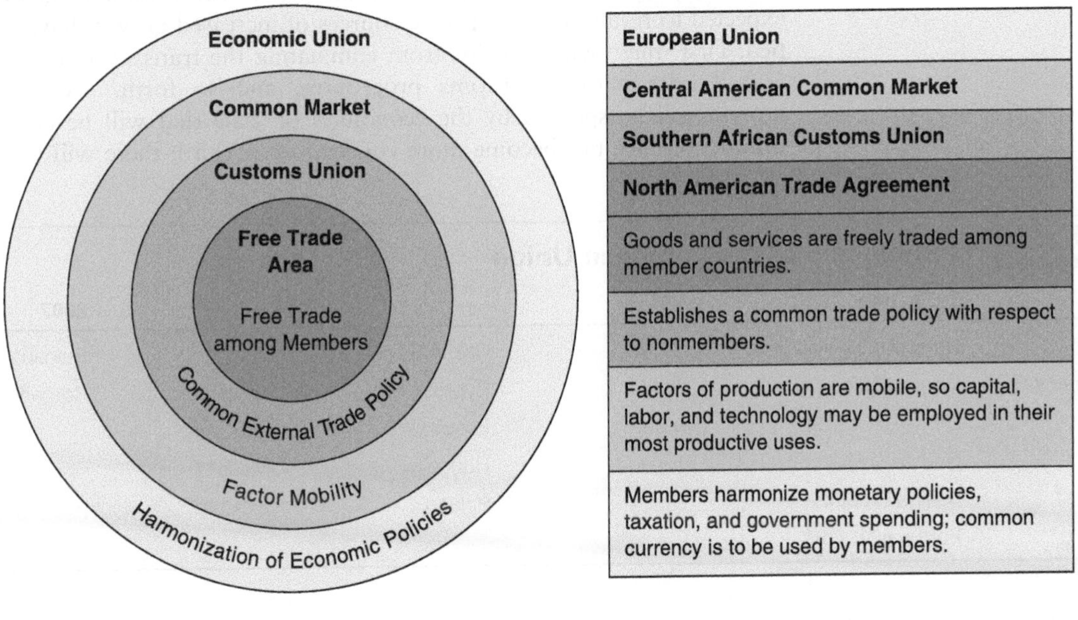

SOURCE: © Cengage Learning 2013.

Altogether, the possible members of the Trans-Pacific Partnership (TPP) produce 40 percent of world GDP—far more than the European Union. With an impasse in the Doha Round of WTO negotiations, more countries are turning to bilateral agreements, with 205 of them in effect.[25]

Success of these blocs, from their establishment to future expansion institutionally and geographically, will depend on (1) the leadership of selected countries (i.e., every bloc needs an "engine"); (2) their proximity in terms of geography, culture, administrative dimensions, and basic economic factors; and (3) their commitment to regional cooperation. For example, the biggest trading partners for any of the European Union member nations are other EU countries. Countries that have traditionally not traded with each other or have relations driven by animosities (e.g., in the South Asian Association for Regional Cooperation, or SAARC) have a more challenging time in implementing economic integration.

European Integration

In 1957, the European Economic Community (EEC) was formally established by the Treaty of Rome. The cooperative spirit apparent throughout the treaty was based on the premise that the mobility of goods, services, labor, and capital—the "four freedoms"—was of paramount importance for the economic prosperity of the region. Founding members envisioned that the successful integration of the European economies would result in an economic power to rival that of the United States. Exhibit 4.10 shows the founding members of the community in 1957 and members who have joined since, as well as those invited to join early in the twenty-first century, comprising the European Union.

The enlargement of the European Union has become one of the most debated issues. The EU has most recently expanded to 27 members, accepting 10 Central European and two Mediterranean countries to the Union. Despite some uncertainties about the future cohesiveness of the EU, new nations want to join. Currently, there are five candidate countries: Croatia, the former Yugoslav Republic of Macedonia (fYROM), Iceland, Montenegro, and Turkey. Potential candidates are Albania, Bosnia-Herzegovina, Kosovo, and Serbia. The agreement on the European Economic Area (EEA) extends the single market of the EU to three of the four European Free Trade Association (EFTA) countries (Iceland, Liechtenstein, and Norway, with Switzerland opting to develop its relationship with the EU through bilateral agreements).[26]

The most important implication of the freedom of movement for products, services, people, and capital within the EU is the economic growth that is expected to result. Several specific sources of increased growth have been identified. First, there will be gains from eliminating the transaction costs associated with border patrols, customs procedures, and so forth. Second, economic growth will be spurred by the economies of scale that will be achieved when production facilities become more concentrated. Third, there will be gains from

EXHIBIT 4.10 Membership of the European Union

1957	1973–1986	1995	2004		2007
France*	Great Britain (1973)	Austria*	Czech Republic	Slovenia*	Bulgaria
West Germany*	Ireland (1973)*	Finland*	Cyprus*	Latvia	Romania
Italy*	Denmark (1973)	Sweden	Estonia*	Lithuania	
Belgium*	Greece (1981)*		Hungary	Malta*	
Netherlands*	Spain (1986)*		Poland	Slovakia*	
Luxembourg*	Portugal (1986)*				

*Euro users

SOURCE: © Cengage Learning 2013.

more intense competition among European companies. Firms that were monopolists in one country will now be subject to competition from firms in other member countries. The introduction of the euro (symbol €) is expected to add to the efficiencies, especially in terms of consolidation of firms across industries and across countries. Furthermore, countries in Euro land will enjoy cheaper transaction costs and reduced currency risks, and consumers and businesses will enjoy price transparency and increased price-based competition.[27] The euro is used daily by some 332 million Europeans.

The EU's Economic and Monetary Union (EMU), a single monetary policy for the 17 euro-area member states, combined with coordinated national fiscal policies, has helped foster macroeconomic stability, precipitated the economic integration of Europe, and boosted cross-border trade, financial integration, and investment. The EMU has also increased the EU's resilience to adverse shocks. The EU addressed the sovereign debt crises in several euro-area countries by creating new instruments to provide financial assistance to a euro-area country should this become necessary. In 2011 and 2012, fears have emerged about whether the governments in Greece, Portugal, Ireland, Spain, and Italy will honor their €3 trillion of borrowing. The uncertainty has wreaked havoc on European banks, which also own the sovereign debts, further weakening the banks.[28]

The integration has important implications for firms within and outside Europe because it poses both threats and opportunities, benefits and costs. There will be substantial benefits for those firms already operating in Europe. These firms will gain because their operations in one country can now be freely expanded into others, and their products may be freely sold across borders. In a borderless Europe, firms have access to approximately 501 million consumers. Substantial economies of scale in production and marketing will also result. The extent of these economies of scale will depend on the ability of the marketers to find panregional segments or to homogenize tastes across borders through promotional activity. There are challenges as well. For instance, phone manufacturing should focus on those locations with optimal proximity to suppliers and key markets. As a result, Nokia plans to close its manufacturing facility in Cluj, Romania, by the end of 2011, as Nokia's high-volume Asian factories provide greater scale and proximity benefits.[29]

Progress toward the goal of free movement of goods has been achieved largely due to the move from a "common standards approach" to a "mutual recognition approach." Under the common standards approach, EU members were forced to negotiate the specifications for literally thousands of products, often unsuccessfully. For example, because of differences in tastes, agreement was never reached on specifications for beer, sausage, or mayonnaise. Under the mutual recognition approach, the laborious quest for common standards is, in most cases, no longer necessary. Instead, as long as a product meets legal and specification requirements in one member country, it may be freely exported to any other, and customers serve as the final arbiters of success. Less progress toward free movement of people in Europe has been made than toward free movement of goods.

The North American Free Trade Agreement

After three failed tries last century, the United States and Canada signed a free trade agreement that went into effect January 1, 1989. The two countries had already had sectoral free trade arrangements; for example, one for automotive products had existed for over 30 years. Even before the agreement, however, the United States and Canada were already the world's largest trading partners, and there were relatively few trade barriers. Trade between the United States and Canada exceeded $527 billion in 2010.

Negotiations on a North American Free Trade Agreement (NAFTA) began in 1994 to create the world's largest free market, with currently more than 460 million consumers and a total output of nearly 17.5 trillion.[30] The pact marked a bold departure: never before had industrialized countries created such a massive free trade area with a developing-country neighbor. Because Canada stood to gain very little from NAFTA (its trade with Mexico is 1 percent of its trade with the United States), much of the controversy centered on the gains and losses for the United States and Mexico. Proponents argued that the agreement would give U.S. firms access to a huge pool of relatively low-cost Mexican labor at a time when demographic trends indicate labor shortages in many parts of the United States. At the same time, many new jobs would be created in Mexico. The agreement gave firms in both countries access to millions of additional consumers, and the liberalized trade flows should result in faster economic growth in both countries. The top 20 exports and imports between Mexico and the United States are in virtually the same industries, indicating intraindustry specialization and building of economies of scale for global competitiveness.[31]

Opposition to NAFTA has centered on issues relating to labor and the environment. Unions in particular worried about job loss to Mexico given lower wages and work standards, with some estimating that six million U.S. workers were vulnerable to job loss. A distinctive feature of NAFTA is the two side agreements that were worked out to correct perceived abuses in labor and in the environment in Mexico. The North American Agreement on Labor Cooperation (NAALC) was set up to hear complaints about worker abuse. Similarly, the Commission on Environmental Compliance was established to act as a public advocate for the environment. The side agreements have, however, had little impact, mainly because the mechanisms they created have almost no enforcement power.[32]

Trade among Canada, Mexico, and the United States has increased dramatically since NAFTA took effect, with total trade exceeding $939.4 billion in 2010. Reforms have turned Mexico into an attractive market in its own right. Mexico's domestic product has been expanding by more than 3 percent every year since 1989, and exports to the United States have risen 20 percent a year to $163.5 billion in 2010. By institutionalizing the nation's turn to open markets, the free trade agreement has attracted considerable new foreign investment. The United States has benefited from Mexico's success. U.S. exports to Mexico are nearly double those to Japan at $121.5 billion in 2010. While the surplus of $1.3 billion in 1994 has turned to a deficit of $66.4 billion in 2010, these imports have helped Mexico's growth and will, therefore, strengthen NAFTA in the long term. Furthermore, U.S. imports from Mexico have been shown to have much higher U.S. content than imports from other countries.[33] At present, cooperation between Mexico and the United States is taking new forms beyond trade and investment; for example, binational bodies have been established to tackle issues such as migration, border control, and drug trafficking.[34]

Among the U.S. industries to benefit are computers, autos, petrochemicals, financial services, and aerospace. Aerospace companies such as Boeing, Honeywell, Airbus Industries, and GE Aircraft Engines have recently made Mexico a center for both parts manufacture and assembly. Aerospace is now one of Mexico's largest industries, second only to electronics, with 20,000 workers employed.[35] In Mexico's growth toward a more advanced society, manufacturers of consumer goods will also stand to benefit. NAFTA has already had a major impact in the emergence of new retail chains, many established to handle new products from abroad (see *The International Marketplace 4.2*).[36]

Free trade does produce both winners and losers. Although opponents concede that the agreement spurs economic growth, they point out that segments of the U.S. economy are harmed by the agreement. Wages and employment for unskilled workers in the United States decreased because of Mexico's low-cost labor pool. U.S. companies have been moving operations to Mexico since the

THE INTERNATIONAL MARKETPLACE 4.2

NAFTA Reshaping Retail Markets

Walmart saw the promise of the Mexican market in 1991 when it stepped outside of the United States for the first time by launching Sam's Clubs in 50–50 partnership with Cifra, Mexico's largest retailer at that time. The local partner was needed to provide operational expertise in a market significantly different in culture and income from Walmart's domestic one. Within months, the first outlet—a bare-bones unit that sold bulk items at just above wholesale prices—was breaking all Walmart records in sales. "Save money, live better" may translate into many languages where Walmart operates, but the message behind the mission is universal: Walmart has 5,366 locations, 740,000 people, and total sales of $405 billion worldwide.

Behind Walmart's success are increasingly price-conscious consumers. The greater economic security of NAFTA has helped tame Mexico's once fierce inflation. The resulting price stability has made it easier for Mexican consumers to spot bargains. In addition, Walmart's clean, brightly lit interiors, orderly and well-stocked aisles, and consistent pricing policies are a relief from the chaotic atmosphere that still prevails in many local stores.

Mexican retailers are not just playing a defensive game, either. Gigante has opened nine stores in the Los Angeles area and aims to become the most popular supermarket among California's 11 million Latinos, most of whom are from Mexico and connect with the stores. Latinos boast a collective disposable income of $450 billion a year, with much of it going toward food. Given that food tastes are the last things to change with immigrants, Gigante's product choices (e.g., chorizo and carnitas), placements (e.g., produce close by the entrance), and décor have made it a success. Some local players are focusing on relatively uncontested rural markets in a similar fashion to the way Walmart was able to grow in the United States against Kmart and Sears in its time. Soriana and Chedraui have avoided Mexico City until recently, opting instead to build a presence and refine their approaches in rural areas, where their knowledge of the customer is most valuable.

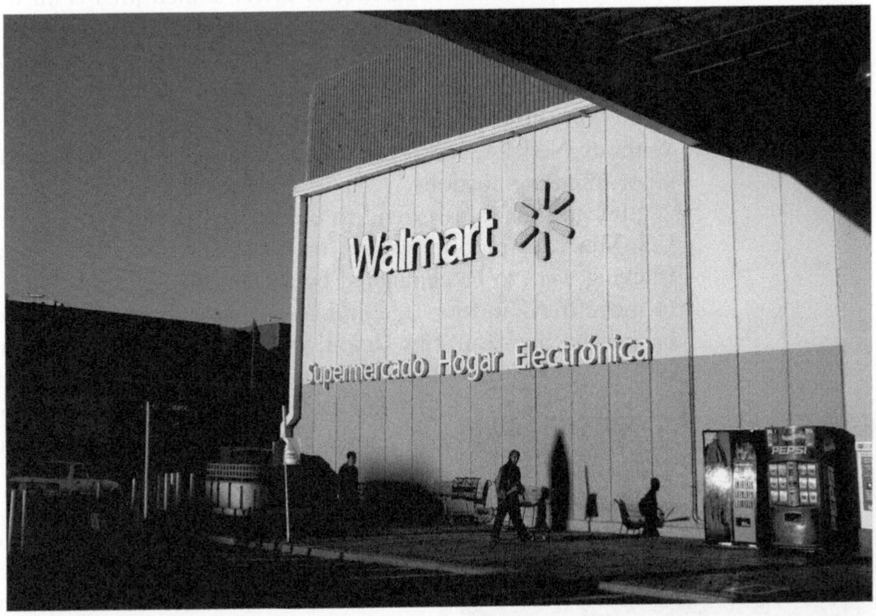

© David Rochkind/Bloomberg via Getty Images

A Walmart store in Mexico.

SOURCES: Walmart, *2011 Annual Report*, www.walmart.com; and Dante Di Gregorio, Douglas Thomas, and Fernan Gonzalez de Castilla, "Competition between Emerging Market and Multinational Firms: Walmart and Mexican Retailers," *International Journal of Management* 25 (September 2008): 532–45.

1960s. The door was opened when Mexico liberalized export restrictions to allow for more so-called **maquiladoras**, plants that make goods and parts or process food for export back to the United States.[37] The supply of labor is plentiful, the pay and benefits are low, and the work regulations are lax by U.S. standards. In the past two decades, maquiladoras have evolved from low-end garment or small-appliance assembly outfits to higher-end manufacturing of big-screen TVs, computers, and auto parts. The factories shipped $100 billion worth of goods (half of all Mexican exports), almost all of it to the United States. Wages have also been rising to $2.10 an hour, resulting in some low-end manufacturers of apparel and toys moving production to Asia.

While the Mexican government is eager to attract maquiladora investment, it is also keen to move away from using cheap labor as a central element of competitiveness. Mexico also stands to benefit from a subtle but steady shift in strategic thinking by U.S. manufacturers, who are reassessing their reliance on Asia and focusing more on near-shore options. Rising Chinese costs and fears of higher trans-Pacific shipping prices if oil spikes again are part of the shift. With capital scarce and markets hard to forecast, companies do not want to tie up cash in inventory as they wait for their cargo to arrive.[38] Such reasons are driving precision manufacturers like GKN Aerospace, a maker of aircraft engine components, to cluster close to the border in cities like Mexicali.

The U.S. Labor Department has certified 316,000 jobs as threatened or lost due to trade with Mexico and Canada. At the same time, the U.S. economy has added some 20 million jobs in the years since NAFTA. The fact that job losses have been in more heavily unionized sectors has made these losses politically charged. In most cases, high Mexican shipping and inventory costs will continue to make it more efficient for many U.S. industries to serve their home market from U.S. plants. Outsourcing of lower-skilled jobs is an unstoppable trend for developed economies such as the United States. However, NAFTA has given U.S. firms a way to take advantage of cheaper labor while still keeping close links to U.S. suppliers. Mexican assembly plants get 82 percent of their parts from U.S. suppliers, while factories in Asia are using only a fraction of that.[39] Without NAFTA, entire industries might be lost to Asia rather than just the labor-intensive portions.

Integration pains extend to other areas as well. Approximately 85 percent of U.S.-Mexican trade moves on trucks. Under NAFTA, cross-border controls on trucking were to be eliminated by the end of 1995, allowing commercial vehicles to move freely in four U.S. and six Mexican border states. But the U.S. truckers, backed by the Teamsters Union, would have none of this, arguing that Mexican trucks were dangerous and exceeded weight limits. The union also worried that opening the border would depress wages because it would allow U.S. trucking companies to team up with lower-cost counterparts in Mexico. In 2001, however, the NAFTA Arbitration Panel ruled that Mexican trucks must be allowed to cross U.S. borders and the United States. Senate approved a measure that allows Mexican truckers to haul cargo provided they meet strict inspection and safety rules. On the Mexican side, truckers are worried that if the border opens, U.S. firms will simply take over the trucking industry in Mexico.[40]

© Sandy Huffaker/Stringer/Getty Images

A truck enters the United States from Mexico at the Otay Mesa Customs Entry in Otay Mesa, California.

Countries dependent on trade with NAFTA countries are concerned that the agreement diverts trade and imposes significant losses on their economies. Asia's continuing economic success depends largely on easy access to the North American markets, which account for more than 25 percent of annual export revenue for many Asian countries. Lower-cost producers in Asia are likely to lose some exports to the United States if they are subject to tariffs while Mexican firms are not and may, therefore, have to invest in NAFTA. Similarly, many in the Caribbean and Central America fear that the apparel industries of their regions are threatened, as are much-needed investments.

Integration in Latin America

Mercado Común del Sur (MERCOSUR) was created in 1991 and includes Brazil, Argentina, Paraguay, and Uruguay. Bolivia, Chile, Colombia, Ecuador, Peru, and Venezuela have joined this South American trading bloc as associate members. MERCOSUR has three main objectives: (1) establishment of a free trade zone; (2) creation of a common external tariff system (i.e., a customs union); and (3) free movement of capital, labor, and services.

MERCOSUR has been likened to the European Union, but with an area of 12 million square kilometers (4.6 million square miles), it is four times as big. The bloc's combined market encompasses more than 266 million people and accounts for more than three-quarters of the economic activity on the continent. MERCOSUR is the world's fourth-largest trading bloc.[41]

Of the four MERCOSUR countries, Brazil is the most advanced in manufacturing and technology. Sao Paulo is one of the world's major industrial cities and is home to the affiliates and subsidiaries of many foreign corporations. Even with its significant industrial base, vast interior areas of Brazil and their rich resources remain virtually untapped. Major infrastructure improvements are under way to permit these resources to be brought to market in a cost-efficient manner. Infrastructure and transportation improvements throughout member nations and in other parts of South America are an important outgrowth of MERCOSUR. Intra-MERCOSUR exports now account for only 13 percent of its members' total exports (intra-EU exports are 60 percent). Brazil's exports to Argentina, for example, its main partner in the MERCOSUR bloc, amount to only about 1 percent of its GDP.

EU–MERCOSUR trade represents as much as EU trade with the rest of Latin America taken together. The EU is MERCOSUR's second largest trading partner after the United States. The EU and MERCOSUR plan to build a transatlantic free trade zone in the early part of the twenty-first century. Since 1995, when South America began to open up its markets, Europeans have won many of the top privatization deals. Spain's Telefonica de Espana spent $5 billion buying telephone companies in Brazil, Chile, Peru, and Argentina, where French Telecom and STET of Italy are active as well. In Brazil, 7 of the 10 largest private companies are European-owned, while just two are controlled by U.S. interests. Europeans dominate huge sectors in the economy, from automakers Volkswagen and Fiat to French supermarket chain Carrefour to Anglo-Dutch personal-care products group Lever.

The Andean Common Market (ANCOM) was founded in 1969 and currently comprises four countries that straddle the Andes: Bolivia, Colombia, Ecuador, and Peru. ANCOM and MERCOSUR leaders have discussed the possibility of allying to form a South American Community of Nations, modeled on the European Union, but those talks have not progressed quickly. The Andean Trade Preference Act (ATPA) was enacted to help four Andean countries in their fight against drug production and trafficking by expanding their economic alternatives.[42]

As a matter of fact, an alternative has arisen in opposition to the U.S.-led Free Trade Area of the Americas (FTAA). The Bolivarian Alternative for the People of Our America (ALBA), led by Cuba and Venezuela, focuses more on social welfare and economic aid than trade liberalization. Ideally, the larger countries would have agreed to consider giving smaller and less-developed countries more time to reduce tariffs, to open their economies to foreign investment, and to adopt effective laws in areas such as antitrust, intellectual property rights, bank regulation, and prohibitions on corrupt business practices. At the same time, the less-developed countries would agree to include labor and environmental standards in the negotiations.

The Central American Common Market (CACM) was formed by the Treaty of Managua in 1960. Its members are Costa Rica, El Salvador, Guatemala, Honduras, and Nicaragua. The group anticipates the eventual liberalization of interregional trade and the establishment of a free trade zone. The CACM has often been cited as a model integrative effort for other developing countries. By the end of the 1960s, the CACM had succeeded in eliminating restrictions on 80 percent of trade among members. A continuing source of difficulty, however, is that the benefits of integration have fallen disproportionately to the richer and more developed members. Political difficulties in the area have also hampered progress. However, the member countries renewed their commitment to integration in 1990. A major change occurred in 2005 with the signing of the Central America–Dominican Republic–United States Free Trade Agreement (CAFTA-DR). CAFTA-DR created the second largest U.S. export market in Latin America, behind only Mexico, and the 13th largest U.S. export market in the world. The United States exported $24.3 billion in goods to the five Central American countries and the Dominican Republic in 2010, more than all exports to Russia, India, and Indonesia combined. At the same time, U.S. imports amounted to $23.7 billion.

Integration efforts in the Caribbean have focused on the Caribbean Community and Common Market (CARICOM) formed in 1968. Its primary mandate is to provide a framework for regional political and economic integration. The following 15 nations make up the Caribbean Community: Antigua and Barbuda, Bahamas, Barbados, Belize, Dominica, Grenada, Guyana, Haiti, Jamaica, Montserrat, St. Kitts-Nevis, St. Lucia, St. Vincent and the Grenadines, Suriname, and Trinidad and Tobago. Among CARICOM's objectives are the strengthening of economic and trade regulations among member states, the expansion and integration of economic activities, and the achievement of a greater measure of economic independence for member states. Before NAFTA, CARICOM members (excluding Suriname) benefited from the Caribbean Basin Initiative (CBI), which, since 1983, extended trade preferences and granted access to the U.S. market. Under NAFTA, such preferences were lost, which means that the member countries have to cooperate more closely.

Integration in Asia

Development in Asia has been quite different from that in Europe and in the Americas. While European and North American arrangements have been driven by political will, market forces may force more formal integration on Asian politicians. The fact that regional integration is increasing around the world may drive Asian interest to it for pragmatic reasons. First, European and American markets are significant for the Asian producers, and some type of organization or bloc may be needed to maintain leverage and balance against the two other blocs. Second, given that much of the Asian trade growth is from intraregional trade, having common understandings and policies will become necessary.

Future integration will most likely use the frame of the most established arrangement in the region, the Association of Southeast Asian Nations (ASEAN). Before late 1991, ASEAN had no real structures, and consensus was reached through informal consultations. In October 1991, ASEAN members announced the formation of a customs union called the ASEAN Free Trade Area (AFTA). The 10 member countries agreed to reduce tariffs to a maximum level of 5 percent by 2005 and to create a customs union by 2020.[43] Even a common currency has been proposed. Skepticism about the lofty targets has been raised regarding the group's ability to follow the example of the European Union given the widely divergent levels of economic development (e.g., Singapore versus Laos) and the lack of democratic institutions (especially in Myanmar). ASEAN has also agreed to economic cooperation with China, Japan, and South Korea (the so-called ASEAN + 1 and ASEAN + 3 arrangements), as well as with India. Integrating

Southeast Asia, China has recently signed agreements to build new rail lines in Laos and Thailand, while it extends its network from Kunming to the China–Laos border. These lines are meant to be ready by 2015.[44]

The Malaysians have pushed for the formation of the East Asia Economic Group (EAEG), which would add Hong Kong, Japan, South Korea, and Taiwan to the membership list. This proposal makes sense because without Japan and the rapidly industrializing countries of the region such as South Korea and Taiwan, the effect of the arrangement would be nominal. Japan's reaction has been generally negative toward all types of regionalization efforts, mainly because it has the most to gain from free trade. However, part of what has been driving regionalization has been Japan's reluctance to foster some of the elements that promote free trade, for example, reciprocity. Should the other trading blocs turn against Japan, its only resort may be to work toward a more formal trade arrangement in the Asia–Pacific area.

Another formal proposal for cooperation would start building bridges between two emerging trade blocs. Some individuals have publicly called for a U.S.-Japan common market. Given the differences on all fronts between the two countries, the proposal may be quite unrealistic at this time. Negotiated trade liberalization will not open Japanese markets because of major institutional differences, as seen in many rounds of successful negotiations but totally unsatisfactory results. The only solution, especially for the U.S. government, is to forge better cooperation between the government and the private sector to improve competitiveness.

In 1989, Australia proposed the Asia Pacific Economic Cooperation (APEC) as an annual forum. The proposal called for ASEAN members to be joined by Australia, New Zealand, Japan, China, Hong Kong, Taiwan, South Korea, Canada, and the United States. It was initially modeled after the OECD, which is a center for research and high-level discussion. Since then, APEC's goals have become more ambitious. At present, APEC has members with a combined 55 percent of global GDP, 58 percent of U.S. goods exports, and nearly 43 percent of global trade. APEC is the third largest economy of the world. The key objectives of APEC are to liberalize trade by 2020, to facilitate trade by harmonizing standards, and to build human capacities for realizing the region's ambitions. The trade-driven economies of the region have the world's largest pool of savings, the most advanced technologies, and growing markets.[45]

Economic integration has also taken place on the Indian subcontinent. In 1985, seven nations of the region (India, Pakistan, Bangladesh, Sri Lanka, Nepal, Bhutan, and the Maldives) launched the South Asian Association for Regional Cooperation (SAARC). Cooperation has been limited to relatively noncontroversial areas, such as agriculture and regional development, and is hampered by political disagreements. India exported $2.33 billion of goods to Pakistan. In 2011, Pakistan sold goods valued at $332.5 million in India. By comparison, two-way trade between India and China is valued at more than $60 billion annually.[46]

Integration in Africa and the Middle East

Africa's economic groupings range from currency unions between European nations and their former colonies to customs unions among neighboring states. In addition to wanting to liberalize trade among members, African countries want to gain better access to European and North American markets for farm and textile products. Given that most of the countries are too small to negotiate with the other blocs, alliances have been the solution. In 1975, 16 West African nations attempted to create a megamarket large enough to interest investors from the industrialized world and reduce hardship through economic integration. The objective of the Economic Community of West African States (ECOWAS) was to form a customs union and eventual common market. Although many of its objectives have not been reached, its combined population of 160 million represents the largest economic entity in sub-Saharan Africa. Other entities in Africa include the Common Market for Eastern and Southern Africa (COMESA), the Economic Community of Central African States (CEEAC), the Southern African Customs Union, the Southern African

Development Community (SADC), and some smaller, less globally oriented blocs such as the Economic Community of the Great Lakes Countries (ECGLC), the Mano River Union (MRU), and the East African Community (EAC).

Most member countries are part of more than one bloc (for example, Tanzania is a member in both the EAC and SADC). The blocs, for the most part, have not been successful due to the small size of the members and the lack of economic infrastructure to produce goods to be traded inside the blocs. Moreover, some of the blocs have been relatively inactive for substantial periods of time while their members endure internal political turmoil or even warfare among each other. In 2002, African nations established the African Union (AU) for regional cooperation. Eventually, plans call for a pan-African parliament, a court of justice, a central bank, and a shared currency by 2023.[47]

Countries in the Arab world have made some progress in economic integration. The Arab Maghreb Union ties together Algeria, Libya, Mauritania, Morocco, and Tunisia in northern Africa. The Gulf Cooperation Council (GCC) is one of the most powerful, economically speaking, of any trade groups. The per capita income of its six member states (Bahrain, Kuwait, Oman, Qatar, Saudi Arabia, and the United Arab Emirates) is in the 90th percentile in the world. Significant progress has already been made in regional economic integration. The GCC countries have largely unrestricted intraregional mobility of goods, labor, and capital; regulation of the banking sector is being harmonized; and in 2008, the countries established a common market. Further, most of the convergence criteria established for entry into a monetary union have already been achieved. In establishing a monetary union, however, the GCC countries must decide on the exchange rate regime for the single currency. A proposal among GCC members calls for the creation of a common currency by 2013.[48] This area has some of the fastest-growing economies in the world, mostly due to a boom in oil and natural gas revenues coupled with a building and investment boom backed by decades of saved petroleum revenues. In an effort to build a tax base and economic foundation before the reserves run out, the UAE's Abu Dhabi Investment Authority retained more than $875 billion in assets. In recent years, the ratio of private to government expenditure in GCC countries has been below the OECD average, suggesting strong potential for more private-sector involvement in infrastructure development. GCC governments have already made efforts to encourage that investment, privatizing government assets and completing initial public offerings of public-sector infrastructure.[49] The growth in international opportunities is leading to a rapid internationalization as shown in *The International Marketplace 4.3*.

A listing of the major regional trade agreements is provided in Exhibit 4.11.

EMERGING MARKETS

Broadly defined, an emerging market is a country making an effort to change and improve its economy with the goal of raising its performance to that of the world's more advanced nations.[50] Improved economies can benefit emerging-market countries through higher personal income levels and better standards of living, more exports, increased foreign direct investment, and more stable political structures. Developed countries benefit from the development of human and natural resources in emerging markets through increased international trading.

Although opinions on which countries are emerging markets differ, the major emerging markets are China, India, Brazil, Russia, Argentina, and Indonesia. The data provided in Exhibit 4.12 compare selected emerging markets with each other on dimensions indicating market potential. The biggest

THE INTERNATIONAL MARKETPLACE 4.3

The Gulf Economies Are Linked East and West

The countries of the GCC—Bahrain, Kuwait, Oman, Qatar, Saudi Arabia, and the UAE—represent one regional powerhouse whose relationships with emerging peers can offer valuable insights into the way such alliances are forming. The nations of the GCC look around the world to develop their network of relationships, and they will find many opportunities with partners in both developed and developing nations. The BRIC and Next 11 nations are growing stronger—a development that Western countries to date have viewed with trepidation, fearing that a zero-sum game will leave them cut off from increasingly significant consumer markets and sources of natural resources, goods, and services. The GCC countries face four major factors in pursuing economic integration:

1. *More than oil.* The top item on the strategic agenda for every GCC country is to diversify its economy and thus decrease its dependence on oil. Despite significant efforts, achieving this goal has so far proven challenging: oil and gas accounted for 39 percent of GDP in the GCC in 2010. Saudi Arabia's exports to the United States still revolve around oil, whereas its exports to BRIC countries include chemicals, plastics, and minerals.
2. *Rich in talent.* As goods and services flow across the borders of the GCC and other emerging markets, so do people. The most significant aspect of this change is the skill level of many of the people entering the GCC. No longer do executives come from the West and laborers from the East; instead, skilled individuals from emerging markets are deepening their impact on the GCC with influential positions in the region's financial, energy, transportation, and public sectors. India, in particular, has a large community of professional expatriates in the region.
3. *New sources of capital.* GCC nations have long been investors in other countries—primarily in the United States and Europe—via their sovereign wealth funds and other state-owned entities. In light of the strong role that GCC governments play in determining the direction of their countries' capital investments, this trend could accelerate if GCC governments decide that other emerging markets are a better strategic destination—both economically and politically—for their riyals, dirhams, and dinars. The state-owned airlines in the UAE and Qatar have quickly achieved global prominence.
4. *Getting connected.* As GCC countries seek to branch out and build relationships with other emerging markets, they have found one point of entry in the information and communications technology (ICT) sector. The nations of the Gulf and their partners in other emerging markets have collaborated to boost their ICT development in ways that they might not have been able to do alone. Chinese companies Huawei and ZTE have provided equipment for GCC telecom networks.

GCC countries will need to keep pushing forward on economic integration within the region, which will bolster their presence on the world stage. The countries of the GCC have much more clout as an economic bloc than as six separate entities, and the GCC must continue to implement policies that reflect this perspective.

GCC Capital Outflows by Destination

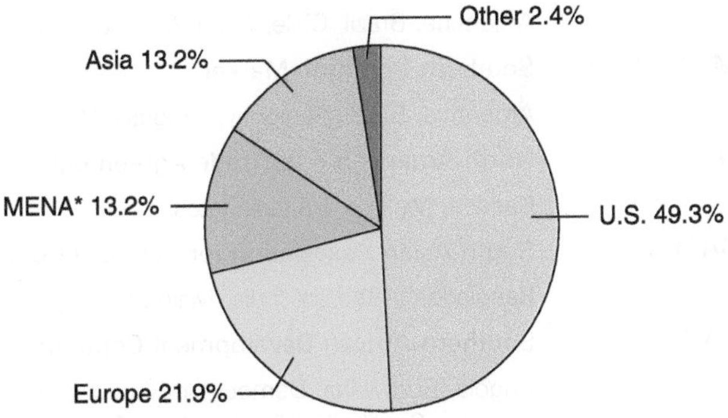

*Middle East and North Africa

SOURCE: © Cengage Learning 2013.

SOURCES: Joe Saddi, Karim Sabbagh, and Richard Shediac, "The New Web of World Trade," *Strategy+Business* no. 64 (Autumn 2011); Joe Saddi, Karim Sabbagh, and Richard Shediac, "The Challenges of Balance," *Strategy+Business* no. 55 (Summer 2009); and Joe Saddi, Karim Sabbagh, and Richard Shediac, "Oasis Economics," *Strategy+Business* no. 50 (Spring 2008).

EXHIBIT 4.11 Major Regional Trade Agreements

AFTA	ASEAN Free Trade Area
	Brunei, Cambodia, Indonesia, Laos, Malaysia, Myanmar, Philippines, Singapore, Thailand, Vietnam
ANCOM	Andean Common Market
	Bolivia, Colombia, Ecuador, Peru
APEC	Asia Pacific Economic Cooperation
	Australia, Brunei, Canada, Indonesia, Japan, Republic of Korea, Malaysia, New Zealand, Philippines, Singapore, Thailand, United States, Chinese Taipei, Hong Kong, People's Republic of China, Mexico, Papua New Guinea, Chile, Peru, Russia, Vietnam
CACM	Central American Common Market
	Costa Rica, El Salvador, Guatemala, Honduras, Nicaragua, Panama
CARICOM	Caribbean Community
	Antigua and Barbuda, Bahamas, Barbados, Belize, Dominica, Grenada, Guyana, Haiti, Jamaica, Montserrat, Saint Kitts and Nevis, Saint Lucia, Saint Vincent and the Grenadines, Suriname, Trinidad and Tobago
EAC	East African Community
	Burundi, Kenya, Rwanda, Tanzania, Uganda
ECOWAS	Economic Community of West African States
	Benin, Burkina Faso, Cape Verde, Côte d'Ivoire, Gambia, Ghana, Guinea, Guinea-Bissau, Liberia, Mali, Niger, Nigeria, Senegal, Sierra Leone, Togo
EFTA	European Free Trade Association
	Iceland, Liechtenstein, Norway, Switzerland
EU	European Union
	Austria, Belgium, Bulgaria, Cyprus, Czech Republic, Denmark, Estonia, Finland, France, Germany, Greece, Hungary, Ireland, Italy, Latvia, Lithuania, Luxembourg, Malta, Netherlands, Poland, Portugal, Romania, Slovakia, Slovenia, Spain, Sweden, United Kingdom
GCC	Gulf Cooperation Council
	Bahrain, Kuwait, Oman, Qatar, Saudi Arabia, United Arab Emirates
LAIA	Latin American Integration Association
	Argentina, Brazil, Chile, Cuba, Mexico, Paraguay, Peru, Uruguay, Bolivia, Colombia, Ecuador, Venezuela
MERCOSUR	Southern Common Market
	Argentina, Brazil, Paraguay, Uruguay, Venezuela
NAFTA	North American Free Trade Agreement
	Canada, Mexico, United States
SAARC	South Asian Association for Regional Cooperation
	Bangladesh, Bhutan, India, Maldives, Nepal, Pakistan, Sri Lanka, Afghanistan
SADC	Southern African Development Community
	Angola, Botswana, Democratic Republic of the Congo, Lesotho, Madagascar, Malawi, Mauritius, Mozambique, Namibia, Seychelles, South Africa, Swaziland, Tanzania, Zambia, Zimbabwe

SOURCE: © Cengage Learning 2013.

emerging markets display the factors that make them strategically important: favorable consumer demographics, rising household incomes, and increasing availability of credit, as well as increasing productivity resulting in more attractive prices.[51] As computer-factory workers in China and software programmers in India increase their incomes, they become consumers. The number of people with the equivalent of $10,000 in annual income will double to 2 billion by 2015—and 900 million of those newcomers to the consumer class will be in emerging markets. GE, for example, expects to get as much as 60 percent of its revenue growth from emerging markets over the next decade.[52]

EXHIBIT 4.12 Market Potential of Twenty-Six Emerging Markets, 2010

Countries	Market Size		Market Growth Rate		Market Intensity		Market Consumption Capacity		Commercial Infrastructure		Economic Freedom		Market Receptivity		Country Risk		Overall Index	
	Rank	Index	Rank	Index	Rank	Index	Rank	Index	Rank	Index	Rank	Index	Rank	Index	Rank	Index	Rank	Index
Hong Kong	24	1	6	45	1	100	17	48	1	100	2	93	2	81	1	100	1	100
China	1	100	1	100	26	1	13	60	21	33	25	2	23	2	8	64	2	92
Singapore	26	1	17	25	2	81	14	57	3	89	8	77	1	100	2	98	3	90
South Korea	7	10	16	31	6	64	1	100	4	85	4	83	9	15	4	73	4	71
Czech Republic	22	1	24	13	13	51	2	94	2	91	3	88	10	13	3	78	5	56
Poland	15	4	13	33	10	60	5	78	6	79	7	77	14	5	9	63	6	51
Israel	23	1	20	22	4	70	7	74	7	72	6	79	5	19	7	66	7	51
Hungary	25	1	25	1	3	71	3	90	5	82	5	82	6	17	10	60	8	49
India	2	38	2	78	24	26	11	60	25	9	18	47	20	3	13	50	9	48
Turkey	8	6	10	36	5	67	9	65	15	48	12	58	13	10	17	40	10	36
Brazil	4	21	11	36	17	47	23	20	13	52	14	55	25	1	12	50	11	28
Indonesia	5	11	4	53	19	41	10	63	20	33	15	50	24	1	22	33	12	27
Mexico	6	10	22	18	8	61	21	27	16	46	9	70	7	17	11	51	13	27
Malaysia	19	3	21	19	23	29	8	73	9	59	16	49	4	28	20	37	14	26
Chile	20	2	23	13	14	50	22	24	14	50	1	100	12	11	6	71	15	26
Egypt	13	4	7	45	11	58	6	75	19	39	22	25	17	4	21	34	16	25
Saudi Arabia	14	4	5	49	25	17	-	-	11	54	23	22	11	12	5	71	17	23
Thailand	16	4	14	33	22	36	15	52	12	54	19	43	8	16	19	38	18	21
Argentina	12	4	8	43	12	52	19	45	10	57	17	48	19	3	24	14	19	19
Peru	21	2	9	41	15	50	20	36	22	33	10	69	18	3	16	41	20	17
Russia	3	24	26	1	20	40	16	49	8	65	24	11	22	2	15	44	21	17
Pakistan	10	6	3	58	9	61	4	79	26	1	21	29	26	1	26	1	22	14
Philippines	11	5	18	24	7	62	18	48	23	31	20	41	15	5	23	26	23	12
South Africa	9	6	19	24	18	46	25	1	24	12	11	67	3	29	14	48	24	8
Colombia	18	3	15	32	16	48	24	9	17	45	13	55	21	2	18	39	25	7
Venezuela	17	3	12	34	21	40	12	60	18	43	26	1	16	4	25	6	26	1

SOURCE: "Market Potential Index (MPI) for Emerging Markets - 2010," available at http://globaledge.msu.edu/resourceDesk/mpi. Reprinted with permission from globalEDGE.

Mere size and growth do not guarantee an emerging market's overall appeal and potential. The growth rates may be consistently higher than in developed markets, but they may be subject to greater volatility. For example, Russia, Brazil, and Argentina all faced severe financial crises between the years of 1999 and 2001. Evident in the data is the role of political risk; that is, government interference in entry and market development situations. The Russian government blocked a landmark investment of German engineering company Siemens in OAO Power Machines on antitrust grounds as the government tightened its control on industries it deems vital to the country's interests. The Russian government has also barred foreign-owned companies from bidding for its oil and metal deposits.[53] In other instances, emerging-market governments have leveraged their position as hosts to foreign investors. The Chinese government has tried to impose its own standards on new technologies, such as EVD for video-disc players and Red Flag Linux for operating systems. The rationale behind this "techno-nationalism" is that China is tired of foreign patent fees for products made and sold domestically (in this case, $4.50 per unit to six Japanese companies that developed the underlying DVD technology).[54] In Brazil, it took a Dutch telecommunications company six months and eight government agency approvals before obtaining a temporary business license.[55]

Another concern is the current and future competition from emerging-market companies. Chinese companies have been able to develop powerful global brands in a very short period of time. Some have been developed from the domestic base in a step-by-step manner (e.g., Haier in appliances and Geely in cars) or through acquisitions of existing global brands (such as TCL in TVs and Lenovo in computers).[56] Another concern is based on economic and national security. Companies such as GE, Microsoft, Cisco, and Intel all have established R&D operations in China, thereby training foreign scientists and possibly giving the omnipresent Chinese government access to proprietary technologies.[57]

Given that emerging markets differ from each other in substantial ways, appropriate strategies have to be developed for each. As shown in Exhibit 4.13, Brazil, China, India, and Russia are quite different when measured on marketing-related dimensions. Surveys show that Chinese consumers value convenience, followed by spaciousness and comfort of stores and selection they offer. Carrefour, Walmart, and Metro have all done very well in China's new retail environment.[58] In Latin America, however, companies that have tried to export supermarket and hypermarket models from developed markets have faced strong competition from small-scale retailers—the shops, street markets, and small independent supermarkets that are an integral part of Latin culture.[59] In 2011, India-led foreign firms could now own 51 percent of multibrand retailers, such as supermarkets (up from zero), and 100 percent of single-brand chains (up from 51 percent).[60]

A number of strategic choices are available, but most of them require recognizing the idiosyncracies of the market. Whatever the strategy, the marketer has to make sure to secure the company's core competencies while being innovative.[61] For example, with half of its population under 21, Saudi Arabia needs to create millions of jobs to absorb those entering the labor force and build a modern economy. Cisco has agreed to invest $265 million in the country over five years. Most of that is going to establish Networking Academy training centers where locals learn everything from repairing routers to network design.[62]

Adjust Entry Strategy

GM entered the Russian market to produce SUVs in a joint venture with Avto-VAZ, Russia's largest automaker. Russia is one of the eight large markets that

EXHIBIT 4.13 Marketing Contexts for Key Emerging Markets

Brazil	China	India	Russia
Modes of Entry			
Both greenfield investments and acquisitions are possible. Companies team up with local partners to gain local expertise.	Government permits both greenfield investments and acquisitions. Acquired companies may have been state-owned and have hidden liabilities. Alliances allow for aligning interests with all levels of government.	Restrictions in some sectors make joint ventures necessary. Red tape hinders companies in sectors where the government does not allow foreign investment.	Both greenfield investments and acquisitions are possible but difficult. Companies form alliances to gain access to government and local inputs.
Product Development and Intellectual Property			
Local design capability exists. Intellectual property rights disputes with the United States exist in some sectors.	Imitation and piracy abound. Penalties for violation vary by province and level of corruption.	Some local design capability is available. Intellectual property rights problems with the United States exist in some industries. Regulatory bodies monitor product quality and fraud.	Strong local design capability but an ambivalent attitude toward intellectual property rights. Sufficient regulatory authority exists, but enforcement is patchy.
Supplier Base and Logistics			
Suppliers are available with MERCOSUR. A good network of highways, airports, and ports exists.	Several suppliers have strong manufacturing capabilities, but few vendors have advanced technical capabilities. Road network is well developed and port facilities are excellent.	Suppliers are available, but their quality and dependability vary greatly. Roads are in poor condition. Ports and airports are underdeveloped.	Companies can rely on local companies for basic supplies. The European region has decent logistics networks; trans-Ural area does not.
Brand Perceptions and Management			
Consumers accept both local and global brands. Global as well as local agencies are present.	Consumers prefer to buy products from American, European, and Japanese companies. Multinational ad agencies exist.	Consumers buy both local and global brands. Global ad agencies are present, but they have been less successful than locals.	Consumers prefer global brands in automobiles and high tech. Local brands thrive in food and beverages. Some local and global ad agencies are present.

SOURCE: Adapted from Tarun Khanna, Keishna Palepu, and Jayant Sinha, "Strategies That Fit Emerging Markets," *Harvard Business Review* 83 (June 2005): 68, 69.

will grow substantially in the future. GM chose to use a joint venture to secure a local engineering source to eliminate many of the risks that lead to failure in emerging markets. Since the car, the Niva, is 100 percent designed in Russia, the cost of engineering is substantially lower than what GM would have had to pay in Europe. Relying completely on local content protects GM from any protective scheme that the government may impose. Controlling the costs allows GM in turn to provide a car at the pricing point (approximately $12,000) that consumers are willing to pay for a GM-branded vehicle. Another benefit of GM's strategy is securing an existing dealer network. A third benefit for GM is its ability to export the Niva to other emerging markets using the Daewoo network (acquired by GM earlier).[63]

As another example, Chinese consumers typically want to lay their hands on computers before they buy them. That means the best way to reach them is via vast retailing operations, the strength of local players Lenovo and Founder

Electronics, which both rank ahead of Dell. Dell's computers are sold in nearly 3,000 outlets of the Gome and Suning electronics store chains. To maintain its core approach, Dell set up kiosks to demonstrate its SmartPC and other products and allow for orders from these kiosks.[64]

Manage Affordability

Volkswagen, which arrived in 1984, and General Motors, which established its operations in 1997, have dominated the Chinese auto markets. However, they are now facing competition offering more economically priced cars. The reason for the shift in purchasing preferences is that the typical buyer has changed. Only a few years ago, the majority of purchases were made by state-owned companies, for whom price was not the critical criterion. Currently, most buyers are individuals who want the best deal for their money. To respond, GM has introduced the $8,000 Chevy Spark but will focus on the higher-end market with its Cadillac line.[65] A critical battleground is emerging for companies in the "good-enough" market segment, home of reliable-enough products at low-enough prices to attract the fastest-growing segment of midlevel Chinese customers. This may mean that rather than paying a 70 to 100 percent premium for a global brand, the customer is only willing to pay 20 to 30 percent.[66]

Invest in Distribution

Kodak has nearly 8,000 photo stores across China, one of the country's largest retail operations. The company taps the desire of many Chinese to run their own businesses while helping them negotiate setting up their operations. One Kodak campaign offered all of the necessary photo-development equipment, training, and a store license for 99,000 yuan ($12,000). Kodak negotiated a deal with the Bank of China and other big banks to arrange financing for individuals lacking capital. These programs are part of Kodak's big bet when it bought three debt-laden state enterprises and many of their workers for $1 billion. In return, no other companies in the industry were allowed into China for four years.[67]

Build Strong Brands

A common characteristic across all emerging markets is the appeal of recognizable brands. While it is easiest for international marketers to extend their global brands to emerging markets, some companies such as Danone acquire companies but continue selling the products under the original names. Consumer loyalty is ensured by adding a new quality dimension to well-established brands. Furthermore, this strategy can generate favor among Chinese officials who may not want to see local brands go under. Brands in the packaged goods, beverages, and retail categories operate in extremely crowded spaces, where brand building can play a critical role in differentiation.[68] Retail sportswear and clothing brands also stand out, including Li-Ning, Metersbonwe, Anta, and 361 Degrees. An Olympic sponsor, the Anta brand promotes the Olympic spirit and sports development in China. The new slogan for Anta is "keep moving."

Courtesy of Anta Sports Products Limited

Chinese ANTA ad celebrating the Olympic spirit.

DEVELOPING MARKETS

The time may have come to look at the four billion people in the world who live in poverty, subsisting on less than $2,000 a year.[69] Not only is this segment a full two-thirds of the current marketplace, but it is expected to grow to six billion by 2040. Despite initial skepticism about access and purchasing power, marketers are finding that they can make profits while having a positive effect on the sustainable livelihoods of people not normally considered potential customers. However, doing so will require radical departures from traditional business models—for example, new partnerships (ranging from local governments to nonprofits) and new pricing structures (allowing customers to rent or lease rather than buy and providing new financing choices for purchases). Hewlett-Packard has an initiative called World e-Inclusion that, working with a range of global and local partners, aims to sell, lease, or donate a billion dollars' worth of satellite-powered computer products and services to markets in Africa, Asia, Eastern Europe, Latin America, and the Middle East.[70] To engage with beta communities in Senegal, Hewlett-Packard partnered with Joko, Inc., a company founded by revered Senegalese pop star Youssou n'Dour.

Five elements of success are required for an international marketer to take advantage of and thrive in developing markets.[71]

Research

The first order of business is to learn about the needs, aspirations, and habits of targeted populations for whom traditional intelligence gathering may not be the most effective means. For example, just because the demand for land lines in developing countries was low, it would have been wrong to assume that little demand for phones existed. The real reasons were that land lines were expensive, subscribers had to wait for months to get hooked up, and lines often went down due to bad maintenance, flooding, and theft of copper cables. Mobile phones have been a solution to that problem. Africa has more than 600 million mobile-phone users—more than America or Europe. Since roads are generally dreadful, advances in communications, with mobile banking and telephonic agro-info, have been a huge boon.[72]

Create Buying Power

Without credit, it is impossible for many developing-country consumers to make major purchases. Programs in microfinance have allowed consumers, with no property as collateral, to borrow sums averaging $100 to make purchases and have retail banking services available to them. Lenders such as Grameen Bank in Bangladesh and Compartamos in Mexico have helped millions of families to escape poverty. Excellent payment records (e.g., only 0.56 percent of the loans are even days late at Compartamos) have started attracting companies such as Citicorp to microfinancing through underwriting microfinance bonds in markets such as Peru.[73]

Tailor Local Solutions

In the product area, companies must combine advanced technology with local insights. Hindustan Lever (part of Unilever) learned that low-income Indians, usually forced to settle for low-quality products, wanted to buy high-end detergents and personal care products but could not afford them in the quantities available. In response, the company developed extremely low-cost packaging material and other innovations that allowed for a product priced in pennies instead of the $4 to $15 price of the regular containers. The same brand is on all of the product forms regardless of packaging. Given that these consumers do not shop at supermarkets, Lever employs local residents with pushcarts who take small quantities of the sachets to kiosks.[74]

Improve Access

Due to the economic and physical isolation of poor communities, providing access can lead to a thriving business. In Bangladesh (with income levels of $200), GrameenPhone Ltd. leases access to wireless phones to villagers. Every phone is used by an average of 100 people and generates $90 in revenue a month—two or three times the revenues generated by wealthier users who own their phones in urban areas.[75] Similarly, the Jhai Foundation, an American–Laotian foundation, is helping villagers in Laos with Internet access. The first step, however, was to develop an inexpensive and robust computer. The computer has no moving parts and very few delicate ones. Instead of a hard disk, it relies on flash-memory chips, and instead of an energy-guzzling glass cathode-ray tube, its screen is a liquid-crystal display. The XO-1, previously known as the $100 Laptop, is an inexpensive laptop computer intended to be distributed to 150 million children in developing countries around the world. The laptop was developed by One Laptop Per Child (OLPC), a nonprofit organization, and manufactured by Quanta Computer. Originally intended to run on open-source software, OLPC has reached an agreement for the use of Microsoft's Windows XP operating system. The agreement with OLPC underscores Microsoft's eagerness to market its software in emerging markets, where it has tried to seed Windows in schools—the target of OLPC's machines. The $3 price represents a big discount to what the company charges in the United States. Recently, Microsoft has also done $3 software deals in Russia, Libya, and Egypt.[76]

Shape Aspirations

The biggest challenges in developing markets are in providing essential services. In this sense, developing markets can be ideal settings for commercial and technological innovation. With significant demand for mobile handsets in developing countries, both Nokia and Motorola have developed models that sell for as little as $25. They are ideally suited to match consumer demand for inexpensive phones with the features, quality, and brand names consumers want. Emerging low-cost producers from China cannot match the volume or the brand franchises of the global players. While gross margins on these phones may be as little as 15 percent (as compared with 33 percent at the high end), the big volumes can establish scale economies that reduce costs even for high-end models. Global marketers are very often the only ones that can realistically make a difference in solving some of the problems in developing markets. Developing new technologies or products is a resource-intensive task and requires knowledge transfer from one market to another. Without multinationals as catalysts, nongovernmental organizations, local governments, and communities will continue to flounder in their attempts to bring development to the poorest nations in the world.[77]

The emergence of these markets presents a great growth opportunity for companies. It also creates a chance for business, government, and civil society to join together in a common cause to help the aspiring poor to join the world market economy. Lifting billions of people from poverty may help avert social decay, political chaos, terrorism, and environmental deterioration that is certain to continue if the gap between the rich and poor countries continues to widen. For example, Coca-Cola has introduced "Project Mission" in Botswana to launch a drink to combat anemia, blindness, and other afflictions common in poorer parts of the world. The drink, called Vitango, is like the company's Hi-C orange-flavored drink, but it contains 12 vitamins and minerals chronically lacking in the diets of people in developing countries. The project satisfies multiple objectives for Coca-Cola. First, it could help boost sales at a time when global sales of carbonated drinks are slowing, and, second, it will help in establishing relationships with governments and other local constituents that will serve as a positive platform for brand Coca-Cola. The market for such nutritional drinks may be limited, but they are meant to offer Coca-Cola a role as a good corporate citizen at a time when being perceived as such is increasingly important for multinational corporations.[78]

ECONOMIC INTEGRATION AND THE INTERNATIONAL MARKETER

Regional economic integration creates opportunities and potential problems for the international marketer. It may have an impact on a company's entry mode by favoring direct investment because one of the basic rationales of integration is to generate favorable conditions for local production and intraregional trade. By design, larger markets are created with more potential opportunity. Harmonization efforts may result in standardized regulations, which in turn affect production and marketing efforts in a positive manner.

Decisions regarding integrating markets must be assessed from four different perspectives: the range and impact of changes resulting from integration, development of strategies to relate to these changes, organizational changes needed to exploit these changes, and strategies to influence change in a more favorable direction.

Effects of Change

The first task is to envision the outcome of the change. Change in the competitive landscape can be dramatic if scale opportunities can be exploited in relatively homogeneous demand conditions. This could be the case, for example, for industrial goods, consumer durables such as cameras and watches, and professional services. The international marketer will have to take into consideration varying degrees of change readiness within the markets themselves. That is, governments and other stakeholders, such as labor unions, may oppose the liberalization of competition, especially when national champions such as airlines, automobiles, energy, and telecommunications are concerned.[79]

Strategic Planning

After determining the effects of change, the international marketer will then have to develop a strategic response to the new environment to maintain a sustainable long-term competitive advantage. Those companies already present in an integrated market should fill in gaps in European product and market portfolios through acquisitions or alliances to create a regional or global company. It is increasingly evident that even regional presence is not sufficient; companies need to set their sights on presence beyond that. In industries such as automobiles, mobile communications, and retailing, blocs in the twenty-first century may be dominated by two or three giants, leaving room only for niche players. Those with currently weak positions, or no presence at all, will have to create alliances for market entry and development with established firms. Tesco entered the US$270-billion-a-year grocery market in China in 2004 through a joint venture with Taiwan's Hymall, of which it now owns 90 percent. Today, Tesco operates 60 stores in China, with 95 percent of products sourced within the country. Global reach is key to local effectiveness: Tesco believes that in China it can use the experience it has gained from operating around the world to localize its food offerings.[80]

Reorganization

Whatever changes are made, they will require company reorganization. Structurally, authority will have to become more centralized to execute regional programs. In staffing, the focus will have to be on individuals who understand the subtleties of consumer behavior across markets and are therefore able to evaluate the similarities and differences between cultures and markets. In developing systems for the planning and implementation of regional programs, adjustments have to be made to incorporate views throughout the organization. If, for example, decisions on regional advertising campaigns are made at headquarters without consultation with country operations, resentment from the local marketing staff could lead to less-than-optimal execution. The introduction of the euro means increased coordination in pricing as compared to the relative autonomy in price setting enjoyed by country organizations in the past. Companies may even move corporate or divisional headquarters from the domestic market to be closer to the customer or centers of innovation. Forum Nokia, a portal available in English, Chinese, and Japanese, gives outside developers access to resources to help them design, test, certify, market, and sell their own applications, content, services, or websites to mobile uses via Nokia devices.[81]

Lobbying

International managers, as change agents, must constantly seek ways to influence the regulatory environment in which they have to operate. Economic integration will create its own powers and procedures similar to those of the EU commission and its directives. The international marketer is not powerless to influence EU; as a matter of fact, a passive approach may result in competitors gaining an advantage or may put the company at a disadvantage. For example, it was very important for the U.S. pharmaceutical industry to obtain tight patent protection as part of the NAFTA agreement; therefore, substantial time and money were spent on lobbying both the executive and legislative branches of the U.S. government. Often, policymakers rely heavily on the knowledge and experience of the private sector to carry out their own work. Influencing change will therefore mean providing industry information, such as test results, to the policymakers.

Many marketers consider lobbying a public relations activity and therefore go beyond the traditional approaches. Lobbying will usually have to take place at multiple levels simultaneously; within the EU, this means the European Commission in Brussels, the European Parliament in Strasbourg, or the national governments within the EU. Marketers with substantial resources have established their own lobbying offices in Brussels, while smaller companies get their voices heard through joint offices or their industry associations. In terms of lobbying, U.S. firms have an advantage because of their experience in their home market; however, for many European firms, lobbying is a new, yet necessary, skill to be acquired. Culture does play a role in lobbying in Brussels as opposed to lobbying in Washington, DC. One does not have to grapple with 20 different languages in Washington as one does in Brussels. Although English is increasingly imposing itself as the *lingua franca* in Brussels, significantly, many members of the European Parliament still value being approached in their native language. Internal political cultures are starkly different too. While U.S.-style politics tend to be polarized around bipartisanship and highly adversarial, Brussels politics draw on a wider array of parties and specific national issues that are often deeply rooted in a country's governance culture (e.g., British laissez-faire versus French command and control).[82] At the same time, marketers operating in two or more major markets (such as the EU and North America) can work to produce more efficient trade through, for example, mutual recognition agreements on standards.

SUMMARY

Economic variables relating to the various markets' characteristics—population, income, consumption patterns, infrastructure, geography, and attitudes toward foreign involvement in the economy—form a starting point for assessment of market potential for the international marketer. These data are readily available but should be used in conjunction with other, more interpretive data because the marketer's plans often require a long-term approach. Data on the economic environment produce a snapshot of the past; in some cases, old data are used to make decisions affecting operations two years in the future. Even if the data are recent, they cannot themselves indicate the growth and the intensity of development. Some economies remain stagnant, plagued by natural calamities, internal problems, and lack of export markets, whereas some witness booming economic development.

Economic data provide a baseline from which other more market- or product-specific and even experiential data can be collected. Understanding the composition and interrelationships between economic indicators is essential for the assessment of the other environments and their joint impact on market potential. The international marketer needs to understand the impact of the economic environment on social development.

The emergence of economic integration in the world economy poses unique opportunities for and challenges to the international marketer. Eliminating barriers between member markets and erecting new ones vis-à-vis nonmembers will call for adjustments in past strategies to fully exploit the new situations. In the late 1980s and the twenty-first century, economic integration increased substantially. New trading blocs and the expansion of the existing ones will largely depend on future trade liberalization and political will within and among countries.

As developed markets have matured, marketers are looking at both emerging and developing markets for their future growth. To succeed, marketers will have to be innovative, pioneer new ways of doing business, and outmaneuver local competitors, many of them intent on becoming global players themselves.

KEY TERMS

Group of Five
Group of Seven
Group of Ten
Group of Twenty
household
urbanization
purchasing power parities (PPP)
inflation
Physical Quality of Life Index (PQLI)
maquiladoras
microfinance

QUESTIONS FOR DISCUSSION

1. Place these markets in the framework that follows.

a. Indonesia	g. Turkey	m. Peru
b. Mozambique	h. Spain	n. Jamaica
c. India	i. Singapore	o. Poland
d. Bangladesh	j. Nigeria	p. United Kingdom
e. Niger	k. Algeria	q. Iraq
f. Brazil	l. Zambia	r. Saudi Arabia

	Income Level		
	Low	Middle	High
TRADE STRUCTURE			
Developed			
Emerging			
Developing			
• Semi-industrial			
• Oil-exporting			
• Primary producing			
• Populous South Asia			
• Least developed			

2. Using available data, assess the market potential for (a) power generators and (b) consumer appliances in (1) the Philippines, (2) Jordan, and (3) Portugal.
3. From the international marketer's point of view, what are the opportunities and problems caused by increased urbanization in emerging and developing countries?
4. In addition to Brazil, Russia, India, and China, identify three other emerging markets that make sense for international business growth. Why?
5. What can a marketer do to advance regional economic integration?
6. Explain the difference between a free trade area and a common market. Speculate why negotiations were held for a North American Free Trade Agreement rather than for a North American Common Market.

INTERNET EXERCISES

1. Compare and contrast two different points of view on expanding trade by accessing the websites of the U.S. Chamber of Commerce, an industry coalition promoting increased access to and from world markets (www.uschamber.com), and the American Federation of Labor–Congress of Industrial Organizations (AFL–CIO) (www.aflcio.org).
2. Alibaba.com (www.alibaba.com) is a business-to-business e-commerce company. It operates two marketplaces: the first is an international marketplace based in English and tailored to global importers and exporters in China; the second is a Chinese marketplace that focuses on suppliers and buyers trading domestically in China. Is a company able to operate in both capacities?

CHALLENGE US

Africa's Growing Middle Class

Over the past decade, the number of middle-class consumers in Africa has expanded more than 60 percent to 313 million, according to the African Development Bank Group. Two-thirds of that supposed new middle class have just $2 to $4 to spend per day. They may be able to buy a telephone or washing machine or television, but often not all three.

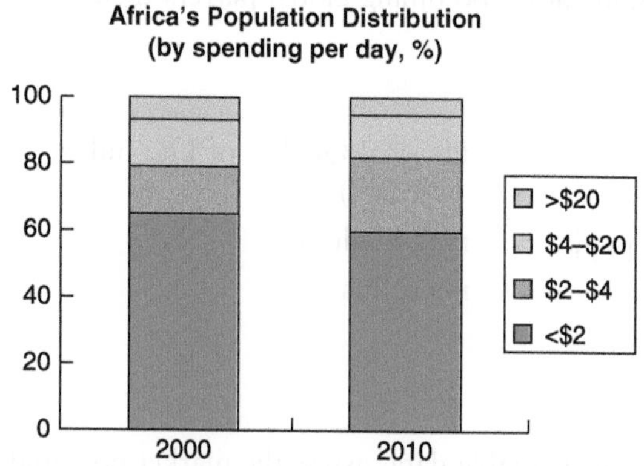

SOURCE: *The Economist*, "Pleased to Be Bourgeois," © The Economist Newspaper Limited, London (May 14, 2011). Reprinted with permission.

Sharp geographical variations persist. North Africans top the rankings. In sub-Saharan Africa, the better the governance, the bigger a country's middle-income bulge. In Botswana, Namibia, Ghana, Kenya, and South Africa, almost half the populations earn more than $2 per day, whereas in the worst-governed countries, less than a fifth have managed to cross that barrier. About 100,000 of the richest Africans had a collective net worth totaling 60 percent of the continent's gross domestic product.

The continent's prospects have proved alluring for Walmart Stores, Inc., which has agreed to pay roughly $2.4 billion to buy 51 percent of South Africa's Massmart Holdings Ltd., with plans to use the discount retailer as a foothold for continental expansion. Yum Brands, Inc., recently said it wants to double its KFC outlets in the next few years to 1,200. In South Africa, Google and Microsoft Corp. are behind efforts to fund entrepreneurs, with the hope that seeding African technology firms will help grow their own businesses.

Many Africans are joining the ranks of the world's consumers. Rising consumption will create more demand for local products, sparking a cycle of increasing domestic growth.

For Discussion

1. The African Development Bank says a third of Africans are now "middle-class," defined as having between $2 and $20 to spend a day. Does $2 a day really mean middle-class?
2. Africa: is the hopeless continent or an emergent opportunities for the future?

SOURCES: "Pleased to Be Bourgeois," *Economist*, May 14, 2011, 55; Peter Wonacott, "A New Class of Consumers Grows in Africa," *Wall Street Journal*, May 2, 2011, A8; and Acha Leke, Susan Lund, Charles Roxburgh, and Arend van Wamelen, "What's Driving Africa's Growth," *McKinsey Quarterly*, June 9, 2010, 1–17.

RECOMMENDED READINGS

Council on Foreign Relations. *Crisis Guide: The Global Economy* (multimedia interactive presentation), October 18, 2011, www.cfr.org/economics/crisis-guide-global-economy/p19710.

Current issues of *Country Monitor, Business Europe, Business East Europe, Business Asia, Business Latin America, Business China.*

The European Union: A Guide for Americans, 2011 edition. Available at www.eurunion.org/eu/EU-US-Relations/EU-US-Facts-Figures.html.

Folsom, Ralph H. *NAFTA and Free Trade in the Americas in a Nutshell*. St. Paul, MN: Thomson/West, 2008.

International Marketing Data and Statistics 2011. London: Euromonitor, 2011.

Ohmae, Kenichi. *Next Global Stage: Challenges and Opportunities in Our Borderless World*. Philadelphia: Wharton School Publishing, 2005.

Spence, Michael. *The Next Convergence: The Future of Economic Growth in a Multispeed World*. New York: Farrar, Straus and Giroux, 2011.

Tse, Edward. *The China Strategy: Harnessing the Power of the World's Fastest-Growing Economy*. New York: Basic Books, 2010.

World Development Report 2011. New York: Oxford University Press, 2011.

The World in Figures. London: Economist Publications, 2011.

Yearbook of International Trade Statistics. New York: United Nations, 2011.

ENDNOTES

1. "Pocket World in Figures 2012 Edition," *Economist*, 208.
2. Vitaly Klintsov, Irene Shvakman, and Yennolai Solzhenitsyn, "How Russia Could Be More Productive," *McKinsey Quarterly*, September 2009.
3. Edward Tse, Bill Russo, and Ronald Haddock, "Competing for the Global Middle Class," *Strategy+Business*, Autumn 2011.
4. "Introducing 'Growth Markets,'" Goldman Sachs, April 2011, www2.goldmansachs.com/our-thinking/global-economic-outlook/intro-growth-markets/index.html.
5. "Increased Investment Rapidly Changing Africa's IT Landscape," *Africa: The Good News*, March 3, 2011.
6. "Now We Are Seven Billion," *Economist*, October 22, 2011.
7. Wayne D. Hoyer and Deborah J. MacInnis, *Consumer Behavior* (Mason, OH: Thomson, 2008), 361–63.
8. William A. Haviland, Harald E. L. Prins, Bunny McBride, and Dana Walrath, *Cultural Anthropology: The Human Challenge* Mason, OH (Wadsworth Publishing, 2010), 214–44.
9. Average size of households (most recent) by country, www.nationmaster.com/graph/peo_ave_siz_of_hou-people-average-size-of-households.
10. GDP per capita, The World Bank, http://data.worldbank.org/indicator/NY.GDP.PCAP.CD.
11. Shanoo Bijlani and Regan Luis, "Indian Luxury Market Difficult to Ignore," *Solitaire*, May 2011.
12. Gartner, "Forecast Analysis: PCs, Asia/Pacific," June 2010 Update.
13. Claudia Penteado, "Brazil's Northeast Goes from 'Land of Laziness' to Next China," *Advertising Age*, June 13, 2011, 11.
14. "Here Comes Anyware; Technology and Society," *Economist*, October 8, 2011, 19.
15. "As China Builds, Too Much 'Boom'?" *Washington Post*, October 23, 2011, G1–G7.
16. Ian Mansfield, "Worldwide Mobile Subscriptions Number More Than Five Billion," *Cellular-News*, October 24, 2010, www.cellular-news.com/story/46050.php.
17. Ian Mansfield, "Africa Crosses 500 Million Mobile Subscriptions Mark," *Cellular-News*, November 11, 2010.
18. "World Internet Usage," Internet World Stats, http://internetworldstats.com/stats.htm.
19. "Internet Usage in the European Union," Internet World Stats, www.internetworldstats.com/stats9.htm.
20. IMT-Advanced, ITU, www.itu.int/ITU-R/index.asp?category=information&rlink=imt-advanced&lang=en.
21. Global Business Policy Council, *Globalization Ledger* (Washington, DC: A.T. Kearney, April 2000).
22. Derek Gregory, Ron Johnston, Geraldine Pratt, et al., eds., "Quality of Life," in *Dictionary of Human Geography* (Oxford, England: Wiley-Blackwell, 2009).
23. "The Adolescent Girls Initiative: Investing in Young Women as Smart Economics," World Bank, April 2011.
24. Ed Diener and Eunkook Suh, eds., *Culture and Subjective Well-Being* (Boston: MIT Press, 2003), Chapter 1; and "In Bhutan, Happiness Is King," *Wall Street Journal*, October 13, 2004, A14.
25. "Free Trade in the Pacific," *Economist*, November 19, 2011, 18; Michael R. Czinkota and Ilkka A. Ronkainen, "A Forecast of Globalization, International Business and Trade: Report from a Delphi Study," *Journal of World Business*, 40 (May 2005): 111–23; and Ilkka A. Ronkainen, "Trading Blocs: Opportunity or Demise for International Trade?" *Multinational Business Review* 1 (Spring 1993): 1–9.
26. EFTA, http://secretariat.efta.int.
27. "Facts and figures," European Union, http://europa.eu/about-eu/facts-figures/index_en.htm.
28. "Staring into the Abyss," *Economist*, November 12, 2011, 1–16.
29. "Nokia continues to align its workforce and operations," Nokia press release, September 29, 2011, http://press.nokia.com/2011/09/29/nokia-continues-to-align-its-workforce-and-operations.
30. U.S. International Trade in Goods and Services - Annual Revision for 2010," U.S. Census Bureau, June 9, 2011, Exhibit 13, www.census.gov/foreign-trade/Press-Release/2010pr/final_revisions/exh13tl.pdf.
31. Gary Clyde Hufbauer and Jeffrey J. Schott, *NAFTA Revisited: Achievements and Challenges* (Washington, DC: Institute for International Economics, 2005), Chapter 1.
32. John Cavanagh, Sarah Anderson, Jaime Serra, and J. Enrique Espinosa, "Happily Ever NAFTA," *Foreign Policy*, September/October 2002, 58–65.
33. Sidney Weintraub, *NAFTA's Impact on North America: The First Decade* (Washington, DC: CSIS Press, 2004).
34. "Fox and Bush, for Richer, for Poorer," *Economist*, February 3, 2001, 37–38.
35. "Aerospace Industry Migrating to Mexico in Greater Numbers," *Republic*, April 2, 2008.
36. Dante Di Gregorio, Douglas Thomas, and Fernan Gonzalez de Castilla, "Competition between Emerging

Market and Multinational Firms: Walmart and Mexican Retailers," *International Journal of Management* 25 (September 2008): 532–45.
37. See, for example, CREA, www.crea-inc.org; and the Maquila Solidarity Network (MSN), www .maquilasolidarity.org.
38. Lara Sowinki, "NAFTA: Two Sides of the Coin," *World Trade*, August 2009; and "Mexico: Business Is Standing Its Ground," *BusinessWeek*, April 20, 2009.
39. "Americas: Critics Aside, NAFTA Has Been a Boon to Mexico," *Wall Street Journal*, January 9, 2004, A11.
40. David Alexander, Adriana Barrera, Mica Rosenberg, and Xavier Briand, "Obama Hopeful of Fixing Truck Dispute with Mexico," Reuters, April, 17, 2009.
41. Congressional Research Service, *MERCOSUR: Evolution and Implications for U.S. Trade Policy* (Washington, DC, January 5, 2007).
42. Office of the United States Trade Representative, *Third Report to the Congress of the Operations of the Andean Trade Preferences Act as Amended* (Washington, DC, April 30, 2007).
43. ASEAN, www.aseansec.org/64.htm.
44. "China Coming Down the Tracks," *Economist*, January 22, 2011, 49.
45. Background APEC 2011, www.apec2011.gov/about /background.
46. "Pakistan to Boost Trade with India: Rare Goodwill Gesture Shows Small Thaw in Relations despite Tension on Kashmir, Mumbai Attacks," *Wall Street Journal*, November 3, 2011, A16.
47. "Profile: African Union," *BBC News*, March 26, 2009.
48. Ibrahim El-Husseini, Fadi Majdalani, and Alessandro Borgogna, "Filling the Gulf States' Infrastructure Gap," *Strategy+Business*, September 22, 2009.
49. Mohsin S. Khan, "The GCC Monetary Union: Choice of Exchange Rate Regime," Peterson Institute for International Economics, April 2009.
50. "Market Potential Index (MPI) for Emerging Markets - 2011," globalEDGE, March 16, 2012, http://globaledge .msu.edu/resourceDesk/mpi.
51. Yuval Atsmon, Ari Kertesz, and Ireena Vitta, "Is Your Emerging-Market Strategy Local Enough?" *McKinsey Quarterly*, April 2011.
52. "GE Pins Hopes on Emerging Markets," *Wall Street Journal*, April 14, 2005, A3, A10.
53. "Kremlin Blocks Big Acquisition by Siemens AG," *Wall Street Journal*, April 14, 2005, A14, A16.
54. "China Seeks Its Own High-Tech Standards," *CNN.com*, May 27, 2004; and "Despite Shelving WAPI, China Stands Firm on Chip Tax," *InfoWorld*, April 22, 2004.
55. "In Brazil, Thicket of Red Tape Spoils Recipe for Growth," *Wall Street Journal*, May 24, 2005, A1, A9.
56. Kevin Lane, Ian St-Maurice, and Claudia Süssmuth Dyckerhoff, "Building Brands in China," *McKinsey Quarterly*, June 2006.
57. "The High-Tech Threat from China," *BusinessWeek*, January 31, 2005, 22.
58. "Let the Retail Wars Begin," *BusinessWeek*, January 17, 2005, 44–45.
59. Guillermo D'Andrea, E. Alejandro Stengel, and Anne Goebel-Krstelj, "Six Truths about Emerging-Market Consumers," *Strategy+Business* 34 (Spring 2004): 58–69.
60. "Business: The Supermarket's Last Frontier: Indian Retail," *Economist*, December 3, 2011, 75–76.
61. This section builds on Tarun Khanna, Krishna Palepu, and Jayant Sinha, "Strategies That Fit Emerging Markets," *Harvard Business Review* 83 (June 2005): 63–76; and James A. Gingrich, "Five Rules for Winning Emerging Market Consumers," *Strategy+Business* (second quarter, 1999): 19–33.
62. "Cisco's Brave New World," *Businessweek*, November 24, 2008, 56–68.
63. Jason Bush, "GM: Learning the Ropes in Russia," *Businessweek*, February 8, 2007, 67.
64. "Dell Unveils New Computers Targeting Emerging Markets," *Marketing News*, September 15, 2008, 32.
65. "GM and VW: How Not to Succeed in China," *Businessweek*, May 9, 2005, 94.
66. Orit Gadiesh, Philip Leung, and Til Vestring, "The Battle for China's Good-Enough Market," *Harvard Business Review* 85 (September 2007): 81–89.
67. "Cracking China's Market," *Wall Street Journal*, January 9, 2003, B1, B4.
68. BrandZ, Millard Brown, www.millwardbrown.com /BrandZ.
69. The World Bank considers $2,000 to be the minimum to sustain a decent life.
70. HP e-inclusion, www.hp.com/e-inclusion/en/vision/ faq.html.
71. This framework is adapted from C. K. Prahalad and Stuart L. Hart, "The Fortune at the Bottom of the Pyramid," *Strategy+Business* (first quarter, 2002), 35–47.
72. "Africa Rising," *Economist*, December 3, 2011, 15.
73. "Major Victories for Micro-finance," *Financial Times*, May 18, 2005, 10. See also PlaNet Finance, www .planetfinance.org.
74. Cait Murphy, "The Hunt for Globalization That Works," *Fortune*, October 28, 2002, 163–76.
75. "And the Winners Are … ," *Economist*, September 18, 2004, 17; "The Digital Village," *BusinessWeek*, June 28, 2004, 60–62; and Arundhati Parmar, "Indian Farmers Reap Web Harvest," *Marketing News*, June 1, 2004, 27, 31.
76. "Laptop Program for Kids in Poor Countries Teams Up with Microsoft Windows," *Wall Street Journal*, May 16, 2008, B1.
77. C. K. Prahalad and Allen Hammond, "Serving the World's Poor, Profitably," *Harvard Business Review* 80 (September 2002): 48–59.
78. The Coca-Cola Africa Foundation, http://tccaf.org/coca -cola-africa-foundation-partners.asp.
79. Ronald Haddock and John Jullens, "The Best Years of the Auto Industry Are Still to Come," *Strategy+Business*, May 26, 2009.
80. "City Focus: Tesco Takes on China," *Daily Mail*, August 12, 2008.
81. Nokia Developer, www.forum.nokia.com.
82. "EU and US Approaches to Lobbying," *Euractiv.com*, February 15, 2005.

CHAPTER 5

The Political and Legal Environment

LEARNING OBJECTIVES

By the time you complete this chapter, you will be able to:

- Appreciate the importance of politics and laws for the international firm.
- Understand the effect of government regulations legislation.
- Search for conflicts between home and host country legal conditions.
- Link different actions to different levels of risk.
- Be more alert to the nefarious effects of terrorism.

THE INTERNATIONAL MARKETPLACE 5.1

"Of Course I'm a Principal Player"

As globalization has increased and created more interconnection and interdependence in the world economy, the leading industrialized nations have developed various mechanisms to facilitate cooperation for the promotion of economic growth and the avoidance of economic catastrophe. Among these mechanisms are the various informal "groups" of major economies. The G6 was created in 1975 by France to assure representation in economic negotiations for leading industrialized nations in addition to the United States. This group was expanded the following year to the G7, which then included Canada, and in 1997 to the G8, incorporating Russia.

All of these groups were subject to the criticism that they did not include powerful new economies such as China, India, Brazil, and others. The Asian financial crisis of the late 1990s led to the creation of a separate G20. Still, many nations feel excluded. As U.S. president Barack Obama stated, "What I've noticed is everybody wants the smallest possible group, smallest possible organization that includes them. So if they're the 21st-largest nation in the world, then they want the G21, and think it's highly unfair if they've been cut out."

Although the G8 continues as a major economic group, hosted by France in 2011 and the United States in 2012, the G20 has emerged as the premier forum for the financial ministers and leaders of the leading economies. The London G20 summit of 2009 demonstrated that the world's leaders were willing to work together to mitigate the financial crisis and create reforms in the global financial system.

The broadening of the G summits has also introduced more complexity in achieving actionable results. The G7 represented a community of nations with more commonality in economic development and purpose. The G20 is a much more cumbersome group. The G20 France 2011 website states that "we believe that today's key economic challenges require a collective and ambitious action which the G20 is able to impulse." The question remains whether that conviction will lead to coordinated action.

SOURCES: G20 France 2011, www.g20.org; and Jake Tapper, "G-20 to Replace G-8 as Primary International Economic Summit," ABC News, September 24, 2009.

As much as most managers would like to ignore them, political and legal factors often play a critical role in international marketing activities. The interpretation and application of regulations can sometimes lead to conflicting and even misleading results. Even the best business plans can go awry as a result of unexpected political or legal influences, and the failure to anticipate these factors can be the undoing of an otherwise successful business venture. Exhibit 5.1 ranks the factors that affect a country's investment climate; note that inefficient government bureaucracy dominates the concerns of firms. However, variations in political and legal environments can also offer new opportunities to international marketers, as *The International Marketplace 5.1* shows.

Of course, a single international political and legal environment does not exist. The business executive must be aware of political and legal factors on a variety of levels. For example, although it is useful to understand the complexities of a host country's legal system, such knowledge does not protect against a home-country-imposed export embargo.

The study of the international political and legal environment must therefore be broken down into several subsegments. Many researchers do this by separating the legal from the political. This separation—although perhaps

EXHIBIT 5.1 Environmental Shortcomings of the Investment Climate

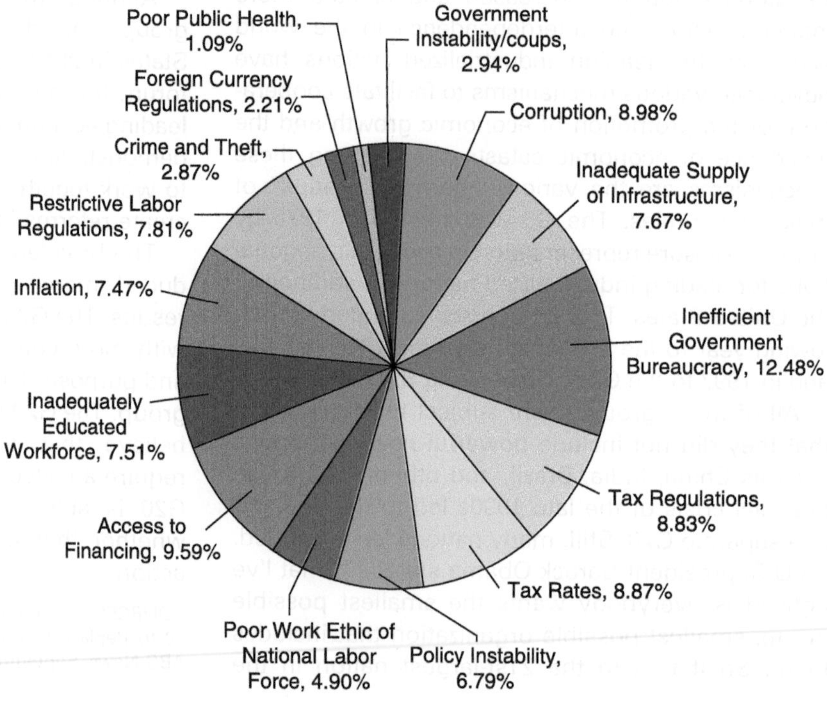

SOURCE: Klaus Schwab and Michael E. Porter, *The Global Competitiveness Report 2008–2009* (Geneva, Switzerland: 2008 World Economic Forum), www.weforum.org/pdf/GCR08/GCR08.pdf, accessed November 3, 2008.

analytically useful—is somewhat artificial because laws are generally the result of political decisions. Here no attempt will be made to separate legal and political factors, except when such a separation is essential.

Instead, this chapter will examine the political and legal environment from the manager's point of view. In making decisions about his or her firm's international marketing activities, the manager will need to concentrate on three areas: the political and legal circumstances of the home country; those of the host country; and the bilateral and multilateral agreements, treaties, and laws governing the relations between host and home countries.

HOME-COUNTRY POLITICAL AND LEGAL ENVIRONMENT

No manager can afford to ignore the policies and regulations of the country from which he or she conducts international marketing transactions. Wherever a firm is located, it will be affected by government policies and the legal system.

Many of these laws and regulations may not be designed specifically to address international marketing transactions, yet they can have a major impact on a firm's opportunities abroad. Minimum wage legislation, for example, affects the international competitiveness of a firm using production processes that are highly labor intensive. The cost of domestic safety regulations may significantly affect the pricing policies of firms in their international marketing efforts. For example, U.S. legislation that created the **Environmental Superfund** requires payment by chemical firms based on their production volume regardless of whether the production is sold domestically or exported. As a result, these firms are at a disadvantage internationally when exporting their commodity-type products because they must compete against foreign firms that are not required to make such a payment in their home countries and therefore have a cost advantage.

Other legal and regulatory measures, however, are clearly aimed at international marketing activities. Some may be designed to help firms in their international efforts. The lack of enforcement of others may hurt the international marketer. For instance, many firms are concerned about the lack of safeguards for **intellectual property rights** in developing countries, an issue discussed later in this chapter.

Another area in which governments may attempt to aid and protect the international marketing efforts of companies is **gray market** activities. Gray market goods are products that enter markets in ways not desired by their manufacturers. Companies may be hurt by their own products if they reach the consumer via uncontrolled distribution channels.

Apart from specific areas that result in government involvement, the political environment in most countries tends to provide general support for the international marketing efforts of the country's firms. For example, a government may work to reduce trade barriers or to increase trade opportunities through bilateral and multilateral negotiations. Such actions will affect individual firms to the extent that they affect the international climate for free trade.

Often, however, governments also have specific rules and regulations restricting international marketing. Such regulations are frequently political in nature and are based on the fact that governments believe commerce to be only one objective among others, such as foreign policy and national security. Four main areas of governmental activities are of major concern to the international marketer here: embargoes or trade sanctions, export controls, import controls, and the regulation of international business behavior.

Embargoes and Sanctions

The terms trade sanctions and embargoes as used here refer to governmental actions that distort the free flow of trade in goods, services, or ideas for decidedly adversarial and political, rather than strictly economic, purposes. Exhibit 5.2 illustrates the sanctions currently maintained by the United States against China. Human rights conditions in the country, as well as the threat of weapons proliferation, are the concerns of the U.S. administration that help maintain these sanctions in place. Advocates of sanctions regard them as an important weapon of foreign policy. Skeptics question whether sanctions are effective and whether the costs they impose are worth the benefits.[1]

Trade sanctions were already used in the thirteenth century by the Hansa league, an association of northern German merchants with grievances against Norway. Over the years, economic sanctions and embargoes have become an often-used foreign policy tool for many countries. Reasons for the impositions are varied, ranging from human rights to nuclear nonproliferation to terrorism (see the section on terrorism later in this chapter). The range of sanctions imposed can be quite broad. Examples are elimination of credits and prohibition of financial transactions. Typically, the intent is to bring commercial interchange to a complete halt.

The League of Nations set a precedent for the international legal justification of economic sanctions by subscribing to a covenant that provided for penalties or sanctions for breaching its provisions. The members of the League of Nations did not intend to use military or economic measures separately, but the success of the blockades of World War I fostered the opinion that "the economic weapon, conceived not as an instrument of war but as a means of peaceful pressure, is the greatest discovery and most precious possession of the League."[2] The basic idea was that economic sanctions could force countries to behave peacefully in the international community.

The idea of the multilateral use of economic sanctions was again incorporated into international law under the charter of the United Nations, but greater emphasis was placed on the enforcement process. Once decided upon, sanctions are mandatory, even though each permanent member of the Security Council can veto efforts to impose sanctions. The charter also allows for sanctions as an enforcement action by regional agencies such as the Organization of American States, the Arab League, and the Organization of African Unity, but only with the Security Council's authorization.

The apparent strength of the United Nations enforcement system soon turned out to be flawed. Stalemates in the Security Council and vetoes by permanent members often led to a shift of emphasis to the General Assembly, which

EXHIBIT 5.2 U.S. Economic Sanctions in Place against China

Since 1969, when the process of normalization began under President Nixon, U.S.-Chinese relations have advanced to a point that relatively few restrictions remain. Today, U.S. economic sanctions against China include:

- Limits on U.S. foreign assistance
- U.S. "No" votes or abstention on China issues in the international banks
- Ban on Overseas Private Investment Corporation (OPIC) programs
- Ban on export of defense articles or defense services
- Ban on import of munitions or ammunition
- Substantial export controls on dual-use items, particularly satellites, nuclear technology, and computers
- Export and licensing restrictions on targeted entities found to have engaged in proliferation of missiles and weapons of mass destruction (or related technology)
- Presidential authority to restrict Chinese military companies and Chinese government–affiliated businesses from developing commercial activities inside the United States

SOURCE: Adapted from Dianne E Rennack, "China: Economic Sanctions," Congressional Research Service Report, p. 1, updated February 1, 2006, www.au.af.mil/au/awc/awcgate/crs/rl31910.pdf, accessed December 5, 2011.

does not have the power to enforce. Further, concepts such as "peace" and "breach of peace" are seldom perceived in the same way by all members, and thus no systematic sanctioning policy developed in the United Nations. As a result, sanctions have frequently been imposed unilaterally in the hope of changing a particular country's government, or at least its policies. Unilateral imposition, however, tends to have major negative effects on the firms in the country that is exercising sanctions because the only result is often a simple shift in trade.

Another key problem with unilateral imposition of sanctions is that they typically do not produce the desired result. Sanctions may make the obtaining of goods more difficult or expensive for the sanctioned country, yet achievement of the purported objective almost never occurs. In order to work, sanctions need to be imposed multilaterally. Only when virtually all nations in which a product is produced agree to deny it to a target can there be a true deprivation effect. Without such denial, sanctions do not have much bite. Yet to get all producing nations to agree can be quite difficult. Typically, individual countries have different relationships with the country subject to the sanctions due to geographic or historic reasons, and therefore some cannot or do not want to terminate trade relations.

Somalia is a poignant example of the importance of a unified sanctions regime. For years, news of persistent violence, acts of piracy, and armed robbery at sea have been splashed across TV screens all over the world. The United States imposed sanctions, effective in May 2010, with a trade embargo and an asset freeze against Somalia. The goal was to reduce the Somali crime wave against the shipping industry and to encourage the country to develop law and order.[3]

One key concern with sanctions is the fact that governments often consider them as being free of cost. However, even though they may not affect the budget of governments, sanctions imposed by governments can mean significant loss of business to firms. One estimate claims that the economic sanctions held in place by the United States annually costs the country some $20 billion in lost exports and that the success rate of all U.S. sanctions where the United States was part of a sanction coalition approached 30 percent.[4]

Due to these costs, the issue of compensating the domestic firms and industries affected by these sanctions needs to be raised. Yet trying to impose sanctions slowly or making them less expensive to ease the burden on these firms undercuts their ultimate chance for success. The international marketing manager is often caught in this political web and loses business as a result. Frequently, firms try to anticipate sanctions based on their evaluations of the international political climate. Even when substantial precautions are taken, firms may still suffer substantial losses due to contract cancellations. However, this can be seen as the cost of one's government's support for an open global trading and investing environment.

Export Controls

Many nations have **export control systems**, which are designed to deny or at least delay the acquisition of strategically important goods by adversaries. Most of these systems make controls the exception rather than the rule, with exports taking place independently from politics. The United States, however, differs substantially from this perspective in that exports are considered to be a privilege rather than a right, and exporting is seen as an extension of foreign policy.

The legal basis for export controls varies across nations. For example, in Germany, armament exports are covered in the so-called War Weapons List, which is a part of the War Weapons Control Law. The exports of other goods are covered by the German Export List. **Dual-use items**, which are goods useful for both military and civilian purposes, are then controlled by the Joint List of the European Union.[5]

U.S. laws control all exports of goods, services, and ideas. It is important to note here that an export of goods occurs whenever goods are physically transferred from the United States. Services and ideas, however, are deemed exported whenever transferred to a foreign national, regardless of location. Permitting a foreign national from a controlled country to have access to a highly sensitive computer program in the United States is therefore deemed to be an export. The effect of such a perspective can be major, particularly on universities and for international students.

The U.S. export control system is based on the Export Administration Act, administered by the Department of Commerce, and the Arms Export Control Act, administered by the Department of State. The Commerce Department focuses on exports in general, while the State Department covers products designed or modified for military use, even if such products have commercial applicability. The determinants for controls are national security, foreign policy, short supply, and nuclear nonproliferation.

In order for any export from the United States to take place, the exporter needs to obtain an export license. The administering government agencies have, in consultation with other government departments, drawn up a list of commodities whose export is considered particularly sensitive. In addition, a list of countries differentiates nations according to their political relationship with the United States. Finally, a list of individual firms that are considered to be unreliable trading partners because of past trade-diversion activities exists for each country.

After an export license application has been filed, government specialists match the commodity to be exported with the commerce control list, a file containing information about products that are either particularly sensitive to national security or controlled for other purposes. The product is then matched with the country of destination and the recipient company. If no concerns regarding any of the three exist, an export license is issued. Control determinants and the steps in the decision process are summarized in Exhibit 5.3.

This process may sound overly cumbersome, but it does not apply in equal measure to all exports. Most international business activities can be carried out under NLR, which stands for "no license required," conditions. NLR provides blanket permission to export. Products can be freely shipped to most trading partners provided that neither the end user nor the end use involved are considered sensitive. However, the process becomes more complicated when products incorporating high-level technologies and countries not friendly to the United States are involved. The exporter must then obtain an **export license**, which consists of written authorization to send a product abroad.

The international marketing repercussions of export controls are important. It is one thing to design an export control system that is effective and that restricts those international business activities subject to important national concerns. It is, however, quite another when controls lose their effectiveness and

EXHIBIT 5.3 The U.S. Export Control System

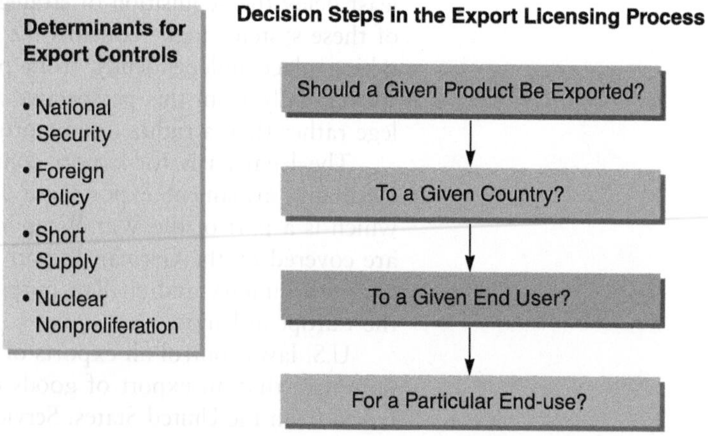

when one country's firms are placed at a competitive disadvantage with firms in other countries whose control systems are less extensive or even nonexistent.

In some instances, the heavy-handed implementation of export regulations can have dramatic and far-reaching effects. The government of Argentina has learned this lesson the hard way with its efforts to pressure farmers and ranchers to sell agricultural products domestically at lower prices. Following a controversial tax increase on grain exports in addition to previous price controls and heavy state intervention, farmers and antigovernment protesters took to the streets. This, in turn, caused fuel and food shortages in parts of the country. Considering that soy accounts for a quarter of Argentina's total exports and has largely been the backbone of its economic growth over the last five years, the new tax was controversial at best. In addition to eroding the government's popularity, it led to a crash in the Argentinean stock and bond markets and drove up the global price of soybeans.[6] When a government sets out to impose export restrictions in an attempt to "redistribute the wealth," as was the case with Argentina, it needs to pay careful attention to the Pandora's box of economic inefficiencies and social unrest that it could unleash.

A New Environment for Export Controls

Today's international environment continues to highlight the importance of export controls. Restricting the flow of materials can be crucial in avoiding the proliferation of weapons of mass destruction; reducing flows of technological knowledge can reduce the sophistication of armaments used by insurgent groups; financial controls can inhibit funding for terrorist training.

Nowadays, the principal focus of export controls rests on the Third World. A number of countries from this region want chemical and nuclear weapons, as well as the technology to make use of them. Even if a country already has dangerous weaponry, export controls can reduce the opportunity for its deployment. Today's export controls use a "tactical balance" approach affecting specific hotspots rather than the "strategic balance" approach exercised during the era of U.S.-Soviet global deterrence. Iran is a prominent example of export control issues. Its efforts to implement a nuclear program have caused much consternation in the global community. Intense negotiations included threats of

Export restrictions can also be imposed in the form of sales curtailment in order to combat low supplies. India tried to restrict exports of its cotton due to possible supply problems but was forced to quickly reverse the ban due to complaints and protests by its trading partners.

additional controls and sanctions. The UN Security Council's five permanent members and Germany pledged to establish full relations and economic cooperation with Iran in exchange for suspension of enrichment-related and reprocessing activities. While this commitment diffused the crisis, most analysts believe that this is not the last the world has seen of Iran's nuclear ambitions.[7] Export controls are likely to remain an important tool in the arsenal of international policymakers as they strive to contain dangers in the world at large.

Major change has also resulted from the increased foreign availability of high-technology products. In the past decade, the number of participants in the international trade field has grown rapidly. In earlier decades, industrializing countries mainly participated in world trade due to wage-based competition. Today, they are increasingly focused on technology-based competition. As a result, high-technology products are available worldwide from many sources. The broad availability makes any product denial more difficult to enforce. If a nation does control the exports of widely available products, it imposes a major competitive burden on its firms.

Enormous technical progress has also brought about a radical change in computer architecture. Instead of having to replace a personal computer or a workstation with a new computer, one can simply exchange microprocessors or motherboards with new, more efficient ones. Furthermore, today's machines can be connected to more than one microprocessor, and users can customize and update configurations almost at will. A user simply acquires additional chips from whomever and uses expansion slots to enhance the capacity of his or her computer.

The question arises as to how much of the latest technology is required for a country to engage in "dangerous" activity. For example, nuclear weapons and sophisticated delivery systems were developed by the United States and the Soviet Union long before supercomputers became available. Therefore, it is reasonable to assert that researchers in countries working with equipment that is less than state-of-the-art, or even obsolete, may well be able to achieve a threat capability that can result in major destruction and affect world safety.

From a control perspective, there is also the issue of equipment size. Supercomputers and high-technology items used to be fairly difficult to hide, and any movement of such products was easily detectable. Nowadays, state-of-the-art technology has been miniaturized. Much leading-edge technological equipment is so small that it can fit into a briefcase, and most equipment is no larger than the luggage compartment of a car. Given these circumstances, it has become difficult to closely supervise the transfer of such equipment.

There is a continuing debate about what constitutes military-use products, civilian-use products, and dual-use products, and the achievement of multilateral agreement on such classifications. Increasingly, goods are of a dual-use nature, meaning that they are commercial products that have potential military applications.[8] Examples are exported trucks that can be used to transport troops, or the exports of supplies to a pesticide factory that, some years later, is revealed to be a poison gas factory.[9] It is difficult enough to define weapons clearly. It is even more problematic to achieve consensus among nations regarding dual-use goods.

Conflicts can result from the desire of nations to safeguard their own economic interests. Due to different industrial structures, these interests vary across nations. For example, Germany, with a strong world market position in machine tools, motors, and chemical raw materials, will think differently about controls than the United States, which sees computers as an area of its competitive advantage.

The rise in international awareness of the threat of terrorism has led to a renewed importance of global export controls as *The International Marketplace 5.2* shows. In recent years, many policies have been targeted to better focus on the dangers of proliferation and terrorist attack. This has helped to differentiate more sharply between those high-tech products that need to be controlled and those that do not; an overall easing of export control policies in the technology field has resulted. U.S. administration export control policy is increasingly based on a "stick and carrot" approach, showing preferential treatment to countries better aligned with U.S. policy goals. It can therefore be said that the role of export controls, as well as their sophistication, has intensified.

THE INTERNATIONAL MARKETPLACE 5.2

International Export Controls

Export controls are a principal means of defending a nation's high-technology advantage over potential adversaries. It has been 23 years since the last major rewrite of the U.S. Export Administration Act, the legislation that provides the basic authority for the president to control exports. In the interim, U.S. practices have become ineffective and inefficient. Unless there is an update of the export control system, lack of coordination will decrease international manufacturing competitiveness.

During the Cold War, the export controls of the United States and its allies successfully isolated the Soviet Union and denied—or at least delayed—its acquisition of the high technology necessary to strengthen its military. Today, there is no longer unanimity among allies about the nature of the threats faced. Nor is there any longer a U.S. veto that can be wielded when there is disagreement. The current export control forum, the Wassenaar Group, is mostly concerned with keeping dangerous technology out of the hands of terrorists and rogue states.

At present, U.S. government restrictions are consistently more limiting than those of European countries with regard to licenses for products and technologies destined for markets like China. Delays combined with foreign availability of products have meant lost business for U.S. firms and trade frictions with China.

Take an example: China is the largest and fastest-growing machine-tool market in the world. The United States still tightly licenses five-axis machine tools because they are considered to be the most sophisticated. U.S. export licenses can take from six months to a year to gain government approval. The Swiss, Germans, and Italians readily take advantage of this delay by licensing products with identical capabilities in weeks. Over the past decade, the United States has lost 50 percent of its share in this fast-growing market, with domestic Chinese and foreign producers grabbing the lost market share. At the same time, the domestic U.S. market has shrunk by 50 percent. The effect on the U.S. defense industrial base has been predictably negative.

Similar problems have occurred in semiconductor manufacturing equipment and scientific instruments. Without the cooperation between allies, the export control system cannot work. It costs American jobs and does not accomplish its objectives.

The U.S. government may view China as a potential threat and seek to deny it the highest levels of technology, but many countries stand ready to supply China with whatever products and technology it wishes to acquire. The key issue is to develop an effective export control system that also receives support from other high-technology-exporting nations.

The U.S. government is now working on reforms to provide a better definition of items on the military-oriented Munitions List and those that constitute dual-use technologies. Other reform plans deal with encryption, the mechanics of license processing, speeding up licensing time and, most importantly, with shortening the list of products that require an individual validated license.

These reforms are a good first step. Export controls can be more relevant and effective if they are targeted and administered better. But more needs to be done by Congress in concert with the administration:

1. The United States needs a better defined purpose for export controls that U.S. allies are willing to support.
2. The United States needs to broaden the list of countries regarding which it has few or no controls, so that it can concentrate its efforts on rogue nations such as Iran and North Korea.
3. Export control implementation must be restructured. Combining and better defining the control lists should reduce endless interagency debates and shorten company waiting periods.

The current U.S. system is not sufficient for the twenty-first century. For the sake of a revitalized manufacturing sector, this is one of the few issues upon which both political parties, as well as the executive and legislative branches, should be able to agree.

SOURCES: Paul Freedenberg and Michael Czinkota, "International Export Control Systems Need Updating," *Japan Today*, June 11, 2011; and www.exportcontrol.org, accessed February 20, 2012.

Import Controls

In these countries, either all imports or the imports of particular products are controlled through tariff and nontariff mechanisms. Tariffs place a tax on imports and raise prices. Nontariff barriers like voluntary restraint agreements are self-imposed restrictions and cutbacks aimed at avoiding punitive trade actions from the host. Quota systems reduce the volume of imports accepted by a country. The final effect of all these actions is a quantitative reduction of imports.

For the international marketer, such restrictions may mean that the most efficient sources of supply are not available because government regulations restrict importation from those sources. The result is either second-best products or higher costs for restricted supplies. This in turn means that the customer receives inferior service and often has to pay significantly higher prices and that the firm is less competitive when trying to market its products internationally.

Policymakers are faced with several problems when trying to administer import controls. First, most of the time such controls exact a huge price from domestic consumers. Even though the wide distribution of the burden among many consumers may result in a less obvious burden, the social cost of these controls may be damaging to the economy and subject to severe attack by individuals. However, these attacks are counteracted by pressures from protected groups that benefit from import restrictions. For example, although citizens of the European Union may be forced—because of import controls—to pay an elevated price for all agricultural products they consume, agricultural producers in the region benefit from higher levels of income. Achieving a proper trade-off is often difficult, if not impossible, for the policymaker.

A second major problem resulting from import controls is the downstream change in import composition that results from these controls. For example, if the import of copper ore is restricted, either through voluntary restraints or through quotas, firms in copper-producing countries may opt to shift their production systems and produce copper wire instead, which they then export. As a

© Imaginechina via AP Images

Taiwanese inspectors checking imported sports drinks contaminated by cancer-causing chemicals.

result, initially narrowly defined protectionist measures may have to snowball in order to protect one downstream industry after another.

A final major problem that confronts the policymaker is that of efficiency. Import controls, which are frequently designed to provide breathing room to a domestic industry either to grow or to recapture its competitive position, often turn out not to work. Rather than improve the productivity of an industry, such controls provide it with a level of safety and a cushion of increased income yet let the drive for technological advancement fall behind. Alternatively, supply may respond to artificial stimulation and grow far beyond demand.

Regulation of International Business Behavior

Home countries may implement special laws and regulations to ensure that the international business behavior of their firms is conducted within the legal, moral, and ethical boundaries considered appropriate. The definition of appropriateness may vary from country to country and from government to government. Therefore, such regulations, their enforcement, and their impact on firms can differ substantially among nations.

Several major areas in which nations attempt to govern the international marketing activities of its firms are **boycotts**, whereby firms refuse to do business with someone, often for political reasons; antitrust measures, wherein firms are seen as restricting competition; and corruption, which occurs when firms obtain contracts with bribes rather than through performance. Arab nations, for example, have developed a blacklist of companies that deal with Israel. Even though enforcement of the blacklisting has decreased, some Arab customers still demand from their suppliers assurances that the source of the products purchased is not Israel and that the company does not do any business with Israel. The goal of these actions clearly is to impose a boycott on business with Israel. The U.S. government, because of U.S. political ties to Israel, has in turn adopted a variety of laws to prevent U.S. firms from complying with the Arab boycott. These laws include a provision to deny foreign income tax benefits to companies that comply with the boycott and also require notification of the U.S. government in case any boycott requests are received. U.S. firms that comply with the boycott are subject to heavy fines and denial of export privileges.

Boycott measures put firms in a difficult position. Caught in a web of governmental activity, they may be forced to either lose business or pay fines. This is particularly the case if a firm's products are competitive yet not unique, so that the supplier can opt to purchase them elsewhere. Heightening of such conflict can sometimes force companies to withdraw operations entirely from a country.

The second area of regulatory activity affecting international marketing efforts of firms is antitrust laws. These can apply to the international operations of firms as well as to domestic business. In the European Union, for example, the European Commission watches closely when any firm buys an overseas company, engages in a joint venture with a foreign firm, or makes an agreement with a competing firm. The commission evaluates the effect these activities will have on competition and has the right to disapprove such transactions. However, given the increased globalization of national economies, some substantial rethinking is going on regarding the current approach to antitrust enforcement. One could question whether any country can still afford to define the competition only in a domestic sense or whether competition has to be seen on a worldwide scale. Similarly, one can wonder whether countries will accept the infringement on their sovereignty that results from the extraterritorial application of any nation's law abroad.

There are precedents for making special allowances for international marketers with regard to antitrust laws. In the United States, for example, the Webb-Pomerene Act of 1918 excludes from antitrust prosecution those firms that are cooperating to develop foreign markets. The Export Trading Company Act of 1982 was specifically designed to assist small- and medium-sized firms with their exports by permitting them to join forces in their international market development activities. Due to ongoing globalization of production, competition, and supply and demand, it would appear that over time the application of antitrust laws to international marketing activities must be revised to reflect global rather than national dimensions.

Governments also regulate corporate marketing actions regarding bribery and corruption. The effects of such governmental intervention are explored later in this chapter.

HOST-COUNTRY POLITICAL AND LEGAL ENVIRONMENT

The host country environment, both political and legal, affects the international marketing operations of firms in a variety of ways. A good manager will understand the country in which the firm operates so that he or she is able to work within the existing parameters and can anticipate and plan for changes that may occur.

Political Action and Risk

Firms usually prefer to conduct business in a country with a stable and friendly government, but such governments are not always easy to find. Managers must therefore continually monitor the government, its policies, and its stability to determine the potential for political change that could adversely affect corporate operations.

There is political risk in every nation, but the range of risks varies widely from country to country. **Political risk** is defined as the risk of loss when investing in a given country caused by changes in a country's political structure or policies, such as tax laws, tariffs, expropriation of assets, or restriction in repatriation of profits. For example, a company may suffer from such loss in the case of expropriation or tightened foreign exchange repatriation rules, or from increased credit risk if the government changes policies to make it difficult for the company to pay creditors.[10] In general, political risk is lowest in countries that have a history of stability and consistency. Political risk tends to be highest in nations that do not have this sort of history. In a number of countries, however, consistency and stability that were apparent on the surface have been quickly swept away by major popular movements that drew on the bottled-up frustrations of the population. Three major types of political risk can be encountered: **ownership risk**, which exposes property and life; **operating risk**, which refers to interference with the ongoing operations of a firm; and **transfer risk**, which is mainly encountered when attempts are made to shift funds between countries. Political risk can be the result of government action, but it can also be outside the control of government.

A major political risk in many countries involves conflict and violent change. A manager will want to think twice before conducting business in a country in which the likelihood of such change is high. To begin with, if conflict breaks out, violence directed toward the firm's property and employees is a strong possibility. Guerrilla warfare, civil disturbances, and terrorism often take an anti-industry bent, making companies and their employees potential targets. Oil workers appear to be especially vulnerable and have frequently been the victims of murder and kidnapping because some of their operations are located in politically volatile parts of the globe, such as Nigeria, Sudan, and Colombia. For example, in May 2008, guerrillas in Nigeria's oil-rich Niger Delta kidnapped a Chevron transport tanker and its 11-member crew. Nigeria is Africa's biggest oil-producing nation, but pipeline bombings and attacks against oil workers by militants demanding a bigger share of the profits have reduced output by a quarter over the past 10 years.[11]

In many countries, particularly in the developing world, coups d'état can result in drastic changes in government. The new government may attack foreign multinational corporations as remnants of the Western-dominated colonial past, as has happened in Cuba, Nicaragua, and Iran. Even if such changes do not represent an immediate physical threat to firms and their employees, they can have drastic effects. The past few decades have seen such coups in the countries of Ghana, Ethiopia, and Venezuela, to name a few. These coups have seriously impeded the conduct of international marketing.

Less dramatic but still worrisome are changes in government policies that are caused not by changes in the government itself but by pressure from nationalist or religious factions or widespread anti-Western feeling. As local businesses become more developed, patriotic feelings can breed new enterprises to compete with global corporations, as *The International Marketplace 5.3* shows. Managers need to anticipate these changes and plan for ways to cope with them.

What sort of changes in policy result from the various events described? The range of possible actions is broad. All of them can affect international marketing operations, but not all are equal in weight. We have learned that companies have to fear violence against employees and that violence against company property is quite common. Also common are changes in policy that take a strong nationalist and anti–foreign investment stance. The most drastic steps resulting from such policy changes are usually confiscation and expropriation.

An important governmental action is **expropriation**, which is the seizure of foreign assets by a government with payment of compensation to the owners. In Venezuela, for example, the government of President Hugo Chávez nationalized more than 960 companies between 2005 and 2010. In 2010, almost two dozen U.S. companies, including Cargill, Coca-Cola, ExxonMobil, and Owens-Illinois, have been seized or threatened with expropriation.[12] Expropriation has appealed to some countries because it demonstrated nationalism and immediately transferred a certain amount of wealth and resources from foreign companies to the host country. It did have costs to the host country, however, to the extent that it made other firms more hesitant to invest in the country. Expropriation does provide compensation to the former owners. However, compensation negotiations are often protracted and result in settlements that are frequently unsatisfactory to the owners. For example, governments may offer compensation in the form of local, nontransferable currency or may base the compensation on the book value of the firm. Even though firms that are expropriated may deplore the low levels of payment obtained, they frequently accept them in the absence of better alternatives.

The use of expropriation as a policy tool has sharply decreased over time. Apparently, governments have come to recognize that the damage inflicted on themselves through expropriation exceeds the benefits.[13]

Confiscation is similar to expropriation in that it results in a transfer of ownership from the foreign firm to the host country. However, its effects are even harsher in that it does not involve compensation for the firm. Some industries are more vulnerable than others to confiscation and expropriation because of their importance to the host country's economy and their lack of ability to shift operations. For this reason, sectors such as mining, energy, public utilities, and banking have been targets of such government actions.

Confiscation and expropriation constitute major political risks for foreign investors. Other government actions, however, are nearly as damaging. Many countries are turning from confiscation and expropriation to more subtle forms of control such as **domestication**. The goal of domestication is the same, to gain control over foreign investment, but the method is different. Through domestication, the government demands partial transfer of ownership and management

THE INTERNATIONAL MARKETPLACE **5.3**

Baidu, Not Google, Is Keyword for Search in China

Google has established itself as the dominant global search engine, but it has not been as successful in China. While China is considered by most global corporations as a vital country for strategic growth and is the largest and fastest-growing Internet market in the world, the U.S. search giant chose to pull its search engine operations out of the country in 2010. After first developing a Chinese-language interface for its website in 2000 and introducing Google.cn in 2006, Google encountered a host-country environment with challenging operating risk.

Among the first challenges that Google faced in China was a requirement that its China-based search site conform to Chinese censorship laws. This meant that Google was required to censor searches for information by Chinese users in order to accommodate government political sensitivities. Yet Google experienced a series of problems with the Chinese government ranging from having its operating license declared invalid to experiencing hacking incidents and the blocking of its YouTube video site and Gmail services.

The disruptions affected Google's Chinese consumers as well, who found rival search site Baidu to be a more reliable engine. Market share loss to Baidu and Chinese government demands for increased censorship caused internal debate at Google, where managers found that the censorship policies ran contrary to the company's "Don't be evil" philosophy. After serious hacking incidents, Google announced in January 2010 that it would no longer censor searches in China. In March 2010, Google announced that it would begin rerouting searches to its Hong Kong–based site. Hong Kong, although part of China, is considered a separate economic region with its own laws and regulations.

As a result of its withdrawal from China-based searches, Google's share of the China search market fell to approximately 26 percent in 2010 as Baidu's share rose to 73 percent. However, Google has not given up on China and has chosen to focus on other businesses including Internet advertising, which is a thriving business there.

© Feng Li/Getty Images

Chinese Google users created a memorial in front of Google's China headquarters in 2010.

SOURCES: Steven Levy, "Inside Google's China Misfortune," *Fortune*, April 15, 2011; Melanie Lee, "Analysis: A Year after China Retreat, Google Plots New Growth," Reuters, January 13, 2011, www.reuters.com/article/2011/01/13/us-google-china-idUSTRE70C1X820110113; Melanie Lee, "Timeline—China Approves Google Search Page," Reuters, July 9, 2010; and Owen Fletcher, "Google's China Market Share Down in 2Q, Baidu's Up—Research Firm," Fox Business, July 15, 2011, www.foxbusiness.com/industries/2011/07/15/googles-china-market-share-down-in-2q-baidus-up-research-firm.

responsibility and imposes regulations to ensure that a large share of the product is locally produced and a larger share of the profit is retained in the country.

Domestication can have profound effects on the international marketer for a number of reasons. First, if a firm is forced to hire nationals as managers, poor cooperation and communication can result. If the domestication is imposed within a very short time span, corporate operations overseas may have to be headed by poorly trained and inexperienced local managers. Further, domestic content requirements may force a firm to purchase supplies and parts locally, which can result in increased costs, inefficiency, and lower-quality products, thus further damaging a firm's competitiveness. Export requirements imposed on companies may also create havoc for the international distribution plan of a corporation and force it to change or even shut down operations in other countries. Finally, domestication will usually shield the industry within one country from foreign competition. As a result, inefficiencies will be allowed to grow due to a lack of market discipline. In the long run, this will affect the international competitiveness of an operation abroad and may become a major problem when, years later, the removal of domestication is considered by the government.

Most businesses operating abroad face a number of other risks that are less dangerous, but probably more common, than the drastic ones already described. Host governments that face a shortage of foreign currency sometimes will impose controls on the movement of capital in and out of the country. Such controls may make it difficult for a firm to remove its profits or investments from the host country. Sometimes, exchange controls are also levied selectively against certain products or companies in an effort to reduce the importation of goods that are considered to be a luxury or unnecessary. Such regulations are often difficult to deal with because they may affect the importation of parts, components, or supplies that are vital for production operations. Restrictions on such imports may force a firm either to alter its production program or, worse yet, to shut down its entire plant. Prolonged negotiations with government officials may be necessary in order to reach a compromise agreement on what constitutes a valid expenditure of foreign currency resources. Because the goals of government officials and corporate managers may often be quite different, such compromises, even when they can be reached, may result in substantial damage to the international marketing operations of a firm.

Countries may also raise the tax rates applied to foreign investors in an effort to control the firms and their capital. On occasion, different or stricter applications of the host country's tax codes are implemented for foreign investors. The rationale for such measures is often an apparent underpayment of taxes by such investors when comparing their payments to those of long-established domestic competitors. Overlooked is the fact that new investors in foreign lands tend to **overinvest** by initially buying more land, space, and equipment than is needed and by spending heavily so that facilities are state-of-the-art. This desire to accommodate future growth and to be highly competitive in the early investment stages will, in turn, produce lower profits and lower tax payments. Yet over time these investment activities should be very successful, competitive, and job-creating. Selective tax increases for foreign investors may result in much-needed revenue for the coffers of the host country, but they can severely damage the operations of the foreign investors. This damage, in turn, may result in decreased income for the host country in the long run.

The international marketing manager must also worry about **price controls**. In many countries, domestic political pressures can force governments to control the prices of imported products or services, particularly in sectors that are considered to be highly sensitive from a political perspective, such as food or health care. Also, in times of severe currency fluctuations and interest rate manipulations, the value of firms' assets and activities can be adversely affected. If a foreign firm is involved in these areas, it is a vulnerable target of government policies because the host government can play on its people's nationalistic tendencies to enforce the controls. Particularly in countries that suffer from high inflation and frequent devaluations, the international marketer may be forced to choose between shutting down the operation or continuing production at a loss in the hope of recouping that loss once the government chooses to loosen or remove its price restrictions. How a firm can adjust to price controls is discussed in greater detail later in the book.

Managers face political and economic risk whenever they conduct business overseas, but there may be ways to lessen the risk. Obviously, if a new government that is dedicated to the removal of all foreign influences comes into power, a firm can do little. In less extreme cases, however, managers can take actions to reduce the risk if they understand the root causes of the host-country policies. Most important is the accumulation and appreciation of factual information about a country's history, political background, and culture before making a long-term investment decision. Also, a high degree of sensitivity by a firm and its employees to country-specific approaches and concerns are important dimensions that help a firm to blend into the local landscape rather than stand out as a foreign object.

Adverse governmental actions are usually the result of a host country's nationalism, desire for independence, and opposition to colonial remnants. If a country's citizens feel exploited by foreign firms, government officials are more likely to take antiforeign action. To reduce the risk of government intervention, a firm needs to demonstrate that it is concerned with the host country's society and that it considers itself an integral part of the host country rather than simply an exploitative foreign corporation. Ways to do this include intensive local hiring and training practices, good pay, philanthropy, and more societally useful investment. In addition, a company can form joint ventures with local partners to demonstrate a willingness to share its benefits with nationals. Although such actions will not guarantee freedom from risk, they will certainly lessen the exposure to it.

Corporations can also protect against political risk by closely monitoring political developments. Increasingly, private-sector firms offer assistance in such monitoring activities, permitting the overseas corporation to discover potential trouble spots as early as possible and react quickly to prevent major losses. Firms can also take out insurance to cover losses due to political risk. Most industrialized countries offer insurance programs for their firms doing business abroad. In Germany, for example, Hermes Kreditanstalt provides exporters with insurance. In the United States, the Overseas Private Investment Corporation (OPIC) can cover three types of risk: (1) currency inconvertibility insurance, which covers the inability to convert profits, debt service, and other remittances from local currency into U.S. dollars; (2) expropriation insurance, which covers the loss of an investment due to expropriation, nationalization, or confiscation by a foreign government; and (3) political violence insurance, which covers the loss of assets or income due to war, revolution, insurrection, or politically motivated civil strife, terrorism, and sabotage. Rates vary by country and industry, but for $100 of coverage per year for a manufacturing project, the base rate is $0.18 to $0.42 for protection against inconvertibility, $0.28 to $0.60 to protect against expropriation, and $0.21 to $0.53 to protect assets against political violence.[14] Usually, insurance policies do not cover commercial risks and, in the event of a claim, cover only the actual loss—not lost profits. In the event of a major political upheaval, however, risk insurance can be critical to a firm's survival.

Clearly, the international marketer must consider the likelihood of negative political factors in making decisions on conducting business overseas. On the other hand, host-country political and legal systems can have a positive impact on the conduct of international business. Many governments, for example, encourage foreign investments, especially if they believe that the investment will produce economic and political benefits domestically. Some governments have opened up their economy to foreign investors, placing only minimal constraints on them, in the hope that such policies will lead to rapid economic development. Others have provided for substantial subsidization of new investment activities in the hope that investments will generate additional employment. The international marketer, in his or her investment decision, can and should therefore also pay close attention to the extent and forms of incentives available from foreign governments. Although international marketing decisions should be driven by free market forces, these decisions may change if incentives are offered.

In this discussion of the political environment, laws have been mentioned only to the extent that they appear to be the direct result of political changes. However, each nation has laws regarding marketing, and the international manager must understand their effects on the firm's efforts.

Legal Differences and Restraints

Countries differ in their laws as well as in their implementation of these laws. For example, the United States has developed into an increasingly litigious society in which institutions and individuals are quick to take a case to court. As a result, court battles are often protracted and costly, and simply the threat of a court case can reduce marketing opportunities. In contrast, Japan's legal tradition tends to minimize the role of the law and of lawyers. Some possible reasons include the relatively small number of courts and attorneys; the delays, the costs, and the uncertainties associated with litigation; the limited doctrines of plaintiffs' standing and rights to bring class-action suits; the tendency of judges to encourage out-of-court settlements; and the easy availability of arbitration and mediation for dispute resolution.

Some estimates suggest that the number of lawyers in the United States is as much as 25 times higher per capita than in Japan, based on the fact that Japan has only about 23,000 fully licensed lawyers.[15] However, comparisons can be misleading because officially registered lawyers in Japan perform only a small fraction of the duties performed by American lawyers. Different perceptions and legal practices can lead to substantially different approaches to communication and conflict resolution.

Over the millennia of civilization, many different laws and legal systems have emerged. King Hammurabi of Babylon codified a series of judges' decisions into a body of law. Hebrew law was the result of the dictates of God. Legal issues in many African tribes were settled through the verdicts of clansmen. A key legal perspective that survives today is that of theocracy, which has faith and belief as its key focus and is a mix of societal, legal, and spiritual guidelines. Examples are Hebrew law and Islamic law (*shari'ah*)—see *The International Marketplace 5.4*—which are the result of scripture, prophetic utterances and practices, and scholarly interpretations.[16]

While these legal systems are important to society locally, from an international business perspective the two major legal systems worldwide can be categorized into common law and code law. Common law is based on tradition and depends less on written statutes and codes than on precedent and custom. Common law originated in England and is the system of law found today in the United States.

On the other hand, code law is based on a comprehensive set of written statutes. Countries with code law try to spell out all possible legal rules explicitly. Code law is based on Roman law and is found in the majority of the nations of the world. In general, countries with the code law system have much more rigid laws than those with the common law system. In the latter, courts adopt precedents and customs to fit the cases, allowing the marketer a better idea of the basic judgment likely to be rendered in new situations.

Although wide in theory, the differences between code law and common law and their impact on the international marketer are not always as broad in practice. For example, many common law countries, including the United States, have adopted commercial codes to govern the conduct of business.

Host countries may adopt a number of laws that affect a company's ability to market. To begin with, there can be laws affecting the entry of goods, such as tariffs and quotas. Also in this category are antidumping laws, which prohibit below-cost sales of products, and laws that require export and import licensing. In addition, many countries have health and safety standards that may, by design or by accident, restrict the entry of foreign goods. Japan, for example, has

THE INTERNATIONAL MARKETPLACE 5.4

The Archbishop and the Law

Rowan Williams is the archbishop of Canterbury and the spiritual leader of the approximately 80-million-member global Anglican Church. He stirred up some controversy when he examined the role of *shari'ah* in British life. *Shari'ah* is the body of Islamic religious law that is based on the Koran, the words and actions of the Prophet Mohammad, and the rulings of Islamic scholars. It typically finds its application mainly in Muslim countries.

The archbishop suggested that, with a population of more than 2 million Muslims in Great Britain, *shari'ah* already figures prominently in the lives of many. For example, informal neighborhood councils provide rulings on family issues such as divorce; banks, such as HSBC, already market mortgages that comply with *shari'ah* rules of lending. Perhaps Muslims in Britain would be more comfortable and willing to build a more constructive relationship with their fellow citizens if they could choose *shari'ah* law for the settling of civil disputes. The archbishop has said that *shari'ah* law in Britain is "unavoidable."

Many commentators, including the British prime minister, David Cameron, strongly opposed such thinking. There was the feeling that illegal immigration of Muslims into Britain and their unwillingness to adapt to British customs would undermine British values and laws and substantially weaken the position of women. Cameron has said that "multiculturalism has been responsible for fostering Islamic extremism in the United Kingdom" and has pledged to reduce immigration to Britain from non-European countries. Perhaps not since Thomas Becket ran afoul of King Henry II in 1170 was there such controversy surrounding the archbishop and the law.

SOURCES: Soeren Kern, "Britain vs. Muslim Immigration," Hudson Institute, New York, April 21, 2011; Karla Adam, "Archbishop Defends Remarks on Islamic Law in Britain," *Washington Post*, February 12, 2008, A11; and "Archbishop of Canterbury: Sharia Law Unavoidable in Britain," *Christian Today*, February 7, 2008.

particularly strict health standards that affect the import of pharmaceuticals. Rather than accepting test results from other nations, the Japanese government insists on conducting its own tests, which are time consuming and costly. It claims that these tests are necessary to reflect Japanese peculiarities. Yet some importers and their governments see these practices as thinly veiled protectionist barriers.

A growing global controversy surrounds the use of genetic technology. Governments are increasingly devising new rules that affect trade in genetically modified products. For example, Australia introduced a mandatory standard for foods

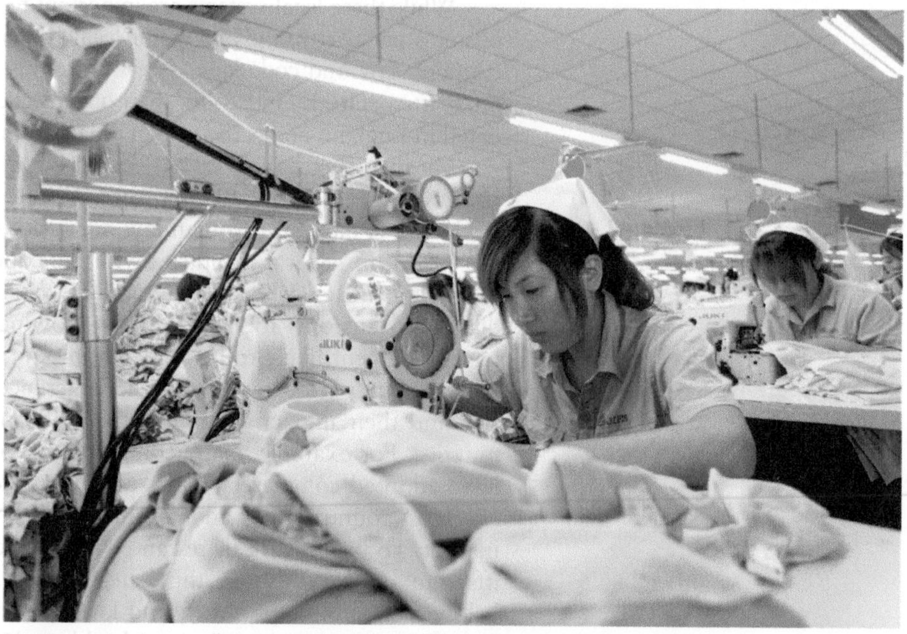

Large production and export volumes can threaten producers in recipient countries who sometimes retaliate by filing anti-dumping actions.

produced using biotechnology, which prohibits the sale of such products unless the food has been assessed by the Australia New Zealand Food Authority.

Other laws may be designed to protect domestic industries and reduce imports. For example, Russia assesses high excise taxes on goods such as cigarettes, automobiles, and alcoholic beverages—and provides a burdensome import licensing and quotas regime for alcohol to depress Russian demand for imports. In the case of alcohol alone, the United States believes that it is losing more than $10 million in annual sales due to these barriers.[17]

Very specific legislation may also exist to regulate where a firm can advertise or what constitutes deceptive advertising. Many countries prohibit specific claims by marketers comparing their product to that of the competition and restrict the use of promotional devices. Some countries regulate the names of companies or the foreign-language content of a product's label. Even when no laws exist, the marketer may be hampered by regulations. For example, in many countries, governments require a firm to join the local chamber of commerce or become a member of the national trade association. These institutions in turn may have internal regulations that set standards for the conduct of business and may be seen as quite confining to the international marketer.

Finally, the enforcement of laws may have a different effect on national and on foreign marketers. For example, the simple requirement that an executive has to stay in a country until a business conflict is resolved may be a major burden for the international marketer.

Influencing Politics and Laws

To succeed in a market, the international marketer needs much more than business know-how. He or she must also deal with the intricacies of national politics and laws. Although a full understanding of another country's legal and political system will rarely be possible, the good manager will be aware of the importance of this system and will work with people who do understand how to operate within the system.

Many areas of politics and law are not immutable. Viewpoints can be modified or even reversed, and new laws can supersede old ones. Therefore, existing political and legal restraints do not always need to be accepted. To achieve change, however, there must be some impetus for it, such as the clamors of a constituency. Otherwise, systemic inertia is likely to allow the status quo to prevail.

The international marketer has various options. One approach may be to simply ignore prevailing rules and expect to get away with it. Pursuing this option is a high-risk strategy because of the possibility of objection and even prosecution. A second, traditional option is to provide input to trade negotiators and expect any problem areas to be resolved in multilateral negotiations. The drawback to this option is, of course, the quite time-consuming process involved.

A third option involves the development of coalitions or constituencies that can motivate legislators and politicians to consider and ultimately implement change. This option can be pursued in various ways. One direction can be the recasting or redefinition of issues. Often, specific **terminology** leads to conditioned but inappropriate responses. For example, before China's accession to the WTO, the country's trade status with the United States had been highly controversial for many years. The U.S. Congress had to decide annually whether to grant most-favored nation (MFN) status to China. The debate on this decision was always very contentious and acerbic and was often framed around the question of why China deserved to be treated the "most favored way." Lost in the debate was the fact that the term "most favored" was simply taken from WTO terminology and indicated only that trade with China would be treated no worse than with any other country. Only when the terminology was changed from MFN to NTR, or "normal trade relations," was the controversy about special treatment eliminated.[18]

Beyond terminology, marketers can also highlight the direct linkages and their cost and benefit to legislators and politicians. For example, the manager can explain the employment and economic effects of certain laws and regulations and demonstrate the benefits of change. Suppliers, customers, and distributors can also be asked to communicate their feelings to decision makers. Such groups can be quite influential. For example, it has been suggested that Indian businesses, fearing hostile U.S. reactions, exerted substantial pressure on their government to resolve the Kashmiri conflict. If so, this is an encouraging example of the benefits of globalization.[19]

Developing such coalitions is not an easy task. Companies often seek assistance to influence the government decision-making process. Such assistance usually is particularly beneficial when narrow economic objectives or single-issue campaigns are needed. Typical providers of this assistance are **lobbyists**. Usually, these are well-connected individuals and firms that can provide access to policymakers and legislators.

Lobbying firms tend to be located in state, national, or regional capitals. Their experience and networks can help in presenting corporate concerns to decision makers. In doing so, new information and insights can be provided to policymakers, and decisions can be precipitated more rapidly.

Lobbying is very valuable to the international marketer, as is evidenced by the large number of global lobbyists and their high compensation. In Washington, DC, alone, there were 12,964 registered lobbyists in 2010, many of whom represented international interests.[20]

A key factor in successful lobbying is the involvement of local citizens and companies. Typically, legislators are only willing to take positions on important issues if they are supported by or at least not opposed by their constituents. Therefore, it is important to demonstrate how a particular issue affects a decision maker's domestic constituents. For example, to ward off negative legislation it may be helpful to point out how many jobs are created by a firm's foreign investment or how export-intensive such an investment can be.

Although representation of the firm's interests to government decision makers and legislators is entirely appropriate, the international marketer must also consider any potential side effects. Major questions can be raised if such representation becomes very strong or is seen as reflecting a conflict of interest. For example, former chancellor Gerhard Schröder of Germany took on the representation of a Russian pipeline corporation. There was substantial concern about his representing a cause that he had championed and approved as chancellor only months before. There is unease with revolving-door issues involving former policy makers working on behalf of clients who were subject to their previous official decisions, or of lobbyists spending large amounts of money to further their cause. Due to the reality or perception of inappropriateness, some countries have passed legislation that restricts lobbying activities. In the United States, for example, policy makers are limited in the extent of hospitality they can accept, ex-policy makers are barred from approaching their former colleagues for at least one year, and involvement in former decision areas is restricted even longer. The American League of Lobbyists has a published code of ethics to provide basic guidelines for the conduct of its members.[21] It is important to abide by these rules and guidelines and to ensure that public perception sees the process as reasonable and fair. Otherwise, short-term gains may be far outweighed by long-term negative repercussions if the international marketer is perceived as exerting too much political influence.

INTERNATIONAL RELATIONSHIPS

In addition to the politics and laws of both the home and the host countries, the international marketer must consider the overall international political and legal environment. Relations between countries can have a profound impact on firms trying to do business internationally.

International Politics

The effect of politics on international marketing is determined by both the bilateral political relations between home and host countries and the multilateral agreements governing the relations among groups of countries.

The government-to-government relationship can have a profound effect, particularly if it becomes hostile. Numerous examples exist of the linkage between international politics and international marketing. One such example involves British–Icelandic relations following the Icelandic government's 2008 decision to assume control of three of the country's largest banks, which were hit hard by the global credit crunch. Iceland initiated a deposit freeze that affected deposits of approximately £4.5 billion from British citizens. The British government promptly used its antiterror law to seize an estimated £4 billion of Icelandic resources, which, in turn, forced Iceland to cover the losses of British depositors at a cost to Icelandic taxpayers of more than £2.2 billion. With a population base of only 300,000 people, such new debt was huge. While the United Kingdom chose to adopt this "stick" approach, the Dutch government secured a commitment from Iceland to pay back its savers using a different tactic, perhaps more conducive to long-term good neighborly relations. It offered to loan Iceland the money.[22]

Another example was the 2010 Chinese two-month ban on exports of rare earth elements. This occurred after the Japanese government arrested the crew of a Chinese fishing boat that had collided with Japanese coast guard vessels. Rare earths are a collection of 17 elements that are critical ingredients in many high-technology military and commercial products. Commercial applications include cell phones, computers, MRI machines, and green technology products. Because 97 percent of 2010 production of rare earths was in China, Japanese marketers were subject to a political crisis.[23]

International political relations do not always have harmful effects on international marketers. If bilateral political relations between countries improve, business can benefit. A good example is the thawing of relations between the West and the countries of the former Soviet bloc. Political warming has opened up completely new frontiers for U.S. international marketers in Hungary, Poland, and Russia. Activities such as selling computers, which would have been considered treasonous only a few years ago, are now routine.

The international marketer needs to be aware of political currents worldwide and attempt to anticipate changes in the international political environment, good or bad, so that his or her firm can plan for them. Sometimes, however, management can only wait until the emotional fervor of conflict has subsided and hope that rational governmental negotiations will let cooler heads prevail.

International Law

International law plays an important role in the conduct of international business. Although no enforceable body of international law exists, certain treaties and agreements respected by a number of countries profoundly influence international business operations. As an example, the WTO defines internationally acceptable economic practices for its member nations. Although it does not deal directly with individual firms, it does influence them indirectly by providing a more stable and predictable international market environment.

In addition to multilateral agreements, firms are affected by bilateral treaties and conventions. The United States, for example, has signed bilateral treaties of friendship, commerce, and navigation with a wide variety of countries. These agreements generally define the rights of U.S. firms doing business in the host country. They normally guarantee that the U.S. firms will be treated by the host country in the same manner in which domestic firms are treated. Although these treaties provide for some stability, they can be canceled when relationships worsen.

The international legal environment also affects the marketer to the extent that firms must concern themselves with jurisdictional disputes. Because no single body of international law exists, firms usually are restricted by both home- and host-country laws. If a conflict occurs between contracting parties in two different countries, a question arises concerning which country's laws will be followed. Sometimes the contract will contain a jurisdictional clause, which settles the matter. If not, the parties to the dispute can follow either the laws of the country in which the agreement was made or those of the country in which the contract will have to be fulfilled. Deciding on the laws to be followed and the location to settle the dispute are two different decisions. As a result, a dispute between a U.S. exporter and a French importer could be resolved in Paris with the resolution based on New York state law. In light of the spillover of corporate missteps onto multiple countries, there is increasing consideration of developing regulations to supervise **stateless corporations**.

The parties to a business transaction can also choose either arbitration or litigation. Litigation is usually avoided for several reasons. It often involves extensive delays and is very costly. In addition, firms may fear discrimination in foreign countries. Companies therefore tend to prefer conciliation and arbitration because these processes result in much quicker decisions. Arbitration procedures are often spelled out in the original contract and usually provide for an intermediary who is judged to be impartial by both parties. Frequently, intermediaries will be representatives of chambers of commerce, trade associations, or third-country institutions. For example, the rules of the international chamber of commerce in Paris are frequently used for arbitration purposes.

International Terrorism and Marketing

Terrorism is the systematic use (or threat) of violence aimed at attaining a political goal and conveying a political message. International terrorism seeks to do this across national borders.[24] While it has existed for centuries, terrorism's global impact has changed significantly in recent years: improved means of transportation lead to an omnipresence never previously experienced. The rise of terrorist incidents in Western nations, often carried out by foreign nationals, brings terrorism to countries once considered immune. Global mass media, meanwhile, have ensured the visibility of terrorist events, spreading fear and creating irrational expectations of localized attacks.

Terrorists direct their strikes at business far more than any other target.[25] Businesses need to be easily accessible and able to conduct transactions with many new persons every day; this introduces a level of vulnerability that is not typically encountered by government offices. Exhibit 5.4 shows the frequency of terrorist attacks in different geographic regions. Bombings are most common, followed by armed assaults, kidnapping, vandalism, and hijacking.

While always regrettable, terrorism nevertheless creates new opportunities for firms in a few industries like construction, security, and information technology. For most companies, however, terrorism results in reduced revenues or increased costs, and managers must prepare for this. Terrorists intend to affect supply and demand in order to shatter existing economic systems; this brings about both direct and indirect effects. The direct consequences to business are the immediate costs levied on individual firms. While harm is clear to individual firms, from a societal perspective the direct effects tend to be less consequential than the indirect ones. The latter accumulate over time and are often not apparent immediately.

The indirect negative consequences of terrorism begin with macroeconomic phenomena, such as the real or perceived decline in per capita income, purchasing power, and stock market values. In the wake of a terror event, these trends cause a fall in the subjective (perceived) security of the nation. Buyers become

EXHIBIT 5.4 **Lethality of Attacks**

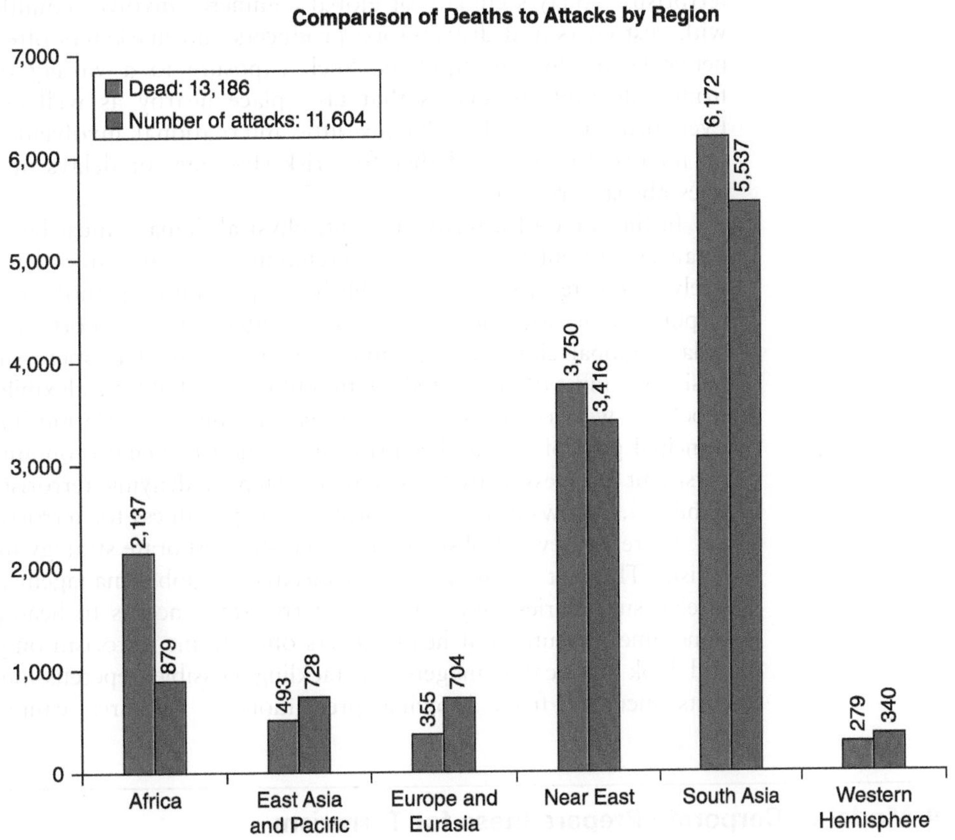

SOURCE: National Counterterrorism Center, *Report on Terrorism*, April 30, 2011, www.nctc.gov/witsbanner/docs/2010_report_on_terrorism.pdf, accessed December 5, 2011.

uncertain about the state of their nation's economy, and a sharp reduction in demand for both consumer and industrial goods follows—a phenomenon that we call the **chill effect**.

A further effect on enterprises may be the failures in power, communication, transport, and other infrastructure due to actual physical damage incurred at the terrorists' hands. Indirectly, this leads to unpredictable shifts and interruption in the supply of inputs, resources, and services. Finally, international terrorism often causes tension between the countries whose citizens or property is involved; the deterioration of transnational relationships can affect foreign buyer and seller attitudes and thus the marketing activities of firms doing business abroad. "In Europe, the radicalization of individuals and groups, motivated by ideology, religion, or economics, threatens local cooperation and social harmony."[26]

One key side effect of terrorism can be the government policies and laws it brings about. In order to make a country less vulnerable, politicians often enact restrictions on the business environment. New regulations in customs clearance may delay the supply of inputs, increase the administrative burden, and require firms to invest in new procedures. Transaction costs generally increase, and the commercial environment may be altered in ways that are more harmful to business than the terrorist attack itself might have been. For example, stricter regulations and increased security measures in the United States following 9/11 have generated large losses in cross-border trade and tourism. Also, "European business schools have benefited from tighter restrictions on international student enrollments in the U.S."[27]

From a global perspective, these effects are present for many firms, even those that are geographically remote from any location directly affected by terrorism. Today's climate of global commerce involves countless interactions with customers and distributors; producers and marketers often rely on entire networks of diverse suppliers. Such exposure to a variety of actors leaves firms vulnerable to events that take place nearby as well as at a distance. Even firms perceived as having little international involvement may depend on imported goods, and therefore risk shortages or delays of input if economies abroad are disrupted.

In the wake of a terrorist event, physical damage must be undone, security arrangements enhanced, and risk premiums reassessed. In order to do this effectively, an enterprise must establish its priorities, quantify risk, and outline response scenarios ahead of an actual attack. It is important to note that in today's global climate, firms must aim for more than mere survival. Instead, businesses must offer assured continuity to stakeholders. Flexibility to withstand shock, as well as the continuity of existing business relationships, must be the principal goal of any global firm. In addition to being economically necessary, persistent business activity is a major step in denying terrorists their goals.[28] Exhibit 5.5 shows a model of corporate preparedness for terrorist attack.

There are several obstacles to successful corporate strategy in mitigating terrorism. The first lies in a frequent mistake of global management: managers of foreign subsidiaries may shunt any terrorism concerns to headquarters. At the same time, executives at headquarters often frame terrorism only in local terms and look to local managers for tackling possible repercussions. As a result, costs incurred from growing precautionary measures cannot be defrayed

EXHIBIT 5.5 A Model of Corporate Preparedness for Terrorism

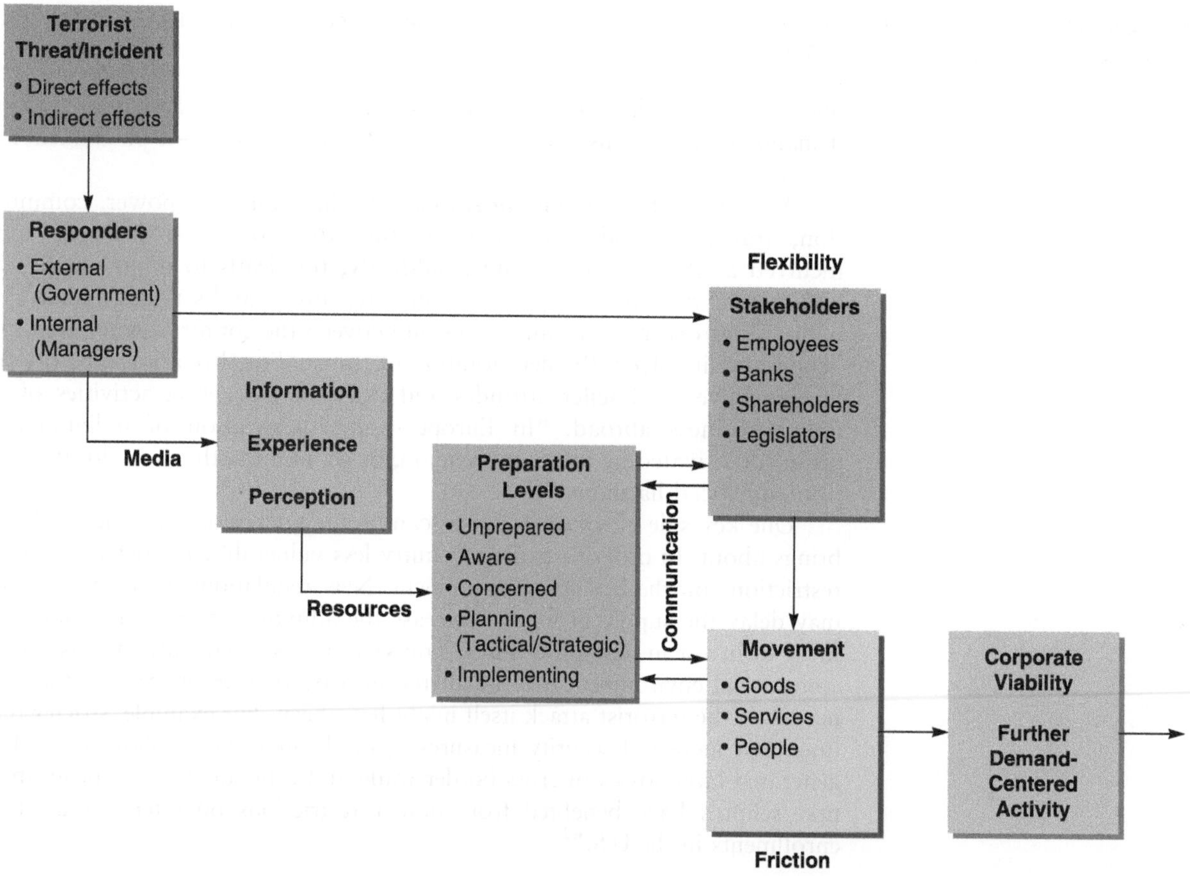

efficiently throughout the enterprise, and wholesale closure of international operations may follow.

In addition, terrorist risk is difficult to assess in an integrated global economy. If supply chains are complex and multinational, the effects of terrorism can potentially spread across the globe from an initially local focus. For most firms, the costs of averting terrorism are hard to quantify and even harder to justify to key stakeholders. In an era when the mandates of the Sarbanes-Oxley Act (see upcoming section on corporate governance) are straining corporate budgets, top executives put a greater premium on meeting financial performance benchmarks than on addressing vague political risks.

An important consideration is that individual assessment of vulnerability changes based on individual information, experience, and perception of an event. Over time, these impressions shift, resulting in potentially faulty managerial decisions. Ironically, the greater the tragedy, the more likely people are to discount it as an aberration once confidence is restored and normal activities are resumed. Widespread underestimation of the likelihood of future recurrences results. Managers are therefore tempted to rest comfortably in the belief that any future attack will not affect their company and not lead to widespread personal repercussions.

Over time, terrorism will increasingly influence the evaluation and selection of markets. Thus far, for instance, developing nations have proven to be most vulnerable to economic and consumption downturns following terror events.

In a volatile world, marketing managers are the frontline response to business disruption. Although all corporate areas are likely to be affected by terrorist activity, the marketing field, which constitutes a key liaison with the world outside the firm, is likely to be under the most pressure. Marketers deal specifically with the activities of supply and demand that terrorists aim to destroy and are thus confronted with terrorism on a daily basis. Devising new distribution and logistics avenues in the case of attack, responding with pricing strategies to dislocations, and communicating the firm's position to buyers and suppliers are all marketing activities.[29]

In some cases, marketers may choose to pursue a strategy of working with customer segments less sensitive to terrorism. For instance, in the months following September 11, marketers in the hotel industry focused their selling efforts on regional rather than national or international business. Oftentimes, sales are perceived to be safer in domestic and thus familiar markets. However, staying domestic is becoming difficult as a long-term strategy in our increasingly globalized world.

Marketers tend to have the clearest understanding of the mutual corporate dependence so critical for effective planning. For example, when determining the need for specific emergency inputs, marketers will not only look for the source of such inputs. They will also be able to analyze the existing relationships and networks and devise incentives to ensure that the supplier will actually provide goods and services to the firm. Dry runs and simulations can be used by marketers to develop expectations about long-term effects and to see whether the system works as planned. Otherwise, a plan is akin to identifying the location of gas stations as the principal remedy for a fuel shortage without keeping in mind that the stations need to be resupplied to stay open and need to be willing to provide the gasoline for a client pulling in.

On the supply side, marketers deal with communication with customers and suppliers, devise campaigns to present information, provide direction, and alter any misperceptions. Marketers are the experts who implement steps to address imbalances and create new incentives by changing corporate pricing, packaging, or sizing. Goods or services whose price is strongly affected by changing information flows and perceptions of risk are highly susceptible to the indirect consequences of terrorism. Insurance coverage is an example. Actual or perceived terrorist threats tend to create upward pressure on the pricing of particularly vulnerable offerings. Prices may also experience a certain "stickiness," that is, under conditions of inability to predict the occurrence of terrorism or its indirect effects, once raised, prices may not be decreased. Conversely, firms in certain industries may feel pressure to lower prices in order to induce reluctant buyers to maintain or increase their buying activities.

Through their actions, marketers can reverse an emerging softness in demand, rally joint responses, and avoid the occurrence of unintended consequences. With their understanding of the long-term repercussions of terrorism, marketers can also be instrumental in formulating alternative corporate strategies, for example the shift from an investment-based foreign market expansion to an export-based one.

> Companies have placed more emphasis on terrorism risk considerations when choosing how to enter foreign markets. In the last century, foreign direct investment (FDI) was the preferred approach. But terrorism has shifted the balance. Now many more firms favor entry through exporting, which permits broad and rapid coverage of world markets, reduces dependence on highly visible physical facilities, and offers much flexibility for making rapid adjustments. In terms of economies of scale and transaction costs, FDI is generally superior, but the risks of exporting are judged to be lower. Markets tend to punish failure more harshly than they reward success, which makes risk-minimizing strategies more effective.[30]

Every world region is vulnerable, and most attacks are directed at businesses and business-related infrastructure. Terrorism requires decision making and behaviors that support vigilance and development of appropriate strategies. Managers who fail to prepare run the risk of weaker performance or even loss of the firm. While we can no longer choose the lowest cost option, 10 years after 9/11 companies are more aware, less exposed, and less vulnerable to the risk of terrorism. But in the next 10 years comes the really big task: what can and should we do collectively and individually to reduce the causes of terrorism?

The continuing efforts of marketers to understand cultural issues are also highly useful for devising terminology and persuasive encouragement. Studies tell us that there are major cultural differences between and even within nations. International marketing, through its linkages via goods, services, ideas, and communications, can achieve important assimilations of value systems. Marketers know that culture and values are learned, not genetically implanted. As life's experiences grow more international and more similar, so do values. Therefore, every time international marketing forges a new linkage in thinking and provides for new exchanges of goods or services, new progress is made in shaping a greater global commonality in values. It may well be that international marketing's ability to align global values, and the subsequent greater ease of countries, companies, and individuals to build bridges among themselves, may eventually become the field's greatest gift to the world.[31]

ETHICAL ISSUES

Corporate governance, responsibility, intellectual property rights, and corruption all fall under the ethical obligations experienced by multinational enterprises today. Whether following the most ethical route in business dealings matters in the long run is, in many ways, a difficult question. Historically, the answer has depended on the environment and outcomes. Nineteenth-century textile mills in the United States, for instance, flagrantly violated today's standards for workers' rights (including living wages, maximum weekly working hours, and safe working conditions). However, they did much to move U.S. industrialization forward. It was a fire in one such mill in New York—in which 146 workers died because employers had locked all the exits from the factory—that spurred safety drives by U.S. labor unions. Similarly, the credit conflagration that started in the United States in 2007 provoked considerable global public debate and legislation concerning responsible and ethical lending practices and banking oversight.

Today, one issue concerning corporate ethics is the divide between the "first world" and less-developed countries. Should emerging economies follow the same course experienced by the United States and Europe in their industrial history? Or should they be aided and, on occasion, forced by developed nations to skip the mishaps of the Western experience, and industrialize under more stringent modern-day standards? The key question remains: who will bear the cost?

Restrictions may hinder progress by excessively curbing business practices with ethical requirements. In addition, corporate practices are far from perfect in the world's most advanced countries themselves. Some even claim that a focus on ethics is a thin disguise for protectionism. Finally, globalization raises an interesting concern: When investing abroad, should firms from a developed country with stringent ethical laws be allowed to use looser local principles to their advantage?

The following sections may shed some light on the nature, focus, and concerns of the ethical dimension in modern-day businesses abroad.

Corporate Governance and Responsibility

The relationships among stakeholders that determine and control the strategic direction and performance of an organization are called **corporate governance**.[32] A system of corporate governance must be established to ensure that decisions are made and interests are represented properly for all stakeholders. The structure, conduct, and methods used in the assessment of company behavior vary dramatically across countries. Key elements of corporate governance, however, remain the transparency of a firm's operations, its financial results, and the principles by which it measures sales, expenses, assets, and liabilities.

For some, the overriding objective of corporate governance is to optimize returns to shareholders over time. In order to achieve this, good governance practices focus the attention of the company's board of directors on strategies that ensure corporate growth and increase equity value. In addition, corporate governance frameworks typically protect shareholders' rights and ensure their equitable treatment, provide for timely and accurate disclosure of all the company's material matters, and ensure the board of directors' accountability to the company and its shareholders.

Others interpret corporate governance as dealing with stakeholders (such as employees, customers, banks, etc.) who are affected by corporate decisions. For them, the providers of capital are only one of various constituencies to satisfy.

The separation of ownership from management, and the various cultural views on stakeholders' identity and significance, all affect corporate governance and lead to different practices across countries, economies, and cultures. Exhibit 5.6 illustrates variants of corporate governance structures classified by regime and ownership. The major factors driving global corporate governance

EXHIBIT 5.6 Comparative Corporate Governance Regimes

Regime Basis	Characteristics	Examples
Market-based	Efficient equity markets; Dispersed ownership	United States, United Kingdom, Canada, Australia
Family-based	Management & ownership is combined; Family/majority and minority shareholders	Hong Kong, Indonesia, Malaysia, Singapore, Taiwan, France
Bank-based	Government influence in bank lending; Lack of transparency; Family control	Korea, Germany
Government affiliated	State ownership of enterprise; Lack of transparency; No minority influence	China, Russia

SOURCE: Based on J. Tsui and T. Shieh, "Corporate Governance in Emerging Markets: An Asian Perspective," in *International Finance and Accounting Handbook*, 3rd ed., Frederick D. S. Choi, ed. (Hoboken, NJ: Wiley, 2004), 244–246.

principles and practices are financial market development, the degree of separation between management and ownership, and transparency.

Proponents of a market-based regime emphasize the benefit of forces that result from interplaying supply and demand. Price signals adjust activities instead of government intervention and create an environment of respect for profitability and private property. In exchange for the chance to derive proceeds, investors allocate resources to the most productive and efficient uses. In order for such allocations to take place, however, trust must exist between managers and investors. In return for their financial inputs, managers must provide stakeholders with their best efforts to secure gains on the supplied capital.

In this sense, managers can be seen as marketing their corporate virtue, vision, and potential for economic gain to potential investors. It is therefore of vital interest to them that bribery, corruption, and obscurity be eliminated, allowing relationships of trust and commitment to be forged between firms and individual sources of money.[33] This takes on additional importance as investment experiences globalization. Transparency must reign not only within a country but also across borders to foreign business partners.

As firms become increasingly multinational, governments respond by increasing global cooperation to achieve the same principles of taxation and corporate ethics laws across nations. This serves to slowly eliminate tax issues like the shifting of income from high- to low-tax countries or the shielding of income from taxation by holding profits in tax havens.

Aside from responsibility to stakeholders, corporations are often expected to fulfill certain obligations and exhibit conscientious behavior toward the societies in which they operate. Such obligations often include environmental safety and efficiency, reasonable working conditions and wages, and concerns about layoffs, health care, and family care. The EU has surpassed most of the world in both cultural friendliness to and actual implementation of such programs. In 1995, the president of the European Commission joined with leading European companies to found CSR Europe, a business network aimed at helping companies integrate corporate social responsibility (CSR) with daily business practices. Meanwhile, *The International Marketplace 5.5* illustrates that environmental concerns are often important not only for ethical but also for practical reasons.

THE INTERNATIONAL MARKETPLACE 5.5

ENVIRONMENT & SUSTAINABILITY

Does Pollution Matter?

Economic development in China leads to numerous benefits, like a rise in GDP and popular welfare levels. However, it has also caused significant environmental challenges. To fuel its rapid industrialization, China consumes record amounts of coal as it builds new factories and energy plants. It has become the world's second largest emitter of greenhouse gases; in the next 10 years, it is even expected to surpass the United States, which holds first place.

This may seem like a concern mainly for the Chinese government and for international environmental protection agencies. However, lately the destruction of China's ecosystem has become a threat for multinational corporations as well. A lack of transparent laws concerning the environment has caused instability in the local workforce. The latter, in turn, creates uncertainty about the future and increases the risk faced by any multinational enterprise wishing to enter a developing market. Recent events in the northern Chinese province of Shanxi have presented an example.

In 2004 and 2005, Taiyuan, the capital of Shanxi province, offered incentives to electronic manufacturers to locate production facilities there as companies began to look for lower costs in inland provinces. Among the companies that moved to Taiyuan is Foxconn, one of Apple's suppliers of components of iPhones and iPads. Environmental groups have accused Foxconn, and a number of global companies with factories in Taiyuan, of not only emitting dangerous substances into the air but also discharging harmful chemicals into local water systems. The pollution of waterways, in turn, threatens both the health and lifestyle of local farmers: crops grown with

© AP Images/Kin Cheung, File

Students protesting Foxconn, known for its air and water pollution, at its Taiwanese Apple factories.

contaminated irrigation become substandard in quality and low in quantity.

Local officials, meanwhile, can be bribed into turning a blind eye to polluters to spur economic growth. Such laxity on their part could be viewed as an opportunity for foreign companies to utilize China's resources and cheap labor force without the limits and costs of environmental protection. However, employees and the local populace are increasingly unwilling to live with the environmental decision. In May 2011, a fire caused by a buildup of flammable dust in a Foxconn factory assembling iPads killed three workers. Already challenged by employee groups for substandard labor conditions, Foxconn needs to be concerned about embarrassing Apple, its major customer.

A multinational firm must carefully manage its supply chain to avoid tarnishing its brand and risking operational continuity. If local interests are capable of manipulating regulations, a multinational's production facility could easily be closed. A sudden change in laws (or their implementation) could threaten the entire input supply structure of an international company, particularly if its international subsidiaries depend on each other for resources and inputs.

Is it therefore better that an international corporation comes into China with stricter environmental laws than those existent in China itself? Should a firm adopt the local culture (including bribing) to be more in tune with local customs? Even with government support corporations are vulnerable to the concerns of other stakeholders.

SOURCES: Kathrin Hille and Leslie Hook, "Chinese Electronics Makers Fail to Keep It Clean," *Financial Times*, August 31, 2011; Emily Rauhala, "The Richest Reds in China," *Time*, April 4, 2008, www.time.com/time/world/article/0,8599,1728126,00.html, accessed February 20, 2012; and Cindy Sui, "China's Economic Development Creating Dire Consequences on Environment."

Intellectual Property

The development of a new product or technique by a corporation can be a lucrative endeavor, opening the door to a variety of benefits, such as a larger customer base, increased market share, or a reduction in production costs. However, innovation is also a vulnerable process. Statistics regarding the survival rates of new businesses vary from source to source; however, the probability for a new enterprise to fail in the first three years of existence can be as high as 85 percent.[34] This makes it important that an enterprise be able to recoup its investments into new products, including its research and development costs. However, competitors can make this more difficult if they are able to copy the innovation, thereby reducing the originator's market share and ability to profit. Finally, as "copycat" enterprises often try to beat the originator through lower prices, they wind up producing inferior products.

The term **intellectual property (IP)** refers to a legal entitlement of exclusive rights to use an idea, piece of knowledge, or invention. The subject of such legal claims must be a product of the mind—an intangible but potentially profitable form of property. In the past, intellectual property laws were usually territorial, meaning that the registration and enforcement of rights to certain knowledge had to be pursued separately in each country. Recently, however, IP laws have become increasingly harmonized across nations. TRIPs, or the WTO *Agreement on Trade-Related Aspects of Intellectual Property Rights,* was a significant step in this direction. Adopted in 1994, it introduced intellectual property law into the international trade system for the first time; included were minimum standards for copyrights, appellations of geographic origin, industrial designs, trademarks, and even trade secrets. Unlike other international agreements on the subject, TRIPS has powerful enforcement mechanisms (like trade sanctions) at its disposal. Its requirements apply equally to all WTO member states; developing countries are given more time to implement necessary changes. However, the act's fairness with regards to developing nations and their ability to patent is frequently contested.

Intellectual property is of key concern to various industries. For several years, the EU had struggled to reach a consensus regarding online music copyright laws—something it was finally able to achieve in 2008. Up to that point, music rights were sold separately in each European country, effectively preventing online music retailers, such as iTunes, from setting up a single service store for all of Europe. Instead, separate licenses had to be obtained from each member state, forcing iTunes to make considerable adjustments for each market in Europe. The change in regulations removed a major obstacle to iTunes' expansion. Not everybody is excited about the possibility of a pan-European music market. Some artists have protested that selling music rights across the EU might reduce their royalties. They have threatened to boycott the reform by refusing to allow their work to be played. More than 220 singers, musicians, and composers, including Sade, Julio Iglesias, and Mark Knopfler, have signed a petition stating that pan-European music licensing will stifle creativity.[35]

Another, more ethically charged issue with intellectual property rights is the availability of medicine. Many life-saving vaccines and remedies were initially developed by private enterprises; examples include the AIDS cocktail and Tamiflu (today's only bird flu–fighting drug). The issue, then, is whether a corporation ought to retain all rights to manufacture the drug even in times when its supply cannot satisfy world demand or when its prices are too high for those who need its product. Most patent laws permit, for a limited period of time, a corporation to refuse the manufacture of generic versions of its product. This provides it with the benefit of monopolizing an indispensable commodity.

Multinational corporations have been criticized for exercising this right, particularly in the case of the AIDS cocktail, given the numbers and the typical poverty of those infected with the disease. Cipla, India's third largest drug company, is one of many third-world producers who has offered to make the cocktail at a "humanitarian price"—one significantly lower than that negotiated by the United Nations for impoverished African countries. However, three large multinationals (one British, one German, and one American) hold the patents for the drugs involved. In South Africa, the country with the largest number of HIV infections, the firms have filed lawsuits against local generic producers of the cocktail. However, in light of mounting public outrage, they were forced to drop the lawsuits in order to extricate themselves from what had become a large-scale public relations morass. An unidentified drug company representative reportedly said: "People ask me, how we could have been so stupid as to sue Nelson Mandela?"[36]

Bribery and Corruption

In many countries, payments or favors are a way of life, and a "greasing of the wheels" is expected in return for government services. In the past, many U.S. companies doing business internationally routinely paid bribes or did favors for foreign officials in order to gain contracts. In the 1970s, major national debates erupted over these business practices, led by arguments that U.S. firms should provide ethical and moral leadership and that contracts won through bribes do not reflect competitive market activity. As a result, the Foreign Corrupt Practices Act (FCPA) was passed in 1977, making it a crime for U.S. firms to bribe foreign officials for business purposes.

A number of U.S. firms have complained about the act, arguing that it hinders their efforts to compete internationally against companies from countries that have no such antibribery laws. In-depth research supports this claim by indicating that in the years after the antibribery legislation was enacted, U.S. business activity in those countries in which government officials routinely received bribes declined significantly.[37] The problem is one of ethics versus practical needs and, to some extent, of the amounts involved. For example, it may be difficult to draw the line between providing a generous tip and paying a bribe in order to speed up a business transaction. Many business managers argue that one country should not apply its moral principles to other societies and cultures in which bribery and corruption are endemic. If they are to compete internationally, these managers argue, they must be free to use the most common methods of competition in the host country. Particularly in industries that face limited or even shrinking markets, such stiff competition forces firms to find any edge possible to obtain a contract.

On the other hand, applying different standards to management and firms depending on whether they do business abroad or domestically is difficult to envision. Also, bribes may open the way for shoddy performance and loose moral standards among managers and employees and may result in a spreading of generally unethical business practices. Unrestricted bribery could result in a concentration on how best to bribe rather than on how best to produce and market products.

The international manager must carefully distinguish between reasonable ways of doing business internationally—including compliance with foreign expectations—and outright bribery and corruption. To assist the manager in this task, revisions were made in the 1988 Trade Act to clarify the applicability of the Foreign Corrupt Practices legislation. These revisions clarify when a manager is expected to know about violation of the act, and a distinction is drawn between the facilitation of routine governmental actions and governmental policy decisions. Routine actions concern issues such as obtaining permits and licenses, processing governmental papers such as visas and work orders, providing mail and phone service, and loading and unloading cargo. Policy decisions refer mainly to situations in which obtaining or retaining contracts is at stake. One researcher differentiates between **functional lubrication** and individual greed. With regard to functional lubrication, he reports the "express fee" charged in many countries, which has several characteristics: the amount is small, it is standardized, and it does not stay in the hands of the official who receives it but is passed on to others involved in the processing of the documents. The express service is available to anyone, with few exceptions. By contrast, in the process driven by "individual greed," the amount depends on the individual official and is for the official's own personal use.[38] Although the facilitation of routine actions is not prohibited, the illegal influencing of policy decisions can result in the imposition of severe fines and penalties.

The issue of global bribery prevention has taken on new momentum. In 1995, the Organization of American States (OAS; **www.oas.org**) officially condemned bribery. The Organization for Economic Cooperation and Development

(OECD; www.oecd.org) in 2009 released a Recommendation for Further Combating Bribery of Foreign Public Officials to mark the 10th anniversary of the entry into force of its Anti-Bribery Convention. Following up on its previous efforts to change the bribery regulations among its member countries not only to prohibit the tax deductibility of improper payments but to prohibit such payments altogether, the OECD now provides guidelines for corporate good practices to combat bribery.[39] Similarly, the WTO has, for the first time, decided to consider placing bribery rules on its agenda. A good portion of this progress can be attributed to the public work done by Transparency International (TI). This nonprofit organization regularly publishes information about the perception of corruption in countries around the globe. In addition, TI also measures the perceived levels of public sector corruption as shown in Exhibit 5.7.

The Sarbanes-Oxley Act of 2002 is intended to protect investors by improving the accuracy and reliability of corporate disclosures. The act covers issues like corporate responsibility, financial transparency, and accounting oversight. Major provisions include the certification of financial reports by CEOs and CFOs and a requirement for publicly traded companies to furnish annual reports on the reliability of their internal financial reporting structures. This was considered a highly significant change to U.S. security laws.

There are questions regarding the law's effectiveness and the cost-benefit rationale for compliance. Some estimate that the cost of being a publicly traded company doubled within a few months of the law's enactment, from $1.3 million to $2.5 million. Business leaders have also expressed concerns about disclosing too much information to the competition.[40]

The act seems to be effective in changing the way companies operate in the developing world—a fortunate and unexpected side effect of a law targeting domestic business relations. By requiring corporate directors and CEOs to personally certify their companies' internal controls and by making executives who provide false certifications criminally liable, the law inadvertently led to the emergence of an entire industry of global compliance auditors. These auditors are effective in finding the "offshore intermediaries" that help companies to sidestep the 1977 Foreign Corrupt Practices Act (which prohibited payoffs to foreign

EXHIBIT 5.7 Corruption Perceptions Index 2010*

Least Corrupt			Most Corrupt		
Rank	**Country**	**CPI Score**	**Rank**	**Country**	**CPI Score**
1	Denmark	9.3	178	Somalia	1.1
1	New Zealand	9.3	176	Myanmar	1.4
1	Singapore	9.3	176	Afghanistan	1.4
4	Finland	9.2	175	Iraq	1.5
4	Sweden	9.2	172	Uzbekistan	1.6
6	Canada	8.9	172	Turkmenistan	1.6
7	Netherlands	8.8	172	Sudan	1.6
8	Australia	8.7	171	Chad	1.7
8	Switzerland	8.7	170	Burundi	1.8
10	Norway	8.6	168	Equatorial Guinea	1.9

*A country's Corruption Perception Index score shows the degree of public sector corruption perceived by businesspeople and country analysts. Possible scores range from 10 (very clean) to 0 (highly corrupt). The top 10 least corrupt and most corrupt countries are shown above along with their world ranks and CPI scores.

SOURCE: Transparency International, *Corruption Perceptions Index 2010* (University of Passau, Germany: Transparency International), www.transparency.org, accessed August 3, 2011.

officials). The result has been a sharp increase in the number of companies cleaning up their overseas procedures and self-reporting illegal payments overseas.

The United States is not the only country with strict laws against corrupt practices overseas. In 2010, the U.K. Parliament passed the Anti-Bribery Reform Law, an even more stringent act that extends liability to organizations that do not have adequate programs to prevent bribery. Companies operating in the United Kingdom now need to ensure that their antibribery compliance programs are rigorous enough to prevent exposure to legal liability.[41]

A critical issue for international marketers is general standards of behavior and ethics. Increasingly, public concerns are raised about such issues as global warming, pollution, and moral behavior. However, these issues are not of the same importance in every country. What may be frowned on or even illegal in one nation may be customary or at least acceptable in others. For example, cutting down the Brazilian rainforest may be acceptable to the government of Brazil, but scientists, concerned consumers, and environmentalists may object vehemently because of the effect of global warming and other climatic changes. The export of U.S. tobacco products may be legal but results in accusations of exporting death to developing nations. China may use prison labor in producing products for export, but U.S. law prohibits the importation of such products. Mexico may permit the use of low safety standards for workers, but the buyers of Mexican products may object to the resulting dangers. In the area of moral behavior, firms are increasingly not just subject to government rules but are also held accountable by the public at large. For example, issues such as child labor, inappropriately low wages, or the running of sweatshops are raised by concerned individuals and communicated to customers. Firms can then be subject to public scorn, consumer boycotts, and investor scrutiny if their actions are seen as reprehensible, and they run the danger of losing much more money than they gained by engaging in such practices.

One major development in Europe, particularly in Germany, is an effort to return to the concept of **ehrbarer Kaufmann** (honorable merchant). This concept, which emerged in the sixteenth century, focuses on maintaining long-term successful international trade efforts with distant and often unfamiliar people. Key requirements are a good understanding of other cultures, dedicated research and planning for opportunities (one could not afford to have a ship travel home empty), and scrupulous honesty so that there always would be the ability to return for more business. There is no room for bribery and corruption with the honorable merchant.

SUMMARY

The political and legal environment in the home country, the environment in the host country, and the laws and agreements governing relationships among nations are all important to the international marketer. Compliance with them is mandatory in order to successfully do business abroad. Such laws can control exports and imports both directly and indirectly and can also regulate the international business behavior of firms, particularly in the areas of boycotts, antitrust, corruption, and ethics.

To avoid the problems that can result from changes in the political and legal environment, the international marketer must anticipate changes and develop strategies for coping with them. Whenever possible, the manager must avoid being taken by surprise and thus not let events control business decisions.

On occasion, the international marketer may be caught between clashing home- and host-country laws. In such instances, the firm needs to conduct a dialogue with the governments in order to seek a compromise solution. Alternatively, managers can encourage their government to engage in government-to-government negotiations to settle the dispute. By demonstrating the business volume at stake and the employment that may be lost through such governmental disputes, government negotiators can often be motivated to press hard for a settlement of such intergovernmental difficulties. Finally, the firm can seek redress in court. Such international legal action, however, may be quite slow and, even if it results in a favorable judgment for the firm, may not be adhered to by the government against which the judgment is rendered.

In the final analysis, a firm conducting business internationally is subject to the vagaries of political and legal changes and may lose business as a result. The best the manager can do is to be aware of political influences and laws and strive to adopt them as far as possible.

KEY TERMS

Environmental Superfund
intellectual property rights
gray market
trade sanctions
embargo
export control system
dual-use item
export license
foreign availability
tariffs
voluntary restraint agreement
quota system
downstream change
boycott
political risk
ownership risk
operating risk
transfer risk
expropriation
confiscation
domestication
overinvest
price controls
theocracy
common law
code law
antidumping law
terminology
lobbyist
stateless corporation
chill effect
corporate governance
intellectual property (IP)
functional lubrication
Sarbanes-Oxley Act
ehrbarer Kaufmann

QUESTIONS FOR DISCUSSION

1. Discuss this statement: "High political risk requires companies to seek a quick payback on their investments. Striving for such a quick payback, however, exposes firms to charges of exploitation and results in increased political risk."
2. Can countries effectively control rising prices of domestic agricultural production through export controls?
3. How appropriate is it for governments to help drum up business for their companies abroad? Should commerce be completely separate from politics?
4. Discuss this statement: "The national security that export control laws seek to protect may be threatened by the resulting lack of international competitiveness of firms."
5. After you hand your passport to the immigration officer in country X, he misplaces it. A small "donation" would certainly help him find it again. Should you give him money? Is this a business expense to be charged to your company? Should it be tax deductible?
6. Discuss the advantages and disadvantages of common versus code law for the international marketer.
7. Are global corporations subject to international law?
8. The United States has been described as a litigious society. How does frequent litigation affect the international marketer, particularly in comparison with the situation in other countries?
9. What are your views on lobbying efforts by foreign firms?
10. Discuss how changes in technology have affected the effectiveness of U.S. export control policy.
11. What attributes should an "ehrbarer Kaufmann" possess today?

INTERNET EXERCISES

1. Summarize the U.S. export licensing policy toward Cuba. What countries are the most restricted destinations for U.S. exports? (Go to the Business of Industry and Security site www.bis.doc.gov.)
2. What are the key components of the anticorruption agreements passed by the European Union, the Organization of American States, and the United Nations? (Go to the OECD at www.oecd.org

or Transparency International at www.transparency.org.)

3. What are the key provisions of the U Bribery Act of 2010? (View the Act at www.justice.gov.uk/guidance/docs/bribery-act-2010-guidance.pdf.)
4. What South American countries are currently rated as high-risk countries for payment transfers and payment default? (Consult Euler Hermes, the leading German credit insurer, at www.eulerhermes-aktuell.de/en/country-ratings/south-america.html.)

CHALLENGE US

Bribery and Corruption

Bribery and corruption continues to be a major international business challenge. Some firms claim that in many countries, public sector contracts can simply not be obtained unless major payments are made to government officials. Furthermore, the Foreign Corrupt Practices Act of the United States (FCPA) exposes companies and their managers doing business in the U.S. to harsh financial penalties and prison sentences if they violate the FCPA. On the other hand, many competing firms are said to bribe their way to the contract. Such action is particularly onerous, when a specific project serves as the entryway into subsequent, much larger business activities.

In consequence, some firms keep at a distance from their foreign appointed middlemen and agents, since they do not want to know the details how the contract was won. Others develop in-house formal antibribery programs which all employees must learn about.

For Discussion

1. As a shareholder, how do you evaluate the need for companies to go beyond the letter of the law?

RECOMMENDED READINGS

Fergusson, Ian F., and Paul K. Kerr. "The U.S. Export Control System and the President's Reform Initiative." Congressional Research Service report for Congress, 2011. Available at www.hsdl.org/?view&did=682402.

Hirschhorn, Eric. *The Export Control and Embargo Handbook*, 3rd ed. Oxford University Press, 2010.

Howard, Russell, Reid Sawyer, and Natasha Bajema, *Terrorism and Counterterrorism: Understanding the New Security Environment, Readings and Interpretations*, 4th ed. New York: Graw-Hill/Dushkin, 2011.

Hufbauer, Gary C., Jeffrey J. Schott, Kimberly Ann Elliott, and Barbara Oegg. *Economic Sanctions Reconsidered*, 3rd ed. Washington, DC: Peterson Institute, 2009.

Lambsdorff, Johann Graf. *The Institutional Economics of Corruption and Reform: Theory, Evidence and Policy.* Cambridge, UK: Cambridge University Press, 2008.

Organization for Economic Co-operation and Development (OECD), Working Group on Bribery. *2010 Annual Report*. Available at www.oecd.org/dataoecd/7/15/47628703.pdf.

U.S. Department of Commerce, Bureau of Industry and Security. *Annual Report 2010*. Available at www.bis.doc.gov/news/2011/bis_annual_report_2010.pdf.

United Nations Conference on Trade and Development (UNCTAD). *World Investment Report 2011*. Available online at www.unctad.org/Templates/WebFlyer.asp?intItemID=6018&lang=1.

World Economic Forum. *Global Risks Report 2011*. [Interactive multimedia report]. Available at http://riskreport.weforum.org.

ENDNOTES

1. Gary C. Hufbauer, Jeffrey J. Schott, Kimberly Ann Elliott, and Barbara Oegg. *Economic Sanctions Reconsidered*, 3rd ed. (Washington, DC: Peterson Institute, 2008).
2. Robin Renwick, *Economic Sanctions* (Cambridge, MA: Harvard University Press, 1981), 11.
3. U.S. Department of the Treasury, Office of Foreign Assets Control, "Somalia: What You Need to Know about Sanctions against Persons Contributing to the Conflict in Somalia," September 2010.
4. Gary C. Hufbauer, Jeffery J. Schott, Kimberly Ann Elliott, and Barbara Oegg, *op. cit.*
5. Michael R. Czinkota and Erwin Dichtl, "Export Controls and Global Changes," *Der Markt* 37, no. 5 (1996): 148–55.
6. Kevin Gray, "Argentina Defends Export Taxes in Farm Conflict," Reuters, June 17, 2008, http://uk.reuters.com/article/2008/06/17/idUKN1738140020080617.

7. Warren Hoge and Elaine Sciolino, "Security Council Adds Sanctions against Iran," *New York Times*, March 4, 2008, www.nytimes.com/2008/03/04/world/middleeast/04nations.html.
8. We are grateful to David Danjczek for his helpful comments.
9. E. M. Hucko, *Aussenwirtschaftsrecht-Kriegswaffenkontrollrecht, Textsammlungmit Einführung*, 4th ed. (Köln, Germany: Bundesanzeiger, 1993).
10. www.investorwords.com, accessed December 3, 2011.
11. "Oil Ship Hijacked on the Niger Delta," *BBC News*, May 14, 2008, http://news.bbc.co.uk/2/hi/africa/7400263.stm.
12. Richard Miniter, "Obama, Chavez and the American Shareholder," Forbes.com, January 12, 2011.
13. See Trade Related Aspects of International Property Rights (TRIPS), www.wto.org/english/tratop_e/trips_e/trips_e.htm.
14. Overseas Private Investment Corporation (OPIC), www.opic.gov, accessed August 30, 2011.
15. Stephen P. Magee, "The Optimum Number of Lawyers," working paper (University of Texas, Austin, December 2010).
16. Surya Prakash Sinha, *What Is Law? The Differing Theories of Jurisprudence* (New York: Paragon House, 1989).
17. *National Trade Estimate Report on Foreign Trade Barriers* (Washington, DC: Office of the United States Trade Representative, 2010), www.ustr.gov/about-us/press-office/reports-and-publications/2010.
18. See Office of the United States Trade Representative, Document Library, www.ustr.gov.
19. We are grateful to Professor Ed Soule of Georgetown University for this example.
20. Center for Responsive Politics, www.opensecrets.org, accessed August 30, 2011.
21. American League of Lobbyists, www.alldc.org/ethicscode.cfm, accessed August 9, 2011.
22. "Brown Condemns Iceland over Banks," *BBC News*, October 10, 2008, http://news.bbc.co.uk/2/hi/uk_news/politics/7662027.stm.
23. Lee Levkowitz and Nathan Beauchamp-Mustafaga, "China Rare Earths Industry and Its Role in the International Market," U.S.-China Economic and Security Review Commission, November 3, 2010, www.uscc.gov/researchpapers/2011/RareEarthsBackgrounderFINAL.pdf.
24. Michael R. Czinkota and Gary Knight, "The Effects of Terrorism on International Marketing," in *Anthology on Global Marketing*, ed. G. Svensson (Honolulu, HI: Anthology Marketing Group, 2009).
25. National Counterterrorism Center, *2010 Report on Terrorism*, April 30, 2011, www.nctc.gov/witsbanner/docs/2010_report_on_terrorism.pdf.
26. Michael R. Czinkota, Gary Knight, and Gabriele Suder, "Terrorism and International Business: Looking Back and Striving Forward," *Japan Today*, September 8, 2011.
27. Ibid.
28. Sheffi Jossi, *The Resilient Enterprise* (Cambridge, MA: MIT Press, 2005).
29. Michael R. Czinkota and Gary Knight, "On the Front Line: Marketers Combat Global Terrorism," *Marketing Management*, May/June 2005, 33–39.
30. Michael R. Czinkota, Gary Knight, and Gabriele Suder, *op. cit.*
31. Michael R. Czinkota, "International Marketing and Terrorism Preparedness," Testimony before the Congress of the United States, 109th Congress, Committee on Small Business, Washington, DC, November 1, 2005.
32. We are very grateful for input within this section from Professor Michael Moffett of Thunderbird University.
33. Michael R. Czinkota, Ilkka A. Ronkainen, and Bob Donath, *Mastering Global Markets* (Mason, OH: Thomson South-Western, 2004), 362.
34. Robert Sullivan, *Small Business Start-Up Guide*, Chapter 1: Prologue, www.isquare.com/prologue.cfm, accessed December 4, 2011.
35. Amy Kapczynski, "Strict International Patent Laws Hurt Developing Countries," *Yale Global*, http://yaleglobal.yale.edu/content/strict-international-patent-laws-hurt-developing-countries, accessed December 4, 2011.
36. Aoife White, "E.U. Changes Music Copyright Rules, Benefiting Online Stores," *Washington Post*, July 17, 2008, D07.
37. James R. Hines, Jr., *Forbidden Payment: Foreign Bribery and American Business after 1977*, working paper 5266 (Cambridge, MA: National Bureau of Economic Research, September 1995), 1.
38. Magoroh Maruyama, "Bribing in Historical Context: The Case of Japan," *Human Systems Management* 15 (1996): 138–42.
39. OECD Convention on Combating Bribery of Foreign Public Officials in International Business Transactions, www.oecd.org, accessed October 4, 2011.
40. Alix Stuart, "Keeping It to Themselves," *CFO magazine*, April 1, 2008, www.cfo.com/article.cfm/10941670/c_10941875?f=insidecfo.
41. PWC, "The UK Bribery Act," www.pwc.co.uk/eng/issues/bribery_act.html, accessed August 3, 2011.

CASES

PART 1

Super Foods: Camu Camu in Peru

"Superfoods" is a new term attributed to physician Steven Pratt[1] who used it as a title for his book in 2003. He pointed out that there are certain types of foods that are beneficial to human health beyond the conventional nutritional values. Although there is no legal or technical definition, the term "superfoods" has become a trendy topic. A Google search yields more than six million results.[2] Superfoods promise an ideal goal sought by many consumers: a product that improves life expectancy and also combats increasing obesity that developed countries, like the United States, are facing.[3] Superfoods originated in Japan in the 1980s. Health authorities recognized that an increased life expectancy should be accompanied by improved quality of life for the expanding elderly population. Also, health care costs could be controlled through the consumption of healthy food.[4] Superfoods are a dynamic product within a larger market, called the function foods market. According to Health Canada:

> *A functional food is similar in appearance to, or may be, a conventional food that is consumed as part of a usual diet, and is demonstrated to have physiological benefits and/or reduce the risk of chronic disease beyond basic nutritional functions, i.e. they contain bioactive compounds.*[5]

Functional foods and beverages account for roughly $40 billion of U.S. retail sales.[6] For the past decade, several products have been showcased in the market with emphasis on their nutritional properties. For example, Oprah Winfrey and Dr. Oz raised the antioxidant properties of acai berries.[7] Supermodel Miranda Kerr explained her consumption of maca powder along with noni juice and acai berry powder[8] as part of her daily diet. In global terms, Japan is the leading market for these products, followed by the United States. The functional food and drink market is outpacing the conventional food and drink market in terms of global growth by about 4 percent per year, according to a Leatherhead Food Research report from June 2011.[9] The fastest growing category within the functional foods market are beverages.

However, in spite of its growth, this segment suffers from a high rate of product failure for newcomers; as many as 80 percent of product launches fail to catch on due to inadequate marketing, consumer, and trade education.[10]

THE POTENTIAL OF NATIVE PRODUCTS: CAMU CAMU

Camu camu (*Myrciaria dubia*) is a small tree or shrub that grows in the Amazon regions of Peru. It typically grows in the flooded areas near the river. Its fruit contains high levels of natural vitamin C, ranging from 1,500 to 2,000, and in some exceptional cases 3,130 mg of ascorbic acid per 100 grs of fresh pulp.[11] To put this into context, camu camu contains up to 30 times more vitamin C than an orange. (An interesting video about this fruit can be found at www.youtube.com/watch?v=CYCUdy0ljGc.[12]) In addition to its antioxidative power, this fruit has proven to have anti-inflammatory properties,[13] making it effective at promoting a healthy diet. Other key properties include astringent, anti-viral, emollient, and nutritive properties, and it contains natural beta-carotene, calcium, iron, niacin, phosphorus, protein, riboflavin, thiamin, and the amino acids valine, leucine, and serine.[14] Camu camu has the potential to be used as a dietary supplement as well as for functional beverages such as Coca Cola's Minute Maid "Camu Camu & Vitamin" drink in Japan[15] and the Super Fruits Mix variety of the Fanta brand that includes a blend of camu camu with other fruits like pomegranate, mangosteen, and white grape.[16] Companies in the natural ingredients sector are starting to capitalize on the potential of camu camu as a "super-fruit." An example of this trend comes from Navitas Naturals, a U.S. company that started with maca (another Peruvian ingredient) and now sells a range of 25 products, all of which are functional foods. (To see camu camu's possible uses in food

SOURCE: Written by Guadalupe Amésquita, biotrade specialist, Universidad Nacional Mayor de San Marcos; and Juan Carlos Schiappa-Pietra, marketing advisor of small business, Lima, Peru.

you can take a look at www.youtube.com/watch?v=nun5oIFXj94&feature=related.)

UNDERSTANDING MARKET BARRIERS

Although accessing international markets is not an easy path for "superfoods," success also has its complications. Even when a superfood, like camu camu, is known in its country of origin, it is not necessarily easily accepted in other countries. The following are examples of market access barriers that represent a challenge for making camu camu a bigger star. The same rules apply to any other exotic food.

U.S. Market

When entering the U.S., all products for human consumption must have an FDA authorization for the commercialization of that product. The FDA's website provides for an interesting compilation of warning letters regarding compliance or misclassification of products.[17] The main barrier occurs when marketing the product: If a company which wants to sell the product makes health claims, it must request permission to sell the product as a drug with all paperwork and information that comes with that request (such as scientific support). However, if the company sells it as a food, or eventually as a dietary supplement under the Dietary Supplement Health and Education Act of 1994 (DSHEA),[18] then permissions are handled on a different basis.

Camu camu is currently sold in the U.S. as a dietary supplement in the form of liquid concentrate, extract in capsules, juices, powder, as well as in chocolate bars and shakes.

The European Union Market

Camu camu is considered a novel food in the European Union according to Regulation EC258/97, which states the following: *Foods and food ingredients that have not been used for human consumption to a significant degree in the EU before 15 May 1997 are "novel foods" and "novel food ingredients."*[19] The above statement covers all exotic foods coming from countries with a rich biodiversity. This regulation represents a considerable challenge to any company that wants to sell novel foods or beverages in any EU country. It must present a dossier of the product in its specific presentation with supporting evidence of its safety. The cost of preparing a novel food dossier ranges between US$390,000 and US$780,000,[20] a sum unattainable for small businesses. The novel food regulation does not cover uses of specific ingredients or products such as camu camu as a dietary supplement. The latter category is monitored under Directive 2009/39/EC. Firms need to recognize that:

- The role of governments to assure safety for their citizens, as well as the prevention of false claims, is getting stronger.
- Consumers are increasingly informed. The Internet has become not only a good source of information but also a place where many people can find reports or scientific support.
- The "newer" the product in a market, the more it will have to support its properties with sufficient evidence or historical record of usage. Many products are based on tradition and use by the native population for centuries.

NAVITAS NATURALS' BET ON FUNCTIONAL FOOD

Navitas is the Latin word for "energy" and "zest." According to its founder, Zach Adelman, this word embodies the company spirit of bringing ancient power foods to the modern consumer, and also how consumers feel after consuming these products.

Back in 2003, Incan nutritional wisdom was an unexpected discovery for Adelman. His first encounter was with maca, an Andean tuber that grows in the high-altitude regions of the Peruvian Andes. The promise of its nutritional value and properties made it a commercial success.

The company began to grow rapidly. To remain true to its vision, it searched the world for functional foods that have been used by traditional cultures for both medicinal and nourishment purposes. Many of these foods have been consumed for thousands of years.

New additions were like cacao nibs, goji berries, and incan berries by 2005. Increasing demand grew the product range to 26 over the past five years. Camu-camu did not go unnoticed. Navitas added the miraculous superfruit to its products list in 2010 and named it "Camu Powder."

In July 2011, the company launched a healthy snacks line, combining the power of all superfoods within their product range with camu camu as part of one combination: the *Citrus Chia Power Snack*, along with chia seeds, maca, and lucuma superfoods, as well as apricot, raisin, cashew, and coconut flakes.

Navitas started in a tiny facility on Hamilton Drive in Novato, California, back in 2003, but the steady growth forced it to move to larger quarters in Pamaron Way in the same city in 2011. The firm achieved GMP/HACCP third-party certifications in 2009.[21]

Nowadays, Navitas Naturals imports foods from Peru (maca, camu camu, lucuma, yacon, and cacao), Colombia (incan berries), Brazil (acai), China (goji berries), Mexico (chia seeds), and Turkey (mulberries), while expanding its sales throughout North America. Distribution channels not only include retailers like Whole Foods or Mrs. Green's in the U.S., but also dietary supplement stores like Manna Foods or Canadian National Nutrition.

IDENTIFYING A STRATEGY

It is important to note that with the increasing demand for healthy foods, consumers are also seeking products with special certifications, such as organic, that ensure truly natural products. Functional foods comprise most often these types of products, as well as fairtrade products, which add social sustainability into the equation.

© Ildi Papp/Shutterstock.com

Navitas Naturals' strategy to capitalize on the functional foods market is clearly aligned with the company's philosophy:

- Provide high-quality superfoods.
- Special certifications as a differentiation element: Organic, Raw, Fairtrade, and Kosher.
- Social responsibility approach.
- Consumer education in order to sustain market growth. As an example, the company took advantage of Internet tools such as YouTube to spread the company's story and values with short videos about its products.[22]
- Mostly Wild Crafted (as an added-value feature).

Navitas' mission is "*to provide premium organic functional foods that increase energy and enhance health.*"[23] Along with a healthy lifestyle comes also the responsibility of buying from local businesses to give back to the communities providing these resources. "An essential part of our mission is to create economic opportunities among indigenous people in developing countries," says Zach. The company's support of native agriculture helps to expand the development of global organic farming practices and economic development among indigenous people by increasing demand for the health-enhancing foods they produce. Thus the firm creates a virtuous cycle for suppliers, consumers, and itself.

QUESTIONS FOR DISCUSSION

1. If no immediate change regarding the Novel Food Regulation (EU) is foreseen, what could be an alternate use of camu camu?
2. What brand strategy is Navitas following to "adapt" camu camu to the U.S. market?
3. Would you recommend that Peru use the same brand strategy Navitas is using in the U.S. and in other international markets?
4. Amazon Herbs follows the U.S. camu camu importation strategy. Would you recommend this strategy to other American importers of camu camu?
5. What international marketing strategy would you recommend to Peru in order to promote camu camu in the North American market?

ENDNOTES

1. http://newhope360.com/functional/natural-and-organic-food-glossary.
2. As of January 29, 2011.
3. Almost two-thirds of the adult population in the U.S. present overweight problems. with one-third being obese; see http://thevisualmd.com/health_centers/nutrition_and_metabolism_health/obesity/obesity_video.
4. www.eufic.org/article/en/expid/basics-functional-foods.
5. www4.agr.gc.ca/AAFC-AAC/display-afficher.do?id=1171305207040&lang=eng.
6. www.nutraceuticalsworld.com/issues/2011-07/view_features/formulation-trends-in-functional-foods-amp-beverag.
7. www.oprah.com/health/Acai-Dr-Perricones-No-1-Superfood.
8. www.koraorganics.com/blog/live-in-my-skin/all-things-organic/organic-certification/some-of-my-favourite-supplements-2.
9. www.nutritionaloutlook.com/news/leatherhead-functional-foods-market-grow-228-2014.
10. www.foodproductdesign.com/galleries/2011/06/functional-foods-report.aspx.
11. "Camu Camu Factsheets," Nicolas Dostert, José Roque, Grischa Brokamp, Asunción Cano, María I. La Torre and Maximilian Weigend/botconsult GMBH. Museo de Historia Natural Universidad Nacional Mayor de San Marcos, May 2009.
12. See also www.youtube.com/watch?v=ONsd7Uzcrfo.
13. "Tropical Fruit Camu-camu (*Myrciaria dubia*) Has Anti-oxidative and Anti-inflammatory Properties," *Journal of*

Cardiology 52 (2008), 127–32, www.ititropicals.com/News_Library/camu-camu.pdf.
14. www.sgn80.com/UserUploads/documents/Camu_Camu_Lit.pdf.
15. www.asiafoodjournal.com/article/camu-camu-beverage-japan/4665.
16. www.foodbev.com/gallery/new-drinks-in-japan-december-2010.
17. www.fda.gov/ICECI/EnforcementActions/WarningLetters/default.htm.
18. www.fda.gov/food/dietarysupplements/default.htm.
19. http://ec.europa.eu/food/food/biotechnology/novelfood/index_en.htm.
20. www.foodbev.com/article/novel-foods-now-and-in-the-future.
21. Implementation of HACCP in the U.S. is compulsory only for some food categories.
22. To watch some of their videos as part of their strategy please refer to www.youtube.com/watch?v=otIPmd2oeZA.
23. As stated in www.amazon.com/Navitas-Naturals-Crafted-Rainforest-Superfruit/dp/B001CGRNME.

African Producers in the Cut Flower and Foliage Trade

The floriculture trade constitutes the production, export, and consumption of cut flowers, foliage, young plants, and trees. It is one of the flourishing industries between the developed and developing countries in recent times.

When the trade started in the seventeenth century, both production and consumption concentrated at and around the same destinations; i.e., the consumers themselves mostly produced the product. The leading actors included Germany, France, and Japan. In the last 30 years, the trade has gradually grown to involve other participating countries. Now a new trend has evolved where much of the production is carried out in new emerging production centres mostly in developing countries, which have better climatic conditions and cheaper labour and energy supplies. These countries include Ethiopia, Kenya, Zimbabwe, and Ghana in Africa, and Colombia, Ecuador, and Israel.

Cut flowers and foliage are considered together because both of them have similar uses; they could be combined to make bouquets. Additionally they both have the same markets and same or similar marketing channels. The factors leading to the involvement of African producers in both the flower and foliage trade and concludes on what African producers can do to sustain their place in the chain. It will focus mostly on Kenyan, Ethiopian, and Ghanaian producers (Kenya and Ethiopia are already advanced producers whilst Ghana has a very young industry) and the Netherlands, which is the main market for African producers.

The products under review are described by the Combined Nomenclature (CN) for statistics in the European Union as follows:

- Cut flowers and flower buds of a kind suitable for bouquets or for ornamental purposes (060310).
- Foliage, branches, and other parts of plants, without flowers or flower buds, suitable for bouquets or for ornamental purposes (0604).

CUT FLOWERS

In 2009 the exported value of fresh cut flowers amounted to over $6.4 billion according to the International Trade Centre (ITC) Trade Map Statistics (COMTRADE). The Netherlands was the leading exporter with a value of $3.4 billion, followed by Colombia ($1 billion), Ecuador ($498,489), Kenya ($245,692), Belgium ($164,632), Ethiopia ($131,440), and Zimbabwe ($115,565). The main product traded was roses. Anthurium and heliconias are, however, gaining importance as tropical flowers from Africa.

FOLIAGE

Foliage cultivation and exports from Africa do not command the same significant place as cut flowers. They are relatively lower and less attractive than flowers because of high transportation costs (due to the exceptionally heavy weight or volume of many tropical species) and relative monotony of their colours. Additionally, they can be replaced by other flora products in a bouquet. In 2009, total foliage exports according to the ITC Trade Map amounted to US$1.1 billion with Netherlands being the main exporter. Ghana exported only US$519,000.

MARKET FOR AFRICA'S CUT FLOWERS AND FOLIAGE

The main market for cut flowers and foliage from Africa is the European Union, as it is for much of its horticulture product. The obvious reasons are proximity to the market, lower cost of transportation, and longer shelf life of these delicate products. (It is for these same reasons that Colombia is the major market for the United States of America.)

The total value of exports of all cut flowers, foliage and cut greens, and pot plants amounted to €10 billion worldwide in 2009 according to the Union Fleurs International Flowers Association, whose membership accounts for around 80 percent of this value. Here again, the major players in the worldwide export and import floricultural trade, e.g., the Netherlands, Colombia, Kenya, Ecuador, Germany, and Italy, are represented in the organization.

Foliage and tropical flowers constitute a growing niche market for African producers. Bouquets enjoy comparative advantage because as a speciality product, they involve a labor-intensive process, which is cheaper and more available in Africa and other developing countries. However, this is still not a captive market for

---

SOURCE: Agnes Gifty Adgei-Sam, principal export development officer and head of Ghana Export Trade Information Centre, Ghana Export Promotion Council, http://cbi.nl/marketinfo/cbi/products/cut_flowers_and_foliage.

EXHIBIT 1 List of Exporters of Fresh Cut Flowers and Flower Buds for Bouquet or Ornamental Purposes

Exporters	Trade Indicators
	Value exported in 2009 (USD thousand)
World	6,466,810
Netherlands	3,464,203
Colombia	1,040,382
Ecuador	498,489
Kenya	245,692
Belgium	164,623
Ethiopia	131,440
Zimbabwe	116,565

SOURCE: ITC calculations based on COMTRADE statistics.

EXHIBIT 2 List of Exporters of Foliage and Branches

Exporters	Trade Indicators
	Value exported in 2009 (USD thousand)
World	1,139,966
Netherlands	221,078
Denmark	165,691
USA	115,473
Colombia	3,471
Kenya	1,041
Ecuador	998
Ghana	519 (Mirror Statistics)

SOURCE: ITC Calculations based on COMTRADE statistics.

developing countries because of two major challenges: the ever-changing fashions/trends with regards to colors and combinations; and the strong negative influence on quality of dense packing of foliage for transportation in order to reduce freight costs.

Demand for different foliage varieties (particularly small-leafed foliage to make cheap bouquets) is becoming a trend for importers who use tropical foliage. Price competition has become a strong determinant toward growing flowers and foliage in low-cost countries, in particular developing countries enjoying duty-free status. However, with a view to minimizing high air freight costs it is more economical to send large quantities to one single destination, primarily Amsterdam when it comes to exports into Europe. This is why the Netherlands has become an important trade destination for Africa for the flower trade. Through the auction markets, the Netherlands imports large quantities of cut flowers and reexports to other countries in the European Union. In the same vein, producers from Africa do less direct exports to wholesalers because of high air freight costs.

USAGE OF FLOWERS AND BOUQUETS IN AFRICA

It is noteworthy that the local consumption of flowers in Africa (apart from South Africa) is almost nil; flower usage is not a cultural practice in most African countries. Many Africans do not value and therefore do not use flowers the way they are used in the developed countries. According to a grower in Ghana, Ghanaians are not familiar with fresh cut flowers. Out of the 300,000 kilos of heliconias the company produced in 2010, the local market consumed less than 1 percent. Indeed, the little that were bought were not for individual use in homes nor given as gifts. They were rather bought by hotels, by government institutions for use during the organization of international programs, and the rest for wreaths during funerals. Some affluent people may grow some flowers and foliage in their homes and keep nice landscapes and large potted plants which are prepared to last for years. During occasions like Mothers' Day, Christmas, and Valentine's Day, people prefer to give and receive "multi-purpose" gifts such as dresses, shoes, and sometimes chocolates. The story is not very different from Kenya, Ethiopia, and Tanzania.

This low to nil competition between the local and international consumption of African-produced flowers is significant; it could be considered as one of the reasons why exports of cut flowers from Africa to the European Union is flourishing. South Africa produces flowers and foliage, but it also consumes much of its own production. China also has become one of the largest cut flower producing as well as consuming countries in recent years. Kenya, Ethiopia, and Ghana export almost all of the flowers and foliage they produce.

In spite of not being familiar with the use of flowers to express emotion, the men and women who work in flower fields in Africa have been trained to understand the intricacies involved in producing good quality and nice flowers, which must reach the final consumers in good time and condition.

THE CUT FLOWER CHAIN

Cut flowers are highly perishable and very quickly lose their usefulness if their production and handling is not properly done. The chain process is therefore marked by a highly efficient coordination of activities between the producers from Africa and the final consumers in homes and offices in Europe.

EXHIBIT 3 **Cut Flower Chain**

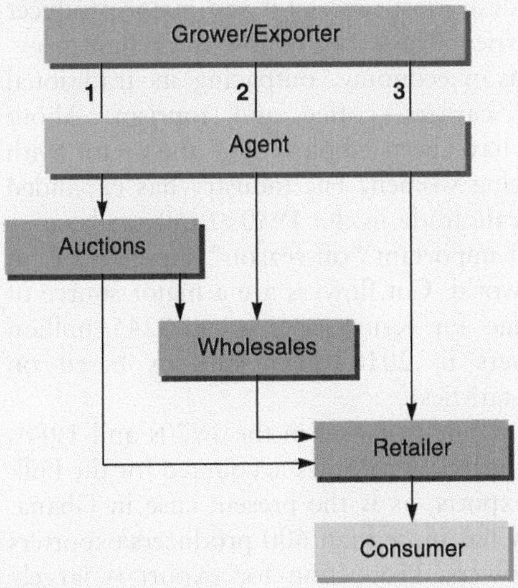

The Structure of the Production

The participation of African producers in the cut flower trade is as a buyer-driven commodity chain. Buyer-driven commodity chains are those industries in which large retailers, marketers, and branded manufacturers play the pivotal roles in setting up decentralized production networks in a variety of exporting countries, typically located in the Third World. This pattern of trade-led industrialization has become common in labor-intensive, consumer goods industries such as garments, footwear, toys, housewares, consumer electronics, and a variety of handicrafts. Production is generally carried out by tiered networks of Third World contractors that make finished goods for foreign buyers. The specifications are supplied by the large retailers or marketers that order the goods.

Many of the successful flower and foliage producers in Africa are part of the production process of bigger chains in Europe. Even though cut flower farming cannot be said to be as industrialized as the garment industry, it is a very labor-intensive industry. The production processes cannot be mechanized; humans are needed to plant, weed, water, nurse, harvest, sort, clean, and pack the products for the market. Close to 60,000 people are employed in the Kenya cut flower industry. MDK in Ghana currently employs 100 workers on its 15-hectare farm. This kind of labor is definitely not available or cheap in Europe.

As in a typical buyer-driven commodity chain, it is also the buyers that determine and dictate the "design" and trends in the trade. Codes and quality requirements are given by the market and must be complied with by flower producers. In Kenya, small holder cut flower farming is decreasing because of the inability of these farmers to comply with the many ever changing quality requirements.

Ghana

The floriculture industry is relatively young in Ghana even though endogenous factors like good climate, strategic location on the equator to guarantee all year-round production, and cheap labor exist to facilitate production of the product. Many Ghanaian producers are interested in products that could also be eaten in the event of their not being exported. Some local flower farm workers in Ghana expressed their initial skepticism about the industry as follows: "… why produce cut flowers if you also can produce rice which at least you can eat!" Consequently, many indigenous Ghanaian farmers have invested in other horticultural products like pineapple, mangoes, and papaya.

Two of the known cut flower and foliage farms belong to Dutch investors. There are no flower associations and clusters in Ghana as in Kenya. The government has also not injected any conscious support for the flora industry as it has done for mangoes and pineapples for example. Currently, only one farm is fully operational—MDK Ghana. This company produces exclusive foliage such as monstera, philodendron, and anthurium. The parent company in Holland undertakes all the sales and marketing activities, 90 percent through the auction market and 10 percent directly to wholesalers in Germany.

MDK Ghana was established in 2007 and produced and sold mono bouquets. Currently, it has reached a much higher level of professionalism which allows it to produce fresh bouquets composed of many different flowers in various styles. It has a 15-hectare farm with access to large areas of water bodies. It employs 100 permanent workers, many of whom were originally rice farmers. At the beginning of 2010, it introduced a new line of tropical flower bouquets. The flowers are grown in the open fields by locals trained to turn the products into bunches and mixed sprays and sold as such in European supermarkets. Consumption of mixed bouquets is gaining a lot of popularity.

Cultivation of the products is done under shades and some in the open field. The company has its own refrigerated van which transports finished products to the airport within one hour. The farm is headed by an experienced Dutch cut flower farmer who has worked in other farms in Africa.

Another farm, Gold Coast Foliage, which is currently not in operation, was also established and fully funded by Dutch investors who themselves were traditional growers of flowers in the Netherlands. They have other flower farms in Ethiopia. Products from the farm were marketed and sold by a buyer called Flueriplus in the Netherlands, who was one of three investors of the farm in Ghana.

Unlike MDK, this farm cultivated just two types of foliage—monstera and asparagus virigatus. Unfortunately, the asparagus virigatus was attacked by a fungus which became difficult to fight. Additionally, the farms were located very far away from the airport, more than three hours drive away. Even though the farm invested in a lot of infrastructure, it did not have a refrigerated van of its own to expeditiously transport finished products to the airport. All these were compounded by the river it depended on to irrigate the farms becoming salty in the dry season. The Ghanaian manager of the farm had no previous knowledge in floriculture farming.

ETHIOPIA

Ethiopia is the second-largest producer of roses in Africa, with Kenya leading and sixth in the world after Holland, Colombia, Ecuador, Kenya, and Israel. Ethiopia has earned US$186 million from horticulture exports out of which 80 percent was generated by flower exports in 2008. The flower farms employ between 30,000 employees and 60,000 according to the Ministry of Trade and Industry. Seventy percent of the flowers produced in Ethiopia go to the Netherlands, and the rest to Russia, the U.S., and Japan.

The first private flower companies, Meskel Flower and Ethio-flora, started activities around 1997 on a few hectares of land. As of 2008 the investment authority had given permits to 251 investors, many of whom are traditional growers from the Netherlands. The sector is governed by the Ethiopian Horticulture Producers and Exporters, which offers tremendous support to its members.

KENYA

Kenya is the oldest, most successful and major producer of flowers in Africa. The sector is now the fastest growing in the Kenyan economy, outpacing its traditional hard currency earners—coffee and tourism. About 60,000 people have been employed by the sector with the majority being women. The industry has expanded from a small scale trade in the 1950s/1960s to become one of the most important "off-season" suppliers of cut flowers in the world. Cut flowers are a major source of foreign exchange for Kenya, exporting $245 million worth of flowers in 2010 (ITC statistics based on COMTRADE statistics).

In contrast to the situation in the 1970s and 1980s when only one or two companies accounted for the bulk of cut flower exports, as is the present case in Ghana, Kenya currently has more than 600 producers/exporters growing cut flowers. Production for export is largely concentrated on some 60 or so medium to large scale flower operations, of which the 25 largest producers account for over 80 percent of total exports. The larger flower operations range in size from 20 to over 120 hectares employing between 250 and 6,000 people.

Many of Kenya's farms (50 to 70 percent) are located around the Lake Naivasha. Lake Naivasha District is situated about 100 kilometer northwest of Nairobi, in the Great Rift Valley, at an altitude of 1,800 to 2,000 meter above sea level, and it comprises an area of 2,000 hectare. The management of these farms is usually by foreigners with extensive knowledge

EXHIBIT 4 Kenyan Cut Flower Producers

Category	Approximate Production Area/Crop	Typical Features
Large Producer Exporter	>20 ha of protected production plus open field production Sophisticated infrastructure, expatriate management Rose + carnation + open field flowers	Manage own export operations May buy in from out growers Diversified markets including direct sales to supermarkets Large employers (250–6,000 staff)
Small- to Medium-sized Producers	2–20 ha, including up to 10 ha of protected production Sophisticated infrastructure Mostly rose + some open field flowers	Own export and/or act as out growers May in turn buy in from out growers Sell through auction system, limited direct sales Employment ~100 staff Account for 20–30 percent of exports
Small-holder Producers	0.25–2 ha, open field crops, particularly Alstromeria	Act as out growers Product sold through auctions Low input system with very little investment Mostly family labor Account for 5–10 percent of exports

SOURCE: Updated from Mick Blowfield, "Ethical Trade and Organic Agriculture," *Tropical Agriculture Association Newsletters*, 22–26.

in the sector. These farms have also invested heavily in infrastructure to support their operations. Over the years, the number of smallholders in Kenya who are mostly indigenous farmers is decreasing rapidly owing to their inability to comply with the many production codes and requirements. The category of farmers in Kenya is represented in Exhibit 4. Ghana can learn from the experience of Kenya and Ethiopia to increase its share in the flora trade.

SUCCESS FACTORS

The rapid growth of floriculture in Africa is due to different factors like suitable climatic and natural resources, high level of support by the government, favorable investment laws and incentives, proximity to the global market, efficiency of the transport system, and availability of abundant and cheap labor.

Another important factor is access to water. Flower farming requires more water than conventional farming, because a flower is said to be 90 percent water. Many of the African flower farms are located near rivers and water bodies. The farms further invest in irrigation equipment for consistent supply and distribution of water for the plants. It is important for these water bodies to be nourishing and clean and free from harmful materials. One of the main factors which adversely affected a foliage farm in Ghana was the presence of salt in the river, River Okye in the Mankessim District in the Central Region of Ghana, where it was located. It is ironic that cut flowers compete with humans for clean sources of water.

THE CUT FLOWER TRADE IN EUROPE

The EU is the largest market for trade in fresh cut flowers in the world. A *CBI Market Intelligence Survey on Cut Flowers* reports that in 2008, the total EU flower market amounted to approximately €13 billion. The largest flower markets in the EU were: Germany (23 percent market share), the United Kingdom (15 percent), France (15 percent), Italy (11 percent), the Netherlands (7.6 percent), Spain (5.7 percent), Belgium (3.3 percent), and Poland (3.2 percent).

Despite sub-optimal climatic conditions, EU companies can grow top-quality flowers using heating and advanced cultivation technologies like assimilation lighting and additional carbon dioxide (CO_2). The value of cut flower production in the EU amounts to approximately €9.5 billion. The Netherlands is by far the major producer in the EU, accounting for 40 percent of total production value. Other major producers are Italy, Germany, and France. In recent years, a larger number of countries report a decline in the number of active growers.

As a result of the increasing competition and search for lower costs, some European growers (particularly in the Netherlands) have relocated their production to lower cost countries, which offer favorable cultivation circumstances. An increasing number of rosa and summer flower growers have set up flower farms in countries such as Kenya and Ethiopia.

Since the mid-nineties, imports of traditional flowers have been dominated by rosa. Nearly all EU countries increased their imports of rosa in the period 2005–2009. This indicates that (1) the increased popularity of rosa was widespread and sustained and that (2) rosa is the leading product for which production has shifted out of the EU. Kenya is one such low-cost suppliers of rosa.

Other new products like heliconia are mostly imported. Heliconias are true exotics, unable to withstand prolonged periods of temperatures below 15°C. The flower comes in many different shapes and sizes, of which heliconia caribea accounts for about 40 percent of traded heliconias. Heliconia is one the products MDK Ghana produces and supplies at the auction market.

Also, the floral industry is essentially a labor-intensive one, which is why although the biggest market still is the Dutch one at Aalsmeer, the flowers are from Third World producers in Kenya, Ethiopia, Ecuador, Colombia, and India.

THE ROLE OF THE NETHERLANDS AND THE AUCTION MARKET IN THE FLOWER CHAIN

Despite the advent of direct buying by supermarkets, the bulk of the world flower trade is channelled through auction houses in Holland. The Dutch auctions have a strong position in the flower chain—over 60 percent of world trade in flowers and plants takes place via Dutch auctions. They process around 40 million blooms a day, taking them in from Dutch growers and from exporters like Kenya, Zimbabwe, Israel, Colombia, and Ecuador.

The Flora Holland flower auction house in Naaldwijk is the largest cut flower and plant auction house in the world and is responsible for over 90 percent of Dutch trade in those products. It has a turnover of €1.9 billion, 3,000 employees, and a market share of 56 percent in the Netherlands and 52.3 percent worldwide. It is specialized in cut flowers (70 percent of the turnover) and pot plants (30 percent). About 7.6 billion products are sold in this marketplace, mainly Dutch products (5.8 billion) but also a growing number of imported products (1.8 billion). Flora Holland does business with about 16,000 suppliers, 4,600 traders, and 2,600 exporters. Many African producers use the auction market to distribute their products.

TO WHAT EXTENT CAN AFRICAN PRODUCERS SUSTAIN THEIR PRESENCE IN THIS CHAIN?

Apart from 2009 during the global crises, the cut flowers trade has been growing since the last 30 years. The trade is characterized by an efficient and flourishing production and consumption chain between the main importers in Europe and producers from developing countries. Factors like the high cost of labor and energy, concern for environmental pollution, the quest for new exotic tropical plants and perhaps the need to promote trade between the north and south led to this shift. The chain process has been facilitated by the proximity of producing countries to the import markets as well as favorable trade agreements between these countries.

In Africa, Kenya and Ethiopia have taken a lead in this sector. They both enjoy support from their governments; they have organized the trade into strong clusters and associations that team up to support each other, and they are able to comply with the codes and standards required by the market. Another characteristic of these successful farms is that they are usually owned and/or managed by traditional European growers who have relocated to Africa. Young producing countries like Ghana can learn from this practice to increase their market share.

However, like fashion, the flower industry is "subjected" to seasonal colors, shapes, and varieties. Consumers continually are seeking products which offer diversity in flower and leaf color, good texture and form, as well as better performance in interior environments. This makes research and development an important aspect of the chain. Much of this is dictated by the buyers, who also have the resources to undertake the research. In Holland, the *Rijnplant* has lately developed a new variety of anthurium plant, which it has patented for 20 years. Research and development costs a lot of money, which indigenous producers from Africa cannot afford. The ability to introduce new varieties or lines of a product is a critical success factor for flower producers.

The Netherlands is an important player for African producers. More than 50 percent of flowers produced in Africa pass through the flower auction markets in the Netherlands. However, Poland, Belgium, and Sweden imports are becoming leading growth markets in the EU, importing traditional flowers directly from Africa and other developing countries. If this trend continues, the Netherlands could lose some of its market share of products from Africa and other developing countries.

If Africa has to sustain its participation in the trade, she must make efforts to develop techniques which will reduce its production costs and ultimate cost to the consumer. The industry is capital-intensive; as such there must be efforts to identify and use low cost production technologies and reorientation of imported technology to suit Africans' requirements. There is also an urgent need for African producers to identify varieties that are most tolerant of the stresses of long shipping and storage in order to remain competitive and sustain their position in the chain.

Another pertinent issue is the continuous supply of clean water to feed the floriculture industry. A flower is 90 percent water, needing more water than conventional horticulture products. This water must also be free from contamination and be fit for human consumption. How long can the water bodies in Africa continue to feed flower production and still have enough for human consumption and, importantly, remain unpolluted?

QUESTIONS FOR DISCUSSION

1. One of the challenges for African flower and foliage producers is the need to ensure that the products reach the final consumers in good quality. Must they then produce and market their own products that are more tolerant to the stresses of long shipping or continue to produce traditional European flowers which are difficult and expensive to transport?
2. What types of upgrading can producers in Africa conveniently adopt to ensure increased recognition and participation in the floriculture chain?
3. How much value does the agent or distributor add to a bouquet of flowers or bunch of roses from Africa before it reaches the final consumers? How can this be accurately calculated to ensure fair prices to the men and women who work on flower farms in Africa?
4. Knowing that flower production depends on availability of water, how long can the water bodies in Africa continue to feed flower production and still have enough for human consumption and, importantly, remain unpolluted?

PART TWO

Finding Global Customers

Part Two examines how to find global customers by first analyzing the global consumer in detail, and then presenting the overall strategic options and their implementation by the firm, which provides the framework for the subsequent development of the text. This setting of the stage is followed by the development of the knowledge base through marketing research, which ensures that the company not only does things right but also does the right things. Then we concentrate on market entry, primarily through exporting and other low-cost, low-risk international expansion alternatives, followed by the systematic multinational expansion of internationally more experienced firms.

CHAPTER 6

Consumer, Industrial, and Government Markets

LEARNING OBJECTIVES

By the time you complete this chapter, you will be able to:

- Comprehend drivers of the global consumer.
- Understand characteristics of the global consumer.
- Recognize influences on the global consumer.
- Comprehend country-of-origin effects.
- Understand characteristics of the industrial buyer.
- Understand characteristics of the government buyer.
- Undertake marketing to global consumers.

THE INTERNATIONAL MARKETPLACE 6.1

Apple Targets Global Consumers

Globalization, advanced technologies, and other trends herald the emergence of the global consumer. Global consumers share similar needs and tastes in the products and services they buy, wherever they are located worldwide. Global marketing is characterized by uniformity of branding, packaging, marketing communications, and distribution channels. Consistency in products is more cost effective than marketing that aims to adapt offerings to needs in individual countries. Companies enjoy substantial cost advantages when they can offer similar products, using similar packaging, to consumers around the world. Global brands help consumers demonstrate their modernity, affiliation with social elites, higher living standards, and values that appeal to shoppers everywhere.

Younger consumers in particular are sensitive to world trends and cosmopolitan culture in areas such as music, film, fashion, and technology. Contemporary consumers are less attached to national tradition and customs; they are more flexible, open to new developments, and want to adopt global brands. Global consumers access a wider variety of products at lower prices than ever before. Global consumers want the latest technologies. Compared to previous generations, today's consumers are more successful at satisfying their needs and wants. They aspire for higher living standards and exciting lifestyles. Many are better educated and more worldly than average consumers.

Apple has tapped into the global consumer market through its best-selling brand of smartphones. Upon its release, the iPhone triggered a revolution in cell phones and mobile computing. Apple receives more than 60 percent of its sales from international markets. Apple's enormous success is attributable to aggressive marketing and distribution strategies worldwide. iPhones are characterized by innovativeness, imaginative designs, and utility that appeals to consumers around the world. In marketing communications, Apple positions the iPhone as cool, hip, and trendy—qualities that appeal to the global segment of youthful and cosmopolitan consumers.

Apple's global appeal includes strong innovativeness, great brand image, and a design that suits buyers' aspirations. The iPhone 4 offered a dramatic, slim design, with a radically sharper screen, superior camera, long battery life, and a fast processor. Apple owes much of its success to a global branding strategy that has captured consumer loyalty across the globe. The iPhone scores very well on values that global consumers embrace, including convenience, performance, and confidence that the purchase will impress peers. To increase global diffusion, the iPhone 4 was introduced in 88 countries in the space of about three months. The social influence of users showing off or publicly "consuming" their phone enhanced iPhone adoption worldwide.

SOURCES: Hoovers.com profile of Apple, www.hoovers.com/company/Apple_Inc/rtjcci-1-1njht4-1njfaq.html; Michael Mallin and Todd Finkle, "Apple Inc.: Product Portfolio Analysis," *Journal of the International Academy for Case Studies* 17, no. 7 (2011): 63–74; and Valerie Vaccaro, Sucheta Ahlawat, and Deborah Cohn, "Diffusion of Innovation, Marketing Strategies, and Global Consumer Values for a High Technology Product," *International Journal of Business Strategy* 10, no. 3 (2010): 113–28.

Globalization and technological advances have coincided with the diffusion of world culture, rising living standards, and enhanced opportunities for companies to market their brands around the world. In this contemporary environment, companies target various types of customers. Globalization stimulates interest in and facilitates the ability to acquire products and services from the broadest range of companies worldwide. It seems that wherever people live today, they encounter global brands—Airbus, Coca-Cola, Madonna, McDonald's, Samsung, Siemens, Toyota, and countless others. As highlighted in *The International Marketplace 6.1*, globalization, improving technologies, and other trends have led to the emergence of the "global consumer," who is relatively sophisticated, often more demanding, and comfortable with buying international brands.

In addition, recent trends have made possible the ability of companies to source needed inputs from the best suppliers worldwide. From alternators to zippers, purchasing managers scour the world to find the raw materials, parts, supplies, and services their firms need to fulfill their business needs. Likewise, governments count on multinational firms to supply them with the products and services they use to serve constituents and perform their administrative tasks. Growing consumerism and global sourcing in emerging markets has opened opportunities for firms to target billions of buyers worldwide who, only a few decades ago, were relatively inaccessible.

Exhibit 6.1 displays three levels of factors that shape the world of consumers today. At the outermost level are supranational factors, which transcend national borders and affect the global consumer at a macro, international level. As explained in the next section, the influence of globalization and information and communications technologies on the emergence and nature of the global consumer has been pervasive. Trade institutions and policy refer to global entities such as the WTO, IMF, and others that influence the evolution of trade and investment at a global level, as discussed in Chapter 2. In terms of national-level factors (the middle circle in the exhibit), consumers everywhere are affected by the economic, political, legal, technological, infrastructural, and cultural conditions that characterize the nations where they live. These dimensions are addressed in Chapter 3.

EXHIBIT 6.1 Three Levels of the Global Consumer

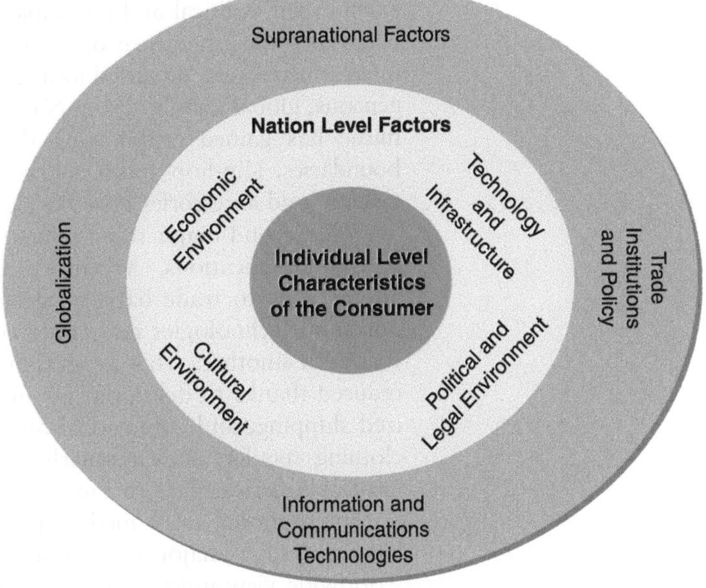

The inner circle in the exhibit represents the consumer, whose preferences are determined to a large extent by personality traits, personal situational factors, and other conditions that exist at the individual level.

Consumers are the focus of marketing activity. Marketing programs are designed to influence them to purchase the firm's products or services. Sales people are fond of saying that "nothing happens in business unless someone buys something." In this chapter, we examine the various types of buyers in international marketing—retail consumers, industrial buyers, and governments. We explore the characteristics of buyers around the world and the factors that influence global consumers to behave the way they do. We contrast buyers affected by where a product is made and those who embrace global brands. We then examine the managerial requirements for marketing success with global consumers.

DRIVERS OF THE GLOBAL CONSUMER

The emergence of the global consumer coincides with two important driving trends: globalization and advancing information and communications technologies.

Globalization refers to the growing interconnectedness of nations, the organization of life on a global scale, and the consolidation of world society. Growing integration of world markets enables individuals, companies, and nations to reach around the world more deeply and efficiently than ever before. Globalization is characterized by a combination of falling trade barriers and the industrialization and modernization of nations worldwide. Today many trade barriers have declined almost to zero, particularly among the advanced economies and emerging markets. In this way, globalization reflects the spread of free-market capitalism, which both fosters and is fostered by massive growth in international trade and investment.

Globalization is a revolution in progress, a historic transformation in world economies, living standards, and modes of existence. Globalization also implies that many nations are losing some autonomy as larger countries and corporations extend their political and economic power around the world. Globalization coincides with the emergence of "world culture," which is marked by the growing interconnectedness of varied local cultures or the appearance of a relatively homogeneous, global culture. From Nairobi to Paris to Shanghai, for example, hip-hop music has gained a following that spans cultural, linguistic, and geographic boundaries. Hip-hop youth culture affects nearly every country. Hip-hop music, fashion, and accessories have flooded markets worldwide.[1]

The second major trend refers to technological developments in information and communications. A century ago, nations were largely cut off from one another due to trade barriers, geographic distance, and lack of efficient transportation technologies that could convey goods quickly from one corner of the world to another. This geographic distance, however, has been dramatically reduced thanks to developments in transportation, such as fast ships, containerized shipping, and commercial aircraft. For example, electronics, furniture, and clothing retailers now regularly source their offerings from factories in Asia, Central America, Eastern Europe, and other far-flung localities worldwide.

International mass media—primarily television, movies, and the Internet—have played a major role in the emergence of the global consumer. People worldwide view much of the same media programming, often flowing from the United States. The enjoyment by people in much of the world of TV shows such as *Friends*, *House*, and *CSI Miami* has coincided with the tendency of buyers to acquire similar characteristics. Many international shows have also been adapted to the United States—*The Office* and *Who Wants to Be a Millionaire* are examples. In a related trend, more than two-thirds of the movies shown around the world are produced in Hollywood in the United States. Such media project a lifestyle and living standard that increasingly transcends national boundaries, representing a way of life that myriad people wish to embrace.[2]

THE GLOBAL CONSUMER

In conjunction with the above trends, the past few decades have seen the emergence of the **global consumer**. Global consumers are individuals or organizational buyers that exhibit similar needs and tastes worldwide. Global market segments (discussed later in this chapter) are groupings of consumers that exist in multiple countries and display similar characteristics regarding preferences and consumption of specific product or service categories.[3] Globalization and global diffusion of media give rise to a desire by people everywhere to participate in an idealized and relatively universal consumer culture. Various product categories have become signs of global cosmopolitanism and modernity, such as air conditioners, automobiles, consumer electronics, and hamburgers. Multinational firms seek to capitalize on world culture by developing global products and positioning their brands in the global consumer culture.

Simultaneously, industrial markets in virtually every economic sector have acquired global characteristics. The rise of multinational corporations has stimulated widespread competitive pressures on firms to reduce costs and seek customers wherever they can be found. Increasingly, companies internationalize their value chains, offering products and services to the world. Many firms cut costs by minimizing the variety of parts, components, and other inputs used to produce finished products and services. Using standardized parts results in economies of scale and the ability to minimize variety in factory inventories. For example, Dell manufactures its laptop computers in only a handful of factories. Ensuring scale economies and just-in-time production requires Dell to minimize the variety of parts and components used to assemble computers. Reducing

© Dongliu/Shutterstock.com

Thanks to international marketing and the rise of the global consumer, Ford can sell its line of pickup trucks around the world.

manufacturing to a few large factories helps ensure consistent, standardized production at minimal cost. In business-to-business markets, global customers seek to centralize and standardize their purchasing of raw materials, parts, components, and finished goods.[4]

Today, fresh strawberries are available around the world, even in winter. Consumers drive Toyota cars made in America and Ford trucks made in Brazil. More products travel greater distances than ever before. MNCs employ similar marketing, often adapted for local languages and cultures, to promote their offerings worldwide. Just as Japanese animation (*manga*) has gained a wide audience in Western countries, American rap music has gained a big following in Asia. One can find Western-style shopping malls in Egypt, Bollywood movies in Europe, and Christmas gift-giving celebrations in China.[5] The diffusion of the Internet, television, radio, and various print media helps firms undertake marketing in the far reaches of the world.

In each country, the existence of a consumer culture is characterized by (1) emphasis on marketing-based exchange relationships; (2) a large proportion of the population achieving an improved standard of living; (3) a perception of consumption as an acceptable, and even desirable, activity; and (4) level and quality of consumption as an important criterion for judging others.[6] The United States is an archetypical consumer culture, where the average citizen spends thousands of dollars annually on consumer goods purchased through a wide range of retail and online stores. Consumerism is practiced with much conviction, and Americans tend to judge their friends and neighbors based on the products they own. Based on its "winner takes all" and "growth at all costs" approach, the marketing discipline has on occasion led individuals and society astray. Such transgressions need to be addressed via the introduction of curative or healing marketing, which compensates for past ills (see Chapter 17). In what might be called a consumption addiction, individuals tend to derive part of their identity from the things they consume. In France, for example, people are often judged by the clothing brands they wear. In South Korea, young people typecast others based on the quality of cell phones they use. In the United States, people make inferences based on the size and location of each other's homes.

In international marketing, demand for certain product categories remains relatively specialized, requiring adaptation to nation-level needs and tastes. This includes food, books, music, and, to a lesser extent, cosmetics and clothing styles. Take the grocery industry as an example. The food preferred by Chinese, Mexicans, Italians, and Russians varies substantially. Food processors understand these differences and tailor their offerings accordingly. However, for fast food, people worldwide increasingly prefer offerings by KFC, McDonald's, or their local Chinese restaurant. People also prefer to read books in their native languages. Music remains a relatively culture-specific experience. Goods and services that depend on language tend to remain relatively local.

Simultaneously, however, products in most other categories have become increasingly standardized. These standardized items include automobiles, consumer electronics, furniture, home appliances, office supplies and furnishing, industrial and scientific equipment, and most types of products and services purchased by firms and governments. For example, no matter where you travel today, you can usually find Toyota Corollas, Dell computers, and Gillette razors. The world's largest furniture retailer, IKEA, offers mostly similar products to consumers in China, Germany, Turkey, and numerous other nations where the firm does business. Honda sells the same basic models of cars around the world.

For several decades, the European Union has undergone integration along political and economic lines. This trend has coincided with growing similarity in consumption patterns throughout Europe.[7] Emerging markets are developing economies such as Brazil, China, India, and Russia. Today, just like people in the advanced economies, consumers in emerging markets purchase dishwashers, microwave ovens, refrigerators, and numerous other household goods.[8] Among the most important factors spurring increased consumption are rising income levels and participation in global free trade.[9]

Internationally, market researchers can observe much similarity in the consumption patterns of young professionals, business executives, teenagers, or the wealthy. The global market segment is based on cross-national similarities in lifestyle and demographics. The emergence of global consumers facilitates companies' ability to target buyers worldwide with very similar products and services.

INFLUENCES ON THE GLOBAL CONSUMER

In international marketing, certain factors are known to influence the preferences and buying behavior of consumers. These factors are summarized in Exhibit 6.2 and explained in detail in the following sections.

Economic Status

The ability to purchase goods and services is strongly influenced by income level.[10] Comparisons can be based on the level of each nation's per-capita gross domestic product (GDP). Only about one billion consumers worldwide are in the highest income category, earning an average annual income of $34,000. An additional two billion consumers are in the middle income category, about $13,000 per year. Known as *emerging markets*, they are typified by countries such as China, Mexico, and Poland. At the lowest income level, people typically

EXHIBIT 6.2 Influences on the Global Consumer

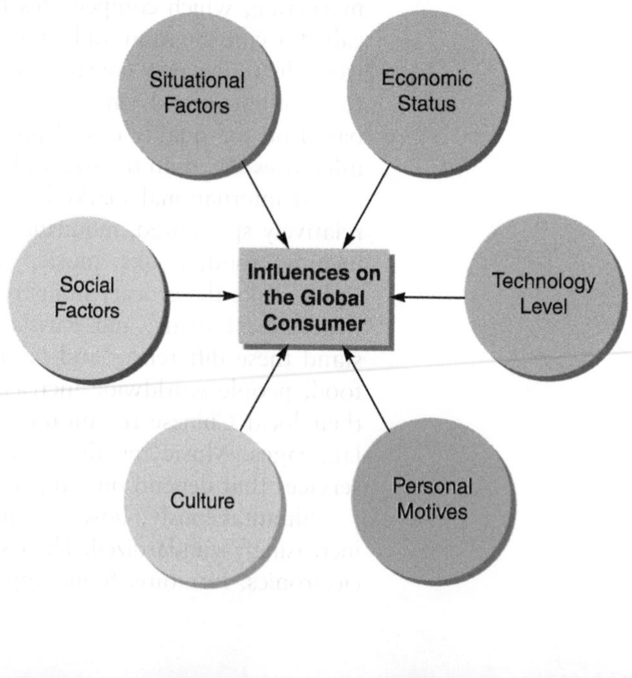

earn an average of $5,000 per year. Many consumers in this group have incomes well below this level.

Historically, international marketers targeted the low-hanging fruit—meaning developed markets and their high-income consumers. Increasingly, firms are also targeting the emerging markets. Most of these countries have rapidly rising incomes and represent promising market opportunities. Numerous companies are now also targeting the developing markets. Most countries in Africa, and some in Asia and Latin America, are in this category. Despite very low incomes, the countries at the bottom of the pyramid collectively represent huge potential markets and can be targeted with numerous goods and services. However, infrastructure is often very poor in developing markets. Consequently, firms usually must devise novel business strategies, which usually include offering low-cost products via innovative marketing communications and distribution approaches.[11]

Countries in the developed and emerging markets often have numerous highly profitable firms. High income at the individual and corporate levels implies a superior ability to purchase products and services. The consumption tendency extends even to relatively poor countries. In rural parts of China, for example, annual per-capita income levels may be less than $5,000. However, consumers are still willing to spend hundreds of dollars to acquire cell phones and personal computers.[12] In China by the year 2016, mobile-phone handset sales and personal computer sales are expected to exceed $50 billion and $100 billion, respectively. Already more than one-quarter of China's population, about 330 million people, owns a personal computer.[13]

Income levels are related to the size of the *middle class*, the people located in the middle of each country's economic hierarchy. The size of the middle class reflects how wealth is distributed. In many countries, income distribution is quite skewed, with a small upper class holding most of the wealth. In spending-power terms, a sizeable middle class represents an important target market. In each of Brazil and Russia, for example, the middle class amounts to more than 65 million people with per-capita incomes greater than $10,000.[14] Collectively, these segments represent an attractive target market. *The International Marketplace 6.2* examines the rise of the middle class in emerging-market countries.

Growing convergence of income levels has coincided with the emergence of consumers with similar tastes around the world. As consumers attain higher levels of affluence, they want to buy more, and they increasingly aspire for the same types of products and services.[15] Mass media expose consumers in less developed economies to the lifestyles of people in Europe, North America, and other advanced economies. Such exposure triggers growing desire for many of the same types of goods and promotes the emergence of a consumer class with similar needs and tastes.

Economic status is also related to occupation. In countries whose economies are still rooted in agriculture or manufacturing (such as China, India, and most of Africa), workers need rugged clothing suitable for farming or factory jobs. By contrast, when the largest proportion of people is employed in the service sector, they are more likely to wear business attire. Recent decades have seen a convergence of clothing styles among those employed in the global corporate world.

Technology Level

Technology refers to knowledge and usage of tools, machines, techniques, or methods of organization applied to solving problems or performing particular functions. Technology varies across all areas of human endeavor and includes computers, factory equipment, communications systems, and accumulated knowledge about specific industries. Advanced technologies are characteristic of economically developed nations. In the absence of advanced technologies, a nation's productivity level and living standards are relatively limited. People in poor countries usually have little access to advanced technologies or knowledge of how to use such tools. Many are employed in subsistence farming or other low-value-adding activities. Their ability to work in most industrial fields, and

THE INTERNATIONAL **MARKETPLACE** 6.2

Rise of the Global Middle Class

Historically, multinational firms have preferred targeting affluent buyers in the advanced economies with their products and services. However, the past two decades have seen the rise of middle-class market segments in emerging-market countries worldwide. Today the middle class in emerging markets amounts to nearly two billion people spending trillions of dollars annually. These markets are on track to far outpace consumption in the United States, which historically has been the largest consumer market.

The buying power of the emergent middle class is changing the landscape of marketing opportunities around the world. In the global apparel sector, Brazil's large population and growing middle class offer attractive prospects. Brazil is the world's fifth largest apparel market and is growing rapidly. Women are fashion conscious, and a credit market enables them to shop for designer clothes.

Brazil's apparel market is serviced mainly by local retailers, which suggests opportunities for the entry of global firms. However, foreign retailers face several challenges in Brazil. First, Brazilians have relatively distinctive needs and tastes in clothing. Second, Brazilians tend to prefer local brands. Third, the consumer credit market in Brazil is underdeveloped, which limits consumer purchasing power. Mango, Zara, and other international retailers are active in the market. However, they primarily serve the nation's wealthy segment. Brazil is served mostly by small, home-grown stores or local, single-format retailers. The typical mass-market clothing buyer in Brazil earns more than $10,000 per year. A recent McKinsey survey of 900 women consumers in Brazil revealed clothing buyer characteristics (see Exhibit 6.3). It found that Brazilian women are very fond of shopping for clothes. About 79 percent say they look forward to shopping, a higher percentage than in most countries. Some 81 percent of Brazilian women favor local brands, a very high percentage. Brazilian women seem to regard foreign brands poorly. More than half stated they buy clothing mainly to go out with family and friends. This response was chosen much more than "buying clothing for work," which indicates that clothing is very important to Brazilians' sense of fashion and style.

Brazilian shoppers indicated they are willing to buy clothing on credit using credit cards. However, the system for general-purpose credit cards—such as Visa and MasterCard—is very limited. Thus, some retailers issue their own credit cards, which many Brazilian shoppers are keen to use. Such private-label credit cards finance about two-thirds of sales by Brazil's larger apparel retailers.

Brazil is typical of many emerging markets. It is quickly developing a huge middle class, hungry for goods from around the world. Multinational

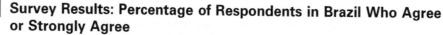

EXHIBIT 6.3 Survey Results: Percentage of Respondents in Brazil Who Agree or Strongly Agree

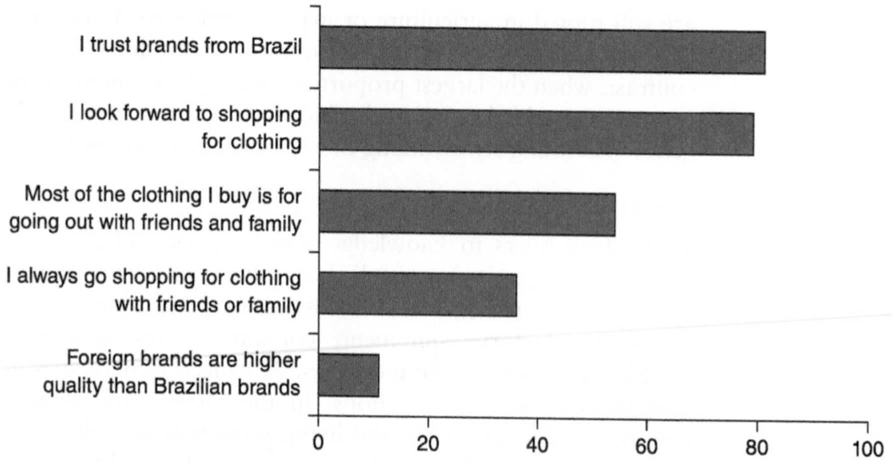

SOURCE: Manuela Artigas and Nicola Calicchio, "How Half the World Shops: Apparel in Brazil, China, and India," *McKinsey Quarterly*, October 2010, www.mckinseyquarterly.com.

retailers need to devise new business models and adapt their approaches to the large Brazilian market.

SOURCES: Manuela Artigas and Nicola Calicchio, "How Half the World Shops: Apparel in Brazil, China, and India," *McKinsey Quarterly*, October 2010, www.mckinseyquarterly.com; David Court and Laxman Narasimhan, "Capturing the World's Emerging Middle Class," *McKinsey Quarterly*, July 2010, www.mckinseyquarterly.com; Donald Gold, "Emerging Markets Will Vie vs. G-7: Economist," *Investors Business Daily*, May 2, 2011, B10; and Silvina Moronta, "Big Brand Ideas Inspire Huge Emerging Market," *Market Leader*, Spring 2011, 56.

resultant prospects for earning a good living, is limited. As consumers, their needs are relatively simple, often restricted to acquiring the basics of food, clothing, and shelter.

Technology level is strongly influenced by the nature of education systems in individual countries. In the United States, Australia, Canada, and most European countries, education is compulsory through about age 16. In Africa, Latin America, and other less economically developed areas, school may end at age 14 or younger. This tendency affects literacy rates, the ability of citizens to deal with advanced technologies, and ultimately earnings potential.

Personal Motives

A *motive* is an internal force that orients a person's activities toward satisfying a need or achieving a goal. Perhaps the most recognized explanation on the formation of motives is that of the psychologist Abraham Maslow.[16] Maslow's "hierarchy of needs" suggests that people are motivated to fulfill basic needs before moving on to other needs, all of which motivate ultimate behavior. Let us review the needs, from most basic to most advanced.

1. *Physiological needs* describe the needs vital to survival, such as the need for food, water, and sleep. All subsequent needs are secondary until physiological needs are met.
2. *Safety needs* refer to people's need for safety and security. They include the desire for steady employment, health care, safe neighborhoods, and shelter from the environment.
3. *Love and belonging needs* are basic to everyone and represent the desire for friendships, romantic attachments, and families, fulfilling a need for acceptance and companionship.
4. *Esteem needs* are sought once the first three needs have been met. Esteem needs describe the desire for objects and activities that enhance self-esteem, personal worth, social recognition, and accomplishment.
5. *Self-actualization needs* represent the highest level in the hierarchy of needs and refer to the desire for personal growth and the ability to achieve one's full potential. Most people worldwide tend to neglect self-actualization because they are so occupied with achieving the four prior needs.

Two points about the hierarchy of needs are especially relevant to international marketing. First, need levels vary worldwide as a function of economic status, technology level, and other factors. Most countries are characterized by substantial poverty, in which the focus is on satisfying physiological and safety needs. Second, worldwide, people do not consistently follow Maslow's hierarchy of needs. In developing economies, for example, people may forgo meeting some physiological needs (such as eating three meals a day) or safety needs (such as living in a safe neighborhood) in order to purchase higher-level products such as cell phones and automobiles. Emergent research suggests esteem and self-actualization needs tend to vary by country. For example, the need for esteem and self-actualization may be less important in collectivist countries such as China.[17] *The International Marketplace 6.3* reviews other characteristics of consumers in China.

THE INTERNATIONAL MARKETPLACE 6.3

China's Huge Consumer Market

China's population is more than 1.3 billion people, and the country is emerging as the world's biggest market for consumer goods. Today, Chinese consumers behave increasingly like their counterparts in the advanced economies. They are more demanding and pragmatic and are willing to pay for better value and quality. They spend more time exploring and researching product information. In the past, companies could get away with selling basic goods to the Chinese, offering them at low prices throughout the country. Now, the Chinese demand increasingly sophisticated and differentiated products.

As Chinese consumers have become more affluent, they tend to shop less and buy more during each shopping trip. This trend is consistent with rising affluence as people work more and time gains value. The tendency to fill shopping baskets also results from the rise in China of supermarkets and warehouse-style stores, such as Carrefour and Walmart. Compared to Western consumers, Chinese shoppers often view shopping as a leisure activity. They focus heavily on the needs or interests of their family members. Shopping is an important family excursion, and many families trek to shopping districts on weekends.

Increasingly, shoppers rely on the advice of family and friends to help them make purchase decisions. Given China's strong culture of social media, word of mouth is an important product information source. The most successful companies develop sophisticated websites that foster social media and viral marketing. In some categories, text messaging via Twitter and similar services accounts for a substantial proportion of the influence on the choice of brands. The Chinese are also becoming more sophisticated consumers. In the past, the demand was for a car or TV that functioned well. Today, consumers are concerned not only with product quality but also with aesthetic appeal and innovative features.

China is geographically diverse, with consumers in eastern cities exhibiting needs very different from those in the rural west. The country has a wide variety of markets and segments, which require differentiated marketing approaches. For example, *status* is a key factor influencing buyer behavior in Shanghai, but this tendency is much less evident in Wuhan. Word of mouth is a key marketing phenomenon in Beijing but is less important in Shenzhen, where consumers rely more on TV ads for product information.

A huge, emergent segment in China is the luxury goods market. It accounts for nearly 20 percent, or 180 billion renminbi ($27 billion), of the global luxury goods market. The business consultancy *McKinsey* surveyed some 1,500 luxury consumers in 17 Chinese cities. "Wealthy consumers" are those with incomes above about $46,000. *McKinsey* expects to see 76 million households in this income range by 2015, which is larger than the populations of most European countries. Such consumers opt for luxury handbags, jewelry, and fashion as well as wellness activities and leisure pursuits. Consumers increasingly desire noncounterfeit products, especially internationally known brands. Most luxury goods buyers reside in China's cities, making it easier for companies to develop distribution channels and organize logistics. Most wealthy Chinese learn about luxury goods through the Internet, foreign travel, and first-hand experience. Many are savvy about global luxury brands such as DKNY, Rolex, and Louis Vuitton.

Companies cannot apply a one-size-fits-all approach to their marketing efforts in China. Consumer behavior patterns differ widely across geography and income groups. Firms will need to tailor their product portfolios to suit local tastes and conduct research to skillfully segment the huge consumer market that constitutes China today.

SOURCES: Yuval Atsmon, Vinay Dixit, and Cathy Wu, "Tapping China's Luxury-Goods Market," *McKinsey Quarterly*, April 2011, www.mckinseyquarterly.com; Yuval Atsmon, Vinay Dixit, Max Magni, and Ian St-Maurice, "China's New Pragmatic Consumers," *McKinsey Quarterly*, October 2010, www.mckinseyquarterly.com; Bob Froehlich, China's Consumer Generation—Down on the Farm No More," *Bank Investment Consultant*, October 2011, 14–16; and Sylvie Laforet and Junsong Chen, "Chinese and British Consumers' Evaluation of Chinese and International Brands and Factors Affecting Their Choice," *Journal of World Business*, January 2012, 54–63.

Culture

Culture is the integrated system of learned behavior patterns that distinguish the members of a given society. It represents basic beliefs, values, and behavioral tendencies that are learned from family and other important institutions. As such, culture strongly influences consumption in each country. Culture is characterized by **norms**, which are accepted behaviors within a society or group.

They may be explicit or implicit and define the rules of behavior regarding interactions with others.[18]

Norms vary substantially from country to country. Product and service purchases deemed acceptable in one country may not be accepted in another. Within countries, norms also differ through time and across social classes and groups. Because they determine one's acceptance and popularity within particular groups, norms are especially important in cultures with a strong collectivist orientation, such as countries in Asia. In the luxury goods market in China, for example, young shoppers feel pressure to purchase internationally well-known brands.[19] Due to increased emphasis on sustainability, many Europeans buy hybrid cars, superefficient heating systems, and other products that save energy and protect the natural environment.

Other cultural norms that affect consumers and their purchase behaviors include *conservatism*, the tendency to prefer traditions and choices that have stood the test of time, and *materialism*, a belief about the importance of possessions in one's life.[20] Conservative consumers tend to remain loyal to existing brands and product types. Thus, markets with numerous conservative consumers can be difficult to enter. Materialistic consumers are relatively anxious to purchase products that demonstrate their affluence, including many new and differentiated goods. As income levels improve, marketers perceive growing numbers of consumers wishing to acquire products typical of affluent consumers in the advanced economies, such as large home appliances, automobiles, and big-screen TVs.

Countries are characterized by *subcultures*, groups of people with shared value systems based on common life experiences and situations. Subcultures may be distinguished by differences in nationality, religion, racial group, or geographic region. Many subcultures constitute important market segments. Religion is a major dimension of culture known to affect consumer behavior. For instance, Islam places various limitations on what or when people should buy. In Islamic countries, consumers may go on shopping sprees to buy new clothes and specialty foods following the fasting phase in the holy month of Ramadan.[21] Religion strongly influences the dietary choices of Orthodox Jews. A *kosher* diet implies one should avoid pork and follow dietary rules described in Jewish scripture. Both Buddhism and Hinduism are characterized by numerous tenets and holidays that affect consumption patterns. Among various influences, Christianity affects store opening hours and the tendency of Christians to shop for gifts during the Christmas season.

© Omar Salem/AFP/Getty Images

Religion can strongly influence shopping habits worldwide. Here consumers shop for food following the fasting phase in the holy month of Ramadan.

Social Factors

Family and social groups strongly influence consumer behavior. In many countries, the family is the center of social life. In Asia, family members may exert considerable influence on the consumption patterns of individuals. The family may serve as a buying unit as purchase decisions are made by two or more family members. In some European countries where the draft has been abolished, parents place their children into school earlier, and the number of school years has been reduced, universities now have to prepare for first-year male students aged 17 rather than the traditional age of 21. The effect on housing, self-sufficiency, teaching, and learning approaches are significant.

North America and Europe have seen elevated levels of divorce, late marriage, and lifestyles that diminish the historic role of the nuclear family. The growth of single-parent and single-occupant households, as well as dual-career couples, has coincided with the emergence of a mass market for convenience goods (such as frozen dinners and microwave ovens) and services that substitute for traditional family roles (such as child care centers). In addition to family members, consumer behavior is often determined by secondary groups, such as friends, neighbors, and coworkers.

In each society, people develop beliefs and attitudes based on the norms of their *reference groups*. These include religious groups, professional associations, and trade unions. In Latin America, for example, most people belong to the Catholic faith. Members of the church that one normally attends are an important reference group and influence purchases regarding food, clothing, and educational pursuits. A buyer may develop a purchase decision based on consulting a single individual, who would be considered a reference individual. The effect of reference groups is particularly strong for purchases that are "public" or conspicuous—such as clothing and automobiles.

Situational Factors

Situational factors are environmental or locational conditions that affect how consumers behave.[22] *Physical surroundings* include geographical location and climate. The buying experience differs between Mexico and the United Kingdom simply due to differences in geography, landscape, and weather. The rainy season in Thailand affects tourism and consumers' likelihood to shop. In Russia, consumers minimize automobile shopping during periods of severe cold and snow. Physical surroundings also vary at individual stores and include retail settings, store locations, and "atmospherics" inside stores, such as music and lighting. To save energy in Mexico, for example, grocery stores often use limited lighting in aisles, which can affect consumer decision making. In Australia, Canada, and the United States, store locations are influenced by the tendency of consumers to drive to shopping destinations, while in Europe and Japan stores are more often located at sites well served by public transportation.

The *institutional environment* refers to the public organizations and constraints that societies create to give structure to human interactions.[23] Institutions include government and legal systems. Laws, regulations, and other formal institutions determine the structure and efficiency of marketing systems. Most developing economies are characterized by weak institutions, which deters many multinational enterprises (MNEs) from entering such countries. In nations with weak institutional guidelines, corruption is often a factor that affects the purchase behavior of organizational buyers. By contrast, extensive rules and regulations may constrain consumer behavior. In Greece, for example, the government regulates the opening hours of retail stores, which are usually required to close at 9:00 P.M. or earlier. In India, government outlays on physical education are very limited, which reduces selling prospects for sports-related equipment and apparel.[24]

COUNTRY-OF-ORIGIN EFFECTS

Buyer behavior is affected by the national origin of products and services. Many consumers are relatively indifferent to where a product is made. Other consumers favor goods produced in their home country. Country of origin (COO) refers to the nation where a product is produced or branded. Origin is usually indicated by means of a product label, such as "Made in China." When consumers are aware of a product's COO, they may react positively or negatively. For example, many people favor cars produced in Japan but would be less upbeat about cars made in Russia. Most people feel confident about buying clothing made in Italy but would be less receptive to clothing from Mexico. Such attitudes arise because consumers hold particular images or conceptions about specific countries. Consumers assume that Japan produces high-quality cars and that Russia makes low-quality cars. While such beliefs are often rooted in reality, many are simplified opinions, false stereotypes, or effects of the slowness of learning about or accepting change.

Exhibit 6.4 shows results of a survey by Hakuhodo, an ad agency in Japan, on the percentage of consumers who view different categories of Japanese products as being of "excellent quality." As shown, consumers in Brazil, China, Russia, and South Korea have a very positive impression of Japanese consumer electronics. Consumers in China and Russia think very well of Japanese cars. But many in Germany, India, and Korea hold a negative view of such goods. When it comes to Japanese music and medical care, consumers in all the locations have a poor impression of offerings from Japan. These results exemplify the importance of COO, which varies over a wide range of goods and service categories. Firms may need to use substantial resources to convince foreign consumers to buy their goods and services or to change their perceptions.[25]

Buyer reactions to COO are influenced by various factors. First, as reflected in the exhibit, COO stereotypes vary depending on the origin of the judge and on the category of the product being judged. For instance, while Japanese cars are disdained by Indians, they are prized by Russians. While people in Brazil love Japanese consumer electronics, they spurn Japanese apparel.

Second, opinion varies depending on the national origin of the firm and the location where its product is actually made. Many consumers love German Volkswagens, even if the cars are produced in China, Poland, or some other location outside Germany. Occasionally, companies take advantage of this tendency in their advertising, as did Toyota, which promoted the Camry as the "best car built in America."[26] Toyota benefited from U.S. customer preferences for Japanese car brands as well as for cars made in the United States.

EXHIBIT 6.4 Percentage of Surveyed Consumers in Each City Who View Japanese Products as Being of "Excellent Quality," by Product Category

Product Category	Beijing, China	Frankfurt, Germany	Moscow, Russia	Mumbai, India	New York, USA	Sao Paolo, Brazil	Seoul, South Korea
Consumer electronics	71%	41%	78%	38%	48%	87%	82%
Automobiles	70	44	73	30	58	59	46
Fashion, apparel	30	24	17	25	18	9	25
Music	15	23	15	8	9	4	21
Medical care	8	8	–	3	5	17	7

SOURCE: Hakuhodo, "Hakuhodo Global HABIT: Worldwide 18-City Comparison of Japanese and Korean Products Image," Hakuhodo Corporation, March 1, 2011, www.hakuhodo.jp/news/year/?t=11.

Third, as the capacity of countries to perform well in specific industries improves, the COO phenomenon varies over time. Until recently, for example, few Westerners would have visited India to undergo surgery. However, many now perceive India as an excellent value for obtaining medical care for various conditions and spend the time and money to travel there to receive heart operations, cosmetic surgery, and other procedures.[27]

Finally, the tendency of consumers to discriminate against foreign products varies by demographic factors. For example, senior citizens and people with limited education tend to shun products that originate abroad.[28]

Consumer ethnocentrism is the tendency to view domestically produced goods as superior to those produced in other countries.[29] Some people believe it inappropriate, and possibly even immoral, to buy products from other countries. In Japan and the United States, for example, buying foreign goods may be seen as unpatriotic or causing job losses. In India, activists tried to dissuade local consumers from buying Coca-Cola, believing it offends traditional and national Indian values.[30]

In contrast to consumer ethnocentrism, **world mindedness** refers to a consumer's interest in, and openness to, acquiring goods from other countries.[31] World mindedness both arises from and contributes to the emergence of a global consumer culture. The more consumers are exposed to products, services, and ideas from abroad, the more likely they may be to adopt world-minded tendencies. A *cosmopolitan* is someone who maintains a network of links and personal contacts with those outside the immediate community and is willing to venture into other cultures.[32] Cosmopolitans are especially attractive targets for MNEs launching new products. Firms may develop advertising that incorporates foreign and global cultural positioning to appeal to world-minded consumers.[33] For example, both Apple and BMW benefit enormously from consumer perceptions of these firms as offering global, worldly brands.

THE INDUSTRIAL BUYER

Also known as organizational buyers or businesses, *industrial buyers* differ substantially from retail consumers. Industrial buyers purchase raw materials, parts, components, and supplies in order to produce other products or run a business. Some industrial buyers function as wholesalers or retailers who purchase unfinished or finished goods to sell and distribute to other industrial buyers or to retail consumers. Industrial buyers may have substantial face-to-face contact with vendors, with whom they often develop long-term relationships. Purchases are usually based on specifications and technical data, with buyers applying relatively scientific and rational approaches to the buying process. Buying is performed by professional purchasing managers who may buy enormous quantities of goods. Industrial buyers often employ competitive bidding and negotiations during the buying process.

Industrial buyers are strongly influenced by globalization. Segmenting markets on a global scale is generally more feasible for industrial products than for retail goods. For example, industrial goods such as bulk metals, semiconductors, and pressure valves require less differentiation to meet industrial buyer needs. Industrial buyers prefer using standardized inputs whenever possible to minimize costs. For example, while Swedish appliance manufacturer Electrolux might sell dozens of distinctive refrigerator models to retail consumers, the firm prefers to source only a limited variety of thermostats, compressors, and other parts to make refrigerators. Their approach helps minimize the costs of purchasing, inventory, manufacturing, and quality control. Chrysler, Honda, and other automakers emphasize modular architecture, where suppliers manufacture single component modules, which are then bolted into a car or truck body rolling down assembly lines. The modular approach minimizes the total cost of vehicle manufacturing.

Industrial buying is associated with two important concepts: derived demand and cost-performance. *Derived demand* refers to demand for raw materials, parts, and other inputs that depends on demand for some other good. For example, demand for antennas used in building Airbus A320 commercial jetliners depends on demand for the jetliners themselves—the more A320s that Airbus sells, the more antennas it buys from vendors. *Cost-performance* refers to the expected performance of a product relative to the cost to buy and use it. Cost-performance is emphasized because organizations aim to maximize profitability. Profits hinge on ensuring the firm obtains maximal performance from input goods for a given level of cost. Firms from developing economies usually have limited resources and give greater weight to the cost-performance relationship when buying industrial goods.

INFLUENCES ON THE GLOBAL INDUSTRIAL BUYER

Decision making on industrial buying varies around the world. For large-scale purchases, firms usually undertake buying as managerial teams, consisting of experts on issues such as engineering and manufacturing. Purchasing managers are empowered to choose suppliers and arrange the terms of purchase but ultimately answer to others in the firm, who, based on their expertise, strongly influence what goods are bought. Many people in the firm may become involved in the buying process. As with retail consumers, industrial buyers are influenced by various factors, especially culture, stage of economic development, and national situational factors.

Culture

Cultural influences occur at the level of the nation, the industry, and the firm. Most companies have a distinctive set of norms, values, and modes of behavior. Marketing goods to such buyers necessitates skills in dealing with organizational and national cultural factors. For example, industrial buyers in Asia and Latin America put much stock in the quality of relationships with individual vendors. In China and Japan, buyers and vendors routinely exchange gifts to build trust and familiarity. In Europe and the Americas, such gifts can be construed as a form of bribery. While a retail consumer might have little direct interaction with retailers and no interaction with manufacturers, industrial buyers work closely with their suppliers. In business-to-business deals, negotiations are common, placing much importance on the quality of relations between buyers and sellers. In such settings, cultural attitudes and values can play a major role.

Industrial buyers vary based on their *attitude toward risk*, which differs cross-nationally. As noted in Chapter 3, uncertainty avoidance refers to the capacity of people in different countries to tolerate risk. High uncertainty-avoidance countries are risk averse and favor rules, regulations, and control mechanisms to minimize risk taking. In such countries, marketers often must work harder to convince purchasing managers to accept proposals from new vendors. Purchase decisions may be driven by consensus, and projects are carefully planned. By contrast, low uncertainty avoidance cultures are usually more innovative and open to new approaches. In such countries, industrial buyers are more willing to try new offerings or goods from new market entrants.[34]

The industrial buying process typically tends to be systematic and stepwise as purchasing professionals identify, evaluate, and choose among alternative brands and suppliers. Initially, the process is guided by the organization's goals and constraints. The buying task is determined by the structure and size of the firm, structure of the organization, and technology available and relevant to purchasing. When management recognizes a need, it undertakes a process of specifying the features of the desired good. The firm will search for suppliers and solicit proposals from suitable vendors. Purchasing will select the most appropriate supplier, place an order, and, eventually, review the performance of the supplier and its goods or service. The nature of these steps varies from country to country. For example, firms in Northern Europe usually have flat organizational structures and purchasing managers employ systematic approaches, with substantial consistency and transparency. In Southeast Asia, by contrast, firms are often hierarchical, and purchasing activities may entail significant complexity or ambiguity. Rules and practices may be somewhat unpredictable and dictated by government regulation.

Stage of Economic Development

Countries pass through various stages of economic development. The level of development determines, to a large extent, the nature and quantity of demand for industrial products. The typical developmental stages are as follows:[35]

1. *Traditional society.* At the most basic level, many countries are characterized by subsistence activity in which output is consumed by producers rather than traded. The stage is most associated with subsistence farming, the most common economic activity in the world's poorest countries. Example regions include South Asia and sub-Saharan Africa.
2. *Transitional stage.* Countries evolve beyond dependence on agriculture and begin to engage in simple manufacturing of value-added goods. The stage coincides with development of infrastructure in transportation, communications, and other areas. Entrepreneurs emerge who launch small firms that require basic inputs and trade in natural resources and other primary products. Many late-stage developing economies—for example, Honduras, Vietnam, and Zimbabwe—are in the transitional phase.
3. *Take-off.* Here workers progress from agriculture to manufacturing. Producers specialize and begin to mass produce goods that can be exchanged with trading partners worldwide. Most emerging market countries—such as Brazil, China, and Russia—have attained this stage. Rising incomes stimulate investment and development of a thriving consumer economy.
4. *Drive to maturity.* In this stage, countries emphasize the production of high-technology products and development of a strong services sector. Late-stage emerging markets such as Poland, Saudi Arabia, and South Korea are examples.
5. *Mass consumption.* Most countries have not reached this stage, which is characterized by a thriving consumer and industrial economy with a substantial services sector. Numerous advanced economies are in this category.

Today most countries have advanced beyond Stage 1, and consequently there are vast opportunities worldwide for various industrial goods. The firm must investigate each nation's specific circumstances to determine what types of products and services are in most demand.

Growing global consumerism is straining resources and pressuring natural environments. *The International Marketplace 6.4* addresses the emergent tension between rising global consumption and *sustainability*, meeting humanity's needs without harming future generations.

National Situational Factors

Numerous situational factors influence industrial buying. Initially, countries have differing levels of technological development. The *technology acceptance model* describes how individuals and firms accept and use given technologies.[36] A firm may be reluctant to embrace an innovation or advanced technological product if the offering exceeds the firm's level of relevant experience or

THE INTERNATIONAL **MARKETPLACE** 6.4

Global Consumerism and Sustainability

Between 1980 and 2010, the middle class worldwide nearly doubled in size, growing to almost two billion people. By the year 2030, it is likely to reach nearly five billion people. The middle class is the largest demographic group in terms of consumers of various products and services. However, the growth of the middle class puts pressures on the natural environment and increases demand for resources, such as energy, food, and raw materials. Rising world population and increased production and consumption raise concerns about *sustainability*, which refers to meeting humanity's needs without harming future generations. On the one hand, rising consumerism is a sign that living standards are improving worldwide; billions of people are emerging from the poverty that besets humanity. On the other hand, a growing population and consumerism pose important challenges to planetary well-being.

The World Economic Forum has proposed various ideas for addressing sustainability while ensuring people can obtain the products and services they need. Some of these ideas are:

1. *Emphasizing durable over disposable.* Firms and consumers alike benefit from products that are relatively durable, as opposed to disposable goods that use more resources and fill up landfills.
2. *Using renewable versus disappearing resources.* Renewable resources are usually more cost effective and encourage sustainability. For example, energy generated from solar and wind sources can be maintained indefinitely, while fossil fuels are dwindling over time.
3. *Sharing resources.* Firms and consumers must think increasingly about developing and using goods that they share with others. For example, homeowners tend to use lawn mowers, snowblowers, and other home-care equipment only intermittently. Economies result when such resources are shared among several households.
4. *Favoring virtual products and delivery methods.* Online product vendors use resources more efficiently than physical, brick-and-mortar retailers. Some products can be offered electronically, which saves paper. For example, many consumers opt for digital books they can read on Kindles, iPads, and similar devices. Such approaches help reduce the destruction of forests and other resources.
5. *Consuming locally grown goods.* Many agricultural products must be transported long distances, which contributes to air pollution and needless resource usage. An emphasis on consuming locally grown farm products can help increase resource sustainability and decrease pollution.

To thrive while preserving natural resources, companies will need to include sustainability in their strategy making. Managers need to improve their understanding of how resources create new risks but also produce new opportunities. Firms must devise sophisticated approaches for conserving resources and offering sustainable products and services.

For example, Otis makes the Gen2 elevator, which uses up to 75 percent less energy than conventional elevators. Recently, Otis established a green manufacturing facility to produce Gen2 elevators in Tianjin, China, which reduced site energy use by more than 25 percent. Builders are also adopting Gen2 elevators and escalators to save energy and help the environment. In another example, the Dutch consumer products company Unilever is cutting water usage and greenhouse gas emissions in its factories. The firm aims to increase recycling and recovery efforts in manufacturing and to reduce by one-third the use of materials in its product packaging by 2020. Also, the Swiss food company Nestlé works with farmers around the world to help them increase crop yields while minimizing their water usage and pollution. Nestlé has allied with nongovernmental organizations such as the Rainforest Alliance to focus on how farmers can improve access to clean water and sanitation.

SOURCES: "Food and Beverage Companies Serve Up Sustainability," *Business & the Environment*, October 2011, 1–3; Richard Dobbs, Jeremy Oppenheim, and Fraser Thompson, "Mobilizing for a Resource Revolution," *McKinsey Quarterly*, January 2012, www.mckinseyquarterly.com; and World Economic Forum, *Consumer Industry Emerging Trends and Issues* (Geneva, Switzerland: World Economic Forum, 2011), www.weforum.org.

knowledge. Acceptance of technological innovations depends on the level of economic or social development in a firm or a nation.

In terms of economic variables, most countries use a currency that is different from the currency of the selling firm. Fluctuating exchange rates affect the attractiveness of foreign goods, either making them relatively costly or inexpensive from the industrial buyer's perspective. Inflation may cause prices to rise over time. Argentina, Israel, Russia, and numerous other countries have experienced high inflation, occasionally exceeding 1,000 percent annually. Inflation complicates the international buying process by distorting exchange rates and the cost of capital and by producing uncertainty in international transactions. Inflation is especially burdensome for industrial goods, which are often sold under long-term contracts.

THE GOVERNMENT BUYER

Governments are important targets for sales of goods and services. Governments at both federal and local levels purchase nearly every kind of good, from aircraft to thumbtacks, from construction services to training services. Many seemingly private companies are actually government-owned enterprises. Some of the largest firms in China, for example, are state owned. Most are energy utilities, oil companies, railways, and others in industries considered vital to China's national security or serving China's huge market with essential products and services. State-owned enterprises are found in all countries but are the norm in developing economies.

Exhibit 6.5 shows the governments with the highest level of expenditures. These countries tend to also be among the best government customers for international marketers. For example, Japan had government expenditures of $2,483 billion. China and Brazil are both notable as emerging markets. The governments of these countries spend huge sums every year and, at the same time, have substantial infrastructure development needs. Thus, China and Brazil would make excellent target markets for companies in the construction, energy, and telecommunications industries.

Most governments have a system, often required by international agreements or treaties, for opening government purchases that exceed a certain dollar value to international bids. The aim of competitive bidding is to ensure the government pays a competitive price, receives quality goods, and avoids the corruption that may accompany choosing suppliers based on personal relationships. Procurement opportunities are huge, with governments spending up to

EXHIBIT 6.5 Government Expenditures, 2011

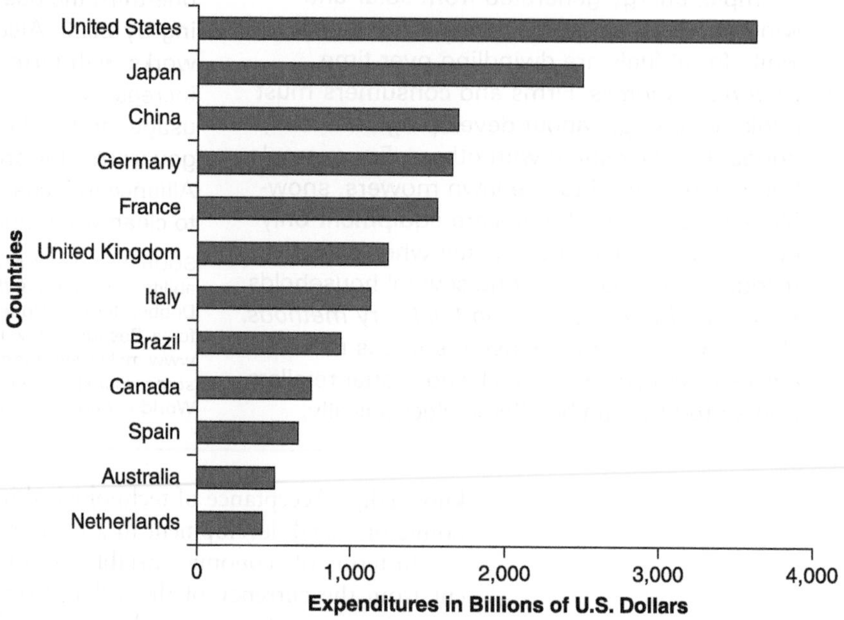

SOURCE: Central Intelligence Agency, *CIA World Factbook 2012*, www.cia.gov.

15 percent of national GDP on purchasing in the advanced economies and up to 20 percent of GDP in the developing economies.

The nature of government procurement varies worldwide. Compared to industrial sales, selling to governments can be highly bureaucratic. For example, India has an extensive, burdensome bureaucracy with formidable obstacles to closing the sale, particularly for foreign firms. Negotiating with foreign governments is often arduous and requires much skill and experience. Many governments have regulations that limit purchases to domestic producers. In many procurement situations, nations discriminate against nonnative suppliers. In Saudi Arabia, for example, contractors must subcontract 30 percent of the value of any government contract to firms owned by Saudi nationals. The EU countries require open, competitive bidding but usually discriminate against bids with less than 50 percent EU content. The content requirement applies to foreign suppliers of goods and services related to water, energy, urban transport, and postal services.[37]

In Brazil, foreign firms face obstacles in public procurement deals unless they are associated with a local firm.[38] The U.S. government favors home-country suppliers for supplying goods deemed vital to national security. In addition, the United States and other countries often prohibit their own citizens from selling certain product categories abroad, especially those related to national security.

Most advanced economies and a few emerging markets are party to the Agreement on Government Procurement (GPA) of the World Trade Organization. The GPA's main goal is to open government procurement to international competition. It also aims to ensure procurement laws, regulations, and procedures are transparent and do not protect domestic products or suppliers nor discriminate against foreign products or suppliers. However, in many industries, developing economies lack a substantial supplier base and, consequently, are relatively open to receiving bids from foreign vendors. In fact, very few countries can supply all the inputs needed to develop large-scale public projects, such as building computer systems, railway lines, and power plants.

MARKETING TO GLOBAL CONSUMERS

In this section, we discuss key managerial implications, including targeting global customers, managing COO issues, customer relationship management, and selling to governments.

Targeting Global Customers

In many ways the task of the international marketer today is less complex than in the past. In earlier times, when countries differed sharply in terms of culture, income, legal systems, and other factors, marketers found themselves devising a wide range of marketing programs to suit diverse needs and tastes around the world. Today, thanks to globalization and related trends, market needs worldwide have grown similar in most industries. Take the food and beverage industry as an example. While there is still much variance in food menus around the world, today people are more open to a variety of international cuisines. Just as the Japanese have acquired a taste for hamburgers and pizza, so too people in the United States increasingly consume sushi and tofu. Cultural observers have noted that many Northern Europeans, who historically favored beer as their alcoholic drink, have acquired a taste for wine. Simultaneously, Southern Europeans, who historically preferred wine, have acquired a taste for beer.

A **global market segment** is a group of customers who share common characteristics across numerous national markets. Marketers target these buyers with relatively standardized marketing programs. Ideally, the marketer should create a unique positioning of its offerings in the minds of target customers.

The Apple iPad has captured the attention of the global market segment of consumers who buy the latest in information technology products.

Many international firms aim for a *global positioning strategy*, that is, one in which the offering is positioned similarly in the minds of buyers across an entire region or worldwide. The strategy reduces international marketing costs by minimizing the need to adapt elements of the marketing program for individual markets. People who use smartphones have emerged as a promising global market segment. Mobile TeleSystems (MTS) is a Russian telecommunications firm that operates mobile and fixed-access networks in Russia, Ukraine, Belarus, Uzbekistan, and Armenia. MTS used a global market segmentation approach to create a common language and consistent platform for its marketing activities across these markets. Market research revealed retail users of its mobile telephone services tend to be price sensitive (given lower incomes in the region), young and trendy, lovers of new technology, and status seeking. Once the key segment characteristics were known, MTS developed its services to serve its customers optimally.[39]

Many firms organize dealings with key global industrial buyers through *global account management* (GAM).[40] Companies worldwide have long used national account management to handle their most important accounts. Recently, globalization has created the need for coordinating top accounts at multinational firms on a global scale. For example, Toyota expects its many suppliers to provide Toyota factories with the same high-quality parts, components, and services at Toyota plants worldwide. In each of Toyota's suppliers, for each category of part or component that Toyota buys, a single manager is charged with all aspects of Toyota's business on a global scale. In this way, a given supplier treats each of Toyota's numerous plants as one single entity, providing consistent and seamless support across all the countries where Toyota manufactures vehicles. Similarly, in the global retailing sector, vendors that supply Walmart provide the firm's many stores with the same products, pricing, and technical support.

GAM benefits customers like Toyota and Walmart in various ways. First, by sourcing the same products and services for its worldwide operations, the customer gains economies of scale and scope that translate into lower costs and more efficiencies. Second, GAM ensures the supplier speaks to the customer with one voice, reducing the possibility for miscommunication or mishap. Third, the customer need deal only with a single contact point, a global account executive or team focused on its specific needs, who knows best how to provide consistent worldwide support.

Country-of-Origin Challenges

Multinational firms employ various strategies to overcome consumer ethnocentrism and the COO phenomenon. First, when contemplating a new marketing venture in a given foreign country, management should conduct market research to learn about the presence and nature of any COO effects. Research also should aim to ascertain the presence of any potentially moderating variables, such as product quality or price, whose manipulation can serve to reduce the impact of a negative COO effect. When management knows that consumers hold a positive image of a given COO, the national origin should be emphasized in marketing efforts.

In the event the COO image is negative, the firm may attempt to conceal the national origin or position the offering as made in the targeted country. In

Japan, McDonald's positioned itself as a Japanese restaurant chain because the Japanese sometimes avoid offerings that are not perceived as made in Japan. Numerous clothing manufacturers in China adopt an Italian-sounding brand name, hoping consumers will assume the apparel is from Italy, which enjoys a strong image in the fashion trade. However, such positioning is difficult when the brand—such as American Express and Deutsche Bank—is closely identified with a particular COO. In addition, many countries require producers to explicitly identify the COO of brands via a "Made in ..." label stamped on products.

Perhaps the best approach to overcoming negative stereotypes is to offer products of such superior quality that consumers take little notice of the goods' national origin. All else being equal, consumers prefer high-quality products. In addition, the firm might undertake marketing aimed at debunking negative images. For example, many consumers hesitate to buy wines from Chile based on misconceptions about Chile's ability to produce superior wines. In reality, Chile produces excellent wines, and Chilean winemakers have conveyed this image through skillful marketing. South Korean automakers recently have applied similar marketing techniques to convince buyers worldwide about the superior quality of their offerings and to launch new lines of Korean luxury cars.

Another strategy for minimizing the impact of a negative COO is to offer the product at a relatively low price. This approach tends to attract value-conscious consumers, even if they usually prefer local brands. However, discount pricing works only if the firm enjoys a cost advantage. For certain types of goods, a company might succeed in charging a relatively high price as a means of signaling superior quality. In the long run, however, the approach will work only if the product is indeed of high quality or has other attributes that justify charging a high price.

Lastly, the firm might overcome a negative COO by having its product distributed through a well-respected intermediary in the target market. For example, the Czech automaker Skoda entered a joint venture with Volkswagen to market Skoda cars in Germany. The arrangement allowed Skoda to achieve substantial sales in the German market and overcome a popular perception of Eastern European cars as being of low quality.[41]

In a world of globalizing production, determining where a product is made is increasingly difficult. Many products with a brand associated with a given country are in fact produced in another country. For example, most consumers know Toyota is a Japanese brand, but Toyota cars and trucks are manufactured in Brazil, Turkey, and numerous other countries worldwide. A typical car is made from parts and components that originate in dozens of different countries. Retailers worldwide now routinely offer products made in countless countries. Increasingly, consumers are understanding and accepting of this globalization of production. Educated consumers tend to hold few biases regarding the national origins of various products.

Global Customer Relationship Management

The customer is the ultimate focus of marketing. Historically, transactional marketing focused on increasing the number of individual sales. Today, experienced marketers know it is more effective to maintain long-term relationships with good customers than to constantly search for and find new customers. In many ways, the historic transactional orientation of marketing has given way to a focus on relationships and relationship marketing. Thus, firms that emphasize **relationship marketing** seek to build long-term relationships with key customers. This is most typically achieved by emphasizing activities that ensure consistent customer satisfaction. Relationship marketing not only is important for key customers but also applies to acquiring quality relations with supply chain partners, collaborative venture partners, and other key connections in the firm's value chains worldwide. Relationship marketing has special relevance to international marketing because the firm often finds itself particularly dependent on partners and facilitators located abroad, such as distribution channel intermediaries, suppliers, and customer service representatives.[42]

Relationship marketing is especially important in industrial sales because of the tendency of large-scale buyers to source goods from sellers whom they trust and with whom they have built up a record of ongoing purchases. Marketers usually succeed best when they develop personal rapport with purchasing managers and other key contacts in target organizations. The development of quality relationships particularly influences industrial buyer-seller relationships in Africa, Asia, and Latin America—regions where much emphasis is placed on social bonds in business. In Japan, for example, offering the lowest cost and best quality product is usually insufficient to ensure a sale if the seller does not have an established relationship with the buyer.

Customer relationship management (CRM) refers to collecting, storing, and analyzing customer data to develop and maintain two-way relations between the firm and key customers. The ultimate goal of CRM is to maximize value to the firm's most important customers so they remain customers indefinitely. CRM is also related to providing superior customer service. *Customer service* includes activities such as training (e.g., teaching customers how to use a product), repair of damaged or malfunctioning products, financing to assist customers in purchasing products, and complaint resolution. Regarding data analysis, there is growing concern about privacy issues and fear of companies simply knowing too much.

Selling to Governments

One of the most lucrative market opportunities when selling to foreign governments is infrastructure development. Nations need basic infrastructure—energy grids, transportation networks, communications systems—in order to function well and develop dynamic economies. Exhibit 6.6 shows the population and electricity consumption of a collection of countries. For example, note how electricity consumption in Norway and South Korea are high relative to their population. By contrast, electricity consumption is low relative to population in Mexico and Brazil, and very low in India and China. These findings suggest a substantial need for goods and services related to developing power plants and other infrastructure for producing energy in those countries.

Broadly, government procurement, or public tendering, is the purchasing of products and services on behalf of a government agency or other public entity. Governments usually designate a central office to serve as a point of contact for publicizing procurement opportunities and receiving bids. Tendering involves several steps. Initially, a government desires to purchase a given product or service. If the anticipated cost is over a minimum threshold amount (for example, $200,000), the government is typically required to open the contract to a public bidding process. Next, companies (whether domestic or foreign) bid on the right to provide the product or service for a price they determine. Once all bids have been received, the government usually chooses the lowest bidder, unless the bidder is deemed incompetent or likely to provide an inferior good. Successful bidders are usually firms with substantial experience in government procurement. They are usually skilled in international negotiations, which are undertaken to address specifications, supplementary services, price, delivery, and payment procedure of the desired good.

Several factors are of paramount importance to ensuring success in selling to foreign governments. First, it is essential to *know one's strengths and weaknesses*. The firm must assess its core competencies and areas of expertise, and then match these to the needs and opportunities that present themselves in government agencies abroad. Second, it is critical for the firm to *develop the right resources* to secure sales and fulfill orders. For example, when approaching the Russian government, the firm should engage personnel familiar with Russia and its complex public sector. Third, it is important to *develop the appropriate*

EXHIBIT 6.6 **Total Population and Electric Power Consumption per Capita for Selected Countries (kWh)**

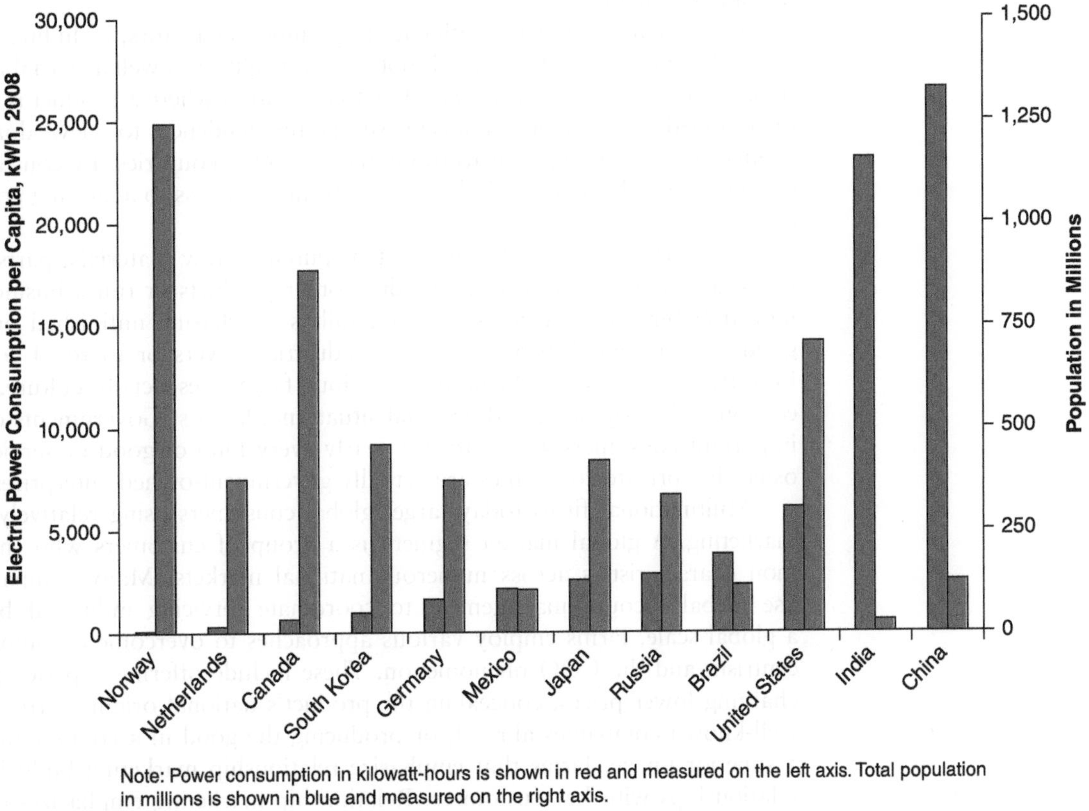

SOURCES: International Monetary Fund, *World Economic Outlook Database 2011*, www.imf.org; and World Bank, *World Development Indicators 2011* (Washington, DC: World Bank, 2011).

relationships. For marketing to foreign governments, having the right contacts is often just as important as specific industry knowledge. Developing key relationships is a time-consuming, painstaking process and often involves networking with the right people for months or years in advance of selling opportunities. It may be necessary to partner with local experts who possess such contacts. Fourth, it is essential to *engage in planning* to help ensure success. The firm will want to devise a plan that identifies key goals, strategies and tactics for achieving them, and a timetable for reaching goals and performing tasks.[43]

Throughout this process, the marketer cannot underestimate the importance of research. The firm should acquire factual and interpretive knowledge about the target government and the opportunity at hand. Successful companies develop a base of knowledge that ensures they are not caught off guard in negotiations and in the preparation of bids and proposals. Knowledge about the political and economic background of target countries—their history, current national affairs, and perceptions about other cultures—is very useful. Such knowledge facilitates understanding about the mindset, organization, and objectives of the target agency. Decisions and events are much easier to interpret when the firm is equipped with the appropriate information.

SUMMARY

Globalization and technological advances are associated with the rise of the global consumer, individuals or organizations that exhibit similar needs and tastes worldwide. Demand for some product categories remains relatively specialized, requiring adaptation. However, products in most categories have become increasingly standardized. Accordingly, firms can employ global marketing, which emphasizes uniformity of branding, packaging, marketing communications, and distribution channels.

The global consumer is influenced by numerous factors, including economic status, technology level, personal motives, and culture as well as social and situational factors. *Country of origin* refers to the nation where a product is produced or branded. Consumer ethnocentrism is the tendency to view domestically produced goods as superior to those made in other countries. By contrast, many consumers exhibit world mindedness, a strong openness to acquiring goods from other countries.

Industrial buyers are businesses that purchase raw materials, parts, components, and supplies in order to produce other products or run a business. Some industrial buyers are wholesalers or retailers purchasing unfinished or finished goods to sell and distribute to other industrial buyers or to retail consumers. Industrial buyers are influenced by various factors, especially culture, stage of economic development, and national situational factors. Governments constitute important consumers and purchase nearly every kind of good or service. Many ostensibly private companies are actually government-owned enterprises.

Multinational firms today target global consumers using relatively uniform marketing. A global market segment is a group of customers who share common characteristics across numerous national markets. Many companies now use global account management to coordinate servicing industrial buyers on a global scale. Firms employ various approaches to overcome consumer ethnocentrism and the COO phenomenon. These include offering superior products, charging lower prices, concealing the product's national origin, partnering with well-known companies abroad, or producing the good in a country that enjoys a superior image. Firms that emphasize relationship marketing build long-term relationships with key customers. Relationship marketing emphasizes consistent customer satisfaction and is important not only for key customers but also for the firm's partners in its worldwide value chains. Government procurement, or public tendering, is the purchasing of goods and services on behalf of a government agency or other public entity. Selling to governments requires the firm to submit bids and vie to be the lowest bidder. Successful government suppliers develop key resources and relationships and engage in skillful planning.

KEY TERMS

global consumer
norms
country of origin (COO)
consumer ethnocentrism
world mindedness
global market segment
relationship marketing
customer relationship management (CRM)

QUESTIONS FOR DISCUSSION

1. Describe the main characteristics of the global consumer.
2. Explain the three levels of the global consumer.
3. Explain the drivers of the contemporary global buyer marketplace.
4. What are the main influences on the global consumer?
5. What are country-of-origin effects? Define *consumer ethnocentrism* and *world mindedness*.
6. Describe the main characteristics of the industrial buyer.
7. What factors influence the global industrial buyer?
8. Explain the typical stages of national economic development.
9. What are the main characteristics of the government buyer?
10. Explain what firms can do to succeed at targeting global consumers.
11. What is global customer relationship management?
12. Explain the major steps in selling to governments.

INTERNET EXERCISES

1. The European Union is home to more than 500 million (mostly well-heeled) consumers, making it one of the largest and most attractive markets worldwide. As firms contemplate selling goods in the EU, they conduct market research using secondary data. An excellent source of secondary data and site for learning about the EU is http://europa.eu, the official website of the EU. Visit the various links at this site and develop a profile of consumers in the EU.
2. Governments are important consumers of products and services. Suppose you work for a firm seeking to market its offerings to the governments of Mexico and Norway. You can learn a lot about the governments in these countries by visiting www.doingbusiness.org, a site sponsored by the World Bank. Visit this site and research the governments in these countries. Write a report on your findings.

CHALLENGE US

Marketing Tobacco and Alcohol to Consumers in Developing Economies

Sales of cigarettes and other tobacco products have declined in the advanced economies in recent decades. Today, only 20 percent of consumers in the United States smoke, down from more than 50 percent in the 1950s. As people in advanced economies learned about smoking's harmful health effects, tobacco companies such as Philip Morris and British American Tobacco increased their marketing efforts in developing economies. In China, for example, 60 percent of all men smoke. A pack of cigarettes sells for $2, even though most Chinese earn less than $600 per month. In Russia, where 70 percent of men smoke, the average lifespan is 65 years.

Global tobacco firms oppose efforts to print warnings on cigarette packages. In developing economies, smoking bans or antismoking activism are rare. Most people endure severe poverty and know little about smoking's link to ailments like cancer. At the same time, however, life in poor countries is hard, and smoking is one of few pleasures that people enjoy. Governments also benefit from the tax revenue they receive from cigarette sales.

Another group that earns big profits in developing economies is the global beer, wine, and liquor industry, typified by companies such as Diageo and Constellation Brands. In much of Africa and Latin America, for example, multinational liquor firms use persuasive advertising to attract consumers to their brands. Ads are often designed to link drinking alcohol with virility, sexual success, or high-class lifestyles. Companies place alcohol billboards in front of schools and playgrounds. Advertising often depicts images and music that appeal to teenagers. Some global alcohol firms use cartoons to market their products on television in Africa. Much research points to excessive alcohol usage as a key predictor of poverty. At the same time, just as with smoking, drinking is one of life's few pleasures in much of the developing world.

For Discussion

1. Should global tobacco and alcohol firms be strictly regulated in developing economies?
2. What steps should be taken, if any, to ensure social responsibility in the marketing of tobacco and alcohol in developing economies?
3. Should governments ban ads directed at young people?
4. What is the appropriate role of governments, activist groups, and companies in marketing and controlling of these types of substances?

RECOMMENDED READINGS

Amtower, Mark. *Selling to the Government: What It Takes to Compete and Win in the World's Largest Market.* Hoboken, NJ: Wiley, 2011.

de Mooij, Marieke. *Consumer Behavior and Culture: Consequences for Global Marketing and Advertising.* Thousand Oaks, CA: Sage, 2011.

Lucas, Robert. *Please Every Customer: Delivering Stellar Customer Service across Cultures.* Burr Ridge, IL: McGraw Hill, 2011.

Martins, Jo, Farhat Yusuf, and David Swanson. *Consumer Demographics and Behaviour: Markets Are People.* London: Springer, 2011.

Morrison, Terri, and Wayne Conaway. *Kiss, Bow, or Shake Hands, Sales and Marketing: The Essential Cultural Guide—From Presentations and Promotions to Communicating and Closing.* Burr Ridge, IL: McGraw Hill, 2012.

ENDNOTES

1. Carol Motley and Geraldine Rosa, "The Global Hip-Hop Diaspora: Understanding the Culture," *Journal of Business Research* 61, no. 3 (2008): 243–53.
2. "Culture Wars," *Economist*, September 12, 1998, 97–99.
3. Dana Alden, Jan-Benedict Steenkamp, and Rajeev Batra, "Brand Positioning through Advertising in Asia, North America, and Europe: The Role of Global Consumer Culture," *Journal of Marketing* 63, no. 1 (1999): 75–87.
4. George Yip and G. Tomas Hult, *Total Global Strategy*, 3rd ed. (Upper Saddle River, NJ: Prentice Hall, 2011).
5. Russell Belk, "Global Consumerism and Consumption," in *International Marketing*, D. Bello and D. Griffith, eds. (West Sussex, UK: John Wiley, 2011), 67–72.
6. Ibid.
7. Jan Nowak and Olena Kochkova, "Income, Culture, and Household Consumption Expenditure Patterns in the European Union: Convergence or Divergence?" *Journal of International Consumer Marketing* 23, no. 3/4 (2011): 260–75.
8. A. Waheeduzzaman, "Are Emerging Markets Catching Up with the Developed Markets in Terms of Consumption?" *Journal of Global Marketing* 24, no. 2 (2011): 136–51.
9. Vijay Mahajan and Kamini Banga, *The 86% Solution: How to Succeed in the Biggest Market Opportunity of the 21st Century* (Upper Saddle River, NJ: Wharton School Publishing, 2006).
10. C. K. Prahalad, *The Fortune at the Bottom of the Pyramid* (Upper Saddle River, NJ: Wharton School Publishing, 2006).
11. Peter Walters and Saeed Samiee, "Executive Insights: Marketing Strategy in Emerging Markets," *Journal of International Marketing* 11, no. 1 (2003): 97–106.
12. Edmond Lococo, "China Unicom's Smart Call on Cheap Phones," *Businessweek*, January 26, 2012, www.businessweek.com/magazine/china-unicoms-smart-call-on-cheap-phones-01262012.html.
13. "Consumer Electronics Market," *China Consumer Electronics Report* 4, no. 1 (2012): 17–28.
14. International Monetary Fund, *World Economic Outlook Database 2011*, www.imf.org, accessed February 2, 2012.
15. Jose Villaverde and Adolfo Maza, "Globalisation, Growth and Convergence," *World Economy* 34, no. 6 (2011): 952–71.
16. Abraham Maslow, *Motivation and Personality* (New York: Harper and Row, 1954).
17. Shigehiro Oishi, Ed Diener, Richard Lucas, and Eunkook Suh, "Cross-Cultural Variations in Predictors of Life Satisfaction: Perspectives from Needs and Values," in *Culture and Well-Being*, Ed Diener, ed. (New York: Springer, 2009).
18. R. Cialdini, "Descriptive Social Norms as Underappreciated Sources of Social Control," *Psychometrika* 72, no. 2 (2007): 263–68; and Michale Hechter and Karl-Dieter Opp, eds., *Social Norms* (New York: Russell Sage Foundation, 2001).
19. Yuval Atsmon, Vinay Dixit, Glenn Liebowitz, and Cathy Wu, "Understanding China's Growing Love for Luxury," *McKinsey Insights China*, April 2011, www.mckinseyquarterly.com, accessed December 4, 2011.
20. Mahesh Shankarmahesh, "Consumer Ethnocentrism: An Integrative Review of Its Antecedents and Consequences," *International Marketing Review* 23, no. 2 (2006): 146–72.
21. Triwik Kurniasari, "Ramadan: Shopping Time?" *Jakarta Post*, August 15, 2010, www.thejakartapost.com.
22. Barbara Krahe, *Personality and Social Psychology: Towards a Synthesis* (London: Sage, 1993).
23. Mike Peng, Denis Wang, and Yi Jiang, "An Institution-Based View of International Business Strategy: A Focus on Emerging Economies," *Journal of International Business Studies* 20, no. 3 (2008): 920–36.
24. Arpita Mukherjee, Ramneet Goswami, Tanu M. Goyal, and Divya Satija, *Sports Retailing in India: Opportunities, Constraints and Way Forward*, Working Paper No. 250, Indian Council for Research on International Economic Relations, New Delhi, 2010, www.icrier.org.
25. Gary Knight, Richard Spreng, and Attila Yaprak, "Cross-national Development and Validation of an International Business Measurement Scale: The COISCALE," *International Business Review* 12, no. 5 (2003): 581–99.
26. *Pittsburgh Post-Gazette*, November 2, 1996, B13.
27. Michael Guiry and David Vequist, "Traveling Abroad for Medical Care: U.S. Medical Tourists' Expectations and Perceptions of Service Quality," *Health Marketing Quarterly* 28, no. 3 (2011): 253–69.
28. T. Shimp and S. Sharma, "Consumer Ethnocentrism: Construction and Validation of the CETSCALE," *Journal of Marketing Research* 24, no. 3 (1987): 280–89.
29. Ibid.
30. Rohit Varman and Russell Belk, "Nationalism and Ideology in an Anticonsumption Movement," *Journal of Consumer Research* 36, no. 4 (2009): 686–700.
31. Edwin Nijssen and Susan Douglas, "Consumer World-Mindedness and Attitudes toward Product Positioning in Advertising: An Examination of Global versus Foreign versus Local Positioning," *Journal of International Marketing* 19, no. 3 (2011): 113–33.
32. Mark Cleveland, Nicholas Papadopoulos, and Michel Laroche, "Identity, Demographics, and Consumer Behaviors," *International Marketing Review* 28, no. 3 (2011): 244–66.
33. Nijssen and Douglas, 2011.
34. Ronald Batenburg, "E-Procurement Adoption by European Firms: A Quantitative Analysis," *Journal of Purchasing & Supply Management* 13, no. 4 (2007): 182–92.
35. Walt Rostow, *The Stages of Economic Growth* (Cambridge, UK: Cambridge University Press, 1990).
36. Fred Davis, "Perceived Usefulness, Perceived Ease of Use, and User Acceptance of Information Technology," *MIS Quarterly* 13, no. 3 (1989): 319–40.
37. United States Trade Representative, *2011 National Trade Estimate Report on Foreign Trade Barriers* (Washington, DC: Office of the United States Trade Representative), www.ustr.gov/about-us/press-office/reports-and-publications/2011-0.
38. Ibid.
39. Marc O'Regan, Kalidas Ashok, Olga Maksimova, and Oleg Reshetin, "Optimizing Market Segmentation for a

Global Mobile Phone Provider for Both Targeting and Insight," *Journal of Advertising Research* 51, no. 4 (2011): 571–77.
40. Tao Gao and Linda Shi, "How Do Multinational Suppliers Formulate Mechanisms of Global Account Coordination? An Integrative Framework and Empirical Study," *Journal of International Marketing* 19, no. 4 (2011): 61–87.
41. "Skoda's Steady Sales Growth," *Country Monitor*, February 10, 1999, 8.
42. Edwin Nijssen and Hester van Herk, "Conjoining International Marketing and Relationship Marketing: Exploring Consumers' Cross-Border Service Relationships," *Journal of International Marketing* 17, no. 1 (2009): 91–115.
43. Mark Amtower, *Selling to the Government* (Hoboken, NJ: John Wiley, 2011).

CHAPTER 7

Strategic Planning

LEARNING OBJECTIVES

By the time you complete this chapter, you will be able to:

- Outline the process of strategic planning in the context of the global marketplace.
- Examine both the external and internal factors that determine the conditions for development of strategy and resource allocation.
- Illustrate how best to utilize the environmental conditions within the competitive challenges and resources of the firm to develop effective programs.
- Suggest how to achieve a balance between local and regional or global priorities and concerns in the implementation of strategy.

THE INTERNATIONAL MARKETPLACE 7.1

Powering Growth in Emerging Markets

China, Brazil, India, Russia, and Indonesia are very different from the Western European and North American markets, but they represent the future growth markets for Heinz. The new emerging middle classes in these countries are going to want the same kind of variety and conveniences. To provide it, Heinz has embraced a long-term marketing strategy called the Four A's. The first A is *applicability*. Suitability to local culture is key when deciding to invest in a new market. Although Heinz sells some ketchup in China, soy sauce is the dominant condiment there. When entering new markets, it is important to be aware as to how the product may be used differently.

The second A is *availability*. Are there channels to distribute products to the relevant local population? The United States markets have modern grocery stores and supercenters in which a company can get shelf space. In Indonesia, less than one-third of the population visits modern grocery stores, leaving the rest to purchase from tiny corner stores and open-air markets. In China, chain grocers have a 50 percent share; Russia's grocers have a 40 percent share; and in India, it is less than a 15 percent share.

The third A is *affordability*. Price is key when entering a new market, with a realistic view of what the markets can afford. Different-size packaging can address this issue. In Indonesia, small packets of soy sauce are sold (about 3 cents apiece), making them convenient for people without refrigerators or pantries.

The fourth A is *affinity*. Local managers for emerging markets are critical in establishing local employee and customer brand awareness and loyalty while communicating with corporate on local standards of living. When necessary, companies can send an emerging markets capability team—a group of senior people from Western businesses—to coach local managers on how to implement a particular way of doing business, such as in marketing or finance.

In 2010 and 2011, Heinz acquired two new platforms in China and Brazil to meet the growing food demands in countries where billions of consumers are discovering packaged foods. In China, Heinz acquired Foodstar, a leading maker of soy sauce and fermented bean curd with annual sales of $100 million. Foodstar offers a solid platform into China's $2 billion retail soy sauce market, where its Master brand holds a strong brand image. Heinz plans to continue the growth momentum by launching new products, expanding distribution across China, and completing a new Foodstar factory in Shanghai to meet demand.

Courtesy of the H.J. Heinz Company

A sampling of Heinz international brands.

In Brazil, the world's fifth most populated country, Heinz purchased an 80 percent stake in the manufacturer of Quero. Quero, a growing brand of tomato-based sauces, ketchup, condiments, and vegetables with annual sales around $325 million, gives Heinz a door to market products in a rapidly expanding economy. Heinz plans to expand the brand and its distribution.

Emerging markets such as Brazil and China should generate more than 20 percent of company sales in fiscal year 2012. This is in line with Heinz's "buy and build" strategy for emerging markets, acquiring strong brands and businesses in key markets.

SOURCES: Bill Johnson, "The CEO of Heinz on Powering Growth in Emerging Markets," *Harvard Business Review* 89 (October 2011), 47–50; and Heinz, www.heinz.com/heinz.aspx.

GLOBAL MARKETING

Many marketing managers have to face the increasing globalization of markets and competition described in *The International Marketplace 7.1*. The rules of survival have changed since the beginning of the 1980s when Theodore Levitt first coined the phrase *global marketing*.[1] Even the biggest companies in the biggest home markets cannot survive on domestic sales alone if they are in global industries such as banking, cars, consumer electronics, entertainment, home appliances, mobile devices, pharmaceuticals, publishing, or travel services. They have to be in all major markets to survive the shakeouts expected to leave three to five players per industry at the beginning of the twenty-first century.[2]

Globalization reflects a business orientation based on the belief that the world is becoming more homogeneous and that distinctions between national markets are not only fading but, for some products, will eventually disappear. As a result, companies need to globalize their international strategies by formulating them across markets to take advantage of underlying market, cost, environmental, and competitive factors. This has meant, for example, that Chinese and Indian companies (ranging from China Mobile to Tata Communications) have entered the main markets of the world, such as Europe and North America, to become global powerhouses.[3] Having a global presence ensures viability against other players, both local and global, in the home market as well.

As shown in Exhibit 7.1, global marketing can be seen as the culmination of a process of international market entry and expansion. Before globalization, marketers utilized a country-by-country multidomestic strategy to a great extent, with each country organization operated as a profit center. Each national entity marketed a range of different products and services targeted to different customer segments, utilizing different marketing strategies with little or no coordination of operations between countries.

However, as national markets become increasingly similar and scale economies become increasingly important, the inefficiencies of duplicating product development and manufacture in each country become more apparent and the pressure to leverage resources and coordinate activities across borders gains

EXHIBIT 7.1 Global Marketing Evolution

Phase 1	Phase 2	Phase 3
Leverage of domestic capabilities: foreign market entry	Expansion of foreign market presence	Coordination of global operations
Objective: economies of scale	Objective: economies of scope	Objective: exploit synergies throughout network
	Corporate Actions	
Driven opportunistically, often by approach of distributor or customer	Slower domestic growth creates greater pressure for foreign sales growth	Product is the broadened, new emphasis on full-line service rather than proprietary technology
Constrained by lack of funding (domestic growth still priority investment), so low-cost entry	New lines carried, sales mix broadens and reflects national market	Global account management
Risk minimized by entering close markets (geographically, culturally, economically)	Search for new customer segments requiring new management skills	Coordination mechanisms (global task forces)
Entry based on core products with technical superiority	Countries develop own marketing programs	Learning transferred between countries
	New applications sought	Headquarters introduces global branding and packaging
	Decentralization of R&D	Requires common culture
	Regional management reflects foreign experience	

SOURCES: Adapted from Susan P. Douglas and C. Samuel Craig, "Evolution of Global Marketing Strategy: Scale, Scope, and Synergy," *Columbia Journal of World Business* 24 (Fall 1989): 47–58; Accenture, "From Global Connection to Global Orchestration: Future Business Models for High Performance Where Technology and the Multi-Polar World Meet," September 30, 2010; and George S. Yip and G. Tomas Hult, *Total Global Strategy* (Prentice Hall, 2011), Chapter 1.

urgency. Similarly, the increasing number of customers operating globally, as well as the demands of facing the same or similar competitors throughout the major markets, adds to the need for strategy integration.

It should be noted that global leverage means balancing three interests: global, regional, and local. In many cases, the exploitation of commonalities is best executed on a regional basis, given that some differences remain between groups of markets.[4] The same strategic principles apply to developing and implementing global and regional strategy. Naturally, the more a marketer can include the local dimension in efforts in each individual market, the more effective the strategy tends to be.[5] For example, consumers may prefer a global brand that has been adapted to local usage conditions. Coke, for instance, uses cane sugar as a sweetener in some countries and corn syrup in others. While the approach is localized, the global resources of a marketer provide the brand with a winning edge (e.g., in terms of quality or quality perceptions).

GLOBALIZATION DRIVERS

Both external and internal factors will create the favorable conditions for development of strategy and resource allocation on a global basis. These factors can be divided into market, cost, environmental, and competitive factors.

Market Factors

With over one billion consumers worldwide, these consumers have similar educational backgrounds, income levels, lifestyles, use of leisure time, and aspirations. One reason given for the similarities in their demand is a level of purchasing power (10 times greater than that of the developing markets or even emerging economies) that translates into higher diffusion rates for certain products. Another reason is that developed infrastructures—diffusion of telecommunication and common platforms such as Microsoft Windows and the Internet—lead to attractive markets for other goods and services. Emerging and developing markets have been able to leapfrog into the newest technologies, closing significant gaps of the past. Products can therefore be designed to meet similar demand conditions throughout the triad and beyond. These similarities also enhance the transferability of other marketing elements. For example, mobile subscribers in BRIC countries rank entertainment, gaming, and music sites among their top categories, while European and U.S. users rank e-mail, weather and news, and sports highest. The reason for the difference is that BRIC residents often do not have the home PCs, cable TV, and iPods that Westerners do, and thus use phones for entertainment purposes.[6] And in Indonesia, BlackBerry handsets made by Canada's Research in Motion (RIM) have become a status symbol among the country's fast-growing middle class.[7]

At the same time, channels of distribution are becoming more global; that is, a growing number of retailers are now showing great flexibility in their strategies for entering new geographic markets.[8] Some are already world powers (e.g., Zara and McDonald's), whereas others are pursuing aggressive growth (e.g., ALDI, Toys 'Я' Us, and IKEA). Also noteworthy are cross-border retail alliances, which expand the presence of retailers to new markets quite rapidly. The presence of global and regional channels makes it more necessary for marketers to rationalize marketing efforts.

Cost Factors

Avoiding cost inefficiencies and duplication of effort are two of the most powerful globalization drivers. A single-country approach may not be large enough for the local business to achieve all possible economies of scale and scope as well as synergies, especially given the dramatic changes in the marketplace. Take, for example, pharmaceuticals. In the 1970s, developing a new drug cost about $16 million and took 4 years. Now, developing a drug costs as much as $1 billion and takes as long as 15 years, with competitive efforts close behind. For the leading companies, annual R&D budgets can run to $5 billion. Only global products for global markets can support that much risk.[9]

Size has become a major asset, which partly explains the many mergers and acquisitions in industries such as aerospace, pharmaceuticals, and telecommunications. We are entering what some in the technology industry refer to as a post-PC era. This does not mean that the personal computer is about to disappear. But, according to estimates from Gartner, a research firm, combined shipments of web-connected smartphones and tablet computers are likely to exceed those of desktop and laptop computers for the first time this year, as shown in Exhibit 7.2.[10]

When General Electric (GE) announced it would spin off its appliance unit for up to $8 billion, five possible buyers emerged, each wanting to boost its global position: LG, a South Korean electronics and telecommunications giant; Haier (China), which is already the second largest maker of refrigerators in the world and ranks sixth in overall appliance sales; Contoladora Mabe, a successful Mexico-based appliance firm that is partly owned by GE and that already makes appliances for other brand-name firms, including GE; Electrolux AB, a Stockholm-based company that parlayed its success in high-end vacuum cleaners into a broader success in home appliances; and Arcelik Anonim Sirketi, an Istanbul, Turkey-based appliance maker that does business throughout the

EXHIBIT 7.2 The Personal Computer versus Mobile Technology

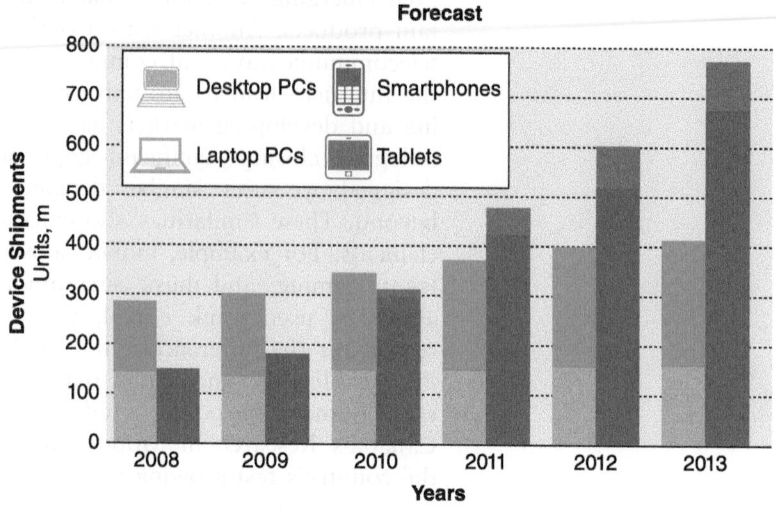

SOURCE: *The Economist*, "Beyond the PC." © The Economist Newspaper Limited, London (October 8, 2011). Reprinted with permission.

world—including in the United States. Even if GE does spin off the consumer unit, it does not mean that it will become a small company.[11]

Environmental Factors

Government barriers have fallen dramatically in the last years to further facilitate the globalization of markets and the activities of marketers within them. For example, the forces pushing toward a pan-European market are very powerful: the increasing wealth and mobility of European consumers (favored by relaxed immigration controls), the accelerating flow of information across borders, the introduction of new products where local preferences are not well established, and the common currency.[12] The resulting removal of physical, fiscal, and technical barriers indicates the changes that are taking place around the world on a greater scale.

At the same time, rapid technological evolution is contributing to the process. With operations spread across different continents, companies regularly use teleconferencing, videoconferencing, and knowledge networks, as well as travel, and are always on the lookout for innovative methods to share information and knowledge. IBM was named one of *CIO* magazine's 2009 CIO 100 award winners for its IBM Virtual Event Space, which allows more IBM employees to virtually attend company events. IBM estimates that this technology saved the company approximately $1 million, including travel, meeting, and venue costs.[13] Newly emerging markets will benefit from advanced communications by being able to leapfrog stages of economic development. Places that until recently were incommunicado in China, Vietnam, or Brazil are rapidly acquiring state-of-the-art telecommunications, especially in mobile telephony, that will let them foster both internal and external development.[14]

A new group of global players is taking advantage of today's more open trading regions and newer technologies. **Mini-nationals** or "born globals" (newer companies with sales between $200 million and $1 billion) are able to serve the world from a handful of bases, compared with having to build a presence in every country as the established multinational corporations once had to do. Their smaller bureaucracies have also allowed these mini-nationals to move swiftly to seize new markets and develop new products—a key to global success.[15] But some, like Skype (from Estonia) or Rovio, the maker of the popular mobile-device game "Angry Birds" (from Finland), have become household names.[16]

The lessons from these new-generation global players are to (1) keep focused and concentrate on being number one or two in a niche; (2) stay lean by having a small headquarters to save on costs and to accelerate decision making; (3) take ideas from wherever they can be found and solutions to wherever they are needed; (4) take advantage, regardless of nationality, of employees' ideas and experience to globalize thinking; and (5) solve customers' problems by involving them rather than pushing standardized solutions on them.[17] For example, Cochlear, an Australian firm specializing in implants for the profoundly deaf, exports 65 percent of its output and maintains its technological lead through strong links with hospitals and research units around the world.[18]

An example of this phenomenon in the area of social marketing is provided in *The International Marketplace 7.2*.

Competitive Factors

Many industries are already dominated by global competitors that are trying to take advantage of the three sets of factors mentioned earlier. To remain competitive, the marketer may have to be the first to do something or to be able to match or preempt competitors' moves. Products are now introduced, upgraded, and distributed at rates unimaginable a decade ago. Without a global network, a marketer may run the risk of seeing carefully researched ideas picked off by other global players.

With the triad markets often both flat in terms of growth and fiercely competitive, many global marketers are looking for new markets and zeroing in on the best product categories for growth. Pepsi, for example, sees a strong opportunity to drive sales in emerging and developing markets where per-capita consumption of its products is still relatively low. The company announced significant investment, capacity expansion, and business building in key countries like Brazil, India, Mexico, and China. Pepsi expanded its beverage business by acquiring Lebedyansky, the number-one juice brand in Russia, and V Water in the United Kingdom. It also expanded its snack business by acquiring Bulgaria's leading nuts and seeds producer and introducing new extensions of global brands in Russia, China, and India.[19]

Market presence may be necessary to execute global strategies and to prevent others from having undue advantage in unchallenged markets. Caterpillar faced mounting global competition from Komatsu but found out that strengthening its products and operations was not enough to meet the challenge. Although Japan was a small part of the world market, as a secure home base (no serious competitors), it generated 80 percent of Komatsu's cash flow. To put a check on its major global competitor's market share and cash flow, Caterpillar formed a heavy-equipment joint venture with Mitsubishi to serve the Japanese market.[20] Similarly, International Paper prevented Finland's United Paper Mills from acquiring Champion International to protect its market position as the leading paper maker in North America and the world.

In another example, Sara Lee accepted Unilever's buyout offer for its global body care business. The global body care and European detergents businesses encompass a wide variety of popular brands, including Sanex, Radox, and Duschdas. Procter & Gamble, however, was mainly interested in the division's air-care business, which makes Ambi Pur air fresheners. Sara Lee's other units may also draw interest from companies such as Godrej Consumer Products Ltd., India's second-biggest soap maker, which may acquire some of Sara Lee's international businesses, including the U.S. company's stake in its Indian joint ventures.[21]

THE INTERNATIONAL MARKETPLACE 7.2

Born Globals and Social Entrepreneurs

Social enterprises are born global for three reasons. First, social problems (such as disease, malnutrition, poverty, and illiteracy) exist on a large scale in many developing countries. Second, the resources (such as funds, institutions, and governance systems) are mainly in the developed world. Third, global for-profit social enterprises that tackle specific conditions can often be adapted to other similar countries and situations. These enterprises are attracting talented and creative leaders, and their work is changing the game in critical industries.

Consider the housing industry. Currently, one-sixth of the world's population lives in slums and squatter cities—that is a billion people who are shut out of the formal housing market. If you are a cement company, a tile maker, a brick manufacturer, a banker, a developer, or a utility, just think: what would it mean for your business if you could unlock the potential of a trillion-dollar housing market? Until recently, that was nearly impossible because the business world acting alone—with its existing cost structures and limited understanding of local markets—could not reach those customers. Nor, for their part, had governments or citizen-sector organizations (CSOs) figured out how to serve them. But look what happened when a for-profit ceramic tile maker partnered with a South American CSO.

Colcerámica women

Colcerámica (a Colombian subsidiary of Corona, one of the largest building-materials retailers in South America) wanted to learn more about the low-income market for ceramics and home products. The company's executives were introduced to Haidy Duque, a cofounder of Kairos, which grew out of a human-rights organization that works with people displaced by armed conflict. They collaborated on market research and developed a business plan.

Colcerámica provided the product—its Iberica tile line—and the technical and business know-how (sales and marketing techniques, for instance). Kairos, in return for fees, recruited and managed a female sales force. That model generated income for previously unemployed women and pushed the product into the hands of potential customers rather than waiting for a storefront to pull them in. It reduced Colcerámica's distribution costs by a third, so the company could afford to pay a percentage of its profits to the sales promoters and community partners. Other local CSOs performed administrative functions in return for a percentage of revenues, which they reinvested in community projects.

The program, now called Viste Tu Casa (Dress Your Home), launched in January 2006. In 2009, its sales reached nearly $12 million as it expanded to five of the six largest cities in Colombia in partnership with five CSOs. It has helped more than 28,000 families improve their living conditions, and 179 saleswomen are each earning $230 a month.

SOURCES: Pierre Omidyar, "EBay's Founder on Innovating the Business Model of Social Change," *Harvard Business Review* 89 (September 2011): 41–44; Bill Drayton and Valeria Budinich, "A New Alliance for Global Change," *Harvard Business Review* 88 (September 2010): 56–64; Stacy Perman, "Making a Profit and a Difference," *Businessweek*, April 3, 2009; Daniel J. Isenberg, "How Social Entrepreneurs Think Global," *Harvard Business Review* 86 (December 2008): 110; MFIC, www.mfi-corp.com; Ashoka, www.ashoka.org; and Colcerámica, www.corona.com.co/colceramica/index.html.

The Outcome

The four globalization drivers have affected countries and industrial sectors differently. While some industries are truly globally contested, such as paper and soft drinks, some others, such as government procurement, are still quite closed and will open up as a decades-long evolution. Commodities and manufactured goods are already in a globalized state, while many consumer goods are accelerating toward more globalization. Similarly, the leading trading nations of the world display far more openness than low-income countries, thus advancing the state of globalization in general.

EXHIBIT 7.3 The Global Landscape by Industry and Market

Industry (Global ← → Local); Country (Less Globalized ↔ More Globalized)

Country	Commodities and Scale-Driven Goods	Consumer Goods and Locally Delivered Goods and Services	Government Services
Triad*	Old arena Globalized in 1980s		
Emerging Countries†	Growing arena Globally contestable today		
Low-Income Countries‡	Closed arena Still blocked or lacking significant opportunity		

*30 OECD countries from North America, Western Europe, and Asia; Japan and Australia included.
†70 countries with middle income per capita, plus China and India.
‡100 countries of small absolute size and low income per capita.

SOURCES: Adapted and updated from Jane Fraser and Jeremy Oppenheim, "What's New about Globalization," *McKinsey Quarterly* 33, no. 2 (1997): 173; and Jagdish N. Sheth and Atul Parkatiyar, "The Antecedents and Consequences of Integrated Global Marketing," *International Marketing Review* 18, no. 1 (2001): 16–29.

The expansion of the global trade arena is summarized in Exhibit 7.3. Emerging countries are increasingly moving toward more globalization as they liberalize their trading environment, even while low-income markets may be financially unattractive. For example, while financially unattractive in the short to medium term, low-income markets may be beneficial in terms of learning the business climate, developing relationships, and building brands for the future. Hewlett-Packard is looking at speech interfaces for the Internet, solar applications, and cheap devices that connect with the web.[22] Danone works with Grameen in Bangladesh in its Grameen Danone Foods joint venture to produce and sell an enriched yoghurt product at a price affordable to the very poor.[23] Nestlé is rolling out a variety of affordable fortified milk products, with brands like Nido and Ideal, in developing and emerging markets to address local nutrition needs. "Nestlé has various approaches for making these milks affordable, such as sourcing milk from local farmers, manufacturing products locally, and using local distribution networks."[24]

Leading companies by their very actions drive the globalization process. There is no structural reason why soft drinks should be at a more advanced stage of globalization than beer and spirits, which remain more local, except for the opportunistic behavior of Coca-Cola. Similarly, Nike and Adidas have driven their businesses in a global direction by creating global brands, a global customer segment, and a global supply chain.

THE STRATEGIC PLANNING PROCESS

Given the opportunities and challenges provided by the new realities of the marketplace, decision makers have to engage in strategic planning to match markets with products and other corporate resources more effectively and efficiently to strengthen the company's long-term competitive advantage. While the process has been summarized as a sequence of steps in Exhibit 7.4, many of the stages can occur simultaneously. Furthermore, feedback as a result of evaluation and control may restart the process at any stage.

EXHIBIT 7.4 Global Strategy Formulation

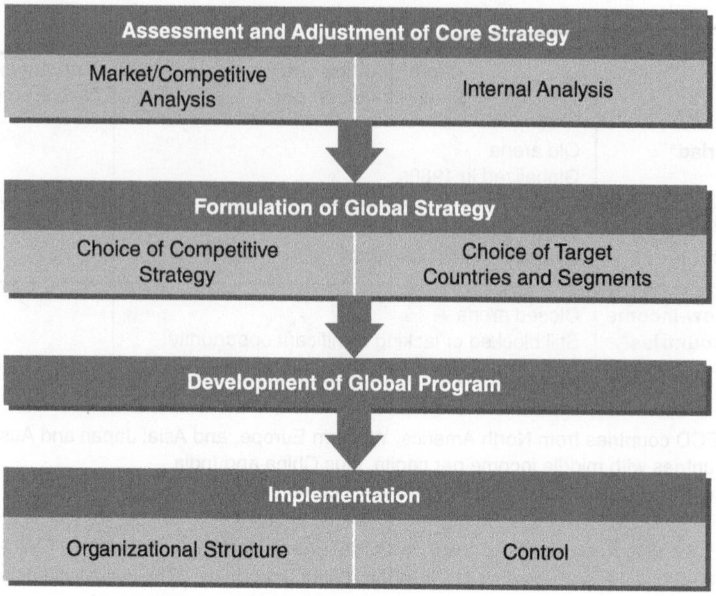

SOURCE: The authors appreciate the contributions of Robert M. Grant in the preparation of this figure.

It has been shown that for globally committed marketers, formal strategic planning contributes to both financial performance and nonfinancial objectives. These benefits include raising the efficacy of new-product launches, enhancing cost reduction efforts, and improving product quality and market share performance. Internally, these efforts increase cohesion and improve on understanding different units' points of view. The process will have to keep three broad dimensions in mind: (1) the potential benefits for the company in the short versus the long term; (2) the costs in terms of management time and process realignment; and (3) the presence of the necessary management resources to undertake the endeavor.[25]

Imbedded in this planning has to be the selection of the types of power the company wants to exercise in the global marketplace. In business, *hard power* refers to the use of scale, financial might, or the use of a low-cost position to win market access and share. Increasingly, marketers will also have to incorporate *soft power* into their tool kits. Soft power refers to the capability of attracting and influencing all stakeholders, whether through energetic brands, heroic missions, distinctive talent development, or an inspirational corporate culture.[26]

Understanding and Adjusting the Core Strategy

The planning process has to start with a clear definition of the business for which strategy is to be developed. Generally, the strategic business unit (SBU) is the unit around which decisions are based. In practice, SBUs represent groupings organized around market similarities based on (1) needs or wants to be met, (2) end user customers to be targeted, or (3) the product or service used to meet the needs of specific customers. For a global marketer such as Stanley Black & Decker, the options may be to define the business to be analyzed as the home improvement business, the do-it-yourself business, or the power tool business. Ideally, these SBUs should have primary responsibility and authority in managing their basic business functions.

This phase of the planning process requires the participation of executives from different functions, especially marketing, production, finance, distribution, and procurement. Geographic representation should be from the major markets or regions as well as from the smaller, emerging markets. With appropriate members, the committee can focus on product and markets as well as competitors whom they face in different markets, whether global, regional, or purely local. Heading this effort should be an executive with highest-level experience in regional or global markets; for example, one global firm called on the president of its European operations to come back to headquarters to head the global planning effort. This effort calls for commitment by the company itself, both in calling on the best talent to participate in the planning effort and later in implementing the proposals.

It should be noted that an assessment of global operations against environmental realities may mean a dramatic change in direction and approach. For example, the once-separate sectors of computing and mobile telephony will be colliding, and the direction of future products is still uncertain. Application software, also known as an app, is computer software designed to help the user to perform specific tasks. The first app store was opened by Apple in 2008, and by 2013 the number of apps available will have risen to 49 billion. Many are games such as "Tap Tap Revenge" and "Angry Birds," in which a bunch of enraged digital fowl wage war against evil pigs who have pinched their eggs. However, there are also plenty with a more serious purpose, such as the Federal Bureau of Investigation's Child ID iPhone app, which lets parents store information about their kids and send it to the authorities if a child goes missing.[27]

Market and Competitive Analysis

For global marketers, planning on a country-by-country basis can result in spotty worldwide market performance. The starting point for global strategic planning is to understand that the underlying forces that determine business success are common to the different countries that the firm competes in. Planning processes that focus simultaneously across a broad range of markets provide global marketers with tools to help balance risks, resource requirements, competitive economies of scale, and profitability to gain stronger long-term positions.[28] On the demand side this requires an understanding of the common features of customer requirements and choice factors. In terms of competition, the key is to understand the structure of the global industry in order to identify the forces that will drive competition and determine profitability.[29]

For any automobile company, for example, strategy begins not with individual national markets but with understanding trends and sources of profit in the global automobile market. What are the trends in world demand? What are the underlying trends in lifestyles and transportation patterns that will shape customer expectations and preferences with respect to safety, economy, design, and performance? What is the emerging structure of the industry, especially with regard to consolidation among both automakers and their suppliers? What will determine the intensity of competition between the different automakers? The level of excess-capacity industry (the total global capacity for light vehicles was 87 million in 2008, with actual utilization at 76 percent) is likely to be a key influence. If competition is likely to intensify, which companies will emerge as winners? An understanding of scale economies, the state of technology, and the other factors that determine cost efficiency is likely to be critically important. Hybrid vehicles are a small number at over 2 million over the last 4 years but gaining ground.[30]

Internal Analysis

Organizational resources have to be used as a reality check for any strategic choice because they determine a company's capacity for establishing and sustaining competitive advantage within global markets. Industrial giants with deep pockets may be able to establish a presence in any market they wish, while more thinly capitalized companies may have to move cautiously. Human resources may also present a challenge for market expansion. A survey of multinational corporations revealed that good marketing managers, skilled technicians, and production managers were especially difficult to find. This difficulty is further compounded when the search is for people with cross-cultural experience to run future regional operations.[31]

At this stage, it is imperative that the company assess its own readiness for the necessary moves. This means a rigorous assessment of organizational commitment to global or regional expansion as well as an assessment of the product's readiness to face the competitive environment. In many cases this has meant painful decisions to focus on certain industries and leave others. For example, Nokia, the world's largest manufacturer of mobile phones, started its rise in the industry when a decision was made at the company in 1992 to focus on digital cellular phones and to sell off dozens of other product lines (such as personal computers, automotive tires, and toilet tissue). By focusing its efforts on this line, the company was able to bring new products to market quickly, build scale economies into its manufacturing, and concentrate on its customers, thereby communicating a commitment to their needs. Its size also allowed it to deal with low-cost challengers in an aggressive manner. In China, which is the company's single largest market, it faced a challenge from Ningbo Bird: appealing new designs for the country's young target audience. In response, Nokia developed trendier phones and, in order to sell them, radically expanded its sales and distribution network.[32]

Formulating Global Marketing Strategy

The first step in the formulation of global strategy is the choice of competitive strategy to be employed, followed by the choice of country markets to be entered or penetrated further.

Choice of Competitive Strategy

In dealing with the global markets, the marketing manager has three general choices of strategy, as shown in Exhibit 7.5: (1) cost leadership, (2) differentiation, or (3) focus.[33] A focus strategy is defined by its emphasis on a single industry segment, within which the orientation may be toward either low cost or differentiation. Any one of these strategies can be pursued on a global or regional basis, or the marketer may decide to mix and match strategies as a function of market or product dimensions.

In pursuing cost leadership, the global marketer offers an identical product or service at a lower cost than the competition. This often means investment in scale economies and strict control of costs, such as overhead, research and development, and logistics. Differentiation, whether it is industry-wide or focused

EXHIBIT 7.5 Competitive Strategies

Competitive Scope	Source of Competitive Advantage: Low Cost	Source of Competitive Advantage: Differentiation
Industry-wide	Cost Leadership	Differentiation
Single Segment	Focus	

SOURCE: Michael Porter, *Competitive Advantage: Creating and Sustaining Superior Performance* (Harvard Business School Press, 2008), chapter 1.

on a single segment, takes advantage of the marketer's real or perceived uniqueness in elements such as design or after-sales service. It should be noted, however, that a low-price, low-cost strategy does not imply a commodity situation.[34] Although Japanese, U.S., and European technical standards differ, mobile manufacturers like Motorola, Nokia, and Samsung design their phones to be as similar as possible to hold down manufacturing costs. As a result, they can all be made on the same production line, allowing the manufacturers to shift rapidly from one model to another to meet changes in demand and customer requirements. In the case of IKEA, the low-price approach is associated with clear positioning and a unique brand image focused on a clearly defined target audience of "young people of all ages." Similarly, marketers who opt for high differentiation cannot forget the monitoring of costs. One common denominator of consumers around the world is their quest for value for their money. With the availability of information increasing and levels of education improving, customers are poised to demand even more of their suppliers.

Most global marketers combine high differentiation with cost containment to enter markets and to expand their market shares. Flexible manufacturing systems using mostly standard components and total quality management measures that reduce the occurrence of defects are allowing marketers to customize an increasing amount of their production while saving on costs. Global activities will in themselves permit the exploitation of scale economies not only in production but also in marketing activities, such as advertising.

Country-Market Choice

A global strategy does not imply that a company should serve the entire globe. Critical choices relate to the allocation of a company's resources among different countries and segments.

The usual approach is first to start with regions and further split the analysis by country. Many marketers use multiple levels of regional groupings to follow the organizational structure of the company, for instance, splitting Europe into northern, central, and southern regions that display similarities in demographic and behavioral traits. An important consideration is that data may be more readily available if existing structures and frameworks are used.

Various portfolio models have been proposed as tools for this analysis. They typically involve two measures—internal strength and external attractiveness.[35] As indicators of internal strength, the following variables have been used: relative market share, product fit, contribution margin, and market presence, which incorporates the level of support by constituents as well as resources allocated by the company itself. Country attractiveness has been measured using market size, market growth rate, number and type of competitors, and governmental regulation, as well as economic and political stability.

An example of such a matrix is provided in Exhibit 7.6. The 3 × 3 matrix on country attractiveness and company strength is applied to the European markets. Markets in the invest/grow position will require continued commitment by management in research and development, investment in facilities, and the training of personnel at the country level. In cases of relative weakness in growing markets, the company's position may have to be strengthened (through acquisitions or strategic alliances), or a decision to divest may be necessary. For example, General Mills signed a complementary marketing arrangement with Nestlé to enter the European market dominated by its main global rival, Kellogg's. This arrangement allowed General Mills effective market entry and Nestlé more efficient utilization of its distribution channels in Europe as well as entry to a new product market. The alliance has since resulted in the formation of Cereal Partners Worldwide, which has a combined worldwide market share of 21 percent and sells its products in more than 130 countries.[36]

EXHIBIT 7.6 Example of a Market-Portfolio Matrix

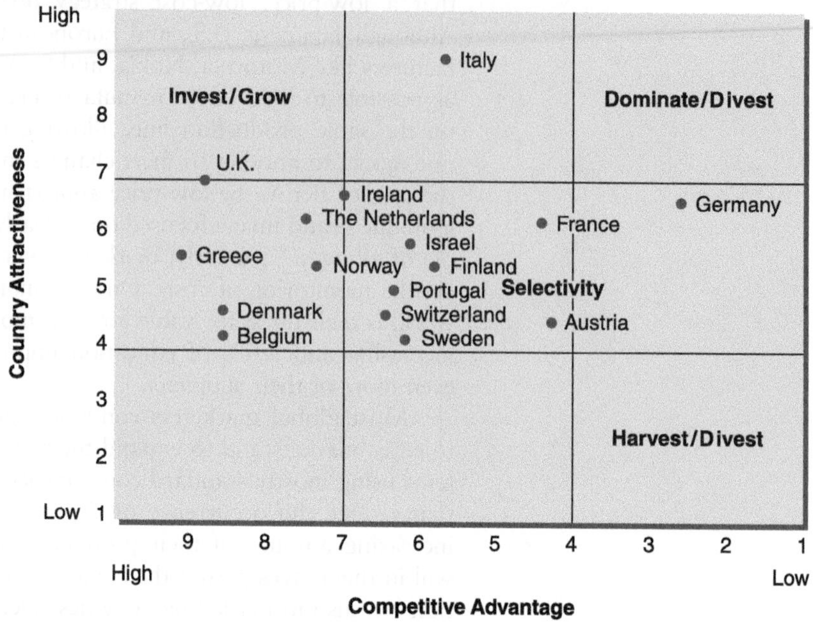

SOURCES: Kevin Coyne, "Enduring Ideas: The GE–McKinsey Nine-Box Matrix," *McKinsey Quarterly*, September 2008; and Gilbert D. Harrell and Richard O. Kiefer, "Multinational Market Portfolios in Global Strategy Development," *International Marketing Review* 10, no. 1 (1993): 60–72.

In choosing country markets, a company must make decisions beyond those relating to market attractiveness and company position. A market expansion policy will determine the allocation of resources among various markets. The basic alternatives are **concentration** on a small number of markets and **diversification**, which is characterized by growth in a relatively large number of markets. Facing high, stable growth rates only in certain markets, the firm will likely opt for a concentration strategy, which is often the case for innovative products early in their life cycle. If demand is strong worldwide, as the case may be for consumer goods, diversification may be attractive. If markets respond to marketing efforts at increasing rates, concentration will occur; however, when the cost of market share points in any one market becomes too high, marketers tend to begin looking for diversification opportunities.

The uniqueness of the product offering with respect to competition is also a factor in expansion strategy. If lead time over competition is considerable, the decision to diversify may not seem urgent. Very few products, however, afford such a luxury. In many product categories, marketers will be affected by spillover effects. Consider, for example, the impact of satellite channels on advertising in Europe or in Asia, where ads for a product now reach most of the market. The greater the degree to which marketing-mix elements can be standardized, the more diversification is probable. Overall savings through economies of scale can then be used in marketing efforts. Finally, the objectives and policies of the company itself will guide the decision making regarding expansion. If extensive interaction with intermediaries and clients is called for, efforts are most likely to be concentrated because of resource constraints.

The conventional wisdom of globalization requires a presence in all of the major markets of the world. In some cases, markets may not be attractive in their own right but may have some other significance, such as being the home market of the most demanding customers (thereby aiding in product development), or being the home market of a significant competitor (a preemptive rationale).

Segmentation

Effective use of segmentation, that is, the recognition that groups within markets differ sufficiently enough to warrant individual marketing mixes, allows global marketers to take advantage of the benefits of standardization (such as economies of scale and consistency in positioning) while addressing the unique needs and expectations of a specific target group. This approach means looking at markets on a global or regional basis, thereby ignoring the political boundaries that otherwise define markets in many cases. The identification and cultivation of such intermarket segments is necessary for any standardization of marketing programs to work.[37] The possible bases for segmentation are summarized in Exhibit 7.7.

The emergence of segments that span markets is already evident in the world marketplace. Global marketers have successfully targeted the teenage segment, which is converging as a result of common tastes in sports and music fueled by teenagers' computer literacy, travels abroad, and, in many countries, financial independence. Furthermore, a media revolution is creating a common fabric of attitudes and tastes among teenagers.[38] For example, Habbo Hotel, founded in 2000, is the world's largest online community and social game site for teenagers, with over 200 million registered users to date. Brands play a key part of how teenagers define their interest and beliefs on- and offline. Brands that engage and involve teens are likely to become a part of both their digital personas as well as their real-life identities.[39]

Similarly, two other distinct segments have been identified as ready for a panregional approach. One includes trendsetters, who are wealthier and better educated than average and tend to value independence, refuse consumer stereotypes, and appreciate exclusive products. The second segment includes

EXHIBIT 7.7 Bases for Global Market Segmentation

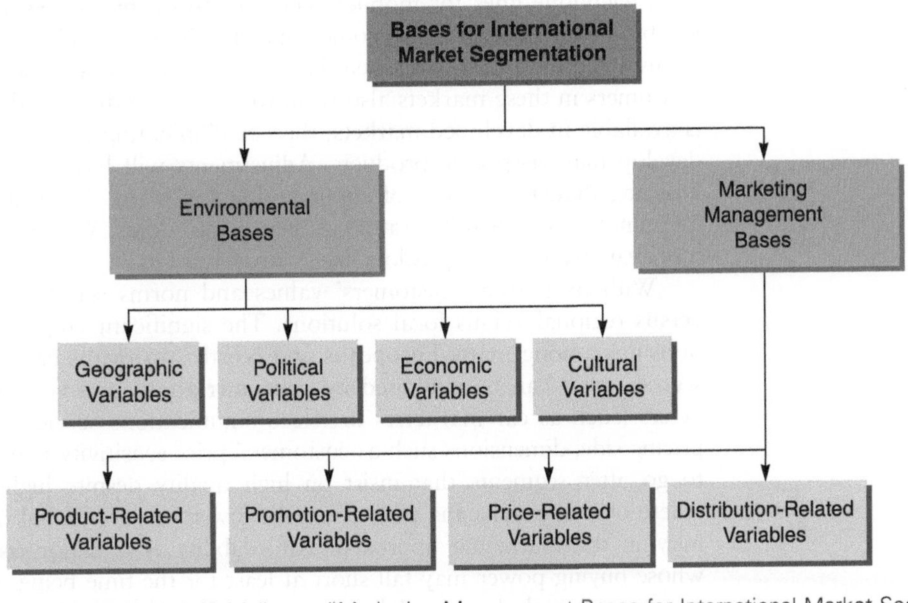

SOURCE: Imad B. Baalbaki and Naresh K. Malhotra, "Marketing Management Bases for International Market Segmentation: An Alternate Look at the Standardization/Customization Debate," *International Marketing Review* 10, no. 1 (1993): 19–44. Reprinted with permission.

businesspeople who are well-to-do, regularly travel abroad, and have a taste for luxury goods.

Despite convergence, global marketers still have to make adjustments in some of the marketing mix elements for maximum impact. For example, while Levi's jeans are globally accepted by the teenage segment, European teens reacted negatively to the urban realism of Levi's U.S. ads. Levi's converted its ads in Europe, drawing on images of a mythical America.[40] Similarly, segment sizes vary from one market to another even in cohesive regions such as Europe. The value-oriented segment accounts for 32 percent of the grocery sales in Germany but for only 9 percent in the United Kingdom and 8 percent in France.[41]

Marketers have traditionally used environmental bases for segmentation. However, using geographic proximity, political system characteristics, economic standing, or cultural traits as a stand-alone basis may not provide relevant data for decision making. Using a combination of them, however, may produce more meaningful results. One of the segments pursued by global marketers around the world is the middle-class family. Defining the composition of this global middle class is tricky, given the varying levels of development among nations in Latin America and Asia. However, some experts estimate that 25 percent of the world population enjoys a middle-class life, with some 300 million in India alone.[42] Using household income alone may be quite a poor gauge of class. Income figures ignore vast differences in international purchasing power. Chinese consumers, for example, spend less than 5 percent of their total outlays on rent, transportation, and health, while a typical U.S. household spends 45 to 50 percent. Additionally, income distinctions do not reflect education or values—two increasingly important barometers of middle-class status. A global segmentation effort using cultural values is provided in *The International Marketplace 7.3*.

It has also been proposed that markets that reflect a high degree of homogeneity with respect to marketing mix variables could be grouped into segments and thereby targeted with a largely standardized marketing strategy. Whether bases related to product, promotion, pricing, or distribution are used, their influence should be related to environmentally based variables. Product-related bases include the degree to which products are culturally based, which stage of the life cycle they occupy, consumption patterns, and attitudes toward product attributes (such as country of origin), as well as consumption infrastructure (e.g., telephone lines for mobile). The growth of microwave sales, for example, has been surprising in low-income countries; however, microwaves have become status symbols, and buying them has become more of an emotional issue. Many consumers in these markets also want to make sure they get the same product as is available in developed markets, thereby eliminating the need in many cases to develop market-specific products. Adjustments will have to be made, however. Noticing that, for reasons of status and space, many Asian and Latin American consumers put their refrigerators in their living rooms, Whirlpool makes refrigerators available in striking colors such as red and blue.

With promotion, customers' values and norms set the baseline for global versus regional versus local solutions. The significant emphasis on family relationships among many Europeans and North Americans creates a multiregional segment that can be exploited by consumer-goods and consumer-services marketers (such as car marketers or telecommunications service providers). On the pricing side, dimensions such as customers' price sensitivity may lead the marketer to go after segments that insist on high quality despite high price in markets where overall purchasing power may be low to ensure global or regional uniformity in the marketing approach. Affordability is a major issue for customers whose buying power may fall short at least for the time being. Offering only one option may exclude potential customers who are not yet part of a targeted segment. Chinese beverage maker Hangzhou Wahaha, for example, has built a $5.2 billion business against global competitors such as Coca-Cola and PepsiCo by targeting rural areas, filling product gaps that meet local needs, keeping costs low,

THE INTERNATIONAL MARKETPLACE 7.3

Mood of the World

GfK Roper Consulting, a division of GfK Custom Research North America, in its first Global Consumer Recession Index, highlights the ranking of the impact of the current economic climate on individuals worldwide based on their level of concern, distress, and reaction. Segmenting the countries by high, medium, and low impact, the index reveals that consumers in the United States, Taiwan, Canada, Korea, the United Kingdom, France, and Australia are feeling most affected. Comparatively, India, Japan, Russia, Indonesia, South Africa, and Argentina all landed low on the impact scale. What is clear is that the global recession is not equally distributed. To truly understand the impact of today's economic environment, it is vital to view this not as one blanket fiscal storm but rather as a series of localized recessions.

Based on GfK Roper Consulting's GfK Roper Mood of the World Study, the index was created by averaging, weighting, and combining the following three measures to calculate an overall score in terms of how consumers are feeling:

1. *Distress.* Consumers indicate which positive and negative finance-related events they have experienced from a list of eight. Globally, 62 percent say they faced a negative event (e.g., losing their job or having difficulty paying their bills) in the past 12 months; the United States clocked in higher at 77 percent, with Canada not far behind at 72 percent. Americans are among the most distressed, following only Turkey.
2. *Reaction.* Participants report where they have cut back from a list of 26 items and activities as well as which of 10 money-saving strategies they have employed. Consumers in English-speaking nations such as the United States, Australia, Canada, and the United Kingdom are the most likely to be doing things to cut back and save money.
3. *Concern.* Respondents list their top three worries from a selection of 21 economic, social, and political issues. "Recession" ranked as the top concern globally. Regarding the highest levels of economic concern, Asian consumers topped the list, while the United States landed in 15th place, just behind its northern neighbor Canada (14th).

Gfk Roper Consulting: Global Consumer Recession Index

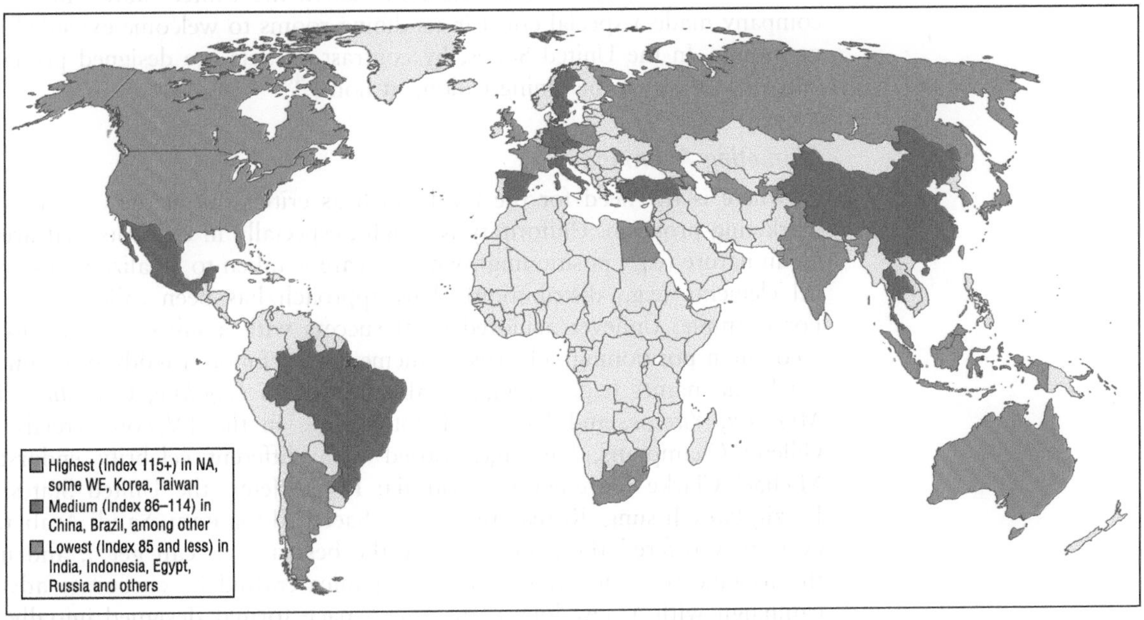

SOURCES: © Cengage Learning 2013; www.gfkamerica.com/practice_areas/roper_consulting/moodoftheworld/index.en.html.

and appealing to patriotism.[43] As distribution systems converge, for example with the increase of global chains, markets can also be segmented by outlet types that reach environmentally defined groups. For example, toy manufacturers may look at markets not only in terms of numbers of children but by how effectively and efficiently they can be reached by global chains such as Toys 'Я' Us as opposed to purely local outlets.

Developing the Global Marketing Program

Decisions need to be made regarding how best to utilize the conditions set by globalization drivers within the framework of competitive challenges and the resources of the firm. Marketing-related decisions will have to be made in four areas: (1) the degree of standardization in the product offering, (2) the marketing program beyond the product variable, (3) the location and extent of value-adding activities, and (4) competitive moves to be made.

Product Offering

Globalization is not the same as standardization except in the case of the core product or the technology used to produce the product. The need to localize varies by product. Fashion or fashion products depend for their appeal on sameness. Information technology products are susceptible to power requirements, keyboard configurations (e.g., Europe alone may require 20 different keyboards), instruction-manual language, and warning labels compliant with local regulations.[44] Product standardization may result in significant cost savings upstream. For example, Stanley Works' compromise between French preferences for handsaws with plastic handles and "soft" teeth and British preferences for wooden handles and "hard" teeth—to produce a plastic-handled saw with "hard" teeth—allowed consolidation for production and resulted in substantial economies of scale. Most automakers have reduced the number of platforms they offer worldwide to achieve greater economies of scale. For example, Jaguar has reduced the number of its platforms from six to two. This is not to reduce variety but to deliver it more cost effectively.[45] KFC China's menus typically include 50 items, compared with about 29 in the United States. In China, the company made a special effort in its dining rooms to welcome extended families or groups. In the United States, by contrast, outlets are designed primarily for take-out—most of the dining is done at home.[46]

Marketing Approach

Nowhere is the need for the local touch as critical as in the execution of the marketing program. Uniformity is sought, especially in elements that are strategic in nature (e.g., positioning), whereas care is taken to localize necessary tactical elements (e.g., distribution). This approach has been called glocalization. For example, Unilever achieved great success with a fabric softener that used a common positioning, advertising theme, and symbol (a teddy bear) but differing brand names (e.g., Snuggle is also known as *Cajoline*, *Coccolino*, *Robijn*, *Mimosin*, *Yumos*, and *Fofo*) and bottle sizes. In the TV commercials for the Gillette Champions, languages varied with different celebrity endorsements: Michael Clarke representing Australia; Derek Jeter, the United States; Kaka, Brazil; Park Ji-sung, Korea; and Yasser Saeed Al-Qahtani, Saudi Arabia. However, they offered the same theme ("the best a man can get"), and most of the footage was the same. Starr Companies crafted its corporate advertising campaign with a new long-copy, small-space format designed initially to run exclusively opposite the editorial page in targeted financial, business, and thought leader publications. Starr's international heritage and global experience has fueled the company's enduring expertise in global investment markets, with particular proficiency in Asian and emerging markets (see Exhibit 7.8).

EXHIBIT 7.8 Corporate Advertising Campaign

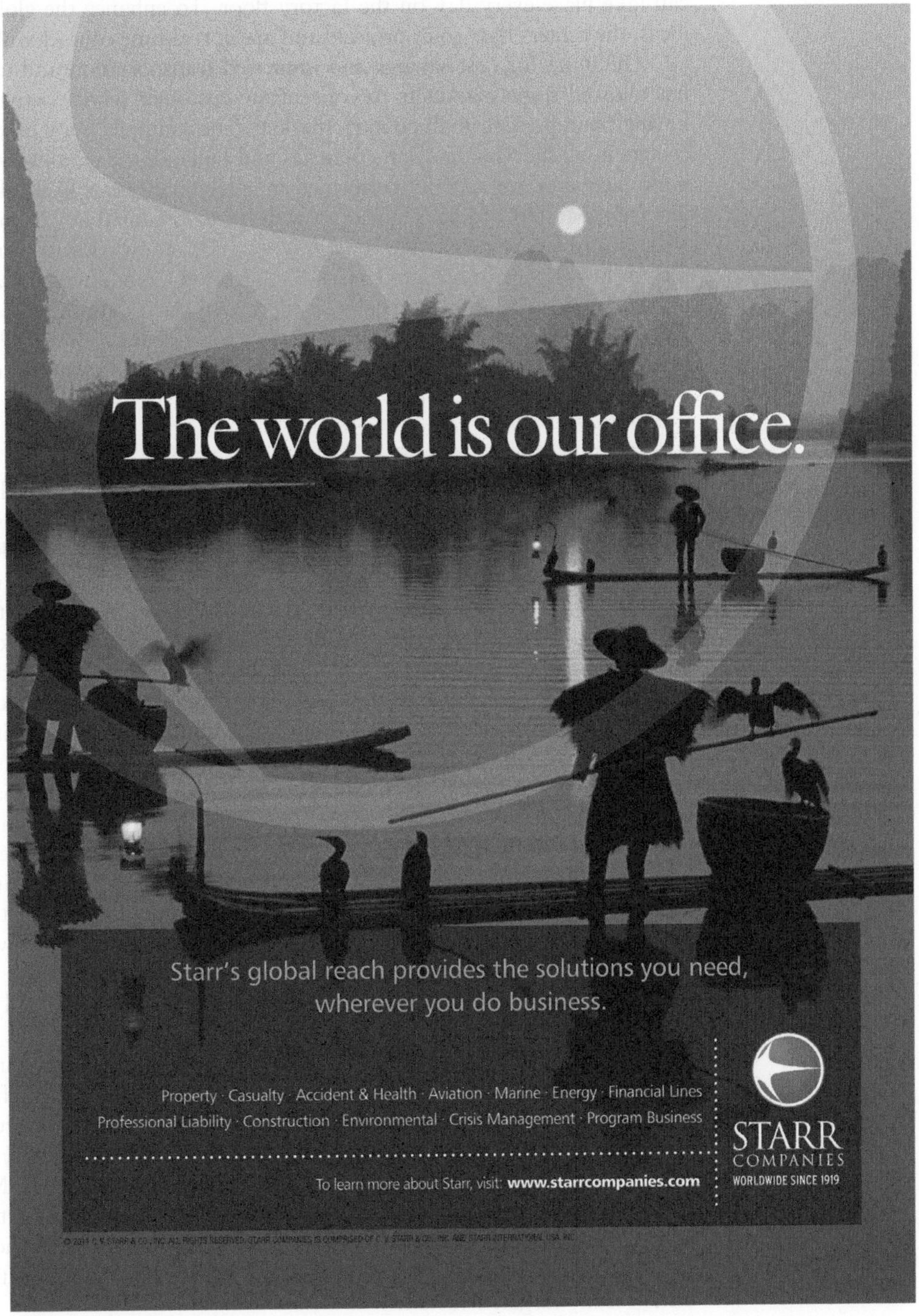
The world is our office.
Starr's global reach provides the solutions you need, wherever you do business.
Property · Casualty · Accident & Health · Aviation · Marine · Energy · Financial Lines
Professional Liability · Construction · Environmental · Crisis Management · Program Business
To learn more about Starr, visit: www.starrcompanies.com
STARR
COMPANIES
WORLDWIDE SINCE 1919

SOURCE: © Courtesy of Starr Companies.

Location of Value-Adding Activities

Globalization strives to reduce costs by pooling production or other activities or exploiting factor costs or capabilities within a system. Rather than duplicating activities in multiple, or even all, country organizations, a firm concentrates its activities. Nokia's over 20,000 R&D people work in centers in 13 different countries, including Bangalore, Beijing, Cambridge (U.K.), Cambridge (U.S.), Helsinki, Lausanne, Nairobi, and Shenzhen. The company has also entered into development agreements with operators (such as France Telecom and Vodafone) to bring innovations to market more efficiently.[47] Many global marketers have established R&D centers next to key production facilities so that concurrent engineering can take place every day on the factory floor. To enhance the global exchange of ideas, the centers have joint projects and are in real-time contact with each other.

The quest for cost savings and improved transportation and transfer methods has allowed some marketers to concentrate customer service activities rather than having them present in all country markets. For example, Sony used to have repair centers in all the Scandinavian countries and Finland; today, all service and maintenance activities are actually performed in a regional center in Stockholm, Sweden. Similarly, MasterCard has teamed up with Mascon Global in Chennai, India, where MasterCard's core processing functions—authorization, clearing, and settlement—for worldwide operations are handled.[48] To show commitment to a given market, both economically and politically, centers may be established in these markets. Philips has chosen China as its Asian center for global product research and development and moved the global headquarters of domestic appliances to Shanghai.[49]

Competitive Moves

A company with a regional or global presence will not have to respond to competitive moves only in the market where it is being attacked. A competitor may be attacked in its profit sanctuary to drain its resources, or its position in its home market may be challenged.[50] When Fuji began cutting into Kodak's market share in the United States, Kodak responded by drastically increasing its advertising in Japan and creating a new subsidiary to deal strictly with that market.

Cross-subsidization, or the use of resources accumulated in one part of the world to fight a competitive battle in another, may be the competitive advantage needed for the long term.[51] One major market lost may mean losses in others, resulting in a domino effect. Jockeying for overall global leadership may result in competitive action in any part of the world. This has manifested itself in the form of "wars" between major global players in industries such as appliances, automotive tires, computers, mobile technology, and soft drinks. Given their multiple bases of operation, global marketers may defend against a competitive attack in one country by countering in another country or, if the competitors operate in multiple businesses, countering in a different product category altogether. In the mobile phone category, the winners in the future will be those who can better attack developing and emerging markets with cheaper phones.

Haier put in place three successive strategic initiatives, aimed respectively at improving product quality, expanding globally, and diversifying the company's product line (e.g., offering washers at a range of price points for consumers in different income segments). Haier stopped shipping products from China to the rest of the world; instead, it designs and manufactures products elsewhere, customizing them for specific national and regional markets. Haier produces extra-large-capacity washers that can accommodate the robes of Middle Eastern consumers; electronically sophisticated washers that can cope with the frequent power fluctuations in India; whisper-quiet, timer-equipped washers for Italians who want to take advantage of the lower power rates available late at night; and other locally targeted variants.[52]

Implementing Global Marketing

The successful global marketers of the future will be those who can achieve a balance between local and regional or global concerns. Marketers who have tried the global concept have often run into problems with local differences. Especially early on, global marketing was seen as a standardized marketing effort dictated to the country organizations by headquarters.

Challenges of Global Marketing

Pitfalls that handicap global marketing programs and contribute to their suboptimal performance include market-related concerns, such as insufficient research and a tendency to overstandardize, as well as internal problems, such as inflexibility in planning and implementation.

If a product is to be launched on a broader scale without formal research as to regional or local differences, the result may be failure. For example, when Coca-Cola re-entered the Indian market in 1993, it invested most heavily in its Coke brand, using its typical global positioning, and saw its market leadership slip to Pepsi. Recognizing the mistake, Coke re-emphasized a popular local cola brand (Thums Up) and refocused the Coke brand advertising to be more relevant to the local Indian consumer. In the past 10 years, Coca-Cola has been acquiring local soft-drink brands, such as Inca Coca in Peru, which it makes available in Peru, Chile, Ecuador, and United States.[53]

Globalization by design requires a balance between sensitivity to local needs and deployment of technologies and concepts globally. This means that neither headquarters nor independent country managers alone can call the shots. If country organizations are not part of the planning process, or if adoption is forced on them by headquarters, local resistance in the form of the **not-invented-here (NIH) syndrome** may lead to the demise of the global program or, worse still, to an overall decline in morale. Subsidiary resistance may stem from resistance to any idea originating from the outside or from valid concerns about the applicability of a concept to that particular market. Without local commitment, no global program will survive.

Localizing Global Marketing

Successful global marketers achieve a balance between country managers and global product managers at headquarters. This balance may be achieved by a series of actions to improve a company's ability to develop and implement global strategy. These actions relate to management processes, organization structures, and overall corporate culture, all of which should ensure cross-fertilization within the firm.[54]

Management Processes In the multidomestic approach, country organizations had very little need to exchange ideas. Globalization, however, requires transfer of information not only between headquarters and country organizations but also among the country organizations themselves. By facilitating the flow of information, ideas are exchanged and organizational values strengthened. Information exchange can be achieved through periodic meetings of marketing managers or through worldwide conferences to allow employees to discuss their issues and local approaches to solving them. The IBM Institute for Business Value is composed of more than 50 consultants who conduct research and analysis across multiple industries and functional disciplines. The institute has a worldwide presence, drawing on consultants in 11 countries to identify issues of global interest and to develop practical recommendations with local relevance.[55] IBM has found that some country organizations find it easier to accept input from other country organizations than input coming directly from headquarters.

Part of the preparation for becoming global has to be personnel interchange. Many companies encourage (or even require) midlevel managers to gain experience abroad during the early or middle stages of their careers. The more experience people have in working with others from different nationalities—getting to know other markets and surroundings—the better a company's global philosophy, strategy, and actions will be integrated locally.

The role of headquarters staff should be that of coordination and leveraging the resources of the corporation. For example, this may mean activities focused on combining good ideas that come from different parts of the company to be fed into global planning. Many global companies also employ world-class advertising and market research staffs, whose role should be to consult subsidiaries by upgrading their technical skills and to focus their attention not only on local issues but also on those with global impact.

Globalization calls for the centralization of decision-making authority far beyond that of the multidomestic approach. Once a strategy has been jointly developed, headquarters may want to permit local managers to develop their own programs within specified parameters and subject to approval rather than forcing them to adhere strictly to the formulated strategy. For example, Colgate Palmolive allows local units to use their own ads, but only if they can prove they beat the global "benchmark" version. With a properly managed approval process, effective control can be exerted without unduly dampening a country manager's creativity.

Overall, the best approach against the emergence of the NIH syndrome is utilizing various motivational policies, such as (1) ensuring that local managers participate in the development of marketing strategies and programs for global brands, (2) encouraging local managers to generate ideas for possible regional or global use, (3) maintaining a product portfolio that includes local as well as regional and global brands, and (4) allowing local managers control over their marketing budgets so that they can respond to local customer needs and counter global competition (rather than depleting budgets by forcing them to participate only in uniform campaigns). Acknowledging this local potential, global marketers can pick up successful brands in one country and make them cross-border stars. Since Nestlé acquired British candy maker Rowntree Mackintosh, it has increased its exports by 60 percent and made formerly local brands, such as After Eight dinner mints, into pan-European hits. When global marketers get their hands on an innovation or a product with global potential, rolling it out in other regions or worldwide is important.

Organization Structures Various organization structures have emerged to support the globalization effort. Some companies have established global or regional product managers and their support groups at headquarters. Their tasks are to develop long-term strategies for product categories on a worldwide basis and to act as the support system for the country organizations. This matrix structure focused on customers, which has replaced the traditional country-by-country approach, is considered more effective in today's global marketplace according to companies that have adopted it.

Whenever a product group has global potential, firms such as Procter & Gamble, 3M, and Henkel create strategic planning units to work on the programs. These units consist of members from the country organizations that market the products, managers from both global and regional headquarters, and technical specialists. For Procter & Gamble, the technology entrepreneurs work out of six connect-and-develop hubs in China, India, Japan, Western Europe, Latin America, and the United States. Each hub focuses on finding products and technologies that, in a sense, are specialties of its region. The China hub, for example, looks in particular for new high-quality materials and cost innovations (products that exploit China's unique ability to make things at low cost). The India hub seeks out local talent in the sciences to solve problems—in manufacturing processes, for instance—using tools like computer modeling.[56]

To deal with the globalization of customers, marketers are extending national account management programs across countries, typically for the most important customers.[57] In a study of 165 multinational companies, 13 percent of their revenues came from global customers (revenues from all international customers were 46 percent). While relatively small, this 13 percent comes from the most important customers, who cannot be ignored.[58] AT&T, for example, distinguishes between international and global customers and provides the global customers with special services, including a single point of contact for domestic and international operations and consistent worldwide service. Honeywell provides global account services for multinational customers who want to specify the types of process-control equipment that can be installed in their facilities worldwide in order to ensure common quality standards and minimize variations in operating and training procedures.

Executing global account management programs not only builds relationships with important customers but also allows for the development of internal systems and interaction. However, it requires a new organizational overlay and demands new ways of working for anyone involved in marketing to global customers. One of the main challenges is in evaluating and rewarding sales efforts. If Nokia sells equipment to Telefonica in Brazil, should the sale be credited to the sales manager in Brazil or to the global account manager for Telefonica? The answer in most cases is to double-count the credit.[59]

Corporate Culture Corporate culture affects and is affected by two dimensions: the overall way in which the company holds its operations together and makes them a single entity, and the commitment to the global marketplace. For example, Panasonic (formerly Matsushita) has a corporate vision of being a "possibility-searching company" with four specific objectives: (1) business that creates new lifestyles based on creativity and convenience; (2) technology based on artificial intelligence, fuzzy logic, and networking technology; (3) a culture based on heterogeneity; and (4) a structure to enable both localization and global synergy. Overall, this would mean a company in which individuals with rich and diversified knowledge share similar ideals and values.[60]

An example of a manifestation of global commitment is a global identity that favors no specific country (especially the "home country" of the company). The management features several nationalities, and whenever teams are assembled, people from various country organizations get represented. The management development system has to be transparent, allowing nonnational executives an equal chance for the fast track to top management.[61] Whirlpool's corporate profile states the following: "Beyond selling products around the world, being a global home-appliance company means identifying and respecting genuine national and regional differences in customer expectations, but also recognizing and responding to similarities in product development, engineering, purchasing, manufacturing, marketing and sales, distribution, and other areas." Companies that exploit the efficiencies from these similarities will outperform others in terms of market share, cost, quality, productivity, innovation, and return to shareholders. In truly global companies, very little decision making occurs that does not support the goal of treating the world as a single market. Planning for and executing programs takes place on a worldwide basis.

The pressure to be global and local at the same time has to be addressed through developing talent. Leading companies systematically identify global talent sources while building name recognition in the labor market to assist in wooing potential recruits. They also develop global training programs and manage careers carefully over many years (including expatriate assignments). Finally, the companies have to implement appropriate compensation and mobility policies to ensure that the best talent is always available regardless of a job's location.[62]

For marketers from emerging markets, achieving cultural integration to facilitate market penetration on a global scale can be a daunting task. Many Chinese managers have limited fluency in English, which is increasingly the language of global business. Also, Chinese cultural traits—such as avoiding direct confrontation, having few boundaries between work and personal life, and maintaining an emphasis on seniority and relationships—have to be addressed through approaches such as regular meetings and training programs.[63]

THE LOCAL COMPANY IN THE GLOBAL ENVIRONMENT

The global marketplace presents significant challenges but also opportunities for local firms.[64] As global marketers such as Boeing, Honda, McDonald's, and Volkswagen expand their presence, there are local companies that must defend their positions or lose out. They can no longer rely on the government to protect or support them. If selling out or becoming a part of a bigger global entity is not an acceptable option, the local marketer will have to build on an existing competitive advantage or adopt a creative growth strategy globally. To counter the significant resources of global marketers (such as powerful brands and sizable promotional budgets), the local company can compete successfully in the local market by emphasizing the perceived advantages of its product and marketing.[65] More proactively, the local company can pursue its own globalization strategy through segments that have similar features to the local marketer's home market or segments that global marketers have not catered to.

Strategies available to the local company depend on both external and internal realities. The degree and strength of globalization in an industry will determine the pressure that the local marketer will be under. Internally, the extent to which the company's assets are transferable (as opposed to having only local relevance) will determine the opportunity dimension. Exhibit 7.9 provides a summary of the options to be considered.

In markets where a local company has enjoyed government protection, the liberalization of markets as a result of economic integration or WTO membership may mean hardship for the local company. A **dodger** may have to rethink its entire strategy. With the collapse of communism and introduction of free-market reforms, the Czech carmaker Škoda found its models to be outdated and with little appeal in comparison to Western makes that became available for consumers. The company became part of one of the largest privatization deals in Eastern Europe in its sale to Volkswagen in 1991. Rather than being merged with VW's operations, Škoda has followed VW's formula for success: performance-oriented management, cooperative labor relations, utilitarian marketing, and an emphasis on design. It has benefited from wholesale implementation of the latest technologies and working practices and has been able to leapfrog into leaner and more intelligent supply and distribution networks. With sales in 85 countries, Škoda is a leading emerging global brand in one of the most competitive industries.[66] In another example Robust Group used to be the leading brand of healthy food and drink in China. In early 2000, facing fierce competition from other Chinese manufacturers and declining profit, the company was sold to Danone, the French food and drink giant.

A **defender** is a local company that has assets that gives it a competitive advantage only in its home market. Ideally, this asset is something that an entering global marketer cannot easily replicate, for instance, channel penetration or a product line that has a strong local-customer franchise. Many believed that small local retailers in Latin America would be swept away with the sector's consolidation and the entry of global players such as Carrefour. This has been the case in developed markets, where small retailers have retained only 10 to 20 percent of the consumer packaged-goods market as large retailers have expanded. In Latin America, their share has remained at 45 to 61 percent because they are not only meeting the needs of emerging consumers but in many ways are serving them better. For emerging-market consumers price is not the determining factor of retailer choice; it is the total cost of purchases (including cost of transportation, time, the burden of carrying purchases, and ability to store purchased items).[67] Similarly, U.S. chocolate

EXHIBIT 7.9 Competitive Strategies for Local Companies

		Competitive Assets	
		Customized to Home Market	Transferable Abroad
Pressures to Globalize in the Industry	High	**Dodger** Sells out to a global player or becomes part of an alliance	**Contender** Upgrades capabilities to match globals in niches
	Low	**Defender** Leverages local assets in segments where globals are weak	**Extender** Expands into markets similar to home base

SOURCES: Jack Neff, "Emerging-Market Growth War Pits Global Brand Giants against Scrappy Local Rivals," *Advertising Age*, June 13, 2011, 4: and adapted from Niraj Dawar and Tony Frost, "Competing with the Giants: Survival Strategies for Local Companies in Emerging Markets," *Harvard Business Review* 77 (March–April 1999): 119–129.

companies Mars and Hershey's have established only a marginal presence in Latin America with their larger chocolate bars; Arcor and Nacional de Chocolates have maintained their businesses selling bite-sized chocolates that are affordable to low-income consumers, cater to their tastes, and can be bought in remote rural stores.[68]

If a local company's assets are transferable, the company may be able to compete head-on with the established global players worldwide. While Airbus and Boeing have been competing by developing and launching ever-bigger aircraft, the niche for jets that carry 70 to 110 passengers has been left open for others. In the last 10 years, the number of regional jet routes has grown 1,000 percent in Europe and 1,400 percent in North America. Much of that increase has come from commuter airlines that the majors own or contract with to connect smaller markets with their hubs. The **contender** that has taken advantage of the increased demand is Brazil's Embraer, which has challenged the market leader, Canada's Bombardier. When demand took off faster than expected, Bombardier could not meet demand, thus opening the door for Embraer. Currently, Brazil's lower labor costs allow Embraer to undercut its competitor on prices.[69]

Extenders are able to exploit their success at home as a platform for expansion elsewhere. This calls for markets or segments that are similar in terms of customer preferences; for instance, sizable expatriate communities. The number of Indians in the United States has doubled in the last 10 years to 2.5 million, making them the largest and fastest-growing Asian minority.[70] This will provide an opportunity for Bollywood to extend its marketing beyond India. Televisa from Mexico, Venevisíon from Venezuela, and Globo TV from Brazil have emerged as leading producers and marketers of telenovelas, especially to culturally close markets in Europe.[71] Some local marketers have been seasoned in competing against global players and subsequently extended their market presence to new markets abroad. Jollibee Foods Corporation challenged McDonald's in its home market of the Philippines, with its products and services customized to local tastes, and has subsequently expanded its presence to other markets with sizable Filipino communities, such as Hong Kong, Qatar, and California. Jollibee now has 600 restaurants operating in six countries and continues to grow.[72]

Multiple strategies are available to the local marketers when global markets and marketers challenge them. The key is to innovate rather than imitate and to exploit inherent competitive advantages over global players. A six-part strategy for success has been proposed.[73] First, given that local companies have an inherent familiarity with their own marketplace, they should create customized products and services. E-commerce site Dangdang edged out Amazon in China by recognizing the country's poor credit-card payment infrastructure and developing the best cash-settlement system. Second, the local marketer can develop approaches that overcome key obstacles. Grupo Elektra, a leading Mexican retailer, provides consumer financing to cater to low-income Mexican consumers (as well as those in Peru, Guatemala, Honduras, and El Salvador). The retailer has 4,000 loan officers to visit prospective borrowers' homes to establish creditworthiness. Third, local companies can utilize the latest technologies for advantage. Brazil Gol airline issues e-tickets and promotes online sales for cost efficiency. Customers without Internet access can use kiosks or approach attendants with wireless-enabled pocket PCs to process check-ins. Fourth, local companies scale up swiftly, not only locally but also regionally and even globally. Chinese auto parts company Wanxiang has used the production know-how it gained in China to revive a number of U.S. producers. Fifth, local companies can often exploit low-cost labor. Chinese dairy companies such as Mengniu and Yili are examples of successes in categories where a relatively high proportion of the cost structure and capital goes to production and logistics and where customer needs change infrequently. Finally, local companies need to invest in talent to sustain their growth and expansion. The successful players promise and deliver accelerated careers, a chance to contribute meaningfully, and a meritocratic corporate culture.[74] An example of giants against local rivals is seen in *The International Marketplace 7.4*.

THE INTERNATIONAL **MARKETPLACE** **7.4**

Emerging-Market Growth War Pits Global Brand Giants against Local Rivals

In March 2011, a Goldman Sachs report said the focus on Goliath-on-Goliath combat overlooks how the multinational "Goliaths" are increasingly overtaking emerging-market "Davids." After locally based competitors outperformed multinationals for much of the past decade, the tide has begun to turn. History has shown that you can just come in and beat up on the local competitors. The local rivals typically understand the local consumer better and have already mastered distribution in a complex distribution environment. For multinationals versus local players, the game is changing, as shown in the table below, which shows sales of household and personal-care products.

	Local Players	**Multinationals**
China	\$2.0 billion	\$6.0 billion
Russia	\$0.4 billion	\$4.1 billion
Brazil	\$2.5 billion	\$6.2 billion
India	\$1.0 billion	\$2.9 billion

Brazil's Natura is already the number 1 cosmetic company in Latin America. Natura focuses on its image as an ecofriendly, sustainable company (using natural products and working toward sustainable environment and social support) while building an international brand. The company also prides itself on strong research and development. Natura prides itself as creating products for "ordinary" women rather than supermodels in its advertisements. Before becoming a global brand, Natura wants to establish global quality. It follows a successful direct-sales model, working with 1 million consultants (resellers) in Brazil and another 200,000 in Mexico, Colombia, Peru, Argentina, and Chile; but it splurged on a concept store in Paris, plus an additional 50-person research-and-development unit there, to take advantage of the sophisticated French consumer's knowledge of and interest in beauty products. French women's magazine *Madame Figaro* rated Natura exfoliating cream, whose active ingredient is Brazilian acai fruit, as a "must have." Natura has always been concerned about using natural ingredients. French consumers are highly aware, and their demands have helped the company improve.

Natura has been traded on the São Paulo Stock Exchange since 2004 and posted a 20 percent increase in revenue to \$2.9 billion in 2010. According to Euromonitor, Natura gained market share during the first quarter of 2011 in each of its Latin American markets, including Brazil, where the company has a 24 percent share in its core business of cosmetic, fragrance, and personal-care products. In 2006, Natura surpassed Avon in sales in Brazil.

Ads are done by São Paulo agency Taterka, which adapts campaigns for Latin America, where the focus is mostly on the Natura umbrella brand. While within Brazil, it promotes Natura's seven different brands.

SOURCES: Claudia Penteado, "Brazil's Natura Building Global Brand," *Advertising Age*, June 4, 13, 2011; Natura, www.natura.net; and Goldman Sachs, www.goldmansachs.com.

© imagebroker/Alamy

SUMMARY

Globalization continues to be one of the most important strategy issues for managers. Many forces, both external and internal, are driving companies to further globalize their markets and operations. As companies look to expand and coordinate their participation in foreign markets, they must consider various factors such as where they will find markets for accelerated growth or opportunities to realize scale efficiencies. Standardization, although attractive to managers for its cost benefits, is not the answer. Managers may indeed occasionally be able to take identical concepts and approaches around the world, but most often they must be customized to local tastes. Internally, companies must make sure that country organizations around the world are ready to launch global products and programs as if they had been developed only for their markets. Firms that are able to exploit commonalities across borders and to do so with competent marketing managers in country organizations are able to see the benefits in their overall performance.

Managers need to engage in strategic planning to better adjust to the realities of the new marketplace. Understanding the firm's core strategy (i.e., what business it is really in) starts the process, and this assessment may lead to adjustments in what business the company may want to be in. In formulating a global strategy for the chosen business, the decision makers have to assess and make choices about markets and competitive strategies to be used in penetrating them. This may result in the choice of one particular segment across markets or the targeting of multiple segments in which the company has a competitive advantage. Managers must decide how to allocate resources across the most desirable countries and segments. Once that focus is achieved, the old adage "think globally, act locally" becomes a critical guiding principle both as far as customers are concerned and in terms of country organization motivation.

KEY TERMS

triad
mini-national
soft power
portfolio model
concentration
diversification
glocalization
cross-subsidization
not-invented-here (NIH) syndrome
global account management
dodger
defender
contender
extender

QUESTIONS FOR DISCUSSION

1. What is the danger in oversimplifying the globalization approach? Would you agree with the statement that "if something is working in a big way in one market, you better assume it will work in all markets"?
2. In addition to teenagers as a global segment, are there possibly other such groups with similar traits and behaviors that have emerged worldwide?
3. The concept dubbed "reverse innovation" encompasses any innovation that is adopted first in the developing world and then migrates into mature markets. Why?
4. Carrefour has adapted many aspects of its product offerings and processes to fit the different consumer demands in various countries. Why?
5. What is the key to a successful global assignment? Why do some assignments fail?
6. What are the basic reasons why country operations would not embrace a new regional or global plan (i.e., why the not-invented-here syndrome might emerge)?

INTERNET EXERCISES

1. Whirlpool's goal is "a Whirlpool product in every home, everywhere." Using its website, www.whirlpoolcorp.com/about/strategy.aspx, describe what needs to take place for this vision to become a reality.

2. Innovators solve problems in two key ways: by acquiring or developing technologies and by altering business models or capabilities. In India, IT-based software and service providers used off-the-shelf hardware from the West but devised new ways of organizing work. Tata Motors focused on technology as well as capabilities when it set out to create the world's cheapest car (www.tatamotors.com/products-services/passenger.php?ref=worldwide). Examine the advantages of both of these methods.

CHALLENGE US

Cruise Ship Building: Europe and Asia

For a long time, Italy, France, Germany, Finland, and very occasionally Japan, have been the only serious builders in the world to produce large cruise ships. But with recent shipbuilding takeovers, this may now be changing.

In Italy, Fincantieri's biggest customers are Carnival Cruise Lines, Holland America Line, and Princess Cruises, all of whom have taken most of their new deliveries from the Italian shipbuilders. To these can now be added Cunard and P&O. In 2010, Fincantieri delivered the *Queen Elizabeth*, the new flagship of Cunard Line. Carnival's new 130,000-ton *Carnival Magic* became Fincantieri's largest product when it was delivered in 2011. Fincantieri, one of the largest shipbuilders in the world, designs and produces cruise ships, ferries, naval vessels, offshore units, and megayachts. With nine shipyards—eight in Italy—it has 10,000 employees. Fincantieri, a world leader in the sector, has built 59 cruise ships.

STX Group, the South Korean conglomerate, last year had a daring swoop on Aker Yards (a Finnish-based company) that will see it take two-thirds of Aker Yards and leave the French with 34 to 25 percent already held by Alstom and another 9 percent STX will now sell to the French government. Aker Yards gives STX Group, a conglomerate involved in shipbuilding and energy production, specialized cruise ship and offshore vessel capabilities. STX is presently the sixth largest shipbuilder worldwide, with its strength in bulk carriers and container ships. Aker Yards, meanwhile, controls 13 shipyards and has 15 cruise- and ferry-type vessels on its order book. However, Aker Yards has suffered losses, and building cruise ships is vulnerable not only to the economic downturn but also to changes in the dollar–euro exchange rates. However, Aker Yards' advanced technologies in cruise ships, icebreakers, and specialized ships should put it less head-to-head with its national competitors.

In a generally difficult context, the European shipbuilding industry is in a very weak position. The main shipbuilding groups have had to face a drastic reduction in their order backlogs and requests by many ship owners to postpone deliveries. This has led to underutilization of production capacity, with the consequent job losses in the shipyards estimated at some 20 percent of the total workforce of 180,000. In view of the difficult market conditions, STX Europe, Fincantieri's main competitor (together with Meyer Werft shipyards in Germany), purchased by STX Shipbuilding of Korea in 2007, has considered the option of partially refocusing its cruise and ferries business unit on other segments. In the meantime, the absence of new orders led the company in 2009 first to temporarily lay off workers from its French and Finnish shipyards, and later to significantly reduce headcount, with a consequent downsizing of production capacity. Germany was one of the countries hardest hit by the shipbuilding crisis: many shipyards are about to go bankrupt, others have already failed or shut down, and others have been or are about to be sold.

For Discussion

1. The leadership gained with a distinctive product "Made in Italy," is the result of top quality and a privileged relationship with the best international customers. Why?
2. STX offers a wide variety of ships including icebreakers. Will this variation allow them to retain their market share?

SOURCES: Fincantieri Annual Report 2009, www.fincantieri.it/cms/data/pages/files/000128_resource1_orig.pdf; "Top 90 Cruise Ships in the World," *Condé Nast Traveler*, February 2009, 66; Robert Anderson, "Korea's STX Takes Control of Aker Yards," *Financial Times*, August 19, 2008, 17; and "Cruise Ship Building: Asia Invades Europe," Cybercruises.com, January 9, 2008, www.cybercruises.com/cruisecolumn_sep2.htm.

RECOMMENDED READINGS

Arnold, David. *Mirage of Global Markets: How Globalizing Companies Can Succeed as Markets Localize.* Englewood Cliffs, NJ: Prentice Hall, 2003.

Birkinshaw, Julian, and Michael Mol. *Giant Steps in Management: Innovations That Change the Way You Work.* Englewood Cliffs, NJ: Prentice Hall, 2009.

Grant, Robert M. *Cases in Contemporary Strategy Analysis.* 7th ed. New York: Wiley, 2010.

Inkpen, Andrew, and Kannan Ramaswamy. *Global Strategy: Creating and Sustaining Advantage across Borders.* Oxford, England: Oxford University Press, 2005.

Irwin, Douglas A. *Free Trade Under Fire.* Princeton, NJ: Princeton University Press, 2009.

Prahalad, C. K., and M. S. Krishnan. *The New Age of Innovation: Driving Co-Created Value through Global Networks.* New York: McGraw-Hill, 2008.

Rosensweig, Jeffrey. *Winning the Global Game: A Strategy for Linking People and Profits.* New York: Free Press, 2007.

Schwab, Klaus, Michael Porter, and Xavier Sala-Martin. *The Global Competitiveness Report 2007–2008.* Oxford, England: Oxford University Press, 2007.

Scott, Allen J., and Gioacchino Garofoli. *Development on the Ground: Clusters, Networks and Regions in Emerging Economies.* Oxford, England: Routledge, 2007.

Stiglitz, Joseph E. *Making Globalization Work.* New York: W.W. Norton & Co., 2010.

ENDNOTES

1. Theodore Levitt, *The Marketing Imagination* (New York: Free Press, 1983), 20–49.
2. Michael R. Czinkota and Ilkka A. Ronkainen, "A Forecast of Globalization, International Business and Trade: Report from a Delphi Study," *Journal of World Business* 40 (Winter 2005): 111–23.
3. George Stalk and David Michael, "What the West Doesn't Get about China,"*Harvard Business Review* 89 (June 2011), 25–27; and "Business in India: Building India Inc.," *Economist*, October 22, 2011, 14.
4. Pankaj Ghemawat, "Regional Strategies for Global Leadership," *Harvard Business Review* 83 (December 2005): 98–108.
5. Bruce Greenwald and Judd Kahn, "All Strategy Is Local," *Harvard Business Review* 83 (September 2005): 94–107.
6. "BRICs and the Mobile Web," *Businessweek*, October 13, 2008, 72.
7. "Black Berry's Maker Finds Fertile Ground in Indonesia," *Wall Street Journal*, September 12, 2011, B1–B10.
8. Manuela Artigas and Nicola Calicchio, "How Half the World Shops: Apparel in Brazil, China, and India," *McKinsey Quarterly* 43, no. 3 (2007), 43–48.
9. Laleh Safinia, "Future of Drug Discovery: Why Are Eastern European Destinations so Appealing?" *Frost & Sullivan*, March 2008.
10. "Personal Technology," *Economist*, October 8, 2011, 1–20.
11. "Will GE's Appliances Suffer under a New Owner?" *Wall Street Journal*, June 16, 2008, A11; and William Patalon III, "GE Home Appliance Unit Sale Underscores Again That Corporations and Investors Alike Must Go Global to Succeed," *Money Morning*, May 29, 2008, available at www.moneymorning.com.
12. "Europe and You: A Snapshot of EU Acheivements," 2011 edition, http://ec.europa.eu/publications/booklets/others/92/en.pdf.
13. "The 2009 CIO 100 Winners: Driving Future Business Growth with Technology Innovation," *CIO Magazine*, June 1, 2009.
14. "Talk Is Cheaper; Telecommunications," *Economist*, May 17, 2011, 54–55.
15. Daniel J. Isenberg, "The Global Entrepreneur," *Harvard Business Review* 86 (December 2008): 107–111.
16. Hal Varian, "Micromultinationals Will Run the World," *Foreign Policy*, September/October 2011, 70–71.
17. Gary Knight, Tage Koed Madsen, and Per Servais, "An Inquiry into Born-Global Firms in Europe and the USA," *International Marketing Review* 21 (November 6, 2004): 645–66; and Oystein Moen and Per Servais, "Born Global or Gradual Global?" *Journal of International Marketing* 10, no. 3 (2002): 49–72.
18. Cochlear, www.cochlear.com.
19. *Pepsico 2008 Annual Report*, Indra K. Nooyi, Chairman and Chief Executive Officer, Letter to Shareholders, 2.
20. Jordan D. Lewis, *Trusted Partners: How Companies Build Mutual Trust and Win Together* (New York: The Free Press, 2000), 157.
21. "Sara Lee Receives Binding Offer of 1.275 Euros Billion from Unilever for Its Global Body Care Business," *Sara Lee Corporation*, September 25, 2009.
22. "Making the most of information in a connected world," HP, www.hp.com/hpinfo/globalcitizenship/global_issues/a_connected_world.html.
23. The Grameen Creative Lab, www.grameencreativelab.com/live-examples/grameen-danone-foods.html.
24. Nestlé presentation, "Bernstein Pan-European Strategic Conference," www.nestle.com/NestleResearch/Innovations/Present/Present.htm, accessed October 22, 2009.
25. Marcus Alexander and Harry Korine, "When You Shouldn't Go Global," *Harvard Business Review* 86 (December 2008): 70–77.
26. Edward Tse, Andrew Cainey, and Ronald Haddock, "Evolution on the Global Stage," *Strategy+Business Leading Ideas*, October 9, 2007.
27. "Apps on Tap," *Economist*, October 8, 2011, 9.
28. C. Samuel Craig and Susan P. Douglas, "Configural Advantage in Global Markets," *Journal of International Marketing* 8, no. 1(2000): 6–26.
29. Michael E. Porter, *Competitive Strategy: Techniques for Analyzing Industries and Competitors* (Harvard Business School Press, 2008), chapter 1.
30. "TMC's Hybrid Vehicles Sold 2 Million," Toyota, September 18, 2009.
31. "Developing Your Global Know-How," *Harvard Business Review* 89 (March 2011): 71–75.

32. Pankaj Ghemawat and Thomas Hout, "Tomorrow's Global Giants? Not the Usual Suspects," *Harvard Business Review* 86 (November 2008): 80–89.
33. Michael Porter, *Competitive Advantage: Creating and Sustaining Superior Performance* (Harvard Business School Press, 2008), chapter 1.
34. Robert M. Grant, *Contemporary Strategy Analysis: Concepts, Techniques, Applications* (Oxford, England: Blackwell, 2005), chapter 7.
35. The models referred to are GE/McKinsey, Shell International, and A. D. Little portfolio models; see also Kevin Coyne, "Enduring Ideas: The GE–McKinsey Nine-Box Matrix," *McKinsey Quarterly*, September 2008.
36. Cereal Partners Worldwide, General Mills, www.generalmills.com.
37. Constantine S. Katsikeas, Saeed Samiee, and Marios Theodosiou, "Strategy Fit and Performance Consequences of International Marketing Standardization," *Strategic Management Journal*, September 2006, 867–90.
38. Dannie Kjeldgaard and Soren Askegaard, "The Glocalization of Youth Culture: The Global Youth Segment as Structures of Common Difference," *Journal of Consumer Research*, September 2006, 231–47.
39. "Global Teen Segmentation Shows Digital Opportunities," *Strategy Analytics*, May 20, 2009.
40. "The American Connection," *Washington Post*, May 25, 2002, E1–E2.
41. Peter N. Child, Suzanne Heywood, and Michael Liger, "Do Retail Brands Travel?" *McKinsey Quarterly*, 38, no. 1 (2001): 73–77.
42. "The Middle Class in India," *Deutsche Bank Research*, February 15, 2010.
43. David Court and Laxman Narasimham, "Capturing the World's Emerging Middle Class," *McKinsey Quarterly*, July 2010.
44. Pascal Cagni, "Think Global, Act European," *Developments in Strategy+Business*, August 30, 2004, www.strategy-business.com/export/export.php?article_id=4510703.
45. Pankaj Ghemawat, "Regional Strategies for Global Leadership," *Harvard Business Review* 83 (December 2005): 98–108.
46. David Bell and Mary Shelman, "KFC's Radical Approach to China," *Harvard Business Review* 89 (November 2011): 137–42.
47. Nokia Research Center, http://research.nokia.com.
48. MGL, http://mgl.com.
49. Philips Annual Report 2010, www.philips.com/shared/assets/Investor_relations/pdf/Annual_Report_English_2010.pdf.
50. W. Chan Kim, and Renee Mauborgne, "Blue Ocean Strategy," *Harvard Business Review* 82 (October 2004): 76–84.
51. Gary Hamel and C. K. Prahalad, "Do You Really Have a Global Strategy?" *Harvard Business Review* 63 (July–August 1985): 75–82.
52. "China Isn't Golden for Whirlpool," *Wall Street Journal*, April 28, 2011.
53. Coca-Cola Brand Fact Sheet, www.virtualvendor.coca-cola.com/ft/index.jsp?brand_id=250.
54. Nathan Washburn and Tom Hunsaker, "Finding Great Ideas in Emerging Markets," *Harvard Business Review* 89 (September 2011): 115–20.
55. IBM Institute for Business Value, www-935.ibm.com/services/us/gbs/bus/html/bcs_whatwethink.html.
56. Larry Huson and Nabil Sakkab, "Connect and Develop: Inside Procter and Gamble's New Model for Innovation," *Harvard Business Review* 84 (March 2006): 46–58.
57. George Yip and Audrey Bink, "Managing Global Accounts," *Harvard Business Review* 85 (September 2007): 103–111.
58. David B. Montgomery and George S. Yip, "The Challenge of Global Customer Management," *Marketing Management* (Winter 2000): 22–29.
59. Julian Birkinshaw, "Global Account Management: New Structures, New Tasks," *FTMastering Management* (2001), www.ftmastering.com/mmo/mmo05_2.htm.
60. Venkat Ramaswamy and Francis Gouilart, "Building the Co-Creative Enterprise," *Harvard Business Review* 88 (October 2010): 100–109.
61. John A. Quelch and Helen Bloom, "Ten Steps to Global Human Resources Strategy," *Strategy+Business* 4 (first quarter 1999): 18–29.
62. Pablo Haberer and Adrian Kohan, "Building Global Champions in Latin America," *McKinsey Quarterly* (March 2007): 35–41.
63. Meagan Dietz, Gordon Orr, and Jane Xing, "How Chinese Companies Can Succeed Abroad," *McKinsey Quarterly* (May 2008): 23–31.
64. This section draws from Jack Neff, "Emerging-Market Growth War Pits Global Brand Giants against Scrappy Local Rivals," *Advertising Age*, June 13, 2011, 4; Niraj Dawar and Tony Frost, "Competing with the Giants: Survival Strategies for Local Companies in Emerging Markets," *Harvard Business Review* 77 (March–April 1999): 119–29; and Güliz Ger, "Localizing in the Global Village: Local Firms Competing in Global Markets," *California Management Review* 41 (Summer 1999): 64–83.
65. John H. Roberts, "Defensive Marketing: How a Strong Incumbent Can Protect Its Position," *Harvard Business Review* 83 (November 2005): 150–163.
66. Jonathan Ledgard, "Škoda Leaps to Market," *Strategy+Business* 10 (Fall 2005): 1–12.
67. Guillermo D'Andrea, E. Alejandro Stengel, and Anne Goebel-Krstelj, "6 Truths about Emerging-Market Consumers," *Strategy+Business* 10 (Spring 2004): 59–69.
68. Alonso Martinez, Ivan De Souza, and Francis Liu, "Multinationals vs. Multilatinas," *Strategy+Business* 9 (Fall 2003): 56–67.
69. "The Little Aircraft Company That Could," *Fortune*, November 14, 2005, 201–208.
70. "Chasing Desi Dollars," *Time Inside Business*, August 2005, A22–A24.
71. Ibsen Martínez, "Romancing the Globe," *Foreign Policy* (November/December 2005): 48–56.
72. Jollibee Foods Corporation International, www.jollibee.com.ph/corporate/international.htm.
73. Arindam Bhattacharya and David Michael, "How Local Companies Keep Multinationals at Bay," *Harvard Business Review* 86 (March 2008): 85–95.
74. Douglas Ready, Linda Hill, and Jay Conger, "Winning the Race for Talent in Emerging Markets," *Harvard Business Review* 86 (November 2008): 62–71.

CHAPTER 8

Analyzing People and Markets

LEARNING OBJECTIVES

By the time you complete this chapter, you will be able to:

- Develop an understanding of the importance and necessity of research.
- Compare and contrast domestic and international research.
- Learn how to obtain research objectives through secondary information.
- Access information through primary sources.

THE INTERNATIONAL MARKETPLACE 8.1

Research in Business and Soccer

Strong, relevant research has the potential to make or break an international business deal. Deciding between your potential business decisions carries a lot of importance. Favorable statistics, past experiences, and in-depth knowledge are all vital for the success of an international business decision.

On a smaller scale, international business decisions can be seen as parallel to penalty shoot-outs in a soccer match. In a shoot-out, each team takes a turn sending one player to shoot against their opponent's goalie. Whether the shooter aims for the top right or top left of the goal is what the goalie is aiming to predict. If the goalie dives in the wrong direction, that important goal is lost—and the game is likely lost, as well.

Today, because of research, it is increasingly easy to predict where a striker will aim the ball in a shoot-out. *Financial Times* writer Simon Kuper notes that Argentine national and Real Madrid striker Gonzalo Higuain consistently shoots to the right during a shoot-out. Many players suffer from an utterly consistent shooting style. Most soccer stars are unable to bend the ball in the infamous style of David Beckham. Though a few players, like English midfielder Frank Lampard, have perfected the art of random, unpredictable striking during a shoot-out, most footballers make predictable decisions during shoot-outs. As soccer research increases and team managers increasingly begin to utilize this information, the final moments of a tight soccer match will be determined by research and knowledge rather than pure skill.

Ignacio Palacios-Huerta, a professor in the Management Department at the London School of Economics, has conducted much of the foundational research on soccer shoot-outs. Since 1995, Palacios-Huerta has analyzed shoot-outs in soccer matches. Every five years, there are about 1,500 penalty kicks total within all of the European league matches. In his research, Palacios-Huerta has uncovered the shooting habits of many of the world's premiere soccer players. He spoke with *Financial Times*' Kuper and said, "I don't think serious analysis of the data has arrived yet in football, but it's coming. I think the [football] world will be a different place in a decade or so."

Research is already making its mark on soccer. In the coming years, it is likely that most teams will have a database of statistics and video based on their opponents' shooting habits. The analysis of soccer teams and players is similar to the analysis of international businesses in that research done right in either of these sectors can affect contenders' success.

SOURCES: Simon Kuper, "Teams That Don't Do Their Research Pay the Penalty," *Financial Times* (London), July 1, 2010; and Ignacio Palacios-Huerta, "Professionals Play Minimax," *Review of Economic Studies* 70, no. 2 (April 2003): 395–415.

Even though most managers recognize the need for domestic marketing research, the single most important cause for failure in the international marketplace is insufficient preparation and information. Major mistakes often occur because the firm and its managers do not have an adequate understanding of the business environment. Hindsight, however, does not lead to an automatic increase in international marketing research. Many firms either do not believe that international market research is worthwhile or face manpower and resource bottlenecks that impede such research. The increase in international marketing practice is also not reflected in the orientation of the articles published in key research journals.[1] Yet building a good knowledge base is a key condition for subsequent marketing success. To do so, one needs to accumulate data and information through research. As the opening vignette shows, data can then be used to perform better. Knowledge is power. Two basic forms of research are available to the firm: primary research, where data are collected for specific research purposes, and secondary research, where data that have already been collected are used.

This chapter will first outline secondary research issues, focusing primarily on ways to obtain basic information quickly, ensuring that the information is reasonably accurate, and doing so with limited corporate resources. Later, primary research and its ways of answering more in-depth questions for the firm are covered together with the development of a decision-support system.

DEFINING THE ISSUE

The American Marketing Association (AMA) defines marketing research as

> the function that links the consumer, customer, and public to the marketer through information—information used to identify and define marketing opportunities and problems; generate, refine, and evaluate marketing actions; monitor marketing performance; and improve understanding of marketing as a process. Marketing research specifies the information required to address these issues, designs the method for collecting information, manages and implements the data collection process, analyzes the results, and communicates the findings and their implications.[2]

This very broad statement highlights the fact that research is the link between marketer and market without which marketing cannot function. It also emphasizes the fact that marketing actions need to be monitored and outlines the key steps of the research process.

Another definition states that marketing research is the "systematic and objective identification, collection, analysis and dissemination for the purpose of improving decision making related to the identification and solution of problems and opportunities in marketing."[3] This statement is more specific to research activities for several reasons: It highlights the need for systematic work, indicating that research should be the result of planned and organized activity rather than coincidence. It stresses the need for objectivity and information, reducing the roles of bias, emotions, and subjective judgment. Finally, it addresses the need for the information to relate to specific problems. Marketing research cannot take place in a void; rather, it must have a business purpose.

International marketing research must also be linked to the decision-making process within the firm. The recognition that a situation requires action is the factor that initiates the decision-making process. The problem must then be defined. Often, symptoms are mistaken for causes; as a result, action determined by symptoms may be oriented in the wrong direction.

INTERNATIONAL AND DOMESTIC RESEARCH

The tools and techniques of international marketing research are said by some to be exactly the same as those of domestic marketing research, and only the environment differs. However, the environment is precisely what determines how well the tools, techniques, and concepts apply to the international market. Although the objectives of marketing research may be the same, the execution of international research may differ substantially from the process of domestic research. As a result, entirely new tools and techniques may need to be developed. The four primary differences are new parameters, new environments, an increase in the number of factors involved, and a broader definition of competition.

New Parameters

In crossing national borders, a firm encounters parameters not found in domestic marketing. Examples include duties, foreign currencies and changes in their value, different modes of transportation, international documentation, and port facilities. A firm that has done business only domestically will have had little or no prior experience with these requirements and conditions. Information about each of them must be obtained in order for management to make appropriate business decisions. New parameters also emerge because of differing forms of international operations. For example, a firm can export, it can license its products, it can engage in a joint venture, or it can carry out foreign direct investment.

New Environments

When deciding to go international in its marketing activities, a firm exposes itself to an unfamiliar environment. Many of the assumptions on which the firm was founded and on which its domestic activities were based may not hold true internationally. Firms need to learn about the culture of the host country and its demographics, understand its political system, determine its stability, and appreciate differences in societal structures and language. In addition, they must fully comprehend pertinent legal issues in the host country to avoid operating contrary to local legislation. They should also incorporate the technological level of the society in the marketing plan and understand the economic environment. In short, all the assumptions formulated over the years in the domestic market must be reevaluated. This crucial point has often been neglected because most managers were born into the environment of their domestic operations and have subconsciously learned to understand the constraints and opportunities of their business activities. The process is analogous to learning one's native language. Growing up with a language makes speaking it seem easy. Only in attempting to learn a foreign language do we begin to appreciate the complex structure of languages, the need for rules, and the existence of different patterns.

Number of Factors Involved

Going international often means entering into more than one market. As a result, the number of changing dimensions increases geometrically. Even if every dimension is understood, management must also appreciate the interaction between them. Because of the sheer number of factors, coordination of the interaction becomes increasingly difficult. The international marketing research process can help management with this undertaking.

Broader Definition of Competition

By entering the international market, the firm exposes itself to a much greater variety of competition than existed in the domestic market. For example, when expanding the analysis of an island's food production from a local to an international level, fishery products compete not only with other fishery products but also with meat or even vegetarian substitutes. Similarly, firms that offer labor-saving devices in the domestic marketplace may suddenly face competition from cheap manual labor abroad. Therefore, the firm must, on an ongoing basis, determine the breadth of the competition, track the competitive activities, and, finally, evaluate the actual and potential impact on its own operations.

RECOGNIZING THE NEED FOR RESEARCH

To serve a market efficiently, firms must learn what customers want, why they want it, and how they go about filling their needs. To enter a market without conducting marketing research places firms, their assets, and their entire operation at risk. Even though most firms recognize the need for domestic marketing research, this need is not fully understood for international marketing activities. Often, decisions concerning entry and expansion into overseas markets and the selection and appointment of distributors are made after a cursory, subjective assessment of the situation. The research done is less rigorous, less formal, and less quantitative than for domestic marketing activities. Many business executives appear to view foreign market research as relatively unimportant.

A major reason that firms are reluctant to engage in international marketing activities is the lack of sensitivity to differences in consumer tastes and preferences. Managers tend to assume that their methods are both best and acceptable to all others. This is fortunately not true. What a boring place the world would be if it were!

A second reason is a limited appreciation for the different marketing environments abroad. Often, managers incorrectly believe that national or geographic boundaries indicate cultural homogeneity. In addition, firms are not prepared to accept that distribution systems, industrial applications and uses, the availability of media, or advertising regulations may be entirely different from those in the home market. Barely aware of the differences, many firms are unwilling to spend money to find out about them.

A third reason is the lack of familiarity with national and international data sources and the inability to use them if obtained. As a result, the cost of conducting international marketing research is seen as prohibitively high and therefore not a worthwhile investment relative to the benefits to be gained.[4] Now, however, there is wider information collection and more data availability than in the past, and the expanding research base also includes more countries than those traditionally researched in marketing, namely, the United States and Europe. In addition, the Internet makes international marketing research much easier and much less expensive. Therefore, growing access to the Internet around the world has made research more accessible as well.

Finally, firms often build up their international marketing activities gradually, frequently on the basis of unsolicited orders. Over time, actual business experience in a country or with specific firms may be used as a substitute for organized research.

Yet international marketing research is important. It permits management to identify and develop strategies for internationalization. This task includes the identification, evaluation, and comparison of potential foreign market opportunities and subsequent market selection. Second, research is necessary for the development of a marketing plan. The requirements for successful market entry and market penetration need to be determined. Subsequently, the research should define the appropriate marketing mix for each international market and should maintain continuous feedback in order to fine-tune the various marketing elements.

Finally, research can provide management with foreign market intelligence to help it anticipate events, take appropriate action, and prepare for global changes.

THE BENEFITS OF RESEARCH

To carry out international research, firms require resources in terms of both time and money. For the typical smaller firm, those two types of resources are its most precious and scarce commodities. To make a justifiable case for allocating resources to international marketing research, management must understand what that value of research will be. This is even more important for international market research than for domestic market research because the cost tends to be higher. The value of research in making a particular decision may be determined by applying the following equation:

$$V(dr) - V(d) > C(r)$$

where

$V(dr)$ is the value of the decision with the benefit of research;
$V(d)$ is the value of the decision without the benefit of research; and
$C(r)$ is the cost of research.

Obviously, the value of the decision with the benefit of research should be greater than the value of the decision without research, and the value increase should exceed the cost of the research. Otherwise, international marketing research would be a waste of resources. It may be difficult to quantify the individual values because often the risks and benefits are not easy to ascertain. Realistically, companies and their marketing researchers are often quite pragmatic: their research decisions are guided by research objectives but constrained by resources.[5] The use of decision theory permits a comparison of alternative research strategies.[6]

DETERMINING RESEARCH OBJECTIVES

Research objectives will vary from firm to firm because of the views of management, the corporate mission, and the marketing situation. In addition, the information needs of firms are closely linked with the level of existing international expertise. The firm may therefore wish to start out by determining its internal level of readiness to participate in the global market. This includes a general review of corporate capabilities such as personnel resources and the degree of financial exposure and risk that the firm is willing and able to tolerate. Existing diagnostic tools can be used to compare a firm's current preparedness on a broad-based level.[7] Knowing its internal readiness, the firm can then pursue its objectives with more confidence.

Going International: Exporting

The most frequent objective of international market research is that of foreign-market opportunity analysis. When a firm launches its international activities, basic information is needed to identify and compare key alternatives. The aim is not to conduct a painstaking and detailed analysis of the world on a market-by-market basis but instead to utilize a broad-brush approach. Accomplished quickly at low cost, this can narrow down the possibilities for international marketing activities. As of 2012, there are 196 countries in the world,[8] and an evaluation of each one is difficult and time-consuming. There are two ways to evaluate foreign markets, country ranking and clustering, and both should be used. Indexing and ranking countries by their market appeal to a specific business or project is the first step. Clustering countries into similar groups for screening and evaluation is essential for further development and planning of strategies once a specific country is chosen.[9]

Such an approach should begin with a cursory analysis of general market variables such as total and per capita GDP, GDP growth, mortality rates, and population figures. Although these factors in themselves will not provide detailed market information, they will enable the researcher to determine whether the corporation's objectives might be met in those markets. For example, expensive labor-saving consumer products may not be successful in the People's Republic of China because their price may be a significant proportion of the annual salary of the customer and the perceived benefit to the customer may be only minimal. Such cursory evaluation will help reduce the number of markets to be considered to a more manageable number—for example, from 196 to 25.

Next, the researcher will require information about each individual market for a preliminary evaluation. This information typically identifies the fastest-growing markets, the largest markets for a particular product, market trends, and market restrictions. Although precise and detailed information for each product probably cannot be obtained, it is available for general product categories.

Government restrictions on markets must also be considered. For example, the large population of China would have presented a great market for citrus imports from its relatively close neighbor Australia. However, due to a citrus canker outbreak in Australia, the importation of its citrus fruit was prohibited by the Chinese government.[10] A cursory overview will screen markets quickly and reduce the number of markets subject to closer investigation.

At this stage, the researcher must select appropriate markets. The emphasis will shift to focus on market opportunities for a specific product or brand, including existing, latent, and incipient markets. Even though the aggregate industry data have already been obtained, general information is insufficient to make company-specific decisions. For example, the market demand for medical equipment should not be confused with the potential demand for a specific brand. In addition, the research should identify demand-and-supply patterns and evaluate any regulations and standards. Finally, a competitive assessment needs to be made that matches markets with corporate strengths and provides an analysis of the best market potential for specific products. Exhibit 8.1 offers a summary of the various stages in the determination of market potential.

Going International: Importing

When importing, firms shift their major focus from supplying to sourcing. Management must identify markets that produce desired supplies or materials or that have the potential to do so. Foreign firms must be evaluated in terms of their capabilities and competitive standing.

The importer needs to know, for example, about the reliability of a foreign supplier, the consistency of its product or service quality, and the length of delivery time. Information obtained through the subsidiary office of a bank or through one's embassy can be very helpful. Information from business rating services and recommendations from current customers are also very useful in evaluating the potential business partner.

Firms must consider a number of important issues when deciding to import or export within a foreign country.

In addition, government rules must be scrutinized as to whether exportation from the source country is possible. For example, India may set limits on the cobra handbags it allows to be exported, and laws protecting cultural heritage may prevent the exportation of pre-Columbian artifacts from Latin American countries. The international manager must also analyze domestic restrictions and legislation that may prohibit the importation of certain goods into the home country. Even though a market may exist in the United States for foreign

EXHIBIT 8.1 A Sequential Process of Researching Foreign Market Potentials

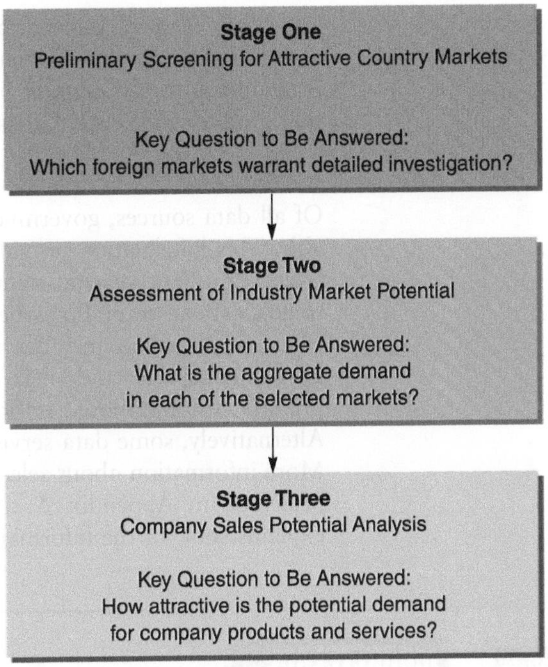
Stage One
Preliminary Screening for Attractive Country Markets
Key Question to Be Answered:
Which foreign markets warrant detailed investigation?
Stage Two
Assessment of Industry Market Potential
Key Question to Be Answered:
What is the aggregate demand
in each of the selected markets?
Stage Three
Company Sales Potential Analysis
Key Question to Be Answered:
How attractive is the potential demand
for company products and services?

SOURCE: Reprinted from *Business Horizons*, 28(6), S. Tamer Cavusgil, "Guidelines for Export Market Research," p. 29, Copyright 1985, with permission from Elsevier.

umbrella handles, for example, quotas may restrict their importation in order to protect domestic industries. Similarly, even though domestic demand may exist for ivory, its importation may be illegal because of worldwide legislation enacted to protect wildlife. Firms must also consider the risks of imports, such as disruption or terrorism. Such occurrences can cause major dislocations in corporate planning and order fulfillment.

Market Expansion

Research objectives may include obtaining detailed information for penetrating a market, for designing and fine-tuning the marketing mix, or for monitoring the political climate of a country so that the firm can expand its operation successfully. The better defined the research objective is, the better the researcher will be able to determine the information requirements and thus conserve the time and financial resources of the firm.

DETERMINING SECONDARY INFORMATION REQUIREMENTS

Using the research objective as a guide, the researcher will be able to pinpoint the type of information needed. For example, if only general, initial market information is required, macro level data such as world population statistics will be sufficient. If research is to identify market restraints, then information is required about international accords and negotiations in the WTO. Alternatively, broad product category, production, and trade figures may be desired in order to pinpoint general market activities. For the fine-tuning of a marketing mix, very specific detailed product data may be necessary. This often entails gathering data on both a macro and micro level. On the macro level, these are typically tariff and nontariff information and data on government trade policy.

On the micro level, these tend to be data on local laws and regulations, local standards and specifications, distribution systems, and competitive activities.

Sources of Data

Secondary data for international marketing research purposes are available from a wide variety of sources. The major ones are briefly reviewed here. In addition, Appendix A to this chapter lists a wide variety of publications and organizations that monitor international issues.

Governments

Of all data sources, governments typically have the greatest variety of data available. This information provided by governments addresses either macro or micro issues or offers specific data services. Macro information includes population trends, general trade flows between countries, and world agricultural production. Micro information includes materials on specific industries in a country, their growth prospects, and their foreign trade activities. Specific data services might provide custom-tailored information responding to the detailed needs of a firm. Alternatively, some data services may concentrate on a specific geographic region. More information about selected government publications and research services is presented in Appendix A to this chapter. *The International Marketplace 8.2* explains some of the information services offered by the European Union.

THE INTERNATIONAL MARKETPLACE 8.2

What if You Need Information on Europe?

With the expanding economic and political union within Europe, official information resources are becoming more centralized. A short sampling of government sources of information helpful to international managers targeting the EU are reviewed below. All of them are accessible through EUROPA (http://europa.eu), the portal site of the European Union.

How the EU Works
Provides an overview of the EU, including basic information, facts and figures, member countries, institutions and bodies, and more.

Your Life in the EU
Aimed at residents of the EU, this section gives an overview on work life and pensions, education and training, health care systems, consumer rights, and travel in Europe, including clearing customs.

Publications and Documents
Offers access to the official documents of the EU, the legislation and treaties, statistics, and opinion polls. Included are conclusions of European Councils, the *General Report* on the activities of the European Union, and the *Bulletin of the European Union*. Other documents, such as the *Official Journal*, the treaties, and documents on current legislation and legislation under preparation, can be ordered or downloaded.

Policies and Activities
This section sets out the EU's activities by subject, giving an overview of the policies as well as more detailed information for students and professionals.

Take Part!
Provides a portal to EU citizens where they can provide opinion on EU policies, read blogs, visit EU institutions, connect with the EU on social networks, and vie for prizes and competitions.

Media Center
Aimed principally at journalists and other people professionally involved in the information industry. Contains links to the virtual press rooms of the various EU institutions and information on major upcoming events. Provides links to videos, photos, podcasts, RSS feeds, and press events.

Information about the EU for Young People and Teachers
Aimed at learners and instructors, the section provides various educational materials and aims to provide clear answers to key questions concerning such things as the objectives of the European Union, European citizens' rights, and the history of the EU.

SOURCE: EUROPA—Gateway to the European Union, http://europa.eu/index_en.htm, accessed January 29, 2012.

Most countries have a wide array of national and international trade data available. Increasingly these data are available on the Internet, which makes them much more current than ever before. Closer collaboration between governmental statistical agencies also makes the data more accurate and reliable because it is now much easier to compare data such as bilateral exports and imports to each other. These information sources are often available at embassies and consulates, whose mission includes the enhancement of trade activities. A country's commercial counselor or commercial attaché can provide the information available from these sources.

International Organizations

International organizations often provide useful data for the researcher. The *Statistical Yearbook* produced by the UN contains international trade data on products and provides information on exports and imports by country. Because of the time needed for worldwide data collection, the information is often dated. Additional information is compiled and made available by specialized substructures of the UN. Some of these are the UN Conference on Trade and Development (www.unctad.org), which concentrates primarily on international issues surrounding developing nations, such as debt and market access; the UN Center on Transnational Corporations; and the International Trade Centre (www.intracen.org). The *World Atlas*, published by the World Bank (www.worldbank.org), provides useful general data on population, growth trends, and GDP figures. The WTO (www.wto.org) and the OECD (www.oecd.org) also publish quarterly and annual trade data on their member countries. Organizations such as the IMF (www.imf.org) and the World Bank publish summary economic data and occasional staff papers that evaluate region- or country-specific issues in depth.

Service Organizations

A wide variety of service organizations that may provide information include banks, accounting firms, freight forwarders, airlines, and international trade consultants. Frequently, they are able to provide data on business practices, legislative or regulatory requirements, and political stability as well as basic trade data. Although some of this information is available without charge, its basic intent is to serve as an "appetizer." Much of the initial information is quite general in nature; more detailed answers often require an appropriate fee.

Trade Associations

Associations such as world trade clubs and domestic and international chambers of commerce (e.g., the American Chamber of Commerce abroad) can provide valuable information about local markets. Often, files are maintained on international trade issues and trends affecting international marketers. Useful information can also be obtained from industry associations. These groups, formed to represent entire industry segments, often collect from their members a wide variety of data that are then published in an aggregate form. The information provided is often quite general in nature because of the wide variety of clients served. It can provide valuable initial insights into international markets because it permits a benchmarking effort through which the international marketer can establish how it is faring when compared to its competition. For example, an industry summary that indicates firm average exports to be 10 percent of sales, and export sales growth to take place mainly in Asia, allows a better evaluation of a specific firm's performance by the international marketer.

Directories and Newsletters

Many industry directories are available on local, national, and international levels. These directories primarily serve to identify firms and to provide very general background information such as the name of the chief executive officer, the address and telephone number, and some information about a firm's products. The quality of a directory depends, of course, on the quality of input and the frequency of updates. Some of the directories are becoming increasingly sophisticated and can provide quite detailed information to the researcher.

Many newsletters are devoted to specific international issues such as international trade finance, international contracting, bartering, countertrade, international payment flows, and customs news. Published by banks or accounting firms in order to keep their clientele current on international developments, newsletters usually cater to narrow audiences but can provide important information to the firm interested in a specific area.

Electronic Information Services

When information is needed, managers often cannot spend a lot of time, energy, or money finding, sifting through, and categorizing existing materials. Consider laboring through every copy of a trade publication to find out the latest news on how environmental concerns are affecting marketing decisions in Mexico. With electronic information services, search results can be obtained almost immediately. International online computer database services, numbering in the thousands, can be purchased to supply information external to the firm, such as exchange rates, international news, and import restrictions. Most database hosts do not charge any sign-up fee and request payment only for actual use. The selection of initial database hosts depends on the choice of relevant databases, taking into account their product and market limitations, language used, and geographical location.

A large number of databases and search engines provide information about products and markets. Many of the main news agencies, through online databases, provide information about events that affect certain markets. Some databases cover extensive lists of companies in given countries and the products they buy and sell. A large number of databases exist that cover various categories of trade statistics. The main economic indicators of the UN, IMF, OECD, and EU are available online. Standards institutes in most of the G8 nations (Canada, France, Germany, Italy, Japan, Russia, the United Kingdom, and the United States) provide online access to their databases of technical standards and trade regulations on specific products.

In the United States, "opportunities" and "solutions" are available through the U.S. Department of Commerce (www.export.gov). These sections contain information on international commerce from federal agencies, including trade leads, exchange rates, market and country research, and contact databases. Country commercial guides report the political, economic, and commercial environment of foreign countries. "Opportunities" gives detailed information on industries, countries, trade events, trade leads, and market research. "Solutions" provides detailed information on international sales and marketing, financing, logistics, licenses and regulations, and trade data and analysis.[11]

Using data services for research means that researchers do not have to leave their offices, going from library to library to locate the facts they need. Many online services have late-breaking information available within 24 hours. These research techniques are cost-effective as well. Stocking a company's library with all the books needed to have the same amount of data that is available online or on a CD would be too expensive and space-consuming. However, there are also drawbacks. In spite of the ease of access to data on the Internet, search engines cover only a portion of international publications. Also, they are heavily biased toward the English language. As a result, sole reliance on electronic information may cause the researcher to lose out on valuable input.[12] Electronic databases should therefore be seen as only one important dimension of research scrutiny.

Other Firms

Often, other firms can provide useful information for international marketing purposes. Firms appear to be more open about their international than about their domestic marketing activities. On some occasions, valuable information can also be obtained from foreign firms and distributors.

Evaluating Data

Before obtaining secondary data, the researcher needs to evaluate their appropriateness for the task at hand. As the first step of such an evaluation, the quality of the data source needs to be considered with a primary focus on the purpose and method of the original data collection. Next, the quality of the actual data needs to be assessed, which should include a determination of data accuracy, reliability, and recency. Obviously, outdated data may mislead rather than improve the decision-making process. In addition, the compatibility and comparability of the data need to be considered. Because they were collected with another purpose in mind, we need to determine whether the data can help with the issue of concern to the firm. In international research it is also important to ensure that data categories are comparable to each other in order to avoid misleading conclusions. For example, the term *middle class* is likely to have very different implications for income and consumption patterns in different parts of the world.

Analyzing and Interpreting Secondary Data

After the data have been obtained, the researcher must use his or her research creativity to make good use of them. This often requires the combination and cross-tabulation of various sets of data or the use of proxy information in order to arrive at conclusions that address the research objectives. A **proxy variable** is a substitute for a variable that one cannot directly measure. For example, the market penetration of personal music devices, such as the iPod, can be used as an indicator of the number of tracks that can be sold online. Similarly, in an industrial setting, information about plans for new port facilities may be useful in determining future containerization requirements. Also, the level of computerization of a society may indicate the future need for software.

The researcher must go beyond the scope of the data and use creative inferences to arrive at knowledge useful to the firm. However, such creativity brings risks. Once the interpretation and analysis have taken place, a consistency check must be conducted. The researcher should always cross-check the results with other possible sources of information or with experts.

In addition, the researcher should take another look at the research methods employed and, based on their usefulness, determine any necessary modifications for future projects. This will make possible the continuous improvement of international market research activities and enable the corporation to learn from experience.

Data Privacy

The attitude of society toward obtaining and using both secondary and primary data must be taken into account. Many societies are increasingly sensitive to the issue of data privacy, and the concern has grown exponentially as a result of e-business. Readily accessible databases may contain information valuable to marketers, but they may also be considered privileged by individuals who have provided the data. The European Union has passed a number of regulations on privacy and electronic communications. These maintain high standards of data privacy to ensure the free flow of data throughout its member states.

For example, the European Union requires member states to block transmission of data to non-EU countries if these countries do not have domestic legislation that provides for a level of protection judged adequate by the European Union. These laws restrict access to lifestyle information and its use for segmentation purposes. It is particularly difficult for direct marketers to obtain international access to voter rolls, birth records, or mortgage information. There are key differences between the European and the U.S. perspective on data privacy.

The EU law permits companies to collect personal data only if the individuals consent to the collection, know how the data will be used, and have access to databases to correct or erase their information. The U.S. approach strictly safeguards data collected by banks and government agencies. However, it also recognizes that most personal data such as age or zip code are collected because someone is trying to sell something. Consumers who are annoyed by such data requests or sales pitches can only refuse to provide the information, throw out the junk mail, or request to be taken off telemarketers' call list.

Increasingly, however, the desire for personal privacy, particularly in the context of business contacts, is growing in value in the United States. Firms must inform their customers of privacy policies and inform them of the right to deny the use of their personal information. Therefore, the gap in policies is likely to shrink.

In order to settle conflicts between divergent government policies, companies are increasingly likely to encourage global privacy rules for managing information online and to seek international certification to assure users. Overall, the international marketer must pay careful attention to the privacy laws and expectations in different nations and to possible consumer reactions to the use of data in the marketing effort.

THE PRIMARY RESEARCH PROCESS

Primary research is conducted to fill specific information needs. The research may not actually be conducted by the firm with the need, but the work must be carried out for a specific research purpose. Primary research therefore goes beyond the activities of secondary data collection, which often cannot supply answers to the specific questions posed. Conducting primary research internationally can be complex due to different environments, attitudes, and market conditions. Yet it is precisely because of these differences that such research is necessary. Nonetheless, at this time, marketing research is still mainly concentrated in the industrialized nations of the world. Global marketing research expenditures were estimated to be approximately $23 billion in 2010. Of that amount, more than 80 percent was spent in the United States and in the European Union.[13]

Primary research is essential for the formulation of strategic marketing plans. One particular area of research interest is international market segmentation. Historically, firms segmented international markets based on macro variables such as income per capita or consumer spending on certain product categories. Increasingly, however, firms recognize that segmentation variables, such as lifestyles, attitudes, or personality, can play a major role in identifying similar consumer groups in different countries, which can then be targeted across borders. One such group could consist, for example, of educationally elite readers who read *Scientific American, The Financial Times*, and *The Economist*. Members in this group are likely to have more in common with one another than with their fellow citizens.[14] Alternatively, in marketing to women, it is important to understand the degree to which they have entered the workforce in a country and how women in different economic segments make or influence purchase decisions. In order to identify these groups and to devise ways of meeting their needs, primary international market research is indispensable.

Determining Information Requirements

Specific research questions must be formulated to determine precisely the information that is sought. The following are examples of such marketing questions:

- What is the market potential for our furniture in Indonesia?
- How much does the typical Nigerian consumer spend on soft drinks?

- What will happen to demand in Brazil if we raise our product price along monthly inflation levels?
- What packaging is expected by our "green" consumers in Germany, France, and England?

Only when information requirements are determined as precisely as possible will the researcher be able to develop a research program that will deliver a useful product.

Industrial versus Consumer Research

The researcher must decide whether to conduct research with consumers or with industrial users. This decision will in part determine the size of the research universe and respondent accessibility. For example, consumers are usually a very large group and can be reached through interviews at home or through intercept techniques. On the other hand, the total population of industrial users may be smaller and more difficult to reach. Further, cooperation by respondents may be quite different, ranging from very helpful to very limited. In the industrial setting, differentiating between users and decision makers may be much more important because their personality, their outlook, and their evaluative criteria may differ widely.

Determining Research Administration

The major issues in determining who will do the research are whether to use a centralized, coordinated, or decentralized approach and whether to engage an outside research service.

Degree of Research Centralization

The level of control that corporation headquarters exercises over international marketing research activities is a function of the overall organizational structure of the firm and the nature and importance of the decision to be made. The three major approaches to international research organization are the centralized, coordinated, and decentralized approaches.

The centralized approach clearly affords the most control to headquarters. All research specifications such as focus, thrust, and design are directed by the home office and are forwarded to the local country operations for implementation. The subsequent analysis of gathered information again takes place at headquarters. Such an approach can be quite valuable when international marketing research is intended to influence corporate policies and strategy. It also ensures that all international marketing studies remain comparable to one another. On the other hand, some risks exist. For example, headquarters management may not be sufficiently familiar with the local market situation to be able to adapt the research appropriately. Also, headquarters cultural bias may influence the research activities. Finally, headquarters staff may be too small or insufficiently skilled to provide proper guidance for multiple international marketing research studies.

A coordinated research approach uses an intermediary such as an outside research agency to bring headquarters and country operations together. This approach provides for more interaction and review of the international marketing research plan by both headquarters and the local operations and ensures more responsiveness to both strategic and local concerns. If the intermediary used is of high quality, the research capabilities of a corporation can be greatly enhanced through a coordinated approach.

The decentralized approach requires corporate headquarters to establish the broad thrust of research activities and to then delegate the further design and implementation to the specific countries. The entire research is then carried out locally under the supervision of the specific country operation, and only a final report is provided to headquarters. This approach has particular value when international markets differ significantly because it permits detailed adaptation to local circumstances. However, implementing research activities on a country-by-country basis may cause unnecessary duplication, lack of knowledge transference, and lack of comparable results.

A country's operations may not be aware of research carried out by corporate units in other countries and may reinvent the wheel. This problem can be avoided if a proper intracorporate flow of information exists so that local units can check whether similar information has already been collected elsewhere within the firm. Corporate units that operate in markets similar to one another can then benefit from the exchange of research findings.

Local units may also develop their own research thrusts, tools, and analyses. A researcher in one country may, for example, develop a creative way of dealing with a nonresponse problem. This new technique could be valuable to company researchers who face similar difficulties in other countries. However, for the technique to become widely known, systems must be in place to circulate information to the firm as a whole.

Finally, if left to their own devices, researchers will develop different ways of collecting and tabulating data. As a result, findings in different markets may not be comparable, and potentially valuable information about major changes and trends may be lost to the corporation.

International marketing research activities will always be carried out subject to the organizational structure of a firm. Ideally, a middle ground between centralization and decentralization will be found, one that permits local flexibility together with an ongoing exchange of information within the corporation. As the extent of a firm's international activities grows, the exchange of information becomes particularly important because global rather than local optimization is the major goal of the multinational corporation.

Outside Research Services

One major factor in deciding whether or not to use outside research services is, of course, the size of the international operations of a firm. No matter how large a firm is, however, it is unlikely to possess specialized expertise in international marketing research for every single market it currently serves or is planning to serve. Rather than overstretch the capabilities of its staff or assert a degree of expertise that does not exist, a corporation may wish to delegate the research task to outside groups. This is particularly the case when corporate headquarters have little or no familiarity with the local research environment. Exhibit 8.2 provides an example of such a situation. The use of outside research agencies may be especially appropriate for large-scale international marketing research or when highly specialized research skills are required. Increasingly, marketing research agencies operate worldwide in order to accommodate the research needs of their clients. Exhibit 8.3 provides information about the top 25 global research organizations and their international activities. More than half of these are non-U.S. firms, demonstrating the growing global importance of marketing research.

The selection process for outside research providers should emphasize the quality of information rather than the cost. Low price is no substitute for data pertinence or accuracy.

Before a decision is made, the capabilities of an outside organization should be carefully evaluated and compared with the capabilities available in house and from competing firms. Although general technical capabilities are important, the prime selection criterion should be previous research experience in a particular country and a particular industry. Some experience is transferable from one industry or country to another; however, the more the corporation's research needs overlap with an agency's past research accomplishment, the more likely it is that the research task will be carried out satisfactorily. Although the research may be more difficult to administer, multinational corporations should consider subcontracting each major international marketing research task to specialists, even if research

EXHIBIT 8.2 Research Agencies Understand the Importance of Cultural Adaptation

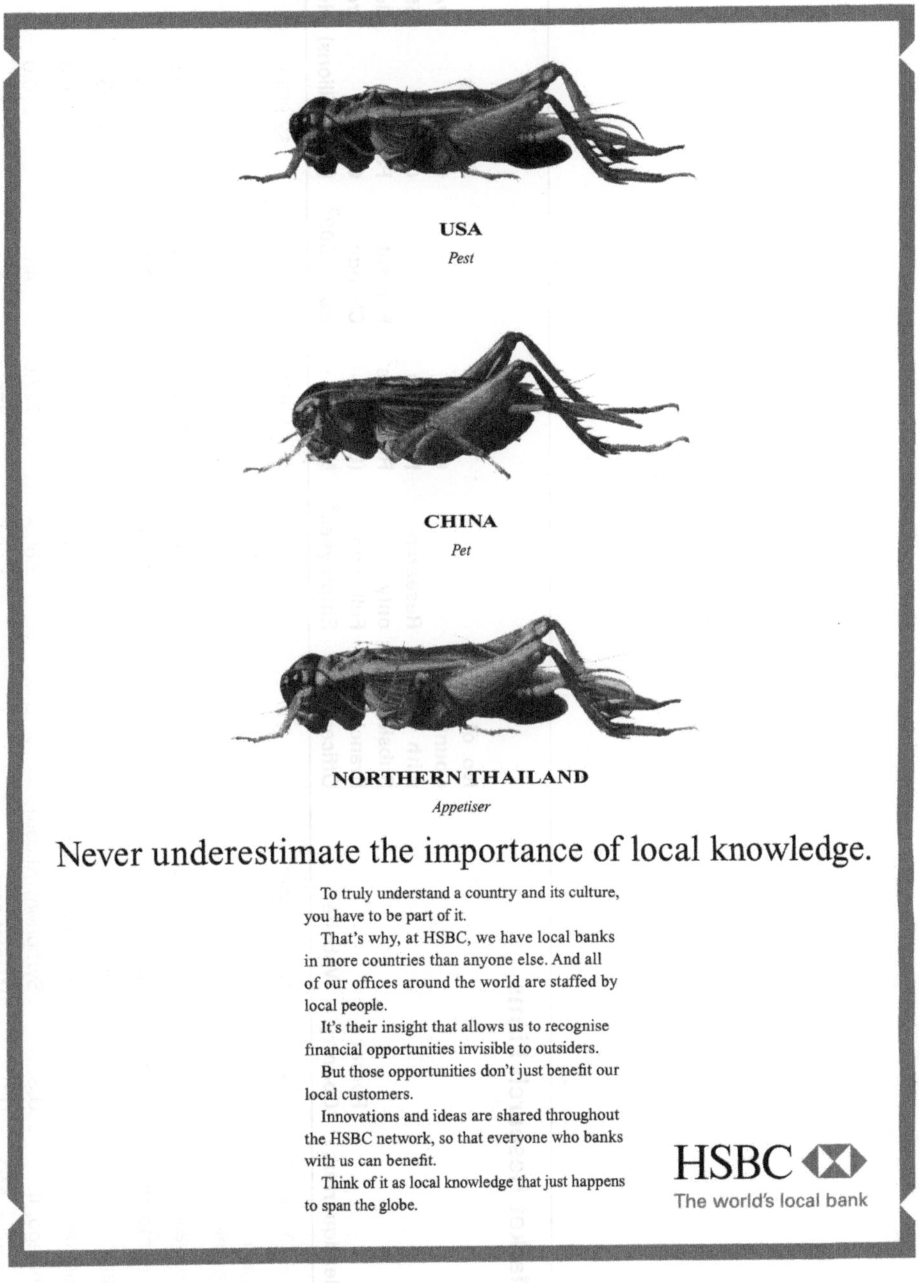
USA
Pest
CHINA
Pet
NORTHERN THAILAND
Appetiser
Never underestimate the importance of local knowledge.
To truly understand a country and its culture, you have to be part of it.
That's why, at HSBC, we have local banks in more countries than anyone else. And all of our offices around the world are staffed by local people.
It's their insight that allows us to recognise financial opportunities invisible to outsiders.
But those opportunities don't just benefit our local customers.
Innovations and ideas are shared throughout the HSBC network, so that everyone who banks with us can benefit.
Think of it as local knowledge that just happens to span the globe.
HSBC
The world's local bank

Advertisement issued by HSBC Holdings PLC

within one country is carried out by various international marketing research agencies as a result. To have experts working on a problem is usually more efficient than to conserve corporate resources by centralizing all research activities with one service provider, who is only marginally familiar with key aspects of the research. However, if different firms carry out the research, it becomes very important to ensure that data are comparable. Otherwise, the international firm will not be able to transfer lessons learned from one market to another.

Determining the Research Technique

Selection of the research technique depends on a variety of factors. First, the objectivity of the data sought must be determined. Standardized techniques are more useful in the collection of objective data than of subjective data. *Unstructured data* will require more open-ended questions and more time

EXHIBIT 8.3 Top 25 Global Market Research Firms

U.S Rank 2010	U.S Rank 2009	Organization	Headquarters	Parent Country	Website	No. of Countries with Subsidiaries/ Branch Offices[1]	Research-only Full-time Employees[4]	Global Research Revenues[2] (US$ Millions)	Percent Change from 2009[3]	Revenues from Outside Parent Country (US $ Millions)	Percentage of Global Revenues from Outside Home Country
1	1	**The Nielson Co.**	New York, NY	U.S.	Nielson.com	100	32,900	$4,958.0	6.5%	$2,551.0	51.5%
2	2	**Kantar***	London & Fairfield, CT	U.K.	Kantar.com	80	21,800	3,183.6	3.9	2,387.7	75.0
3	3	**IMS Health, Inc.***	Norwalk, CT	U.S.	IMSHealth.com	74	7,000	2,211.6	0.3	1,410.5	63.8
4	4	**GfK SE**	Nuremberg	Germany	GfK.com	65	10,546	1,716.2	7.3	1,265.4	73.7
5	5	**Ipsos SA**	Paris	France	Ipsos.com	67	9,498	1,512.8	8.3	1,383.0	91.4
6	6	**Synovate**	London	U.K.	Synovate.com	64	5,902	884.8	5.9	776.3	87.7
7	7	**SymphonyIRI Group**	Chicago, IL	U.S.	SymphonyIRI.com	8	3,600	727.0	4.6	270.0	37.1
8	8	**Westat, Inc.**	Rockville, MD	U.S.	Westat.com	1	1,964	455.3	−9.4	—	—
9	10	**INTAGE, Inc.****	Tokyo	Japan	Intage.co.jp	3	1,997	416.2	4.7	12.7	3.1
10	9	**Arbitron, Inc.**	Columbia, MD	U.S.	Arbitron.com	2	1,113	395.4	2.6	5.0	1.3
11	12	**The NPD Group, Inc.**	Port Washington, NY	U.S.	NPD.com	14	1,135	240.1	5.5	66.4	27.7
12	11	**J.D. Power and Associates***	Westlake Village, CA	U.S.	JDPower.com	10	730	231.4	−5.4	84.1	36.3
13	14	**Video Research Ltd.****	Tokyo	Japan	VideoR.co.jp	3	393	212.0	−1.2	—	—
14	17	**IBOPE Group**	Sao Paulo	Brazil	IBOPE.com.br	15	2,259	210.8	25.8	38.8	18.4
15	–	**ICF International, Inc.**	Fairfax, VA	U.S.	ICFI.com	7	1,107	200.1	9.5	46.9	23.4
16	18	**comScore, Inc.**	Reston, VA	U.S.	comScore.com	18	922	175.0	15.0	32.7	18.7

(continued)

17	15	**Harris Interactive, Inc.**	New York, NY	U.S.	Harrisinteractive.com	7	853	166.8	−0.6	72.9	43.7
18	16	**Maritz Research**	Fenton, MO	U.S.	MaritzResearch.com	5	743	162.1	4.8	21.2	13.1
19	20	**Abt SRBI, Inc.**	Cambridge, MA	U.S.	AbtAssociates.com	37	819	129.4	17.9	42.6	32.9
20	25	**Macromill, Inc.**	Tokyo	Japan	Macromill.com	2	553	115.0	16.2	—	—
21	22	**Lieberman Research Worldwide**	Los Angeles, CA	U.S.	LRWonline.com	3	368	100.8	14.5	18.5	18.4
22	19	**ORC International**	Princeton, NJ	U.S.	ORCInternational.com	6	444	98.0	−1.9	34.1	34.8
23	21	**Mediametrie**	Paris	France	Mediametrie.com	1	547	92.3	9.4	8.5	9.2
24	23	**Cello Research & Consulting**	London	U.K.	CelloGroup.co.uk	2	353	84.5	4.8	37.2	44.0
25	24	**Market Strategies International**	Livonia, MI	U.S.	MarketStrategies.com	3	257	80.7	1.7	13.1	16.2
		Total					107,803	**$18,759.9**	4.9%	$10,578.6	56.4%

*Estimated by Top 25 authors.

**For fiscal year ending March 2011.

[1]Includes countries that have subsidiaries with an equity interest or branch offices, or both.

[2]Total revenues that include nonresearch activities for some companies are significantly higher. This information is given in the individual company profiles.

[3]Rate of growth from year to year has been adjusted so as not to include revenue gains or losses from acquisitions or divestitures. See company profiles for explanation. Rate of growth is based on home country currency and excludes currency exchange effects.

[4]Includes some nonresearch employees.

SOURCE: Jack Honomichl, "2011 Honomichl Global Top 25 Research Report," *Marketing News*, August 30, 2011, www.marketingpower.com/AboutAMA/Pages/Honomichl Reports.aspx.

than structured data. Because the willingness and ability of respondents to spend the time and provide a free-form response are heavily influenced by factors such as culture and education, the prevailing conditions in the country and segments to be studied need to be understood in making these decisions. Whether the data are to be collected in the real world or in a controlled environment also must be decided. Finally, a decision needs to be made as to whether the research is to collect historical facts or gather information about future developments. This is particularly important for consumer research because firms frequently desire to determine consumers' future intentions to purchase a certain product.

Cultural and individual preferences, which vary significantly among nations, play a major role in determining research techniques. U.S. managers frequently prefer to gather large quantities of hard data through surveys, which provide numbers that can be manipulated statistically and directly compared to other sets of data. In some other countries managers appear to prefer the "soft" approach. For example, much of Japanese-style market research relies heavily on two kinds of information: soft data obtained from visits to dealers and other channel members and hard data about shipments, inventory levels, and retail sales.

Once the structure of the type of data sought has been determined, a choice must be made among the types of research instruments available. Each provides a different depth of information and has its unique strengths and weaknesses.

Interviews

Interviews with knowledgeable persons can be of great value to a corporation desiring international marketing information. Because bias from the individual may be part of the findings, the intent should be to obtain in-depth information rather than a wide variety of data. Interviews can be most useful, particularly when specific answers are sought to very narrow questions.

Focus Groups

Focus groups are a useful research tool resulting in interactive interviews. A group of informed persons is gathered for a limited period of time (two to four hours). Usually, the ideal size for a focus group is 7 to 10 participants. A specific topic is introduced and thoroughly discussed by all group members. Because of the interaction, hidden issues are sometimes raised that would not have been addressed in an individual interview.

The skill of the group leader in stimulating discussion is crucial to the success of a focus group. Discussions are often recorded on tape and subsequently analyzed in detail. Focus groups, like in-depth interviews, do not provide statistically significant information; however, they can be helpful in providing information about perceptions, emotions, and other nonovert factors. In addition, once individuals are gathered, focus groups are highly efficient in terms of rapidly accumulating a substantial amount of information. With the advances occurring in the communications field, focus groups can also be carried out internationally, with interaction between groups. When conducting international research via focus groups, the researcher must be aware of the importance of culture in the discussion process. Not all societies encourage frank and open exchange and disagreement among individuals. Status consciousness may result in situations in which the opinion of one is reflected by all other participants. Disagreement may be seen as impolite, or certain topics may be taboo.

Observation

Observation techniques require the researcher to play the role of a nonparticipating observer of activity and behavior. Observation can be personal or impersonal—for example, mechanical. Observation can be obtrusive or unobtrusive, depending on whether the subject is aware or unaware of being observed. In international marketing research, observation can be extremely useful in shedding light on practices not previously encountered or understood.

This aspect is particularly valuable for the researcher who is totally unfamiliar with a market or market situation, and can be quickly achieved through, for example, participation in a trade mission. Finding employees with personal experience and observations about international markets can be very beneficial for employers. *The International Marketplace 8.3* shows how the state of Utah is benefiting from the international exposure of its citizens.

Observation can also help in understanding phenomena that would have been difficult to assess with other techniques. For example, Toyota sent a group of its engineers and designers to southern California to unobtrusively observe how women get into and operate their cars. They found that women with long fingernails have trouble opening the door and operating various knobs on the dashboard. Based on their observations, Toyota engineers and designers were able to observe the women's plight and redraw some of the automobile exterior and interior designs.[15]

Conducting observations can also have its pitfalls. For example, people may react differently to the discovery that their behavior has been observed. The degree to which the observer has to be familiarized or introduced to other participants may vary. The complexity of the task may differ due to the use of multiple languages. To conduct in-store research in Europe, for example, store checks, photo audits of shelves, and store interviews must be scheduled well in

THE INTERNATIONAL MARKETPLACE 8.3

Excellence in International Research

The Church of Jesus Christ of Latter-day Saints, commonly known as the Mormon Church, was organized by Joseph Smith in 1830 in New York. It has grown into an organization with more than 14 million members and congregations throughout the world and is currently increasing at an average rate of about one million new members every few years. It generates close to $6 billion in annual income from its non-church-related businesses and enterprises and has $30 billion in assets. One of its key growth strategies is to send many of its members abroad as missionaries. Therefore, the church has thousands of young and experienced travelers returning with foreign language skills and intercultural understanding. Indeed Utah, where the Mormon population is highly concentrated, has speakers fluent in 90 percent of the world's written languages, and 30 percent of its U.S.-born adult males speak a second language. Due to its large and globally educated workforce, Utah is successfully attracting businesses such as Intel, eBay, American Express, and Goldman Sachs.

Young Mormon followers, 19 to 22 years of age, are expected to go on a mission abroad for 18 to 24 months. There are currently approximately 60,000 full-time missionaries serving in more than 330 mission districts around the world. Most missionaries learn new languages during their brief stay at the missionary training centers, where about 50 different languages are taught, and become fully proficient during their stay abroad. In any country in which they are located, missionaries go door to door promoting their religion and indirectly developing their sales skills. Young individuals are completely immersed in the host culture, live among local families, and therefore have a personal understanding of the people of the country. Individuals with such extensive experience abroad can be great resources to their companies as sources of global knowledge. Their personal insight into local cultures can help enlighten employers about marketing abroad. Many Mormons undertake international ventures in the countries where they once served as missionaries.

CEOs in Utah note the diverse foreign language experience, high ethics, and family-oriented attitudes of the Mormon workforce as significant factors in the success of their businesses. Employers look for individuals who are not only well rounded but have a specific area of expertise. Having a workforce that knows foreign languages and has the experience of living abroad adds to a company's ability to research international markets.

SOURCES: "Utah CEOs Cite Cost Advantages, Ethics and Local Workforce as Top Reasons to Locate Companies Here," *PR Newswire US*, November 3, 2005; Earl Fry, Wallace McCarlie, Derek Wride, and Stacey Sears, "Mapping Globalization along the Wasatch Front," Pacific Council on International Policy, www.pacificcouncil.org, accessed February 19, 2008; Eric Johnson, "Get The Fire: Young Mormon Missionaries Abroad," Mormonism Research Ministry, www.mrm.org, accessed March 12, 2012; and Walter Kirn, McKay Coppins, Andrew Romano, and David Graham, "Mormons Rock!" *Newsweek*, June 13, 2011, pp. 38–45.

advance and need to be preceded by a full round of introductions of the researchers to store management and personnel. In some countries, such as Belgium, a researcher must remember that four different languages are spoken and their use may change from store to store.

The research instruments discussed so far—interviews, focus groups, and observation—are useful primarily for gathering qualitative data. The intent is not to amass data or to search for statistical significance but rather to obtain a better understanding of given situations, behavioral patterns, or underlying dimensions. The researcher using these instruments must be cautioned that even frequent repetition of the measurements will not lead to a statistically valid result. Yet statistical validity often is not the major focus of corporate international marketing research. Rather, it is the better understanding, description, and prediction of events that have an impact on marketing decision making. When quantitative data are desired, surveys are appropriate research instruments.

Surveys

Survey research is useful in providing the opportunity to quantify concepts. In the social sciences, the cross-cultural survey is generally accepted as a powerful method of hypothesis testing. Surveys are usually conducted via questionnaires that are administered personally, by mail, or by telephone. Use of the survey technique presupposes that the population under study is able to comprehend and respond to the questions posed. Also, particularly in the case of mail and telephone surveys, a major precondition is the feasibility of using the postal system or the widespread availability of telephones. In many countries, only limited records are available about dwellings, their location, and their occupants. In Venezuela, for example, most houses are not numbered but rather are given individual names like "Casa Rosa" or "El Retiro." In some countries, street maps are not even available. As a result, it becomes virtually impossible to reach respondents by mail.

In other countries, obtaining a correct address may be easy, but the postal system may not function well. The Italian postal service, for example, has suffered from scandals that exposed such practices as selling undelivered mail to paper mills for recycling.

Telephone surveys may also be inappropriate if telephone ownership is rare. In such instances, any information obtained would be highly biased even if the researcher randomizes the calls. In some instances, telephone networks and systems

© STUART WALKER/Alamy

The Scotland's Census 2011, conducted by the government, is an example of a large-scale survey.

may also prevent the researcher from conducting surveys. Frequent line congestion and a lack of telephone directories are examples. There are also great variations between countries or regions of countries in terms of unlisted telephone numbers or numbers for cellular phones. For example, the percentage of households with unlisted telephone numbers varies widely by country and even city.

Surveys can be hampered by social and cultural constraints. Recipients of letters may be illiterate or may be reluctant to respond in writing. In some nations, entire population segments—for example, women—may be totally inaccessible to interviewers. One must also assess the purpose of the survey in the context of the population surveyed. It has been argued, for example, that one should not rely on consumer surveys for new product development information. Key reasons are the absence of responsibility—the consumer is sincere when spending but not when talking; conservative attitudes—ordinary consumers are conservative and tend to react negatively to a new product; vanity—it is human nature to exaggerate and put on a good appearance; and insufficient information—the research results depend on the product characteristics information that is given to survey participants and that may be incomplete or unabsorbed.[16]

In spite of all these difficulties, however, the survey technique remains a useful one because it allows the researcher to rapidly accumulate a large quantity of data amenable to statistical analysis. Even though quite difficult, **international comparative research** has been carried out very successfully between nations, particularly if the environments studied are sufficiently similar that the impact of uncontrollable macrovariables is limited. However, even in environments that are quite dissimilar, in-depth comparative research can be carried out.[17] Doing so may require a country-by-country adjustment of details while preserving the similarity of research thrust. For example, researchers have reported good results in mail surveys conducted simultaneously in Japan and the United States after adjusting the size of the return envelope, outgoing envelope, address style, signature, and cover letter to meet specific societal expectations.[18] With constantly expanding technological capabilities, international marketers will be able to use the survey technique more frequently in the future. Exhibit 8.4 provides an overview of the extent of the Internet technology available to help the international research process.

EXHIBIT 8.4 Internet Penetration by Language

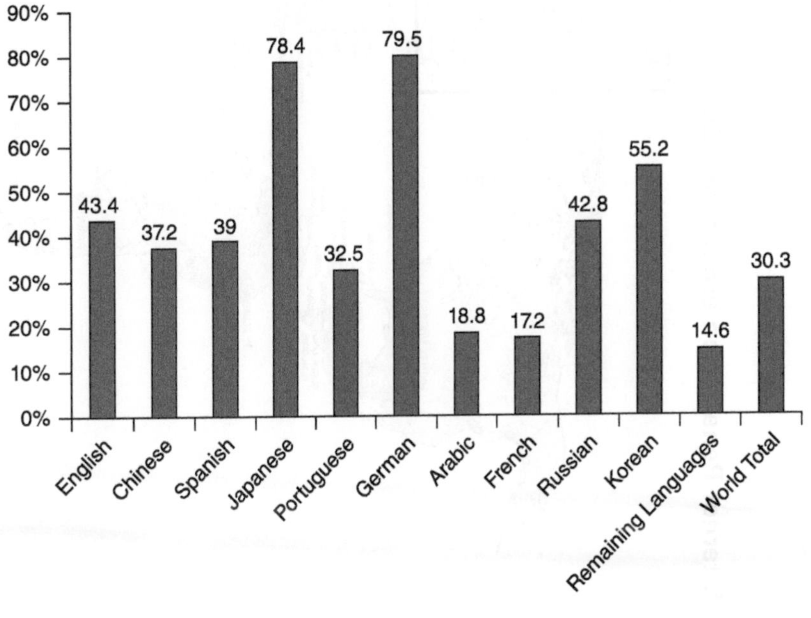

SOURCE: Internet World Stats, www.internetworldstats.com, accessed February 6, 2012.

Internet Penetration around the Globe

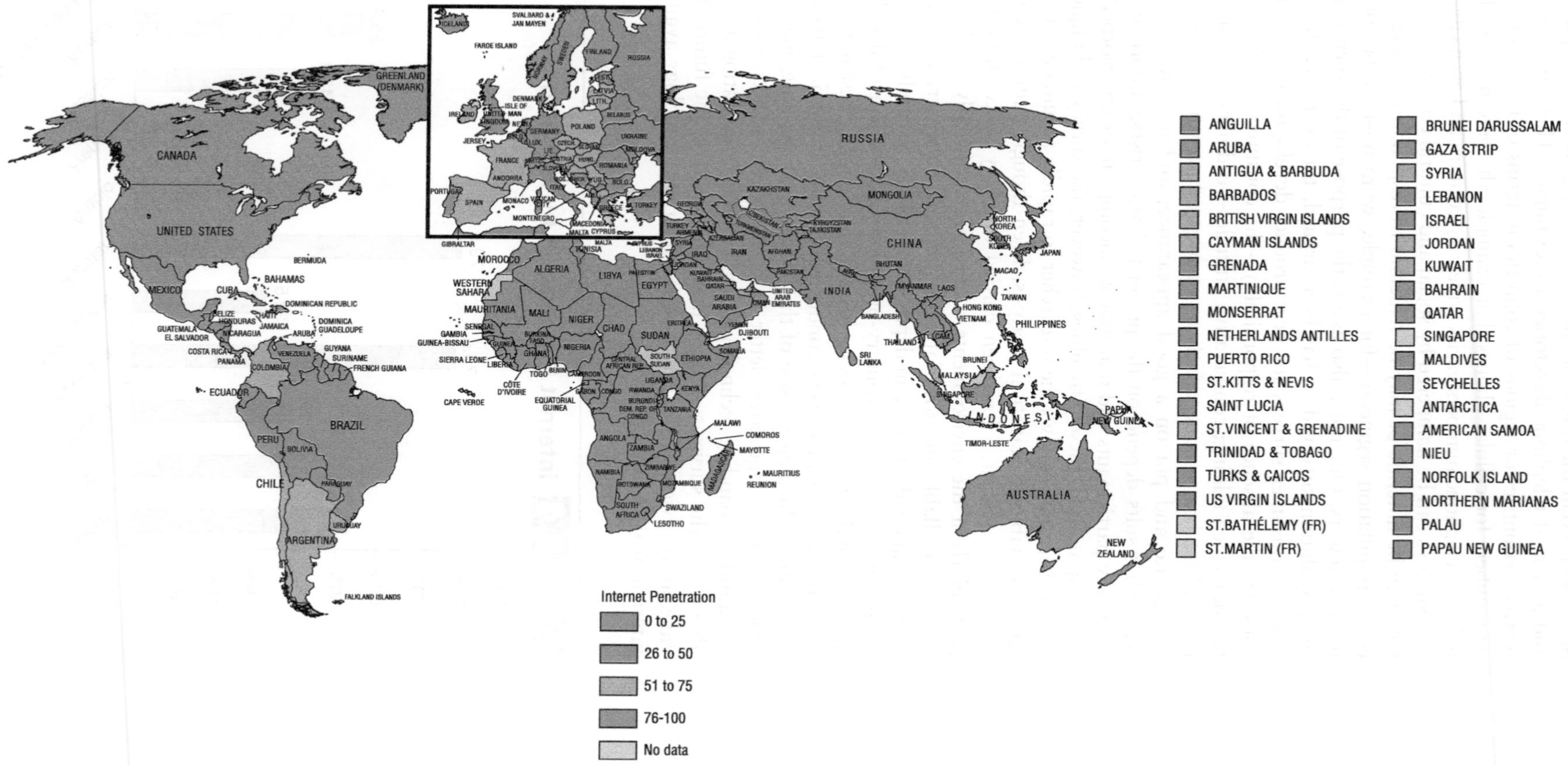

SOURCES: © Cengage Learning 2013; Data from Internet World Stats, www.internetworldstats.com/stats.htm.

Designing the Survey Questionnaire

International marketing surveys are usually conducted with questionnaires. These questionnaires should contain questions that are clear and easy to comprehend by the respondents, as well as easy for the data collector to administer. Much attention must therefore be paid to question format, content, and wording.

Question Format

Questions can be structured or unstructured. Structured questions typically allow the respondents only limited choice options. Unstructured (or open-ended) questions permit the capture of more in-depth information, but they also increase the potential for interviewer bias. Even at the cost of potential bias, however, open-ended questions are quite useful in cross-cultural surveys because they make allowance for the frame of reference of the respondents and can even permit the respondents to set their own frame of reference.

Another question format decision is the choice between direct and indirect questions. Societies have different degrees of sensitivity to certain questions. Questions related to the income or age of a respondent may be accepted differently in different countries. Also, the social desirability of answers may vary. In some cultures, questions about employees, performance, standards, and financing are asked directly of a respondent, while in others, particularly in Asia or the Middle East, these questions are thought to be rude and insulting.[19] As a result, the researcher must be sure that the questions are culturally acceptable. This may mean that questions that can be asked directly in some cultures will have to be asked indirectly in others. For example, rather than ask, "How old are you?" one could ask, "In what year were you born?"

The researcher must also be sure to adapt the complexity of the question to the level of understanding of the respondent. For example, a multipoint scaling method, which may be effectively used in a developed country to discover the attitudes and attributes of company executives, may be a very poor instrument if used among rural entrepreneurs. It has been found that demonstration aids are useful in surveys among poorly educated respondents.[20]

The question format should also ensure data equivalence in international marketing research. This requires categories used in questionnaires to be comparatively structured. In a developed country, for example, a white-collar worker may be part of the middle class, whereas in a less-developed country the same person would be part of the upper class. Before using categories in a questionnaire, the researcher must therefore determine their appropriateness in different environments. This is particularly important for questions that attempt to collect attitudinal, psychographic, or lifestyle data because cultural variations are most pronounced in these areas. For example, pizza may be chic in Asia but a convenience food in the United States, or a bicycle may be recreational in some regions while being a basic mode of transportation in others.[21]

Question Content

Major consideration must be given to the ability and willingness of respondents to supply the answers. The knowledge and information available to respondents may vary substantially because of different educational levels and may affect their ability to answer questions. Further, societal demands and restrictions may influence the willingness of respondents to answer certain questions. For various reasons, respondents may also be motivated to supply incorrect answers. For example, in countries where the tax collection system is consistently eluded by taxpayers, questions regarding level of income may deliberately be answered inaccurately. Distrust in the researcher, and the fear that research results may be passed on to the government, may also lead individuals to consistently understate their assets. Because of government restrictions in Brazil, for example, individuals will rarely admit to owning an imported car. Nevertheless, when one observes the streets of Rio de Janeiro, a substantial number of foreign cars are seen. The international market researcher is unlikely to change the societal context of a country. The objective of the content planning process should therefore be to adapt the questions to societal constraints.

Question Wording

The impact of language and culture is of particular importance when wording questions. The goal for the international marketing researcher should be to ensure that the potential for misunderstandings and misinterpretations of spoken or written words is minimized. Both language and cultural differences make this issue an extremely sensitive one in the international marketing research process. As a result, attention must be paid to the translation equivalence of verbal and nonverbal questions that can change in the course of translation. One of this book's authors, for example, used the term *group discussion* in a questionnaire for Russian executives, only to learn that the translated meaning of the term was "political indoctrination session."

The key is to keep questions clear by using simple rather than complex words, by avoiding ambiguous words and questions, by omitting leading questions, and by asking questions in specific terms, thus avoiding generalizations and estimates.[22] To reduce problems of question wording, it is helpful to use a translation–retranslation approach. The researcher formulates the questions, has them translated into the language of the country under investigation, and subsequently has a second translator return the foreign text to the researcher's native language. Through the use of this method, the researcher can hope to detect possible blunders. As demonstrated in *The International Marketplace 8.4*, translation mistakes are easy to make. An additional safeguard is the use of alternative wording. Here the researcher uses questions that address the same issue but are worded differently and that resurface at various points in the questionnaire in order to check for consistency in question interpretation by the respondents.

In spite of superb research planning, a poorly designed instrument will yield poor results. No matter how comfortable and experienced the researcher is in international research activities, an instrument should always be pretested. Ideally, such a pretest is carried out with a subset of the population under study. At least a pretest with knowledgeable experts and individuals should be conducted. Even though a pretest may mean delays and additional cost, the risks of poor research are simply too great for this process to be omitted.

Developing the Sampling Plan

To obtain representative results, the researcher must reach representative members of the population under study. Many methods that have been developed in industrialized countries for this purpose are useless abroad. For example, address directories may simply not be available. Multiple families may live in one dwelling. Differences between population groups living, for example, in highlands and lowlands may make it imperative to differentiate these segments. Lack of basic demographic information may prevent the design of a sampling frame. In instances in which comparative research addresses very different areas, for example China and North America, it may be virtually impossible to match samples.[23]

The international marketing researcher must keep in mind the complexities of the market under study and prepare his or her sampling plan accordingly. Often, samples need to be stratified to reflect different population groups, and innovative sampling methods need to be devised in order to assure representative and relevant responses. For example, a survey concerning grocery shopping habits might require data from housewives in one country but from domestic help in another.[24]

Data Collection

The international marketing researcher must check the quality of the data collection process. In some cultures, questionnaire administration is seen as useless by the local population. Instruments are administered primarily to humor the

THE INTERNATIONAL MARKETPLACE 8.4

Check Your Translations!

All sorts of things can go wrong when a company translates its advertising into foreign languages. Kentucky Fried Chicken's slogan "Finger-lickin' good" was translated into the less appetizing "Eat your fingers off" in Chinese. Ford launched the Ford Fiera in Spanish-speaking Latin American countries not knowing that *fiera* means "ugly old woman." The Italian brand of mineral water Traficante didn't sell so well either, being translated into "drug dealer" in Spanish. Advertising mistakes receive a fair amount of attention in the media and the international business world when they occur, but many people never stop to think about what would happen if a company unknowingly committed translation errors much earlier—in the research phase.

The possibility of disaster due to such errors is in many ways even greater than in the advertising stage because research findings are often used to determine a firm's strategy or for new product development. A translation blunder that goes undiscovered at this stage could set a company on the wrong track entirely. Imagine spending millions of dollars to develop a new product or to enter a new market only to find that your company's surveys had asked the wrong questions!

Researchers at the Pew Research Center for the People and the Press in Washington, DC, are not new to international research. They have been conducting public opinion research around the globe for more than a decade. Their findings related to attitudes toward the press, politics, and public policy issues are regularly cited in the media. However, the company received an unwelcome surprise when it translated one of its worldwide polls into 63 languages and then back into English. As it turns out, the ride to the foreign languages and back again was bumpier than they had imagined.

For example, in Ghana, the original phrase "married or living with a partner" was first translated into one of the country's tribal languages as "married but have a girlfriend," and the category "separated" became "There's a misunderstanding between me and my spouse." The original version of a questionnaire to be used in Nigeria had similar problems: "American ideas and customs" came out "the ideology of America and border guards" (get it—customs? border guards?) and the phrase "success in life is pretty much determined by forces outside our control" initially read "Goodness in life starts with blessings from one's personal god." In the original Nigerian Yoruba version, "fast food" had been translated to "microwave food," and "the military" became "herbalist/medicine man." Not quite the same thing, is it?

Fortunately, the meanings were corrected in the final translation of the questionnaire, said the Center's director, Andrew Kohut. The lesson? Multinational researchers, check your translations!

SOURCES: Terri Morrison and Wayne Conaway, *Kiss, Bow, or Shake Hands: Sales and Marketing* (New York: McGraw-Hill, 2012); Richard Morin, "Words Matter," *Washington Post*, January 19, 2003, B5; Ian Dow, "Your Ad Is a Tad Mad," *Scottish Daily Record*, October 5, 2002, 8; and Global Attitude Report, "What the World Thinks in 2002," December 4, 2002 (from the Pew Research Center for the People and the Press).

researcher. In such cases, interviewers may cheat quite frequently. Spot checks on the administration procedures are vital to ensure reasonable data quality. A realism check of data should also be used. For example, if marketing research in Italy reports that very little spaghetti is consumed, the researcher should perhaps consider whether individuals responded to their use of purchased spaghetti rather than homemade spaghetti. The collected data should therefore be compared with secondary information and with analogous information from a similar market in order to obtain a preliminary understanding of data quality.

Analyzing and Interpreting Primary Data

Interpretation and analysis of accumulated information are required to answer the research questions that were posed initially. The researcher should, of course, use the best tools available and appropriate for analysis. The fact that a market may be in a less-developed country does not preclude the collection of good data and the use of good analytical methods. On the other hand, international researchers should be cautioned against using overly sophisticated tools for unsophisticated data. Even the best of tools will not improve data quality. The quality of data must be matched with the quality of the research tools to achieve appropriately sophisticated analysis and yet not overstate the value of the data.

Presenting Research Results

The primary focus in the presentation of research results must be communication. In multinational marketing research, communication must take place not only with management at headquarters but also with managers in the local operations. Otherwise, little or no transference of research results will occur, and the synergistic benefits of a multinational operation are lost. To minimize time devoted to reading reports, the researcher must present results clearly and concisely. In the worldwide operations of a firm, particularly in the communication efforts, lengthy data and analytical demonstrations should be avoided. The availability of data and the techniques used should be mentioned, however, so that subsidiary operations can receive the information on request.

The researcher should also demonstrate in the presentation how research results relate to the original research objective and fit with overall corporate strategy. At least schematically, possibilities for analogous application should be highlighted. These possibilities should then also be communicated to local subsidiaries, perhaps through a short monthly newsletter. A newsletter format, ideally distributed through an intranet, can be used regardless of whether the research process is centralized, coordinated, or decentralized. The only difference will be the person or group providing the input for the newsletter. It is important to maintain such communication in order for the entire organization to learn and to improve its international marketing research capabilities.

Follow-Up and Review

Now that the research has been carried out, appropriate managerial decisions must be made based on the research, and the organization must absorb the research. For example, if it has been found that a product needs to have certain attributes to sell well in Latin America, the manager must determine whether the product development area is aware of this finding and the degree to which the knowledge is now incorporated into new product projects. Without such follow-up, the role of research tends to become a mere "staff" function, increasingly isolated from corporate "line" activity and lacking major impact on corporate activity. If that is the case, research will diminish and even be disregarded—resulting in an organization at risk.

Research on the Web

The growing use of technology has given rise to new marketing research approaches that allow consumers to be heard more often and permit firms to work much more effectively at their customer-listening skills. The evolution of marketing research on the web has been both dramatic and rapid. The rise in Internet usage and capabilities has catapulted marketing research from a Web 1.0 model in which researchers have taken traditional primary data collection methods online (e.g., surveys or questionnaires in which specific questions are asked) to a Web 2.0 model in which users generate the content of the data collected.[25]

The increasing degree to which everyone uses the Internet is making it possible for international marketers to use this medium in their research efforts. With low barriers to entry, understanding consumers worldwide is now an option for almost any company. For a market researcher, the Internet serves as a portal to reach out to consumers in a low-cost fashion. For example, product details, pictures of products, brand logos, and shopping environments can be portrayed with graphics and sounds—thus bringing the issues to be researched much closer to the respondent.

In the Web 1.0 online research model, surveys can be administered either through e-mail or via a website. An e-mail survey format eliminates the need for printing and postage. This is especially critical due to the fact that mailing surveys internationally can be very costly. As a result, larger and geographically diverse audiences can be the focus of inquiry. If surveys are posted on a site, they can be of the pop-up nature, where visitors can be targeted specifically. Companies that utilize the web for administering traditional surveys internationally are Qualtrics (www.qualtrics.com), Zoomerang (www.zoomerang.com), Zogby International (www.zogby.com), and Harris (www.harrisinteractive.com). Research indicates that there is a higher and faster response rate to electronic inquiries. In addition, the process of data entry can be structured so that responses are automatically fed into data analysis software.[26]

However, it would be too simplistic to assume that the digitalization of survey content is all that it takes to go global on the web. There are cultural differences that must be taken into account by the researcher. Global visitors to a site should encounter research that is embedded in their own cultural values, rituals, and symbols. Testimonials or encouragement should be delivered by culture-specific heroes. For example, a website might first offer a visitor from Korea the opportunity to become part of a product user community. A low-context visitor from the United States may in turn be exposed immediately to product features.[27] Other suggestions for constructing successful web surveys are to include only the most important questions, keep the total number of questions to 30 or fewer, limit the number of screens respondents have to navigate through, keep response time to less than 10 to 15 minutes, inform each respondent of the time needed to complete the survey, and give an incentive to take the survey that relates directly to the company's product that respondents are being asked to evaluate.[28]

Another trend in the Web 2.0 world has been the use of social networks to access particular consumer groups. With the popularity and growth in the number of social networking sites, market researchers can post pop-up and banner ads on these sites directing particular target audiences to online surveys. There are a number of worldwide social networking sites, such as Facebook, MySpace, Twitter, Bebo, LinkedIn, Ning, Classmates, and Flickr. The benefits for market research on these social networking sites are numerous: highly targeted markets (can specify demographics of respondent), real-time results (results within an hour), simple interface and ease of use, over millions of potential users for less than US$50, open-source software to allow researchers to customize surveys, and the ability to recruit respondents actively or passively. The major benefit to the networking site is a fee for each completed survey.[29]

The recent company acquisitions and geographical expansion within the social networking marketplace signal the importance that businesses are placing on the wealth of interactions within these sites. For example, Goldman Sachs purchased a big stake in Facebook, and Google acquired YouTube. Facebook, headquartered in California (USA), opened an international headquarters in Ireland because it has millions of users in Britain, Italy, France, Germany, Spain, and the Netherlands.[30]

In one of the first Web 2.0 moves, Facebook and Vizu[31] challenged traditional research methods by offering polling, which is a new way to find quick answers to simple questions. With Facebook Poll or Vizu's Web Polls, all a user has to do is create a question and specify a sample size. For as little as US$50 per 100 interviews, users can have results in their account in just a few hours. In this paradigm, the research is not designed before it begins but occurs over a series of polls.[32] Unlike the use of social networks to *access* respondents, the online survey is moved *into the existing* social network. Users can actually view real-time results, which increase their perception of value with respect to the interaction.[33] Herein, however, lie some of the limitations of Web 2.0 market research efforts: reliability (lack of respondent screening), sampling (are the right people answering?), and methodology (single-response poll format, does not currently offer statistically significant results).[34]

Communispace was one of the first online market researchers to fully engage in the Web 2.0 research space. This company established a new online community dedicated solely to market research. These online communities mimic traditional focus groups in the amount of qualitative information made available to the market researcher.[35] The company touts some of its biggest success stories as those related to Hallmark's Shoebox cards, Unilever's AXE products, GlaxoSmithKline's launch of alli, and Kraft's South Beach Diet products.[36]

The future of online marketing research is evolving as the capabilities of the Internet evolve. While traditional marketing research tools will not be replaced in the near term by online research methods, the world is the marketplace in the twenty-first century, and access to consumer opinions worldwide is critical for business success. Web-based research is a natural means for gathering consumer information quickly and cost-effectively.

THE INTERNATIONAL INFORMATION SYSTEM

Many organizations have data needs going beyond specific international marketing research projects. Most of the time, daily decisions must be made, and there is neither time nor money for special research. An information system already in place is needed to provide the decision maker with basic data for most ongoing decisions. Corporations have responded by developing marketing decision support systems. Defined as "an integrated system of data, statistical analysis, modeling, and display formats using computer hardware and software technology," such a system serves as a mechanism to coordinate the flow of information to corporate managers for decision-making purposes.[37]

To be useful to the decision maker, the system needs various attributes. First, the information must be *relevant*. The data gathered must have meaning for the manager's decision-making process. Second, the information must be *timely*. It is of little benefit to the manager if decision information help that is needed today does not become available until a month from now. To be of use to the international decision maker, the system must therefore feed from a variety of international sources and be updated frequently. For multinational corporations, this means a real-time linkage between international subsidiaries and a broad-based, ongoing data input operation.

Third, information must be *flexible*—that is, it must be available in the forms needed by management. A marketing decision support system must therefore permit manipulation of the format and combining of the data. Therefore, great effort must be expended to make diverse international data compatible with and comparable to each other. Fourth, information contained in the system must be *accurate*. This attribute is particularly relevant in the international field because information quickly becomes outdated as a result of major changes. Obviously, a system is of no value if it provides incorrect information that leads to poor decisions. Fifth, the system's information bank must be reasonably *exhaustive*. Because of the interrelationship between variables, factors that may influence a particular decision must be appropriately represented in the information system. This means that the marketing decision support system must be based on a broad variety of factors. Finally, to be useful to managers, the system must be *convenient* both to use and to access. Systems that are cumbersome and time-consuming to reach and to use will not be used enough to justify corporate expenditures to build and maintain them.

More international information systems are being developed successfully due to progress in computer technology in both hardware and software. To build an information system, corporations use the internal data that are available from divisions such as accounting and finance and also from their subsidiaries. In addition, many organizations put mechanisms in place to enrich the basic data flow. Three such tools are environmental scanning, Delphi studies, and scenario building.

Environmental Scanning

Any changes in the business environment, whether domestic or foreign, may have serious repercussions on the marketing activities of the firm. Corporations therefore should understand the necessity for tracking new developments and obtaining continuous updates. To carry out this task, some large multinational organizations have formed environmental scanning groups.

Environmental scanning activities are useful to continuously receive information on political, social, and economic affairs internationally; on changes of attitudes held by public institutions and private citizens; and on possible upcoming alterations in international markets.

The precision required for environmental scanning varies with its purpose. Whether the information is to be used for mind stretching or for budgeting, for example, must be taken into account when constructing the framework and variables that will enter the scanning process. The more immediate and precise the exercise is to be in its application within the corporation, the greater the need for detailed information. At the same time, such heightened precision may lessen the utility of environmental scanning for the strategic corporate purpose, which is more long term in its orientation.

Environmental scanning can be performed in various ways. One method consists of obtaining factual input regarding many variables. For example, the U.S. Census Bureau collects, evaluates, and adjusts a wide variety of demographic, social, and economic characteristics of foreign countries. Estimates for all countries of the world are developed, particularly on economic variables, such as labor force statistics, GDP, and income statistics, but also on health and nutrition variables. Similar factual information can be obtained from international organizations such as the World Bank or the United Nations.

Frequently, corporations believe that such factual data alone are insufficient for their information needs and use other methods to capture underlying dimensions of social change. One significant method is **content analysis**. This technique investigates the content of communication in a society and entails literally counting the number of times preselected words, themes, symbols, or pictures appear in a given medium. It can be used productively in international marketing to monitor the social, economic, cultural, and technological environment in which the marketing organization is operating.

Corporations can use content analysis to pinpoint upcoming changes in their line of business, and new opportunities, by attempting to identify trendsetting events. For example, the BP oil spill in the Gulf of Mexico resulted in entirely new international concern about environmental protection and safety reaching far beyond the incident itself.

Environmental scanning is conducted by a variety of groups within and outside the corporation. Frequently, small corporate staffs are created at headquarters to coordinate the information flow. In addition, subsidiary staff can be used to provide occasional intelligence reports. Groups of volunteers are also formed to gather and analyze information worldwide and feed individual analyses back to corporate headquarters, where they can be used to form the "big picture."

Finally, it should be kept in mind that internationally there may be a fine line between tracking and obtaining information and misappropriating corporate secrets. With growing frequency, governments and firms claim that their trade secrets are being obtained and abused by foreign competitors. The perceived threat from economic espionage has led to accusations of government spying networks trying to undermine the commercial interests of companies.[38] Information gatherers must be sensitive to these issues in order to avoid conflict or controversy.

Delphi Studies

To enrich the information obtained from factual data, corporations resort to the use of creative and highly qualitative data-gathering methods. Delphi studies are one such method. These studies are particularly useful in the international marketing environment because they are "a means for aggregating the judgments of a number of ... experts ... who cannot come together physically."[39] This type of research approach clearly aims at qualitative rather than quantitative measures by aggregating the information of a group of experts. It seeks to obtain answers from those who know instead of seeking the average responses of many with only limited knowledge.

Typically, Delphi studies are carried out with groups of about 30 well-chosen participants who possess particular in-depth expertise in an area of concern, such as future developments in the international trade environment. These participants are asked via mail to identify the major issues in the area of concern. They are also requested to rank their statements according to importance and explain the rationale behind the order. Next, the aggregated information is returned to all participants, who are encouraged to state clearly their agreements or disagreements with the various rank orders and comments. Statements can be challenged, and in another round participants can respond to the challenges. After several rounds of challenge and response, a reasonably coherent consensus is developed.

The Delphi technique is particularly valuable because it uses the mail or facsimile method of communication to bridge large distances and therefore makes individuals quite accessible at a reasonable cost. It does not suffer from the drawback of ordinary mail investigations: lack of interaction among the participants. One drawback of the technique is that it requires several steps, and therefore months may elapse before the information is obtained. Even though the increasing availability of e-mail may hasten the process, the researcher must be cautious to factor in the different penetration and acceptance levels of such technology. One should not let the research process be driven by technology to the exclusion of valuable key informants who utilize less sophisticated methods of communication.

Also, substantial effort must be expended in selecting the appropriate participants and in motivating them to participate in this exercise with enthusiasm and continuity. When obtained on a regular basis, Delphi information can provide crucial additions to the factual data available for the marketing information system. In this book, the final chapter has largely been designed based on a Delphi study carried out by the authors.

Scenario Building

Some companies use **scenario analysis** to look at different configurations of key variables in the international market. For example, economic growth rates, import penetration, population growth, and political stability can be varied. By projecting such variations for medium- to long-term periods, companies can envision completely new environmental conditions. These conditions are then analyzed for their potential domestic and international impact on corporate strategy.

Of major importance in scenario building is the identification of crucial trend variables and the degree of their variation. Frequently, key experts are used to gain information about potential variations and the viability of certain scenarios.

A wide variety of scenarios must be built to expose corporate executives to multiple potential occurrences. Ideally, even far-fetched variables deserve some consideration, if only to build worst-case scenarios.

Scenario builders also need to recognize the nonlinearity of factors. To simply extrapolate from currently existing situations is insufficient. Frequently, extraneous factors may enter the picture with a significant impact. Finally, in scenario building, the possibility of joint occurrences must be recognized because changes may not come about in an isolated fashion but may be spread over wide regions. An example of a joint occurrence is the indebtedness of developing nations. Although the inability of any one country to pay its debts would not present a major problem for the international banking community, large and simultaneous indebtedness may well pose a problem of major severity. Similarly, given large technological advances, the possibility of obsolescence of current technology must also be considered. For example, quantum leaps in computer development and new generations of computers may render obsolete the technological investment of a corporation or even a country.

For scenarios to be useful, management must analyze and respond to them by formulating contingency plans. Such planning will broaden horizons and may prepare management for unexpected situations. Familiarization in turn can result in shorter response times to actual occurrences by honing response capability. The difficulty, of course, is to devise scenarios that are unusual enough to trigger new thinking yet sufficiently realistic to be taken seriously by management.[40]

The development of an international information system is of major importance to the multinational corporation. It aids the ongoing decision process and becomes a vital corporate tool in carrying out the strategic planning task. Only by observing global trends and changes will the firm be able to maintain and increase its international competitive position. Many of the data available are quantitative in nature, but attention must also be paid to qualitative dimensions. Quantitative analysis will continue to improve as the ability to collect, store, analyze, and retrieve data increases through the use of high-speed computers. Nevertheless, qualitative analysis should remain a major component of corporate research and strategic planning.

SUMMARY

Constraints of time, resources, and expertise are the major inhibitors of international marketing research. Nevertheless, firms need to carry out planned and organized research in order to explore global market alternatives successfully. Such research needs to be closely linked to the decision-making process.

International market research differs from domestic research in that the environment, which determines how well tools, techniques, and concepts apply, is different abroad. In addition, the manager needs to deal with new parameters, such as duties, exchange rates, and international documentation; a greater number of interacting factors; and a much broader definition of the concept of competition.

Given the scarcity of resources, companies beginning their international effort often need to use data that have already been collected—that is, secondary data. Such data are available from governments, international organizations, directories, trade associations, or online databases.

To respond to specific information requirements, firms frequently need primary research. The researcher needs to select an appropriate research technique to collect the information needed. Sensitivity to different international environments and cultures will guide the researcher in deciding whether to use interviews, focus groups, observation, surveys, or experimentation as data-collection techniques. In addition to traditional data-gathering tools, web-based surveys can be faster at bringing better quality results. The same sensitivity applies to the design of the research instrument, where issues such as question format, content, and wording are decided. Also, the sampling plan needs to be appropriate for the local environment in order to ensure representative and useful responses.

Once the data have been collected, care must be taken to use analytical tools appropriate for the quality of data collected so that management is not misled about the sophistication of the research. Finally, the research results must be presented in a concise and useful form so that management can benefit in its decision making, and implementation of the research needs to be tracked.

To provide ongoing information to management, an international information support system is useful. Such a system will provide for the systematic and continuous gathering, analysis, and reporting of data for decision-making purposes. It uses a firm's internal information and gathers data via environmental scanning, Delphi studies, or scenario building, thus enabling management to prepare for the future and hone its decision-making skills.

KEY TERMS

foreign-market opportunity analysis
proxy variable
research specification
qualitative data
quantitative data
international comparative research
structured question
unstructured question
direct question
indirect question
social desirability
data equivalence
translation–retranslation approach
realism check
web-based research
content analysis
scenario analysis

QUESTIONS FOR DISCUSSION

1. Discuss the possible shortcomings and benefits of secondary data.
2. Explore the trade-offs between centralized and decentralized international marketing research.
3. What implications does language have for international market research?
4. Compare and contrast the various research techniques explained in this chapter.
5. What effects has information technology had on international marketing research?

INTERNET EXERCISES

1. Who are the European Union's main trade partners? Which of these countries are members of the Organization for Economic Cooperation and Development? (Check both the WTO website, www.wto.org and the OECD website, www.oecd.org.)
2. Against what industries and countries did the United States file antidumping actions last year? (Check the U.S. International Trade Commission at www.usitc.gov.)

CHALLENGE US

Doctored Data Cast Doubt on Argentina's Inflation Rate

Over the past 50 years, Argentina has often achieved the highest inflation rate in the world. Recently, there has evolved a severe disagreement between politicians and business executives regarding the publication of data and research of inflation levels.

Businesses (and researchers) want accurate reporting so that they can adjust their prices and forecasts accordingly. However, higher inflation numbers have severe economic repercussions for government, since there were commitments made to adjust many government payments. In the budget, it makes a big difference whether the inflation rate is reported as 40 percent or as 8 percent.

In the country's statistical office, starting in early 2007, the government replaced several statisticians, clerks, and field workers who collect consumer prices. Subsequently, starkly lower inflation figures began to be reported. Workers at the National Institute of Statistics protested Argentina's miraculous declines in inflation and poverty rates. For example, the government numbers report an official poverty figure of 15.3 percent while the Catholic Church says it is near 40 percent.

Such discrepancies lead to controversy. Economists and political analysts say the allegations hurt the country's credibility in terms of investments. In speeches, though, President De Kirchner and other officials have defended the country's unorthodox economic policies, including high taxes on agricultural exports, heavy spending and energy subsidies. "Our different way of doing things has permitted growth and the creation of jobs," Vice President Amado Boudou recently told reporters. "Argentines can be proud we did things our way." Also, the government budget is less strained due to lower adjustment payments.

For Discussion

1. Who is right—the accuracy side, which is said to be particularly short term oriented, or the adjustment side, which claims there are other things than just numbers to worry about?

SOURCES: Juan Forero, "Doctored Data Cast Doubt on Argentina," *The Washington Post*, August 16, 2009, www.washingtonpost.com/wp-dyn/content/article/2009/08/15/AR2009081502758.html; and Juan Forero, "Fight over Argentina's inflation rate pits government against private economists," *The Washington Post*, October 31, 2011.

RECOMMENDED READINGS

Baker, H. Kent, J. Clay Singleton, and E. Theodore Veit. *Survey Research in Corporate Finance: Bridging the Gap between Theory and Practice*. Oxford, UK: Oxford University Press, 2011.

Barker, Donald, Melissa Barker, and Katherine Pinard. *Internet Research*. 5th ed. Stamfort, CT: Course Technology, 2011.

Bradley, Nigel. *Marketing Research: Tools and Techniques*. Oxford, UK: Oxford University Press, 2010.

Delphos, William A. *Inside Washington: Government Resources for International Business*. 6th ed. New York: Business Expert Press, 2011.

Hair Joseph, Jr. *Essentials of Marketing Research*. 2nd ed. New York: McGraw-Hill Higher Education, 2010.

Roberts, Mary Lou, and Debra Zahay. *Internet Marketing*. 3rd ed. Cincinnati, OH: South-Western College, 2012.

Scott, David Meerman. *The New Rules of Marketing and PR: How to Use News Releases, Blogs, Podcasting, Viral Marketing, and Online Media to Reach Buyers Directly*. 3rd ed. New York: Wiley, 2011.

Zikmund, William, and Barry Babin. *Essentials of Marketing Research*. 5th ed. Cincinnati, OH: South-Western College, 2012.

ENDNOTES

1. Naresh K. Malhotra, Mark Peterson, and Susan Bardi Kleiser, "Marketing Research: A State-of-the-Art Review and Directions for the Twenty-First Century," *Journal of the Academy of Marketing Science* 27, no. 2 (1999): 160–83.
2. "Marketing Definitions," American Marketing Association, www.marketingpower.com, accessed January 28, 2012.
3. Naresh Malhotra, *Marketing Research: An Applied Orientation and SPSS 14.0 Student CD*, 5th ed. (Upper Saddle River, NJ: Prentice Hall, 2006).
4. C. Samuel Craig and Susan P. Douglas, *International Marketing Research*, 3rd ed. (Chichester: John Wiley and Sons, 2006).
5. Nina L. Reynolds, "Benchmarking International Marketing Research Practice in UK Agencies—Preliminary Evidence," *Benchmarking* 7, no. 5 (2000): 343–59.
6. For an excellent exposition on measuring the value of research, see Gilbert A. Churchill, Jr., and Dawn Iacobucci, *Marketing Research: Methodological Foundations*, 10th ed. (Mason, OH: South-Western, 2010).
7. For an excellent online diagnostic tool, see Tamer S. Cavusgil's CORE (Company Readiness to Export), Michigan State University, http://globaledge.msu.edu/diagtools, accessed January 29, 2012.
8. "Geography," About.com, www.geograpy.about.com, accessed February 29, 2012.
9. Tamer S. Cavusgil, Tunga Kiyak, and Sengun Yeniyurt, "Complementary Approaches to Preliminary Foreign Market Opportunity Assessment: Country Clustering and Country Ranking," *Industrial Marketing Management*, December 24, 2003, 616.
10. "MP Backs Federal Action over China Fruit Trade Stance," Australian Broadcasting Corporation, www.abc.net.au/news/stories/2005/09/15/1460594.htm, accessed December 2, 2008.
11. Michael R. Czinkota, *International Marketing and Accessibility* (Washington, DC: U.S. Department of Commerce, 2007).
12. Michael R. Czinkota, "International Information Cross-Fertilization in Marketing: An Empirical Assessment," *European Journal of Marketing* 34 (2000).
13. European Society for Opinion and Marketing Research (ESOMAR), "Marketing Research Expenditures Up Worldwide by 5.1%," www.esomar.nl, accessed December 2, 2008; and Jack Honomichl, "2011 Honomichl Global Top 25 Research Report," *Marketing News*, August 30, 2011, 12–47.
14. Salah S. Hassan and A. Coskun Samli, "The New Frontiers of Intermarket Segmentation," in *Global Marketing:*

Perspectives and Cases, eds. Salah S. Hassan and Roger D. Blackwell (Fort Worth, TX: The Dryden Press, 1994), 76–100.
15. Michael R. Czinkota and Masaaki Kotabe, "Product Development the Japanese Way," in *Trends in International Business: Critical Perspectives*, eds. M. Czinkota and M. Kotabe (Oxford, England: Blackwell Publishers, 1998), 153–58.
16. R. Nishikawa, "New Product Planning at Hitachi," *Long Range Planning* 22 (1989): 20–24.
17. For an excellent example, see Alan Dubinsky, Marvin Jolson, Masaaki Kotabe, and Chae Lim, "A Cross-National Investigation of Industrial Salespeople's Ethical Perceptions," *Journal of International Business Studies* 22 (1991): 651–70.
18. Raymond A. Jussaume, Jr., and Yoshiharu Yamada, "A Comparison of the Viability of Mail Surveys in Japan and the United States," *Public Opinion Quarterly* 54 (1990): 219–28.
19. Camille P. Schuster and Michael J. Copeland, "Global Business Exchanges: Similarities and Differences around the World," *Journal of International Marketing* 2 (1999): 63–80.
20. Kavil Ramachandran, "Data Collection for Management Research in Developing Countries," in *The Management Research Handbook*, eds. N. Craig Smith and Paul Dainty (London: Routledge, 1991), 304.
21. Tamer S. Cavusgil, Seyda Deligonul, and Attila Yaprak, "International Marketing as a Field of Study: A Critical Assessment of Earlier Development and a Look Forward," *Journal of International Marketing* 13, no. 4 (2005): 1–27.
22. Gilbert A. Churchill, Jr., and Dawn Iacobucci, *Marketing Research: Methodological Foundations*, 10th ed. (Mason, OH: South-Western, 2010).
23. Kathleen Brewer Doran, "Lessons Learned in Cross-Cultural Research of Chinese and North American Consumers," *Journal of Business Research* 55 (2002): 823–29.
24. C. Samuel Craig and Susan P. Douglas, *International Marketing Research*, 3rd ed. (Chichester, England: John Wiley and Sons, 2006).
25. Jason Freedman, Evan Konwiser, Emily Nielsten, and Colin Van Ostern, "Market Research: Web 1.0 in a Web 2.0 World. How Can We Listen Instead of Asking Questions?" Glassmeyer/McNamee Center for Digital Strategies, Tuck School of Business at Dartmouth, March 2008, http://mba.tuck.dartmouth.edu/digital/Research/ResearchProjects/ResearchMarketWeb.pdf.
26. Janet Ilieva, Steve Baron, and Nigel M. Healey, "On-line Surveys in Marketing Research: Pros and Cons," *International Journal of Marketing Research* 44, no. 3 (2002): 361–76.
27. David Luna, Laura A. Peracchio, and Maria D. de Juan, "Cross-Cultural and Cognitive Aspects of Web Site Navigation," *Journal of the Academy of Marketing Science* 30, no. 4 (2002): 397–410.
28. "Web-based Surveys Help Customers Evolve with Your Products," *ATX Dialogue*, February 2004, www.broadviewnet.com/BVN/Default.asp, accessed December 2, 2008.
29. Michael Stanat, "Facebook: The Future of Market Research?" *Market Intelligence, Research Trends*, October 2007, http://marketintelligences.com/2007/10/19/the-future-of-market-research.aspx.
30. Eric Pfanner, "AOL to Buy Social Networking Site Bebo," *International Herald Tribune*, March 13, 2008, www.iht.com/articles/2008/03/13/technology/aol.php; and Halah Touryalai, "Facebook Will Go Public in Second Quarter 2012," *Forbes.com*, February 29, 2012, www.forbes.com/sites/halahtouryalai/2011/11/28/facebook-will-go-public-in-second-quarter-2012-report.
31. Vizu Facebook Polls, http://vizu.typepad.com/facebook_polls/2007/07/create-a-poll-o.html, accessed February 29, 2012.
32. Ray Poynter, "Facebook: The Future of Networking with Customers," *International Journal of Market Research* 50, no. 1 (2008), www.mrs.org.uk/publications/ijmr_viewpoints/poynter.htm, accessed February 29, 2012.
33. Freedman, Konwiser, Nielsten, and Ostern, op. cit.
34. Stanat, 2007; and Freedman, Konwiser, Nielsten, and Ostern, 2008.
35. Freedman, Konwiser, Nielsten, and Ostern, 2008.
36. Communispace, www.communispace.com.
37. Fred M. Feinberg, Thomas C. Kinnear, and James R. Taylor, *Modern Marketing Research: Concepts, Methods and Cases,* 2nd ed. (Cincinnati, OH: South Western, 2012).
38. Peter Clarke, "The Echelon Questions," *Electronic Engineering Times*, March 6, 2000, 36.
39. Andre L. Delbecq, Andrew H. Van de Ven, and David H. Gustafson, *Group Techniques for Program Planning* (Glenview, IL: Scott, Foresman, 1975), 83.
40. David Rutenberg, "Playful Plans," Queen's University working paper, 1991.

APPENDIX A

Information Sources for Marketing Issues

EUROPEAN UNION

EUROPA
The umbrella server for all institutions
http://europa.eu

CORDIS: Community Research and Development Information Service
Information on EU research programs
www.cordis.europa.eu

Council of the European Union
Information and news from the council, with sections covering common foreign and security policy (CFSP) and justice and home affairs
http://ue.eu.int

Court of Auditors
Information notes, annual reports, and other publications
http://eca.europa.eu

Court of Justice
Overview, press releases, publications, and full-text proceedings of the court
http://curia.europa.eu

Citizens of Europe
Covers rights of citizens of EU member states
http://panorama.citizens-of-europe.eu

Delegation of the European Commission to the United States
Press releases, EURECOM: economic and financial news, EU–U.S. relations, information on EU policies, and delegation programs
www.eurunion.org/eu

Euro
The single currency
http://ec.europa.eu/economy_finance/euro

ERBD: European Bank for Reconstruction and Development
Assists in the development of market economies across Europe and in parts of Asia
www.ebrd.com

CEDEFOP: European Centre for the Development of Vocational Training
Information on the center and contact information
www.cedefop.europa.eu

EEA: European Environment Agency
Information on the mission, products and services, and organizations and staff of the EEA
www.eea.europa.eu

EIB: European Investment Bank
Press releases and information on borrowing and loan operations, staff, and publications
www.eib.org

European Medicines Agency
Information on drug approval procedures and documents of the Committee for Proprietary Medicinal Products and the Committee for Veterinary Medicinal Products
www.ema.europa.eu/ema

European Monetary Institute
European Central Bank
The central bank for the euro; Identifies its primary mission as promoting and preserving economic stability in the Eurozone
www.ecb.int

EuroStat
Statistical information on Europe
http://epp.eurostat.ec.europa.eu

European Training Foundation
Information on vocational education and training programs in Central and Eastern Europe and Central Asia
www.etf.europa.eu

EU: European Union
200 Rue de la Loi
1049 Brussels, Belgium
and
2300 M Street NW
Washington, DC 20037
www.eurunion.org

OHIM: Office of Harmonization for the Internal Market
Guidelines, application forms, and other information for registering an EU trademark
www.oami.europa.eu

UNITED NATIONS

UNCTAD: Conference of Trade and Development
Palais des Nations
8-14, Av. de la Paix
1211 Geneva 10
Switzerland
www.unctad.org

UNDESA: Department of Economic and Social Affairs
2 United Nations Plaza
New York, NY 10017
www.un.org/desa

UNIDO: Industrial Development Organization
1 United Nations Plaza
Room DC1–1118
New York, NY 10017
and
Vienna International Centre
Wagramerstr. 5
P.O. Box 300
A-1400 Vienna
Austria
www.unido.org

ITC: International Trade Centre
Palais des Nations
1211 Geneva 10
Switzerland
www.intracen.org

UNESCO: Educational, Scientific and Cultural Organization
2 United Nations Plaza
Room 900
New York, NY 10017
www.unesco.org

United Nations Publications
2 United Nations Plaza
Room DC2-853
New York, NY 10017
http://unp.un.org

U.S. GOVERNMENT

USAID: Agency for International Development
Office of Press Relations
Ronald Reagan Building
Washington, DC 20523
www.usaid.gov

Census Bureau
4600 Silver Hill Road
Washington, DC 20233
www.census.gov

CPB: Customs and Border Protection
1300 Pennsylvania Avenue NW
Washington, DC 20229
www.cbp.gov

USDA: Department of Agriculture
1400 Independence Avenue SW
Washington, DC 20250
www.usda.gov

Department of Commerce
1401 Constitution Avenue NW
Washington, DC 20230
www.commerce.gov

Department of State
2201 C Street NW
Washington, DC 20520
www.state.gov

Department of the Treasury
1500 Pennsylvania Avenue NW
Washington, DC 20220
www.ustreas.gov

FTC: Federal Trade Commission
600 Pennsylvania Avenue NW
Washington, DC 20580
www.ftc.gov

FedStats
www.fedstats.gov

ITC: International Trade Commission
500 E Street SW
Washington, DC 20436
www.usitc.gov

Small Business Administration
409 Third Street SW
Washington, DC 20416
www.sbaonline.sba.gov

USTDA: Trade and Development Agency
1000 Wilson Blvd.
Suite 1600
Arlington, VA 22209
www.ustda.gov

The World Factbook
www.cia.gov/library/publications/the-world-factbook

WTCA: World Trade Centers Association
420 Lexington Avenue
Suite 518
New York, NY 10170
www.wtca.org

CEA: Council of Economic Advisers
www.whitehouse.gov/administration/eop/cea

DOD: Department of Defense
1400 Defense Pentagon
Washington, DC 20301
www.defense.gov

Department of Energy
1000 Independence Avenue SW
Washington, DC 20585
www.energy.gov

Department of Interior
1849 C Street NW
Washington, DC 20240
www.doi.gov

Department of Labor
200 Constitution Avenue NW
Washington, DC 20210
www.dol.gov

Department of Transportation
1200 New Jersey Avenue SE
Washington, DC 20590
www.dot.gov

EPA: Environmental Protection Agency
1200 Pennsylvania Avenue NW
Washington, DC 20460
www.epa.gov

National Economic Council
www.whitehouse.gov/nec

Office of Management and Budget
725 17th Street NW
Washington, DC 20503
www.whitehouse.gov/omb

Office of the U.S. Trade Representative
600 17th Street NW
Washington, DC 20508
www.ustr.gov

OPIC: Overseas Private Investment Corporation
1100 New York Avenue NW
Washington, DC 20527
www.opic.gov

SELECTED ORGANIZATIONS

FHI 360
1825 Connecticut Avenue NW
Washington, DC 20009
www.aed.org

American Bankers Association
1120 Connecticut Avenue NW
Washington, DC 20036
www.aba.com

American Bar Association: Section of International Law and Practice
321 North Clark Street
Chicago, IL 60654
and
740 15th Street NW
Washington, DC 20005
http://apps.americanbar.org/intlaw

AMA: American Management Association
1601 Broadway
New York, NY 10019
www.amanet.org

American Marketing Association
311 South Wacker Drive
Suite 5800
Chicago, IL 60606
www.marketingpower.com

API: American Petroleum Institute
1220 L Street NW
Washington, DC 20005
www.api.org

APEC: Asia-Pacific Economic Cooperation Secretariat
35 Heng Mui Keng Terrace
Singapore 1196169
www.apec.org

ADB: Asian Development Bank
6 ADB Avenue
Mandaluyong City 1550
Metro Manila, Philippines
www.adb.org

ASEAN: Association of South East Asian Nations
70A, Jalan Sisingamangaraja
Jakarta 12110
Indonesia
www.aseansec.org

BBB: Better Business Bureau
3033 Wilson Blvd, Suite 600
Arlington, VA 22201
www.bbb.org

Industry Canada
Canadian market data
www.strategis.ic.gc.ca/ic_wp-pa.htm

U.S. Chamber of Commerce
1615 H Street NW
Washington, DC 20062
www.uschamber.com

Delegation of the European Union to the United States
2175 K Street NW
Washington, DC 20037
www.eurunion.org/eu

The Conference Board
845 Third Avenue
New York, NY 10022
www.conference-board.org

Deutsche Bundesbank
Postfach 10 06 02
D—60047 Frankfurt am Main
Germany
www.bundesbank.de

Export-Import Bank of the United States
811 Vermont Avenue NW
Washington, DC 20571
www.exim.gov

Federal Reserve Bank of New York
33 Liberty Street
New York, NY 10045
www.newyorkfed.org

Gallup Organization
www.gallup.com

Greenpeace
702 H Street, NW
Suite 300
Washington, DC 20001
www.greenpeace.org

Iconoculture
244 First Avenue North
Minneapolis, MN 55401
http://iconoculture.com

IDB: Inter-American Development Bank
1300 New York Avenue NW
Washington, DC 20577
www.iadb.org

International Bank for Reconstruction and Development
(The World Bank)
1818 H Street NW
Washington, DC 20433
www.worldbank.org

IMF: International Monetary Fund
700 19th Street NW
Washington, DC 20431
www.imf.org

ITU: International Telecommunication Union
Place des Nations
1211 Geneva 20
Switzerland
www.itu.int

Odom Institute for Research in Social Science
Manning Hall, CB #3355
University of North Carolina at Chapel Hill
Chapel Hill, NC 27599
www.irss.unc.edu

LANIC: Latin American Network Information Center
Teresa Lozano Long Institute of Latin American
Studies
SRH 1.310
1 University Station D0800
Austin, TX 78712
www1.lanic.utexas.edu

globalEDGE
International business research site
http://globaledge.msu.edu

National Association of Manufacturers
1331 Pennsylvania Avenue NW
Suite 600
Washington, DC 20004
www.nam.org

NFIB: National Federation of Independent Business
53 Century Blvd, Suite 250
Nashville, TN 37214
www.nfib.com

OECD: Organization for Economic Cooperation and
Development
2, rue André Pascal
75775 Paris Cedex 16
France
and
2001 L Street NW, Suite 650
Washington, DC 20036
www.oecd.org

Organization of American States
17th Street and Constitution Avenue NW
Washington, DC 20006
www.oas.org

The Roper Center for Public Opinion Research
University of Connecticut
Homer Babbidge Library
369 Fairfield Way, Unit 2164
Storrs, CT 06269
www.ropercenter.uconn.edu

Transparency International
Alt-Moabit 96
10559 Berlin
Germany
www.transparency.org

INDEXES TO LITERATURE

Business Periodicals Index
H.W. Wilson Co.
950 University Avenue
Bronx, NY 10452

The New York Times Index
www.nytimes.com

The Virtual Reference Desk
www.virtualref.com

The Wall Street Journal Index
http://online.wsj.com

DIRECTORIES

American Register of Exporters and Importers
38 Park Row
New York, NY 10038

Arabian Year Book
Dar Al-Seuassam Est. Box 42480
Shuwahk, Kuwait

Directories of American Firms Operating in Foreign Countries
World Trade Academy Press
Uniworld Business Publications, Inc.
50 E. 42nd Street
New York, NY 10017

The Directory of International Sources of Business Information
Pitman
128 Long Acre
London WC2E 9AN
England

Encyclopedia of Associations
Gale Research Co.
Book Tower
Detroit, MI 48226

Polk's World Bank Directory
R.C. Polk & Co.
2001 Elm Hill Pike
P.O. Box 1340
Nashville, TN 37202

Verified Directory of Manufacturer's Representatives
MacRae's Blue Book, Inc.
817 Broadway
New York, NY 10003

World Guide to Trade Associations
K.G. Saur & Co.
175 Fifth Avenue
New York, NY 10010

PERIODIC REPORTS, NEWSPAPERS, AND MAGAZINES

Advertising Age
711 Third Avenue
New York, NY 10017
www.adage.com

Barron's
1211 Avenue of the Americas
New York, NY 10036
http://online.barrons.com

Bloomberg Businessweek
www.businessweek.com

UN Comtrade
United Nations Commodity Trade Statistics Database
United Nations Publications
2 United Nations Plaza
Room DC2-853
New York, NY 10017
http://comtrade.un.org

Conference Board Record
The Conference Board, Inc.
845 Third Avenue
New York, NY 10022

Customs and Border Protection Bulletin
U.S. Customs and Border Protection
130 Pennsylvania Avenue NW
Washington, DC 20229
http://cbp.gov/xp/cgov/trade/legal/bulletins_decisions

The Dismal Scientist
www.economy.com/dismal

The Economist
Economist Newspaper Ltd.
25 St. James Street
London SWIA 1HG
England
www.economist.com

The Financial Times
The Financial Times, Ltd.
One Southwark Bridge
London
England
www.ft.com

Forbes
Forbes, Inc.
90 Fifth Avenue
New York, NY 10011
www.forbes.com

Fortune
Time, Inc.
1 Time Warner Center
New York, NY 10036
www.fortune.com

Global Trade and Transportation
North American Publishing Co.
401 N. Broad Street
Philadelphia, PA 19108

Industrial Marketing Management
Elsevier
Reed Elsevier, Inc.
125 Park Avenue
23rd Floor
New York, NY 10017
www.journals.elsevier.com/industrial-marketing-management

International Encyclopedia of the Social Sciences
Gale, Cengage Learning
27500 Drake Road
Farmington Hills, MI 48331

International Financial Statistics
International Monetary Fund
Publications Unit
700 19th Street NW
Washington, DC 20431
www.imf.org

Investor's Daily
Investor's Business Daily, Inc.
www.investors.com

The Journal of Commerce
2 Penn Plaza East
Newark, NJ 07105
www.joc.com

Michie's Legal Resources
Lexis-Nexis
www.michie.com

Sales and Marketing Management
http://salesandmarketing.com

Trade Finance
Euromoney Institutional Investor
225 Park Avenue South
7th Floor
New York, NY 10003
www.tradefinancemagazine.com

The Wall Street Journal
Dow Jones & Company, Inc.
1211 Avenue of the Americas
New York, NY 10036
http://online.wsj.com

The WWW Virtual Library: Law
www.vlib.org/Law

World Trade Center Association (WTCA) Directory
World Trade Centers Association
420 Lexington Avenue
Suite 518
New York, NY 10170
www.wtca.org

SELECTED TRADE DATABASES

Trade Publication References with Bibliographic Keywords

Agris
Biocommerce Abstracts & Directory
Findex
Frost (short) Sullivan Market
Research Reports
Marketing Surveys Index
McCarthy Press Cuttings Service
Paperchem
PTS F & S Indexes
Trade and Industry Index

Trade Publication References with Summaries

ABI/Inform
Arab Information Bank
Asia-Pacific
BFAI
Biobusiness
CAB Abstracts
Chemical Business Newbase
Chemical Industry Notes
Caffeeline
Delphes
InfoSouth Latin American Information System
Management Contents
NTIS Bibliographic Data Base
Paperchem
PIRA Abstract
PSTA
PTS Marketing & Advertising
Reference Service
PTS PromtRapra Abstracts
Textline
Trade & Industry ASAP
World Textiles

Full Text of Trade Publications

Datamonitor Market Reports
Dow Jones News

Euromonitor Market Direction
Federal News Service
Financial Times Business Report File
Financial Times Fulltext
Globefish
ICC Key Notes Market Research
Investext
McCarthy Press Cuttings Service
PTS Promt
Textline
Trade & Industry ASAP

Statistics

Agrostat (diskette only)
Arab Information Bank
ARI Network/CNS
Comext/Eurostat
Comtrade
FAKT-German Statistics
Globefish
IMF Data
OECD Data
Piers Imports
PTS Forecasts
PTS Time Series
Reuters Monitor
Trade Statistics
Tradstat World Trade Statistics
TRAINS (CD-ROM being developed)
U.S. I/E Maritime Bills of Lading
U.S. Imports for Consumption
World Bank Statistics

Price Information

ARI Network/CNS
Chemical Business Newsbase
COLEACP
Commodity Options
Commodities 2000
Market News Service of ITC
Nikkei Shimbun News Database
Reuters Monitor
UPI
U.S. Wholesale Prices

Company Registers

ABC Europe Production Europe
Biocommerce Abstracts & Directory
CD-Export (CD-ROM only)
Company Intelligence
D&B Dun's Market Identifiers (U.S.A.)
D&B European Marketing File
D&B Eastern Europe
Dun's Electronic Business Directory
Firmexport/Firmimport
Hoppenstedt Austria
Hoppenstedt Benelux
Hoppenstedt Germany
Huco-Hungarian Companies
ICC Directory of Companies
Kompass Asia/Pacific
Kompass Europe (EKOD)
Mexican Exporters/Importers
Piers Imports
Polu-Polish Companies
SDOE
Thomas Register
TRAINS (CD-ROM being developed)
UK Importers
UK Importers (DECTA)
U.S. Directory of Importers
U.S. I/E Maritime Bills of Lading
World Trade Center Network

Trade Opportunities, Tenders

Business
Federal News Service
Huntech-Hungarian Technique
Scan-a-Bid
Tenders Electronic Daily
World Trade Center Network

Tariffs and Trade Regulations

Celex
ECLAS
Justis Eastern Europe (CD-ROM only)
Scad
Spearhead
Spicer's Centre for Europe
TRAINS (CD-ROM being developed)
U.S. Code of Federal Regulations
U.S. Federal Register
U.S. Harmonized Tariff Schedule

Standards

BSI Standardline
Noriane/Perinorm
NTIS Bibliographic Data Base
Standards Infodisk ILI (CD-ROM only)

Shipping Information

Piers Imports
Tradstat World Trade Statistics
U.S. I/E Maritime Bills of Lading

Others

Fairbase
Ibiscus

APPENDIX B

The Structure of a Country Commercial Guide

THE U.S. COMMERCIAL SERVICE

The following is an example of governmental research made available to firms. Country commercial guides provide a condensed and business-focused overview of business customs, conditions, contacts, and opportunities. Using such guides can be of major help in getting started in unfamiliar territory.

DOING BUSINESS IN CHINA

Table of Contents

Chapter 4 Leading Sectors for U.S. Exports and Investment

A. Commercial Sectors
- Education and Training
- Marine Industries
- Air Pollution
- Green Building
- Renewable Energy—Solar and Wind
- Safety/Security
- Aviation Market
- Automotive Components Market
- Healthcare Market
- Travel and Tourism Sector
- Agricultural Sectors

B. Agricultural Sectors
- Agricultural Sectors
- Soybeans
- Cotton
- Hides and Skins
- Corn
- Fish and Fish Products
- Tobacco
- Wood and Wood Products

Chapter 5 Trade Regulations, Customs, and Standards

A. Import Tariffs
B. Trade Barriers
C. Import Requirements and Documentation
D. U.S. Export Controls
E. Temporary Entry
F. Labeling and Marking Requirements
G. Prohibited and Restricted Imports
H. Customs Regulations and Contact Information
I. Standards
J. Trade Agreements
K. Web Resources

Chapter 6 Investment Climate

A. Introduction
B. Openness to Foreign Investment
C. Conversion and Transfer Policies
D. Expropriation and Compensation
E. Dispute Settlement
F. Performance Requirements/Incentives
G. Right to Private Ownership and Establishment
H. Protection of Property Rights
I. Transparency of the Regulatory System
J. Efficient Capital Markets and Portfolio Investment
K. Political Violence
L. Corruption
M. Bilateral Investment Agreements
N. OPIC and Other Investment Insurance Programs
O. Labor
P. Foreign Trade Zones/Free Ports
Q. Foreign Direct Investment Statistics
R. List of Major Foreign Investors
S. Web Resources

Chapter 7 Trade and Project Financing
- A. How Do I Get Paid? (Method of Payment)
- B. How Does the Banking System Operate?
- C. Foreign-Exchange Controls
- D. U.S. Banks and Local Correspondent Banks
- E. Project Financing
- F. Web Resources

Chapter 8 Business Travel
- A. Business Customs
- B. Travel Advisory
- C. Visa Requirements
- D. Telecommunication
- E. Transportation
- F. Language
- G. Health
- H. Local Time, Business Hours, and Holidays
- I. Temporary Entry of Materials and Personal Belongings
- J. Web Resources

Chapter 9 Contacts, Market Research, and Trade Events
- A. Contacts
  - Chinese Government Agencies
  - Chinese Trade Associations/Chambers of Commerce
  - Chinese Commercial Banks/Branch Offices of Austrian Banks in the U.S.
  - Washington-Based U.S. Government Contacts
- B. Market Research
- C. Trade Events

SOURCE: *Doing Business in China*, U.S. Department of Commerce and U.S. Department of State, Washington, DC, 2011, http://export.gov/china/doingbizinchina/index.asp.

CHAPTER 9

Market Entry and Expansion

LEARNING OBJECTIVES

By the time you complete this chapter, you will be able to:

- Know how firms continuously progress through a process of internationalization.
- Understand the effects—benefits and repercussions—of entering international markets.
- Study different means for entering international markets.
- Understand the responsibility of international intermediaries.
- Learn about the opportunities and challenges of cooperative market development.
- Comprehend how firms overcome market barriers through various means.

THE INTERNATIONAL MARKETPLACE 9.1

Product Innovation May Come Mainly from China

Since the 2007–2008 global recession, confidence in the American model of economic development has decreased significantly. Economists are eager to draw conclusions from China's continued economic growth even through the economic slowdown, which affected much of the developed world. Many assert that Chinese economic policy is more stable because of the government's large role. However, it may also be the demand of Chinese consumers that shapes innovation and supply.

The American toilet company Kohler has just released the state-of-the-art Numi toilet. This toilet, designed and marketed primarily for the United States and China, has many features included especially for the Chinese market. The toilet's feet-warming system is a solution to infamously cold Chinese bathrooms. Other Chinese market features include the Numi's music system, Skype capabilities, and bidet. This toilet suggests that even an American company must keep the Chinese populace in mind when developing products. In an editorial in the *Financial Times*, Christopher Caldwell concluded that the Numi toilet suggests more than just an increase in Chinese-centered goods. He claims that this toilet "is a sign that this era of US advantage is spiraling towards its close."

Caldwell is not alone in his belief that Beijing will soon begin its reign of prominence. The Numi is not the only special global product marketed for China. In 2005, GM's luxury sedan the Buick LaCrosse was redesigned especially for the Chinese market. Joe Qiu, designer of the Chinese version of the LaCrosse, told Fara Warner of *Fast Company* how he created a car that would sell well in the Chinese market. The interior of the car is meant to recreate the soft, luxurious environment of Chinese nightclubs and upscale Shanghai homes. The car's exterior is sleek and trendy, targeting the chicest Chinese clientele. Since then, sales of the LaCrosse in China have outperformed those in the United States. In 2010, GM released the updated version of the Buick LaCrosse globally. Much to U.S. GM's chagrin, the car's interior was designed by Qiu. The U.S. team took the lead role in developing the car's interior but had to take into account the input and edits from the Chinese design team. This move displayed how Chinese preferences trumped American ones. As a result, China gained more clout within the powerful American company.

With the second largest economy in the world and an envy-inducing continued growth, China is beginning to rival the United States' position as the world's economic leader. Whether the twenty-first century will become the age of China will be determined over time. Right now, Chinese preferences are beginning to share the lead in the development of new global products.

SOURCES: Christopher Caldwell, "Telling Lessons for the Future from China's Bathrooms," *Financial Times* (London), June 4, 2011; Patti Waldmeir, "The Numi Toilet: Chinese Design for a Global Market," *Globe and Mail* (Toronto), May 30, 2011; and Fara Warner, "Made in China," *Fast Company*, April 1, 2007.

As *The International Marketplace 9.1* shows, doing business internationally provides opportunities for companies to bring innovations to the world. International expansion may turn out to be the key to prosperity for corporations and employees. Firms that export grow faster, are more productive, and have employees who tend to earn more.[1] Even though some firms go international from the start, most of them do so gradually. New activities in an unfamiliar environment increase a firm's risk. Therefore, companies must prepare their activities and adjust to the needs and opportunities of international markets in order to become long-term participants.

This chapter discusses the activities that take place within the firm preparing to enter the international market. It focuses on the basic stimuli for internationalization and on the internal and external change agents that activate these stimuli. The concerns and preoccupations of firms as they begin their international marketing operations are discussed. Finally, expansion strategies, such as franchising, licensing, and foreign direct investment, are presented. Exhibit 9.1 provides a model of the international entry and expansion process. It shows what triggers and inhibits international expansion and outlines the subsequent discussion of this chapter.

EXHIBIT 9.1 A Model of International Entry and Expansion

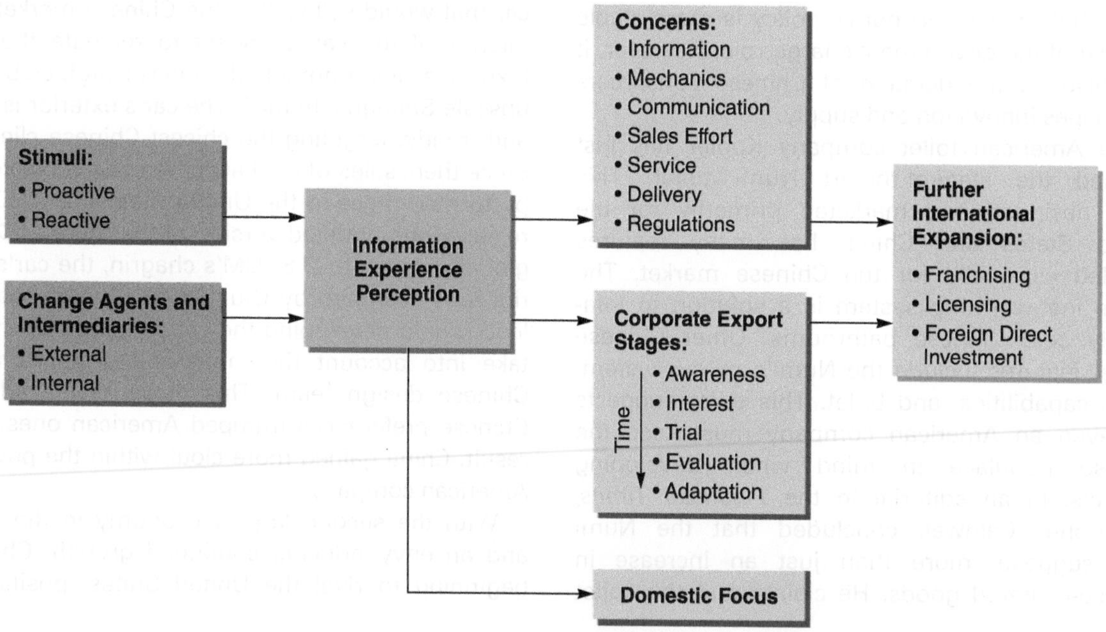

STIMULI TO INTERNATIONALIZE

In most business activities, one factor alone rarely accounts for any given action. Usually a mixture of factors results in firms taking steps in a given direction. This is true of internationalization; there are a variety of stimuli both pushing and pulling firms along the international path. Exhibit 9.2 lists the major motivations to go international, differentiated into proactive and reactive motivations. Proactive motivations represent stimuli to attempt strategic change. Reactive motivations influence firms that respond to environmental shifts by changing their activities over time. In other words, proactive firms go international because they want to, while reactive ones go international because they have to.

Proactive Stimuli

Profits provide the strongest incentive to become involved in international marketing. Management may perceive international sales as a potential source of higher profit margins or of additional profits. Of course, the perceived profitability from going international may not match actual profitability because of such factors as high start-up costs, sudden shifts in exchange rates, or insufficient market research.

A second major stimulus results either from *unique products* or a *technological advantage*. A firm's goods or services may not be widely available from international competitors or may offer technological advances in a specialized field. Uniqueness can provide a competitive edge and result in major business success abroad. Again, real and perceived advantages should be differentiated. Many firms believe that theirs are unique products or services, even though on a global level this may not be the case. The intensity of marketing's interaction with the research and development function, as well as the level of investment into R&D, has been shown to have a major effect on the success of exported products.[2] One issue to consider is how long such a technological or product advantage will continue. Historically, a firm with a competitive edge could count on being the sole supplier to international markets for years to come. This type of advantage, however, has shrunk dramatically because of competing technologies and imitation due to insufficient protection of intellectual property rights.

Exclusive market information is another proactive stimulus. This includes knowledge about foreign customers, marketplaces, or market situations that is not widely shared by other firms. Such knowledge may result from a firm's international research, special contacts, or being in the right place at the right time (for example, recognizing a good business situation during a vacation trip). Although exclusivity can serve well as an initial stimulus to go international, it rarely provides for sustained motivation. Over time competitors will catch up

EXHIBIT 9.2 Why Firms Go International

Proactive Stimuli	Reactive Stimuli
• Profit advantage	• Competitive pressures
• Unique products	• Overproduction
• Technological advantage	• Declining domestic sales
• Exclusive information	• Excess capacity
• Economies of scale	• Saturated domestic markets
• Market size	• Proximity to customers and ports

© Imaginechina via AP Images

The world's largest convenience store franchise, 7-Eleven, recently tapped into the Chinese market for the first time, debuting stores in Shanghai, China, with the hopes of expanding to eastern China.

with the information advantage of the firm, particularly in light of the growing ease of global information access.

A major proactive motivation is *economies of scale*. The *size* of the international market may enable the firm to increase its output and slide more rapidly on the learning curve. Increased production for the international market can also help reduce the cost of production for domestic sales. Research by the Boston Consulting Group showed that a doubling of output can reduce production costs up to 30 percent![3]

Reactive Stimuli

Here firms respond to changes and pressures in the business environment rather than blaze new trails. In reaction to *competitive pressures*, a firm may fear losing domestic market share to competing firms or losing foreign markets permanently to new competitors. However, insufficient preparation may result in a hasty market entry and a quick withdrawal.

Overproduction is a major reactive motivation. Historically, during downturns in the domestic business cycle, markets abroad provided an ideal outlet for high inventories. Such market expansion often does not represent commitment by management but rather a temporary safety-valve activity. Instead of developing an international marketing perspective by adjusting the marketing mix to needs abroad, firms stimulate export sales with short-term price cuts.[4] As soon as the domestic market demand returns to previous levels, international marketing activities are curtailed or even terminated. Firms that have used such a strategy once may encounter difficulties when trying it again because many foreign customers are not interested in temporary or sporadic business relationships. The lessons learned, and the increased synchronization of the major industrial economies, may well decrease the importance of this motivation over time.

Stable or declining domestic sales, whether measured in sales volume or market share, also stimulate firms to expand internationally. Products marketed by the firm domestically may be in the declining stage of the product life cycle; thus, the firm may opt to prolong the life of the product by expanding the market. In the past, such efforts often met with success in developing nations because their customers only gradually reached a level of need already attained by customers in industrialized nations. Increasingly, however, global lag times are quite short. Nevertheless, developing nations often still have very good use for products for which the demand in the industrialized world is already on the decline. This holds particularly true for high-technology items that are outdated by the latest innovations. Such "just-dated" technology—for example, slightly obsolete medical equipment—can be highly useful to economic development and offer vast progress.

Excess capacity can be a powerful motivation. If equipment is not fully utilized, international expansion can help achieve broader distribution of fixed costs. Alternatively, if all fixed costs are assigned to domestic production, the firm can penetrate international markets with a pricing scheme that focuses mainly on variable costs. Such a strategy may result in the offering of products abroad at a cost lower than at home, which may trigger dumping charges. In the long run, fixed-cost recovery needs to ensure the replacement of production equipment used for international marketing activities.

The stimulus of a *saturated domestic market* is similar to that of declining domestic sales. Again, firms can use the international market to prolong the life cycle of their product and of their organization.

A final major reactive motivation is *proximity to customers and ports*. Physical closeness to foreign markets can encourage the international activities of a firm. This factor is much less prevalent in North American nations than in many other countries, since most American firms are situated far away from the border. Consider a typical 200-mile activity radius of U.S. firms, which would likely mean doing business in another state. In Europe, however, such a radius makes most firms international simply because their neighbors are so close. As an example, a European company operating in the heart of Belgium needs to go only 50 miles to be in multiple foreign markets.

In this context, the concept of **psychological distance** needs to be understood. Psychological distance refers to the lack of symmetry between growing international markets with respect to cultural variables, legal factors, and other societal norms. Geographic closeness to foreign markets may not translate into real or perceived closeness to the foreign customers because a foreign market that is geographically close may be psychologically distant. For example, research has shown that U.S. firms perceive Canada to be much closer psychologically than Mexico. Two major issues frame the context of psychological distance. First, some of the distance seen by firms is based on perception rather than reality. For example, German firms may view the Austrian market simply as an extension of their home market due to so many superficial similarities, just as many U.S. firms may see the United Kingdom as psychologically very close due to the similarity in language. However, the attitudes and values of managers and customers may vary substantially between markets. Too much of a focus on the similarities may let the firm lose sight of the differences. Many Canadian firms have incurred high costs in learning this lesson when entering the United States.[5] Second, at the same time, closer psychological proximity does make it easier for firms to enter markets. Therefore, for firms new to international marketing, it may be advantageous to begin this new activity by entering the psychologically closer markets first in order to gather experience before venturing into markets that are farther away.[6]

Overall, the more successful international firms are motivated by proactive—that is, firm-internal—factors. The motivations of firms do not seem to shift dramatically over the short term but are rather stable. For the reader who seeks involvement in international markets and searches for good corporate opportunities, an important consideration should be whether a firm is proactive or reactive.

CHANGE AGENTS

Someone or something within the firm must initiate change and shepherd it through to implementation. This intervening individual or variable is here called a **change agent**. Change agents in the internationalization process are shown in Exhibit 9.3.

EXHIBIT 9.3 Change Agents in the Internationalization Process

Internal	External
• Enlightened management	• Demand
• New management	• Competition
• Significant internal event	• Domestic distributors
	• Service firms
	• Business associations
	• Governmental activities
	• Export intermediaries
	• Export management companies
	• Trading companies

Internal Change Agents

The type and quality of *management* is key to a firm's international activities. Dynamic management is important when firms take their first international steps. Over the long term, management commitment and management's perceptions and attitudes are also good predictors of export success.[7] Also key are the international experience and exposure of management.[8] Managers who have lived abroad, know foreign languages, or are particularly interested in foreign cultures are likely, sooner rather than later, to investigate whether international marketing opportunities would be appropriate for their firm. Managerial urge reflects the desire, drive, and enthusiasm toward international marketing activities. This enthusiasm can exist simply because managers like to be part of a firm that operates internationally. They may like international travel—for example, to call on a major customer in the Bahamas during a cold winter month. Or the urge to internationalize may simply reflect entrepreneurial zeal—a desire for continuous market growth and expansion.[9]

This conclusion has largely been formulated by reverse deduction: the managers of firms that are unsuccessful or inactive in the international marketplace usually exhibit a lack of commitment to international marketing. International markets cannot be penetrated overnight—to succeed in them requires substantial market development activity, market research, and identification of and response to new market factors. Therefore, a high level of commitment is crucial to endure setbacks and failure. It is important to involve all levels of management early on in the international planning process. Any international venture must be incorporated into the firm's strategic management process. A firm that sets no strategic goals is less likely to achieve long-term success.[10] It is also important to establish a specific structure in which someone has the responsibility for international activities. Without such responsibility, the focus necessary for success is lost. Just one person assigned part time can explore international opportunities successfully.

Another major change agent is a *significant internal event*. The development of a new product that can be useful abroad can serve as such an event, as can the receipt of new information about current product uses. As an example, a manufacturer of hospital beds learned that beds it was selling domestically were being resold in a foreign country. Further, the beds sold abroad for more than twice the price that they were fetching at home. This new information triggered a strong interest by the company's management to enter international markets.

In small- and medium-sized firms (firms with fewer than 250 employees), the initial decision to go international is usually made by the president, with substantial input from the marketing department. The implementation of this decision usually becomes primarily the responsibility of marketing personnel. The strategic evaluation of international marketing activities is typically carried out again by the president of the firm. This makes the president and the marketing department the leading internal change agents.

External Change Agents

The primary outside influence on a firm's decision to go international is foreign *demand*. Inquiries from abroad and other expressions of demand have a powerful effect on initial interest in entering the international marketplace. Unsolicited international orders are one major factor that encourages firms to begin exporting. In the United States, such orders have been found to account for more than half of all cases of export initiation by small- and medium-sized firms. Through their websites, firms can easily become unplanned participants in the international market. Customers from abroad can visit the site and place an international order, even though a firm's plans may have been strictly domestic. Thus, a company can unexpectedly find itself an exporter.[11] We call such firms **accidental exporters**. While good fortune may have initiated the export activity, over the longer term the firm must start planning how to systematically increase its international expansion, or at least how to make more of these accidents happen.

Another major change agent may actually be the *competition*. Just as firms respond to competitive pressures from other companies, statements by executives from competing firms may serve as change agents. Therefore, formal and informal meetings among managers from different firms at trade association meetings, conventions, or business roundtables often trigger major change.

Domestic distributors also initiate change. To increase their international distribution volume, they encourage purely domestic clients to participate in the international market. This is true not only for exports but also for imports.

Banks and other *service firms*, such as accounting offices, can alert domestic clients to international opportunities. Although these service providers have historically followed their major multinational clients abroad, increasingly they are establishing a foreign presence and then urging domestic clients to expand their market reach.

Chambers of commerce and other *business associations* that interact with firms locally can frequently heighten international marketing interests. These organizations function as secondary intermediaries by sponsoring the presence and encouragement of other managers.

Government efforts on the national or local level can also serve as a major change agent. In light of the contributions exports make to growth, employment, and tax revenue, governments are active in encouraging and supporting exports. In the United States, the Department of Commerce is particularly involved in export promotion. Frequently, district officers, with the help of voluntary groups such as District Export Councils, visit firms and analyze their international marketing opportunities. In addition, many states have formed economic development agencies that assist companies by providing information, displaying products abroad, and sometimes even helping with financing.

GOING INTERNATIONAL

For many firms, internationalization is a gradual process. Particularly in small markets, however, firms may very well be **born global**, founded for the explicit purpose of marketing abroad because the domestic economy is too small to support their activities. There are three major methods to enter new markets. These are export, licensing and franchising, and foreign direct investment.

EXPORT

In some countries, more than a third of exporting firms commenced their export activities within two years of establishment.[12] Such start-up or innate exporters play a growing role in an economy's international trade involvement. In addition, firms with a strong e-commerce focus may also be gaining rapid global exposure due to the ease of outreach and access. Such rapid exposure, however, should not be confused with actual internationalization because it may often take a substantial amount of time to translate exposure into international business activities and strategic corporate acceptance.

In most instances today, firms begin their operations in the domestic market. From their home location, they gradually expand, and, over time, some of them become interested in the international market. The development of this interest typically appears to proceed in several stages, as shown in Exhibit 9.4.

In each one of these stages, firms are measurably different in their capabilities, problems, and needs.[13] Initially, the vast majority of firms are not even aware of the international marketplace. Frequently, management will not even fill an unsolicited export order. Should unsolicited orders or other international market stimuli continue over time, however, a firm may gradually become aware of international market opportunities. While such awareness is unlikely to trigger much business activity, it can lead management to gradually become interested in international activities. Eventually, firms will answer inquiries, participate in export counseling sessions, attend international trade fairs and seminars, and even begin to fill unsolicited export orders.

Prime candidates among firms to make this transition from aware to interested are those companies that have a track record of domestic market expansion. In the next stage, the firm gradually begins to explore international markets. Management is willing to consider the feasibility of exporting. In this trial, or exploratory, stage, the firm begins to export systematically, usually to psychologically close countries. However, management is still far from being committed to international marketing activities.

After some export activity, typically within two years of the initial export, management is likely to conduct an evaluation of its export efforts. Key questions concern the fulfillment of expectations: are our products as unique as we thought they were, and are we making enough money on our exports? If a firm is disappointed with its international performance it may withdraw from these activities. Alternatively, it can continue as an experienced small exporter. Success can also lead to the process of export adaptation. Here a firm is an experienced exporter to a particular country and adjusts its activities to changing exchange rates, tariffs, and other variables. Management is ready to explore the feasibility of exporting to additional countries that are psychologically farther away. Frequently, this level of adaptation is reached once export transactions comprise 15 percent of overall sales volume. Planning for export marketing becomes incorporated into the strategy of the firm.

The population of exporting firms within these stages does not remain stable. Researchers of U.S. firms have found that in any given year, 15 percent of exporters will stop exporting by the next year, while 10 percent of nonexporters

EXHIBIT 9.4 Key Corporate Export Stages

- Awareness
- Interest
- Trial
- Evaluation
- Demand
- Adaptation

will enter the foreign market. The most critical junctures for the firm are the points at which it begins or ceases exporting.[14]

As can be expected, firms in different stages are faced with different problems. Firms at the export awareness and interest stages are primarily concerned with operational matters such as information flow and the mechanics of carrying out international business transactions. They understand that a totally new body of knowledge and expertise is needed and try to acquire it. Companies that have already had some exposure to international markets via trial or evaluation begin to think about tactical marketing issues such as communication and sales effort. Finally, firms that have reached the export adaptation phase are mainly strategy- and service-oriented. They worry about longer-range issues such as service delivery and regulatory changes. Increased sophistication in international markets translates into increased application of marketing knowledge on the part of firms. The more they become active in international markets, the more firms recognize that a marketing orientation is just as essential internationally as it is in the domestic market.

Firms who choose to export their products may do so in a number of different ways. They may export directly or use export intermediaries such as export management companies or trading companies. They can also sell to a domestic firm that in turn sells abroad. For example, many products sold to multinational corporations are used as input for their global sales.

Market intermediaries specialize in bringing firms or their goods and services to the global market. Often, they have detailed information about the competitive conditions in certain markets or have personal contacts with potential buyers abroad. They can also evaluate credit risk, call on customers abroad, and manage the physical delivery of the product. Two key intermediaries are export management companies and trading companies.

Export Management Companies

Export management companies (EMCs) are domestic firms that perform international marketing services as commissioned representatives or as distributors for several other firms. Most EMCs are quite small. They are frequently formed by one or two principals with experience in international marketing or in a particular geographic area.

EMCs have two primary forms of operation. They either take title to goods and operate internationally on their own account, or they perform services as agents. As an agent, an EMC is likely to have a contractual relationship that specifies exclusivity agreements and sales quotas. In addition, price arrangements and promotional support payments are agreed on.[15] Because EMCs often serve a variety of clients, their mode of operation may vary from client to client and from transaction to transaction. An EMC may act as an agent for one client, whereas for another client, or even for the same one on a different occasion, it may operate as a distributor.

For the EMC concept to work, both parties must recognize the delegation of responsibilities, the costs associated with these activities, and the need for information sharing and cooperation. On the manufacturer's side, use of an EMC is a major channel commitment. This requires a thorough investigation of the intermediary, a willingness to cooperate on a prolonged basis, and proper rewards. The EMC in turn must adopt a flexible approach to the export relationship. As access to the Internet is making customers increasingly sophisticated, EMCs must ensure that they continue to deliver true value added assets. They must acquire, develop, and deploy resources, such as new knowledge about foreign markets or about export processes, in order to lower their client firm's export-related transaction costs.[16] The EMC must show that the service is worth the cost.

Trading Companies

Another major exporting intermediary is the trading company. The concept was originated by European trading houses, such as the Fuggers, and was soon formalized by the monarchs. Hoping to expand their power and wealth, kings chartered traders with exclusive trading rights and protection by the naval forces in exchange for tax payments. Today, the most famous trading companies are the **sogoshosha** of Japan. Names like Sumitomo, Mitsubishi, Mitsui, and C. Itoh have become household words around the world. These general trading companies play a unique role in world commerce by importing, exporting, countertrading, investing, and manufacturing. Because of their vast size, they can benefit from economies of scale and survive on very low profit margins.

Four major reasons have been given for the success of the Japanese *sogoshosha*. First, these firms are organized to gather, evaluate, and translate market information into business opportunities. By making large investments in their information systems, these firms have developed a strategic information advantage. Second, their vast transaction volume provides them with cost advantages. For example, they can negotiate preferential transportation rates. Third, these firms serve large markets around the world and have transaction advantages. They can benefit from unique opportunities, such as barter trade in which they exchange goods for goods. Finally, *sogoshosha* have access to vast quantities of capital, both within Japan and in the international capital markets. With their financial advantage they can carry out transactions that are larger and riskier than is feasible for other firms.

For many decades, the emergence of trading companies was commonly believed to be a Japan-specific phenomenon. Over time, however, prodded by government legislation, successful trading companies have also emerged in countries as diverse as Brazil, South Korea, and Turkey.

Export trading company (ETC) legislation designed to improve the export performance of small and medium-sized firms in the United States permits bank participation in trading companies and reduces the antitrust threat to joint export efforts. An ETC can apply for a certificate of review from the U.S. Department of Commerce that provides antitrust preclearance for specific export activities. Businesses are encouraged to join together for a certificate to export or offer export services.

Bank participation in ETCs was intended to allow better access to capital. The relaxation of antitrust provisions in turn was to enable firms to share the cost of international market entry. As an example, in case a warehouse is needed to support foreign-market penetration, one firm alone does not have to bear all the costs.

Although ETCs seem to offer major benefits to U.S. firms wishing to penetrate international markets, they have not been used very extensively. By 2012, certificates were held by hundreds of individuals, companies, and associations. In total, the certificates cover more than 3,000 firms, mainly because the various trade associations have applied for certification for all of their members.[17]

Firms participating in trading companies by joining or forming them need to consider the difference between product- and market-driven activities. Firms have a tendency to use a trading company to dispose of their existing merchandise. International success, however, depends primarily on market demand. Trading companies must therefore accomplish a balance between the demands of the market and the supply of the members in order to be successful. Information must be collected on the needs and wants of foreign customers. It must then be disseminated to participating firms, and help must be provided in implementing change. Otherwise, lack of responsiveness to market demand will limit international success.

E-Commerce

Many companies increasingly choose to market their products internationally through **e-commerce**, the ability to offer goods and services over the web. The growth of e-commerce has led to increased revenue for many companies. There are a variety of ways in which companies can market their products over the Internet. One key option is the development of corporate websites. Many companies initially become exporters because of unsolicited international orders. In order to encourage more orders from foreign consumers, companies should accept international means of payment and have the ability to ship their product internationally. In addition, companies need to consider the ever-growing population of non-English speakers on the web. Websites should be offered in several different languages. However, having a website translated and kept up to date may be costly and time-consuming. If the site is well developed, it will naturally lead to the expectations that order fulfillment will be of equal caliber. Therefore, any web strategy has to be tied closely to the company's overall growth strategy in world markets.

Companies can also enter e-commerce by exporting through a variety of business-to-consumer and business-to-business forums. For example, consumers and businesses alike can sell their products on the online auction site eBay (www.ebay.com). Businesses that would like to target the Chinese market can use China's Alibaba (www.alibaba.com), whose slogan is "Global trade starts here." Alibaba, in particular, targets small and medium-sized businesses that aim to export to China and Chinese businesses looking to expand domestically. In 2012, Alibaba.com Limited was the world's leading business-to-business e-commerce company with more than 70 million registered users from over 240 countries and regions.[18]

There are a variety of new concerns if a firm uses e-commerce to enter the international marketplace. Due to international time differences, firms must be ready to provide 24-hour order-taking and customer-support service, have the regulatory and customs-handling expertise to deliver internationally, and have an understanding of global marketing environments for the further development of business relationships. Many companies choose to use the capabilities of air carriers such as UPS, DHL, and FedEx, who offer a range of support services such as order fulfillment, delivery, customs clearance, and supply chain management. There are some legal concerns for e-businesses, such as export control laws, especially if they market strategically important products or software. Firms must also consider privacy, security, and intellectual property regulations. The EU's privacy measures are much more stringent than those of the United States and thus may impact U.S. companies looking to do business in Europe. Furthermore, companies need to be able to protect their customers from identity theft and other online scams.

As seen in Exhibit 9.5, Internet usage worldwide is growing rapidly. Africa and the Middle East have experienced substantial increase in usage since the beginning of the twenty-first century. But each of those regions still has significant room for growth, as do other regions around the world. As use of the Internet grows, e-commerce will become an even more important venue for commercial activity. It can be expected that countries will implement more laws concerning business transactions over the Internet and that the international community as a whole will develop standards, either outside or inside the WTO, for conducting e-commerce.

EXHIBIT 9.5 Internet Usage Statistics

World Regions	Population (2011 Est.)	Internet Users Dec. 2000	Internet Users March 2011	% Population (Penetration)	Users % of World	% Usage Growth 2000–2011
Africa	1,037,524,058	4,514,400	118,609,620	11.5	5.7	2,627.4
Asia	3,879,740,877	114,304,000	922,329,554	23.8	44.0	806.9
Europe	816,426,346	105,096,093	476,213,935	58.3	22.7	453.1
Middle East	216,258,843	3,284,800	68,553,666	31.7	3.3	2,087.0
North America	347,394,870	108,096,800	272,066,000	78.3	13.0	251.7
Latin America/ Caribbean	597,283,165	18,068,919	215,939,400	36.2	10.3	1,195.1
Oceania/Australia	35,426,995	7,620,480	21,293,830	60.1	1.0	279.4
WORLD TOTAL	6,930,055,154	360,985,492	2,095,006,005	30.2	100	580.4

SOURCE: Compiled from Global Market Information Database.

LICENSING AND FRANCHISING

Licensing and franchising are market expansion alternatives used by all types of firms, large and small. They offer flexibility and reflect the needs of the firm and the market. A small firm, for example, uses licensing to access intellectual property owned by a foreign business or to expand without much capital investment. A multinational corporation may use the same strategy to rapidly enter foreign markets in order to take advantage of new conditions and foreclose opportunities for its competition.

Licensing

Under a licensing agreement, one firm, the licensor, permits another to use its intellectual property in exchange for compensation designated as a royalty. The recipient firm is the licensee. The property might include patents, trademarks, copyrights, technology, technical know-how, or specific marketing skills. *The International Marketplace 9.2* describes how three companies have entered into a licensing agreement that brings together one company's established customer base, another company's distribution expertise, and yet another's product knowledge.

THE INTERNATIONAL MARKETPLACE 9.2

Will a Manufacturing, Marketing, and Distribution Licensing Agreement Grow the International Market for Tazo Tea?

Tea is one of the oldest beverages in the world and the second most consumed beverage worldwide (water being the first). Approaches to drinking tea have evolved from as far back as 2372 B.C. In 1904, teabags largely replaced loose tea leaves; in the 1940s instant tea and mixes appeared; and the 1980s saw the advent of ready-to-drink (RTD) tea. For aesthetic reasons, RTD teas have been sold in glass bottles. However, the future appears to lie with plastic and aluminum packaging, and packaging attributes are critical to the growth of the RTD tea market because convenience and availability will be the critical demand drivers of this market. Along with these packaging attributes, however, is the fact that tea is perceived to be healthful, and the consumption of healthy products is a trend that has worldwide appeal. In 2011, the global tea market was estimated at $87 billion.

Tapping into this underdeveloped and potential growth market are major international players Unilever, PepsiCo, and Starbucks. In 1991, Unilever and PepsiCo entered into a joint venture, the Pepsi/Lipton Tea Partnership (PLP), with each company having 50 percent ownership. The PLP quickly became the leading distributor of RTD tea in the United States. In 2003, the Pepsi Lipton International joint venture took the RTD tea product into over 40 countries and experienced double-digit volume growth. Building on these two joint ventures, the two companies expanded on their international partnership in 2007. The intent with the 2007 expansion of the international joint venture was to further leverage complementary strengths of Unilever's Lipton brand and tea product knowledge with PepsiCo's bottling and distribution network. The expansion added 11 new countries to Unilever and Lipton's RTD tea business, essentially more than doubling the RTD tea volume and propelling the partnership into the leadership spot in the global RTD tea business.

With strong growth expected in the RTD tea marketplace, neither company was, however, taking any time to bask in the leadership spot. In 2008, PepsiCo and Unilever entered into a licensing agreement for the manufacturing, marketing, and distribution of Starbucks Tazo Tea RTD beverages. In 1994, Starbucks and PepsiCo formed the North American Coffee Partnership. This joint venture focused on the RTD coffee business in the United States via the development and distribution of Starbucks bottled products such as Frappuccino, Doubleshot Espresso, and Doubleshot Energy + Coffee. With over 100 unique tea, fruit, and herbal beverages, Tazo was acquired by Starbucks in 1999, and Tazo is the exclusive tea offered in Starbucks coffeehouses.

Starbucks has been successful in building an established base of Tazo consumers. A licensing agreement with PLP for the manufacturing, marketing, and distribution of the Tazo brand of tea in RTD packaging sets the stage for all three companies to take advantage of a worldwide growing tea marketplace.

© Terri Miller/E-Visual Communications, Inc.

Starbucks has been successful with creating an established base of Tazo consumers.

SOURCES: Heather Landi, "High Tea," *Beverage World*, July 15, 2011, 18–22; *Marketing Week*; "Starbucks in Overhaul to Boost Global Brand Growth," July 14, 2011, 4; Aninditta Savitry, "The US Ready-to-Drink Team Market: Trends and Compe-tea-tion," *Beverage Aisle*, April 1, 2001; "Tea and the Ready-to-Drink Tea in the U.S.," *Packaged Facts*, November 1, 2007; "Starbucks, Pepsi, and Unilever Partner to Grow the Tazo Tea Ready-to-Drink Business," *istockAnalyst*, August 19, 2008, www.istockanalyst.com/article/viewiStockNews/articleid/2527986; "Unilever and PepsiCo to Expand Ready-to-Drink Tea Joint Venture," September 14, 2007, www.unilever.com/mediacentre/pressreleases/2007/UnileverPepsicotoexpand.aspx; and "Starbucks, Pepsi and Unilever Partner to Grow the Tazo Tea Ready-to-Drink Business," August 19, 2008, http://news.starbucks.com/article_print.cfm?article_id=30.

Assessment of Licensing

As an international entry strategy, licensing requires neither capital investment nor knowledge or marketing strength in foreign markets. Royalty income provides an opportunity to obtain an additional return on R&D investments already incurred. Licensing offers a proven concept that reduces the risk of R&D failures, the cost of designing around the licensor's patents, or the fear of patent-infringement litigation. Furthermore, ongoing licensing cooperation and support enables the licensee to benefit from new developments.

Licensing reduces the exposure to both government intervention and terrorism because the licensee is typically a local company. It allows a firm to test a foreign market without major investment of capital or management time. It can also preempt a market for the competition, especially if the licensor's resources permit full-scale involvement only in selected markets. A final reason for growing licensing activities is the increase in global protection of intellectual property rights, which makes companies more willing to transfer proprietary knowledge internationally.[19] A strong foreign partner then becomes a local force with a distinct interest in rooting out unlicensed activities.

Licensing is not without disadvantages. It leaves most international marketing functions to the licensee. As a result, the licensor gains only limited expertise and may not even gain any advantages when it comes to market entry itself. In exchange for the royalty, the licensor may actually create its own competitor not only in the markets for which the agreement was made but also in third markets.

Licensing has come under criticism from supranational organizations, such as the United Nations Conference on Trade and Development (UNCTAD). It has been alleged that licensing lets multinational corporations (MNCs) capitalize on older technology. Such technology, however, may be in the best interest of the recipient. Guinness Brewery, for example, in order to produce Guinness Stout in Nigeria, licensed equipment that had been used in Ireland at the turn of the twentieth century. This equipment had additional economic life in Nigeria because it presented a good fit with local needs.

Principal Issues in Negotiating Licensing Agreements

The key issues in negotiating licensing agreements include the scope of the rights conveyed, compensation, licensee compliance, dispute resolution, and the term and termination of the agreement.[20] Clear agreements reduce trouble down the road.

The rights conveyed are product or patent rights. Defining their scope involves specifying the technology, know-how, or show-how to be included, the format, and guarantees. An example of format specification is an agreement on whether manuals will be translated into the licensee's language.

Compensation issues may be heavily argued. The licensor wants to cover (1) **transfer costs**, which are all variable costs incurred in transferring technology to a licensee and all ongoing costs of maintaining the agreement, (2) **R&D costs** incurred in researching and developing the licensed technology, and (3) **opportunity costs** incurred in the foreclosure of other sources of profit, such as exports or direct investment. To cover these costs, the licensor wants a share of the profits generated from the use of the license.

Compensation can take the form of running royalties, such as 5 percent of the licensee sales, and up-front payments, service fees, and disclosure fees (for proprietary data). Sometimes, government regulations restrict royalty payments. In such instances, the know-how transferred can be capitalized and payments can be profits or dividends.

Licensee compliance in the agreement should address (1) export control regulations, (2) confidentiality of the intellectual property and technology provided, and (3) record keeping and provisions for licensor audits. Finally, the term, termination, and survival of rights must be specified.

Trademark Licensing

Trademark licensing permits use of the names or logos of designers, literary characters, sports teams, and movie stars on merchandise such as clothing. British designer Laura Ashley started the first major furniture licensing program. Coca-Cola licensed its name to Murjani to be used on blue jeans, sweatshirts, and windbreakers. The licensors can obtain large revenues with little effort, whereas the licensees can produce a branded product that consumers will recognize immediately. Fees can range between 7 to 12 percent of net sales for merchandising license agreements.[21]

Both licensor and licensee may run into difficulty if the trademark is used for a product too far removed from the original success or if the licensed product casts a shadow on the reputation of the licensor. In licensing a trademark, consumer perceptions have to be researched to understand the effect on the brand's position.

Franchising

In **franchising**, a parent company (the franchiser) grants another, independent entity (the franchisee) the right to do business in a specified manner. This right can take the form of selling the franchiser's products or using its name; its production, preparation, and marketing techniques; or its business approach. The

EXHIBIT 9.6 Fast Food Franchise in New Delhi, India

SOURCE: © AFP/Douglas E. Curran/Getty Images.

major forms of franchising are manufacturer–retailer systems (such as car dealerships), manufacturer–wholesaler systems (such as soft drink companies), and service firm–retailer systems (such as lodging services and fast food outlets). Product or trade franchising emphasizes the product or commodity to be sold, while business-format franchising focuses on ways of doing business.

Franchising's origins are in Bavaria, but it has been adopted by various types of businesses in many countries. Franchises exist across many different industries, but the ones perhaps most visible to consumers are in the restaurant and food service industry. Exhibit 9.6 shows an example of a U.S. fast food franchise that has successfully entered Indonesia. Franchisers from around the world are penetrating international markets. For example, 24 percent of British and 30 percent of French franchisers are active outside their home countries.[22] In Vietnam, after the government established a legal framework for franchising, the number of domestic and international franchises soared, increasing to more than 100 franchises by 2011. Today in Vietnam, one can find many foreign-owned franchises such as Thailand's Five Star Chicken, Britain's Body Shop, and Japan's Lotto Burger.[23]

The typical reasons for the international expansion of franchise systems are market potential, financial gain, and saturated domestic markets. From a franchisee's perspective, the franchise is beneficial because it reduces risk by implementing a proven concept. In Spain, for example, the success rate in the franchise business is about 70 percent, compared to a 20 percent success rate of all new businesses.[24]

From a government perspective, franchising does not replace exports or export jobs. From a recipient-country view, franchising requires little outflow of foreign exchange, and the bulk of the profit generated remains within the country. However, many countries have complex laws that regulate franchising, which international franchisers must obey.[25]

One key franchising concern is the need for standardization, without which many of the benefits of the transferred know-how are lost. Typically, such standardization will include the use of a common business name, similar layout, and similar production or service processes. Apart from leading to efficient operations, all of these factors also help make franchises more recognizable. Standardization, however, does not mean 100 percent uniformity. Adjustments in the final product need to take local market conditions into account. For example, fast-food outlets in Europe often need to serve beer and wine to be attractive to the local clientele. In order to enter the Indian market, where cows are considered sacred, McDonald's has developed nonbeef burgers.

Another issue is the protection of the total business system that a franchise offers. Once a business concept catches on, local competition may emerge quite quickly with an imitation of the product, the general style of operation, and even with a similar name.

Selection and training of franchisees present another concern. Although the local franchisee knows the market best, the franchiser still needs to understand the market for product adaptation purposes and operational details. There may be complications in selecting appropriate advertising media, effective copy testing, effective translation of the franchiser's message, and the use of appropriate sales promotion tools.

To encourage better-organized and more successful growth, many companies turn to the master franchising system, wherein foreign partners are selected and awarded the rights to a large territory in which they can subfranchise in turn. As a result, the franchiser gains market expertise and an effective screening mechanism for new franchises while reducing costly mistakes.[26]

Foreign Direct Investment

Foreign direct investment (FDI) represents international investment flows that acquire properties and plants. The international marketer makes such investments to create or expand a long-term interest in an enterprise with some degree of control. Portfolio investment in turn focuses on the purchase of stocks and bonds internationally. Portfolio investment is of primary concern to the international financial community.

FDIs have grown rapidly. With financial investments alone burgeoning from billions in the late 1960s to trillions by the mid-2000s, it is not surprising that FDI is the largest source of external finance for developing countries. This amounts to around 33 percent of GDP, compared to approximately 10 percent in 1980. Additionally, the impact on overall productivity is phenomenal. For example, the foreign affiliates of close to 64,000 transnational corporations (TNCs) generate 53 million jobs.[27] The United States plays a major role in global investments. At the end of 2010, U.S.-owned assets abroad were $20.3 billion, compared to $14.4 billion at the end of 2006. Foreign-owned assets in the United States were $22.8 billion at the end of 2010, compared to $16.6 billion in 2006.[28] Exhibit 9.7 shows how the U.S. net international investment position has changed over time. Note that FDI dipped in 2009 due to the global recession. Broadly, however, FDI has clearly become a major avenue for international market entry and expansion.

Major Foreign Investors

The United Nations defines multinational corporations as "enterprises which own or control production or service facilities outside the country in which they are based."[29] This definition makes all foreign direct investors multinational corporations. Yet large corporations are the key players. Exhibit 9.8 lists 50 of the world's biggest and most important companies according to the Forbes Global 2000 list of companies. These 50 companies have the best composite ranking based on sales, profits, assets, and market value. Overall, 60 countries and 72 million people are represented in Forbes's Global 2000 list. The Global 2000 companies account for $32 trillion in revenues, $2.4 trillion in profits, and $138 trillion in assets.[30] Their

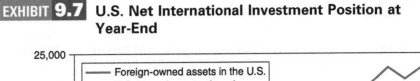

EXHIBIT 9.7 **U.S. Net International Investment Position at Year-End**

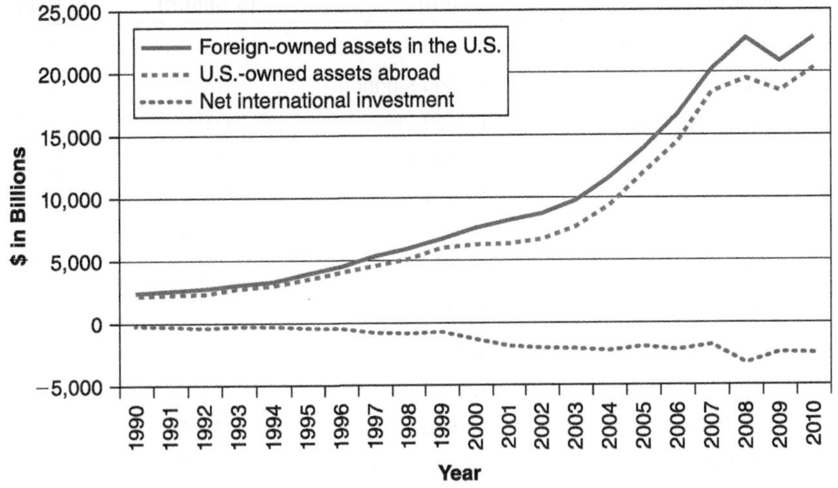

SOURCE: Based on Elena Nguyen, "The International Investment Position of the United States at Yearend 2010," *Survey of Current Business*, July 2011 (Washington, DC: Bureau of Economic Analysis), accessed at www.bea.gov.

market value exceeds the equivalent of more than half of global GDP. These firms appear to benefit from a greater ability to cope with new, unfamiliar situations.[31]

Exhibit 9.8 suggests a couple of notable trends. First, about 15 percent of the firms in the top 50 list are from China, reflecting the growing role of Chinese companies in global commerce. Second, about half the firms in the list are in the services sector. Recently, numerous companies in banking, retailing, telephone services, and other such industries have expanded abroad, underscoring widespread internationalization of the services sector.

Many of the large multinationals operate in well over 100 countries. For some, their original home market accounts for only a fraction of their sales. For example, the Dutch company Philips, the Swedish SKF, and the Swiss Nestlé each sell less than 5 percent of their total sales in their home country. In some firms, even the terms *domestic* and *foreign* have fallen into disuse. Others are working to consider issues only from a global perspective. For example, in management meetings of ABB (Asea Brown Boveri), individuals get fined $100 every time the words *foreign* and *domestic* are used.

Through their investment, multinational corporations bring economic vitality and jobs to their host countries and often pay higher wages than the average domestically oriented firms.[32] At the same time, however, trade follows investment. This means that foreign direct investors often bring with them imports on an ongoing basis. The flow of imports in turn may contribute to the weakening of a nation's international trade position.

Reasons for Foreign Direct Investment

Marketing Factors

Marketing considerations and the corporate desire for growth are major causes for the increase in FDI. Even large domestic markets limit growth, which typically means greater responsibilities and more pay for those who contribute to it. Corporations therefore seek wider market access in order to maintain and increase their sales. This objective can be achieved most quickly through acquisitions abroad.

EXHIBIT 9.8 Top Global Performers

Rank	Company	Country	Sales ($ Billion)	Profits ($ Billion)	Assets ($ Billion)	Market Value ($ Billion)
1	JPMorgan Chase	United States	115.5	17.4	2,117.6	182.2
2	HSBC Holdings	United Kingdom	103.3	13.3	2,467.9	186.5
3	General Electric	United States	150.2	11.6	751.2	216.2
4	ExxonMobil	United States	341.6	30.5	302.5	407.2
5	Royal Dutch Shell	Netherlands	369.1	20.1	317.2	212.9
6	PetroChina	China	222.3	21.2	251.3	320.8
7	ICBC	China	69.2	18.8	1,723.5	239.5
8	Berkshire Hathaway	United States	136.2	13.0	372.2	211.0
8	Petrobras-Petróleo	Brazil	121.3	21.2	313.2	238.8
10	Citigroup	United States	111.5	10.6	1,913.9	132.8
11	BNP Paribas	France	130.4	10.5	2,680.7	88.0
11	Wells Fargo	United States	93.2	12.4	1,258.1	170.6
13	Banco Santander	Spain	109.7	12.8	1,570.6	94.7
14	AT&T	United States	124.3	19.9	268.5	168.2
15	Gazprom	Russia	98.7	25.7	275.9	172.9
16	Chevron	United States	189.6	19.0	184.8	200.6
17	China Construction Bank	China	58.2	15.6	1,408.0	224.8
18	Wal-Mart Stores	United States	421.8	16.4	180.7	187.3
19	Total	France	188.1	14.2	192.8	138.0
20	Allianz	Germany	142.9	6.7	838.4	62.7
21	Bank of China	China	49.4	11.9	1,277.8	143.0
22	ConocoPhillips	United States	175.8	11.4	156.3	109.1
22	Sinopec-China Petroleum	China	284.8	10.9	148.7	107.7
24	Volkswagen Group	Germany	168.3	9.1	267.5	70.3
25	Agricultural Bank of China	China	49.4	9.5	1,298.2	134.0
26	Nestlé	Switzerland	112.0	36.7	117.7	181.1
27	Vodafone	United Kingdom	67.5	13.1	236.6	148.2
28	ENI	Italy	130.5	8.4	176.1	96.8
29	American Intl Group	United States	77.3	7.8	683.4	67.1
29	GDF Suez	France	113.1	6.2	245.5	85.2
31	IBM	United States	99.9	14.8	113.4	198.1
31	Telefónica	Spain	81.3	13.6	166.5	113.3
33	Samsung Electronics	South Korea	133.8	13.7	119.3	112.9
34	China Mobile	Hong Kong–China	71.8	17.7	129.3	192.1
35	Procter & Gamble	United States	79.6	11.2	134.3	172.2
36	Pfizer	United States	67.8	8.3	195.0	155.7
37	Goldman Sachs Group	United States	46.0	8.4	911.3	90.0
38	E.ON	Germany	124.6	7.9	205.1	64.0
39	ING Group	Netherlands	149.2	4.3	1,665.3	46.8
40	UBS	Switzerland	49.8	7.7	1,403.0	70.8
41	Barclays	United Kingdom	63.9	5.6	2,328.3	58.3
42	Hewlett-Packard	United States	127.2	9.1	119.9	90.3
43	Daimler	Germany	130.9	6.0	178.7	70.5

EXHIBIT 9.8 Top Global Performers (*continued*)

Rank	Company	Country	Sales ($ Billion)	Profits ($ Billion)	Assets ($ Billion)	Market Value ($ Billion)
44	Société Générale	France	85.4	5.3	1,518.7	46.9
45	Siemens	Germany	103.5	5.3	135.0	110.2
46	Banco Bradesco	Brazil	70.1	6.0	373.5	63.3
47	Apple	United States	76.3	16.6	86.7	324.3
48	AXA Group	France	162.4	3.7	981.8	46.4
49	Nippon Telegraph & Tel	Japan	108.9	5.3	193.8	70.3
50	Microsoft	United States	66.7	20.6	92.3	215.8

SOURCE: Forbes, "The World's Biggest Public Companies." Reprinted by Permission of Forbes Media LLC © 2011.

Corporations also attempt to obtain low-cost resources and ensure their sources of supply. Finally, once the decision is made to invest internationally, the investment climate plays a major role. Firms will seek to invest where their investment is most protected and has the best chance to flourish.

FDI permits corporations to circumvent current barriers to trade and operate abroad as a domestic firm, unaffected by duties, tariffs, or other import restrictions. For example, research on Japanese FDI in Europe found that a substantial number of firms have invested there in order to counteract future trade friction.[33]

Customers may insist on domestic goods and services as a result of nationalistic tendencies, as a function of cultural differences, or for strategic planning and security purposes.[34] Having the origin of a product associated with a specific country may also bring positive effects with it, particularly if the country is known for the particular product category. An investment in a Swiss dairy firm by a cheese producer is an example.

Firms have been categorized as resource seekers, market seekers, and efficiency seekers.[35] **Resource seekers** search for either natural resources or human resources. Natural resources typically are based on mineral, agricultural, or oceanographic advantages. Companies seeking human resources typically search for either low-cost labor or highly skilled labor. The value of labor resources may change over time and lead to corporate relocations. For example, in the 1980s, many non-European firms invested in the low-wage countries of Portugal, Spain, and Greece. The major political changes of the 1990s, however, shifted the investment interest to Hungary, the former East Germany, and the Czech Republic, where wages were even lower.

Corporations primarily in search of better opportunities to enter and expand within markets are **market seekers**. Particularly when markets are closed or access is restricted, corporations have a major incentive to invest rather than export. **Efficiency seekers** attempt to obtain the most economic sources of production. They frequently have affiliates in multiple markets with highly specialized product lines or components, and exchange their production in order to maximize the benefits to the corporation. The reasons why firms engage in foreign investment can change over time.

A second major cause for the increase in foreign direct investment is **derived demand**, which is the result of the move abroad by established customers. Large multinational firms like to maintain their established business relationships and, therefore, frequently encourage their suppliers to follow them abroad. As a result, a few initial investments can lead to a series of additional investments. For example, advertising agencies may move to service foreign affiliates of their domestic clients. Similarly, engineering firms, insurance companies, and law firms may provide their services abroad. Some suppliers invest abroad out of fear that their clients might find better sources abroad and therefore begin to import the products or services they currently supply.

Government Incentives

Governments are under pressure to provide jobs for their citizens. Foreign direct investment can increase employment and income. Countries such as Ireland have been promoting government incentive schemes for FDI for decades. Increasingly, state and local governments promote investment by sending out investment missions or opening offices abroad in order to inform local businesses about the beneficial investment climate at home.

Government incentives are mainly of three types: fiscal, financial, and nonfinancial. **Fiscal incentives** are specific tax measures designed to attract the foreign investor. They typically consist of special depreciation allowances, tax credits or rebates, special deductions for capital expenditures, tax holidays, and other reductions of the tax burden on the investor. **Financial incentives** offer special funding for the investor by providing land or buildings, loans, loan guarantees, or wage subsidies. **Nonfinancial incentives** consist of guaranteed government purchases; special protection from competition through tariffs, import quotas, and local content requirements; and investments in infrastructure facilities.

Incentives may slightly alter the advantage of a region. By themselves, they are unlikely to spur an investment decision if proper market conditions do not exist. Consequently, when individual states or regions within a country offer special incentives to foreign direct investors, they may be competing against each other for a limited pie rather than increasing the size of the pie. Furthermore, a question exists about the extent to which new jobs are actually created by FDI. Because many foreign investors import equipment, parts, and even personnel, the expected benefits in terms of job creation may often be either less than initially envisioned or only temporary. One additional concern arises from domestic firms already in existence. Because their "old" investments typically do not benefit from incentives designed to attract new investment, established firms may feel disadvantaged when competing against the newcomer.

A Perspective on Foreign Direct Investors

Foreign direct investors, and particularly multinational corporations, are viewed with a mixture of awe and dismay. Governments and individuals praise them for bringing capital, economic activity, and employment and for transferring technology and managerial skills. These actions encourage competition, market choice, and competitiveness.

At the same time, investment may lead to dependence. Just as the establishment of a corporation can create all sorts of benefits, its disappearance can also take them away again. Very often, international direct investors are accused of draining resources from their host countries. By employing the best and the brightest, they are said to deprive domestic firms of talent, thus causing a **brain drain**. Once they have hired locals, multinational firms are often accused of not promoting them high enough.

By raising money locally, multinationals can starve smaller capital markets. By bringing in foreign technology, they are viewed either as discouraging local technology development or as perhaps transferring only outmoded knowledge. By increasing competition, they are declared the enemy of domestic firms. There are concerns about foreign investors' economic and political loyalty toward their host government and a fear that such investors will always protect only their own interests and those of their home governments. And, of course, their sheer size, which sometimes exceeds the financial assets of the government, makes foreign investors suspect.

EXHIBIT 9.9 The American International Automobile Dealers Association

SOURCE: © AP Images/PRNewsFoto/American International Automobile Dealers Association.

Clearly, a love–hate relationship can exist between governments and the foreign investor. Corporate experts may be more knowledgeable than government employees. Particularly in developing countries, this knowledge advantage may offer opportunities for exploitation. There seems to be a distinct "liability of foreignness" affecting both firms and governments. As Exhibit 9.9 shows, there are firms that try to inform markets and governments about foreign companies' contributions to the local economy.

An array of guidelines for international corporate behavior have been published by organizations such as the United Nations, the OECD, and the International Labor Organization. They address the behavior of foreign investors in such areas as employment practices, consumer and environmental protection, political activity, and human rights. While the social acceptability of certain practices may vary among nations, the foreign investor should transfer the best business practices across nations. The multinational firm should be a leader in improving standards of living around the world. It will be managerial virtue, vision, and veracity combined with corporate openness, responsiveness, long-term thinking, and truthfulness that will determine the degrees of freedom and success of global business in the future.[36] *The International Marketplace 9.3* describes how Vietnam is mandating that all foreign direct investors now adhere to strict laws regarding sustainable projects.

Types of Ownership

A corporation's ownership choices can range from 100 percent ownership to a minority interest. The different levels of ownership will affect corporate flexibility, ability to control business plans and strategy, and exposure to risk. Some firms appear to select specific foreign ownership structures based on their experience with similar structures in the past.[37] In other words, they tend to keep using the same ownership model. However, the ownership decision should be a strategic response to corporate needs or a consequence of government regulation.

Full Ownership

Many firms prefer to have 100 percent ownership. Sometimes, this is the result of ethnocentric considerations based on the belief that no outside entity should have an impact on management. At other times, the issue is one of principle.

THE INTERNATIONAL MARKETPLACE 9.3

Foreign Direct Investments in Vietnam: The Good and the Bad

Often referred to as the "next Asian Tiger," Vietnam had 13,644 FDI projects worth $198 billion as of December 2011. Newly registered capital in 2011 reached $14.7 billion. The top investors in Vietnam were firms from Singapore, South Korea, Japan, and Taiwan. The move to a market economy is positioning Vietnam as a dynamic and influential player in Southeast Asia. Inflow of FDI is considered an important resource for national economic development.

Typical large FDI projects include: (1) the *Son Duong Port and Steel Complex* by Formosa, a Taiwanese group; (2) a project by a Brunei company called the *New City Vietnam Tourism Project*, a complex of hotels, office buildings, restaurants, health care centers, and sports clubs; (3) the *Ho Tram Tourism and Resort Complex* under development by Asian Coast Development Ltd., based in Canada; (4) the *Vietnam International University Township Project* through Malaysian-based Berjaya Land Berhad; (5) a resort by an affiliate of U.S.-based Starbay Holding Group, called *Cua Dai Beach Resort*; (6) a tourism complex, the *5-Star Complex*, by the American group Good Choice; (7) the *TA Associates International Project*, office buildings and living facilities by a group out of Singapore; and (8) the *Urban, Hotel, Trade and Service Complex* by Water Front Ltd., based in Singapore.

Such rapid FDI activity, however, has not been without oversight. The Ministry of Planning and Investment's Foreign Investment Agency has stated clearly that it appreciates foreign companies that contribute to Vietnam's social activities and adhere to environmental protection regulations. As such, 40 foreign investment companies are selected annually as recipients of the *Sai Gon Times* Top 40 Awards, where the selection criteria include a contribution to community development through social, charitable, and environmental preservation programs. The companies come from a variety of industries, with four actually receiving the award in consecutive years. My Duc Ceramics is a leading tile manufacturer and was the first company in Vietnam to be certified with ISO 9001:2000 and ISO 14001:2004 quality assurance. My Duc Ceramics' staff members are trained in Europe, with Italian technicians present in the Vietnamese factory developing breakthrough products. Nam Con Son Pipeline is a partnership among three companies: ONGC-Videsh, BP, and Statoil. This FDI has formulated a plan for successful development of gas reserves. Hikosen Cara produces clothing, home accessories, and other textile-related products. The company's head office is in Japan. Phu My 3 BOT Power, Vietnam's first build-operate-transfer power plant, is one of Vietnam's most important power projects and plays a critical role in the government's plan to develop a clean and dependable power generation sector. The Phu My 3 BOT Power Company is a consortium of BP, Sojitz Corp., SembCorp Utilities of Singapore, and Kyushu Electric Power of Japan.

Unfortunately, not all of Vietnam's FDI projects operate in a sustainable manner. In 2008, a large Taiwanese-owned factory, Vedan Vietnam, was closed after it was found to be dumping over 80,000 cubic feet of untreated wastewater daily into the Thi Vai River. This 14-year producer of monosodium glutamate (MSG) was discovered to have an underground pipeline network that pumped the untreated water into the river. This waste water contained high contents of molasses and chemicals, which is in violation of the country's Environmental Protection Law. The damage to the river's ecosystem was deemed almost irreversible.

In any developing country, there are risks associated with rapid industrialization. Yet it appears that the Vietnamese government recognizes the need for sustainable economic growth and is preparing itself to welcome only environmentally friendly investors by imposing strong sanctions against violators.

SOURCES: "Vietnam Expects $15b FDI Capital Attraction in 2012," *Vietnam Business News*, January 12, 2012, http://vietnambusiness.asia/vietnam-expects-15b-fdi-capital-attraction-in-2012; "FDI into Vietnam Nears $200 Billion," *Vietnam Business News*, January 3, 2012, http://vietnambusiness.asia/fdi-into-vietnam-nears-200-billion; "Vietnam—Programming Framework 2004–2009," *Canadian International Development Agency*, http://publications.gc.ca/site/eng/269212/publication.html; *My Duc Ceramics*, http://myduc.com; John Mueller, "Nam Con Son Players Step on the Gas," *Asian Oil and Gas*, January 1, 2002; *Hikosen Cara*, http://hikosen-cara.com; Chua Siew Joo, "Vietnam Implements Regulations for Environmental Sustainability," *Vietnam Briefing*, October 8, 2008; and Tran Van Minh, "Vietnam Shuts Taiwanese Plant for Dumping Wastewater," *The China Post*, October 8, 2008, www.chinapost.com.tw/asia/vietnam/2008/10/08/177829/Vietnam-shuts.htm.

To make a rational decision about the extent of ownership, management must evaluate how important total control is for the success of its international marketing activities. Often, full ownership may be a desirable, but not a necessary, prerequisite for international success. At other times, interdependencies between local operations and headquarters may require total control. Because the international environment is quite hostile to full ownership by multinational firms, it is important to determine whether these reasons are important enough to warrant a sole ownership policy or whether the needs of the firm can be accommodated with other arrangements.

Commercial activities under the control of foreigners are frequently believed to reflect the wishes, desires, and needs of headquarters abroad much more than those of the domestic economy. Governments fear that domestic economic policies may be counteracted by such firms, and employees are afraid that little local responsibility and empathy exist at headquarters. A major concern is the "fairness" of **profit repatriation**, or transfer of profits, and the extent to which firms reinvest into their foreign operations. Governments often believe that transfer pricing mechanisms are used to amass profits in a place most advantageous for the firm and that, as a consequence, local operations often show very low levels of performance. By reducing the foreign control of firms, they hope to put an end to such practices.

Ownership can be limited either through outright legal restrictions or through measures designed to make foreign ownership less attractive—such as limitations on profit repatriation. The international marketer is therefore frequently faced with the choice of either accepting a reduction in control or of losing the opportunity to operate in the country.

General market instability can also serve as a major deterrent to full ownership of FDI. Instability may result from political upheavals or changes in regimes. More often, it results from threats of political action, complex and drawn-out bureaucratic procedures, and the prospect of arbitrary and unpredictable alterations in regulations after the investment decision has been made.[38]

Joint Ventures

Joint ventures are collaborations of two or more organizations for more than a transitory period.[39] As equity-stake participants, the partners share assets, risks, and profits, though equality of partners is not necessary. The partners' contributions to the joint venture can vary widely and can consist of funds, technology, know-how, sales organizations, or plants and equipment.

Advantages of Joint Ventures The two major reasons for joint ventures are governmental and commercial. Government restrictions are designed to reduce the extent of control that foreign firms can exercise over local operations. As a basis for defining control, most countries have employed percentage levels of ownership. Over time, the thresholds of ownership that define control have decreased as it became apparent that even small, organized groups of stockholders may influence control of an enterprise. At the same time, many countries also recognize the competitive benefits of FDI and permit more control of local firms by foreign entities.

Equally important to the formation of joint ventures are commercial considerations. Joint ventures can pool resources and lead to a better outcome for each partner than if they worked individually. This is particularly the case when each partner has a specialized advantage in areas that benefit the joint venture. For example, a firm may have new technology available yet lack sufficient capital to carry out FDI on its own. By linking efforts with a partner, the technology can be used more quickly and market penetration is made easier. Similarly, if one of the partners has an established distribution system, a greater volume of sales can be achieved more rapidly.

Joint ventures also permit better relationships with local organizations—government, local authorities, or labor unions. If the local partner can bring political influence to the undertaking, the new venture may be eligible for tax incentives, grants, and government support and may be less vulnerable to political risk. Negotiations for certifications or licenses may be easier with authorities. Relationships with the local financial establishment may enable the joint venture to tap local capital markets. The greater experience—and therefore greater familiarity—with the culture and environment of the local partner may enable the joint venture to be more aware of cultural sensitivities and to benefit from greater insights into changing market conditions and needs.

Disadvantages of Joint Ventures Problem areas in joint ventures, as in all partnerships, involve implementing the concept and maintaining the relationship. Joint venture regulations are often subject to substantial interpretation and arbitrariness. Major problems can arise due to conflicts of interest, problems with disclosure of sensitive information, and disagreement over how profits are to be shared; these are typically the result of a lack of communication and planning before, during, and after the formation of the venture. In some cases, managers are interested in launching the venture but are too little concerned with actually running the enterprise. In other instances, managers dispatched to the joint venture by the partners may feel differing degrees of loyalty to the venture and its partners.[40] The joint venture may, for example, identify a particular market as a profitable target, yet the headquarters of one of the partners may already have plans for serving this market that would require competing against its own joint venture. Reconciling such conflicts of loyalty is one of the greatest human resource challenges for joint ventures.[41]

Strategic Alliances

One special form of joint ventures consists of strategic alliances, or partnerships, which are arrangements between two or more companies with a common business objective. Unlike the more rigid joint venture, the great advantage of strategic alliances is their ongoing flexibility, as they can be formed, adjusted, and dissolved rapidly in response to changing conditions. In essence, strategic alliances are networks of companies that collaborate in the achievement of a given project or objective. Partners for one project may well be fierce competitors for another.

© AP Images/PRNewsFoto/Royal Caribbean International

Royal Caribbean International's strategic alliance with DreamWorks Animation (in this ad featuring the Donkey from "Shrek") brings family programming and entertainment to the cruise world.

Alliances can range from information cooperation in the market development area to joint ownership of worldwide operations. For example, Texas Instruments has reported agreements with companies such as IBM, Hyundai, Fujitsu, Alcatel, and L. M. Ericsson, using such terms as *joint development agreement*, *cooperative technical effort*, *joint program for development*, *alternative sourcing agreement*, and *design/exchange agreement for cooperative product development and exchange of technical data*.

Market development is one reason for the growth in such alliances. In Japan, Motorola is sharing chip designs and manufacturing facilities with Toshiba to gain greater access to the Japanese market. Another focus is spreading the cost and risk inherent in production and development efforts. Texas Instruments and Hitachi have teamed up to develop the next generation of memory chips. The costs of developing new jet engines are so vast that they force aerospace companies into collaboration; one such consortium was formed by United Technologies' Pratt & Whitney division, Britain's Rolls Royce, Motoren-und-Turbinen Union from Germany, Fiat of Italy, and Japanese Aero Engines. Some alliances are also formed to block or co-opt competitors.[42] For example, Caterpillar formed a heavy equipment joint venture with Mitsubishi in Japan to strike back at its main global rival, Komatsu, in its home market.

Companies must carefully evaluate the effects of entering such a coalition, particularly with regard to strategy and competitiveness. The most successful alliances are those that match the complementary strengths of partners to satisfy a joint objective. Often the partners have different product, geographic, or functional strengths, which the alliance can build on in order to achieve success with a new strategy or in a new market. They can then either operate jointly as equals or have one partner piggyback by making use of the other's strengths. For example, Pepsi has combined its marketing prowess for canned beverages with Lipton's strong brand position for tea in order to jointly sell canned iced tea beverages.[43] Firms also can have a reciprocal arrangement whereby each partner provides the other access to its market. The New York Yankees and Manchester United sell each others' licensed products and develop joint sponsorship programs. International airlines have started to share hubs, coordinate schedules, and simplify ticketing. Star Alliance (joining airlines such as United and Lufthansa) and Oneworld (British Airways and American Airlines) provide worldwide coverage for their customers both in the travel and shipping communities.

In a management contract, the supplier brings together a package of skills that will provide an integrated service to the client without incurring the risk and benefit of ownership. The activity is quite different from other contractual arrangements because people actually move and directly implement the relevant skills and knowledge in the client organization.[44]

Management contracts have clear benefits for the client. They can provide organizational skills that are not available locally, expertise that is immediately available rather than built up, and management assistance in the form of support services that would be difficult and costly to replicate locally. In addition, the outside involvement is clearly limited. When a turnkey project is online, the system will be totally owned, controlled, and operated by the customer. As a result, management contracts are seen by many governments as a useful alternative to FDI and the resulting control by nondomestic entities.

Similar advantages exist for the supplier. The risk of participating in an international venture is substantially lowered because no equity capital is at stake. At the same time, a significant amount of operational control can be exercised. Being on the inside represents a strategic advantage in influencing decisions. In addition, existing know-how that has been built up with significant investment can be commercialized. Frequently, the impact of fluctuations in business volume can be reduced by making use of experienced personnel who otherwise would have to be laid off. Accumulated service knowledge and comparative advantage should be used internationally. Management contracts permit a firm to do so.

In a dynamic business environment, alliances must be able to adjust to market conditions. Any agreement should therefore provide for changes in the original concept so that the venture can grow and flourish. In light of growing international competition and the rising cost of innovation in technology, strategic alliances are likely to continue their growth in the future.

Government Consortia

One form of cooperation takes place at the industry level and is typically characterized by government support or even subsidization. Usually, it is a reflection of escalating cost and a governmental goal of developing or maintaining global leadership in a particular sector. A new drug, computer, or telecommunication switch can cost more than $1 billion to develop and bring to market. To combat the high costs and risks of research and development, **research consortia** have emerged in the United States, Japan, and Europe. Since the passage of the Joint Research and Development Act of 1984 (which allows both domestic and foreign firms to participate in joint basic research efforts without the fear of antitrust action), well over 100 consortia have been registered in the United States. These consortia pool their resources for research into technologies ranging from artificial intelligence and electric car batteries to semiconductor manufacturing.

The European Union has undertaken several megaprojects to develop new technologies under names such as BRITE, COMET, ESPRIT, EUREKA, and SOKRATES. Japanese consortia have worked on producing the world's highest-capacity memory chip and other advanced computer technologies. On the manufacturing side, the formation of Airbus Industries secured European production of commercial jets. The consortium of the European Aeronautic Defence and Space Company, which emerged from the link-up of the German Daimler-Chrysler Aerospace AG, the French Aerospatiale Matra, and CASA of Spain, has become a prime global competitor.[45]

SUMMARY

Most companies become gradually involved in international markets, though some are born global. A variety of internal and external factors expose them to the international market. Employees and management serve as particularly important change agents. After becoming aware of international marketing opportunities, companies progress through the corporate export stages and may choose to retreat to a purely domestic focus or to increase the scope of their international activities through a variety of different means.

Firms may employ third parties, such as export management companies or trading companies, or they may break into the global marketplace using the technology of the Internet. If a firm wants to establish an international presence, it can also license its products, open global franchises, or directly invest into a region of the world. These expansion alternatives involve varying degrees of risk and varying degrees of control that a company may exercise over its international ventures. Firms' involvement in international markets may also be legally limited by the extent to which a country allows foreign ownership of assets. Companies looking to go abroad need to consider a variety of factors—such as mechanics, corporate structure, strategic goals, logistics, cost, and regulations—before they expand.

KEY TERMS

safety-valve activity
psychological distance
change agent
accidental exporter
born global
innate exporter
awareness
interest
trial
evaluation
adaptation
sogoshosha
export trading company (ETC)
e-commerce
licensing
transfer cost
R&D cost
opportunity cost
trademark licensing
franchising
master franchising system
foreign direct investment (FDI)
portfolio investment
resource seeker
market seeker
efficiency seeker
derived demand
fiscal incentive
financial incentive
nonfinancial incentive
brain drain
profit repatriation
joint venture
strategic alliance
complementary strengths
piggyback
management contract
research consortia

QUESTIONS FOR DISCUSSION

1. Why do firms enter the global market?
2. What is meant by the term *born global*?
3. What relationship exists between governments and foreign investors? Why are foreign investors important?
4. Discuss the impact of the Internet and e-commerce in making a firm global.
5. Discuss the various advantages and disadvantages of full ownership versus joint ventures.

INTERNET EXERCISES

1. What programs does the Export-Import Bank (www.exim.gov) offer that specifically benefit small businesses trying to export? What benefits can be derived from each?
2. Use the United National Conference on Trade and Development FDI Database (available under the Statistics option at www.unctad.org) to research the foreign direct investment profile of a country or region of your choice.

CHALLENGE US

Chopstick-Lickin' Dishes: KFC in China

KFC, owned by Kentucky-based Yum! Brands, started out as the quintessential American fast food company, originally being named Kentucky Fried Chicken. What could be more patriotic than deep-fried chicken wings with special roots in the U.S. south?

In 1973, the company opened 11 restaurants in the British colony of Hong Kong but closed them within two years because it couldn't win over local consumers. Decades later, KFC returned, opening up stores in Beijing and slowly adapting its model to the Chinese system.

KFC's Chinese managers staff is young and hip. College-aged employees are encouraged to socialize over company-provided video games on their breaks. The goal is to create lifelong Yum! Brand customers. These practices helped to make the individual restaurant feel localized, even family oriented.

Besides serving some American fare like dark-meat chicken and corn on the cob, KFC sells more Chinese-styled fast food to appeal to local tastes. Offerings include Dragon Twister, a chicken wrap in Peking duck-type sauce, spicy tofu chicken rice based on the cuisine of Sichuan province, home of China's hottest dishes, as well as fried dough sticks, egg tarts, shrimp burgers, and soymilk drinks.

KFC also actively advertises to appeal to Chinese culture. For example, in Urumqi, capital of the Xinjiang province, a Muslim region of China, KFC advertises parties for family boys who have just undergone the religious ritual of circumcision, instead of just birthday parties like they do in the United States.

Some claim that every day KFC in China moves further away from its U.S. roots. They believe that Chinese customers eating in a KFC establishment really want the U.S. experience—with the Colonel watching over them. Others think that adapting to local preferences means KFC needs to drop forks for chopsticks. KFC-China, with a focus on a consistent appreciation for the culture and unique needs of its consumers, might even become the birthplace of a new cuisine all together.

For Discussion

1. Discuss the claims made in the last paragraph. Do you agree or disagree?
2. How far should KFC China go to keep its U.S.-based roots or to adapt to it's location's culture?

SOURCES: William Mellor, "The Secret to KFC's Success in China," *The Washington Post*, February 20, 2011, G; and Maggie Starvish "KFC's Explosive Growth in China," Harvard Business School Working Knowledge, June 17, 2011, http://hbswk.hbs.edu.6704.html.

RECOMMENDED READINGS

Alon, Ilon. *Global Franchising Operations Management: Cases in International and Emerging Markets Operations*. Upper Saddle River, NJ: Financial Times Press, 2012.

Cavusgil, S. Tamer, and Gary Knight. *Born Global Firms: A New International Enterprise*. New York: Business Expert Press, 2009.

Griffith, D., and M. R. Czinkota, "Release the Constraints: Working to Solve the Problems of Expert Financing in Troublesome Times," *Business Horizons*, February 2, 2012, www.sciencedirect.com/science/article/pii/S000 7681312000043.

Kukral, Jim. *Internet Marketing for Business Answers: Interviews with the Experts Edition*. Digital Book Launch, July 2011.

Meiners, Roger E., Al H. Ringleb, and Frances L. Edwards. *The Legal Environment of Business*. Washington, DC: South-Western Cengage Learning, 2012.

Moran, Theodore H. *Foreign Direct Investment and Development: Reevaluating Policies for Developed and Developing Countries*. Washington, DC: Peterson Institute, 2011.

Yeung, Arthur, Katherine Xin, Waldemar Pfoertsch, and Shengjun Liu. *The Globalization of Chinese Companies: Strategies for Conquering International Markets*. Hoboken, NJ: Wiley, 2011.

ENDNOTES

1. Howard Lewis III and J. David Richardson, *Why Global Commitment Really Matters!* (Washington, DC: Institute for International Economics, 2001).
2. Tiger Li, "The Impact of the Marketing-R&D Interface on New Product Export Performance: A Contingency Analysis," *Journal of International Marketing* 7, no. 1 (1999): 10–33.
3. Michael L. Ursic and Michael R. Czinkota, "An Experience Curve Explanation of Export Expansion," in *International Marketing Strategy: Environmental Assessment and Entry Strategies*, edited by Michael R. Czinkota and Ilkka Ronkainen (Fort Worth, TX: Dryden Press, 1994), 133–41.
4. C. P. Rao, M. Krishna Erramilli, and Gopala K. Ganesh, "Impact of Domestic Recession on Export Marketing Behaviour," *International Marketing Review* 7 (1990): 54–65.
5. Shawna O'Grady and Henry W. Lane, "The Psychic Distance Paradox," *Journal of International Business Studies* 27, no. 2 (1996): 309–33.
6. Aviv Shoham and Gerald S. Albaum, "Reducing the Impact of Barriers to Exporting: A Managerial Perspective," *Journal of International Marketing* 3, no. 4 (1995): 85–105.
7. Michael R. Czinkota, "How Government Can Help Increase U.S. Export Performance," Testimony before the House Committee on Small Business, 111th Congress of the United States, Second Session, Washington, DC, April 28, 2010.
8. Shaoming Zou and S. Tamer Cavusgil, "The GMS: A Broad Conceptualization of Global Marketing Strategy and Its Effect on Firm Performance," *Journal of Marketing*, October 2002, 40–56.
9. Yoo S. Yang, Robert P. Leone, and Dana L. Alden, "A Market Expansion Ability Approach to Identify Potential Exporters," *Journal of Marketing* 56 (January 1992): 84–96.
10. S. Tamer Cavusgil and Shaoming Zou, "Marketing Strategy–Performance Relationship: An Investigation of the Empirical Link in Export Marketing Ventures," *Journal of Marketing* 58, no. 1 (1994): 1–21.
11. Michael R. Czinkota, "Export Promotion: A Framework for Finding Opportunity in Change," *Thunderbird International Business Review*, May–June 2002, 315–24.
12. Oystein Moen and Per Servais, "Born Global or Gradual Global? Examining the Export Behavior of Small and Medium-Sized Enterprises," *Journal of International Marketing* 10, no. 3 (2002): 49–72.
13. Masaaki Kotabe and Michael R. Czinkota, "State Government Promotion of Manufacturing Exports: A Gap Analysis," *Journal of International Business Studies*, Winter 1992, 637–58.
14. Andrew B. Bernard and J. Bradford Jensen, *Exceptional Exporter Performance: Cause, Effect, or Both*, Census Research Data Center, Pittsburgh, Carnegie Mellon University, 1997.
15. Daniel C. Bello and Nicholas C. Williamson, "Contractual Arrangement and Marketing Practices in the Indirect Export

Channel," *Journal of International Business Studies* 16 (Summer 1985): 65–82.
16. Mike W. Peng and Anne Y. Ilinitch, "Export Intermediary Firms: A Note on Export Development Research," *Journal of International Business Studies* 3 (1998): 609–20.
17. Export Trade Certificate of Review, www.federalregister.gov/articles/2012/01/13/2012-523/export-trade-certificate-of-review, accessed January 22, 2012.
18. Alibaba corporate company overview, www.alibaba.com, accessed January 23, 2012.
19. Farok J. Contractor and Sumit K. Kundu, "Franchising versus Company-Run Operations: Modal Choice in the Global Hotel Sector," *Journal of International Marketing* 6, no. 2 (1998): 28–53.
20. Martin F. Connor, "International Technology Licensing," Seminars in International Trade, National Center for Export-Import Studies, Washington, DC.
21. Pamela M. Deese and Sean Wooden, "Managing Intellectual Property in Licensing Agreements," *Franchising World* 33 (September 2001): 66–67.
22. Josh Martin, "Profitable Supply Chain Supporting Franchises," *Journal of Commerce*, Global Commerce Section, March 11, 1998, 1C.
23. Nguyen Ba Binh and Andrew Terry, "Good Morning, Vietnam! Opportunities and Challenges in a Developing Franchise Sector," *Journal of Marketing Channels* 18, no. 2 (2011): 147–63.
24. Victoria Bordonaba-Juste, Laura Lucia-Palacios, and Yolando Polo-Redondo, "An Analysis of Franchisor Failure Risk: Evidence from Spain," *Journal of Business & Industrial Marketing* 26, no. 6 (2011): 407–20.
25. Margaret McEntire, "Best Practices for International Franchising: Be Aware of Cultural Differences," *Franchising World*, March 2011, 29.
26. Marko Grünhagen and Carl L. Witte, "Franchising as an Export Product and Its Role as an Economic Development Tool for Emerging Economies," *Enhancing Knowledge Development in Marketing*, vol. 13, eds. W. Kehoe and J. Lindgren, Jr. (Chicago, IL: American Marketing Association, 2002), 414–15.
27. United Nations, Foreign Direct Investment, www.unctad.org, accessed January 16, 2012.
28. "2007 Year-end U.S. Net Investment Position," Bureau of Economic Analysis, U.S. Department of Commerce, Washington, DC, June 27, 2008.
29. *Multinational Corporations in World Development* (New York, NY: United Nations, 1973), 23.
30. Scott DeCarlo, "The World's Biggest Companies," *Forbes*, April 20, 2011, www.forbes.com, accessed January 22, 2012.
31. Bernard L. Simonin, "Transfer of Marketing Know-How in International Strategic Alliances: An Empirical Investigation of the Role and Antecedents of Knowledge Ambiguity," *Journal of International Business Studies* 30, no. 3 (1999): 463–90.
32. Howard Lewis III and David Richardson, *Why Global Commitment Really Matters!* (Washington, DC: Institute for International Economics, 2001).
33. Detlev Nitsch, Paul Beamish, and Shige Makino, "Characteristics and Performance of Japanese Foreign Direct Investment in Europe," *European Management Journal* 13, no. 3 (1995): 276–85.
34. Michael R. Czinkota, "From Bowling Alone to Standing Together," *Marketing Management*, March/April 2002, 12–16.
35. Jack N. Behrman, "Transnational Corporations in the New International Economic Order," *Journal of International Business Studies* 12 (Spring–Summer 1981): 29–42.
36. Michael R. Czinkota, "Success of Globalization Rests on Good Business Reputations," *Japan Times*, October 12, 2002, 19.
37. Prasad Padmanabhan and Kang Rae Cho, "Decision Specific Experience in Foreign Ownership and Establishment Strategies: Evidence from Japanese Firms," *Journal of International Business Studies* 30, no. 1 (1999): 25–44.
38. Isaiah Frank, *Foreign Enterprise in Developing Countries* (Baltimore, MD: Johns Hopkins University, 1980).
39. W. G. Friedman and G. Kalmanoff, *Joint International Business Ventures* (New York, NY: Columbia University Press, 1961).
40. R.H. Holton, "Making International Joint Ventures Work," in L. Otterbeck (ed.), *The Management of Headquarters-Subsidiary Relationships in Multinational* Corporations, Aldershot, England: Gower, 1981.
41. Oded Shenkar and Shmuel Ellis, "Death of the 'Organization Man': Temporal Relations in Strategic Alliances," *International Executive* 37, no. 6 (November/December 1995): 537–53.
42. Jordan D. Lewis, *Partnerships for Profit: Structuring and Managing Strategic Alliances* (New York, NY: Free Press, 1990), 85–87.
43. PepsiCo, www.pepsico.com, accessed January 28, 2012.
44. Lawrence S. Welch and Anubis Pacifico, "Management Contracts: A Role in Internationalization?" *International Marketing Review* 7 (1990): 64–74.
45. EADS, *EADS Annual Review 2010: Flight into the Future* (Leiden, The Netherlands: European Aeronautic Defence and Space Company EADS N.V., 2010), www.eads.com, accessed January 23, 2012.

CHAPTER 10

Marketing Organization, Implementation, and Control

LEARNING OBJECTIVES

By the time you complete this chapter, you will be able to:

- Describe alternative organizational structures for international operations.
- Highlight factors affecting decisions about the structure of international organizations.
- Indicate roles for country organizations in the development of strategy and implementation of programs.
- Outline the need for and challenges of controls in international operations.

THE INTERNATIONAL MARKETPLACE 10.1

Touch and Improve People's Everyday Lives

For Procter & Gamble (P&G), globalization's unique organizational structure offers the global-scale benefits of an international company and the local focus to be relevant for consumers in more than 180 countries where P&G brands are sold. This global structure replaced a region-driven apparatus with the goal of making employees stretch themselves and speed up innovation as well as moving products and processes across borders.

Four pillars—global business units, global operations, global business services, and corporate functions—form the heart of P&G's organizational structure:

- Global business units (GBUs) build major global brands with robust business strategies.
- Market development organizations (MDOs) build local understanding as a foundation for marketing campaigns.
- Global business services (GBSs) provide business technology and services that drive business success.
- Corporate functions (CFs) work to maintain P&G's place as a leader of its industries.

How the organization works can be highlighted with an example. The GBUs define the equity, or what a brand stands for. The Pantene brand, for example, gives a customer healthy, shiny hair, and a Pantene team within the Beauty Care GBU is charged with building on this. It starts with product initiatives or upgrades, which ideally would be launched simultaneously around the world. It includes a marketing campaign that communicates the same fundamental benefit around the world, and it includes manufacturing the product against global formula and package specifications. The MDOs then ensure Pantene excels in their region. In the United States, this could mean focusing on club stores, which might entail partnering with the GBU to develop the large-size packaging the outlets demand to maximize value for their shoppers. Conversely, the focus in Latin America might be to develop the smallest possible package, such as a sachet, as consumers in that region want to minimize their out-of-pocket costs. The outcome should be the same overall brand equity but very different

© Imaginechina via AP Images

Head & Shoulders line.

executions by region. The GBS center in Costa Rica would be providing support for both the U.S. and Latin America MDOs in this example (and for any other brand business team from these regions). Some of the services would include accounting, employee benefits and payroll, order management and product logistics, and systems operations. Those working directly on the business teams would likely determine the amount of CF support. Each function would want to ensure that they are capitalizing on the latest thinking or methodologies for each discipline. In this capacity, think of CFs as consulting groups ready to provide service if called upon.

P&G currently competes in a total of 38 product categories. Today, on average, the company competes in 19 categories in any given country. In P&G's most developed market, the United States, it competes in all 38 product categories. In Russia and Mexico, the number of categories is in the 20s; in China, Brazil, and India, it is in the mid-to-high teens; and in Nigeria, that number is in the mid–single digits. The five-year plan, from 2011 to 2015, will increase the average number of categories from 19 to 24. This will result in developing markets, with the aggregate (35 percent) in CEEMEA, Latin America, AAIK, and Greater China and the rest (65 percent) is comprised of North America, Western Europe, and Japan.

SOURCES: Procter & Gamble Annual Report, 2011; and Lafley, A. G., "What Only the CEO Can Do," *Harvard Business Review* 87 (May 2009): 54–62. See also P&G, www.pg.com.

As companies evolve from purely domestic entities to multinationals, their organizational structure and control systems must change to reflect new strategies. With growth comes diversity in terms of products and services, geographic markets, and personnel, leading to a set of challenges for the company. Three critical issues are basic to addressing these challenges: (1) the type of organization that provides the best framework for operational effectiveness; (2) the optimal approach to implementing corporate strategy globally, regionally, and locally; and (3) the type and degree of control to be exercised from headquarters to maximize total effort.[1] Organizational structures and control systems have to be adjusted as market conditions change, as seen in *The International Marketplace 10.1*. While some units are charged with the development of strong global brands, others are charged with local adaptation and creating synergies across programs.

ORGANIZATIONAL STRUCTURE

The basic functions of an organization are to provide (1) a route and locus of decision making and coordination, and (2) a system for reporting and communications. Increasingly, the coordination and communication dimensions have to include learning from the global marketplace through the company's different units.[2] These networks are typically depicted in the organizational chart.

Organizational Designs

The basic configurations of international organizations correspond to those of purely domestic ones; the greater the degree of internationalization, the more complex the structures can become. The core building block is the individual company operating in its particular market. However, these individual companies need to work together for maximum effectiveness—thus the need for organizational design. The types of structures that companies use to manage foreign activities can be divided into three categories based on the degree of internationalization:

1. *Little or no formal organizational recognition of international activities of the firm.* This category ranges from domestic operations handling an occasional international transaction on an ad hoc basis to separate export departments.
2. *International division.* Firms in this category recognize the ever-growing importance of international involvement.
3. *Global organizations.* These can be structured by product, area, function, process, or customer.

Hybrid structures may exist as well, in which one market may be structured by product and another by area. Matrix organizations have emerged in large multinational corporations to combine product, regional, and functional expertise. As worldwide competition has increased dramatically in many industries, the latest organizational response is networked global organizations in which heavy flows of technology, personnel, and communication take place between strategically interdependent units to establish greater global integration. The ability to identify and disseminate best practices throughout the organization is an important competitive advantage for global companies. For example, Essilor International, a global maker of ophthalmic lenses, has created an internal training program that mixes in-person and Web 2.0 formats to transmit best practices among 102 sites in 40 countries. A lens-processing center in Thailand, for example, developed a game to teach new workers how to understand the shape of a given kind of lens; now it is used in Brazil too.[3] The increasing enthusiasm for outsourcing has put new demands on managing relationships with independent partners. Boeing, for example, holds a partners' council meeting every six weeks and has set up a network that makes it possible for designers (both at Boeing and its suppliers) to work on the same up-to-the-minute database. Virtual meetings with colleagues in different time zones take place throughout the day.[4]

Little or No Formal Organization

In the very early stages of international involvement, domestic operations assume responsibility for international marketing activities. The share of international operations in the sales and profits of the corporation is initially so minor that no organizational adjustment takes place. No consolidation of information or authority over international sales is undertaken or is necessary. Transactions are conducted on a case-by-case basis either by the resident expert or quite often with the help of facilitating agents, such as freight forwarders.

As demand from the international marketplace grows and interest within the firm expands, the organizational structure will reflect it. An export department appears as a separate entity. This may be an outside export management

EXHIBIT 10.1 The Export Department Structure (TAL)

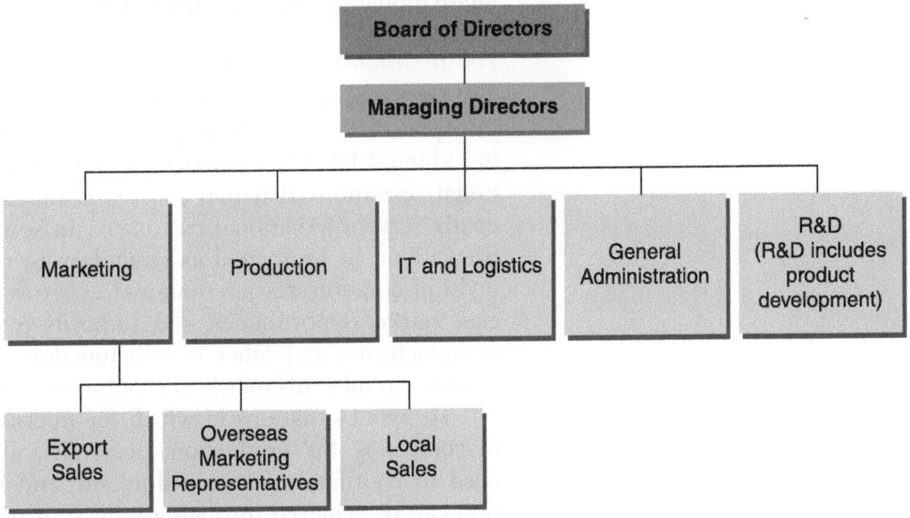

SOURCE: Hong Kong Chamber of Commerce.

company—that is, an independent company that becomes the de facto export department of the firm. This is an indirect approach to international involvement in that very little experience is accumulated within the firm itself. Alternatively, a firm may establish its own export department, hiring a few seasoned individuals to take full responsibility for international activities. Organizationally, the department may be a subdepartment of marketing (as shown in Exhibit 10.1) or may have equal ranking with the various functional departments. This choice will depend on the importance assigned to overseas activities by the firm. Because the export department is the first real step for internationalizing the organizational structure, it should be a full-fledged marketing organization and not merely a sales organization; that is, it should have the resources for market research and market-development activities (such as trade show participation).

Headquartered in Hong Kong, TAL is an innovative garment manufacturer for the world's leading brands, including Banana Republic, Calvin Klein, Giordano, and LL Bean. The United States has traditionally been TAL's main market, taking 80 percent of its production, but emerging markets are now playing a larger role, with demand for branded garments increasing dramatically in China and other countries. Presently, its customers in the United States and other countries report back to TAL's sales team what has been sold on a daily basis. Within the week, garments are delivered directly to stores to replenish their stocks. TAL is centrally managed in Hong Kong with operations in the United States, China, Thailand, Indonesia, Vietnam, and Malaysia.

Licensing is the international entry mode for some firms. Responsibility for licensing may be assigned to the R&D function despite its importance to the overall international strategy of the firm. A formal liaison among the export, marketing, production, and R&D functions should be formed for the maximum utilization of licensing.[5] A separate manager should be appointed if licensing becomes a major activity for the firm.

As the firm becomes more involved in foreign markets, the export department structure will become obsolete. The firm may then undertake joint ventures or direct foreign investment, which require those involved to have functional experience. The firm therefore typically establishes an international division.

Some firms that acquire foreign production facilities pass through an additional stage in which foreign subsidiaries report directly to the president or to a manager specifically assigned this duty. However, the amount of coordination and control that is required quickly establishes the need for a more formal international organization in the firm.

The International Division

The international division centralizes in one entity, with or without separate incorporation, all of the responsibility for international activities, as illustrated in Exhibit 10.2. The approach aims to eliminate a possible bias against international operations that may exist if domestic divisions are allowed to independently serve international customers. In some cases, international markets have been found to be treated as secondary to domestic markets. The international division concentrates international expertise, information flows concerning foreign market opportunities, and authority over international activities. However, manufacturing and other related functions remain with the domestic divisions in order to take advantage of economies of scale.

To avoid situations in which the international division is at a disadvantage in competing for production, personnel, and corporate services, corporations need to coordinate between domestic and international operations. Coordination can be achieved through a joint staff or by requiring domestic and international divisions to interact in strategic planning and to submit the plans to headquarters. Further, many corporations require and encourage frequent interaction between domestic and international personnel to discuss common challenges in areas such as product planning. Coordination is also important because domestic operations may be organized along product or functional lines, whereas international divisions are geographically oriented.

International divisions best serve firms with few products that do not vary significantly in terms of their environmental sensitivity, and when international sales and profits are still quite insignificant compared with those of the domestic

EXHIBIT 10.2 The International Division Structure (General Mills)

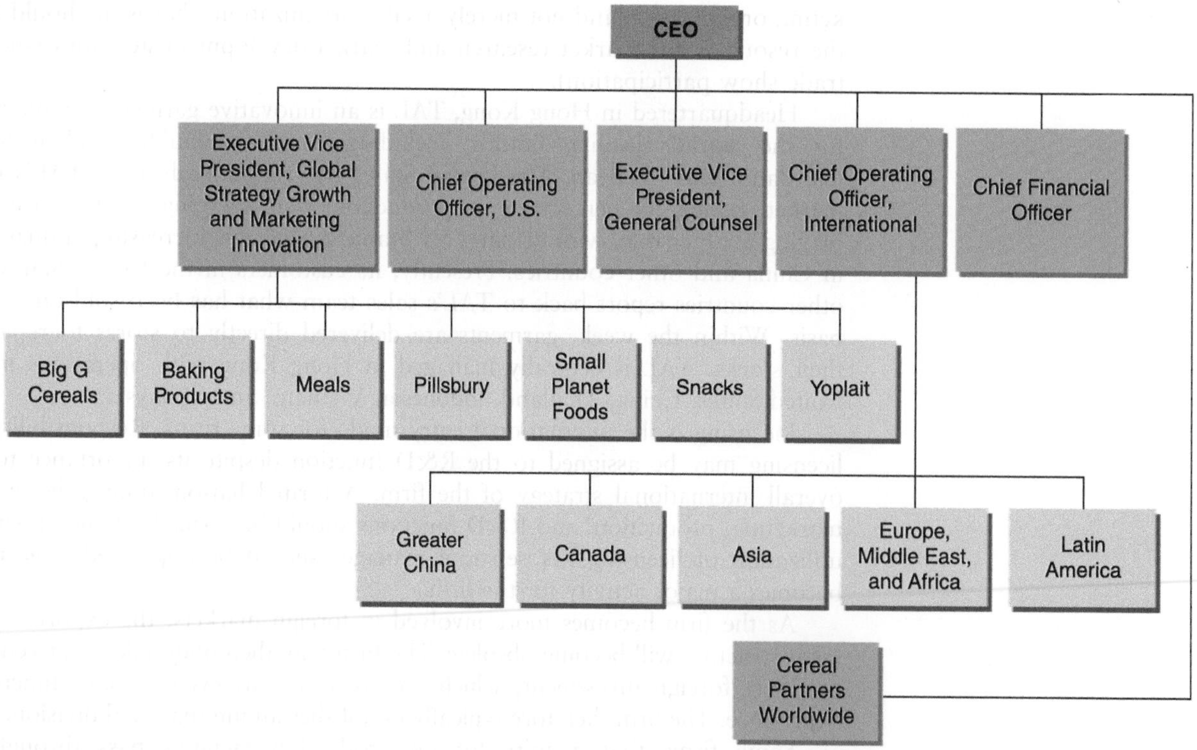

SOURCE: General Mills, www.generalmills.com/en/Company/Businesses.aspx.

divisions.[6] Companies may outgrow their international divisions as their international sales grow in significance, diversity, and complexity. European companies used international divisions far less than their U.S. counterparts due to the relatively small size of their domestic markets. Royal Dutch Shell and Nestlé, for example, would have never grown to their current prominence by relying on the Dutch market alone. General Mills, a notable exception among consumer-goods companies, was still using the international division structure with sales from international customers at approximately 20 percent. In addition to their global brands (e.g., Pillsbury and Betty Crocker), General Mills also offers several local brands such as La Salteña pastas and tapas in Argentina and Jus-Rol pastries in the United Kingdom. General Mills participates in two international joint ventures: Cereal Partners Worldwide (Nestlé) and Häagen-Dazs Japan.[7]

Global Organizational Structures

Global structures have grown out of competitive necessity. In many industries, competition is on a global basis, with the result that companies must have a high degree of reactive capability.

Six basic types of global structures are available:

1. Global product structure, in which product divisions are responsible for all manufacturing and marketing worldwide
2. Global area structure, in which geographic divisions are responsible for all manufacturing and marketing in their respective areas
3. Global functional structure, in which the functional areas (such as production, marketing, finance, and personnel) are responsible for worldwide operations of their own functional areas
4. Global customer structure, in which operations are structured based on distinct worldwide customer groups
5. Mixed—or hybrid—structure, which may combine the other alternatives
6. Matrix structures, in which operations have reporting responsibility to more than one group (typically, product, area, or functions)

Product Structure Some form of a **product structure** is most commonly used by multinational corporations, whether in its pure form or as the driver in a more complex matrix structure. The pure product structure approach gives worldwide responsibility to strategic business units for the marketing of their product lines. Most consumer-product firms use some form of this approach, mainly because of the diversity of their product lines. One of the major benefits of this approach is improved cost efficiency through centralization of manufacturing facilities. This is crucial in industries in which competitive position is determined by world market share, which in turn is often determined by the degree to which manufacturing is rationalized.[8] Adaptation to this approach has historically been associated with consolidation of operations and plant closings. A good example is Stanley Black & Decker, which groups its brands under consumer products, industrial products, and fastening and assembly systems groups and which rationalized many of its operations in its worldwide competitive effort against Makita, the Japanese power-tool manufacturer.

In a similar move, Ford merged its large and culturally distinct European, North American, and Chinese auto operations by vehicle platform type to make more efficient use of its engineering and product development resources against rapidly globalizing rivals.[9] The Ford Fusion was designed by one team of engineers for worldwide markets. With competitive pressures on the automotive industry intensifying, many automotive companies have consolidated and reorganized for greater efficiency. U.S.-based Dura Automotive Systems announced its shift from a regional organization structure to four global business units, each headquartered in either the United States or Germany. These four units are organized around product lines for sales to global automakers including cable systems, shifter systems, glass and trim systems, and structural and safety systems.[10]

Another benefit is the ability to balance the functional inputs needed by a product and to react quickly to product-specific problems in the marketplace. Even smaller brands receive individual attention. Product-specific attention is important because products vary in terms of the adaptation they need for different foreign markets. All in all, the product approach ideally brings about the development of a global strategic focus in response to global competition.

At the same time, this structure fragments international expertise within the firm because a central pool of international experience no longer exists. The structure assumes that managers will have adequate regional experience or advice to allow them to make balanced decisions. Coordination of activities among the various product groups operating in the same markets is crucial to avoid unnecessary duplication of basic tasks. For some of these tasks, such as market research, special staff functions may be created and then hired by the product divisions when needed. If product managers lack an appreciation for the international dimension, they may focus their attention on only the larger markets, often with emphasis on the domestic markets, and fail to take the long-term view.

Area Structure The second most frequently adopted approach is the area structure. The firm is organized on the basis of geographical areas; for example, operations may be divided into those dealing with North America, the Far East, Latin America, and Europe. Ideally, no special preference is given to the region in which the headquarters is located—for example, North America or Europe. Central staffs are responsible for providing coordination support for worldwide planning and control activities performed at headquarters.

Regional integration continues to play a major role in area restructuring; for example, many multinational corporations have located their European headquarters in Brussels, where the EU has its headquarters. Brussels is a top choice for law and lobbying firms, consulting companies, accounting firms, and nongovernmental organizations. For some companies, economic integration as a result of NAFTA has led to the formation of North American divisions in place of specific U.S. divisions. German manufacturing companies like Schneider Electric and Trumpf have created North American operational units that operate across the United States, Mexico, and Canada.

The driver of structural choices may also be cultural similarity, such as in the case of Asia, or historic connections between countries, such as in the case of combining Europe with the Middle East and Africa. As new markets emerge, they may be first delegated to an established country organization for guidance with the ultimate objective of having them be equal partners with others in the organization.

The area approach follows the marketing concept most closely because individual areas and markets are given concentrated attention. If market conditions with respect to product acceptance and operating conditions vary dramatically, the area approach is the one to choose. Companies opting for this alternative typically have relatively narrow product lines with similar end uses and end users. However, expertise is most needed in adapting the product and its marketing to local market conditions. Once again, to avoid duplication of effort in product management and in functional areas, staff specialists—for product categories, for example—may be used.

Without appropriate coordination from the staff, essential information and experience may not be transferred from one regional entity to another. Also, if the company expands in terms of product lines and if end markets begin to diversify, the area structure may become inappropriate.

Some marketers may feel that going into a global product structure may be too much too quickly and opt, therefore, to have a regional organization for planning and reporting purposes. The objective may also be to keep profit or sales centers of similar size at similar levels in the corporate hierarchy. If a group of countries has small sales compared with other country operations, they can be consolidated into a region. The benefits of a regional operation and regional headquarters are more efficient coordination of programs across the region (as opposed to globally), a management more sensitized to country-market operations in the region, and the ability for the region's voice to be heard more clearly at global headquarters (as compared to what an individual, especially smaller, country operation could achieve).[11]

Functional Structure Of all the global organization approaches, the functional structure is the most simple from the administrative viewpoint because it emphasizes the basic tasks of the firm—for example, manufacturing, sales, and research and development. This approach works best when both products and customers are relatively few and similar in nature. Because coordination is typically the key problem, staff functions have been created to interact between the functional areas. Otherwise, the company's marketing and regional expertise may not be exploited to the fullest extent.

A variation of this approach is one that uses processes as a basis for structure. The process structure is common in the energy and mining industries, where one corporate entity may be in charge of exploration worldwide and another may be responsible for the actual mining operation.

Customer Structure Firms may also organize their operations using the customer structure, especially if the customer groups they serve are dramatically different—for example, consumers versus businesses versus governments. Catering to these diverse groups may require the concentration of specialists in particular divisions. The product may be the same, but the buying processes of the various customer groups may differ. Governmental buying is characterized by bidding, in which price plays a larger role than when businesses are the buyers. However, products and solutions are increasingly developed around capabilities, such as networked communications, that can be used by more than one service or agency.[12] Similarly, in financial institutions, it is important to know whether customers who signed up for one service are already customers for other services being provided by the institution.[13]

Mixed Structure In some cases, mixed, or hybrid, organizations exist. A mixed structure combines two or more organizational dimensions simultaneously. It permits adequate attention to product, area, or functional needs as required by the company. The approach may only be a result of a transitional period after a merger or an acquisition, or it may come about due to unique market characteristics or product lines. It may also provide a useful structure before the implementation of a worldwide matrix structure.

Naturally, organizational structures are never as clear-cut and simple as presented here. Whatever the basic format, product, functional, and area inputs are needed. Alternatives could include an initial product structure that would subsequently have regional groupings or an initial regional structure with subsequent product groupings. However, in the long term, coordination and control across such structures become tedious. The Nestlé Group is managed by geographies (Europe, Americas, and Asia/Oceania/Africa) for most of the food and beverage business, with the exceptions of Nestlé Waters, Nestlé Nutrition, Nestlé Purina Petcare, Nespresso, Nestlé Professional, and Nestlé Health Science, which are managed on a global basis (see Exhibit 10.3).[14]

Matrix Structure Many multinational corporations—in an attempt to facilitate planning, organizing, and controlling interdependent businesses, critical resources, strategies, and geographic regions—have adopted the matrix structure.[15] Business is driven by a worldwide business unit (e.g., photographic products or commercial

EXHIBIT 10.3 The Global Division Structure (Nestlé)

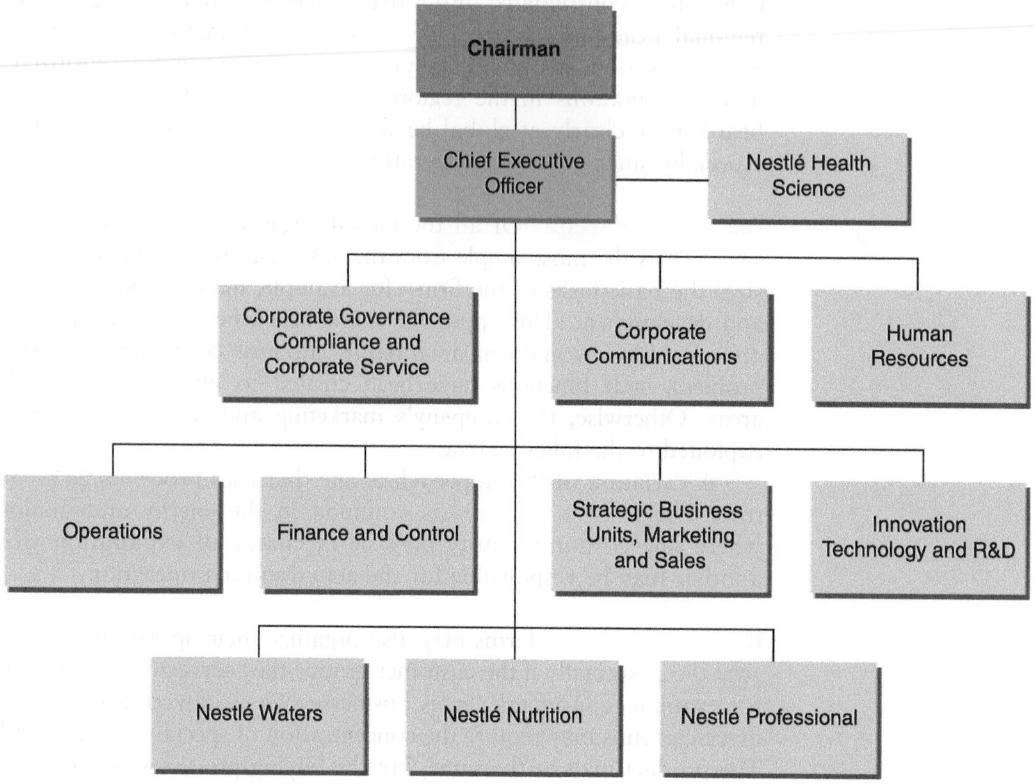

SOURCE: Nestlé, General Organization chart (www.nestle.com/ABOUTUS/MANAGEMENT/Pages/Management-landing.aspx). © 2012 Nestlé. Reprinted with permission.

and information systems) and implemented by a geographic unit (e.g., Europe or Latin America). The geographical units, as well as their country subsidiaries, serve as the "glue" between autonomous product operations.

Organizational matrices integrate the various approaches already discussed, as the example in Exhibit 10.4 illustrates. Matrices vary in terms of their areas of emphasis and the number of dimensions. ABB, a Swiss-Swedish engineering firm, has a multidimensional matrix consisting of eight geographic areas, five operating segments, and the new ABB business services group that provides global support capabilities to the operating segments. Each of the operating segments has sales and marketing, research and development, engineering and manufacturing, and finance functions. These provide operational support in focused service functions that include group functions reporting to the CEO, group functions reporting to the CFO, group functions reporting to the head of marketing and customer solutions, group functions reporting to the general counsel, and group functions reporting to the head of human resources.[16]

The matrix approach helps cut through enormous organizational complexities in making business managers, functional managers, and strategy managers cooperate. However, the matrix requires sensitive, well-trained middle managers who can cope with problems that arise from reporting to two bosses—for example, a product-line manager and an area manager. For example, every management unit may have a multidimensional reporting relationship, which may cross functional, regional, or operational lines. On a regional basis, group managers in Europe, for example, report administratively to a vice president of operations for Europe but report functionally to group vice presidents at global headquarters.

Many companies have found the matrix structure problematic. The dual reporting channel easily causes conflict; complex issues are forced into a

EXHIBIT 10.4 The Global Matrix Structure (ABB)

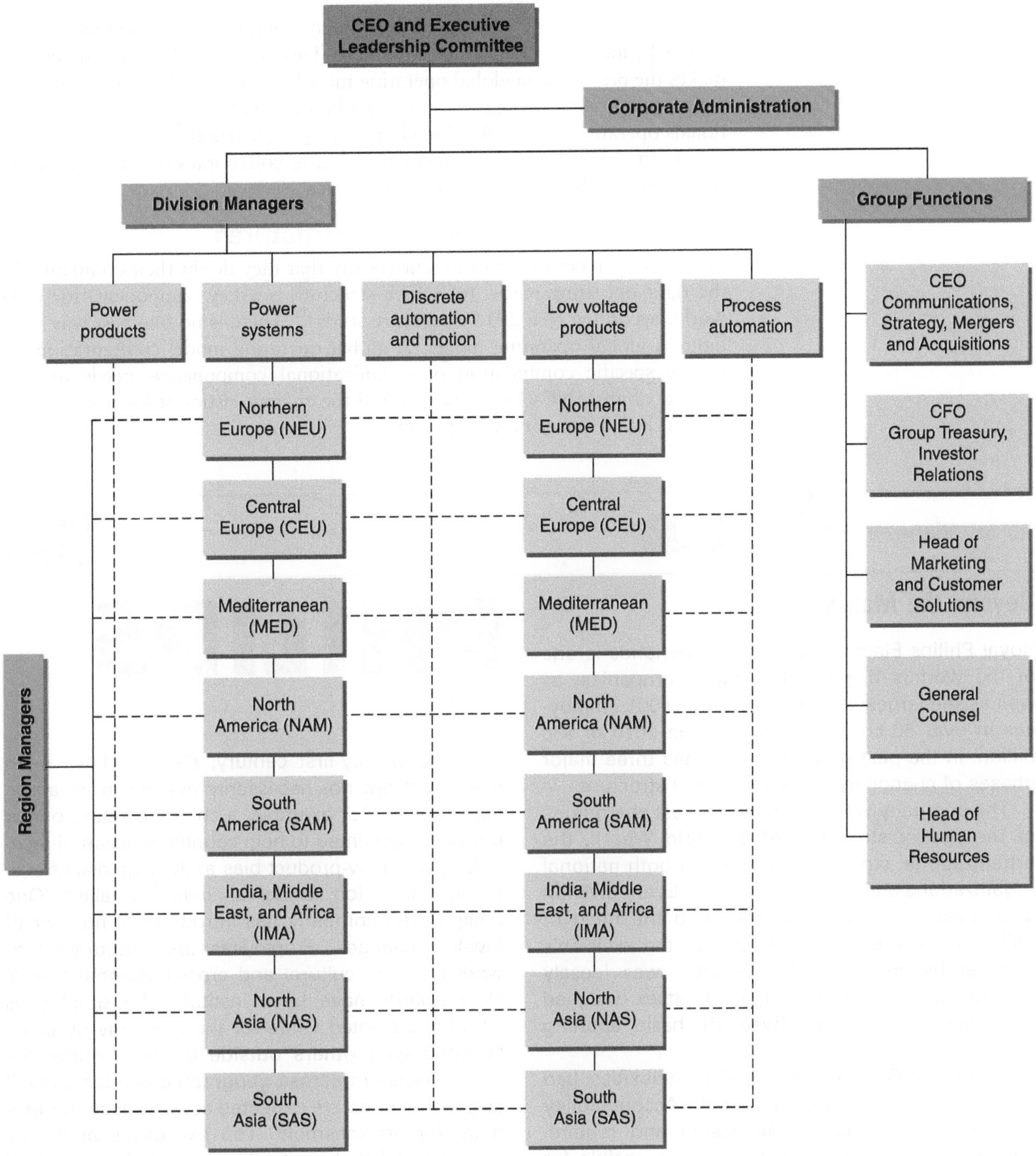

SOURCE: ABB, www.abb.com.

two-dimensional decision framework; and even minor issues may have to be resolved through committee discussion.[17] Ideally, managers should solve problems themselves through formal and informal communication; however, physical and psychic distance often make that impossible. Especially when competitive conditions require quick reaction, the matrix, with its inherent complexity, may actually lower the reaction speed of the company. As a result, authority has started to shift in many organizations from area to product, although the matrix may still officially be used.

Transnational Structure MNEs need to build synergies and economies of scale as well as be locally responsive and adaptive. This double and conflicting challenge makes the pressures on global operating models more acute because transnational forces will become stronger as industries become more multipolar, with multinationals operating in both developed and emerging markets.[18]

At the same time, approaches to increase collaboration have been focused on, as seen in *The International Marketplace 10.2.*

Evolution of Organizational Structures

In fact, 95 percent of senior executives say that they doubt their companies have the right operating model (of which structure is a key component) for today's world, according to a 2011 Accenture study.[19] There is no one best way to configure a global operating model. A global operating model configuration—that is, the specific combination of organizational components—needs to fit the context of an MNE's home market and the characteristics of its host markets as defined by its international strategy.

THE INTERNATIONAL **MARKETPLACE** **10.2**

Beyond the Matrix

Royal Philips Electronics of the Netherlands is one of the world's biggest electronics companies, as well as the largest in Europe, with 119,001 employees in over 60 countries and sales in 2010 of $36 billion. In the past 65 years, it has had three major phases of change in its organizational structure.

The company was one of the earliest champions of the matrix structure. After World War II, the organizational structure consisted of both national organizations and product divisions. Every division in a given country would report to the head of Philips in that country but also to the division's head at headquarters. This network was loosely held together by coordinating committees designed to resolve any conflicts between the basic reporting structures.

By the 1990s, environmental complexities had rendered the structure inefficient. Accountability and credit were difficult to assign and require. For example, who was to be held responsible for the profit-and-loss account—the country manager or the product head? The subsequent reorganization created a number of units with worldwide responsibility for groups of the company's businesses (e.g., consumer electronics and lighting products). The national offices became subservient to these units, built around products and based at headquarters.

PHILIPS

Philips logo.

In the twenty-first century, changes have been made that are not necessarily evident in organizational charts. For example, a chief marketing officer has been appointed to help counter criticism of technology and new-product bias at the expense of customer orientation. Under an initiative called "One Philips," the company has introduced a number of low-key changes. Employees are encouraged to work on cross-cultural and cross-functional teams. New awards have been instituted for employees who have created value for the company by collaborating with others outside of their immediate units. Transfers across geographic entities as well as product units are expected as an explicit requirement for advancement. Top executives at Philips have argued that up to 80 percent of the desired changes will come about through readjustment of attitudes and the rest from using appropriate incentives, most of them not directly monetary. To accelerate these changes, Philips brought together its top 1,000 managers for a series of workshops designed to find ways to cut through organizational barriers.

SOURCE: "The Matrix Master," *Economist*, January 21, 2006, 4. See also Philips, www.philips.com.

Ideally, the structure allows a corporation to best meet the challenges of global markets: to be global and local, big and small, decentralized with centralized reporting, by allowing the optimization of businesses globally and maximizing performance in every country of operation. Companies develop new structures in stages as their product diversity develops and the share of foreign sales increases.

A new structure called the T-shaped organization is now emerging. Multinational subsidiaries in emerging markets must reorganize themselves so that they can better cope with two sets of pressures. One, the customer side, needs them to move faster, make more decisions locally, and alter the incentives and career opportunities offered to employees. In other words, their front-end operations must become highly localized. Given the size of emerging markets like China and India, a high level of localization does not preclude economies of scale. General Electric (GE) develops new jet engines, but they rely on their China unit's designs to manufacture them; the India unit adds the analytical and materials aspects, while the German labs use the wind-tunnel testing. GE R&D design engineers from around the world collaborate effectively, all speaking the same language of Six Sigma.[20]

The evolutionary process of global structures is summarized in Exhibit 10.5.

A gateway model to reduce the tension between global integration and local responsiveness has been proposed.[21] As new markets emerge, the need to manage increased complexity is necessary. For example, 10 gateway countries could serve as hubs for the developed markets and another 10 countries might perform the same role for emerging markets. Each hub would serve the gateway market as well as other similar markets. For example, the German hub might manage Austria, Hungary, and Switzerland; Brazil would support Argentina, Bolivia, Chile, Paraguay, and Uruguay. The nonhub countries would usually feature only customer contact and service. Some countries would cover all aspects of corporate activity, while others might gradually build capabilities beyond sales. The executive committee of the company would consist of leaders with diverse experience from all of the hubs across the key countries of the developed and developing world.

EXHIBIT 10.5 Evolution of Global Structures

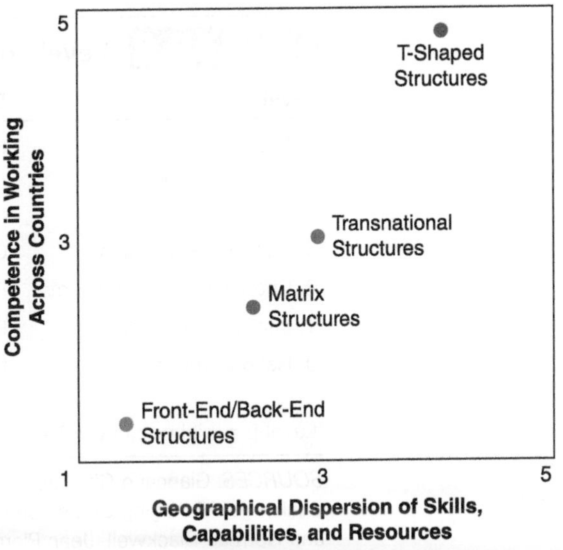

SOURCE: Nirmalya Kumar and Phanish Puranam, "Have You Restructured for Global Success?" *Harvard Business Review* 89 (October 2011): 123–28.

Whatever the choice of organizational arrangement may be, the challenge of people having to work in silos remains. Employee knowledge tends to be fragmented, with one unit's experience and know-how inaccessible to other units. Therefore, the wheel gets reinvented at considerable cost to the company and frustration to those charged with tasks. Information technology can be used to synchronize knowledge across even the most complicated and diverse organizations.[22] At Procter & Gamble, for example, brand managers have use of a standardized, worldwide ad-testing system that allows them access to every ad the company has ever run, providing examples for the needs that may have to be met at a particular time. Once knowledge transfer is established, what may be needed is a form of organization in which individuals and teams decide for themselves what to do but are accountable for the results.[23]

IMPLEMENTATION

Organizational structures provide the framework for carrying out marketing decision making. However, for marketing to be effective, a series of organizational initiatives are needed to develop marketing strategy to its full potential: secure implementation of such strategies at the national level and across markets.[24]

Locus of Decision Making

Organizational structures themselves do not indicate where the authority for decision making and control rests within the organization, nor do they reveal the level of coordination among units. The different levels of coordination between country units are summarized in Exhibit 10.6. Once a suitable form of structure has been found, it has to be made to work by finding a balance between the center and the country organizations.

If subsidiaries are granted a high degree of autonomy, the result is termed **decentralization**. In decentralized systems, controls are relatively loose and simple and the flows between headquarters and subsidiaries are mainly financial; that is, each subsidiary operates as a profit center. On the other hand, if controls are tight and if strategic decision making is concentrated at headquarters, the result is termed **centralization**. Firms are typically neither totally centralized nor totally decentralized. Increasingly, companies do not want constituents to

EXHIBIT 10.6 Levels of Coordination

Level	Description
5. Central control	No national structures
4. Central direction	Central functional heads have line authority over national functions
3. Central coordination	Central staff functions in coordinating role
2. Coordinating mechanisms	Formal committees and systems
1. Informal cooperation	Functional meetings: exchange of information
0. National autonomy	No coordination between decentralized units, which may even compete in export markets
Level 5 = highest; Level 0 = lowest. Most commonly found levels are 1–4.	

SOURCES: Giancarlo Ghislanzoni, Risto Penttinen, and David Turnbull, "The Multilocal Challenge: Managing Cross-border Functions," *McKinsey Quarterly*, March 2008, 70–81; and Norman Blackwell, Jean-Pierre Bizet, Peter Child, and David Hensley, "Creating European Organizations That Work," in *Readings in Global Marketing*, edited by Michael R. Czinkota and Ilkka A. Ronkainen (London: The Dryden Press, 1995), 376–85.

think they are from anywhere in particular, nor do they want to be perceived as having a home base in each of the markets where they operate. For example, Lenovo's main corporate functions are divided among Beijing, Singapore, and Raleigh, North Carolina.[25] Some functions, such as finance, lend themselves to more centralized decision making, whereas other functions, such as promotional decisions, lend themselves to far less. Research and development is typically centralized in terms of both decision making and location, especially when basic research work is involved. In many cases, however, variations in decision making are product- and market-based; for example, in Unilever's new organization, managers of global business units are responsible for brand management and product development, and managers of regional market development organizations are responsible for sales, trade marketing, and media choices.[26]

Allowing maximum flexibility at the country-market level takes advantage of the fact that subsidiary management knows its market and can react to changes quickly. Problems of motivation and acceptance are avoided when decision makers are also the implementers of the strategy. On the other hand, many marketers, faced with global competitive threats and opportunities, have adopted global strategy formulation, which by definition requires some degree of centralization. What has emerged as a result can be called **coordinated decentralization**. This means that overall corporate strategy is provided from global or regional headquarters, but subsidiaries are free to implement it within the range established in consultation between headquarters and the subsidiaries.

However, moving into this new mode may raise significant challenges. Among these systemic difficulties is a lack of widespread commitment to dismantling traditional national structures, driven by an inadequate understanding of the larger, global forces at work. Power barriers—especially if the personal roles of national managers are under threat of being consolidated into regional organizations—can lead to proposals being challenged without valid reason. Finally, some organizational initiatives (such as multicultural teams or corporate chat rooms) may be jeopardized by the fact that people do not have the necessary skills (e.g., language ability) or that an infrastructure (e.g., intranet) may not exist in an appropriate format.[27]

One particular case is of special interest. Organizationally, the forces of globalization are changing the country manager's role significantly. With profit-and-loss responsibility, oversight of multiple functions, and the benefit of distance from headquarters, country managers in the past enjoyed considerable decision-making autonomy as well as entrepreneurial initiative. Today, however, many companies have to emphasize the product dimension of the product-geography matrix, which means that the power has to shift at least to some extent from country managers to worldwide strategic-business-unit and product-line managers. Many of the previously local decisions are now subordinated to global strategic moves. However, regional and local brands still require an effective local management component. Therefore, the future country manager will have to have diverse skills (such as government relations and managing entrepreneurial teamwork) and wear many hats in balancing the needs of the operation for which the manager is directly responsible with those of the entire region or strategic business unit.[28] To emphasize the importance of the global/regional dimension in the country manager's portfolio, many companies have tied the country manager's compensation to the way the company performs globally or regionally, not just in the market for which the manager is responsible.

Factors Affecting Structure and Decision Making

The organizational structure and locus of decision making in multinational corporations are determined by a number of factors. They include (1) the degree of involvement in international operations, (2) the business(es) in which the firm is engaged (in terms, for example, of products marketed), (3) the size and importance of the markets, and (4) the human resource capability of the firm.[29]

The effect of the degree of involvement on structure and decision making was discussed earlier in the chapter. With low degrees of involvement by the parent company, subsidiaries can enjoy high degrees of autonomy as long as they meet their profit targets. The same situation can occur even with the most globally oriented companies, but within a different framework. Consider, for example, Alcatel Lucent, which generates 30 percent of its worldwide revenues from North America, mostly from the United States. The company is organized into three geographies (Americas, Europe–Middle East–Africa, and Asia-Pacific) and three corporate functions (customer care, solutions and marketing, and quality assurance). However, its U.S.-based Bell Labs, the company's "innovation engine," enjoys considerable autonomy because it is at the leading edge of communications technology development, although it is still within the parent company's planning and control system.

The firm's country of origin and the political history of the area can also affect organizational structure and decision making. For example, Swiss-based Nestlé, with only 3 to 4 percent of its sales in the small domestic market, has traditionally had a highly decentralized organization. Moreover, events of the past 90 years, particularly during the two world wars, have often forced subsidiaries of European-based companies to act independently in order to survive.

The type and variety of products marketed will have an effect on organizational decisions. Companies that market consumer products typically have product organizations with high degrees of decentralization, allowing for maximum local flexibility. On the other hand, companies that market technologically sophisticated products, such as General Electric's turbines, display centralized organizations with worldwide product responsibilities.

Going global has recently meant transferring world headquarters of important business units abroad. For example, Halliburton opened a second corporate headquarters office in Dubai, United Arab Emirates, in 2007 to align with the oil and gas business moving its focus to the Eastern Hemisphere in order to "provide new manufacturing capacity, move closer to key markets, and help reduce the costs of moving materials, products, tools and people."[30]

Apart from situations that require the development of an area structure, the unique characteristics of particular markets or regions may require separate and specific considerations for the firm. For example, Yum Brands has a structure that emphasizes its individual brands, including KFC, Pizza Hut, Taco Bell, and Long John Silver's, but also has three operational units: one for the U.S. market, an international division, and a separate China division (covering mainland China, Thailand, and KFC Taiwan) because of the size and strategic importance of China.[31]

The human factor in any organization is critical. Managers both at headquarters and in the subsidiaries must bridge the physical and psychic distances separating them. If subsidiaries have competent managers who rarely need to consult headquarters about their problems, they may be granted high degrees of autonomy. In the case of global organizations, subsidiary management must understand the corporate culture because subsidiaries must sometimes make decisions that meet the long-term objectives of the firm as a whole but that are not optimal for the local market.

The Networked Global Organization

No international structure is ideal, and some have challenged the wisdom of even looking for one. They have recommended attention to new processes that would, in a given structure, help to develop new perspectives and attitudes that reflect and respond to the complex, opposing demands of global integration and local responsiveness. The question thus changes from which structural alternative is best to how the different perspectives of various corporate entities can better be taken into account when making decisions. In structural terms, little

EXHIBIT 10.7 The Networked Global Organization

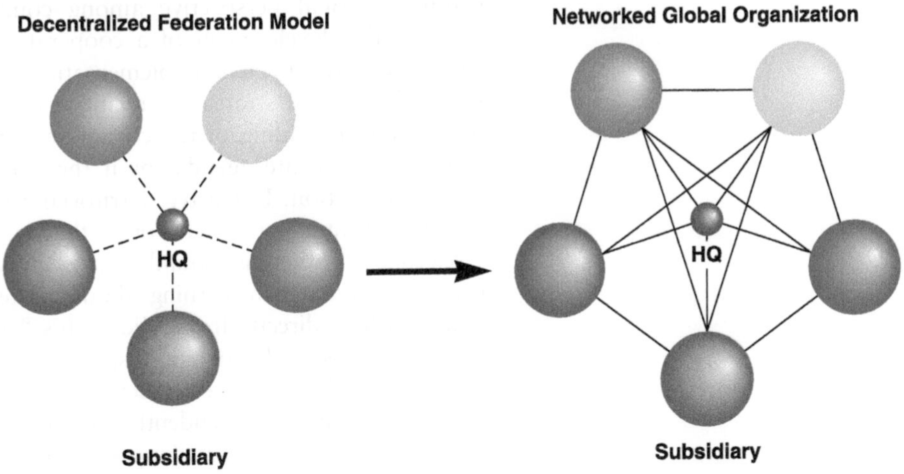

SOURCES: Stéphane J.G. Girod, Joshua B. Bellin, and Robert J. Thomas, "Are Emerging-Market Multinationals Creating the Global Operating Models of the Future?" Accenture, May 2009, www.accenture.com/us-en/Pages/insight-emerging-market-multinationals-creating-global-operating-models-future-summary.aspx; and Thomas Gross, Ernie Turner, and Lars Cederholm, "Building Teams for Global Operations," *Management Review*, June 1987, 34.

may change. Philips, for example, has not changed its basic matrix structure, yet major changes have occurred in its functional sectors and its internal relations. Philips has organized on an operating-sector basis with each of its three sectors—healthcare, consumer lifestyle, and lighting—responsible for the management of its businesses globally. In addition, Philips created an innovation and emerging businesses sector to invest in future-oriented projects outside of the operating sectors, and a group management and services sector to provide support in areas such as brand management for the operating sectors. Philips operates as a networked global organization rather than a decentralized federation model, as depicted in Exhibit 10.7.

Many of the most successful global companies have adopted an organizational approach that provides clear global strategic direction along with the flexibility to adapt to local opportunities and requirements. The term *glocalization* has been coined to describe this approach. Kraft International describes the company's strategy as "to win locally and leverage globally." A Dow Chemical executive explained his company's approach: "You simply cannot develop or initiate a market penetration strategy, in an emerging country from a location thousands of miles away in which no one has seen and still be successful ... period. You need to 'Think and Act Globally but Implement Locally.'"[32]

Companies that have adopted this approach have incorporated the following three dimensions into their organizations: (1) the development and communication of a clear corporate vision, (2) the effective management of human resource tools to broaden individual perspectives and develop identification with corporate goals, and (3) the integration of individual thinking and activities into the broad corporate agenda. The first dimension relates to a clear and consistent long-term corporate mission that guides individuals wherever they work in the organization. IBM established three values for the twenty-first century: dedication to every client's success, innovation that matters (for the company and the world), and trust and personal responsibility in all relationships.[33] Other examples of this are Johnson & Johnson's corporate credo of customer focus, Coca Cola's mission of leveraging global beverage brand leadership "to refresh the world," and Nestlé's vision to make the company the "reference for nutrition, health, and wellness."[34]

The second dimension relates both to the development of global managers who can find opportunities in spite of environmental challenges as well as to creating a global perspective among country managers. The last dimension relates to the development of a cooperative mindset among country organizations to ensure effective implementation of global strategies. Managers may believe that global strategies are intrusions on their operations if they do not have an understanding of the corporate vision, if they have not contributed to the global corporate agenda, or if they are not given direct responsibility for its implementation. Defensive, territorial attitudes can lead to the emergence of the "not-invented-here" syndrome, that is, country organizations objecting to or rejecting an otherwise sound strategy. Research showed that Microsoft's audience was interested in learning about the technology they would work on and wanted to hear directly from Microsoft's "core tech" team. Microsoft knew this site needed to be authentic and display the realities of working at Microsoft.[35]

For example, in an area structure, units (such as Europe and North America) may operate quite independently, sharing little expertise and information with the others. While they are supposed to build links to headquarters and other units, they may actually be building walls. To tackle this problem, Nissan established four management committees, meeting once a month, to supervise regional operations. Each committee includes representatives of the major functions (e.g., manufacturing, marketing, and finance), and the committees (for Japan, Europe, the United States, and general overseas markets) are chaired by Nissan executive vice presidents based in Japan. The CEO attends the committee meetings periodically but regularly.[36]

The network avoids the problems of duplication of effort, inefficiency, and resistance to ideas developed elsewhere by giving subsidiaries the latitude, encouragement, and tools to pursue local business development within the framework of the global strategy. Headquarters considers each unit as a source of ideas, skills, capabilities, and knowledge that can be utilized for the benefit of the entire organization. This means that the subsidiaries must be upgraded from the role of implementation and adaptation to that of contribution and partnership in the development and execution of worldwide strategies. Efficient plants may be converted into international production centers, innovative R&D units may become centers of excellence (and thus role models), and leading subsidiary groups may be given a leadership role in developing new strategies for the entire corporation.

Centers of excellence can emerge in three formats: charismatic, focused, or virtual. Charismatic centers of excellence are individuals who are internationally recognized for their expertise in a function or an area. The objective is primarily to build through an expert, via a mentoring relationship, a capability in the firm that has been lacking. The most common types are focused centers of excellence that are based on a single area of expertise, be it technological or product-based. The center has an identifiable location from which members provide advice and training. In virtual centers of excellence, the core individuals live and work around the world and keep in touch through electronic means and meetings. The knowledge of dispersed individuals is brought together, integrated into a coherent whole, and disseminated throughout the firm.[37]

Promoting Global Internal Cooperation

In today's environment, the global business entity can be successful only if it is able to move intellectual capital within the organization; that is, transmit ideas and information in real time. If there are impediments to the free flow of information across organizational boundaries, important updates about changes in the competitive environment might not be communicated in a timely fashion to those tasked with incorporating them into strategy.[38]

One of the tools is teaching through educational programs and executive development. The focus is on teachable points of view, that is, an explanation of what a person knows and believes about what it takes to succeed in his or her business. For example, Procter & Gamble makes recruiting and teaching future leaders a priority for its top executives. All of the top officers at the company teach in the company's executive education programs and act as mentors and coaches for younger managers. P&G takes global executive development seriously and grooms its top management prospects through a series of career-building assignments across business units and geographies. Eighty-five percent of the company's top management has had one or more international assignment.[39] WPP, the global marketing services group, has developed a graduate marketing fellowship program for promising global managers, comprising three one-year rotations with individual companies within the group's global network and requiring an international assignment.

Former GE CEO Jack Welch coined the term *boundarylessness*, which means that people can act without regard to status or functional loyalty and can look for better ideas from anywhere. Top leadership of GE spends considerable time at GE training centers interacting with up-and-comers from all over the company. Each training class is given a real, current company problem to solve, and the reports can be career makers (or breakers). GE claimed that its 191 top executives had each spent at least one year in training and development programs in their first 15 years at GE.[40] With this approach, a powerful, teachable point of view can reach the entire company within a reasonable period by having students become teachers themselves. At PepsiCo, for instance, the CEO passed his teachable point onto 110 executives, who then passed it to 20,000 people within 18 months.

Another method to promote internal cooperation for global strategy implementation is the use of international teams or councils. In the case of a new product or program, an international team of managers may be assembled to develop strategy. While final direction may come from headquarters, it has been informed of local conditions, and implementation of the strategy is enhanced because local-country managers were involved in its development. The approach has worked even in cases involving seemingly impossible market differences. Both Procter & Gamble and Henkel have successfully introduced pan-European brands for which strategy was developed by European teams. These teams consisted of country managers and staff personnel to smooth eventual implementation and to avoid unnecessarily long and disruptive discussions about the fit of a new product to individual markets.

On a broader and longer-term basis, companies use councils to share **best practice**; for instance, an idea that may have saved money or time, or a process that is more efficient than existing ones. Most professionals at the leading global companies are members of multiple councils. In some cases, it is important to bring in members of other constituencies (e.g., suppliers, intermediaries, service providers) to such meetings to share their views and experiences and make available their own best practice for benchmarking. In some major production undertakings, technology allows ongoing participation by numerous internal and external team members. For the production of the Boeing 787, Boeing created the Global Collaborative Environment (GCE), a set of computer and networking capabilities made available via the web to every member of the 787 team around the world.[41] ABB created two group R&D laboratories—Global Lab Automation and Global Lab Power—to link and integrate its global R&D operations in Germany, Switzerland, Sweden, the United States, Poland, China, and India with universities and other external partners in a fully networked online environment.[42]

While technology has made such teamwork possible wherever the individual participants may be, relying only on technology may not bring about the desired results; "high-tech" approaches inherently mean "low touch," at the expense of results. Human relationships are still paramount. A common purpose is what binds team members to a particular task, which can only be achieved through trust, which in turn is achievable through face-to-face meetings.[43]

The term *network* also implies two-way communications between headquarters and subsidiaries themselves. This translates into intercultural communication efforts focused on developing relationships.[44] While this communication has traditionally taken the form of newsletters, traveling executive "road shows," or regular and periodic meetings of appropriate personnel, new technologies are allowing businesses to link far-flung entities and eliminate the traditional barriers of time and distance. Companies now use regular audio podcasts to transmit seminars and conferences to employees globally. Streaming media technology allows live webcasts for important company meetings. TBWA Worldwide conducts three live webcasts every year, showing recent creative work and taking questions from agency employees around the world. TBWA also offers the webcast three times during the day to allow staffers from different time zones the ability to conveniently participate.[45] Intranets integrate a company's information assets into a single, globally accessible system that allows more efficient collaboration and the formation of virtual teams. For example, employees at Levi Strauss & Co. can join an electronic discussion group with colleagues around the world, watch the latest Levi's commercials, or comment on the latest business programs or plans. The benefits of intranets are: (1) increased productivity in that there is no longer a time lag between an idea and the information needed to assess and implement it; (2) enhanced knowledge capital, which is constantly updated and upgraded; (3) facilitated teamwork-enabling online communication at insignificant expense; and (4) incorporation of best practice at a moment's notice by allowing managers and functional-area personnel to make to-the-minute decisions anywhere in the world. For consumer goods companies, intranets allow global brand management teams access to consumer research, product development timelines, international creative concepts, individual country campaigns, media planning and buying information, international pricing structures, new packaging ideas, and much more. The challenge becomes one of efficient design interface, usage stimulation, and training.[46]

As can be seen from this discussion, the networked approach is not a structural adaptation but a procedural one, calling for a change in management mentality. It requires adjustment mainly in the coordination and control functions of the firm. And while there is still considerable disagreement as to which of the approaches work best, some measures have been shown to correlate with success. Of the many initiatives developed to enhance the workings of a networked global organization, such as cross-border task forces and establishment of centers of excellence, the most significant was the use of electronic networking capabilities.

Further adjustment in organizational approaches is required as businesses face new challenges such as emerging markets, global accounts, the digitization of business, and cyber-security.[47] Emerging markets present the company with unique opportunities but also challenges such as product counterfeiters and informal competitors who ignore local labor and tax laws. How these issues are addressed may require organizational rethinking. Increasingly, companies are organizing their business not just regionally but also to focus on emerging markets as a group. Global account managers need to have skills and the empowerment to work across functional areas and borders to deliver quality service to the company's largest clients. Also, digital business, such as business-to-business and business-to-consumer Internet-based activities, will continue to be brought into the mainstay of the business's activities and structures and not just segregated as a separate activity. Finally, cyber-security has surfaced as an issue of critical importance as increased global team collaboration can expose the company to risks from hackers and spies. U.S. government agencies and defense contractors had been "the victims of an unprecedented rash of [*sic*] cyber attacks over the last two years" and linked those attacks to Chinese sources.[48] The Accenture report related this problem to a corporate organizational issue as it discussed the tendencies of young "millennial generation" workers within corporations to ignore corporate CIO policies about data protection and to share work outside of corporate "firewalls" through e-mail, Google apps, and other networking practices because it is easier and faster. Companies must adapt to new technologies and networking options to balance the need for easy and vast informational flow with that of security.[49]

The Role of Country Organizations

Country organizations should be treated as a source of supply as much as they are considered a source of demand. Quite often, however, headquarters managers see their role as the coordinators of key decisions and controllers of resources and perceive subsidiaries as implementers and adapters of global strategy in their respective local markets. Furthermore, all country organizations may be seen as the same. This view severely limits the use of the firm's resources by not using country organizations as resources and by depriving country managers of possibilities of exercising their creativity.[50]

The role that a particular country organization can play depends naturally on that market's overall strategic importance as well as the competencies of its organization. From these criteria, four different roles emerge (see Exhibit 10.8).

The role of strategic leader can be played by a highly competent national subsidiary located in a strategically critical market. The country organization serves as a partner of headquarters in developing and implementing strategy. For example, a strategic leader market may have products designed specifically with it in mind. Nissan's Z-cars have always been designated primarily for the U.S. market, starting with the 240Z in the 1970s to the 350Z and 370Z in the 2000s. The new model was designed by the company's La Jolla, California, studio. The Mercedes-Benz Design Studios—in Sindelfingen (Germany), Irvine (California), Yokohama (Japan), and a fourth studio in Como (Italy) that focuses exclusively on interior vehicle design—regularly share ideas. They function as one seismograph for influences emerging from art, culture, and architecture.[51] Global automotive companies like GM and Volkswagen have joint ventures with

EXHIBIT 10.8 Roles for Country Organization

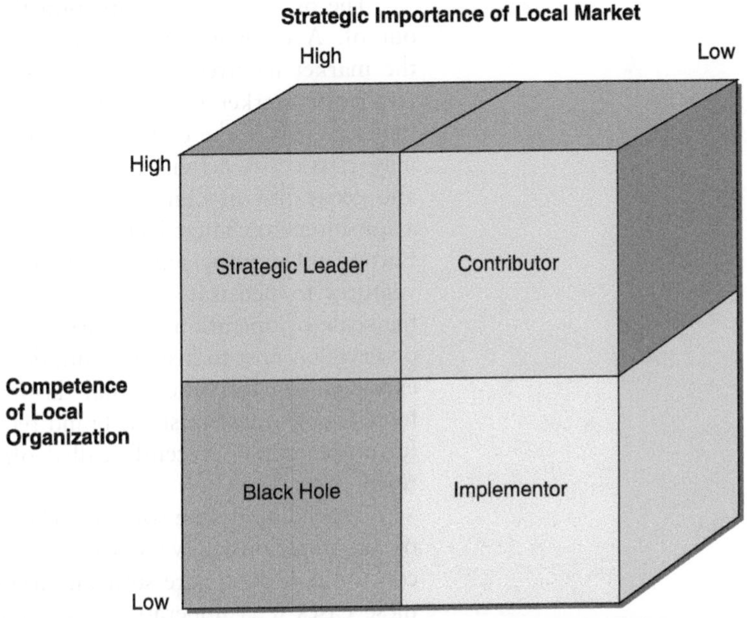

SOURCE: Reprinted by permission of *Harvard Business Review*. An exhibit from "Tap Your Subsidiaries for Global Reach," by Christopher A. Bartlett and Sumantra Ghoshal, 64 (November/December 1986), 90. Copyright © 1986 Harvard Business School Publishing Corporation; all rights reserved.

Chinese auto manufacturer SAIC to produce cars specifically for the Chinese market. Since China is the largest automobile market in the world, it is logical that the country's management team plays an important strategic role in the company's global planning.

A **contributor** is a country organization with a distinctive competence, such as product development or regional expertise. Increasingly, country organizations are the source of new products. These range from high-end innovations, like IBM scientists (Zurich) being the first to image the "anatomy" of a molecule, opening new possibilities for exploring the building blocks of future microprocessors and other nanodevices,[52] to low-end innovations such as Procter & Gamble's country team in Turkey developing new seal-tight polyethylene bags for shipping Ariel detergent that are entirely recyclable and use significantly less packing material. P&G is expanding the use of these shipping materials across different regions. A contributor designation may be a function of geography as well. The development of new markets such as the "Stans" (e.g., Kazakhstan and Azerbaijan) has been delegated to country organizations in Russia, Turkey, and Dubai. For products or technologies with multiple applications, leadership may be divided among different country operations. For example, INVISTA delegates responsibility for each different application of Lycra to managers in a country where the application is strongest, that is, Brazil for swimwear and France for fashion. The global brand manager for Lycra ensures that those applications come together in an overall strategy.

The critical mass for the international marketing effort is provided by **implementers**. These country organizations may exist in smaller, less-established markets in which corporate commitment to market development is lower. The presence in these markets is typically through a sales organization. Although most entities fill this role, it should not be slighted. Implementers provide the opportunity to capture economies of scale and scope that are the basis of a global strategy. With a few notable exceptions, most subsidiary managers would argue they do not get the level of attention they need or deserve. But they are important nonetheless because they provide clear evidence that parent companies can view initiative-taking and profile-building efforts positively (rather than as unnecessary or annoying lobbying).[53]

The **black hole** is a situation that the international marketer has to work out of. A company may be in a "black hole" situation because it has read the market incorrectly (e.g., Philips focused its marketing efforts in the North American market on less-expensive items instead of the up-market products that have made the company's reputation worldwide)[54] or because government may restrict its activities (e.g., Citibank being restricted in terms of activities and geography in China). If possible, the marketer can use strategic alliances or acquisitions to change its competitive position. Whirlpool established itself in the European Union by acquiring Philips's white-goods operation and has used joint ventures to penetrate the Chinese market. If governmental regulations hinder the scale of operations, the firm may use its presence in a major market as an observation post to keep up with developments before a major thrust for entry is executed. On the other hand, the Indian government has been careful to limit foreign investment in single-brand retailers. Sweden's IKEA, the world's biggest furniture retailer, recently called off a $1 billion investment plan due to the restrictions.[55]

Depending on the role, the relationship between headquarters and the country organization will vary from loose control based mostly on support to tighter control in making sure strategies are implemented appropriately. Yet in each of these cases it is imperative that country organizations have enough operating independence to cater to local needs and to provide motivation to the country managers. For example, an implementer should provide input in the development of a regional or a global strategy or program. Strategy formulation should ensure that appropriate implementation can be achieved at the country level.

Good ideas can, and should, come from any country organization. To take full advantage of this, individuals at the country level have to feel that they have the authority to pursue ideas in the first place and that they can see their concepts through to commercialization.[56] In some cases, this may mean that subsidiaries are allowed to experiment with projects that would not be seen as feasible by headquarters. For example, developing products for small-scale power generation using renewable resources may not generate interest in Honeywell's major markets and subsidiaries but may well be something that one of its developing-country subsidiaries should investigate.

CONTROL

The function of the organizational structure is to provide a framework in which objectives can be met. A set of instruments and processes is needed, however, to influence the behavior and performance of organization members to meet the goals. Controls focus on actions to verify and correct activities that differ from established plans. Compliance needs to be secured from subordinates through various means of coordinating specialized and interdependent parts of the organization.[57] Within an organization, control serves as an integrating mechanism. Controls are designed to reduce uncertainty, increase predictability, and ensure that behaviors originating in separate parts of the organization are compatible and in support of common organizational goals despite physical, psychic, and temporal distances.

The critical issue is the same as with organizational structure: what is the ideal amount of control? On the one hand, headquarters needs information to ensure that international activities contribute maximum benefit to the overall organization. On the other hand, controls should not be construed as a code of law and allowed to stifle local initiative.

This section will focus on the design and functioning of control instruments available for the international marketer, along with an assessment of their appropriateness. Emphasis will be placed on the degree of formality of controls used.

Types of Controls

Most organizations display some administrative flexibility, as demonstrated by variations in the application of management directives, corporate objectives, or measurement systems. A distinction should be made, however, between variations that have emerged by design and those that are the result of autonomy. The one is the result of management decision, whereas the other has typically grown without central direction and is based on emerging practices. In both instances, some type of control will be exercised. Here, we are concerned only with controls that are the result of headquarters initiative rather than consequences of tolerated practices. Firms that wait for self-emerging controls often find that such an orientation may lead to rapid international growth but may eventually result in problems in areas of product-line performance, program coordination, and strategic planning.[58]

Whatever the system, it is important in today's competitive environment to have internal benchmarking. Benchmarking relays organizational learning and sharing of best practices throughout the corporate system to avoid the costs of reinventing solutions that have already been discovered. A description of the knowledge transfer process by which this occurs is provided in *The International Marketplace 10.3*.

Three critical features are necessary in sharing best practice. First, there needs to be a device for organizational memory. For example, at Xerox, contributors to solutions can send their ideas to an electronic library where they are indexed and provided to potential adopters in the corporate family.

THE INTERNATIONAL **MARKETPLACE** 10.3

International Best Practice Exchange

As growing competitive pressures challenge many global firms, strategies to improve the transfer of best practice across geographically dispersed units and time zones becomes critical. The premise is that a company with the same product range targeting the same markets panregionally should be able to use knowledge gained in one market throughout the organization. The fact is, however, that companies use only 20 percent of their most precious resource—knowledge, in the form of technical information, market data, internal know-how, and processes and procedures. Trying to transfer best practice internationally amplifies the problem even more. However, a corporate environment that creates informal cooperation, in addition to the more formal linkages, builds the necessary trust—and subsequently the critical mass—to share knowledge.

Copier maker Xerox, with over 60 subsidiaries, is working hard to make better use of its knowledge corporation-wide. A 35-person group identified nine practices that could be applicable throughout the group. These ranged from the way the Australian subsidiary retains customers to Italy's method of gathering competitive intelligence to a procedure for handling new major accounts in Spain. These practices were thought to be easier to "sell" to other operating companies, were considered easy to implement, and would provide a good return on investment.

Three countries were much quicker in introducing new products successfully than others. In the case of France, this was related to the training given to employees. The subsidiary gave its sales staff three days of hands-on practice, including competitive benchmarking. Before they attended the course, salespeople were given reading materials and were tested when they arrived. Those remaining were evaluated again at the end of the course, and performance reports were sent to their managers.

The difficult task is to achieve buy-in from the other country organizations. Six months might be spent in making detailed presentations of the best practice to all the companies and an additional three years helping them implement the needed changes. It is imperative that the country manager is behind the proposal in each subsidiary's case. However, implementation cannot be left to the country organizations after the concept has been presented. This may result in the dilution of both time and urgency and in possible country-specific customization that negates comparisons and jeopardizes the success of the change.

With time, these projects become codified into programs. Focus 500 allows the company's top 500 executives to share information on their interactions with customers and industry partners. Project Library details costs, resources, and cycle times of more than 2,000 projects, making it a vital resource in assuring Six Sigma in project management. PROFIT allows salespeople to submit hot selling tips—with cash incentives for doing so.

SOURCES: Philip Evans and Bob Wolf, "Collaboration Rules," *Harvard Business Review* 83 (July–August 2005): 96–104; Kristine Ellis, "Sharing Best Practices Globally," *Training*, July 2001, 34–38; and Xerox, www.xerox.com.

Second, best practice must be updated and adjusted to new situations. For example, best practice adopted by the company's Chinese office will be modified and customized, and this learning should then become part of the database. Finally, best practice must be legitimized. This calls for a shared understanding that exchanging knowledge across units is valued in the organization and that these systems are important mechanisms for knowledge exchange. An assessment of how effectively employees share information with colleagues and utilize the databases can also be included in employee performance evaluations.

In the design of the control system, a major decision concerns the object of control. Two major objects are typically identified: output and behavior. Output controls consist of balance sheets, sales data, production data, product line growth, or a performance review of personnel. Measures of output are accumulated at regular intervals and forwarded from the foreign operation to headquarters, where they are evaluated and critiqued based on comparisons to the plan or budget. Behavioral controls require the exertion of influence over behavior after, or ideally before, it leads to action. This influence can be achieved, for example, by providing sales manuals to subsidiary personnel or by fitting new employees into the corporate culture.

EXHIBIT 10.9 Comparison of Bureaucratic and Cultural Control Mechanisms

	Type of Control		
Object of Control	**Pure Bureaucratic/ Formalized Control**	**Pure Cultural Control**	**Characteristics of Control**
Output	Formal performance reports	Shared norms of performance	HQ sets short-term performance target and requires frequent reports from subsidiaries
Behavior	Company policies, manuals	Shared philosophy of management	Active participation of HQ in strategy formulation of subsidiaries

SOURCES: Peter J. Kidger, "Management Structure in Multinational Enterprises: Responding to Globalization," *Employee Relations*, August 2001, 69–85; and B. R. Baliga and Alfred M. Jaeger, "Multinational Corporations: Control Systems and Delegation Issues," *Journal of International Business Studies* 15 (Fall 1984): 28.

To institute either of these measures, corporate officials must decide on instruments of control. The general alternatives are bureaucratic (formalized) control or cultural control. Bureaucratic controls consist of a limited and explicit set of regulations and rules that outline desired levels of performance. Cultural controls, on the other hand, are much less formal and are the result of shared beliefs and expectations among the members of an organization. A comparison of the two types of controls and their objectives is provided in Exhibit 10.9. It can be argued that instilling the marketing approach (i.e., customer orientation) will have to rely more on behavioral dimensions because an approach focused on outputs may put undue pressure on short-term profits.[59]

Bureaucratic or Formalized Control

The elements of bureaucratic or formalized controls are (1) an international budget and planning system, (2) the functional reporting system, and (3) policy manuals used to direct functional performance. Budgets are short-term guidelines in such areas as investment, cash, and personnel, whereas plans are formalized, long-range programs with more than a one-year horizon. The budget and planning process is the major control instrument in headquarters–subsidiary relationships. Although systems and their execution vary, the objective is to achieve the best fit possible with the objectives and characteristics of the firm and its environment.

The budgetary period is typically one year because budgets are tied to the accounting systems of the company. The budget system is used for four main purposes: (1) allocation of funds among subsidiaries; (2) planning and coordination of global production capacity and supplies; (3) evaluation of subsidiary performance; and (4) communication and information exchange among subsidiaries, product organizations, and corporate headquarters. Long-range plans, on the other hand, extend over periods of two to ten years, and their content is more qualitative and judgmental in nature than that of budgets. Shorter periods, such as two years, are the norm because of the uncertainty of diverse foreign environments.

Although firms strive for uniformity, this may be comparable to trying to design a suit to fit the average person. The budget and planning processes themselves are formalized in terms of the schedules to be followed.

Control can also be seen as a mechanism to secure cooperation of local units. For example, while a company may grant substantial autonomy to a country organization in terms of strategies, headquarters may use allocation of production volume as a powerful tool to ensure compliance. Some of the ways for headquarters to gain cooperation of country organizations are summarized in Exhibit 10.10. Some of the methods used are formal, such as approval of strategic plans and personnel selection, while some are more informal, including personal contact and relationships as well as international networking.[60]

EXHIBIT 10.10 Securing Country-Organization Cooperation

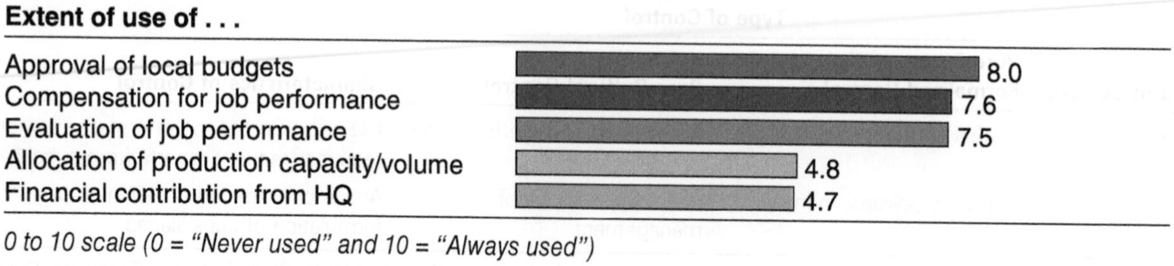

SOURCE: Henry P. Conn and George S. Yip, "Global Transfer of Critical Capabilities," in *Best Practices in International Business*, edited by Michael R. Czinkota and Ilkka A. Ronkainen (Mason, OH: South-Western, 2001): 256–74.

Since the frequency and types of reports to be furnished by subsidiaries are likely to increase due to globalization, it is essential that subsidiaries see the rationale for the often time-consuming task. Two approaches, used in tandem, can facilitate the process: participation and feedback. Involving the preparers of reports in their ultimate use serves to avoid the perception at subsidiary levels that reports are "art for art's sake." When this is not possible, feedback about results and consequences is an alternative. Through this process, communication is also enhanced.

On the behavioral front, headquarters may want to guide the way in which subsidiaries make decisions and implement agreed-upon strategies. U.S.-based multinational companies, relying heavily on manuals for all major functions, tend to be far more formalized than their Asian and European counterparts. The manuals are for functions such as personnel policies for recruitment, training, motivation, and dismissal. The use of policy manuals as a control instrument correlates with the level of reports required from subsidiaries.

Cultural Control

In countries other than the United States, less emphasis is placed on formal controls, which are viewed as rigid and too quantitatively oriented. Rather, the emphasis is on corporate values and culture, and evaluations are based on the extent to which an individual or entity fits in. Cultural controls require an extensive socialization process, and informal, personal interaction is central to the process. Substantial resources must be spent to train the individual to share the corporate culture, that is, "the way things are done at the company." Adding to this need is the increasing cultural diversity at companies. For example, people of 115 different nationalities work at Nokia, and 45 percent of senior management are not Finnish.[61] To build common vision and values, managers spend a substantial amount of their first months at Matsushita in what the company calls "cultural and spiritual training." They study the company credo, the "Seven Spirits of Matsushita," and the philosophy of the founder, Konosuke Matsushita. Then they learn how to translate these internalized lessons into daily behavior and operational decisions. Many Western entities have similar programs, for example, Philip's "organization cohesion training" and Unilever's "indoctrination." This corporate acculturation will be critical to achieve the acceptance of possible transfers of best practice within the organization, as seen in *The International Marketplace 10.4*.

The primary instruments of cultural control are the careful selection and training of corporate personnel and the institution of self-control. The choice of cultural controls rather than bureaucratic controls can be justified if the company enjoys a low turnover rate. Cultural controls are thus applied, for example, when companies offer lifetime or long-term employment, as many Japanese firms do.

THE INTERNATIONAL **MARKETPLACE** **10.4**

Corporate Acculturation

A Toyota concept car.

Toyota has 26 different companies with 317,716 employees around the world, 50 factories outside of Japan, and sells 8,557,351 cars in more than 170 countries. What holds these operations together and makes them part of a cohesive entity is a strong corporate culture.

The "Toyota Way" has seven distinct elements: (1) *Kaizen*, the process of continuous improvement, which has Toyota employees coming back to work each day determined to performing better than the day before; (2) *Genchigenbustu*, which expects fact-based consensus building on defining challenges; (3) *Kakushin*, which focuses on radical innovation in terms of technologies and models; (4) *Challenge*, getting employees to see challenges not as something undesirable but as way to help reach improvements; (5) *Teamwork* to share knowledge with others in the team and to put the company's interests before those of the individual; (6) *Respect* for other people, not just as people but for their skills and special knowledge; and (7) *Customers first, dealers second—and manufacturer last* with the realization that customers pay the salaries, not the company.

Before "hybrid" was in common use, Toyota launched a project to investigate what type of vehicles would be best for the twenty-first century. The scope of research was expanded to include areas such as ease of boarding and exiting, body size, design, and fuel efficiency, as well as twenty-first-century themes including societal issues; and a process of reviewing from the very beginning what a vehicle is and its manufacturing processes was repeatedly carried out.

Between 2009 and 2011, after two separate recalls covering 7.5 million vehicles, Toyota was forced to announce it was suspending the sale of eight of its best-selling vehicles, a move that will cost the company and its dealers a minimum of $54 million a day in lost sales revenue. How did a company that became the world's largest and most profitable automaker on the back of a rock-solid reputation for quality and dependability find itself at the center of the biggest product recall? The challenge is created by two elements of the culture: first, an obsession with quality, which means that anything less than perfection is seen as shameful and embarrassing. As a consequence, problems with quality are literally inconceivable, and denial takes over. The second interlinked element of culture is a hierarchical approach to management and a lack of open communication. Where this exists, junior employees, who are best placed to spot early signs of crisis, feel unable to point out flaws. As a result, problems go unnoticed and unresolved until they explode into a major crisis.

SOURCES: "U.S. Points to Toyota Driver Error," *Wall Street Journal*, February 9, 2011, B1; Jonathan Hemus, "Accelerating towards Crisis: A PR View of Toyota's Recall," *Guardian*, February 9, 2010, 25; Angus MacKenzie and Scott Evans, "The Toyota Recall Crisis," *Motor Trend*, January, 2010; Hirotaka Takeuchi, Emi Osono, and Norihiko Shimizu, "The Contradictions That Drive Toyota's Success," *Harvard Business Review* 86 (June 2008): 96–105; Thomas A. Stewart and Anand P. Raman, "Lessons from Toyota's Long Drive," *Harvard Business Review* 85 (July/August 2007): 74–82; and "Inculcating Culture," *Economist*, January 21, 2006, 11. See also Toyota, www.toyota.co.jp/en/index_company.html.

In selecting home country nationals and, to some extent, third-country nationals, global companies are exercising cultural control. They assume that these managers have already internalized the norms and values of the company and that they tend to run a country operation with a more global view. In some cases, the use of headquarters personnel to ensure uniformity in decision making may be advisable. Expatriates are used in subsidiaries not only for control purposes but also for initiating change and to develop local talent. Companies control the efforts of management specifically through compensation, promotion, and replacement policies.

Management training programs for overseas managers, as well as visits to headquarters, will indoctrinate individuals to the company's way of doing things. Similarly, visits to subsidiaries by headquarters teams will promote a sense of belonging. These may be on a formal basis, as for a strategy audit, or less formal—for example, to launch a new product. Some innovative global marketers assemble temporary teams of their best talent to build local skills. Multinational companies will increasingly have to move people from emerging markets, especially Chinese and Indian managers, into leadership positions. Companies in financial services, consulting, and technology, where opportunities have migrated quickly to China and India, have been among the first to do so. As a bridging mechanism, companies like P&G rotate non-U.S. executives in and out of headquarters. Many corporations, including P&G and Unilever, have asked the China and India heads to report directly to the worldwide CEO or have accorded them the status of regional heads. Samsung's China CEO, for instance, is regarded as one of the company's top three executives worldwide.[62]

Corporations rarely use one pure control mechanism. Rather, emphasis is placed on both quantitative and qualitative measures. Corporations are likely, however, to place different levels of emphasis on the types of performance measures and on the way the measures are taken. To generate global buy-in, annual bonuses have shifted away from the employee's individual unit and towards the company as a whole. This sends a strong signal in favor of collaboration across all boundaries. Other similar approaches exist to motivate and generate changes in thinking. For example, in the past, Kraft has given incentives to the general manager of a country (e.g., China) based on the total performance. Now, bonuses are calculated by weighing the performance of their individual businesses (e.g., China) at 70 percent and the next higher level of aggregation (e.g., Asia-Pacific) at 30 percent. That is just enough to encourage the managers to support the greater good, not just their own individual performance.[63] At BP, for another example, individual performance assessments exclude the effects of the price of oil and foreign exchange because they are outside of the employee's control.[64]

Exercising Control

Within most corporations, different functional areas are subject to different guidelines. The reason is that each function is subject to different constraints and varying degrees of those constraints. For example, marketing as a function has traditionally been seen as incorporating many more behavioral dimensions than do manufacturing or finance. As a result, many multinational corporations employ control systems that are responsive to the needs of the function. Yet such differentiation is sometimes based less on appropriateness than on personality. For example, since Malaysia is an emerging economy in which managerial talent is in short supply, headquarters may want to participate more in all facets of decision making. If a country market witnesses economic or political turmoil, controls may also be tightened to ensure the management of risk.[65]

In their international operations, U.S.-based multinational corporations place major emphasis on obtaining quantitative data. Although this allows for good centralized comparisons against standards and benchmarks, or cross-comparisons between different corporate units, several drawbacks are associated with the undertaking. In the international environment, new dimensions—such as inflation, differing rates of taxation, and exchange rate fluctuations—may distort the performance evaluation of any given individual or organizational unit.

For the global corporation, measuring whether a business unit in a particular country is earning a superior return on investment relative to risk may be irrelevant to the contribution an investment may make worldwide or to the long-term results of the firm. In the short term, the return may even be negative. Therefore, the control mechanism may quite inappropriately indicate reward or punishment. Standardizing the information received may be difficult if the environment fluctuates and requires frequent and major adaptations. Further complicating the issue is the fact that, although quantitative information may be collected monthly or at least quarterly, environmental data may be acquired annually or "now and then," especially when crisis seems to loom on the horizon.

To design a control system that is acceptable not only to headquarters but also to the organization and individuals abroad, a firm must take great care to use only relevant data. Major concerns, therefore, are the data collection process and the analysis and use of data. Evaluators need management information systems that provide for maximum comparability and equity in administering controls. The more behaviorally based and culture-oriented controls are, the more care that needs to be taken.

In designing a control system, management must consider the costs of establishing and maintaining it and weigh the costs against the benefits to be gained. Any control system will require investment in a management structure and in systems design. As an example, consider the costs associated with cultural controls: personal interaction, use of expatriates, and training programs are all quite expensive. Yet these expenses may be justified in savings through lower employee turnover, an extensive worldwide information system, and a potentially improved control system. Moreover, the impact goes beyond the administrative component. If controls are erroneous or too time-consuming, they can slow or misguide the strategy implementation process and thus the overall capability of the firm. The result will be lost opportunity or, worse, increased threats. In addition, time spent on reporting takes time away from other tasks. If reports are seen as marginally useful, the motivation to prepare them will be low. A parsimonious design is therefore imperative. The control system should collect all the information required and trigger all the intervention necessary but should not create a situation that resembles the pulling of strings by a puppeteer.

The impact of the environment must also be taken into account when designing controls. First, the control system should measure only dimensions over which the organization has control. Rewards or sanctions make little sense if they are based on dimensions that may be relevant for overall corporate performance but over which no influence can be exerted—for example, price controls. Neglecting the factor of individual performance capability would send the wrong signals and severely impede the motivation of personnel. Second, control systems should harmonize with local regulations and customs. In some cases, however, corporate behavioral controls have to be exercised against local customs even though overall operations may be affected negatively. This type of situation occurs, for example, when a subsidiary operates in markets where unauthorized facilitating payments are a common business practice.

Corporations are faced with major challenges to adequately control systems in today's business environment. With an increase in local (government) demands for a share in the control of companies established, controls can become tedious, especially if the multinational company is a minority partner. Even in a merger, such as the one between Air France and KLM—or in a new entity formed by two companies, as when Toyota and GM formed NUMMI—the backgrounds of the partners may be sufficiently different to cause problems in terms of the controls.

SUMMARY

The structures, implementation, and control mechanisms needed to operate internationally define relationships between the firm's headquarters and subsidiaries and provide the channels through which these relationships develop. The most fundamental test of organizational design is whether there is a fit with the company's overall marketing strategy and whether it reflects the strengths of the entities within the organization.[66]

International firms can choose from a variety of organizational structures, ranging from a domestic operation that handles ad hoc export orders to a full-fledged global organization. The choice will depend primarily on the degree of internationalization of the firm, the diversity of international activities, and the relative importance of product, area, function, and customer variables in the process. Whatever the choice on structure may be, implementation of the planned strategies is a critical factor determining success. Companies typically realize only 60 percent of their strategies' potential value due to factors such as organizational silos and culture blocking execution.[67] What is critical is that the framework establish a common language for the dialogue between the corporate center and the units, one that the strategy, marketing, and finance teams all understand and use.

The control function is of increasing importance because of the high variability in performance that results from divergent local environments and the need to reconcile local objectives with the corporate goal of synergism. It is important to grant autonomy to country organizations so that they can be responsive to local market needs, but it is equally important to ensure close cooperation between units.

Control can be exercised through bureaucratic means, emphasizing formal reporting and evaluation of benchmark data. It can also be exercised through a cultural control process in which norms and values are understood by individuals and entities that compose the corporation. U.S. firms typically rely more on bureaucratic controls, whereas multinational corporations headquartered in other countries frequently control operations abroad through informal means and rely less on stringent measures.

The implementation of controls requires great sensitivity to behavioral dimensions and to the environment. The measurements used must be appropriate and must reflect actual performance rather than marketplace vagaries. Entities should be measured only on factors over which they have some degree of control.

KEY TERMS

product structure
area structure
functional structure
process structure
customer structure
mixed structure
matrix structure
transnational structure
T-shaped organization
decentralization
centralization
coordinated decentralization
best practice
podcast
webcast
intranet
virtual team
strategic leader
contributor
implementer
black hole
bureaucratic control
cultural control
budget
plan

QUESTIONS FOR DISCUSSION

1. Firms differ, often substantially, in their organizational structures even within the same industry. What accounts for these differences in their approaches?
2. Discuss the benefits gained in adopting a matrix approach in terms of organizational structure.
3. Video Collaboration Studios (VCS) is continually growing new studios globally. The immersive environment created by VCS allows employees to connect face to face from any part of the world as if they were in the same room. These studios greatly reduce the need for travel—saving money and time and reducing carbon footprint. What factors are overlooked?
4. Is there more to the "not-invented-here" syndrome than simply hurt feelings on the part of those who believe they are being dictated to by headquarters?
5. How can systems that are built for global knowledge transfer be used as control tools?
6. "Implementers are the most important country organizations in terms of buy-in for effective global marketing strategy implementation." Comment.

INTERNET EXERCISES

1. Every big company has in-house experts. So why do they not use them more? Search systems that apply social-computing tools such as internal blogs, wikis, and social networks can fill these critical gaps. Posted comments and communication between users help reveal not only who knows what but who is approachable. Cemex (www.cemex.com/AboutUs/OurApproach.aspx) invited 400 employees involved with its ready-mix products to help figure out which products worked best and which were redundant. The result is a slimmed-down product line offered in a constantly updated catalog available globally.
2. See how Dow's "solutionism" (www.dow.com/about/index.htm) is addressing some of the world's biggest challenges. The more we talk together, the more we solve together. Wind turbines today are truly revolutionizing energy generation across the globe. The Orkney Islands provide a glimpse of a renewable future. Cutting-edge wave and tidal technology is regenerating island communities and bringing new jobs and new skills.

CHALLENGE US

Just Right Globalization?

Too little attention to foreign markets seems to result in missed opportunities for sales growth, operational inefficiencies, and the risk of being blindsided by fast-moving international competitors. In companies with large international operations, senior executives who gave too little attention to global issues tended to follow one of two approaches. In the first instance, they forced head-office solutions on overseas subsidiaries using a kind of "my way or the highway" mentality. In the second approach, they delegated primary strategic and operating decision-making authority to foreign subsidiary managers, employing a sort of "it's not my job to worry about these things" mindset. While both approaches may be efficient from a head-office perspective, neither maximizes company performance. Both fail to tap the rich resources of the global company. Both also fail to achieve the learning and best-practice benefits that come through global knowledge sharing and skill generation.

On the other hand, an excessive level of attention to opportunities and threats abroad seems to create even bigger problems. It can lead senior executives to take their minds off potentially more critical issues at home or interfere with the smooth functioning of foreign operations that do not need intense scrutiny from head-office managers. This can also lead to mental overload and exhaustion on the part of members of the top management team. Given the complexity of global markets, staying abreast of and interpreting world events is taxing.

The greater the international experience levels of managers, the greater the benefits that come from global attention. Managers with more international

experience generally had greater ability not only to make sense of rather complex international stimuli but also to process them quickly and in ways that improved the quality of their decision making. Bottom line: if you want to get the most benefit from global attention, put people in place with lots of international experience.

For Discussion

1. What works best if executives want to increase the level of attention their subordinates give to global issues?
2. Managers who use the "Goldilocks scenario" to solve problems may exhaust themselves as they encounter new issues. What can managers do to avoid exhaustion while managing their international offices?

SOURCES: Allen Morrison and Cyril Bouquet, "Are You Giving Globalization the Right Amount of Attention?" *MIT Sloan Management Review* (Winter 2011): 14–16; and Cyril Bouquet, Allen Morrison, and Julian Birkinshaw, "International Attention and Multinational Enterprise Performance," *Journal of International Business Studies* 40, no. 1 (2009): 108–131.

RECOMMENDED READINGS

Bartlett, Christopher, and Paul Beamish. *Transnational Management: Text, Cases, and Readings in Cross-Border Management.* New York: McGraw-Hill, 2010.

Bartlett, Christopher, and Sumantra Ghoshal. *Managing across Borders.* Cambridge, MA: Harvard Business School Press, 2002.

Doz, Yves, and Mikko Kosonen. *Fast Strategy.* New York: Pearson Prentice Hall, 2008.

Galbraith, Jay R. *Designing Matrix Organizations That Actually Work: How IBM, Procter & Gamble, and Others Design for Success.* New York: Jossey-Bass, 2008.

Ghemawat Pankaj. *Redefining Global Strategy: Crossing Borders in a World Where Differences Still Matter.* Cambridge, MA: Harvard Business School Press, 2007.

Govindarajan, Vijay, and Robert Anthony. *Management Control Systems.* New York: McGraw-Hill/Irwin, 2006.

Gupta, Anil K., Vijay Govindarajan, and Haiyan Wang. *The Quest for Global Dominance: Transforming Global Presence into Global Competitive Advantage.* New York: Jossey-Bass, 2008.

ENDNOTES

1. Jonathan D. Day, "The Value of Organizing," *McKinsey Quarterly*, June 2003; and Jonathan D. Day, "Organizing for Growth," *McKinsey Quarterly*, May 2001.
2. Lawrence M. Fischer, "Thought Leader," *Strategy+Business* 7 (fourth quarter, 2002): 115–23.
3. "Social Technologies on the Front Line: The Management 2.0 M-Prize Winners," *McKinsey Quarterly*, September 2011.
4. "Partners in Wealth," *Economist*, January 21, 2006, 16–17.
5. LIMA, www.licensing.org.
6. Jay R. Galbraith, *Designing the Global Corporation* (New York: Jossey-Bass, 2005), chapter 3.
7. General Mills, www.generalmills.com/en/Company.aspx.
8. Anil K. Gupta, Vijay Govindarajan, and Haiyan Wang, *The Quest for Global Dominance: Transforming Global Presence into Global Competitive Advantage* (New York: Jossey-Bass, 2008), chapters 1 and 2.
9. "Ford Tries a Global Campaign for Its Global Car," *New York Times*, February 24, 2011, B4; and Ford, www.ford.com.
10. Dura Automotive Systems, Inc. "DURA Automotive Systems Announces Global Reorganization and Other Business Updates," press release, October 13, 2008.
11. Pankaj Ghemawat, "Regional Strategies for Global Leadership," *Harvard Business Review* 83 (December 2005): 98–105.
12. "Boeing's Defense Unit to Divide Its Operations into 3 Segments," *Wall Street Journal*, January 28, 2006, A5.
13. "The New Organization," *Economist*, January 21, 2006, 3–5.
14. Nestlé, www.nestle.com/AboutUs/GlobalPresence/Pages/Global-Presence.aspx.
15. Christopher A. Bartlett and Sumantra Ghoshal, *Managing across Borders* (Cambridge, MA: Harvard Business School Press, 2002), chapter 10.
16. ABB, www.abb.com/cawp/abbzh252/9c53e7b73aa42f7ec1256ae700541c35.aspx.
17. Milton Harris and Artur Raviv, "Organization Design," *Management Science* 48 (July 2002): 852–65.
18. Transnational Organization, www.enotes.com/management-encyclopedia/transnational-organization.
19. Stéphane J. G. Girod, Joshua B. Bellin, and Robert J. Thomas, "Are Emerging-Market Multinationals Creating the Global Operating Models of the Future?" *Accenture*, May 26, 2009, www.accenture.com/us-en/Pages/insight-emerging-market-multinationals-creating-global-operating-models-future-summary.aspx.
20. Nirmalya Kumar and Phanish Puranam, "Have You Restructured for Global Success?" *Harvard Business Review* 89 (October 2011): 123–28.
21. C.K. Prahalad and Hrishi Bhattacharyya, "Twenty Hubs and No HQ," *Strategy+Business*, Spring 2008, 1–6.
22. Mohanbir Sawhney, "Don't Homogenize, Synchronize," *Harvard Business Review* 79 (July–August 2001): 100–108.
23. Gerard Fairtlough, *The Three Ways of Getting Things Done* (London: Triarchy Press, 2005), chapters 3 and 4.
24. Ilkka A. Ronkainen, "Thinking Globally, Implementing Successfully," *International Marketing Review* 13, no. 3 (1996): 4–6.

25. "Why Multiple Headquarters Multiply," *Wall Street Journal*, November 19, 2007, B1, B3.
26. Andrew Campbell, Sven Kunisch, and Günter Müller-Stewens, "To Centralize or Not to Centralize?" *McKinsey Quarterly* 41, no. 3 (2011): 97–102; Jack Neff, "Unilever Reorganization Shifts P&L Responsibility," *Advertising Age*, February 28, 2005, 13; and "Despite Revamp, Unwieldy Unilever Falls Behind Rivals," *Wall Street Journal*, January 3, 2005, A1, A5.
27. Russell Eisenstat, Nathaniel Foote, Jay Galbraith, and Danny Miller, "Beyond the Business Unit," *McKinsey Quarterly* 37, no. 1 (2001): 180–95.
28. Giancarlo Ghislanzoni, Risto Penttinen, and David Turnbull, "The Multilocal Challenge: Managing Cross-border Functions," *McKinsey Quarterly*, March 2008, 70–81.
29. Stéphane J.G. Girod, Joshua B. Bellin, and Robert J. Thomas, "Are Emerging-Market Multinationals Creating the Global Operating Models of the Future?" Accenture, research report, May 2009.
30. Halliburton, www.halliburton.com.
31. Yum! Brands, www.yum.com.
32. Sanjay Khosla, Kraft International presentation at McDonough, Georgetown University, November 4, 2009; and Mike Gambrell, Dow Chemical Company, speech at Emerging Markets Summit 2008, September 23, 2008.
33. "Big and No Longer Blue," *Economist*, January 21, 2006, 15; and "Beyond Blue," *Businessweek*, April 18, 2005, 68–76.
34. The Coca Cola Company, 2011 annual review; and Nestlé, www.nestle.com.
35. JWT Inside, www.jwt.com/search/case+studies.
36. Carlos Ghosn, "Saving the Business without Losing the Company," *Harvard Business Review* 80 (January 2002): 37–45.
37. Julian Birkinshaw and Tony Sheehan, "Managing the Knowledge Life Cycle," *Sloan Management Review* 44 (Fall 2002): 75–83.
38. Gary L. Neilson, Karla L. Martin, and Elizabeth Powers, "The Secrets to Successful Strategy Execution," *Harvard Business Review* 86 (June 2008): 61–70.
39. Procter and Gamble, 2009 annual report, http://annualreport.pg.com/annualreport2009/leadership/index.shtml, accessed November 22, 2009.
40. General Electric, www.ge.com/company/leadership/executives.html, accessed November 22, 2009.
41. Beth Stackpole, "Boeing's Global Collaboration Environment Pioneers Groundbreaking 787 Dreamliner Development Effort," *Design News*, May 14, 2007.
42. The ABB Group, www.abb.com, accessed September 22, 2011.
43. Mark Little, "Using Rivalry to Spur Innovation," *McKinsey Quarterly*, May 2010, 113–17.
44. Lowell L. Bryan, Eric Matson, and Leigh M. Weiss, "Harnessing the Power of Informal Employee Networks," *McKinsey Quarterly*, June 2007, 32–37; and "GE Mentoring Program Turns Underlings into Teachers of the Web," *Wall Street Journal*, February 15, 2000, B1, B16.
45. Laurel Wentz, "TBWA Worldwide: How to Behave as a Network," *Advertising Age*, January 9, 2009.
46. Linda S. Sanford and Dave Taylor, *Let Go to Grow* (Englewood Cliffs, NJ: Prentice Hall, 2007), chapter 1.
47. David A. Griffith and Michael G. Harvey, "An Intercultural Communication Model for Use in Global Interorganizational Networks," *Journal of International Marketing* 9, no. 3 (2001): 87–103.
48. Keith Epstein Grow and Chi-Dhu Tschang, "The New E-spionage Threat," *BusinessWeek*, April 10, 2008.
49. Gary A. Curtis, Kelly Dempski, and Catherine S. Farley, "Does Your Company Have an IT Generation Gap?" Accenture report, October 2009.
50. Arindan Bhattacharya and David Michael, "How Local Companies Keep Multinationals at Bay," *Harvard Business Review* 86 (March 2008): 85–95
51. "Mercedes-Benz Advanced Design Studio—Irvine, California," *Car Body Design*, June 2, 2008.
52. IBM, "IBM Scientists First to Image the 'Anatomy' of a Molecule," www.zurich.ibm.com/news/09/pentacene.html.
53. Cyril Bouquet and Julian Birkinshaw, "Weight versus Voice: How Foreign Subsidiaries Gain Attention from Corporate Headquarters," *Academy of Management Journal* 51 (June 2008): 577–601.
54. "A European Electronics Giant Races to Undo Mistakes in the U.S.," *Wall Street Journal*, January 7, 2004, A1, A10.
55. "India's First Wal-Mart Draws Excitement, Not Protest: Venture Comes with Limits That Protect Merchants," *Washington Post*, July 13, 2009.
56. Julian Birkinshaw and Neil Hood, "Unleash Innovation in Foreign Subsidiaries," *Harvard Business Review* 79 (March 2001): 131–37; and Julian Birkinshaw and Nick Fry, "Subsidiary Initiatives to Develop New Markets," *Sloan Management Review* 39 (Spring 1998): 51–61.
57. Robert Newton and Vijay Govindarajan, *Management Control Systems* (New York: McGraw-Hill/Irwin, 2006), chapter 1.
58. Kenneth Merchant and Wim Van der Stede, *Management Control Systems: Performance Measurement, Evaluation and Incentives* (New York: Prentice Hall, 2007).
59. Cheryl Nakata, "Activating the Marketing Concept in a Global Context," *International Marketing Review* 19, no. 1 (2002): 39–64.
60. Henry P. Conn and George S. Yip, "Global Transfer of Critical Capabilities," in *Best Practices in International Business*, edited by Michael R. Czinkota and Ilkka A. Ronkainen (Mason, OH: South-Western, 2001): 256–74.
61. Nokia, www.nokia.com/global/about-nokia/about-us/culture/our-people-and-culture.
62. Nirmalya Kumar and Phanish Puranam, "Have You Restructured for Global Success?" *Harvard Business Review* 89 (October 2011): 123–28.
63. Introduced by Chairman and CEO Irene Rosenfeld, "Inside the Kraft Foods Transformation," *Strategy+Business*, August 27, 2009.
64. "Thinking for a Living," *Economist*, January 21, 2006, 9–12.
65. Ron Edwards, Adlina Ahmad, and Simon Moss, "Subsidiary Autonomy: The Case of Multinational Subsidiaries in Malaysia," *Journal of International Business Studies* 33, no. 1 (2002): 183–91.
66. Michael Goold and Andrew Campbell, "Do You Have a Well-Designed Organization?" *Harvard Business Review* 80 (March 2002): 117–24.
67. Michael C. Mankins and Richard Steele, "Turning Great Strategy into Great Performance," *Harvard Business Review* 83 (July–August 2005): 65–72.

CASES

PART 2

Working towards Better Vision

Since 1992, Essilor had been the world leader in corrective lenses with €3.8 billion annual revenue (approximately $5.6 billion). Although the global market was growing slowly at approximately 3 to 4 percent, Essilor was able to achieve high profits and sales growth. The economic downturn in the U.S. and Europe did not affect its financial performance. In 2010, many large optical lens manufacturers faced financial hardship, but Essilor earned net profits of 11 percent. The company planned to maintain its leading position as well as its sales growth and profits.

COMPANY BACKGROUND

Essilor International S.A. was a French company that manufactured ophthalmic lenses and ophthalmic optical equipment. Formed in 1972, Essilor was formed from a merger between Essel, a small network of eyeglass assembly workshops, and Silor, a lens manufacturer. In the late 1970s, Essilor started to pursue a geographical expansion strategy by acquiring manufacturing plants in the U.S., Ireland, and the Philippines. Subsequently, Essilor transferred part of its lens production to emerging markets and expanded its sales in other countries. Geographical expansion was achieved by acquiring the local distributor, setting up new subsidiaries, or partnering with local companies. Since 2003, Essilor had acquired close to 100 companies, primarily in the prescription laboratory market, and formed partnerships with more than 60 companies worldwide. In 2010, the company operated in over 100 countries by owning three R&D centers, 14 manufacturing facilities, 332 prescription laboratories, and 12 distribution centers.

The scope of its business operations was rather concentrated. Essilor was heavily dependent on its corrective lens segment, which contributed 93 percent of the company's total revenues. In the fragmented global ophthalmic industry, Essilor was the market leader with only 27 percent share. Europe and the U.S. were its major markets, contributing over 80 percent of its revenue.

EXHIBIT 1 Essilor's Financial Performance

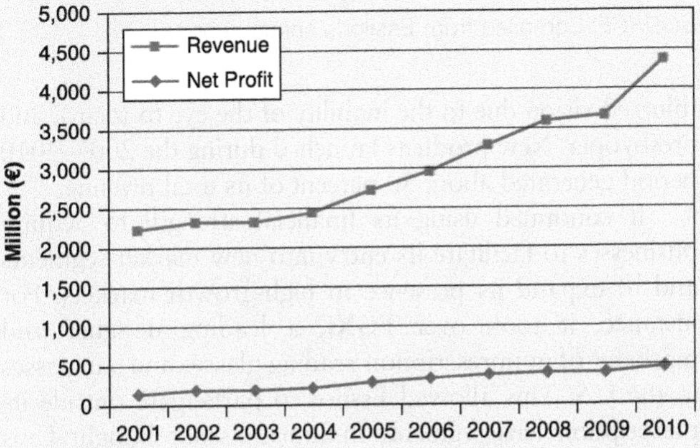

SOURCE: Compiled from Essilor's annual reports.

ESSILOR'S STRATEGY

The success of Essilor rested on its product innovation, efficient distribution network, and production tooling. To meet the demands of customers (both optical professionals and consumers), it developed a large number of new products combining different materials, optical surfaces, and coatings. For instance, sun protection lenses were designed for athletic presbyopes (people with farsightedness due to aging), and computer lenses for those presbyopic glass wearers who experience tired eyes, blurred vision, headaches, or neck and shoulder pain. Essilor had the largest product offering in the market with 580,000 product items. Through a broad range of lenses, Essilor could provide solutions for correcting myopia (nearsightedness), hypermetropia (farsightedness caused by eye imperfections), astigmatism

SOURCE: This case was prepared by associate professor Nittaya Wongtada, NIDA Business School, National Institute of Development Administration (NIDA), Thailand; and Philippe Bonnet, vice president North Asia, group HR director, and global head for learning and education, Essilor International. It is for classroom discussion only and does not intend to reflect the ability of the management.

EXHIBIT 2 Essilor's Revenue from Different Markets

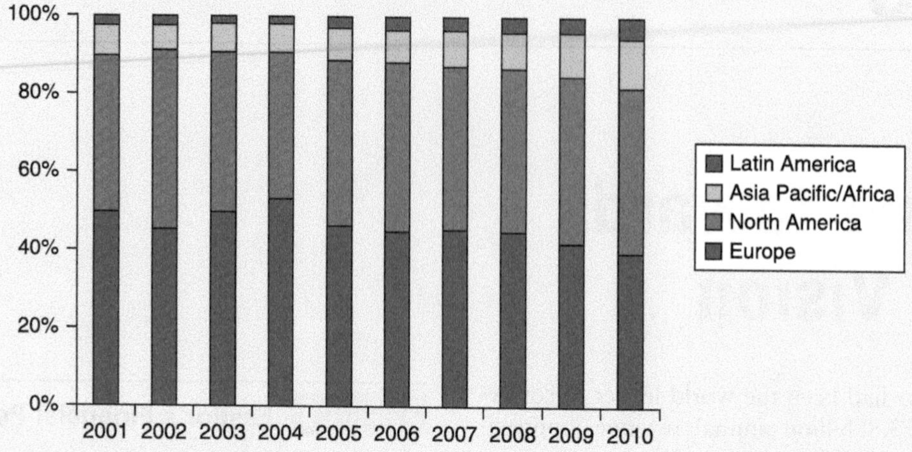

SOURCE: Compiled from Essilor's annual reports.

(blurred vision due to the inability of the eye to focus), and presbyopia. New products launched during the 2007–2010 period generated about 50 percent of its total revenue.

It continued using its financial strength to acquire businesses to facilitate its entry into new market segments and to expand its presence in high-growth markets. For instance, it took over FGXI, a leading designer and marketer of nonprescription reading glasses and sunglasses in the U.S. This allowed Essilor to participate outside its prescription lens segment. In India, Essilor bought Lens and Spects Inc., a distributor with two prescription laboratories in four cities in western India. This helped Essilor to gain a strong foothold in one of the fastest growing markets. The company also invested heavily in logistics to distribute lenses to retailers.

BUSINESS SEGMENTS

Essilor operated in three business segments: optical lenses and instruments, equipment, and nonprescription glasses. For optical lenses and instruments, the company designed, manufactured, and customized corrective lenses to meet individual users' vision requirements. It also sold lens edging instruments to opticians and prescription laboratories, and vision screening instruments to eye care professionals, schools, and other institutional users. The nonprescription glasses segment consisted of premade vision-corrective glasses that users purchased without a prescription. Many nonophthalmic stores sold these glasses on an over-the-counter basis. In 2010, the lens and optical instruments business represented 93 percent of Essilor's revenue.

Exhibit 3 classifies the optical lens market based on price levels, life-styles, and product benefits. For the high-end market, Essilor offered several brands covering various situations as part of the "modern-life and aging," "outdoor," and "active" lifestyles. For example, Varilux Progressive lenses provided clear natural vision at all distances. The Crizal brand had the benefits of antireflective lenses, and antiscratch and antistatic surface coatings. Antifatigue lenses were advanced single vision lenses specially designed to relieve the symptoms of visual fatigue from reading or computer usage. In the mid-range price and entry level segments, Essilor had more limited product choices.

Approximately half of Essilor's revenue derived from selling antireflective lenses, followed by easy cleaning and progressive lenses. For antireflective lenses, some countries like Japan and Germany had reached a high saturation level while penetration rate was low in, for example, France and the U.S. Other new premium lenses such as antifatigue lenses and those for computer use still accounted for only a small fraction of Essilor's total lens production. (View an example of Essilor's commercial on a new lens at: www.youtube.com/watch?v=aEW42M0X534.)

THE OPHTHALMIC LENS INDUSTRY STRUCTURE

Eyeglasses were distributed through two major channels—the channel for prescription lenses (RX), and another for premade over-the-counter glasses (OTC glasses). The market size for prescription lenses was larger with about 1 billion RX lenses produced annually while the OTC market was only 200 million lenses.

In acquiring prescription lenses, users visit an optical eyeglass store to select frames and semifinished lenses, have their eyes tested, and pick up new glasses at the store after the lenses are returned from a prescription laboratory. A prescription laboratory finishes semifinished lenses based on individual specifications. For the OTC market, users can obtain premade glasses immediately.

EXHIBIT 3 **Essilor's Brands and Markets**

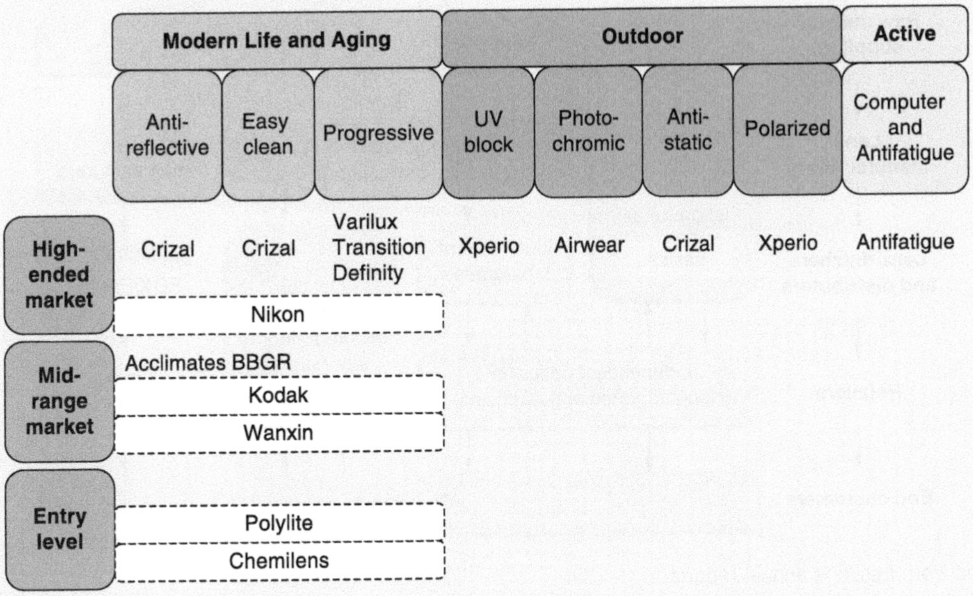

SOURCE: Adapted from Essilor's annual reports.

The global prescription lens industry was organized into four distinct businesses according to the stages in fitting lenses to individual needs: raw materials suppliers, lens manufacturers, lens finishers and distributors, and retailers.

Raw Materials Suppliers

Basic materials were composed of glass and polymerizable thermoset resins and injectable thermoplastic resins. Glass manufacturers developed and made glass lenses. Chemical companies sold polymerizable thermoset resins and injectable thermoplastic resins for plastic lenses.

Lens Manufacturers

Using these raw materials, lens manufacturers produced single-vision finished lenses and a variety of semifinished lenses. There were about 150 to 200 small operators for prescription glasses worldwide and 200 to 300 manufacturers for nonprescription lens manufacturers.

Lens Finishers and Distributors

Based on the specifications from a retail optical shop, a prescription laboratory polished the semifinished lenses and then applied coatings. The coating options included tinting, anti-UV, scratch-proofing, antireflective, smudge-proofing, antistatic, light-filtering, and others. Approximately 1,500 to 2,000 operators worldwide served as laboratories and distributors.

Retailers

There were a large number of optical outlets in the world, and the retail structures in different countries varied. For instance, there were 14,000 optical stores and 16,000 optometrist's offices in the U.S. The opticians' stores in the U.S. were rather concentrated, controlled by the 50 largest optical chains, such as Luxottica (LensCrafters and Pearle Vision), U.S. Vision, and Eye Care Centers of America.[1] Together they held about 60 percent of the market share. In India, the retail optical sector was more fragmented with more than 3.5 million outlets. These outlets were small, and large optical chains accounted for less than 4 percent. Indians living in remote areas did not have access to optical shops.

Essilor bought chemicals and glass from manufacturers around the world. It functioned as a lens manufacturer and owned prescription laboratories in various parts of the globe. It supplied ophthalmic lenses to optical retailers and chains worldwide and sold edging-mounting instruments and laboratory equipment to prescription laboratories. It also helped retailers in promoting its lenses to customers. It did not acquire retail operations since this would compete directly with independent retailers who influenced consumers' choices of lenses. Nevertheless, in some emerging economies like India where retail outlets were limited, Essilor cooperated with a not-for-profit charitable eye hospital to send mobile eye clinics to villages in rural south India. These mobile units were equipped with modern comprehensive eye examination instruments. (View Essilor India's Rural Marketing Initiatives at: www.youtube.com/watch?v=KJbMsCZPLnA.)

For the nonprescription market, spectacles were sold in pharmacies, grocery stores, mass merchandisers, other retail outlets, and eyeglass websites without a prescription. By acquiring FGX International in 2010, Essilor had entered into this market segment. FGX was the North American leader in the design and sale of reading glasses and sun glasses. Its glasses were distributed in North

EXHIBIT 4 Ophthalmic Lens Industry Structure

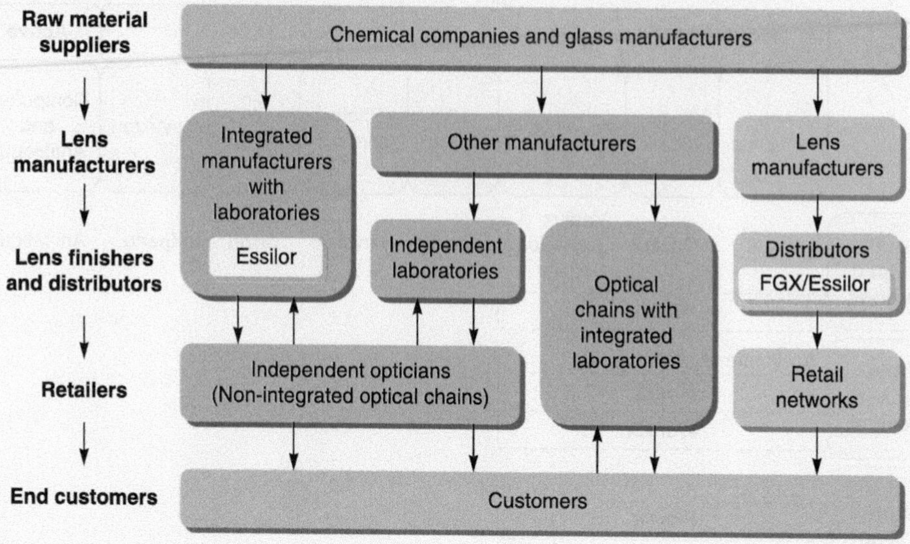

SOURCE: Adapted from Essilor's annual reports.

America (the U.S., Canada, and Mexico) and the United Kingdom. The customers of FGX International were large retail companies (Walmart, Target, etc.), pharmacies (Walgreens, CVS, etc.), specialized retail outlets (Barnes & Noble, etc.), and airport and rail station boutiques.

TRENDS IN THE OPTICAL INDUSTRY

The ophthalmic optical market was affected by several trends, which would influence the growth of this industry.

Demographics

Numerous demographic factors favored the increasing need for eyeglasses. Several factors contributed to this potential industry growth. Nearsightedness, especially in younger adults, was caused by hereditary factors and the visual stress of too much close work. In 2010, there were approximately 2 billion people with nearsightedness; this was projected to be 2.1 billion in 2050. The size of the older population with farsightedness was about 2 billion, expected to grow to 3.8 billion by 2050. Corrective lenses were the cheapest option for age-related farsightedness. Other vision problems also increased as the world's population expanded.

Retailing

The retail market for optical products in developed countries was facing some structural changes. Retail chains already controlled about half of the U.S. market. In Europe, chains and buying groups together accounted for the majority of the market. For example, in Germany, Fielman was estimated to control 25 percent of the market in terms of value and 45 percent in terms of volume. This trend could spread to other parts of the world. The ongoing retail consolidation would further reduce the bargaining power of lens manufacturers. Typically, gross margins of lens manufacturers were lower for products distributed through chains. Although the volume of corrective lenses sold through the Internet was still relatively low, purchasing eyeglasses through this new outlet had gained more acceptance among price conscious buyers. A buyer could get her eyes tested and send her prescription to an online vendor.

Geographic Locations

The number of lenses and selling prices were related closely to GDP per capita. Low-income countries tended to use cheap mineral lenses. As incomes rose, mineral lenses were replaced by basic plastic lenses and, subsequently, by premium lenses such as those with multicoating layers and antiglare lenses. Developed countries with a high GDP per capita such as the U.S., France, the UK, Germany, and Spain were the primary markets for glasses. Although these countries would continue to be important, their market growth rates were low. In contrast, emerging markets like China, India, Indonesia, Mexico, and Brazil had more growth potential. However, much of the population in developing countries who needed eyeglasses did not have access to eye care or were unable to afford eyeglasses.

Substitute Products

Instead of wearing glasses, contact lenses and Lasik surgery to correct eyesight were alternatives. The worldwide contact lens market was estimated at $6.1 billion in 2010 and projected to be $11.7 billion by 2015. Despite the popularity of contact lenses, many users still wore both contacts and glasses. Also, there were more than 18 million people who had Lasik surgery. However, the operation was still costly, and not all eyeglass wearers were good candidates for Lasik surgery. Only those who did not have problems with cornea disease, dry eyes, unstable diabetes, or arthritis were appropriate for the Lasik procedure.

Replacement Markets

Replacements controlled the majority of the industry sales volume. Eyeglasses needed to be maintained and inspected regularly. If there were scratches on the surface of a lens, its optical corrective performance would deteriorate. However, many people kept their eyeglasses beyond their service life, especially during times of economic hardship. They waited until the eyeglasses broke or could not be used anymore.

Insurance Programs

In several developed countries, state social security systems partially reimbursed prescriptions. The high government deficits in these countries may lead to the removal of prescription lenses from the list of reimbursable items. This would affect the demand for eyeglasses and corrective lenses in these lucrative markets.

COMPETITION

Although the optical market was fragmented, composed of a large number of small local players, there were several multinational optical companies operating in this industry such as Hoya, Carl Zeiss-Sola, Rodenstock, Seiko, and Indo. As the market leader, Essilor was more than three times larger than the second largest operator, Hoya. Essilor operated only in the corrective lens segment, while most of its competitors had expanded into related industries.

Hoya

It was the first specialized manufacturer of optical glass products in Japan. Its businesses were in the areas of optical technology, including electronics, photonics, eye care, and health care. For visual care, Hoya was a manufacturer of specialty lens designs that incorporated optics with high-end materials and coatings. Revenue from visual care products accounted for a quarter of its revenue. Like Essilor, Hoya took pride in innovation. For instance, its measuring devices and software were installed at eyeglass retailers to help customers get lenses customized for their prescriptions, frame and face shapes, and individual lifestyles. It also owned a chain of contact lens specialty stores in Japan. Although Hoya was represented in over 30 countries worldwide, Japan and other Asian countries were its main markets. The company controlled the largest market share in Japan but was the second largest player in the global market. In 2010, Hoya experienced lower revenues as a result of the declining population in Japan and falling prices in several countries.

Carl Zeiss-Sola

The company was established from the merger between Sola Optical and the ophthalmic lens division of German manufacturer Carl Zeiss in 2005. It operated in 30 countries. In addition to producing ophthalmic lenses and lens coatings, Carl Zeiss was in the business of semiconductor technology, medical systems, and microscopy. While Hoya and Essilor had acquired prescription laboratories, Carl Zeiss did not enter the lab business. Instead, it supported independent laboratories to compete with the integrated laboratories.

Rodenstock

The company was a German manufacturer of ophthalmic lenses and spectacle frames. It specialized in producing high-quality optical lenses for cameras and enlargers. It was the fourth largest lens manufacturer in the global market, operating in more than 80 countries with sales subsidiaries and distribution partners. Rodenstock had 14 production sites for ophthalmic lenses in 12 countries. In 2009, Rodenstock achieved record annual revenue of €345 million.

QUESTIONS FOR DISCUSSION

1. How was Essilor able to achieve outstanding financial performance? Did it employ strategies differently from other lens manufacturers?
2. What were the opportunities and threats in the optical industry? How did these trends affect industry growth?
3. In order to sustain strong financial performance, what options did Essilor have? How should it expand geographically, if at all? Should its marketing strategies differ between advanced and lesser developed countries?

ENDNOTES

The information on this case is extracted from annual reports of Essilor, Hoya, Carl Zeiss-Sola, and Rodenstock.

1. An optometrist is a general eye doctor who can do eye exams and prescribe corrective lenses. An optician adjusts and fits glasses according to the optometrist's prescription.

La Casa de Las Botas

What do the following people have in common: the founder of a world famous Italian fashion brand (Luciano Benetton), a U.S. actress and wildlife preservationist (Stephanie Powers), the Prime Minister of Malaysia (Dato' Sri Mohd Najib), the two daughters of a former U.S. President (Jenna and Barbara Bush), and Olympic athletes from around the world (e.g., Frederic Cottier and Martin Mallo)? Imagine boots, but beautiful leather boots, custom-made by La Casa de Las Botas. There is nowhere better in the world to buy exquisitely handcrafted riding boots than in the Argentine capital.

Because of the high profile of their customers, La Casa de Las Botas could be one of these fancy companies with luxurious retail space in downtown Buenos Aires. Far from being the case, the little workshop is located about 10 kilometers to the West. Contrasting with chaotic parts of town, this quiet side of the Palermo neighborhood offers the charms of old-fashioned cobbled streets, shaded by tall *jacaranda* trees. With an utterly unnoticeable façade and a 160 square foot showroom, La Casa de Las Botas is nothing but modest and traditional. Almost every day of the year, el Señor Jorge Da Silva Villagrán, the company founder and owner, supervises the ten highly trained craftsmen he employs in a little workshop, at the back of the showroom. One of his two sons regularly comes and gives a hand in marketing and selling their luxury boots. Being the only one in the company who speaks English, the young man is especially helpful with foreign customers. Even though the walls of the showroom are covered with autographed pictures from the many celebrities among their customers, it is hard to imagine the international success of this small company, shipping products to over 15 countries.

BEGINNINGS AND BUSINESS PHILOSOPHY

Jorge Da Silva Villagrán was born in Uruguay in 1952. In his early twenties, Jorge decided to make the three hour-boat trip from Montevideo to Buenos Aires and try his luck at working in the large neighboring country. He first started as an apprentice for the Pierri Company, a renowned workshop for equestrian boots. During the following 15 years, Jorge learned all of the techniques and secrets for manufacturing first-class leather boots, from European (mainly French and Italian) emigrants. In 1989, Jorge Da Silva Villagrán chose to buy the business from Mr. Pierri who was retiring along with several of his employees. Jorge renamed the firm La Casa de Las Botas and first specialized in riding boots. Soon, he created a new line of fashion boots to attract non-horse-riding customers. From the beginning, Jorge applied a business philosophy entirely oriented towards product quality and customer satisfaction.

> *"I keep telling my employees that the work they do must always be beyond reproach. I tell them: do not forget that what you are making a living out of are the boots. Remember to always respect the client's money. [...] We cannot tell a client that his boots are not ready. The company's response to customer requests after delivery is also very important; we have to respect the client. Respect is essential to growth."* [Interview, May 2010]

THE INTERNATIONALIZATION OF A SMALL COMPANY

Starting in 2000 with the set-up of the company website, La Casa de Las Botas internationalized. Using a predesigned form, customers from any location in the world could order a pair of custom boots. By 2010, about 60 percent of overall sales were made outside of Argentina. Customers reside in all of Latin America (especially in Mexico, Costa Rica, Panama, Bolivia, Ecuador, Chile, and Brazil) but also in Europe, the United States, Japan, Hong Kong, and the United Arab Emirates. Jorge mainly saw further growth opportunities further penetrating first-world markets. Emerging markets (such as Russia, India, South Africa, and Turkey) could also represent avenues for future development. Indeed, new elite classes with high purchasing power all around the world were eagerly "westernizing" their lifestyle and consuming fashionable and luxury products, such as equestrian boots. Yet, the issue for La Casa de Las Botas was not simply to acquire and retain customers. In 2010, a thoughtful strategic marketing plan was needed to maintain the benefits from international expansion while avoiding its pitfalls.

On the one hand, Jorge was not interested in expanding his business significantly. Selling better, yes, but not necessarily selling more. Moving production up to larger quantities risked going against La Casa de Las Botas' high standards of quality and customer service. The products could not be standardized and their

SOURCE: This case was written by Aurelia Durand, Universidad DiTella, Argentina (now at HEC Montréal, Canada). Jorge Da Silva Villagrán, interview April, May, July 2010, www.casadelasbotas.com.ar.

exclusivity was part of the company's positioning. In addition, expanding foreign sales would continue to strain limited production capacities. Because good employees for manufacturing boots were difficult to find and took a long time to train (about five years are needed to reach the required "savoir-faire") and because of current space limitations (which may require ultimately a move to a new facility), Jorge was not willing to hire and increase the workforce. A common belief in Argentina is that the economy will collapse every 8 to 10 years. The 2001 economic meltdown was still very memorable. For Jorge, maintaining his business in the long run was far more important than any spectacular short term peak in business development. Finally, none of Jorge's sons were interested in taking over the family business. Considering all these elements and his retirement sometime within the next decade, Jorge was not highly motivated to undergo major changes.

On the other hand, production capacity could still be improved (by some 20 percent) with current resources. Furthermore, the foreign markets which contributed to stabilizing incomes over the year were especially attractive. Indeed, some seasonality in the riding boots business could be observed with slower sales in the equestrian "offseason" in the Southern hemisphere offset by increased sales in the Northern hemisphere. The company could therefore benefit from complementary foreign markets and exploit the link between climate and intensity of equestrian activities. In addition, international sales helped mitigate fluctuations due to economic slowdowns around the world.

> *"The way of marketing products has changed with globalization and the Internet. For some companies, globalization has been hurtful, for others—like us—it has been beneficial. For those who have found a way to enter international markets, the Internet has been a real work tool. [...] All countries do not experience economic turndowns the same way or at the same time. Despite the current world crisis and demand slowing down in many of our markets, we have received a wealth of orders from Australia. Apparently, Australia was not impacted as hard as others and we have received many orders from this country last year."* [Interview, April 2010]

ON EXPLAINING SUCCESS FROM ARGENTINA

In the custom-made boot business, key success factors revolve around product quality and a good corporate reputation, maintained over time. The quality of boots is dependent on two main elements: skins and skills. Surprisingly, Argentina did not seem to produce the kind of superior quality in skins suggested by its worldwide leadership in meat exports. Leather treatment and availability were certainly not the issue. Instead, volume-oriented techniques used to raise the cattle and a fragmented supply chain impeded the development of a strong competitive advantage in leather (against world famous Italian leathers, for instance). To produce superior quality, upstream supply chain actors in Argentina needed to understand the value of abandoning both barbed wires for fences and the use of branding irons for marking the cattle. A more efficient control of ticks and other parasites would contribute to obtain better skins without scratches and marks. The quality of skins and of cuts was indeed of central importance for boot making as well as for other specialty leather-based manufacturing. For instance, stories abounded of Brazilian and Argentinean saddle manufacturers importing leather from Italy for their production. Exhibit 1 illustrates the main activities and actors involved in the value chain.

Las Botas had managed to develop reliable local procurement sources. Skills in selecting the leather and in measuring for a perfect fit of the boots were fundamental for being competitive in the custom-made business. Finally, the creativity and know-how to interpret customers' personal desires were also considered key factors in producing high-value boots.

In terms of corporate reputation, the quality of products as described previously was an obvious primary success factor. In addition, customer service and personalized attention were critical for both the Equestrian and Fashion segments. Service to customers often took the form of answering questions in the pre-purchase phase (about the quality of the boots, how they were made, what were the payment options, what would happen if the boots did not fit perfectly) and in addressing after-sale situations (adjusting the boots to weight loss or gain, for instance). Business stability over time was the key to build trust and long-term relationships with customers. Since the lifetime of boots was of about ten to fifteen years, a long-term horizon was most important for capturing re-purchases and building up word-of- mouth recommendations.

All these factors explained the international competitiveness of La Casa de Las Botas. Yet, when compared to direct competitors, the company hardly differentiated its offer. Full customization, technical know-how and innovative designs in products, as well as personalized attention in customer service, were also offered by most competitors in Italy, the U.K., and Russia. In this case, a positive "country of origin" effect seemed to play an important role in explaining the company's international success. Indeed, Argentina is well-known for some products, places, and activities such as quality meat and wine, polo, tango music and dancing, clothing and design, soccer champions and fervor, and last but not least, Patagonia and "Pampa" field with their many cows, horses and gauchos. Interestingly, wearing boots like the classy ones produced by La Casa de las Botas is highly relevant in most "typical" contexts (let alone playing soccer and dancing tango, for obvious reasons). The company's products somehow encapsulated authentic Argentine experiences.

EXHIBIT 1 An Illustration of the Value Chain for Custom Leather Boots

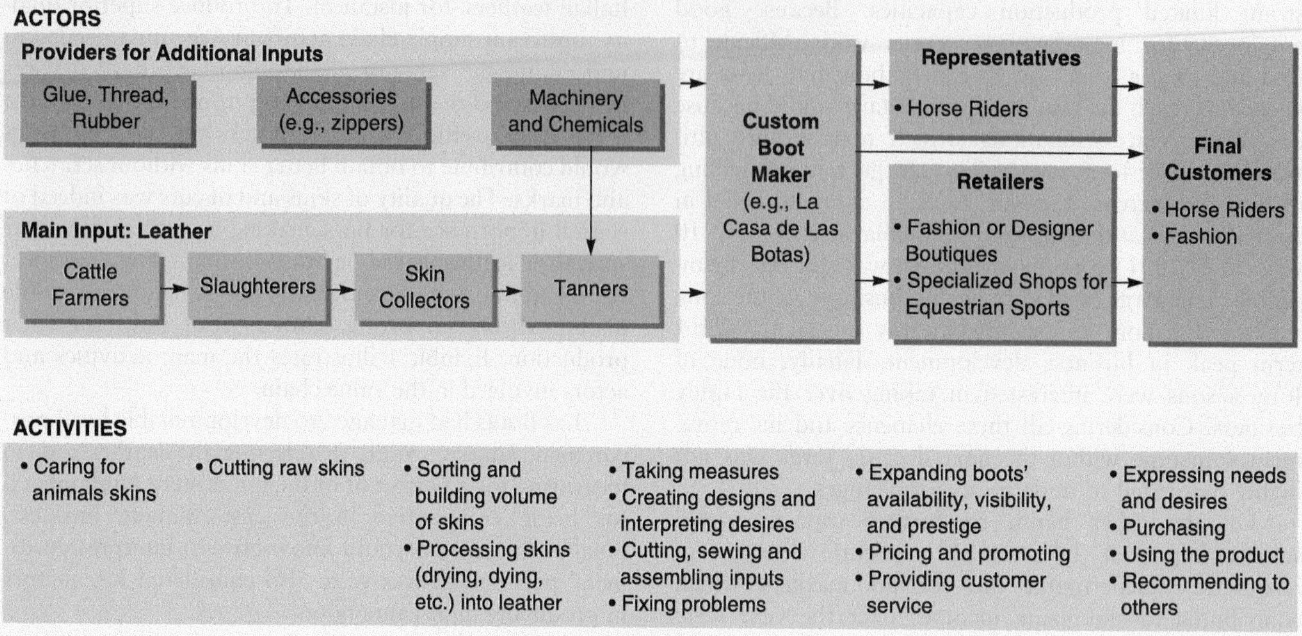

SOURCE: Aurelia Durand.

TWO HIGH-END CUSTOMER SEGMENTS

In 2010, the customer base of La Casa de Las Botas included more than 1,000 end-users. The niche market for custom-made boots could be segmented based on psychographic and demographic characteristics e.g., the product's use (purpose and frequency) as well as gender and purchasing power.

Traditionally, La Casa de Las Botas has targeted the "Equestrian" segment (70 percent of overall sales). This segment is composed of adults, teenagers, and children of both genders passionately undertaking equestrian activities and sports. In this segment, professional users need to be distinguished from recreational users because of the high frequency of use, and the intensity of their practice of specific activities (e.g., polo, horse ball, jumping, dressage, endurance, cross-country jumping, hunting). Usually, dedicated horse-riders own two pairs of boots and wear them alternately in order to spare them the strain of daily use. Although professionals make a very minor contribution to overall sales (less than 1 percent), they are very important to the company because of their advocacy power. Like in any sport, recreational users strongly look to professionals and are motivated to purchase the equipment "as seen on TV" in major competitions. Generally, professionals put emphasis on the boots' technical qualities (such as comfort, durability, flexibility, and quality of contact with the horse).

In recent years, the "Fashion" segment has grown to represent about 30 percent of overall sales. This segment is mainly composed of women with superior purchasing power who like the equestrian boots style but use the products for regular pedestrian activities. These customers tend to look for unique designs and color combinations rather than for technical qualities. Jorge has started to wonder if his company should further attend to the demand from this segment. First, the number of potential buyers was much larger than in the Equestrian segment. In addition, margins could even be more interesting considering the lack of direct competition (impeding price comparisons, for instance) for products falling entirely into the luxury category. However, doing so would represent a significant move away from La Casa de Las Botas core business. Furthermore, Jorge was unsure of how much strain a strategic move in this direction would place on the company's production capacity.

PRODUCT HIGH-VALUE BOOTS

La Casa de Las Botas were considered high-value products for their quality and durability, as well as for their high degrees of customization. Not only were the boots entirely adapted to the customers' legs and feet (according to eight specific measures for each leg) but they were also entirely customized to individual needs and tastes.

Depending on the activity for which the boots were used (e.g., polo, dressage, jumping, country, or multipurpose), clients were advised to choose among an unlimited number of colors and shades and various attribute combinations. These attributes related to the finish of leather ("thick," "regular," "soft," "polo"), the type of piping/upper top design ("regular," "dressage," "Italian"), the type of sole ("grooved rubber,"

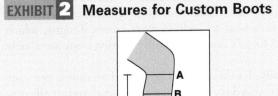

EXHIBIT 2 Measures for Custom Boots

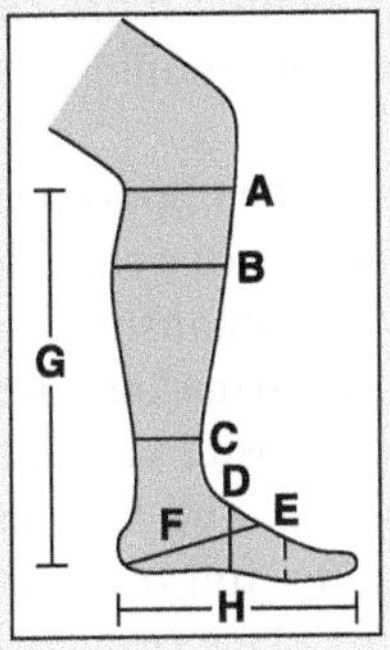

SOURCE: Aurelia Durand.

"rimless rubber," "classic rubber"), toe style (square or round), the vamp design/toe cap design ("straight," "double line," "line with circles"), spurs rest (with, without), and thin leather straps (with, without).

The labor-intensive production process for a pair of boots lasted for about a week and included the steps of setting up the boot shape according to measurements, humidifying the leather to make it fit and hand-sewing each shoe. Production could not be standardized and therefore capacity was strongly tied to the number of craftsmen employed. This represented an important limitation for La Casa de Las Botas in considering automated sales over the Internet or to further target the Fashion segment, for instance. The company could quickly become unable to fill the demand for its products. For Jorge, this situation needed to be avoided by all means. Maintaining customer satisfaction and a certain exclusivity to his business corresponded to the strategic positioning of La Casa de Las Botas.

> *"You cannot be selling to be selling and then lose prestige."* [Interview, April 2010]

DIRECT AND INDIRECT DISTRIBUTION CHANNELS

End users could purchase La Casa de Las Botas' boots through several direct and indirect channels. First, they could buy products directly at the workshop store in Buenos Aires or else at stands at local and regional equestrian events staffed personally by Jorge or his son. Second, customers could order their boots by phone or through the company website. In this case, the boots were shipped via international couriers (such as FedEx and UPS) and customers were charged with the additional shipping costs (typically USD 200 for U.S. or Europe residents). Usually, they received the boots about a month after placing the order. Third, exports took a more indirect form through sales to distributors around the world. The nature and number of these intermediaries varied according to the targeted segment and evolved largely over time.

For the fashion segment, retailers and designer boutiques have shown an interest in offering the custom-made boots service. For instance, a French footwear retailer with presence in the Parisian upscale department store "Le Bon Marché" had engaged in displaying some of La Casa de Las Botas' models at € 735. For the Equestrian segment, distribution has been established historically through individual representatives. In 2010, La Casa de Las Botas counted about 11 active representatives in: France (2), Spain (1), Italy (1), U.S.A. (3), Venezuela (2), Costa Rica (1), and the Dominican Republic (1). These people were mostly competitive horse-riders who had first purchased boots as end users and then personally approached Jorge to manifest their interest in distributing the products in their own country. International riders also offered a more extensive geographic coverage, selling products in the various countries hosting competitions. Requirements for being a representative for La Casa de Las Botas included: high credibility (i.e., being knowledgeable about equestrian practice to advise customers); strong visibility (attendance at events and participation in competitions); and a good reputation. The company also asked representatives to work with local shoemakers to reduce delays and costs in the case of minor repair. Once awarded the exclusive representation for La Casa de Las Botas (through verbal agreements), these individuals were delegated many marketing tasks, from promotion to pricing. They typically started by taking with them a couple of previously purchased boot models to the many competitions they attended for display on-site. They were also in charge of taking the clients' measurement and communicating them to the manufacturer in Argentina. Finally, they received and delivered the products in person or else the boots were sent directly to the buyer's home address.

Because they are part of the equestrian "milieu," representatives are well-informed about local market conditions for leather boots. They know the type of quality and prices of products available to their potential clients. For this reason, they are entrusted with determining their own mark up above the price they pay for each pair of boots.

Generally, exports were not much of a hassle once the paperwork for customs requirements in each country was well understood. Yet, experience had sometimes reserved unpleasant surprises such as in Mexico where several pair of boots had arrived lacerated. Indeed, custom officers at the Los Cabos entry point were in the habit of conducting content verification with a big knife, not taking much care for what was in the package.

LITTLE ADVERTISING, LOTS OF WORD OF MOUTH PROMOTION

Advertising efforts by La Casa de Las Botas were limited compared to the coverage obtained in paper and online media. The only expenses incurred were for a half-page ad renewed yearly in *Ecuestrian*, a specialized Argentinean magazine. Beyond this, La Casa de Las Botas receive free publicity from a significant number of specialized on-line portals and directories about equestrian activities as well as magazines, newspapers, guides and reviews addressed to travelers, such as *The New York Times, The Wall Street Journal, Forbes*, and *National Geographic* in the United States or *Marie-Claire* in the United Kingdom.

The writers of these notes mentioning La Casa de Las Botas could take pride in making suggestions to their readers and displaying their flair for finding genuine local specialties and offering an exclusive experience. This experience could later result in the story telling of how they had visited an old-fashioned little shop, had a true boot maker take their measures and handcraft precious boots just for them.

Boots by La Casa de Las Botas are regularly promoted by local representatives at competitions, fairs and exhibitions held around the world. For instance, the company has been represented at the 1999 Salon du Cheval in Paris, the largest annual equestrian fair in France, and at the 2010 World Equestrian Games (the rough equivalent of the world cup for soccer), in Kentucky (USA). Referring to work ethics, Jorge Da Silva Villagrán has been vigilant to avoid 'short cutting' his distributors by attending these events himself. Indeed, with his presence at a fair stand, consumers would certainly be interested in placing direct orders with the manufacturer in Argentina. Jorge considers this as unfair to the distributors, who have invested and spent large sums for their commercial presence at such events. Maintaining healthy distributor relationships also comes with some opportunity costs. Indeed, the branch of the government in charge of promoting exports of national products (the "Ministerio de Relaciones Exteriores, Comercio Internacional y Culto" also called "Cancillería"), has offered twice to finance a direct presence for La Casa de Las Botas. For the 2010 Games in Kentucky, Jorge was invited at the Palacio San Martín along with other craftsmen enjoying international recognition and whose products would contribute to promote the brand "Argentina." They were offered a booth valued at USD 40,000 to share among six companies. For the second time in recent years, Jorge declined this offer for the above-mentioned reasons.

The only promotional paper material developed by La Casa de las Botas is a small-format catalog. Set to inform clients about the wide array of customization possibilities and inspire them into 'designing' their very own pair of boots, it presented glossy pictures of about 30 models of boots. Many models were named after famous riders, like Katty Kitterman who agreed to pose in the 2010 edition, wearing "her" boot model. In addition, each picture was accompanied by sophisticated short texts, describing with a somewhat poetic touch the model's specifics in Spanish, English, and French. The catalog was made available to visitors at the workshop and to distributors in large quantities. It was re-edited every year to include more recent designs, which followed Jorge's creativity in interpreting customers' new ideas.

Finally, La Casa de Las Botas had an online presence which conveyed the image of a traditional and small company dedicated to craftsmanship (www.casadelasbotas.com.ar). In addition, a page on Facebook was also created mid-2010. The website contents were available in Spanish, English, French, and German. The website was not equipped to conduct full transactions but included a form for customers to place orders (by email, phone, or fax) with all the required measures of their two legs and feet. According to the company owner, the reasons why online payments were not possible was due to the high costs of the system, the inflationary risk, the willingness to keep a certain control over the number of accepted orders (for production limitation), and finally, a sense of comfort with the current payment system, as described hereafter.

A MONTH'S PAY FOR A PAIR OF BOOTS?

End users could pay for their boots directly in the store in cash or by bank draft, the only option for foreign customers. Sales to distributors for several pairs of boots were not concluded through formal contracts but by simple verbal agreements. Once the distributors had passed on an order, they had to make a deposit for the amount due with the Central Bank of Argentina. In order to retrieve the funds, La Casa de Las Botas had to prove to the Bank that the merchandise had been shipped abroad (notably showing customs certifications). This system provided some reassurance to foreign distributors. For instance, they could cancel an order even after having deposited the money and be sure to be fully reimbursed by the Central Bank. In this sense, the Central Bank of Argentina intervened as a risk moderator.

Price determination for international markets is generally delegated to distributors who are knowledgeable about local conditions. Representatives are only asked to fix their prices to end-customers above USD 800 in order to preserve their margins in case the manufacturer in Argentina should face unexpected cost increases. For instance, it happened in the past that increased transportation costs of raw materials to the workshop (due to erratic increases of oil prices) had to be incorporated into the prices of boots sold to distributors. By absorbing minor adjustments of costs, distributors avoided temporary price fluctuations for international final customers, and contributed to stability. The margin charged by distributors depends on the country where they are located and usually ranges from 30 percent to 100 percent. In 2010, a pair of boots made by La Casa de Las Botas was sold by representatives, on average for: €700 in Spain, €1,000 in France, and USD 1,250 in the United States. In Argentina, these boots were sold for AR$ 1,600, the equivalent of USD 400. Jorge saw a direct relation between the price of his boots and the local minimum wage.

> *"The price is defined according to the purchasing power in each country. Even though people who ride horses usually tend to have a high purchasing power [...] the criteria used is more or less that of a blue collar worker's monthly earnings. [...] Typically, a pair of boots costs a month's pay at the minimum wage level. [...] There is always a relation with the minimum wage which varies from country to country.* [Interview, April 2010]

QUESTIONS FOR DISCUSSION

1. Should La Casa de las Botas embrace expansion or should it maintain the status quo? If you think Jorge should expand his business (perhaps to better sell the company when he retires), which geographic markets and which customer segments should he focus on? That is, should La Casa de las Botas further penetrate existing markets or develop new markets, and in this case which ones? Should the company further develop the fashion segment or should it stick to its core business, the equestrian segment? Building upon your recommendations, establish an international marketing plan for the company.
2. How can the demand for custom-made boots be estimated in an underserved foreign market?
3. How should La Casa de las Botas address online ordering and customer payment methods for both individual customers and distributors?
4. Do you think Jorge should modify his views about promotion at fairs and exhibition and establish a direct presence or is he right to give priority to his distributors' interests? List the possible advantages and disadvantages of his policy in this regard on the short and the long term. For instance, how would La Casa de las Botas benefit from further participating in the Government's efforts to promote the "Industria Argentina" label abroad?

PART THREE

The Global Marketing Mix

Part Three deals with global marketing activities. The core marketing concerns of the beginning internationalist and the multinational corporation are the same. Yet experienced marketers face challenges and opportunities that are different from those encountered by new entrants. They are able to expend more resources on international marketing effort than are small and medium-sized firms. In addition, their perspective can be more globally oriented. Multinational corporations also have more impact on individuals, economies, and governments. Therefore, they are much more subject to public scrutiny and need to be more concerned about repercussions from their activities. Yet their very size often enables them to be more influential in setting international marketing rules.

LEARNING OBJECTIVES

By the time you complete this chapter, you will be able to:

- Understand the complex combination of tangible and intangible elements that distinguishes goods from other products or services.
- Comprehend the importance of designing, modifying, or developing a product to meet the needs of a regional or global basis.
- Know how to develop a global approach that will increase growth and profitability to reach the world's megamarkets.
- Recognize unauthorized uses of a trademark, patent, or copyright good, which take advantage of a superior value.

CHAPTER 11

Product Management and Global Brands

THE INTERNATIONAL MARKETPLACE 11.1

Are Global Brands the Way to Go?

Pressure is on marketing managers to develop global approaches that increase growth and profit potential while maintaining local appeal. If these two seemingly opposite demands could be coupled and the goal of being "global locally" could be met, one of the greatest challenges facing marketers could be solved. The cost of developing global programs is high in terms of intellectual and monetary investment, and the marketing challenges are commensurate. Externally, customer behavior similarities may not be sufficient. Internally, country management may object to cross-border efforts as an encroachment on decision making.

In the last few years, the global/local controversy has been most evident in branded consumer products. A number of companies have engaged in brand pruning efforts with the aim of reducing brand portfolios to manageable sizes. Preference has naturally been given to global brands given their prominent positions. (For example, according to Unilever executives, three-fourths of the company's business comes from 25 global brands.) Many local brands are being evaluated according to their potential as global candidates or as examples of best practice that could be applied elsewhere. The bottom line for global companies is that there are not enough resources for managing scores of local brands that are not truly different.

Global brands, like any facet of global marketing, are supposed to benefit from the scale and the scope that having a presence in multiple markets brings. As global retailers gain more power, marketers may feel more pressure to have brands that can travel with their customers. Another justification for a global presence is the increasing similarity that consumers are displaying in terms of their consumption habits and preferences. It has also been argued that global brands are perceived to have more value added for the consumer, either through better quality (as a function of worldwide acceptance) or by enhancing the consumer's self-perception as being cosmopolitan, sophisticated, and modern.

Internally, global branding can be seen as a tool to tighten organizational relationships using the transfer of best practice in brand management, as well as programs like brand stewardship through brand management teams at headquarters or designated centers of excellence. Concentrating resources and efforts on a limited number of brands is likely to bring improved results. For example, Unilever has singled out six brands for special attention in the personal care category, all of which have shown double-digit growth in the last years.

While the level and effects of globalization can be disputed, the critical question is whether a brand's image will carry over effectively to other markets. Efforts to standardize brand names by eliminating local brand names have met with consumer hostility, and globally branded items introduced into product lines have not always received the enthusiastic support of country managers. Consumers' behavior may have converged, but some markets continue to have their own idiosyncrasies that can prove fatal to globalization efforts. The ability of a global product to penetrate individual markets is determined to some extent by the product category in question. Global brands may have more success in high-profile, high-involvement categories, while consumers may still give local brands preference in purchasing everyday products.

© Boniface Mwangi/Bloomberg via Getty Images

Unilever detergents Lifebouy, Omo, Sunlight, and Geisah line the shelves of a supermarket in Nairobi, Kenya.

SOURCES: Claudiu V. Dimofte, Johny K. Johansson, and Ilkka A. Ronkainen, "Cognitive and Affective Reactions of U.S. Consumers to Global Brands," *Journal of International Marketing* 16 (December 2008): 113–23; Johny K. Johansson and Ilkka A. Ronkainen, "The Esteem of Global Brands," *Journal of Brand Management* 12, no. 5 (2005): 339–54; and Johny K. Johansson and Ilkka A. Ronkainen, "Are Global Brands the Right Choice for Your Company?" *Marketing Management*, March/April 2004, 53–56.

Because meeting and satisfying customer needs and expectations is the key to successful marketing, research findings on market traits and potential should be used to determine the optimal degree of customization needed in products and product lines relative to the incremental cost of the effort. As seen in *The International Marketplace 11.1*, mass customization is a growing option. Adapting to new markets should be seen not only in the context of one market but also with attention to how these changes can contribute to operations elsewhere. A new feature for a product or a new line item may have applicability on a broader scale, including the market that originated the product.[1]

Take the Boeing 737, for example. Due to saturated markets and competitive pressures, Boeing started to look for new markets in the Middle East,

Africa, and Latin America for the 737 rather than kill the program altogether. To adjust to the idiosyncrasies of these markets, such as softer and shorter runways, the company redesigned the wings to allow for shorter landings and added thrust to the engines for quicker takeoffs. To make sure that the planes would not bounce even if piloted by less experienced captains, Boeing redesigned the landing gear and installed low-pressure tires to ensure that the plane would stick to the ground after initial touchdown. In addition to becoming a success in the intended markets, the new product features met with approval around the world and made the Boeing 737 the best-selling commercial jet in history.

This chapter is concerned with how the international marketer should adjust the firm's product offering to the marketplace, and it discusses the influence of an array of both external and internal variables. A delicate balance has to be achieved between the advantages of standardization and those of localization to maximize performance. Focus will be on how the product development process can take into account the globalization of markets without compromising dimensions considered essential by local markets. Many strategic product decisions, such as branding, will benefit from worldwide experience and exposure applied to the local context. The challenge of intellectual property violation will be focused on as a specialty topic. International marketers must be ready to defend themselves against theft of their ideas and innovations.

PRODUCT VARIABLES

The core of a firm's international operations is a product or service. This product or service can be defined as the complex combination of tangible and intangible elements that distinguishes it from the other entities in the marketplace, as shown in Exhibit 11.1. The firm's success depends on how good its product or service is and on how well the firm is able to differentiate the product from the offerings of competitors. Products can be differentiated by their composition, by their country of origin, by their tangible features such as packaging or quality, or by their augmented features such as warranties. Further, the positioning of the product in consumers' minds (e.g., Volvo's reputation for safety) will add to its perceived value. The core product—for example, the component of a personal computer or the recipe for a soup—may indeed be the same as or highly similar to those of competitors, leaving the marketer with the other tangible and augmented features of the product with which to achieve differentiation. Winnebago Industries, a leading exporter of motor homes, is finding increased interest in China, the United Kingdom, and Japan for its "American-styled" recreation vehicles, or RVs, that offer more features and options, such as automatic transmissions and air conditioning, than those made available by local competitors. Furthermore, buyers are assured that they will receive the same quality of product and service as customers in the United States.[2]

To the potential buyer, a product is a complete cluster of value satisfactions. A customer attaches value to a product in proportion to its perceived ability to help solve problems or meet needs. This will go beyond the technical capabilities of the product to include intangible benefits sought. In Latin America, for

EXHIBIT 11.1 Elements of a Product

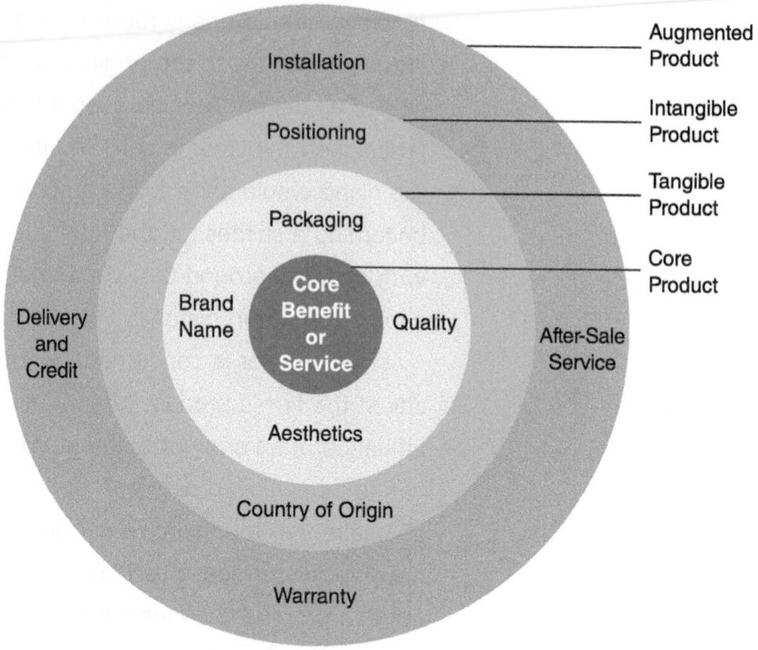

SOURCE: Adapted from Philip Kotler and Gary Armstrong, *Principles of Marketing,* 14th ed. (Pearson, 2012), p. 226.

example, great value is placed on products made in the United States. If packaging is localized, then the product may no longer have the "EEUU" (*EstadosUnidos,* or United States) appeal that motivates customers to choose the product over others, especially over local competitors. In some cases, customer behavior has to be understood from a broader perspective. For example, while Chinese customers may view Japanese products quite positively regarding their quality, historic animosity toward Japan may prevent them from buying Japanese goods or cause them to prefer goods from other sources.[3] Given such dramatic variation from market to market, careful assessment of product dimensions is called for.

Standardization versus Adaptation

The first question, after the internationalization decision has been made, concerns the product modifications that are needed or warranted. A firm has four basic alternatives in approaching international markets: (1) selling the product as is in the international marketplace, (2) modifying products for different countries or regions, (3) designing new products for foreign markets, and (4) incorporating all the differences into one flexible product design and introducing a global product.

Different approaches for implementing these alternatives exist. For example, a firm may identify only target markets where products can be marketed with little or no modification. A large consumer products marketer may have global products, regional products, and purely local products in its product line for any given market. Some of the products developed for one market may later be introduced elsewhere, including the global marketer's "home" market. The Dockers line of casual wear originated at Levi Strauss's Argentine unit and was applied to loosely cut pants by Levi's Japanese subsidiary. The company's U.S. operation later adopted both, making Dockers the number one brand in the category in the United States. Similar success has followed in over

50 country markets entered.[4] Occasionally, the international marketplace may want something that the domestic market discards. By exporting chicken cuts that are unpopular (e.g., dark meat) or would be hauled off to landfills (such as chicken feet), U.S. poultry producers earn well over $1 billion annually from Russian and Chinese markets.[5]

Coca-Cola and the iPhone have been cited as evidence that universal product and marketing strategies can work. Yet the argument that the world is becoming more homogenized may actually be true for only a limited number of products that have universal brand recognition and minimal product knowledge requirements for use.[6] Although product standardization is generally increasing, there are still substantial differences in company practices, depending on the products marketed and where they are marketed.

Even companies that are noted for following the same methods worldwide have made numerous changes in their product offerings. Coca-Cola introduces 30 to 40 new products per year, the majority of which are never marketed outside of the country of introduction.[7] McDonald's serves the same menu of hamburgers, soft drinks, and other foods abroad that it does in the United States, and the restaurants look the same. But McDonald's has also tried to tailor its products to local styles. For example, in Japan, the chain's trademark character, known as Ronald McDonald in the United States, is called Donald McDonald because it is easier to pronounce. Menu adjustments include rice and beans in Costa Rica; McLaks, a sandwich made of grilled salmon and dill sauce, in Norway; and Ruis McFeast rye bread burgers in Finland. McDonald's also offers a gluten-free bun in Spain, Sweden, Finland, and Norway but not in the litigious U.S. market yet.[8]

Factors Affecting Adaptation

In deciding the form in which the product is to be marketed abroad, the firm should consider three sets of factors: (1) the market(s) that have been targeted, (2) the product and its characteristics, and (3) company characteristics, such as resources and policy. For most firms, the key question linked to adaptation is whether the effort is worth the cost involved—in adjusting production runs, stock control, or servicing, for example—and the investigative research involved in determining, for example, features that would be most appealing. For most firms, the expense of modifying products should be moderate. In practice, this may mean, however, that the expense is moderate when modifications are considered and acted on, whereas modifications are considered but rejected when the projected cost is substantial.

There is no panacea for resolving questions of adaptation. Many firms are formulating decision-support systems to aid in product adaptation, and some consider every situation independently. Exhibit 11.2 provides a summary of the factors that determine the need for either **mandatory** or **discretionary product adaptation**. All products have to conform to the prevailing environmental conditions, over which the marketer has no control. These relate to legal, economic, and climatic conditions in the market. Further adaptation decisions are made to enhance the exporter's competitiveness in the marketplace. This is achieved by matching competitive offers, catering to customer preferences, and meeting demands of local distribution systems.

The adaptation decision will also have to be assessed as a function of time and market involvement. The more exporters learn about local market characteristics in individual markets, the more they are able to establish similarities and, as a result, standardize their marketing approach, especially across similar markets. This market insight will give the exporters legitimacy with the local representatives in developing a common understanding of the extent of standardization versus adaptation.[9]

EXHIBIT 11.2 Factors Affecting Product-Adaptation Decisions

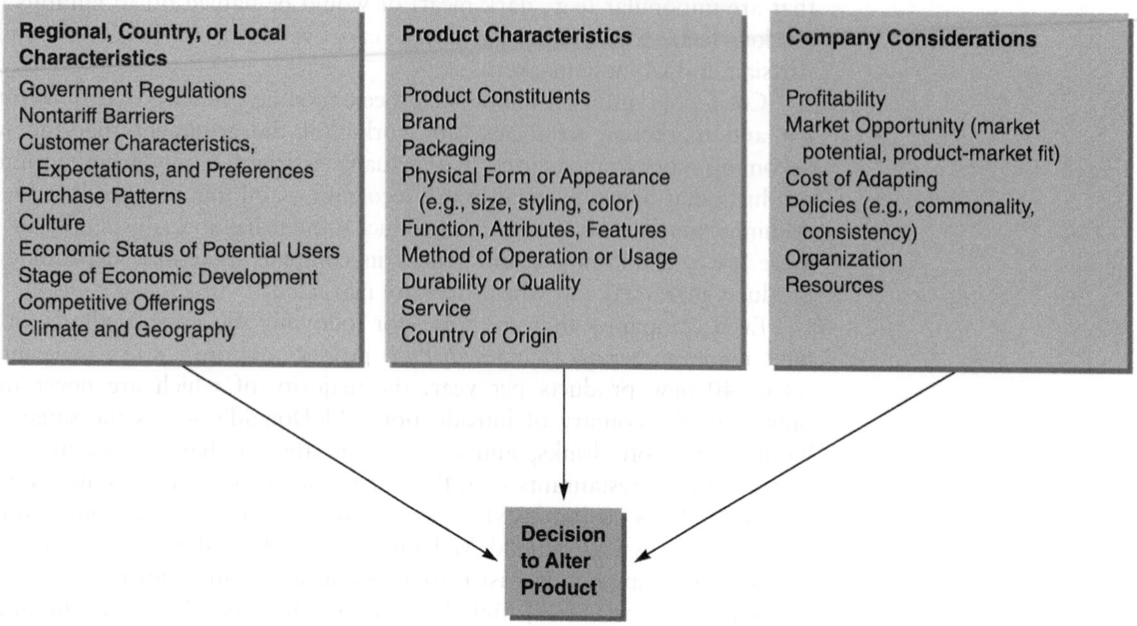

Regional, Country, or Local Characteristics
Government Regulations
Nontariff Barriers
Customer Characteristics, Expectations, and Preferences
Purchase Patterns
Culture
Economic Status of Potential Users
Stage of Economic Development
Competitive Offerings
Climate and Geography
Product Characteristics
Product Constituents
Brand
Packaging
Physical Form or Appearance (e.g., size, styling, color)
Function, Attributes, Features
Method of Operation or Usage
Durability or Quality
Service
Country of Origin
Company Considerations
Profitability
Market Opportunity (market potential, product-market fit)
Cost of Adapting
Policies (e.g., commonality, consistency)
Organization
Resources
Decision to Alter Product

SOURCE: Reproduced with permission from *The Conference Board*, Inc. Adapting Products for Export by Virginia Vario © 1983, *The Conference Board*, Inc.

THE MARKET ENVIRONMENT

Government Regulations

Government regulations often present the most stringent requirements. Some of the requirements may serve no purpose other than the political (such as protection of domestic industry or response to political pressures). Because of the sovereignty of nations, individual firms need to comply but can influence the situation by lobbying, directly or through their industry associations, for the issue to be raised during trade negotiations. Government regulations may be spelled out, but firms need to be ever vigilant in terms of changes and exceptions.

Sweden was the first country in the world to enact legislation against most aerosol sprays on the grounds that they may harm the atmosphere. The ban covers thousands of hair sprays, deodorants, air fresheners, insecticides, paints, waxes, and assorted sprays that use Freon gases as propellants. It does not apply to certain medical sprays, especially those used by people who suffer from asthma. An international treaty banning aerosols, the Montreal Protocol, is now ratified by 196 countries.[10] As a matter of fact, certain markets, such as Sweden and California, often serve as precursors of changes to come in broader markets and should, therefore, be monitored by marketers.

Although economic integration usually reduces discriminatory governmental regulation, some national environmental restrictions may stay in place. For example, a ruling by the European Court of Justice let stand Danish laws that require returnable containers for all beer and soft drinks. These laws seriously restrict foreign brewers, whose businesses are not on a scale large enough to justify the logistics system necessary to handle returnables. Fiji consumes some 50 million containers of beverage per year; few of these containers are recycled, and millions are discarded improperly. The beverage tax from the producers and importers will be paid into a revolving fund to be managed by the Managing Agency.[11]

Government regulations are probably the single most important factor contributing to product adaptation and, because of bureaucratic red tape, often the most cumbersome and frustrating factor to deal with. In some cases, government regulations have been passed and are enforced to protect local industry from competition from abroad. A poll of 4,000 European companies found that burdensome regulatory requirements (e.g., need to ensure that products conform to national requirements) affecting exports made the United Kingdom the most difficult market in which to trade within the EU.[12] The EU decided to limit the use of older commercial aircraft that have "hush kit" mufflers on their engines to cut down airplane noise. U.S. marketers saw a two-dimensional threat in this new regulation: what the EU was really trying to do was keep out U.S. goods (hush kits are typically made in the United States) and, in forcing airlines to buy new aircraft, to direct them to buy European Airbus rather than U.S. Boeing planes.[13]

Some government regulations for adaptation may be controversial both within the company and with some of its constituents, including home governments. Google was forced by the Chinese government to establish a new site, Google.cn, the contents of which were censored by Google in accordance with government preferences. Although a warning label informed the user of the arrangement, the company was criticized for its collaboration to curtail the free flow of information.[14] Google now redirects users to its Hong Kong–based search engine (www.google.com.hk), and the censorship has little direct impact. Chinese users are already accustomed to using circumvention technology, which means an uncensored, overseas version of Google remains accessible from the mainland.

Nontariff Barriers

Nontariff barriers include product standards, testing or approval procedures, subsidies for local products, and bureaucratic red tape. The nontariff barriers affecting product adjustments usually concern elements outside the core product. For example, France requires the use of the French language in any offer, presentation, or advertisement, whether written or spoken; in instructions for use; and in specification or guarantee terms for goods or services, as well as for invoices and receipts.

Small companies with limited resources may simply give up in the face of seemingly arbitrary harassment. For example, product testing and certification requirements have made the entry of many foreign companies into Japanese markets quite difficult, if not impossible.[15] Japan requires testing of all pharmaceutical products in Japanese laboratories, maintaining that these tests are needed because the Japanese may be physiologically different from Americans or Swiss.

With a substantial decrease in tariff barriers, nontariff forms of protectionism have increased. On volume alone, agriculture dominates the list. The United States and the EU have fought over beef produced with the aid of hormones. Although it was declared safe for consumption by UN health authorities, the Europeans have banned the importation of such beef and demand appropriate labeling as a precondition for market entry. In a similar debate, an international trade agreement requires the labeling of genetically modified food in the world market. This means that U.S. farmers have to separate the increasingly controversial foods from the overall supply.[16]

One way to keep a particular product or producer out of a market is to insist on particular standards. Since the EU chose ISO 9000 as a basis to harmonize varying technical norms of its member states, some of its trading partners have accused it of erecting a new trade barrier against outsiders.[17] ISO 9000, created by the International Organization for Standardization (ISO), is a set of technical standards designed to offer a uniform way of determining whether manufacturing plants and service organizations implement and document sound quality procedures. The ISO itself does not administer or regulate these standards; that job is left to the 178 countries that have voluntarily adopted them.

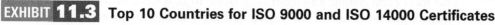

EXHIBIT 11.3 Top 10 Countries for ISO 9000 and ISO 14000 Certificates

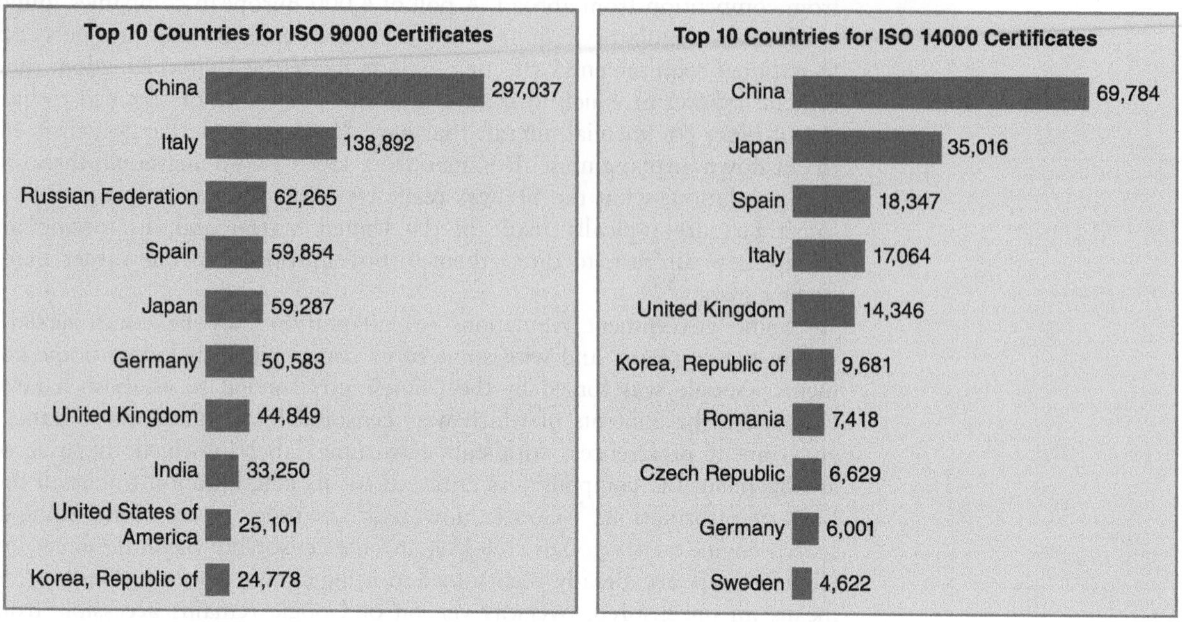

SOURCE: The ISO Survey 2010, www.iso.org/iso/iso-survey2010.pdf.

There were 1,457,912 certificates of ISO registration by 2010, and the five-year period between 2005 and 2010 experienced a near doubling of certificates worldwide.[18] There is no legal requirement to adopt the standards; however, many agree that these guidelines are already determining what may be sold to and within the EU and increasingly around the world. This is especially true for products for which there are safety or liability issues or that require exact measurements or calibration, such as medical or exercise equipment.

The ISO also issued the first standards on environmental management, the ISO 14000 series, in 1996. The standards, which basically require that a firm design an environmental management system, do provide benefits for the adopters such as substantial efficiencies in pollution control (e.g., packaging) and a better public image.[19] However, these standards can also serve as a nontariff barrier if advanced nations impose their own requirements and systems on developing countries that often lack the knowledge and resources to meet such conditions. The adoption rate has increased more rapidly in the last few years to 250,972 by 2010. Exhibit 11.3 provides an overview of the top 10 countries worldwide in terms of ISO 9000 and ISO 14000 certificates at the end of 2011. The ISO 9000 and 14000 international standards have been widely accepted by many organizations across all industrial sectors in China.

Customer Characteristics, Expectations, and Preferences

The characteristics and behavior of intended customer groups are as important as governmental influences on the product adaptation decision. Even when the benefits sought are quite similar, the physical characteristics of customers may dictate product adaptation. For example, Kraft Foods' Oreo cookie was first introduced in China in the 1990s, but it was not until the company began actively engaging with consumers that sales began to take off. In communicating with customers, Kraft found that the original Oreo was too sweet for local palates and the package too big for small Chinese families. To ease one of these concerns, Kraft introduced packages containing fewer Oreos for just US$0.29.

Then in 2006, after testing 20 different prototypes, Kraft reformulated both the cookie and its packaging.[20] To reintroduce the Oreo, Kraft capitalized on the desire of Chinese citizens to interact with national celebrities and their affinity for digital media. Mothers in China, the ultimate audience, were encouraged to share 40 million "Oreo Moments" in an online diary on China's popular QZone social network.[21]

Product decisions of consumer-product marketers are especially affected by local behavior, tastes, attitudes, and traditions—all reflecting the marketers' need to gain customers' approval. This group of variables is critical in that it is the most difficult to quantify but is nevertheless essential in making a go/no-go decision. The reason most Europeans who wear western-style boots buy those made in Spain may be that U.S. footwear manufacturers are unaware of style-conscious Europeans' preference for pointed toes and narrow heels. They view U.S.-made boots as "practical, but not interesting." Similarly, the U.S. Mint has been unable to penetrate the Asian market with its gold coins, which are 22 carat (.916 pure), because customers there value pure gold (i.e., 24 carat, .999 pure).

Three groups of factors determine cultural and psychological specificity in relation to products and services: consumption patterns, psychosocial characteristics, and general cultural criteria. The types of questions asked in Exhibit 11.4

EXHIBIT 11.4 Cultural and Psychological Factors Affecting Product Adaptation

I. Consumption Patterns

A. Pattern of Purchase

1. Is the product or service purchased by relatively the same consumer income group from one country to another?
2. Do the same family members motivate the purchase in all target countries?
3. Do the same family members dictate brand choice in all target countries?
4. Do most consumers expect a product to have the same appearance?
5. Is the purchase rate the same regardless of the country?
6. Are most of the purchases made at the same kind of retail outlet?
7. Do most consumers spend the same amount of time making the purchase?

B. Pattern of Usage

1. Do most consumers use the product or service for the same purpose or purposes?
2. Is the product or service used in different amounts from one target area or country to another?
3. Is the method of preparation the same in all target countries?
4. Is the product or service used along with other products or services?

II. Psychosocial Characteristics

A. Attitudes toward the Product or Service

1. Are the basic psychological, social, and economic factors motivating the purchase and use of the product the same for all target countries?
2. Are the advantages and disadvantages of the product or service in the minds of consumers basically the same from one country to another?
3. Does the symbolic content of the product or service differ from one country to another?
4. Is the psychic cost of purchasing or using the product or service the same, whatever the country?
5. Does the appeal of the product or service for a cosmopolitan market differ from one market to another?

B. Attitudes toward the Brand

1. Is the brand name equally known and accepted in all target countries?
2. Are customer attitudes toward the package basically the same?
3. Are customer attitudes toward pricing basically the same?
4. Is brand loyalty the same throughout target countries for the product or service under consideration?

III. Cultural Criteria

1. Does society restrict the purchase or use of the product or service to a particular group?
2. Is there a stigma attached to the product or service?
3. Does the usage of the product or service interfere with tradition in one or more of the targeted markets?

SOURCE: Adapted from Steuart Henderson Britt, "Standardizing Marketing for the International Market," *Columbia Journal of World Business* 9 (Winter 1974): 32–40.

should be answered and systematically recorded for every product under consideration.

Since Brazilians are rarely breakfast eaters, Dunkin' Donuts markets doughnuts in Brazil as snacks and desserts and for parties. To further appeal to Brazilians, the company makes doughnuts with local fruit fillings like papaya and guava. Campbell Soup Company failed in Brazil with its offerings of vegetable and beef combinations, mainly because Brazilians prefer the dehydrated products of competitors such as Knorr and Maggi; Brazilians could use these products as soup starters but still add their own flair and ingredients. The only way of solving this problem is through proper customer testing, which can be formidably expensive for a company interested only in exports.

Often, no concrete product changes are needed, only a change in the product's positioning. **Positioning** refers to consumers' perception of a brand as compared with competitors' brands—the mental image that a brand, or the company as a whole, evokes. A brand's positioning, however, may have to change to reflect the differing lifestyles of the targeted market. Coca-Cola has renamed Diet Coke in many countries to Coke Light and has subtly shifted the promotional approach from "weight loss" to "figure maintenance."

Even the export of TV culture, which is considered by many as a local product, can succeed abroad if concepts are adjusted to reflect local values. By 2011, the Muppets were being seen in over 140 countries, including 21 co-productions reflecting local languages, customs, and educational needs. The Russian version of *Sesame Street* is 70 percent locally produced and features Aunt Dasha, a quintessential Russian character who lives in a traditional cottage and spouts folklore and homespun wisdom. In China, new characters were added for local color (such as Little Berry, "Xiao Mei").[22] When the Arab satellite network MBC started broadcasting the Simpsons, "Al Shamsoon" had replaced Homer's Duff beer with soda, hot dogs with Egyptian beef sausages, and donuts with cookies called *kahk*; Moe's Bar had been written out completely.[23]

Economic Development

Management must take into account the present stage of economic development of the overseas market. As a country's economy advances, buyers are in a better position to buy and to demand more sophisticated products and product versions. With broad country considerations in mind, the firm can determine potentials for selling certain kinds of products and services. This means managing affordability in a way that makes the marketer's products accessible. For example, C&A, an apparel retailer from Holland, has been able to build a successful business in Latin American countries because it offers reasonable-quality goods at various price points—the best \$10, \$20, and \$30 dresses on the market. In Brazil, two-thirds of its sales are to families with incomes below \$8,000 per year.[24]

Companies have described how they have adapted to the new global era through a process they call **reverse innovation**. For example, in India, General Electric developed a handheld electrocardiogram device that it sells for \$1,000, about one-tenth of the price of the original (and much bulkier) U.S.-developed machine. Similarly, in China, the company introduced a portable ultrasound machine with a price tag of \$15,000, again vastly cheaper than the model GE used to try to sell to the Chinese market. Both these innovations have not only been successful in emerging markets but have also found new customers back in the United States with ambulance teams and in emergency rooms.[25]

There is also a great need to develop new products for people with little money who aspire to a taste of the better life. For example, Tata Motors' \$2,200 Nano (a small vehicle analogous to the American SMART car) is specifically designed for India's poor. Similarly, because fewer than one in five Indian homes has a refrigerator, a refrigerator manufacturer could attract a huge new group of consumers if it could get the price right. Mumbai's Godrej & Boyce Manufacturing Co. developed a small, inexpensive refrigerator called Little Cool. By keeping it small and reducing the number of parts to around 20 instead of the 200 that go into regular refrigerators, it has been able to sell it for only $70, which is less than one-third of the price of a regular bottom-of-the-line fridge.[26]

Competitive Offerings

Monitoring competitors' product features, as well as determining what has to be done to meet and beat them, is critical. Competitive offerings may provide a baseline against which the firm's resources can be measured—for example, what it takes to reach a critical market share in a given competitive situation. An analysis of competitors' offerings may reveal holes in the market or suggest avoiding certain market segments. Huawei's expanding device business has found a niche with American consumers. The devices have given lower-income consumers—who may not have wired Internet access at home—a new path online. As carriers set their sights on one of the last sources of growth in U.S. telecom—smartphone adoption among lower-income consumers—Huawei has been there with some of the cheapest phones available, and these gains have come at the expense of companies like Nokia.[27]

Climate and Geography

Climate and geography will usually have an effect on the total product offering: the core product; tangible elements, mainly packaging; and the augmented features. Some products, by design, are vulnerable to the elements. Marketing of chocolate products is challenging in hot climates, which may restrict companies' options.[28] Kraft has its own display cases in shops, and Toblerone has confined its distribution to air-conditioned outlets. With a large section of Indians still choosing traditional sweets over chocolates, an offering was required that would seed chocolate consumption amongst non-users and help increase consumption frequency amongst fringe chocolate users. Kraft's Cadbury saw the potential. However, even at its lowest price point, Cadbury chocolate was still inaccessible to the majority of the rural population. So Cadbury launched Dairy Milk Shots, which are ball shaped candy that is milk with a chocolate cover.

The international marketer must consider two, sometimes contradictory, aspects of packaging for the international market. On the one hand, the product itself has to be protected against longer transit times and possibly for longer shelf life; on the other hand, care has to be taken that no non-allowed preservatives are used. The packaging must be able to withstand the longer distribution channels and the longer time required for distribution, so the product will not arrive in stores in poor condition and can be sold properly. If a product is exposed to a lot of sunshine and heat as a result of being sold on street corners, as may be the case in developing countries, marketers are advised to use special varnishing or to gloss the product wrappers. Without this, the coloring may fade and make the product unattractive to the customer.

Courtesy of Cadbury India Ltd. Inc.

An innovative format of sugar coated chocolate made to withstand the rural temperature fluctuations.

PRODUCT CHARACTERISTICS

Product characteristics are the inherent features of the product offering, whether actual or perceived. The inherent characteristics of products and the benefits they provide to consumers in the various markets make certain products good candidates for standardization, others not. Consumer nondurables, such as food products, generally show the highest amount of sensitivity toward differences in national tastes and habits. Consumer durables, such as cameras and home electronics, are subject to far more homogeneous demand and more predictable adjustment (e.g., adjustment to a different technical system in television sets). Industrial products tend to be more shielded from cultural influences. However, substantial modifications may sometimes be required—in the telecommunications industry, for example—as a result of government regulations and restraints.

Product Constituents and Content

The international marketer must make sure products do not contain ingredients that might be in violation of legal requirements or religious or social customs. As an example, Schwarzkopf & DEP Corporation, a Los Angeles manufacturer, in its sales of hair and skin products, takes particular pains to make sure that no Japan-bound products contain formaldehyde—an ingredient commonly used in the United States but illegal in Japan. To ensure the purity of the Japanese batches, the company repeatedly cleans and sterilizes the chemical vats, checks all ingredients for traces of formaldehyde, and checks the finished product before shipment. When religion or custom determines consumption, ingredients may have to be replaced in order for the product to be acceptable. In Islamic countries, for example, animal fats have to be replaced by ingredients such as vegetable shortening. In deference to Hindu and Muslim beliefs, McDonald's "Maharaja Mac" is made with mutton in India.

Digital technology is making it easy and inexpensive to substitute product placements in country or region-specific versions of the same movie. Dr Pepper's logo appeared on a refrigerator in the U.S. version of *Spider-Man 2*, whereas overseas the logo belonged to Mirinda, a fruit-flavored soft drink brand that PepsiCo markets outside the United States.[29]

Branding

Brand names convey the image of the product or service. The term **brand** refers to a name, term, symbol, sign, or design used by a firm to differentiate its offerings from those of its competitors. Brands are one of the most easily standardized items in the product offering; they may allow further standardization of other marketing elements such as promotional items. The brand name is the vocalizable part of the brand, the brand mark the nonvocalizable part (e.g., Twitter " "). The brand mark may become invaluable when the product itself cannot be promoted but the symbol can be used. As an example, Marlboro cannot be advertised in most European countries because of legal restrictions on cigarette advertising; however, Philip Morris features advertisements showing only the Marlboro cowboy, who is known throughout the world. Unfortunately, most brands do not have such recognition. The term *trademark* refers to the legally protected part of the brand, indicated by the symbol ®. Increasingly, international markets have found their trademarks violated by counterfeiters who are illegally using or abusing the brand name of the marketer.

The international marketer has a number of options in choosing a branding strategy. The marketer may choose to be a contract manufacturer to a distributor (the generics approach) or to establish national, regional, or worldwide brands. The use of standardization in branding is strongest in culturally similar markets; for example, for U.S. marketers this means Canada and the United Kingdom. Standardization of product and brand do not necessarily move hand in hand; a regional brand may well have local features, or a highly standardized product may have local brand names. PepsiCo adapts its products to the idiosyncrasies of its customers from around the world. The soda maker advertised itself as "Pecsi" in Argentina to much success, and it is trying to do the same in Mexico and Spain. Many Spanish-speaking people would feel more comfortable pronouncing "Pecsi" or "Pesi" rather than "Pepsi."[30]

The establishment of worldwide brands is difficult; how can a consumer marketer establish world brands when it sells 800 products in more than 200 countries, most of them under different names? A global or regional brand may well have local features (such as Ford's Escort), or a highly standardized product may have local brand names (e.g., Kuschelweich or Mimosin). Standardizing names to reap promotional benefits can be difficult because a particular name may already be established in each market and the action may raise objections from local constituents. Despite the opposition, globalizing brands presents huge opportunities to cut costs and achieve new economies of scale.[31] To avoid problems with brand names in foreign markets, NameLab, a California-based laboratory for name development and testing, suggests these approaches:

1. *Translation*. Little Pen Inc. would become La Petite Plume, S.A., for example.
2. *Transliteration*. This requires the testing of an existing brand name for connotative meaning in the language of the intended market. Toyota's MR2 brand faced a challenge in French-speaking countries due to the pronunciation of "MR2" and emphasized the Spyder designation to defuse the connotation. In other instances, positive connotations are sought, as shown in *The International Marketplace 11.2*.
3. *Transparency*. This can be used to develop a new, essentially meaningless brand name to minimize trademark complexities, transliteration problems, and translation complexities. "Sony" is an example.
4. *Transculture*. This means using a foreign-language name for a brand. Vodkas, regardless of where they originate, should have Russian-sounding names or at least Russian lettering, whereas perfumes should sound French.[32]

Packaging

Packaging serves three major functions: protection, promotion, and user convenience. The major consideration for the international marketer is making sure the product reaches the ultimate user in the form intended. Packaging will vary as a function of transportation mode, transit conditions, and length of time in transit. Because of the longer time that products spend in channels of distribution, firms in the international marketplace, especially those exporting food products, have had to use more expensive packaging materials or more expensive transportation modes. The solution of food processors has been to utilize airtight, reclosable containers that reject moisture and other contaminants.

Pilferage is a problem in a number of markets and has forced companies to use only shipping codes on outside packaging.[33] With larger shipments, containerization has helped alleviate the theft problem. An exporter should anticipate inadequate, careless, or primitive loading methods. The labels and loading instructions should be not only in English but also in the market's language as well as in symbols.

The promotional aspect of packaging relates mostly to labeling. The major adjustments concern bilingual legal requirements. Even when the same language is spoken across markets, nuances will exist, requiring labeling adaptation. Ace Hardware's paint division had to be careful in translating the word *plaster* into Spanish. In Venezuela, *friso* is used, while Mexicans use *yeso*. In the end, *yeso* was used for the paint labels because the word was understood in all of Latin America.[34] Governmental requirements include more informative labeling on products. Inadequate identification, failure to use the needed languages, or inadequate or incorrect descriptions printed on the labels may cause problems.

THE INTERNATIONAL MARKETPLACE 11.2

When There Is More to a Name

Products in Asia often carry brand names that are translated from their original names. They are either direct translations (which result in a different-sounding but same-meaning name in the local language) or phonetic translations (which result in the same sound but likely different meaning). Given the globalization of markets, marketers not only need to decide whether to translate their brand names but also must consider the form, content, style, and image of such translations.

In Europe and the Americas, brand names such as Subway and Sharp have no meaning in themselves, and few are even aware of the origins of the name. But to Chinese-speaking consumers, brand names include an additional dimension: meaning. Subway means "tastes better than others" and Sharp stands for "treasure of sound."

Chinese and Western consumers share similar standards when it comes to evaluating brand names. Both appreciate a brand name that is catchy, memorable, distinct, and says something indicative of the product. But because of cultural and linguistic factors, Chinese consumers expect more in terms of how the names are spelled, written, and styled and whether they are considered lucky. When Frito-Lay introduced Cheetos in the Chinese market, it did so under a Chinese name that translates as "Many Surprises," in Chinese *qi duo*—roughly pronounced "chee-do."

Other similar examples include:

BMW: 宝马—precious horse
Budweiser: 百威—hundreds of power and influence
Heineken: 喜力—happy and powerful
Rejoice: 飘柔—waving and softening
Windows: 视窗—a window of vision
J&J: 强生—strong life
Gucci: 古姿—classic pose
Ikea: 宜家—pleasant home
Canon: 佳能—perfect capability
E-land: 衣恋—love the clothes
Land Rover: 陆虎—tiger on the road
Haier: 海尔—sounds like "higher"

A name is like a work of art, and the art of writing (*shufa*—calligraphy) has had a long tradition all over Asia. Reading Chinese relies more on the visual processes, whereas reading English is dominated by phonological processes (affecting, for example, the processing of features such as font style and color). A name has to look good and be rendered in appealing writing, thereby functioning like a logo or trademark. Companies will consequently have to take into account this dimension of Chinese and Chinese-based languages such as Korean, Japanese, and Vietnamese when they create corporate and brand names and related communications strategies.

Courtesy of SUBWAY

Subway Ad in Both Chinese and English.

SOURCES: Nader T. Tavassoli, "Would a 'Rose' in Chinese Smell as Sweet?" *Business Strategy Review*, Summer 2007, 35–39; Nader Tavassoli and Jin K. Han, "Auditory and Visual Brand Identifiers in Chinese and English," *Journal of International Marketing* 10, no. 2 (2002): 13–28; F. C. Hong, Anthony Pecotich, and Clifford J. Schultz, "Brand Name Translation: Language Constraints, Product Attributes, and Consumer Perceptions in East and Southeast Asia," *Journal of International Marketing* 10, no. 2 (2002): 29–45; and June N. P. Francis, Janet P. Y. Lam, and Jan Walls, "The Impact of Linguistic Differences on International Brand Name Standardization," *Journal of International Marketing* 10, no. 1 (2002): 98–116.

Package aesthetics must be a consideration in terms of the promotional role of packaging. This mainly involves the prudent choice of colors and package shapes. African nations, for example, often prefer bold colors, but flag colors may be alternately preferred or disallowed. Red is associated with death or witchcraft in some countries. Color in packaging may be faddish. White is losing popularity in industrialized countries because name brands do not want to be confused with generic products, usually packaged in white. Black, on the other hand, is increasingly popular and is now used to suggest quality, excellence, and "class."

Package size varies according to purchasing patterns and market conditions. For instance, a six-pack format for soft drinks may not be feasible in certain markets because of the lack of refrigeration capacity in households. Quite often, overseas consumers with modest or low discretionary purchasing power buy smaller sizes or even single units in order to stretch a limited budget. For example, the smallest size of laundry detergent available in Latin American supermarkets is 500 grams, while sizes as small as 150 grams may be in demand (and carried by small retailers).[35] The marketer also has to take into consideration perceptions concerning product multiples. In the West, the number 7 is considered lucky, whereas 13 is its opposite.

Finally, the consumer mandate for marketers to make products more environmentally friendly also affects the packaging dimension, especially in terms of the Four *R*s: redesign, reduce, recycle, and reuse. The EU has strict policies on the amounts of packaging waste that are generated and the levels of recycling of such materials.[36] Depending on the packaging materials (20 percent for plastics and 60 percent for glass), producers, importers, distributors, wholesalers, and retailers are held responsible for generating the waste. In Germany, which has the toughest requirements, all packaging must be reusable or recyclable, and packaging must be kept to a minimum needed for proper protection and marketing of the product. Exporters to the EU must find distributors who can fulfill such requirements and agree how to split the costs.

Appearance

Adaptations in product styling, color, size, and other appearance features are more common in consumer marketing than in industrial marketing. Color plays an important role in the way consumers perceive a product, and marketers must be aware of the signal being sent by the product's color.[37] Color can be used for brand identification—for example, the yellow of Hertz, red of Avis, and green of National. It can be used for feature reinforcement; for example, Honda adopted the color black to give its motorcycles a Darth Vader look, whereas Rolls Royce uses a dazzling silver paint that denotes luxury. Colors communicate in a subtle way in developed societies; they have direct meaning in more traditional societies. IKEA has found that Latin families prefer bold colors to the more subdued Scandinavian preferences, and want to display numerous pictures in elaborate frames.[38] AVG Inc., a California-based provider of technology for theme-park rides, had to change the proposed colors of a ride it designed for a park outside Beijing because the client felt they conveyed the wrong attitude for the ride. Instead the client wanted the colors to be "happy" ones.[39] The only way companies can protect themselves against incidents of this kind is through thorough on-site testing, or, as in AVG's case, on-site production.

Method of Operation or Usage

The product as it is offered in the domestic market may not be operable in the foreign market. One of the major differences faced by appliance manufacturers is electrical power systems. In some cases, variations may exist even within a country, such as Brazil. An exporter can learn about these differences through local government representatives or various trade publications such as the *Electric Current Abroad*.[40] However, exporters should determine for themselves the adjustments that are required by observing competitive products or having their product tested by a local entity.

Many complicating factors may be eliminated in the future through standardization efforts by international organizations and by the conversion of most countries to the metric system. When Canada adopted the metric system in 1977 and 1978, many U.S. companies were affected. More than 2,000 U.S.

businesses use the metric system in research and development (e.g., General Electric) and marketing (e.g., Procter & Gamble's Scope mouthwash is sold in incremental liter bottles) to take advantage of global economies of scale.

Products that rely heavily on the written or spoken language have to be adapted for better penetration of the market. For example, IBM SPSS, the marketer of statistical software, localizes Windows, Mac OS X, and Unix for Chinese, German, English, Japanese *kanji*, and Spanish. Producing software in the local language has also proven to be a weapon in the fight against software piracy.

An exporter may also have to adapt the product to different uses. 3M Touch Systems, which produces touch-activated computer screens for video poker machines and ATMs, makes a series of adjustments in this regard. Ticket vending machines for the French subway need to be waterproof because they are hosed down. Similarly, for the Australian market, video poker screens are built to take a beating because gamblers there take losing more personally than anywhere else.[41]

Quality

Many Western exporters must emphasize quality in their strategies because they cannot compete on price alone. Many new exporters compete on value in the particular segments they have chosen. In some cases, producers of cheaper Asian products have forced international marketers to reexamine their strategies, allowing them to win contracts on the basis of technical advantage. To maintain a position of product superiority, exporting firms must invest in research and development for new products as well as manufacturing methods.

Marketers themselves may seek endorsement of their efforts from governmental or consumer organizations. Many car exporters to the United States (e.g., the Koreans) have become more popular in the market by doing well in the J.D. Power and other car rankings, a fact that may then be used in promotional efforts. However, China's initial efforts to sell cars to the European Union and the United States is drawing scrutiny regarding the quality, especially the safety, of its exports.[42]

Many exporters may overlook the importance of product quality, especially when entering an emerging market. While Fedders, the largest U.S. manufacturer of room air conditioners, had planned to market its most up-to-date air conditioners in China, it quickly discovered that even that was not going to be enough. The reason was that many Chinese buyers want a more sophisticated product than the standard unit sold in the United States. In China, it is a major purchase and therefore often a status symbol. The Chinese also want special features such as remote control and an automatic air-sweeping mechanism.[43]

Service

When a product sold overseas requires repairs, parts, or service, the problem of obtaining, training, and holding a sophisticated engineering or repair staff is not easy. If the product breaks down and the repair arrangements are not up to standard, the image of the product will suffer. In some cases, products abroad may not even be used for their intended purpose and may thus require modifications not only in product configuration but also in service frequency. For instance, snow plows exported from the United States are used to remove sand from driveways in Saudi Arabia. Closely related to servicing is the issue of product warranties. Warranties are not only instructions to customers about what to do if the product fails within a specified period of time but are also effective promotional tools.

Country-of-Origin Effects

The country of origin of a product, typically communicated by the phrase "Made in (country)," has a considerable influence on the quality perceptions of a product. The manufacture of products in certain countries is affected by a built-in positive or negative stereotype of product quality. These stereotypes become important when important dimensions of a product category are also associated with a country's image.[44] For example, if an exporter has a positive match of quality and performance for its exports, the country of origin should be a prominent feature in promotional campaigns. If there is a mismatch, the country of origin may have to be hidden through the adoption of a carefully crafted brand name (e.g., a Hong Kong–based apparel company chose the name Giordano), or the product may be sold with the help of prestigious partners whose image overshadows concerns about negative country-of-origin perceptions. This issue may be especially important to emerging countries, which need to increase exports, and for importers, who source products from countries different from those where they are sold.

When the country of origin does matter to consumers, it is in the exporter's best interest to monitor consumers' perceptions. For example, many consumers around the world perceive Nokia as a Japanese brand, which does not have a negative impact on the company despite the incorrect appropriation and which has led to no action by Nokia. However, Japanese car maker Daihatsu suffered in the U.S. market at the time of its launch because it was perceived as a Korean brand. For this and other reasons, Daihatsu is no longer in the United States but concentrates its efforts on Latin America.[45] French and Italian trade and consumer groups are lobbying the European Union to require mandatory place-of-origin labels. The issue has become a sensitive one for high-end European fashion houses that are starting to make products overseas in low-cost countries.[46]

Countries also argue with the labeling standards of other countries. Mexico, for example, argued that the U.S. dolphin-safe standards are misleading and discriminate against the controversial fishing techniques that Mexico employs to catch tuna. Canada argued that the U.S. Department of Agriculture's mandatory country-of-origin labeling (COOL) program discriminates against imported cattle and hogs.[47]

COMPANY CONSIDERATIONS

Product adaptation is an international marketing tool that serves a variety of strategic needs. In addition to the need to cater to market differences and to compete effectively with others in these markets, the role of product adaptation is also to reach internal goals more effectively.[48]

The issue of product adaptation most often climaxes in the question "Is it worth it?" The answer depends on the firm's ability to control costs, correctly estimate market potential, and finally secure profitability, especially in the long term. The costs of product adaptation may be recouped through higher export performance. Arguments to the contrary exist as well. While new markets, such as those in Central Europe, may at present require product adaptation, some marketers may feel that the markets are too small to warrant such adjustments and may quite soon converge with Western European ones, especially in light of their EU membership. Sales of a standard product may be smaller in the short term, but long-term benefits will justify the adoption of this approach. However, the question that used to be posed as "Can we afford to do it?" should now be "Can we afford not to do it?"

The decision to adapt should be preceded by a thorough analysis of the market. Formal market research with primary data collection or testing is warranted. From the financial standpoint, some firms have specific return-on-investment levels to be satisfied before adaptation (for instance, 25 percent), whereas some let the requirement vary as a function of the market considered and also the time in the market—that is, profitability may be initially compromised for proper market entry.

Most companies aim for consistency in their marketing efforts. This translates into the requirement that all products fit in terms of quality, price, and user perceptions. An example of where consistency may be difficult to control is in the area of warranties. Warranties can be uniform only if the use conditions do not vary drastically and if the company is able to deliver equally on its promise anywhere it has a presence.

Individuals are needed who are willing to make risky decisions and who know about existing market conditions. Many companies benefit from having managers from different (types of) countries, giving them the experience and the expertise to make decisions between standardization and adaptation.

GLOBAL PRODUCT DEVELOPMENT

Product development is at the heart of the global marketing process. New products should be developed, or old ones modified, to cater to new or changing customer needs on a global or regional basis. At the same time, corporate objectives of technical feasibility and financial profitability must be satisfied.

To illustrate, Stanley Black & Decker, manufacturer of power tools for do-it-yourself household repairs, had done some remodeling of its own. The company earlier was the consummate customizer: the Italian subsidiary made tools for Italians, the British subsidiary for the British. At the same time, Japanese power-tool makers, such as Makita Electric Works Ltd., saw the world differently. Makita was Stanley Black & Decker's first competitor with a global strategy. Makita management did not care that Germans prefer high-powered, heavy-duty drills and that U.S. consumers want everything lighter. Using this strategy, Makita effectively cut into Stanley Black & Decker's market share. As a result, Stanley Black & Decker unveiled each new product standardized for world production. The company's current objective is to establish itself as the preeminent global manufacturer and marketer in its field.[49]

With competition increasingly able to react quickly when new products are introduced, worldwide planning at the product level provides a number of tangible benefits. A firm that adopts a worldwide approach is better able to develop products with specifications compatible on a worldwide scale. A firm that leaves product development to independent units will incur greater difficulties in transferring its experience and technology.

In many global corporations, each product is developed for potential worldwide usage, and unique market requirements are incorporated whenever technically feasible. Some design their products to meet the regulations and other key requirements in their major markets, and then, if necessary, smaller markets' requirements are met on a country-by-country basis. Companies like 3M and Xerox develop most of their products with this objective in mind, just as Ford has done, as shown in *The International Marketplace 11.3*.

In a world economy where most of the growth is occurring in emerging markets, the traditional approach of introducing a global product may keep new products out of the hands of consumers due to their premium price. As a result, Procter & Gamble figures out what consumers in various countries can afford and then develops products they can pay for. For example, in Brazil, the company introduced a diaper called Simply Dry, a less-expensive version of its mainstream product. The strategy is to create price tiers, generating brand loyalty early and then encouraging customers to trade up as their incomes and desire for better products grow.[50]

The main goal of the product development process, therefore, is not to develop a standard product or product line but to build adaptability into products and product lines that are being developed to achieve worldwide appeal. To accomplish the right balance, marketers need to develop basic capability for capturing consumer information within their country organizations. If consumers are willing to talk about their preferences, traditional approaches such as focus groups and interviews work well.[51]

THE INTERNATIONAL MARKETPLACE 11.3

New World Car Strategy

Ford Motor has lifted the veil on a new sport-utility vehicle, which illustrates exactly how much the auto maker has changed the way it now looks at developing and making cars. The 2012 Escape, which is due to arrive in showrooms this spring, will be made from a common set of parts and components that Ford will also use to make its Focus compact car, two future minivans, and at least six other models. Those same components, known in the industry as a "platform," will pop up in vehicles assembled and sold in North and South America, Europe, and Asia. Ford has said that it will cost about two-thirds less to engineer a new vehicle using shared platforms than developing a wholly new one.

Ford hopes to produce more than two million vehicles a year around the globe that are all made from the same basic parts and assembled in plants that use the same type of tooling. The goal is to leverage design and manufacturing economies of scale to wring huge savings from its $50 billion annual budget for auto parts. There are so many facets to the savings that it is hard to put a number to it. Companies save money in literally every area of development, from engineering time, to parts and service, to tooling and machinery.

The sharing goes far beyond the new Escape. All told, Ford is betting on five common platforms to deliver sales of more than six million vehicles by the middle of the decade. Five years ago, Ford had 15 platforms that accounted for sales of 6.6 million vehicles. By sharing parts, Ford expects to produce a raft of new, cost-competitive vehicles that the company can sell in emerging markets including China and India. The company is aiming to boost global sales to more than eight million vehicles a year, up from 5.5 million last year.

Ford is not alone in its pursuit of common platforms. Rival General Motors Co. is charging in the same direction. It now shares parts between the Chevrolet Cruze and most of the other compact cars it makes around the world. Chrysler Group is farther behind, although it hopes to do this with its partner Fiat SpA.

Already, the Focus now serves as the underpinning for all of Ford's small cars. Another set of parts is used for all of its subcompacts and related models that it makes around the world. Subcompact production is expected to exceed two million vehicles a year. In 2012, Ford will introduce a new Fusion mid-sized car also based on a global platform shared by an expected one million vehicles. The current version of the Fusion shares almost no parts with Ford's European mid-sized car, the Mondeo. Ford has also finished or is working on platforms for small pickup trucks and commercial vans to be produced and sold globally.

Markets like China, India, and Brazil are buying low-cost cars that generate slim profits. While past global car strategies have failed, Ford's designs have helped the auto maker carve bigger inroads in one of the fastest growing auto markets in the world. The small utility vehicle, called the EcoSport, will be built on the same underpinnings as the auto maker's subcompact Ford Fiesta and likely will be sold first in Asia and South America. By 2020, it expects one-third of its global sales will be from Asia, as opposed to about one-sixth today. The industry also has been forced to find new savings to offset the rising cost of commodities like steel and plastics and has had to develop expensive new technologies to boost fuel economy and cut tailpipe emissions.

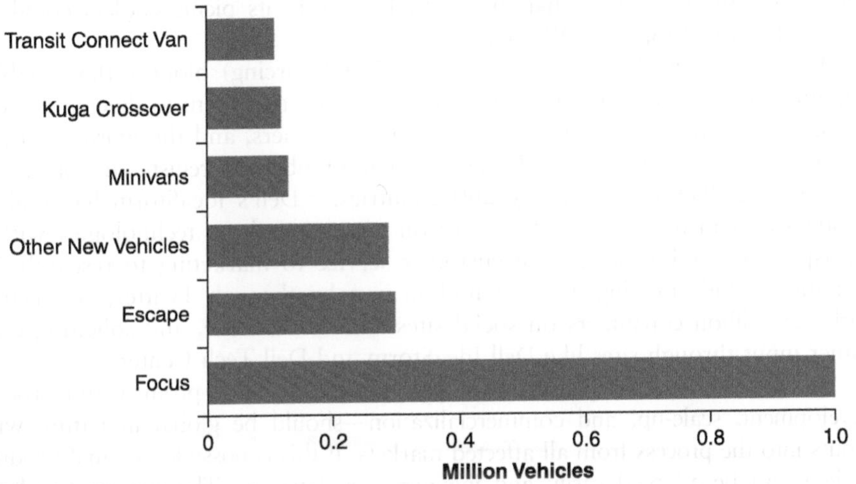

By 2016, Ford expects to produce 1.9 million vehicles from the basic parts that go into its new Escape.

SOURCE: Ford.

SOURCES: Mike Ramsey, "Ford to Unveil SUV in India," *Wall Street Journal*, January 4, 2012, B4; Mike Ramsey, "Ford SUV Marks New World Car Strategy," *Wall Street Journal*, November 16, 2011, B1; and Mike Ramsey, "Higher Costs Hit Ford," *Wall Street Journal*, October 27, 2011, B5.

The Product Development Process

The product development process begins with idea generation. Ideas may come from within the company—from the research and development staff, sales personnel, or almost anyone who becomes involved in the company's efforts. In a recent IBM survey, 750 global CEOs reported that only 14 percent of their innovation ideas came from traditional R&D. Instead, 41 percent came from employees and 36 percent came from customers.[52]

Via an internal R&D process, companies can pick the brains of their employees, and many companies have developed new-product ideas based on employee feedback. For example, Cisco makes it everyone's business to come up with great ideas. It set up an internal wiki called Idea Zone, through which any Cisco employee can propose an idea for a new product or comment on or modify someone else's proposed idea. Since its inception, Idea Zone has generated hundreds of ideas, leading to the formation of four new Cisco business units. In the end, more than 2,500 innovators from 104 countries submitted some 1,200 distinct ideas.[53]

Customers provide the best source of ideas for new products. Many new commercially important products are initially thought of and even prototyped by users rather than originators via the external R&D process. They tend to be developed by **lead users**—companies, organizations, or individuals who are ahead of trends or have needs that go beyond what is available at present. For example, a car company in need of a new braking system may look for ideas from racing teams or even the aerospace industry, which has a strong incentive to stop its vehicles before they run out of runway. Of the 30 products with the highest world sales, 70 percent trace their origins to manufacturing and marketing (rather than laboratories) via customer input. Many companies work together with complementary-goods producers in developing new solutions; for instance, Whirlpool and Procter & Gamble developed new solutions for keeping people's clothes clean. With the increased diffusion of the Internet, chat rooms about products and features will become an important source of information pertinent to product development and adjustment. For example, Sony set up a website to support hackers who are interested in exploring and developing new types of games that could be played on the Sony PlayStation. In the field of industrial products, users are invited to use toolkits to design products and services that fit their own needs precisely.[54]

For some companies, procurement requisitions from governments and supranational organizations (e.g., the United Nations) are a good source of new product ideas. When the United Nations Children's Fund (UNICEF) was looking for containers to transport temperature-sensitive vaccines in tropical climates, Igloo Corporation noticed that the technology from its picnic coolers could be used and adapted for UNICEF's use.[55]

InnoCentive is the **open innovation** (crowdsourcing) pioneer that enables organizations to solve their key problems by connecting them to diverse sources of innovation including employees, customers, partners, and the world's largest problem-solving marketplace. It has a total number of registered solvers of more than 250,000 from nearly 200 countries.[56] Dell's IdeaStorm has built a strong social media team that focuses on entwining those technologies within all aspects of its business, from customer service to marketing to research. Its activities include racking up $6.5 million in sales through Twitter, connecting with 3.5 million consumers on social sites and its own site, and soliciting consumer input through sites like Dell IdeaStorm and Dell Tech Center.[57]

All the development phases—idea generation, screening, product and process development, scale-up, and commercialization—should be global in nature with inputs into the process from all affected markets. If this is possible, original product designs can be adapted easily and inexpensively later on. The process has been greatly facilitated through the use of **computer-aided design (CAD)**. Some companies are able to design their products so that they meet most standards and requirements around the world, with minor modifications on a country-by-country basis.

Global companies may have an advantage in being able to utilize resources from around the world. Otis Elevator Inc.'s product for high-rises, the Elevonic, is a good example of this. The elevator was developed by six research centers in five countries. Otis's group in Farmington, Connecticut, handled the systems integration; Japan designed the special motor drives that make the elevators ride smoothly; France perfected the door systems; Germany handled the electronics; and Spain took care of the small-geared components. The international effort saved more than $10 million in design costs and cut the development cycle from four years to two.[58]

The activities of a typical global program are summarized in Exhibit 11.5. The managing unit has prime responsibility for accomplishing (1) single-point worldwide technical development and design of a new product that conforms to the global design standard and global manufacturing and procurement

EXHIBIT 11.5 Global Program Management

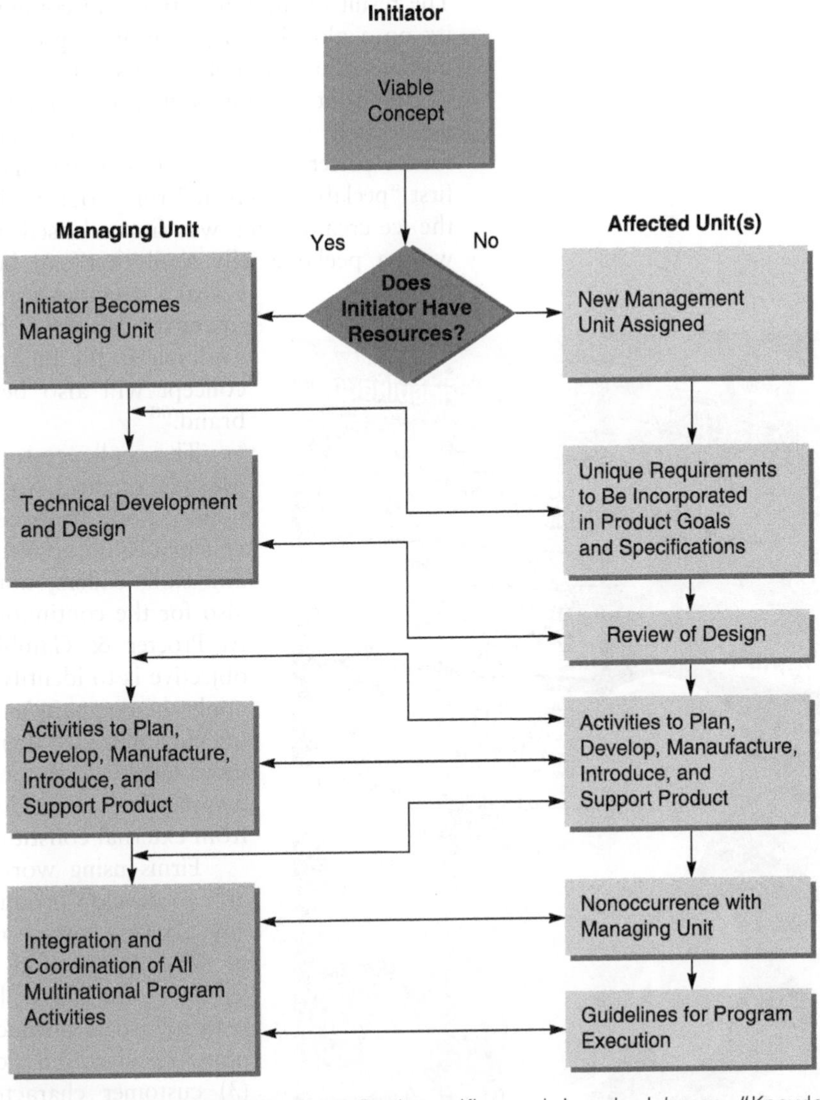

SOURCES: Ruby P. Lee, Qimei Chen, Daekwan Kim, and Jean L. Johnson, "Knowledge Transfer between Multinational Corporations' Headquarters and Their Subsidiaries: Influences on and Implications for New Product Outcomes," *Journal of International Marketing* 16, no. 2 (2008): 1–31; and Ilkka A. Ronkainen, "Product Development in the Multinational Firm," *International Marketing Review* 1 (Winter 1983): 57–65.

standards, as well as transmittal of the completed design to each affected unit; (2) all other activities necessary to plan, develop, originate, introduce, and support the product in the managing unit, as well as direction and support to affected units to ensure that concurrent introductions are achieved; and (3) integration and coordination of all global program activities.

The affected units, on the other hand, have prime responsibility for achieving (1) identification of unique requirements to be incorporated in the product goals and specifications as well as in the managing unit's technical effort; (2) all other activities necessary to plan, originate, introduce, and support products in affected units; and (3) identification of any nonconcurrence with the managing unit's plans and activities.

During the early stages of the product development process, the global emphasis is on identifying and evaluating the requirements of both the managing unit and the affected units and incorporating them into the plan. During the later stages, the emphasis is on the efficient development and design of a global product with a minimum of configuration differences and on the development of supporting systems' capabilities in each of the participating units. The result of the interaction and communication is product development activity on a global basis, as well as products developed primarily to serve world markets. For example, Fiat's Palio is designed for the rough roads of the Brazilian interior rather than the smooth motorways of Italy. The car was also deliberately overengineered because market research revealed that customers' future preferences were developing that way.[59] In another example, Nestlé's first "peelable ice cream" rolled out worldwide in 2011. Called Eskimo Monkey, the ice cream snack was first released in Thailand and is eaten like a banana, with a peelable jelly shell that can be rolled down like a banana skin to reveal a delicious ice cream core. First extended to Malaysia under the Mat kool brand, the ice cream snack will now be available in the Philippines as Krazy Banana. The ice cream concept will also be on sale in Europe under the Pirulo brand.[60]

Courtesy of NESTLE PEELABLE ICE CREAM ®

NESTLE PEELABLE ICE CREAM ® is marketed across the world.

The challenge today is that no internal R&D effort can possibly predict, evaluate, and cover all possible configurations. Taking these new realities to heart, companies need to systematically tap into the capabilities of external knowledge and skill leaders, not just for state-of-the-art products but also for the continuous innovation and evolution of ideas.[61] At Procter & Gamble, the "connect-and-develop" model's objective is to identify promising ideas around the world and apply the company's own R&D, manufacturing, and marketing capabilities to them to create better and cheaper products more quickly.[62] A total of 45 percent of the initiatives in the company's product-development portfolio have key elements from external constituents.

Firms using worldwide product management are better able to develop products that can be quickly introduced into any market. Foreign-market introduction can take the form of either production or marketing abroad. In general, the length of the lag will depend on (1) the product involved, with industrial products having shorter lags because of their more standardized general nature; (2) degree of newness; (3) customer characteristics—both demographics and psychographics; (4) geographic proximity; (5) firm-related variables—the number and type of foreign affiliations as well as overall experience in global marketing; and (6) degree of commitments of resources.

The Location of R&D Activities

In the past, many corporations located most of their product-development operations within the parent corporation. However, a significant number of companies have started using foreign-based resources to improve their ability to compete internationally. At ABB, for example, 80 percent of research was carried out in the company's Swiss, Swedish, and German offices only a few years ago, but now it is only half of the total. The company has established new research units in countries such as India and China to stay closer to markets to meet customer needs.[63] Dutch electronics giant Philips has 15 R&D centers in China as part of the company's strategy aiming at satisfying demand for its products (such as low-end mobile phones) in China, India, Africa, South America, and Eastern Europe. These centers are integrated with the efforts of the R&D centers in Europe and the company's Innovation Campus in India.[64]

Investments for R&D abroad are made for four general reasons: (1) to aid technology transfer from parent to subsidiary, (2) to develop new and improved products expressly for global markets, (3) to develop new products and processes for simultaneous application in world markets of the firm, and (4) to generate new technology of a long-term, exploratory nature. In most cases, companies want to be closer to the customers they intend to serve. Caterpillar's labs scattered around the world allow the company to work on urgent projects around the clock, passing them from one time zone to another. Caterpillar's largest R&D center by far is near Peoria, Illinois. Other research sites are in Chennai, India; Peterborough, England; and Ono, Japan, as well as Wuxi, China.[65]

In truly global companies, the location of R&D is determined by the existence of specific skills. A **center of excellence** is defined as an organizational unit that incorporates a set of capabilities that have been identified as an important source of value creation with the explicit intention that these capabilities be leveraged by and disseminated to other parts of the firm. Procter & Gamble has six development hubs that are focused on finding products and technologies that are specialties of their regions. The China hub looks for new high-quality materials and cost innovations, while the India hub seeks out local talent in the sciences to solve problems using tools such as computer modeling. Unilever has installed a network of innovation centers in 19 countries, many of which are emerging markets (such as Brazil, China, and Thailand).[66]

The United States is rapidly losing high-technology jobs as American companies expand their R&D labs in China and elsewhere in Asia. U.S. companies generally are not closing labs at home but rather focusing their expansion abroad. Total U.S. spending on R&D in 2009 was about $400 billion. The total for China, India, Japan, and seven other Asian countries came to $399 billion. The European Union total was about $300 billion.[67]

Booz & Co. makes an annual study of the 1,000 publicly traded companies globally that spend the most on R&D, based on their public disclosures. Roche Holding AG had the biggest spending total in 2010, at $9.64 billion. It was followed by Pfizer with $9.41 billion and Novartis at $9.07 billion (see Exhibit 11.6).

Booz also found that heavy spending on R&D does not necessarily lead to recognition as a technology leader. In a survey of more than 450 "innovation executives" from 400 companies representing $150 billion in annual R&D spending, Booz asked them to name the companies they considered most innovative. The three most frequently chosen by respondents were Apple, Google, and 3M, none of which was among the 10 biggest spenders on R&D.[68]

R&D centers are seen as highly desirable investments by host governments. Developing countries are increasingly demanding R&D facilities as a condition of investment or continued operation, to the extent that some companies have left countries where they saw no need for the added expense. Countries that

EXHIBIT 11.6 The Global Innovation 1000

Rank			R&D Spending			
2010	**2009**	**Company**	**2010, US$ Millions**	**As a Percent of Sales**	**Headquarters Location**	**Industry**
1	1	Roche Holding	9,646	21.1	Europe	Healthcare
2	5	Pfizer	9,413	13.9	North America	Healthcare
3	6	Novartis	9,070	17.9	Europe	Healthcare
4	2	Microsoft	8,714	14.0	North America	Software and Internet
5	14	Merck	8,591	18.7	North America	Healthcare
6	4	Toyota	8,546	3.9	Asia	Auto
7	10	Samsung	7,873	5.9	Asia	Computing and electronics
8	3	Nokia	7,778	13.8	Europe	Computing and electronics
9	11	General Motors	6,962	5.1	North America	Auto
10	7	Johnson & Johnson	6,844	11.1	North America	Healthcare
11	13	Intel	6,576	15.1	North America	Computing and electronics
12	18	Panasonic	6,176	6.1	Asia	Computing and electronics
13	9	GlaxoSmithKline	6,127	14.0	Europe	Healthcare
14	15	Volkswagen	6,089	3.6	Europe	Auto
15	12	IBM	6,026	6.0	North America	Computing and electronics
16	8	Sanofi-Aventis	5,838	14.5	Europe	Healthcare
17	19	Honda	5,704	5.5	Asia	Auto
18	22	AstraZeneca	5,318	16.0	Europe	Healthcare
19	17	Cisco Systems	5,273	13.2	North America	Computing and electronics
20	16	Siemens	5,217	5.1	Europe	Industrials

SOURCE: Adapted and reprinted with permission from "The Global Innovation 1000: Why Culture Is Key" by Barry Jaruzelski, John Loehr, and Richard Holman from the Winter 2011 issue of *strategy+business* magazine, published by Booz & Company Inc. Copyright © 2011. All rights reserved. www.strategy-business.com.

have been known to attempt to influence multinational corporations are Japan, India, Brazil, and France. The Chinese government has maintained a preference for foreign investors who have promised a commitment to technology transfer, especially in the form of R&D centers; Volkswagen's ability to develop its business in China is largely due to its willingness to do so.

In companies that still employ multidomestic strategies, product-development efforts amount to product modifications—for example, making sure that a product satisfies local regulations. In these cases, local technical people identify alternate, domestically available ingredients and prepare initial tests. More involved testing usually takes place at a regional laboratory or at headquarters.

The Organization of Global Product Development

The product-development activity is undertaken by specific teams, whose task is to subject new products to tough scrutiny at specified points in the development cycle to eliminate weak products before too much is invested in them and to guide promising prototypes from labs to the market.[69] Representatives of all the affected functional areas serve on each team to ensure the integrity of the project. A marketing team member is needed to assess the customer base for the new product, an engineering member to make sure that the product can be produced in the intended format, and a finance member to keep costs in control. An international team member should be assigned a permanent role in the product-development process and not simply be called in when a need arises. Organizational relationships have to be such that the firm's knowledge-based assets are easily transferable and transferred.[70]

In addition to having international representation on each product-development team, some multinational corporations hold periodic meetings of purely international teams. A typical international team may consist of five members, each of whom also has a product responsibility (such as cable accessories) as well as a geographical responsibility (such as the Far East). Others may be from central R&D and domestic marketing planning. The function of international teams is to provide both support to subsidiaries and international input to overall planning efforts. A critical part of this effort is customer input before a new product design is finalized. This is achieved by requiring team members to visit key customers throughout the process. A key input of international team members is the potential for universal features that can be used worldwide as well as unique features that may be required for individual markets.

Such multidisciplinary teams maximize the payoff from R&D by streamlining decision making; that is, they reduce the need for elaborate reporting mechanisms and layers of committee approvals. With the need to slash development time, reduce overall material costs, and trim manufacturing processes, these teams can be useful. For example, in response to competition, LG and Honeywell set up a multidisciplinary "tiger team" to build a thermostat in 12 months rather than the usual four years.

Language and cultural barriers are often challenges to using teams or approaches that require cooperation between R&D centers. For example, pragmatic engineers in the United States may distrust their more theoretically thinking European counterparts. National rivalries may also inhibit the acceptance by others of solutions developed by one entity of the organization. Many companies have solved these problems with increased communication and exchange of personnel.[71]

With the costs of basic research rising and product life cycles shortening, many companies have joined forces in R&D. The EU and U.S. government and multinational corporations have seen this approach as necessary to restore technological competitiveness. Since then, **R&D consortia** have been established to develop technologies ranging from artificial intelligence to those in semiconductor manufacturing, such as Sematech. Sematech's focus is on accelerating the commercialization of technology innovations into manufacturing solutions in semiconductors and emerging technologies.[72] The United States Council for Automotive Research was set up by GM, Ford, and Chrysler to work on new concepts for use in the automotive sector, such as new battery technology, safety features, and recyclability. A key focus of this collaboration is on the development of hybrid technology designed to improve efficiency and conserve energy.[73] Similar consortia in the European Union are often heavily supported by the European Commission.

The Testing of New Product Concepts

The final stages of the product-development process involve testing the product in terms of both its performance and its projected market acceptance. Depending on the product, testing procedures range from reliability tests in the pilot plant to minilaunches, from which the product's performance in world markets will be estimated. Any testing will prolong full-scale commercialization and increase the possibility of competitive reaction.

Because of the high rate of new product failure (estimated at 67 to 95 percent and usually attributed to market or marketing reasons), most companies want to be assured that their product will gain customer acceptance.[74] They therefore engage in testing or a limited launch of the product. This may involve introducing the product in one country—for instance, Belgium or Ireland—and basing the go-ahead decision for the rest of Europe on the performance of the product in that test market. Some countries are emerging as test markets for global products. Brazil is a test market used by Procter & Gamble, and Unilever uses Thailand as a test market for the Asian market.

Reasons for product failure are a lack of product distinctiveness, unexpected technical problems, and mismatches between functions.[75] Mismatches between functions may occur not only between, for example, engineering and marketing but within the marketing function as well. Engineering may design features in the product that established distribution channels or selling approaches cannot exploit. Advertising may promise the customer something that the other functions within marketing cannot deliver.

The trend is toward a complete testing of the marketing mix. All the components of the brand are tested, including formulation, packaging, advertising, and pricing. Test marketing is indispensable because prelaunch testing is an artificial situation; it tells the researcher what people say they will do, not what they will actually do. Test marketing carries major financial risks, which can be limited only if the testing can be conducted in a limited area. Ideally, this would utilize localized advertising media—that is, broadcast and print media to which only a limited region would be exposed.

Because test marketing is risky or even impossible, researchers have developed three research methods to cope with the difficulty. **Controlled market tests** allow companies to assess an item's sales potential in a real-world environment with real consumers making real purchases. With a controlled market test design, the marketing plan can be replicated and year-one sales volume is forecasted from a robust sample of recognized food, drug, or mass merchandise retailers. **Simulated test markets** offer simulation under realistic conditions from a 360° marketing vantage point. Innovations need to establish themselves against the competition in terms of advertising, shelf placement, price, and product experience. A third method, the **vitality lab**, provides a directional gauge of the initiative's potential in a real-world environment, with real consumers making real purchases. Sales rates and consumer responses to the initiative can determine if another, more precise level of in-store testing is warranted or if a particular issue needs to be addressed prior to rollout. Either saleable or unsaleable products can be utilized based on production capabilities.[76]

The Global Product Launch

The impact of an effective global product launch can be great, but so can the cost of one that is poorly executed.[77] High development costs as well as competitive pressures are forcing companies to rush products into as many markets as possible. But at the same time, a company can ill afford new products that are not effectively introduced, marketed, and supported in each market the company competes in.

A global product launch means introducing a product into countries in three or more regions within a narrow time frame. To achieve this, a company must undertake a number of measures. The country managers should be involved in the first stage of product strategy formulation to ensure that local and regional considerations are part of the overall corporate and product messages. More important, intercountry coordination of the rollout preparations will ultimately determine the level of success in the introduction. A product launch team (consisting of product, marketing, manufacturing, sales, service, engineering, and communication representatives) can also approach problems from an industry standpoint, as opposed to a home-country perspective, enhancing product competitiveness in all markets.

Adequate consideration should be given to localization and translation requirements before the launch. This means that the right messages are formulated and transmitted to key internal and external audiences. Support materials have to take into account both cultural and technical differences. The advantage of a simultaneous launch is that it boosts the overall momentum and attractiveness of the product by making it immediately available in key geographic markets.

A successfully executed global launch offers several benefits. First, it permits the company to showcase its technology in all major markets at the same time. Setting a single date for the launch functions as a strict discipline to force the entire organization to gear up quickly for a successful worldwide effort. A simultaneous worldwide introduction also solves the "lame duck" dilemma of having old models available in some markets while customers know of the existence of the new product. If margins are most lucrative at the early stages of the new product's life cycle, they should be exploited by getting the product to as many markets as possible from the outset. With product development costs increasing and product life cycles shortening, marketers have to consider this approach seriously. An additional benefit of a worldwide launch may be added publicity to benefit the marketer's efforts, as happened with the worldwide introductions of Microsoft's Windows 95, 98, 2000, XP, Vista, and 7 versions.

MANAGING THE BRAND PORTFOLIO

Branding is one of the major beneficiaries of a well-conducted portfolio analysis. Brands are important because they shape customer decisions and, ultimately, create economic value. The brand is a key factor behind the decision to purchase in both consumer and business-to-business situations. On the average, the brand is responsible for 18 percent of total purchase decisions, and the majority of studies reveal a brand-loyal segment of individuals for whom the brand is the major influencing factor. In addition, strong brands are able to charge a price premium of 19 percent.[78] Gillette's Mach3, although priced more than 50 percent above its predecessor (Sensor Excel), was able to increase sales by 30 percent since rollout.[79] Research into the connection of brand strength and corporate performance at 130 multinational companies revealed that strong brands generate total returns to shareholders that are 1.9 percent above the industry average, while weaker brands lag behind the average by 3.1 percent.[80]

The BrandAsset Consulting model for valuing brands is based on four key pillars that measure consumer sentiment and usage. "Energized differentiation" contributes to pricing power and consideration, "relevance" builds consideration and trial, "esteem" builds loyalty and, along with "knowledge," moves sales. With measurements in 50 countries, the BrandAsset Valuator uniquely gauges the nature of international marketing opportunities. The research indicates that there are two dimensions to global brands: (1) consistency of brand strength (differentiation, relevance) and brand stature (esteem and knowledge) together; and (2) consistency of brand meaning. Preliminary analyses suggest that brands that are strong around the world and have a consistent meaning globally perform better financially than strong brands with inconsistent meaning. Not surprisingly, Disney is the brand with the most consistent meaning from country to country. In each country, Disney's "imagery profile" falls into the category of "fun."[81]

Global marketers have three choices for branding within the global, regional, and local dimensions: (1) have brands that feature the corporate name; (2) have family brands for a wide range of products or product variations; or (3) have individual brands for each item in the product line. With the increase in strategic alliances, cobranding—in which two or more well-known brands are combined in an offer—has also become popular. Examples of these approaches include Heinz, which has a policy of using its corporate name in all its products; Procter & Gamble, which has a policy of stand-alone products or product lines; and Nestlé, which uses a mixture of Nestlé and Nes-designated brands and stand-alones. In the case of marketing alliances, the brand portfolio may be a combination of both partners' brands. General Mills' alliance with

Nestlé in cereals, Cereal Partners Worldwide, features General Mills brands such as Trix and Nestlé brands such as Chocapic.[82]

Market power is usually in the hands of brand-name companies that have to determine the most effective use of this asset across markets. The value of brands can be seen in recent acquisitions where prices have been many times over the book value of the company purchased. Nestlé, for example, paid five times the book value for the British Rowntree, the owner of such brands as Kit Kat and After Eight. Many of the world's leading brands command high brand equity values, that is, the price premium the brand commands times the extra volume it moves over what an average brand commands.[83]

An example of global rankings of brands is provided in Exhibit 11.7. This Interbrand-sponsored study rates brands on their value and their strength. Each ranked brand had to derive at least one-third of its earnings outside its home country, be recognizable beyond its established customer base, and have publicly available marketing and financial data. The ranking is truly on the strength of individual brands, not a portfolio of brands. Of the top 25 global brands in terms of brand value in 2011, three are Asian, six are European, and 16 are based in the United States.

EXHIBIT 11.7 25 Most Valuable Global Brands

Rank			Brand Value ($millions)			
2011	**2010**	**Brand**	**2011**	**2010**	**Sector**	**Region/Country**
1	1	Coca-Cola	71,861	70,452	Beverages	United States
2	2	IBM	69,905	64,727	Business services	United States
3	3	Microsoft	59,087	60,895	Computer software	United States
4	4	Google	55,317	43,557	Internet services	United States
5	5	GE	42,808	42,808	Diversified	United States
6	6	McDonald's	35,593	33,578	Restaurants	United States
7	7	Intel	35,217	32,015	Electronics	United States
8	17	Apple	33,492	21,143	Electronics	United States
9	9	Disney	29,018	28,731	Media	United States
10	10	Hewlett-Packard	28,479	26,867	Electronics	United States
11	11	Toyota	27,764	26,192	Automotive	Japan
12	12	Mercedes-Benz	27,445	25,179	Automotive	Germany
13	14	Cisco	25,309	23,219	Business services	United States
14	8	Nokia	25,071	29,495	Electronics	Finland
15	15	BMW	24,554	22,322	Automotive	Germany
16	13	Gillette	23,997	23,298	Fast-moving consumer goods	United States
17	19	Samsung	23,430	19,491	Electronics	South Korea
18	16	Louis Vuitton	23,172	21,860	Luxury	France
19	20	Honda	19,431	18,506	Automotive	Japan
20	22	Oracle	17,262	14,881	Business services	United States
21	21	H&M	16,459	16,136	Apparel	Sweden
22	23	Pepsi	14,590	14,061	Beverages	United States
23	24	American Express	14,572	13,944	Financial services	United States
24	26	SAP	14,542	12,756	Business services	Germany
25	25	Nike	14,528	13,706	Sporting goods	United States

SOURCE: "Best Global Brands," www.interbrand.com, December 7, 2011.

Brand Strategy Decisions

The goal of many marketers currently is to create consistency and impact, both of which are easier to manage with a single worldwide identity. Global brands are a key way of reaching this goal. Global brands are those that reach the world's megamarkets and are perceived as the same brand by consumers and internal constituents.[84] While some of the global brands are completely standardized, some elements of the product may be adapted to local conditions. These adjustments include brand names (e.g., Tide, Whisper, and Clairol in North America are Ariel, Allways, and Wella in Europe), positioning (e.g., Ford Fiesta as a small car in Germany but a family vehicle in Portugal), or product versions sold under the same brand name (e.g., 9 to 13 different types of coffee sold under the Nescafé name in Northern Europe alone).[85]

Consumers all over the world associate global brands with three characteristics and evaluate their performance on them when making purchase decisions.[86] Global brands carry a strong quality signal suggested by their success across markets. Part of this is that great brands often represent great ideas and leading-edge technological solutions. Second, global brands compete on emotion, catering to aspirations that cut across cultural differences. Global brands may cater to needs to feel cosmopolitan, something that local brands cannot deliver. Global brands may also convey that their users have reached a certain status both professionally and personally. This type of recognition represents both perception and reality, enabling brands to establish credibility in markets.[87] The third reason consumers choose global brands is involvement in solving social problems linked to what they are marketing and how they conduct their business. Expectations that global marketers use their monetary and human resources to benefit society are uniform from developed to developing markets.

There are three main implications for the marketing manager to consider. (1) Don't hide globality. Given the benefits of globality, marketers should not be shy in communicating this feature of a brand. Creatively, this may mean referring to the leadership position of the brand around the world or referring to the extent of innovation or features that are possible only for a brand with considerable reach. Marketers intent on scaling down their brand portfolios and focusing on global offerings are able to invest in more marketing muscle and creative effort behind the sleeker set of offerings. (2) Tackle home-country bias. One of the marketing mantras is "being local on a global scale." Because some markets feature substantial preference for home-grown brands, it is imperative to localize some features of the marketing approach, possibly including even the brand name. One approach could be that a brand has a consistent global positioning but the name varies according to country language. An example is Mr. Clean becoming Mr. Proper in Germany, Austria, and Switzerland; Mr. Propre in France; Don Limpio in Spain; and MastroLindo in Italy. Many global brands have already localized to neutralize the home-country effect. (3) Satisfy the basics. Global brands signal quality and aspiration. However, taking a global approach to branding is not in itself the critical factor. What is critical is creating differentiation and familiarity as well as the needed margins and growth. The greater esteem that global brands enjoy is not sufficient in itself for pursuing this strategy. However, this dimension may tip the balance in the ultimate strategy choice. At the same time, it is evident that globality should not be pursued at the cost of alienating local consumers by preemptively eliminating purely local brands or converging them under a global brand.[88]

Branding is an integral part of the overall identity management of the firm. Global brands need to achieve a high degree of consistency in their delivery of customer service and how it is communicated across all consumer points of touch. Therefore, it is typically a centralized function to exploit to the fullest the brand's assets as well as to protect the asset from dilution by, for example, extending the brand to inappropriate new lines. The role of headquarters, strategic business unit management, global teams, or global managers charged with a product is to provide guidelines for the effort without hampering local initiative.[89] The "glocal" dimension can only be achieved by giving regional and local managers the power to interpret and express the message. In addition to the use of a global brand name from the very beginning, many marketers are consolidating their previously different brand names (often for the same or similar products) with global or regional brand names. For example, Mars replaced its Treets and Bonitas names with M&M worldwide and renamed its British best-seller, Marathon, with the Snickers name it uses in North and South America. The benefits in global branding are in marketing economies and higher acceptance of products by consumers and intermediaries. The drawbacks are in the loss of local flavor, especially when a local brand is replaced by a regional or global brand name. At these times, internal marketing becomes critical to instill ownership of the global brands in the personnel of the country organizations.[90]

Nestlé has been dedicated to enhancing lives by establishing four levels of brands: worldwide corporate brands (e.g., Maggi and Perrier), worldwide strategic brands (e.g., KitKat and Smarties), regional strategic brands (e.g., Stouffer's and Alpo), and local brands (e.g., Estrelitas and Thomy). The worldwide brands are under the responsibility of SBUs and general management, which establish a framework for each in the form of a planning policy document. These policies lay out the brand's positioning, labeling standards, packaging features, and other related marketing mix issues, such as a communications platform. The same principle applies to regional brands, where guidelines are issued and decisions made by the SBU and regional management. Among the 7,500 local brands are 700 local strategic brands, such as Chambinho in Brazil, which are monitored by the SBUs for positioning and labeling standards. Nestlé is consolidating its efforts behind its corporate and strategic brands. This is taking place in various ways. When Nestlé acquired Rowntree, which had had a one-product, one-brand policy, it added its corporate name to some of the products, such as Nestlé Kit Kat. Its refrigerated products line under the Chambourcy brand is undergoing a name change to Nestlé. Some of the products that do not carry the corporate name feature a Nestlé "seal of guarantee" on the back. About 40 percent of the company's sales come from products covered by the corporate brand.

Carefully crafted brand portfolios allow marketers to serve defined parts of specific markets. At Whirlpool, the Whirlpool brand name will be used as the global brand to serve the broad middle-market segment, while regional and local brands will cover the others. For example, throughout Europe, the Bauknecht brand is targeted at the upper end of the market seeking a reputable German brand. Ignis and Laden are positioned as price-value brands, Ignis Europe-wide, Laden in France. This approach applies to Whirlpool's other markets as well: in Latin America, Consul is the major regional brand.

The brand portfolio needs to be periodically and regularly assessed. A number of global marketers are focusing their attention on "A" brands with the greatest growth potential. By continuing to dispose of noncore brands, the marketer can concentrate on the global ones and reduce production, marketing, storage, and distribution costs. It is increasingly difficult for the global company to manage purely local brands. The surge of private-label products has also put additional pressure on "B" brands.[91]

However, before disposing of a brand, managers need to assess it in terms of current sales, loyalty, potential, and trends. For example, eliminating a local brand that may have a strong and loyal following, has been created by local management, and shows potential to be extended to nearby markets is not necessarily in the best interests of the company. Three approaches for purely local brands may work: a penetration price approach, a cultural approach positioning the product as a true defender of local culture, and a "chameleon" approach in which the brand tries not to look local.[92]

Private Brand Policies

The emergence of strong intermediaries has led to the significant increase in private-brand goods, that is, the intermediaries' own branded products or "store brands." Two general approaches have been used: umbrella branding, where a number of products are covered using the same brand (often the intermediary's name), and separate brand names for individual products or product lines.

With price sensitivity increasing and brand loyalty decreasing, private-brand goods have achieved a significant penetration in many countries. The overall penetration of private-brand goods in Switzerland is 53 percent, in the United Kingdom 47 percent, in Germany 37 percent, and in France 36 percent.[93] Over the past 20 years, private-brand sales in the United States have averaged 22 to 30 percent of supermarket sales. As both the trades and consumers become more sophisticated, private brands' market share is expected to reach U.K. levels in many parts of Europe and the world.

While private-brand success has been shown to be affected strongly by economic conditions and the self-interest of retailers who want to improve their bottom lines through the contribution of private-label goods, new factors have emerged to make the phenomenon more long-lived and significant in changing product choices worldwide. The level of private-brand share will vary by country and by product category, reflecting variations in customer perceptions, intermediary strength, and behavior of leading branders.[94] The improved quality of private-brand products and the development of segmented private-brand products have been major changes in the last 20 years. Moreover, in one study, 39 percent of respondents who identify themselves as the primary grocery shopper of their household say they would recommend a store-brand product. Meanwhile, 34 percent say they do not feel like they are giving anything up (such as flavor or prestige) by using store brands. Only 19 percent believe it is worth paying more for name-brand products.[95]

Beyond just offering products, many retailers are focusing on a broader approach. For example, Tesco in the United Kingdom has focused on the design of its own-label products with the goal of projecting a more uniform image across product categories. Some premium private-brand products have been developed to reposition manufacturer's brands. In Canada, for example, Loblaw's President's Choice brand and its regular private-brand line squeeze national brands in between the two. Some U.S. chains have also started carrying this line of premium products.

European supermarket chains have had enormous success with private brands, mainly due to their power over manufacturers. While the five largest operators in the United States command only 21 percent of supermarket sales, the figure in the United Kingdom is 80 percent, and in Finland the three leading wholesaler-led chains control over 90 percent.[96] With the emergence of new types of intermediaries, such as mass merchandisers and warehouse clubs, this phenomenon will expand as these players exercise their procurement clout over manufacturers. Furthermore, many retailers believe that strong private-brand programs can successfully differentiate their outlets and solidify shoppers' loyalty, thereby strengthening their position vis-à-vis manufacturers and resulting in increasing profitability.[97]

The internationalization of retailers carrying or even focusing solely on private labels has given an additional boost to the phenomenon, such as German ALDI, which sells only its own private-label goods in its stores throughout Europe, the United States (with over 1,000 stores in 31 states), and Australia.[98] ALDI's focus is on cutting costs rather than sacrificing quality, permitting it to drive out low-quality brands that trade only on price.

With the increasing opportunities in the private-brand categories, the marketing manager will have to make critical strategic choices, which are summarized in Exhibit 11.8.[99] If the marketer operates in an environment where consumers have an absolute preference for manufacturers' brands and where

EXHIBIT 11.8 Private Brand Strategies

Strategy	Rationale	Circumstance
No participation	Refusal to produce private label	Heavily branded markets; high distinctiveness; technological advantage
Capacity filling	Opportunistic	
Market control	Influence category sales	High brand shares where distinctiveness is lower; more switching by consumers
Competitive leverage	Stake in both markets	
Chief source of business	Major focus	Little or no differentiation by consumers
Dedicated producer	Leading cost position	

SOURCES: Adapted from Jan-Benedict E. M. Steenkamp and Nirmalya Kumar, "Don't Be Undersold!" *Harvard Business Review* 87 (December 2009): 90–95; and Sabine Bonnot, Emma Carr, and Michael J. Reyner, "Fighting Brawn with Brains," *McKinsey Quarterly* 40, no. 2 (2000): 85–92.

product innovation is a critical factor of success, the marketer can refuse to participate. Brand leaders can attack private brands and thereby direct their ambitions on smaller competitors, which often may be local-only players. The argument for strategic participation is that because the phenomenon cannot be eliminated, it is best to be involved. For example, Nestlé sells ice cream called Grandessa for ALDI through an acquired unit called Scholler.[100] Reasons include capacity filling, economies of scale, improved relationships with trade, and valuable information about consumer behavior and costs. The argument that profits from private-brand manufacture can be used for promotion of the manufacturer's own brands may be eliminated by the relatively thin margins and the costs of having to set up a separate private-brand manufacturing and marketing organization. Participation in the private-brand category may, however, be inconsistent with the marketer's global brand and product strategy by raising questions about quality standards, by diluting management attention, and by affecting consumers' perception of the main branded business. Many marketers pursue a mixture of these strategies as a function of marketing and market conditions. While H. J. Heinz produces insignificant amounts for private-brand distributors in the United States, most of its U.K. production is for private brands.

PRODUCT COUNTERFEITING

Counterfeit goods are any goods bearing an unauthorized representation of a trademark, patented invention, or copyrighted work that is legally protected in the country where it is marketed. Companies lose a total of $657.76 billion every year because of product counterfeiting and other infringement of intellectual property.[101] Hardest hit are the most innovative, fastest-growing industries, such as computer software, pharmaceuticals, and entertainment. In 2011, the software, publishing, and distribution industries lost more than $59 billion due to software theft.[102] Worldwide, more than 42 percent of all software is illegally copied, with the percentage rising to over 90 percent in countries such as Georgia, Bangladesh, Yemen, Zimbabwe, and Moldova. For the first time, PC shipments to emerging economies outpaced those to mature markets, 174 million to 173 million. The United States (20 percent), European Union (35 percent), and BRIC countries (71 percent) account for the commercial value of PC software piracy.

The practice of product counterfeiting has spread to high-technology products and services from the traditionally counterfeited products: high-visibility, strong-brand-name consumer goods. In addition, previously the only concern was whether a company's product was being counterfeited; now, companies have to worry about whether the raw materials and components purchased for production are themselves real. The European Union estimates that trade in counterfeit goods now accounts for 2 percent of total world trade. The International Chamber of Commerce estimates the figure at 5 to 7 percent. In general, countries with lower per capita incomes, higher levels of corruption in government, and lower levels of involvement in the international trade community tend to have higher levels of intellectual property violation.[103]

Counterfeiting problems occur in three ways and, depending on the origin of the products and where they are marketed, require different courses of action. Approximately 75 percent of counterfeit goods are estimated to be manufactured outside the United States, and 25 percent are either made in this country or imported and then labeled here. Problems originating in the United States can be resolved through infringement actions brought up in federal courts. Counterfeit products that originate overseas and that are marketed in the United States should be stopped by the customs barrier. Enforcement has been problematic because of the lack of adequate personnel and the increasingly high-tech character of the products. When an infringement occurs overseas, action can be brought under the laws of the country in which it occurs. The sources of the largest numbers of counterfeit goods are China, Brazil, Taiwan, Korea, and India, which are a problem to the legitimate owners of intellectual property on two accounts: the size of these countries' own markets and their capability to export. For example, Nintendo estimates its annual losses to video-game piracy at $975 million, with the origin of the counterfeits mainly in China.[104] Countries in Central America and the Middle East are typically not sources but rather markets for counterfeit goods. Counterfeiting is a pervasive problem in terms not only of geographic reach but of the ability of the counterfeiters to deliver products and the market's willingness to buy them.

The first task in fighting intellectual property violation is to use patent applications or registration of trademarks or mask works (for semiconductors). The rights granted by a patent, trademark, copyright, or mask work registration in the United States confer no protection in a foreign country. There is no such thing as an international patent, trademark, or copyright. Although there is no shortcut to worldwide protection, some advantages exist under treaties or other international agreements. These treaties are all under the World Intellectual Property Organization (WIPO). Applicants are typically granted international protection throughout the member countries of the organization.[105]

After securing valuable intellectual property rights, the international marketer must act to enforce, and have enforced, these rights. Four types of action against counterfeiting are legislative action, bilateral and multilateral negotiations, joint private-sector action, and measures taken by individual companies, as shown in Exhibit 11.9. It is essential that all the parties interact to gain the most effect. For example, the pharmaceutical industry lobbied to make sure that provisions for patent protection in the NAFTA agreement were meticulously spelled out.

In the legislative arena, the Omnibus Tariff and Trade Act of 1984 amended Section 301 of the Trade Act of 1974 to clarify that the violation of intellectual property rights is an unreasonable practice within the statute. The act also introduced a major carrot-and-stick policy: the adequacy of protection of intellectual property rights of U.S. manufacturers is a factor that will be considered in the designation of Generalized System of Preferences (GSP) benefits to countries. The United States has denied selected countries duty-free treatment on goods because of lax enforcement of intellectual property laws.

EXHIBIT 11.9 Measures to Combat Counterfeiting

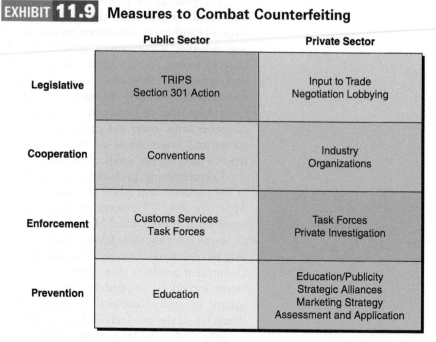

	Public Sector	Private Sector
Legislative	TRIPS Section 301 Action	Input to Trade Negotiation Lobbying
Cooperation	Conventions	Industry Organizations
Enforcement	Customs Services Task Forces	Task Forces Private Investigation
Prevention	Education	Education/Publicity Strategic Alliances Marketing Strategy Assessment and Application

SOURCE: Ilkka A. Ronkainen, "Protecting Intellectual Property Rights: Public and Private Sector Interaction," working paper, Georgetown University, February 2011.

The Trademark Counterfeiting Act of 1984 made trading in goods and services using a counterfeit trademark a criminal rather than a civil offense, establishing stiff penalties for the practice. The Semiconductor Chip Protection Act of 1984 clarified the status and protection afforded to semiconductor masks, which determine the capabilities of the chip. Protection will be available to foreign-designed masks in the United States only if the home country of the manufacturer also maintains a viable system of mask protection. The Intellectual Property Rights Improvement Act requires the U.S. trade representative to set country-specific negotiating objectives for reciprocity and consideration of retaliatory options to ensure intellectual property protection. The United States imposed punitive tariffs on $39 million of Brazilian imports to retaliate against Brazil's refusal to protect U.S. pharmaceutical patents. The United States has threatened to take China's lack of progress against piracy to the World Trade Organization.[106]

The U.S. government is seeking to limit counterfeiting practices through bilateral and multilateral negotiations as well as education. A joint International Trade Administration and Patent and Trademark Office action seeks to assess the adequacy of foreign countries' intellectual property laws and practices, to offer educational programs and technical assistance to countries wishing to establish adequate systems of intellectual property protection, to offer educational services to the industry, and to review the adequacy of U.S. legislation in the area. Major legislative changes have occurred in the past few years in, for example, Taiwan and Singapore, where penalties for violations have been toughened. The WTO agreement includes new rules on intellectual property protection under the Trade-Related Aspects of Intellectual Property Rights (TRIPS) agreement. Under these rules, trade-related intellectual property will enjoy 20 years of protection. More than 100 countries have indicated they will amend their laws and improve enforcement. Violators of intellectual property will face retaliation not only in this sector but in others as well.[107]

© Nelson Ching/Bloomberg via Getty Images

A pedestrian walks past a sign depicting counterfeit Rolex Group watches at a commercial development in Xian, Shaanxi province, China.

A number of private-sector joint efforts have emerged in the battle against counterfeit goods. In 1978, the International Anti-Counterfeiting Coalition was founded to lobby for stronger legal sanctions worldwide. The coalition consists of 150 members. The International Chamber of Commerce established the Counterfeit Intelligence Bureau in London, which acts as a clearinghouse capable of synthesizing global data on counterfeiting.

In today's environment, companies are taking more aggressive steps to protect themselves. The victimized companies are losing not only sales but also goodwill in the longer term if customers believe they have the real product rather than a copy of inferior quality. In addition to the normal measures of registering trademarks and copyrights, companies are taking steps in product development to prevent knockoffs of trademarked goods. For example, new authentication materials in labeling are extremely difficult to duplicate. Some companies, such as Disney, have tried to legitimize offenders by converting them into authorized licensees. These local companies would then be a part of the fight against counterfeiters because their profits would be the most affected by fakes.

Many companies maintain close contact with the government and the various agencies charged with helping them. Computer makers, for example, loan testing equipment to Customs officers at all major U.S. ports, and company attorneys regularly conduct seminars on how to detect pirated software and hardware. Other companies retain outside investigators to monitor the market and stage raids with the help of law enforcement officers. For example, when executives at WD-40 Co., the maker of an all-purpose lubricant, realized a counterfeit version of their product was being sold in China, they launched an investigation and then approached local authorities about the problem.[108]

SUMMARY

Marketers may routinely exaggerate the attractiveness of international markets, especially in terms of their similarity. Despite the dramatic impact of globalization as far as market convergence is concerned, distances, especially cultural and economic, challenge the marketer to be vigilant.[109] The international marketer must pay careful attention to variables that may call for an adaptation in the product offering.

Firms entering or participating in the international marketplace will certainly find it difficult to cope with the conflicting needs of the domestic and international markets. They will be certain to ask whether adjustments in their product offerings, if the marketplace requires them, are worthwhile. There are, unfortunately, no magic formulas for addressing the problem of product adaptation. The answer seems to lie in adopting formal procedures to assess products in terms of the markets' and the company's own needs.

In product development, marketers are increasingly striving toward finding common denominators to rationalize worldwide production. This is achieved through careful coordination of the product development process by worldwide or regional development teams. No longer is the parent company the only source of new products. New product ideas emerge throughout the system and are developed by the entity most qualified to do so.

Global marketers will also have to determine the extent to which they will use one of their greatest assets, brands, across national markets. Marketers will have to choose among global brands, regional brands, and purely local approaches as well as forgoing their own branding in favor of becoming a supplier for the private-brand efforts of retailers. Efficiencies of standardization must be balanced with customer preferences and internal issues of motivation at the country-market level.

The theft of intellectual property—ideas and innovations protected by copyrights, patents, and trademarks—is a critical problem for many industries and countries, accelerating with the pace of market globalization.[110] Governments have long argued about intellectual property protection, but the lack of results in some parts of the world has forced companies themselves to take action on this front.

KEY TERMS

core product
augmented feature
mandatory product adaptation
discretionary product adaptation
positioning
reverse innovation
brand
lead user
open innovation
computer-aided design (CAD)
center of excellence
R&D consortium
controlled market test
simulated test market
vitality lab
global brand
Generalized System of Preferences (GSP)

QUESTIONS FOR DISCUSSION

1. Are standards like those promoted by the International Organization for Standardization (see www.iso.org) a hindrance or an opportunity for exporters?
2. How can marketers satisfy the Four *R*s of environmentally correct practice? See, for example, the approaches proposed by the Duales System Deuschland (see www.gruener-punkt.de).
3. The software industry is the hardest hit by piracy. Using the website of the Business Software Alliance (www.bsa.org), assess how this problem is being tackled.
4. What factors should be considered when deciding on the location of research and development facilities?
5. What are the benefits of a coordinated global product launch? What factors will have to be taken into consideration before the actual launch?
6. Argue for and against the use of the corporate name in global branding.

INTERNET EXERCISES

1. The elements that make up a truly innovative company are many: a focused innovation strategy, a winning overall business strategy, deep customer insight, great talent, and the right set of capabilities to achieve successful execution. How do those key goals and attributes aid and abet the efforts of companies in each strategy to develop the capabilities they need to succeed? (See *Strategy+Business* article, "The Global Innovation 1000: Why Culture Is Key," at www.strategy-business.com/article/11404?gko=dfbfc.)
2. Using the list of the world's leading brands (available at Interbrand, www.interbrand.com) evaluate why certain brands place high and some lower.

CHALLENGE US

Newcomers Were Chinese Brands

China's economy is now at a tipping point—consumers have an increasing number of brands to choose from and therefore are becoming more sophisticated in their choices. Chinese companies understand that good brand building is a powerful way to develop and maintain a competitive edge in a market evolving as quickly as China's.

The Giants

State-owned enterprises (SOEs) dominate, benefiting from strong government support, relatively few competitors, and a growing commitment to brand building. Some SOEs, such as China Mobile, have taken advantage of favorable market conditions to adopt sophisticated brand strategies and market-segmentation approaches. These steps should position these brands well as they are expected to face increased competition in the future.

The Innovators

Innovator brands have developed great products and great product experiences. The technology sector ranked highly, with online entertainment platform TencentQQ ranked at number eight and search engine Baidu close behind at number nine. Other brands have also demonstrated high levels of innovation: China Merchants Bank (rank 11), which has invested heavily in branding and rolling out new customer offerings; domestic automotive manufacturer BYD (rank 19), known for its electric car designs and green technology; and Haier (rank 29), recognized for its energy-efficient product designs and consistent branding.

The Image Builders

Brands in the packaged-goods, beverages, and retail categories operate in extremely crowded spaces, where brand building can play a critical role in differentiation. In this group, trust and product performance are key factors in successful branding. Wine and beer brands Changyu (rank 22), Tsingtao (rank 35), and Great Wall (rank 50) all recorded strong brand contribution. COFCO's Fulinmen food brand also claimed a spot at number 49. Retail/sportswear/clothing brands also stand out, with Li Ning (rank 24), Metersbonwe (rank 31), Anta (rank 43), and 361 Degrees (rank 44) placing in the top 50.

Rank	Brand Value (in US$ millions)	Brand
1	56,074	China Mobile
2	38,090	Industrial & Commercial Bank of China
3	22,344	Bank of China
4	21,676	China Construction Bank
5	18,320	China Life (insurance provider)
6	16,494	Agricultural Bank of China
7	14,223	Petrochina (oil and gas)
8	12,199	Tencent/QQ (Internet service portal)
9	9,715	Baidu (search engine)
10	8,443	Ping An (insurance provider)

For Discussion

1. Brands based in North America still account for a disproportionate amount of brand value. The brand value of the leaders based in North America totaled about $830 billion, or roughly 55 percent of the roughly $1.5 trillion in value for all brand leaders ranked in the regional charts. China appeared with only two brands in 2006 and increased to 12 in 2011. How many brands will China have by 2015?
2. Will the expanding presence of Chinese brands reflect the transformation of China from a center for low-cost production to a nation capable of product innovation and marketing originality?

SOURCE: Millward Brown, www.millwardbrown.com/BrandZ/Default/Categories.aspx.

RECOMMENDED READINGS

Adamson, Allen P., and Martin Sorrell. *BrandSimple: How the Best Brands Keep It Simple and Succeed.* Hampshire, England: Palgrave-Macmillan, 2007.

Czinkota, Michael R., and Ilkka A. Ronkainen. *Global Business: Positioning Ventures Ahead.* New York: Routledge, 2011.

Czinkota, Michael R., Masaaki Kotabe, and Ilkka A. Ronkainen. *The Future of Global Business.* New York: Routledge, 2011.

Kapferer, Jean-Noel. *The New Strategic Brand Management: Creating and Sustaining Brand Equity Long Term.* London: Kogan Page, 2012.

Phillips, Tim. *Knockoff: The Deadly Trade in Counterfeit Goods: The True Story of the World's Fastest Growing Crime Wave*. London: Kogan Page, 2007.

Prahalad, C.K., and M.S. Krishnan. *The New Age of Innovation: Driving Cocreated Value through Global Networks*. Columbus, OH: McGraw-Hill, 2008.

Rein, Shaun. *The End of Cheap China*. Hoboken, NJ: Wiley, 2012. Skarzynski, Peter, and Rowan Gibson. *Innovation to the Core: A Blueprint for Transforming the Way Your Company Innovates*. Boston: Harvard Business School Press, 2008.

Tisch, Jonathan M. *Chocolates on the Pillow Aren't Enough: Reinventing the Customer Experience*. Hoboken, NJ: Wiley, 2009.

ENDNOTES

1. David Martin and Simon McLain, "Fortresses and Footholds: Emerging Market Growth Strategies, Practices and Outlook," *Deloitte*, 2011, 2–3.
2. Itasca Motor Homes, www.goitasca.com/company.
3. Guan Xiaomeng, "Survey: Sino-Japan Animosity Lessens," *China Daily*, August 26, 2009.
4. Levi Strauss & Co., www.levistrauss.com/brands/dockers.
5. Shruti Date Singh, "China and Russia Are Snubbing American Chicken," *BusinessWeek*, August 1, 2011, 53.
6. Thomas L. Friedman, *The Lexus and the Olive Tree: Understanding Globalization* (New York: Anchor Books, 2000), chapters 3 and 15.
7. "Star Power," *Fortune*, February 6, 2006, 61.
8. "Fast Food Goes Gluten-Free," *Fortune*, January 16, 2012, 11.
9. Carl A. Sohlberg, "The Perennial Issue of Adaptation or Standardization of International Marketing Communication: Organizational Contingencies and Performance," *Journal of International Marketing* 10, no. 3 (2002): 1–21.
10. Matthew Cimitile, "The Fight for the First Climate Change Treaty," *Solutions*, October 2011.
11. Ministry of Information, "Cabinet Approves Environment Management (Waste Disposal and Recycling) Regulations 2011," *Fiji*, September 29, 2011.
12. "Trading Places," *Economist*, November 22, 2001, 58.
13. "Making Future Commercial Aircraft Quieter," NASA Glenn Research Center, November 22, 2004.
14. Lara Farrar, "Google.cn: R.I.P or Good Riddance?" *CNN*, January 12, 2011; "Google Under the Gun," *Time*, February 13, 2006, 53–54; "Microsoft Revises Policy on Shutting Down Blogs," *Wall Street Journal*, February 1, 2006, B10; and "Here Be Dragons," *Economist*, January 28, 2006, 59.
15. James D. Southwick, "Addressing Market Access Barriers in Japan through the WTO: A Survey of Typical Japan Market Access Issues and the Possibility to Address Them through WTP Dispute Resolution Procedures," *Law and Policy in International Business* 31 (Spring 2000): 923–76.
16. Cinnamon Carlarne, "From the USA with Love: Sharing Home-grown Hormones, GMOs, and Clones with a Reluctant Europe," *Environmental Law*, March 22, 2007, 159–78.
17. Daniel I. Prajogo, "The Roles of Firms' Motives in Affecting the Outcomes of ISO 9000 Adoption," *International Journal of Operations & Production Management* 31, no. 1 (2011): 78–100.
18. ISO Survey of Certifications, 2010, www.iso.org/iso/pressrelease.htm?refid=Ref1491.
19. Iñaki Heras-Saizarbitoria, German Arana Landín, Molina-Azorín, and José Francisco, "Do Drivers Matter for the Benefits of ISO 14001?" *International Journal of Operations & Production Management* 31, no. 2 (2011): 192–216.
20. Julie Jargon, "Kraft Reformulates Oreo, Scores in China," *Wall Street Journal*, May 1, 2008, B1.
21. Eden Estopace, "Study Revisits the Marketing Landscape: It's Complicated," *Enterprise Innovation*, January 10, 2012.
22. Sesame Workshop, www.sesameworkshop.org/aroundtheworld.
23. "The Simpsons Exported to Middle East—Minus Bacon, Beer," *ABC News*, October 18, 2005.
24. C&A, www.cea.com.br.
25. Jeffrey R. Immelt, Chris Trimble, and Vijay Govindarajan, "How GE Is Disrupting Itself," *Harvard Business Review* 87 (October 2009): 56–63.
26. "Indian Firms Shift Focus to the Poor," *Wall Street Journal*, October 20, 2009, A1, 18.
27. Anton Troianovski, "Can You Say 'WAH-wey'? Low-Cost Phones Find Niche," *Wall Street Journal*, January 11, 2012, B1–2.
28. Bhaskar Chakravorti, "Finding Competitive Advantage in Adversity," *Harvard Business Review* 88 (November 2010): 102–108.
29. "Dubbing in Product Plugs," *Wall Street Journal*, December 6, 2004, B1, B5.
30. "Pepsi Mexico's 'Pecsi' Campaign Recognized for Innovation and Strong Results," November 30, 2011, www.pepsico.com/Story/Pepsi-Mexicos-Pecsi-campaign-recognized-for-innovation-and-strong-results11302011.html.
31. Jean-Noël Kapferer, "Is There Really No Hope for Local Brands?" *Journal of Brand Management* 9 (January 2002): 163–70.
32. NameLab, Inc., www.namelab.com.
33. Lawrence Fennelly, *Handbook of Loss Prevention and Crime Prevention* (Waltham, MA: Butterworth-Heinemann, 2012), 281.
34. Chanin Ballance, "Effective Multicultural Communication," *World Trade* 17 (July 2006): 54, 56, 58.
35. Guillermo D'Andrea, E. Alejandro Stengel, and Anne Goebel-Krstelj, "Six Truths about Emerging-Market Consumers," *Strategy+Business* 34 (Spring 2004): 58–69.
36. European Commission, http://ec.europa.eu/environment/waste/index.htm.

37. Thomas J. Madden, Kelly Hewett, and Martin S. Roth, "Managing Images in Different Cultures: A Cross-National Study of Color Meanings and Preferences," *Journal of International Marketing* 8, no. 4 (2000): 90–107.
38. "How the Swedish Retailer Became a Global Cult Brand," *BusinessWeek*, November 14, 2005, 96–106.
39. AVG Technologies, http://a-v-g.com/index1.html.
40. Electric Current Worldwide, www.trade.gov/mas/ian/ecw.
41. 3M, http://solutions.3m.com/wps/portal/3M/en_US/TouchSystems/TouchScreen.
42. "EU Lifts the Hood on Chinese Autos," *Wall Street Journal*, October 7, 2005, A14.
43. "Fedders: Made in China for the World," *Appliance Magazine*, February 2005.
44. Adamantios Diamantopoulos, Bodo Schlegelmilch, and Dayananda Palihawadana, "The Relationship Between Country-of-origin Image and Brand Image as Drivers of Purchase Intentions," *International Marketing Review* 27, no. 5 (2011): 508–24.
45. Peter Magnusson, Stanford A. Westjohn, and Srdan Zdravkovic,"'What? I Thought Samsung Was Japanese': Accurate or Not, Perceived Country of Origin Matters," *International Marketing Review* 28, no. 5 (2011): 454–72.
46. "Push for 'Made In' Tags Grows in EU," *Wall Street Journal*, November 7, 2005, A6; and "Breaking a Taboo, High Fashion Starts Making Goods Overseas," *Wall Street Journal*, September 27, 2005, A1, A10.
47. Tim Carman, "Tuna, Meat Labeling Disputes Highlight WTO Control," *Washington Post*, January 11, 2012, E1, E3.
48. Roger J. Calantone, Daekwan Kim, Jeffrey B. Schmidt, and S. Tamer Cavusgil, "The Influence of Internal and External Firm Factors on International Product Adaptation Strategy and Export Performance: A Three-Country Comparison," *Journal of Business Research* 59, no. 2 (2006): 176–85.
49. Stanley Black & Decker Investor Overview, December 19, 2011, http://ir.stanleyblackanddecker.com/phoenix.zhtml?c=114416&p=irol-presentations.
50. Natalie Zmuda, "P&G, Levi's, GE Innovate by Thinking in Reverse," *Advertising Age*, June 13, 2011, 2–3.
51. C. K. Prahalad and Hrishi Bhattacharyya, "How to Be a Truly Global Company," *Strategy+Business* 64 (Autumn 2011): 18.
52. John Peppers and Martha Rogers, "The Buzz on Customer-Driven Innovation," *Sales and Marketing Management* 159 (June 2007): 13
53. Guido Jouret, "Inside Cisco's Search for the Next Big Idea," *Harvard Business Review* 87 (September 2009): 43–45.
54. Eric von Hippel and Ralph Katz, "Shifting Innovation to Users via Toolkits," *Management Science* 48 (July 2002): 821–33.
55. Igloo, www.igloocoolers.com/Igloo-Cool-Facts.
56. Innocentive, www.innocentive.com/about-innocentive/facts-stats.
57. Brian Morrissey, "Does Social Sell?" *Mediaweek* 20 (February 15, 2010): 8–9.
58. Otis, www.otis.com/site/us/Pages/ElevonicClass.aspx,
59. Vikas Yogi, "New Generation Fiat Palio Launched in Brazil," *Cartrade India*, November 9, 2011.
60. "Nestlé's First Peelable Ice Cream Rolls Out Worldwide," *Nestle*, February 16, 2011.
61. Nitin Nohria, "Feed R&D—or Farm It Out," *Harvard Business Review* 83 (July/August 2005): 17–27.
62. Larry Huston and Nabil Sakkab, "Connect and Develop: Inside Procter & Gamble's Model for Innovation," *Harvard Business Review* 84 (March 2006): 58–66.
63. "ABB Opens R&D Center in Beijing," *China Business Daily News*, April 4, 2005; and "Imperial and ABB Set to Pool R&D Expertise," *Professional Engineering* 17, no. 21 (2004): 45.
64. "8 Multinationals Found R&D Centers in Shanghai," *China Business Daily News*, May 27, 2005.
65. James Hagerty, "U.S. Loses High-Tech Jobs as R&D Shifts toward Asia," *Wall Street Journal*, January 18, 2012, 1–2.
66. C. K. Prahalad and Allen Hammond, "Serving the World's Poor, Profitably," *Harvard Business Review* 80 (September 2002): 48–57.
67. "New Report Outlines Trends in U.S. Global Competitiveness in Science and Technology," *National Science Board*, January 17, 2012.
68. Barry Jaruzelski, John Loehr, and Richard Holman, "The Global Innovation 1000: Why Culture Is Key," *Strategy+Business*, October 25, 2011.
69. Rajesh Sethi, Daniel Smith, and C. Whan Park, "Cross-Functional Product Development Teams, Creativity, and the Innovativeness of New Consumer Products," *Journal of Marketing Research* 38 (February 2001): 73–85.
70. Julian Birkinshaw, "Managing Internal R&D Networks in Global Firms—What Sort of Knowledge Is Involved?" *Long Range Planning* 35 (June 2002): 245–67.
71. Gloria Barczak and Edward McDonough III, "Leading Global Product Development Teams," *Research Technology Management* 46, no. 6 (2003): 14–22.
72. Sematech, "Letter from the CEO," www.sematech.org/corporate/ceo_letter.htm.
73. USCAR, www.uscar.org/guest/index.php#3.
74. Robert G. Cooper, *Winning at New Products: Creating Value through Innovation* (New York: Basic Books, 2011), chapter 8.
75. Eric Berggren and Thomas Nacher, "Introducing New Products Can Be Hazardous to Your Company," *Academy of Management Executive* 15 (August 2001): 92–101.
76. Integrated Research Associates, "Controlled Market Tests," http://integratedresearch.com/techniques/controlledmarkettest.htm; and GfK MarketingLab, "Simulated Test Markets," www.gfk.com/marktforschung/marketing_topics/market_launch/simulated_test_market/index.en.html.
77. Margaret Bruce, Lucy Daly, and Kenneth B. Kahn, "Delineating Design Factors that Influence the Global Product Launch Process," *Journal of Product Innovation Management* 24 (September 2007): 456–70; and Veronica Wong, "Antecedents of International New Product Rollout Timeliness," *International Marketing Review* 19, no. 2 (2002): 120–32.

78. David C. Court, Anthony Freeling, Mark G. Leiter, and Andrew J. Parsons, "Uncovering the Value of Brands," *McKinsey Quarterly* 32, no. 4 (1996): 176–78.
79. Sean Poulter, "Sharp Practice? The Razor Heads that Cost just 5p to Make, but Sell for £2.43 Each," *Mail*, June 8, 2009.
80. David C. Court, Mark G. Leiter, and Mark A. Loch, "Brand Leverage," *McKinsey Quarterly* 35, no. 2 (1999): 100–10.
81. BrandAsset Valuator's PowerGrid, www.brandasset consulting.com/site_pages/max_intangible_value.
82. Nestlé, "Nestlé Acquisition of Uncle Tobys in Australia Enhances Group's Nutrition, Health and Wellness Dimension," May 23, 2006, www.nestle.com/Media /PressReleases/Pages/AllPressRelease.aspx?PageId=57& PageName=2006.aspx.
83. David A. Aaker, *Brand Relevance: Making Competitors Irrelevant* (New York: Jossey-Bass, 2011), 1–46.
84. Johny K. Johansson and Ilkka A. Ronkainen, "Are Global Brands the Right Choice for Your Company?" *Marketing Management*, March/April, 2004, 53–56.
85. Jean-Noël Kapferer, "The Post-Global Brand," *Journal of Brand Management* 12, no. 5 (2005): 319–24.
86. Douglas B. Holt, John A. Quelch, and Earl L. Taylor, "How Global Brands Compete," *Harvard Business Review* 82 (September 2004): 68–75.
87. Interbrand, *Going Global: Global Branding-Risks and Rewards* (New York: Interbrand, October 2005): 1–7.
88. Johny K. Johansson and Ilkka A. Ronkainen, "The Esteem of Global Brands," *Journal of Brand Management* 12, no. 5 (2005): 339–54.
89. Anand P. Raman, "The Global Brand Face-Off," *Harvard Business Review* 81 (June 2003): 35–45.
90. Colin Mitchell, "Selling the Brand Inside," *Harvard Business Review* 80 (January 2002): 99–105.
91. "Unilever's Goal: Power Brands," *Advertising Age*, January 3, 2000, 1, 12.
92. Jean-Noël Kapferer, "Is There Really No Hope for Local Brands?" *Journal of Brand Management* 9 (January 2002): 163–70.
93. Private Label Manufacturers Association, www .plmainternational.com/en/private_label_en.htm.
94. Yongchuan Bao, Yeqing Bao, and Shibin Sheng, "Motivating Purchase of Private Brands: Effects of Store Image, Product Signatureness, and Quality Variation," *Journal of Business Research* 64 (2011): 220–26.
95. Mintel, "Private Label Gets a Quality Reputation, Causing Consumers to Change Their Buying Habits," press release, January 2011, www.mintel.com/press-centre /press-releases/653/private-label-gets-a-quality-reputation -causing-consumers-to-change-their-buying-habits.
96. Barbara Farfan, "2011 World's Largest UK Retailers—The Biggest United Kingdom Retail Chains," *About.com—Retail Industry*, July 7, 2011.
97. Fu-Ling Hu and Chao Chao Chuang, "How Can Different Brand Strategies Lead to Retailers' Success?" *Journal of Global Business Issues* 3 (Spring 2009): 129–35.
98. ALDI, http://aldi.us/index_ENU_HTML.htm.
99. Nirmalya Kumar, "Strategies to Fight Low-Cost Rivals," *Harvard Business Review* 84 (December 2006): 104–12.
100. "Nestlé Set to Enter Euro Own-Label Market," *Marketing Week*, August 9, 2001, 7.
101. Havocscope Black Markets, "Counterfeit Markets Ranking," www.havocscope.com/black-market/counterfeit -goods/counterfeit-goods-market-ranking.
102. Business Software Alliance, www.bsa.org/country/Anti -Piracy.aspx.
103. Ilkka A. Ronkainen and Jose-Luis Guerrero-Cusumano, "Correlates of Intellectual Property Violation," *Multinational Business Review* 9, no. 1 (2001): 59–65.
104. Nintendo Anti-Piracy Program, https://ap.nintendo.com /_pdf/Nintendo_Antipiracy_Training_Manual.pdf.
105. World Intellectual Property Organization, www.wipo.int /portal/index.html.en.
106. Kevin E. Noonan, "U.S. Trade Representative Issues Report on China's Compliance with WTO and TRIPS," December 29, 2011, www.patentdocs.org/2011/12/us -trade-representative-issues-report-on-chinas-compli ance-with-wto-and-trips.html.
107. Daniele Archibugi and Andrea Filippetti, "The Globalisation of Intellectual Property Rights: Four Learned Lessons and Four Theses," *Global Policy*, May 2010, 139–49.
108. "WD-40's China Strategy," *Technomic Asia News*, January 2, 2007, www.technomicasia.com/blog/2007 /01/02/kent-kedl-interviews-geoff-holdsworth-managing.
109. Pankaj Ghemawat, "Distance Still Matters: The Hard Reality of Global Expansion," *Harvard Business Review* 79 (September 2001): 137–47.
110. Kenneth Cukier, "In Defence of Creativity," *RSA Journal*, December 2005, 18–21.

CHAPTER 12

Global Marketing of Services

LEARNING OBJECTIVES

By the time you complete this chapter, you will be able to:

- Understand the differences and linkages between goods and services.
- Appreciate the growing role of services in the global economy.
- Be informed about business strategies needed specifically for services.
- Anticipate the further internationalization of domestic services.
- Understand how new technology contributes to the global providing of services.

THE INTERNATIONAL **MARKETPLACE** 12.1

Marketing "The Cloud": Computing as a Service

How to manage the dramatic growth in data has become an issue of critical importance to companies around the world. In 2011, most companies managed, stored, and manipulated their data on their premises with a relatively expensive system infrastructure of hardware, operating systems, networks, and data storage capabilities. Anyone who has ever stepped into a corporate data center lined with banks of servers and storers will not only need a sweater to keep warm but will quickly understand the significant physical space, power, and cooling that are required for these operations. With increasing pressure to cut costs and to make their operations more sustainable, chief information officers (CIOs) are actively seeking new ideas for future data-management planning.

"Cloud computing," or the remote management of information as a service via the Internet rather than a product, is becoming increasingly attractive to global CIOs worldwide. *Cloud computing* covers broad business applications with solution providers, like IBM, HP, Microsoft, NetSuite, Taleo, and Salesforce.com, offering various consulting, software, platform, and infrastructure computing applications as a service. Technology research firm Gartner identifies cloud computing as the number one technology priority of global CIOs in 2011 and estimates annual global revenues from cloud services in 2011 at $81.3 billion, compared to $68.3 billion in 2010.

Google Trends tracks the usage of terms over time. First referenced in late 2007, *cloud computing* climbed steeply as the new buzzword after major companies began to market cloud services. Globally, the top search queries for *cloud computing* have been in India, Singapore, and Hong Kong.

The United States has been the top market for cloud computing, with fast growth in Asia, particularly in India. Europe has lagged behind in global sales of cloud services, partly because of European Union concerns about data privacy and restrictions on cross-border data transfers. Many of the larger information technology firms are lobbying in Europe for legal revisions, and Gartner predicts that Europe will account for 29 percent of cloud-services sales in 2012 because of the cost and energy savings. As organizations shift computing functions that are not mission critical to the "cloud," Gartner predicts that data-center space requirements will be reduced by 60 percent of what they were in 2011. The forecast for information technology is "cloudy."

For interactive research, visit IBMCloud's YouTube channel at www.youtube.com/user/IBMCloud.

© ODD ANDERSEN/AFP/Getty Images

SOURCES: Kevin J. O'Brien, "Europe Turns to the Cloud," *New York Times*, July 24, 2011; Gartner Research, "Gartner Highlights Four Forces to Have a Significant Impact on Data Centers during the Next Five Years," press release, March 15, 2011; Tim Ferguson, "Cloud Computing: Why 2011 Is the Year to Say 'Do It,'" *Silicon.com*, January 13, 2011; and Google Trends, www.google.com/trends?q=cloud+computing, accessed August 19, 2011.

International services marketing is a major component of world business. This chapter will highlight marketing dimensions that are specific to services, with particular attention given to their international aspects. A discussion of the differences between the marketing of services and of goods will be followed by insights on the role of services in the United States and in the world economy. The chapter will explore the opportunities and new problems that have arisen from the increase in international services marketing, focusing particularly on the worldwide transformations of industries as a result of profound changes in the environment and in technology. The strategic responses to these transformations by both governments and firms will be described. Finally, the chapter will outline the initial steps that firms need to undertake in order to offer services internationally and will look at the future of international services marketing.

DIFFERENCES BETWEEN SERVICES AND GOODS

We rarely contemplate or analyze the precise role of services in our lives. As *The International Marketplace 12.1* shows, companies are recognizing that the race for global success demands service innovations. Services often accompany goods, but they are also, by themselves, an increasingly important part of our economy, domestically and internationally. One writer has contrasted services and products by stating that "a good is an object, a device, a thing; a service is a deed, a performance, an effort."[1] This definition, although quite general, captures the essence of the difference between goods and services. Services tend to be more intangible, personalized, and custom-made than goods. Services are also often marketed differently than goods. While goods are typically distributed to the customer through various intermediaries, services can be transferred directly across borders or originated abroad. The service provider can be transferred to the customer or the customer can be transferred to the service territory. Services also typically use a different approach to customer satisfaction. It has been stated that "service firms do not have products in the form of preproduced solutions to customers' problems; they have processes as solutions to such problems."[2]

Services are the fastest-growing sector of world trade, far outpacing the growth in the trade of goods. These major differences add dimensions to services that are not present in goods and thus call for a major differentiation.

Linkage between Services and Goods

Services may complement goods; at other times, goods may complement services. Offering goods that are in need of substantial technological support and maintenance may be useless if no proper assurance for service can be provided. For this reason, the initial contract of sale often includes important service dimensions. This practice is common in aircraft sales. When an aircraft is purchased, the buyer often contracts not only for the physical good—namely the plane—but also for training of personnel, maintenance service, and the promise of continuous technological updates. Similarly, the sale of computer hardware is critically linked to the availability of proper servicing and software.

This linkage between goods and services can make international marketing efforts quite difficult. A foreign buyer, for example, may wish to purchase helicopters and contract for service support over a period of 10 years. If the sale involves a U.S. firm, both the helicopter and the service sale will require an export license. Such licenses, however, are issued only for an immediate sale. Therefore, over the 10 years, the seller will have to apply for an export license each time service is to be provided. Because the issuance of a license is often dependent on the political climate, the buyer and seller are haunted by uncertainty. As a result, sales may be lost to firms in countries that can unconditionally guarantee the long-term supply of support services.

Services can be just as dependent on goods. For example, an airline that prides itself on providing an efficient reservation system and excellent linkups with rental cars and hotel reservations could not survive without its airplanes. As a result, many offerings in the marketplace consist of a combination of goods and services. A graphic illustration of the tangible and intangible elements in the market offering of an airline is provided in Exhibit 12.1.

The simple knowledge that services and goods interact, however, is not enough. Successful managers must recognize that different customer groups will frequently view the service/goods combination differently. The type of use and usage conditions will also affect evaluations of the market offering. For example, the intangible dimension of "on-time arrival" by airlines may be valued differently by college students than by business executives. Similarly, a 20-minute delay will be judged differently by a passenger arriving at her final destination than by one who has just missed an overseas connection. As a result, adjustment possibilities in both the service and the goods area can be used as strategic tools to stimulate demand and increase profitability. For different offerings, service and goods elements may vary substantially. The marketer must identify the role of each and adjust all of them to meet the desires of the target customer group.

Stand-Alone Services

Services do not always come in unison with goods. Increasingly, they compete against goods and become an alternative offering. For example, rather than buy

Services as a Portion of Gross Domestic Product

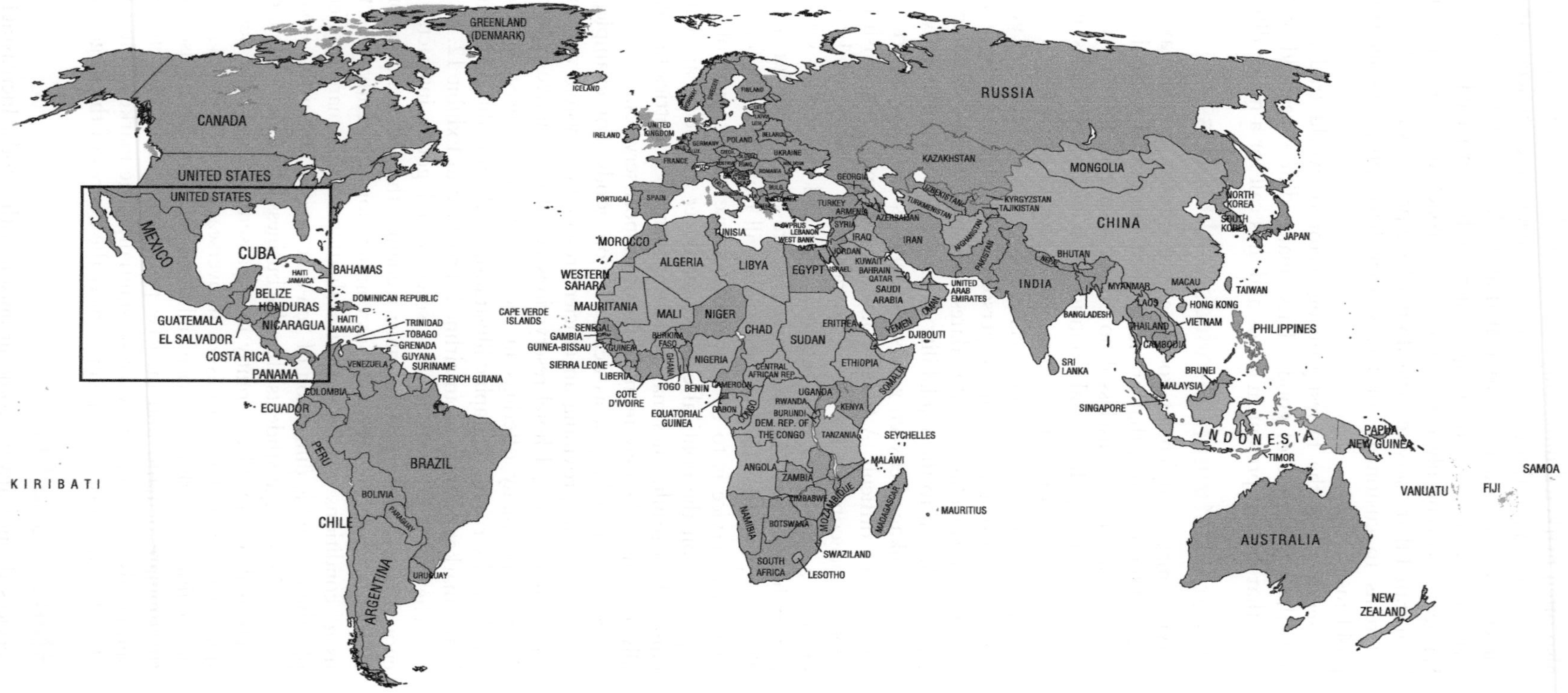

Services as a percentage of GDP

- 61% to 85%
- 41% to 60%
- 21% to 40%
- 0% to 20%
- No current data available

SOURCES: © Cengage Learning 2013; Based on the World Bank, http://data.worldbank.org/indicator/BG.GSR.NFSV.GD.ZS.

EXHIBIT 12.1 Tangible and Intangible Offerings of Airlines

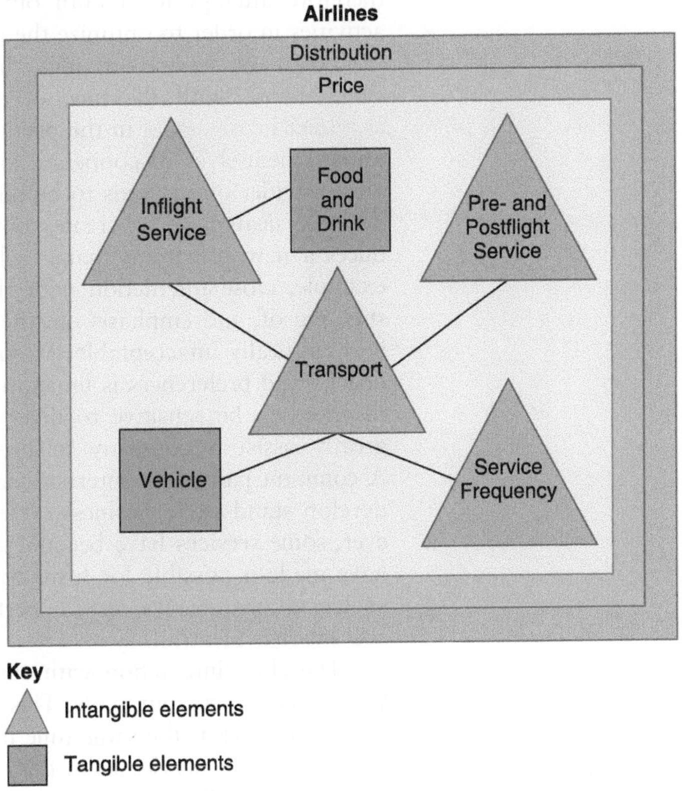

SOURCE: Adapted from G. Lynn Shostack, "Breaking Free from Product Marketing," in *Services Marketing*, ed. Christopher H. Lovelock (Englewood Cliffs, NJ: Prentice-Hall, 1984), 40.

an in-house computer, the business executive can contract computing work to a local or foreign service firm. Similarly, the purchase of a car (a good) can be converted into the purchase of a service by leasing the car from an agency.

Services may also compete against each other. As an example, a store may have the option of offering full service to consumers who purchase there or of converting to the self-service format. With automated checkout services, consumers may self-serve all activities such as selection, transportation, packaging, and pricing.

Services differ from goods most strongly in their **intangibility**: they are frequently consumed rather than possessed. Even though the intangibility of services is a primary differentiating criterion, it is not always present. For example, publishing services ultimately result in a tangible good, namely a book or an article. Similarly, construction services eventually result in a building, a subway, or a bridge. Even in those instances, however, the intangible component that leads to the final product is of major concern to both the producer of the service and the recipient of the ultimate output because it brings with it major considerations that are not traditional to goods.

One major difference concerns the storing of services. Because of their nature, services are difficult to inventory. If they are not used, the "brown around the edges" syndrome tends to result in high services **perishability**. Unused capacity in the form of an empty seat on an airplane, for example, becomes nonsalable quickly. Once the plane has taken off, selling an empty seat is virtually impossible—except for an in-flight upgrade from coach to first class—and the capacity cannot be stored for future usage. Similarly, the difficulty of keeping services in inventory makes it troublesome to provide service backup for peak demand. Constantly maintaining service capacity at levels necessary to satisfy peak demand would be very expensive. The marketer must therefore attempt to smooth out demand levels through price or promotion activities in order to optimize the use of capacity.

For many service offerings, the time of production is very close to or even simultaneous with the time of consumption. This fact points toward close customer involvement in the production of services. Customers frequently either service themselves or cooperate in the delivery of services. As a result, the service provider often needs to be physically present when the service is delivered. This physical presence creates both problems and opportunities, and it introduces a new constraint that is seldom present in the marketing of goods. For example, close interaction with the customer requires a much greater understanding of, and emphasis on, the cultural dimension. A good service delivered in a culturally unacceptable fashion is doomed to failure. Sensitivity to culture, beliefs, and preferences is imperative in the services industry. In some instances, the need to be sensitive to diverse customer groups in domestic markets can greatly assist a company in preparing for international market expansion. A common pattern of internationalization for service businesses is therefore to develop stand-alone business systems in each country. At the same time, however, some services have become delocalized as advances in modern technology have made it possible for firms to delink production and service processes and switch labor-intensive service performance to countries where qualified, low-cost labor is plentiful.

The close interaction with customers also points toward the fact that services often are custom made. This contradicts the desire of a firm to standardize its offering, yet at the same time it offers the service provider an opportunity to differentiate the service from the competition. The concomitant problem is that in order to fulfill customer expectations, service consistency is required. As with anything offered in real time, however, consistency is difficult to maintain over the long run. The human element in the service offering therefore takes on a much greater role than in the offering of goods. Errors can enter the system, and unpredictable individual influences can affect the outcome of the service delivery. The issue of quality control affects the provider as well as the recipient of services. Efforts to increase such control through uniformity may sometimes be seen by customers as a reduction in service choices. The quality perception of service customers is largely determined by the behavior of the employees they contact. Customer-contact workers are therefore a key internal group whose skills must be addressed systematically through internal marketing, which takes place between firms and employees. The target groups of internal marketing are managers and employees of all levels who handle customer concerns. They must first be convinced that complaints contain business opportunities rather than dangers and must therefore be handled in a positive and proactive manner. Second, achievement-based rewards should be established to create complaint-management incentives for employees.[3]

Buyers have more problems in observing and evaluating services than goods. This is particularly true when a shopper tries to choose intelligently among service providers. Even when sellers of services are willing and able to provide more market transparency where the details of the service are clear, comparable, and available to all interested parties, the buyer's problem is complicated: Customers receiving the same service may use it differently, and service quality may vary for each delivery. Because production lines cannot be established to deliver an identical service each time and the quality of a service cannot be tightly controlled, the problem of service heterogeneity emerges, meaning that services may never be the same from one delivery to another.[4] For example, a teacher's advice, even if it is provided on the same day by the same person, may vary substantially depending on the student. Over time, even for the same student, the counseling may change. As a result, service offerings are not directly comparable, which makes quality measurements quite challenging. Therefore, the reputation of the service provider plays an overwhelming role in the customer choice process.

Services may require entirely new forms of distribution. Traditional channels are typically multitiered and long and therefore slow. They often cannot be used because of the perishability of services. A weather news service, for example, either reaches its audience quickly or rapidly loses its value. As a result, direct delivery and short distribution channels are often required. When they do not exist—which is often the case domestically and even more so internationally—service providers need to be distribution innovators in order to reach their market.

All these aspects of services exist in both international and domestic settings. Their impact, however, takes on greater importance for the international marketer. For example, because of the longer distances involved, service perishability that may be an obstacle in domestic business becomes a barrier internationally. Similarly, the issue of quality control for international services may be much more difficult to deal with due to different service uses, changing expectations, and varying national regulations.

Because services are delivered directly to the user, they are frequently much more sensitive to cultural factors than are products. Sometimes their influence on the individual may even be considered with hostility abroad. For example, the showing of U.S. films in cinemas or on television abroad is often attacked as an imposition of U.S. culture. National leaders who place strong emphasis on national cultural identity frequently denounce foreign services and attempt to hinder their market penetration. Even dimensions that one thinks to be highly standardized around the globe may need to be adapted. For an example, see Exhibit 12.2. As you can tell, many nations have developed their own meanings for the symbol. Similarly, services are subject to many political vagaries occurring almost daily. Yet coping with these changes can become the service provider's competitive advantage.

THE ROLE OF SERVICES IN THE U.S. ECONOMY

Since the Industrial Revolution, the United States has seen itself as a primary international competitor in the area of production of goods. There has been a shift in this thinking, however, as the U.S. economy has increasingly become service oriented over time, as shown in Exhibit 12.3. The United States is now the world's largest services market and the world's largest exporter and importer of services.[5] The service sector in 2008 produced 80 percent of the U.S. GDP, employing 80 percent of the American workforce.[6] The shift from goods-producing to service-providing employment is expected to account for almost 16 million new service-related jobs between 2006 and 2016, while the goods-producing industries are expected to experience an overall job loss.[7] **Infrastructure services** are a significant component of the overall services trade and are comprised of telecommunications, insurance, banking, and logistics.

Services trade means that people, information, and money cross national borders during the exchange process. This exchange is referred to as **cross-border transactions**. Total U.S. service exports grew from $6 billion in 1958 to $560 billion in 2010.[8] With total cross-border exports at $3.6 trillion in 2010, the United States accounted for 15 percent of services exports worldwide.[9] International service trade has had very beneficial results for many firms and industries. For example, management consulting firms may derive more than half of their revenue from international sources, while large and small advertising agencies serve customers around the globe. The leading U.S. services exported in 2010 were (1) business, professional, and technical services (46 percent of services exports); (2) travel services (19 percent of services exports); and

EXHIBIT 12.2 Symbolism

What do people around the world call the "@" symbol, so prevalent in e-mail addresses? While in the United States most people say "at," in other countries it's referred to by different, and often humorous, names associated with what the @ reminds speakers of.

DOG

In Russia, the most common word for @ is *sobaka* or *sobachka*, meaning "dog" and "little doggie," respectively.

MONKEY

In countries such as Bulgaria, Poland, and Serbia, the @ symbol seems to remind speakers of a monkey with a long tail. They refer to it as *alpa* (Polish), *majmunkso* (Bulgarian), and *majmun* (Serbian). Another variation is "ape's tail," said as *aapstert* in Afrikaans, *apestaart* in Dutch, and *apsvans* in Swedish.

SNAIL

While traditional stamp and envelope mail is often referred to as "snail mail," many speakers insert a snail into their e-mail addresses. In Korea, @ is known as *dalphaengi* and in Italian it's *chiocciola* (both literally meaning "snail").

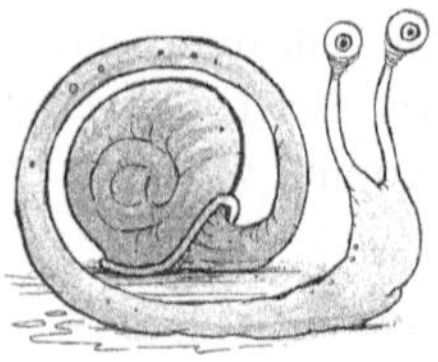

CAT

When Poles aren't referring to @ as a monkey, they know it as a curled up kitten (*kotek*). Similarly, Finns use the phrase *miuku mauku*.

FISH

A quite creative name for the @ is *zavinac*, or "rolled-up pickled herring," in Slovakia and the Czech Republic.

ELEPHANT

In Denmark, you would refer to @ as *snabel*, or elephant's trunk.

MOUSE

In China, the word "mouse" used in reference to a computer means more than that object you click and point with. *Xiao lao shu* ("little mouse") is also used for the symbol @.

WORM

In Hungary, the mental image of a *kukac* (literally "worm") is associated with @.

SOURCES: Images © David Clark, used with permission; Text is based on Nancy Szokan, "Where It's At, and Where It's Not," *Washington Post,* 2 October 2005, p. B2.

EXHIBIT 12.3 Employment in Industry as Percentage of the Total Labor Force

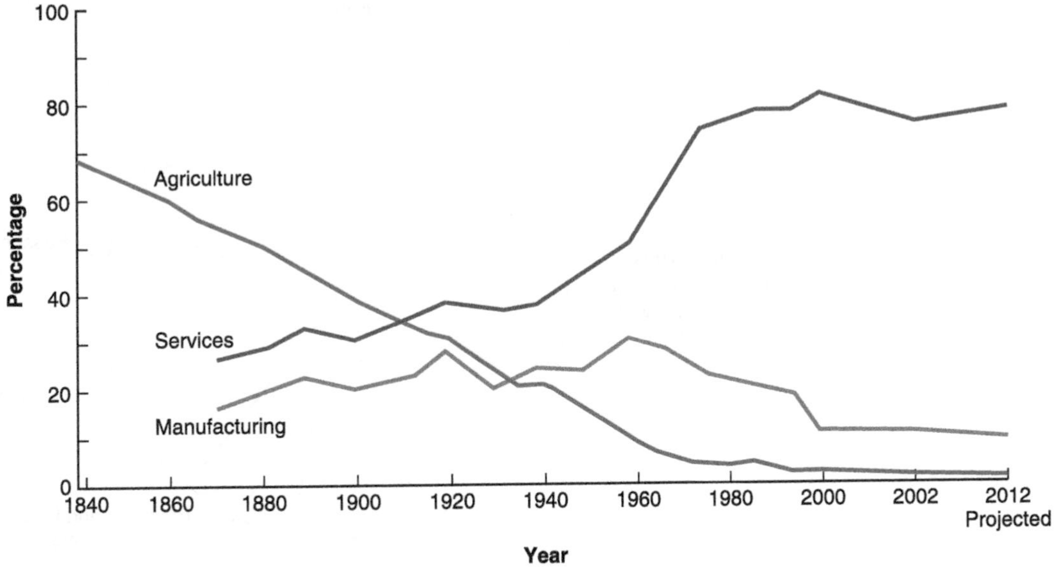

SOURCES: Bureau of Labor Statistics, "2002–12 Employment Projections," www.bls.gov, accessed May 18, 2006; Coalition of Service Industries, and Office of Service Industries, U.S. Department of Commerce, July 2002; *Quarterly Labor Force Statistics*, Paris, Organization for Economic Cooperation and Development, 1996, no. 2; and J. B. Quinn, "The Impacts of Technology on the Services Sector," *Technology and Global Industry: Companies and Nations in the World Economy*, by the National Academy of Sciences, Washington, DC.

(3) royalties and license fees (19 percent of services exports).[10] Exhibit 12.4 shows U.S. services exports.

Large international growth and cross-border transactions, however, are not confined to U.S. service imports. The import of services into the United States is also high relative to other countries. Total services imported into the United

EXHIBIT 12.4 U.S. Exports of Services by Industry, 2010

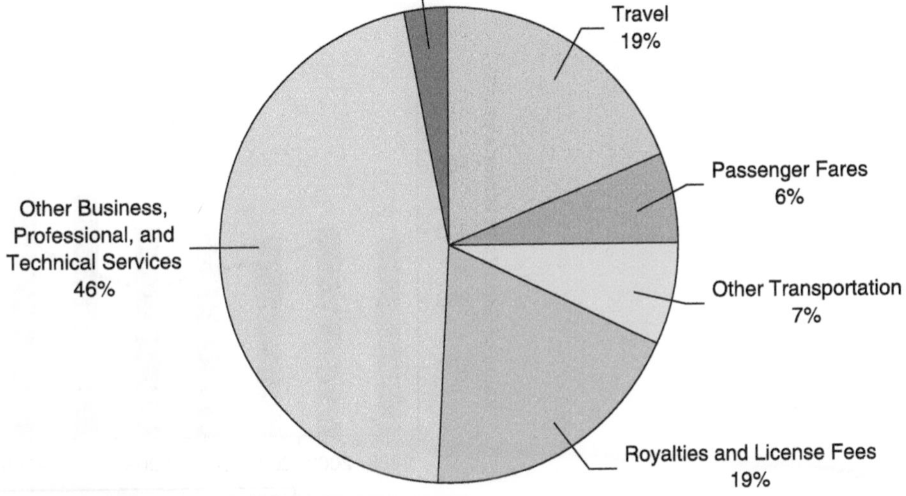

SOURCE: "FT-900 U.S. International Trade in Goods and Services," Census Bureau and the Bureau of Economic Analysis, Prepared by International Trade Administration, Office of Trade and Industry Information, 2011.

EXHIBIT 12.5 U.S. Imports of Services by Industry, 2010

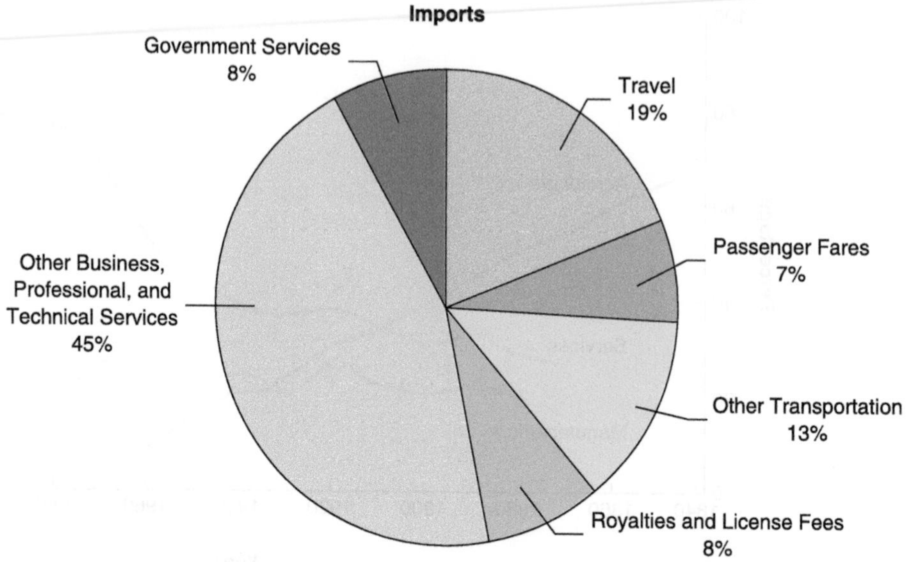

SOURCE: "FT-900 U.S. International Trade in Goods and Services," Census Bureau and the Bureau of Economic Analysis, Prepared by International Trade Administration, Office of Trade and Industry Information, 2011.

States in 2010 were almost $403 billion.[11] The growth in service imports was comprised largely of business, professional, and technical services (43 percent of service imports), travel services (19 percent of service imports), and transportation (13 percent of service imports). Exhibit 12.5 shows U.S. imports.[12]

As seen in Exhibit 12.6, the United States had a services trade surplus in 2009 of $132 billion. As a reminder, a **trade surplus** is a positive difference between exports and imports, while a **trade deficit** occurs if imports are greater than exports. The services trade surplus of 2009 was the largest service trade surplus globally.[13]

EXHIBIT 12.6 U.S. Services Exports and Services Trade Surplus, 1999–2010

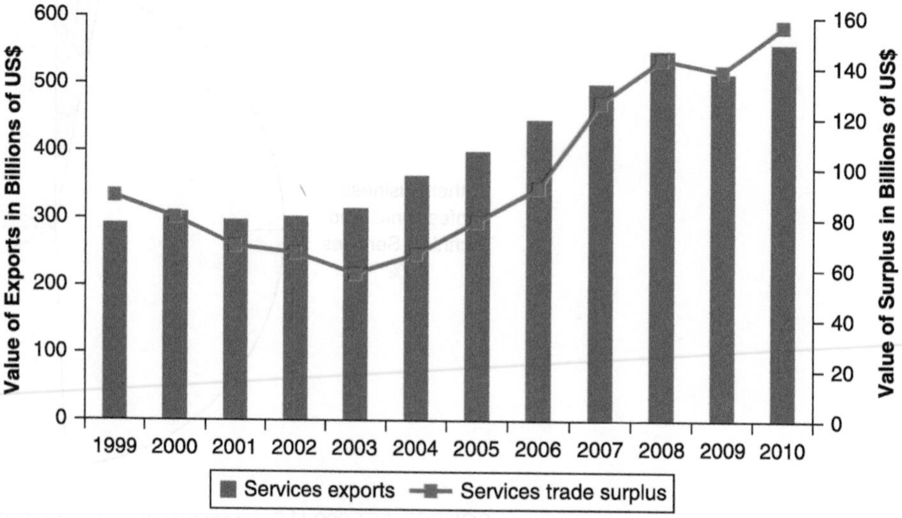

SOURCE: NIPA Table 1.1.5, Bureau of Economic Analysis, Prepared by International Trade Administration, Office of Trade and Industry Information, 2011.

THE ROLE OF SERVICES IN THE WORLD ECONOMY

The rise of the service sector is a global phenomenon. According to the WTO, cross-border exports of services globally totaled $3.6 trillion in 2010.[14] Exhibit 12.7 shows world exports of merchandise and commercial services from 2005 to 2010. After declining precipitously in 2009, world commercial services exports grew by 8 percent in 2010. Although trade in services grew more slowly than merchandise goods trade in 2010, it declined less than merchandise goods in 2009 and did not need as dramatic a recovery pace.[15] Exhibit 12.8 shows how trade in services has become increasingly important worldwide.

Unfortunately, the global credit crisis, as experienced in 2008 and 2009, hit smaller countries particularly hard. *The International Marketplace 12.2* describes the impact difficult economic times have had on a relatively small country that depends upon the service sector for almost 70 percent of its GDP.

The hard hit taken by Iceland is not surprising given the role of banking in the global services sector. As late as 2006, conditions for global banks appeared favorable, with the global banking industry valued at $68.2 trillion. With profits at an all-time high of $788 billion, the industry had the highest absolute profits in the worldwide services sector.[16] Other large service industries worldwide include insurance, telecommunications, retail, and logistics.

EXHIBIT 12.7 World Exports of Merchandise and Commercial Services

	Value	Annual Percentage Change			
	2010	2008	2009	2010	2005–2010
Merchandise	15,237.6	15	−22	22	8
Commercial services	3,663.8	13	−12	8	8
Transport	782.8	16	−23	14	7
Travel	935.7	10	−9	8	6
Other commercial services	1,945.3	13	−8	6	9

SOURCE: WTO Secretariat, Geneva, 2011.

EXHIBIT 12.8 The Global Importance of the Service Sector (countries ranked by size of GDP)

Country	Service as Percentage of GDP
United States	76.7
China	43.6
Japan	75.9
Germany	71.3
France	79.0
United Kingdom	77.1
Brazil	67.5
Italy	73.3
Canada	78.0
India	55.3

SOURCE: CIA World Factbook 2010, "GDP–Composition by Sector–Services."

THE INTERNATIONAL MARKETPLACE 12.2

Iceland Goes Bankrupt

Only around 304,000 people live in the small country of Iceland. But the country became one of the largest casualties in the global financial crisis of 2008. In October of 2008, Iceland's government took control of the three major banks and shut down the country's stock exchange. At the same time, Iceland's prime minister began to raise the notion of "national bankruptcy."

Worldwide, people began to question what it meant for a country to go into bankruptcy. Essentially, Iceland could not pay its debts or raise foreign currency to pay for imports. For a country that relies heavily on the importation of necessary goods and services, this in and of itself evoked national panic. And Iceland's currency, the krona, was devalued to the point of 340 krona to the euro! As the financial collapse was unfolding, the British government even invoked antiterrorism laws (placing Iceland in the same category as Al Qaeda) in an effort to get money back that their citizens had deposited with Icelandic institutions.

Observers worldwide began to question how something like this could happen. Most people had never even considered the notion that a country could file for bankruptcy. Analysts attributed the problem to the fact that the Icelandic banking system, which was privatized in 2000, relied too heavily on external financing. The banks used such wholesale funding to gain entry into the local mortgage market and to acquire foreign financial firms. Most of the acquisitions took place in Britain and Scandinavia. By the beginning of 2007, this aggressive expansion had amassed $150 billion in the country's three main banks (Kaupthing Bank hf, Glithnir Banki hf, and Landsbanki Islands hf). This was eight times Iceland's GDP. The country had been transformed from one of Europe's poorest countries to one of the wealthiest.

Iceland is not a major player in any of the large currency trading blocs. Thus, there was very little incentive for a country or financial intermediary to step in and save it. Iceland looked to Russia for a €4 billion loan but was also very quick to clarify that there could be no strings attached (e.g., possible military cooperation). In November of 2008, the International Monetary Fund approved a $2 billion loan as part of an assistance package totaling approximately $10 billion.

In looking at the Iceland financial crisis, one has to wonder how such a small country acquired so much debt. Some now suggest that aggressive spenders in Iceland got caught up in a whirlwind of high-risk ventures. In doing so, they also began buying the best food, the best clothes, the best cars, the best vacations, and the best of everything—all on borrowed funds. The banks gave away too much money and landed everyone in a big mess with the devaluation of the krona. Unfortunately, all Icelanders, as well as many international investors and foreign banks, had to pay the price for these profligate Vikings.

But perhaps the collapse of Iceland's financial system and the necessity for Iceland to allow its banks to go bankrupt effectively purged the system and provided for a speedier recovery than

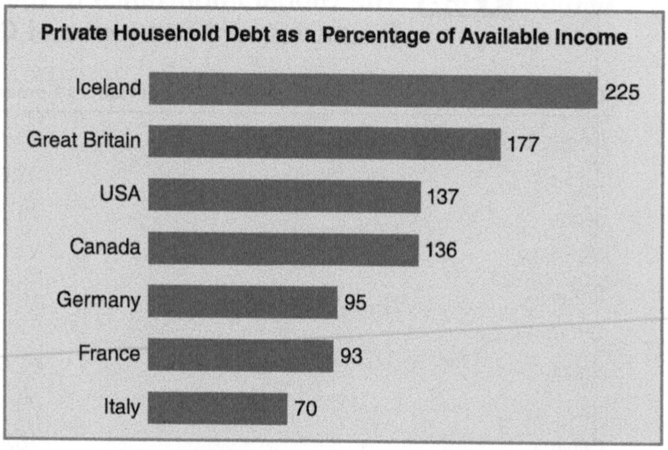

SOURCES: Data from OECD 2010; and Central Bank of Iceland.

other European countries. Iceland's exports, including fisheries and tourism, became cheaper, and by 2011, Iceland was showing signs of recovery with a stabilized krona, economic growth expected to be above 2 percent, and low inflation. However, Icelanders would be wise to hold off on raising their glasses of Brennivin in celebration because the country continues to hold one of the highest levels of private household debt in the world.

SOURCES: Eric Pfanner, "Iceland, in Financial Collapse, Is Likely to Need I.M.F. Help," *New York Times*, October 10, 2008, www.nytimes.comf/2008/10/10/business/worldbusiness/10icebank.html?_r=1; Kerry Capell, "The Stunning Collapse of Iceland," *Businessweek*, October 9, 2008, www.businessweek.com/globalbiz/content/oct2008/gb2008109_947306.htm; "FACTBOX–Iceland Crisis: What Does 'National Bankruptcy' Mean?" *Reuters*, October 14, 2008, www.reuters.com/article/idUSLE43838820081014; Jan Puhl, "Mountains of Debt Temper Hopes despite Recovery," December 8, 2011, *Spiegel Online*, www.spiegel.de/international/europe/0,1518,802285,00.html; and Stephen Beard, "Iceland Strongly Recovering from Bankruptcy," *Marketplace*, August 2, 2011, www.marketplace.org/topics/world/iceland-strongly-recovering-bankruptcy, retrieved December 14, 2011.

GLOBAL TRANSFORMATIONS OF SERVICES

The rapid rise in international services marketing has been the result of major shifts in the business environment and innovations in technology. One primary change in the past decades has been the reduction of governmental regulation of services. In the mid-1970s, many governments made a philosophical decision in favor of **deregulation**, which reduced government interference in the marketplace, in the hope that this would enhance competitive activity. Some service sectors have benefited, and others have suffered, from the withdrawal of government intervention. The primary deregulated industries in the United States have been transportation, banking, and telecommunications. As a result, new competitors participate in the marketplace. Regulatory changes were initially thought to have primarily domestic effects, but they have rapidly spread internationally. For example, the 1984 deregulation of AT&T has given rise to the deregulation of Japan's telecommunications monopoly, NTT. European deregulation followed in the mid-1990s.

Similarly, deregulatory efforts in the transportation sector have had international repercussions. New air carriers have entered the market to compete against established trunk carriers and have done so successfully by pricing their services lower both nationally and internationally. In doing so, these airlines also affected the regulatory climate abroad. Obviously, a British airline can count only to a limited extent on government support to remain competitive with new low-priced fares offered by other carriers also serving the British market. As a result, the deregulatory movement has spread internationally and has fostered the emergence of new competition and new competitive practices. Because many of these changes resulted in lower prices, demand has been stimulated, leading to a rise in the volume of international service trade.

Another major change has been the decreased regulation of service industries by their industry groups. For example, business practices in fields such as health care, law, and accounting are becoming more competitive and aggressive. New economic realities require firms in these industries to search for new ways to attract market share. International markets are one frequently untapped possibility for market expansion and have therefore become a prime target for such service firms.

Technological advancement is another major factor in increasing service trade. Progress in technology offers new ways of doing business and permits businesses to expand their horizons internationally. For example, more rapid transmission of data has permitted financial institutions to expand their service delivery through a worldwide network. Again, were it not for advances in technology, such expansion would rarely have been possible or cost effective.

© Mark Boulton/Alamy
Global Internet services is one factor in increasing global trade services.

Another result of these developments is that service industry expansion has not been confined to the traditional services that are labor-intensive and could therefore have been performed better in areas of the world where labor possesses a comparative advantage because of lower prices. Rather, technology-intensive services are the sunrise industries of the new century. Increasingly, firms can reconfigure their service delivery in order to escape the location-bound dimension. Banks, for example, can offer their services through automatic teller machines or online banking. Consultants can advise via video conferences, and teachers can teach the world through webinars. Physicians can perform operations from a distance if proper computer linkages can drive roboticized medical equipment.

As a result, many service providers can become truly global marketers. To them, the traditional international market barrier of distance no longer matters. Knowledge, the core of many service activities, can offer a global reach without requiring a local presence. Service providers therefore may have only a minor need for a local establishment because they can operate without premises. You don't have to be there to do business! The effect of such a shift in service activities is major. Insurance and bank buildings in the downtowns of the world may soon become obsolete. Talented service providers see the demand for their performance increase while less capable ones suffer from increased competition. Most important, consumers and society have a much broader range and quality of service choices available, and often at a lower cost.

INTERNATIONAL TRADE PROBLEMS IN SERVICES

Together with the increasing importance of service marketing, new problems have beset the service sector. Even though many of these problems have been characterized as affecting mainly the negotiations between nations, they are of sufficient importance to the firm in its international activities to merit a brief review.

Data Collection Problems

The data collected on service trade are inadequate. Service transactions are often invisible statistically as well as physically. The fact that governments have precise data on the number of trucks exported, down to the last bolt, but little information on reinsurance flows, reflects past governmental inattention to services.

Only recently have policymakers recognized that the income generated and the jobs created through the sale of services abroad are just as important as income and jobs resulting from the production and exportation of goods. As a result, many governments are beginning to develop improved measuring techniques for the services sector. For example, the U.S. government has improved its estimates of services by covering more business, professional, and technical services and incorporating improved measurement of telecommunications services and insurance services. New data are also developed on travel and passenger fares, foreign students' expenditures in the United States, repairs and alterations of equipment, and noninterest income of banks.

It is easy to imagine how many data collection problems are encountered in countries lacking elaborate systems and unwilling to allocate funds for such efforts. The gathering of information is, of course, made substantially more difficult because services are intangible and therefore more difficult to measure and to trace than goods. The lack of service homogeneity does not make the task any easier. In an international setting, of course, an additional major headache is the lack of comparability between services categories as used by different national statistical systems. For example, while gas and electricity production and distribution are classified as goods by most governments, they are classified as services in the United States.[17]

Insufficient knowledge and information have led to a lack of transparency. As a result, governments have great difficulty gauging the effect of service transactions internationally or influencing service trade. Consequently, international service negotiations progress only slowly, and governmental regulations are often put into place without precise information as to their repercussions on actual trade performance.

Regulations and Service Trade Negotiations

Typical obstacles to service trade can be categorized into two major types: barriers to entry and problems in performing services. Governments often justify **barriers to entry** by referring to **national security** and economic security. For example, the impact of banking on domestic economic activity is given as a reason why banking should be carried out only by nationals or indeed be operated entirely under government control. Sometimes, the protection of service users is cited, particularly of bank depositors and insurance policyholders. Some countries claim that competition in societally important services is unnecessary, wasteful, and should be avoided. Another justification for barriers is the frequently used **infant industry** argument: "With sufficient time to develop on our own, we can compete in world markets." Often, however, this argument is used simply to prolong the ample licensing profits generated by restricted entry. Impediments to services consist of either tariff or nontariff barriers. Tariff barriers typically restrict or inhibit market entry for the service provider or consumer, while nontariff barriers tend to impede service performance. Yet defining a barrier to service marketing is not always easy. For example, Germany gives an extensive written examination to prospective accountants (as do most countries) to ensure that licensed accountants are qualified to practice. Naturally, the examination is given in German. The fact that few U.S. accountants read and write German does not necessarily constitute a barrier to trade in accountancy services.

© Kyodo via AP Images

Political organizations, such as the BRICS, which consists of Brazil, Russia, India, China, and South Africa, reduce trade regulations to help promote trade between their nations.

Even if barriers to entry are nonexistent or can be overcome, service companies have difficulty in performing effectively abroad once they have achieved access to the local market. One reason is that rules and regulations based on tradition may inhibit innovation. A more important reason is that governments aim to pursue social or cultural objectives through national regulations. Of primary importance here is the distinction between discriminatory and nondiscriminatory regulations. Regulations that impose larger operating costs on foreign service providers than on the local competitors, that provide subsidies to local firms only, or that deny competitive opportunities to foreign suppliers are a proper cause for international concern. The discrimination problem becomes even more acute when foreign firms face competition from government-owned or government-controlled enterprises. On the other hand, nondiscriminatory regulations may be inconvenient and may hamper business operations, but they offer less opportunity for international criticism.

For example, barriers to services destined for the U.S. market result mainly from regulatory practices. The fields of banking, insurance, and accounting provide some examples. These industries are regulated at both the federal and state levels, and the regulations often pose formidable barriers to potential entrants from abroad. The chief complaint of foreign countries is not that the United States discriminates against foreign service providers but rather that the United States places more severe restrictions on them than do other countries. These barriers are, of course, a reflection of the decision-making process within the U.S. domestic economy and are unlikely to change in the near future. A coherent approach toward international commerce in services is hardly likely to emerge from the disparate decisions of agencies such as the Interstate Commerce Commission (ICC), the Federal Communications Commission (FCC), the Securities and Exchange Commission (SEC), and the many licensing agencies at the state level.

All these regulations make it difficult for the international service marketer to penetrate world markets. At the governmental level, services frequently are not recognized as a major facet of world trade or are viewed with suspicion because of a lack of understanding, and barriers to entry often result. To make progress in tearing them down, much educational work needs to be done. Unfortunately, the Doha Round WTO service negotiations have not yet achieved success.[18]

CORPORATE INVOLVEMENT IN INTERNATIONAL SERVICES MARKETING

Services and E-Commerce

Electronic commerce has opened up new horizons for global services reach and has drastically reduced the meaning of distance. For example, when geographic obstacles make the establishment of retail outlets cumbersome and expensive, firms can approach their customers via the Internet. Government regulations that might be prohibitive to a transfer of goods may not have any effect on the international marketing of services. Also, regardless of size, companies are finding it increasingly easy to appeal to a global marketplace. The Internet can help service firms develop, and transitional economies overcome two of the biggest tasks they face: gaining credibility in international markets and saving on travel costs. Little-known firms can become instantly visible on the Internet. Even a small firm can develop a polished and sophisticated web presence and promotion strategy. Customers are less concerned about geographic location if they feel the firm is electronically accessible. An increasing number of service providers have never met their foreign customers except virtually, online.[19]

Nonetheless, several notes of caution must be kept in mind. First, the penetration of the Internet has occurred at different rates in different countries. There are still many businesses and consumers who do not have access to electronic business media. Unless they are to be excluded from a company's focus, more traditional ways of reaching them must be considered. Also, firms need to prepare their Internet presence for global visitors. A multilingual website is a necessity in today's global world because the Internet has become the default port of call for finding goods and services. Ten reasons for having a multilingual website are to:

1. Facilitate a shift toward non-English-speaking Internet users
2. Use as a cost-effective marketing tool
3. Access new customers
4. Increase sales with little investment
5. Demonstrate that the company is customer-centric
6. Generate trust by providing services in a customer's native language
7. Demonstrate cultural sensitivity
8. Beat competition
9. Show that company thinks, works, and deals internationally
10. Be picked up by more search engines[20]

© sjscreens/Alamy

It is important for companies to have an Internet presence in many different countries, without also alienating their global visitors; having multilingual sites help accomplish both these goals.

With today's web technology, it is rather straightforward to publish in many different languages. A survey of 225 corporate websites across 21 industry categories found that it takes 20 languages to reach 90 percent of the web's worldwide users.[21] The most common website languages are (in decreasing order):

- English
- French
- German
- Japanese
- Spanish (Spain)
- Chinese (simplified)
- Italian
- Spanish (Latin America)
- Korean
- Dutch
- Portuguese (Brazil)
- Polish
- Russian
- Chinese (traditional)
- French (Canada)
- Swedish
- Danish
- Portuguese (Portugal)
- Norwegian
- Czech
- Finnish[22]

A new development in 2011 has been the emergence of internationalized domain names (IDNs) or full-length URLs in non-Latin scripts such as Arabic, Hebrew, Greek, Cyrillic, and Chinese.[23] Exhibit 12.9 lists the top 20 global websites (both goods and services providers) for 2010.

Services and Academia

In the context of international services, we briefly review here the position of higher education.[24] Academia has staunchly resisted accepting the notion of being part of any services sector. University presidents, deans, and professors from around the world consistently assure the trade community that the problems they face are so specific and unique that wholesale approaches to anything in higher education would be heresy. However, academia is not exempt

EXHIBIT 12.9 Top 20 Global Websites, 2010

1. Facebook	11. Autodesk
2. Google	12. Wikipedia
3. Cisco Systems	13. Microsoft
4. 3M	14. Nokia
5. LG	15. Panasonic
6. Philips	16. Volkswagen
7. Samsung	17. Hotels.com
8. NIVEA	18. Adobe
9. Symantec	19. Volvo Group
10. HP	20. Deloitte Touche Tohmatsu

SOURCE: "Best Global Web Sites of 2011," Byte Level Research, www.bytelevel.com.

from the factors that affect other global services, such as demand and supply. Higher education is one of the largest service exports in the United States, with international students contributing $21 billion to the U.S. economy in the 2011 academic year.[25]

Over 723,000 international students studied in the United States during the 2011 academic year. The top 10 countries tapping into this sector of U.S. services are:

1. China
2. India
3. South Korea
4. Canada
5. Taiwan
6. Saudi Arabia
7. Japan
8. Vietnam
9. Mexico
10. Turkey[26]

Business management is the most popular field of study for international students, followed closely by engineering. The most prominent locations of interest in the United States are California, New York, Texas, Massachusetts, Illinois, Pennsylvania, Florida, Ohio, Michigan, and Indiana.[27]

Students from the United States also require international knowledge acquisition. During the 2009–2010 academic year, 270,604 U.S. students studied abroad.[28] Keep in mind that only a decade before less than 100,000 students did so. The most popular destination point for U.S. students is Europe, with the United Kingdom drawing almost 32,683 U.S. students, followed closely by Italy, Spain, France, and China.[29] The second most popular destination is Latin America, drawing 15 percent of American students, with Asia (12 percent), and Oceania—Australia, New Zealand, and the South Pacific Islands—(5 percent) close behind as destination points.[30]

Typical International Services

Although many firms are active in the international service arena, many often do not perceive their existing competitive advantage. Numerous services have great potential for internationalization.

Financial institutions can offer some functions very competitively in the international field of banking services. Increased mergers and acquisitions on a global basis have led to the emergence of financial giants in Europe, Japan, and the United States. With the increased reach made possible by electronic commerce, they can develop direct linkages to clients around the world, offering tailor-made financial services and reductions in intermediation cost. Exhibit 12.10 provides an example of the international positioning of a bank.

Another area with great international potential consists of construction, design, and engineering services. Economies of scale work not only for machinery and material but also for areas such as personnel management and the overall management of projects. Particularly for international projects that are large scale and long term, the experience advantage could weigh heavily in favor of seasoned firms. The economic significance of these services far exceeds their direct turnover because they encourage subsequent demand for capital goods. For example, having an engineering consultant of a certain nationality increases the chances that contracts for the supply of equipment, technology, and know-how will be won by an enterprise of the same nationality, given the advantages enjoyed in terms of information, language, and technical specification.[31]

Law and accounting firms can aid their domestic clients abroad through support activities; they can also consult with foreign firms and governments abroad, though in some instances they may have to work under the umbrella of

EXHIBIT 12.10 Financial Services Firm Positions Itself

EN ESPAÑA SOMOS ESPAÑOLES.
IN DEUTSCHLAND SIND WIR DEUTSCHE.
IN AUSTRALIA, WE ARE AUSTRALIAN.
日本では、日本人。
IN CANADA, WE ARE CANADIAN.
IN NEDERLAND ZIJN WE NEDERLANDS.
IN ENGLAND, WE ARE ENGLISH.
IN DER SCHWEIZ SIND WIR SCHWEIZER.
在香港我們是中國人。
IN AMERICA, WE ARE AMERICAN.
DI SINGAPURA KAMI IALAH ORANG SINGAPURA.
EN FRANCE, NOUS SOMMES FRANÇAIS.

AROUND THE WORLD WE ARE THE
CS FIRST BOSTON GROUP.

Announcing a worldwide investment banking firm that draws its strength from established investment banks in the world's financial capitals.

Operating as First Boston in the Americas, Credit Suisse First Boston in Europe and the Middle East, and CS First Boston Pacific in the Far East and Asia, the CS First Boston Group – together with Credit Suisse – offers unparalleled expertise in capital raising, mergers and acquisitions, securities sales, trading and research, asset management, and merchant banking.

So regardless of what language you speak, the words for powerful investment banking are the same all over the world – CS First Boston Group.

CS First Boston Group First Boston Credit Suisse First Boston CS First Boston Pacific

SOURCE: Courtesy of Credit Suisse First Boston LLC, www.csfb.com.

an authorized local firm. In computer and data services, international activities are growing rapidly. Knowledge of computer operations, data manipulations, data transmission, and data analysis are insufficiently exploited internationally by many small- and medium-sized firms. For example, India is increasingly participating in the provision of international data services. Although some aspects of the data field are high-technology intensive, many operations still require skilled human service input. The coding and entering of data often has to be performed manually because appropriate machine-readable forms may be unavailable or not usable. Because of lower wages, Indian companies can offer data-entry services at a rate much lower than in more industrialized countries. As a result, data are transmitted in raw form to India where they are encoded on a proper medium and returned to the ultimate user. To some extent, this transformation can be equated to the value-added steps that take place in the transformation of a raw commodity into a finished product. Obviously, using its comparative advantage for this labor-intensive task, India can compete in the field of international services. While the global economic slowdown did slow the growth of India's information technology sector somewhat, the industry itself was expected to become a $72 billion industry in 2011.[32]

Many opportunities exist in the field of teaching services. Both the academic and the corporate education sectors have concentrated their work in the domestic market. Yet the teaching of knowledge is in high global demand and offers new opportunities for growth. Technology allows teachers to go global via video conferences, e-mail office hours, and Internet-relayed teaching materials. Removing the confinement of the classroom may well trigger the largest surge in learning that humankind has ever known.

Management consulting services can be provided by firms to institutions and corporations around the globe. Of particular value is management expertise in areas where firms possess global leadership, be it in manufacturing or process activities. For example, companies with highly refined transportation or logistics activities can sell their management experience abroad. Yet consulting services are particularly sensitive to the cultural environment, and their use varies significantly by country and field of expertise.

All domestic service expenditures funded from abroad by foreign citizens represent a service export. This makes tourism an increasingly important area of services trade. For example, every foreign visitor who spends foreign currency in a country contributes to an improvement in that nation's current account. The natural resources and beauty offered by so many countries contribute to travel and tourism becoming one of the world's leading growth service sectors.[33] While still expecting growth, real GDP sector growth was expected to slow with the economic conditions of 2011.[34] Overall, the contribution of the travel and tourism economy to employment is expected to continue in a positive direction.

A proper mix in international services might also be achieved by pairing the strengths of different partners. For example, information technology expertise from one country could be combined with financial resources from another. The strengths of both partners can then be used to obtain maximum benefits. As seen in *The International Marketplace 12.3*, partnerships among service providers are even contributing to the future of greening the industry.

Combining international advantages in services may ultimately result in the development of an even newer and more drastic comparative lead. For example, if a firm has an international head start in such areas as high technology, information gathering, information processing, and information analysis, the major thrust of its international service might not rely on providing these service components individually but rather on enabling clients, based on all resources, to make better decisions. If better decision making is transferable to a wide variety of international situations, that in itself might become the overriding future competitive advantage of the firm in the international market.

Starting to Market Services Internationally

For many firms, participation on the Internet will offer the most attractive starting point in marketing services internationally. Setting up a website will allow visitors from any place on the globe to come see the offering. Of course, the most important problem will be communicating the existence of the site and enticing visitors to come. For that, very traditional advertising and communication approaches often need to be used. In some countries, for example, rolling billboards announce websites and their benefits. Overall, however, we need to keep in mind that not everywhere do firms and individuals have access to or make use of the new e-commerce opportunities.

For services that are delivered mainly in the support of or in conjunction with goods, the most sensible approach for the international novice is to follow the path of the good. For years, many large accounting and banking firms have done so by determining where their major multinational clients have set up new operations and then following them. Smaller service marketers who cooperate

THE INTERNATIONAL MARKETPLACE 12.3

Service Contractor Offers Sustainability in Trade Shows and Exhibitions

GES, with operations in 16 cities in the United States, eight cities in Canada, and four cities in the United Kingdom, provides exhibition and event services to a variety of companies worldwide. GES produces some of the world's leading trade shows and exhibitions, such as:

- International CES (consumer technology)
- Spring Fair Birmingham (launch for a variety of new products and trends)
- Canadian International Auto Show (largest auto show in Canada)
- International Council of Shopping Centers (global trade association for shopping centers)
- MAGIC (fashion)
- WSA Show (footwear and accessories)
- CONEXPO-CON/AGG (construction industry)
- IFPE (power transmissions and motion control technologies)

GES is at the forefront in sustainability. The service contractor is dedicated to decreasing waste and using environmentally friendly products as much as possible. As early as 1990, the company began recycling the carpet from its trade shows and exhibitions. Importantly, the company works closely with its vendors and clients to develop and use more ecofriendly, cost-effective alternatives.

One of the first company partners in the contractor's greening efforts was Nielsen Business Media's Sports Group. Nielsen Business Media, a part of the Nielsen Company, runs over 135 trade shows and conferences in over 30 industries across the globe. Events include the Outdoor Retailer Summer and Winter Markets, Action Sports Retailer September World Trade Expo, Health and Fitness Business Expo and Conference, Fly-Fishing Retailer World Trade Expo, and Interbike International Bicycle Expo.

The Sports Group at Nielsen Business Media was a natural sustainability partner because the environment and sustainability already figured in the mindset of the exhibitors and the attendees of various trade shows. All of the shows run by the Sports Group now have 100 percent recycled aisle carpet, recyclable badges for exhibitors (made with recycled paper and soy ink), biodegradable can liners, LED lighting for signs and backlighting, and recycling programs for exhibitors' materials. GES is dedicated to offering exhibitor services and products that decrease the carbon footprint.

Initially, GES found that sourcing the desired recyclable materials was neither easy nor inexpensive. However, raised awareness of environmental concerns has now made it easier to find the necessary resources. As a service provider, GES had to keep in mind that offering environmentally sustainable contractor services also meant that it had to be able to acquire the necessary supplies to do so. The goal for the company is to provide a service that offers environmentally friendly booth-rental packages for all of its trade shows and exhibits around the world.

SOURCES: Stephanie Corbin and Rachel Wimberly, "Service Contractors: Sustainability on the Floor," *Tradeshow Week*, April 21, 2008, www.tradeshowweek.com/article/CA6552183.html, accessed February 2, 2009; and GES, www.ges.com, accessed December 15, 2011.

closely with manufacturing firms can determine where the manufacturing firms are operating internationally. Ideally, of course, it would be possible to follow clusters of manufacturers in order to obtain economies of scale internationally while looking for entirely new client groups abroad.

For service providers whose activities are independent from goods, a different strategy is needed. These individuals and firms must search for market situations abroad that are similar to the domestic market. Such a search should concentrate in their area of expertise. For example, a design firm learning about construction projects abroad can investigate the possibility of rendering its design services. Similarly, a management consultant learning about the plans of a foreign country or firm to computerize operations can explore the possibility of overseeing a smooth transition from manual to computerized activities. What is required is the understanding that similar problems are likely to occur in similar situations.

Another opportunity consists in identifying and understanding points of transition abroad. Just as U.S. society has undergone change, foreign societies

© Andia/Alamy

International services, such as logistics providers, need to market their services globally.

are subject to a changing domestic environment. If, for example, new transportation services are introduced, an expert in containerization may wish to consider whether to offer service to improve the efficiency of the new system.

Leads for international service opportunities can also be gained by staying informed about international projects sponsored by domestic organizations such as the U.S. Agency for International Development, as well as international organizations such as the United Nations, the International Finance Corporation, or the World Bank. Very frequently, such projects are in need of support through services. Overall, the international service marketer needs to search for familiar situations or similar problems requiring similar solutions in order to formulate an effective international expansion strategy.

Strategic Implications of International Services Marketing

To be successful, the international service marketer must first determine the nature and the aim of the service offering—that is, whether the service will be aimed at people or at things, and whether the service act in itself will result in tangible or intangible actions. Exhibit 12.11 provides examples of such a classification that will help the marketer to better determine the position of the services effort.

During this determination, the marketer must consider other tactical variables that have an impact on the preparation of the service offering. The measurement of service capacity and delivery efficiency often remains highly qualitative rather than quantitative. In the field of communications, the intangibility of the service reduces the marketer's ability to provide samples. This makes communicating the service offer much more difficult than communicating an offer for a good. Brochures or catalogs explaining services often must show a proxy for the service in order to provide the prospective customer with tangible clues. A cleaning service, for instance, can show a picture of an individual removing trash or cleaning a window. Yet the picture will not fully communicate the performance of the service. Because of the different needs and requirements of individual consumers, the marketer must pay very close attention to the two-way flow of communication. Mass communication must often be supported by intimate one-on-one follow up.

The role of personnel deserves special consideration in the international marketing of services. Because the customer interface is intense, proper provisions

EXHIBIT 12.11 Understanding the Service Act

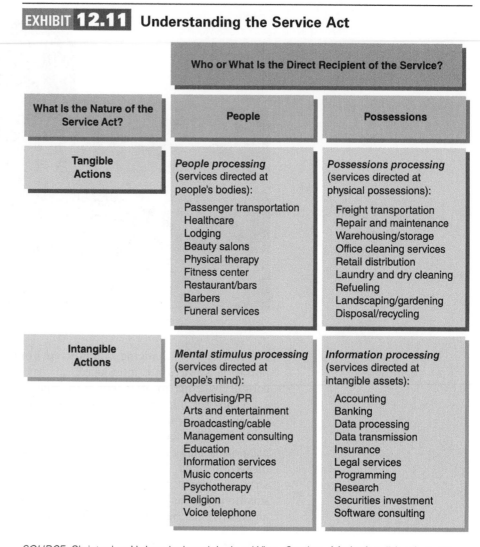

What Is the Nature of the Service Act?	Who or What Is the Direct Recipient of the Service? People	Possessions
Tangible Actions	*People processing* (services directed at people's bodies): Passenger transportation Healthcare Lodging Beauty salons Physical therapy Fitness center Restaurant/bars Barbers Funeral services	*Possessions processing* (services directed at physical possessions): Freight transportation Repair and maintenance Warehousing/storage Office cleaning services Retail distribution Laundry and dry cleaning Refueling Landscaping/gardening Disposal/recycling
Intangible Actions	*Mental stimulus processing* (services directed at people's mind): Advertising/PR Arts and entertainment Broadcasting/cable Management consulting Education Information services Music concerts Psychotherapy Religion Voice telephone	*Information processing* (services directed at intangible assets): Accounting Banking Data processing Data transmission Insurance Legal services Programming Research Securities investment Software consulting

SOURCE: Christopher H. Lovelock and Jochen Wirtz, *Services Marketing*, 5th ed., p. 15. © 2004. Reprinted by permission of Pearson Education, Inc., Upper Saddle River, NJ.

need to be made for training personnel both domestically and internationally. Major emphasis must be placed on appearance. The person delivering the service—rather than the service itself—will communicate the spirit, value, and attitudes of the service corporation. The service person is both the producer and the marketer of the service. Therefore, recruitment and training techniques must focus on dimensions such as customer relationship management and image projection as well as competence in the design and delivery of the service.[35]

This close interaction with the consumer will also have organizational implications. Whereas tight control over personnel may be desired, the individual interaction that is required points toward the need for an international decentralization of service delivery. This, in turn, requires both delegation of large amounts of responsibility to individuals and service "subsidiaries" and a great deal of trust in all organizational units. This trust, of course, can be greatly enhanced through proper methods of training and supervision. Sole ownership also helps strengthen trust. Research has shown that service firms, in their international expansion, tend greatly to prefer the establishment of full-control ventures. Only when costs escalate and the company-specific advantage diminishes will service firms seek out shared-control ventures.[36]

The areas of pricing and financing require special attention. Because services cannot be stored, much greater responsiveness to demand fluctuation must exist, and therefore much greater pricing flexibility must be maintained. At the same time, flexibility is countered by the desire to provide transparency for both the seller and the buyer of services in order to foster an ongoing relationship. The intangibility of services also makes financing more difficult. Frequently, even financial institutions with large amounts of international experience are less willing to provide financial support for international services than for products. The reasons are that the value of services is more difficult to assess, service performance is more difficult to monitor, and services are difficult to repossess. Therefore, customer complaints and difficulties in receiving payments are much more troublesome for a lender to evaluate for services than for products.

Finally, the distribution implications of international services must be considered. Usually, short and direct channels are required. Within these channels, closeness to the customer is of overriding importance in order to understand what the customer really wants, to trace the use of the service, and to aid the consumer in obtaining a truly tailor-made service.

SUMMARY

Services are taking on an increasing importance in international marketing. They need to be considered separately from the marketing of goods because they no longer simply complement goods. Increasingly, goods complement services or are in competition with them. Because of service attributes such as intangibility, perishability, customization, and cultural sensitivity, the international marketing of services is frequently more complex than that of goods.

Services play a growing role in the global economy. As a result, international growth and competition in this sector outstrips that of merchandise trade and is likely to intensify in the future. Even though services are unlikely to replace production, the sector will account for the shaping of new comparative advantages internationally, particularly in light of new facilitating technologies that encourage electronic commerce.

The many service firms now operating domestically need to investigate the possibility of going global. The historical patterns in which service providers followed manufacturers abroad have become obsolete as stand-alone services have become more important to world trade. Management must therefore assess its vulnerability to international service competition and explore opportunities to provide its services around the world.

KEY TERMS

intangibility
perishability
service capacity
customer involvement
service consistency
quality perception
market transparency
infrastructure services
cross-border transactions
trade surplus
trade deficit
deregulation
barrier to entry
national security
infant industry
discriminatory regulations
nondiscriminatory regulations
regulatory practice

QUESTIONS FOR DISCUSSION

1. Should electronic commerce be considered a good or a service?
2. What percentage of your books do you purchase via e-commerce? How will that change in the next few years?
3. Discuss the major reasons for the growth of international services.
4. How does the international sale of services differ from the sale of goods?

5. What are some of the international marketing implications of service intangibility?
6. Discuss the effects of cultural sensitivity on international services.
7. What are some ways for a firm to expand its services internationally?
8. How can a firm in a developing country participate in the international services boom?
9. Which services would be expected to migrate globally in the next decade? Why?
10. How will increased use of cloud computing affect the global technology services industry? Which firms are likely to benefit or suffer?

INTERNET EXERCISES

1. Find the most current data on the five leading export and import countries for commercial services. (The information is available on the World Trade Organization site at www.wto.org. Click the statistics button.)
2. What are the key U.S. services exports and imports? What is the current services trade balance? (See the Bureau of Economic Analysis website at www.bea.gov).
3. How do Indian government regulations affect the ability of global banks to offer services there? (Consult the latest India report on the U.S. Trade Representative site at www.ustr.gov.)

CHALLENGE US

Services

"Services" often have the connotation of low level, servant-like activities. So, such services as cleaning, food provision, delivery, and protective actions are often seen as unsophisticated and marginally participatory in the economy. It is said that there is no need to internationalize when others abroad can do it so easily as well, and often at a much lower price.

Yet, others identify top notch trained people as leading service providers—be it as astronauts, international lenders, or masters of drone airplanes. They claim that the future belongs to service providers, and that proper understanding and dispersion of services will make the difference between winners and losers. Some even feel that the entire agricultural sector will, eventually, change into a service rather than a production field.

For Discussion

1. Where do you see employment and growth occurring?

RECOMMENDED READINGS

Alexander, Kern, and Mads Andenas. *The World Trade Organization and Trade in Services*. Leiden, The Netherlands: Martinus Nijhoff/Brill Academic, 2008.

Hefley, Bill, and Wendy Murphy. *Service Science, Management, and Engineering: Education for the 21st Century*. New York: Springer, 2010.

Jensen, J. Bradford. *Global Trade in Services: Fear, Facts, and Offshoring*. Washington, DC: Peterson Institute of International Economics, 2011.

Lovelock, Christopher, and Jochen Wirtz. *Services Marketing: People, Technology, Strategy*. Upper Saddle River, NJ: Prentice Hall, 2011.

Marchetti, Juan A., and Martin Roy. *Opening Markets for Trade in Services: Countries and Sectors in Bilateral and WTO Negotiations*. Cambridge, England: Cambridge University Press, 2009.

Saez, Sebastian, ed. *Trade in Services Negotiation: A Guide for Developing Countries*. Washington, DC: World Bank, 2010.

ENDNOTES

1. Leonard L. Berry, "Services Marketing Is Different," in *Services Marketing*, ed. Christopher H. Lovelock (Englewood Cliffs, NY: Prentice-Hall, 1984), 30.
2. Christian Grönroos, "Marketing Services: The Case of a Missing Product," *Journal of Business & Industrial Marketing* 13, no. 4/5 (1998): 322–38.
3. Bernd Stauss and Wolfgang Seidel, *Complaint Management: The Heart of CRM* (Chicago: American Marketing Association, 2005): 232–34.
4. Pierre Berthon, Leyland Pitt, Constantine S. Katsikeas, and Jean Paul Berthon, "Virtual Services Go International: International Services in the Marketspace," *Journal of International Marketing* 7, no. 3 (1999): 84–106.
5. United States International Trade Commission, "Recent Trends in U.S. Services Trade," *Annual Report*, June 2011.
6. United States International Trade Commission, "Recent Trends in U.S. Services Trade," *Annual Report*, June 2010.

7. Bureau of Labor Statistics, "Tomorrow's Jobs," *Occupational Handbook, 2008–09 Edition*, United States Department of Labor, www.bls.gov/oco/ocotjt1.htm, accessed November 30, 2011.
8. United States International Trade Administration, "U.S. Trade Overview," June 24, 2011, www.ita.gov.
9. World Trade Organization, press release, April 7, 2011, www.wto.org.
10. United States International Trade Administration, "Trade Overview," June 24, 2011, www.ita.gov.
11. United States International Trade Administration, "Top U.S. Trade Partners," April 2011, www.ita.gov.
12. United States International Trade Administration, "Trade Overview," June 24, 2011, www.ita.gov.
13. United States International Trade Commission, www.usitc.gov.
14. World Trade Organization, press release, April 7, 2011, www.wto.org.
15. Ibid.
16. United States International Trade Commission, www.usitc.gov.
17. Terry Clark, Daniel Rajaratnam, and Timothy Smith, "Toward a Theory of International Services: Marketing Intangibles in a World of Nations," *Journal of International Marketing* 4, no. 2 (1995): 2–28.
18. United States International Trade Commission, www.usitc.gov.
19. Dorothy Riddle, "Using the Internet for Service Exporting: Tips for Service Firms," *International Trade Forum* 1 (1999): 19–21.
20. Neil Payne, "10 Reasons Why You Need a Multilingual Website," May 10, 2008, www.kwintessential.co.uk/translation/articles/multilingual-website.html, accessed November 30, 2011.
21. Byte Level Research LLC, "Byte Level Research Announces Best Global Web Sites of 2008," March 12, 2008, http://bytelevel.com/news/reportcard2008.html.
22. Jim DeLaHunt, "Web 2.0 goes to Babel: Multilingual Websites and User-Supplied Content," September 9, 2008, http://jdlh.com/en/doc/2008/web2babel.html.
23. John Yunker, "A URL in Any Language: Getting to Know the Next Generation of URLs," *UX Magazine*, August 16, 2011.
24. Michael R. Czinkota, "Loosening the Shackles: The Future of Global Higher Education," testimony at WTO Symposium on Cross-Border Supply of Services, Geneva, 2005, www.wto.org/english/tratop_e/serv_e/sym_april05_e/sym_april05_e.htm.
25. Institute of International Education, "International Student Enrollment Increased by 5 Percent in 2010–2011," www.iie.org, accessed December 14, 2011.
26. Fast Facts, December 14, 2011.
27. Ibid.
28. Institute of International Education, "Open Doors 2011: Study Abroad by U.S. Students Rose in 2009/10 with More Students Going to Less Traditional Destinations," press release, www.iie.org/Who-We-Are/News-and-Events/Press-Center/Press-Releases/2011/2011-11-14-Open-Doors-Study-Abroad, accessed November 30, 2011.
29. Ibid.
30. Ibid.
31. "Engineering, Technical, and Other Services to Industry," Synthesis Report, Organization for Economic Cooperation and Development, Paris, 1988.
32. Gartner Research, "Gartner Says Indian ITC Spending to Grow 10.3 Percent in 2011," press release, November 23, 2010.
33. World Travel and Tourism Council, "Economic Impact of Travel & Tourism: Update November 2011," www.wttc.org/site_media/uploads/downloads/4pp_document_for_WTM_RGB.pdf.
34. Benjamin Jones, "UNWTO: World Tourism Growth Will Slow in 2011," HotelNewsNow.com, January 18, 2011.
35. Paul G. Patterson and Muris Cicic, "A Typology of Services Firms in International Markets: An Empirical Investigation," *Journal of International Marketing* 3, no. 4 (1995): 19–38.
36. M. Krishna Erramilli and C. P. Rao, "Service Firms' International Entry-Mode Choice: A Modified Transaction-Cost Analysis Approach," *Journal of Marketing* 57 (July 1993): 19–38.

CHAPTER 13

Advertising, Promotion, and Sales

LEARNING OBJECTIVES

By the time you complete this chapter, you will be able to:

- Understand the message channel in which the message moves from the sender to the receiver and then back to the sender.
- Manage the different elements of a promotional campaign.
- Understand the most effective way to use a sales force.
- Seek a direct connection between target consumers and businesses.
- Identify the use of short-term incentives to encourage the purchase or sales of a product or service.
- Recognize the importance of the relationship between and perception of a corporation and its constituents.

THE INTERNATIONAL **MARKETPLACE** 13.1

Global Sponsorship

In any given country, the majority of corporate sponsorship goes to sports. Of the $51.0 billion spent worldwide for sponsorships in 2012, 69 percent was allocated to sports. Within sports, the two flagship events are the World Cup in soccer and the Olympic Games (both summer and winter). Sponsors want to align themselves with—and create—meaningful sports-related moments for consumers. At the same time, consumers associate sponsors of sports events with leadership, teamwork, and pursuit of excellence, as well as friendship.

As a global partner, a country or corporation must strike the right mix of color and culture to represent both the event and the global partner. There may be a fine line to project all these dimensions. The 2014 FIFA World Cup Brazilian logo was able to combine the vibrant colors of Brazil along with a sense of the country's emergence as one of the world's most modern and influential economies into a strong visual representation.

© GIANLUIGI GUERCIA/AFP/Getty Images/Newscom

Sponsorships have been a cornerstone of the Coca-Cola Company's marketing efforts for 100 years, having started with using sports stars such as world champion cyclist Bobby Walthour in ads in 1903. Presently, the company is the world's biggest sports sponsor, with total sponsorship-related expenses at $1 billion annually. These activities span different types of sports and various geographies. Each country organization within Coca-Cola decides which programs it wants to use during sponsorship depending on its goals, which are jointly set by local managers and headquarters.

While measurement of the return on such investments is challenging, Coca-Cola evaluates such dimensions as the number of new corporate customers that sell Coke in their stores, the incremental amount of promotional and display activity, and new vending placement. The influence on the brand is the most difficult to establish. The World Cup sponsorship has been suggested to have boosted Coca-Cola's presence, especially in the emerging and developing markets. In soccer, Coca-Cola's involvement includes the following:

- FIFA partner since 1974—signed landmark 15-year agreement through 2022 to be official soft or sports drink at Men's World Cup, Women's World Cup, Confederation Cup competitions, and under 20/under 17 World Youth Championships.
- Also sponsors Copa America, Asian Football Confederation, and over 40 national teams.

SOURCES: FIFA, www.fifa.com; Coca-Cola, www.coca-cola.com/en/index.html; and IEG, www.sponsorship.com.

The general requirements of effective marketing communications apply to global marketers as well as their domestic counterparts; however, the environments and the situations usually are more numerous and call for coordination of the promotional effort. Increasingly, marketers opt for varying degrees of panregional and integrative approaches to take advantage of similarities in markets they serve, as seen in *The International Marketplace 13.1*. All possible points of touch that the customer has with the marketer's brands have to be incorporated into the communications plan.

The technology is in place for global communication efforts, but difficult challenges still remain in the form of cultural, economic, ethnic, regulatory, and demographic differences in the various countries and regions. Standardization of any magnitude requires sound management systems and excellent communication to ensure uniform strategic and tactical thinking of all the professionals in the overseas marketing chain.[1]

This chapter will analyze the elements to be managed in promotional efforts in terms of environmental opportunities and constraints. A framework is provided for the planning of promotional campaigns. Although the discussion focuses mostly on advertising, other elements of the promotion mix, especially sales promotion and publicity, fit integrally into the planning model. Naturally, all of the mass selling methods have to be planned in conjunction with personal selling efforts.

THE MARKETING COMMUNICATIONS PROCESS

As shown in the communications model presented in Exhibit 13.1, effective communications requires three elements—the sender, the message, and the receiver—connected by a message channel. The process may begin with an unsolicited inquiry from a potential customer or as a planned effort by the marketer. Whatever the goal of the communications process, the sender needs to study receiver characteristics before encoding the message in order to achieve maximum impact. **Encoding** the message simply means converting it into a

EXHIBIT 13.1 The Marketing Communications Process

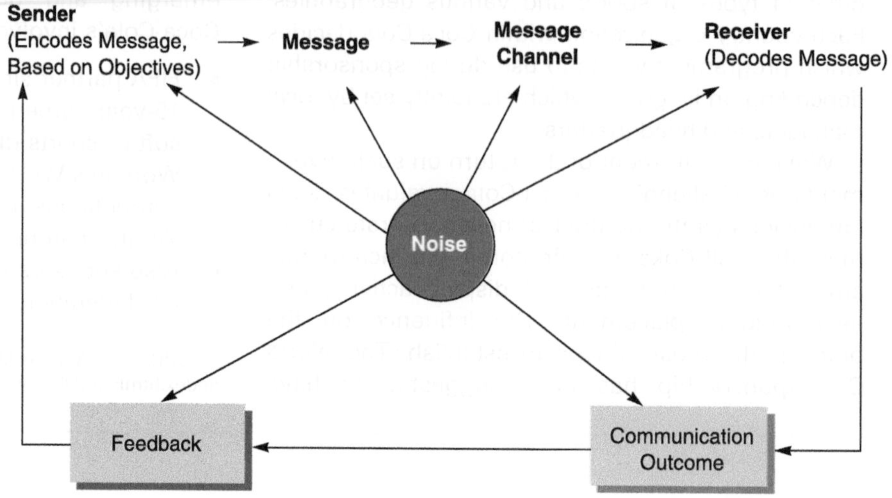

SOURCES: © Cengage Learning 2013; Adapted from Terence A. Shimp, and J. Craig Andrews, *Advertising, Promotion, and Other Aspects of Integrated Marketing Communications* (Mason, OH: South-Western, 2012), 82.

symbolic form that is properly understood by the receiver. This is not a simple task, however. For example, if an e-commerce site's order form asks only for typical U.S.-type address information, such as a zip code, and does not include anything for other countries, the would-be buyer abroad will interpret this as unwillingness to do business outside the United States.

The message channel is the path through which the message moves from sender (source) to receiver. This link that ties the receiver to the sender ranges from sound waves conveying the human voice in personal selling to transceivers or intermediaries such as print and broadcast media. Although technological advances (for example, video conferencing and the Internet) may have made buyer–seller negotiations more efficient, the fundamental process and its purpose have remained unchanged. Face-to-face contact is still necessary for two basic reasons. The first is the need for detailed discussion and explanation, and the second is the need to establish the rapport that forms the basis of lasting business relationships. Technology will then support in the maintenance of the relationship.

The message channel also exists in mass communications. Complications in international marketing may arise if a particular medium does not reach the targeted audience, which is currently the case for Internet communications, for example, due to varying online penetration rates around the world. Other examples of complications are the banning of advertising for certain product categories, such as for cigarettes in most of Europe. Many direct sellers in China have been accused of operating sophisticated pyramid schemes and other sales swindles. Big direct-selling companies disputed those claims, saying regulators simply misunderstood their business model. In 2006, after heavy lobbying from American companies, China lifted its ban. And since then, direct selling, with some modifications, has flourished in China, growing into an $8 billion industry that now markets products as diverse as health supplements, cosmetics, toothpaste, and dishwashing liquid.

Once a sender has placed a message into a channel or a set of channels and directed it to the intended destination, the completion of the process is dependent on the receiver's **decoding**—that is, transforming the message symbols back into thought. If there is an adequate amount of overlap between sender characteristics and needs reflected in the encoded message and receiver characteristics and needs reflected in the decoded message, the communications process has worked.

A message moving through a channel is subject to the influence of extraneous and distracting stimuli, which interfere with the intended accurate reception of the message. This interference is referred to as noise. In the international marketing context, noise might be failure to express a quotation in the inquirer's system of currency and measurement, or lack of understanding of the recipient's environment—for example, having only an English-language website. A U.S. company got a message from its Thai client complaining of an incomplete delivery: an order of 85,000 units was four short! When the U.S. company shipped in bulk, the number of units was estimated by weight. In Thailand, however, labor is cheap and materials expensive, allowing the client to hand-count shipments. The solution was to provide a slight overage in each shipment without incurring a major expense but achieving customer satisfaction.

The international marketer should be most alert to cultural noise. The lack of language skills may hinder successful negotiations, whereas translation errors may render a promotional campaign or brochure useless. Similarly, nonverbal language and its improper interpretation may cause problems. While eye contact in North America and Europe may be direct, the cultural style of the Japanese may involve markedly less eye contact.

The success of the outcome is determined by how well objectives have been met in generating more awareness, a more positive attitude, or increased purchases. For example, the development of sales literature in the local language and reflective of the product line offered may result in increased inquiries or even more sales. While call centers abroad may provide significant cost savings, their use has to be benchmarked against customer-service standards, expectations, and overall goodwill towards the company.[2]

Regardless of whether the situation calls for interpersonal or mass communications, the collection and observation of feedback is necessary to analyze the success of the communications effort. The initial sender–receiver relationship is transposed, and interpretative skills similar to those needed in developing messages are needed. To make effective and efficient use of communications requires considerable strategic planning. Examples of concrete ways in which feedback can be collected are inquiry cards and toll-free numbers distributed at trade shows to gather additional information. Similarly, the Internet allows marketers to track traffic flows and to install registration procedures that identify individuals and track their purchases over time.

PLANNING PROMOTIONAL CAMPAIGNS

The planning for promotional campaigns consists of the following seven stages, which usually overlap or take place concurrently, especially after the basics of the campaign have been agreed on:

1. Determine the target audience
2. Determine specific campaign objectives
3. Determine the budget
4. Determine media strategy
5. Determine the message
6. Determine the campaign approach
7. Determine campaign effectiveness[3]

The actual content of these stages will change by type of campaign situation; compare, for example, a local campaign for which headquarters provides support versus a global corporate image campaign.

The Target Audience

Global marketers face multiple audiences beyond customers. The expectations of these audiences have to be researched to ensure the appropriateness of campaign decision making. Consider the following publics with whom communication is necessary: suppliers, intermediaries, government, the local community, bankers and creditors, media organizations, shareholders, and employees. Each can be reached with an appropriate mix of tools. A multinational corporation that wants to boost its image with the government and the local community may sponsor events. One of the approaches available is cause-related marketing, in which the company, or one of its brands, is linked with a cause such as environmental protection or children's health. For example, TOMS gave its one-millionth pair of new shoes to a needy child in September 2010. TOMS now gives in over 20 countries and works with charitable partners in the field who incorporate shoes. As another example, Microsoft launched a website in Singapore to further the use of information technology. For every page hit within the site, Microsoft donates one cent to three local charities. This type of activity can benefit a brand but must be backed by a genuine effort within the company to behave responsibly. Corporate cause sponsorship will grow to hit $1.73 billion in 2012.[4]

An important aspect of research is to determine multimarket target audience similarities. If such exist, panregional or global campaigns can be attempted. Grey Advertising checks for commonalities in variables such as economic expectations, demographics, income, and education. Consumer needs and wants are assessed for common features. An increasing number of companies are engaging in corporate image advertising in support of their more traditional, tactical, product-specific, and local advertising efforts. Especially for multidivisional companies, an umbrella campaign may help either to boost the image of lesser-known product lines or make the company itself be understood correctly or perceived more positively. Companies may announce repositioning strategies through image campaigns to both external and internal constituents. GE's campaign, branded Ecomagination, is a company-wide initiative to push environmentally friendly products. The plan is to double company revenues from ecosafe products to $20 billion. To go beyond the campaign, each of GE's 11 business units are to come up with at least five big environmental ideas capable of generating $100 million of revenue.[5] Itaú, in an example of corporate image advertising, wants to show its vision of Latin America to the world, reinforcing its Latin roots and demonstrating that it is the bank that understands this region best (see Exhibit 13.2). Itaú is an international bank with operations in the Americas, Europe, and Asia, providing services in a wide range of business segments.

In some cases, the product may be standard across markets but the product's positioning, and subsequently marketing communication, has to change. For example, Mars is a meal substitute in Britain but an energizer in continental Europe. The Ford Fiesta is a small car for the German market but a family car in Portugal.[6] Audience similarities are more easily found in business markets.

Campaign Objectives

Nothing is more essential to the planning of international promotional campaigns than the establishment of clearly defined, measurable objectives. These objectives can be divided into overall global and regional objectives as well as local objectives. The objectives that are set at the local level are more specific and set measurable targets for individual markets. These objectives may be product- or service-related or related to the entity itself. Typical goals are to increase awareness, enhance image, and improve market share in a particular market. Whatever the objective, it has to be measurable for control purposes.

FedEx has introduced a series of service-enhancement initiatives in Asian markets to further strengthen its products and services for shippers. The company wanted to increase brand awareness among its target audience of small- and medium-sized international shippers. Among large corporate clients, FedEx has no concerns, and marketing to them is usually done through personal visits by the FedEx sales force. The core creative concept is a response to an observation that in today's ever-more-demanding world, every delivery is important.

EXHIBIT 13.2 **An Example of a Corporate Image Campaign**

SOURCE: Courtesy of Itaú Unibanco.

Developed in Asia for customers in Asia, the campaign was inspired by Hollywood blockbuster movies to convey how FedEx "takes the drama out of delivery."[7]

There is a move by many governments to influence how their countries are perceived in order to gain commercial or political advantage. The United States has needed to build a new level of understanding of how its values and policies are understood, especially in countries where resentment of its power and influence may be high. Part of this effort was a $10 million advertising campaign from McCann Erickson featuring stories of Muslim life in the United States. It ran on TV and radio from Indonesia through the Middle East. The campaign was based on the premise that Arab and U.S. cultures share family as a common core value. The Business for Diplomatic Action was founded by leading global companies on the premise that anti-American feelings would eventually hurt U.S. brands overseas.[8] The global economic debacle that struck in 2008 undermined substantially the trust the public had for government, firms, and the market economy. There may be, therefore, a substantial need for a future global campaign exercise to restore the belief of individuals in a newly devised corporate and government cooperation.

Local objectives are typically developed as a combination of headquarters (global or regional) and country organization involvement. Basic guidelines are initiated by headquarters, whereas local organizations set the actual country-specific goals. These goals are subject to headquarters approval, mainly to ensure consistency. Although some campaigns, especially global ones, may have more headquarters involvement than usual, local input is still quite important, especially to ensure appropriate implementation of the subsequent programs at the local level.

The Budget

The promotional budget links established objectives with media, message, and control decisions.[9] Ideally, the budget would be set as a response to the objectives to be met, but resource constraints often preclude this approach. Many marketers use judgmental and an objective-and-task method; however, realities may force compromises between ideal choices and resources available (see Exhibit 13.3).[10] As a matter of fact, available funds may dictate the basis from which the objective-and-task method can start. Furthermore, advertising budgets should be set on a market-by-market basis because of competitive differences across markets. When it comes to global image campaigns, for example, headquarters should provide country organizations extra funds for their implementation.

Budgets can also be used as a control mechanism if headquarters retains final budget approval. In these cases, headquarters decision makers must have a clear understanding of cost and market differences to be able to make rational decisions.

In terms of worldwide ad spending, the leaders in 2010 were Procter & Gamble ($11.4 billion), Unilever ($6.6 billion), L'Oreal ($4.9 billion), General Motors ($3.5 billion), Nestlé ($3.1 billion), Toyota ($2.8 billion), Coca-Cola ($2.4 billion), Reckitt Benckiser ($2.4 billion), Kraft ($2.3 billion), and Johnson & Johnson ($2.3 billion).[11] Geographic differences exist in spending; for example, while Procter & Gamble spent 38 percent of its budget in the United States, Unilever's spending there was only 15 percent. The top 100 advertisers incurred one-third (33.4 percent) of their spending in the United States, with Europe second at 27.8 percent. Asia-Pacific was a distant third, commanding only 26 percent of measured media bought.[12]

EXHIBIT 13.3 Budgeting Methods for Promotional Programs

Budgeting Method	Percentage of Respondents Using This Method*	Major Differences: Lowest Percentages	Major Differences: Highest Percentages
Objective and task	64	Sweden (36) Argentina (44)	Canada (87) Singapore (86)
Percentage of sales	48	Germany (31)	Brazil (73) Hong Kong (70)
Executive judgment	33	Finland (8) Germany (8)	United States (64) Denmark (51) Brazil (46) Great Britain (46)
All-you-can-afford	12	Argentina (0) Israel (0)	Sweden (30) Germany (25) Great Britain (24)
Matched competitors	12	Denmark (0) Israel (0)	Germany (33) Sweden (33) Great Britain (22)

*Total exceeds 100 percent because respondents checked all budgeting methods that they used.

SOURCES: Douglas West and Gerard Prendergast, "Advertising and Promotions Budgeting and the Role of Risk," *European Journal of Marketing* 43, no. 11/12 (2009): 1457–76; and Nicolaos E. Synodinos, Charles F. Keown, and Laurence W. Jacobs, "Transnational Advertising Practices," *Journal of Advertising Research* 29 (April–May 1989): 43–50.

Media Strategy

Target audience characteristics, campaign objectives, and the budget form the basis for the choice between media vehicles and the development of a media schedule. The major factors determining the choice of the media vehicles to be used are (1) the availability of the media in a given market, (2) the product or service itself, and (3) media habits of the intended audience.

Media Availability

Media spending, which totaled $464 billion in 2011, varies dramatically around the world. In absolute terms, the United States spends more money on advertising than most of the other major advertising nations combined. Other major spenders are Japan, China, Germany, the United Kingdom, and Brazil.[13] China is increasingly the emerging market of choice, although it only represents 3 to 4 percent of total spending. Five global marketers, Procter & Gamble, Yum Brands, PernodRicard, Avon Products, and Colgate-Palmolive, already invest more than 10 percent of their budgets in China.[14]

Naturally, media spending varies by market. Countries devoting the highest proportions to television were Serbia (hours/minutes: 5:39), Macedonia (5:19), and the United States (5:04). In some countries, the spending devoted to print is still high: India (109.9 million in circulation), China (109 million), and Japan (50.353 million). Radio accounts for more than 20 percent of total measured media in only a few countries, such as Trinidad and Tobago, Nepal, and Honduras. Outdoor and transit advertising accounted for 48 percent of Bolivia's media spending but only 3 percent in Germany. Cinema advertising is important in countries such as India and Nigeria. Today, the Internet is well on the way to establishing itself as a complementary advertising medium worldwide. The projection is that the Internet may have a 21.2 percent market share in world advertising by 2014. Internet advertising constitutes 97 percent of advertising in Iceland and 94.4 percent in Norway. China accounts for half of the Asia-Pacific region's Internet advertising and will constitute 52 percent of its projected growth. In addition to PCs, mobile phones and interactive TV are becoming delivery mechanisms for the Internet.[15] The rapid spread of Internet connectivity is making Facebook accessible to ever more people. The Boston Consulting Group estimates that around three billion people will be online by 2016, up from 1.6 billion in 2010. Already more than 425 million people are tapping into Facebook on mobile devices, and in the future most of the social network's growth will come from the mobile web. Together, these trends could propel the number of web users beyond 1 billion.[16]

The media available to the international marketer in major ad markets are summarized in Exhibit 13.4. The breakdown by media points to the enormous diversity in how media are used in a given market. These figures do not tell the whole story, however, which emphasizes the need for careful homework on the part of the international manager charged with media strategy. As an example, Brazil has five television networks, but one of them—TV Globo—corners 50 percent of all television advertising spending. Throughout Latin America, the tendency is to allocate half or more of total advertising budgets to television, with the most coveted spots on prime-time soap operas that attract viewers from Mexico to Brazil. In general, advertising in Latin America requires flexibility and creativity. Inflation rates have caused advertising rates to increase dramatically in countries like Argentina.

The major problems affecting global promotional efforts involve conflicting national regulations. Even within the EU there is no uniform legal standard. Conditions do vary from country to country, and ads must comply with national regulation. Most European countries either observe the 2011 revision of the ICC Consolidated Code of Advertising and Marketing or have their guidelines based on it.[17] Some of the regulations include limits on the amount of time available for advertisements; for example, in Italy, the state channels allow a maximum of

EXHIBIT 13.4 Global Advertising Expenditure by Medium (in $ millions)

	2010	2011	2012	2013	2014
Newspapers	94,600	91,495	89,868	88,785	88,446
Magazines	43,741	43,122	42,681	42,464	42,186
Television	176,627	184,290	193,735	203,608	215,737
Radio	32,017	32,903	33,667	34,827	35,923
Cinema	2,313	2,442	2,564	2,732	2,916
Outdoor	29,824	31,291	32,928	34,559	36,350
Internet	63,979	72,842	84,267	97,764	113,281
Total	443,100	458,385	479,710	504,738	534,839

SOURCE: Based on ZenithOptimedia, www.zenithoptimedia.com.

12 percent advertising per hour and 4 percent per week, and commercial stations allow 18 percent per hour and 15 percent per week. Furthermore, the leading Italian stations do not guarantee audience delivery when spots are bought. Strict separation between programs and commercials is almost a universal requirement, preventing U.S.-style sponsored programs. Restrictions on items such as comparative claims and gender stereotypes are prevalent; for example, Germany prohibits the use of superlatives such as "best." Although the German courts have been less stringent in cases as recently as 2009, the courts can find comparative advertising to be illegal if as little as 15 percent of consumers are "misled" by the advertising.

Currently, however, approximately half of the homes in Europe have access to additional television broadcasts through either cable or direct satellite, and television will no longer be restricted by national boundaries. The implications of this for global marketers are significant. The viewer's choice will be expanded, leading to competition among government-run public channels, competing state channels from neighboring countries, private channels, and pan-European channels. This means that marketers need to make sure that advertising works not only within markets but across countries as well. As a consequence, media buying will become more challenging.

Product Influences

Marketers and advertising agencies are currently frustrated by wildly differing restrictions on how products can be advertised. Agencies often have to produce several separate versions to comply with various national regulations. Changing and standardizing these regulations, even in an area like the EU, is a long and difficult process. While some countries have banned tobacco advertising altogether (e.g., France), some have voluntary restriction systems in place. For example, in the United Kingdom, tobacco advertising is not allowed in magazines aimed at very young women, but it is permitted in other women's magazines. Starting in 2003, tobacco companies were required to print vivid pictures of lung cancer victims and diseased organs on cigarette packets sold in the United Kingdom. The EU has developed union-wide regulations and has banned all forms of cross-border tobacco advertising, effective since 2005. This means no tobacco advertising in print, as well as on radio, the Internet, and Formula One racing. Existing regulations ban TV advertising. Tobacco marketers are allowed to advertise on cinema, poster, and billboard sites, but can still be banned by national laws.[18] A summary of product-related regulations found in selected European countries is provided in Exhibit 13.5. Tobacco products, alcoholic beverages, and pharmaceuticals are the most heavily regulated products in terms of promotion.

EXHIBIT 13.5 Restrictions on Advertisements for Specific Products

Country	Cigarette and Tobacco Products	Alcoholic Beverages	Pharmaceutical Products
United Kingdom	Banned in broadcast; approval required for showing brands of tobacco companies in any sponsored events	Banned in broadcast during or adjacent to children's programs Broadcast permitted in non–children's program airtime, with many regulations	Advertisements for prescription drugs prohibited Restrictions apply; e.g., no promotion by celebrities allowed
Ireland	Banned for all cigarette and tobacco products in all forms of advertising, including any sponsorship of events	Broadcast targeting adults is allowed with many rules	Advertisements for prescription drugs prohibited Strict guideline applies to non-prescription drugs
Denmark	Banned in all forms of advertising	Permitted for beverages with alcohol content of less than 2.8% Strict conditions apply	Banned in TV broadcast for both prescription-only and nonprescription medicines Radio broadcast is permitted with strict guidelines
Portugal	Banned in all forms of advertising, except in automobile sports events with international prestige	Banned in TV and radio broadcast between 7 A.M. and 10:30 P.M. Banned in sponsoring events in which minors participate	Advertisements for prescription drugs prohibited Strict guideline applies to non-prescription drugs

SOURCE: "Study on the Evolution of New Advertising Techniques in UK, Ireland, Denmark, and Portugal," *Bird & Bird Brussels*, June 17, 2002.

However, the manufacturers of these products have not abandoned their promotional efforts. Altria Group (formerly Philip Morris) engages in corporate image advertising using its cowboy spokesperson. Some European cigarette manufacturers have diversified into the entertainment business (restaurants, lounges, movie theaters) and named them after their cigarette brands. AstraZeneca, a leading global pharmaceutical, funded a TV campaign run by the French Migraine Association, which discussed medical advances but made no mention of the company. Novo Nordisk has set up an Internet page on diabetes separate from its home page and established the World Diabetes Foundation awareness group.[19]

Beyond the traditional media, the international marketer may also consider **product placement** in movies, TV shows, videogames, or Internet sites. Although there is disagreement about the effectiveness of the method beyond creating brand awareness, products from makers such as BMW, Omega, Nokia, and Heineken have been placed in movies to help both parties to the deal: to create a brand definition for the product and a dimension of reality for the film. The estimated size of the product-placement market in 2010 was $3.61 billion.[20] This is driven partly by the success of reality television and partly by more empowered consumers who use PCs and mobile devices and can skip traditional ads with the touch of a button. In China, placing products in soap operas, such as *Too Late to Say I Love You*, has been found to be an effective way to reach the burgeoning middle class in the world's most populous country. However, calls have been made to ban product placements or at the very least clearly disclose them in credits. The European Commission allows product placement in fiction (not in news or factual material) and requires clear labeling.[21]

Audience Characteristics

A major objective of media strategy is to reach the intended target audience with a minimum of waste. As an example, BP wanted to launch a corporate image campaign in China in the hope of receiving drilling contracts. Identifying the appropriate decision makers was not difficult because they all work for the government. The selection of appropriate media proved to be equally simple because most of the decision makers overseeing petroleum exploration were found to read the vertical trade publications: *International Industrial Review*, *Petroleum Production*, and *Offshore Petroleum*.

If conditions are ideal, and they seldom are in international markets, the media strategist would need data on (1) media distribution, that is, the number of copies of the print medium or the number of sets for broadcast; (2) media audiences; and (3) advertising exposure. For instance, an advertiser interested in using television in Brazil would like to know that the top adult TV program is *Caminhodas Índias* with an average audience share of 34 percent and a 30-second ad rate of $100,000. In markets where more sophisticated market research services are available, data on advertising perception and consumer response may be available. In many cases, advertisers have found circulation figures to be unreliable or even fabricated.

Global Media

Global media vehicles have been developed that have target audiences on at least three continents and for which the media buying takes place through a centralized office. These media have traditionally been publications that, in addition to the worldwide edition, have provided advertisers the option of using regional editions. For example, *Time* publishes regional editions for the United States, Asia, the South Pacific, Europe, the Middle East, and Africa. For each region, *Time* publishes subregional editions. In Asia, for example, there are 19 geographic sub-editions available for advertisers to reach country-specific audiences. Other global publications include the *International Herald Tribune*, the *Wall Street Journal* (as well as the *Asian Wall Street Journal*), *National Geographic*, the *Financial Times*, and the *Economist*. The Internet provides the international marketer with an extremely versatile global medium. Online editions of publications, as well as mobile editions and podcasts, can be used in tandem with print publications and broadcast media or can stand separately. Advertisers who want to reach business travelers, for example, can buy advertising packages from *CNN* that include, for example, *CNN* regional programming in Africa, the Middle East, Europe, the United States, Latin America (*CNN en Español*), or Asia; *CNN.com*; and *CNN* mobile services. Advertisers in the Middle East might look to Al Jazeera as a very attractive medium. AlJazeera TV claims 40 million viewers, and Aljazeera.net is the most visited website in the Arab world.[22] Globally, National Geographic Channel (including NGC U.S., which is a joint venture of NGV and Fox Cable Networks Group) is available in 435 million homes in 173 countries and 37 languages (see Exhibit 13.6).

A smart approach to global marketing over the Internet might start with search engine optimization or paid placement in search marketing. In 2012, Google sites dominated global search properties with an 85.5 percent share, followed by Yahoo sites with a 5.4 percent share. Baidu, the Chinese search engine, was third with 4.7 percent of global searches.[23] In Japan, however, Yahoo continues to be the leading search engine with 56.5 percent of the Japanese market compared to Google's 33.7 percent share. Yahoo has proven particularly adept at customizing its product to the needs of the Japanese consumer, while Google has had a more difficult time in penetrating the market.[24]

With the rapid growth in the use of social media such as Facebook, LinkedIn, Twitter, YouTube, and blogs, marketers are increasingly integrating public relations and viral marketing ideas into their media planning. Word-of-mouth and grassroots brand advocacy can have a powerful effect, particularly for the launch of new products and services or a new marketing push. T-Mobile staged an event in Liverpool Station where 350 hired dancers began dancing to popular music to amplify the launch of T-Mobile's "Life's for Sharing" television campaign. Hidden cameras captured the reaction of surprised commuters, many of whom joined in the fun. The news quickly spread through social media and was covered by multiple news organizations.[25]

EXHIBIT 13.6 Example of a Panregional Medium

SOURCE: Courtesy of National Geographic Channels International.

The Promotional Message

Developing the promotional message is referred to as *creative strategy*. The marketer must determine what the consumer is really buying—that is, the consumer's motivations. These will vary depending on:

- *The diffusion of the product, service, or concept into the market.* For example, to enter China with online sales requires an understanding of the variances in Internet penetration and online shopping by region. With overall Internet penetration in China at approximately 25 percent and online shopping penetration at less than 7 percent in 2009, half of Beijing and Shanghai Internet users are online shoppers, while only 35 percent of users in Guangzhou and 29 percent in Chengdu shop online.[26]
- *The criteria on which the consumer will evaluate the product.* For example, Hyundai Motors spent considerable time researching its Indian customers. After determining that Indian consumers most valued the lifetime ownership cost of a vehicle, Hyundai implemented this criterion in its Santro automobile with a reduced engine output, keeping the car fuel efficient. Hyundai also considered India's less-than-optimum road conditions when designing the car. Hyundai also priced its spare parts reasonably and tailored dozens more product specifications to the Indian market. As a result, the Santro has been a success with the Indian consumers, far outselling the other foreign brands.[27]
- *The product's positioning.* For example, Parker Pen's upscale image may not be profitable enough in a market that is more or less a commodity business. The solution is to create an image for a commodity product and make the public pay for it. In 2008, FIJI Water received Elle Magazine's Green Award and Oracle Corporation's "Empower the Green Enterprise" Award.[28]

The ideal situation in developing message strategy is to have a world brand—a product that is manufactured, packaged, and positioned the same around the world. Companies that have been successful with the global approach have shown flexibility in the execution of the campaigns. The idea may be global, but overseas subsidiaries then tailor the message to suit local market conditions and regulations. Executing an advertising campaign in multiple markets requires a balance between conveying the message and allowing for local nuances. The localization of global ideas can be achieved by various tactics, such as adopting a modular approach, localizing international symbols, and using international advertising agencies.

Toyota's 2011 Corolla campaign for the Asian American market announced a new partnership with HatsuneMiku, a unique musical artist known for her songs, dance moves, and long blue pigtails. U.S. Toyota Corolla served as the proud sponsor of HatsuneMiku's first U.S. concert performance at the Nokia Theatre in Los Angeles during Anime Expo 2011. Working with its Asian American advertising agency, Toyota has built an integrated marketing campaign that includes TV, print, out-of-home, digital, and social media, primarily targeted to the Asian American market. Not only are commercials in English, but it has also been translated to Cantonese, Mandarin, Korean, and Vietnamese. An example of local adjustment in a global campaign for Toyota is provided in Exhibit 13.7.

Marketers may also want to localize their international symbols. Some of the most effective global advertising campaigns have capitalized on the popularity of pop music worldwide and used well-known artists in the commercials, such as Lady Gaga, Beyoncé, and Shakira. In some versions, local stars have been included with the international stars to localize the campaign. Aesthetics plays a role in localizing campaigns. The global marketer does not want to

EXHIBIT 13.7 Local Adjustments in a Global Campaign

SOURCE: Courtesy of Imprint Venture Lab.

chance the censoring of the company's ads or risk offending customers. For example, even though importers of perfumes into Saudi Arabia want to use the same campaigns as are used in Europe, they occasionally have to make adjustments dictated by moral standards. In one case, the European version shows a man's hand clutching a perfume bottle and a woman's hand seizing his bare forearm. In the Saudi Arabian version, the man's arm is clothed in a dark suit sleeve, and the woman's hand is merely brushing his hand.

The use of one agency—or only a few agencies—ensures consistency. The use of one agency allows for coordination, especially when the global marketer's operations are decentralized. It also makes the exchange of ideas easier and may therefore lead, for example, to wider application of a modification or a new idea. For example, BP uses Ogilvy & Mather for its largely corporate-image-based advertising. Companies such as Procter & Gamble and Unilever have each of their global brands under a single agency, such as Pampers handled by Saatchi & Saatchi, and Old Spice by Wieden + Kennedy.[29]

The environmental influences that call for these modifications, or in some cases totally unique approaches, are culture, economic development, and lifestyles. It is quite evident that customers prefer localized to foreign-sourced advertising.[30] Of the cultural variables, language is most apparent in its influence on promotional campaigns. The European Union alone has 23 languages. Advertisers in the Arab world have sometimes found that the voices in a TV commercial speak in the wrong Arabic dialect. The challenge of language is often most pronounced in translating themes. For example, Coca-Cola's worldwide theme "Can't Beat the Feeling" is the equivalent of "I Feel Coke" in Japan, "Unique Sensation" in Italy, and "The Feeling of Life" in Chile. In Germany, where no translation really worked, the original English-language theme was used. One way of getting around this is to have no copy or very little copy and to use innovative approaches, such as pantomime. Using any type of symbolism will naturally require adequate copy testing to determine how the target market perceives the message.

The Campaign Approach

Many multinational corporations are staffed and equipped to perform the full range of promotional activities. In most cases, however, they will rely on the outside expertise of advertising agencies and other promotions-related companies such as media-buying companies and specialty marketing firms. In the organization of promotional efforts, a company has two basic decisions to make: (1) what type of outside services to use and (2) how to establish decision-making authority for promotional efforts.

Outside Services

Of all the outside promotion-related services, advertising agencies are by far the most significant. A list of the world's top 25 agencies and agency groups is given in Exhibit 13.8. Of the top 25 agencies, 12 are based in the United States, 6 in the European Union, 6 in Japan and Korea, 2 in Australia, and 1 in Latin America. Size is typically measured in terms of revenue and billings. Billings are the cost of advertising time and space placed by the agency plus fees for certain extra services, which are converted by formula to correspond to media billings in terms of value of services performed. Agencies do not receive billings as income; in general, agency income is approximately 15 percent of billing.

Agencies form world groups for better coverage. One of the largest world holding groups, WPP Group, includes such entities as Ogilvy & Mather, J. Walter Thompson, Young & Rubicam, and Grey. Smaller advertising agencies have affiliated local agencies in foreign markets.

The choice of an agency will largely depend on the quality of coverage the agency will be able to give the multinational company. Global marketing requires global advertising, according to proponents of the globalization trend.

EXHIBIT 13.8 Top 25 Marketing Organizations (worldwide revenue in 2010, $ in millions)

Rank	Company	Headquarters	Net Revenue in 2010	Percentage Change
1	WPP	Dublin, Ireland	14,416	6.0
2	Omnicom Group	New York, NY	12,543	7.0
3	PublicisGroupe	Paris, France	7,175	14.1
4	Interpublic Group of Cos.	New York, NY	6,532	8.4
5	Dentsu Inc.	Tokyo, Japan	3,600	15.6
6	Aegis Group	London, England	2,257	7.0
7	Havas	Suresnes, France	2,069	3.0
8	Hakuhodo DY Holdings	Tokyo, Japan	1,674	10.7
9	Acxiom Corp.	Little Rock, AK	785	0.4
10	MDC Partners	Toronto, Canada/New York, NY	698	28.0
11	Alliance Data Systems Corp.'s Epsilon	Plano, TX	613	19.3
12	GroupeAeroplan's Carlson Marketing	Minneapolis, MN	593	3.0
13	Daniel J.Edelman	Chicago, IL	544	18.8
14	Sapient Corp.'s Sapient Nitro	Boston, MA	515	27.2
15	Asatsu-DK	Tokyo, Japan	484	7.3
16	Media Consulta	Berlin, Germany	408	1.6
17	Cheil World	Seoul, South Korea	386	23.8
18	IBM Corp.'s IBM Interactive	Chicago, IL	368	14.1
19	Grupo ABC	Sao Paulo, Brazil	362	30.5
20	Photon Group	Sydney, Australia	334	1.3
21	In Ventiv Group Holdings	Somerset, NJ	313	15.0
22	STW Group	St. Leonards, Australia	280	31.2
23	Huntsworth	London, England	268	9.7
24	Merkle	Columbia, MD	254	13.9
25	Aspen Marketing Services	West Chicago, IL	244	8.4

SOURCE: "Top 25 Marketing Organizations," *Advertising Age*, April 25, 2011, 20.

The reason is not that significant cost savings can be realized through a single worldwide ad campaign but that such a global campaign is inseparable from the idea of global marketing. Some predict that the whole industry will be concentrated into a few huge, multinational agencies. Agencies with networks too small to compete have become prime takeover targets in the creation of worldwide mega-agencies. Many believe that local, midsized agencies can compete in the face of globalization by developing local solutions or joining international networks.[31]

Advertising agencies have gone through major geographic expansion in the last five years. The leader is McCann-Erickson, with advertising running in 111 countries, compared with 72 countries in 1991. McCann Worldgroup is one of the world's largest marketing communications networks, boasting a roster of eight best-in-class companies collaborating toward the transformation of their clients' brands and growth of their businesses.[32] Some agencies, such as DDB Worldwide, were domestically focused in the early 1990s but have been forced to rethink their strategy with the globalization of their clients. As a result, by 2011 DDB Worldwide had more than 200 offices in over 90 countries.[33] New markets are also emerging, and agencies are establishing their presence in them. WPP's priority, in the long term or over the next 5 to 10 years, is to gain in the faster-growing markets of Asia-Pacific, Latin America, Africa, the Middle East, and Central and Eastern Europe, from around 27 percent to 35–40 percent.[34]

In a study of 40 multinational marketers, 32.5 percent are using a single agency worldwide, 20 percent are using two, 5 percent are using three, 10 percent are using four, and 32.5 percent are using more than four agencies. Euro RSCG Worldwide, Oglivy Group, and McCann Worldgroup have the numbers 72, 37, and 34, respectively, of global clients companies in the Top 100 global marketers—including accounts handled in five countries—as well as networks handling major clients.[35] On the client side, Unilever assigns more business on an international basis than any other global marketers, working with eight agency networks from four holding groups.

The main concern arising from the use of mega-agencies is conflict. With only a few giant agencies to choose from, the global marketer may end up with the same agency as its main competitor. The mega-agencies believe they can meet any objections by structuring their companies as rigidly separate, watertight agency networks (such as the Interpublic Group) under the umbrella of a holding group. Following that logic, Procter & Gamble, a client of Saatchi & Saatchi, and Colgate-Palmolive, a client of TBWA, should not worry about falling into the same network's client base. However, when the Saatchi & Saatchi network purchased TBWA, Colgate-Palmolive left the agency.

Despite the globalization trend, local agencies will survive as a result of governmental regulations. In Peru, for example, a law mandates that any commercial aired on Peruvian television must be 100 percent nationally produced. Local agencies also tend to forge ties with foreign agencies for better coverage and customer service and thus become part of the general globalization effort. A basic fear in the advertising industry is that accounts will be taken away from agencies that cannot handle world brands. An additional factor is contributing to the fear of losing accounts. In the past, many multinational corporations allowed local subsidiaries to make advertising decisions entirely on their own. Others gave subsidiaries an approved list of agencies and some guidance. Still others allowed local decisions subject only to headquarters' approval. Now the trend is toward centralization of all advertising decisions, including those concerning the creative product.

Decision-Making Authority

The alternatives for allocating decision-making authority range from complete centralization to decentralization. With complete centralization, the headquarters level is perceived to have all the right answers and has adequate power to impose its suggestions on all of its operating units. Decentralization involves relaxing most of the controls over foreign affiliates and allowing them to pursue their own promotional approaches.

Of 40 multinational marketers, 26 percent have centralized their advertising strategies, citing as their rationale the search for economies of scale, synergies, and brand consistency.[36] Xerox's reason is that its technology is universal and opportunities abound for global messages. Centralization is also occurring at the regional level. GM's Opel division in Europe is seeking to unify its brand-building efforts with central direction.[37] A total of 34 percent of the companies favor decentralization with regional input. This approach benefits from proximity to markets, flexibility, cultural sensitivity, and faster response time. FedEx allows local teams to make advertising decisions as needed. The majority of marketers use central coordination with local input. While Ford Motor Company conceives brand strategy on a global level, ad execution is done at the regional level. However, multinational corporations are at various stages in their quest for centralization. Procter & Gamble and Gillette generally have an approved list of agencies, whereas Quaker Oats and Johnson & Johnson give autonomy to their local subsidiaries but will veto those decisions occasionally.

The important question is not who should make decisions but how advertising quality can be improved at the local level. Gaining approval in multinational corporations is an interactive approach using coordinated decentralization. This nine-step program, which is summarized in Exhibit 13.9, strives for development

EXHIBIT 13.9 **Coordinated Approach to Panregional Campaign Development**

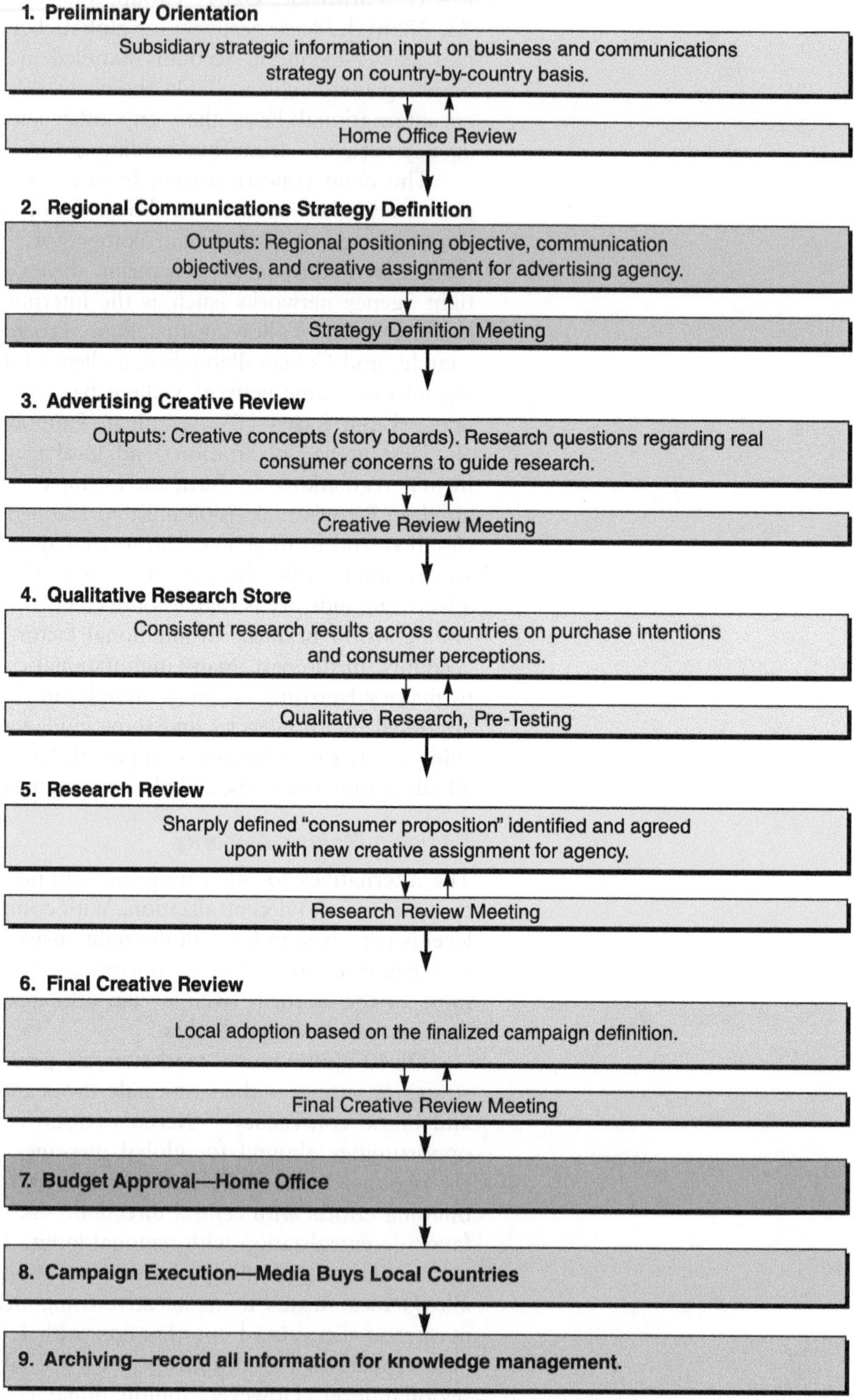
1. Preliminary Orientation
Subsidiary strategic information input on business and communications strategy on country-by-country basis.
Home Office Review
2. Regional Communications Strategy Definition
Outputs: Regional positioning objective, communication objectives, and creative assignment for advertising agency.
Strategy Definition Meeting
3. Advertising Creative Review
Outputs: Creative concepts (story boards). Research questions regarding real consumer concerns to guide research.
Creative Review Meeting
4. Qualitative Research Store
Consistent research results across countries on purchase intentions and consumer perceptions.
Qualitative Research, Pre-Testing
5. Research Review
Sharply defined "consumer proposition" identified and agreed upon with new creative assignment for agency.
Research Review Meeting
6. Final Creative Review
Local adoption based on the finalized campaign definition.
Final Creative Review Meeting
7. Budget Approval—Home Office
8. Campaign Execution—Media Buys Local Countries
9. Archiving—record all information for knowledge management.

SOURCES: Jae H. Pae, Saeed Samiee, and Susan Tai, "Global Advertising Strategy: The Moderating Role of Brand Familiarity and Execution Style," *International Marketing Review* 19, no. 2 (2002): 176–89; Clive Nancarrow and Chris Woolston, "Pre-Testing International Press Advertising," *Qualitative Market Research: An International Journal* (1998): 25–38; and David A. Hanni, John K. Ryans, Jr., and Ivan R. Vernon, "Coordinating International Advertising: The Goodyear Case Revisited for Latin America," *Journal of International Marketing* 3, no. 2 (1995): 83–98.

of a common strategy but flexible execution. The approach maintains strong central control but at the same time capitalizes on the greatest asset of the individual markets: market knowledge. Interaction between the central authority and the local levels takes place at every single stage of the planning process. The central authority is charged with finding the commonalities in the data provided by the individual market areas. This procedure will avoid one of the most common problems associated with acceptance of plans—the not-invented-here (NIH) syndrome—by allowing for local participation by the eventual implementers.

Agencies are adjusting their operations to centrally run client operations. Many accounts are now handled by a lead agency, usually in the country where the client is based. More and more agencies are moving to a strong international supervisor for global accounts. This supervisor can overrule local agencies and make personnel changes. Specialty units have emerged as well. For example, Ogilvy & Mather established the Worldwide Client Service organization at headquarters in New York, specializing in developing global campaigns for its clients.[38]

Measurement of Advertising Effectiveness

John Wanamaker reportedly said, "I know half the money I spend on advertising is wasted. Now, if I only knew which half." Whether or not advertising effectiveness can be measured, most companies engage in the attempt. Measures of advertising effectiveness should range from pretesting of copy appeal and recognition, to posttesting of recognition, all the way to measuring sales effects. The measures most used are sales, awareness, recall, executive judgment, intention to buy, and profitability, regardless of the medium used.

The technical side of these measurement efforts does not differ from that in the domestic market, but the conditions are different. Very often, syndicated services, such as A.C. Nielsen, are not available to the global marketer. If available, their quality may not be at an acceptable level. Testing is also quite expensive and may not be undertaken for the smaller markets.

Compared with costs in the U.S. market, the costs of research in the international market are higher in relation to the overall expenditure on advertising. The biggest challenge to advertising research will come from the increase of global and regional campaigns. Comprehensive and reliable measures of campaigns for a mass European market, for example, are difficult because audience measurement techniques and analysis differ for each country. Advertisers are pushing for universally accepted parameters to compare audiences in one country to those in another.

OTHER PROMOTIONAL ELEMENTS

Personal Selling

Personal selling, unlike advertising or sales promotion, involves direct relations between the seller and the prospective buyer or customer. Personal selling can be defined as a two-way flow of communication between a potential buyer and a salesperson and is designed to accomplish at least three tasks: (1) identify the buyer's needs; (2) match these needs to one or more of the firm's products; and (3) on the basis of this match, convince the buyer to purchase the product.

Personal selling is the most effective of the promotional tools available to the marketer; however, its costs per contact are high. The average cost of sales calls may vary from $200 to $1,100, depending on the industry and the product or service (per industry, with a low of $276 in the food industry and a high of $354 in electronics).[39] Personal selling allows for immediate feedback on customer reaction as well as information on markets.

The sales effort is determined by the degree of internationalization, as shown in Exhibit 13.10. As the degree of globalization advances, so will the marketer's own role in carrying out or controlling the sales function.

EXHIBIT 13.10 Levels of Involvement in Global Sales

Type of Involvement	Level of Involvement	Target of Sales Effort	Advantage/Disadvantage
Indirect exports	Low	Home-country–based intermediary	+ No major investment in international sales
			– Minor learning from/control of effort
Direct exports	Medium	Locally based intermediary	+ Direct contact with local market
			– Possible gatekeeping by intermediary
Integrated solutions	High	Customer	+ Generation of market-specific assets
			– Cost/risk

SOURCE: Framework adapted from Reijo Luostarinen and Lawrence Welch, *International Operations of the Firm* (Helsinki, Finland: Helsinki School of Economics, 1990), chapter 1.

Indirect Exports

When the exporter uses indirect exports to reach international markets, the export process is externalized; in other words, the intermediary, such as an EMC, will take care of the international sales effort. While there is no investment in international sales by the marketer, there is also no, or very little, learning about sales in the markets that buy the product. The sales effort is basically a domestic one directed at the local intermediary. This may change somewhat if the marketer becomes party to an ETC with other similar producers. Even in that case, the ETC will have its own sales force, and exposure to the effort may be limited. Any learning that takes place is indirect; for example, the intermediary may advise the marketer of product adaptation requirements to enhance sales.

Direct Exports

At some stage, the exporter may find it necessary to establish direct contact with the target market(s), although the ultimate customer contact is still handled by locally based intermediaries, such as agents or distributors. Communication with intermediaries must ensure both that they are satisfied with the arrangement and that they are equipped to market and promote the exporter's product appropriately. Whatever the distribution arrangement, the exporter must provide basic selling-aid communications, such as product specification and data literature, catalogs, the results of product testing, and demonstrated performance information—everything needed to present products to potential customers. In some cases, the exporter has to provide the intermediaries with incentives to engage in local advertising efforts. These may include special discounts, push money, or cooperative advertising. Cooperative advertising will give the exporter's product local flavor and increase the overall promotional budget for the product. However, the exporter needs to be concerned that the advertising is of sufficient quality and that the funds are spent as agreed.

For the marketer–intermediary interaction to work, four general guidelines have to be satisfied.

1. *Know the sales scene.* Often what works in the exporter's home market will not work somewhere else. This is true especially in terms of compensation schemes. In U.S. firms, incentives and commission play a significant role, while in most other markets salaries are the major share of compensation. The best way to approach this is to study the salary structures and incentive plans in other competitive organizations in the market in question.
2. *Research the customer.* Customer behavior will vary across markets, meaning the sales effort must adjust as well. ECA International, which sells marketing information worldwide based on a membership concept (companies

purchase memberships to both participate in information gathering and receive appropriate data), found that its partners' sales forces could not sell the concept in Asia. Customers wanted instead to purchase information piece by piece. Only after research and modification of the sales effort was ECA able to sell the membership idea to customers.[40]

3. *Work with the culture.* Realistic objectives have to be set for the salespeople based on their cultural expectations. This is especially true in setting goals and establishing measures such as quotas. If either of these is set unrealistically, the result will be frustration for both parties. Cultural sensitivity also is required in situations where the exporter has to interact with the intermediary's sales force—in training situations, for example.[41] In some cultures, such as those in Asia, the exporter is expected to act as a teacher and more or less dictate how things are done, while in some others, such as in Northern Europe, training sessions may be conducted in a seminar-like atmosphere of give and take.
4. *Learn from your local representatives.* If the sales force perceives a lack of fit between the marketer's product and the market, as well as an inability to do anything about it, the result will be suboptimal. A local sales force is an asset to the exporter, given its close contact with customers. Beyond daily feedback, the exporter is wise to undertake two additional approaches to exploit the experience of local salespeople. First, the exporter should have a program by which local salespeople can visit the exporter's operations and interact with the staff. If the exporter is active in multiple markets of the same region, it is advisable to develop ways to put salespeople in charge of the exporter's products in different markets to exchange ideas and best practice. Naturally, it is in the best interest of the exporter also to make regular, periodic visits to markets entered.

An approach that requires more commitment from the exporter is to employ its own sales representatives, whose main function is to represent the firm abroad to existing and potential customers and to seek new leads. It is also important to sell with intermediaries by supporting and augmenting their efforts. This type of presence is essential at some stage of the firm's international involvement. Other promotional tools can facilitate foreign market entry, but eventually some personal selling must take place. A cooperative effort with the intermediaries is important at this stage, in that some of them may be concerned about the motives of the exporter in the long term. For example, an intermediary may worry that once the exporter has learned enough about the market, it will no longer need the services of the intermediary. If these suspicions become prevalent, sales information may no longer flow to the exporter in the quantity and quality needed.

Integrated Solutions

The final stage of globalization involves either a sales office in the target market or a direct contact with the buyer from home base. This is part of the exporter's perceived need for increased customer relationship management, where the sales effort is linked to call-center technologies, customer-service departments, and the company's website. Advancements in 4G networks, voice-over-Internet protocol (VoIP), and dual-mode handsets will bring new opportunities to account management, and real-time reporting tools will enable managers to gain insight into the sales process. This may include also automating the sales force, as seen in *The International Marketplace 13.2*.

The establishment of a sales office does not have to mean an end to the use of intermediaries; the exporter's salespeople may be dedicated to supporting intermediaries' sales efforts. At this stage, expatriate sales personnel, especially those needed to manage the effort locally or regionally, may be used. The benefits of expatriates are their better understanding of the company and its products and

THE INTERNATIONAL MARKETPLACE 13.2

Automation of the Sales Force

Dataram, a company delivering computer solutions to businesses, made a critical decision over 10 years ago to automate its sales force. The automated system is used to manage database marketing activity, such as lead generation and tracking, trade shows, telemarketing, advertising tracking, product support, and customer service. Management can also spot emerging trends, avert impending disasters, and forecast sales with the help of the system. When a sales rep can answer a question in one to five minutes instead of three days, the company is perceived as a consultant as much as a vendor. Recruiting salespeople may be easier when a company can offer state-of-the-art support. Furthermore, if turnover takes place, important customer information is not lost but preserved in the database.

Sales-force automation (SFA), like anything else in marketing, is subject to the realities of the international environment: borders, time zones, languages, and cultures. Sales professionals may see their customer accounts as proprietary and may not be willing to share information for fear of losing their leverage. Furthermore, in markets in which personal relationships drive sales practices, such as in Latin America, technological wizardry may be frowned upon. Representatives in every country may want to do things slightly differently, which requires a system that can be localized. This localization may be as comprehensive as complete language translations or as minor as changing address fields in the database. Another issue to be considered is hardware costs are higher in Europe, and telecommunications costs have to be factored in. Finally, with transoceanic support needs, the company may want to look for local support or invest in keeping desk personnel on board at offhours.

A significant concern is the cost. A Latin American company may face a price tag of $2 million for a large company or $700,000 for a mid- or small-sized firm. However, according to a recent study, automated companies have realized sales increases of 10 to 30 percent, and in some cases as much as 100 percent.

Complaints are also heard. While initial reactions to the use of technology are normally high, six months after implementation some companies report negative job-related perceptions by salespeople, some even going so far as to reject the technology. Poor results are especially likely when salespeople feel that their jobs or role is being threatened. These facts need to be incorporated into the implementation plan of any SFA program.

SOURCES: Kevin Roebuck, *SaaS Sales Force Automation: High-impact Emerging Technology—What You Need to Know: Definitions, Adoptions, Impact, Benefits, Maturity, Vendors* (Tebbo, 2011), 1–5; "How Sales Teams Should Use CRM," *Customer Relationship Management* 10 (February 2006): 30–35; and Cheri Speier and Viswanath Venkatesh, "The Hidden Minefields in the Adoption of Sales Force Automation Techniques," *Journal of Marketing* 66 (July 2002): 98–111.

their ability to transfer best practice to the local operation. With expatriate management, the exporter can exercise a high amount of control over the sales function. Customers may also see the sales office and its expatriate staff as a long-term commitment to the market. The challenges lie mostly in the fit of the chosen individual to the new situation. The cost of having expatriate staff is considerable, approximately 2.5 times the cost of maintaining staff at home, and the availability of suitable talent may be a problem, especially if the exporting organization is relatively small.[42]

The role of personal selling is greatest when the marketer sells directly to the end user or to governmental agencies, such as foreign trade organizations. Firms selling products with high price tags (such as Boeing commercial aircraft) or companies selling to monopsonies (such as Seagrams liquor to certain Northern European countries, where all liquor sales are through state-controlled outlets) must rely heavily on person-to-person communication, oral presentations, and direct-marketing efforts. Many of these firms can expand their business only if their markets are knowledgeable about what they do. This may require corporate advertising and publicity generation through extensive public relations efforts.

Whatever the sales task, effectiveness is determined by a number of interrelated factors. One of the keys to personal selling is the salesperson's ability to adapt to the customer and the selling situation.[43] This aspect of selling requires cultural knowledge and empathy; for example, in the Middle East, sales presentations may be broken up by long discussions of topics that have little or nothing to do with the transaction at hand. The characteristics of the buying task, whether routine or unique, have a bearing on the sales presentation. The marketer may be faced by a situation in which the idea of buying from a foreign entity is the biggest obstacle in terms of the risks perceived. If the product does not provide a clear-cut relative advantage over that of competitors, the analytical, interpersonal skills of the salesperson are needed to assist in the differentiation. A salesperson, regardless of the market, must have a thorough knowledge of the product or service. The more the salesperson is able to apply that knowledge to the particular situation, the more likely it is that he or she will obtain a positive result. The salesperson usually has front-line responsibility for the firm's customer relations, having to handle conflict situations such as the parent firm's bias for domestic markets.

Direct Marketing

The purpose of direct marketing is to establish a relationship with a customer in order to initiate immediate and measurable responses.[44] In the past, this was accomplished through direct mail, catalogs, and telemarketing. Today, spurred by mobile and Internet technologies, direct marketing can be found on places like Facebook, Google, Twitter, TripAdvisor, and Yelp.

Direct mail is by far the dominant direct-response medium and includes letters, catalogs, ads, brochures, samples, and DVDs. Direct mail can be a highly personalized tool of communication if the target audience is identified and narrowly defined. Ranging from notices to actual samples, it allows for flexibility in the amount of information conveyed. Catalogs are typically distributed to overseas customers through direct mail, although many catalogs have online versions as well. Their function is to make a marketer known, generate requests for further information, stimulate orders, and serve as a reminder between transactions. Catalogs are particularly useful if a firm's products are in a highly specialized field such as technology with direct interface with specialists. In the past, U.S. marketers thought that country-specific offices were almost essential to bringing their companies closer to overseas customers. With the deregulation of the telecommunication industry, telemarketing (including sales, customer service, and helpdesk–related support) is flourishing throughout the world. A growing number of countries in Latin America, Asia, and Europe are experiencing growth in this area as consumers are becoming more accustomed to calling toll-free numbers and more willing to receive calls from marketers.

The Internet connects users of all types all around the world to each other and contains an amazingly large information repository. It offers five main advantages: First, it allows the company to increase its presence in the marketplace and to communicate its overall mission and information about its marketing mix. Second, the Internet allows 24-hour access to customers and prospects. Providing important information during decision making can help the customer clarify the search. The potential interactivity of the website (e.g., in providing tailor-made solutions to the customer's concerns) may provide a competitive advantage as the customer compares alternative sites. For example, the website for apparel marketer Lands' End allows consumers to identify their body type and then mix and match clothing items that suit them. Interactivity is also critical when the site is designed, in determining what features to include (e.g., whether sites should adjust to different dialects of a language in a region).

Third, the Internet can improve customer service by allowing customers to serve themselves when and where they choose. This is an area where an exporter's web presence can reduce overall communications costs in the most significant way. Naturally, the exporter must have the necessary capacity to serve all interested customers through the website, especially if there is an increase in interest and demand. An important dimension of customer service is after-sales service to solve consumer problems and to facilitate the formation of consumer groups. A web forum where customers can exchange news and views on product use will not only facilitate product research but will also build loyalty among consumers.

The fourth advantage is the ability of the marketers to gather information, which has its uses not only in research but also in database development for subsequent marketing efforts. While the data collected may be biased, they are also very inexpensive to collect. If the data are used to better cater to existing customers, then data collected through Internet interaction are the best possible.

The fifth advantage of the Internet is the opportunity to actually close sales. This function is within the realm of e-commerce. It will require a significant commitment on the part of the exporter in terms of investment in infrastructure to deliver not only information but also the product to the customer. E-commerce is discussed in more detail in Chapter 15.[45]

Database marketing allows the creation of an individual relationship with each customer or prospect. There are two main types of marketing databases: consumer databases and business databases. For example, a call center operator will know a customer's background with the company or overall purchasing habits. Care has to be taken not to violate privacy regulations or sensitivities. The development of the needed databases through direct mail or the Internet will advance the use of telemarketing.

A **social networking service** is an online service, platform, or site that focuses on building and reflecting social networks that share interests or activities. Facebook, Google+, Twitter, and YouTube have grabbed most of the headlines. Popular services in other countries now are Draugiem (Latvia), Odnoklassniki (Russia), Qzone (China), VKonkakte (Russia), and Zing Me (China). Social media have had an enormous impact on buying behavior. Thinking about such media as digital word-of-mouth enables salespeople to appreciate just how crucial it is. Many U.S. companies claim to have a social media strategy, but only 27 percent of U.S. salespeople say their company trains or educates them on the use of social media for sales. This stands in stark contrast to Brazil, where 65 percent of salespeople surveyed receive training on social media usage. Seventy-three percent of the salespeople surveyed in China use personal blogs in their selling process.[46]

Sales Promotion

Sales promotion has been used as the catch-all term for promotion that does not fall under advertising, personal selling, or publicity. Sales promotion directed at consumers involves such activities as couponing, sampling, premiums, consumer education and demonstration activities, cents-off packs, point-of-purchase materials, and direct mail. Sales promotion directed at intermediaries, also known as trade promotion, includes activities such as trade shows and exhibits, trade discounts, and cooperative advertising. The use of sales promotions as alternatives to and as support for advertising is increasing worldwide. Mobile marketing messages, for example, can include text with numeric short codes that customers dial to receive a promotion, bar-coded digital coupons, website links, and display advertisements.[47] The appeal is related to several factors: cost and clutter of media advertising, simpler targeting of customers compared with advertising, and easier tracking of promotional effectiveness (for example, coupon returns provide a clear measure of effectiveness).

The success in Latin America of Tang, Kraft Foods' presweetened powder juice substitute, is for the most part traceable to successful sales promotion efforts. Tang in Brazil is offering a promotion trading Tang pouches for free glasses, prizes, and pitchers. Kraft Brazil launched a Club Tang website in 2011 for kids in Spanish and Portuguese. Club Tang encourages recycling and sends reusable Tang shopping bags when consumers register. Children are able to win Tang pouches and are even eligible to win a game system.

For sales promotion to be effective, the campaign planned by manufacturers, or their agencies, must gain the support of the local retailer population. Coupons from consumers, for example, have to be redeemed and sent to the manufacturer or to the company handling the promotion. A.C. Nielsen tried to introduce cents-off coupons in Chile and ran into trouble with the nation's supermarket union, which notified its members that it opposed the project and recommended that coupons not be accepted. The main complaint was that an intermediary, like Nielsen, would unnecessarily raise costs and thus the prices to be charged to consumers. Also, some critics felt that coupons would limit individual negotiations because Chileans often bargain for their purchases.

Global marketers are well advised to take advantage of local or regional opportunities. In Brazil, gas delivery people are used to distribute product samples to households by companies such as Nestlé, Johnson & Johnson, and Unilever. The delivery people are usually assigned to the same district for years and have, therefore, earned their clientele's trust. For the marketers, distributing samples this way is not only effective, it is very economical: they are charged five cents for each unit distributed. The gas companies benefit as well in that their relationship with customers is enhanced through these "presents."[48]

Sales promotion tools fall under varying regulations. A particular level of incentive may be permissible in one market but illegal in another. The Northern European countries present the greatest difficulties in this respect because every promotion has to be approved by a government body. In France, a gift cannot be worth more than 4 percent of the retail value of the product being promoted, making certain promotions virtually impossible. Although competitions are allowed in most of Europe, to insist on receiving proofs of purchase as a condition of entry is not permitted in Germany.

Regulations such as these make truly global sales promotions rare and difficult to launch. Although only a few multinational brands have been promoted on a multiterritory basis, the approach can work. In general, such multicountry promotions may be suitable for products such as soft drinks, liquor, airlines, credit cards, and jeans, which span cultural divides. Naturally, local laws and cultural differences have to be taken into account at the planning stage. Although many of the promotions may be funded centrally, they will be implemented differently in each market so that they can be tied with the local company's other promotional activities. For example, Johnson & Johnson Vision Care offered trials of its one-day Acuvue contact lens throughout Europe, Africa, and the Middle East. The aim was to deliver the brand message of "Enhancing Everyday Experiences" and encourage consumers to book a sight test. The venue was a road-show event that adapted well to local market conditions. Professional lens fitters offered on-the-spot trials at gyms, sports clubs, and leisure centers. The program was devised and tested in Germany and has since been executed in 18 different countries. The creative materials were translated into 14 languages, and a virtual network using intranets ensured that all offices shared information and best practice.[49]

In the province of Quebec in Canada, advertisers must pay a tax on the value of the prizes they offer in a contest, whether the prize is a trip, money, or a car. The amount of the tax depends on the geographical extent of the contest. If it is open only to residents of Quebec, the tax is 10 percent; if open to all of Canada, 3 percent; if worldwide, 1 percent. Subtle distinctions are drawn in the regulations between a premium and a prize. As an example, the Manic soccer team was involved with both McDonald's and Provigo Food stores. The team offered a dollar off the price of four tickets, and the stubs could be cashed for a special at McDonald's. Provigo was involved in a contest offering a year's supply of groceries. The Manic–McDonald's offer was a premium that involved no special tax; Provigo, however, was taxed because it was involved in a contest. According to the regulation, a premium is available to everyone, whereas a prize is available to a certain number of people among those who participate. In some cases, industries may self-regulate the use of promotional items.

Trade Shows and Missions

Marketing goods and services through trade shows is a European tradition that dates back at least as far as A.D. 1240. After sales-force costs, trade shows are one of the most significant cost items in marketing budgets. Although they are usually associated with industrial firms, some consumer products firms are represented as well. Typically, a trade show is an event at which manufacturers, distributors, and other vendors display their products or describe their services to current and prospective customers, suppliers, other business associates, and the press.[50] The Consumer Electronics (Las Vegas) and Consumer and Industry Products (Guangzhou) trade shows, for example, run eight hours a day for three days, plus one or two preview days, and register 200,000 attendees. In the consumer goods area, expositions are the most common type of show. Tickets are usually sold; typical expositions include home and garden, boat, auto, consumer electronics, and antiques. Although a typical trade show or typical participant does not exist, an estimated $75,000 is allocated for each show, and the median manufacturer or distributor attends 9 or 10 shows annually. The number of days spent at trade shows averages 2.2, and the hours per day are 8.1.[51]

Whether an exporter should participate in a trade show depends largely on the type of business relationship it wants to develop with a particular country. More than 19,500 trade shows create an annual $50 billion in business worldwide.[52] A company looking only for one-time or short-term sales might find the expense prohibitive, but a firm looking for long-term involvement may find the investment worthwhile. Arguments in favor of participation include the following:

- Some products, by their very nature, are difficult to market without providing the potential customer a chance to examine them or see them in action. Trade fairs provide an excellent opportunity to introduce, promote, and demonstrate new products. Auto shows, such as the ones in Detroit, Geneva, and Tokyo, feature "concept" cars to gauge industry and public opinion. Recently, many of these new models have been environmentally friendly, such as being 90 percent recyclable. The world's premier mobile event, Mobile World Congress, has nearly 1,000 marketers showcasing their latest mobile products, services, and solutions.[53]
- An appearance at a show produces goodwill and allows for periodic cultivation of contacts. Beyond the impact of displaying specific products, many firms place strong emphasis on "waving the company flag" against competition. This facet also includes morale boosting of the firm's sales personnel and distributors.
- The opportunity to find an intermediary may be one of the best reasons to attend a trade show. A show is a cost-effective way to solicit and screen candidates to represent the firm, especially in a new market. Copylite Products of Ft. Lauderdale used the CeBIT computer-and-automation show in Hannover, Germany, to establish itself in Europe. The result was a distribution center in Rotterdam and six distributors covering eight countries. Its $40,000 investment in the trade show has reaped millions in new business.[54]

- Attendance is one of the best ways to contact government officials and decision makers, especially in China. For example, participation in the Chinese Export Commodities Fair, which is held twice a year in Guangzhou, China, is expected by the host government and companies.
- Trade fairs provide an excellent chance for market research and collecting competitive intelligence. The exporter is able to view most rivals at the same time and to test comparative buyer reactions. Trade fairs provide one of the most inexpensive ways of obtaining evaluative data on the effectiveness of a promotional campaign.
- Exporters are able to reach a sizable number of sales prospects in a brief time period at a reasonable cost per contact. According to research by Hannover Messe, more than 86 percent of all attendees represent buying influences (managers with direct responsibility for purchasing products and services). Of equal significance is the fact that trade show visitors are there because they have a specific interest in the exhibits.[55]

On the other hand, the following are among the reasons cited for nonparticipation in trade fairs:

- *High costs.* These can be avoided by participating in events sponsored by the U.S. Department of Commerce or exhibiting at U.S. trade centers or export development offices. An exporter can also lower costs by sharing expenses with distributors or representatives. Further, the costs of closing a sale through trade shows are estimated to be much lower than for a sale closed through personal representation.
- *Difficulty in choosing the appropriate trade fairs for participation.* This is a critical decision. Because of scarce resources, many firms rely on suggestions from their foreign distributors on which fairs to attend and what specifically to exhibit. Caterpillar, for example, usually allows its foreign dealers to make the selections for themselves. In markets where conditions are more restricted for exporters, such as China, Caterpillar in effect serves as the dealer and thus participates itself.
- *For larger exporters with multiple divisions, the problem of coordination.* Several divisions may be required to participate in the same fair under the company banner. Similarly, coordination is required with distributors and agents if joint participation is desired, which requires joint planning.

Trade show participation is too expensive to be limited to the exhibit alone. A clear set of promotional objectives would include targeting accounts and attracting them to the show with preshow promotion using mailings, advertisements in the trade journals, or website information. Contests and giveaways are effective in attracting participants to the company's exhibition area. Major customers and attractive prospects often attend, and they should be acknowledged, for example by arranging for a hospitality suite. Finally, a system is needed to evaluate post show performance and to track qualified leads.

Exporters may participate in general or specialized trade shows. General trade fairs are held in Hannover, Germany (see *The International Marketplace 13.3*), and Milan, Italy. An example of a specialized one is Retail Solutions, a four-day trade show on store automation held in London. Participants planning to exhibit at large trade shows may elect to do so independently or as part of a national pavilion. For small- and medium-sized companies, the benefit of a group pavilion is in both cost and ease of the arrangements. These pavilions are often part of governmental export-promotion programs. Other promotional events that the exporter can use are trade missions, seminar missions, solo exhibitions, video or catalog exhibitions, and virtual trade shows.

THE INTERNATIONAL MARKETPLACE 13.3

At the Fair

CeBIT is the "Olympic Games" exposition for the international ICT industry. Around 339,000 visitors attended in 2011, including 54,240 from abroad (42,850 from the rest of Europe; 2,170 from the Americas; 4,882 from the Middle East and Africa; and 4,339 from East Asia). Moreover, more than 4,200 companies from over 70 countries participated at CeBIT 2011, and the event was covered by some 5,000 accredited journalists from 58 nations.

CeBIT's Exhibition Grounds comprise approximately 496,000 square meters of covered indoor space (i.e., over 5.3 million square feet), 58,000 square meters of open-air space, and 27 halls and pavilions.

The 2011 fair keynote theme was "Work and Life in the Cloud," which intended to provide attendees with a comprehensive overview of cloud applications and services already on the market, and also with the best-practice examples in the industry. There was also a clear focus on tablet PCs and smartphones, business solutions and applications for the new German identity card, 3D (with and without glasses), IT security, cloud-based print technologies, intelligent networking for health and traffic applications, and sustainable energy concepts for businesses and households.

Courtesy of Deutsche Messe

CeBit's promotion of their Hannover event.

International branding is taking Deutsche Messe to new markets. As a result, CeBIT events are no longer based solely in Hannover but have found their way to Turkey, Australia, and Brazil. This means global exhibitors can benefit from new trade fair platforms and the added demand this brings.

SOURCE: CeBIT, www.cebit.de.

Public Relations

Image—the way a multinational corporation relates to and is perceived by its key constituents—is a bottom-line issue for management. Public relations is the marketing communications function charged with executing programs to earn public understanding and acceptance, which means both internal and external communication. The function can further be divided into proactive and reactive forms.

Internal Public Relations

Especially in multinational corporations, internal communication is important to create an appropriate corporate culture.[56] The Japanese have perfected this in achieving a *wa* ("we") spirit. Everyone in an organization is, in one way or another, in marketing and will require additional targeted information on issues not necessarily related to his or her day-to-day functions. A basic part of most internal programs is the employee publication produced and edited typically by the company's public relations or advertising department and usually provided in both hard-copy and electronic formats. More often, as at ExxonMobil, each affiliate publishes its own employee publication. The better this vehicle can satisfy the information needs of employees, the less they will have to rely on others, especially informal sources such as the grapevine. Audiovisual media in the form of e-mails and videoconferencing are being used, especially for training purposes. Some of the materials that are used internally can be provided to other publics as well; for example, booklets, manuals, and handbooks are provided to employees, distributors, and visitors to the company.

External Public Relations

External public relations (also known as marketing public relations) is focused on the interactions with customers. In the proactive context, marketers are concerned about establishing global identities to increase sales, differentiate products and services, and attract employees. These activities have been seen as necessary to compete against companies with strong local identities. External campaigns can be achieved through the use of corporate symbols, corporate advertising, customer-relations programs, and publicity. For example, Stanley Black & Decker's corporate logo, which is in the shape and color of an orange hexagon, is used for all Black & Decker products. Specific brand books are developed to guide marketing personnel worldwide on the proper use of these symbols to ensure a consistent global image. Exhibit 13.11 depicts an agricultural marketing publication, *The Furrow*, which is available in 15 different language versions. *The Furrow* is the award-winning customer magazine produced by John Deere. Total circulation is 1.5 million in more than 100 countries. *The Furrow* has covered many articles on new farming practices and the latest equipment within the agricultural industry.

Publicity, in particular, is of interest to the multinational corporation. Publicity is the securing of editorial space (as opposed to paid advertising) to further marketing objectives. Because it is editorial in content, the consuming public perceives it as more trustworthy than advertising. A good example of how publicity can be used to aid in advertising efforts was the introduction by Carnival of a new liner, the *Carnival Breeze*. Because of its innovative design and size, the *Breeze* was granted substantial press coverage, which was especially beneficial in the travel and leisure magazines. Such coverage does not come automatically but has to be coordinated and initiated by the public relations staff of the company.

Unanticipated developments in the marketplace can place the company in a position that requires *reactive* public relations, including anticipating and countering criticism. The criticisms range from general ones against all multinational corporations to more specific ones. They may be based on a market; for example, problems are as varied as onerous work environments and serious safety problems in China. Apple is not the only electronics company doing business within a troubling supply system. Bleak working conditions have been documented at factories manufacturing products for Dell, Hewlett-Packard, IBM, Lenovo, Motorola, Nokia, Sony, and Toshiba. Companies have a supplier code of conduct that details standards on labor issues and safety protections. In fact, Apple has mounted a vigorous auditing campaign, and when abuses are discovered, corrections are demanded.[57]

Crisis management is becoming more formalized in companies, with specially assigned task forces ready to step in if problems arise. In general, companies must adopt policies that will allow them to effectively respond to pressure and criticism, which will continue to surface. Crisis management policies should have the following traits: (1) openness about corporate activities, with a focus on how these activities enhance social and economic performance; (2) preparedness to utilize the tremendous power of the multinational corporation in a responsible manner and, in the case of pressure, to counter criticisms swiftly; (3) integrity, which often means that the marketer must avoid not only actual wrongdoing but also the mere appearance of it; and (4) clarity, which will help ameliorate hostility if a common language is used with those pressuring the corporation.[58]

EXHIBIT 13.11 **External Media: *The Furrow***

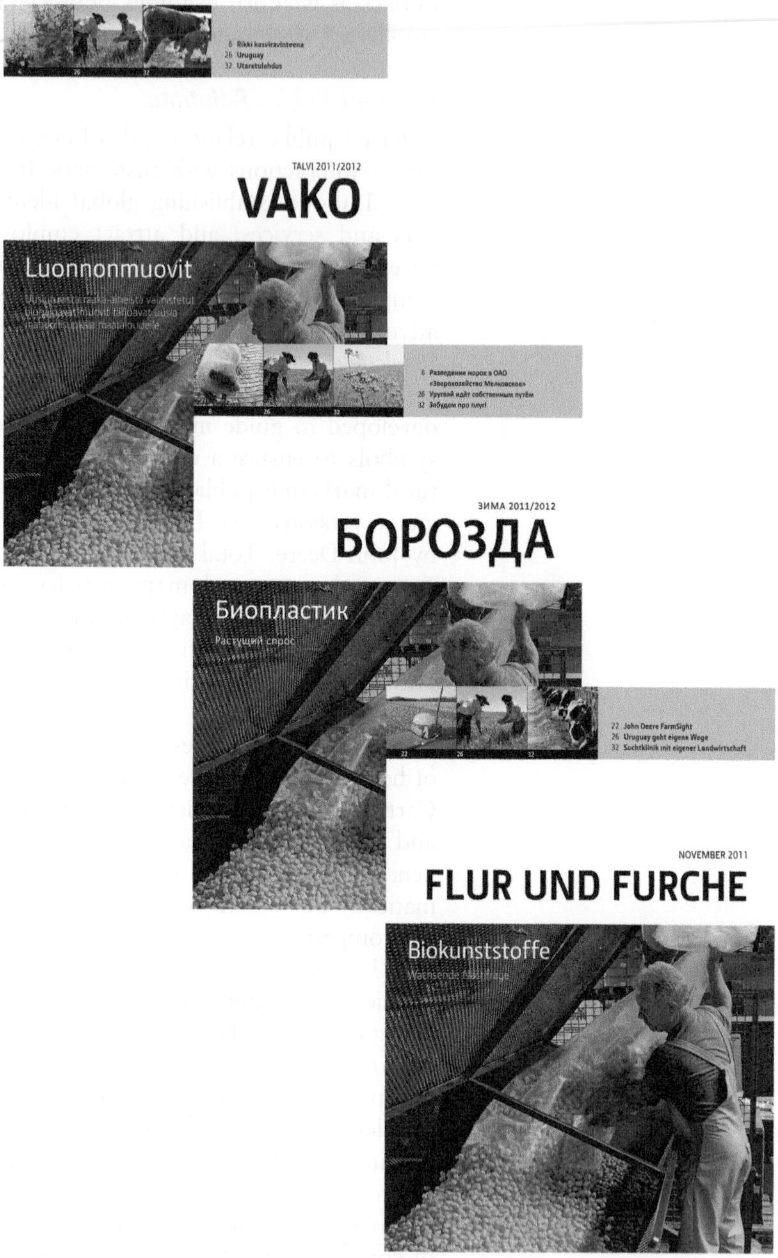

SOURCE: Courtesy of Deere & Company European Office.

With growing and evolving interactive technology, consumers can find or initiate topics of interest on the web and engage in online discussions that strongly affect their and others' views. This new form of communication, consumer-generated media (CGM), is growing at 30 percent per year. While these media can take multiple forms, the most prominent are online bulletin boards, blogs, podcasts, and websites for consumers to post complaints and compliments. The challenges for the global marketer include the new media's limitless reach, fast diffusion of news, and very expressive and influential nature. To leverage CGM to the marketer's advantage, someone in the company needs to be put in charge of the phenomenon: to monitor the relevant information and then disseminate the important findings and take action when needed.[59]

EXHIBIT 13.12 Worldwide Fees of Independent Firms with Major U.S. Operation

Rank	Firm	2011 Net Fees	Employees	% Fee Change from 2010
1.	Edelman: New York, NY	$604,740,732	4,120	+15.9
2.	APCO Worldwide: Washington, DC	120,701,000	603	+6.4
3.	Waggener Edstrom: Bellevue, WA	115,832,000	878	+3.5
4.	Ruder Finn: New York, NY	81,281,000	644	0
5.	Text 100 Global PR: San Francisco, CA	50,425,771	108	+10.0
6.	WCG: San Francisco, CA	47,577,000	231	+29.0
7.	MWW Group: East Rutherford, NJ	38,626,000	202	+11.0
8.	ICR: Norwalk, CT	32,030,483	92	+21.0
9.	Qorvis Communications: Washington, DC	29,500,000	102	0
10.	DKC Public Relations, New York, NY	26,800,000	150	+12.1

SOURCE: www.odwyerpr.com/pr_firm_rankings/independents.htm, accessed May 31, 2012.

Marketers are incorporating consumer-generated content into their promotion mixes. For example, Mercedes Benz encourages drivers to send digital photos of themselves living the Mercedes-Benz lifestyle for posting on the company's website.[60]

The public relations function can be handled inhouse or with the assistance of an agency. The largest agencies are presented in Exhibit 13.12. The use and extent of public relations activity will vary by company and the type of activity needed. Product-marketing public relations may work best with a strong component of control at the local level and a local public relations firm, while crisis management—given the potential for worldwide adverse impact—will probably be controlled principally from a global center. This has meant that global marketers funnel short-term projects to single offices for their local expertise while maintaining contact with the global agencies for their worldwide reach when a universal message is needed. Some global corporations maintain public relations staffs in their main offices around the world, while others use the services of firms that are part of large worldwide agency groups.

Sponsorship Marketing

Sponsorship involves the marketer's investment in events or causes. Sponsorship funds worldwide are directed for the most part at sports events (both individual and team sports) and cultural events (both in the popular and high-culture categories). Sponsorship spending is relatively even around the world: of the nearly $51.0 billion spent in 2011, North America contributed $30.5 billion, Europe $13.5 billion, Asia-Pacific $11.2 billion, Latin America $3.7 billion, and all other countries $2.1 billion.[61] The Coca-Cola Company, for example, is proud to be the longest-standing continuous corporate partner of the Olympic Games. Sponsorship of events such as the Olympics is driven by the desire to be associated with a worldwide event that has a positive image, global reach, and a proven strategic positioning of excellence. The rising costs of sponsorship and the difficulty of establishing return on the investment has forced some marketers to bow out; for example, IBM after Sydney in 2000, and Xerox after Athens in 2004.[62]

The challenge is that an event may become embroiled in controversy, thus hurting the sponsors' images as well. Furthermore, in light of the high expense of sponsorship, marketers worry about **ambush marketing** by competitors. Ambush marketing is the use of an event without the permission of the event owner. For example, an advertising campaign could suggest a presumed sponsorship relationship. During the Atlanta Olympic Games in 1996, some of the sponsors' competitors garnered a higher profile than the sponsors themselves. For example, Pepsi erected stands outside venues and plastered the town with signs. Nike secured substantial amounts of airtime on radio and TV stations. Fuji bought billboards on the route from the airport into downtown Atlanta. None of the three contributed anything to the International Olympic Committee during this time. In London in 2012, total costs are estimated to be $7 billion, and big sponsors may expect to pay as much as $80 million apiece. The ambush-marketing provisions of the London Olympics Bill will prohibit the uses of terms such as *gold*, *summer*, and *2012* in advertisements by nonsponsors.[63]

Cause-related marketing is a combination of public relations, sales promotion, and corporate philanthropy. This activity should not be developed merely as a response to a crisis, nor should it be a fuzzy, piecemeal effort to generate publicity; instead, marketers should have a social vision and a planned long-term social policy. For example, in Casanare, Colombia, where it is developing oil interests, British Petroleum invests in activities that support its business plan and contribute to the region's development. This has meant an investment of $10 million in setting up a loan fund for entrepreneurs, giving students technical training, supporting a center for pregnant women and nursing mothers, working on reforestation, building aqueducts, and helping to create jobs outside the oil industry.[64] Cisco Systems' Networking Academy is an example of how a marketer can link philanthropic strategy, its competitive advantage, and broader social good. To address a chronic deficit in information-technology job applicants, the company created the Network Academy concept, whereby it contributes networking equipment to schools. Cisco now operates 10,000 academies in secondary schools, community colleges, and community-based organizations in 150 countries. As the leading player in the field, Cisco stands to benefit the most from this improved labor pool. At the same time, Cisco has attracted worldwide recognition for this program, boosted its employee morale and partner goodwill, and generated a reputation for leadership in philanthropy.[65] Cisco partners with public and private organizations to promote socioeconomic development through increased access to Information and communications technology resources, education, and career opportunities (see Exhibit 13.13).

Increasingly, the United Nations is promoting programs to partner multinationals and nongovernmental organizations (NGOs) to tackle issues such as healthcare, energy, and biodiversity. For example, Merck and GlaxoSmithKline have partnered with UNICEF and the World Bank to improve access to AIDS care in the hardest-hit regions of the world.[66]

Public relations activity also includes anticipating and countering criticism. First-party certification is the most common variety, whereby a single firm develops its own rules and reports on compliance. This certification includes prohibitions on child labor and forced labor and guarantees of nondiscrimination in the workplace. Second-party certification involves an industry or trade association fashioning a code of conduct and implementing reporting mechanisms. The chemical industry's global Responsible Care program provides developed environmental, health, and safety principles and codes; requires participating firms to submit implementation reports; and reports aggregated industry progress. Third-party certification involves an external group, often an NGO, imposing its rules and compliance methods onto a particular firm or industry. The Council on Economic Priorities (CEP),

EXHIBIT 13.13 Global Community Relations

SOURCE: Courtesy of Cisco Systems.

the pioneering New York–based NGO, has collected data on corporate activities since its creation in 1969 and publishes reports on corporate behavior. Fourth-party certification involves government or multilateral agencies. The United Nations Global Compact, for instance, lists environmental, labor, and human rights principles for companies to follow; participating corporations must submit online updates of their progress for NGOs to scrutinize.[67]

SUMMARY

As global marketers manage the various elements of the promotions mix in differing environmental conditions, decisions must be made about channels to be used in communication, the message, who is to execute or help execute the program, and how the success of the endeavor is to be measured. The trend is toward more harmonization of strategy, at the same time allowing for flexibility at the local level and early incorporation of local needs into the promotional plans.

The effective implementation of the promotional program is a key ingredient in the marketing success of the firm. The promotional tools must be used within the opportunities and constraints posed by the communications channels as well as by the laws and regulations governing marketing communications.

Advertising agencies are key facilitators in communicating with the firm's constituent groups. Many marketers are realigning their accounts worldwide in an attempt to streamline their promotional efforts and achieve a global approach.

The use of other promotional tools, especially personal selling, tends to be more localized to fit the conditions of the individual markets. Decisions concerning recruitment, training, motivation, and evaluation must be made at the affiliate level, with general guidance from headquarters. Personal selling brings the marketer face-to-face with the targeted customer.

An area of increasing challenge for global marketers is public relations. The best interest of the marketer lies in anticipating problems with both internal and external constituencies and managing them, through communications, to the satisfaction of all parties. Community relations and cause-related marketing play important roles in this process.

KEY TERMS

encoding
decoding
noise
outcome
feedback
cause-related marketing
corporate image advertising
product placement
global media
database marketing
social networking service
consumer-generated media (CGM)
ambush marketing

QUESTIONS FOR DISCUSSION

1. For over 30 years, wildlife rescuers have used Dawn dishwashing liquid to gently remove oil and help save wildlife affected by oil spills. The Wildlife Champions' Facebook page lets you choose your own unique way to help. How will you help and what do you care about?
2. Mobile phone users worldwide are projected to be 4.85 billion by 2015. Suggest which consumer features (e.g., GPS and social networking) will be the most valued.
3. What type of adjustments must advertising agencies make as more companies want "one sight, one sound, one sell" campaigns?
4. Assess the programmed management approach for coordinating global advertising efforts.
5. Some exporters report that they value above all the broad exposure afforded through exhibiting at a trade show, regardless of whether they are able to sell directly at the event. Comment on this philosophy.
6. What is the role of community relations for a global marketer? How can the marketer treat even the antiglobals as customers?

INTERNET EXERCISES

1. Working with its Asian American advertising agency, Toyota has built an integrated marketing campaign that includes TV, print, out-of-home, digital, and social media, primarily targeted to the Asian American market. Not only are commercials in English, but they have also been translated to Cantonese, Mandarin, Korean, and Vietnamese. The campaign launched on May 5, 2011, with commercial spots on YouTube, garnering over half a million views in less than three days. With big dreams in a compact package, both the Corolla and HatsuneMiku are driving straight to the top. The updated exterior and interior design and technology features allow the Corolla—the best-selling compact car—to stand out from the compact vehicle category, much like HatsuneMiku does in her field. No wonder it was HatsuneMiku's top choice for her first vehicle in the United States. Read more at www.channelapa.com/2011/05/toyota-corolla-use-virtual-pop-diva-hatsune-miku-in-us-market.html#ixzz1Mo1qwNyr.
2. The global advertising industry has experienced significant consolidation, with a few giant communications companies owning most of the major advertising, branding, public relations, digital marketing, marketing research, and other marketing services agencies. Visit the websites of the four largest communications groups, www.wpp.com, www.omnicom.com, www.interpublic.com, and www.publicis.com. From the information they provide about their companies, create a short list of 5 to 10 global advertising agencies that a global marketer might consider working with to create a global advertising campaign and to provide advertising services in most major countries.

CHALLENGE US

Ambush Strategy

The definition of ambush marketing as a marketing strategy is when a competing brand connects itself with a major sporting event without paying a sponsorship fee. Ambush marketing occurs when one brand pays to become an official sponsor of an event and another competing brand attempts to cleverly connect itself with the event without paying the sponsorship fee and without breaking any laws. FIFA (the International Federation of Association Football) is adamant about the protection of its sponsors and their legal resources and has the wherewithal to defend and enforce its rights and fulfill its commitment to tournament sponsors.

FIFA is considering legal action against a Dutch brewery it accuses of using women fans to advertise its beer at the World Cup. Stewards ejected 36 Dutch supporters during the match between the Netherlands and Denmark midway through the second half in Johannesburg. All were dressed identically in tight-fitting, short orange dresses sold as part of a gift pack by a Dutch brewery. A brewery representative dismissed FIFA's concerns as "ridiculous."

The World Cup's authorized beer, Budweiser, has paid millions of dollars for the privilege of being its sponsor. With a large chunk of FIFA's revenue coming from selling marketing rights, it vigorously pursues anyone who tries to associate themselves with the World Cup without paying the tournament for those marketing rights. "What seems to have happened is that there was a clear ambush marketing activity by a Dutch brewery company," said a FIFA spokesman. No charges have been filed against the ejected orange-clad Dutch supporters, FIFA said in an e-mailed statement.

The World Cup generated $1.6 billion in sponsorship revenue from 2007 to 2010. The weak economy has led some companies to turn to ambush marketing at sporting events as a way to get their message out in a less costly manner and successfully avoid sponsorship fees.

For Discussion

1. "FIFA does not have the monopoly on orange, and people have the freedom to wear what they want." Why?
2. The World Cup's authorized beer is Budweiser, which pays millions of dollars for the privilege. Why?

© David Cannon/Getty Images

Crowd shot of Dutch women wearing orange dresses during the World Cup 2010, appearing to support a Dutch brewery, which was not the official sponsor of the Cup.

SOURCES: "FIFA Files Charges over World Cup Ambush Marketing (Update1)," *Bloomberg Businessweek*, June 16, 2010, 45; "World Cup 2010 for Ambush Marketing," *Guardian*, June 15, 2010, 6; and "FIFA Acts after 'Ambush Marketing' by Dutch Brewery," *BBC News Africa*, June 15, 2010, www.bbc.co.uk/news/10321668.

RECOMMENDED READINGS

Beckwith, Sandra. *Publicity for Nonprofits*. Chicago: Kaplan, 2006.

De Mooij, Marieke K. *Global Marketing and Advertising: Understanding Cultural Paradoxes*. San Francisco: Sage, 2009.

Hawk, Keith, and Michael Boland. *Get-Real Selling: Your Personal Coach for Real Sales Excellence*. New York: Nova Vista, 2010.

Mullin, Roddy. *Sales Promotion: How to Create, Implement and Integrate Campaigns That Really Work*. London: Kogan, 2010.

Musgrove, Linda. *The Complete Idiot's Guide to Trade Shows*. New York: Alpha Books, 2009.

Scotts, David Meerman. *The New Rules of Marketing & PR: How to Use Social Media, Online Video, Mobile Applications, Blogs, News Releases, and Viral Marketing to Reach Buyers Directly*. Hoboken, NJ: Wiley, 2011.

Shimp, Terence A., and J. Craig Andrews. *Advertising, Promotions, and Other Aspects of Integrated Marketing Communications*. Cincinnati, OH: South-Western, 2012.

Stengel, Jim. *Grow: How Ideals Power Growth and Profit at the World's Greatest Companies*. New York: Crown Business, 2011.

Zenith Media. *Advertising Expenditure Forecasts*. London: Zenith Media, December 2011.

ENDNOTES

1. Demetris Vrontis, Alkis Thrassou, and Iasonas Lamprianou, "International Marketing Adaptation versus Standardisation of Multinational Companies," *International Marketing Review* 26, no. 4/5 (2009): 477–500.
2. "Overseas Call Centers Can Cost Firms Goodwill," *Marketing News*, April 15, 2004, 21; and "Lost in Translation," *Economist*, November 29, 2003, 58.
3. Framework adapted from Thomas O'Guinn, Chris Allen, and Richard Semenik, *Advertising and Integrated Brand Promotion* (Cincinnati, OH: South-Western, 2011), 2–158; and Dean M. Peebles and John K. Ryans, *Management of International Advertising: A Marketing Approach* (Boston: Allyn & Bacon, 1984), 72–73.
4. Cause Marketing Research and Reports, www.causemarketingforum.com/site/c.bkLUKcOTLkK4E/b.6448351/k.4B30/Cause_Marketing_Research_and_Reports.htm.
5. Jonah Bloom, "GE: The Marketing Giant Lights Up with Imagination," *Creativity*, October 2005, 63; and Matthew Creamer, "GE Sets Aside Big Bucks to Show Off Some Green," *Advertising Age*, May 9, 2005, 7.
6. Jean-Noël Kapferer, "The Post-Global Brand," *Journal of Brand Management* 12, no. 5 (2005): 319–24.
7. "Take the Drama Out of Delivery: New FedEx Advertising Campaign Emphasizes Reliability in a Demanding World," *FedEx News*, September 19, 2011, 1.
8. "Brand America," *Marketing News*, April 15, 2005, 33; and Ira Tenowitz, "Beers Draws Mixed Reviews after One Year," *Advertising Age*, September 23, 2002, 3, 57.
9. Data Center, "2007 Advertising to Sales Ratios for 200 Largest Ad Spending Industries," *Advertising Age*, September 2007, 1.
10. Douglas West and Gerard Prendergast, "Advertising and Promotions Budgeting and the Role of Risk," *European Journal of Marketing* 43, no. 11/12 (2009): 1457–76.
11. "Advertisers Spending," *Advertising Age*, December 19, 2011, 4.
12. Data Center, "Global Marketers 2011," *Ad Age*, December 5, 2011, 5.
13. Bradley Johnson, "Where's the Growth in Marketing? Follow the BRIC Road," *Advertising Age*, December 5, 2011, 1, 8.
14. Laurel Wentz and Bradley Johnson, "Top 100 Global Advertisers Heap Their Spending Abroad," *Advertising Age*, November 30, 2009.
15. "The Media Issue: Content Is King," *Advertising Age*, October 3, 2011, 1–52.
16. "The Value of Friendship," *Economist*, February 4, 2012, 23–26.
17. "Advertising and Marketing Communication Practice," *International Chamber of Commerce*, August 2011, 1–48.
18. "Tobacco Advertising: European Commission Takes Action against Two Noncompliant EU Member States," *European Commission Press Releases*, February 1, 2006.
19. "Pushing Pills: In Europe, Prescription-Drug Ads Are Banned," *Wall Street Journal*, March 15, 2002, B1.
20. PQ Media, "New PQ Media Report Finds U.S. Branded Entertainment Spending on Consumer Events & Product Placement Dipped Only 1.3% to $24.63 Billion in 2009 & on Pace to Grow 5.3% in 2010, Exceeding Most Advertising & Marketing Segments," press release, June 29, 2010, www.pqmedia.com/about-press-20100629-gbem2010.html.
21. "Lights, Camera, Brands," *Economist*, October 29, 2005, 61–62.
22. Allied Media, "Al Jazeera Television: Viewers Demographics," www.allied-media.com/aljazeera/al_jazeera_viewers_demographics.html.
23. Abbey Klaasen, "Search Marketing," *Advertising Age*, November 2, 2009.
24. Karma Snack, "Search Engine Market Share," www.karmasnack.com/about/search-engine-market-share.
25. Tom Warren, "T-Mobile Invades Busy London Rail Station," www.neowin.net, January 17, 2009.
26. Rocky Fu, "China Online Shopping Statistics 2009 Part 1—Penetration Rate by City," *Online Shopping*, December 9, 2009.
27. Lulu Raghavan, "Lessons from the Maharaja Mac," *Landor*, December 2007.
28. Anna Lenzer, "Fiji Water: Spin the Bottle," *Mother Jones*, September/October 2009, http://motherjones.com/politics/2009/09/fiji-spin-bottle.
29. R. Craig Endicott, "Global Marketing," *Advertising Age*, November 14, 2005, 17; Jack Neff, "P&G Flexes Muscle for Global Branding," *Advertising Age*, June 3, 2002, 53; and Wieden + Kennedy, www.wk.com/office/portland/client/old_spice.
30. Jae H. Pae, Saeed Samiee, and Susan Tai, "Global Advertising Strategy: The Moderating Role of Brand Familiarity

and Execution Style," *International Marketing Review* 19, no. 2 (2002): 176–89.
31. AdAge, "Agency Report 2011 Index," April 25, 2011, http://adage.com/datacenter/article?article_id=226900.
32. McCann Worldgroup, www.mccann.com.
33. DDB, www.ddb.com.
34. "Annual Report 2010," *WPP*, 2010.
35. "Agency Networks," *Ad Age Insights*, December 6, 2010, 3.
36. "Centralization," *Advertising Age International*, June 1999, 40.
37. Tim Higgins and Alex Webb, "GM Seen Accelerating Opel Restructuring as Sales Plunge: Cars," *Bloomberg Businessweek*, January 31, 2012, 45.
38. OgilvyOne Worldwide, www.ogilvy.com/About/Network/OgilvyOne-Worldwide.aspx.
39. Brandi Newman, "The Costs of Personal Selling," www.seekarticle.com/business-sales/personal-selling.html, April 13, 2011.
40. ECA International, "About ECA," www.eca-international.com/about_eca.
41. Sergio Román and Salvador Ruiz, "A Comparative Analysis of Sales Training in Europe: Implications for International Sales Negotiations," *International Marketing Review* 20, no. 3 (2003): 304–26.
42. For a detailed discussion of the expatriate phenomenon, see Michael R. Czinkota, Ilkka A. Ronkainen, and Michael H. Moffett, *International Business* (Hoboken, NJ: Wiley, 2011), chapter 18.
43. Lisa Bertagnoli, "Selling Overseas Complex Endeavor," *Marketing News*, July 30, 2001, 4.
44. Anna Chernis, *DMA 2011 Statistical Fact Book: The Definitive Source for Direct Marketing Benchmarks* (DMA, 2011).
45. For a discussion on marketing on the Internet, see K. Douglas Hoffman, *Marketing: Best Practices* (Mason, OH: South-Western, 2006), chapter 15.
46. "Future of Selling," *OgilvyOne*, October 2010, 8.
47. Cellfire, http://biz.cellfire.com.
48. "Fuel and Freebies," *Wall Street Journal*, June 10, 2002, B1, B6.
49. Robert McLuhan, "Face to Face with Global Consumers," *Marketing*, August 22, 2002, 34.
50. Ruth Stevens, *Trade Show & Event Marketing: Plan, Promote & Profit*, (Mason, OH: South-Western Educational, 2005), 3–32.
51. Exhibit Surveys, Inc., "All-Show Averages," www2.exhibitsurveys.com/trends.
52. Trade Show News Network, "About Us," www.tsnn.com/about-us.
53. Mobile World Congress, www.mobileworldcongress.com.
54. Copylite, www.copylite.com/Departments.aspx?dpt=IS.
55. Messe Frankfurt, "You Want Your Event to Achieve Something," www.messefrankfurt.com/frankfurt/en/veranstalter/veranstaltungsarten.html.
56. Alison Theaker, *The Public Relations Handbook* (New York: Routledge, 2011), 131–47.
57. Charles Duhigg and David Barboza, "In China, Human Costs Are Built Into an iPad," *New York Times*, January 25, 2012, D3.
58. Oliver Williams, "Who Cast the First Stone?" *Harvard Business Review* 62 (September/October 1984): 151–60.
59. Christopher Hart and Pete Blackshaw, "Internet Inferno," *Marketing Management*, January/February 2006, 19–25; and Christopher Hart and Pete Blackshaw, "Communication Breakdown," *Marketing Management*, November/December 2005, 24–30.
60. Allison Enright, "Spin (Out of) Control," *Marketing News*, February 15, 2006, 19–20.
61. "Economic Uncertainty to Slow Sponsorship Growth in 2012," *IEG Sponsorship Report*, January 3, 2012, 5.
62. Rich Thomaselli, "No Fun in Games," *Advertising Age*, August 9, 2004, 1, 21.
63. Barry Janoff, "London 2012 Olympics Doing Its Best to Ambush Ambush Marketers," *BigLeadSports*, November 25, 2011, 1; and "War Minus the Shooting," *Economist*, February 18, 2006, 62–63.
64. Bradley K. Googins, "Why Community Relations Is a Strategic Imperative," *Strategy+Business* 2 (third quarter, 1997): 64–67.
65. Michael E. Porter and Mark R. Kramer, "The Competitive Advantage of Corporate Philanthropy," *Harvard Business Review* 80 (December 2002): 56–68. See also Cisco, "Networking Academies," www.cisco.com/web/about/ac227/about_cisco_corp_citi_net_academies.html.
66. Blanche Gatt and Jason Gale, "Glaxo, Merck Support Effort to Boost Vaccine Access," *Bloomberg*, June 6, 2011, 1; and "Business Scales World Summit," *Wall Street Journal*, August 28, 2002, A12, A13.
67. Gary Gereffi, Ronnie Garcia-Johnson, and Erika Sasser, "The NGO-Industrial Complex," *Foreign Policy*, July/August 2001, 56–66.

CHAPTER

14

Pricing Strategies and Tactics

LEARNING OBJECTIVES

By the time you complete this chapter, you will be able to:

- Understand how pricing can serve as a means of strategy or as a competitive tool with buyers.
- Determine complete and accurate quotations, choosing the terms of the sale and selecting the payment method in selling a product or service overseas.
- Understand the global, decentralized financial market for trading currencies in commercial banks and trade finance.
- Determine market pricing using corporate objectives, costs, customer behavior and market conditions, market structure, and environmental constraints.
- Place value within an organization as a means to set charges between related parties for goods, services, or property usage.
- Analyze the process of using goods and services as a medium of exchange in addition to money to international marketing.

THE INTERNATIONAL **MARKETPLACE** 14.1

Now for the Hard Part: Getting Paid for Exports

Smaller exporters often do not have the luxury that big corporations have to weigh the risks of doing business abroad and to investigate the creditworthiness of foreign customers. The result may be a hard lesson about the global economy: foreign sales do not help much when you cannot collect the bill.

More often than not, exporters will do less checking on an international account than they will on a domestic customer. For example, a U.S. fan blade manufacturer with less than $10 million in revenue was left with an overdue payment of $127,000 owed by an African customer. Before shipping the goods, the company had failed to call any of the customer's credit references. These turned out to be nonexistent—just like the company itself.

The simple guideline of selling only in countries where you are most likely to get paid may not be enough, given that collection periods for some of the more attractive markets may be long (see table). However, in many cases, basic information about the economic and political conditions in markets may be enough to warrant caution. Old World Industries, LLC, a large manufacturer of

© Courtesy of Old World Industries, LLC

Global Antifreeze.

Country	No Delay	Less than 30 days	30–60 days	60–90 days	More than 90 days
Germany	9	11	2	0	0
Ireland	3	12	1	0	0
Italy	3	13	5	1	0
Portugal	0	12	2	2	0
Spain	3	11	4	1	0
Turkey	3	9	2	1	1
Canada	12	27	2	0	1
Costa Rica	7	9	3	1	1
Mexico	3	19	9	2	3
Panama	7	13	4	1	0
United States	15	22	6	0	0

antifreeze, found that out after selling 500,000 gallons of antifreeze to a customer in a newly emerging market. After two years, Old World was still waiting to be paid in full because the foreign bank it dealt with had trouble obtaining U.S. dollars despite the country's strengthening foreign reserve position.

The length of time required for companies in different industries to collect on the average bill varies dramatically. The data in the table are for the second half of 2011 as reported by members of the Foreign Credit Interchange Bureau (FCIB).

SOURCES: Data updated by interview with FCIB, May 2011; and Old World Industries, www.oldworldind.com.

Successful pricing is a key element in the marketing mix. Many executives believe that developing a pricing capability is essential to business survival; they rank pricing as second only to the product variable in importance among the concerns to marketing managers.[1] The setting of export prices is complicated by factors such as increased distance from the markets, currency fluctuations, governmental policies such as duties, and typically longer and different types of channels of distribution. In spite of new factors influencing the pricing decision, the objective remains the same: to create demand for the marketer's offerings and to do so profitably in the long term. In achieving this, financing arrangements for export transactions are critical for two reasons: to secure sales and to combat various types of risk. This involves the pricing of sales to members of the corporate family as well as pricing within the individual markets in which the company operates. With increased economic integration and globalization of markets, the coordination of pricing strategies between markets becomes more important. As *The International Marketplace 14.1* shows, the most crucial assurance a firm will want in its export process is getting paid.

PRICE DYNAMICS

Price is the only element of the marketing mix that generates revenue; all the others are costs. It should therefore be used as an active instrument of strategy in the major areas of marketing decision making. Price serves as a means of communication with the buyer by providing a basis for judging the attractiveness of the offer. It is a major competitive tool in meeting and beating close rivals and substitutes. Competition will often force prices down, whereas intracompany financial considerations have an opposite effect. Prices, along with costs, will determine the long-term viability of the enterprise.[2]

Price should not be determined in isolation from the other marketing mix elements. It may be used effectively in positioning the product in the marketplace—for example, JLG, the world leader in self-propelled aerial work platforms used at construction sites, is able to charge premium prices because its products are powered by nonpolluting hydrogen fuel cells.[3] The feasibility

EXHIBIT 14.1 International Pricing Situations

Pricing Situation	International Involvement		
	Exporting	Foreign-Market Pricing	Intracompany Pricing
First-Time Pricing			
Changing Pricing			
Multiple-Product Pricing			

SOURCE: Elements of the model adopted from http://members.pricingsociety.com/articles/international-industrial-pricing.pdf.

range for price setting established by demand, competition, costs, and legal considerations may be narrow or wide in a given situation (e.g., the pricing of a commodity versus an innovation). The marketer's ultimate goal is to make the customer as inelastic as possible; the customer should prefer the marketer's offer even at a price premium.

Similarly, pricing decisions cannot be made in isolation from the other functions of the firm. Effective financial arrangements can significantly support the marketing program if they are carefully formulated between the finance and marketing areas. Sales are often won or lost on the basis of favorable credit terms to the buyer. With large numbers of competent firms active in international markets, financing packages—often put together with the help of governmental support—have become more important.

A summary of international pricing situations is provided in Exhibit 14.1. Pricing challenges—such as pricing for a new market entry, changing price either as an attack strategy or in response to competitive changes, and multiple-product coordination in cases of related demand—are technically the same as problems encountered in domestic markets.

In first-time pricing, the general alternatives are (1) skimming, (2) market pricing, and (3) penetration pricing. The objective of **skimming** is to achieve the highest possible contribution in a short time period. The product has to be unique, and some segments of the market must be willing to pay the high price. As more segments are targeted and more of the product is made available, the price is gradually lowered. The success depends on the ability and speed of reaction.

© China Photos/Stringer/Getty Images

Inside an IKEA store in China.

If similar products already exist in the target market, **market pricing** can be used. The final customer price is determined based on competitive prices, and then both production and marketing must be adjusted to the price. This approach requires the exporter to have a thorough knowledge of product costs as well as confidence that the product life cycle is long enough to warrant entry into the market. It is a reactive approach and may lead to problems if sales volumes never rise to sufficient levels to produce a satisfactory return. Although firms use pricing as a differentiation tool, the marketing manager may have no choice but to accept the prevailing world market price.

When **penetration pricing** is used, the product is offered at a low price intended to generate volume sales and achieve high market share, which would compensate for a lower per-unit return. IKEA found that a 70 percent reduction in average pricing roughly doubled the demand for its product.[4] This approach typically requires mass markets, price-sensitive customers, and decreasing production and marketing costs as sales volumes increase. This approach can be used to discourage other marketers from entering the market.

Price changes are called for when a new product is launched, when a change occurs in overall market conditions (such as a change in the value of the billing currency), or when there is a change in the internal situation, such as costs of production. A firm may elect not to change price even though the result may be lower profitability. However, if a decision is made to change prices, related changes must also be considered.

With multiple-product pricing, the various items in the line may be differentiated by pricing them appropriately to indicate an economy version, a standard version, and a top-of-the-line version.[5] One of the products in the line may be priced to protect against competitors or to gain market share from existing competitors. The other items in the line are then expected to make up for the lost contribution of such a "fighting brand."

THE SETTING OF EXPORT PRICES

In setting the export price, a company can use a process like the one illustrated in Exhibit 14.2.

As in all marketing decisions, the intended target market will establish the basic premise for pricing.[6] Factors to be considered include the importance of price in customer decision making (in particular, the ability to pay), the strength of perceived price–quality relationships, and potential reactions to marketing-mix manipulation by marketers. For example, an exporter extending a first-world product to an emerging market may find its potential unnecessarily limited and thus opt for a new version of a product that costs a fraction of the original version. Customers' demands will also have to be considered in terms of support required by the intermediary. The marketing mix must be planned to match the characteristics of the target market. Pricing will be a major factor in determining the desired brand image as well as the distribution channels to be used and the level of promotional support required. Conversely, mix elements affect pricing's degrees of freedom. If the use of specialty channels is needed to maintain product positioning, price will be affected.

Pricing policies follow from the overall objectives of the firm for a particular target market and involve general principles or rules that a firm follows in making pricing decisions.[7] Objectives include profit maximization, market share, survival, percentage return on investment, and various competitive policies such as copying competitors' prices, following a particular competitor's prices, or pricing so as to discourage competitors from entering the market.

Where and how decisions are made is also an important part of an exporter's pricing policy. The degree to which the pricing decision should be localized is a function of competitive conditions and economic conditions, such as inflation. The more dissimilarity and uncertainty a market displays, the more a local pricing decision has to be pushed. The inherent conflicts between local sales (focused on volume generation) and upper management (focused on profitability) have to be settled as well.[8]

Export Pricing Strategy

There are three general price-setting strategies in global marketing: (1) setting a standard worldwide price; (2) dual pricing, which differentiates between domestic and export prices; and (3) market-differentiated pricing. The first two methods are cost-oriented methods that are relatively simple to establish and easy to understand. The third strategy is based on a demand orientation and thus may be more consistent with the marketing concept.

EXHIBIT 14.2 Stages in Setting Export Prices

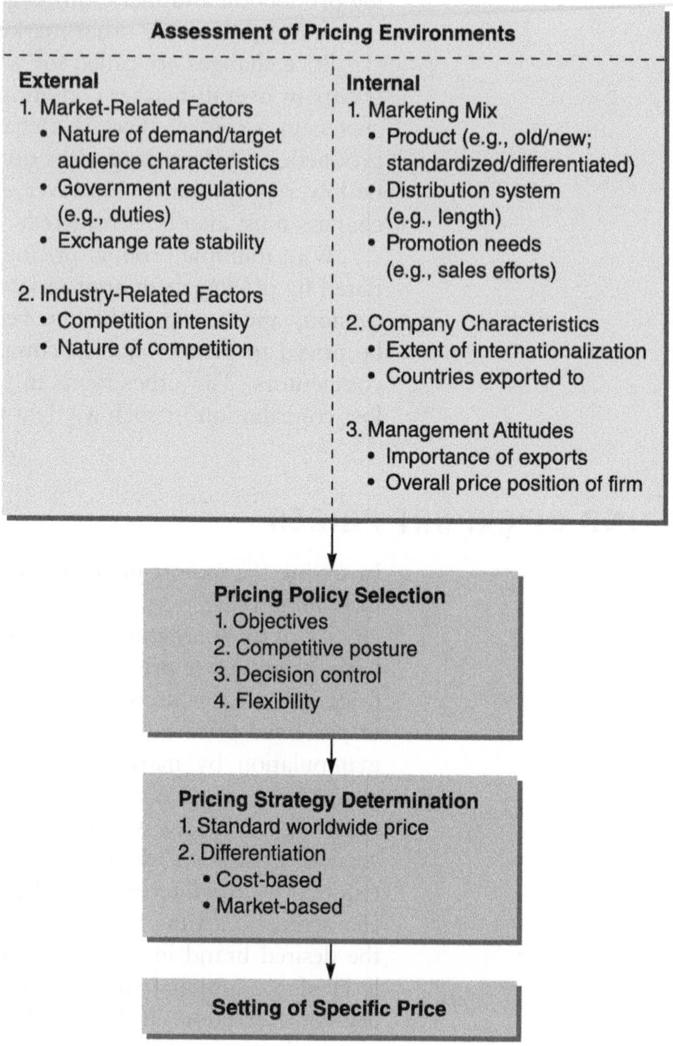

Assessment of Pricing Environments
External
1. Market-Related Factors
• Nature of demand/target audience characteristics
• Government regulations (e.g., duties)
• Exchange rate stability
2. Industry-Related Factors
• Competition intensity
• Nature of competition
Internal
1. Marketing Mix
• Product (e.g., old/new; standardized/differentiated)
• Distribution system (e.g., length)
• Promotion needs (e.g., sales efforts)
2. Company Characteristics
• Extent of internationalization
• Countries exported to
3. Management Attitudes
• Importance of exports
• Overall price position of firm
Pricing Policy Selection
1. Objectives
2. Competitive posture
3. Decision control
4. Flexibility
Pricing Strategy Determination
1. Standard worldwide price
2. Differentiation
• Cost-based
• Market-based
Setting of Specific Price

SOURCES: Elements of model adopted from Matthew Myers, S. Tamer Cavusgil, and Adamantios Diamantopoulos, "Antecedents and Actions of Export Pricing Strategy: A Conceptual Framework and Research Propositions," *European Journal of Marketing* 36, nos. 1/2 (2002): 159–89; and Barbara Stöttinger, "Strategic Export Pricing: A Long and Winding Road," *Journal of International Marketing* 9, no. 1 (2001): *S* 40–63.

The standard worldwide price may be the same price regardless of the buyer (if foreign product or foreign marketing costs are negligible) or may be based on average unit costs of fixed, variable, and export-related costs. Uniform pricing is advisable when customers worldwide are aware of the prices charged and when there is little chance of differentiating the product or the service to warrant price differences.

In dual pricing, domestic and export prices are differentiated, and two approaches to pricing products for export are available: cost-driven and market-driven methods. If a cost-based approach is decided upon, the marketer can choose between the cost-plus method and the marginal cost method. The cost-plus strategy is the true cost, fully allocating domestic and foreign costs to the product. Although this type of pricing ensures margins, the final price may be so high that the firm's competitiveness is compromised. This may cause some exporters to consider a flexible cost-plus strategy, which allows for variations in special circumstances. Discounts may be granted depending on the customer, the size of the order, or the intensity of competition. Changes in prices may also be put into effect to counter exchange rate fluctuations. Despite these allowances, profit is still a driving motive, and pricing is more static.

The marginal cost method considers the direct costs of producing and selling products for export as the floor beneath which prices cannot be set. Fixed costs for plants, R&D, and domestic overhead as well as domestic marketing costs are disregarded. An exporter can thus lower export prices to be competitive in markets that otherwise might have been beyond access. On certain occasions, especially if the exporter is large, this may open a company to dumping charges because determination of dumping may be based on average total costs, which are typically considerably higher. A comparison of the cost-oriented methods is provided in Exhibit 14.3.

Market-differentiated pricing calls for pricing exports according to the dynamic conditions of the marketplace. For these firms, the marginal cost strategy provides a basis, and prices may change frequently due to changes in competition, exchange rate changes, or other environmental changes. The need for information and controls becomes crucial if this pricing alternative is to be attempted. Exporters are likely to use market-based pricing to gain entry or better penetration in a new market, ignoring many of the cost elements, at least in the short term.

While most exporters, especially in the early stages of their internationalization, use cost-plus pricing, it usually does not lead to desired performance.[9] It typically leads to pricing too high in weak markets and too low in strong markets by not reflecting prevailing market conditions. But as experience is accumulated, the process allows for more flexibility and is more market-driven. Care has to be taken, however, that the cost of implementing a pricing-adaptation strategy does not outweigh the advantages of having a more adapted price.[10]

Overall, exporters see the pricing decision as a critical one, which means that it is typically made centrally under the supervision of top-level management.

EXHIBIT 14.3 Export Pricing Alternatives

Production Costs	Standard	Cost-Plus	Marginal Cost
Materials	2.00	2.00	2.00
Fixed costs	1.00	1.00	0.00
Additional foreign product costs	0.00	0.10	0.10
Production overhead	0.50	0.50	0.00
Total production costs	**3.50**	**3.60**	**2.10**
U.S. marketing costs	1.50	0.00	0.00
General and administrative	0.75	0.75	0.00
Foreign marketing	0.00	1.00	1.00
Other foreign costs	0.00	1.25	1.25
Subtotal	**5.75**	**6.60**	**4.35**
Profit margin (25%)	1.44	1.65	1.09
Selling price	7.19	8.25	5.44

In addition to product quality, correct pricing is seen as the major determinant of marketing success.[11]

Export-Related Costs

In preparing a quotation, the exporter must be careful to take into account and, if possible, include unique export-related costs. These are in addition to the normal costs shared with the domestic side. They include the following:

- The cost of modifying the product for foreign markets
- Operational costs of the export operation: personnel, market research, additional shipping and insurance costs, communications costs
- Costs incurred in entering the foreign markets: tariffs and taxes, risks associated with a buyer in a different market (mainly commercial credit and political risks), and risks from dealing in other than the exporter's domestic currency

The combined effect of both clear-cut and hidden costs results in export prices that far exceed domestic prices. The cause is termed **price escalation**. In the case of Geochron, the marketer of world time indicators, the multilayered distribution system with its excessive markups makes the price of a $1,300 clock exceed $3,800 in Japan.[12] A **value-added tax (VAT)**, such as those used within the European Union, is included in the calculations.

Complicating price escalation in today's environment may be the fact that price increases are of different sizes across markets. If customers are willing to shop around before purchasing, the problem of price differentials will make distributors unhappy and could result in a particular market being abandoned altogether.

Price escalation can be overcome through creative strategies, depending on what the demand elasticities in the market are. Typical methods, such as the following, focus on cost cutting:

- *Reorganize the channel of distribution.* Based on import channels for spaghetti in Japan, wholesalers show how the flow of merchandise through the various wholesaling levels has been reduced to only an internal wholesale distribution center, resulting in savings of 25 percent and increasing the **overall** potential for imports. Shortening of channels may, however, bring about other costs such as demands for better discounts.
- *Adapt the product.* The product itself can be reformulated by including less expensive ingredients or unbundling costly features, which can be made optional. Remaining features, such as packaging, can also be made less expensive. If price escalation causes price differentials between markets, the product can be altered to avoid cross-border price shopping by customers. For example, Geochron alters its clocks' appearance from one region to another.
- *Use new or more economical tariff or tax classifications.* In many cases, products may qualify for entry under different categories that have different charges levied against them. The marketer may have to engage in a lobbying effort to get changes made in existing systems, but the result may be considerable savings.
- *Assemble or produce overseas.* In the longer term, the exporter may resort to overseas sourcing or eventually production. Through foreign sourcing, the exporter may accrue an additional benefit to lower cost: **duty drawbacks**. A firm may be refunded up to 99 percent of duties paid on imported goods when they are exported or incorporated in articles that are subsequently exported within five years of the importation.[13]

If the marketer is able to convey a premium image, it may then be able to pass the increased amounts to the final price.

Appropriate export pricing requires the establishment of accounting procedures to assess export performance. Without such a process, hidden costs may bring surprises. For example, negotiations in the Middle Eastern countries or Russia may last three times longer than the average domestic negotiations, dramatically increasing the costs.

TERMS OF SALE

The responsibilities of the buyer and the seller should be spelled out as they relate to what is and what is not included in the price quotation and when ownership of goods passes from seller to buyer. Incoterms are the internationally accepted standard definitions for terms of sale set by the International Chamber of Commerce (ICC) since 1936. The Incoterms 2010 (for the next 10 years) went into effect on January 1, 2011, with significant revisions to better reflect changing transportation technologies and the increased use of electronic communications.[14] Although the same terms may be used in domestic transactions, they gain new meaning in the international arena. Incoterms 2010 are subdivided into two categories based only on method of delivery. The larger group of seven rules applies regardless of the method of transport, with the smaller group of four being applicable only to sales that solely involve transportation over water. Incoterms are available in 31 languages. The most common of the Incoterms used in international marketing are summarized in Exhibit 14.4.

Prices quoted *ex-works* (EXW) apply only at the point of origin, and the seller agrees to place the goods at the disposal of the buyer at the specified place on the date stated or within a fixed period. All other charges are for the account of the buyer.

One of the newer Incoterms is *free carrier* (FCA), which replaced a variety of "FOB" terms for all modes of transportation except vessel. FCA (named inland point) applies only at a designated inland shipping point. The seller is responsible for loading goods into the means of transportation; the buyer is responsible for all subsequent expenses. Under *carriage paid to* (CPT) terms, the seller's risk and responsibility for the condition of cargo end when the goods are delivered to the first carrier. The seller must bear all transportation costs to the named destination on the buyer's side.

Carriage and insurance paid to (CIP) indicates that the seller's risk and responsibility for the condition of the cargo end when the goods are delivered to the first carrier. The seller must bear all transportation costs to the named destination on the buyer's side. The seller is responsible to provide insurance. The seller is obligated to provide minimum insurance only, so we recommend the buyer obtain additional insurance coverage.

Delivered at terminal (DAT) indicates that the seller's obligation ends when it has delivered the goods to the disposal of the buyer and they are unloaded from the arriving carrier at the named destination terminal, cleared for export but not cleared for import.

Delivered at place (DAP) means the seller's obligation ends when it has delivered the goods to the disposal of the buyer at the named destination place and they are cleared for export but not cleared for import. The seller and buyer should agree which party will be responsible for unloading.

With *delivered duty paid* (DDP), the seller delivers the goods with import duties paid, including inland transportation from import point to the buyer's

EXHIBIT 14.4 Selected Trade Terms

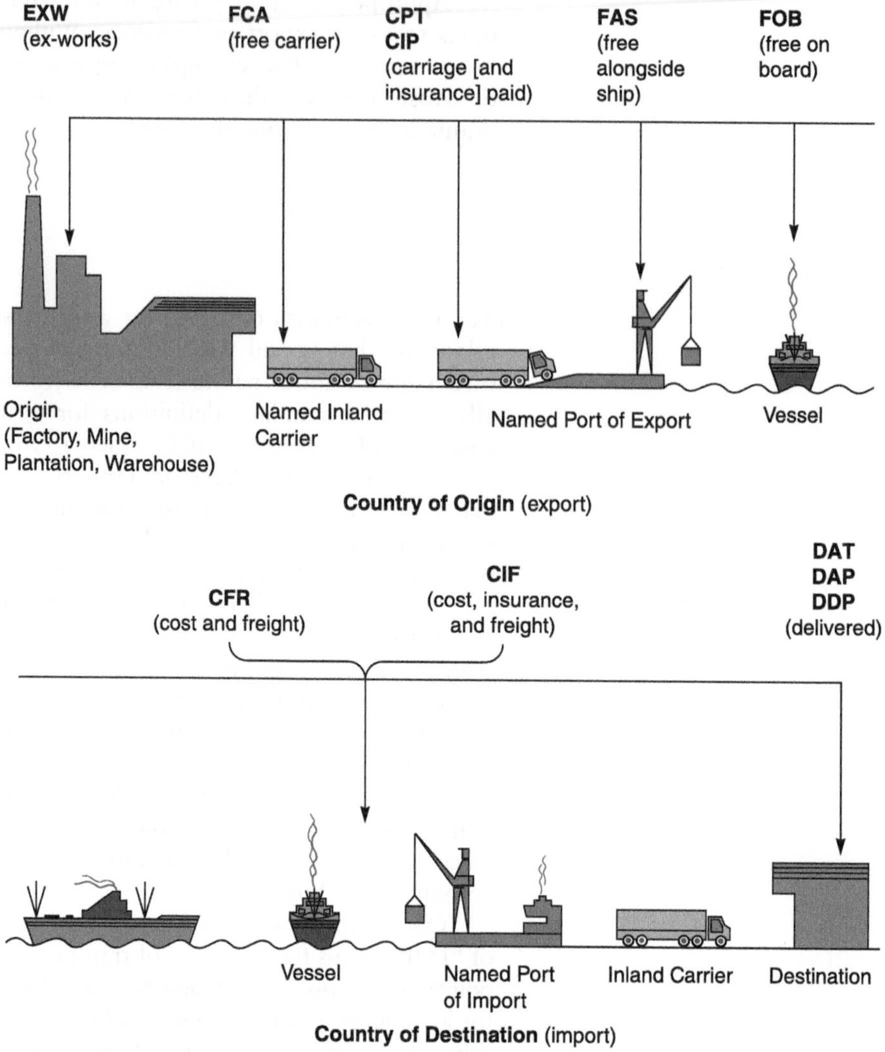

SOURCE: © Cengage Learning 2013.

premises. The buyer is responsible to take delivery of the goods at the named place of destination. *Ex-works* signifies the maximum obligation for the buyer; *delivered duty paid* puts the maximum burden on the seller.

Free alongside ship (FAS) at a named port of export means that the exporter quotes a price for the goods, including charges for delivery of the goods alongside a vessel at the port. The seller handles the cost of unloading and wharfage; loading, ocean transportation, and insurance are left to the buyer.

Free on board (FOB) applies only to vessel shipments. The seller quotes a price covering all expenses up to and including delivery of goods on an overseas vessel provided by or for the buyer.

Under *cost and freight* (CFR) to a named overseas port of import, the seller quotes a price for the goods including the cost of transportation to the named port of debarkation. The cost of insurance and the choice of insurer are left to the buyer.

With *cost, insurance, and freight* (CIF) to a named overseas port of import, the seller quotes a price including insurance, all transportation, and miscellaneous charges to the point of debarkation from the vessel. If other than waterway transport is used, the terms are *CPT* or *CIP*.

Careful determination and clear understanding of terms used, and their acceptance by the parties involved, are vital if subsequent misunderstandings and disputes are to be avoided not only between the parties but also within the marketer's own organization.[15] These terms are also powerful competitive tools. The exporter should therefore learn what importers usually prefer in the particular market and what the specific transaction may require.

Increasingly, exporters are quoting more inclusive terms. The benefits of taking charge of the transportation on either a CIF or DDP basis include the following: (1) exporters can offer foreign buyers an easy-to-understand "delivered cost" for the deal; (2) by getting discounts on volume purchases for transportation services, exporters cut shipping costs and can offer lower overall prices to prospective buyers; (3) control of product quality and service is extended to transport, enabling the exporter to ensure that goods arrive to the buyer in good condition; and (4) administrative procedures are cut for both the exporter and the buyer.[16] These benefits are highlighted in *The International Marketplace 14.2.*

THE INTERNATIONAL MARKETPLACE 14.2

Penetrating Foreign Markets by Controlling Export Transport

Companies that once sought short-term customers to smooth out recessions are searching for every means to get an edge over rivals in foreign markets. To achieve that, they are increasingly concerned about controlling quality and costs at every step, including the transportation process.

International transport costs are far higher than domestic shipping expenses. International ocean transport typically accounts for 4 to 20 percent of the product's delivered cost but can reach as high as 50 percent for commodity items. That makes transport a factor in situations in which a single price disadvantage can cause a sale to be lost to a competitor.

Still, most U.S. companies continue to abdicate responsibility for export shipping—either because they lack sophistication or simply because they do not want to be bothered. Increasingly, however, companies like Deere & Co. are paying for, controlling, and often insuring transport from their factories either to foreign ports or to the purchasing companies' doorsteps. This means that they are shipping on a DDP basis.

Deere exports premium-quality farm and lawn equipment worldwide. For years, it has insisted on overseeing transportation because it boosts sales, cuts costs, and ensures quality.

One goal of Deere's approach to transportation is to ensure that equipment is delivered to customers in good condition—a factor that Deere considers central to its image as a quality producer. The goal is to avoid cases like the one in which an inexperienced customer insisted on shipping a tractor himself. The tractor was unwittingly put on a ship's deck during a long, stormy sea voyage and arrived in terrible shape. The process also helps when Deere tractor windows are inadvertently broken during transport. Because Deere closely monitors the tractors, it can quickly install new windows at the port and avoid the huge cost of flying replacements to a customer.

Deere announces plans to build a new manufacturing, distribution, replacement-parts, and training center in Russia, a European Technology and Innovation Center in Germany, and a marketing office in Kiev, Ukraine. Deere will invest $100 million to build five tractor and five harvester models at a plant in the farming province of Santa Fe, Argentina. Argentina is also a big importer of farm machinery. But the government has been prodding foreign manufacturers that currently import products to make those goods locally as part of its import substitution policy.

SOURCES: Bob Tita, "Deere's Earnings Offer Few Clues," *Wall Street Journal*, August 18, 2011, B10; Scott Kilman, "Farmers Sense the End of the Big Boom," *Wall Street Journal*, October 22, 2011, A3; Deere & Company Annual Report 2010, www.deere.com/en_US/docs/Corporate/investor_relations/pdf/financialdata/reports/2011/2010annualreport.pdf; and ICC, www.iccwbo.org.

TERMS OF PAYMENT

Export credit and terms add another dimension to the profitability of an export transaction. The exporter has in all likelihood already formulated a credit policy that determines the degree of risk the firm is willing to assume and the preferred selling terms. The main objective is to meet the importer's requirements without jeopardizing the firm's financial goals. The exporter will be concerned over being paid for the goods shipped and will therefore consider the following factors in negotiating terms of payment: (1) the amount of payment and the need for protection, (2) terms offered by competitors, (3) practices in the industry, (4) capacity for financing international transactions, and (5) relative strength of the parties involved.[17] If the exporter is well established in the market with a unique product and accompanying service, price and terms of trade can be set to fit the exporter's desires. If, on the other hand, the exporter is breaking into a new market or if competitive pressures call for action, pricing and selling terms should be used as major competitive tools. Both parties have their own concerns and sensitivities; therefore, this very basic issue should be put on the negotiating table at the very beginning of the relationship.[18]

The basic methods of payment for exports vary in terms of their attractiveness to the buyer and the seller, from cash in advance to open account or consignment selling. Neither of the extremes is feasible for longer-term relationships, but they do have their use in certain situations. For example, in the 2009 period, very few companies were exporting into sub-Saharan Africa except on a cash-in-advance basis due to the countries' financial turmoil.[19] A marketer may use multiple methods of payment with the same buyer. For example, in a distributor relationship, the distributor may purchase samples on open account, but orders have to be paid for with a letter of credit. These methods are depicted in the risk triangle presented in Exhibit 14.5.

The most favorable term to the exporter is **cash in advance** because it relieves the exporter of all risk and allows for immediate use of the money.

EXHIBIT 14.5 Methods of Payment for Exports

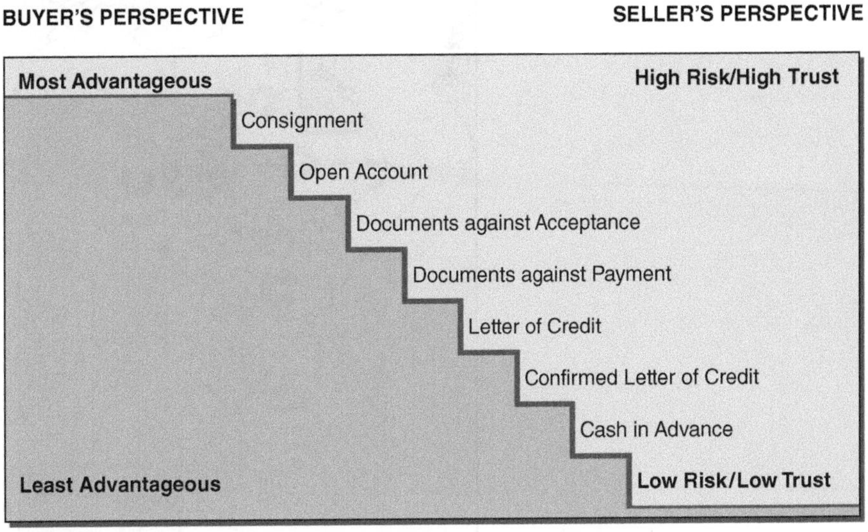

It is not widely used, however, except for smaller, first-time transactions or situations in which the exporter has reason to doubt the importer's ability to pay. Cash-in-advance terms are also found when orders are for custom-made products because the risk to the exporter is beyond that of a normal transaction. In some instances, the importer may not be able to buy on a cash-in-advance basis because of insufficient funds or government restrictions.

A **letter of credit** is an instrument issued by a bank at the request of a buyer. The bank promises to pay a specified amount of money on presentation of documents stipulated in the letter of credit, usually the bill of lading, consular invoice, and a description of the goods.[20] Letters of credit are one of the most frequently used methods of payment in international transactions. Exhibit 14.6 summarizes the process of obtaining a letter of credit and the relationship between the parties involved.

Letters of credit can be classified along three dimensions:

1. *Irrevocable versus revocable.* An irrevocable letter of credit can neither be canceled nor modified without the consent of the beneficiary (exporter), thus guaranteeing payment. According to the new rules drawn by the ICC, all letters of credit are considered irrevocable unless otherwise stated.[21]
2. *Confirmed versus unconfirmed.* In the case of a U.S. exporter, a U.S. bank might confirm the letter of credit and thus assume the risk, including the transaction (exchange) risk. The single best method of payment for the exporter in most cases is a confirmed, irrevocable letter of credit. Banks may also assume an advisory role.
3. *Revolving versus nonrevolving.* Most letters of credit are nonrevolving, that is, they are valid for the one transaction only. In case of established relationships, a revolving letter of credit may be issued.

The major caveat is that the exporter has to comply with all the terms of the letter of credit. For example, if the documents state that shipment is made in crates measuring 4 × 4 × 4 and the goods are shipped in crates measuring 4 × 3 × 4, the bank will not honor the letter of credit. If there are changes, the letter of credit can be amended to ensure payment. Importers have occasionally been accused of creating discrepancies to slow down the payment process or to drive down the agreed-upon price. In some cases, the exporter must watch out for fraudulent letters of credit, especially in the case of less-developed countries.

EXHIBIT 14.6 Letter of Credit: Process and Parties

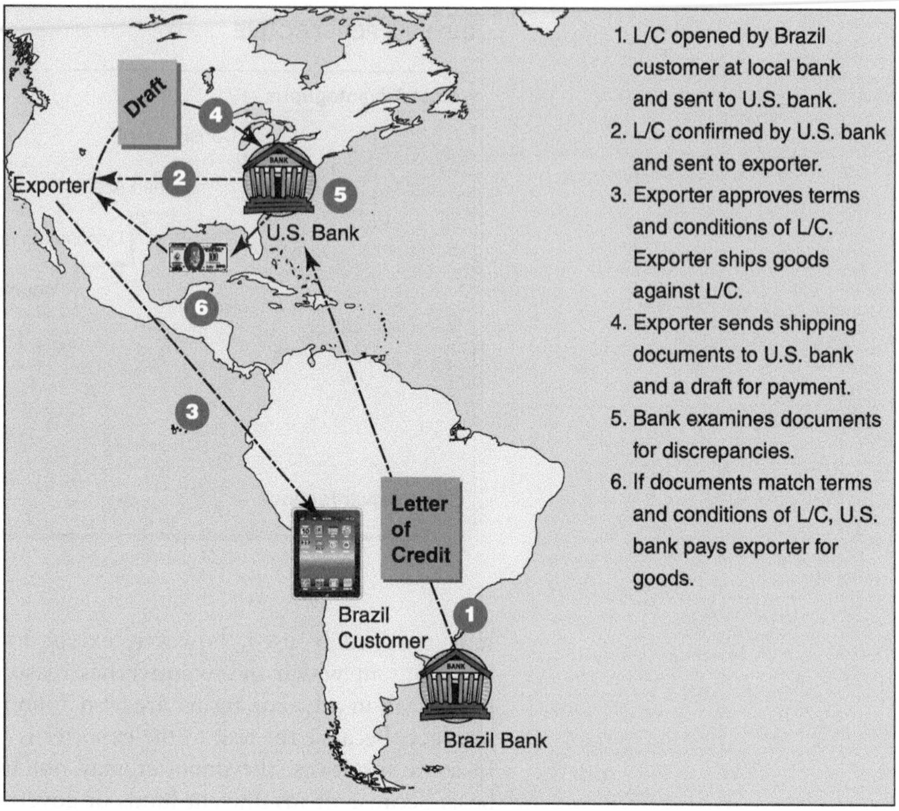
Draft
Exporter
U.S. Bank
Letter of Credit
Brazil Customer
Brazil Bank
1. L/C opened by Brazil customer at local bank and sent to U.S. bank.
2. L/C confirmed by U.S. bank and sent to exporter.
3. Exporter approves terms and conditions of L/C. Exporter ships goods against L/C.
4. Exporter sends shipping documents to U.S. bank and a draft for payment.
5. Bank examines documents for discrepancies.
6. If documents match terms and conditions of L/C, U.S. bank pays exporter for goods.

SOURCES: © Cengage Learning 2013; Based on Faren L. Foster and Lynn S. Hutchins, "Six Steps to Quicker Collection of Export Letters of Credit," *Export Today* 9 (November–December 1993): 26–30.

With the increasing amount of e-commerce, things will have to change. Solutions include online issuance and status reporting on letters of credit, creating a worldwide network of electronic trade hubs, and offering a smart card that will allow participating companies to transact financial business online.[22] For example, TradeCard is an online service for B2B (business-to-business) exchanges. Once an exporter and importer have agreed on the terms, the buyer creates an electronic purchase order, which specifies the terms and conditions. Once it is in electronic format, the seller formally agrees to the contract. The purchase order is stored in TradeCard's database.[23]

The letter of credit is a promise to pay but not a means of payment. Actual payment is accomplished by means of a draft, which is similar to a personal check. Like a check, it is an order by one party to pay another. Most drafts are documentary, which means that the buyer must obtain possession of various shipping documents before obtaining possession of the goods involved in the transaction. Clean drafts—orders to pay without any other documents—are mainly used by multinational corporations in their dealings with their own subsidiaries and in well-established business relationships.

In documentary collection situations, the seller ships the goods, and the shipping documents and the draft demanding payment are presented to the importer through banks acting as the seller's agent. The draft, also known as the bill of exchange, may be either a sight draft or a time draft. A sight draft documents against payment and is payable on presentation to the drawee, that is, the party to whom the draft is addressed. A time draft documents against acceptance and allows for a delay of 30, 60, 90, 120, or 180 days. When a time draft is drawn on and accepted by a bank, it becomes a banker's acceptance, which is sold in the short-term money market. Time drafts drawn on and accepted by a business firm become trader's acceptances, which are normally not marketable. A draft is presented to the drawee, who accepts it by writing or stamping a notice of acceptance on it. With both sight and time drafts, the buyer can effectively extend the period of credit by avoiding receipt of the goods. A date draft requires payment on a specified date regardless of the date on which the goods and the draft are accepted by the buyer.

Even if the draft is not sold in the secondary market, the exporter may convert it into cash by discounting. To discount the draft simply means that the draft is sold to a bank at a discount from face value. If the discounting is with recourse, the exporter is liable for the payment to the bank if the importer defaults. If the discounting is without recourse, the exporter will not be liable even if the importer does not pay the bank.

The normal manner of doing business in the domestic market is open account (open terms). The exporter selling on open account removes both real and psychological barriers to importing. However, no written evidence of the debt exists, and the exporter has to put full faith in the references contacted. Worst of all, there is no guarantee of payment. If the debt turns bad, the problems of overseas litigation are considerable. Bad debts are normally easier to avoid than to rectify. For more involved marketers with units abroad, internal transactions are normally handled on an open-account basis.

The most favorable term to the importer is consignment selling, which allows the importer to defer payment until the goods are actually sold. This approach places all the burden on the exporter, and its use should be carefully weighed against the objectives of the transaction. If the goods are not sold, returning them will be costly and time-consuming. Due to its burdensome characteristics, consignment is not widely used.

GETTING PAID FOR EXPORTS

The exporter needs to minimize the risk of not being paid if a transaction occurs. The term commercial risk refers primarily to the insolvency of, or protracted payment default by, an overseas buyer. Commercial defaults, in turn, usually result from deterioration of conditions in the buyer's market, fluctuations in demand, unanticipated competition, or technological changes. These naturally emerge domestically as well, but the geographic and cultural distances in international markets make these changes more severe and more difficult to anticipate. In addition, noncommercial or political risk is completely beyond the control of either the buyer or the seller. For example, the foreign buyer may be willing to pay but the local government may use every trick in the book to delay payment as far into the future as possible.

These challenges must be addressed through actions by either the company itself or its support systems. The decision must be an informed one, based on detailed and up-to-date information on international credit and country conditions. In many respects, the assessment of a buyer's creditworthiness requires the same attention to credit checking and financial analysis as for domestic buyers; however, the assessment of a foreign private buyer is complicated by some of the following factors:

- Credit reports may not be reliable.
- Audited reports may not be available.
- Financial reports may have been prepared according to a different format.
- Many governments require that assets be annually reevaluated upward, which can distort results.
- Statements are in local currency.
- The buyer may have the financial resources in local currency but may be precluded from converting to dollars because of exchange controls and other government actions.

EXHIBIT 14.7 Providers of International Credit Information

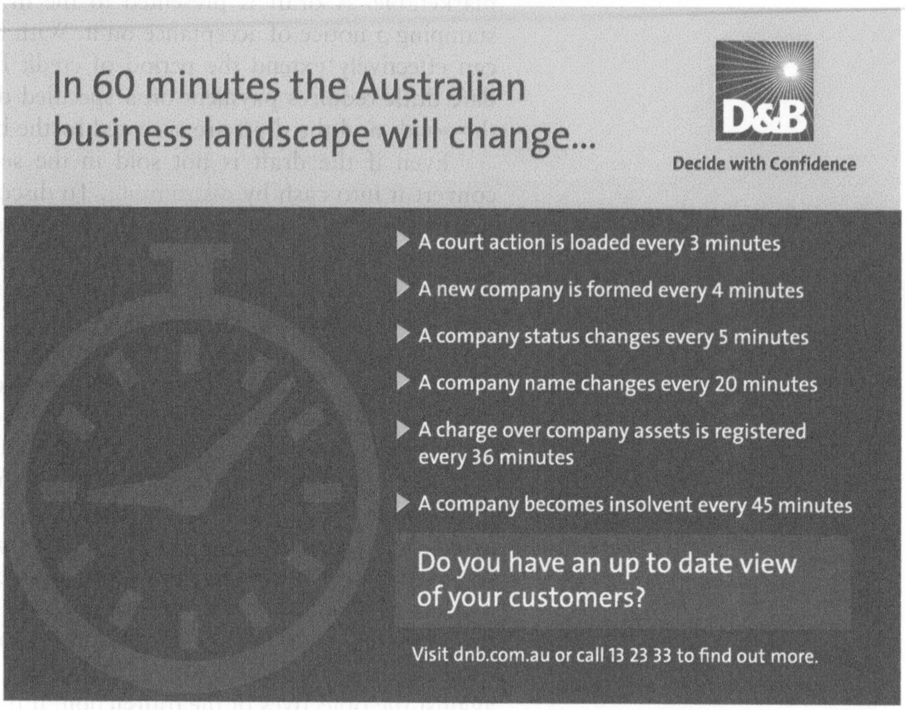

SOURCE: © D&B - Dun & Bradstreet.

More than one credit report should be obtained (from sources such as the one in Exhibit 14.7), and it should be determined how each credit agency obtains its reports. They may use the same correspondent agency, in which case it does the exporter no good to obtain the same information from two sources and to pay for it twice. Where private-sector companies (such as Dun & Bradstreet or Veritas) are able to provide the needed credit information, the services of the U.S. Department of Commerce's International Company Profiles (ICPs) are not available. Local credit reporting agencies, such as Profancresa in Mexico, may also provide regional services (in this case, throughout Latin America). With the growth of e-commerce, a company may want to demonstrate its creditworthiness to customers and suppliers in a rapid and secure fashion. The Coface Group (of which Veritas is the information arm in the Americas) introduced the "@rating" system, designed to assess a company's performance in paying its commercial obligations.[24]

Beyond protecting oneself by establishing creditworthiness, an exporter can match payment terms to the customer. In the short term, an exporter may require payment terms that guarantee payment. In the long term, the best approach is to establish a relationship of mutual trust, which will ensure payment even if complications arise during a transaction. Payment terms need to be stated clearly and followed up effectively. If prompt payment is not stressed and enforced, some customers will assume they can procrastinate.

Should a default situation occur in spite of the preparatory measures discussed above, the exporter's first recourse is the customer. Communication with the customer may reveal a misunderstanding or error regarding the shipment. If the customer has financial or other concerns or objections, rescheduling the payment terms may be considered. Third-party intervention through a collection agency may be needed if the customer disputes the charges. For example, the Total Credit Management Group, a cooperative of leading credit and collection companies in 150 countries, can be employed. Only when further amicable demands are unwarranted should an attorney be used.[25]

MANAGING FOREIGN EXCHANGE RISK

Unless the exporter and the importer share the same currency (as is the case in the 17 countries of Euroland), exchange rate movements may harm or benefit one or the other of the parties. If the price is quoted in the exporter's currency, the exporter will get exactly the price it wants but may lose some sales due to lack of customer orientation. If the exporter needs the sale, the invoice may be in the importer's currency, and the exchange risk will be the burden of the exporter. Some exporters, if they are unable to secure payment in their own currency, try to minimize the risk by negotiating shorter terms of payment, such as 10 or 15 days. Exchange risks may be a result of an appreciating or depreciating currency or result from a revaluation or devaluation of a currency by a central bank. Assume that a U.S. importer bought $250,000, or €208,750, worth of goods from a German company, which agreed to accept U.S. dollars for payment in 90 days. At the time of the quotation, the exchange rate for $1 was €0.835, whereas at the time of payment it had changed to €0.820. This means that the German exporter, instead of receiving €208,750, winds up with €206,250.

Two types of approaches to protect against currency-related risk exist: (1) risk shifting, such as foreign currency contractual hedging, and (2) risk modifying, such as manipulating prices and other elements of a marketing strategy.

When invoicing in foreign currencies, an exporter cannot insulate itself from the problems of currency movements, but it can at least know how much it will eventually receive by using the mechanism of the **forward market exchange**. In essence, the exporter gets a bank to agree to a rate at which it will buy the foreign currency the exporter will receive when the importer makes payment. The rate is expressed as either a premium or a discount on the current spot rate. A fixed rate allows the exporter to budget effectively without currency fluctuations eroding profit margins.[26] The risk still remains if the exchange rate does not move as anticipated, and the exporter may be worse off than if it had not bought forward. Although forward contracts are the most common foreign currency contractual hedge, other financial instruments and derivatives, such as currency options and futures, are available.

An **option** gives the holder the right to buy or sell foreign currency at a prespecified price on or up to a prespecified date. The difference between the currency options market and the forward market is that a transaction in the former gives the participant the right to buy or sell, whereas a transaction in the forward market entails a contractual obligation to buy or sell. This means that if an exporter does not have any or the appropriate amount of currency when the contract comes due, it would have to go into the foreign exchange markets to buy the currency, potentially exposing itself to major losses if the currency has appreciated in the meanwhile. The greater flexibility in the options contract makes it more expensive, however.

The currency **futures** market is conceptually similar to the forward market; that is, to buy futures on the British pound sterling implies an obligation to buy in the future at a prespecified price. However, the minimum transaction sizes are considerably smaller on the futures market. Forward quotes apply to transactions of $1 million or more, whereas on the futures market transactions will typically be well below $100,000. The market, therefore, allows relatively small firms engaged in international trade to lock in exchange rates and lower their risk. Forward contracts, options, and futures are available from banks (such as UBS and JPMorgan Chase), the Chicago Mercantile Exchange, and the Philadelphia Stock Exchange. OANDA Corporation is a financial services provider of currency conversion, online retail foreign exchange (forex) trading, online foreign currency transfers, and forex information (see in Exhibit 14.8).

U.S. exporters have faced both high and low values of the dollar with respect to other currencies in the past 20 years: low values in the early to mid-1990s, high values from then until early 2002, and lower values of as much as 30 percent

EXHIBIT 14.8 Trade Forex

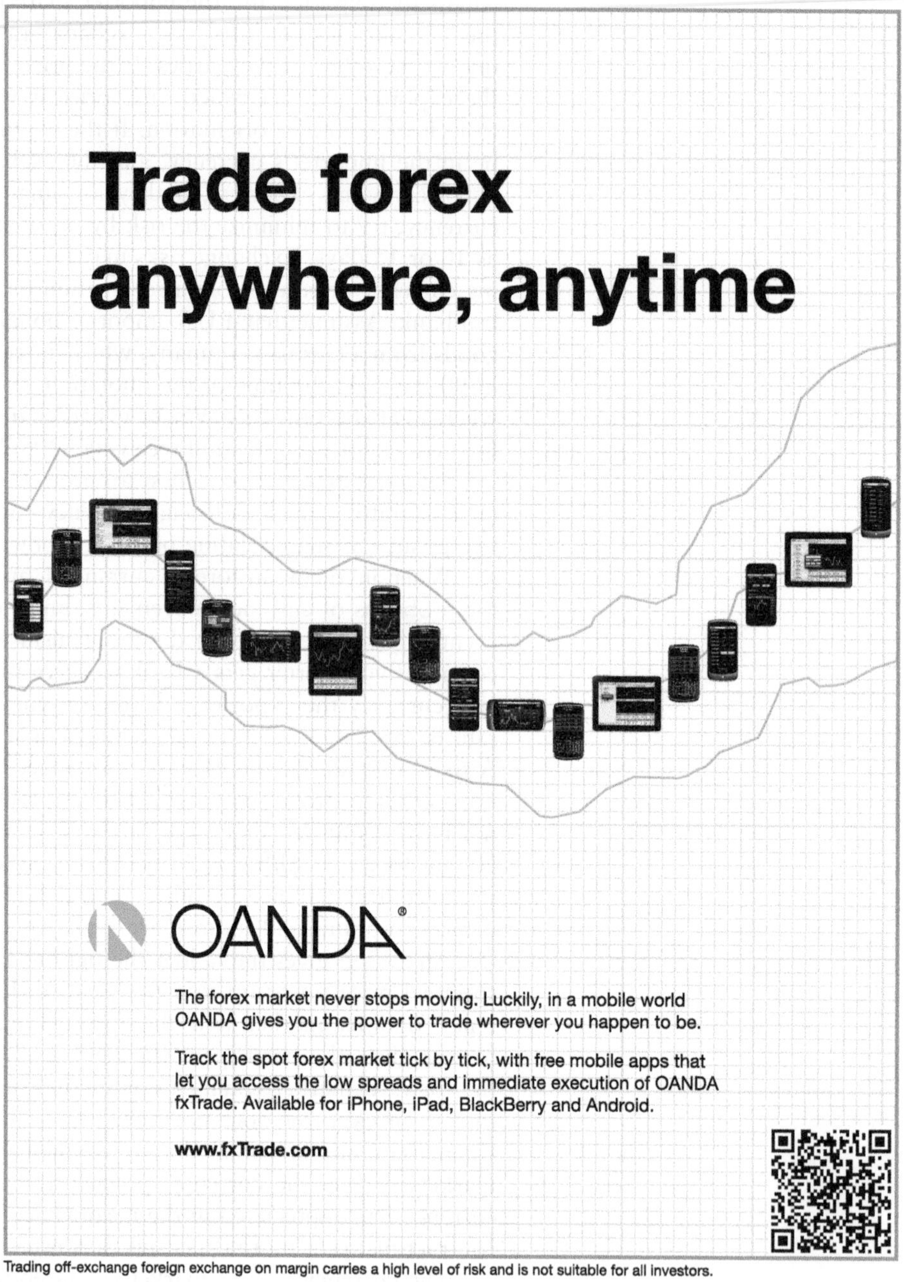

SOURCE: © Courtesy of OANDA Corporation.

from then on. When the exporter's domestic currency is weak, strategies should include stressing the price advantage to customers and expanding the scale and scope of the export operation. Sourcing can be shifted to domestic markets, and the export price can be subjected to full costing. However, under the opposite scenario, the exporter needs to engage in nonprice competition, minimizing the price dimension as much as possible. Costs should be reduced by every means, including enhancing productivity. At this time, the exporter should prioritize efforts to markets that show the greatest returns. Marketers may also attempt to protect themselves by manipulating leads and lags in export and import payments or receivables in anticipation of either currency revaluations or devaluations. This, however, will require thorough market knowledge and leverage over overseas partners. Strategies available to marketers under differing conditions are listed in Exhibit 14.9.

EXHIBIT 14.9 Exporter Strategies under Varying Currency Conditions

Weak	Strong
1. Stress price benefits	1. Use nonprice competition
2. Expand product line	2. Improve productivity/cost reduction
3. Shift sourcing to domestic market	3. Source overseas
4. Exploit all possible export opportunities	4. Prioritize exports
5. Make cash-for-goods trade	5. Countertrade with weak-currency countries
6. Use full costing	6. Use marginal-cost pricing
7. Speed repatriation	7. Slow collections
8. Minimize expenditure in local currency	8. Buy needed services abroad
	9. Maximize expenditures in home currency

SOURCE: Adapted from S. Tamer Cavusgil, "Unraveling the Mystique of Export Pricing," *Business Horizons* 31 (May–June 1988): 54–63.

Whatever the currency movements are, the marketer needs to decide how to adjust pricing to international customers in view of either a more favorable or an unfavorable domestic currency rate. This first alternative is pass-through, while the second alternative features the absorption approach; that is, the increase in the price is absorbed into the margin of the product, possibly even resulting in a loss. For pass-through to work, customers have to have a high level of preference for the exporter's product. In some cases, exporters may have no choice but to pass most of the increase to the customer due to the cost structure of the firm. Exporters using the absorption approach have as their goal long-term market-share maintenance, especially in a highly competitive environment.

The strategic response depends on market conditions and may result in different strategies for each market or product. Destination-specific adjustment of markups in response to exchange-rate changes have been referred to as pricing-to-market.[27] For example, a markup change will be more substantial in a price-sensitive market or product category. In addition, the exporter needs to consider the reactions of local competitors, who may either keep their prices stable (hoping that price increases in imports will improve their position) or increase their prices along with those of imports in search of more profits. U.S. automakers were criticized for raising their domestic prices at a time when Japanese imports were forced up by the higher value of the yen. Instead of trying to capture more market share, the automakers went for more profits. If the exporter faces a favorable domestic currency rate, pass-through means providing international customers with a more favorable price, while absorption means that the exporter keeps the export price stable and pockets a higher level of profits.

Beyond price manipulation, other adjustment strategies exist. They include the following:

- *Market refocus.* If lower values of the target-market currencies make exporting more difficult by, for example, making collection times longer, marketers may start looking at other markets for growth. In some cases, the emphasis may switch to the domestic market, where market-share gain at the expense of imports may be the most efficient way to grow. Currency appreciation does not always lead to a dire situation for the exporter. Domestic competitors may depend very heavily on imported components and may not able to take advantage of the currency-related price pressure on the exporter.
- *Streamlined operations.* The marketer may start using more aggressive methods of collection, insisting on letters of credit and insurance to guarantee payments. Some have tightened control of their distribution networks by

cutting layers or taking over the responsibility from independent intermediaries. On the product side, marketers may focus on offerings that are less sensitive to exchange-rate changes.

- *Shift in production*. Especially when currency shifts are seen as long-term, marketers will increase direct investment. With the high value of the yen, Japanese companies shifted production bases to lower-cost locations or closer to final customers. Panasonic, for example, moved a substantial share of its production to Southeast Asian countries. Remaining units in Japan will focus on research and development, design, software, and high-precision manufactured goods.[28]

SOURCES OF EXPORT FINANCING

Except in the case of larger companies that may have their own financing entities, most international marketers assist their customers abroad in securing appropriate financing. Export financing terms can significantly affect the final price paid by buyers. Consider, for example, two competitors for a $1 million sale. Exporter A offers a 3 percent interest rate over a 10-year payment period, while B offers 4 percent for the same term. Over the 10 years, the difference in interest is $55,000. In some cases, buyers will award a contract to the provider of cheaper credit and overlook differences in quality and price.

Commercial Banks

Commercial banks around the world provide trade financing depending on their relationship with the exporter, the nature of the transaction, the country of the borrower, and the availability of export insurance. This usually means that financing assistance is provided only to first-rate credit risks, leaving many U.S. exporters to report major problems in enlisting assistance from U.S. commercial banks. Furthermore, some U.S. banks do not see international trade finance as part of their core competence. Although the situation has improved, exporters still continue to complain about lack of export financing as it pertains to developing countries, financing high technology, or lending against foreign receivables. Many exporters complain that banks will not deal with them without a guarantee from the Export-Import Bank of the United States (Ex-Im Bank) of rock-solid collateral, such as property or equipment.

However, as the share of international sales and reach of companies increases, banking relationships become all the more important, a fact that is also noted by banks themselves. Many banks offer enhanced services, such as electronic services, which help exporters monitor and expedite their international transactions to customers who do a certain amount of business with them. As with all suppliers, the more business is done with a bank, the higher the level of service, usually at a better price. As the relationship builds, the more comfortable bankers feel about the exporter's business and the more likely they will go out of their way to help, particularly with difficult transactions. It is clear that the development of an effective credit policy requires teamwork between the company's marketing and finance staffs and its bankers.

In addition to using the types of services a bank can provide as a criterion of choice, an exporter should assess the bank's overseas reach. This is a combination of the bank's own network of facilities and correspondent relationships. While money-center banks can provide the greatest amount of coverage through their own offices and staff, they still use correspondents in regions outside the main banking or political centers of foreign markets.

Some banks have formed alliances to extend their reach to markets that their customers are entering. Some regional banks develop relationships with global banks that have strong correspondent networks in place in emerging markets. Other banks have no intention of establishing branches abroad and rely only on strong alliances with, or ownership by, foreign banks. Foreign banks can provide a competitive advantage to exporters because of their home-country connections and their strong global networks. For example, Commerzbank, Germany's second-largest private-sector bank, has 5,000 banks in 50 countries in North America, the Far East, Latin America, South America, Africa, and Eastern Europe to support its international trade financing activities.[29] Regardless of the arrangement, the bank's own branches or correspondents play an important role at all stages of the international transaction, from gathering market intelligence about potential new customers to actually processing payments.

Forfaiting and Factoring

Forfaiting provides the exporter with cash at the time of the shipment. In a typical forfait deal, the importer pays the exporter with bills of exchange or promissory notes guaranteed by a leading bank in the importer's country. The exporter can sell them to a third party (e.g., Citicorp) at a discount from their face value for immediate cash. The sale is without recourse to the exporter, and the buyer of the notes assumes all the risks. The discount rate takes into account the buyer's creditworthiness and country, the quality of the guaranteeing bank, and the interest cost over the term of the credit.

The benefits to the exporter are the reduction of risk, simplicity of documentation (because the documents used are well known in the market), and 100 percent coverage, which official sources such as export-import banks do not provide. In addition, forfaiting does not involve either content or country restrictions, which many of the official trade financing sources may have.[30] The major complaints about forfaiting center on availability and cost. Forfaiting is not available where exporters need it most, that is, the high-risk countries. Furthermore, it is usually a little more expensive than public sources of trade insurance.

Certain companies, known as **factoring** houses, may purchase an exporter's receivables for a discounted price (2 to 4 percent less than face value). Factors not only buy receivables but also provide the exporter with a complete financial package that combines credit protection, accounts-receivable bookkeeping, and collection services to take away many of the challenges that come with doing business overseas.[31] Arrangements are typically with recourse, leaving the exporter ultimately liable for repaying the factor in case of a default. Some factors accept export receivables without recourse but require a large discount.

Official Trade Finance

Official financing can take the form of either a loan or a guarantee, including credit insurance. In a loan, the government provides funds to finance the sale and charges interest on those funds at a stated fixed rate. The government lender accepts the risk of a possible default. In a guarantee, a private-sector lender provides the funds and sets the interest rate, with the government assuring that it will reimburse the lender if the loan is unpaid. The government is providing not funds but rather risk protection. The programs provide assurance that the governmental agency will pay for a major portion of the loss should the foreign buyer default on payment. The advantages are significant: (1) protection in the riskiest part of an exporter's business (foreign sales receivables), (2) protection against political and commercial risks over which the exporter does not have control, (3) encouragement to exporters to make competitive offers by extending terms of payment, (4) broadening of potential markets by minimizing exporter risks, (5) the possibility of leveraging exporter accounts receivable, and (6) through the government guarantee, the opportunity for commercial banks to remain active in the international finance arena.[32]

Because credit has emerged as an increasingly important component in export selling, the governments of most industrialized countries have established entities that insure credit risks for exports. Officially supported export credit agencies

EXHIBIT 14.10 Solar Power Panels

SOURCE: © Digital Vision/Getty Images.

(ECAs), such as the French Coface or German Hermes, are organizations whose central purpose is to promote national trade objectives by providing financial support for national exports. ECAs benefit from varying degrees of explicit or implicit support from national governments. Some ECAs are divisions of government trade missions. Other ECAs operate as autonomous or even private institutions, but most require a degree of recourse to national government support.

The Ex-Im Bank was created in 1934 and established as an independent U.S. government agency in 1945. The purpose of the bank is "to aid in financing and facilitating exports." Since its inception, Ex-Im Bank has supported more than $400 billion in U.S. export sales. The Ex-Im Bank supports short-, medium-, and long-term financing to creditworthy international customers (both in the private and public sectors) as well as working-capital guarantees to U.S. exporters. Special initiatives exist for environmental exports, small businesses, and lending directly to municipalities in certain countries. Ex-Im Bank has been actively pursuing financing opportunities in India since opening for business over 20 years ago.

LEASING

Organizational customers frequently prefer to lease major equipment, making it a $220 billion industry. About 30 percent of all capital goods (50 percent of commercial aircraft) are leased in the United States, with eight out of ten companies involved in leasing.[33] Although a major force in the United States, Japan, and Germany, leasing has grown significantly elsewhere as well; for example, one of the major international trade activities of Russia, in addition to shipping and oil, is equipment leasing. The Russians view leasing not only as a potential source of hard currency but also as a way of attracting customers who would be reluctant to buy an unfamiliar product.

In today's competitive business climate, traditional financial considerations are often only part of the asset-financing formula. Many leasing companies have become more than a source of capital, developing new value-added services that have taken them from asset financiers to asset managers, or forming relationships with others who can provide these services. In some cases, lessors have even evolved into partners in business activities. El Camino Resources, Ltd., targets high-growth, technology-dependent companies such as Internet providers and software developers for their hardware, software, and technical services needs, including e-commerce as well as Internet and intranet development.[34]

PRICING WITHIN INDIVIDUAL MARKETS

Pricing within the individual markets in which the company operates is determined by (1) corporate objectives, (2) costs, (3) customer behavior and market conditions, (4) market structure, and (5) environmental constraints.[35] Because all these factors vary among the countries in which the multinational corporation might have a presence, the pricing policy is under pressure to vary as well. With price holding a position of importance with customers, a market-driven firm must be informed and sensitive to customer views and realities. This is especially critical for those marketers wanting to position their products as premium alternatives.

Although many global marketers emphasize nonprice methods of competition, they rank pricing high as a marketing tool overseas, even though the nondomestic pricing decisions are made at the middle management level in a majority of firms. Pricing decisions also tend to be made more at the local level, with coordination from headquarters in more strategic decision situations.[36] With increased trade liberalization and advanced economic integration, this coordination is becoming more important.

Corporate Objectives

Global marketers must set and adjust their objectives, both financial (such as return on investment) and marketing-related (such as maintaining or increasing market share), based on the prevailing conditions in each of their markets. Pricing may well influence the overall strategic moves of the company as a whole. This is well illustrated by the decision of many companies—automakers for example—to begin production in the United States rather than to continue exporting. To remain competitive in the market, many have had to increase the dollar component of their output. Apart from trade barriers, many have had their market shares erode because of higher wages in their home markets, increasing shipping costs, and unfavorable exchange rates. Market share very often plays a major role in pricing decisions in that marketers may be willing to sacrifice immediate earnings for market-share gain or maintenance.

Pricing decisions will also vary depending on the pricing situation. The basics of first-time pricing, price adjustment, and product line pricing as discussed earlier apply to pricing within nondomestic situations as well. For example, companies such as Kodak and Xerox, which introduce all of their new products worldwide within a very short time period, have an option of either skimming or penetration pricing. If the product is an innovation, the marketer may decide to charge a premium for the product. If, however, competition is keen or expected to increase in the near future, lower prices may be used to make the product more attractive to the buyers and the market less attractive to the competition. The Korean conglomerates (such as Daewoo, Hyundai, LG, and Samsung) were able to penetrate and capture the low end of many consumer goods markets in both the United States and Europe based on price competitiveness over the past 20 years (as shown in Exhibit 14.11). For example, Samsung is about to enter another transition and is positioning itself for the future. Its Galaxy smartphone has sold more than 30 million units, despite Samsung only entering the smartphone market a year ago. It beat Apple in global smartphone sales, grabbing 24 percent of the market to Apple's 15 percent. It is now the number two overall smartphone seller by volume.[37]

EXHIBIT 14.11 The Price Edge Game

Product	Korean Brand			Japanese Brand			Chinese Brand	
	1996	2008	2011	1996	2008	2011	2008	2011
Subcompact autos	Excel/Accent (Hyundai)			Sentra (Nissan)			Chery QQ (Chery)	
	$9,079	$12,971	$9,899	$11,499	$15,483	$16,060	$7,500	$7,000
DVD/videocassette recorders	Samsung			Toshiba			Cyberhome	
	$206	$99	$74	$430	$49	$87	$48	$69
Compact refrigerators	Goldstar	Daewoo	Daewoo	Sanyo			Haier	
	$150	$80	$109	$180	$130	$132	$90	$80
13-inchcolor TVs	Samsung			Hitachi/Sony			Haier	
	$179	$159	$141	$229	$159	$199	$100	$129
Microwave ovens	Goldstar			Toshiba		Panasonic	Haier	
	$120	$95	$149	$140	$100	$155	$85	$55

SOURCE: Direct manufacturer and retailer inquiries, December 1996, December 2008, November 2011. In the absence of information or availability, a similar make and model has been used based on Consumer Reports data, www.consumerreports.org. The lowest price for each model was taken.

In the last few years, Chinese marketers have used similar pricing strategies to establish market positions. For example, Shanghai-based SVA Group sells LCD and plasma TV sets through channels such as Costco and Target at prices that are 30 percent below those of Panasonic from Japan.[38]

Price changes may be frequent if the company's objective is to undersell a major competitor. A marketer may, for example, decide to maintain a price level 10 to 20 percent below that of a major competitor; price changes would be necessary whenever the competitor made significant changes in its prices. Price changes may also be required because of changes in foreign exchange rates.

Product line pricing occurs typically in conjunction with positioning decisions. The global marketer may have a premium line as well as a standard line and, in some cases, may sell directly to retailers for their private-label sales. Products facing mass markets have keener competition and smaller profit margins than premium products, which may well be priced more liberally because there is less competition. For example, for decades, Caterpillar's big-ticket items virtually sold themselves. Company executive Rich Lavin says, "It's difficult to replicate our dealer network or the individual aspects of our business model that include product support, logistics, rental and used equipment, remanufacturing, and financing." Multinational companies are competing for the business as well as dozens of small, regional companies trying to get into the business. They are producing low-cost machines that are popular with many customers in China (as well as India, ASEAN, and CIS [Commonwealth of Independent States]).[39]

Costs

Costs are frequently used as a basis for price determination largely because they are easily measured and provide a floor under which prices cannot go in the long term. These costs include procurement, manufacturing, logistics, and marketing costs as well as overhead. Quality at an affordable price drives most procurement systems. The decision to turn to offshore suppliers may often be influenced by their lower prices, which enable the marketer to remain competitive.[40] Locating manufacturing facilities in different parts of the world may lower various costs, such as labor or distribution costs, although this may create new challenges. While a market may be attractive as far as labor costs are concerned, issues such as productivity, additional costs (such as logistics), and political risk will have to be factored in. Furthermore, a country may lose its attraction due to increasing costs, and the marketer may have to start the cycle anew by going to new markets (such as Indonesia or Vietnam).

Varying inflation rates will have a major impact on the administration of prices, especially because they are usually accompanied by government controls. The task of the parent company is to aid subsidiaries in their planning to ensure reaching margin targets despite unfavorable market conditions. Most experienced companies in the emerging markets generally have strong country managers who create significant value through their understanding of the local environment. Their ability to be more agile in a turbulent environment is a significant competitive advantage. Inflationary environments call for constant price adjustments; in markets with hyperinflation, pricing may be in a stable currency such as the U.S. dollar or the euro with daily translation into the local currency. In such volatile environments, the marketer may want to shift supply arrangements to cost-effective alternatives, pursue rapid inventory turnovers, shorten credit terms, and make sure contracts have appropriate safety mechanisms against inflation (e.g., choice of currency or escalator clause).

The opposite scenario may also be encountered; that is, prices cannot be increased due to economic conditions. Inflation has been kept in check in developed economies for a number of reasons. Globalization has increased the number of competitors, and the Internet has made it easy for customers to shop for the lowest prices. Big intermediaries, such as Walmart, are demanding prices at near cost from their suppliers. A survey of executives from 134 countries revealed that 59 percent of the respondents did not expect to be able to raise prices in the coming year.[41] Strategies for thriving in disinflationary times may include (1) target pricing, in which efficiencies are sought in production and marketing to meet price-driven costing; (2) value pricing to move away from coupons, discounts, and promotions to everyday low prices; (3) stripping down products to offer quality without all the frills; (4) adding value by introducing innovative products sold at a modest premium (accompanied by strong merchandising and promotion) but perceived by customers to be worth it; and (5) getting close to customers by using new technologies (such as the Internet and electronic data interchange [EDI]) to track their needs and company costs more closely.

Internally, controversy may arise in determining which manufacturing and marketing costs to include. For example, controversy may arise over the amounts of research and development to charge to subsidiaries or over how to divide the costs of a panregional advertising campaign when costs are incurred primarily on satellite channels and viewership varies dramatically from one market to the next.

Demand and Market Factors

Demand will set a price ceiling in a given market. Despite the difficulties in obtaining data on foreign markets and forecasting potential demand, the global marketer must make judgments concerning the quantities that can be sold at different prices in each foreign market. The global marketer must understand the **price elasticity of consumer demand** to determine appropriate price levels, especially if cost structures change. A status-conscious market that insists on products with established reputations will be inelastic, allowing for far more pricing freedom than a market where price-consciousness drives demand. Many U.S. and European companies have regarded Asia as a place to sell premium products at premium prices. Parker Pen Company has found a new prestige market in China for special edition pens with added Chinese characters costing between about $82 and $7,500 while its Western market has been fading.[42]

The marketer's freedom in making pricing decisions is closely tied to customer perceptions of the product offering and the marketing communication tied to it. Toyota's Corolla is able to outsell Chevrolet's Prizm, which is identical (both are produced by NUMMI Inc., which is a joint venture between Toyota and GM), even though the Corolla is priced $2,000 higher on the average.[43]

Similarly, Korean automakers have had a challenging time in shedding their image as a risky purchase. For example, consumers who liked the Hyundai Santa Fe said they would pay $10,000 less because it was a Hyundai. Hyundai has made major inroads into improving quality perceptions with its 10-year drive train warranty policy (which is very expensive, however).

Prices have to be set keeping in mind not only the ultimate consumers but also the intermediaries involved. The success of a particular pricing strategy will depend on the willingness of both the manufacturer and the intermediary to cooperate. For example, if the marketer wants to undercut its competition, it has to make sure that retailers' margins remain adequate and competitive to ensure appropriate implementation. At the same time, there is enormous pressure on manufacturers' margins from the side of intermediaries who are growing in both size and global presence. These intermediaries, such as Carrefour and Marks & Spencer, demand low-cost, direct-supply contracts, which many manufacturers may not be willing or able to furnish. The only other option may be to resort to alternate distribution modes, which may be impossible.

Market Structure and Competition

Competition helps set the price within the parameters of cost and demand. Depending on the marketer's objectives and competitive position, it may choose to compete directly on price or elect for nonprice measures. If a pricing response is sought, the marketer can offer bundled prices (e.g., value deals on a combination of products) or loyalty programs to insulate the firm from a price war. Price cuts can also be executed selectively rather than across the board. New products can be introduced to counter price challenges.

Faced with continuing losses in share, Kodak, for example, launched a fighter brand of camera film called Funtime, which sold at the same price as Fuji's offering. In an attempt to avoid cannibalization, Kodak manufactured Funtime using an older, less effective formula emulsion that made it significantly inferior to Gold Plus. But what appeared, from a corporate standpoint, to represent a genuine product distinction was lost in the subjective world of consumer interpretation. Already a low-involvement purchase, film had increasingly become a commodity, and most consumers were unaware of the differences in product quality. They simply saw Funtime as Kodak film at a lower price, and the fighter brand ate into Gold Plus sales more than it damaged Fuji's. Kodak withdrew Funtime from the market after only two years and began to experiment with other alternatives.[44]

If a company's position is being eroded by competitors who focus on price, the marketer may have no choice but to respond. Motorola and Nokia, the leading mobile phone makers, are facing tough conditions in the world market. In addition to being competitive in price and quality, local companies such as Ningbo Bird are quick to come up with new models to satisfy the fast-changing needs of consumers while providing better after-sales service free of charge or at a marginal price.

Procter & Gamble and Unilever, for example, have been particularly effective at developing strategies to keep product prices low, offering micropacks for items including shampoo, soaps, cigarettes, and food. Although buying in small quantities, or sachets, is not the most economical way to purchase such goods, it does allow consumers to stay within their budgets. They buy the products through the Philippines small sari-sari stores, which survive on high-turnover, low-value transactions. Indeed, buying goods in small amounts is part of daily life.[45] At $40 to $60, jeans are not affordable to the masses in developing countries. Arvind Mills, the world's fifth-largest denim maker, introduced Ruf & Tuf jeans—a ready-to-make kit of jeans components priced at $6 that could be assembled inexpensively by a local tailor.[46]

The pricing behavior of a global marketer may come under scrutiny in important market sectors, such as automobiles or retailing. If local companies lose significant market share to outsiders as a result of lower prices, they may ask for government interference against alleged dumping. Walmart resigned from

Mexico's National Retailers Association to protest an ethics code that members approved prohibiting price comparisons in ads by their members (on the basis of negative publicity for other retailers). Since ad campaigns are the key to Walmart's "everyday low prices" strategy, it had no choice but to leave the organization.[47]

Environmental Constraints

Governments influence prices and pricing directly as well. In addition to policy measures, such as tariffs and taxes, governments may also elect to directly control price levels. Once under price controls, the global marketer has to operate as it would in a regulated industry. Setting maximum prices has been defended primarily on political grounds: it stops inflation and an accelerating wage–price spiral, and consumers want it. Supporters also maintain that price controls raise the income of the poor. Operating in such circumstances is difficult. Achieving change in prices can be frustrating; for example, a company may wait 30 to 45 days for an acknowledgment of a price-increase petition.

To fight price controls, multinational corporations can demonstrate that they are getting an unacceptable return on investment and that, without an acceptable profit opportunity, future investments will not be made and production perhaps will be stopped. These have been the arguments of U.S. and European pharmaceutical marketers in China.[48] At one time, Coca-Cola and PepsiCo withdrew their products from the shelves in Mexico until they received a price increase. Pakistani milk producers terminated their business when they could not raise prices, and GlaxoSmithKline, a pharmaceutical manufacturer, canceled its expansion plans in Pakistan because of price controls.

PRICING COORDINATION

The issue of standard worldwide pricing has been mostly a theoretical one because of the influence of the factors already discussed. However, coordination of the pricing function is necessary, especially in larger, regional markets such as the European Union. With the increasing level of integration efforts around the world, and even discussion of common currency elsewhere, control and coordination of global and regional pricing takes on a new meaning.

With more global and regional brands in the global marketer's offering, control in pricing is increasingly important. Of course, this has to be balanced against the need for allowing subsidiaries latitude in pricing so that they may quickly react to specific market conditions.

Studies have shown that foreign-based multinational corporations allow their U.S. subsidiaries considerable freedom in pricing. This has been explained by the size and unique features of the market. Further, it has been argued that these subsidiaries often control the North American market (that is, a Canadian customer cannot get a better deal in the United States, and vice versa) and that distances create a natural barrier against arbitrage practices that would be more likely to emerge in Europe—although, even with the common currency, different rules and standards, economic disparities, and information differences may make deal-hunting difficult.[49] However, recent experience has shown that pricing coordination has to be on a worldwide basis because parallel imports will surface in any markets in which price discrepancies exist, regardless of distances. Marketers who mainly sell to organizational customers, such as Nokia to telecommunications operators, have started using standard worldwide pricing.

TRANSFER PRICING

Transfer pricing, or intracorporate pricing, is the pricing of sales to members of the extended corporate family. With rapid globalization and consolidation across borders, estimates have up to two-thirds of world trade taking place between related parties, including shipments and transfers from parent company to affiliates as well as trade between alliance partners.[50] This means that transfer pricing has to be managed in a world characterized by different tax rates, different foreign exchange rates, varying governmental regulations, and other economic and social challenges. Even in regions that are increasingly integrated, price differentials can play a pivotal role. Allocation of resources among the various units of the multinational corporation requires the central management of the corporation to establish the appropriate transfer price to achieve the following objectives:

- Competitiveness in the international marketplace
- Reduction of taxes and tariffs
- Management of cash flows
- Minimization of foreign exchange risks
- Avoidance of conflicts with home and host governments
- Internal concerns such as goal congruence and motivation of subsidiary managers[51]

Intracorporate sales can so easily change the consolidated global results that they compose one of the most important ongoing decision areas in the company. This is quite a change from the past when many executives dismissed internal pricing as the sole responsibility of the accounting department and as a compliance matter. Transfer pricing, when viewed from a company-wide perspective, enhances operational performance (including marketing), minimizes the overall tax burden, and reduces legal exposure both at home and abroad. According to an annual survey, the portion of multinationals citing transfer pricing as the most important issue in terms of taxation has grown from one-half to two-thirds, and at the subsidiary level this importance is even more pronounced.[52]

Transfer prices can be based on costs or on market prices.[53] The cost approach uses an internally calculated cost with a percentage markup added. The market price approach is based on an established market selling price, and the products are usually sold at that price minus a discount to allow some margin of profit for the buying division. In general, cost-based prices are easier to manipulate because the cost base itself may be any one of these three: full cost, variable cost, or marginal cost.

Market conditions in general, and those relating to the competitive situation in particular, are typically mentioned as key variables in balancing operational goals and tax considerations. In some markets, especially in the Far East, competition may prevent the international marketer from pricing at will. Prices may have to be adjusted to meet local competition with lower labor costs. This practice may provide entry to the market and a reasonable profit to the affiliate. However, in the long term, it may also become a subsidy to an inefficient business. Further, tax and customs authorities may object because underpricing means that the seller is earning less income than it would otherwise receive in the country of origin and is paying duties on a lower base price on entry to the destination country.

Economic conditions in a market, especially the imposition of controls on movements of funds, may require the use of transfer pricing to allow the company to repatriate revenues. Take a beverage company located in Mexico that has a subsidiary in France. Taxes are owed in France based on the French subsidiary's results. The higher the royalties paid by the French subsidiary, the lower the taxable profits in France. The French tax authorities will be satisfied if they see that the royalties paid by the French company to its headquarters in Mexico are not higher than those that would be paid to an independent enterprise for a similar transaction. But if the royalties are too high, there is a possibility that profits are being shifted out of France to reduce tax liabilities there.[54]

A new dimension is emerging with the increase in e-commerce activity. Given a lack of clear understanding and agreement of tax authorities on taxation of electronic transfer pricing activities, companies have to be particularly explicit on how pricing decisions are made to avoid transfer-price audits.[55]

International transfer pricing objectives may lead to conflicting objectives, especially if the influencing factors vary dramatically from one market to another. For example, it may be quite difficult to perfectly match subsidiary goals with the global goals of the multinational corporation. Specific policies should therefore exist that would motivate subsidiary managers to avoid making decisions that would be in conflict with overall corporate goals. If transfer pricing policies lead to an inaccurate financial measure of the subsidiary's performance, this should be taken into account when a performance evaluation is made.

Use of Transfer Prices to Achieve Corporate Objectives

Three philosophies of transfer pricing have emerged over time: (1) cost-based price (direct cost or cost-plus), (2) market-based price (discounted "dealer" price derived from end-market prices), and (3) **arm's-length price**, or the price that unrelated parties would have reached on the same transaction. The rationale for transferring at cost is that it increases the profits of affiliates, and their profitability will eventually benefit the entire corporation. In most cases, cost-plus is used, requiring every affiliate to be a profit center. Deriving transfer prices from the market is the most marketing-oriented method because it takes local conditions into account. Arm's-length pricing is favored by many constituents, such as governments, to ensure proper intracompany pricing. However, the method becomes difficult when sales to outside parties do not occur in a product category. Additionally, it is often difficult to convince external authorities that true negotiation occurs between two entities controlled by the same parent. In a study of 32 U.S.-based multinational corporations operating in Latin America, a total of 57 percent stated that they use a strategy of arm's-length pricing for their shipments, while the others used negotiated prices, cost-plus, or some other method.[56] Generally tax authorities will honor agreements among companies provided those agreements are commercially reasonable and the companies abide by the agreements consistently.

The effect of environmental influences in overseas markets can be alleviated by manipulating transfer prices, at least in principle. High transfer prices on goods shipped to a subsidiary and low ones on goods imported from it will result in minimizing the tax liability of a subsidiary operating in a country with a high income tax. The effective corporate tax rate in the United States is 40 percent, while the average rate in the EU is 20.12 percent, in Latin America 25.06 percent, and in Asia 22.78 percent.[57] Many of the new members of the European Union have cut their rates the most—for example, Bulgaria (10 percent) and Poland (19 percent). This may give multinationals a reason to report higher profits outside of the United States. On the other hand, a higher transfer price may have an effect on the import duty, especially if it is assessed on an ad valorem basis. Exceeding a certain threshold may boost the duty substantially when the product is considered a luxury, and it will have a negative impact on the subsidiary's competitive posture. Adjusting transfer prices for the opposite effects of taxes and duties is, therefore, a delicate balancing act.

Transfer prices may be adjusted to balance the effects of fluctuating currencies when one partner is operating in a low-inflation environment and the other in one of rampant inflation. Economic restrictions such as controls on dividend remittances and allowable deductions for expenses incurred can also be blunted. For example, if certain services performed by corporate headquarters (such as product development or strategic planning assistance) cannot be charged to the subsidiaries, costs for these services can be recouped by increases in the transfer prices of other product components. A subsidiary's financial and competitive position can be manipulated by the use of lower transfer prices. Start-up costs can be lowered, a market niche carved more quickly, and long-term survival guaranteed. Ultimately, the entire transfer price and taxation question is best dealt with at a time when the company is considering a major expansion or restructuring of operations. For example, if it fits the overall plan, a portion of a unit's R&D and marketing activities could be funded in a relatively low-tax jurisdiction.

Transfer pricing problems grow geometrically as all of the subsidiaries with differing environmental concerns are added to the planning exercise, calling for more detailed intracompany data for decision making. Further, fluctuating exchange rates make the planning even more challenging. However, to prevent double taxation and meet arm's-length requirements, it is essential that the corporation's pricing practices be uniform. Many have adopted a philosophy that calls for an obligation to maintain a good-citizen fiscal approach (that is, recognizing the liability to pay taxes and duties in every country of operation and to avoid artificial tax-avoidance schemes) and a belief that the primary goal of transfer pricing is to support and develop commercial activities. Some companies make explicit mention of this obligation of good citizenship in their corporate codes of conduct.

Transfer Pricing Challenges

Transfer pricing policies face two general types of challenges. The first is internal to the multinational corporation and concerns the motivation of those affected by the pricing policies of the corporation. The second, an external one, deals with relations between the corporation and tax authorities in both the home country and the host countries.

Performance Measurement

Manipulating intracorporate prices complicates internal control measures and, without proper documentation, will cause major problems. If the firm operates on a profit center basis, some consideration must be given to the effect of transfer pricing on the subsidiary's apparent profit performance and its actual performance. To judge a subsidiary's profit performance as unsatisfactory when it was targeted to be a net source of funds can easily create morale problems. The situation may be further complicated by cultural differences in the subsidiary's management, especially if the need to subsidize less-efficient members of the corporate family is not made clear. An adjustment in the control mechanism is called for to give appropriate credit to divisions for their actual contributions. The method may range from dual bookkeeping to compensation in budgets and profit plans. Regardless of the method, proper organizational communication is necessary to avoid conflict between subsidiaries and headquarters.

Taxation

Transfer prices will by definition involve the tax and regulatory jurisdictions of the countries in which the company does business. Sales and transfers of tangible properties and transfers of intangibles such as patent rights and manufacturing know-how are subject to close review and to determinations about the adequacy of compensation received. This quite often puts the multinational corporation in a difficult position. U.S. authorities may think the transfer price is too low, whereas it may be perceived as too high by the foreign entity, especially if a less-developed country is involved. Section 482 of the Internal Revenue Code gives the commissioner of the IRS vast authority to reallocate income between controlled foreign operations and U.S. parents and between U.S. operations of foreign corporations.

Since 1962, the U.S. government has attempted to stop U.S. companies from shifting U.S. income to their foreign subsidiaries in low- or no-tax jurisdictions and has affirmed the arm's-length standard as the principal basis for transfer pricing. Because unrelated parties normally sell products and services at a profit, an arm's-length price normally involves a profit to the seller. Guidelines of the OECD for transfer pricing are similar to those used by U.S. authorities (as are those of an increasing number of non-OECD countries, such as Argentina, China, India, Russia, Singapore, and South Africa). Some experts who argue that the arm's-length standard is only applicable for commodities businesses have proposed a simpler system that allocates profits by a formula such as that of the state of California, which factors in percentages of world sales, assets, and other indicators. The rapid changes in international marketing caused by e-business will also have an impact on transfer pricing. Although transactions involving e-commerce represent new ways of conducting business, the fundamental economic relationships will remain the same. As a result, the existing principle of arm's length will probably be retained and adapted to address cross-border activities in a virtual economy.

According to Section 482, there are methods of determining an arm's-length price. The starting point for testing the appropriateness of transfer prices is a comparison with *comparable uncontrolled* transactions involving unrelated parties. Uncontrolled prices exist when (1) sales are made by members of the multinational corporation to unrelated parties, (2) purchases are made by members of the multinational corporation from unrelated parties, and (3) sales are made between two unrelated parties, neither of which is a member of the multinational corporation. In some cases, marketers have created third-party trading where none existed before. Instead of selling 100 percent of the product in a market to a related party, the seller can arrange a small number of direct transactions with unrelated parties to create a benchmark against which to measure related-party transactions.

If this method does not apply, the *resale* method can be used. This usually applies best to transfers to sales subsidiaries for ultimate distribution. The arm's-length approximation is arrived at by subtracting the subsidiary's profit from an uncontrolled selling price. The appropriateness of the amount is determined by comparison with a similar product being marketed by the multinational corporation.

The *cost-plus* approach is most applicable for transfers of components or unfinished goods to overseas subsidiaries. The arm's-length approximation is achieved by adding an appropriate markup for profit to the seller's total cost of the product. The key is to apply such markups consistently over time and across markets.

The two methods focused on profits are based on the *functional analysis approach*. Functional analysis measures the profits of each of the related companies and compares them with the proportionate contribution to total income of the corporate group or comparable multinational marketers. It addresses the question of what profit would have been reported if the intercorporate transactions had involved unrelated parties. Understanding the functional interrelationships of the various parties (that is, which entity does what) is basic to determining each entity's economic contribution vis-à-vis total income of the corporate group.

Since 1991, the Internal Revenue Service has been signing advance pricing agreements (APAs) with multinational corporations to stem the tide of unpaid U.S. income taxes. By 2010, a total of 1,523 such agreements were completed and 973 were under negotiation.[58] Since 1998, special provisions have been made for small- and medium-sized companies to negotiate such arrangements. Agreement on transfer pricing is set ahead of time, thus eliminating court challenges and costly audits. The harsh penalties have also caused companies to consider APAs. In the United States, a transfer pricing violation can result in a 40 percent penalty on the amount of underpayment, whereas in Mexico the penalty can reach 100 percent. The main criticism of this approach is the exorbitant amount of staff time that each agreement requires as well as the amount of information that may have to be disclosed. In cases in which a company is doing business in a country that has a bilateral tax treaty with the home government (e.g., the United States and Germany), the company can seek a bilateral APA that is negotiated simultaneously with the tax authorities of both countries.

The most difficult of cases are those involving intangibles because comparables are absent in most cases.[59] The IRS requires that the price or royalty rate for any cross-border transfer be commensurate with income; that is, it must result in a fair distribution of income between the units. Needless to say, many of the analyses have to be quite subjective, especially in cases that involve the transfer of intellectual property, and may lead to controversies and disputes with tax authorities (see *The International Marketplace 14.3*).[60]

THE INTERNATIONAL MARKETPLACE 14.3

The Tax Haven That Is Saving Google Billions

All of the following arrangements are legal. Google's practices are very similar to those at countless other global companies operating across a wide range of industries. A company's obligation to its shareholders is to try to minimize its taxes and all costs, but to do so legally.

The setup lowers Google's overseas tax bill, but it also affects U.S. tax revenues as the government struggles to close a projected $1.4 trillion budget gap. Google Ireland licenses its search and advertising technology from Google headquarters in Mountain View, California. The licensing agreement allows Google to attribute its overseas profits to its Irish operations instead of the United States, where most of the technology was developed. The subsidiary is supposed to pay an arm's-length price for the rights, or the same amount an unrelated company would. Yet, because licensing fees from the Irish subsidiary generate income that is taxed at 35 percent, one of the highest corporate rates in the world, Google has an incentive to set the licensing price as low as possible. The effect is to shift some of its profits overseas in an arrangement known as transfer pricing. This, too, is legal. In 2006, the IRS approved Google's transfer pricing arrangements, which had begun in 2003, according to Google's SEC disclosures.

Transfer pricing arrangements are popular with technology and pharmaceutical companies in particular because they rely on intellectual property, which is easily transportable across borders. Facebook is preparing a structure similar to Google's that will send earnings from Ireland to the Cayman Islands, according to company filings and a person familiar with the arrangement. Microsoft and Forest Laboratories, maker of the blockbuster antidepressant Lexapro, have used a similar Irish–Bermuda transfer pricing arrangement.

The government has made halting steps to change the rules that let multinationals shift income overseas. The Treasury Department proposed levying taxes on certain payments between U.S. companies' foreign subsidiaries, potentially including Google's transfers from Ireland to Bermuda. The idea was dropped after Congress and Treasury officials were lobbied by companies including General Electric, Hewlett-Packard, and Starbucks, according to federal disclosures compiled by the nonprofit Center for Responsive Politics. In February 2010, the Obama administration proposed measures to curb companies' ability to shift profits offshore, but they have largely stalled.

SOURCES: "Cisco, Human Genome, Google, Viacom: Intellectual Property," *Businessweek*, November 03, 2011; and Jesse Drucker, "The Tax Haven That's Saving Google Billions," *Businessweek*, October 21, 2010.

Want a Lower Tax Bill? Just Google It

Google's elaborate international network allowed the company to cut its overseas tax rate to just 2.4% between 2007 and 2009.

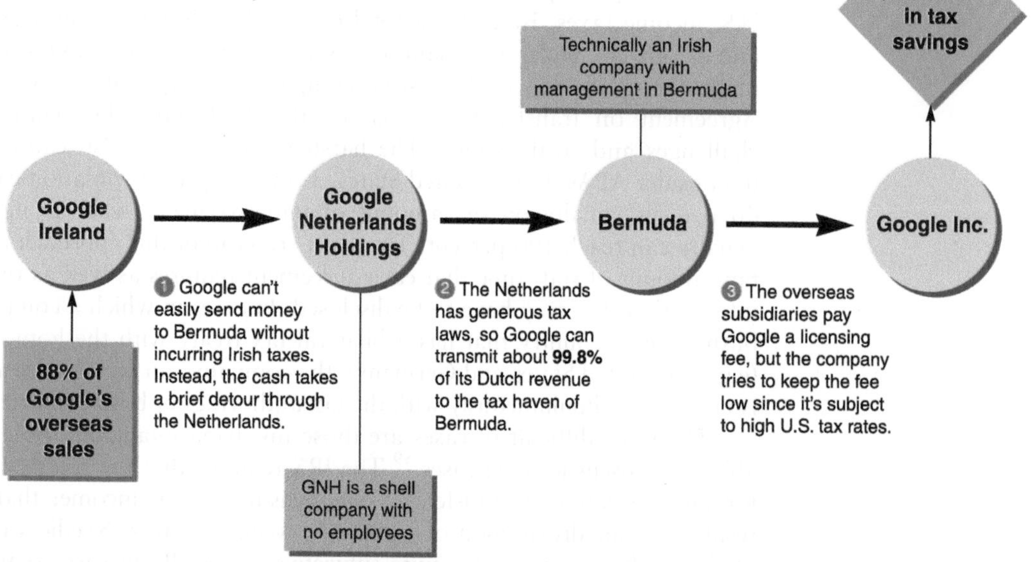

SOURCE: Jesse Drucker, "The Tax Haven That's Saving Google Billions," *Businessweek*, October 21, 2010. Used with permission of Bloomberg L.P. Copyright © 2012. All rights reserved.

COUNTERTRADE

Poland's use of defense offsets illustrates how a foreign government can use such arrangements to quickly advance the development of its industrial base. The $3.8 billion deal for F-16s between Lockheed Martin and the government of Poland included subcontracts with Polish firms to produce the Pratt & Whitney engine for the F-16 and commercial jet trainers as well as parts for business aircraft like the Gulfstream and Piper, which would then be exported by Poland back to the United States. The offset package also included a partnership with the University of Texas to start a technology accelerator at the University of Lodz.[61]

Countertrade conditions that support such business activities are a lack of money, lack of value of money, lack of acceptability of money as an exchange medium, or greater ease of transaction by using goods. However, the shrinking of established markets and the existence of a substantial product surplus are also conditions that foster countertrade.

These same reasons prevail in today's resurgence of countertrade activities. By 1983, the countries conducting countertrade transactions numbered 88; by 2011, the number was 130.[62] Estimates of the total global countertrade volume vary widely. The United Nations estimates that countertrade transactions make up about 10 percent of world trade.[63]

Why Countertrade?

Many countries are deciding that countertrade transactions are more beneficial to them than transactions based on financial exchange alone. A primary reason is that world debt crises and exchange rate volatility have made ordinary trade financing very risky. Many in the developing world cannot obtain the trade credit or financial assistance necessary to afford desired imports.

The use of countertrade permits the covert reduction of prices and therefore allows firms and governments to circumvent price and exchange controls. Particularly in commodity markets with operative cartel arrangements, such as oil or agriculture, this benefit may be very useful to a producer. For example, by using oil as a countertraded product for industrial equipment, a surreptitious discount (by using a higher price for the acquired products) may expand market share.

Countertrade is also often viewed by firms and nations alike as an excellent mechanism to gain entry into new markets. When a producer believes that marketing is not its strong suit or that international competition is too strong, it often sees countertrade as useful. The producer often hopes that the party receiving the goods will serve as a new distributor, opening up new international marketing channels and ultimately expanding the original market. Conversely, markets with little cash can provide major opportunities for firms if they are willing to accept countertrade. A firm that welcomes countertrade welcomes new buyers and sets itself apart from the competition.

Countertrade also can provide stability for long-term sales. For example, if a firm is tied to a countertrade agreement, it will need to source the product from a particular supplier, whether or not it wants to do so. This stability is often highly valued because it eliminates, or at least reduces, vast swings in demand and thus allows for better planning.

Under certain conditions, countertrade can ensure the quality of an international transaction. In instances where the seller of technology is paid in output produced by the technology delivered, the seller's revenue depends on the success of the technology transfer and maintenance services in production. Therefore, the seller is more likely to be dedicated in the provision of services, maintenance, and general technology transfer. China has extensively used offset agreements to obtain technology from American and European aerospace firms to build up China's aviation and aerospace industry so that it can independently manufacture its own aerospace products and insisted that portions of commercial passenger jets be manufactured and assembled in China as a condition of purchasing them.[64]

Types of Countertrade

Under the traditional types of barter arrangements, goods are exchanged directly for other goods of approximately equal value. However, simple barter transactions are less often used today.

Increasingly, participants in countertrade have resorted to more sophisticated versions of exchanging goods that often also include some use of money. Exhibit 14.12 provides an overview of the different forms of countertrade that are in use today. One refinement of simple barter is the counterpurchase, or parallel barter, agreement. The participating parties sign two separate contracts that

EXHIBIT 14.12 Classification of Forms of Countertrade

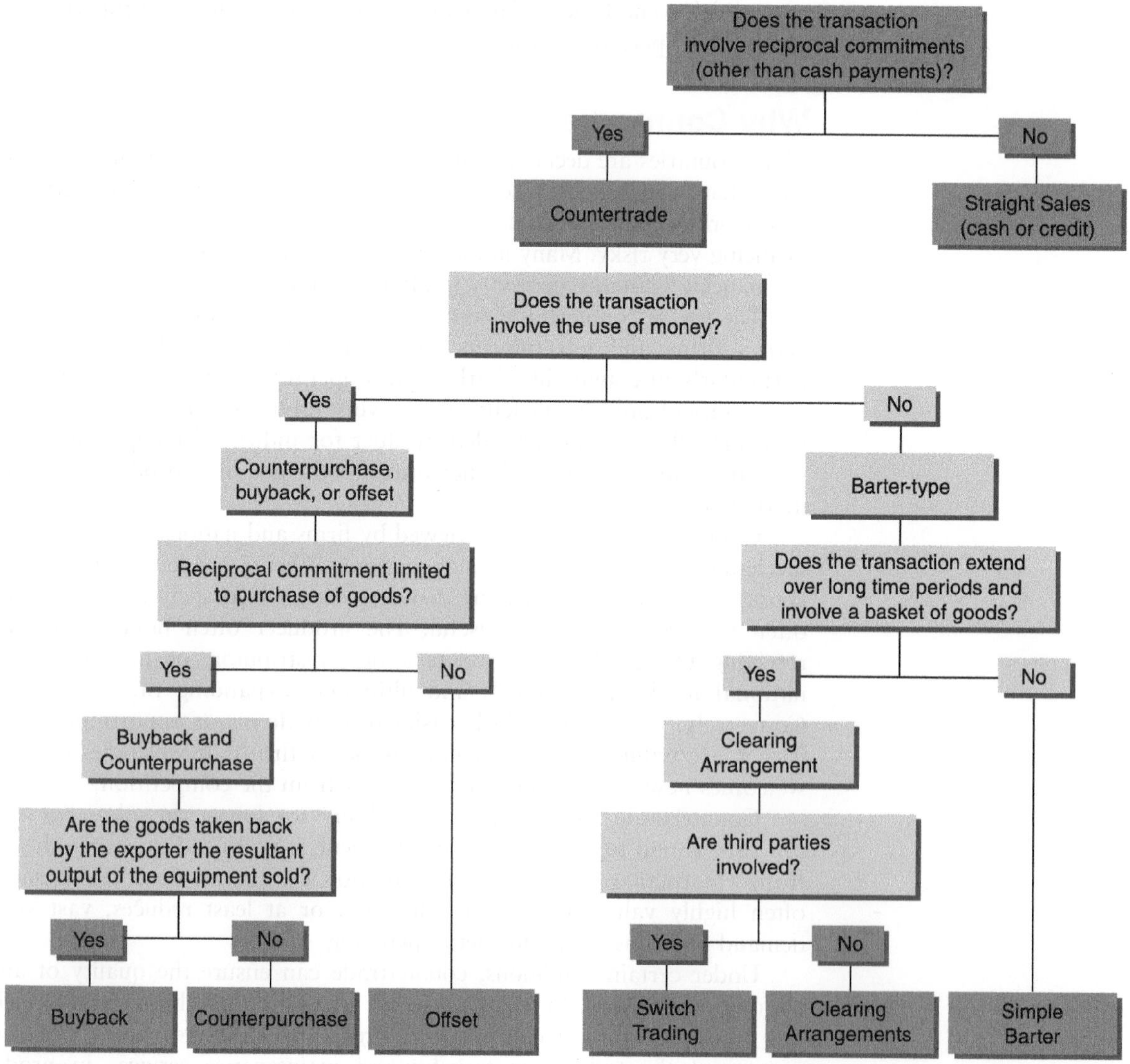

SOURCE: Adapted from Jean-François Hennart, "Some Empirical Dimensions of Countertrade," *Journal of International Business Studies* 21, no. 2 (1990): 245.

specify the goods and services to be exchanged. Frequently, the exchange is not of precisely equal value; therefore, some amount of cash will be involved. However, because an exchange of goods for goods does take place, the transaction can rightfully be called barter.

Another common form of countertrade is the buyback, or compensation, arrangement. One party agrees to supply technology or equipment that enables the other party to produce goods with which the price of the supplied products or technology is repaid. One example of such a buyback arrangement is an agreement entered into by Levi Strauss and Hungary. The company transferred the know-how and the Levi's trademark to Hungary. A Hungarian firm began producing Levi's products and marketing some of them domestically. The rest are marketed abroad by Levi Strauss in compensation for the know-how.

A more refined form of barter, aimed at reducing the effect of the immediacy of the transaction, is called clearing arrangements. Here, clearing accounts are established in which firms can deposit and withdraw the results of their countertrade activities. These currencies merely represent purchasing power, however, and are not directly withdrawable in cash. As a result, each party can agree in a single contract to purchase goods or services of a specified value. Although the account may be out of balance on a transaction-by-transaction basis, the agreement stipulates that over the long term a balance in the account will be restored. Frequently, the goods available for purchase with clearing account funds are tightly stipulated. In fact, funds have on occasion been labeled "apple clearing dollars" or "horseradish clearing funds." Additional flexibility can be given to the clearing account by permitting switch-trading, in which credits in the account can be sold or transferred to a third party. Doing so can provide creative intermediaries with opportunities for deal making by identifying clearing account relationships with major imbalances and structuring business transactions to reduce them.

Another key form of barter arrangement is called offset, which is the industrial compensation mandated by governments when purchasing defense-related goods and services in order to offset or counterbalance the effect of this purchase on the balance of payments. Offsets can include coproduction, licensed production, subcontractor production, technology transfer, or overseas investment. Typically, in order to secure the sale of military equipment, the selling companies have to offset the cost of the arms through investment in nonrelated industries. The offsets frequently reach or exceed the price of the defense equipment, to the delight of the buyer but often to the chagrin of the home country government of the selling firms. U.S. weapons exporters alone are estimated to complete about $4 to $7 billion annually in defense offset transactions, which, according to some, may over time strengthen foreign competitors and adversely affect employment.[65]

SUMMARY

The status of price has changed to that of a dynamic element in the marketing mix. This has resulted from both internal and external pressures on business firms. Management must analyze the interactive effect that pricing has on the other elements of the mix and how pricing can assist in meeting the overall goals of the marketing strategy.

The process of setting an export price must start with the determination of an appropriate cost baseline and should include variables such as export-related costs to avoid compromising the desired profit margin. The quotation needs to spell out the respective responsibilities of the buyer and the seller in getting the goods to the intended destination.

Pricing decisions are typically left to the local managers; however, planning assistance is provided by the parent company. Pricing in individual markets comes under the influence of environmental variables, with each market having its own unique set.

Transfer pricing concerns are both internal and external to the company. Internally, manipulating transfer prices may complicate control procedures and documentation. Externally, problems arise from the tax and regulatory entities of the countries involved.

The individual impact of these environmental variables and their interaction must be thoroughly understood by the global marketer, especially if regional or even worldwide coordination is attempted. Control and coordination are becoming more important with increasing economic integration.

KEY TERMS

skimming
market pricing
penetration pricing
standard worldwide price
dual pricing
cost-plus method
marginal cost method
market-differentiated pricing
price escalation
value-added tax (VAT)
duty drawbacks
Incoterms
cash in advance
letter of credit
draft
documentary collection
banker's acceptance
discounting
open account
consignment selling
commercial risk
political risk
forward market exchange
option
future
pass-through
absorption
pricing-to-market
price manipulation
forfaiting
factoring
price elasticity of consumer demand
price controls
arm's-length price
countertrade
barter
counterpurchase
buyback
clearing arrangement
switch-trading
offset

QUESTIONS FOR DISCUSSION

1. What are the implications of price escalation?
2. The standard worldwide base price is most likely looked on by management as full-cost pricing, including an allowance for manufacturing overhead, general overhead, and selling expenses. What factors are overlooked?
3. Suggest different importer reactions to a price offer and how you, as an exporter, could respond to them.
4. Comment on the pricing philosophy, "Sometimes price should be wrong by design."
5. The arm's-length principle of transfer pricing states that the amount charged by one related party to another for a given product must be the same as if the parties were not related. What would a product cost if transacted by unrelated parties?
6. Discuss the advantages and drawbacks of countertrade.

INTERNET EXERCISES

1. The European Union promotes the benefits of the euro as a common currency for the 17 EU nations that have adopted it (see http://ec.europa.eu/economy_finance/euro/index_en.htm). What are possible disadvantages of it?
2. Compare the services of the Global Offset and Countertrade Organization (www.globaloffset.org) and the Asia-Pacific Countertrade Association (http://apca.net).

CHALLENGE US

Just Swipe It

Ordering food has not changed for 30 to 40 years. Now, McDonald's is ready to change how you pay for your Happy Meal in Europe with touch screens and swipe cards. They will also be revamping their menu and introducing longer opening hours to make it easier for their customers and improve efficiency. McDonald's is also looking forward to harvesting more information about their customers' ordering habits. The people of the United Kingdom will shortly be able to swipe their Visa debit cards as simply as their Oyster cards. (The Oyster card is a form of electronic ticketing used on public transport services within the Greater London area of the United Kingdom.) They may also introduce roving waiters with handheld terminals to assist customers with extra products such as ice cream cones without them having to return to the till. This move has been triggered by the pervasive use of technology in Japan, whose citizens currently use their mobile phone for tickets.

On the bright side, (1) you will not have to repeat your order several times, (2) you can get a McDonald's meal without having cash in your wallet, and (3) the ordering process will speed up, thereby reducing the lines. On the not-so-bright side, (1) expect thousands to lose their jobs, and (2) McDonald's may act like Google and log, monitor, and do analytics of your buying behavior.

At a time when many retail and consumer companies are racking up sluggish or even shrinking sales in Europe, McDonald's like-for-like sales rose 5.7 percent year-on-year in the first quarter and McDonald's North American sales were up 2.9 percent in 2011—the highest growth out of its three main geographic regions. McDonald's reduced the locations in Europe, but the U.S. company is looking for 50,000 new employees.

© RICK WILKING/Reuters/Landov

For Discussion

1. McDonald's new system could face criticism in a sensitive time just months from a global recession when people are still struggling to find jobs. Why?
2. There is no word yet on whether or not McDonald's plans to bring the technology to North America. Why?

SOURCES: Louise Lucas, "McDonald's to Introduce Swipe Cards to Europe," *Financial Times*, May 16, 2011, B4; and Irwin Allen Rivera, "McDonald's goes hi-tech: touch the screen to order, swipe card to pay," May 17th, 2011, http://technoodling.net/mcdonalds-goes-hi-tech-touch-the-screen-to-order-swipe-card-to-pay.

RECOMMENDED READINGS

Ancheoli, Brian, Mark Levey, and Kenneth Parker. *Tax Director's Guide to International Transfer Pricing*. Newton, MA: GBIS, 2008.

Bureau of Industry and Security, U.S. Department of Commerce. *Offsets in Defense Trade, 15th Annual Report*. Washington, DC: December 2010.

Contino, Richard M., and Tony Valmis, eds. *Handbook of Equipment Leasing: A Deal Maker's Guide*. New York: AMACOM, 2006.

Czinkota, Michael R., and Ilkka A. Ronkainen, *Global Business: Positioning Ventures Ahead*. New York: Routledge, 2010.

Hart, Rupert M. *Recession Storming: Thriving in Downturns through Superior Marketing, Pricing, and Product Strategies*. Scotts Valley, CA: Create Space, 2008.

Holden, Reed and Mark Burton. *Pricing with Confidence: 10 Ways to Stop Leaving Money on the Table*. New York: Wiley, 2008.

Li, Jian, and Alan Paisey. *International Transfer Pricing*. New York: Palgrave McMillan, 2008.

Silicon Valley Bank. *A Guide and Overview to Export Financing*. 2009.

U.S. Department of Commerce. *A Basic Guide to Exporting*, 10th edition. Washington DC: International Trade Administration, 2011.

Zale, Joseph, Thomas Nagle, and John Hogan, *Strategy and Tactics of Pricing*. Englewood Cliffs, NJ: Prentice Hall, 2011.

ENDNOTES

1. Julian Birkinshaw, Cyril Bouquet, and Jean-Louis Barsoux, "The 5 Myths of Innovation," *MIT Sloan Management Review*, Winter 2011, 43–50; and Shantanu Dutta, Mark Bergen, Daniel Levy, Mark Ritson, and Mark Zbaracki, "Pricing as a Strategic Capability," *Sloan Management Review* 43 (Spring 2002): 61–66.
2. Julie Demers, "Enhanced Export Pricing Strategies," *CMA Management* 77 (June/July 2003): 52–53.
3. JLG, www.jlg.com.
4. Mei Fong, "IKEA Hits Home in China," *Wall Street Journal*, March 3, 2006, B1.
5. Matthew Myers, S. Tamer Cavusgil, and Adamantios Diamantopoulos, "Antecedents and Actions of Export Pricing Strategy: A Conceptual Framework and Research Propositions," *European Journal of Marketing* 36, nos. 1/2 (2002): 159–89.
6. James C. Anderson, Marc J. F. Wouters, and Wouter van Rossum, "Why the Highest Price Isn't the Best Price," *MIT Sloan Management Review*, Winter 2010, 67–76.
7. Howard Forman and Richard A. Lancioni, "International Industrial Pricing Strategic Decisions and the Pricing Manager: Some Key Issues," *The Journal of Professional Pricing*, http://members.pricingsociety.com/articles/international-industrial-pricing.pdf.
8. Chiranjeev Kohli and Rajneesh Suri, "The Price Is Right? Guidelines for Pricing to Enhance Profitability," *Business Horizons*, November/December 2011, 563–73.
9. Joseph Zale, Thomas T. Nagle, and Reed K. Holden, *The Strategy and Tactics of Pricing: A Guide to Profitable Decision Making* (Englewood Cliffs, NJ: Prentice Hall, 2011), chapter 3.
10. Luis Felipe Lages and David B. Montgomery, "Effects of Export Assistance on Pricing Strategy Adaptation and Export Performance," *MSI Reports*, issue 3 (2004): 67–88.
11. Barbara Stöttinger, "Strategic Export Pricing: A Long and Winding Road," *Journal of International Marketing* 9, no. 1 (2001): 40–63.
12. Geochron, www.geochron.com.
13. FedEx, www.fedex.com/us/services/ftn/drawback.html; and U.S. Customs and Border Protection, www.cbp.gov.
14. International Chambers of Commerce, *Incoterms 2010* (Paris: ICC Publishing, 2010). See also ICC, www.iccwbo.org.
15. Kevin Reilly, "Exporters Must Ensure Coordination of Incoterms and Documentary Requirements for LC Payment," *Business Credit* 107, no. 6 (2005): 48–50.
16. Edward G. Hinkelman, *Dictionary of International Trade* (Novato, CA: World Trade Press, 2008), chapter 10.
17. Silicon Valley Bank, Trade Finance Guide, www.svb.com/pdfs/TradeFinanceGuide.pdf.
18. Claude Cellich, "Business Negotiations: Making the First Offer," *International Trade Forum* 14, no. 2 (2000): 12–16.
19. John Humphrey, "Are Exporters in Africa Facing Reduced Availability of Trade Finance?" (Brighton, UK: Institute of Development Studies, March 2009).
20. David K. Eiteman, Arthur I. Stonehill, and Michael H. Moffett, *Multinational Business Finance* (Reading, MA: Addison-Wesley, 2009), 460–88.
21. International Chamber of Commerce, *Uniform Customs and Practice for Documentary Credits* (New York: ICC Publishing Corp., 2002).
22. Erika Morphy, "Paper's Last Stand," *Global Business*, May 2001, 36–39.
23. TradeCard, www.tradecard.com.
24. Coface, www.coface.com.
25. TCMGroup, http://tcmgroup.com.
26. Guido Schultz, "Foreign Exchange Strategies for Coping with Currency Volatility," *World Trade*, January 2005, 10.
27. Andrew Atkeson and Ariel Burstein, "Pricing-to-Market, Trade Costs, and International Relative Prices," UCLA, January 2008, 1–51; and Paul R. Krugman, "Pricing-to-Market When the Exchange Rate Changes," in *Real-Financial Linkages among Open Economies*, ed. S. W. Arndt and J. D. Robinson (Cambridge, MA: MIT Press, 1987), 49–70.
28. Woei Lo, Han-Jen Niu, Chyan Yang, and Yau-De Wang, "Determinants of Manufacturing Location in China: An Examination of Taiwan-invested Electronics Assembly Plants," *Journal of Contemporary Asia*, November 2010, 638–55.
29. Commerzbank, www.commerzbank.com.
30. Paula L. Green, "In with the Old," *Global Finance*, October 2011, 126–27.
31. Hannah Clark Steiman, "Short on Cash?" *Inc.*, January 2008, 52.
32. The authors acknowledge the assistance of Craig O'Connor of the Export-Import Bank of the United States.
33. Global Insight Advisory Services Group, *The Economic Contribution of Equipment Leasing to the U.S. Economy*, July 25, 2005, 4. See also www.ELFA.online.org.
34. El Camino Resources International Inc., www.fundinguniverse.com/company-histories/El-Camino-Resources-International-Inc-Company-History.html.
35. Kent B. Monroe, *Pricing: Making Profitable Decisions* (New York: McGraw-Hill, 2003), 12.
36. Ranjay Gulati and James B. Oldroyd, "The Quest for Customer Focus," *Harvard Business Review* 83 (April 2005): 92–101.
37. Beth Snyder Bulik, "2011 Marketer A-list: Samsung," *Advertising Age*, November 7, 2011, 28.
38. "The China Price," *Business Week*, December 6, 2004, 102–12.
39. Caterpillar, "What the World Needs," www.caterpillar.com/cda/files/2674611/7/FullReport_FINAL.pdf.
40. Mark Bernstein, "Expanding Capacity while Facing Global Pricing Puts Cummins' Supply Chain to the Test," *World Trade*, February 2006, 34–36.
41. "Global Survey of Business Executives: Inflation and Pricing," *McKinsey Quarterly*, April 2005.
42. Cameron McWhirter and Laurie Burkitt, "In China, the Pen Is Mightier When It's Pricier," *Wall Street Journal*, November 2, 2011, B12.
43. NUMMI, www.insidebayarea.com/nummi.
44. Mark Ritson, "Should You Launch a Fighter Brand?" *Harvard Business Review* 87 (October 2009): 86–95.

45. Jamie Anderson and Costas Markides, "Strategic Innovation at the Base of the Pyramid," *MIT Sloan Management Review*, Fall 2007, 83–89.
46. C. K. Prahalad and Stuart L. Hart, "The Fortune at the Bottom of the Pyramid," *Strategy+Business* 7 (first quarter, 2002): 35–47.
47. "Wal-Mart Quits Retailers Group," *Advertising Age*, October 21, 2002, 16.
48. "Price Controls Hurting China's Pharmaceutical Industry," www.itv-asia.com/article/price-controls-hurting-china's-pharmaceutical-industry.
49. "Not What It Was: European Business Has Improved Out of Recognition," *Economist*, February 8, 2007.
50. OECD, "Transfer Pricing Guidelines for Multinational Enterprises and Tax Administrations," August 18, 2010.
51. Robert Feinschreiber, *Transfer Pricing Handbook* (New York: John Wiley & Sons, 2002), chapter 1; and Wagdy M. Abdallah, "How to Motivate and Evaluate Managers with International Transfer Pricing Systems," *Management International Review* 29 (1989): 65–71.
52. Ernst & Young, *Transfer Pricing 2007–2008 Global Surveys* (New York: Ernst & Young, November 2008), available at www.ey.com.
53. Robert Feinschreiber, *Transfer Pricing Handbook* (New York: John Wiley & Sons, 2002), chapter 2.
54. Caroline Silberztein, "Transfer Pricing: A Challenge for Developing Countries," *OECD Observer*, December 2009/January 2010, 29–31.
55. Wagdy Abdallah, "Global Transfer Pricing of Multinationals and E-Commerce in the 21st Century," *Multinational Business Review* 10 (Fall 2002): 62–71.
56. Robert Grosse, "Financial Transfers in the MNE: The Latin American Case," *Management International Review* 26 (1986): 33–44.
57. KPMG, *Corporate Tax Rate Survey 2010* (New York: KPMG, 2010), available at www.kpmg.com.
58. Internal Revenue Service, *APA Quarterly Report* (Washington, DC: Department of the Treasury, March 29, 2011).
59. Paul Burns, "U.S. Transfer Pricing Developments," *International Tax Review* 13, no. 4 (2002): 48–49.
60. Phillip Beutel, Steven Schwartz, and Bryan Ray, "Beware the Transfer Pricing Gap," *Managing Intellectual Property*, June 2005, 33–38.
61. Herrnstadt, Owen E., *Offsets and the Lack of a Comprehensive U.S. Policy: What Do Other Countries Know That We Don't?* EPI briefing paper. (Washington, DC: Economic Policy Institute, April 17, 2008).
62. APCA, www.apca.net.
63. United Nations, *Trade Facilitation and Electronic Commerce*, available at www.unescap.org/tid/publication/part_six2184.pdf.
64. U.S.-China Economic and Security Review Commission, *2008 Report to Congress*, One Hundred Tenth Congress, Second Session, Washington, DC: November 2008.
65. BIS, "Offsets in Defense Trade," www.bis.doc.gov/news/2011/15th_offsets_defense_trade_report.pdf.

CHAPTER 15

Global Distribution and Logistics

LEARNING OBJECTIVES

By the time you complete this chapter, you will be able to:

- Understand how channels can vary from direct, producer-to-consumer types to elaborate, multilevel channels employing many types of intermediaries.
- Define the term *channel design* and explain the impact of the length and width of the channel employed.
- Describe how to select, manage, and motivate individual channel members.
- Outline the process of buying and selling of products or services over electronic systems such as the Internet.
- Design and manage a system that controls the flow of materials into, through, and out of the international corporation.
- Understand the infrastructure, availability of modes, and shipping rules for international transportation and shipments.
- Design international inventory and storage to mitigate forecasted shortcomings and understand how inventory costs money to maintain.
- Coordinate logistics activities to achieve effectiveness.

THE INTERNATIONAL MARKETPLACE 15.1

Getting the Distribution Job Done in Latin America

Regional trade pacts and free trade are enabling companies both to consider entry and to reformulate their strategies in Latin America. The region, however, is not one homogeneous area (due to, for example, language differences), and three primary markets have emerged: Brazil, Mexico, and Argentina.

In the past, the infrastructure for effective and efficient distribution was largely missing. Underdeveloped and monopolistic distributor networks saw their primary jobs as distributing sales literature, cutting through red tape, and charging invariably high fees. Times are changing for these intermediaries, however. Outside competition has forced distributors to add value to what they do, for example by carrying inventory, providing specialized packaging, participating in the logistics infrastructure, handling shipments when they arrive, or otherwise serving the customers' needs. And if locals do not measure up, companies are willing to look for other solutions, such as using outside captive distribution systems or putting their own people in place.

There are no standard answers as to distribution system design. In many cases, companies have found that a mix of techniques yields the best results and allows greater responsiveness to customer requests, as shown by the following examples.

Motorola in Brazil

Motorola's subsidiary combines in-house systems with an independent distributor network. It uses an in-house sales force to service large manufacturing clients and major end users of its line of imported and domestic semiconductors and portable radios, as well as wireless telephones and pagers. Other customers are served through four large distribution firms. Subrepresentatives are contracted by distributors to provide coverage in areas where they do not have a direct presence. The company has determined that sales made via a distributor at this level are cheaper than direct sales. Distributors can offer fast delivery because in-house inventories are maintained.

AkzoNobel in Mexico

AkzoNobel Car Refinishes Americas has announced that it has bought out its joint-venture partner, Comex, to assume full responsibility for the marketing and distribution of the Sikkens, Lesonal, U-Tech, and Wanda brands in Mexico. During the 15-year joint-venture period, AkzoNobel solidified its presence and advanced refinish technologies with key businesses in the Mexican market. This has been achieved through a network of Comex concessionaries and more than 200 independent distributors.

The long and respected business history of Comex provided AkzoNobel with a solid foundation for establishing itself in the collision-repair industry in Mexico. Access to these products will be available through the current chain of Comex locations and the valued network of independent distributors. AkzoNobel has had significant success with a variety of clients including Toyota, General Motors, the Public Transportation System in Mexico City, and most recently AXA Insurance Company, which awarded Sikkens the status as the preferred paint brand for their affiliated nationwide body-shop network.

Eveready in Argentina

Battery makers sell a large share of their product through small retailers. In Argentina, which is one of the 160 countries in which Energizer and Eveready brands are available, kiosks are one of the most important outlets, and product turnover is high. Eveready reaches thousands of kiosks by selling to

Energizer battery billboards appear in foreign markets.

some 600 independent distributors throughout the country. Distributors are attracted to the firm because of the high product turnover rate and Eveready's strong name recognition. Eveready reaches distributors through a national shipping company that carries products to remote markets.

SOURCES: Motorola, www.motorola.com; AkzoNobel, www.akzonobel.com; Everready, www.eveready.com; and Energizer, www.energizer.com.ar/index.php?option=com_content&view=category&layout=blog&id=65&Itemid=167.

Channels of distribution provide the essential linkages that connect producers and customers. The links are intracompany and extracompany entities that perform a number of functions. Optimal distribution systems are flexible and are able to adjust to market conditions over both the short and long terms. Producers often rely on **intermediaries**, as seen in *The International Marketplace 15.1*, to facilitate the location of companies interested in distributing products.

A channel of distribution should be seen as more than a sequence of marketing institutions connecting producers and consumers; it should be a team working toward a common goal.[1] Too often intermediaries are mistakenly perceived as temporary market-entry vehicles and not the partners with whom marketing efforts are planned and implemented. The intermediary is often the de facto marketing arm of the producer or originator. In today's marketing environment, being close to customers—be they the final consumers or intermediaries—and solving their problems is vital to bringing about success. When its office supplies superstore customer kicked off a joint venture in Australia, 3M dispatched two employees to its Australian subsidiary to educate that division on the special needs of a superstore.

The decisions involved in the structuring and management of the channel of distribution are discussed first, including an evaluation of a distribution challenge presented by parallel imports. The chapter then includes a discussion of the steps needed in preparation for e-commerce.

The remainder of the chapter will focus on international logistics and supply chain management. We will concentrate on the linkages between the firm, its suppliers, and its customers, as well as transportation, inventory, packaging, and storage issues. The logistics management problems and opportunities that are particular to international marketing will also be highlighted.

CHANNEL STRUCTURE

A generalization of channel configurations for consumer and industrial products as well as services is provided in Exhibit 15.1. Channels can vary from direct, producer-to-consumer types to elaborate, multilevel channels employing many types of intermediaries, each serving a particular purpose. For example, Canadian software firms enter international markets by exporting directly from Canada (40 percent), by opening their own sales offices (14 percent), by entering into cooperative arrangements with other exporters (15 percent), by using a local distributor or a value-adding reseller (13 percent), or by a mixture of modes (17 percent).[2]

The channel system in which businesses have traditionally operated has enlarged and become more complex, with more customers, more stakeholders,

EXHIBIT 15.1 Channel Configuration

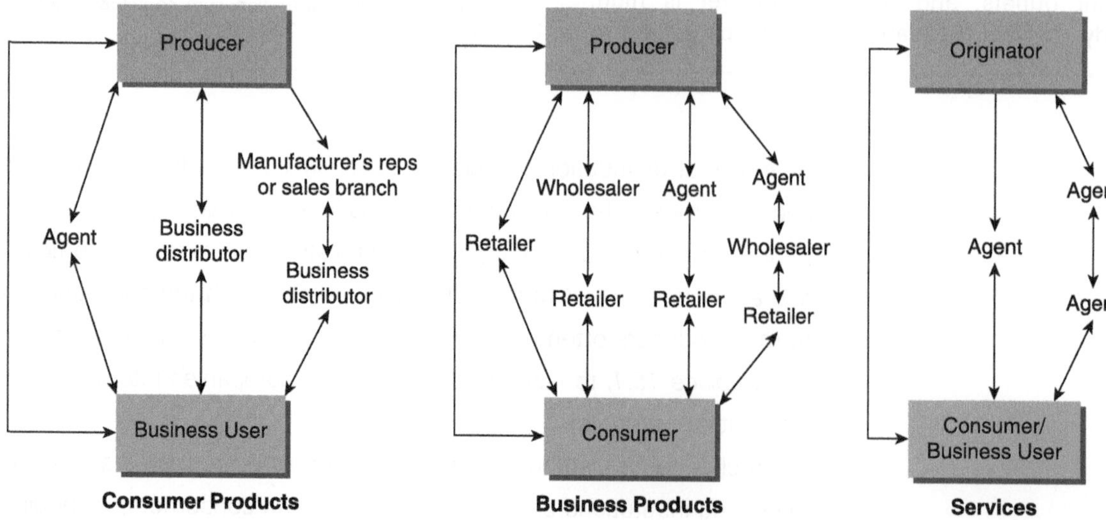

SOURCE: © Cengage Learning 2013.

and more competition spread across more geographic boundaries.[3] In order to help combat the growing complexity, businesses are employing techniques such as:

1. *Creating new bridges between producers and customers.* At Apple's iTunes Store, consumers can purchase over 10 million songs across every music genre. Similarly, retailers and individuals can find large international audiences for their niches using eBay's marketplace. Also, Nokia and Grameen Foundation provide mobile access to remote village communities. The "Village Phone" program, operating in Uganda and Rwanda, involves a local entrepreneur who acquires subscribers, an operator who offers services, and a microfinancier who procures a network access point that supports 70 Nokia handsets. The program can reduce the cost of owning a mobile phone to approximately US$3 per month.
2. *Harnessing customers' ideas, tastes and productive powers.* For example, Danish toy maker Lego has launched an online customization platform site—Design by Me—where enthusiasts assemble components for their own designs, which Lego makes available to other customers. Lego delivers to over 23 countries.
3. *Creating new forms of B2B commerce, including the emergence of specialist horizontal players.* Li & Fung, a multinational exporter for sourcing, distribution, and retail, now provides sophisticated procurement solutions. Acting like a primary global sourcing agent, it provides services for all Liz Claiborne labels, including Lucky Brand, Juicy Couture, and Kate Spade.
4. *Offering consumer-to-consumer (C2C) activity, where participants are sharing information in open, global online forums.* TripAdvisor's website, for example, offers individuals the opportunity to rate and talk about their experiences in hotels and restaurants around the world, giving the traveler a voice.
5. *Focusing on peer-to-peer (P2P), which offers a cooperative interaction among individuals rather than traditional sources of experience and trust.* Zopa, a UK-based company, provides online money exchange services, allowing people who have money to lend to those who wish to borrow it instead of to a traditional bank or lending institution.
6. *Engaging in cooperative consumption by groups of end consumers.* Shanghai-based Liba.com sells items mainly for young families, from building materials to baby products. It has more than four million members and 30,000 transactions on average every month.[4]

The connections made by marketing institutions are not solely for the physical movement of goods. They also serve as transactional title flows and informational communications flows. Rather than being unidirectional, downward from the producer, the flows are usually multidirectional, both vertical and horizontal. Agent intermediaries, for example, act only to facilitate the information flow; they do not take title and often do not physically handle the goods. Similarly, electronic intermediaries, such as Amazon.com, have to rely on facilitating agents to perform the logistics functions of their operation.

CHANNEL DESIGN

The term *channel design* refers to the length and width of the channel employed.[5] Channel design is determined by factors that can be summarized as the 11 Cs: customer, culture, competition, company, character, capital, cost, coverage, control, continuity, and communication. While there are no standard answers to channel design, the international marketer can use the 11 Cs as a checklist to determine the proper approach to reach target audiences before selecting channel members to fill the roles. The first three factors are given because the company must adjust its approach to the existing structures. The other eight are controllable to a certain extent by the marketers.

Customers

The demographic and psychographic characteristics of targeted customers will form the basis for channel-design decisions. Answers to questions such as what customers need as well as why, when, and how they buy are used to determine ways in which products should be made available to generate a competitive advantage. In the three rapidly growing cities of Mumbai, Rio de Janeiro, and Accra (Ghana), Nokia's design team set up open studios where members of the local community could sketch their dream phones. The team gleaned information on participants' tastes, styles, personalities, professions, religions, sense of heritage, and communities.

Culture

The marketer must analyze existing channel structures, or what might be called the **distribution culture** of a market. Many believed small retail players in Latin America would be swept away by the sector's consolidation and the rapid entry of new hypermarkets and supermarkets, as was the case in the United States and Europe, where small retailers have retained only 10 to 20 percent of the consumer packaged-goods market as large retailers have grown. So far, this has not occurred in Latin America. Small-scale, independent supermarkets and traditional stores together still account for between 45 and 61 percent of consumer-goods retailing in Latin American countries. For Curves International Inc. (owned and based in Woodway, Texas, which currently has over 7,000 fitness franchises worldwide), delivering customized marketing tools to Curves international franchisees has not changed—the scope and tools have. The franchises are now in nearly 90 markets, and each has a unique culture and language (see Exhibit 15.2), so Curves now has even more flexible, cost-effective, and dynamic solutions to offer to their franchisees.

EXHIBIT 15.2 Culturally Relevant Marketing Tools

SOURCE: Courtesy of Curves Inc.

Competition

Channels used by competitors may make up the only distribution system that is accepted both by the trade and by consumers. In this case, the international marketer's task is to use the structure more effectively and efficiently. Walmart's investments outside North America have had mixed results: its operations in the United Kingdom, South America, and China are highly successful, while it was forced to pull out of Germany and South Korea when ventures there were unsuccessful. An alternate strategy is to use a totally different distribution approach from the competition and hope to develop a competitive advantage in that manner, as IKEA has been able to do with its use of supermarketing concepts in furniture retail.

Company Objectives

Sometimes, management goals may conflict with the best possible channel design. Fast-food chains have typically rushed into newly opened markets to capitalize on the development. The companies have attempted to establish mass sales as soon as possible by opening numerous restaurants in the busiest sections of several cities. Unfortunately, control has proven to be quite difficult because of the sheer number of openings over a relatively short period of time. Starbucks invests very little capital in international expansion (less than 5 percent of revenue), and local partners bear all business risk.

Character

The type or *character* of the good will have an impact on the design of the channel. Rules of thumb aside, particular products may be distributed in a number of ways even to the same target audience for the PC industry. A dual channel may be used in which both intermediaries and a direct contact with customers are used. In some cases, a channel may extend beyond having one tier of distributors and resellers to include importers or agents. Another alternative—hybrid channels—features sharing of marketing functions, with the manufacturer handling promotion and customer generation and the intermediaries handling sales and distribution. The hybrid strategy is based more on cooperation and partnership, while the dual channel may result in conflict if disagreements arise as to who is to handle a specific customer. In either case, multiple channels are used to enhance sales performance in a foreign market.

Capital

The term *capital* is used to describe the financial requirements in setting up a channel system. The international marketer's financial strength will determine the type of channel and the basis on which channel relationships will be built. The stronger the marketer's finances, the more able the firm is to establish channels it either owns or controls. Intermediaries' requirements for beginning inventories, selling on a consignment basis, preferential loans, and need for training will all have an impact on the type of approach chosen by the international marketer. Coca-Cola, which usually visits its smallest retailers once or twice weekly, has proposed that these retailers receive three to four weeks of consigned inventory in return for exclusivity. When Coca-Cola returns at the end of the period, the retailers pay only for the product sold during that time. For cash-strapped small shop owners, this incentive is extremely attractive. Coca-Cola wins increased sales at the expense of displaced competition and a much lower cost-to-serve, with delivery visits cut by a factor of three or more.

Cost

Closely related to the capital dimension is *cost*—that is, the expenditure incurred in maintaining a channel once it is established. Costs will naturally vary over the life cycle of the relationship as well as over the life cycle of the product marketed. An example of the costs involved is promotional monies spent by a distributor for the marketer's product. Costs may also be incurred in protecting the company's distributors against adverse market conditions. A number of European manufacturers helped their distributors maintain competitive prices through subsidies when the high rate for the U.S. dollar caused pricing problems.[6]

Coverage

The term *coverage* is used to describe both the number of areas in which the marketer's products are represented and the quality of that representation. Coverage, therefore, is two-dimensional in that both horizontal and vertical coverage need to be considered in channel design. The number of areas to be covered depends on the dispersion of demand in the market and also the time elapsed since the product's introduction to the market. A company typically enters a market with one local distributor, but, as volume expands, the distribution base often has to be adjusted. Benetton's marketing strategy was abandoned because of concerns about oversaturation of certain urban areas and overprojection of retail sales. Rather, more emphasis is placed on customer service, and the number of stores in major North American cities totaled 50 in 2011.[7]

Control

The use of intermediaries will automatically lead to loss of some control over the marketing of the firm's products. The looser the relationship is between the marketer and the intermediaries, the less control can be exerted. The longer the channel, the more difficult it becomes for the marketer to have a final say over pricing, promotion, and the types of outlets in which the product will be made available. Sales at TaoBao, China's largest online retailer, have soared to more than $14 billion annually since it was launched in 2003. Lancome reports that its partnership with Baidu, China's largest search engine, helped lift online sales in China by 30 percent. And Amway has become one of China's largest consumer packaged-goods companies by selling its products door-to-door through a network of 300,000 sales representatives.[8]

Continuity

Nurturing continuity rests heavily on the marketer because foreign distributors may have a more short-term view of the relationship. An example is STIHL, a manufacturer of outdoor power equipment that has never sold its products through mass merchants. Instead, the company sells its innovative products through thousands of independently owned servicing dealers across the world. An industry global leader in both market share and profitability, STIHL continues to embrace its founding principle of only selling the company's products through servicing dealers.[9]

Communication

Proper communication performs important roles for the international marketer. It helps convey the marketer's goals to the distributors, helps solve conflict situations, and aids in the overall marketing of the product. Communication is a two-way process that does not permit the marketer to dictate to intermediaries. Sometimes the planned program may not work because of a lack of communication. Prices may not be competitive; promotional materials may be obsolete or inaccurate and not well received overall. It is for this reason that Dell formed the company Customer Experience Council, a group that scrutinizes every aspect of how Dell interacts with customers.[10] However, as seen in *The International Marketplace 15.2*, companies sometimes will take a risk and utilize their own channel strategies in markets.

THE INTERNATIONAL **MARKETPLACE** **15.2**

Tesco: Community Promises and Local Priorities

Based in the United Kingdom, Tesco is the world's third largest grocer, operating more than 3,900 stores in 14 countries. More than 60 percent of Tesco's sales space is now located outside the United Kingdom. The company made its first move abroad in 1994, when it set up in Hungary, followed by Poland, Slovakia, and the Czech Republic. In addition to becoming a clear winner in Eastern Europe, the company is now the market leader in Malaysia. Tesco also planned to double the number of Tesco Express stores in Turkey in 2008 and more than doubled its online grocery sales in South Korea—its second most profitable market—since 2007.

Multipolar Focus

Tesco set out a strategy to grow the core business and diversify with new products and services in existing and new markets. Some of their tactics included

- Partner with local players in emerging markets
- Cater to local shopping preferences
- Source talent globally, staff locally
- Deploy a global operating model for standardization efficiencies
- Pioneer sustainability initiatives

Use Joint Ventures to Enter New Markets

Tesco entered the US$270-billion-a-year grocery market in China in 2004 through a joint venture with Taiwan's Hymall, of which it now owns 90 percent. Today, Tesco operates 60 stores in China, with 95 percent of products sourced within the country. Global reach is key to local effectiveness: Tesco believes that in China it can use the experience it has gained from operating around the world to localize its food offerings better than its two major rivals. In India, Tesco partners with Trent (the retail arm of Tata) to establish wholesale cash-and-carry stores for retailers, restaurants, and caterers and to expand Trent's Star Bazaar hypermarkets by sharing know-how and technology. If current rules that restrict foreign ownership of retail outlets are relaxed in the future, Tesco expects to be well-positioned.

Tailor the Store Experience to Local Preferences

Tesco is highly flexible in its retailing format to respond to different consumer norms and tastes. Tesco entered the market not by opening hypermarkets but by acquiring a discount supermarket operator. The company's stores in Thailand seek to replicate the product selection experience of traditional street markets, with less emphasis on the neatly packaged portions found in many Western markets. Tesco sells live toads and

Tesco's Check-Outs Around the World

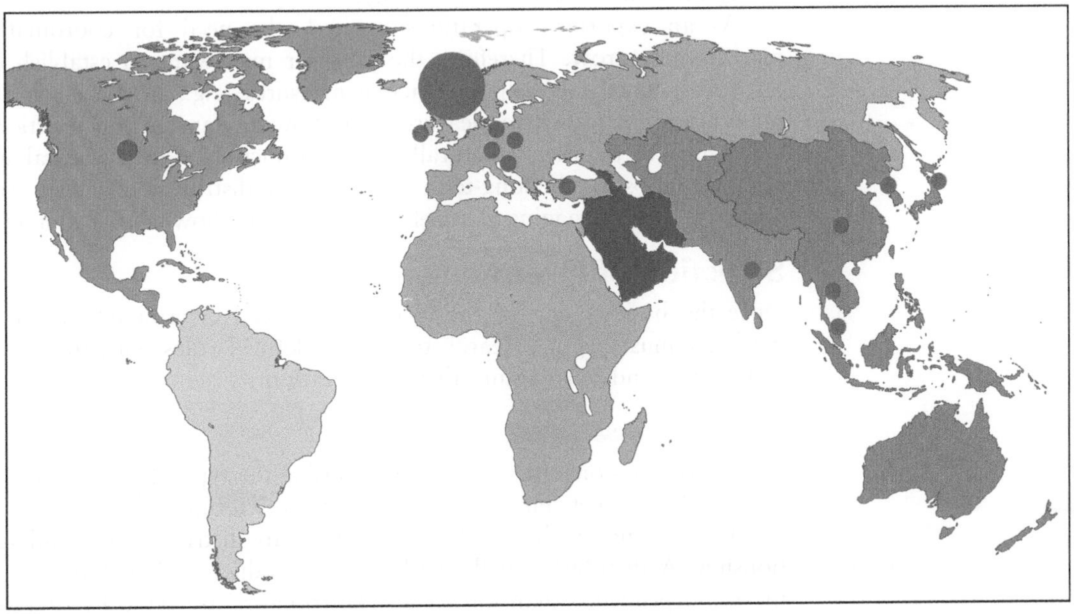

SOURCES: © Cengage Learning 2013; Based on *Telegraph*, http://s.telegraph.co.uk/graphics/hotspotgraphics/175tesco/assets/1390new-tesco-world.jpg.

turtles from tanks in Chinese stores, catering to consumers' preference for shopping in "wet" markets.

Look Locally—and Globally—to Overcome Talent Bottlenecks

Recruiting employees of the right caliber remains a challenge. Tesco views overseas growth as "not about putting flags down in countries, but about the quality of people." The company has filled 80 percent of managerial posts in China with people hired locally, consistent with its strategy of acclimatizing to each country and keeping down the number of expatriate employees. At the same time, the company has recruited MBA degree holders from Indian consulting firms to staff the global function charged with deploying Tesco's new global operating model around the world.

CHANNEL MANAGEMENT

A channel relationship can be likened to a marriage in that it brings together two independent entities that have shared goals.[11] For the relationship to work, each party must be clear about its expectations and openly communicate changes perceived in the other's behavior that might be contrary to the agreement. The closer the relationship is to a distribution partnership, the more likely marketing success will materialize. Conflict will arise, ranging from small grievances (such as billing errors) to major ones (rivalry over channel duties), but it can be managed to enhance the overall channel relationship. In some cases, conflict may be caused by an outside entity, such as gray markets, in which unauthorized intermediaries compete for market share with legitimate importers and exclusive distributors. Nevertheless, the international marketer must solve the problem.

The relationship has to be managed for the long term. An exporter may in some countries have a seller's-market situation that allows it to exert pressure on its intermediaries for concessions, for example. However, if environmental conditions change, the exporter may find that the channel support it needs to succeed is not there because of the manner in which it managed channel relationships in the past.[12] Firms with harmonious relationships are typically those with more experience abroad and those that are proactive in managing the channel relationship. Harmonious relationships are also characterized by more trust, communication, and cooperation between the entities and, as a result, by less conflict and perceived uncertainty.[13]

As an exporter's operations expand, the need for coordination across markets may grow. Therefore, the exporter may want to establish distributor advisory councils to help in reactive measures (e.g., how to combat parallel importation) or proactive measures (e.g., how to transfer best practice from one distributor to another). Naturally, such councils are instrumental in building esprit de corps for the long-term success of the distribution system. An excellent framework for managing channel relationships is shown in Exhibit 15.3.

Selection of Intermediaries

Once the basic design of the channel has been determined, the international marketer must begin a search to fill the defined roles with the best available candidates, and must secure their cooperation.

Types of Intermediaries

Two basic decisions are involved in choosing the type of intermediaries to serve a particular market. First, the marketer must determine the type of relationship to have with intermediaries. The alternatives are distributorship and agency relationship. A **distributor** will purchase the product and will therefore exercise more independence than an agency. Distributors are typically organized along product lines and provide the international marketer with complete marketing services. **Agents** have less freedom of movement than distributors because they

EXHIBIT 15.3 Performance Problems and Remedies When Using Overseas Distributors

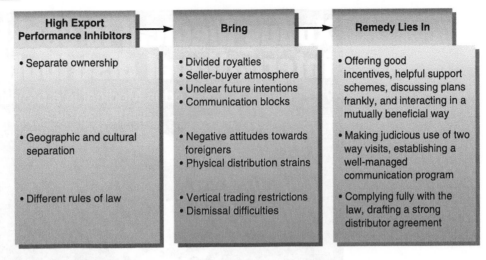

High Export Performance Inhibitors →	Bring →	Remedy Lies In
• Separate ownership	• Divided royalties • Seller-buyer atmosphere • Unclear future intentions • Communication blocks	• Offering good incentives, helpful support schemes, discussing plans frankly, and interacting in a mutually beneficial way
• Geographic and cultural separation	• Negative attitudes towards foreigners • Physical distribution strains	• Making judicious use of two way visits, establishing a well-managed communication program
• Different rules of law	• Vertical trading restrictions • Dismissal difficulties	• Complying fully with the law, drafting a strong distributor agreement

SOURCES: Based on Paul Matthyssens, Pieter Pauwels, and Lieven Quintens, "The Global Purchasing Challenge: A Look Back and a Look Ahead," *Journal of Purchasing & Supply Management* 12 (2006): 167–69; and Philip J. Rosson, "Success Factors in Manufacturer–Overseas Distributor Relationships in International Marketing," in *International Marketing Management*, ed. Erdener Kaynak (New York: Praeger, 1984), 91–107.

operate on a commission basis and do not usually physically handle the goods. This, in turn, allows the marketer control to make sure, for example, that the customer gets the most recent and appropriate product version. In addition to the business implications, the choice of type will have legal implications in terms of what the intermediary can commit its principal to and the ease of terminating of the agreement.

Governmental Agencies

The U.S. Department of Commerce has various services that can assist firms in identifying suitable representatives abroad. Macron Dynamics of Croydon, Pennsylvania, is a complete robotic automation system. For many years, Macron conducted business in Canada through a sole distributor of its products. Macron utilized the Gold Key Matchmaking Service from U.S. Commercial Service (CS) to meet with prescreened distributors and identify a selling agent for Macron products in Mexico. Since 2009, the company has received ongoing CS support to identify distribution channels and selling agents in India, the United Kingdom, Australia, New Zealand, and Mexico and to qualify customers who contact the company unsolicited through the Internet.[14] *Commercial News USA* is a catalog-magazine distributed worldwide six times each year featuring advertisements by U.S. producers. Both sources help producers find export partners and locate export companies, freight forwarders, and other service firms that can facilitate export business. The print version of the magazine reaches more than one-quarter million readers in 178 countries. The North Dakota Trade Office is dedicated to expanding trade opportunities for the mutual benefit of global companies and their worldwide customers and business partners. In 2011, the program brought 40 intercontinental guests to international farmers and agribusiness leaders. In Colombia, Proexport is the entity that promotes international tourism, foreign investment, and nontraditional exports to 18 offices around the world.[15]

Private Sources

The marketer can take an even more direct approach to finding intermediaries by buying space in a source to solicit representation. Advertisements typically indicate the type of support the marketer will be able to give to its distributor. An example of an advertisement for intermediaries placed in a trade medium is

EXHIBIT 15.4 Advertisement for an Intermediary

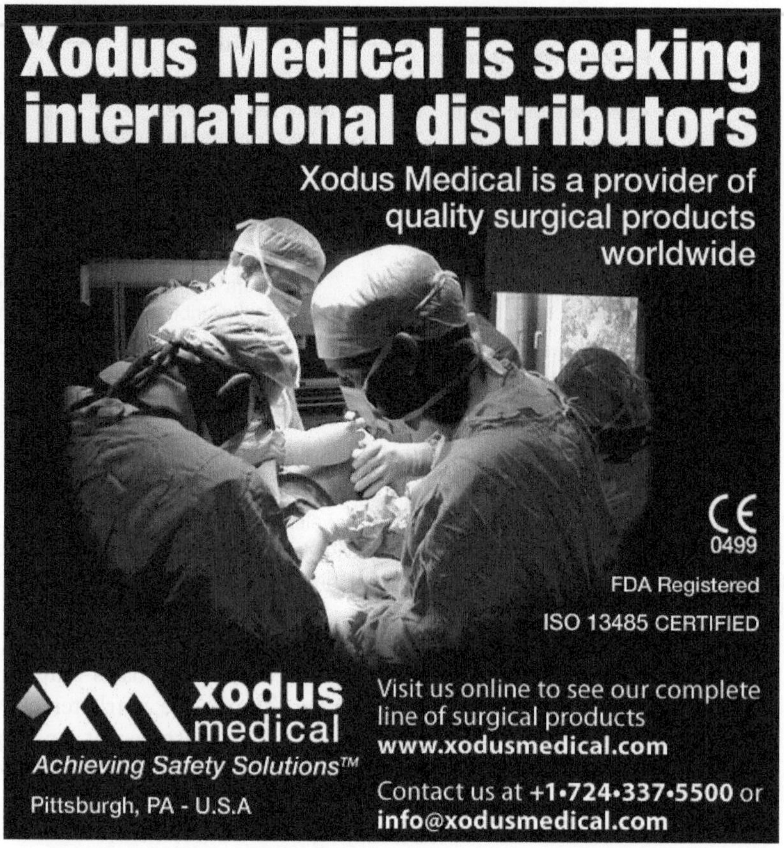

SOURCE: Courtesy of Xodus Medical, Inc.

provided in Exhibit 15.4. Xodus Medical, Inc., a privately held corporation, manufactures medical and surgical products that provide innovative solutions for use in hospital operating rooms and surgery centers. In the past, Xodus developed—and continues to foster—business relationships with medical distributors around the world. All of the company's international distributors are experiencing double-digit growth with Xodus products.[16]

Trade fairs are an important forum to meet potential distributors and to get data on intermediaries in the industry. Increasingly, marketers are using their own websites to attract international distributors and agents. The marketer may also deal directly with contacts from previous applications, launch new mail solicitations, use its own sales organization for the search, or communicate with existing customers to find prospective distributors. The latter may happen after a number of initial (unsolicited) sales to a market, causing the firm to want to enter the market on a more formal basis. If resources permit, the international marketer can use outside service agencies or consultants to generate a list of prospective representatives. For example, interest in China may warrant contacting the American Chamber of Commerce in Beijing, Hong Kong, or Shanghai.

The Distributor Agreement

When the international marketer has found a suitable intermediary, a sales agreement is drawn up.[17] The checklist presented in Appendix 15A is the most comprehensive in stipulating the nature of the contract and the respective rights and responsibilities of the marketer and the distributor.

Contract duration is important, especially when an agreement is signed with a new distributor. In general, distribution agreements should be for a specified, relatively short period (one or two years). The initial contract with a new distributor should stipulate a trial period of either three or six months, possibly with minimum purchase requirements. Duration should be determined with an eye on the local laws and their stipulations on distributor agreements. These will be discussed later in conjunction with distributor termination.[18]

Geographic boundaries for the distributor should be determined with care, especially by smaller firms. Future expansion of the product market might be complicated if a distributor claims rights to certain territories. The marketer should retain the right to distribute products independently, reserving the right to certain customers. For example, many marketers maintain a dual distribution system, dealing directly with certain large accounts. This type of arrangement should be explicitly stated in the agreement. Transshipments, or sales to customers outside the agreed-upon territory or customer type, have to be explicitly prohibited to prevent the occurrence of parallel importation.

The payment section of the contract should stipulate the methods of payment as well as how the distributor or agent is to draw compensation. Distributors derive compensation from various discounts, such as the functional discount, whereas agents earn a specific commission percentage of net sales (such as 15 percent). Given the volatility of currency markets, the agreement should also state the currency to be used. The international marketer also needs to make sure that none of the compensation forwarded to the distributor is in violation of the Foreign Corrupt Practices Act or the OECD guidelines. A violation occurs if a payment is made to influence a foreign official in exchange for business favors, depending on the nature of the action sought. So-called grease or facilitating payments, such as a small fee to expedite paperwork through customs, are not considered violations.

The product and conditions of sale need to be agreed on. The products or product lines included should be stipulated, as well as the functions and responsibilities of the intermediary in terms of carrying the goods in inventory, providing service in conjunction with them, and promoting them. Conditions of sale determine which party is to be responsible for some of the expenses involved, which will in turn have an effect on the price to the distributor. These conditions include credit and shipment terms.

Effective means of communication between the parties must be stipulated in the agreement if a marketer–distributor relationship is to succeed. The marketer should have access to all information concerning the marketing of his or her products in the distributor's territory, including past records, present situation assessments, and marketing research concerning the future. Communication channels should be formal for the distributor to voice formal grievances. The contract should state the confidentiality of the information provided by either party and protect the intellectual property rights (such as patents) involved.

Gray Markets

Gray markets, or parallel importation, refer to authentic and legitimately manufactured trademark items that are produced and purchased abroad but imported or diverted to the market by bypassing designated channels. The IT industry estimates that gray market sales of IT products account for over $40 billion in revenue each year, collectively costing IT manufacturers up to $5 billion annually in lost profits.[19] Gray-marketed products vary from inexpensive consumer goods (such as chewing gum) to expensive capital goods (such as excavation equipment). The phenomenon is not restricted to the United States; Japan, for example, has witnessed gray markets because of the high value of the yen and the subsidization of cheaper exports through high taxes. Japanese marketers thus often found it cheaper to go to Los Angeles to buy export versions of Japanese-made products.

EXHIBIT 15.5 Gray Market

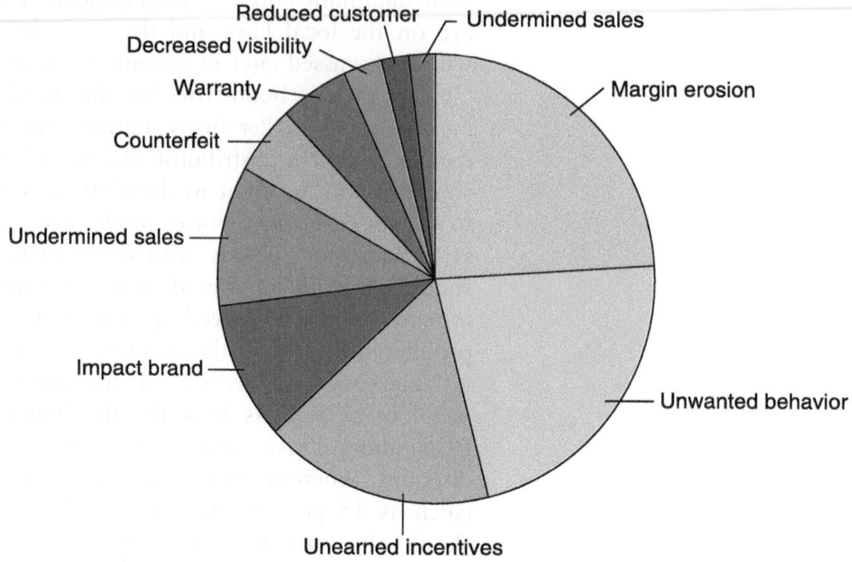

SOURCE: Deloitte, "When Channel Incentives Backfire: Strategies to Help Reduce Gray Market Risks and Improve Profitability," 2011. Reprinted with permission.

Various conditions allow unauthorized resellers to exist (e.g., Exhibit 15.5). The most important are price segmentation and exchange-rate fluctuations. Competitive conditions may require the international marketer to sell essentially the same product at different prices in different markets or to different customers.[20] Because many products are priced higher in, for example, the United States, a gray marketer can purchase them in Europe or the Far East and offer discounts between 10 and 40 percent below list price when reselling them in the U.S. market. Exchange-rate fluctuations can cause price differentials and thus opportunities for gray marketers.

Opponents and supporters of the practice disagree on whether the central issue is price or trade rights. Detractors typically cite the following arguments: (1) the gray market unduly hurts the legitimate owners of trademarks; (2) without protection, trademark owners will have little incentive to invest in product development; (3) gray marketers will "free ride" or take unfair advantage of the trademark owners' marketing and promotional activities; and (4) parallel imports can deceive consumers by not meeting product standards or their normal expectations of aftersale service.[21] The bottom line is that gray-market goods can severely undercut local marketing plans, erode long-term brand images, eat up costly promotion funds, and sour manufacturer–intermediary relations. The opponents scored a major victory when the European Court of Justice ruled in 2001 against Tesco, which imported cheap Levi's jeans from the United States and sold them at prices well below those of other retailers. The decision backed Levi's claim that its image could be harmed if it lost control of import distribution. Tesco can continue sourcing Levi's products within the EU from the cheapest provider, but not from outside it.[22]

Proponents of parallel importation approach the issue from an altogether different point of view. They argue for their right to free trade by pointing to manufacturers that are both overproducing and overpricing in some markets. The main beneficiaries are consumers, who benefit from lower prices, and discount distributors, with whom some of the manufacturers do not want to deal and who have now, because of gray markets, found a profitable market niche.

Gray markets attract consumers with high price sensitivities. However, given the price–quality inference, quality may become a concern for the consumers, especially if they do not have relevant information about the brand and the intermediary. In addition, risk aversion will have a negative influence on consumers' propensity to buy gray-market goods. The likelihood of obtaining a counterfeit version, a deficient guarantee, or no service are the foremost concerns.[23]

A one-price policy can eliminate one of the main reasons for gray markets. This means choosing the most efficient of the distribution channels through which to market the product, but it may also mean selling at the lowest price to all customers regardless of location and size. A meaningful one-price strategy must also include a way to reward the providers of other services, such as warranty repair, in the channel.

Other strategies have included producing different versions of products for different markets. For example, some electronics-goods companies are designing products so they will work only in the market for which they are designated. Some of the latest printers from Hewlett-Packard do not print if they are fed ink cartridges not bought in the same region as the printer. Nintendo's handheld game machines are sold in the United States with power adaptors that do not work in Europe.[24] Some companies have introduced price incentives to consumers. Hasselblad, the Swedish camera manufacturer, offers rebates to purchasers of legally imported, serial-numbered camera bodies, lenses, and roll-fill magazines. Many manufacturers promote the benefits of dealing with authorized dealers (and, thereby, the dangers of dealing with gray-market dealers). Many pharmaceutical companies and the U.S. Food and Drug Administration have embarked on educational and promotional campaigns to call attention to buying drugs from abroad via Internet pharmacies.[25]

Termination of the Channel Relationship

Many reasons exist for the termination of a channel relationship, but the most typical are changes in the international marketer's distribution approach (for example, establishing a sales office) or a (perceived) lack of performance by the intermediary. On occasion, termination may result from either party not honoring agreements, for example by selling outside assigned territories and initiating price wars.

Channel relationships go through a life cycle. The concept of an international distribution life cycle is presented in Exhibit 15.6. Over time, the

EXHIBIT 15.6 International Distribution Life Cycle

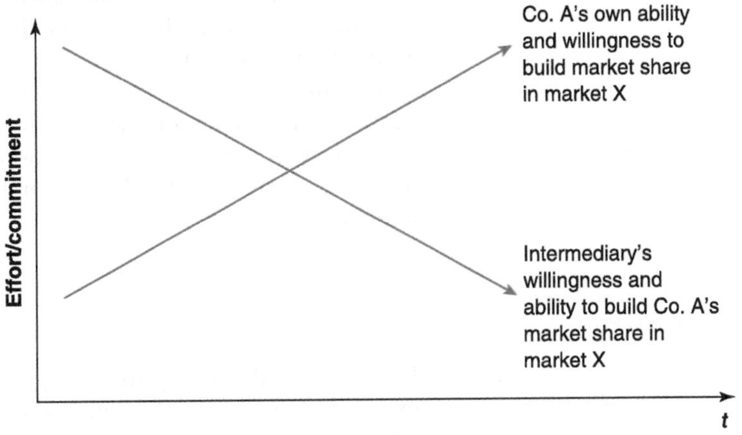

SOURCE: Framework courtesy of Professors David Arnold and John Quelch, Harvard Business School.

marketer's capabilities increase, while a distributor's ability and willingness to grow the business in that market decreases. When a producer expands its market presence, it may expect more of a distributor's effort than the distributor is willing to make available. Furthermore, with expansion, the marketer may want to expand its product line to items that the distributor is neither interested in nor able to support.

In some cases, intermediaries may not be interested in growing the business beyond a certain point (e.g., due to progressive taxation in the country) or as aggressively as the principal may expect (i.e., being more of an order-taker than an order-getter). As a marketer's operations expand, it may want to start to coordinate operations across markets for efficiency and customer-service reasons or to cater to global accounts—thereby needing to control distribution to a degree that independent intermediaries are not willing to accept, or requiring a level of service that they may not be able to deliver.

Independent distributors do remain long-run representatives of originators under certain circumstances. Some markets may not be considered strategic (e.g., due to size) or they may be culturally challenging (e.g., Saudi Arabia). The distributors may carry product lines that are complementary, thus enhancing the originator's efforts, and they may act more as partners by sharing information or undertaking originator-specific projects in their own or nearby markets to become "indispensable."[26]

If termination is a result of a structural change, the situation has to be handled carefully. The effect of termination on the intermediary has to be understood, and open communication is needed to make the transition smooth. For example, the intermediary can be compensated for investments made, and major customers can be visited jointly to assure them that service will be uninterrupted.

Termination conditions are one of the most important considerations in the distributor agreement because the just causes for termination vary and the penalties for the international marketer may be substantial. Just causes include fraud or deceit, damage to the other party's interest, or failure to comply with contract obligations concerning minimum inventory requirements or minimum sales levels. These must be spelled out carefully because local courts are often favorably disposed toward local businesses. In some countries, termination may not even be possible. In the EU and Latin America, terminating an ineffective intermediary is time-consuming and expensive. One year's average commissions are typical for termination without justification. A notice of termination has to be given three to six months in advance. In Austria, termination without just cause or failure to give notice of termination may result in damages amounting to average commissions for between 1 and 15 years.

The time to think about such issues is before the overseas distribution agreement is signed. It is especially prudent to find out what local laws say about termination and to check what type of experience other firms have had in the particular country. Careful preparation can allow the exporter to negotiate a termination without litigation. If the distributor's performance is unsatisfactory, careful documentation and clearly defined performance measures may help show that the distributor has more to gain by going quietly than by fighting.

E-COMMERCE

E-commerce, the ability to offer goods and services over the web, continues to experience rapid growth around the globe as Internet penetration has increased. Global Internet penetration grew at a rate of 409 percent from 2000 to 2011 with further penetration projected as relatively inexpensive mobile 3G devices allow more access in developing countries. The mobile market, in turn, has facilitated the growth of m-commerce, the exchange of goods and services via the use of smart mobile handheld devices that allow web browsing. In 2011, Internet penetration in North America exceeded all other regions at 78.3 percent, followed by Oceania/Australia at 60.1 percent and Europe at 58.3 percent. Latin America (36.2 percent), Asia (23.8 percent), and Africa (11.4 percent) lag behind, but Asia exceeds all other regions in Internet users with 42.6 percent of the worldwide total.[27]

Although many firms still use their websites as marketing and advertising tools without expanding them to order-taking capabilities, worldwide e-commerce revenue is projected to grow at an average rate of 18.9 percent between 2011 and 2013 with the fastest rates of growth occurring in Japan, Asia/Pacific, and in parts of the world outside of the United States and Western Europe.[28] The United States, however, is projected to remain the largest market for e-commerce, followed by Western Europe. Even so, the growth of U.S. e-commerce lags behind spending on online advertising. Global net e-commerce revenue is expected to reach $680 billion in 2011.[29]

Some companies elect to build their own international distribution networks. Both QVC, a televised shopping service, and Amazon.com, an online retailer, have their own distribution centers. For industries such as music and motion pictures, the Internet is both an opportunity and a threat. The web provides a new, efficient method of distribution and customization of products. However, the web can also be a channel for intellectual property violation through unauthorized posting and downloading on other sites. Currently companies lose tens of billions of dollars in sales each year due to such theft.

Many companies entering e-commerce choose to use marketplace sites, like eBay, which bring together buyers, sellers, distributors, and transaction payment processors in one single marketplace, making convenience the key attraction. Amazon.com has broadened its offerings from books and music to include tools, clothing, shows, jewelry, health and beauty products, and electronics, among others. Walmart.com has one million products available online and continues to develop new online services such as music downloads and photo developing. For companies that choose to operate their own e-commerce sites, transaction payment processors like PayPal offer services to facilitate payments around the world. PayPal opened its global payments platform with capabilities that include currency conversion and mobile applications.[30]

To fully serve the needs of its customers via e-commerce, the company itself must be prepared to provide 24-hour order taking and customer service, have the regulatory and customs-handling expertise to deliver internationally, and have an in-depth understanding of marketing environments, as well as customer habits and preferences, for the further development of the business relationship. The instantaneous interactivity users experience will also be translated into an expectation of expedient delivery of answers and products ordered. Many people living outside the United States who purchase online expect U.S.-style service. However, in many cases, these shoppers may find that shipping is not even available.

The challenges faced in terms of response and delivery capabilities can be overcome through outsourcing services or by building international distribution networks. Air express carriers such as DHL, FedEx, and UPS offer full-service packages that leverage their own Internet infrastructure with customs clearance and e-mail shipment notification. If a company needs help in order fulfillment and customer support, logistics centers offer warehousing and inventory management services as well as same-day delivery from in-country stocks. UPS, for example, has 901 supply chain facilities in more than 120 countries and serves more than 200 countries and territories.[31] Some companies elect to build their own international distribution networks, especially as they open country-specific websites. Amazon.com, for example, now has country websites in the United States, the United Kingdom, Germany, France, Japan, China, and

Canada. Amazon offers free shipping options in each of these countries except Canada and China. As the company broadens its product categories, it will require additional facilities and must fulfill more quickly and cheaply the orders generated locally.

Transactions and the information they provide about the buyer allow for more customization and service by region, market, or even by individual customer. Dell Computer does 30 percent of its business via the web; this adds up to $18 million worth of hardware, software, and accessories per day. Dell offers thousands of its corporate customers a Dell premier page site offering procurement and support designed to save these customers money with their IT process. For instance, Iglu.com (UK), a leading online ski holiday retailer, needed to ensure that its main database, containing details of availability and pricing from over 200 suppliers, could scale to cope at times of peak traffic. Its existing technology was struggling to process customer searches quickly enough, and the company was concerned that this would inevitably have an impact on its profitability. Iglu could buy products directly from Dell so they did not waste extra time by dealing with third-party resellers. According to Iglu, "It could have been complicated working with Microsoft, Intel and Dell together, but communication between the companies was seamless."[32]

Although originally English was perceived as the *lingua franca* of the web, increased global Internet penetration has made localization of web content and e-commerce a requirement. In targeting international markets, it is prudent to use a company located in the specific geographic area. It has been shown that web users are three times more likely to buy when the offering is made in their own language.[33] True to the marketing concept, smart marketers will seek to customize commercial websites to meet customer convenience and ease-of-use needs in different countries, starting with language localization. Numerous service providers can assist international businesses with this process, and reliable localization guidance can be found at the Localization Industry Standards Association (**www.lisa.org**) or the Globalization and Localization Association (**www.gala-global.org**).

The marketer has to be sensitive to the governmental role in e-commerce in regard to local regulations and taxation implications. Although some countries require businesses to have a permanent establishment or taxable entity established before they will hold the company responsible for taxes, there are often exceptions and requirements for payments from customers to be withheld from taxes. The U.S. CS offers good counsel for prospective international online merchants: "Electronically delivered goods should be treated like any other sale to a foreign customer. It generally is the responsibility of the customer/importer to declare their purchase and pay any taxes." In addition, marketers should anticipate that a foreign country may require VAT on sales. For example, the EU requires that e-commerce merchants must register with tax authorities in their member states and comply with the VAT regime and rates where the customer is located.[34]

Privacy issues have grown exponentially as a result of e-business as businesses collect and process personally identifiable information. Many countries, including the United States and the member states of the European Union, have specific privacy laws requiring strict compliance by online businesses. In 1998, the EU passed a Directive on Data Protection that introduced high standards of data privacy to ensure the free flow of data throughout its member states. Each individual has the right to review personal data, correct them, and limit their use. But, and more importantly, the directive also requires member states to block transmission of data to countries, including the United States, if those countries' domestic legislation does not provide an adequate level of protection. The comprehensive requirements of the EU directive involve particularly restrictive government approval of databases and data processing, which can pose significant barriers for non-EU firms. To avoid these barriers, the U.S. Department of Commerce and the European Commission created a "safe harbor" process that allows participating companies a simpler and easier means of complying with the requirements of the directive. Information on the "safe harbor" can be found at www.export.gov/safeharbor.

For industries such as music and motion pictures, the Internet has proven to be both an opportunity and a threat. The web provides a new, efficient method of distribution and customization of products that has been enthusiastically embraced by music and film lovers. At the same time, it can be a channel for intellectual property violation through unauthorized distribution methods that threaten the revenue streams to artists and creative industries.[35]

INTERNATIONAL LOGISTICS

International logistics is the design and management of a system that controls the flow of materials into, through, and out of the international corporation. It encompasses the total movement concept by covering the entire range of operations concerned with goods movement, including both exports and imports. A systems approach ensures that the firm reflects the linkages among the traditionally separate logistics components within and outside of the corporation. By incorporating the interaction with outside organizations and individuals such as suppliers and customers, the firm integrates all partners in the areas of performance, quality, and timing. Successful implementation of these systems' consideration allows the firm to develop just-in-time (JIT) delivery for lower inventory costs, electronic data interchange (EDI) for more efficient order processing, and early supplier involvement (ESI) for better planning of goods development and movement. All this will lead to the implementation of effective supply chain management. A firm can also choose to focus on manufacturing and leave all aspects of order filling and delivery to an outside provider. By working closely with customers such as retailers, firms can also develop efficient customer response (ECR) systems, which can track sales activity. As a result, manufacturers can precisely coordinate production in response to actual shelf replenishment needs rather than basing production on forecasts.

Two phases in the movement of materials are of major logistical importance. First is materials management, or the timely movement of raw materials, parts, and supplies into and through the firm. The second phase is physical distribution, which involves the movement of the firm's finished product to its customers. In both phases, movement includes stationary periods (storage and inventory). The goal of logistics management is the effective coordination of both phases and their various components to result in maximum cost effectiveness while maintaining service goals and requirements. Logistics is increasingly concerned with sustainability.

There are three major concepts within logistics: the systems concept, the total cost concept, and the trade-off concept. The systems concept is based on the notion that materials-flow activities within and outside of the firm are so extensive and complex that they can be considered only in the context of their interaction. It stipulates that some components may have to work suboptimally to maximize the benefits of the system as a whole. In order for the systems concept to work, information flows and partnership trust are instrumental. Long-term partnership and trust are required in order to forge closer links between firms and managers.

An outgrowth of the systems concept is the *total cost concept.* To evaluate and optimize logistical activities, the total cost concept is to minimize the firm's overall logistics cost within the entire system. Its implementation requires that the members of the system understand the sources of costs. Activity-based costing is a technique designed to more accurately assign the indirect and direct resources of an organization to the activities performed based on consumption.[36] In the international arena, the total cost concept must also incorporate the consideration of total after-tax profit by taking the impact of national tax policies on the logistics function into account. The objective is to maximize after-tax profits rather than to minimize total cost.

The *trade-off concept* recognizes the linkages within logistics systems that result from the interaction of their components. For example, locating a warehouse near the customer may reduce the cost of transportation. However, the new warehouse will lead to increased storage costs and more inventory. Managers can maximize performance of logistics systems only by formulating decisions based on the recognition and analysis of such trade-offs.

Supply Chain Management

The integration of these three concepts has resulted in the new paradigm of supply chain management, which encompasses the planning and management of all activities involved in sourcing and procurement, conversion, and logistics. It also includes coordination and collaboration with channel partners, which can be suppliers, intermediaries, third-party service providers, and customers. Supply chain management integrates supply and demand management within and across companies.[37]

Advances in information technology have been crucial to progress in supply chain management. Consider the example of Gestamp (Spain's leading supplier of metal components for car manufacturers), which used EDI technology to integrate inbound and outbound logistics between suppliers and customers. The company reports increased manufacturing productivity, reduced investment needs, increased efficiency of the billing process, and a lower rate of logistic errors across the supply process after implementing a supply chain management system.[38] Globalization has opened up supplier relationships for companies outside of the buyer's domestic market; however, the supplier's ability to provide satisfying goods and services will play the most critical role in securing long-term contracts.

The Impact of International Logistics

Logistics costs comprise between 10 and 30 percent of the total landed cost of an international order.[39] International firms experience ongoing increases in their logistics cost. Surging fuel costs show no signs of dropping. Globalization has stretched the length of the value chain. Transportation providers have boosted their prices to offset fuel costs but also as a result of growing demand for their services and constraints in capacity. Increased security requirements for freight also have increased costs.[40]

Close collaboration with suppliers is required in order to develop a JIT inventory system, which in turn may be crucial to maintain manufacturing costs at a globally competitive level. Japan's earthquake cut crucial links in the global supply chain, forcing buyers and suppliers to rethink business relationships; see *The International Marketplace 15.3*. Yet without EDI, such collaborations or alliances are severely handicapped. While most industrialized countries can offer the technological infrastructure for such computer-to-computer exchange of business information, the application of such a system in the global environment may be restricted. Often, it is not just the lack of technology that forms the key obstacle to modern logistics management but rather the entire business infrastructure, ranging from ways of doing business in fields such as accounting and inventory tracking to the willingness of businesses to collaborate with one another.

THE INTERNATIONAL MARKETPLACE 15.3

Supply Chains after the Japanese Earthquake

On March 11, 2011, Japan was hit by one of the largest earthquakes in recorded history, with a magnitude of 8.9. The aftermath left over 13,000 dead and even more lost or displaced. The earthquake also had far-reaching effects on the state of the Japanese economy and its international clientele.

The quake hit Japan's northeastern region, where many manufacturing factories are located. In March and April 2011, there were sharp decreases in output of components for Japanese-made cars, technology, and other goods. Nissan, Honda, Suzuki, Mazda, Mitsubishi, Sony, and Panasonic all had to temporarily shut down production in March. In the following months, prices of Japanese-made goods rose. Just a few months later, output began to increase. The production halt at car factories decreased global supply.

Earthquakes and other unpredictable natural disasters affect more than just their immediate victims. As seen with this example of Japan, the international supply chain was directly affected, as were global consumers.

SOURCES: Joachim Fels, Joseph Lupton, and Andrew Kenningham, "How Much Has Japan's Quake Shaken Supply Chains?" Interview by Financial Times, *Financial Times* (London), April 1, 2011; and Neil Irwin, "Quake Puts Output of Cars, Computer Chips, Other Goods at Risk," *Washington Post*, March 15, 2011.

The New Dimensions of International Logistics

In domestic operations, logistics decisions are guided by the experience of the manager, possible industry comparison, an intimate knowledge of trends, and the development of heuristics, or rules of thumb. The logistics manager in the international firm, on the other hand, frequently has to depend on educated guesses to determine the steps required to obtain a desired service level. Variations in locale mean variations in environment. Lack of familiarity with these variations will lead to uncertainty in the decision-making process. By applying decision rules developed at home, the firm will be unable to adapt well to the new environment, and the result will be inadequate profit performance. The long-term survival of international activities depends on an understanding of the differences inherent in the international logistics field.

Basic differences such as distance, currency variation, and transportation in international logistics emerge because the corporation is active in more than one country. International marketing activities frequently require goods to be shipped farther to reach final customers. These distances in turn result in longer lead times, more opportunities for things to go wrong, and more inventories—in short, greater complexity. Currency variation forces corporations to adjust planning to incorporate different currencies and changes in exchange rates. The border-crossing process brings with it the need for conformance with national regulations, an inspection at customs, and proper documentation. As a result, additional intermediaries participate in the international logistics process. They include freight forwarders, customs agents, customs brokers, banks, and other financial intermediaries, and all of them charge for their services.

INTERNATIONAL TRANSPORTATION ISSUES

International transportation is of major concern to the international firm because transportation determines how and when goods will be received. The transportation issue can be divided into three components: infrastructure, the availability between modes, and the choice between modes.

Transportation Infrastructure

In industrialized nations, firms can count on an established transportation network. Internationally, however, major infrastructural variations may be encountered. Some countries may have excellent inbound and outbound transportation systems but weak transportation links within the country. This is particularly true in former colonies, where the original transportation systems were designed to maximize the extractive potential of the countries. In such instances, shipping to the market may be easy, but distribution within the market may represent a very difficult and time-consuming task. It turns out that it costs more to ship a ton of wheat from Mombassa in Kenya to Kampala in Uganda than it does to ship the same ton of wheat from Chicago to Mombassa.[41] Such differences in logistics cost have a major impact on a firm's ability to participate successfully in international trade.

The international marketer must therefore learn about existing and planned infrastructures abroad. In some countries, for example, railroads may be an excellent transportation mode, far surpassing the performance of trucking, whereas in others the use of railroads for freight distribution may be a gamble at best. The future routing of pipelines must be determined before any major commitments are made to a particular location if the product is amenable to pipeline transportation. The transportation methods used to carry cargo to seaports or airports must also be investigated. Mistakes in the evaluation of transportation options can prove to be very costly. One researcher reported the case of a food processing firm that built a pineapple cannery at the delta of a river in Mexico. Because the pineapple plantation was located upstream, the company planned to float the ripe fruit down to the cannery on barges. To its dismay, the firm discovered that at harvest time the river current was far too strong for barge traffic. Because no other feasible alternative method of transportation existed, the plant was closed and the new equipment was sold for a fraction of its original cost.[42]

Extreme variations also exist in the frequency of transportation services. For example, a particular port may not be visited by a ship for weeks or even months. Sometimes, only carriers with particular characteristics, such as small size, will serve a given location.

Availability of Modes

Goods are shipped abroad by rail or truck, but international transportation frequently requires ocean or airfreight modes, which many corporations only rarely use domestically. In addition, combinations such as land bridges or sea bridges frequently permit the transfer of freight among various modes of transportation, resulting in intermodal movements.

Ocean Shipping

Water transportation is a key mode for international freight movements. Three types of vessels operating in ocean shipping can be distinguished by their service: liner service, bulk service, and tramp or charter service. Liner service offers regularly scheduled passage on established routes. Bulk service mainly provides contractual services for individual voyages or for prolonged periods of time. Tramp service is available for irregular routes and is scheduled only on demand.

In addition to the services offered by ocean carriers, the type of cargo a vessel can carry is also important. Most common are conventional (break-bulk) cargo vessels, container ships, and roll-on-roll-off vessels. Conventional cargo vessels are useful for oversized and unusual cargoes but may be less efficient in their port operations. Among the largest cargo ships in the world is the *Eleonora Maersk*, which can transport about 7,500 40-foot containers, each capable of holding 70,000 t-shirts.[43] The premium assigned to speed and ease of

EXHIBIT 15.7 Container Ship

Some container ships can carry more than 7,500 40-foot containers.

SOURCE: © iStockphoto.com/Dan Barnes.

handling has caused a decline in the use of general cargo vessels and a sharp increase in the growth of container ships. These ships carry standardized containers that greatly facilitate the loading and unloading of cargo and intermodal transfers (see Exhibit 15.7).

Large investments in infrastructure are usually necessary to produce results. Selective allocation of funds to transportation tends to only shift bottlenecks to some other point in the infrastructure. For many products, quick delivery is essential because of required high levels of industry responsiveness to orders. From a regional perspective, maintaining adequate facilities is therefore imperative in order to remain on the list of areas and ports served by international carriers. Investment in leading-edge port technology can also provide an instrumental competitive edge and cause entire distribution systems to be reconfigured to take advantage of possible savings.

Air Shipping

Airfreight is available to and from most countries. The tremendous growth in international airfreight is shown in Exhibit 15.8. Total volume of airfreight in relation to the total volume of shipping in international business remains quite small. Yet 40 percent of the world's manufactured exports by value travel by air.[44] Clearly, high-value items are more likely to be shipped by air, particularly if they have a high density, that is, a high weight-to-volume ratio.

Airlines make major efforts to increase the volume of airfreight by developing better, more efficient ground facilities, introducing airfreight containers, and marketing a wide variety of special services to shippers. Some airfreight companies have specialized and become partners in the international logistics

EXHIBIT 15.8 World Air Cargo Traffic

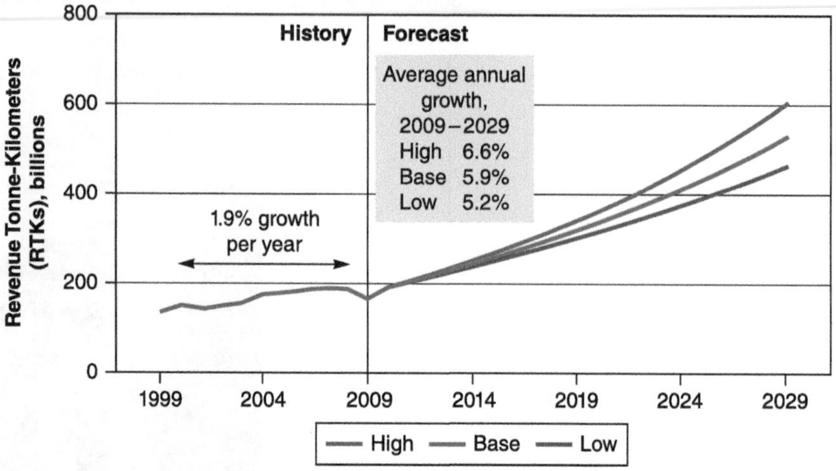

SOURCE: Boeing Corporation, *World Air Cargo Forecast*, www.boeing.com/commercial/cargo, accessed November 28, 2011. Reprinted with permission.

effort. From the shipper's perspective, the products involved must be amenable to air shipment in terms of their size. Airfreight may be needed if a product is perishable or if, for other reasons, it requires a short transit time. The level of customer service needs and expectations can also play a decisive role.

Choice of Transport Modes

The international marketer must make the appropriate selection from the available modes of transportation. The manager must consider the performance of each mode on four dimensions: transit time, predictability, cost, and noneconomic factors.

Transit Time

The period between departure and arrival of the carrier varies significantly between ocean freight and airfreight. The 45-day transit time of an ocean shipment can be reduced to 12 hours if the firm chooses airfreight. The length of transit time will have a major impact on the overall operations of the firm. Inventories can be significantly reduced if they are replenished frequently. As a result, capital can be freed up and used to finance other corporate opportunities. Transit time can also play a major role in emergency situations. If the shipper is about to miss an important delivery date because of production delays, a shipment normally made by ocean freight can be made by air.

Rapid transportation prolongs the shelf life in the foreign market. International sales of cut flowers have reached their current volume only as a result of airfreight. At all times, the international marketing manager must understand the interactions among different components of the logistics process and their effect on transit times. Unless a smooth flow can be assured throughout the entire supply chain, bottlenecks will deny any timing benefits from specific improvements.

Predictability

Providers of both ocean and airfreight service are subject to the vagaries of nature, which may impose delays. Yet because reliability is a relative measure, a delay of one day for airfreight tends to be seen as much more severe and "unreliable" than the same delay for ocean freight. But delays tend to be shorter in absolute time for air shipments. Due to the higher predictability of airfreight, inventory safety stock can be kept at lower levels. Greater predictability can also serve as a useful sales tool for foreign distributors, who are able to make more precise delivery promises to their customers. If inadequate harbor facilities exist, airfreight may again be the better alternative. Finally, merchandise shipped via air is likely to suffer less loss and damage from exposure of the cargo to movement. Therefore, once the merchandise arrives, it is more likely to be ready for immediate delivery.

Cost

A major consideration in choosing international transportation modes is the cost factor. International transportation services are usually priced on the basis of both cost of the service provided and value of the service to the shipper. Because of the high value of the products shipped by air, airfreight is often priced according to the value of the service. In this instance, of course, price becomes a function of market demand and the monopolistic power of the carrier.

The international marketer must decide whether the clearly higher cost of airfreight can be justified. In part, this will depend on the cargo's properties. Bulky products may be too expensive to ship by air, whereas very compact products may be more amenable to airfreight transportation. High-priced items can absorb transportation costs more easily than low-priced goods because the cost of transportation as a percentage of total product cost will be lower. As a result, sending diamonds by airfreight is easier to justify than sending coal by air. In order to keep cost down, a shipper can join groups such as shippers associations, which give the shipper more leverage in negotiations. Alternatively, a shipper can decide to mix modes of transportation in order to reduce overall cost and time delays.

The overall logistical considerations of the firm need to incorporate the product, the competition, and the environment. The manager must determine how important it is for merchandise to arrive on time, which will be different even within a product category—for example, for DVDs of Oscar-nominated movies compared with those that did poorly at the box office. The effect of transportation cost on price and the need for product availability abroad must be considered. Some firms may wish to use airfreight as a new tool for aggressive market expansion. Airfreight may also be considered a good way to begin operations in new markets without making sizable investments for warehouses and distribution centers.

Noneconomic Factors

Often, noneconomic dimensions will enter into the selection process for a proper form of transportation. The transportation sector both benefits and suffers from heavy government involvement. Carriers may be owned or heavily subsidized by governments. As a result, governmental pressure is exerted on shippers to use national carriers, even if more economical alternatives exist. Such preferential policies are most often enforced when government cargo is being transported. For example, in the United States, all government cargo and all official government travelers must use national-flag carriers when available.

For balance-of-payments reasons, international quota systems of transportation have been proposed. UNCTAD has recommended a 40/40/20 treaty whereby 40 percent of the traffic between two nations is allocated to vessels of the exporting country, 40 percent to vessels of the importing country, and 20 percent to third-country vessels (40/40/20). However, stiff international competition among carriers and the price sensitivity of customers frequently render such proposals ineffective, particularly for trade between industrialized countries.

A useful overall comparison between different modes of transportation is provided in Exhibit 15.9.

EXHIBIT 15.9 Evaluating Transportation Choices

Characteristics of Mode of Transportation	Air	Pipeline	Highway	Rail	Water
Speed (1 = fastest)	1	4	2	3	5
Cost (1 = highest)	1	4	2	3	5
Loss and Damage (1 = least)	3	1	4	5	2
Frequency* (1 = best)	3	1	2	4	5
Dependability (1 = best)	5	1	2	3	4
Capacity** (1 = best)	4	5	3	2	1
Availability (1 = best)	3	5	1	2	4

*Number of times mode is available during a given period of time.
**Ability of mode to handle large or heavy goods.

SOURCE: Ballou, Ronald H., *Business Logistics Management*, 5th Edition, © 2004. Adapted by permission of Pearson Education, Inc., Upper Saddle River, NJ.

THE INTERNATIONAL SHIPMENT

International shipments may use multiple types of carriers. The shipment must be routed to the port of export, where it is transferred to another mode of transportation—for example, from truck or rail to vessel. Documentation for international shipments is universally perceived as so complicated, especially by smaller firms, that it can be a trade barrier. Recognizing the impact both in terms of time and money that documentation can have, trading regions such as the European Union have greatly simplified their required documentation for shipments.

Documentation

In the simplest form of exporting, the only documents needed are a bill of lading and an export declaration. In most countries, these documents are available either from the government or from transportation firms. For example, an export declaration can be obtained in the United States from the Census Bureau (www.census.gov). A bill of lading can be obtained in Canada from a shipper, for example, Manitoulin Transport (www.manitoulintransport.com).

Most exports fit under a general license, which is a generalized authorization consisting simply of a number to be shown on the documents. Certain goods and data require a special validated license for export, as discussed under export controls in Chapter 5. For imports, the basic documents are a bill of lading and an invoice.

The bill of lading is the most important document to the shipper, the carrier, and the buyer. It acknowledges receipt of the goods, represents the basic contract between the shipper and the carrier, and serves as evidence of title to the goods for collection by the purchaser. Bills of lading may be negotiable instruments in that they may be endorsed to other parties (order bill) or may be non-negotiable (straight). The shipper's export declaration states proper authorization for export and serves as a means for governmental data-collection efforts.

There are many other documents required, such as the packing list, a shipper's declaration for dangerous goods, a consular invoice or pro forma invoice, and a certificate of origin. The bottom line is that the exporter has to provide the importer with the data needed to obtain the required licenses from governmental authorities. Also, since the terrorist attacks of 2001, governments now expect detailed information about cargo well in advance of its arrival in port.

Improper or missing documents can easily delay payment or cause problems with customs.

Assistance with International Shipments

Several intermediaries provide services in the physical movement of goods. One very important distribution decision an exporter makes is the selection of an international freight forwarder. Such an international freight forwarder acts as an agent for the marketer in moving cargo to an overseas destination. The forwarder advises the marketer on shipping documentation and packing costs and will prepare and review the documents to ensure that they are in order. Forwarders will also book the space aboard a carrier. They will make necessary arrangements to clear outbound goods with customs and, after clearance, forward the documents either to the customer or to the paying bank. A customs broker serves as an agent for an importer with authority to clear inbound goods through customs and ship them on to their destination.

INTERNATIONAL INVENTORY ISSUES

Inventories tie up a major portion of corporate funds. As a result, capital used for inventory is not available for other corporate opportunities. Because annual **inventory carrying costs** (the expense of maintaining inventories) can easily comprise up to 25 percent or more of the value of the inventories themselves, proper inventory policies should be of major concern to the international marketing manager. JIT inventory policies minimize the volume of inventory by making it available only when it is needed for the production process. Firms using such a policy will choose suppliers on the basis of their delivery and inventory performance. Proper inventory management may therefore become a determining variable in obtaining a sale.

In deciding the level of inventory to be maintained, the international marketer must consider three factors: the order cycle time, desired customer service levels, and the use of inventories as a strategic tool.

Order Cycle Time

The total time that passes between the placement of an order and the receipt of the merchandise is the order cycle time. Two dimensions are of major importance to inventory management: the length of the total order cycle and its consistency. In international marketing, the order cycle is frequently longer than in domestic business. It comprises the time involved in order transmission, order filling, packing and preparation for shipment, and transportation. Order transmission time varies greatly internationally depending on whether telephone, fax, mail, or electronic order placement is used in communicating. The order filling time may also be increased because lack of familiarity with a foreign market makes the anticipation of new orders more difficult. As a result, total order cycle time can frequently approach 100 days or more. Larger inventories may have to be maintained both domestically and internationally to bridge these time gaps.

Consistency, the second dimension of order cycle time, is also more difficult to maintain in international marketing. Depending on the choice of transportation mode, delivery times may vary considerably from shipment to shipment. This variation requires the maintenance of larger safety stocks in order to be able to fill demand in periods when delays occur.

The international marketer should attempt to reduce order cycle time and increase its consistency without an increase in total costs. This objective can be accomplished by altering methods of transportation, changing inventory locations, or improving any of the other components of the order cycle time, such as the way orders are transmitted.

Customer Service Levels

The level of customer service denotes the responsiveness that inventory policies permit for any given situation. Customer service is therefore a management-determined constraint within the logistics system. A customer service level of 100 percent could be defined as the ability to fill all orders within a set time—for example, three days. If within these three days only 70 percent of the orders can be filled, the customer service level is 70 percent. The choice of customer service level for the firm has a major impact on the inventories needed. In their domestic operations, U.S. companies frequently aim to achieve customer service levels of 95 to 98 percent.

Different locales have country-specific customer service needs and requirements. Service levels should not be oriented primarily around cost or customary domestic standards. Rather, the level chosen for use internationally should be based on customer expectations encountered in each market. These expectations depend on past performance, product desirability, customer sophistication, the competitive status of the firm, and whether a buyers' or sellers' market exists.

Because high customer service levels are costly, the goal should not be the highest customer service level possible but rather an acceptable level. Different customers have different priorities. In industrial marketing, for example, even an eight-hour delay may be unacceptable for the delivery of a crucial product component as it may mean a shutdown of the production process. Other firms may put a higher value on flexibility, and another group may see low cost as the most important issue. Flexibility and speed are expensive, so it is wasteful to supply them to customers who do not value them highly. The higher prices associated with higher customer service levels may reduce the competitiveness of a firm's product.

Inventory as a Strategic Tool

International inventories can be used by the international corporation as a strategic tool in dealing with currency valuation changes or in hedging against inflation. By increasing inventories before an imminent devaluation of a currency instead of holding cash, the corporation may reduce its exposure to devaluation losses. Similarly, in the case of high inflation, large inventories can provide an important inflation hedge. In such circumstances, the international inventory manager must balance the cost of maintaining high levels of inventories with the benefits accruing to the firm from hedging against inflation or devaluation. Many countries, for example, charge a tax on stored goods. If the increase in tax payments outweighs the hedging benefits to the corporation, it would be unwise to increase inventories before devaluation occurs. Only by recognizing the trade-offs, which may result in less-than-optimal inventory policies, can the corporation maximize the overall benefit.

INTERNATIONAL STORAGE ISSUES

International logistics involves a stationary period when merchandise becomes inventory stored in warehouses. Heated arguments can arise within a firm over the need for and utility of warehousing internationally. Accommodating the customer's expectation may require locating many distribution centers around the world. On the other hand, warehousing space is expensive. In addition, the larger volume of inventory increases the inventory carrying cost. The international marketer must consider the trade-offs between service and cost to determine the appropriate levels of warehousing.

Storage Facilities

The availability of facilities abroad will differ from the domestic situation. For example, whereas public storage is widely available in some countries, such facilities may be scarce or entirely lacking in others. Also, the standards and quality of facilities abroad may often not be comparable to those offered at home. As a result, the storage decision of the firm is often accompanied by the need for large-scale, long-term investments. Despite the high cost, international storage facilities should be established if they support the overall marketing effort.

Once the decision is made to utilize storage facilities abroad, the warehouse conditions must be carefully analyzed. In some countries, warehouses have low ceilings. Packaging developed for the high stacking of products is therefore unnecessary. In other countries, automated warehousing is available. Proper bar coding of products and the use of package dimensions acceptable to the warehousing system are basic requirements. In contrast, in warehouses still stocked manually, weight limitations will be of major concern.

An ABC analysis classifies products that are most sensitive to delivery time as "A" products. "A" products would be stocked in all distribution centers, and safety stock levels would be kept high. Products for which immediate delivery is not urgent are classified as "B" products, stored only at selected distribution centers around the world. For "C" products, short delivery time is not important as there is little demand for them. They are stocked only at headquarters. Classifying products through such an ABC analysis enables the international marketer to substantially reduce total international warehousing requirements and still maintain acceptable service levels.

Outsourcing

For many global firms, the practice of outsourcing—which refers to the shifting of traditional corporate activities to parties outside of the firm and often outside of the country—is on the increase. The decisive factors for choosing to outsource are the desire to reduce and control operating costs, to improve company focus, to gain access to world-class capabilities, and to free internal resources for other purposes.[45]

Our research into the future of outsourcing indicates continued growth and expansion of this practice.[46] An increasing portion of high-end, high-value-added services will be sourced from low-labor-cost but high-labor-skilled countries. To remain competitive, firms in developed economies must change their strategy to focus on their ability to manage, coordinate, and define the interfaces between suppliers and customers.

Often manufacturing jobs move to emerging markets. Firms face the challenge to retain first-mover advantages through continued innovation. When cost pressures force firms to source globally, some will locate their own plants abroad, while others will outsource the needed inputs. Sourcing from abroad through independent suppliers on a contractual basis will have long-term consequences on the processes, competence, and capabilities of firms. When market conditions change, there may be the phenomenon of "onshoring," where firms bring their operations back home.

Foreign Trade Zones

Foreign trade zones can have a major effect on the international logistician because production-cost advantages may require a reconfiguration of storage, processing, and distribution strategies. Trade zones are considered, for purposes of tariff treatment, to be outside the customs territory of the country within which they are located. They are special areas and can be used for warehousing, packaging, inspection, labeling, exhibition, assembly, fabrication, or transshipment of imports without burdening the firm with duties.[47] Trade zones can be found at major ports of entry and also at inland locations near major production facilities. For example, Kansas City, Missouri, has one of the largest foreign trade zones in the United States. (A listing of U.S. trade zones can be found at **http://ia.ita.doc.gov/ftzpage.html**.)

Foreign trade zones are designed to exclude the impact of duties from the location decision. This is done by exempting merchandise in the foreign trade zone from duty payment. The international firm can therefore import merchandise; store it in the foreign trade zone; and process, alter, test, or demonstrate it—all without paying duties. If the merchandise is subsequently shipped abroad (that is, reexported), no duty payments are ever due. Duty payments become due only when the merchandise is shipped into the country from the foreign trade zone.

One country that has used trade zones very successfully for its own economic development is China. Through the creation of *special economic zones* in which there are no tariffs, substantial tax incentives, and low prices for land and labor, the government has attracted many foreign investors bringing in billions of dollars. These investors have brought new equipment, technology, and managerial know-how and have therefore substantially increased the local economic prosperity.

Both parties to the arrangement benefit from foreign trade zones. The government maintaining the trade zone achieves increased employment. The firm using the trade zone obtains a spearhead in or close to the foreign market without incurring all of the costs customarily associated with such an activity.

INTERNATIONAL PACKAGING ISSUES

Packaging is instrumental in getting the merchandise to the ultimate destination in a safe, maintainable, and presentable condition. Packaging that is adequate for domestic shipping may be inadequate for international transportation because the shipment will be subject to the motions of the vessel on which it is carried. Added stress in international shipping also arises from the transfer of goods among different modes of transportation.

The responsibility for appropriate packaging rests with the shipper of goods. The U.S. Carriage of Goods by Sea Act of 1936 states: "Neither the carrier nor the ship shall be responsible for loss or damage arising or resulting from insufficiency of packing." The shipper must therefore ensure that the goods are prepared appropriately for international shipping. This is important because it has been found that "the losses that occur as a result of breakage, pilferage, and theft exceed the losses caused by major maritime casualties, which include fires, sinkings, and collision of vessels. Thus, the largest of these losses is a preventable loss."[48]

Packaging decisions must take into account differences in environmental conditions. When the ultimate destination is very humid or particularly cold, special provisions must be made to prevent damage to the product.

The weight of packaging must be considered, particularly when airfreight is used, because the cost of shipping is often based on weight. At the same time, packaging material must be sufficiently strong to permit stacking in international transportation. Another consideration is that, in some countries, duties are assessed according to the gross weight of shipments, which includes the weight of packaging. The heavier the packaging, the higher the duties will be.

The shipper must pay sufficient attention to instructions provided by the customer for packaging. Often they reflect limitations in transportation or handling facilities at the point of destination.

One solution to packaging issues in international logistics has been intermodal containers—large metal boxes that fit on trucks, ships, railroad cars, and airplanes and ease the frequent transfer of goods in international shipments. In addition, containers offer greater safety from pilferage and damage. Developed in different forms for both sea and air transportation, containers also offer better utilization of carrier space because of standardization of size. The shipper therefore may benefit from lower transportation rates.

Container traffic is heavily dependent on the existence of appropriate handling facilities, both domestically and internationally. In addition, the quality of inland transportation must be considered. If transportation for containers is not available and the merchandise must be removed and reloaded, the expected cost reductions may not materialize.

In some countries, rules for the handling of containers may be designed to maintain employment. For example, U.S. union rules obligate shippers to withhold containers from firms that do not employ members of the International Longshoreman Association for loading and unloading containers within a 50-mile radius of Atlantic or Gulf ports. Such restrictions can result in an onerous cost burden.

Overall, close attention must be paid to international packaging. The customer who ordered and paid for the merchandise expects it to arrive on time and in good condition. Even with replacements and insurance, the customer will not be satisfied if there are delays. This dissatisfaction will usually translate directly into lost sales.

MANAGEMENT OF INTERNATIONAL LOGISTICS

The purpose of a multinational firm is to benefit from system synergism. Therefore the coordination of international logistics at corporate headquarters is important. Without coordination, subsidiaries tend to optimize their individual efficiency but jeopardize the overall performance of the firm.

Centralized Logistics Management

If headquarters exerts control, it must also take the primary responsibility for its decisions. To avoid internal problems, both headquarters staff and local logistics management should report to one person. This person can then become the final arbiter to decide the firm's priorities. Of course, this individual should also be in charge of determining appropriate rewards for managers, both at headquarters and abroad, so that corporate decisions that alter a manager's performance level will not affect the manager's appraisal and evaluation. Further, this individual can contribute an objective view when inevitable conflicts arise in international logistics coordination.

Decentralized Logistics Management

If a firm serves many international markets that are diverse in nature, total centralization would leave the firm unresponsive to local adaptation needs. If each subsidiary is made a profit center in itself, each one carries the full responsibility for its performance, which can lead to greater local management satisfaction and to better adaptation to local market conditions. Yet often such decentralization deprives the logistics function of the benefits of coordination.

Contract Logistics

A growing preference among international firms is to outsource, often referred to as contract or third-party logistics (3PL). Most companies have outsourced at least one major logistics function such as customs clearance, transportation management, freight payment, warehouse management, shipment tracking, or other transportation-related functions. The main thrust behind the idea is that individual firms are experts in their industry and should therefore concentrate only on their operations. 3PL providers are experts at logistics, with the knowledge and means to perform efficient and innovative services for those companies in need. The goal is improved service at equal or lower cost.

Logistics providers' services vary in scope. Some may use their own assets in physical transportation, while others subcontract out portions of the job. Certain other providers are not involved as much with the actual transportation as they are with developing systems and databases or consulting on administrative management services. In many instances, the partnership consists of working closely with established transport providers such as FedEx or UPS.

One of the greatest benefits of contracting out the logistics function in a foreign market is the ability to take advantage of an existing network complete with resources and experience. One of the main arguments leveled against contract logistics is the loss of the firm's control in the supply chain. Yet contract logistics does not and should not require the handing over of control. Rather, it offers concentration on one's specialization—a division of labor.

LOGISTICS AND SECURITY

Firms worldwide have been exposed to the vicissitudes of terrorism, which often aims to disrupt the flow of supply and demand in order to damage economic systems. Logistics systems, the true soft spots of vulnerability for both nations and firms, are often the targets of attacks. For instance, in the issue of sea ports, some 95 percent of all international trade shipments to the United States arrives by sea and is then transferred to truck and rail. In most instances, the containers are secured by nothing more than a low-cost seal that can be easily broken. Similar to imported merchandise, exported products also need to be protected by companies as they leave the country in order to prevent terrorists from contaminating shipments with the goal of destroying foreign markets together with the reputations of the exporting firms.

Security measures instigated by governments will affect the ability of firms to efficiently plan their international shipments. There is now more uncertainty and less control over the timing of arrivals and departures. There is also a much greater need for internal control and supervision of shipments.[49]

Security measures for international shipments affect the ability of firms to efficiently plan their distributions. Increased inspections of containers, new security programs to protect ports, and other new protective policies are decreasing the efficiency and effectiveness of international shipping and logistics. Consequently, the costs of value chain and supply chain activities have increased substantially. There is now more uncertainty and less control over the timing of arrivals and departures. Companies may be inclined to produce more essential products themselves locally instead of relying on outside producers to deliver those products on time.

Similarly, costs may rise if companies choose to purchase goods from suppliers located in close proximity or from suppliers that are more familiar—and therefore more safe—in order to reduce their vulnerability. Companies may also increase their inventory holdings in hopes of protecting against delays caused by sudden heightened security measures against terrorism.[50] Holding more inventory or drawing goods from more than one source will increase the ability to meet the customers' demand at times when an outside producer is unable to deliver on time. Flexibility of supply chains is therefore a necessity when logistics security is at risk from terrorism.[51]

Firms with a JIT regimen are exploring alternative management strategies because the process of moving goods has become more expensive. Some firms are considering replacing international shipments with domestic ones, where transportation via truck would replace transborder movement and eliminate the use of vulnerable international transportation. One key security problem for logistics is piracy. See *The International Marketplace 15.4* for more details on this growing concern.

THE INTERNATIONAL MARKETPLACE 15.4

The Dangers of Somali Pirates

A critical security problem for logistics is shipping piracy. Even though pirates are often seen as legends from the past, piracy is very much a part of today's shipping security concerns. The twenty-first-century freebooters are highly organized and heavily armed. Somali, Indonesian, and Nigerian shores are the most treacherous areas of the world. The 2010 Piracy Map by the International Maritime Bureau (IMB), a department within the ICC, is based on information reported to the IMB Piracy Reporting Centre. This information shows that the largest number of pirate attacks in 2010 were off the coast of eastern Africa. Other regions subject to many of these attacks are the shores off Myanmar (Burma), Thailand, and Cambodia.

By November 2011, the ICC reported that there were 389 total worldwide pirate attacks that year. Total hijackings at sea worldwide were 39. In Somalia alone there had been 219 incidents, 26 hijackings, 450 hostages held, and 15 hostages killed in 2011. In November 2011, Somali pirates held 11 vessels and 194 hostages.

Companies conducting business in the surrounding areas have to face higher costs due to security measures undertaken to prevent severe loss of life and cargo. In order to protect their revenues, shipping companies have been installing electric fences on their cargo ships. In spite of large corporate investments to build security, new attacks happen daily. You can track them at **www.icc-ccs.org/piracy-reporting-centre/imb-live-piracy-map.**

Piracy Map, 2010

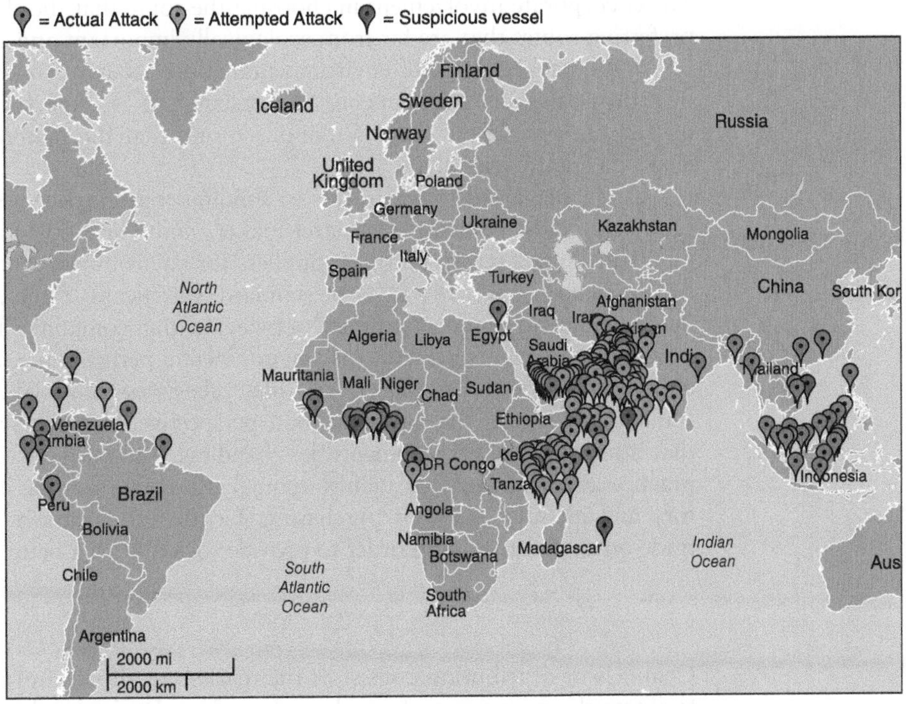

SOURCES: © Cengage Learning 2013; IMB, www.icc-ccs.org/home/piracy-reporting-centre/imb-live-piracy-map-2010/piracy-map-2010.

RECYCLING AND REVERSE LOGISTICS

Environmental laws, social expectations, and self-imposed goals set by firms are difficult to adhere to without a logistics orientation that systematically takes these concerns into account. Because laws and regulations differ across the world, the firm's efforts need to be responsive to a wide variety of requirements. One logistics orientation that has grown in importance due to environmental concerns is the development of reverse distribution systems. Such systems are instrumental in ensuring that the firm not only delivers the product to the market but also can retrieve it from the market for subsequent use, recycling, or disposal. To a growing degree, the ability to develop such reverse logistics is a key determinant for market acceptance and profitability.

Traditionally, businesses have focused on forward logistics even though product returns, an example of reverse logistics, have always been a fact of business life. Similar to forward logistics, reverse logistics require quality information and processes and the ability to track both at all times. Reverse logistics, however, is also a complex customer service, inventory control, information management, cost accounting, and disposal process.[52] Reverse logistics management is highly specialized. Return and reclamation rates vary drastically between industries such as cosmetics or pharmaceuticals.

Society is beginning to recognize that retrieval should not be restricted to short-term consumer goods, such as bottles. Increasingly, governments establish rules that hold the manufacturer responsible for the ultimate disposal of the product at the end of its economic life. In Germany, for example, car manufacturers are required to take back their used vehicles for dismantling and recycling. The design of such long-term systems across the world may well be one of the key challenges and opportunities for the logistician and will require close collaboration with all other functions in the firm, such as design, production, and sales.

On the transportation side, logistics managers will need to expand their involvement in carrier and routing selection. Shippers of oil or other potentially hazardous materials are increasingly expected to ensure that the carriers used have excellent safety records and use only double-hulled ships. Society may even expect corporate involvement in choosing the route that the shipment will travel, preferring routes that are far from ecologically important and sensitive zones.

In the packaging field, environmental concerns are also growing on the part of individuals and governments. Increasingly, it is expected that the amount of packaging materials used is minimized and that the materials used are more environmentally friendly.

Companies need to learn how to simultaneously achieve environmental and economic goals. Esprit, the apparel maker, and The Body Shop, a British cosmetics producer, screen all their suppliers for environmental and socially responsible practices. ISO 14000 is a standard specifically targeted at encouraging international environmental practices by evaluating companies both at the organization level (management systems, environmental performance, and environmental auditing) and at the product level (life-cycle assessment, labeling, and product standards).[53] From the environmental perspective, those practices are desirable that bring about fewer shipments, less handling, and more direct movement. Such practices are to be weighed against optimal efficiency routings, including JIT inventory and quantity discount purchasing. Firms need to assert leadership in such trade-off considerations in order to provide society with a better quality of life.

SUMMARY

Channels of distribution consist of the marketing efforts and intermediaries that facilitate the movement of goods and services. Decisions that must be made to establish an international channel of distribution focus on channel design and the selection of intermediaries for the roles that the international marketer will not perform. The channel must be designed to meet the requirements of the intended customer base, coverage, long-term continuity of the channel once it is established, and the quality of coverage to be achieved. Having determined the basic design of the channel, the international marketer will then decide on the number of different types of intermediaries to use and how many of each type, or whether to use intermediaries at all. The latter would be the case in direct distribution using, for example, sales offices or e-commerce. The process is important because the majority of international sales involve distributors, and channel decisions are the most long-term of all marketing decisions. The more the channel operation resembles a team rather than a collection of independent businesses, the more effective the overall marketing effort will be.

Competitiveness depends on cost efficiency. International logistics and supply chain management are of major importance because distribution comprises between 10 and 30 percent of the total landed cost of an international order.

International logistics is concerned with the flow of materials into, through, and out of the international corporation and includes materials management as well as physical distribution. The logistician must recognize the total systems demands of the firm in order to develop trade-offs between various logistics components. By taking a supply chain perspective, the marketing manager can develop logistics systems that are highly customer-focused and very cost-efficient. Implementation of such a system requires close collaboration between all members of the supply chain.

International logistics differs from domestic activities in that it deals with greater distances, new variables, and greater complexity because of country-specific differences.

International logistics management is growing in importance. The marketer must consider the benefits and the drawbacks that the IT revolution has brought to supply chain and logistics activities. Increasingly, better implementation of change in logistics is key to defining a firm's competitiveness.

Security concerns have also greatly affected the planning and implementation of the logistics interface. In previous decades many governmental efforts were devoted to speeding up transactions across borders. Now national security concerns are forcing governments to construct new barriers to entry and conduct new inspections. Flexibility of supply chains to allow for disruptions caused by terrorism is therefore a necessary component of conducting business in this day and age. Companies also will have to think about the need to build reverse logistics systems when customer returns and recycling activities make such systems a necessity.

KEY TERMS

intermediary
distribution culture
distributor
agent
facilitating payment
parallel importation
m-commerce
international logistics
materials management
physical distribution
systems concept
supply chain management
modes of transportation
inventory carrying cost

QUESTIONS FOR DISCUSSION

1. The international marketer and the distributor will have different expectations concerning the relationship. Why should these expectations be spelled out and clarified in the contract?
2. Channels of distribution tend to vary according to the level of economic development of a market. The more developed the economy, the shorter the channels tend to be. Why?
3. One method of screening candidates is to ask potential distributors for a sample marketing plan. What items would you want included in this plan?

4. The Internet has had a dynamic effect on the supply chain, specifically in terms of speed. Discuss the benefits of the Internet's effect on supply chains. Are there any drawbacks? Explain them.
5. As a consumer, what logistics attribute is most important to you: speed, predictability, cost, or quality? Discuss which are relatively more important to you and why.
6. Track the live number of pirate attacks at www.icc-ccs.org/piracy-reporting-centre/imb-live-piracy-map. Should governments intervene? Why or why not?

INTERNET EXERCISES

1. Using the website of the U.S. Commercial Service (http://trade.gov/cs), assess the types of help available to an exporter in establishing distribution channels and finding partners in this endeavor.
2. Go to the United States Census Bureau's website (www.census.gov/foreign-trade/regulations) and read through the Foreign Trade Regulations. Consider the various logistical obstacles and management issues addressed in this chapter and the implications these government regulations have on them.

CHALLENGE US

Supreme Court Rules against Consumers in Costco versus Omega

The U.S. Supreme Court has upheld a ban on gray-market products sold legally in other countries but not authorized by their maker for sale in the United States. This ruling means that any manufacturer that makes items overseas and uses a copyrighted logo on them can go after importers who do not play by the manufacturer's rules.

Retailing giant Costco acquired Omega watches from gray-market sources and sold them cheaply—without Omega's permission, which prompted Omega to sue for copyright infringement. Because the watches were not made in the United States, Omega claimed that they did not qualify for "first sale" rules. (An earlier Supreme Court case held that "first sale" protections do apply if the item was made in the United States, even if it is then sold overseas and reimported without permission.) In this case, Omega argued that all foreign-made, copyrighted products could only be sold in the United States with the manufacturer's permission.

Omega sells its watches for far less money in some countries than in others, a common enough practice known to economists as *geographical price discrimination.* The U.S. market will generally bear more than the market in a Latin American republic, and so Omega offers its goods to distributors in places such as Paraguay for less than it does to American distributors. Given the difference in prices, there is a tempting arbitrage opportunity in importing Omega watches from Paraguay to the United States. They become watches like those that Costco bought from a stateside importer, allowing the warehouse store to offer an Omega Seamaster for $1,299 when the brand prefers them to sell in the United States for $1,999.

Omega has since fashioned a small globe logo and copyrighted the device in the United States. By engraving the tiny logo on the back of the watch, Omega could claim that it created a copyright on the watch as a whole, one that would give the company more control over when and where the watches are sold.

Collision of copyright law and gray market goods.

For Discussion

1. Why would a retailer go to the trouble of buying something overseas—say, a very expensive Omega Seamaster watch—to resell in the United States?
2. Who pays?

SOURCES: Abigail Field, "Supreme Court Rules Against Consumers in Costco vs. Omega," *Daily Finance*, December 13, 2010; and Eric Felten, "Watch Out for the Omega Copyright Windup," *Wall Street Journal*, July 30, 2010.

RECOMMENDED READINGS

Benfield, Scott, and Stephen D. Griffith. *Disruption in the Channel: The New Realities of Distribution and Manufacturing in a Global Economy*. Camby, IN: Power Publishing, 2008.

Bowersox, Donald, David Closs, and M. Bixby Cooper. *Supply Chain Logistics Management*. New York: McGraw-Hill, 2009.

Christopher, Martin. *Logistics and Supply Chain Management*. London, England: Financial Times, 2011.

Cook, Sarah. *Complaint Management Excellence: Creating Customer Loyalty through Service Recovery*. London, England: Kogan Page, 2012.

Dent, Julian. *Distribution Channels: Understanding and Managing Channels to Market*. London, England: Kogan Page, 2011.

Harvard Business Review on Managing Supply Chains. Cambridge, MA: Harvard Business School Press, 2011.

Lavin, Frank, Peter Cohan, and Gary Locke. *Export Now: Five Keys to Entering New Markets*. Hoboken, NJ: Wiley, 2011.

Murphy, Paul R., Donald Wood, and David Parker. *Contemporary Logistics*, 10th ed. Prentice Hall, 2010.

Rangan, V. Kasturi, and Marie Bell. *Transforming Your Go-to-Market Strategy: The Three Disciplines of Channel Management*. Boston, MA: Harvard Business School Press, 2006.

Raulerson, Peter, Jean-Claude Mairaison, and Antoine Leboyer. *Building Routes to Customers: Proven Strategies for Profitable Growth*. New York: Springer, 2010.

ENDNOTES

1. Andrew R. Thomas and Timothy J. Wilkinson, "The Outsourcing Compulsion," *MIT Sloan Management Review*, Fall 2006, 10–18.
2. Keith J. Perks, "Influences on International Market Entry Method Decisions by European Entrepreneurs," *Journal of International Entrepreneurship* 7, no. 2 (2009): 71–80; Lee Li and Gongming Qian, "Partnership or Self-reliance Entry Modes: Large and Small Technology-based Enterprises' Strategies in Overseas Markets," *Journal of International Entrepreneurship* 6, no. 4 (2008): 188–208; and Rod B. McNaughton, "Foreign Market Channel Integration Decisions of Canadian Computer Software Firms," *International Business Review* 5, no. 1 (1996): 23–52.
3. Accenture, "From Global Connection to Global Orchestration," www.accenture.com/SiteCollectionDocuments/PDF/Accenture_From_Global_Connection_to_Global_Orchestration.pdf.
4. Liba, www.liba.com/index.
5. Erin Anderson, George S. Day, and V. Kasturi Rangan, "Strategic Channel Design," *Sloan Management Review* 39 (Summer 1997): 59–69.
6. Todd Guild, "Think Regionally, Act Locally: Four Steps to Reaching the Asian Consumer," *McKinsey Quarterly*, September 2009, 38–44.
7. United Colors of Benetton, www.benetton.com, accessed February 25, 2011; and Mark J. Barela, "United Colors of Benetton: An Examination of the Triumphs and Controversies of a Multinational Clothing Company," *Journal of International Marketing* 11, no. 4 (2003): 113–28.
8. Expert International GmbH, www.expert.org, accessed February 25, 2011.
9. Andrew R. Thomas and Timothy J. Wilkinson, "The Devolution of Marketing," *Marketing Management*, Spring 2011, 18–25.
10. Scott Kirsner, "The Customer Experience," *Fast Company.com*, December 2007.
11. Keith J. Perks, "Influences on International Market Entry Method Decisions by European Entrepreneurs," *Journal of Entrepreneurship* 7, no. 2 (2009): 71–80; and Lee Li and Gongming Qian, "Partnership or Self-reliance Entry Modes: Large and Small Technology-based Enterprises' Strategies in Overseas Markets," *Journal of International Entrepreneurship* 6, no. 4 (2008): 188–208.
12. Maggie Chuoyan Dong, David K. Tse, and Kineta Hung, "Effective Distributor Governance in Emerging Markets: The Salience of Distributor Role, Relationship Stages, and Market Uncertainty," *Journal of International Marketing* 18, no. 3 (2010): 1–17.
13. Leonidas C. Leonidou, Constantine S. Katsikeas, and John Hadjimarcou, "Building Successful Export Business Relationships: A Behavioral Perspective," *Journal of International Marketing* 10, no. 3 (2002): 96–115.
14. "Macron Dynamics of Pennsylvania," Export.gov, http://export.gov/articles/successstories/eg_main_037217.asp.
15. Proexport Colombia, "Office Network," www.proexport.com.co/en/office-network.
16. Hospital Management, www.hospitalmanagement.net.
17. For a detailed discussion, see International Chambers of Commerce, *The ICC Model Distributorship Contract* (Paris, France: ICC Publishing, 2004), chapters 1–3; and ICC, www.iccwbo.org, accessed May 25, 2011.
18. Keysuk Kim and Changho Oh, "On Distributor Commitment in Marketing Channels for Industrial Products: Contrast between the United States and Japan," *Journal of International Marketing* 10, no. 1 (2002): 72–97.
19. AGMA, www.agmaglobal.org.

20. Deloitte, "When Channel Incentives Backfire: Strategies to Help Reduce Gray Market Risks and Improve Profitability," Deloitte and AGMA, 2011.
21. Frank V. Cespedes, E. Raymond Corey, and V. Kasturi Rangan, "Gray Markets: Causes and Cures," *Harvard Business Review* 66 (July–August 1988): 75–82.
22. "European Court Supports Levi Strauss in Tesco Case," *Wall Street Journal*, November 21, 2001, A11.
23. Jen-Hung Huang, Bruce C. Y. Lee, and Shu Hsun Ho, "Consumer Attitude toward Gray Market Goods," *International Marketing Review* 21, no. 6 (2004): 598–614.
24. "Electronics with Borders: Some Work Only in the U.S.," *Wall Street Journal*, January 17, 2005, B1, B5.
25. See, for example, "Buying Prescription Medicine Online: A Consumer Safety Guide," FDA, www.fda.gov/Drugs/ResourcesForYou/ucm080588.htm.
26. David Arnold, *The Mirage of Global Markets* (Upper Saddle River, NJ: Prentice-Hall, 2003), 149–50.
27. "Internet World Stats," www.internetworldstats.com/stats.htm, accessed October 10, 2011.
28. International Data Corporation (IDC), "Worldwide Digital Marketplace Model and Forecast," November 2009.
29. Leena Rao, "J. P. Morgan: Global E-Commerce Revenue to Grow by 19 Percent in 2011 to $680 bil," *TechCrunch*, January 3, 2011, http://techcrunch.com/2011/01/03/j-p-morgan-global-e-commerce-revenue-to-grow-by-19-percent-in-2011-to-680b.
30. "Step-by-Step Guide to Going Online," Export.gov, www.export.gov/sellingonline/eg_main_020784.asp.
31. "UPS Fact Sheet," UPS, www.ups.com, accessed October 23, 2011.
32. "UK's Leading Online Ski Holiday Retailer Implements High-Performance, Clustered Database Solution and Accelerates Processes by Nine Times," Dell, March 2005, www.dell.com/downloads/global/casestudies/2005_iglu.pdf.
33. "The Best Global Websites in Travel & Hospitality," Byte Level Research, 2011, http://en-us.lionbridge.com/uploadedFiles/Lionbridge/~Files/Landing_Pages/Travel-Hospitality-Global-Websites.pdf.
34. "E-Payments & Taxes," Export.gov, www.export.gov/sellingonline/eg_main_020781.asp.
35. David Kravets, "U.S. Copyright Czar Cozied Up to Content Industry, E-mails Show," *Wired*, October 14, 2011.
36. Bernard LaLonde and James Ginter. "Activity-Based Costing: Best Practices," Paper 606, Supply Chain Management Research Group, Ohio State University, September 1996.
37. Council of Supply Chain Management Professionals, http://cscmp.org, accessed November 22, 2011.
38. "Manufacturing Strategy and Operations: Services Overview," Accenture Global, www.accenture.com/us-en/Pages/service-manufacturing-strategy-operations-overview.aspx, accessed November 22, 2011.
39. Richard T. Hise, "The Implication of Time-Based Consumption on International Logistics Strategies," *Business Horizons*, September/October 1995, 39–45.
40. Tonya Vinas, "IW Value-Chain Survey: A Map of the World," *Industry Week*, September 1, 2005, www.industryweek.com/articles/iw_value-chain_survey_a_map_of_the_world_10629.aspx.
41. "Logistics in Africa," *Economist*, October 18, 2008, 76.
42. David A. Ricks, *Blunders in International Business*, 4th ed. (Oxford, England: Blackwell, 2006).
43. "Economies of Scale Made Steel," *Economist*, November 12, 2011, 72.
44. Latin American Travel Association, www.lata.org, accessed November 22, 2011.
45. "The Top Ten Outsourcing Survey," Outsourcing Institute, www.outsourcing.com/content.asp?page=01b/articles/intelligence/oi_top_ten_survey.html, accessed November 22, 2011.
46. Michael R. Czinkota and Ilkka A. Ronkainen, "A Forecast of Globalization, International Business, and Trade: Report from a Delphi Study," in *Emerging Trends, Threats, and Opportunities in International Marketing*, edited by M. R. Czinkota, I. Ronkainen, and M. Kotabe, pp. 17–41 (Monroe, NY: Business Expert Press, 2010).
47. Patriya S. Tansuhak and George C. Jackson, "Foreign Trade Zones: A Comparative Analysis of Users and Non-Users," *Journal of Business Logistics* 10 (1989): 15–30.
48. Charles A. Taft, *Management of Physical Distribution and Transportation*, 7th ed. (Homewood, IL: Irwin, 1984): 15–30.
49. Michael R. Czinkota with G. Knight, P. Liesch, and J. Steen, "Terrorism and International Business: A Research Agenda," *Journal of International Business Studies* 45, no. 1 (2010).
50. Michael R. Czinkota, "International Marketing and Terrorism Preparedness," testimony before the Congress of the United States, 109th Congress, Washington DC, November 1, 2005.
51. Yossi Sheffi and James B. Rice Jr., "A Supply Chain View of the Resilient Enterprise," *MIT Sloan Management Review* 47, no. 1 (2005): 41–48.
52. Robert Malone, "Reverse Side of Logistics: The Business of Returns," *Forbes*, November 2005.
53. Haw-Jan Wu and Steven C. Dunn, "Environmentally Responsible Logistics Systems," *International Journal of Physical Distribution and Logistics Management* 2 (1995): 20–38.

APPENDIX A

Elements of a Distributor Agreement

A. Basic Components
   1. Parties to the agreement
   2. Statement that the contract supersedes all previous agreements
   3. Duration of the agreement (perhaps a three- or six-month trial period)
   4. Territory:
      a. Exclusive, nonexclusive, sole
      b. Manufacturer's right to sell direct at reduced or no commission to local government and old customers
   5. Products covered
   6. Expression of intent to comply with government regulations
   7. Clauses limiting sales forbidden by U.S. Export Controls or practices forbidden by the Foreign Corrupt Practices Act

B. Manufacturer's Rights
   1. Arbitration:
      a. If possible, in the manufacturer's country
      b. If not, before Chamber of Commerce or American Arbitration Association, or using the London Court of Arbitration rules
      c. Assurance that award will be binding in the distributor's country
   2. Jurisdiction that of the manufacturer's country; if not possible, a neutral site such as Sweden or Switzerland
   3. Termination conditions (e.g., no indemnification if due notice given)
   4. Clarification of tax liabilities
   5. Payment and discount terms
   6. Conditions for delivery of goods
   7. Nonliability for late delivery beyond manufacturer's reasonable control
   8. Limitation on manufacturer's responsibility to provide information
   9. Waiver of manufacturer's responsibility to keep lines manufactured outside the United States (e.g., licensees) outside of covered territory
   10. Right to change prices, terms, and conditions at any time
   11. Right of manufacturer or agent to visit territory and inspect books
   12. Right to repurchase stock
   13. Option to refuse or alter distributor's orders
   14. Training of distributor personnel in the United States subject to:
      a. Practicality
      b. Costs to be paid by the distributor
      c. Waiver of manufacturer's responsibility for U.S. immigration approval

C. Distributor's Limitations and Duties
   1. No disclosure of confidential information
   2. Limitation of distributor's right to assign contract
   3. Limitation of distributor's position as legal agent of manufacturer
   4. Penalty clause for late payment
   5. Limitation of right to handle competing lines
   6. Placement of responsibility for obtaining customs clearance
   7. Distributor to publicize designation as authorized representative in defined area
   8. Requirement to move all signs or evidence identifying distributor with manufacturer if relationship ends
   9. Acknowledgment by distributor of manufacturer's ownership of trademarks, trade names, patents

10. Information to be supplied by the distributor:
    a. Sales reports
    b. Names of active prospects
    c. Competitive products and competitors' activities
    d. Price at which goods are sold
    e. Complete data on other lines carried (on request)
11. Information to be supplied by distributor on purchasers
12. Accounting methods to be used by distributor
13. Requirement to display products appropriately
14. Duties concerning promotional efforts
15. Limitation of distributor's right to grant unapproved warranties, make excessive claims
16. Clarification of responsibility arising from claims and warranties
17. Responsibility of distributor to provide repair and other services
18. Responsibility to maintain suitable place of business
19. Responsibility to supply all prospective customers
20. Understanding that certain sales approaches and sales literature must be approved by manufacturer
21. Requirement to maintain adequate stock, spare parts
22. Prohibition of transshipments

SOURCES: Based on Nevada District Export Council, www.nevadadec.com/reps_checklist.htm; and "Elements of a Distributor Agreement," *Business International*, March 29, 1963, 23–24. Some of the sections have been changed to reflect the present situation.

CASES

PART 3

Toyota Incident

In August 2009, the improper installation of an all-weather floor mat from an SUV into a loaner Lexus sedan by a Toyota dealer led to the vehicle's accelerator getting stuck, causing a tragic, fatal accident and launching the most challenging crisis in Toyota's history. How did a company that became the world's largest and most profitable automaker on the back of a rock-solid reputation for quality and dependability find itself at the center of the biggest product recall? And what does this mean for Toyota's brand image in its largest and most profitable market? Toyota's perceived delay in addressing the situation is central to the problems Toyota is now facing.[1]

TOYOTA HISTORY

The company was founded by Kiichiro Toyoda in 1937 as a spin-off from his father's company, Toyota Industries, to create automobiles. Three years earlier, in 1934, while still a department of Toyota Industries, it created its first product, the Type A engine, and, in 1936, its first passenger car. Toyota Motor Corporation (TMC) group companies are Toyota (including the Scion brand), Lexus, Daihatsu, and Hino Motors. TMC is part of the Toyota Group, one of the largest conglomerates in the world.

The Corona, the first popular Toyota in America, was designed specifically for American drivers. With a powerful engine, factory-installed air conditioning, and an automatic transmission, Corona helped increase U.S. sales of Toyota vehicles threefold in 1966 to more than 20,000 units. The thrifty Corolla was introduced in 1968 and, like the Corona, was a huge success with American drivers. Corolla has since become the world's all-time best-selling passenger car, with 27 million sold in more than 140 countries.

As more Americans discovered the quality and reliability of Toyota products, sales continued to soar. By July 1967, Toyota had become the third-best-selling import brand in the United States. In 1972, Toyota sold its one-millionth vehicle. By the end of 1975, Toyota surpassed Volkswagen to become the number one import brand in the United States. Three years later, in 1978, Toyota won the "Import Triple Crown" by leading all import brands in sales of cars, trucks, and total vehicles.

In 1986, Toyota became the first import automaker to sell more than one million vehicles in America in a single year, racking up sales of 1,025,305 cars and trucks. That year also marked the company's debut as a manufacturer in the United States, with the rollout of the first Toyota car built on American soil. The vehicle, a white Corolla FX16, was produced on October 7, 1986, at the New United Motor Manufacturing, Inc. plant, a joint venture with General Motors. By 2010, Toyota had the annual capacity to build about 2.2 million cars and trucks and 1.45 million engines in 15 plants across North America. In 2007, the Toyota Camry was Car of the Year. The Toyota brand outsold Chevrolet in 2008 to become the top-selling automotive brand in America, and the Camry retained its crown as the top-selling car in the nation for the 11th time in 12 years. Toyota also passed General Motors in global sales to become the world's largest automaker for the first time in history.

In 1989, Toyota branched out by establishing a luxury line of vehicles with the debut of the Lexus LS 400 and the ES 250. Highly acclaimed cars plus exceptional customer service quickly became the hallmark of Lexus. Toyota launched two all-new gas/electric hybrids in 2009: the third-generation Prius with an estimated EPA fuel economy rating of 50 miles per gallon and the first hybrid Lexus, HS 250h.[2]

Toyota ranked eighth on the *Forbes* 2000 list of the world's leading companies for the year 2005 but slid to 55th for 2011.

In a 2010 worldwide ranking of automakers, the International Organization of Motor Vehicle Manufacturing ranked the Toyota Motor Corporation first on the list with 8.6 million units produced globally (market share based on OICA 2010 global total of 77,743,862).

SOURCE: This case was written by Susan C. Ronkainen and Ilkka A. Ronkainen for discussion purposes and not to exemplify correct or incorrect decision making.

By the middle of 2011, Toyota had fallen to third place, with GM moving to first and Volkswagen second.[3]

Top 3 Automakers Global, OICA, 2010		
Group	**Units**	**% Share**
Toyota	8,557,351	11.0
GM	8,476,192	10.9
Volkswagen	7,341,065	9.4

THE "TOYOTA WAY"

The "Toyota Way" has seven distinct elements: (1) *Kaizen*, the process of continuous improvement, which has Toyota employees coming back to work each day determined to perform better than the day before; (2) *Genchi genbustu*, which expects fact-based consensus building on defining challenges; (3) *Kakushin*, which focuses on radical innovation in terms of technologies and models; (4) *Challenge* to get employees to see challenges not as something undesirable but as a way to help reach improvements; (5) *Teamwork* to share knowledge with others in the team and to put the company's interests before those of the individual; (6) *Respect* for other people, not just as people but for their skills and special knowledge; and (7) *Customers first, dealers second—and manufacturer last* with the realization that customers pay the salaries, not the company.[4]

Ultimately, employees reach a point of "emotional fortitude," where their behavior is consistent with the organization's objectives. In the West, where individualism is at a higher level, it is more difficult for employees to absorb this objective. Emulating Toyota is not about copying any one practice; it is about creating a culture. It takes 1.2 American workers to do what one worker in Japan does. They have *kaizen*-ed and *kaizen*-ed and *kaizen*-ed in the jobs in Japan and there is very little waste.[5]

TOYOTA'S HANDLING OF THE CRISIS

Toyota said it received the first complaint about the Prius in August 2007 but some reports go back as far as the early 2000s. In October 2009, Toyota began sending letters to certain Toyota and Lexus owners to notify them of a serious safety risk where improperly installed floor mats could interfere with the accelerator pedal and provoke very high vehicle speeds. As a precaution the company asked owners to take out the mats and not replace them with any other floor mat and to have cars be fixed by the dealers. Additionally there were two more recalls in order to address the potential for sticking accelerator pedals and to update the antilock brake system (ABS) in certain Prius and Lexus 2010 models.

EXHIBIT 1 Installed Floor Mats

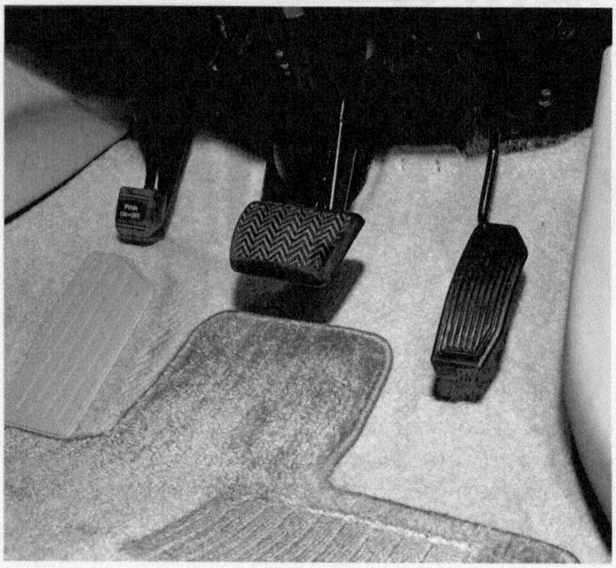

SOURCE: KAZUHIRO NOGI/AFP/Getty Images.

In February 2010, Akio Toyoda, president and CEO of Toyota Motor, made the first public appearance since the sudden acceleration problem started, in a press conference in Nagoya. The president expressed his regret for the inconvenience caused to customers and announced that he would command quality improvement around the world with the establishment of a global quality task force. The action plan of the task force included the enhancement of customer research, the improvement of regional subsidiaries' autonomy, and the support from outside experts.

Later in February 2010, Toyoda, and Yoshimi Inaba, president and CEO of Toyota Motor North America Inc., appeared before the Committee on Oversight and Government Reform to give statements on the subject "Toyota Gas Pedals: Is the Public at Risk?" In this hearing, where family members from people who died in a car accident involving a Toyota vehicle were present, the CEO took full responsibility for the safety of Toyota's vehicles and reminded the audience how seriously the company took the quality and safety of its vehicles. The CEO also explained how the company was going to manage quality control in the future.

Among the proposed measures were setting up a system for customers' voices around the world to reach management in a timely manner and also of a system which will allow each region to make any decisions as necessary. Another measure was the establishment of a quality advisory group composed of respected outside experts from North America and around the world. Finally the CEO announced the following measures in the United States: the establishment of an automotive center of quality excellence; the introduction of a new position (product safety executive), and the sharing of

EXHIBIT 2 Toyota's National Ad on Recall, January 31, 2010

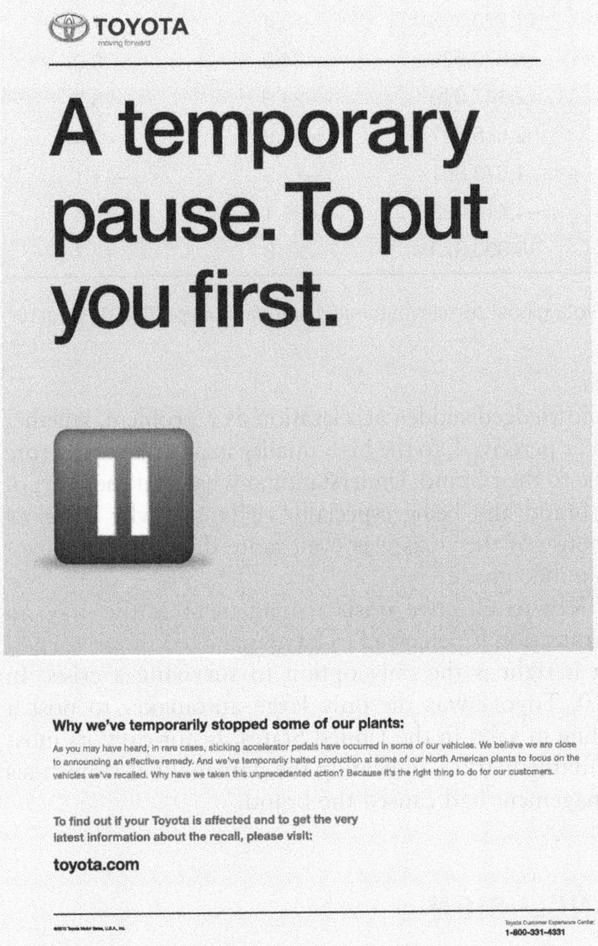

TOYOTA
moving forward
A temporary pause. To put you first.
Why we've temporarily stopped some of our plants:
As you may have heard, in rare cases, sticking accelerator pedals have occurred in some of our vehicles. We believe we are close to announcing an effective remedy. And we've temporarily halted production at some of our North American plants to focus on the vehicles we've recalled. Why have we taken this unprecedented action? Because it's the right thing to do for our customers.
To find out if your Toyota is affected and to get the very latest information about the recall, please visit:
toyota.com
Toyota Customer Experience Center
1-800-331-4331

SOURCE: © Toyota Motor Sales, U.S.A., Inc.

more information and responsibility within the company for product quality decisions, including defects and recalls. The ad says "A temporary pause. To put you first," in very big letters, followed by an explanation as to why the plants were temporarily shut down in comparatively tiny letters. The ad does not give any specifics about the recall, but it directs customers to the automaker's website for information about the Toyota recall.[6]

Additionally, the company also created a section on its website with information about the recall process. The new section included an option for customers to write down their Vehicle Identification Number (VIN) and figure out whether their cars were involved in recent recalls, and postings of all important messages about the recall process.[7] Finally, Toyota also created the Toyota Safety Website in order to inform customers about the technology it is developing to keep its customers safe and the safety features it is implementing in its vehicles.[8]

THE MARKET RESPONSE

The recall came at a difficult time for Toyota, as it was struggling to emerge from the recession and had already suffered from a resultant decrease in sales. Additionally, Toyota Motors as a whole announced that it could face losses totaling as much as US$2 billion from lost output and sales worldwide. Between January 25 and January 29, 2010 Toyota shares fell in value by 15 percent.

TOYOTA'S RESPONSE: ANALYSIS

The key to good crisis management is being prepared for a crisis before it erupts rather than responding to it. The recent Toyota crisis was two-fold: its crisis prevention procedures and its response to the actual crisis.

EXHIBIT 3 Toyota's Worldwide Vehicle Sales per Region (in thousands of units)

	2008	2009	2010	% Change 2009–2008	% Change 2010–2009
Japan	2,188	1,945	2,163	−11.1	11.2
Overseas total	6,725	5,622	5,074	−16.4	−9.7
North America	2,958	2,212	2,098	−25.2	−5.2
Europe	1,284	1,062	858	−17.3	−19.2
Asia	956	905	979	−5.3	8.2
Central and South America	320	279	231	−12.8	−17.2
Oceania	289	261	251	−9.7	−3.8
Africa	314	289	184	−8.0	−36.3
Middle East	597	606	466	1.5	−23.1
Other	7	8	7	14.3	−12.5
Consolidated total	8,913	7,567	7,237	−15.1	−4.4

SOURCE: Toyota Motor Corporation Annual Report 2010, p. 12, www.toyota-global.com/investors/ir_library/annual/pdf/2010/pdf/ar10_e.pdf. Reprinted with permission.

EXHIBIT 4 Toyota's Worldwide Net Revenues per Region (in millions of yen)

	2008	2009	2010	% Change 2009–2008	% Change 2010–2009
Japan	15,315,812	12,186,737	11,220,303	−20.4	−7.9
North America	9,423,258	6,222,914	5,670,526	−34.0	−8.9
Europe	3,993,434	3,013,128	2,147,049	−24.5	−28.7
Asia	3,120,826	2,719,329	2,655,327	−12.9	−2.4
Other	2,294,137	1,882,900	1,673,861	−17.9	−11.1
Intersegment elimination	−7,858,227	−5,495,438	−4,416,093	−30.1	−19.6
Consolidated total	26,289,240	20,529,570	18,950,973	−21.9	−7.7

SOURCE: Toyota Motor Corporation Annual Report 2010, p. 34, www.toyota-global.com/investors/ir_library/annual/pdf/2010/pdf/ar10_e.pdf. Reprinted with permission.

First, its hierarchical approach could be a major reason for its lack of capacity to identify potential crises. If subordinate employees are hesitant about communicating bad news to senior staff, the company's ability to spot flaws will probably be severely hindered. Additionally, the absence of an outside worker on the company's board could be a problem too because this could prevent top management from using fresh ideas to find creative ways to deal with any problem.

At the heart of Toyota's problem is its perceived delay in identifying and addressing the situation in the first place. There was a sense by the public that Toyota ignored the problem until it was forced to take action. It looked like the crisis was managing Toyota rather than vice versa. Corporate denial appears to have been the order of the day. The company was unable to perceive sudden acceleration as a problem due to Toyota's obsession with perfection. At first, it identified the source of the problem with the improper installation of floor mats, but later it shifted the cause to sticking accelerator pedals. Moreover, the fact that the company executed consecutive recalls revealed that it did not have a defined strategy to manage this process.

In regard to the communication strategy, Toyota's president, Akio Toyoda, made the first public appearance more than three months after the first recall of vehicles was made. Although the CEO should be the face of an organization, it may not be the best choice in a crisis. By August 2009, the National Highway Traffic Safety Administration had received over 2,500 driver complaints about sudden acceleration in Toyota's vehicles. The company spokesperson must be trained and practiced to be clear in a crisis and concise in crisis mode and not cause more confusion, as one Toyota spokesperson did in this incident.

During the crisis, Toyota's communication strategy was not the best, especially since people representing it were not quite effective at clearing up the public's doubts and informing them of Toyota's measures to address the issue. With their reputation on the line, Toyota finally acknowledged sudden acceleration as a problem, whether real or perceived, to the high-quality image that is the core value to their brand. Understanding what is at the heart of the brand and being especially vigilant is why the slow response to the crisis was even more damaging to Toyota's public image.[9]

Key to effective crisis management is the way an organization is perceived to have managed the crisis; getting it right is the only option to surviving a crisis. In 2010, Toyota was the only large automaker to post a decline in sales in the United States, historically its most profitable market, indicating the damage that slow crisis management had caused the brand.

CONCLUSION

In February 2011, the Federal Highway Safety Commission absolved the electronics in Toyota Motor Corp. vehicles for unintended acceleration and said driver error was to blame for most of the incidents. Three main causes for the sudden acceleration were found after a 10-month investigation. Two of them were sticky accelerator pedals and floor mats that trapped the throttle in an open position. The third and most common problem was driver errors, called "pedal misapplication."

The report came as Toyota's profits fell 39 percent in the December quarter (2010). Its sales had been hurt by the recalls and continued worries about its vehicles' safety. Ray Lahood, the transportation secretary, who had called previously for Toyota drivers to stop driving their Toyotas, now feels that Toyotas are safe to drive.

Electronically controlled throttle braking, steering, safety, and vehicle stability systems are critical to modern vehicles. Computer-controlled electronic systems have replaced mechanical connections to save weight, improve fuel economy, and enable advanced safety systems such as automatic braking.[10] The Alliance of Automobile Manufacturing hopes that these findings reassure the driving public. The exhaustive study should help Toyota fend off hundreds of lawsuits under litigation in federal courts that blame Toyota for the unintended acceleration that is currently hurting the company's image.

The reality is that Toyota is positioned for recovery about as well as it could be—owing, in large measure, to the reputation for quality products and corporate responsibility it has developed over the last two decades. And that may be one of the biggest lessons for other companies as they study how Toyota emerges from this recall crisis.[11]

QUESTIONS FOR DISCUSSION

1. Toyota had achieved the pinnacle in the U.S market by creating reliable, high-quality, fuel-economic cars. The past three years have seen that brand's superiority erode. What can Toyota do now to recapture its market share? With Toyota's new brands Venza and Yaris, can Toyota attract a new, younger market with new social media? How does Toyota break out of the stodgy styling of past brands—or should it?
2. Toyota is not only having a quality crisis but an internal battle as well, pitting the founding Toyota family against a group of professional managers each blaming the other for the automakers problems. Why?
3. Did the "Toyota Way" get in the way of corporate response?
4. Did Toyota make enough changes to further prevent sales damages and to get the company's reputation back on path?

ENDNOTES

1. Angus MacKenzie and Scott Evans, "The Toyota Recall Crisis," *Motor Trend*, January, 2010, www.motortrend.com/features/auto_news/2010/112_1001_toyota_recall_crisis.
2. Toyota, "Our History," www.toyota.com/about/our_business/our_history.
3. OICA, http://oica.net.
4. Hirotaka Takeuchi, Emi Osono, and Norihiko Shimizu, "The Contradictions That Drive Toyota's Success," *Harvard Business Review* 86 (June 2008): 96–105.
5. Drake Bennett, "Toyota Bets on Japan," *Businessweek*, May 9–15, 2011.
6. Chris Shunk, "Toyota Loses $21B in Market Share in One Week," *Auto News*, January 31, 2010.
7. Toyota Recall Information, www.toyota.com/recall.
8. Toyota Safety, www.toyota.com/safety.
9. Jonathan Hemus, "Accelerating Towards Crisis: A PR View of Toyota's Recall," *Guardian*, February 9, 2010, 25.
10. Mike Ramsey, Josh Mitchell and Chester Dawson, "U.S. Points to Toyota Driver Error," *Wall Street Journal*, February 9, 2011, B1–B2.
11. Michael Connor, "Toyota Recall: Five Critical Lessons," *Business Ethics*, January 31, 2010, http://business-ethics.com/2010/01/31/2123-toyota-recall-five-critical-lessons.

The Bell Boeing V-22

The Bell Boeing V-22 Program, a strategic alliance between Bell Helicopter, a Textron Company, and the Boeing Company,[1,2] announced the V-22 Osprey tiltrotor will be featured at the Dubai International Air Show in the United Arab Emirates (UAE) from November 13 to 17, 2011. The Air Show, held biennially, is organized in cooperation with the government of Dubai, the Department of Civil Aviation, and Dubai International Airport in collaboration with the UAE Union Defense Forces. Now in its 22nd year, the Dubai Air Show is one of the world's fastest growing aerospace events with industry and government participants from around the world.[3] The Air Show offers an excellent opportunity for Bell Boeing to showcase the Osprey's one-of-a-kind tiltrotor capability.

The V-22 is a hybrid aircraft combining helicopter and traditional winged aircraft performance. The engines and rotor blades point vertically up (like a helicopter) to allow the aircraft to take off and land vertically without need of a runway. Once off the ground, the massive engines and rotor blades begin to tilt forward to propel the aircraft upward and forward, gaining lift from the aircraft's wing as it speeds forward. In about a minute, the engines and rotor blades tilt to full forward flight, allowing the aircraft to fly with the speed and the efficiency of a traditional winged airplane. When in flight, the aircraft can slow, tilting its engines and rotor blades back to vertical, so the aircraft can hover or land like a traditional helicopter. This hybrid tiltrotor capability is an attractive solution for customers requiring helicopter-like vertical take-off and landing capability but seeking the longer range, higher speeds, and larger payloads of a traditional winged airplane.

The multicapable V-22 provides operators with tremendous flexibility for military and humanitarian missions. Mission flexibility is the basis of the value proposition for the tiltrotor V-22 Osprey. To understand the mission flexibility value proposition, one only needs to look at the variety of customers considering the V-22. In the United States, the U.S. Marine Corps uses the V-22 as its primary amphibious air assault vehicle to transport troops and equipment from ships to the battlefield. The U.S. Air Force Special Operations uses the V-22 for worldwide deployment of U.S. Special Forces. The United Kingdom's Royal Navy has evaluated the V-22 for maritime airborne surveillance and control operations to replace its aging Sea King helicopters, while the Royal Norwegian Air Force included the Osprey as a candidate for the Norwegian All Weather Search and Rescue Helicopter. Recent media reports suggest the Israeli Defense Forces are considering the V-22 for their own special-operations forces and for combat search-and-rescue missions. This hybrid tiltrotor aircraft is being considered to replace existing helicopters and winged aircraft, as well as to perform missions that helicopters and winged aircraft are not able to perform.

Defense and commercial trade offsets are valued in the tens of billions of dollars each year and often accompany the export of advanced technological goods. An offset is any type of nonmonetary compensation that a procuring government requires an exporting firm to provide as a condition of the sale and generally commits the exporting firm to spend a certain percentage of the value of the sale in the procuring country. Although U.S. defense firms generally see offsets as a reality of the marketplace in order to compete for international defense sales, the U.S. government's lack of a proactive policy that addresses the impact of offsets may undermine its economic and national security interests.[4]

OFFSETS

Obligations are imposed on the seller in major (most often military hardware) purchases by or for foreign governments to minimize any trade imbalance or other adverse economic impact caused by the outflow of currency required to pay for such purchases. In wealthier countries, offsets are often used for establishing infrastructure. Two basic types of offset arrangements exist: direct and indirect (as seen in Exhibit 1). Although offsets have long been associated only with the defense sector, there are now increasing demands for offsets in commercial sales where the government is the purchaser or user.

The Bureau of Industry and Security (BIS) collects data annually from U.S. firms involved in defense exports with associated offset agreements in order to assess the impact of offsets in defense trade. In 2009, U.S. defense contractors reported entering into 56 new offset agreements with 21 countries valued at $6.69 billion. The value of these agreements equaled 62.65 percent of the $10.68 billion in reported contracts for sales of defense articles and services to foreign entities with associated offset agreements. In 2009, U.S. firms reported 664 offset transactions (transactions conducted to fulfill

SOURCE: This case was written by Eugene J. Cunningham and Ilkka A. Ronkainen.

© Jason Phelan/Alamy

EXHIBIT 1 The Offset Process

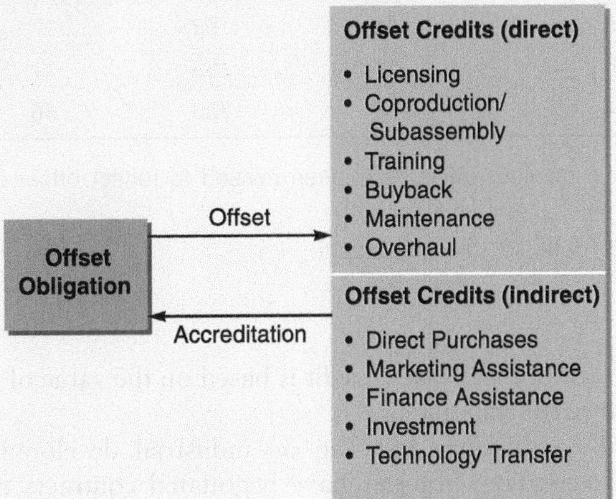

SOURCE: © Cengage Learning 2013.

offset agreement obligations) with 28 countries with an actual value of $3.50 billion and an offset credit value of $4.04 billion. During 2009, reported offset agreements ranged from a low of 9 percent of the defense export sales contract value to a high of 128.6 percent (see Exhibit 2).[5]

Direct offsets consist of product-related manufacturing or assembly either for the purposes of the project in question only or for a longer-term partnership. The purchase, therefore, enables the purchaser to be involved in the manufacturing process. As an example, various Spanish companies produced rudders, fuselage components, and speed brakes for the Spanish Air Force's EF/A-18s. In addition to component coproduction, complete products are produced under license. Examples of these include Egyptian production of U.S. M1-Al tanks, Chinese production of 719 aircraft, and Korean assembly of F-16 fighters. An integral part of these arrangements is the training of the local employees. Training is not only for production and assembly purposes but also for maintenance and overhaul of the equipment in the longer term. Some offsets have buyback provisions; that is, the seller is obligated to purchase output from the facility or operations it has set up or licensed. For example, Westland takes up an agreed level of parts and components from the Korean plant that produces Lynx Helicopters under license. In practice, therefore, direct offsets amount to technology transfer.

Indirect offsets are deals involving products, investments, and so forth that are not to be used in the original sales contract but that will satisfy part of the seller's "local" obligation. Direct purchases of raw materials, equipment, or supplies by the seller or its suppliers from the offset customer country present the clearest case of indirect offsets. These offset arrangements are analogous to counterpurchases and switch trading. Sellers faced with offset obligations work closely with their supplier base, some having goals of increasing supplier participation in excess of 50 percent. Teamwork can make the process more effective and efficient. As an example, a seller or supplier may have a business transaction in a specific country, but the company has no offset obligation in that country. A second seller or supplier, through a credit agreement, may be allowed to use the initial company's transaction to fulfill the second seller's indirect offset obligation.

Many governments see offsets as a mechanism to develop their indigenous business and industrial sectors.

EXHIBIT 2 Defense Export Sale Contract Values

Summary of Defense Export Sale Contract Values with Related Offset Agreements, 1993–2009

Year	Contract Value ($ millions)	Offset Agreement Value ($ millions)	Percentage of Offset Agreement to Contract Value	U.S. Firms (number)	Agreements (number)	Countries (number)
1993	$13,935.00	$4,784.43	34.33	17	28	16
1994	$4,792.42	$2,048.72	42.75	18	49	20
1995	$7,529.92	$6,102.58	81.04	20	47	18
1996	$3,119.67	$2,431.62	77.94	16	53	19
1997	$5,925.47	$3,825.53	64.56	15	60	20
1998	$3,029.20	$1,768.15	58.37	12	41	17
1999	$5,656.62	$3,456.89	61.11	10	45	11
2000	$6,576.21	$5,704.81	86.75	10	43	16
2001	$7,116.00	$5,549.55	77.99	12	35	13
2002	$7,406.23	$6,094.81	82.29	12	41	17
2003	$7,293.05	$9,110.44	124.92	11	32	13
2004	$4,927.51	$4,329.69	87.87	14	40	18
2005	$2,259.87	$1,464.13	64.79	8	25	18
2006	$4,951.97	$3,437.35	69.41	13	45	20
2007	$6,735.74	$5,437.57	80.73	10	43	18
2008	$6,286.16	$3,664.43	58.29	15	53	17
2009	$10,676.53	$6,688.34	62.65	13	56	21
Total	**$108,217.59**	**$75,899.05**	**70.14**	**49**	**736**	**46**

Note: Due to rounding, totals may not add up exactly. Figures for certain previous years have been revised to reflect offset data recently submitted by U.S. firms.

SOURCE: BIS Offset Database, www.bis.doc.gov/news/2011/15th_offsets_defense_trade_report.pdf.

Training in management techniques may be attractive to both parties. The upgrading of skills may be seen by the government as more critical for improving international competitiveness than efforts focused only on hardware. For the seller, training is relatively inexpensive, and training is often perceived to be politically desirable by government buyers.

An important dimension of the developmental effort will relate to exports. This may involve the analysis of business sectors showing the greatest foreign market potential, improving organizational and product readiness, conducting market research (e.g., estimating demand or assessing competition), identifying buyers or partners for foreign market development, or assisting in the export process (e.g., company visits, support in negotiations and reaching a final agreement, facilitating trial/sample shipments, handling documentation needs).

Sales are often won or lost on the availability of financing and favorable credit terms to the buyer. Financing packages put together by one of the seller's entities, if it is critical in winning the bid, will earn offset credits. Sellers also can offer financing assistance to help close third-party transactions for industries in buyer nations. In these cases, credit is based on the value of the third-party transaction.

Buyer nations focusing on industrial development and technology transfer have negotiated contracts that call for offsetting the cost of their purchases through investments. Recently, Saudi Arabian purchases of military technology have been tied to a seller's willingness to invest in manufacturing plants, defense-related industries, or special-interest projects in the country. British Aerospace, for example, has agreed to invest in factories for the production of farm feed and sanitary ware.

Most often, the complete offset package includes a combination of activities, both direct and indirect vis-à-vis the sale, and no two offset deals are alike. With increasing frequency, governments are requiring predeal counterpurchases as a sign of commitment and a demonstration of a seller's ability to deliver a successful offset program should the seller be awarded the contract. Some companies, such as United Technologies, argue there is limited advantage in carrying out offset activities in advance of the contract unless the buyer agrees to a firm commitment. While none of the bidders may like the advanced contract offset requirement, buyer's market conditions give bidders very little leverage to argue. If a bidder loses the deal, it can attempt to sell its offset credits to the winner or bank its credits for a future sale.

While previous deals were executed on a one-on-one basis, the government now wants, through the use of multipliers, direct purchases to certain industries or types of companies. For example, in the case of small- or medium-sized companies, a multiplier of two may be used; that is, a purchase of $500,000 from such a firm will satisfy a $1 million share of the counterpurchaser's requirement. Attractive multipliers also may be used that may generate long-term export opportunities or support indigenous arms or other targeted industry. Similarly, the seller may also insist on the use of multipliers. In the case of technology transfer, the seller may request a high multiplier because of the high initial cost of research and development that may have gone into the technology licensed or provided to the joint venture as well as its relative importance to the recipient country's economic development.

BELL BOEING V-22

With the speed of an airplane and the vertical agility of a helicopter, the V-22 Osprey is a true multimission aircraft (see Exhibit 3). An Osprey can carry 24 combat troops, 20,000 pounds of internal cargo, or 15,000 pounds of external cargo using its vertical takeoff and landing capabilities. On the ground, the rotors can fold and the wings rotate to parallel the fuselage so the aircraft can be stored compactly aboard an aircraft carrier or assault ship. The aircraft also can be refueled in air to provide worldwide self-deployment.

The V-22 provides a significant increase in operational range over the legacy helicopters it will replace. It also is the only vertical-lift platform capable of rapid self-deployment to any theater of operation worldwide. Current variants with the U.S. Marine Corps and U.S. Air Force provide the following multimission capabilities:

- Amphibious assault
- Combat support and transport
- Long-range special ops infiltration and exfiltration
- Combat search and rescue
- Medevac

The Boeing Company is responsible for design and production of the fuselage, the empennage, the avionics, and other subsystems contained in the fuselage. Boeing's partner, Bell Helicopter Textron, Inc., is responsible for the design and production of the wing, transmissions, and rotor systems and for the aircraft final assembly.

IMPACTS ON THE U.S. INDUSTRIAL BASE

The United States government maintains a "hands-off" policy regarding offset negotiation and implementation.[6] This approach creates a situation where offset agreements and the impacts from these agreements are determined by the private sector firms and the international customer nations. Essentially, the federal government has ceded its policymaking and regulatory authority over offsets to market participants. The United States is likely to continue to experience offset arrangements running counter to U.S. interests because the goals of private sector firms and other governments are not necessarily aligned with U.S. economic and national security interests.

Defense offsets can have an adverse impact on national security. First, offsets may undermine national security interests if they exacerbate the decline in the defense industrial base or disrupt critical parts of the defense supply chain. Second, offsets may undermine national security if the offsets result in the loss of critical skills in the defense industry's workforce that cannot later be replaced or expanded quickly. And third, while the United States has export licensing requirements, offsets multiply the chances that "leading edge weapons and the technology for producing them" may go to

EXHIBIT 3 Bell Boeing V-22 General Characteristics

Propulsion	Two Rolls-Royce AE1107C, 6,150 shp (4,586 kW) each
Length	Fuselage: 57.3 ft. (17.48.20 m); Stowed: 63.0 ft. (19.20 m)
Width	Rotors turning: 84.6 ft. (25.78 m); Stowed: 18.4 ft. (5.61 m)
Height	Nacelles vertical: 22.1 ft. (6.73 m); Stabilizer: 17.9 ft. (5.46 m)
Rotor Diameter	38.1 ft. (11.6 m)
Vertical Takeoff Max Gross Weight	52,600 lbs. (23,859 kg)
Max Cruise Speed	275 kts (443 km/h) SL
Mission Radius	430 nm (796 km)—MV-22 Blk B with 24 troops, ramp mounted weapon system, SL STD, 15 min loiter time
Cockpit (crew seats)	2 MV/3 CV

countries that represent a threat to U.S. national security interests.

Despite the risks that are raised by the use of offsets, the United States has yet to develop a proactive offset strategy. Therefore, the Department of Commerce, tasked with monitoring defense offsets, should take the lead in developing a comprehensive, proactive strategy to identify the policies and the actions necessary to address the risks posed by defense and commercial trade offsets. Moreover, this offset strategy should be developed as expeditiously as possible and incorporated in national strategy documents as appropriate.

QUESTIONS FOR DISCUSSION

1. Why would the Bell Boeing team agree to an offset deal rather than insist on a money-based transaction?
2. Why do governments typically take an unsupportive stance on countertrade arrangements?
3. Comment on this statement: "Offset arrangements involving overseas production that permits a foreign government or producer to acquire the technical information to manufacture all or part of a U.S.-origin article trade short-term sales for long-term loss of market position."
4. The international market is key for the V-22, which has been named as one of the programs vulnerable to pending deep cuts in U.S. defense spending. Does the Middle East hold promise for the Osprey? Does Europe?

ENDNOTES

1. Bell Boeing V-22 Osprey, www.boeing.com/rotorcraft/military/v22/index.htm.
2. Bell Helicopter, Press Release, www.bellhelicopter.com/en_US/News/1296722014702.html.
3. Abdul Basit, "Boeing Sees Strong ME Growth," *McClatchy Tribune Business News*, November 13, 2011, 15.
4. Herrnstadt, Owen E. *Offsets and the Lack of a Comprehensive U.S. Policy: What Do Other Countries Know That We Don't?* EPI Briefing Paper, Washington, DC: Economic Policy Institute, April 17, 2008.
5. "Offsets in Defense Trade," BIS, December 2010, www.bis.doc.gov/news/2011/15th_offsets_defense_trade_report.pdf.
6. Carol Dawn Petersen, "Defense and Commercial Trade Offsets: Impacts on the U.S. Industrial Base Raise Economic and National Security Concerns," *Journal of Economic Issues*, June 2011, 487–91.

PART FOUR

Leadership in Global Marketing

Part Four addresses contemporary approaches and directions in global marketing. Many companies today emphasize social networks in their international marketing. Leveraging the power of social media helps the firm reach deeper into existing markets and find new markets worldwide. Simultaneously, international marketers have become sensitized to adopting a more responsible posture in their international activities. Corporate social responsibility reflects company efforts that benefit not only humanity, but also provide important advantages to the firm. By striving for efficient and careful use of organizational resources, a focus on sustainability benefits society, the natural environment, and the firm itself. We conclude the book with a discussion of new directions and challenges confronting companies in the global business environment today.

© LOOK Die Bildagentur der Fotografen GmbH/Alamy

CHAPTER 16

Social Networks and Communication

LEARNING OBJECTIVES

By the time you complete this chapter, you will be able to:

- Understand the nature of social networks and social media.
- Comprehend the marketing dimensions of social media.
- Distinguish the challenges of social media.
- Understand the role of social media in international communications.
- Understand the differences in social media use around the world.
- Use social media success strategies in international marketing.

THE INTERNATIONAL MARKETPLACE 16.1

Volkswagen's Global Social Media Campaigns

German automaker Volkswagen has enjoyed much international marketing success due largely to the power of social networks and social media. Platforms such as Facebook, YouTube, and Twitter facilitate interaction between marketers and consumers. Firms use social media to promote their brands and connect with customers by creating web pages and interactive marketing. For example, Volkswagen used Twitter to tease consumers during the Super Bowl about its live unveiling of the New Beetle, generating substantial buyer interest and engagement. In print ads, Volkswagen featured a long stretch of road in Norway and urged consumers to download an app that lets them "drive" a car by hovering a smartphone over the ad.

In a campaign in Europe, Volkswagen used social media to encourage people to enter a contest to become the brand's official car reviewer. The campaign leveraged the growing influence of peer-to-peer reviews across web-based social networks. Top participants were given a Volkswagen Tiguan and a video camera for a week to carry out their reviews. Volkswagen then posted highlights on a dedicated site for consumers to choose their favorites. The contest generated enormous positive exposure in social networks around Europe.

In its most famous social media campaign, Volkswagen invented a German-accented, dominatrix-type blonde bombshell named Helga. She is an over-the-top parody of a German nightclubbing seductress. She appears in online ads to introduce the latest Volkswagen vehicles, with phrases like "Unpimp Your Auto." Visitors to Volkswagen's social sites can choose an interior, wheels, engine, and the like and take a virtual test drive with the boot-wearing vamp, who remarks on drivers' selections with comments like "I *luf* leather" and "I see from your paddle shifters, you're ready to go." Shortly after its launch, the Helga campaign went viral. For a time, Volkswagen ads were the top download at YouTube. Thousands of fans "friended" and "liked" Helga.

Social media via Helga and other online campaigns are helping make Volkswagen part of pop culture. Increasingly, firms use social media to offer action-oriented experiences that enable consumers to interact with brands. The goal is to develop and maintain meaningful, favorable, and long-lasting consumer–brand relationships.

SOURCES: Charles Child, "Making Brands Relevant," *Automotive News*, September 12, 2011, 1–44; David Kiley, "The Craziest Ad Guys in America," *BusinessWeek*, May 22, 2006, 72–80; Michael Learmonth, "Winning on Twitter," *Advertising Age*, May 9, 2011, 4; Charlotte McEleny, "Volkswagen Seeks 'People's Reviewer' via Social Media," *New Media Age*, July 2, 2009, 3; and E. Vines, "CP+B Offers a Joyride with Helga for GTI Enthusiasts," *SHOOT*, April 7, 2006, 14.

As highlighted in *The International Marketplace 16.1*, Internet-based social networks bring information, photos, video, and other content to an audience that wants to learn or be entertained. Consumers exchange e-mails with companies, personalize web pages, upload videos, rate products, and join networks of like-minded customers who also enjoy the brand. Social networks help raise brand awareness, increase market penetration, maintain customer loyalty, create user advocates, conduct market research, develop viral word-of-mouth advertising, create online buzz, drive consumers to company websites, and generally increase sales.

In this chapter, we examine the nature and impact of social networks in international marketing. For our purposes, a **social network** is a communal structure consisting of individuals or organizations connected with each other through friendship, common interest, commercial transactions, information exchange, or other types of relationship. Social networks play a growing role in society, particularly in marketing, as they serve the needs of consumers and help firms achieve their goals. When a social network converges around shared interests, goals, values, or attitudes, it fosters a common identity among its members, which is called a **social community**.[1]

Social networks provide the context through which marketers create and employ **social media**, which refers to the use of communications technology, such as the Internet and mobile telephones, to facilitate meaningful interaction among individuals and organizations. The intent of firms that use social media is to promote their brands and connect with customers by creating web pages, profiles, and advertising. Social media leverage the power of **electronic word of mouth**, through which any statement made by consumers about a product or company can be made available to a multitude of people via the Internet.[2]

At the time of writing of this chapter, Facebook is the most popular social networking site, followed by LinkedIn, Twitter, MySpace, and YouTube.[3] In 2012, Facebook had nearly one billion members worldwide—about one-seventh of the world's population. Exhibit 16.1 shows the countries where Facebook has more than 10 million members. North America has the highest Facebook penetration rate—the percentage of the country's total population that are Facebook users—at more than 50 percent. This is followed by Oceania and Australia (38 percent penetration), Europe (27 percent), and Latin America (26 percent). About 70 percent of Facebook users are outside the United States. Most of the Global 1,000 companies on *Businessweek*'s list of the 1,000 largest multinational firms have adopted Facebook and other social media to conduct marketing functions ranging from research to customer service.

International communications via social networks are a form of mass marketing. This is not the first time that new technology has given rise to new and intense, game-changing forms of communication and marketing.

EXHIBIT 16.1 Facebook Users and Penetration Rates in Selected Countries (in millions of people)

Region/Country	Number of Users	Facebook Penetration Rate, Percent
Africa	38	3.6
Asia	184	4.7
India	41	3.5
Indonesia	42	17.0
Malaysia	12	42.0
Philippines	27	26.5
Taiwan	12	50.3
Thailand	13	19.9
Europe	223	27.4
France	24	36.2
Germany	22	27.2
Italy	21	34.2
Spain	16	33.5
Turkey	31	39.3
United Kingdom	30	48.6
Latin America	142	25.5
Argentina	18	42.1
Brazil	35	17.3
Colombia	15	35.3
Mexico	31	27.3
Venezuela	10	34.7
North America	175	50.3
Canada	17	50.3
United States	157	50.3
Middle East	18	8.4
The Caribbean	6	15.0
Oceania/Australia	13	37.7
Australia	11	49.3

Note: only those with more than 10 million users are listed
Data as of December 31, 2011

SOURCE: Data from "Internet Usage Statistics" for country, *Internet World Stats*, http://internetworld stats.com, accessed January 8, 2012.

Gutenberg's invention of the printing press in about 1445 eventually facilitated the mass production of flyers, brochures, and magazines. Radio and television emerged in the early 1900s. Each of these media led to novel forms of targeting consumers with advertising and other marketing communications on a massive scale. The Internet, initially developed for use by the military, was commercialized in the early 1990s, leading to the rise of online advertising. Around the same time, firms began to employ *relationship marketing*, which emphasized the importance of developing and maintaining long-term relationships with customers, in order to enhance business performance.

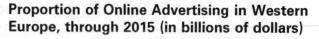

EXHIBIT 16.2 Proportion of Online Advertising in Western Europe, through 2015 (in billions of dollars)

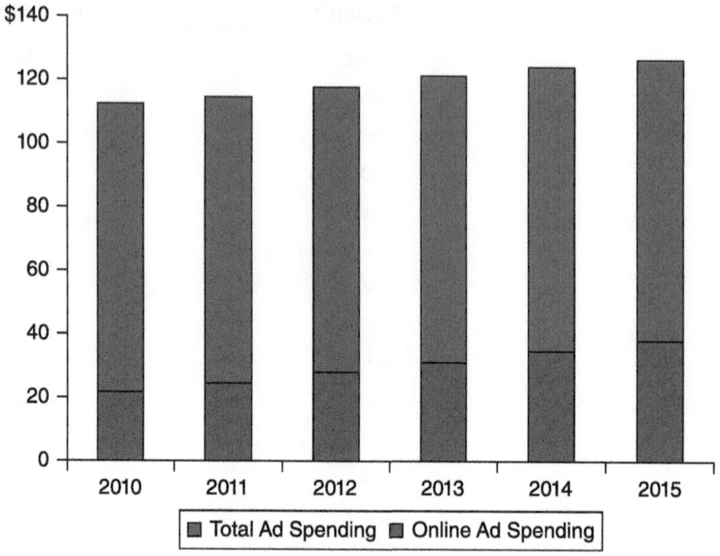

SOURCE: Adapted from "Digital Media Spending Thrives in Western Europe," *Emarketer*, December 15, 2011, www.emarketer.com/Article.aspx?R=1008736.

Recent trends include growth in Internet penetration worldwide. As a percentage of total population, Internet usage exceeds 70 percent in Japan, South Korea, North America, and most European countries. The rate is lower but still substantial in emerging market countries such as Brazil (50 percent), China (36 percent), and Saudi Arabia (44 percent). While traditional mass media continue to account for most advertising spending, Internet-based communications are the fastest growing category of marketing communications.

Online marketing communications take on various forms, including targeted e-mail messages, display advertising, and social media–based approaches. The use of online marketing continues to grow, particularly in the advanced economies. For example, Exhibit 16.2 shows the proportion of online advertising in Western Europe up to 2015. Total advertising spending is expected to grow to about $126 billion across all media, which includes Internet, magazines, newspapers, billboard, radio, and television. At the same time, the proportion of spending on online advertising is growing at a faster rate. Online advertising here represents spending on display, search, and other types of advertising via the Internet. Specifically, the exhibit shows that, while in 2010 online ads represented only 19 percent of total advertising spending, the proportion is expected to rise to more than 30 percent by 2015.

SOCIAL NETWORKS: KEY TO ONLINE RELATIONSHIPS

The effectiveness of social media derives from the power of social networks. A social network is a collection of people and organizations, often termed *actors*, and the *ties* or *relationships* among them. Actors and ties consist of individuals and their friendships, companies and commercial transactions, and so on. Marketers focus primarily on consumers and the ties between them, the firm, and its brands.[4] The strength of the ties depends mainly on the frequency and quality of customer interactions related to the firm's products.[5] Companies leverage social networks to strengthen ties, especially with their best customers, and to generally enhance the effectiveness of marketing activities. For example, marketers seek to ensure that consumers encounter their brands frequently and form meaningful brand relationships, which in turn lead to brand value.

Marketers also note the tendency of consumers to imitate the buying habits of those whom they know or respect. In this way, consumer preferences often depend on social contagion, which connotes the extent to which people are exposed to, and influenced by, the knowledge, attitude, or behavior of others, particularly those in their peer group. For example, teenagers typically consume the same brands preferred by their friends. Social contagion helps make consumers aware of particular brands. It also plays a role in helping them revise preexisting beliefs and misconceptions. For example, consumers with limited experience of a foreign brand will feel more confident about adopting it if they have received positive brand-related information from a friend or other trustworthy source.[6]

A growing number of firms use social networks for international marketing. Social media have gained popularity for several reasons:

- *Traditional marketing communications are "one-way."* Historically, firms have conveyed marketing messages via radio, television, magazines, newspapers, billboards, and direct mail. But such media are one-way, company-to-customer, and interrupt people to induce them to focus on a message. The sole aim is to sell products. Public relations (PR) aims to publish positive news about the firm and its products. But consumers learn about a brand only if journalists publish a story about it.[7]
- *Traditional marketing communications are expensive.* Traditional communications are conducted through expensive advertisements and other forms of compensated media. Celebrities and large firms dominate the news through their fame, connections, and sheer market power. Most firms are small- and medium-sized, with limited resources. Traditional marketing is often ill-suited to smaller firms, which often lack the means to communicate their message to a large audience.
- *Traditional marketing communications are inefficient.* Every day, people are bombarded with an endless stream of marketing messages. But traditional campaigns are static, with a limited life. The barrage has reached saturation levels, especially in the advanced economies. People find most mass advertising either irrelevant or unreliable. The end result is that people "tune out" and even distrust traditional marketing communications. Traditional media do not serve niche markets well. Traditional, nontargeted media work well for goods that are marketed massively, such as Crest toothpaste and Dell computers. But most products do not appeal to the masses; most are intended for specific market segments. For such offerings, broad-based advertising is inefficient.
- *Traditional media are fragmenting.* A few decades ago, only a few TV and radio networks dominated the airwaves; mass advertising reached huge audiences. But audience sizes have fallen sharply due to the advent of satellite radio and TV and a vast increase in the number of channels. Increasingly, people follow only those stations that appeal to their specific interests. Mass media market share has declined, and advertising has grown more complex.

Such tendencies are forcing firms to devise novel ways of communicating their brands to consumers. Today, social network–based marketing is providing a way forward. More than any other approach, social media reach specific markets with targeted messages that cost only a fraction of traditional big-budget media.[8]

Traditional marketing communications bombard consumers with one-way messages, such as these billboards in Japan.

THE RISE OF SOCIAL MEDIA

Social media are an Internet-based communication medium in which extensive conversations and interactions take place among people online. Social media allow people to share and feel connected with each other via brands and organizations they like and trust. Thanks to sites such as Google, Yahoo, and Facebook, the Internet has become a truly global medium. Marketing using social media provides the ability to deliver useful content, at the right time, to the right customers. Online communications are relatively low cost. After all, anyone can launch a Facebook fan page for free. Social media are a revolution in progress, overthrowing traditional marketing. Advertising and PR can be targeted to very specific markets. They target Internet-savvy consumers who opt for authenticity, empowerment, and satisfying relations with the brands they love. Consumers want participation, not propaganda. They want to receive targeted, meaningful marketing communications that focus on their specific needs and wants.[9]

Compared to traditional media, social media provide the means for consumers to voice negative as well as positive views on products and services. Traditional marketing emphasized pushing or cajoling consumers to buy the firm's products. By contrast, social media are interactive, allowing firms and customers to interact and provide information in a mutually shared relationship. Firms use social media to listen to their customers in real time and respond in the most effective way. Consumers are increasingly sophisticated. Younger consumers in particular prefer nontraditional means, especially the Internet, for obtaining news and information.

The constant connectedness created through social media allows firms to continuously remind and update followers about their brands and other offerings. Because followers subscribe only to the sites that interest them most, social media can be substantially more effective for promoting products than conventional marketing communications conducted through traditional media. The efficiency and effectiveness of social media marketing might well signal the decline of traditional media—radio, TV, and print—as vehicles for marketing communications. For example, before launching her tour of concert venues in Europe, pop star Taylor Swift undertook a sophisticated social media campaign that targeted fans in Belgium, France, Germany, and the Netherlands. Swift's highly active social networking presence allowed her promoter, Universal Music Group in London, to send targeted messages to fans in their own language about release dates, awards, fan polls, and tour dates.[10] In the past, pop stars relied exclusively on radio, TV, and print media to market themselves in foreign markets.

Forms of Social Media

Social media can take various forms, including blogs, wikis, forums, and podcasts. A **blog** (short for "web log") is a website on which individuals make regular entries of commentary or descriptions of events. Blogging is the fastest growing medium of personal publishing, individual expression, and opinion on the Internet. Bloggers may upload graphics, video, and other materials. Most blogs are interactive—visitors can leave comments and message each other, facilitating a dynamic website on topics of interest. Companies launch blogs to foster discussion, feedback, testimonials, descriptions, videos, and other material related to particular brands. For example, the book you are reading is accompanied by a blog titled michaelczinkota.com, where you can find updates, comments, and additional insights. Many bloggers write about global brands such as Apple, BMW, and Justin Bieber. Blogging connects firms to customers, facilitating market research. Blog analysis software permits analysis of market phenomena and long-term trends. A positive review or substantial buzz about a product on a popular blog, visible through large increases in traffic, can translate into sizeable sales increases.

A **wiki** is a website developed and maintained by a community of users who add informative content on a variety of topics. The most famous example is Wikipedia. On a smaller scale, many firms use wikis as a form of collaborative software, allowing employees and customers to interact and enhance group learning. Ultimately the wiki can become a database for creating, browsing, and searching through useful information. The consumer products firm Procter & Gamble makes extensive use of wikis to facilitate R&D and market research among its more than 138,000 employees in 160 countries. The firm used a Facebook-like platform called PeopleConnect to accelerate decision making on new product development. For example, a 150-person workgroup of multinational managers launched a new product with unprecedented connectivity, transparency, and speed.[11]

An Internet **forum** is essentially a site where people hold conversations in the form of posted messages. Typically, the conversation deals with a product, a brand, or some other specific topic. The resulting information is usually archived so buyers can conduct searches on issues that interest them. A firm can launch and manage a forum and invite interested consumers and other parties to join in the discussion. For example, video-game vendors employ forums to promote their products in Asia and Europe. The site boardgamegeek.com features a forum that promotes discussions about board games with players around the world.

For many firms, **podcasting** is an important part of the marketing mix. Podcasts started out as purely audio files for the iPod and other MP3 players. Now they are also available in video formats, giving firms more flexibility to provide consumers with useful material, such as do-it-yourself guides and product-use instructions. Historically, customer service departments responded reactively to customer complaints. Today, many firms address product problems proactively through podcasts that consumers download. Podcasts can also raise awareness of new products and ways to use existing products in novel ways. At the Apple iTunes website, for example, customers in Latin America can access podcasts from Mercedes-Benz Financial on purchase options for luxury cars. Subscribers can listen to a podcast on "How to Open a Bottle of Champagne" from a beverage vendor in the United Kingdom. In Japan, they can access podcasts on do-it-yourself repairs for the home.

Why Do Social Media Work?

Social media succeed largely due to three major aspects: opinion seeking, opinion giving, and opinion passing. Consumers with high opinion-seeking needs tend to search for information and advice from others when making purchase decisions. Individuals who exhibit opinion-giving behavior, sometimes known as *opinion leaders*, can exert great influence on others' attitudes and behaviors. Because the Internet facilitates multidirectional communication, social media provide the means for passing or sharing opinions at a very efficient pace. The dynamic nature of cyberspace means that a single person can take on the roles of opinion provider, giver, and sharer. Consumers' tendency to seek, create, and share content online is extremely useful for increasing the relevance and engagement of brands. Opinion seekers tend to regard recommendations by friends or classmates as particularly credible and reliable and thus rely on social media for obtaining information regarding their purchases. Using a few keystrokes, consumers can spread the word, both positive and negative, on brands to a global public.[12]

Social networking via social media has grown in popularity worldwide. Exhibit 16.3 shows the average number of hours spent per month at online social networking sites by world region. These data show that people in Latin America, Europe, and North America are all avid users of social media.

Representing a community of shared interests, social media are inherently social. They perform best when the members participate, interact, share, and recruit new members. One firm that has made such use of social media is Adidas Originals (www.facebook.com/adidasoriginals), which has more than 10 million fans who use Facebook to connect to the Adidas brand, apparel, and sports shoes. If one uses an international medium, one also has to be prepared for an international response. Adidas receives consumer comments in French, Spanish, German, Japanese, and countless other languages. Adidas Originals is a truly global Facebook site. Social media are not only for consumer goods. Firms that market business and industrial products also have substantially hiked their ad spending on social sites.[13]

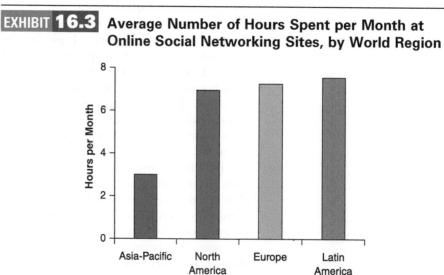

EXHIBIT 16.3 Average Number of Hours Spent per Month at Online Social Networking Sites, by World Region

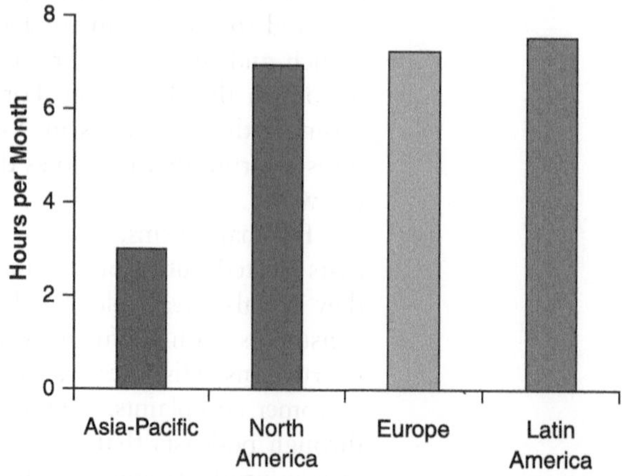

SOURCE: Adapted from ComScore Data Mine, "Women Spend More Time Social Networking than Men Worldwide," December 22, 2011, www.comscoredatamine.com.

Today, social media have become a critical part of marketing communications worldwide. For example, Britain's WPP, the world's largest advertising agency, generates more than 25 percent of its total worldwide revenue from digital activities. Publicis, a leading agency based in France, generates more than one-third of its North American revenues from online marketing.[14] The success of social media–based communications is driven by several factors, including:

- *Consumers' natural social tendencies.* People are naturally social and seek outlets through which to satisfy their needs to socialize and interact with others. The emergence of Internet-based communications, as well as instant messaging and text messaging, allows people to stay in contact with friends and interest sites throughout the day. Social media have taken the ability to socialize to a new level. A survey of 25,000 Internet users in 25 European countries found that social networking was the most popular activity among children aged 9 to 16.[15] Social media give young people countless opportunities to socialize about brands and other topics that interest them.
- *Growth of information and communications technologies.* Computers, mobile phones, tablets, and other such devices facilitate novel ways to create, target, and deliver advertising and communications. Such technologies allow people to socialize online and firms to promote their offerings, track consumers, and measure the effectiveness of their marketing efforts. The advent of smartphones was especially key to the rise of social media. For example, customers use smartphones on "quick response" barcodes to access websites and social sites of Triple-S, the largest medical insurance provider in Puerto Rico.[16]
- *Ability to reach countless consumers in novel and engaging ways.* Consumers are spending an increasing amount of time surfing the Internet. The trend is occurring across all major demographic groups, including elderly consumers. Electronic social communities provide vast opportunities to promote and engage with company brands, particularly those that fit the specific attributes of the communities in question. KLM, a Dutch airline, uses Twitter to instantly respond to customer service issues. KLM has over 200,000 dedicated customers following its Twitter account.
- *Ability to track and measure consumer behavior and target highly specific market segments.* Recent technologies facilitate tracking consumer behavior online. For example, despite some controversy, Google tracks your web-surfing habits, including which sites you visit and how long you spend at each site. Google then posts advertising at its search engine and Gmail sites that suits your specific interests. Sina Weibo, China's biggest web portal, provides the means to measure the most popular keywords on its microblog sites. This capability allows marketers to rapidly understand the hottest trends in China at any given time.

Creating Content via Social Media

Social media marketing emphasizes promotional content that consumers share with their social networks. Sharing implies that members provide content to the community that they themselves have created or co-created with other members. Once content is created, whether by the site owners or the membership, it is then disseminated among the membership and potentially far beyond, through viral means. For example, Gucci used a global, multilingual social networking site to launch a new collection of sunglasses aimed at 18- to 25-year-olds. The site encouraged users to upload and share their photos, rotated over a 3D image of the sunglasses and looking as if they are reflected in the dark lenses. Users can switch among London, Milan, Paris, and Tokyo and share their Gucci photo galleries at each site.[17]

At Facebook, YouTube, and other sites, consumers also generate their own content, facilitating greater engagement with given brands.[18] Every month,

Facebook users share more than 30 billion pieces of content, including web links, news stories, blog posts, notes, and photos. Companies try to stimulate users to post content that supports their brands. Some firms undertake **viral marketing** campaigns, a technique that facilitates and encourages people to pass along a marketing message to other users or sites, leading to potentially exponential growth of communications. Viral marketing can be a highly effective form of word-of-mouth marketing, generating news about company brands or activities and spreading rapidly through the Internet.

Many firms leverage the power of online opinion leaders and trendsetters to create buzz and accelerate product adoption. For example, Ford developed an aggressive social media program that employed 100 bloggers to introduce the new Fiesta automobile. The goal was to get the model's target audience to drive and chatter about the car for months throughout the launch phase. Ford designed the car in Europe and loaned 100 German-built Fiestas to social media trendsetters for six months. The 100 "Fiesta agents," chosen from 4,000 online applicants, blogged about their experiences behind the wheel and updated their friends and followers on Facebook, YouTube, and Twitter. Empowering 100 regular consumers to offer honest thoughts and reviews online was a risky strategy for Ford, requiring a new kind of corporate responsiveness and flexibility. Ford is also leveraging social media to conduct market research aimed at building "global cars" that meet buyer needs in each of Asia, Europe, and the United States.[19]

The *personalization* aspect of social media sites such as Facebook is powerful because it reveals what your friends and your friends' friends are buying and the companies they admire most. If you need to buy a new laptop, for example, you probably care little about what computers are advertised on television. However, if your Facebook friends "like" a particular brand, you will probably prefer it too. Social media succeed as a marketing tool because people usually trust the recommendations of the friends they know, particularly over those of companies they do not know.[20]

Exhibit 16.4 lists the most common reasons given by consumers in various regions for following or "liking" a particular brand or firm on social networking sites. For example, North Americans cited "to receive special offers or discounts" as the number one reason for following or "liking" a particular brand or firm, while Europeans were much less likely to give this reason. Europeans replied that showing support for a brand or company was relatively important to them. For social networkers in the Asia-Pacific region, being "among the first to get news on a brand or company" was an important reason for liking a particular brand or firm, whereas this rationale held relatively little importance to North Americans. In Latin America, many social network users indicated they liked a particular brand or firm after having seen an advertisement for it. By contrast, only half as many social networkers in the Asia-Pacific region cited this as an important reason. These findings underscore how social media usage varies substantially as a marketing medium around the world.

The United States is a leading exemplar of company usage of social media and how it might evolve in other countries. One survey showed that about two-thirds of U.S. firms using social media intend to increase such usage in the future.[21] Most respondents said social media improve marketing effectiveness by increasing awareness and consideration of company brands. About half the firms said it increases customer satisfaction and reduces marketing costs. Half also noted social media's effectiveness for market research and communicating with value-chain members, such as suppliers and distributors. Many noted that social media reduce the time required to launch products in new markets. Heavy users of social media reported significant gains in market share and other performance goals, though the causality is not necessarily one-dimensional.[22] Numerous firms in developing economies have embraced social media via *technological leapfrogging*. That is, many have accelerated marketing

EXHIBIT 16.4 Top Reasons Given for Following or "Liking" a Particular Brand or Firm on Social Networking Sites

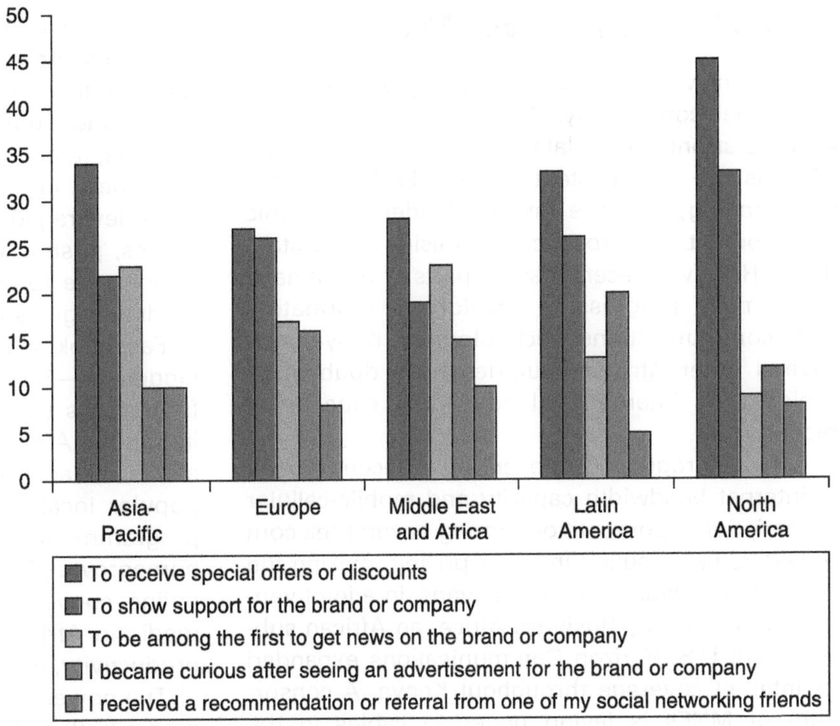

SOURCE: Adapted from Nielsenwire, "Deal with It! Discounts Drive Brand Love on Social Media," November 3, 2011, http://blog.nielsen.com/nielsenwire/global/deal-with-it-discounts-drive-brand-love-on-social-media; and R. Miller and K. Washington, "Chapter 85: Social Marketing," *Consumer Behavior,* 2012, pp. 466–69.

activities by skipping less efficient or more expensive approaches, such as television and market research firms, and embracing cost-effective social media to achieve marketing goals. *The International Marketplace 16.2* highlights Africa's rapid adoption of social media.

As the Internet gains momentum worldwide, firms are using social media to undertake international marketing campaigns. Because social media are cost-effective, even small firms can market offerings to market niches around the world. The media are an important means for establishing product interest in markets where consumers may have little prior experience with the brand. Leveraging social networks can be especially effective in emerging markets and developing economies, where consumers may be less receptive to traditional Western forms of marketing communications, such as TV and print advertising.[23]

Some cultures appear to lend themselves especially well to social media marketing approaches. For example, collectivist cultures characterized by a high need for social affiliation and respect for peers are likely to value the brand-oriented interaction available through social media. China is one of the top users of e-mail and social media worldwide, and the Chinese tend to exhibit a strong preference for online media that enhance social relationships. The market for credit cards in Russia is still emerging, and finding information on the creditworthiness of cardholders is challenging. Banks leverage social media sites, such as Vkontakte and Odnoklassniki, to identify potential users with strong potential credit ratings. Such sites help financial institutions target Russian consumers with higher income levels and graduate degrees, as they are usually more creditworthy than less qualified consumers.[24]

THE INTERNATIONAL MARKETPLACE 16.2

Africa's Blossoming Social Media

Africa is the world's least developed region in terms of Internet connectivity. Access to the Internet in Africa is strongly correlated with income, and most Africans live in persistent poverty. Lack of access to technology and the Internet hinders economic development and prospects for raising living standards. However, recently some parts of Africa have made much progress in developing information and communications technologies. Kenya and several other African countries have doubled or tripled their international bandwidth capacity in recent years.

Kenya's progress is due largely to recent growth in Internet bandwidth capacity and mobile-cellular subscriptions. Competition among several telecom providers has resulted in lower pricing, making the Internet accessible to more Kenyans. In a joint venture with Gateway Business Africa, an African subsidiary of U.S. Verizon Communications expanded its Internet coverage throughout Kenya. A consortium of MNEs is laying undersea cables in the Indian Ocean to upgrade Internet service between Africa and Europe.

Between 2005 and 2010, international Internet bandwidth in Africa increased from 3,500 to 82,000 megabits. Rising connectivity has fostered a flurry of international commerce with the continent. In Kenya, Namibia, and other African countries, cell phones are the usual means for getting online. In many areas, Africans have leapfrogged landline telephone technology by adopting mobile telephony.

More than 80 percent of Internet users in Namibia use social media. Popular providers include Facebook, Twitter, and MXit. Facebook was an important platform for disseminating information during the Arab Spring revolutions in North Africa that began in 2010. Media organizations in South Africa and numerous companies, such as Kenya Airways, are using social media to interact with customers. In Côte d'Ivoire, candidates for national office leveraged social sites for their political campaigns, posting updates on Twitter and Facebook. Pundits are forecasting a "seismic shift" in social media usage as more Africans access the Internet.

Facebook launched versions in major African languages—Swahili, Hausa, and Zulu—and offers free access to its platform to mobile phone users in various African countries. In South Africa, MXit, a free instant messaging application, is the most popular local social networking platform. African programmers are designing and launching new, homegrown platforms and tools to keep the African online conversation going. The growth of social media in Africa signals rising commercial activity, productivity, and business opportunities.

The power of Facebook, Twitter, and other social media is that they cost so little for what they are able to accomplish. In Africa, the economic domain is intertwined with the social and technological spheres. Marketers would do well to understand the revolution that is taking place. Increasingly, social interaction is fundamental to economic activity and market success.

SOURCES: André-Michel Essoungou, "A Social Media Boom Begins in Africa," *Africa Renewal*, December 3, 2010, www.un.org/ecosocdev/geninfo/afrec/vol24no4/social-media-boom.html; John Hagel and John Seely Brown, "Life on the Edge: Learning from Facebook," *BusinessWeek*, April 3, 2008, 14; and International Telecommunications Union, *Measuring the Information Society 2011*, Geneva: United Nations International Telecommunications Union, www.itu.int.

Social media are particularly useful to small- and medium-sized firms, which typically lack substantial resources to launch websites and develop customers around the world. The media are used even by government agencies and NGOs. For example, the international human rights group Amnesty International (AI) uses social media to promote its cause in multiple languages worldwide. AI undertakes campaigns using paid search, online public relations, market research, and other marketing functions. Using social media, AI targets specific groups with its online advertising, including global policy makers and activist groups.[25]

Social media provide a platform for communication, information sharing, and the development of meaningful relationships online. The media enable marketing communications that function much like conversations and shared experiences in a manageable form. Traditional advertising relied on interrupting and even disrupting buyers' lives. Companies and ad agencies controlled the distribution of content targeted at consumers. Through social media, the customer can be involved in promoting products and receiving product-related messages. Thus, consumers may even assume part ownership of a product or process. Consumer-generated media (CGM) refers to publicity and other marketing communications that consumers create themselves. CGM takes many forms, including comments, blogs, videos, and photos. In the United States, nearly half of all Internet users create some form of online content, whether posting entries at fan sites, editing videos, or interacting with blogs. Nearly two-thirds of younger consumers—*millennials*, those born between 1980 and 2000—regard using the Internet for social or personal interests as their favorite media activity.[26]

Among countless sites worldwide, Facebook and MySpace appeal best to retail consumers. LinkedIn is aimed at managers and those developing their careers. LinkedIn has more than 100 million members, including countless company-based groups in industries from finance to pharmaceuticals. Google+ has millions of members in such countries as Brazil, Canada, Germany, India, Taiwan, the United Kingdom, and the United States. Blogging and LinkedIn are often best for business-to-business marketing.[27] YouTube offers a forum where participants broadcast opinions and other information through self-created videos. Blogspot and Wordpress are two of the most popular blog-hosting websites, typically ranking in the top dozen sites worldwide.

Among the millions of websites worldwide, many focus on communities interested in specific topics and brands. Dogster.com, autoblog.com, and engadget.com all provide news and information to people interested in dogs, cars, and consumer electronics, respectively. Muxlim.com appeals to adherents of Islam around the world. Million of Muslims visit the Muxlim site to share their faith and obtain information on music, entertainment, food, culture, and more. Muxlim.com combines interactive video, audio, blogs, and images. Firms employ the Muxlim site to promote products and services to Muslims and to learn about their interests.[28]

Marketing communications using social media represent the new frontier in international marketing. Social networks are considered increasingly critical to any interactive marketing communications program. While much online marketing aims to drive consumers to specific websites where they can obtain product information and make purchases, social media are highly effective for developing customer relationships and building brand equity.[29] Marketers aim for *brand engagement*; that is, they want customers to develop a personal relationship with the brand. Social media represent perhaps the best means for achieving this closeness. A relationship implies developing an emotional connection and communication between the involved parties. The Internet facilitates a hands-on experience, through which customers can read, watch, listen, research, rate, post, purchase, and much more, all through a range of devices across a vast network of millions of collaborators and destinations.

MARKETING DIMENSIONS OF SOCIAL MEDIA

Social media facilitate engaging with online communities to generate exposure, opportunity, and sales. There are some major benefits that firms obtain by using social media in their international marketing activities, which we review in this section.

Generate Exposure for the Firm and Its Products

Perhaps the number one advantage of social media is the ability to draw attention to the firm's products and services. A good website and skillful use of social media lay the foundation for selling products and promoting the firm. Once consumers are exposed to a particular brand, marketers then take additional steps to generate interest and desire and spur potential buyers to action. Online social networks are an important channel through which information on new and existing products diffuse through marketplaces worldwide. For example, millions of consumers in Japan signed up to receive mobile alerts from McDonald's, such as tailored messages, discount coupons, contest opportunities, and special event invitations.[30]

Build Brand Equity

Social media provide myriad opportunities to develop and maintain awareness of the firm's brands.[31] The sites also serve to enhance the reputation and image of well-established brands by engaging consumers in brand experiences. For example, the German athletic shoe maker Reebok launched a digital ad campaign aimed at teenagers in nine major European markets. Reebok leveraged the popularity of rap star 50 Cent to create an online event in which participants engaged the brand. Entrants competed for prizes, with winners attending a 50 Cent concert. Some 180,000 teens visited the Reebok hub, and more than 23,000 took part in the event by uploading their entry to the contest, befriending Reebok and helping build brand equity.[32]

Drive Traffic to Corporate Websites

The best social media sites include links to company websites that provide a range of useful information regarding the firm's brands. Marketers employ various methods to encourage social media participants to visit the main company site. A good corporate website is eye-catching and includes company logos and graphic images. It describes the firm and its products and often contains press releases and links to news articles about the firm. The website should include pages aimed at current and potential customers, generate interest and sales, and indicate a clear reason why people should return to the site later. The global consumer products giant Unilever uses Twitter and Facebook to steer shoppers to its corporate websites, which cover five major regions worldwide.

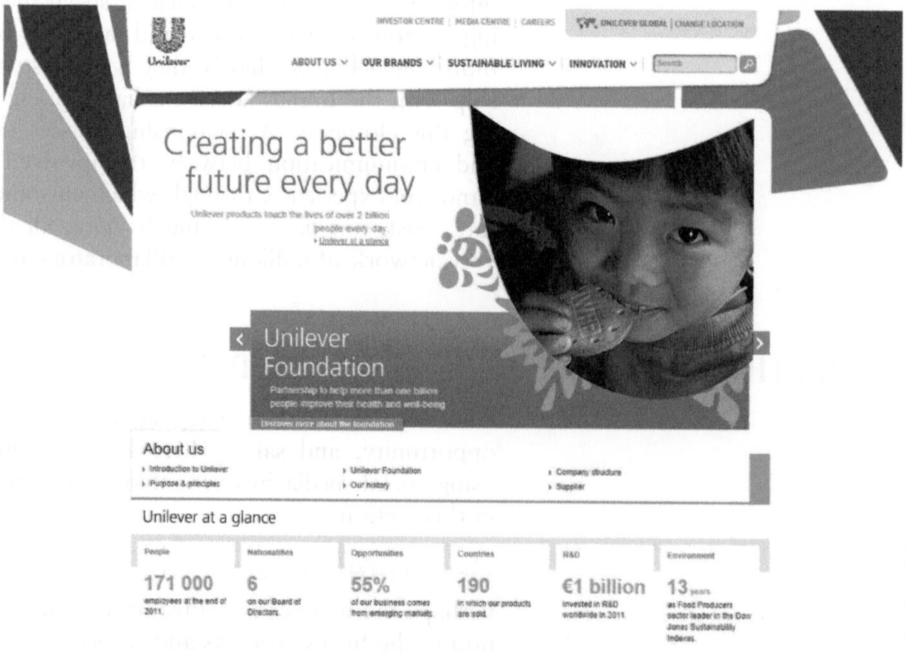

Multinational firms such as Unilever leverage the power of social media to persuade consumers to visit their corporate website.

Link with Other Sites across the Internet

Unlike traditional marketing communications, social media provide the means to obtain information instantly about a given brand, product category, and firm. By embedding links in social media messages, consumers can be taken instantly to their most relevant sites on the Internet. In 2011, Facebook was integrated with more than 2.5 million websites, primarily corporate sites, around the world.

Leverage Social Networks

Social media can quickly tap into consumers' social networks, producing word-of-mouth marketing that can spread at an exponential rate. This leverage is best exemplified by the "Like" button, which Facebook introduced in 2010. Since then, millions of individual firms have added a "Like" button to their websites, allowing nearly one billion Facebook users to express their approval of individual brands. When numerous consumers indicate they "like" a product, their testimonial spreads quickly among their social networks, reaching countless people worldwide. In Europe, Internet advertising has taken off, with substantial growth in social media advertising. Firms in Europe now spend upwards of $20 billion per year for online advertising.[33] Hotel le Seven is a boutique hotel in Paris that has generated much buzz via social media and thousands of "likes" at Facebook. The increased publicity has gone far in making Seven one of the most popular hotels in the French capital.

Generate Buzz and Spread Specific Messages Virally

Viral marketing implies a marketing message that is passed rapidly from person to person via social networks. The goal is to achieve specific marketing objectives, such as creating buzz and excitement about a particular brand. Viral marketing depends on a high pass-along rate. If many recipients forward the message to others, the speed of overall transmission can snowball very quickly. Today, many firms attempt to incorporate deliberate viral messaging into the firm's overall marketing strategy. However, the approach can be risky and controversial. In reality, relatively few viral marketing campaigns are successful. The best approach is sincere advocacy for a particular brand from real customers. By contrast, "astroturfing" is advocacy designed to give the appearance of a grassroots movement that is actually produced behind the scenes by a firm promoting itself or its products. Several organizations have been caught posting self-supportive messages online that they had initially portrayed as originating from enthusiastic customers.

Generate Product Sales

Generating product sales is the ultimate goal of most firms' marketing activities. Social media provide the means to engage target markets more efficiently and effectively. The technology is especially appropriate for niche markets, whether consisting of one thousand or one million individuals or organizations. Social media facilitate buyers' decision-making processes and ultimate purchases. Philips, the Dutch electronics company, has made a big splash via the online community in China. The firm works with leading players across five online categories, including Tudou.com for online video and Renren.com for social networking. Social media sites have helped Philips become the most popular brand across 11 of its product categories, including shavers, coffee makers, and steam irons.[34]

Conduct Market Research

Environmental scanning, data mining, and other forms of research are facilitated by the wealth of information that participants provide about themselves on social sites. At Facebook, for example, members provide various demographic and geographic information, as well as political affiliation, educational level, and psychographic data, such as interests, attitudes, and opinions on various topics, from favorite books and hobbies to contemporary issues. Some sites track members' shopping habits. In addition, marketers mine posts and other information published by members to better understand attitudes and preferences regarding individual brands. Such data lead to strategies for segmentation, targeting, positioning, communications, and other marketing tasks. When consumers signal their preferences for various product features via social media, important intelligence is generated that firms use to refine current offerings and launch new ones. For example, suppose you are targeting your product to baseball fans in Japan making more than $50,000 per year. Suppose your market is single parents who consume high-culture products in each of France, Germany, and Spain. Suppose your target is companies in the industrial equipment sector in Brazil. Social media provide the means to find and engage such markets. Facebook alone facilitates targeting a sizeable proportion of the world using very specific criteria at little or no cost.

Develop Ideas for New Products and Marketing Approaches

Marketers employ social media to develop new products, improve existing ones, and devise new marketing approaches. Crowdsourcing is the act of mining a group of customers for new product ideas, improvements in marketing methods, and other useful outcomes. For example, Cisco Systems enlisted the aid of its online social communities to develop innovative business plans. More than 2,500 people from 104 countries participated, including a three-person team from Germany who won the competition. Facebook leveraged more than 300,000 users of its social network worldwide to create different language versions of its site, leading to site versions more compatible with local cultures.[35]

Garner Publicity from News Media

Today, Internet users consider nontargeted, broadcast sales pitches to be spam. Sophisticated spam filters do not allow such messages to reach their intended audience. Accordingly, news releases and other forms of information dissemination online must be crafted and targeted skillfully. For example, when asked how he manages his e-mail, the chairman of Intel replied that if mail is properly labeled and addresses his interest, then it will get through. The Mexico Tourist Board also uses social media to generate positive buzz about Mexico, seeking to lure North Americans to Mexico to visit its resorts and historic sites. The Tourist Board uses social media to overcome negative press about Mexican crime and to generate positive news in newspaper and magazine outlets. The strategy includes the use of social media to co-opt Americans living in Mexico and reaching out to major media outlets like Bloomberg and CNN.[36] As highlighted in *The International Marketplace 16.3*, numerous international charities use social media to boost their fundraising.

Improve Search Engine Rankings

Search engine marketing is a form of e-commerce that seeks to promote products or services by using search engines to reach buyers directly. For example, when a shopper types a search term into Google—say "laptops"—he or she will be greeted by several ads in the search results from firms such as Dell and Toshiba who have paid Google for the right to display their products in conjunction with a given online search. Dell and Toshiba optimize the likelihood their products will be "found" via online searches, helping find potential customers. Marketers bid to have their ads appear in this way, based on keywords and phrases that consumers enter online.

THE INTERNATIONAL MARKETPLACE 16.3

Social Media for Charity Fundraising

Twitter is a free microblogging social network that enables users to post short messages viewed by other subscribers. "Tweets" of 140 characters or less are sent and received from computers, BlackBerrys, iPhones, and other mobile devices. Facebook is the most popular social networking service. Facebook gets most of its revenue from advertising, and firms use the site to promote their products and services. In 2011, Facebook launched a new portal for marketers and creative agencies to help them develop brand promotions. Hi5.com is giving Facebook a run for its money. The social networking site has become the world's third most trafficked, thanks to a focus on Spanish-speaking countries.

Social media have evolved through Web 2.0, a term that describes a new wave of Internet innovation that enables users to publish and exchange content. More consumers are using social media to obtain information that influences their buying decisions. By creating brand presence in social media, marketers boost people's tendency to imbue products or activities with "personality" or other characteristics they can identify with.

Social media are making a particularly big impact in charitable fundraising, a field that benefits enormously from international marketing. For example, the British charity Oxfam expanded its social media to better engage audiences online. Oxfam recruited a digital specialist to lead the expansion. Video content is preferred because of its emotional impact, moving people to donate at levels that reading a blog or Twitter message cannot. Oxfam is ramping up its Facebook sites and launching a web TV channel.

Charities used social media to conduct fundraising for the Haiti earthquake in 2010. Twitter, Facebook, and other sites made it easier for charities to communicate. The Red Cross uses such media to augment traditional fundraising methods, such as direct mail, e-mail, and telephone. Social media are less effective for contacting older donors, so it makes sense to use a variety of communications methods. Orphan charity SOS Children's Villages prefers social media because of its cost effectiveness over more traditional methods. The charity posts videos on YouTube and makes ample use of Facebook, Hi5, and Twitter. For many charitable organizations, social media are the most effective approach for maximizing returns for the amount of time and money spent on fundraising.

SOURCES: Celina Bublik, "Oxfam Sees Social Media and Video as Way to Increase Aid," *New Media Age*, September 9, 2009, 9; Paul Gillin, "Take Heed of a Developing Digital Divide," *B to B*, January 19, 2009, 9; Eun Sook Kwon and Sung Yongjun Sung, "Follow Me! Global Marketers' Twitter Use," *Journal of Interactive Advertising* 12, no. 1 (2011): 4–16; and Kaye Wiggins, "Charities Ring the Changes in Emergency Fundraising," January 26, 2010, 7.

Achieve Cost Effectiveness

Cost efficiency is a significant rationale for using social media. The firm takes advantage of the large cost gap between traditional media and marketing done online. At the same time, however, marketers need to devote sufficient managerial and financial resources to social sites to ensure visitors of a superior, consistent experience.

CHALLENGES OF SOCIAL MEDIA

Having discussed the benefits of social media, we now examine their shortcomings.

Send the Wrong Message

Social media are a double-edged sword. Just as firms leverage the technology to generate positive exposure for the firm and its brands, consumers and the media use such sites to highlight bad product experiences and other damaging information. Numerous companies have suffered the viral spread of rumors, scandal, and news stories that portray the firm and its brands in a negative light. For example, when cosmetics firm Christian Dior spokeswoman Sharon Stone suggested that an earthquake in Sichuan province was retribution for Beijing "not being nice" to her friend the Dalai Lama, bulletin board systems in China lit up instantly, with countless consumers posting complaints. Christian Dior had to drop Stone from all of its Chinese marketing and issued a statement of apology from her.[37] Canadian musician Dave Carroll complained to United Airlines that his guitar was broken during a trip on the airline in 2008 on a flight from Nova Scotia to Chicago. Carroll complained to the airline but was rebuffed and declared too late in filing his claim. In response, Carroll wrote a protest song about the incident that became a hit on YouTube and iTunes. The media picked up the story, and the song garnered more than 10 million online hits. The incident sent the wrong customer service message to consumers.[38] The ability of social media to damage the firm and its brands underscores the importance of ensuring consumers have consistently positive product experiences across all the firm's brands and marketing activities.[39]

Resource Intensive

Online marketing entails a substantial commitment of time and resources, which may be particularly taxing on smaller firms with extensive international activities across numerous languages. Thus, many companies find they simply lack the resources to undertake social media efforts seriously.[40] Successful strategy starts with ensuring the firm develops a good website and is consistently skillful in its online marketing activities and vigilant in tracking changes or attacks. It is critical to designate a team of managers dedicated to constantly monitoring and maintaining the firm's social sites. Neglected corporate blogs convey the impression the firm cares little about its customers and their needs. The firm should aim for creating a consistent message, which is often challenging with social media.

Results Are Difficult to Measure

Measuring the effectiveness of social media is often difficult because measures used in traditional media do not work for social media. A major problem is that it is often difficult to measure the technology's return on investment to the firm. Without the ability to measure the effectiveness of social media, managers may be reluctant to use it. Senior management may be reluctant to authorize resources for marketing approaches based on social media. As firms shift marketing budgets from traditional advertising (whose effect on sales is relatively easy to quantify) to social media, there is a stronger need to measure the effect of online approaches on profits and marketing performance.[41]

Lack of Access

Internationally, many people and organizations do not have ready access to computer technologies. This "digital divide" also occurs when people lack knowledge on how to use such technologies. The digital divide affects both developed and developing economies alike. However, it is most pronounced in poor countries. For example, it is estimated that about half the world's population lives on only a few dollars per day.[42] Such people cannot afford access to social media, let alone computers or the Internet. One study found there are more Internet subscribers in London alone than in the whole continent of Africa. Despite much progress in economic development in recent years, much of the world remains disconnected from the Internet and social media.[43]

In 2011, the petroleum company BP experienced the wrath of consumers worldwide via its social sites following the company's oil spill in the Gulf of Mexico. The BP episode was one of the first times a firm experienced negative publicity via social media on a global scale. Moreover, environmentalist organizations and other activist groups are using social media to pressure companies regarding practices such groups find objectionable. For example, Greenpeace threatened Nestle regarding its proposed use of a major palm-oil supplier due to concerns over rainforest destruction. The food products giant reportedly received 28,000 e-mails from Australia via Facebook and negative coverage on YouTube. Organizations like Greenpeace now regard social media as important means for undertaking activist campaigns against corporations around the world.[44]

SOCIAL MEDIA AND INTERNATIONAL COMMUNICATIONS

Social media require an approach to marketing communications that is more sophisticated than ever before. In an online environment, consumers widely disseminate their views and brand experiences via e-mail and blogs. In the contemporary online environment, marketers must provide relevant, interesting messages when and where consumers want them and engage users by enticing them to create content and comments that support the marketing goals of the firm. Categories of Internet-based communications include online advertising, banner ads, search ads, classifieds, rich media, e-mail with embedded ads, sponsorships, and of course, social media. We examine how social media affect individual elements of the marketing communications mix.

Advertising

Early attempts at Internet-based communications featured static display advertising and pop-up ads. There were even traditional ads on trucks and sandwich boards encouraging people to look up specific websites. The ads on the websites in turn imitated traditional approaches by emphasizing one-way communication. When first tried in the early 1990s, display ads and pop-ups enjoyed much success because, for nearly everyone, the Internet was new. However, today's consumers are more sophisticated—they usually ignore display ads, and most find pop-ups annoying. Yet marketers continue to use online display ads because they help remind consumers about particular brands and can significantly increase sales when targeted to the right audience. Many firms use Facebook to display advertising that they target to very specific groups. For example, by selecting "Japan" and "cooking" in the ad-creation section of Facebook, a marketer of cookware can quickly identify and target 40,000 Facebook users in Japan who have listed "cooking" as an interest area.

The Internet already has surpassed television as the largest market for advertising. Indeed, firms often end their TV commercials by asking viewers to check them out at Facebook, Twitter, or other sites. Print-media ads feature similar requests to "visit us online," often accompanied by barcodes that consumers scan with their cell phones. For example, in South Korea, the British grocery chain Tesco plastered the walls of subway stations with photos of various meat, dairy, and produce options, each bearing a unique barcode to be scanned with a smartphone. While waiting for the train to arrive, customers fill their virtual shopping carts and pay their bill using a phone app. The goods are then delivered to their front door while they return home at the end of the workday.[45]

Sales

Personal selling typically is most effective when the salesperson visits a prospect directly or by telephone. However, social media are an important adjunct to sales activities. Initially, social media are useful for finding, connecting with, and engaging prospects. Selling usually implies making several calls on prospective customers and being there when they are ready to buy. Social media can go far in facilitating this interaction and in maintaining ongoing relations with current customers. Such activities can be performed using social media at very low cost.

Social media provide the means to deliver the right message to the right audience at the right time. The most sophisticated marketers design social media sites to draw prospective buyers into the sales cycle.[46] Thus, for consumers at the early stage of the buying cycle, the firm should provide basic information about their problems and the ways company brands can solve them. Individuals in a later phase of the buying cycle will prefer technologies that assist them in comparing products and services. They will desire more detailed information about the benefits of the firm's offerings. Some firms provide chat sites and real-time sales assistance online. When consumers are ready to buy, they need easy-to-use mechanisms linked directly from brand content that facilitate quick purchase of the good.

For example, in 2011 Britney Spears used social media to promote her single "Hold It Against Me" and generated massive sales. Four days prior to the song's release, a demo tape was "leaked" to YouTube and posted on Twitter. The posting, combined with the demo tape, resulted in substantial press coverage of the single as well as abundant user-generated buzz. In the first week of its official launch, the single was downloaded 411,000 times from iTunes, the best sales week for a digital song in Britney Spears's history. The song jumped to the top of the iTunes charts in 16 countries: Australia, Belgium, Canada, Denmark, Finland, France, Greece, Ireland, Italy, New Zealand, Norway, Portugal, Spain, Sweden, Switzerland, and the United States. Thanks to skillful use of social media, the song proved to be a smash hit worldwide.[47]

Public Relations

PR, or publicity, consists of nonpaid news or editorial commentary intended to generate goodwill and a positive image for the firm or its products. Historically, PR managers worked closely with journalists in traditional media—newspapers, magazines, radio, and television—to generate publicity about the firm and its activities. Today, compared to traditional media, more people get their main news from online sites such as Yahoo! and CNN. Thus, contemporary PR requires creating a corporate website that offers an attractive portal, relevant and inviting content, and activities that support consumers and society. The best websites also feature a "press room" where journalists and bloggers can quickly access company news. Journalists depend on corporate press-room sites to obtain the latest news on individual firms. The online press room is a critical asset for publicizing the firm and its brands. PR managers at companies and public organizations write online press releases using keywords that help journalists find them when researching stories on given topics. Skillful use of keywords also helps potential customers find specific websites more easily.

In addition to journalists, ordinary citizens also visit corporate websites to obtain information that they include in posts at social sites about companies and their brands. Firms can assist users of Facebook, YouTube, and other sites to generate helpful content by ensuring the corporate website includes plenty of useful news and information. The website should feature engaging, fresh content; exciting videos; attractive photos; and links to useful sites and social media. Having a great corporate website has become a requirement for successful PR activities.

Promotional Activities

Sales promotion refers to short-term inducements that provide extra value and incentives to sales personnel, intermediaries, and consumers. The Internet, and social media in particular, lend themselves well to facilitating sales promotion activities, which include offering coupons, discounts, rebates, product sampling, contests, and premiums (free or low-cost gifts). Firms may offer any or some combination of these to entice buyers to act immediately, such as by visiting a website, registering online, or making a purchase. For example, Avis offers coupon deals at its various websites for car rentals in Europe, Latin America, and other international locales. Offering coupons online significantly lowers the costs of development, distribution, and database creation. Unlike traditional coupons, the firm incurs no printing costs. Many consumers prefer to obtain coupons online because of the time savings in searching for and organizing them.[48]

Some sites allow users to sample digital offerings prior to purchase. This approach is common in international sales of music, software, and many types of online services. Many firms employ social media to engage users in contests, sweepstakes, and games. The goal is typically to create interest, generate excitement, and entice users to visit a retail website. For example, in Europe, Sony regularly uses online contests to draw gamers to its Playstation websites. Contestants vie for prizes by playing various Playstation games.

Integrating Social Media with Traditional Marketing Communications

In terms of the traditional AIDA model of marketing communications, the firm seeks to create Awareness, Interest, Desire, and Action among consumers. Social media are particularly useful for creating awareness of, and interest in, the firm's brands. Social media used in combination with other marketing activities—such as traditional advertising, sales, and promotions—serve to increase desire and ultimate action—that is, purchase—among consumers.

Social media have added an additional dimension to integrated marketing communications. For example, a retail customer might buy a product from the company website, complain about a problem online, and return the product to the brick-and-mortar store. Every point of contact with the firm must provide a satisfying experience because, collectively, each encounter establishes or confirms the image of the firm and its brands. Thus, marketing conducted via social media must be unified and consistent with the firm's other marketing activities to create and support positive brand relationships with customers.

SOCIAL MEDIA AROUND THE WORLD

Social media take on various forms in nations and regions around the world. Exhibit 16.5 reveals the various rationales people use for engaging in particular activities on the Internet in various countries. Differences in culture, economic conditions, technology diffusion, and other factors drive differences in the way social media are used, or whether they are used, around the world.

In North America, social media have already become an integral part of sales and marketing. People of all ages use social networking sites. Social media

EXHIBIT 16.5 Internet and Social Media Activities in Various Countries

Country	Obtaining Information about Products or Services	Posting Information or Instant Messaging	Purchasing or Ordering Products or Services	Internet Banking	Downloading, Listening to, or Watching Music, Video, Images, TV
Brazil	53%	72%	22%	15%	71%
Canada	65	52	49	64	61
Iran	89	17	6	5	–
South Korea	62	53	55	35	34
Russia	64	70	21	6	69
Turkey	53	61	13	16	–
European Union (average of all states)	81	45	45	52	38

Table shows the percent of Internet users who engage in such activities. Data are for 2009 and 2010.

SOURCE: International Telecommunications Union, *Measuring the Information Society 2011* (Geneva: United Nations International Telecommunications Union).

accounts for over one-quarter of all time spent online in the United States. The United States has taken the lead in social media development and innovation. U.S. companies that make substantial use of social media include Apple, Amazon, Microsoft, Nike, and Ford. Numerous firms from other countries also substantially use social media in their international marketing, including LG (South Korea), Sony (Japan), and Blackberry (Canada).[49] In Canada and the United States, numerous colleges and universities have introduced classes on social media practices, preparing students for careers in social media marketing.

About 80 percent of active Internet users visit social network sites and blogs. Nearly half of social media users in the United States access their sites via mobile devices such as smartphones. About three-quarters of active online adult social networkers also use the Internet to do at least some shopping, making them a significant potential target market for generating sales. Most people in North America who use social media also follow at least one brand online. The most popular online activities include social networking, viewing blogs, and playing games. Facebook is by far the most popular social website, followed by Google and YouTube.[50] People from Canada and the United States watch more online videos than any other country.[51]

Europe is characterized by substantial differences in culture, income, and other factors across countries. Consequently, there is much variation in the use of social media across the continent.[52] In total, about 90 percent of all Europeans who use the Internet regularly visit a social networking site. Facebook ranked as the top site, favored by about 70 percent of Europeans online.[53] However, individual European countries favor home-grown social sites, such as Skyrock in France and StudiVZ in Germany. On average, Northern European countries tend to be more advanced in terms of the quality of information and communications technologies infrastructure. However, Southern European countries tend to be the most active on social networks.[54]

European consumers spend more hours surfing the Internet than they do reading newspapers and magazines. More than 80 percent of web surfers in the European Union use the Internet to obtain information about products and services. About half of EU Europeans use the Internet to buy or order products or services online.[55] The countries with the greatest market potential for advertising via social media are Germany, the United Kingdom, France, Italy, and Spain.[56] However, Europe has numerous laws and regulations aimed at protecting the privacy of the individual, which poses challenges for online research using social networks. For example, Google has encountered legal battles in several European countries based on its efforts to collect market data.

China has the most Internet users, about 500 million, far more than any other country. About one-third of Chinese use the Internet, and millions more come online every month. However, fearing the dissemination of content offensive to authorities, the Chinese government has historically blocked Western social media sites, such as Facebook, YouTube, and Wordpress. Chinese Internet users flock instead to local sites, such as Baidu, a web services site headquartered in Beijing and used by 500 million Chinese. Similar to Google, it features a search engine and numerous social and community sites. Tencent QQ.com is the most popular instant messaging service in China, with more than 600 million users, making it among the world's top three online communities. In addition to its chat service, QQ offers various blogs, games, and virtual pets. Sina.com is the largest infotainment web portal in China, featuring news and blogs.[57]

Among the Internet users, more than 230 million Chinese use social media regularly. Over 90 percent of Chinese social media users visit the sites three or more times per week, and the vast majority have friended specific company brands. Thus, about 200 million Chinese regularly follow brands via social media sites; that is more than in the United States. Facebook's penetration of China is relatively low, which has resulted because China is home to numerous Chinese social sites, such as QQ and Renren. Demographically, most Chinese Internet users are under 30 years old, but fully 40 percent are past 30.[58]

Most Chinese go online from home; the average user spends more than two hours surfing the Internet every day. Indeed, Chinese spend far more time on e-mail and the web than they do watching television. Two-thirds of Chinese web users access the Internet through their mobile phones. China has the world's most mobile phone subscribers—about 900 million. Starbucks, Louis Vuitton, and countless firms use social media and other sites to market their products in China. The Chinese web auction and shopping site Taobao generated about US$60 billion in sales in 2010.[59]

Most of the world's top 10 blogging nations are in Asia. Korea is the leader with 77 percent of Internet users reading blogs every week. China is the top market for blog writing. One reason for blogging's popularity in China is that freedom of the press is somewhat restricted. Thus, millions of Chinese get their news from blogs, which face fewer restrictions.[60]

Over time, social media marketing may well help democratize marketing communications around the world. Even a small company in a developing country can succeed in communicating its product to a vast audience by using Facebook and other such media. This results because news about great products spreads quickly online and at very low cost. Positive word of mouth about a superior product spreads quickly through social media, whether the inventor is a large or small firm, based in Beijing, Berlin, Brasilia, or Boston.

SOCIAL MEDIA SUCCESS STRATEGIES IN INTERNATIONAL MARKETING

Creating a substantial social media presence is not simply about making a Facebook page and hoping customers will drop by. In business, successful communities are developed through the use of skillful marketing research, planning, and strategy making. As with any marketing communications, the firm is competing with countless others, hoping to win customers over to its brands. Social media–based marketing succeeds best when the firm offers products and services relevant to the customer, incorporating substantial value, and provided by an organization deemed trustworthy and reliable. This section summarizes important strategies firms should follow to maximize the effectiveness of social media in international marketing.

Understand the Difference between Traditional Approaches and Social Media

In today's Internet environment, marketing communications often consist of unplanned messages created by customers online. Unplanned word of mouth among consumers and publicity in the mass media can do much harm. Thus, firms must focus on creating positive brand experiences so unplanned messages will be positive. You build trust in social channels by being helpful. The quickest way to turn off a community is to deliver a sales pitch. Become a trusted source and the goodness will come back.[61]

Communicate Your Expertise

Sophisticated companies publicize their expertise in various ways online, such as via websites, podcasts, blogs, and social media, all emphasizing buyers' needs. Fundamentally, more than caring about products themselves, consumers seek solutions to their specific problems. By providing expertise online that addresses the specific problems of target markets, the firm gains credibility and loyalty.[62]

Customize the Message to the Audience

Rather than using mass media to offer cookie-cutter solutions to the masses, today's marketers need to identify specific target audiences and customize communications that address their specific problems. For example, when a customer in the United States complains about a defective copy machine, he or she wants it fixed quickly. Alternatively, a Japanese customer expects a quick fix but also desires an explanation of what went wrong and what the manufacturer will do in order to avoid a repeat of the failure. In short, the American and the Japanese each require a different approach and solution.

Target a Specific Market

Most firms will need to target fairly specific audiences with their marketing communications. The audiences already may be known, in which case implementation is a matter of finding each audience and devising social media and other online approaches that cater specifically to the market. For example, a company that makes sporting goods might identify its target market on Facebook and other social sites and create media that appeal to potential customers there. It might devise a blog on sporting goods, develop YouTube videos that highlight various sports and feature its products, and so forth.[63]

Understand Your Markets

The Internet is an excellent tool for understanding specific characteristics of target markets. Marketers need to devise marketing communications only after acquiring substantive knowledge of the characteristics of intended buyers. With such knowledge in hand, the firm should then create and deliver appropriate products and services accordingly. By knowing who is using which social sites, marketers can promote their products to their targeted audience at the appropriate sites. For example, the social network site aSmallWorld targets affluent members and others who are part of the international social jet set. Care2 is a social network site that appeals to environmentalists and others interested in green living from around the world.

Monitor Your Firm's Online Reputation

Trust plays a critical role in the success of social media marketing.[64] In a world of 24-hour news cycles via practically unlimited news and information outlets, firms can fall victim to gossip and the rants of disgruntled consumers, activists, and others. Thus, marketers need to invest efforts every day scanning the Internet to monitor news about the firm and its brands. Continuous scanning helps deal proactively with emergent news stories that can harm the firm's good name. It also allows for deeper understanding of "the mind of the marketplace."[65]

Manage Information about Your Company and Brands

Many firms today use Facebook and other sites to disseminate continuous news releases that provide value to consumers. Buyers respond favorably to information that appeals to their needs and concerns about products and brands they enjoy. News releases online link to the corporate website, where explanations are offered regarding emergent trends and events that interest buyers. Smart companies target their audience with promotions, offers, and requests that inspire consumers to respond in a positive way. The most successful social media sites incorporate numerous useful links to other sites and provide easy means for customers to contact company representatives. It is critical to participate in Facebook, Twitter, and other social sites regularly to ensure a continuous flow of information that benefits consumers.[66] Social media help firms boost speed and agility to adapt quickly to rapidly evolving events and customer needs. For example, Chinese computer giant Lenovo launched a site called "Voices of the Olympic Games" to collect posts from the athletes competing at the 2008 Beijing Olympics. The site allowed Lenovo to link its brand to exciting Olympics events as they developed.

Social media are a revolution in progress. They are changing the face of international marketing. Social media provide a platform for international marketing that is authentic and cost-effective, building satisfying relations with customers around the world.

SUMMARY

In international marketing, companies increasingly leverage the power of social networks, communal structures of individuals or organizations connected with each other through friendship, common interests, commercial transactions, information exchange, or other types of relationships. Firms access social networks to conduct international marketing via social media communications technology, such as the Internet and mobile telephones, to facilitate meaningful interaction with customers. Facebook is the most popular social media site. Social media derive their power from social contagion, the tendency of people to be influenced by the knowledge, attitudes, or behavior of their peers. Firms use social media to bring information, photos, video, and other content to their audiences.

Social media have gained popularity in international marketing due to their relative advantage over conventional marketing methods and the fragmentation of traditional media approaches alongside the rise of information and communications technologies. Social media may take the form of blogs, forums, wikis, podcasts, and video sharing. The media take advantage of people's natural social tendencies, the ability to engage consumers, and the ability to track and research consumer behavior.

Social media provide numerous benefits to internationalizing firms, including the ability to generate exposure and sales for the firm and its products, build brand equity, drive traffic to corporate and other sites, spread messages virally, conduct research, and generally leverage the power of social networks. However, social media also entail disadvantages. They can send the wrong message and require new types of organizational resources. Results are often difficult to measure, and many people worldwide lack access to the Internet.

Firms use social media to conduct sales, advertising, public relations, and promotional activities on a global scale. Firms must be skillful in devising appropriate social media strategies for marketing activities around the world.

KEY TERMS

social network
social community
social media
electronic word of mouth
social contagion
blog
wiki
forum
podcasting
viral marketing
consumer-generated media (CGM)
crowdsourcing

QUESTIONS FOR DISCUSSION

1. Describe the relationship between social networks and social media.
2. What trends have given rise to the emergence of social media as an important international marketing tool?
3. Distinguish between social media and traditional media in international marketing.
4. Describe the various forms of social media.
5. How do consumers create content using social media?
6. What benefits do social media provide firms in their international marketing activities?
7. What disadvantages do social media pose for internationalizing firms?
8. Describe how firms use social media in international marketing communications.
9. How do social media vary around the world?
10. What are the success strategies for using social media in international marketing?

INTERNET EXERCISES

1. Current information on the state of social media worldwide is provided by various websites, including comScore at www.comscoredatamine.com, eMarketer at www.emarketer.com, Nielsen Wire at blog.nielsen.com/nielsenwire, and Internet World Stats at www.internetworldstats.com. Visit these and other sites and develop a profile of the current state of social media in a country or region of your choice.

2. Visit the websites of three multinational firms, for example, Volkswagen at www.vw.com, Sony at www.sony.com, and Nike at www.nike.com. How does each firm use social media to achieve its international marketing goals? Suppose you worked for a small company. Based on your investigation of the above sites, write a memo to your superior in which you describe the most important social media features of corporate websites for facilitating international marketing success.

CHALLENGE US

Up for Debate

In international marketing, social media pose an important dilemma about the privacy of personal information. Around the world, people freely release data about themselves through social networks online. Many teens post thousands of personal messages to social sites every month. Google, MySpace, and countless other sites profit from the client information they supply to marketers and others with commercial goals. But social media facilitate scams and other fraudulent activity online. Information revealed online exposes teenagers to sexual predators. In China, authorities have used data provided online to find and persecute those who criticize the government. In Russia, authorities harass bloggers and others who expose corruption or criticize those in power. In most of the world, privacy laws are lax. Anyone, including criminals and predators, can access confidential data.

Some governments have passed laws protecting private information and prescribing penalties for violators. In Europe, governments may require Internet firms to obtain explicit consent from consumers about using their personal data, delete data at the consumer's request, and face fines for failure to comply. India requires companies to ensure the security of credit card numbers, personal health information, and other private information that consumers may provide online.

Critics claim that online providers are obliged to guard private information. Some assert that the Internet and social media cannot succeed unless private data are protected from misuse. Others argue it is unreasonable to expect information posted to social sites will remain private. Social media's complex network of connections provides seemingly limitless ways to disseminate information far and wide. Social media blur the boundary between private and public.

For Discussion

1. What is your view? Are you careful about the information you provide online?
2. How should privacy issues be managed online? Should governments intervene to ensure private information is not misused? Should firms be required to obtain your consent before posting personal information online?
3. How can governments distinguish personal from public information? Given that websites may link to hundreds of other sites, how can social sites ensure personal communications are not disseminated around the Internet? Where do you draw the line?
4. Should market research using information gleaned online be outlawed?
5. Does Internet privacy imply that all information posted online remains private and confidential?

RECOMMENDED READINGS

Barker, Melissa, Donald Barker, Nicholas Bormann, and Krista Neher. *Social Media Marketing: A Strategic Approach*, 1st ed. Stamford, CT: Cengage, 2013.

Kerpen, David. *Likeable Social Media*. New York: McGraw Hill, 2011.

Klososky, Scott. *Manager's Guide to Social Media*, 1st ed. Burr Ridge, IL: McGraw Hill, 2011.

Scott, David. *The New Rules of Marketing & PR: How to Use Social Media, Online Video, Mobile Applications, Blogs, News Releases, and Viral Marketing to Reach Buyers Directly*. Hoboken, NJ: Wiley, 2011.

Smith, Mari. *The New Relationship Marketing: How to Build a Large, Loyal, Profitable Network Using the Social Web*. Hoboken, NJ: Wiley, 2011.

Van den Bulte, Christoph, and Stefan Wuyts. *Social Networks and Marketing*. Cambridge, MA: Marketing Science Institute, 2007.

ENDNOTES

1. Dave Kerpen, *Likeable Social Media* (New York: McGraw Hill, 2011); Scott Klososky, *Manager's Guide to Social Media*, 1st ed. (Burr Ridge, IL: McGraw Hill 2011); and Christophe Van den Bulte and Stefan Wuyts, *Social Networks and Marketing* (Cambridge, MA: Marketing Science Institute, 2007).
2. "Electronic Word-of-Mouth (eWOM) in Social Networking Sites," *International Journal of Advertising* 30, no. 1 (2011): 47–75; and T. Hennig-Thurau, K. Gwinner, G. Walsh, G. Gremler, and D. Gremler, "Electronic Word-of-Mouth via Consumer-Opinion Platforms," *Journal of Interactive Marketing* 18, no. 1 (2004): 38–52.
3. Emily Banks, "Facebook Is Most Popular Social Network for All Ages; LinkedIn Is Second," Mashable, November 4, 2011, http://mashable.com.
4. Van den Bulte and Wuyts, 2007.
5. J. Brown and P. H. Reingen, "Social Ties and Word-of-Mouth Referral Behavior," *Journal of Consumer Research* 14, no. 3 (1987): 350–62; and Van den Bulte and Wuyts, 2007.
6. Shu-Chuan Chu and Yoojung Kim, "Determinants of Consumer Engagement in Consumer Engagement in Electronic Word-of-Mouth (eWOM) in Social Networking Sites," *International Journal of Advertising* 30, no. 1 (2011): 47–75.
7. David Scott, *The New Rules of Marketing and PR* (Hoboken, NJ: John Wiley, 2007).
8. Ibid.
9. Ibid.
10. "U.K., Europe Embrace Swift," *Billboard*, December 10, 2011, 36.
11. Rick Swanborg, "Procter & Gamble's Social Enterprise," *CIO*, September 1, 2009, 24.
12. Chu and Kim, 2011.
13. Paul Gillin, "Let a Hundred Flowers Bloom," *B to B*, April 4, 2011, S8.
14. Ibid.
15. International Telecommunications Union, *Measuring the Information Society 2011* (Geneva: United Nations International Telecommunications Union).
16. Lilly Sein, "Local Companies Employing QR Codes in New Ad Campaigns," *Caribbean Business*, May 5, 2011, 48.
17. Samantha Conti, "A Growing Conversation: Gucci Latest Luxe Brand Flocking to Social Media," *WWD: Women's Wear Daily*, October 15, 2009, 1.
18. Al Ries, "Social Media Will Usher in a Golden Age of Global Branding—If Marketers Get the Message Right," *Advertising Age*, January 10, 2011, 16.
19. Eric Tegler, "Ford Is Counting on Army of 100 Bloggers to Launch New Fiesta," *Advertising Age*, April 20, 2009, 17.
20. Jacques Bughin and Michael Chui, "The Rise of the Networked Enterprise: Web 2.0 Finds Its Payday," *McKinsey Quarterly*, Spring 2011, www.mckinseyquarterly.com.
21. Ibid.
22. Van den Bulte and Wuyts, 2007.
23. Ibid.
24. Kimberly Maul, "Facebook Marketing: Strategies for Turning 'Likes' into Loyalty," *eMarketer* Webinar, July 29, 2011, www.emarketer.com.
25. Will Cooper, "Amnesty Looks to Utilise Social Media in Latest Global Campaign," *New Media Age*, August 5, 2008, 9.
26. Deloitte Development LLC, *State of the Media Democracy Survey*, 5th ed. (2011), www.deloitte.com, accessed February 3, 2012; and Salvatore Parise, Patricia Guinan, and Bruce Weinberg, "The Secrets of Marketing in a Web 2.0 World," *Wall Street Journal*, December 15, 2008, www.wsj.com.
27. Gillin, 2011.
28. "Marketing 2 Muslims," *Marketing Week*, June 24, 2010, 18.
29. Ries, 2011.
30. David Edelman, "Branding in the Digital Age," *Harvard Business Review*, December 2010, 62–69.
31. Ries, 2011.
32. "Fashion: Reebok," *Revolution*, October 17, 2008, 75.
33. A. Fontevecchia, "Europe's Sizzling Display Ad Market Provides Opportunity for Facebook," *Forbes.com*, June 16, 2011, 18.
34. "Campaign Digital Media Awards: Best Viral Marketing," *Campaign Asia-Pacific*, December 2010, 99; and "Philip's Global Star Eyes China," *Campaign Asia-Pacific*, March 2011, 36.
35. "Facebook Asks Users to Translate New Versions for Free," Fox News, April 20, 2008, www.foxnews.com; and Dave Webb, "Why the Cisco i-Prize Is So Powerful," *itbusiness.ca*, October 22, 2008, www.itbusiness.ca.
36. A. Bruell, "Mexico Leans on PR to Lure Back Tourists," *Advertising Age*, June 27, 2011, 18.
37. "Dior Drops Sharon Stone in China," *BBC News*, May 29, 2008, http://news.bbc.co.uk.
38. Andrew Clancy, "Listen Up," *Smart Business Detroit*, May 2011, 7.
39. Michael Zeisser, "Unlocking the Elusive Potential of Social Networks," *McKinsey Quarterly*, June 2010, www.mckinseyquarterly.com.
40. N. Bussey, "When Consumers Ambush Best-Laid Ad Plans," *Campaign*, March 13, 2009, 12; and "The Scale of the Alignment Challenge," *Marketing*, October 26, 2011, 18–19.
41. Gillin, 2009; and T. Morris, "The ROI on Social Media: Time to Bring in an Accounting Framework," *CMA Magazine,* March 2011, 20–21.
42. World Bank, *World Bank Development Indicators 2012* (Washington, DC: World Bank, 2012).
43. T. Kemeny, "Are International Technology Gaps Growing or Shrinking in the Age of Globalization?" *Journal of Economic Geography* 11, no. 1 (2011): 1–35.
44. O. Millman, "Social Problems for Brands," *B&T Magazine*, July 23, 2010, 8; and Emily Steel, "Nestlé Takes a Beating on Social-Media Sites," *Wall Street Journal*, March 3, 2010, B5.
45. Cigdem Iltan, "Next Stop, Groceries," *Maclean's*, July 25, 2011, 43.
46. Scott, 2007.
47. A. Kaplan and M. Haenlein, "The Britney Spears Universe: Social Media and Viral Marketing at its Best," *Business Horizons* 55, no. 1 (2012): 27–31.

48. Kwon Jung and Boon Young Lee, "Online vs. Offline Coupon Redemption Behaviors," *International Business & Economics Research Journal* 9, no. 12 (2010): 23–36.
49. Matt Carmichael, "Top Brand Ad Spending by Category and Social-Media Ranking," *Ad Age Blogs*, June 19, 2011, http://adage.com.
50. Nielsen, *State of the Media: The Social Media Report 2011*, http://blog.nielsen.com/nielsenwire/social.
51. ComScore Data Mine 1, "Canadians Watch Most Online Videos," December 15, 2011, www.comscoredatamine.com.
52. M. Kemp, "How Social Media Use Varies across Europe," *New Media Age*, July 12, 2007, 8.
53. ComScore Data Mine 2, "Facebook Continues Strong Lead across Europe," December 5, 2011, http://www.comscoredatamine.com.
54. International Telecommunications Union, 2011.
55. Ibid.
56. "The 2011–2016 Outlook for Advertising for Social Media Web Sites in Europe," *Regional Outlook Reports*, January 5, 2011.
57. "Behind the Great Firewall," *Advertising Age*, June 13, 2011, 12; Patrick Keefe, "China's Biannual Internet Demographic Breakdown: 485 Million Users and Climbing!" July 29, 2011, http://shanghaiist.com; and Doug Tsuruoka, "China Ousts U.S. Social Media Firms," *Investors Business Daily*, October 31, 2011, A6.
58. China Internet Watch, "Demographic Profiles of China's Top Social Networking Sites," November 28, 2011, www.chinainternetwatch.com; and Keefe, 2011.
59. "Behind the Great Firewall," 2011; Keefe, 2011; and China Internet Watch, 2011.
60. Asiya Bakht, "Ad Men Fail to Keep Pace as Social Media Takes Off," *Media*, June 12, 2008, 14.
61. Gillin, 2011.
62. Scott, 2007.
63. Ibid.
64. Chu and Kim, 2011.
65. Ibid.
66. Bussey, 2009.

CHAPTER 17

Leadership, Corporate Social Responsibility, and Sustainability

LEARNING OBJECTIVES

By the time you complete this chapter, you will be able to:

- Understand the key role that marketing leaders must play in addressing the evolving and varying needs and requirements of constituencies in global markets.
- Consider the responsibility of international marketers towards society.
- Explore the responsibilities that businesses have for their environmental impact.
- Examine how international marketing can cure the effects of past mistakes for a better future.

THE INTERNATIONAL MARKETPLACE 17.1

Bank Bonuses and Aristotelian Finance

Many in society find it quite difficult to understand the financial community's culture of very large annual bonuses (see Exhibit 17.1). There is public anger over corporate compensation structures, especially after many of the top banks were recipients of government support. Many citizens of developed nations resented perceived "bailouts" of financial firms. Some called for government punitive action against financial industry executives and increased regulation of banks. Others called for curbs or taxes on bonuses during a time when so many people in the greater public were suffering from the lack of a job or wage freezes.

Mervyn King, governor of the Bank of England, addressed the British Parliament in January 2012 on the subject of excessive financial industry rewards:

> We've been through a crisis where the squeeze on real living standards has been unprecedented. And that squeeze on real living standards has been on people who clearly were no way responsible for this crisis. I think the reputation of those institutions will be affected if their senior executives reward themselves, particularly in a period when the performance of the banks in terms of their share prices has hardly been stellar, if they reward themselves with very substantial compensation.

Immediately following the financial collapse in 2009, U.K. finance minister Alistair Darling imposed a "super tax" of 50 percent on bankers' bonuses in response to public anger. This tax angered bankers in turn, who viewed the action as unfair and pandering to short-term populism. The government of Prime Minister David Cameron has not renewed that tax. Critics of the super tax claimed that it damaged the City's attractiveness as a financial center. In a global environment, bankers and banks will look at alternative centers such as Hong Kong, Singapore, Geneva, or even Dublin. Given today's mobility of both industries and employees, banks that are convinced of their righteousness can fight back and move core units to more business-friendly locations.

Businesses, however, need to remember that they are only part of society. Their actions should reflect their firms' long-term best interests within an overall societal context. Business educators without an emphasis on such context and proportionality must revise such shortcomings in their teaching. Legislators and government in turn need to recognize that their actions can trigger a corporate response. Eliminating a comparative advantage and successful clusters without a productive replacement is a risky strategy.

EXHIBIT 17.1 Investment Bank Bonuses

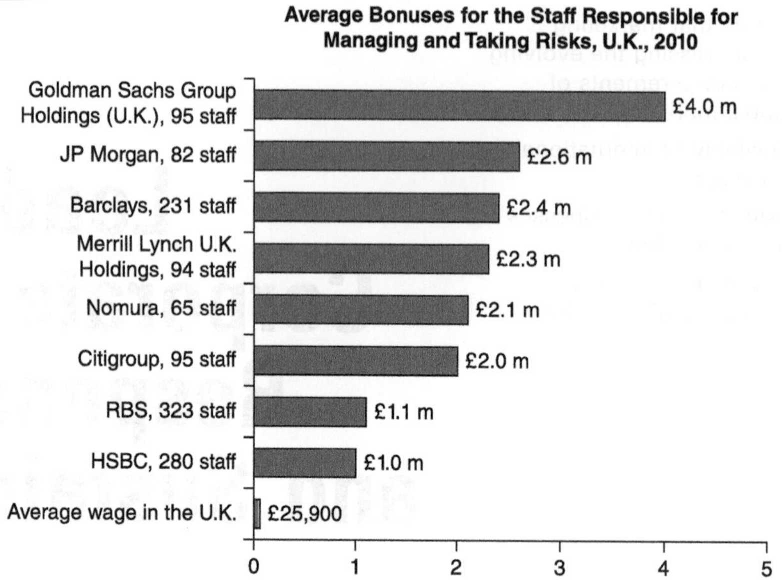

SOURCE: Jill Treanor, "Eight City Banks in 1.8m Pound Pay Spree," *Guardian*, January 22, 2012 Copyright Guardian News & Media Ltd 2012. Reprinted with permission.

In 2011, Martin Sandbu of the *Financial Times* wrote that businessmen and bankers in particular

> would do well to read the great moral philosophers, with the courage to follow their thinking wherever it might lead. Bankers whose inquisitiveness matches their acquisitiveness might, for instance, ponder Aristotle's view that the virtues of a profession are what fulfills its social purpose. That could prompt reflection on how to forge new ethics for investment banking along the lines of the medical or legal professions.

Sandbu went on to suggest that society could benefit from more "philosopher-executives" and that reading Aristotle's works "may be one of the best investments they can make."

In a letter in response to Mr. Sandbu's article published in the *Financial Times*, Professor Charles Skuba of Georgetown University agreed with Sandbu, writing

> at Georgetown, we educate many executives and bankers-to-be. We require them to study Aristotle and other philosophers before they turn to finance and other business disciplines. We seek thought about what constitutes virtue and explore the social purpose of an enterprise to endow our students with a knowledge foundation we hope will make them business and social leaders.

Skuba made the point that

> Aristotle distinguishes between intellectual virtue and moral virtue, ascribing the former to be the result of teaching and the latter of habit. The best banks and businesses work to develop habits that are socially responsible. As a part of the "philosophical inquiry" Mr. Sandbu advocates bankers will benefit from ingraining a culture that values moral virtue, or corporate social responsibility, along with making money and managing risk.

SOURCES: Michael R. Czinkota and Charles J. Skuba, "Government May Put the Financial Industry at Risk," *Roll Call*, February 1, 2010; Martin Sandbu, "Why Aristotle Is the Banker's Best Friend," *Financial Times*, January 13, 2011; Charles J. Skuba, "Best Banks and Businesses Work at Good Habits," letter to the *Financial Times*, January 18, 2011; and Jill Treanor, "Eight City Banks in 1.8m Pound Pay Spree," *Guardian*, January 22, 2012.

International marketing has never been more important or more powerful. As Chapter 1 has indicated, world trade has increased exponentially in the past several decades. The rapid expansion of globalization has been driven by the inclusion of billions of new customers and new competitors in the world marketplace from countries like China, India, and the former Soviet Union, along with revolutionary improvements in communications and transportation, and further economic liberalization. Dramatic growth in disposable income in emerging markets and increasing access to a broad array of media channels allow new audiences much greater access to the many benefits that international marketers offer for a better quality of life.

Yet there are also fears and challenges emanating from the field and its activities. Just like the Roman god Janus, who had two faces and has come to embody the notion of contradiction to modern thinkers, international marketing brings both good and bad to the global marketplace.[1] Exploitation of factory workers by global apparel and footwear marketers in previous decades, or by electronics and computer brands more recently, exemplifies the negative consequences of globalization. While there are operations and management dimensions involved as well, this negative impact is primarily a marketing issue because this discipline interacts closely with customers and suppliers. Unethical and inappropriate actions carry many risks such as negative brand publicity.

The role of global businesses and marketers in the financial crises that began in 2008 has led to public anger and increased scrutiny by society, particularly those who experienced great hardships, as shown in *The International Marketplace 17.1*. Not all markets experienced serious economic setbacks, but some of the poorer nations in the world were profoundly impacted. In its October 2011 "Note on Financial Reform," the Vatican's Pontifical Council for Justice and Peace reported,

> The costs are extremely onerous for millions in the developed countries, but also and above all for billions in the developing ones. In countries and areas where the most elementary goods like health, food and shelter are still lacking, more than a billion people are forced to survive on an average income of less than a dollar a day. Global economic well-being, traditionally measured by national income and also by levels of capacities, grew during the second half of the twentieth century, to an extent and with a speed never experienced in the history of humankind. But the inequalities within and between various countries have also grown significantly. While some of the more industrialized and developed countries and economic zones—the ones that are most industrialized and developed—have seen their income grow considerably, other countries have in fact been excluded from the overall improvement of the economy and their situation has even worsened.[2]

LEADERSHIP

With increased power come increased concerns and responsibility—*noblesse oblige*. International marketers are playing a leading role in societies and in the lives of people around the world. This leadership brings serious social impacts that need consideration. If marketers do not respond to these, governments will impose their own rules.

Recognizing Marketing Challenges and Dilemmas

Janus was not only a god of contradiction but a god whose countenance the Romans put on doors and gates as a symbol of transition. In times of transition, there are many who come new to the market and even new to marketing.

Changes have made life more complex both for marketers and those to whom they market. For example, some slogans offered routinely to markets with an experience of marketing promotion, such as "you may have won a new car," may be interpreted quite differently by newcomers to the marketing world. Their high expectations may lead to disappointments and even hostility. Because marketers are the initiators of new practices, it is the marketers' responsibility to avoid causing harm.

As economic growth in emerging and developing markets allows millions of people to enter the middle class, it brings great new opportunities for them to experience and enjoy a better quality of life with goods and services that help them in many ways. It also exposes them to the challenge of rising aspirations with limited income. Indeed, the gaps between the rich, the rising middle class, and the poor present practical and ethical dilemmas. New international consumers must learn how to manage their aspirations as they experience emotional marketing appeals for products and services that might not be considered practical or "good for them." Philip Kotler has posed two dimensions of the marketing dilemma for all of marketing: (1) What if the customer wants something that is not good for him or her? (2) What if the product or service, while good for the customer, is not good for society or other groups?[3]

How consumers, marketers, and societies manage that dilemma in international markets will need to be resolved on a country-by-country and culture-by-culture basis.

All too often cultures are insufficiently studied or wrongly interpreted by newly entering outsiders. It might seem that responsiveness to cultural differences should be second nature to marketers and therefore virtually reflexive. However, as Chapter 3 has shown, cultural differences continue to challenge marketers and can negatively affect the marketplace. Many times, disregarding local idiosyncrasies is like introducing a virus that may have destructive effects on a culture, if not on a marketer.

Though there is frequent talk about how we understand each other so much better than in the past, the reality looks different. The actual overlap between societies is typically miniscule. There may be a number of Chinese industry leaders who have been to the United States or Europe and have developed a clear understanding of Western cultures, but they represent a very small fraction of the Chinese population. The average Chinese person may knowledgeably understand as much about Columbus, Ohio, as the average Buckeye State resident knows about Tianjin. The consequence of that limitation is a danger of misunderstandings and susceptibility to hostility.

One key Western marketing dimension is the glory of victory in competition. Such an adherence to victory often means that there is no mercy for the vanquished. This plays out particularly harshly in regard to the loss of jobs and feelings of security about one's way of life for many employees of Western firms. Not everywhere are such approaches supported, desired, or accepted. In some regions, the goal becomes for the victor to mend fences, reinvigorating a feeling of togetherness and providing a cause for standing together. In many societies, it is expected that one not take advantage of what could be done but rather consensually do what ought to be done, particularly given the cultural importance of long-term relationships. Such context makes it far less acceptable to practice what we have called "vampire marketing," where the airline or hotel or communications company extracts bloodsucking prices for additional services or products from its captive audience after the major purchase decision has been made. Perhaps marketers can learn valuable lessons from this context and consequently make themselves more valuable to their customers.[4]

International marketing and societal orientation interact closely. For example, in the United States, the individual is considered the key component of society. But such a perspective is not uniformly taken around the world.

In socialist or tribal societies, it is typically the group that receives preference over the individual, and the family is accorded top billing. In such cases, just imagine how different emphases in making financial decisions can be reinterpreted in various settings. What may be corruption and bribery to some may turn out to be filial devotion to others. With the strict administration of the U.S. Foreign Corrupt Practices Act and the new, more stringent U.K. antibribery law, there may be harsh consequences to businesses and individuals who neglect these laws.

The saying goes that "distance makes the heart grow fonder." But in international marketing, distance can also provide temptation for the abdication of responsibility. Marketers sometimes clearly demonstrate their desire not to know. When host-country regulations have been less demanding than those in home countries, some firms sell products that may not meet home-country expectations in terms of quality or benefit. As developing nations develop greater regulatory capability and more expectations of the responsibility of firms, irresponsible marketers may encounter a less tolerant face in host countries. The chairman of a multinational corporation may feel removed from local issues; due to the evolution of a firm through mergers and acquisitions, he or she may see actions as being strictly business. However, the locals take all of the firm's actions very personally. When Olympic Games officials in London selected Dow Chemical as a 2012 sponsor, Indian activists protested vehemently because of outstanding claims against Dow by survivors of the Bhopal chemical disaster of 1984 caused by a leak from the factory owned by Union Carbide, which Dow bought in 1999.[5] Their injured and sick are still with them.

We can use Janus as a god of contradictions and transitions, but we cannot turn to him for guidance in morality, ethics, or even law. International marketers will confront dilemmas and challenges. How well they pursue the confluence of highly effective marketing, ethical practices, and social responsibility will inevitably be reflected in the loyalty of customers and the judgment of host governments.[6]

The Increased Role of Government

Today, there is a substantial transformation characterized by the response of governments to the failures and weaknesses in the global economy and financial system that triggered the economic crisis in 2008. In the developed economies, public anger and frustration that arose from the crisis led to massive government interventions to prevent systemic collapse, stabilize financial markets, and reinvigorate economic activity. Political pressures to correct currency and trade imbalances have also increased in many countries. The policy and regulatory efforts created to reform the system to correct mistakes and abuses that were seen to have caused the crisis will have continuing major implications for the private sector in the coming years.

Governments have increased regulation of complex financial instruments and required greater securitization for banks. There are now limitations on the size of banks and the extent of their activities. Overall governmental control over financial markets continues to grow in the European Union and the United States. For example, the U.S. Consumer Financial Protection Agency was created by the Dodd-Frank Wall Street Reform and Consumer Protection Act, and was launched in 2011 to prevent and correct abuses by marketers of credit cards, mortgages, and other financial products.[7]

Ironically, while the financial and economic crisis caused a loss of confidence in American-style capitalism, it may have also worked to demonstrate the resilience and underlying strength of market economics. It certainly revealed the importance of emerging markets and showed the extent of interconnectedness among markets worldwide. Emerging markets and developing countries have a greater say in the global economic system. This means that they must expect that the system is working in their interests and not just the interests of the developed economies. The gap between rich and poor nations, and the potential for developing countries to close that gap, will play a more important role going forward on the global economic stage.

Leaders of the G20 nations have pledged to work together to grow the global economy, avoid protectionism, and strengthen international systems and institutions. They promised to avoid the mistakes made during the Great Depression of the 1930s, when protectionist legislation in the United States led to similar actions by other countries and escalated trade sanctions. The G20 nations intend to focus on the private sector. In the November 2011 G20 Leaders Summit in Cannes, France, the leaders specifically pledged to work together to reform the financial sector and enhance market integrity. They promised, "We will not allow a return to pre-crisis behaviours in the financial sector and we will strictly monitor the implementation of our commitments regarding banks, OTC markets and compensation practices."[8]

Increased government involvement will also be manifested in interrelated efforts to tackle climate change, energy consumption, environmental damage, poverty, malnutrition, and food security. The G20 leaders have specifically committed to "improving energy markets and pursuing the fight against climate change."[9] Development goals are also on the G20 agenda, and the private sector will play a role in this area:

> We also agree that, over time, new sources of funding need to be found to address development needs and climate change. We discussed a set of options for innovative financing highlighted by Mr Bill Gates. Some of us have implemented or are prepared to explore some of these options. We acknowledge the initiatives in some of our countries to tax the financial sector for various purposes, including a financial transaction tax, inter alia to support development.[10]

Whenever "new sources of funding" comes up in government circles, it is likely to have a major impact on private sector firms because it refers to either higher taxes or greater voluntary funding expectations. Governments cannot be expected, for the sake of the theoretical ideals of free trade and laissez-faire economics, to sit back and watch the disadvantages and detrimental effects that capitalism and international marketing often bring alongside their benefits. In every country, there is deep suspicion among many powerful interest groups about market economics. The most that can be expected from leaders and legislators in the major economies is that they will permit an open-market orientation subject to the needs of domestic policy. Such an open-market orientation will be maintained only if governments can provide reasonable assurances to their own citizens and firms that the openness applies to foreign markets as well. Therefore, unfair trade practices such as governmental subsidization, dumping, and industrial targeting will be examined more closely, and retaliation for such activities is likely to be swift and harsh. When firms are seen to violate societal norms through their labor and environmental practices, they are likely to face stern government reaction and stiff penalties.

Government is now a key player in the international business and marketing environment, much more so than in the past several decades, and is likely to remain that way.

Trust

The size and scope of global corporations in the twenty-first century is unprecedented. Global corporations have vast reach and enormous economic power. The Coca Cola Company sells it branded products in over 200 countries.[11] With operations in 80 countries, Procter & Gamble estimates that four billion of the world's seven billion people buy P&G brands in 180 countries every year.[12] If one were to equate the annual revenues of the largest global corporations with the size of the world's leading economies, many firms would rank among the top economic powers. Exhibit 17.2 shows an analysis of how firms would rank in comparison to the world's leading economies as of 2010.

EXHIBIT 17.2 Economic Power of Global Companies, 2010

Combined Ranking	Company/Country	Revenue (*Fortune* Magazine 2010)/GDP (World Bank 2010) both in millions of U.S. dollars
1	United States	14,582,400
2	China	5,878,629
3	Japan	5,497,813
4	Germany	3,309,669
5	France	2,560,002
6	United Kingdom	2,246,079
7	Brazil	2,087,890
8	Italy	2,051,412
9	India	1,729,010
10	Canada	1,574,052
23	Wal-Mart Stores	421,849
26	Royal Dutch Shell	378,152
31	Exxon Mobil	354,674
35	BP	308,928
38	Sinopec Group	273,422
39	China National Petroleum	240,192
44	State Grid	226,294
47	Toyota Motor	221,760
50	Japan Post Holdings	203,958

SOURCES: World Bank, "Gross Domestic Product 2010," http://siteresources.worldbank.org/DATASTATISTICS/Resources/GDP.pdf; and *Fortune*, "Global 500," 2011, http://money.cnn.com/magazines/fortune/global500/2011/full_list, accessed January 27, 2012. Analysis by Charles J. Skuba and Joao Almeida, McDonough School of Business, Georgetown University.

Walmart Stores, with 2010 revenues of approximately $422 billion, would rank as the 23rd largest economy in the world, ahead of countries like Norway and Venezuela. Royal Dutch Shell would rank 26th, ahead of Austria, Saudi Arabia, Argentina, and South Africa. Exxon Mobil would rank 31st, ahead of Iran, Thailand, and Denmark. BP would rank 35th, ahead of Greece. This analysis reveals that 45 companies would be listed in the top 100 economies.[13]

With such economic power comes greater expectations for corporate governance, responsibility, and ethics across many fronts from many stakeholder audiences. Businesses do not have impunity in the global economy. The capitalist system and the corporations that it creates exist at the will of the societies and nations in which they operate. The tolerance of these nations for allowing market capitalism latitude is always subject to their confidence that good business brings good benefits to societies. Business does not enjoy *carte blanche* at any time and especially when societies evidence distrust in the truthfulness and responsibility of business to perform for the greater good. In an editorial in October 2011, the *Financial Times* advocated that "in order to preserve the capitalist model, it is vital to reform. For without public support, it will not thrive."[14]

Public trust in business may be seen as a measurement that corresponds to the willingness of societies to allow international marketers greater leeway to do business. Since 2000, the public relations firm Edelman has been conducting a global survey of public trust towards government, business, and other institutions called the Edelman Trust Barometer© (see http://trust.edelman.com).[15] Observing the findings of that survey since its inception, one can conclude that trust in business is generally stronger when a greater number of people are realizing the benefits of business. The level of trust in businesses in the developed economies was severely shaken by the economic disruptions caused by the financial crisis and recession. Trust in business in developed economies reached a nadir in the depths of the crisis in early 2009 with less than 40 percent of Informed Publics in the United States, Germany, and France indicating that they trusted business "to do what is right."[16] In 2011 and 2012, overall levels of trust remained low and Edelman reported, "there is still a yawning trust gap for business." Although trust in business rebounded from its 2009 lows, as Exhibit 17.3 shows, trust in government dropped dramatically in many countries since then. Public frustrations resulting from the continuing euro currency crisis, the anemic economic growth rates in the developed economies, the daunting debts of governments, and the inability of political leaders to work together effectively to solve problems in the United States damaged the credibility of governments. In 2011–2012, trust in government leaders to tell the truth was lowest in Europe, especially in Italy, where public scandals, mounting debt concerns, and the need for austerity measures led to the resignation of Prime Minister Silvio Berlusconi.[17]

The problems confronting the world are complex and intimidating. Anxiety over these issues increases when there is a dearth of optimism and no clear direction about how to solve them. So Edelman's findings about lack of trust in government are logical. Though overall trust in business had remained steady

EXHIBIT 17.3 Trust in the Truthfulness of Leaders

How much do you trust leaders to tell you the truth, regardless of how complex or unpopular it is?

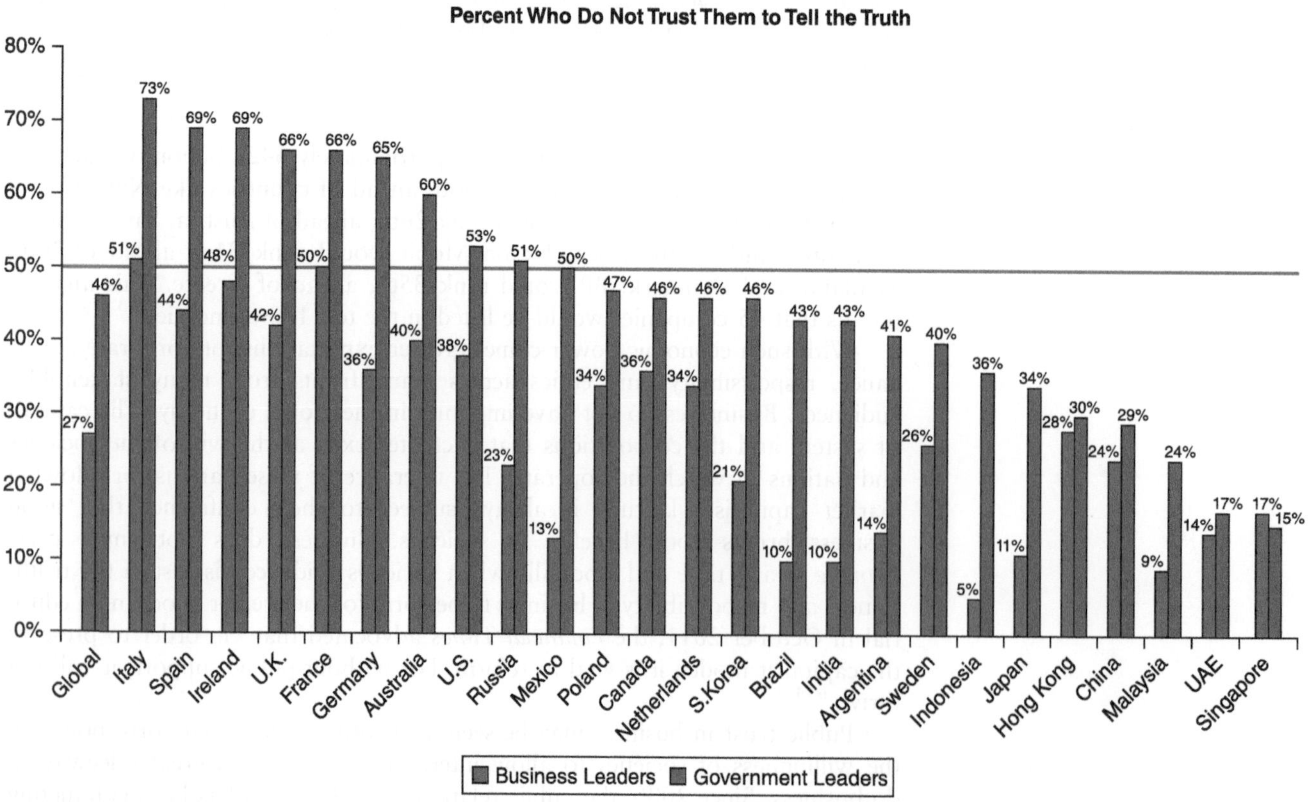

SOURCE: Edelman Trust Barometer © 2012 Annual Global Study.

EXHIBIT 17.4 Trust in Business

How much do you trust business to do what is right?

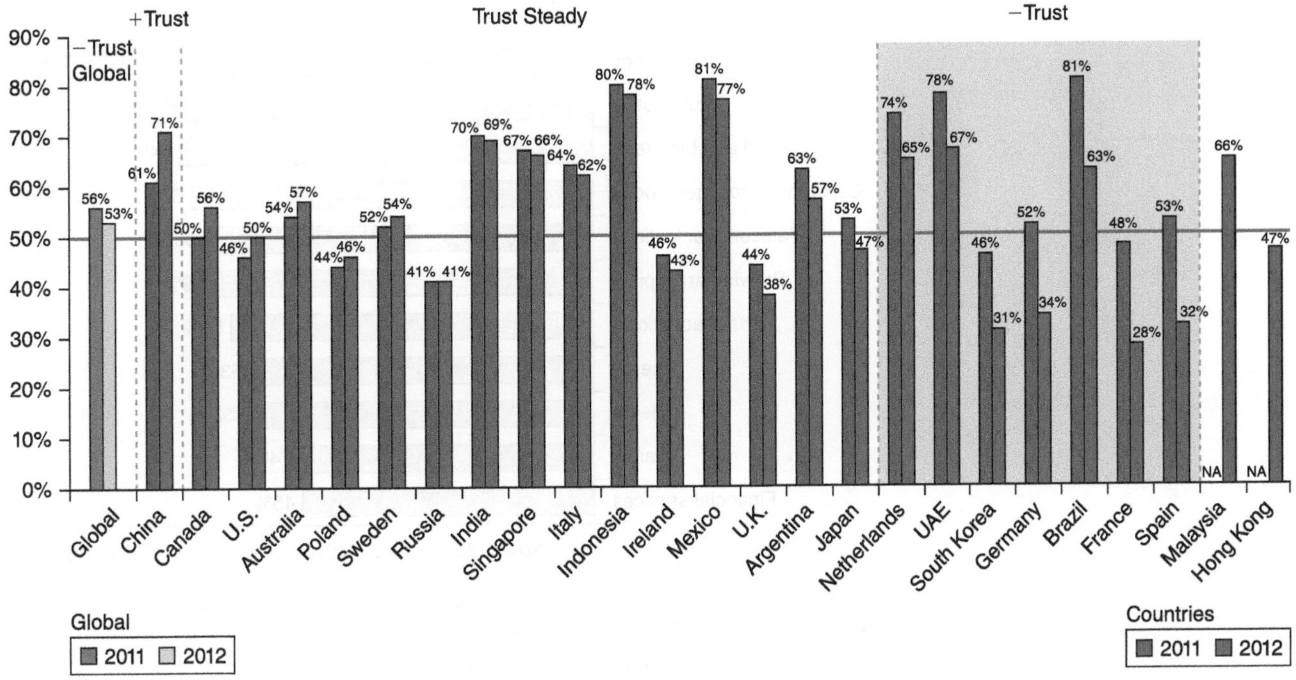

SOURCE: Edelman Trust Barometer © 2012 Annual Global Study.

from 2011–2012 in the developed countries, as shown in Exhibit 17.4, trust in business remained much stronger in emerging markets. With the promises of increased prosperity more tangible and with less exposure to economic problems, trust in business was particularly strong in China, India, Indonesia, UAE, Singapore, Brazil, Mexico, and Malaysia. Overall, Edelman cautions that while trust in business leaders exceeds trust in government officials,

> business leaders should not be cheered by government's ineptitude, especially as trust in the two institutions tend to move in sync. There is still a yawning trust gap for business, as evidenced by one half of informed public respondents saying government does not regulate business enough. Yet what most stakeholders want from the government—consumer protection and regulation ensuring responsible corporate behavior—are actions business can take on its own.[18]

Trust has direct implications for international marketers. Consumers around the world place a great deal of trust in technology companies as well as companies in the automotive, food and beverages, consumer packaged goods, and telecommunications industries—as the results in Exhibit 17.5 illustrate. Marketers will instantly realize where they can exercise a leadership role. Many consumers feel that companies do not pay attention to their interests or concerns. Edelman recommends that listening to customer feedback and putting customers ahead of profits are vital to building future trust. A customer-centric approach is almost religion to the best international marketers.[19] The more trusted industries tend to be more marketing oriented than the banks and financial services companies, which rank at the bottom of the list. Perhaps the financial services industry should learn from other firms about the importance of customer communications. An *Advertising Age* study of the top 100 global marketers by measured media spending reveals that the highest ranked financial services firm is ING Group, which is ranked 77. ING, Visa, MasterCard, and Citigroup are the only financial services firms ranked in the top 100 global marketers.[20]

EXHIBIT 17.5 Trust in Technology Is High While Trust in Finance Is Low

How much do you trust the following industries to do what is right?

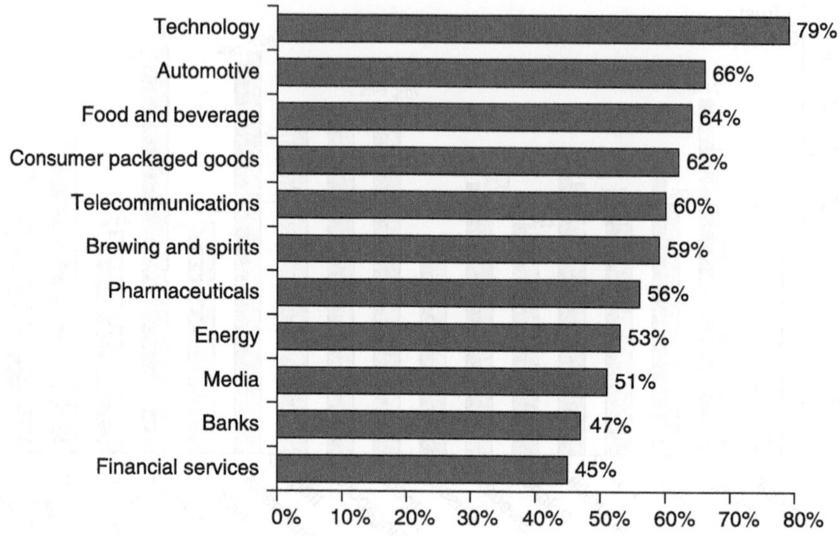

Note: Responses 6 through 9 only on 1 through 9 scale, with 9 highest; question was asked of informed publics ages 25 through 64 in 20 countries.

SOURCE: Edelman Trust Barometer © 2012 Annual Global Study.

Edelman maintains that

> business is now better placed than government to lead the way out of the trust crisis. But the balance must change so that business is seen both as a force for good and an engine for profit.... Business is a force for good. Yes, there are risks in bold decision-making, in telling hard truths, and in structuring business goals that serve investors and society. But the bigger risk for business is in waiting for government to act.[21]

The Leadership Challenge

There are strong forces at work demanding government action, as evidenced by the Occupy Now protest movement that spread across cities around the globe in 2011 or by those angered by the size of bankers' bonuses while many people were out of jobs or underemployed. As *The International Marketplace 17.1* in this chapter captures, there is much strong emotion in England over the size of bonuses. This is especially true in regard to banks that have been "bailed out" and are now largely owned by public taxpayers, such as the Royal Bank of Scotland and Barclay's. Bank and corporate **bailouts** are a highly emotional topic to many who perceive that the same perpetrators of the financial crisis are the beneficiaries of a "rigged system."

Bankers and international marketers must develop a greater understanding that "business as usual" will inevitably be altered as a result of public pressure and the advocacy of other ethical forces. For example, the Vatican has called for specific policies on business in 2011:

> On the basis of this sort of ethical approach, it seems advisable to reflect, for example, on: a) taxation measures on financial transactions through fair but modulated rates with charges proportionate to the complexity of the operations, especially those made on the "secondary" market. Such taxation would be very useful in promoting global development and sustainability according to the principles of social justice and solidarity. It could also contribute to the creation of a world reserve fund to support the economies of the countries hit by crisis as well as the recovery of

> their monetary and financial system; b) forms of recapitalization of banks with public funds making the support conditional on "virtuous" behaviours aimed at developing the "real economy"; c) the definition of the domains of ordinary credit and of Investment Banking. This distinction would allow a more effective management of the "shadow markets" which have no controls and limits. It is sensible and realistic to allow the necessary time to build up broad consensuses, but the goal of the universal common good with its inescapable demands is waiting on the horizon.[22]

The Vatican's proposal has led to calls for a **financial transactions tax** on equity, bond, currency, and financial derivatives transactions in the European Union and the United States. These proposals may all appear to be focused on financial markets and institutions, but there are broader implications for international marketers in all industries. If the private sector does not lead, it will be led.

The leadership challenge extends across many areas beyond the global economy and financial markets. The confluence of multiple trends around the globe such as population growth, demographic shifts, disparity in incomes, endemic poverty, urbanization, resource scarcity, climate change, endemic diseases, cultural clashes, and the threats of terrorism, piracy, and cyber attacks with ongoing technological and scientific advances requires high-level leadership qualities among government, societal, and business leaders. The World Economic Forum poses the problem in terms of the risks that leaders must manage: "We are living in a new world of risk. Globalization, shifting demographics, rapidly accelerating technological change, increased connectivity, economic uncertainty, a growing multiplicity of actors and shifting power structures combine to make operating in this world unprecedentedly complex and challenging for corporations, institutions and states alike."[23]

It is no longer sufficient for a business CEO to "mind the store." Among the major challenges and opportunities for international marketers is the choice of leaders with the skills and capabilities to lead an organization with its multiple customer, employee, and other stakeholder audiences towards a competitive vision for the future. CEOs of corporations who might be labeled as visionaries include many who could be acknowledged as marketing and customer-focused leaders. Robert McDonald of P&G, Muhtar Kent of Coca Cola, the late Steve Jobs of Apple, Richard Branson of Virgin, Jeffrey Immelt of GE, and Sam Palmisano of IBM stand out for their communication of a clear vision for how their companies will succeed and intersect with society in this dynamic global marketplace. *The International Marketplace 17.2* describes how Sam Palmisano led IBM, a company famous both for its computers and its unique corporate culture, towards a dramatically different strategy in the twenty-first century.

THE INTERNATIONAL MARKETPLACE 17.2

For IBM, a "Smarter Planet" Is Smart Business

In global business, no company can rest on the laurels of success. Given the rapidly changing environment, leading companies can quickly lose their position if they fail to foresee the evolution of competitive requirements to satisfy demanding customers with immense needs in a highly complex global environment. Vision and leadership are requirements of the CEO. Perhaps no global business requires more vision and leadership than the hyperdynamic information technology industry.

With the personal computer (PC) business becoming more commoditized and global demand for technological innovation growing, IBM divested its $10 billion PC business to Lenovo in 2004 and shifted its strategic direction increasingly towards business analytics, strategy consulting, and information technology services. Beginning in 2002, IBM's CEO, Samuel Palmisano, charted a new strategic path for "Big Blue" and led a company of more than 425,000 employees around the world through a dramatic transformation process towards a smarter company and "a smarter planet."

Palmisano and IBM had recognized that world megatrends were combining to present challenges for societies, governments, and businesses to operate efficiently. Globalization, population growth, urbanization, and the environmental effects of global growth, together with technology advancements, increasing interconnection, and widespread availability of digital information, were creating needs for smarter information analysis and management. IBM saw opportunity in marketing to customers' needs for smarter data analysis and management to help improve national and municipal electrical grids, water systems, health care, and transportation networks. Tying IBM's strategic future with the future of the planet's governments and societies, Palmisano rallied his employees to transform the company.

In a combination of strategic insight and smart marketing, IBM's "smarter planet" marketing campaign both explains customers' organizational needs and presents IBM's substantial capabilities and credentials through detailed applications and product information. IBM was already a leader in new patent filings with 5,896 patents in 2010 and an investment of over $6 billion a year in research and development. Also, Palmisano drove a series of business acquisitions that complemented IBM's capabilities to "walk the talk" of its marketing.

IBM's initiative seems to be paying off. The firm experienced consistent growth in revenues and earnings per share from 2002 to 2010. In 2010, IBM had $14.8 billion in earnings on nearly $100 billion in revenues. Also, in the BrandZ "Top 100 Most Valuable Global Brands 2011" report, IBM was ranked number 3, and the company was ranked number 12 in *Fortune*'s 2010 list of the most admired companies.

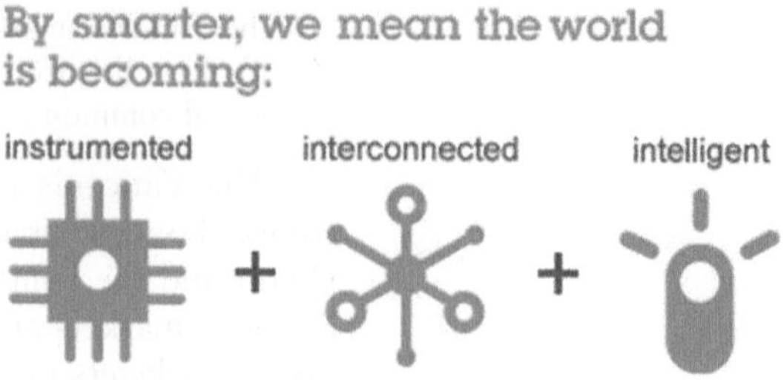
By smarter, we mean the world is becoming:
instrumented
interconnected
intelligent
+
+

SOURCE: Courtesy of International Business Machines Corporation, © International Business Machines Corporation.

In a speech to the Council on Foreign Relations in 2008, Palmisano captured the competitive reality that is driving IBM, saying,

> So, yeah, the world's becoming smaller, yeah, the world is becoming flatter, and of course it's becoming smarter, but as we move to this globally integrated intelligent economy and society, I think the question for all of us that we should reflect upon is what do we do with that? I mean, this world is beckoning us to take advantage of this as an economic opportunity, and I believe it's one we can do and it's one we can build on if we open our minds and we come together and get committed to lead some of the change that's required to make this planet a smarter place.

SOURCES: Jessi Hempel, "IBM's Sam Palmisano: A Super Second Act," *CNN Money*, March 4, 2011; IBM, www.ibm.com, accessed January 22, 2012; and Samuel J. Palmisano, "The Current Economic Environment in the United States," speech to the Council on Foreign Relations, November 6, 2008.

Aligning Strategy, Products, and Societal Interests

Companies like IBM, GE, and Siemens are aligning their corporate strategies as well as their product offerings with societal interests and the global trends that are impacting societies. Many of their largest customers are national, state, and municipal governments that are confronted with complex challenges. With product and service offerings in areas like health care, aviation, energy, electrical distribution, railroad engines, water treatment, and lighting, GE has a large intersection with societal interests. GE's marketing positioning reflects the needs of its government customers and is centered on the notion of using imagination and innovation "to solve the world's biggest problems." GE claims that "GE businesses all share one important trait: each harnesses the power of imagination to make life better for our customers and consumers all around the world."[24] Similarly, as a major competitor to GE, Siemens provides products and services in areas like energy, health care, rail systems, power grids, construction, information technology, transportation and logistics management, and infrastructure logistics. Siemens is a huge global employer with over 360,000 employees from over 140 countries in operations in 190 regions.[25] Siemens positions itself as "a pioneer" that uses innovations "to provide answers to societies' most vital challenges, enabling us to create sustainable value."[26] One of Siemens' newest initiatives is its "infrastructure and cities sector," which is specifically designed to bring its product and service offerings as "answers" to the needs of global urban governments.[27]

Not all companies make products that directly contribute to meeting societal goals. However, all international marketers have an integral relationship with the home and host countries in which they do business. Part of that relationship is a responsibility of the company to act as a responsible citizen. Governments are playing a new and growing role in international marketing. In part, this role has been the outgrowth of global crises that had not been anticipated or addressed by market forces. Today, there are new global regulations and restrictions. However, it has not yet been established what indicators are more accurate—the siren calls of the marketplace with its market signals or the plans and mandates of governments. Governments, however, are not always free from fault and ambition.[28] International marketers must learn the advantages and disadvantages of following one direction over the other. They must understand new paths to follow in order to market successfully in different countries. International marketers in the twenty-first century require a new kind of leader to see and navigate these unfamiliar paths.

CORPORATE SOCIAL RESPONSIBILITY

What Is the Responsibility of Business?

In his famous 1970 *New York Times Magazine* article, Milton Friedman attacked the concept of "social responsibilities of business in a free-enterprise system" in his headline—"The Social Responsibility of Business Is to Increase Its Profits." He described those business executives who spoke in favor of corporate social responsibilities as being "incredibly shortsighted and muddleheaded" and "preaching pure and unadulterated socialism" with their arguments being "notable for their analytical looseness and lack of rigor."[29] To accurately understand Friedman's point of view, one has to understand the political circumstances that were influencing business conditions in the United States at that time and reflect on the issue of wage and price controls and his concerns about its threat to the free enterprise system that he so fiercely championed. At that time, inflationary pressures were causing criticism of the capitalist system and businesses pursuing profits, with some calling for businesses to act responsibly in their pricing policies. Friedman argued that

> the doctrine of "social responsibility" taken seriously would extend the scope of the political mechanism to every human activity. It does not differ in philosophy from the most explicitly collectivist doctrine. It differs only by professing to believe that collectivist ends can be attained without collectivist means.... I have called it a "fundamentally subversive doctrine" in a free society, and ... in such a society, there is one and only one social responsibility of business—to use its resources and engage in activities designed to increase its profits so long as it stays within the rules of the game, which is to say, engages in open and free competition without deception or fraud.[30]

Friedman represented one end of the spectrum of opinion on the responsibility of business in society. A prevailing argument from those who held the Friedman viewpoint was that profitable corporations would create private wealth, which its private owners could then choose to channel towards philanthropic purposes. The United States has a long tradition of philanthropy and is the leading country for private philanthropic donations per capita in the world. The Carnegie Corporation of New York annually awards the Carnegie Medal of Philanthropy. This award is given to those who donate their private wealth to "do real and permanent good for the world."[31] Some believe that a corporation should not be distracted from the efficiency of its primary purpose: maximizing

EXHIBIT 17.6 What Is the Social Responsibility of Business?

Milton Friedman: "The social responsibility of business is to increase its profits."

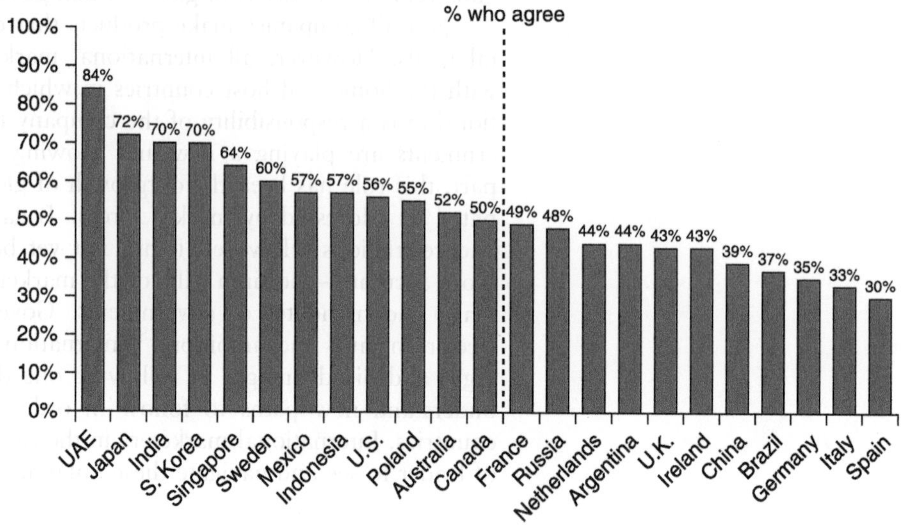

Note: Net of "strong agree" and "somewhat agree" responses only; Informed Publics ages 25–64.

SOURCE: Edelman Trust Barometer © 2011 Annual Global Study.

the return on the shareholders' investment. The other end of the spectrum maintains that the corporation has multiple roles and effects in society other than wealth creation. The corporation exists and operates in nations and communities, employs individuals, uses community resources, creates waste and byproducts through its manufacturing and operations, and has multiple integral relationships with society. For the sake of their own advancement, corporations are treated by governments as persons rather than merely financial entities. So, it seems not far-fetched to expect them to respond to society's needs as persons rather than simply as financial entities.

There is also a spectrum of opinion across the globe regarding Friedman's contention. As Exhibit 17.6 shows, when asked if they agreed with Milton Friedman that "the social responsibility of business is to increase its profits," there were broad differences among national Informed Public respondents. While 84 percent of respondents in the United Arab Emirates, 72 percent in Japan, and 70 percent in India and South Korea agreed with that viewpoint, only 30 percent of respondents in Spain, 33 percent in Italy, and 35 percent in Germany agreed.[32] Whether one agrees precisely with Friedman or not, it is common sense that an international marketer will need to be profitable if it is to practice corporate social responsibility at a high level.

Defining Corporate Social Responsibility

Corporate social responsibility (CSR) carries different meanings to different audiences. Research has shown that many people are confused by the term. In a 2007 study in the United States by the public relations firm Fleishman Hillard and the National Consumers League, most respondents identified either "commitment to community" or "commitment to employees" as the principal meaning of corporate social responsibility. Other meanings included "responsibility to the environment" and "providing quality products." The study found that American consumers expected corporate commitment to encompass more than just charitable and philanthropic giving and that treating and paying employees well was of prime importance.[33]

Corporate social responsibility is a broad term that includes many specific corporate practices. The European Commission defines it as "a concept whereby companies integrate social and environmental concerns in their business operations and in their interaction with stakeholders on a voluntary basis."[34] The broader meaning of the term is also captured by other expressions used by many corporations and individuals such as *corporate citizenship*, *corporate philanthropy*, or *sustainability*. **Corporate citizenship** refers to the fact that, historically, many companies have supported their local and national communities through a variety of roles, including support for nonprofit organizations vital to a community's social development. These associations include board memberships, employee volunteer programs, and charitable donations. Another frequently used term, **corporate philanthropy**, has a narrower context specific to the philanthropic or charitable contributions of a firm. As this chapter will address in a later section under the specific subject of **sustainability**, CSR also includes a range of issues related to the environmental impact of the firm's operations and products.

Corporate citizenship practices have been around for centuries. In Augsburg, Germany, the Fuggerei is a Roman Catholic housing settlement for the poor that Jakob Fugger "the Rich" founded in 1520 and that still exists today through the support of the original charitable trust. The 145 residents of the Fuggerei, many of them elderly widows, pay an annual rent of less than 1 euro to live in the quaint community on the condition that they pray for the Fugger family. (Was he hedging his bets?) Fugger was an international marketer and financier who even financed a trade mission to India.[35] Fugger may be a good example today for international marketers to follow in combining successful business practices with social responsibility.

The International Chamber of Commerce (ICC) defines corporate social responsibility as "the voluntary commitment by business to manage its activities in a responsible way."[36] The ICC encourages its membership to take initiatives on their own volition that make good sense for their company's overall strategy. Corporate social responsibility practices are now encouraged by governments and business associations worldwide as *The International Marketplace 17.3* describes for the United States. European CSR efforts are also leading examples of the practice. To provide such leadership, CSR Europe was founded in 1998 by business leaders across Europe in cooperation with the European Commission in response to an earlier appeal by commission president Jacques Delors to take a more active role in addressing broader social needs. It now includes 80 multinational companies and 35 national partner organizations with outreach to 4,000 companies across Europe.[37] CSR Europe has launched the Enterprise 2020 initiative to help companies collaborate to develop profitable, innovative business practices that lead "the transformation towards a smart, sustainable and inclusive society." The initiative envisions that the "enterprise of the future" will have societal issues at the heart of its strategy.[38]

The Chambers Ireland present CSR awards annually since 2004 to "recognize the work being carried out by Irish and multinational companies to improve the lives of their employees and to enhance the civic environment in which they operate."[39] The Council of British Chambers of Commerce in Europe, in the spirit of William Wilberforce, who convinced the British Parliament to abolish slavery in the nineteenth century, has created a specific CSR initiative to stop human trafficking through educational programs and other efforts.[40]

There have been efforts by governments to more specifically codify what they expect of companies regarding CSR practices. The ICC warns against this kind of "one-size-fits-all" approach and defends the voluntary nature of CSR:

> Government's role is to provide the basic national and international framework of laws and regulations for business operations and that essential role will continue to

THE INTERNATIONAL MARKETPLACE 17.3

"And the Award Goes to..."

CSR efforts by global corporations serve multiple purposes beyond the humanitarian and developmental goals set by the firms. Good citizenship programs empower the employees of companies to effectively channel their own desire to help local communities and to be proud representatives of the companies for which they work. Socially responsible firms are also representatives of their home countries and help to promote good diplomatic relationships as well as conditions that improve the overall business environment in host countries. When consumers and employees in host countries experience extraordinary citizenship efforts, it reflects well on both the companies and the home countries.

Recognizing that good citizenship is also good business for American businesses and the United States government, the U.S. Department of State created the American Corporate Excellence (ACE) award in 1999 to honor the contributions that American businesses make around the world. According to the State Department, "The ACE helps define America as a positive force in the world. It highlights our increasing outreach to the business community, our public-private partnerships, and our public diplomacy efforts."

The 2011 winners of the ACE award were Sahlman Seafoods and Procter & Gamble. A family-owned and operated shrimp company, Sahlman Seafoods runs a shrimp farm on the Pacific coast of Nicaragua. The ACE award recognized Sahlman for its community development and environmental efforts as a small company. Sahlman prioritized hiring local women, rehabilitated the local health clinic, actively promoted improvements at the Escuela Francisco Hernandez de Cordoba local elementary school, created a model waste management system, and actively worked with the Nicaraguan Ministry for Environmental Protection to implement a program to preserve and protect the local ecosystem.

Procter & Gamble was recognized for its corporate and employee efforts in both Nigeria and Pakistan. P&G's corporate purpose is expressed through its motto of "touching lives, improving life." In accepting the ACE award, CEO Bob McDonald explained this motto:

> We improve lives with our brands. We improved lives with our business growth. We improve lives with our employee programs and with our social responsibility efforts. When we improve lives, we grow our business, and by growing our business, we're able to improve even more lives. It's a virtuous cycle and entirely congruent with our growth strategy to improve more lives in more parts of the world more completely.

The company invested in growing its business in Pakistan and Nigeria. Living up to its commitment, P&G provided nearly 350 million liters of clean drinking water to 2010 flood victims through its PUR Purifier of Water sachets, which it had developed in collaboration with the U.S. Centers for Disease Control and Prevention for philanthropic use in the P&G Children's Safe Drinking Water program. In Nigeria, P&G has provided over 44 million liters of clean drinking water. In addition, P&G's Pampers brand runs mobile clinics and hospital programs for Nigerian mothers and children, and its Always brand provides feminine hygiene education for Nigerian girls.

The U.S. business community also realized the importance of recognizing the good work of American companies to improve the quality of life in other countries through the creation of the U.S. Chamber of Commerce's Business Civic Leadership Center (BCLC). Working to improve the image of U.S. businesses abroad, the BCLC has presented awards for corporate citizenship since 1999. In 2011, Pfizer and the Pfizer Foundation received the Best International Ambassador award for its work and $47 million investment in 46 countries "to fight neglected non-communicable diseases and their associated risks, such as tobacco use." Kraft Foods won the BCLC Best Corporate Stewardship award for "its overall culture, its operational practices, and for creating shared value benefitting both the company and society."

Such awards serve to validate and encourage corporate social responsibility practices. The U.S. Chamber maintains that the recognition of efforts will serve as a model for other companies. They may not be glamorous like the Oscars, but these awards are a very important recognition for companies.

SOURCES: U.S. State Department, "2011 ACE Winners Announced," January 18, 2012, www.state.gov/e/eb/ace; "U.S. Chamber Announces Corporate Citizenship Award Winners," U.S. Chamber of Commerce press release, November 18, 2011, www.uschamber.com/press/releases/2011/november/us-chamber-announces-corporate-citizenship-award-winners; and Business Civic Leadership Center, "BCLC Awards Grainger, Kraft, Pfizer and UnitedHealth 2011 'Citizens,'" http://bclc.uschamber.com/blog/2011-11-18/bclc-awards-grainger-kraft-pfizer-and-unitedhealth-2011-citizens, accessed January 22, 2012.

evolve. Beyond this, good corporate practice is usually spread most effectively by strong corporate principles and example, rather than by codes of conduct. A commitment to responsible business conduct requires consensus and conviction within a company. Voluntary business principles have the advantage of bridging cultural diversity within enterprises and offering the flexibility to tailor solutions to particular conditions. Voluntary approaches minimize competitive distortions, transaction costs associated with regulatory compliance, and inspire many companies to go beyond the regulatory baseline, thus often eliminating the need for further legislation.[41]

Strategic Focus

Early corporate citizenship initiatives were often directed at supporting community causes ranging from charitable organizations to cultural institutions like municipal symphonies and operas. Companies have been historically helpful in developing the cultural infrastructure of many communities. Whether these corporate philanthropy efforts were beneficial to the company or only to selected individuals is very subjective. However, many of these early efforts were not scrutinized for their contribution to the strategic objectives of the firm. Michael E. Porter and Mark R. Kramer have argued that a company needs to choose its social initiatives strategically. They have advanced the concept of **shared value**, which they define as "policies and operating practices that enhance the competitiveness of a company while simultaneously advancing the economic and social conditions in the communities in which it operates. Shared value creation focuses on identifying and expanding the connections between societal and economic programs."[42]

Porter and Kramer identify three approaches that apply to international marketers: (1) delivering attractive products that are truly beneficial to society; (2) removing problems in the supply chain that are both costly and socially detrimental, such as reducing greenhouse gases; and (3) enabling local cluster development to help communities become more competitive.[43] They argue that "we need a more sophisticated form of capitalism, one imbued with a social purpose. But that purpose should arise not out of charity but out of a deeper understanding of competition and economic value creation."[44] The best international marketers are driven by the desire to create value and improve their competitive positions, so shared value becomes the right and smart thing to do.

CSR Reporting

Porter and Kramer distinguish between shared value and corporate social responsibility by claiming that the latter mostly focuses on corporate reputation rather than on directly improving a company's profitability and competitive position.[45] This distinction can be misleading. Many companies have certainly used their CSR initiatives to build their reputations through marketing communications, but that is not inimical to a strategic approach to CSR. Crucial is the CEO's commitment to a holistic CSR program. If the CEO takes up the flag in leadership, the company is more likely to rally to the cause and integrate it deeply into the very fabric of the operation. Some deeply committed companies, like GE, reflect this approach by embedding CSR initiatives into their marketing programs as *The International Marketplace 1.1* in the opening chapter illustrates.

How companies communicate their involvement and commitment to CSR is very important. Edelman advocates that companies should "practice radical transparency." This can be done by communicating effectively with various stakeholder groups, especially employees, about their CSR goals and their progress towards meeting them. Enabling employees to take that conversation further with others, individually and through the increasingly important social media channels, can be particularly convincing to other audiences.[46] (See the Edelman report on trust in social media at http://trust.edelman.com/social-media-and-trust.)

The most common means of formal communication is through regular dedicated reports. Most large companies issue annual or periodic reports on their CSR practices. The reporting procedure and the quality of the reports are a good lens to view the actual commitment of the company to responsibility programs. KPMG has analyzed the CSR reporting practices of companies. In its "International Survey of Corporate Responsibility Reporting 2011," KPMG reported that "while CR reporting was once seen as fulfilling a moral obligation to society, many companies are now recognizing it as a business imperative. Today, companies are increasingly demonstrating that CR reporting provides financial value and drives innovation, reflecting the old adage of 'what gets measured gets managed.'"[47]

In a 34-country analysis, shown in Exhibit 17.7, European companies were "leading the pack" in the professionalism of the process they used and the quality of the communication. Many companies in countries like South Africa, Romania, Mexico, Nigeria, and Russia, as well as Denmark and Finland, were "starting behind" in both categories. Companies in the United States, Canada, Brazil, Japan, and Israel, were just "scratching the surface" with quality communications but a low level of process maturity. These companies "had the highest risk of failing to deliver on the promises they make in their CR report and/or targets they have set."[48] Such failure can lead to harsh responses by stakeholders. KPMG reported a dramatic rise in the number of companies reporting on CSR activities. As Exhibit 17.8 illustrates, almost all global companies now have some form of reporting. In 2011, 95 percent of the 250 largest global companies

EXHIBIT 17.7 Reporting on Corporate Social Responsibility: Quality of Communications versus Process Maturity

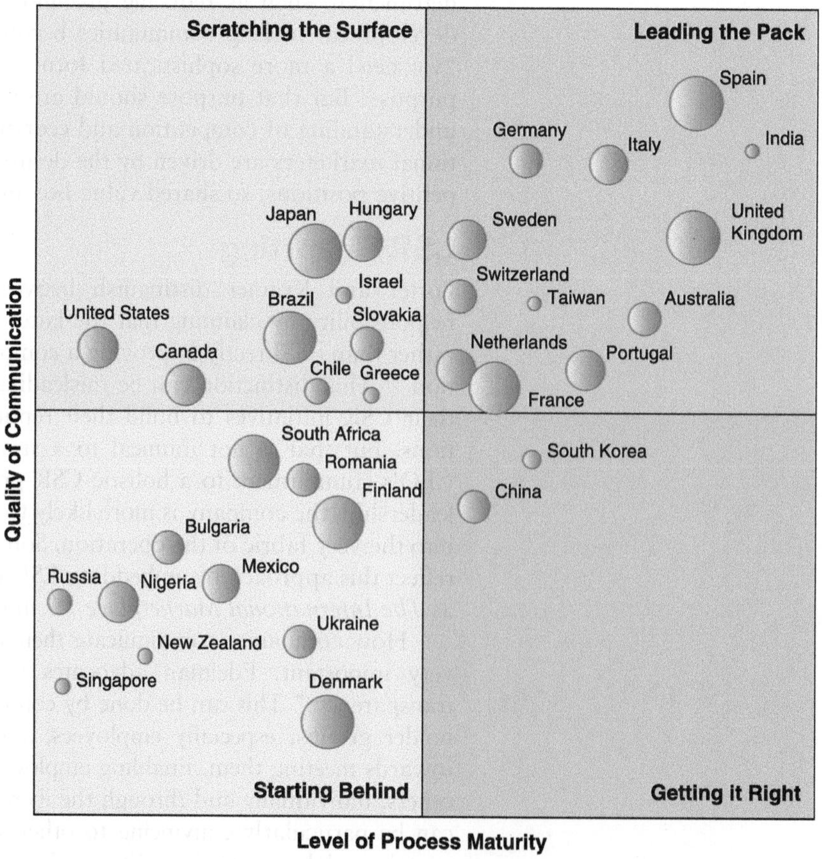

SOURCE: KPMG, "International Survey of Corporate Social Responsibility Reporting 2011."

EXHIBIT 17.8 Companies Reporting on Corporate Social Responsibility

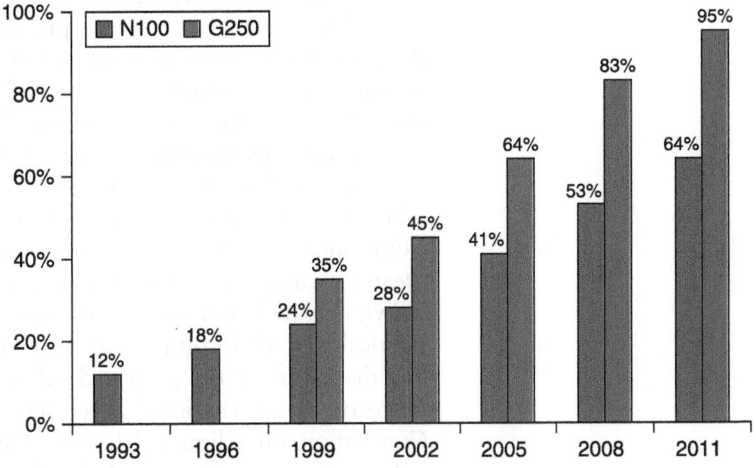

Note: G250 = 250 largest companies in the world; N100 = 100 largest companies in each of the 34 countries in the study.

SOURCE: KPMG, "International Survey of Corporate Social Responsibility Reporting 2011."

(G250) and 64 percent of the 100 largest companies in the 34 countries analyzed (N100) now report on these activities. This kind of reporting only began among global companies around 1999 and picked up dramatically after 2002.[49] A separate Georgetown University analysis of top U.S. companies found that there was a spike in these reports in 2007 and then a rebound in 2010 after a short drop.[50]

One important indicator of a company's CSR commitment is the degree of transparency and honesty in these reports, often expressed through establishing clear goals and reporting on progress towards meeting them. Another important indicator is the quality of the messaging from the CEO, often in the form of a letter. One can tell the difference between sincere conviction and the company merely covering the topic.

SUSTAINABILITY

Issues related to the environment comprise perhaps the most important individual element of CSR. Of the U.S. *Fortune* 100 corporations that issued some form of CSR report since 2010, over one-quarter specifically included some variation of "sustainability" or "environment" in their titles.[51] The focus on these kind of issues is logical when one considers the impact that large companies have upon the environment in relation to water usage and disposal, energy consumption, energy emissions, continued availability of natural ecosystems, the effects of chemical components of products and packaging, product and packaging disposal, and overall wastes from operations. More of the leading global operations have begun to embrace sustainability issues not only to improve their reputation but as a part of their core corporate strategy to improve efficiencies and even increase revenues.

A Sustainable Future?

Just like the broader term of *corporate social responsibility*, *sustainability* also carries multiple meanings to different audiences. Inevitably, groups and organizations that are interested in specific issues related to the environment tend to define the issue in narrow terms. It is helpful to understand the term in its most general sense, which often involves some sense of marrying commercial needs with preserving the natural environment for the future. Several definitions can help. The 1986 World Commission on Environment and Development (Brundtland Commission) definition of sustainable development could reasonably be applied to sustainable business practices: "development that meets the needs of the present without compromising the ability of future generations to meet their own needs."[52] A simple but powerful expression is that of Robert Gillman: "do unto future generations as you would have them do unto you."[53]

Growing population, increased urbanization and industrialization around the world, and dramatic increases in production and consumption all have a significant impact upon the environment. The result has led to increased pressures from nongovernmental organizations and multilateral institutions to create greater awareness and to improve practices by governments, businesses, and individuals to lessen the detrimental impact. This involvement sometimes raises political and philosophical disagreements in regard to the extent of problems and the nature of the proposed solutions. An example of this is the 1997 Kyoto Protocol, an international agreement linked to the United Nations Framework Convention on Climate Change. This agreement sets binding targets for 37 industrialized countries and the European Community for reducing national levels of greenhouse gas emissions.[54] The United States declined to join this agreement because it excludes major developing economies like China, India, and Brazil, which are also major greenhouse gas emitters.

Controversy continues over whether these greenhouse gases are causing climate change or global warming. Within individual nations, political disagreements over the wisdom and necessity of "green" policies and practices often show varying opinions about whether "green is good." For example, the EU announced a carbon emissions tax on all airlines flying into Europe. This ruling has raised protests from the U.S., Indian, Russian, and Chinese governments and those of other countries as well. In another example, U.S. and European regulations that set new standards for the amount of light emitted per watt of power used effectively require the use of compact fluorescent bulbs and make incandescent light bulbs obsolete. Subsequently, concerns have emerged about mercury content in the new bulbs and how to dispose of them, as well as whether they are as effective in illumination. As a result, some people are hoarding old lightbulbs.[55] Similar issues and a secondary market in old toilets have resulted from regulations on low-flow toilets to save water.

International marketers will need to pay attention to multiple regulations governing the environmental impact of products. The EU has implemented REACH (Registration, Evaluation, Authorization, and Restriction of Chemical substances), a set of broad-reaching regulations on the use of chemicals, to motivate businesses to exclude dangerous chemicals like cadmium in products such as personal computers and cell phones.

Where problems exist, business opportunity may exist as well. As we have outlined in this chapter, companies like IBM, GE, and Siemens are adjusting their corporate strategies and their product offerings to address some of the planet's environmental challenges and governmental plans to tackle them. In President Obama's 2011 State of the Union address, he called for the United States to generate 80 percent of its electricity from clean energy sources by 2035. Depending upon the evolving definition of "clean energy," this goal may mean good opportunity for companies that have products and services in renewable energies, nuclear power, efficient natural gas, coal with carbon capture and sequestration, wind power, and solar energy. Some businesses objected, contending that the goal was unachievable because of existing regulatory barriers.[56] Business groups and environmental organizations in many countries often clash over various regulations that affect access to energy supplies. Even "clean energy" can pose environmental disputes as illustrated by the issues of shale gas drilling and pipelines in the United States and by the movement away from nuclear power in Germany.

Sustainable Practices

Irrespective of the many disagreements that exist in relation to the green movement, many large international marketers have realized that sustainable practices can make good business sense. As *The International Marketplace 17.4* illustrates, reduced emissions are often directly related to lower fuel costs and increased operational efficiency. Leading global companies are seeing strategic value in making sustainability a corporate imperative. A 2011 McKinsey survey of companies found that

> a handful of companies are capturing significant value by systematically pursuing the opportunities sustainability offers. We believe the trend is clear: more businesses will have to take a long-term strategic view of sustainability and build it into the key value creation levers that drive returns on capital, growth and risk management as well as the key organizational elements that support the levers. Each company's path to capturing value from sustainability will be unique, but these underlying elements can serve as a universal point from which to get started.[57]

Green practices will become increasingly important as society expects more. The Coca Cola Company provides a good example of the sustainability practices of leading international marketers. Coca Cola identified its priority areas for improving sustainability as water stewardship, energy efficiency and climate protection, sustainable packaging, and healthy communities.[58] One can see how these areas are important to the company and the communities it serves by envisioning the amount of water and agricultural products used in Coca Cola products; the energy usage and climatic impact involved in bottling, refrigerating, and distributing its products; and the relationship of its products to the health and wellness of its customers. Water stewardship is particularly important to the company because Coca Cola uses massive amounts of water in its products and operations. Water is vital to its long-term success as a company. It has been challenged over its water usage practices in some parts of the world. In response, Coca Cola believes that, while it may be successful in securing the legal rights to securing water rights, it must seek a "social license" as well:

> For us to do business—and to be part of the solutions addressing water stress—it is essential to secure the trust and goodwill of the people in the communities where we are located. And that can only come from candid, continual dialogue —an ongoing conversation in which we show residents how much water we are using and how we

© africa924/Shutterstock.com

The Coca Cola Company's Replenish Africa Initiative (RAIN) brings clean water and sanitation to two million Africans.

THE INTERNATIONAL MARKETPLACE 17.4

"Can a War on Carbon Be Good Business?"

In 2010, at the Creating Climate Wealth conference at the Georgetown University McDonough School of Business, Richard Branson, CEO of Virgin Group, along with a group of global entrepreneurs, business leaders, and organizations, officially declared world war on carbon emissions. In defining the nature of the war, Branson said, "I have described the increasing levels of greenhouse gases in the atmosphere as one of the greatest threats to the ongoing prosperity and sustainability of life on the planet. The good news is that creating businesses that will power our growth, and reduce our carbon output while protecting resources, is also the greatest wealth-generating opportunity of our generation." Branson believes that a good profitability opportunity exists in providing fuels and technologies while reducing the harmful effects of greenhouse gases (see **www.carbonwarroom.com**).

As the late Prime Minister Winston Churchill demonstrated, a world war requires a war room to coordinate strategy and direct the battlefront. Branson's Carbon War Room is focused on identifying the key battles:

> To reduce carbon and eliminate the bottlenecks we need to direct capital into the renewable and clean tech sector and take solutions to scale. We aim to bring together business, finance, non-profits and government to unite in tackling this challenge. This way we can combine knowledge, enthusiasm, energy and finance to unlock the potential of the technologies and businesses of the future. We must mobilise expertise and capital from around the world to deliver a sustainable, equitable and prosperous world.

To this aim, Branson assembled a management team of business executives to direct battles across 25 industries such as shipping, information technology, cement, energy, and transport. The team channels its resources to achieve progress in one industry battle after another, similar to Douglas MacArthur's island-hopping strategy in World War II.

One of the first theaters in the Carbon War Room's plan of battle is the shipping sector, a source of one billion tons of carbon emissions annually—about 5 percent of the world's carbon output. Towards the goal of proving that sustainable shipping and efficiency are not incompatible but rather reinforcing, the organization provides information, data analysis, and strategic resources to governments, organizations, and industry. For example, it used data from the European Union and the International Maritime Organization to create a ratings standard for the energy efficiency of ships. Their statistics revealed that the shipping industry could reduce emissions by a third through improved route structures, smarter types of fuel, and better maintenance. Not only would emissions be dramatically reduced but so would costs and fuel usage.

In December 2011, the Carbon War Room launched a new web and information site aimed at the airline industry and the reduction in the use of jet fuels (see **www.carbonwarroom.com/sector/aviation**). The organization also announced its first battle medal winners for outstanding business leadership in carbon emissions reduction, with the Gigaton Prize awarded to renewable energy producer Suntech and a Special Gigaton Prize for "country that has been the most inspiring example for renewable energy and energy efficiency investment and deployment" awarded to Germany.

Can the efforts of the Carbon War Room actually result in significant reductions in carbon emissions? Time will tell, but the Carbon War Room demonstrates that visionary leadership, when combined with a determined, dedicated, and well-resourced effort, improves its chances. As Winston Churchill said, "continuous effort, not strength or intelligence, is the key to unlocking our potential."

SOURCES: Richard Branson, "A letter from Our Founder—If We Don't Act, Mother Nature Will," www.carbonwarroom.com, accessed January 18, 2012; Keren Blankfeld, "Branson's Call to Green Entrepreneurs," *Forbes.com*, April 22, 2010, www.forbes.com/2010/04/22/branson-green-technologies-carbon-war-virgin.html?boxes=businesschannelsections; Fiona Harvey and Robert Wright, "Online Service to Track Shipping Emissions," *Financial Times*, December 6, 2010, www.ft.com/intl/cms/s/0/1add9296-0098-11e0-aa29-00144feab49a.html#axzz17SYKPT5T; and Carbon War Room, "SunTech, Tesco, Philips, Schneider, Swisscom and Centrica Triumph at Gigaton Awards Ceremony During UN Climate Change Talks," press release, December 3, 2011, www.carbonwarroom.com.

> are using it. It comes from telling residents how we are managing water resources and what we are doing to improve them. And it comes from helping to address residents' specific concerns about water.[59]

Sustainable Consumers

In the years leading up to the 2008 recession, there was a significant increase in sustainable or green products. In 2009, *Advertising Age* reported that new package-goods products with claims such as "sustainable," "environmentally friendly," and "eco-friendly" had doubled in 2008 over the previous year.[60] A study by Deloitte on "green shoppers" for grocery products found that

> green shoppers are a great customer target, representing a high value segment who buy more products on each trip, visit the store more regularly, and demonstrate more brand and retailer loyalty in their purchasing behavior. They are active consumers who buy more and shop more often as opposed to the image of an austere minimalist. They are less price sensitive than the average shopper and they are generally not bargain hunters.[61]

At the same time, shoppers were found to be unclear about which products were truly sustainable and how to judge them. While the majority of green shoppers were "looking for green" and 22 percent "bought green" products, only about 2 percent of grocery shoppers were "committed" to green purchases.[62] A 2008 Yankelovich study found that 13 percent of U.S. consumers were "Greenthusiasts" for whom environmental issues were a passionate concern, 15 percent were "Greenspeaks" who had strong environmental attitudes but did not necessarily reflect their attitudes in actual purchases, and 25 percent were "Greensteps" who were "aware, concerned, and taking some action."[63] Major questions remain regarding whether and to what extent consumers reward responsible firms in their purchase decisions. When consumers feel more economic pain, most of them subjugate their attitudes about green products to more fundamental concerns about product quality, effectiveness, shopping convenience, and price. For example, Clorox introduced Greenworks, a line of environmentally friendly cleaning products, in the United States in 2008 and achieved initial success with sales of over $100 million. However, after the recession hit, sales fell by 40 percent as consumers became reluctant to spend higher prices for green products.[64] In the long run, if marketers can offer quality green products at the right price points, they may be rewarded by consumers. Even in periods of good economic conditions, consumers have limits to the price premiums they will pay for secondary benefits.

Those who are motivated to purchase green products may still be challenged by a lack of good and reliable information about the sustainability of products. Good labeling and the availability of certification is helpful. However, perhaps one of the major factors contributing to confusion about which products are truly sustainable or green is the multiplicity of certification authorities. As a sampling in Exhibit 17.9 shows, there are many certification authorities and labels that address sustainability issues, reflecting the wide variety of issues covered under the topic. Over 400 different eco-labels or green certification systems were present in the marketplace in 2011.[65] How is a concerned consumer expected to understand completely what terms such as *organic*, *energy efficient*, *humane*, *dolphin safe*, *bird friendly*, or *fair trade* mean? Which certification authorities are to be trusted, and which products are truly green? This issue is made even more complex by different certification standards across borders. A consumer concerned about buying coffee from producers that follow responsible labor and agricultural practices needs to discern the difference between

EXHIBIT 17.9 Eco-Labels

Rainforest Alliance certification (www.rainforest-alliance.org/multimedia), Fair Trade certification (www.fairtradeusa.org/what-is-fair-trade), and Starbucks' Coffee and Farmer Equity (C.A.F.E.) practices.

One example of governments working together to resolve confusion is the cooperation between the United States, Japan, Korea, Australia, and the European Union to create ENERGY STAR, a voluntary appliance-specific label governing energy efficiency for office equipment.[66] The EU also has voluntary labeling programs that international marketers of products such as consumer appliances, detergents, and paints need to consider. The EU eco-label program sets a variety of ecological criteria that help consumers understand health and environmental impact issues for a number of products and allow them to make an informed purchase decision. Another voluntary environmental program in Germany is the Blue Angel program, the oldest environment-related label in the world, which sets standards of occupational health and safety, ergonomics, economical use of raw materials, service life, and disposal. The Blue Angel seal of approval is awarded to those products that meet the standards, allowing consumer confidence in their choices of products.[67]

Greenwashing

A factor that contributes to consumer confusion and even cynicism about green marketing is that of "greenwashing," or marketers making overblown environmental claims or creating false green imagery. As Exhibit 17.10 shows, about 8 out of 10 Americans are skeptical of corporations promoting their environmental or sustainability behavior.[68] Environmental activists and sympathetic media have become very active in working to expose companies whom they contend follow this practice. The U.K.'s *Guardian* newspaper ran a series of columns under the title "Greenwash" that exposed the "exaggeration, absurd claims or downright lies that big business makes about its green credentials."[69] There are multiple examples of companies being criticized for

EXHIBIT 17.10 **Skepticism about Environmental Marketing Claims**

Green – or Whitewash?

According to Gallup, about 8 in 10 Americans are skeptical of corporations that promote themselves as environmentally responsible, and about 9 in 10 agree that most corporations talk a lot about environmental responsibility but don't make really significant changes.

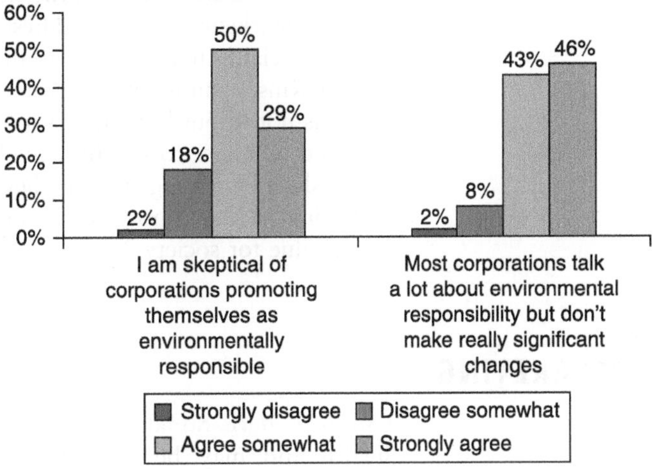

SOURCE: Bryant Ott, "Time to Green Your Business," *Gallup Management Journal*, April 22, 2011, http://gmj.gallup.com/content/147221/time-green-business.aspx.

this greenwashing. Many environmental groups criticized British Petroleum for its "Beyond Petroleum" advertising campaign, particularly after the BP oil spill in the Gulf of Mexico in 2010. Kimberly Clark's Huggies Pure and Natural line of disposable diapers were criticized for overemphasizing their claim of using organic cotton.[70]

Of course, greenwashing can be very subjective. One person's scientific claim may be believed to be false by those who disagree with its policy implications, its source of funding, or the research methodology used to establish it. Perfect standards for judging environmental issues are elusive. One of the effects of the criticism around this issue has been for many international marketers to treat the issue of sustainability relatively quietly in their marketing efforts. Companies may report on sustainability performance but avoid marketing campaigns centered on it.

Growing Importance to Marketing

In the long run, sustainability will be important to international marketers because it will also be important to governments, to consumers, and to employees. Doug Oberhelman, the CEO of Caterpillar, captured the strategic fit of sustainability from an international marketer's customer-centric viewpoint:

> It's a perfect fit. Our strategy is all about serving our customers. And our customers are asking us how we can help make them more efficient and help them meet their sustainability challenges. That pull from customers is really all we need, but our people are also pushing us. Caterpillar employees get really excited about making our products more sustainable and also making our own operations more efficient. And guess what? One of the key groups on our strategy pyramid—stockholders—like sustainability too. I've yet to meet a stockholder that doesn't believe in investing for the future and providing superior products, services and

solutions that meet our customers' needs. And that's what we are doing when we deliver sustainable solutions to our customers."[71]

While we have seen that consumers may lack trust in business and are skeptical of sustainability claims, international marketers must understand the importance of sustainability to a growing number of consumers in the long run. Gallup's 2011 research found that a large majority of consumers "seem willing to reward companies for focusing on the environment" and prefer brands that are "environmentally friendly."[72] As marketers know, when there is significant consumer awareness of an issue, marketing needs to address it. An essential part of marketing is having products and claims that stand up to the test of consumer scrutiny.

McKinsey sums up the issue of sustainability: "The choice for companies today is not if, but how, they should manage their sustainability activities. Companies can choose to see this agenda as a necessary evil—a matter of compliance or a risk to be managed while they get on with the business of business—or they can think of it as a novel way to open up new business opportunities while creating value for society."[73]

CURATIVE MARKETING

Curative international marketing restores and develops international economic health and may be the next step up for marketing. "Restore" indicates something lost that once was there. "Developing" refers to new issues to be addressed with new tools and frames of reference. "Health" in turn positions the issue as important to overall welfare. Marketers must deliver joy, pleasure, fulfillment, safety, personal growth, and advancement towards a better society.

Curative international marketing accepts responsibility for problems to which marketing has contributed. It then uses marketing's capabilities to set things right, to heal past wounds, and to increase the well-being of the individual and society on a global level. Curative marketing's two perspectives consist of looking back to check on what marketing has wrought and making up for past errors with future action.

Global problems require a global approach. Curative international marketing needs to draw on fields like jurisprudence, cultural anthropology, philosophy, and history. Such a perspective acknowledges that marketing is too important to be left to marketers alone, consonant with Keynes's questioning "how and whether economics should rule the world."

International marketers need to focus on past errors and mistakes inflicted by international marketing and sweep these out from under the carpet in the spirit of *Wiedergutmachung*, or restitution.

Marketing's disregard of local idiosyncrasies has sometimes been like the introduction of a destructive virus on a culture, akin to bringing snakes to Guam—which almost exterminated all the local birds—and to how European outsiders brought smallpox, flu, and typhus viruses that decimated the Inca of Peru. More contemporaneous is a current lawsuit:

> The Pine Ridge Indian tribe is suing five beer companies for their role in the alcoholism and fetal alcohol syndrome that plague the tribe's reservation. The Oglala Sioux Tribe claims that the beer companies—which include Anheuser Busch and Molson Coors—sold beer on the perimeter of the teetotalling South Dakota reservation with the knowledge that it would be smuggled in demanding $500 million for healthcare and rehabilitation. Whiteclay, a nearby town in Nebraska with four beer shops and only about a dozen residents, gets most of its customers from the reservation.

> Tom White, the lawyer representing the tribe, told the Associated Press: "You cannot sell 4.9 million 12oz cans of beer and wash your hands like Pontius Pilate, and say we've got nothing to do with it being smuggled."
>
> The reservation, which is about the size of Connecticut, has dealt with poverty and alcoholism for decades. One in four children born suffer from fetal alcohol syndrome, and the life expectancy, between 45 and 52 years, is the lowest in the U.S.[74]

Eastern Europe, in its transition from socialism to market practices, provides another example. Advertisements were taken literally, leading to grave disappointments by consumers because they did not win the "promised" car or look like model Heidi Klum. Local foods (and their producers) disappeared because newly entering chain stores already had suppliers. People were conditioned to increase their consumption of products, which led, for many, to consumption addiction.

Growth is seen by many as the envisioned key accomplishment of marketing. Executives planning only to maintain market share last only for a very short time in their job. More is expected. *Citius, altius, fortius* ("faster, higher, stronger") may be a great motto for the Olympics, but it leads to unexpected repercussions for marketers and their customers.

Consumers' interest in and preparation for marketing are not evenly distributed. Negative effects may result from marketing's misleading of consumers or simply from unawareness or neglect. It is the obligation of international marketers to understand local conditions and to anticipate and limit possible ill effects. Not everything that can be done should be done. There must be a marketing Hippocratic Oath: "First do no harm." Beyond that caveat, marketers need to do everything possible to make people be better off and actually feel better.

A second key concern is the future outlook: how can marketing set things right again? Four core areas are international marketing's pillars for a shining position on the hill: truthfulness, simplicity, expanded participation, and personal responsibility.

Truthfulness

On many occasions, the international marketing community has either actively misled expectations or left its participants with a sense of substantial ambiguity. Marketing must base itself on fact rather than emotion, on insights rather than speculation, and do so within a changing context. Just as human beings change, social science truths may not be eternal but rather subject to change over time. When a customer feels gouged by marketing, the infrastructure of the discipline is weakened. This responsibility for the position of the entire field places a burden of honesty on each marketing actor.

Simplicity

Marketing must find new ways to simplify life because simplicity adds value. The Global Brand Simplicity Index states that up to 19 percent of consumers are willing to spend extra for an uncomplicated experience.[75] Simplification is also crucially linked to truthfulness and making sure that people understand the implications of their decisions. It is hard for front-line marketers to be truthful about something if they do not understand how the system works. Truth and simplicity go hand in hand. The understanding of how a product or even a system works and is interconnected is a valuable product attribute in itself.

Simplicity also means the recognition and elimination of incongruities. It makes little sense to place calling customers on hold and tell them a repeat message that "your call is important to us." If the call were truly important, then the firm would hire more employees to answer phones.

Expanded Participation

International marketing needs to be truly international in its outlook. For example, using only English as the language of business denigrates the use of other language tools and reduces the idiosyncratic participation of other nations and their citizens. If Eskimos had to talk about snow only in the English language, the rich diversity of this theme in their own language would sharply decrease.

Inclusiveness also helps with future change. History indicates that power waxes and wanes. Often, leaders do not prepare for transitions. Just think of the Incas, the Greeks, the Icelanders, the Iraqis, and the Persians. Marketing preparation, however, can convert crashes into soft landings.

More communication with critics is essential. Opponents are a constituency that must be brought into the tent. The human tendency is to focus on and celebrate winners, but not everyone touched by international marketing will come out a winner. International marketing relies on a fundamental belief in the virtues of risk, competition, profit, and private property, yet not everyone considers these four dimensions as crucial or even acceptable. When the rising tide is expected to lift all boats, it becomes crucial that the vessels do not leak, that the crew has been properly trained to cope with a rising sea, and that the sails are tight and strong. Otherwise there is only a winner-takes-all approach.

Personal Responsibility

Personal involvement is crucial in international marketing, where distance can also mean abdication of responsibility. Marketers sometimes demonstrate their desire not to know—by appointing a middleman about whose behavior one can later on be suitably astonished, surprised, and mortified. The best international marketers take things very seriously and actively work as responsible citizens to improve conditions. They know the immediate customer importance of distribution networks, health systems for communities near production facilities, technical education infrastructure, and governance capabilities that benefit both the firm and host countries. Jack Welch, former chairman of GE, always carries light bulbs when traveling so that complaints about early burnout can be attended to.

There need to be reasonable boundaries for firms. A key tenet of marketing is reverence for the customer, yet some firms stray and take a predatory approach. Skuba writes on the phenomenon of vampire marketing to highlight inappropriate, unjust, and ultimately counterproductive actions by firms. Typically, this takes place when the key consumption decision has already been made but circumstances allow for additional offers. High minibar charges in a hotel, or blankets or pillows for rent on an airplane, are examples.[76]

Ultimately, the goal for international marketers is not only to apply existing frameworks to new situations but also to develop new frameworks from the insights that they garner from working in different and diverse environments. They must do so in order to maintain and grow their expertise and its application.

For international marketers, change is a key opportunity. Curative marketing can help us all by overcoming past shortcomings and avoiding future ills. Marketers are the agents of change and need to be directly involved in change. As the great Ludwig von Wittgenstein stated, "A philosopher who is not taking part in discussions is like a boxer who never goes into the ring." It is time for international marketers to enter the ring.

SUMMARY

The international marketplace has changed dramatically during the most recent period of globalization. As new marketplaces and sources of supply have grown for international marketers, firms have become large players on the global stage. The world has become much more interrelated and interdependent, which has led to a greater exposure of countries and societies to new risks. This expansion has in turn placed greater requirements on all to respond to a rapidly changing political, economic, social, technological, and even climatic environment. The stakes have become much higher. Societies and governments are expecting firms to play an ethical and responsible role in the future. A higher standard of leadership is now required for international marketers.

As a 2010 report from the Futures Company states,

> With brands under greater scrutiny, the ways in which brands conduct themselves will matter much more, and not just related to the old labor and environmental issues but conduct related to new issues tied to risks, transparency, compensation and accountability as well. The financial crisis has made it apparent to consumers that these sorts of business ethics can have personal relevance, so the commitment of companies to ethical business practices will become no less important than other brand attributes. As this crisis has shown, sometimes poor ethics can wipe out the brand benefits entirely. An anti-greed spirit will pervade the entire recovery consumer marketplace.[77]

The best international marketers are now transforming themselves to embrace corporate social responsibility and sustainability practices that benefit both the firm and the societies in which it operates. A new generation of leaders is emerging in these companies who embrace these practices as core strategies. Perhaps these new leaders will also begin to embrace curative marketing as the next stage of international marketing.

KEY TERMS

marketing dilemma
bailouts
financial transactions tax
corporate social responsibility (CSR)
corporate citizenship
corporate philanthropy
sustainability
shared value
curative international marketing

QUESTIONS FOR DISCUSSION

1. Why has trust in business dropped in developed countries but remains high in countries like China and India?
2. Is there a need for increased regulation of financial services product marketing to consumers?
3. Will a financial transactions tax on equity, bond, currency, and financial derivatives transactions in the EU and the United States serve a greater social purpose or be bad for business?
4. Do you agree with Milton Friedman's contention that the only responsibility of business is "to use its resources and engage in activities designed to increase its profits so long as it stays within the rules of the game"?
5. Why should businesses be concerned about carbon emissions?
6. Should international marketers embrace a curative international marketing approach and accept responsibility for problems that marketing has generated?

INTERNET EXERCISES

1. Identify 10 non-European-headquartered companies belonging to CSR Europe. Go to www.csreurope.org/members.php.
2. Identify a firm that proves its leadership in sustainability in an industry of your choice. For example, go to the sustainability reports on the websites of leading global brewing companies and compare their metrics for important performance indicators.

CHALLENGE US

Should Customers Care about Apple's Treatment of Chinese Workers?

Apple is admired by consumers worldwide for its consumer-friendly products, its innovative ideas, its stylish approach, and its management. It is regularly listed as one of the strongest brands in international marketing. At the same time, Apple has been criticized for its treatment of workers in its Chinese production facilities, most of which are owned by suppliers outside of the company. The *New York Times* reported in 2012 that

> the workers assembling iPhones, iPads and other devices often labor in harsh conditions, according to employees inside those plants, worker advocates and documents published by companies themselves. Problems are as varied as onerous work environments and serious—sometimes deadly—safety problems. Employees work excessive overtime, in some cases seven days a week, and live in crowded dorms. Some say they stand so long that their legs swell until they can hardly walk.

One of Apple's most important suppliers is Foxconn. From 2009 to 2011, 19 Foxconn employees attempted suicide or fell from buildings in possible suicides. Foxconn has been singled out for criticism of its working conditions and crowded dormitories. In 2011, riots broke out in the company's Chengdu dormitories over workers issues. The *New York Times* reported about Foxconn's official response, which said, "Conditions at Foxconn are anything but harsh.... All assembly line employees are given regular breaks, including one-hour lunch breaks ... Foxconn has a very good safety record.... Foxconn has come a long way in our efforts to lead our industry in China in areas such as workplace conditions and the care and treatment of our employees."

It is important to understand cultural issues when judging Apple's and Foxconn's conduct. Many of the Chinese workers, who often live in dormitories, migrate from rural areas to make as much money as possible to send home to their families. These workers may view their jobs as opportunities to maximize income during a short period of time before returning to their villages to live. Some of these workers are willing to work long hours and may not view the conditions as being as harsh as Westerners would. Still, Apple has a formal code of conduct for its suppliers to follow and regularly conducts audits of facilities. The company actively works to prevent child labor. It trains factory owners and management as well as millions of workers in proper working practices. Apple is increasing its transparency and regularly publishes supplier responsibility progress reports. Under pressure from various nongovernmental organizations and the media, Apple released a list of its suppliers in 2012. Also, Apple has limited control over these independent companies, and good suppliers are hard to find. Strict compliance measures along with ongoing pressures to reduce costs may lead to deceptions and abuses by the suppliers and may inhibit real change. But continued problems may lead to greater concerns among Apple's customers and put the brand at risk.

The *New York Times* summarized the issue by quoting a current Apple executive as follows: "You can either manufacture in comfortable, worker-friendly factories, or you can reinvent the product every year, and make it better and faster and cheaper, which requires factories that seem harsh by American standards ... And right now, customers care more about a new iPhone than working conditions in China."

For Discussion

1. Should Apple continue to work with suppliers like Foxconn?
2. What can Apple do more than it is currently doing to improve worker conditions?
3. Would continued problems prevent you from buying an Apple product?

SOURCES: Charles Duhigg and David Barboza, "In China, Human Costs Are Built into an iPad," *New York Times*, January 25, 2012; and Mia Overall, "CSR Weighs Heavily on Image-Driven Apple," *CSR Asia* 8, no. 5 (January 2, 2012).

RECOMMENDED READINGS

Cramer, Aron, and Zachary Karabell. *Sustainable Excellence: The Future of Business in a Fast Changing World*. New York: Rodale, 2010.

Edelman Trust Barometer, annual updates, http://trust.edelman.com.

KPMG. *KPMG International Corporate Sustainability: A Progress Report*. KPMG, 2011. www.kpmg.com/Global/en/IssuesAndInsights/ArticlesPublications/Documents/corporate-sustainability-v2.pdf.

KPMG. "KPMG International Survey of Corporate Responsibility Reporting 2011." KPMG. http://sustainableindustries.com/sites/default/files/private/cr_report_2011_final.pdf.

Schwartz, Mark S. *Corporate Social Responsibility: An Ethical Approach*. Peterborough. Ontario, Canada: Broadview Press, 2011.

World Economic Forum. *Redefining the Future of Growth: The New Sustainability Champions*. BCG, September 2011. www.bcg.com/about_bcg/social_impact/Corporate_Social_Responsibility/PublicationDetails.aspx?id=tcm:12-86089.

ENDNOTES

1. Michael Czinkota and Charles Skuba, "The Two Faces of International Marketing," *Marketing Management*, Winter 2011, pp. 14, 15.
2. Pontifical Council for Justice and Peace, "Note on Financial Reform," Vatican Information Service, www.news.va/en/news/full-text-note-on-financial-reform-from-the-pontif, accessed January 27, 2012.
3. Jagdish Sheth and Rajendra Sisodia, *Does Marketing Need Reform: Fresh Perspectives on the Future* (Armonk, NY: M.E. Sharpe, 2006).
4. Charles J. Skuba, "Consumers Can Shine Sunlight on Exploitative Vampire Brands," letter to *Financial Times*, July 11, 2011.
5. Shahzeb Jillani, "Indian Anger at Dow Olympics Sponsorship," *BBC News*, August 8, 2011.
6. Michael Czinkota and Charles Skuba, op. cit.
7. Jim Puzzanghera, "Federal Consumer Protection Agency Launching amid Lingering Controversy," *Los Angeles Times*, July 21, 2011.
8. "G20 Leaders Summit–Final Communiqué," November 3–4, 2011, pp. 12–17, www.g20-g8.com/g8-g20/g20/english/for-the-press/news-releases/g20-leaders-summit-final-communique.1554.html, accessed January 25, 2012.
9. Ibid, 20–21.
10. Ibid, 25–27.
11. Coca Cola Company, www.thecoca-colacompany.com/ourcompany/index.html, accessed January 27, 2012.
12. Procter & Gamble, http://za.pg.com/about, accessed January 27, 2012.
13. World Bank, "Gross Domestic Product 2010," http://siteresources.worldbank.org/DATASTATISTICS/Resources/GDP.pdf; and *Fortune*, "Global 500 2011," http://money.cnn.com/magazines/fortune/global500/2011/full_list, accessed January 27, 2012.
14. "Capitalism and Its Global Malcontents," *Financial Times* editorial, October 24, 2011.
15. "Edelman Trust Barometer," http://trust.edelman.com, accessed January 27, 2012.
16. "2010 Edelman Trust Barometer," Executive Summary, www.edelman.com/trust/2010, accessed January 27, 2012.
17. "2012 Edelman Trust Barometer," Executive Summary, http://trust.edelman.com/trust-download/executive-summary, accessed January 27, 2012.
18. Ibid.
19. Ibid.
20. "Top 100 Global Marketers," *Advertising Age*, December 6, 2010.
21. "2012 Edelman Trust Barometer," Executive Summary, http://trust.edelman.com/trust-download/executive-summary, accessed January 27, 2012.
22. Pontifical Council for Justice and Peace, "Note on Financial Reform," Vatican Information Service, www.news.va/en/news/full-text-note-on-financial-reform-from-the-pontif, accessed January 27, 2012.
23. World Economic Forum, "Global Risks 2012," www.weforum.org/issues/global-risks, accessed January 27, 2012.
24. GE, "Products & Services," www.ge.com/products_services/index.html, accessed January 29, 2012.
25. Siemens, "Worldwide Presence," www.siemens.com/about/en/worldwide.htm, accessed January 29, 2012.
26. Siemens, www.siemens.com/about/en/values-vision-strategy/values.htm, accessed January 29, 2012.
27. Siemens, "Values," www.usa.siemens.com/en/about_us/us_business_groups.htm, accessed January 29, 2012.
28. Michael R. Czinkota and Charles J. Skuba, "A Contextual Analysis of Legal Systems and Their Impact on Trade and Foreign Direct Investment," *Journal of Business Research*, 2012.
29. Milton Friedman, "The Social Responsibility of Business Is to Increase Its Profits," *New York Times Magazine*, September 13, 1970.
30. Ibid.
31. "The Carnegie Medal of Philanthropy," www.carnegiemedals.org, accessed February 2, 2012.
32. 2011 Edelman Trust Barometer, www.edelman.com/trust/2011, accessed January 31, 2012.
33. Fleishman–Hillard and National Consumer League, "Rethinking Corporate Social Responsibility," Executive Summary, May 2007.
34. CSR Europe, "History," www.csreurope.org/pages/en/history.html, accessed February 2, 2012.
35. Mike Esterl, "In This Picturesque Village, the Rent Hasn't Been Raised since 1520," *Wall Street Journal*, December 26, 2008.
36. International Chamber of Commerce, "Business in Society: Making a Positive and Responsible Contribution," www.iccwbo.org/policy/society/id1188/index.html, accessed February 3, 2012.
37. CSR Europe, "About Us," www.csreurope.org/pages/en/about_us.html, accessed February 2, 2012.
38. Ibid.
39. Chambers Ireland, "Chambers Ireland's Corporate Social Responsibility Awards," www.csrawards.ie, accessed February 2, 2012.
40. Council of British Chambers of Commerce in Europe, "Corporate Social Responsibility," www.cobcoe.eu/about/corporate-social-responsibility/humtraf, accessed February 2, 2012.
41. The International Chamber of Commerce, "Business in society: making a positive and responsible contribution," May 7, 2002, www.iccwbo.org/policy/society/id1188/index.html.
42. Michael E. Porter and Mark R. Kramer, "Creating Shared Value," *Harvard Business Review*, January–February 2011.

43. Ibid.
44. Ibid.
45. Ibid.
46. "2012 Edelman Trust Barometer," Executive Summary, http://trust.edelman.com/trust-download/executive-summary, accessed January 27, 2012.
47. KPMG, "International Survey of Corporate Responsibility Reporting 2011," Executive Summary, p. 2.
48. Ibid.
49. Ibid.
50. Joao Almeida and Charles Skuba. Internal Research, McDonough School of Business, Georgetown University.
51. Ibid.
52. United Nations Brundtland Report, "Our Common Future," 1987, www.un-documents.net/ocf-02.htm.
53. Robert Gilman, "Sustainability: The State of the Movement," *In Context*, Spring 1990, 10, www.context.org/ICLIB/IC25/Gilman.htm.
54. United Nations Framework Convention on Climate Change, "Kyoto Protocol," http://unfccc.int/kyoto_protocol/items/2830.php, accessed February 5, 2012.
55. Edward Wyatt, "Give Up Familiar Light Bulb? Not without Fight, Some Say," *New York Times*, March 11, 2011.
56. Anne C. Mulkern, "U.S. Chamber, Renewable Groups Clash over Ability to Meet Obama's Clean Energy Goal," *New York Times*, February 2, 2011.
57. McKinsey & Company, "2011 Global Survey Results–The Business of Sustainability," *McKinsey Quarterly*, October 2011, www.mckinseyquarterly.com/The_business_of_sustainability_McKinsey_Global_Survey_results_2867.
58. Coca Cola Company, "2010/2011 Sustainability Report," www.thecoca-colacompany.com/sustainabilityreport/TCCC_2010_2011_Sustainability_Report_Full.pdf.
59. Ibid.
60. Jack Neff, "Green-Marketing Revolution Defies Economic Downturn," *Advertising Age*, April 20, 2009.
61. Deloitte, "Finding the Green in Today's Shoppers," February 2009.
62. Ibid.
63. Yankelovich, "Going Green Bandwagon Stalls among Consumers," *PR Newswire*, August 13, 2008.
64. Stephanie Clifford and Andrew Martin, "As Consumers Cut Spending, 'Green' Products Lose Allure," *New York Times*, April 21, 2011.
65. Jacquie Ottman, "How to Choose the Right Eco-label for Your Brand," *Jacquie Ottman's Green Marketing Blog*, October 19, 2011.
66. EU ENERGY STAR, "Introducing EU ENERGY STAR," www.eu-energystar.org/en/index.html, accessed February 6, 2012.
67. U.S. International Trade Administration, "Trade Regulations and Standards," http://export.gov/germany/MarketResearchonGermany/CountryCommercialGuide/TradeRegulationsandStandards/index.asp, accessed February 7, 2012.
68. Bryant Ott, "Time to Green Your Business," *Gallup Management Journal*, April 22, 2011, http://gmj.gallup.com/content/147221/time-green-business.aspx.
69. "Greenwash: Exposing False Environmental Claims," *Guardian*, www.guardian.co.uk/environment/series/greenwash, accessed February 7, 2012.
70. Business Pundit "The Top 25 Greenwashed Products in America," March 2, 2010, www.businesspundit.com/the-top-25-greenwashed-products-in-america.
71. Caterpillar, "2010 Sustainability Report," Chairman's Message.
72. Bryant Ott, "Time to Green Your Business," *Gallup Management Journal*, April 22, 2011, http://gmj.gallup.com/content/147221/time-green-business.aspx.
73. McKinsey & Company, "2011 Global Survey Results–The Business of Sustainability."
74. Associated Press, "Tribe Sues Beer Companies for Alcoholism on Reservation," *Washington Post*, February 10, 2012.
75. "Global Brand Simplicity Index 2011", Siegel+Gale, www.siegelgale.com/white_paper/2011-global-brand-simplicity-index, accessed May 29, 2012.
76. Charles Skuba, "Consumers Can Shine Sunlight on Exploitative Vampire Brands," *Financial Times*, July 12, 2011.
77. The Futures Company, "A Darwinian Gale," Henley Center Headlight Vision and Yankelovich, 2010, p. 57.

CHAPTER 18

New Directions and Challenges

LEARNING OBJECTIVES

By the time you complete this chapter, you will be able to:

- Understand the trends and environmental factors that will drive international marketing in the future.
- Learn how to identify opportunities in the external environment.
- Comprehend strategic efforts marketers must undertake to stay ahead of key trends.

THE INTERNATIONAL MARKETPLACE 18.1

Marketable Global Business School Models

Business schools across the globe utilize a plethora of different teaching methods. Some have both undergraduate and graduate programs, while others only have the latter. Many European business schools are universities that are solely focused on teaching their students about business. The most important differentiation between business schools is the model that their curriculum follows. The main models are the case study model and the skills-based model.

The *case study model* emphasizes practice and tangible experience as a learning tool. Case studies from a wide array of real business exchanges are read by students. In class, the students must discuss what questions they would ask, what decisions would be most profitable to make, and how to deal with all types of possible complications that may arise in business deals. With this model, professors turn the classroom into the real world so that they can equip their students with knowledge for their futures. The *skills-based method* places importance on problems and solutions. Students take courses in various types of research, international and domestic business, statistics, and more.

Dr. Peter Senge of the Massachusetts Institute of Technology feels that these models need to be pushed further. In an interview with *BizEd Magazine*, Dr. Senge discusses with urgency how business schools need to teach students to focus on the larger picture, with the long-term prospects in mind. He worries that short-term results and the haunting image of quarterly reports have become too important in business schools' curricula and in the minds of their students. Dr. Senge is not alone in his push for change. The Western business school models are continuously being remodeled due to the world's ever-changing economic environment. After the global financial crisis, schools hurried to their classrooms in order to ingrain the importance of making stable, ethical decisions in their students' minds.

As the Western model changes and evolves, it travels in various forms across the globe. Most notably, business schools in Africa have harped on the Western model. With the Western models dominating the African business school world, some local organizations and Western-educated natives are calling for a change. Since 2009, the Global Competitiveness Index conducted by the World Economic Forum has ranked African countries as high as number 32 in the list of the world's most competitive markets. African markets are on the rise, and analysts say that it is critical to improve the African business school programs. The African Association of Business Schools (AABS) has made major strides in recent years to hold all accredited African graduate schools to a level of excellence. It focuses on educating Africans on the continent-specific market. However, there are still many changes that need to be made before African business schools can stop following the Western model entirely.

Dr. Walter Baets, director of the Graduate School of Business within the University of Cape Town, addresses how Africa can and must develop its own model. In an article for the *Financial Times*, Baets wrote that the Western-modeled business schools in Africa import foreign ideas and thinking to a continent that does not approach business in the same way. He writes, "Is it possible to take a success story in one part of the world and transplant it to another?" There is no clear answer, but if Baets has his way, Africa will have the opportunity to create and hone its own business school model—perhaps with aspects included in the various Western models—that will directly address the African business environment.

SOURCES: "Top 100 MBA programs," The Aspen Institute: Center for Business Education, www.beyondgreypinstripes.org/rankings/index.cfm, accessed June 16, 2011; "Association of African Business Schools (AABS)," Global Business School Network, www.gbsnonline.org/the-network-at-gbsn/partners/association-of-african-business-schools-aabs.html, accessed June 16, 2011; Walter Baets, "Africa Deserves Its Own Business School Model," *Financial Times* (London), April 4, 2011; Tricia Bisoux, "Reshaping Business," *BizEd*, May-June 2010, pp. 18-23; "History—Our Story," Global Business School Network, www.gbsnonline.org/our-story/history/history.html, accessed June 16, 2011; and "The Global Competitiveness Index," World Economic Forum, www.weforum.org/reports/global-competitiveness-report-2010-2011-0?fo=1, accessed June 16, 2011.

Worldwide, marketers are faced with major external factors that can dramatically affect efforts toward marketplace success. The fragility of the global marketplace has been seen numerous times over the past few years—from the uprisings that swept through the Middle East and North Africa, to the global financial crisis that beset countries worldwide, to the devastating earthquake in Japan that claimed more than 15,000 lives and devastated countless firms. We have seen how boundaryless the world has become as images of these horrible natural disasters were brought into our homes almost immediately.

We have seen the disasters caused by political instability, marked by conflict in the Middle East, and economic disaster due to the collapse of major financial institutions, perilously high oil prices, and rising unemployment.

© ASAHI SHIMBUN/AFP/Getty Images/Newscom

Earthquakes are one natural disaster which can disrupt international business in a major way.

The job for us, as marketers, is to better understand both the good and the bad of marketplace changes while recognizing that the forces of globalization change rapidly. In a recent study, the functional area of marketing was noted as the second most critical business function for global success (behind logistics).[1] As portrayed in *The International Marketplace 18.1*, the traditional approach to business education may soon become obsolete.

International marketers are faced constantly with global change. This is not a new situation, nor one to be feared, because change provides the opportunity for the emergence of new market positions. Recently, however, changes are occurring more frequently and more rapidly with the potential for more severe impact. Due to growing real-time access to knowledge about customers, suppliers, and competitors, the international marketing environment is increasingly characterized by high speed bordering on instantaneity. The past has lost much of its value as a predictor of the future.

This chapter identifies critical issues that marketers need to understand for future success. The intent is to identify major trends or drivers that will affect a marketer's ability to make sound business decisions as well as suggest critical areas of focus in marketing.

INTERNATIONAL DRIVERS—A MARKETER'S EXTERNAL ENVIRONMENT

The identification of global trends has been the focus of several recent studies. Various methods are used to spot these trends. The Economist Intelligence Unit conducted a survey of more than 260 senior global marketing executives and chief executive officers worldwide to understand challenges faced by global chief marketing officers.[2] The KOF Index of Globalization measures the economic, social, and political dimensions of globalization. The KOF Index can be used to observe the change in globalization in a large number of countries over a long period of time.[3] In the latest of five international Delphi studies involving key global experts in policy, business, and research, Czinkota and Ronkainen identified important international business dimensions subject to change by 2020.[4]

Taken together these studies identify several major trends or drivers that will require considerable marketing attention. These drivers in the international marketplace are demographics, technology, culture, economic development, natural resources, and political and legal issues.

Demographics

Demographic characteristics have long been a foundation for marketing opinions, and trends in demography will remain critical to the future of marketing decisions. According to the Population Reference Bureau (PRB), the **demographic divide** is widening. The demographic divide is the measure of the inequality in the population and health profiles between rich and poor countries. The world's population in 2012 was estimated at more than seven billion and is expected to rise to 9.6 billion by 2050. The PRB estimates that nearly all of the world population growth is now concentrated in the world's poorer countries. Even the small amount of overall growth in the wealthier nations will largely result from immigration.[5] Exhibit 18.1 shows the most populous countries in 2010 and the expected most populous countries in 2050. Exhibit 18.2 lists the countries with the youngest and oldest populations. Such data help marketers target products and services for young people and seniors to the appropriate countries.

EXHIBIT 18.1 Most Populous Countries, 2010 and 2050

2010 Country	2010 Population (in millions)	2050 Country	2050 Population (in millions)
China	1,338	India	1,748
India	1,189	China	1,437
United States	310	United States	423
Indonesia	235	Pakistan	335
Brazil	193	Nigeria	326
Pakistan	185	Indonesia	309
Bangladesh	164	Bangladesh	222
Nigeria	158	Brazil	215
Russia	142	Ethiopia	174
Japan	127	Congo, Dem. Rep.	166

SOURCE: 2010 World Population Data Sheet, 2012 Population Reference Bureau, www.prb.org/Publications/PopulationBulletins/2010/worldpopulationhighlights2010.aspx.

EXHIBIT 18.2 Countries with the Youngest and Oldest Populations, 2011

Youngest	% Ages < 15	Oldest	% Ages 65+
Niger	48.9	Japan	23.2
Uganda	48.3	Germany	20.7
Mali	47.6	Italy	20.2
Angola	47.3	Greece	18.9
Zambia	46.5	Sweden	18.5
Burundi	46.3	Portugal	17.9
Congo, Dem. Rep.	46.0	Bulgaria	17.7
Mozambique	45.3	Austria	17.6
Chad	45.3	Finland	17.5
Burkina Faso	45.2	Latvia	17.4

SOURCE: Population Reference Bureau, "2011 World Population Data Sheet," www.prb.org/Publications/Datasheets/2011/world-population-data-sheet/data-sheet.aspx.

Population numbers are also affected by changes in life expectancy. The longevity of today's population is unprecedented.[6] Life expectancy is increasing, and people have progressively more years to live. The phrase "60 is the new 40" will challenge marketers as never before. Exhibit 18.3 shows current and expected median indices worldwide.

The top 10 most globalized countries according to the Globalization Index 2010 are:

1. Hong Kong
2. Ireland
3. Singapore
4. Denmark
5. Switzerland

EXHIBIT 18.3 **Median Age for Major World Regions**

	2005	2045
WORLD	**28.1**	**37.1**
More developed regions	38.6	45.5
Less developed regions	25.6	35.7
Least developed regions	18.9	26.1
AFRICA	**18.9**	**26.1**
Eastern Africa	17.5	24.3
Middle Africa	16.8	21.6
Northern Africa	23.0	34.6
Southern Africa	23.0	28.6
Western Africa	17.6	25.6
ASIA	**27.7**	**39.0**
Eastern Asia	33.5	45.5
South-central Asia	23.5	35.6
Southeast Asia	25.7	38.8
Western Asia	23.6	34.0
EUROPE	**39.0**	**47.2**
Eastern Europe	37.5	47.3
Northern Europe	38.9	43.8
Southern Europe	39.8	50.4
Western Europe	40.7	46.7
LATIN AMERICA & THE CARIBBEAN	**25.9**	**38.5**
Central America	24.0	38.9
South America	26.4	38.4
NORTH AMERICA	**36.3**	**41.1**

SOURCE: Warren Sanderson and Sergei Scherbov, "Rethinking Age and Aging," *Population Bulletin* 63, no. 4 (2008): 10.

6. Belgium
7. Sweden
8. Netherlands
9. Hungary
10. Finland[7]

Eight of these top 10 have land areas smaller than the state of Indiana in the United States, with seven having fewer than nine million citizens. Mobility is key to such globalization growth.[8] Countries have to be able to step outside their borders to garner resources that might be lacking nationally (e.g., Singapore and the Netherlands lack natural resources) or to tap into larger markets (e.g., Ireland has a limited domestic market size).

Technology

Technological development is today's most critical man-made driver of the world. New routes between and among countries and consumers that were basically impassable or time-restrictive in the late twentieth century have been opened, creating a death of distance[9] with respect to how rapidly information is transferred around the globe. While immigration may be fueling population growth in the wealthiest nations, technology growth is fueling the business world. Historically, worker mobility was a critical human resources variable that involved changing physical environments. Today, worker mobility may mean as little as someone being on their computer at times that coincide with when a customer is on the computer on the other side of the world!

Exhibit 18.4 highlights the number of fixed broadband Internet subscribers per 100 people in a collection of countries in 2010. Broadband Internet subscribers are an indicator of the level of technological development—a high number of subscribers per capita usually indicates a high level of technology. The advanced economies tend to have the most broadband subscribers. By contrast, the number of subscribers in many developing economies, such as Bangladesh and Kenya, is effectively zero.[10] Thus, technologies tend to be most developed in the advanced economies and least developed in the developing economies. The distinction is important because technology is critical to entrepreneurship, productivity, and other factors that support national economic vitality and superior living standards.

Technological developments over the past decade have led to dramatic changes in the way people think about communication and information sharing. Mobile telephone subscriptions worldwide keep rising greatly and contribute the largest share of worldwide sales in the consumer electronics sector. Many mature markets have over 100 percent mobile penetration (meaning that some owners have more than one phone, not that all members of that market's population own a phone).

Technology advances lead to greater information sharing worldwide and allow new equipment to be more sophisticated and perform more functions at a lower cost. More intelligent and accurate control equipment can bring energy efficiency with large cost savings.

EXHIBIT 18.4 Fixed Broadband Internet Subscribers (per 100 people)

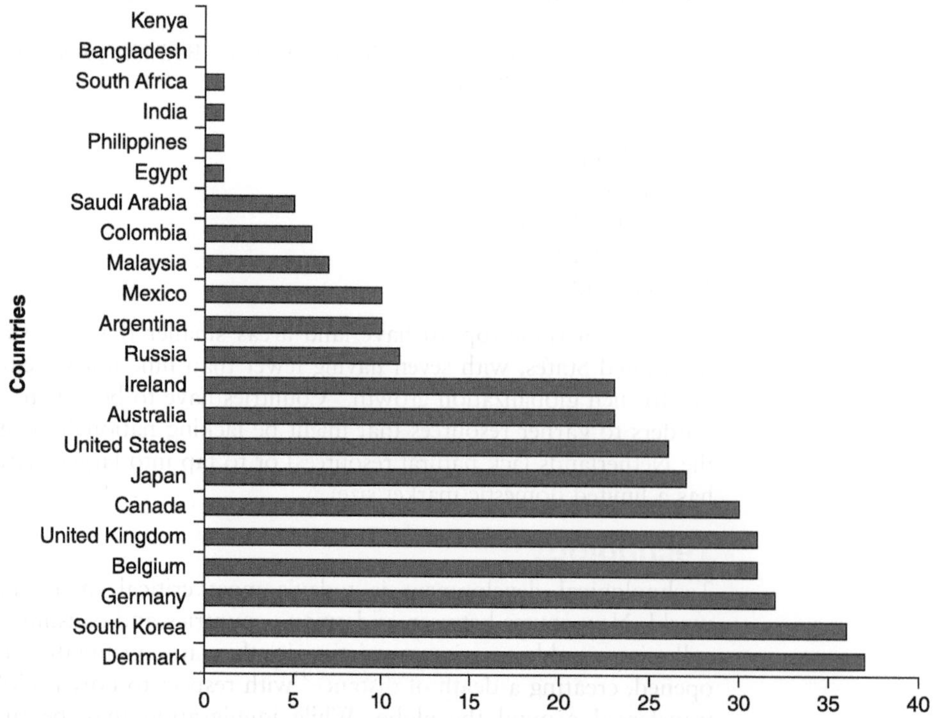

SOURCE: World Bank, http://data.worldbank.org/indicator/IT.NET.BBND.P2, 2011.

Culture

Culture is the result of learned behavior and adjustments to new conditions. Cultures around the globe will become more similar with respect to macro issues such as accountability, performance expectations, freedom accorded within society, and product preferences. However, cultural clashes are expected at the micro level. For example, the United States will have large groups of Latinos, and traditional Caucasians may become a regional minority. Similarly, Western Europeans will see population influx and competitive activity from what used to be their communist neighbors.[11]

Cultural clashes are likely to occur, particularly with respect to religion. For example, there are about three million Muslims now residing in Great Britain.[12] *Shari'ah* is the body of Islamic religious law based on the Koran (the Koran is comprised of the words and actions of the Prophet Mohammad and the rulings of Islamic scholars). *Shari'ah* has begun to enter prominently into British life. Informal neighborhood councils provide rules on family issues such as divorce, and banks offer mortgages that comply with *Shari'ah* rules.[13] As presented in Chapter 5, the Archbishop of Canterbury stirred up much public sentiment when he called for the reexamination of the role of *Shari'ah* in British life. Interestingly, the archbishop faced harsh rejoinders from both sides. Those of Christian heritage were outraged that the archbishop may not have felt strongly enough that British laws should be based on Anglican values, while those in the Muslim community feared that Britain would try to make *Shari'ah* a formal part of law that would disallow the successful informal aspect of the *Shari'ah* councils.

There are many more areas where local culture can inhibit globalization. For example, the French like to insist on home-grown agriculture, and Americans fear foreign management of ports.

One cultural trend that first appeared in 2001 after the terrorist attacks in the United States is cocooning. This trend toward staying at home is now a worldwide phenomenon—from the United States to Australia, people are spending more time at home. They are basically bringing their work and entertainment into their homes rather than going out for these things. Challenging economic times (for example, high gas prices and declines in home values and stock portfolios) are behind this push to cut back on large purchases like traveling, eating out, and viewing movies at the cinema. Retailers in the United States report cocooning trend-related sales in the areas of food shopping, outdoor barbeque equipment, video games, and flat-panel televisions.[14] Similarly, retailers in Australia report the buying or renting of DVDs, meal-preparation ingredients, and outdoor furniture and accessories topping the cocoon-buyer's list of priorities.[15]

Cocooning is, of course, made easier by virtue of technological advances that enable telecocooning. Technology allows people, without leaving their homes, to engage in social exchanges via social networking and matchmaking sites and to communicate with friends and relatives in real time via text and Internet communication.

Economic Development

The economy is an underlying hot spot in the growth and development of any international enterprise. Without a doubt, the economic crisis that began in 2008 rocked the world dramatically! Individuals and nations alike were hit hard by the collapse of financial markets. One of the hardest hit nations was Iceland, home to some 300,000 people. In the wake of the crisis, Iceland's three major banks collapsed. Turmoil in Iceland's financial world had ramifications not only for the well-being of Icelandic citizens but also for world markets. The relationship between Iceland and the United Kingdom was seriously damaged when the U.K. employed the same type of antiterror laws it uses against foes like Al Qaeda to seize Icelandic bank funds.

Emerging markets were vulnerable to the financial crisis in three major ways: (1) exports of goods and services suffered, (2) net imports of capital slowed, and (3) banks had less money to lend. Yet the emerging markets recovered fast from the financial crisis, attaining a GDP growth rate of 6 percent or more by 2012.[16]

At the same time, two-thirds of the world's economy is accounted for by just four major regions: China, Japan, the United States, and the European Union.[17] But the world's economies are intertwined. Thus, economic stimuli put into play by any one nation will rapidly affect other countries and trigger responses.

Looking beyond the turmoil, international service organizations might become weaker. For example, the developmental role of the World Bank could diminish. Poor countries may feel that there is very little for them to gain from the institution. Similarly, the IMF may be outperformed by local and regional lending arrangements. The currently overwhelming power of richer countries in the IMF voting system tends to make the less-developed countries feel that they are not getting the same value as rich members. While all countries and companies have much to gain from strong country economies, they all have much to lose as well!

Natural Resources

A growing concern for planet Earth has prompted much interest and investment in the world's natural resources. Safeguarding the earth refers to protecting Earth's people, plants, animals, and natural systems. This global phenomenon is referred to in a variety of contexts: sustainable development, global warming, climate change, going green, renewable energy, bio-energy, and the green revolution. From a natural resource perspective, futurists predict that we will be stretching our planet's capacity by 2050. Issues such as a growing and aging global population, urbanization, energy demand, and the food and water needed to nourish over nine billion people are close to the hearts and on

© AP Images/Brennan Linsley

Giant ducts carry superheated steam from within a volcanic field to the turbines at a geothermal power plant in Iceland, one way to protect our natural resources.

the minds of organizations around the world. The concern about our natural resources and sustainability has led to a variety of predictions for the future:[18]

- Governments will attempt to put more land into grain production and also use tools such as subsidies and price controls.
- Recycling and recovery will grow as vital business opportunities.
- Farming will regain its attractiveness and profitability as fuel production from food sources accelerates.
- The global shortage of potable water will be rediscovered as a key climate issue, leading to higher government investments in desalination and reverse osmosis technologies and more emphasis on water conservation.
- There will be growing preference for energy-saving technologies and a reduction and limit to energy use.

These concerns will lead to the creation and expansion of sectors worldwide. For example, we can expect to see more focus upon the protection of public health and a growth in biotechnology, genomics, and nanotechnology. Sustainable water-recycling technologies will spawn new industries. Government involvement in the oversight of issues and creation of new industries will be unprecedented.

Political and Legal

The globalization of markets has taken place against a backdrop of political instability and various perspectives on what is and is not legal. Looking ahead politically, the United States witnessed a crucial presidential election in 2012. This process transpired as uprisings and turmoil swept across Egypt, Libya, Syria, and other countries in the Middle East. The 2008 round of the Doha Development Agenda, the latest negotiations of the World Trade Organization on global free trade, failed to reach a positive conclusion because the United States, India, and China could not agree on access to agricultural markets. The U.S. secretary of state listed Mexico and all of Latin America at the bottom of her regional priorities, only ahead of Africa.

In a 2008 Delphi study,[19] the authors identified terrorism as a critical dimension of international business over the upcoming decade. Terrorism was

Trade disruptions can cause a major shortage of supply globally.

THE INTERNATIONAL MARKETPLACE 18.2

Counterfeiting, Software Piracy, and Terrorism

Counterfeiting is a common form of corruption and one that cost businesses well over US$1 trillion in 2012. One of the most highly scrutinized areas of counterfeiting in today's business world is the theft of intellectual property. Intellectual property is the ownership of ideas as well as the control over the tangible or virtual representation of those ideas. The piracy of this intellectual property has become a major form of illegal business.

In 2011, U.S. Department of Homeland Security agents seized counterfeit and pirated products at U.S. borders worth an estimated retail value of more than $1.1 billion. The most frequently counterfeited products included consumer electronics, footwear, and pharmaceuticals. By far the largest source of counterfeit goods was China, which accounted for more than two-thirds of Homeland Security seizures in 2011.

Software is intellectual property, as are books, movies, and music. Music performers, authors, and software developers use copyright laws to protect their work and their investment in the field. Global software piracy has reached financial values of astronomical proportions. According to estimates by the Business Software Alliance (BSA), just under 5 percent of all software purchased annually is pirated, resulting in revenue losses in billions of dollars. IDC, a global market intelligence and information technology and telecommunications advisory firm, estimated that a 10 percent reduction in worldwide software piracy over a four-year period would put US$400 billion back into economic growth. This economic growth would also add more than one million jobs and generate billions in new taxes.

Firms that expand globally with their intellectual property are increasingly mindful of the potential ramifications of software piracy, which range from multimillion-dollar losses to the hindrance of future software development. The accessibility of software and the ease of duplicating it make it highly vulnerable to unauthorized copying.

The BSA delineates five common types of software piracy: end-user piracy, client-server overuse, Internet swapping, hard-disk loading, and commercial counterfeiting. *End-user piracy* occurs when a person reproduces copies of software without authorization. *Client-server overuse* happens when too many people on a network are using a central copy of a program at the same time—a company has to be licensed for the number of users who can access the program simultaneously. *Internet swapping*, or the downloading of unauthorized copies of copyrighted programs from the Internet, is illegal if the software is accessed via pirate websites or peer-to-peer networks. *Hard-disk loading* occurs when a reseller loads software illegally with the aim of

© AP Images/Lynne Sladky

Members of the U.S. Immigration and Customs Enforcement and Homeland Security Investigations holds up a counterfeit handbag seized from U.S. borders.

making the machine more attractive to customers. *Commercial counterfeiting* of software is the illegal duplication of copyrighted programs with the express intent of directly imitating the copyrighted software. Creating, allowing others to create, or obtaining any unauthorized copy of software, regardless of commercial or financial benefit, is considered copyright infringement and can be prosecuted under civil and criminal law in many countries.

Interpol suggests a connection between counterfeiting and both organized crime and terrorism. The secretary general of Interpol has gone so far as to imply that profit from pirated CDs in Central America funded Hezbollah terrorist efforts in the Middle East. Countries considered highly corrupt according to Transparency International tolerate high levels of software piracy.

Given the significant ramifications to the world economy, counterfeiting and the theft of intellectual property will be watched closely in the future. The global electronic village demands a revenue model that ensures adequate income to those developing intellectual property while simultaneously providing consumers with access to such intellectual content.

SOURCES: "Fighting Fakes: Foiling Counterfeit Products," *Businessweek*, May 26, 2007, www.businessweek.com/media-center/video/technology/FEEDROOM196813.html; Frederik Balfour, "Fakes!" *Businessweek*, February 7, 2005, i3919, 54–64; CBP Office of International Trade, *Intellectual Property Rights: Fiscal Year 2011 Seizure Statistics* (Washington, DC: U.S. Immigration and Customs Enforcement, 2012), www.ice.gov/doclib/iprcenter/pdf/ipr-fy-2011-seizure-report.pdf; and William F. Crittenden, Christopher J. Robertson, and Victoria L. Crittenden, "Hard Facts about Software Piracy," *Business Strategy Review*, Winter 2007, pp. 30–33, www.bsa.org.

seen as a facet of international life that would have to be managed, even if it could not be defeated. An extension of this study found the root causes of terrorism to be policies toward immigration and the oftentimes dividing roles taken on by advocates of specific religions, cultures, regions, or races. Consumers worldwide were willing to change their consumption patterns if necessary for security considerations, and corporations expressed an unwillingness to do business in countries that lacked law and order.[20]

Ranking very closely behind terrorism in the Delphi study is **corruption**. Strategic decision makers face pressure from stakeholders when it comes to social and ethical issues in business. Corruption serves as a major barrier to entry as international organizations attempt to move goods and services across borders. Regardless of market potential, corruption is a major detractor with respect to business development and prosperity. There is much concern that corruption breeds corruption.[21] There is also the concern that future business leaders expect laws to guide their actions rather than utilizing a moral compass to determine right and wrong in decision making. Thus, while there are laws governing corruption, such as the U.S. Foreign Corrupt Practices Act, the quality of the business environment is at risk if cheating becomes a norm because "everyone else" is doing it.[22] *The International Marketplace 18.2* describes the impact corruption can have on economic well-being.

THE MARKETER OF THE FUTURE—STRATEGIC EFFORTS

International marketing in the future will have both similarities and differences with that of today. Marketers will still engage in critical marketing-mix decisions and will, as always, need to understand the intricacies of the marketplace in which business is being conducted. Looking ahead, there are five major areas to which marketers will have to be particularly more attentive. These are in balancing global and local expectations, innovation, collaborative partnerships, connecting with the world's customers, and technology-based marketing research.

The Balance between Global and Local

"Think Globally, Act Locally" has long been the mantra in the marketing world. While we are unlikely to see a major shift in this thinking, the balance between global marketing and local marketing has taken on new meaning in the twenty-first century. A major driver behind the precarious balance between global and local has been technology. In particular, the Internet has created a flat world. Customizing for local markets has become more difficult as online viewers access information originating in various countries. Most large companies manage this by asking viewers to select a country upon entry into the corporation's website. The key at the corporate level is to maintain consistency of appearance and product offerings for different country versions.

Within the company, the precarious balance between global and local has a huge impact on the company's organizational structure. If consumers across the globe are becoming more alike, then a centralized structure might make sense from both consistency and budgeting points of view. However, even global consumers have local preferences and, according to the CEO of Interbrand, "One of the big lessons is that in your local market you have a greater duty to stay fresh. People become bored quickly."[23] Thus, the trend is to have a centralized budgeting process with decentralized spending and allocation, centralized development of the marketing message, and decentralization of the marketing mix.[24] Simultaneously, smaller firms will be able to benefit by focusing on niche markets, especially those abandoned by large companies where the global/local imbalance was too great.

Marketers will continue to face pressure from a variety of stakeholders from both governments and NGOs. Accounting systems will have to recognize and develop procedures for calculating worldwide value and performance. Corporate responsibility will be interpreted to include broad-based activities and profit sharing. Stakeholders will demand greater involvement and will play a major role in the global image building of the company. CSR will have to look at global impact because lapses in ethics or social responsibility could affect brand equity in a major way.

Corporate and marketing actions taken locally will be observed globally. It will no longer be "global *versus* local" because the two will have to go hand-in-hand, appealing to consumers globally as well as locally. In thinking about marketing objectives, plans, and programs, marketers will have to begin thinking in terms of "global *and* local."

Innovation

Innovation cannot be emphasized enough when it comes to the future of marketing. Innovation has many meanings and areas of relevance—generating new ideas, exploiting new ideas, creating higher-quality goods and services, sustaining growth, and developing new knowledge are just several examples of what innovation can refer to. Former British prime minister Tony Blair said, "The creativeness and inventiveness of our people is our country's greatest asset in an increasingly global world; our ability to invent, design, and manufacture the goods and services that people want is more vital to our future prosperity than ever before."[25]

The domain of innovation is very broad—it does not just include developing new products and services. Eight different types of innovation have been identified:[26]

1. *Disruptive innovation* gets a great deal of attention and has its roots in technological discontinuities.
2. *Application innovation* takes existing technologies into new markets to serve new purposes.
3. *Product innovation* takes established offers in established markets to the next level.
4. *Process innovation* makes processes for established offers in established markets more effective or efficient.
5. *Experiential innovation* makes surface modifications that improve customers' experiences of established products or processes.
6. *Marketing innovation* improves customer-touching processes.

EXHIBIT 18.5 Aligning Innovation with the Life Cycle

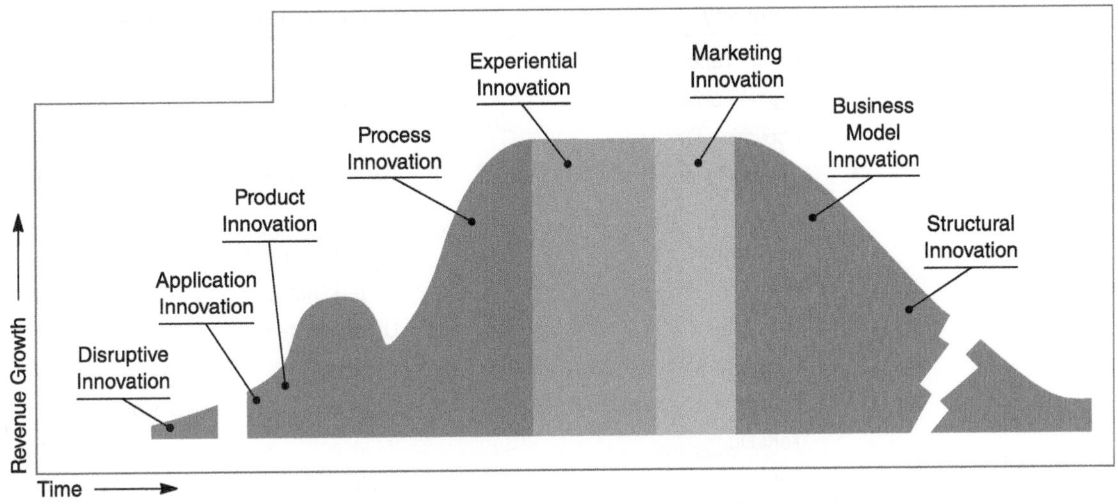

SOURCE: Geoffrey A. Moore, "Darwin and the Demon: Innovating within Established Enterprises," *Harvard Business Review*, July–August 2004, 90–91. Reprinted with permission.

7. *Business model innovation* reframes an established value proposition to the customer or a company's established role in the value chain, or both.
8. *Structural innovation* capitalizes on disruption to restructure industry relationships.

Different types of innovation occur at different points during a product category's life cycle. Exhibit 18.5 maps these eight types of innovation onto the life cycle of a product category. Companies cannot limit themselves to just one type of innovation. Competing in today's global economy demands that companies pursue a range of innovative efforts for continued growth and profitability.

The importance of innovation to the future of world business is stressed by the World Economic Forum. Exhibit 18.6 lists the 31 visionary companies the Forum selected as 2011 technology pioneers. The companies were selected for their accomplishments as innovators of the highest caliber.

Collaborative Partnerships

As described in *The International Marketplace 18.3*, partnering with outside companies in the formulation and implementation of customer-oriented, global marketing strategies is a necessity for companies in the twenty-first century.[27] Doing business in today's economic times is the result of collaboration across country and company boundaries. Companies realize that today's global marketplace requires a diversity of inputs. Those companies that have been able to manage successfully both across geographic and competitive boundaries are the ones that are able to advance in today's fast-paced business world. Collaboration is also crucial in achieving curative marketing, as discussed in Chapter 17. Very often, the desire to deliver recompense for past marketing mistakes inflicted on a society is not sufficient for action unless reinforced and supported by corporate clusters who all feel responsible.

Examples of successful cross-border and cross-company partnerships include:

- *Nokia*. Customer research in Europe and Asia, design skills from Italy and United States, and substitutions for landlines in China and India
- *EADS*. Wing aerodynamics from the United Kingdom, avionics from France, flight-control techniques from the United States, knowledge from regional carriers worldwide

EXHIBIT 18.6 Technology Pioneers, 2011

Company	Home Country	Website
Clean Tech		
Digital Lumens	United States	www.digitallumens.com
Ecovative Design	United States	www.ecovativedesign.com
Ferrate Treatment Technologies	United States	www.ferratetreatment.com
Flexoresearch Group	Thailand	www.flexoresearch.com
Novacem	United Kingdom	www.novacem.com
Onramp Wireless	United States	www.onrampwireless.com
OPOWER	United States	www.opower.com
Ostara Nutrient Recovery Technologies	Canada	www.ostara.com
Quintas Renewable Energy Solutions	Nigeria	www.quintasenergies.com
TaKaDu	Israel	www.takadu.com
Tendril	United States	www.tendrilinc.com
Topell Energy	Netherlands	www.topellenergy.com
Transonic Combustion	United States	www.tscombustion.com
Information Technologies and New Media		
Aster Data	United States	www.asterdata.com
Atlassian	Australia	www.atlassian.com
foursquare	United States	www.foursquare.com
GetJar	Lithuania	www.getjar.com
Knewton	United States	www.knewton.com
Layar	Netherlands	www.layar.com
NetQin Mobile	China	www.netqin.com
OpenDNS	United States	www.opendns.com
ReputationDefender	United States	www.reputationdefender.com
Scribd	United States	www.scribd.com
SecondMarket	United States	www.secondmarket.com
Spotify	United Kingdom	www.spotify.com
Vortex Engineering	India	www.vortexindia.co.in
Life Sciences and Health		
Adimab	United States	www.adimab.com
Ion Torrent	United States	www.iontorrent.com
Medicine in Need (MEND)	South Africa	www.medicineinneed.org
Molecular Partners	Switzerland	www.molecularpartners.com
Neuronetics	United States	www.neuronetics.com

SOURCE: World Economic Forum, www.weforum.org/s?s=pioneers, accessed January 24, 2012.

- *SAP*. Market knowledge from foreign customers to enable language, currency, and accounting differences
- *Starbucks*. Italian technology for espresso coffee roasting, the European concept for the café, U.S. expertise in retail concepts (e.g., fast-food service routines, logistics, staff training, incentive systems), and a preferred supplier program for sustainable development

Companies that innovate across borders and across companies are referred to as **metanational innovators**.[28] Sometimes such partnerships result in

THE INTERNATIONAL MARKETPLACE 18.3

The Body Shop Partners with Daabon

Continuing with its efforts in responsible business practices, The Body Shop became the first cosmetics retailer to introduce sustainable palm oil into the global beauty-product industry. Spurred by growing concerns about the impact of palm oil plantations on biodiversity, The Body Shop partnered with Daabon, a certified organic producer in Colombia, to bring sustainable oil to the marketplace.

Palm oil is one of the world's most popular vegetable oils. It is a common ingredient in items such as cosmetics, household products, and foods. Two countries leading in palm oil production are Malaysia and Indonesia. Unfortunately, rapid expansion of palm oil production has come at the expense of biodiverse rainforests and carbon-rich peatlands that store greenhouse gases. It is estimated that at least 2,000 million tons of carbon dioxide are released annually from just the logged and drained peatlands of Southeast Asia, accounting for 8 percent of global emissions. Over 50 percent of new plantations in Southeast Asia are located on peatlands. As such, palm oil has become a major driver of global CO_2 emissions. In addition to the destruction of rainforests and global emissions issues, expansion of palm oil plantations endangers animal species such as orangutans in Borneo and Sumatra. While the new palm oil plantations create employment opportunities for local people, there is also considerable conflict over human rights violations.

The Body Shop decided that it needed to source its palm oil from a sustainable producer. Producing over 14.5 million bars of soap per annum that contain palm oil, the company needed a reliable source of the raw material—but a source that had concern for the environment in much the same way as The Body Shop.

Certified by the Rainforest Alliance, SA8000, Ecocert, and the Fairtrade Labelling Organization, Daabon is an organic, family-run Colombian company that produces palm oil, coffee, bananas, and cocoa. Daabon's philosophy centers on organic agriculture, social accountability, traceability, and sustainability. It is the only company in the world that has vertically integrated the palm oil production process—from seeding to end products. The company has three organic palm oil plantations for a total of 2,500 hectares of palm trees. The company is also organizing the development of 2,000 hectares owned by cooperatives of local farmers. Both Daabon and The Body Shop are members of the Malaysia-based Roundtable on Sustainable Palm Oil.

Conservation groups applauded the move by The Body Shop. However, it was only through the

© Yuli Seperi/Getty Images

Domestic policy strikes abroad, as Indonesian palm oil producers have been hit by the EPA's declaration that palm oil is not able to join the U.S. renewable fuel program.

partnership with an international company that it was able to engage in such a promising effort. This was not something that the company could have done on its own. Other global consumer products companies, such as Unilever and Marks & Spencer, have undertaken similar partnerships to reduce their use of unsustainable palm oil in the products they offer. The future of sustainability may lie in global partnerships.

SOURCES: Louise Prance, "The Body Shop Produces First Cosmetics using Sustainable Palm Oil," *Decision News Media,* July 12, 2007, www.cosmeticsdesign-europe.com/Formulation-Scuebce?The-Body-Shop-produces-first-cosmetics-using-sustainable-palm-oil; Rhett A. Butler, "Environmental Concerns Mount as Palm Oil Production Surges," Mongabay.com, May 15, 2007, http://news.mongabay.com/2007/0515-palm_oil.html; Greetje Schouten and Pieter Glasbergen, "Creating Legitimacy in Global Private Governance: The Case of the Roundtable on Sustainable Palm Oil," *Ecological Economics,* 70, no. 11 (2011): 1891-99; The Body Shop, www.thebodyshop.com; and Daabon, www.daabon.com.

companies becoming subsidiaries of major multinational companies. For example, Tom's of Maine is a niche-brand product known for its socially responsible production. The company was bought by Colgate-Palmolive in 2006, providing Colgate-Palmolive a much-needed entry into the fast-growing U.S. market for natural personal care products.[29]

Other companies look for new market-entry opportunities by allowing their stocks to be bought and sold publicly. *The International Marketplace 18.4* shows how Facebook going public can change its market and consumer relations drastically.

Connecting with the World's Customers

Historically, connecting with the customer meant that the company had one-way communications (via advertising, packaging, and promotion). In today's world, however, consumers are likely to initiate contact with the company—two-way communication is a must for today's marketer and will become even more important in the future. Curative international marketing, discussed in depth in Chapter 17, is an important way to revise the global standard from an output-centric mentality to one that is focused on quality more than quantity.

Interactive digital media changes the landscape of a marketer's world.[30] Global brand building, channel structure, and marketing messages are only the tip of the iceberg when it comes to the areas in which interactive digital media will impact the future of marketing. The Economist Intelligence Unit explored the idea of the newly empowered individual customer.[31] Over 50 percent of the corporate respondents to the survey reported that their companies were highly customer-centric and expected customers to be directly connected to the brand and the development process. According to the vice president of web strategy of IBM, "We seek to engage with clients in the way they prefer to engage."[32]

Consumers worldwide are now connected to companies in a variety of ways. Marketers and consumers connect via:

- Company websites
- Videoconferencing, webinars, voice-over Internet protocol (VoIP), and podcasts
- Handheld devices for product demonstration and mobile credit-card transaction terminals
- The e-suite of touch processes—e-guests, e-invites, e-reminders, e-magazines, and e-newsletters
- Social networking sites, blogs, text messaging, and YouTube

Nortel utilized connectivity with consumers to highlight their latest product line, engage customers on their website, and underscore the company's focus on sustainability. The company built an interactive energy calculator that allowed visitors to input their own operations variables to calculate energy consumption and costs in 49 countries across the globe.[33]

The future of global marketing lies in connecting with consumers in every corner of the world—and doing so by identifying the consumer-preferred mode and location of connection and outpacing competitors who also want to connect.

THE INTERNATIONAL MARKETPLACE 18.4

Facebook's Initial Public Offering

On February 1, 2012, Facebook founder and CEO Mark Zuckerberg announced his private company's decision to go public. Zuckerberg filed for an initial public offering (IPO) at $5 billion, the largest technology initial offering ever. As of February 2012, experts say that Facebook's IPO could generate up to $100 billion in a full sale. An IPO is made when a privately owned company wishes to have its stocks traded publicly in the stock market. The decision to go public increases the company's available investment capital while also increasing the importance of the opinions of major investors.

Currently, there are about 845 million users on Facebook and growing—projections say that there will be one billion users within one year after going public. Further, its privacy policies clearly inform users that all information shared on the social network platform belongs to the company. As a result, Facebook has amassed what is generally considered to be the largest Internet database of personal data. Previously, Facebook made major efforts to monetize this information, specifically through target advertising. In 2011, 83 percent of all revenue came from advertisers. Facebook has increased its lucrative appearance to potential investors by digitizing and utilizing this aggregate of information.

These potential investors will encourage (effectively if any acquires a large stake in company stock) an increased focus on profits and revenues. This decision to go public will likely have major implications for users, marketers, and the company's current executives. Company executives may succumb to the pressure to expand revenue sources while continuously improving users' Facebook experience. This new pressure could place a lower premium on users' privacy. Marketers may be willing to pay a higher advertising cost if Facebook goes beyond targeted marketing to leads, which allow the advertisers to access further information about the users. The public trading of Facebook will undoubtedly affect Zuckerberg's previous attempts to maintain sole control of and authority over his company. Investor pressure will change the Facebook course to one that is highly profit-centric.

The future of Facebook, as well as other similar social media networks, will be greatly affected as it moves to the public sector. The changes may not come to the surface immediately. However, when the results and repercussions emerge, we will see just how successful and invasive a global service with effective marketing and a drive for profits can be.

SOURCES: Braden Goyette and Elizabeth Lazarowitz, "Facebook Files $5 Billion IPO: What Is an IPO Anyway?" NY Daily News, February, 1, 2012, www.nydailynews.com/news/national/facebook-ipo-coming-ipo-move-change-facebook-article-1.1015241; Lee Spears and Brian Womack, "Facebook's IPO Shares May Be Five Times as Expensive as Google," Businessweek, February 8, 2012, www.businessweek.com/news/2012-02-08/facebook-s-ipo-shares-may-be-five-times-as-expensive-as-google.html; and "Here's the Number That Matters in Facebook's IPO Filing," The Atlantic, February 2, 2012, www.theatlantic.com/technology/archive/2012/02/heres-the-number-that-matters-in-facebooks-ipo-filing/252471.

Facebook founder and CEO Mark Zuckerberg appears in a promotional video ahead of the company's IPO.

Thus, the battle for brand and product allegiance will take place, literally, in the hands of the consumer.

Technology-Based Marketing Research

Marketers will connect with consumers in ways almost unimaginable several years ago. The marketing message has truly become a two-way communication stream, and marketers will be engaging in new and exciting ways of gathering information about consumers. As noted in Chapter 8, traditional methods of marketing research have already migrated to Web 2.0. Polling on social network sites such as Facebook is already mainstream in marketing research.

Companies are moving beyond social networking sites for polling into virtual worlds such as Second Life. Virtual worlds offer many advantages for conducting marketing research.[34] Virtual worlds are truly a worldwide phenomenon, with 60 percent of Second Life users residing outside the United States.[35] As with many Web 2.0 technologies, virtual worlds appeal to a younger audience because this group is used to navigating virtual worlds on game consoles.[36] Exhibit 18.7 lists several marketing research companies that focus largely on virtual worlds for collecting consumer data. Additionally, the nonprofit Social Research Foundation launched a virtual research panel that has millions of registered users.[37]

Another advancement that bodes well for the future of marketing research is video eye-tracking technology. Eye tracking is precisely what the name implies—the technology tracks the eye's movement as it views images on a screen. From a marketing research perspective, the researcher can see what consumers are really viewing when they see an advertisement, a package design, or website. In the eye-tracking methodology, a person sits in front of a specialized computer screen and views marketing material; the computer tracks and records where the person looks and for how long the person looks at something. An eye-tracking marketing research report can provide:[38]

- The real-time scan path or eye movement and areas of focus
- Static plots illustrating where the respondent looked, in what order, and for how long
- What was noticed or not noticed and what seemed to pique interest

Researchers have preliminarily started using eye-tracking research to better understand the impact of specific consumer technologies on advertising. One eye-tracking study found that while an ad placed above the fold ("above the fold" refers to ads that are viewable without having to scroll down) on a website is visible to everyone visiting the site, only about 60 percent of the visitors actually see the ad. Only about 70 percent of visitors actually scroll below the fold and, even then, only about 25 percent of the viewers actually see the ads.[39]

Another groundbreaking study examined the concern that advertisers have with consumers using digital video recorders (DVRs) to fast-forward

EXHIBIT 18.7 Marketing Research Companies in Second Life

Beatenetworks (www.beatenetworks.com)
Market Truths (www.markettruths.com)
Plugged In (www.pluggedin.com)
Sentient Services (www.sentientservices.com)
The Kalypso Agency (www.thekalypsoagency.com)

SOURCE: © Cengage Learning 2013.

through commercials. Results from multiple eye-tracker studies found the following:[40]

- Fast-forwarding viewers constrain their vision to the center of the screen—thus brand information at the center of the screen is viewed more often than information placed elsewhere.
- Brand information found in the center of the screen is a strong predictor of ad recognition.
- Advertisements with branding in the center do lead to increased brand attitude and choice behavior for the centrally placed brand.

Using equipment to gauge consumer responses to stimuli opens the door for yet another piece of equipment to take on a research purpose—the functional magnetic resonance imaging (fMRI) scanning equipment. The fMRI is a noninvasive neural-imaging technique that basically looks inside the brain. By observing blood oxygen signals during an fMRI, marketing researchers can reliably predict, for example, whether a person will purchase a given product or whether the price of a product influences positive or negative responses about a product.[41]

Several global companies have used fMRI to gauge consumers' responses to advertising, branding, and choice behavior.[42] These include Daimler-Chrysler, Delta Airlines, General Motors, Hallmark, Home Depot, Motorola, and Procter & Gamble. But the technique is not without its skeptics. One consumer group in the United States, Commercial Alert, has sought a congressional investigation of the technique. The fear is that marketing researchers will learn too much about neural activity and enable marketers of the future to more adequately trigger desired responses from consumers.[43]

SUMMARY

External factors have always been out of a marketer's control. A good marketer, however, will learn how to identify opportunities in the external environment. Looking ahead, changes in the external environment do present many opportunities for the astute marketer, just as there will be numerous threats that have to be managed accordingly. The international, boundaryless marketplace is changing, and we as marketers have to stay ahead of those changes.

KEY TERMS

demographic divide
death of distance
cultural clashes
cocooning
economic crisis
political instability
terrorism
corruption
innovation
metanational innovators
interactive digital media

QUESTIONS FOR DISCUSSION

1. What are the key drivers that today's marketer has to understand in planning for the international marketplace?
2. Why have smaller countries been able to be some of the top globalized countries?
3. What is the role of each international driver in implementing each of the strategic efforts?
4. Which of the international drivers and strategic efforts are likely to change more often and more rapidly?

INTERNET EXERCISES

1. Identify a global online retail firm and describe how it (1) targets specific countries and (2) engages the consumer in an interactive manner.
2. Identify five social networking sites and prepare a profile of the sites' users in terms of demographic characteristics (for example, gender, age, geographic location). How can an international marketer use this type of information?

CHALLENGE US

The Dilemma of Rising Global Prosperity

Consumers in Europe, North America, and other advanced economies are well off. For decades, such consumers have enjoyed superior living standards and the ability to fulfill all their essential material wants. In population terms, however, the advanced economies represent only about one-sixth of humankind. Fortunately, citizens of emerging markets—for example, Brazil, China, and India—are now experiencing rapid gains in life quality. Economic growth rates have reached a critical momentum in such countries, and, for the first time in history, billions of humanity's poor are beginning to achieve decent living standards. In China and India, real per-capita incomes are now rising much faster than occurred at any time in history. In the coming two decades, up to three billion people will join the global middle class.

Simultaneously, however, the growing global middle class implies the world is entering an era of heightened demand for raw materials, commodities and other resources. Adding billions of consumers to the global marketplace implies the world can expect shortages and higher prices for energy, food, steel, and other precious goods. In addition, rising consumerism poses important challenges for the natural environment. As emerging-market consumers discard products and packaging, waste will pile up in landfills. Increased economic activity will generate pollutants that affect human health and may permanently damage the Earth.

The harmful side effects likely to arise as billions of people emerge from poverty poses one of humanity's greatest dilemmas. On the one hand, eradicating global poverty is a critical goal. On the other hand, the trend poses potentially grave implications for global resources and the natural environment.

For Discussion

1. What can be done to address this dilemma? What are the appropriate roles of governments, corporations, and consumers?
2. Some believe economic development in emerging markets should be delayed in order to reduce resultant harmful effects. What are the moral implications of such a belief? Should consumers in the advanced economies buy fewer products and services in order help reduce the coming threat? Would you be willing to reduce your consumption to help people in poor countries?
3. In the past, technological improvements helped alleviate such challenges. Does technology have a role today, and, if so, what might it be?
4. Do you perceive any opportunities arising from the dilemma?

RECOMMENDED READINGS

Busi, Maroc, and Nancy K. Napier. *Doing Research that Matters: Shaping the Future of Management.* Bradford, England: Emerald Group, 2012.

Carland, Maria, and Candace Faber, eds. *Careers in International Affairs*, 8th ed. Washington, DC: Georgetown University Press, 2009.

Czinkota, Michael. *As I Was Saying: Thoughts on International Business and Trade Policy, Exports, Education, and the Future.* Business Expert Press, 2012.

Daniels, Mitch. *Keeping the Republic: Saving America by Trusting Americans.* New York: Senitel HC, 2011.

Hart, Stuart L. *Capitalism at the Crossroads: Next Generation Business Strategies for a Post-Crisis World*, 3rd ed. Upper Saddle River, NJ: Pearson Prentice Hall, 2010.

Mueller, Sherry, and Mark Overmann. *Working World: Careers in International Education, Exchange, and Development.* Washington, DC: Georgetown University Press, 2008.

Senage, Peter, Bryan Smith, Nina Kruschwitz, Joe Laur, and Sara Schley. *The Necessary Revolution: Working Together to Create a Sustainable World.* New York: Crown Business, 2010.

ENDNOTES

1. Michael R. Czinkota and Ilkka A. Ronkainen, "Trends and Indications in International Business: Topics for Future Research," *Management International Review*, Spring 2009.
2. Rob Garretson, "Future Tense: The Global CMO," Economist Intelligence Unit report, September 2008, www.eiu.com/site_info.asp?info_name=google_CMO& page=noads.
3. "KOF Index of Globalization" (Zürich, Switzerland: ETH, March 2011).
4. Czinkota and Ronkainen, "Trends and Indications."
5. Population Reference Bureau, "2011 World Population Data Sheet," www.prb.org/Publications/Datasheets/2011/world-population-data-sheet/data-sheet.aspx, accessed January 29, 2012.

6. Warren Sanderson and Sergei Scherbov, "Rethinking Age and Aging," *Population Bulletin* 63, no. 4 (2008).
7. Ernst & Young, "The Globalization Index 2010 Summary," www.ey.com/GL/en/Issues/Business-environment/Winning-in-a-polycentric-world–globalization-and-the-changing-world-of-business–The-Globalization-Index-2010-summary, accessed January 25, 2012.
8. Czinkota and Ronkainen, "Trends and Indications."
9. Ron Smith, "7 Revolutions for Global Sustainability," *Delta Farm Press*, December 3, 2008, deltafarmpress.com/news/global-sustainability-1203.
10. A. Zagorchev, G. Vasconcellos, and Y. Bae, "The Long-Run Relation among Financial Development, Technology and GDP: A Panel Cointegration Study," *Applied Financial Economics* 21, no. 14 (2011): 1021–34.
11. Czinkota and Ronkainen, "Trends and Indications."
12. Pew Research Center, "The Future of the Global Muslim Population," January 27, 2011, www.pewforum.org/The-Future-of-the-Global-Muslim-Population.aspx.
13. Karla Adam, "Archbishop Defends Remarks on Islamic Law in Britain," *Washington Post*, February 12, 2008, www.washingtonpost.com/wp-dyn/content/article/2008/02/11/AR2008021102783.html.
14. Tom Ryan, "Turning Point 2008: Cocooning Makes a Comeback," *RetailWire*, December 17, 2008, www.retailwire.com/Discussions/Sngl_Discussion.cfm/13439.
15. Lema Samandar, "Aussies Cocooning in Hard Economic Times," *Sydney Morning Herald*, December 1, 2008, http://news.smh.com.au/business/aussies-cocooning-in-hard-economic-times-20081201-6om3.html.
16. International Monetary Fund, "World Economic Outlook Update," January 24, 2012, www.imf.org/external/pubs/ft/weo/2012/update/01.
17. Michael R. Czinkota and Maureen R. Smith, "Economic Stimulus Plans Must Incorporate International Trade," *Korea Times*, January 20, 2009.
18. Czinkota and Ronkainen, "Trends and Indications."
19. Ibid.
20. M. Czinkota, G. Knight, P. Liesch, and J. Steen, "Terrorism and International Business: A Research Agenda," *Journal of International Business Studies* 45, no. 1 (2010).
21. Victoria L. Crittenden, Richard C. Hanna, and Robert A. Peterson, "Business Students' Attitudes toward Unethical Behavior," *Marketing Letters* 20, no. 1 (2008): 1–14.
22. Victoria L. Crittenden, Richard C. Hanna, and Robert A. Peterson, "The Cheating Culture: A Global Societal Phenomenon," *Business Horizons*, 2009.
23. Jack Ewing, "Brands: Moving Overseas to Move Upmarket," *Businessweek*, September 18, 2008, www.businessweek.com/magazine/content/08_39/b4101060110428.htm?chan=magazine+channel_special+report.
24. Garretson, "Future Tense."
25. Innovation Report, "Competing in the Global Economy: The Innovation Challenge," December 2003, foreword (London: Department of Trade and Industry), www.berr.gov.uk/files/file12093.pdf, accessed May 12, 2012.
26. Geoffrey A. Moore, "Darwin and the Demon: Innovating within Established Enterprises," *Harvard Business Review*, July–August 2004, 86–92.
27. Victoria L. Crittenden, "The Rebuilt Marketing Machine," *Business Horizons*, September 2005, 409–420.
28. José Santos, Yves Doz, and Peter Williamson, "Is Your Innovation Process Global?" *MIT Sloan Management Review*, Summer 2004, 31–37.
29. Chris Reidy, "Colgate Will Buy Tom's of Maine," *Boston Globe*, March 22, 2006, www.boston.com/business/articles/2006/03/22/colgate_will_buy_toms_of_maine.
30. Garretson, "Future Tense."
31. Ibid.
32. Jon Brodkin, "IBM Opens Sales Center in Second Life," *Network World*, May 15, 2007, www.networkworld.com/news/2007/051507-ibm-second-life.html.
33. Garretson, "Future Tense."
34. Tim Ferguson, "Virtual Worlds Set for Second Coming," Silicon.com, October 27, 2008.
35. Arianne Cohen, "The Second Life of Second Life," *Fast Company*, September 17, 2008, www.fastcompany.com/magazine/129/the-second-life-of-second-life.html.
36. C.G. Lynch, "Companies Explore Virtual Worlds as Collaboration Tools," *CIO*, February 6, 2008, www.cio.com/article/180301/Companies_Explore_Virtual_Worlds_As_Collaboration_Tools.
37. Social Research Foundation, http://socialresearchfoundation.org, accessed January 31, 2012.
38. Dave Sattler, "Eye Tracking Marketing Research," *Sattler New Media Marketing*, August 22, 2007, http://davesattler.blogspot.com/2007/08/eye-tracking-marketing-research.html.
39. Tameka Kee, "Only 25% of Viewers See Web Ads below the Fold," *Media Post News*, April 8, 2008, www.mediapost.com/publications/article/80131.
40. S. Adam Brasel and James Gips, "Breaking through Fast-Forwarding: Brand Information and Visual Attention," *Journal of Marketing*, November 2008, 31–48.
41. Joan O'C. Hamilton, "This Is Your Brain on Bargains," *Stanford Magazine*, November/December 2008, www.stanfordalumni.org/news/magazine/2008/novdec/features/brainbuy.html.
42. Hilke Plassman, Tim Ambler, Sven Braeutigam, and Peter Kenning, "What Can Advertisers Learn from Neuroscience?" *International Journal of Advertising* 26, no. 2 (2007): 151–75.
43. Robert Lee Hotz, "You Know You Want It, or Do You? Marketing and the Brain," *Seattle Times*, March 26, 2005, http://seattletimes.nwsource.com/html/nationworld/2002220525_brain26.html.

APPENDIX A

Finding Your Calling: Jobs and Careers in International Marketing

A career in international marketing does not consist only of jet-setting travel among London, Paris, and Rome. Increasingly it means, instead, Ingolstadt, Inchon, and Iguazu. Globalists need to be well versed in the specific business functions and may wish to work at summer internships abroad, take language courses, and travel not simply for pleasure but to observe business operations abroad and to gain a greater understanding of different peoples and cultures. Taking on and successfully completing an international assignment is seen by managers as crucial for the development of professional, managerial, and intercultural skills and is highly likely to affect career advancement.[1]

FURTHER TRAINING

One option to more international involvement for the student on the road is to obtain further in-depth training by enrolling in graduate business school programs that specialize in international business education. A substantial number of universities around the world specialize in training international managers. According to a 2012 study by the Institute of International Education, American students increasingly go abroad for business and economics degrees, not just for a semester or two. At the same time, business and management are the most popular fields of study for the 723,277 international students at American universities during the 2010–2011 school year.[2] A review of college catalogues and of materials from groups such as the Academy of International Business will be useful here.

In addition, as the world becomes more global, more organizations are able to assist students interested in studying abroad or in gathering foreign work experience.

Apart from individual universities and their programs for study abroad, many nonprofit institutions stand ready to help and to provide informative materials. Exhibit 18.A.1 provides information about programs and institutions that can help with finding an international job.

EMPLOYMENT WITH A LARGE FIRM

One career alternative in international marketing is to work for a large multinational corporation. These firms constantly search for personnel to help them in their international operations.

Many multinational firms, while seeking specialized knowledge like languages, expect employees to be firmly grounded in the practice and management of business. They rarely will hire a new employee at the starting level and immediately place him or her in a position of international responsibility. Usually, a new employee is expected to become thoroughly familiar with the company's internal operations before being considered for an international position. The reason a manager is sent abroad is that the company expects him or her to reflect the corporate spirit, to be tightly wed to the corporate culture, and to be able to communicate well with both local and corporate management personnel. In this liaison position, the manager will have to be exceptionally sensitive to both headquarters and local operations. As an intermediary, the expatriate must be empathetic

EXHIBIT 18.A.1 Websites Useful in Gaining International Employment

Advancing Women
321 Kampmann Ave.
San Antonio, TX 78209, USA
(210) 822-8087
Website: www.advancingwomen.com
Provides international networking contacts for women.

Council Exchanges
Council on International Educational Exchange (CIEE)
300 Fore Street
Portland, ME 04101, USA
Telephone: (207) 553-4000
Fax: (207) 553-4299
Email: contact@ciee.org
Website: www.ciee.org
Paid work and internships overseas for college students and recent graduates. Also offers international volunteer projects as well as teaching positions.

Dialogue with Citizens
Internal Market and Services Directorate General
European Commission
B-1049 Brussels, Belgium
Website: http://ec.europa.eu/dgs/internal_market/index_en.htm
Fact sheets on EU citizens' rights regarding residence, education, working conditions and social security, rights as a consumer, ways of enforcing these rights, and so forth. Easy-to-use guides that give a general outline of EU citizens' rights and the possibilities offered by the European Single Market. A signpost service for citizens' practical problems.

The Employment Guide
150 Granby Street
Norfolk, VA 23510, USA
Telephone: (877) 876-4039
Website: www.employmentguide.com
Online employment source with international listings, guides, publications, and so forth.

Escape Artist
EscapeArtist.com Inc.
832–1245 World Trade Center, Republic of Panama
Fax: (+) 507-317-6938
Website: www.escapeartist.com
Website for U.S. expatriates. Contains links on overseas jobs, living abroad, offshore investing, free magazine, and so forth.

EuroJobs
Eurojobs.com Ltd
Upton Fold, Bosley, Macclesfield SK11 0PX, United Kingdom
Telephone: +44 (0)20 3372 4781
Fax: +44 (0) 1260 223145
E-mail: info@eurojobs.com
Website: www.eurojobs.com
Lists vacant jobs all over Europe. Also includes the possibility of submitting curriculum vitae to recruiters, employment tips, and other services.

EUROPA—EURES: The European Job Mobility Portal
European Commission
Employment, Social Affairs & Inclusion
B-1049 Brussels, Belgium
Telephone: 00800 4080 4080
Website: http://ec.europa.eu/eures
Aims to facilitate the free movement of workers within the 31 countries of the European Economic Area. Partners in the network include public employment services, trade unions, and employer organizations. The partnership is coordinated by the European Commission. For citizens of these 31 countries it provides job listings, background information, links to employment services, and other job-related websites in Europe.

Expat Network
19 Bartlett Street
Croydon CR2 6TB, United Kingdom
Telephone: +44 (0)20 8256 0311
Fax: +44 (0)20 8256 0312
Email: expats@expatnetwork.com
Website: www.expatnetwork.com
Dedicated to expatriates worldwide, linking to overseas jobs, country profiles, health care, and expatriate gift and book shop, plus in-depth articles and industry reports on issues that affect expatriates. Access is restricted for nonmembers.

Federation of European Employers (FedEE)
Adam House
7-10 Adam Street
The Strand, London WC2N 6AA, United Kingdom
Telephone: +44 (0)207 520 9264
Fax: +44 (0)207 520 9265
Website: www.fedee.com
FedEE provides a practical HR resource for companies operating internationally across Europe, focusing on employment law, pay, and labor relations.

Jobs.ac.uk
Argent Court, Sir William Lyons Rd.
University of Warwick Science Park
Coventry CV4 7EZ, United Kingdom
Telephone: +44 (0)24 7657 2839
Fax: +44 (0)24 7657 2946
Website: www.jobs.ac.uk
Search jobs in science, research, academic, and administrative employment in the United Kingdom and abroad.

Monster.com
Monster Worldwide, Inc.
622 Third Avenue, 39th Floor
New York, NY 10017, USA
Telephone: (212) 351-7000
Fax: (646) 658-0540
Website: www.monster.com
Global online network for careers and working abroad. Career resources (including message boards and daily chats).

Organization of Women in International Trade (OWIT)
1707 L Street, NW
Suite 570
Washington, DC 20036, USA
Email: info@owit.org
Website: www.owit.org
Offers networking and educational opportunities for women in international trade. Has chapters worldwide.

OverseasJobs.com
AboutJobs.com Network
180 State Road Suite 2U
Sagamore Beach, MA 02562 USA
Website: www.overseasjobs.com
Job seekers can search the database by keywords or locations and post a resume online for employers to view.

PlanetRecruit
Trinity Mirror Digital Recruitment Ltd.
One Canada Square, Canary Wharf
London E14 5AP, United Kingdom
Telephone: 0845 468 0568
Website: www.planetrecruit.com
One of the world's largest UK and international recruitment networks. Features accounting and finance, administrative and clerical, engineering, graduate and trainee, IT, media, new media and sales, marketing, and public relations jobs from about 60 countries.

The Riley Guide
Margaret F. Dikel
11218 Ashley Drive
Rockville, MD 20852 USA
Telephone: (240) 602-6043
Email: margaret@rileyguide.com
Website: www.rileyguide.com
A directory of employment and career information sources and services on the Internet, providing instruction for job seekers and recruiters on how to use the Internet to their best advantage. Includes a section on working abroad, including in Europe.

Service Civil International (SCI-IVS USA)
5505 Walnut Level Rd.
Crozet, VA 22932 USA
Telephone: (434) 336-3545
Fax: (206) 350-6585
Website: www.sci-ivs.org
Through various noncommercial partner organizations worldwide and through SCI international, national, and regional branch development, the U.S. branch of SCI participates in the SCI network, which exchanges over 5,000 volunteers each year in short-term (2–4 week) international group work camps and in long-term (3–12 months) volunteer postings in over 80 countries.

TransitionsAbroad.com
18 Hulst Rd.
Amherst, MA 01002, USA
Telephone: (800) 293-0373
Website: www.transitionsabroad.com
Contains articles from its bimonthly magazine; a listing of work abroad resources (including links); and lists of key employers, internship programs, volunteer programs, and English-teaching openings.

Women in the Academy of International Business (WAIB)
Academy of International Business
7 Eppley Center
East Lansing, MI 48824, USA
Website: www.kelley.iu.edu/waib
Encourages networking, mentoring, and research by linking women faculty, administrators, and Ph.D. students in international business studies.

World Wide Opportunities on Organic Farms (WWOOF International)
Website: www.wwoofinternational.org
WWOOF International is dedicated to helping those who would like to work as volunteers on organic farms internationally.

SOURCE: © Cengage Learning 2013.

and understanding, yet fully prepared to implement the goals set by headquarters.

It is very expensive for companies to send an employee overseas. Typically, the annual cost of maintaining a manager overseas is about three times the cost of hiring a local manager. Companies want to be sure that the expenditure is worth the benefit they will receive, even though certainty is never possible.

Even if a position opens up in international operations, there is some truth in the saying that the best place to be in international business is on the same floor as the chairman at headquarters. Employees of firms that have taken the international route often come back to headquarters to find only a few positions available for them. Such encounters lead, of course, to organizational difficulties as well as to financial pressures and family problems, all of which may add up to significant executive stress. Because family reentry angst is the reason why 25 percent of expatriates quit within one year of their return, companies are paying increasing attention to the spouses and children of employees. For example, about 15 percent of *Fortune* 500 firms offer support for children of employees relocated abroad.[3]

EMPLOYMENT WITH A SMALL- OR MEDIUM-SIZED FIRM

A second alternative is to begin work in a small- or medium-sized firm. Some of these firms have only recently developed an international outlook, and the new employee will arrive on the "ground floor." Initial involvement will normally be in the export field—evaluating potential foreign customers, preparing quotes, and dealing with mundane activities such as shipping and transportation. With a very limited budget, the export manager will only occasionally visit foreign markets to discuss marketing strategy with foreign distributors. Most of the work will be done by e-mail, by fax, or by telephone. The hours are often long because of the need to reach contacts overseas, for example during business hours in Hong Kong. Yet the possibilities for implementing creative business methods are virtually limitless, and the contribution made by the successful export manager will be visible in the firm's growing export volume.

Alternatively, international work in a small firm may involve importing—finding new, low-cost sources for domestically sourced products. Decisions often must be based on limited information, and the import manager is faced with many uncertainties. Often, things do not work out as planned. Shipments are delayed, letters of credit are canceled, and products may not arrive in the form and shape anticipated. Yet the problems are always new and offer an ongoing challenge.

As a training ground for international marketing activities, there is probably no better place than a smaller firm. Ideally, the person with some experience may find work with an export trading or export-management company, concentrating virtually exclusively on the international arena.

OPPORTUNITIES FOR WOMEN IN GLOBAL FIRMS

As firms become more involved in global business activities, the need for skilled global managers is growing. Concurrent with this increase in business activity is the ever-growing presence and managerial role of women in international business.

Research conducted in 2011 indicated that globally women hold about 20 percent of senior management positions, down from 24 percent in 2009. Thailand has the greatest percentage of women in senior management (45 percent). By contrast, in Japan less than 10 percent of senior management positions are held by women. The reason for the low participation of women in global management roles seems to have been the assumption that because of the subservient roles of women in Japan, Latin America, and the Middle East, neither local nor expatriate women would be allowed to succeed as managers. The error is that expatriates are not seen as local women but rather as "foreigners who happen to be women," thus solving many of the problems that would be encountered by a local woman manager.

There appear to be some distinct advantages for a woman in a management position overseas. Among them are the advantages of added visibility and increased access to clients. Clients tend to assume that "expatriate women must be excellent, or else their companies would not have sent them."

It also appears that companies that are larger in terms of sales, assets, income, and employees send more women overseas than smaller organizations. Further, the number of women expatriates is not evenly distributed among industry groups. Industry groups that utilize greater numbers or percentages of women expatriates include banking, electronics, petroleum, publishing, diversified corporations, pharmaceuticals, and retailing and apparel.[4]

For the future, it is anticipated that the upward trend previously cited reflects increased participation of women in global management roles in the future.

SELF-EMPLOYMENT

A third alternative is to hang up a consultant's shingle or to establish a trading firm. Many companies are in dire need of help for their international marketing effort and are quite prepared to part with a portion of their profits to receive it. Yet in-depth knowledge and broad experience are required to make a major contribution to a company's international marketing effort or to run a trading firm successfully. Specialized services that might be offered by a consultant include international market research, international strategic planning, or, particularly desirable, beginning-to-end assistance in international market entry or international marketing negotiations.

The up-front costs in offering such a service are substantial and are not covered by turnover but rather have to be covered by profits. Yet the rewards are there. For an international marketing expert, the hourly billable rate typically is as high as $900 for experienced principals and $400 for staff. Whenever international travel is required, overseas activities are often billed at the daily rate of $6,500 plus expenses. The latter can add up quickly, as the cost-per-diem map in Exhibit 18.A.2 shows. When trading on one's own, income and risk can be limitless. Even at these relatively high rates, solid groundwork must be completed before all the overhead is paid. The advantage is the opportunity to become a true international entrepreneur. Consultants and owners of trading firms work at a higher degree of risk than employees but with the opportunity for higher rewards.

International marketing is complex and difficult, yet it affords many challenges and opportunities. "May you live in interesting times" is an ancient Chinese curse. For the international marketer, this curse is a call to action. Observing changes and analyzing how best to incorporate them into one's plans are the bread and butter of the international marketer. The frequent changes are precisely what makes international marketing so fascinating. It must have been international marketers who were targeted by the old Indian proverb, "When storms come about, little birds seek to shelter, while eagles soar." May you be an eagle!

EXHIBIT 18.A.2 **The Cost per Diem in the World's Major Business Cities (in U.S. dollars)**

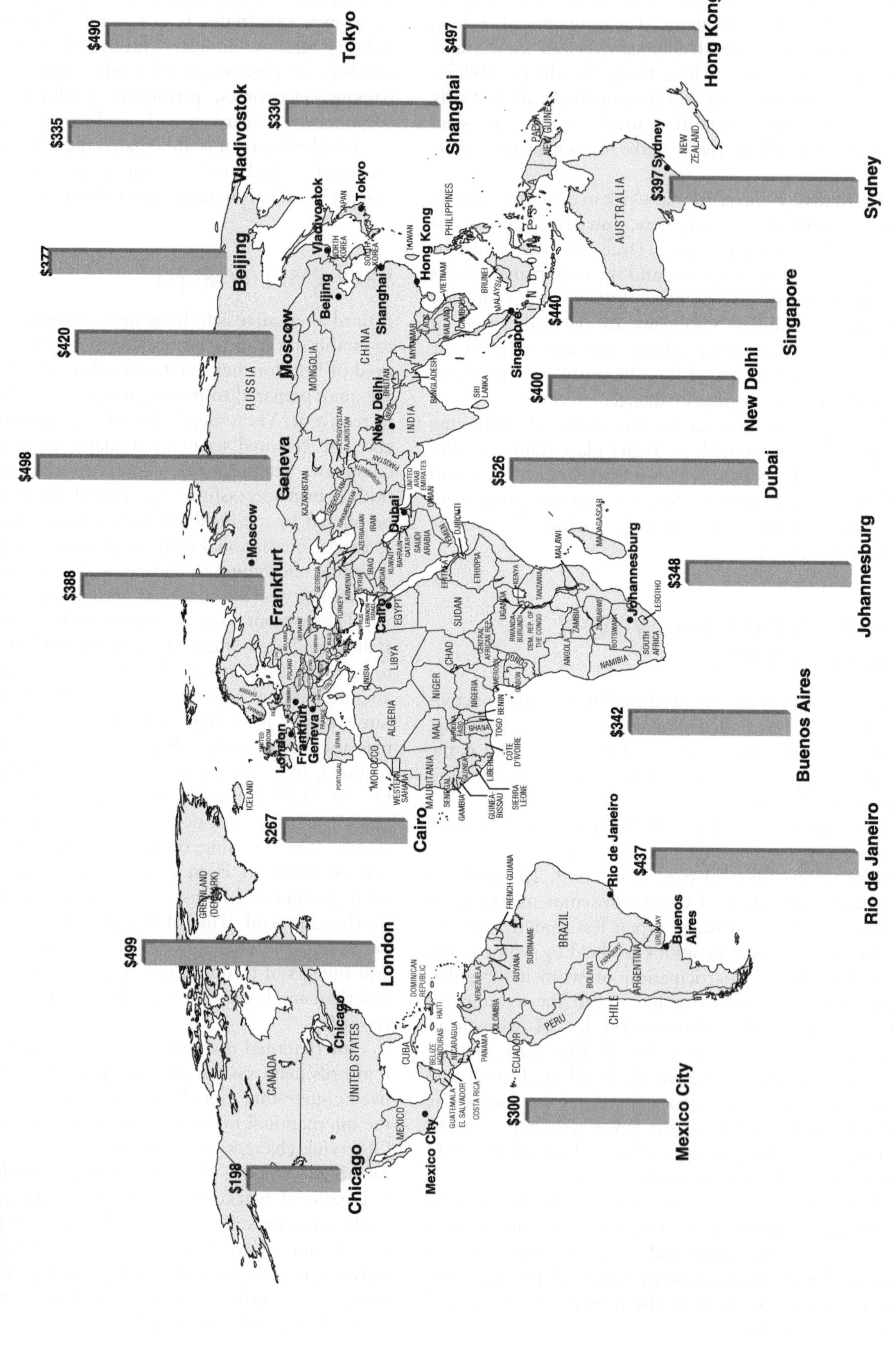

SOURCES: © Cengage Learning 2013; Based on U.S. Department of State, April 2012, http://aoprals.state.gov/web920/per_diem.asp.

ENDNOTES

1. Gunter K. Stahl, Edwin L. Miller, and Rosalie L. Tung, "Toward the Boundaryless Career: A Closer Look at the Expatriate Career Concept and the Perceived Implications of an International Assignment," *Journal of World Business* 37 (2002): 216–27.
2. Institute of International Education, "Open Doors," November 14, 2011, www.iie.org/en/Research-and-Publications/Open-Doors.
3. Joann S. Lublin, "To Smooth a Transfer Abroad, a New Focus on Kids," *Wall Street Journal*, January 26, 1999, B1, B14.
4. Grant Thornton, "International Business Report," www.internationalbusinessreport.com, accessed February 8, 2012.

CASES

PART 4

Thai Food in Europe

Three years after obtaining her MBA, Ampawan Benjathanarak was promoted to be the export manager of Sapanan General Food Co., Ltd., Thailand. The company's exports had grown at rates from 20 to 40 percent annually since 2009. Although the revenue from exporting still accounted for only 10 percent of total sales volume, it was expected to reach 40 percent within a few years. Ampawan anticipated that revenue from the European market would increase significantly. However, many challenges loomed.

THE COMPANY

Sapanan General Food Co., Ltd. was a family business, originally selling cookies and local snacks at train and bus stations. In 2002, the two brothers Adisak and Arnupap Ariyapong took over their family's operation. While studying in Japan, Adisak had noticed a broader selection of beverages than those found in Thailand. Faced with declining sales of Sapanan's local snack business, he searched for new product lines. Subsequently, a Japanese-style fruit drink, Mogu Mogu, was launched. Mogu mogu juice with nata de coco[1] differed from other fruit drinks in Thailand because it contained coconut jelly. The product was so successful that the two brothers set a policy to launch only products that had distinctive characteristics. Nevertheless, not all products were successful. O-Sac, a clear drink with a floating orange sac inside, and Evolution sport drinks were pulled from the market. The brothers' most successful product was Sappé Beauti Drink in the functional drink market.

As soon as they assumed control of the family business, Adisak and Arnupap focused on building exports. The company exported to more than 30 countries in Asia, Europe, and the Middle East. In 2010, however, income from exports represented only 10 percent of Sapanan's total revenue. The European market generated 30 percent of export income. (View the company website at: **www.sapanan.com/en/index.html#/products/overall_products.**)

FUNCTIONAL DRINKS IN THAILAND

Rising health concerns among Thai consumers helped spur the growth of functional products. The functional drink market was expanding rapidly and grew from 800 million baht in 2008 to four billion baht in 2010. Intense competition existed among both local and international companies.

Initially, consumers were unfamiliar with the concept of functional drinks. The Thailand Food and Drug Administration also strictly controlled product-benefit claims. These issues made it difficult to communicate product benefits to consumers. Several brands, including Coca Cola's Alive and Uni iFirm, had left the market in 2004 and 2005 after brief attempts to gain share.

The introduction of Peptein in 2009 illustrates the struggle to launch a functional drink in this market. With a budget of 400 million baht (approximately US$12 million), Peptein tried to educate potential buyers about the benefits of soy products for brain function. The brand achieved a high level of brand awareness, brand recall, and product trial rate. Because of poor product taste, Peptein chose to stress its rational, rather than any emotional, benefit. Consumers viewed Peptein as being too expensive compared to alternative soy bean drinks. In consequence, Peptein did not gain sufficient market share and was still fighting to gain consumer acceptance.[2]

Even though several brands had withdrawn from the market, the functional drink segment was still active as more brands entered and exiting brands were relaunched. Market leadership changed: in 2006, Uni iFirm controlled 71 percent of market sales volume, whereas in 2011 Sappé had a 60 percent share.

SOURCE: This case is prepared by associate professor Nittaya Wongtada, NIDA Business School, National Institute of Development Administration (NIDA), Thailand. It is for classroom discussion and does not intend to reflect effective or ineffective management. The main source of the information for this case is from interviewing the management of the Sapanan General Food Co., Ltd.

EXHIBIT 1 Market Share of Functional Drinks in Thailand

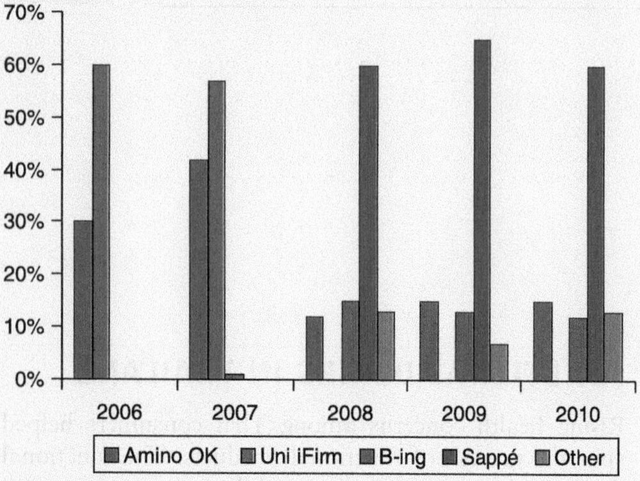

SOURCE: Compiled from various sources and company information.

Sappé Product Line

Sapanan General Food Co., Ltd. entered the functional drink market in 2006 by launching Sappé Beauti Drink, a flavored drink with ingredients for beauty such as collagen, L-carnitine, chlorophyll, and coenzyme Q10. The product offered benefits for women in fighting the harmful effects of sun exposure and in preventing skin aging. Sappé's slogan was "Only Drink ... you can be beautiful!" This was the first time that a functional drink had been directly connected with beauty. The company also launched other brands to serve different segments, including Beauti Shot, Smarti Shot, For One Day, Juice Me, Beauti Drink M for men, and St Anna. However, while the company's sales volume reached over 1,000 million baht in 2009, the largest proportion of sales came from Sappé Beauti Drink for women.

Sappé Beauti Drink was successful beyond the company's expectations. When unveiling this product, Sapanan could not afford mass-marketing activities but had to rely on various other techniques to communicate to potential customers. The name "Beauti drink" suggested the product benefit. In addition, to communicate to its target group of female buyers who were concerned about their figures and beauty, a slim and translucent bottle with a floral design clearly stood out when displayed on a retail shelf. A bottle neck tag also stressed product benefits to consumers unfamiliar with the Sappé Beauti Drink. At 20 baht per bottle, its price was the same as other brands. It was sold mainly in 7-11 convenience stores, the most popular convenience chain in Thailand. After its initial success, the company had sufficient profit to invest in advertising Sappé using mass-media channels and to hire a national celebrity to represent the brand. Phenomenal success resulted in it becoming the leading brand in the functional drink category by 2008. (View the ad at: www.youtube.com/watch?v=fdzVlF6F6XI.)

FUNCTIONAL DRINKS IN EUROPE

Japan was the trendsetter in the global functional food market. Many ingredient trends and product innovations in functional drinks were initiated in Japan and became popular in other Asian countries and subsequently in Europe. The functional drink market in Europe was composed of energy drinks, sports drinks, and nutraceutical drinks. Nutraceutical drinks accounted only for 17.4 percent of the US$8.4 billion market in 2008.[3] Although the market was still small, it was expected to expand rapidly. Consumers in Europe face the same daily situations as those in other parts of the world in terms of increasing time pressures, working longer hours, and having more disposable income to spend on leisure activities. They look for products that can help them to have a better quality of life.

Major suppliers such as Nestlé, Coca-Cola, Danone, and Pepsi-Co participated in the functional food industry in Europe. For instance, Nestlé joined with L'Oréal in introducing Innéov nutritional supplements for skin and hair. Nestlé itself also introduced Glowelle, a dietary supplement in both bottles and stick packs. Coca-Cola launched Glaceau Vitaminwater, while PepsiCo acquired UK vitamin-water brand V Water.

The product benefit claims of functional food and drink products were regulated by the European Commission. Nutraceutical drinks and food could not claim medicinal values. Companies were prohibited from promoting that their products could prevent or cure a disease. They could only advertise that the ingredients might help to improve health. If a direct claim of medicinal benefits was intended, the company had to comply with the regulatory requirements for medicinal products in terms of testing product efficacy and quality and strictly following marketing authorization procedures.

Many companies found that promoting functional products in Europe was rather difficult. For instance, in 2010, Danone withdrew its application for health claims for Activia and Actimel yogurts because of the lack of clarity regarding the European regulation on health and nutrition claims.[4] Nestlé pulled Glowelle out of the market in 2011 without giving a specific reason.[5] The advertisements for Coca-Cola's Glaceau Vitaminwater were banned in the UK in 2009 on the grounds that they could potentially mislead consumers concerning the product's health benefits.[6]

Sappé in Eastern Europe

Exporting Sappé to Eastern Europe was initiated by buyers from the region. For example, a Hungarian engineer who wanted to own a business approached Sapanan during a trade show. When on vacation in Thailand, a beverage distributor from Slovakia contacted Sapanan after buying Sappé drinks from a local convenience store. When the product was widely distributed in Hungary and Slovakia, other importers visiting these countries became interested in representing Sappé in their own countries.

However, not all contacts were fruitful or reliable. For example, at a trade show, a buyer from Eastern Europe requested product samples and specifications. After receiving this requested information, the buyer launched his own brand by imitating the product specifications of Sappé. Also, many importers approaching Sapanan tended to be small entrepreneurs or had no prior experience in international trade. Large, established distributors were more desirable, but they proved to be more difficult business partners. They would demand that their export suppliers provide promotional plans and marketing budgets to support a product launch. In addition, they did not spend much effort to promote new brands because they already represented several products.

Although Sappé products were distributed in numerous countries in Europe, Eastern Europe represented the company's main markets, especially Slovakia and Hungary. From the beginning, the importers in these countries desired to build brands and insisted the company register the Sappé trademark EU-wide (European Community trademark[7]). This turned out to be beneficial for Sapanan. After it had achieved some sales success, a number of imitators entered the market. The company was able to ward off some of these imitators because of its registered brands and unique package design. In addition to the legal protection, modifying machines to produce jelly chunks for Sappé and using raw materials from Thailand reduced copycats significantly.

Sappé Aloe Vera drink was Sapanan's first product in these markets. The company and its importers agreed that Sappé Aloe Vera drink be positioned not as an ultra-healthy drink to avoid being perceived as having poor taste and being associated with older consumers. Instead, they wanted Sappé to be viewed as a modern and stylish brand for those in the younger generation who were health conscious but still wanted fun products with good taste. The product benefit of Sappé Aloe Vera drink relied on the aloe vera ingredient, for which local consumers were already aware of the health benefits, including those relating to the digestive and immune systems, reducing blood sugar, relieving hangovers, and moisturizing the skin.

Since the importers were more familiar with local market conditions, Sapanan had to depend on them to plan marketing activities. Thus, these activities tended to reflect the characteristics of these importers. For example, the importer in Slovakia was a distributor of alcohol and spirits as well as a concert and event organizer. So Sappé Aloe Vera drink was promoted at concerts and in pubs as a drink to be mixed with alcohol. To support the product's positioning as being modern and cool, Sappé Aloe Vera drink was initially advertised by placing its package on a dark background. The importer in Hungary had access to gas stations, and so Sappé was distributed mainly in these outlets. The importer also displayed Sappé Aloe Vera drink on laminated stands, making floating cubes inside the bottle clearly visible in a dark room. Some importers aggressively promoted Sappé Aloe Vera in hypermarkets and faced an out-of-stock problem during a "buy-one-get-one free" promotion, causing friction among retailers, importers, and Sapanan.

Competition in Eastern Europe was negligible. When Sappé was introduced in Eastern Europe, only aloe vera drinks imported from Korea were available. The Korean products had been in the market for a number of years and were sold at a low price. Sappé, on the other hand, was positioned as having superior product quality and so was sold at a much higher price. A 300 ml bottle of Sappé was priced the same as the competitor's 1,000 ml bottle. As consumers switched to buying Sappé, competing products were pulled out of some outlets because of their low sales volume.

MOVING FORWARD

After initial success, Sapanan had sufficient profits to finance brand-building activities in several markets in Eastern Europe. Whether or not to standardize advertising across markets became a key issue. Initial success in Slovakia was achieved partly because of the use of a dark background; it presented Sappé as being hip and different. However, this was not acceptable in other markets. After convincing the Slovakian importer to adopt a lighter-color background in order to gain a wholesome image, the advertisements in Slovakia were gradually adjusted to this new background. Sapanan also tried to coordinate other marketing activities. For example, the same television advertisement was broadcast in Slovakia and Israel. This advertisement portrayed Sappé Aloe Vera drink as being fun and different by using a beautiful transvestite as the presenter. The tone of the commercial was light-hearted, different, and modern. This commercial was well received by the audience in both countries. Because of this success, the company believed that coordinating marketing activities across the European market was viable. (View the ad at: **www.youtube.com/watch?v=QRKNKoR4DA0**.)

Sapanan was expanding into other markets in the region. In 2011, it signed a joint venture with its distributor, Ital Market Slovakia (IMS), to produce Sappé Aloe Vera drink for the European market and set up a representative office in the Czech Republic. The company was searching for additional suitable partners. This was done by selling its products to several importers but without an exclusivity agreement. The company expected that products would be seen by many importers. Some of them might turn out to be more appropriate partners based on their interest in brand building as well as their available resources, market knowledge, and access to extensive distribution networks.

EXHIBIT 2 Export Price Structure to European Markets

	Percent
Shipping costs	10
Import tariffs	15
In-land clearance	4
Importer's operating costs	17
Distribution costs	15
Margins of importer	30–60

Export pricing methods had to be reconsidered. During the initial export arrangement to Eastern Europe, the company set prices very low in order to be attractive to importers. This provided more margins to importers and distributors given the prevailing retail price but caused Sapanan's own margin to be very thin. When importers requested financial support to promote Sapanan's products, it did not have surplus for this activity. In addition, once the price was established, it was difficult to raise it. Thus, a different export pricing structure was needed for new importers and was based on market demand. The average retail price for Sappé Aloe Vera drink (300 ml) was 1.5 euros. In quoting the FOB price for an importer, the company had to consider the various costs incurred when shipping its products to an importer's country. If the retail price was too high, the importer would have little chance to be successful. Typically, a retail price had to cover shipping costs, import tariffs, inland clearance, operating costs, distribution costs, and margin for importers (see Exhibit 2). If the importer did not have direct access to an outlet network, the retail price had to be higher to allow for more margins for distributors. Typically, for a longer channel of distribution, more margins were needed.

Expanding to Western Europe was more complicated than doing business in Eastern Europe since regulations in Western Europe were more stringent. For example, in Eastern Europe, the company could advertise the benefit of L-glutathione in increasing metabolism and weight control. However, all claims had to be clinically proven prior to advertising product benefits in Western European markets. In addition to the EU regulation, each EU member country has its own standards, which are different from those of the EU. Product adaptation in response to these different regulations could become too costly.

As the company was expanding its marketing effort in Europe, different consumer tastes and behaviors became more apparent. Generally, consumers in Western Europe were more conservative and so were less willing to try new products. The demographic mix of a nation's population also influenced product preference. For example, Mogu Mogu juice was successful in the Netherlands because of a large community of Middle Eastern and Asian consumers. Thus the company's attempts to coordinate its marketing activities had to consider the fragmented nature of the EU market.

CHALLENGES IN THE EU MARKET

As the export manager, Ampawan had to cope with the complexities in expanding operations in the EU. The Ariyapong family had encouraged her to think strategically for long-term sustainable success. While walking to a meeting with the management to present her export expansion plan for the European market, she was wondering if she had covered all the important issues.

QUESTIONS FOR DISCUSSION

1. Why was Sappé able to penetrate the Eastern European market? How did the brand's success in its domestic market facilitate this entrance?
2. What challenges did the company face when expanding into other Eastern European markets? How should it deal with these challenges?
3. Was Sapanan's process in searching for and selecting suitable partners appropriate? Are there any other ways to find suitable importers who could support the company's brand building activity?

ENDNOTES

1. Nata de coco is a smooth, clear, jelly-like food product made from the fermentation of coconut water.
2. Pradon Sirakovit, "Food for Thought?" July 30, 2009, QUO blog, www.quo-global.com/thinking/Food-for-Thought-.
3. *Functional Drinks in Europe, Industry Profile 2009*, Datamonitor.
4. Danone withdraws health claims for Actimel and Activia, *BBC News*, April 15, 2010, http://news.bbc.co.uk/2/hi/8622017.stm.
5. Simon Pitman, "Nestlé's Glowelle beauty from within brand 'no longer available for purchase,'" Nutra Ingredients, February 11, 2011, www.nutraingredients.com/Consumer-Trends/Nestle-s-Glowelle-beauty-from-within-brand-no-longer-available-for-purchase.
6. Mark Sweney, "Coca-Cola Ads for Glaceau Vitamin Water Banned," *Guardian*, October 7, 2009, www.guardian.co.uk/media/2009/oct/06/coca-cola-glaceau-ads-banned-asa.
7. There is a unified trademark registration system in Europe. By registering in one country, legal protection is provided for all member states of the EU.

China: The Next Aerospace Giant?

On November 16, 2010, the Chinese-made ARJ21 took off on its first public flight at the Zhuhai air show. The Chinese had already received 240 orders for the ARJ21. The same day China Commercial Aircraft Company announced that 100 orders had been made for its latest aircraft, the large narrow-body C919.[1] With the ARJ21 flying for all to see, it is clear that China has successfully developed and produced a modern aircraft and is in the process of building another to meet the country's insatiable demand for air travel. The significance of China's quest to build a large-body aircraft is far reaching. The global market for large aircraft has consolidated into two major companies: Boeing and Airbus. If China successfully enters the large-body aircraft market, China will enter the global market in a completely new way. China has the opportunity to switch from a market supplier to a market player in the aerospace sector.

CHINESE DEMAND

China is the world's fastest growing economy. As China's economy grows, many of its citizens move to cities. This urbanization, coupled with increasing Chinese incomes, drives an increasing need for regional air travel in China. The increasing demand for air travel in China requires more airports and more aircraft. China has become the world's second largest aviation market, with only the United States having a larger marketplace in commercial aviation.

Chinese passenger traffic has been growing by an average of 20 percent per year. The Chinese aviation market is expected to grow by approximately 14 percent per year in the next 10 years. This means China will require as many as 3,400 new aircraft by 2026 and 116 new airports by 2015. Realizing the large requirement for aircraft, China's government has undergone ambitious plans to build at least a portion of these aircraft in country.

China's goal is to build aircraft, specifically the large narrow-body C919, to supply an ever-increasing market. Internationally, the civil aviation market consists of around 60 percent large, narrow-body aircraft. Currently, two companies supply this market: Boeing with their B737 and Airbus with the A320. In China the percentage of large, narrow-body aircraft in the total market is even higher at about 70 percent. In the near future, 20,000 aircraft in this category will need to be replaced internationally, and China will require over 2,600 large aircraft itself.[2] If the Chinese successfully produce the C919, they will break into a market estimated at US$1.68 trillion over 20 years.[3]

PREVIOUS CHINESE ATTEMPTS

China has attempted to build aircraft indigenously in the past. In the 1970s the Shanghai Aircraft Research Institute developed the Y-10, a four-engine, large-body commercial aircraft. The Y-10 made its first flight in 1980, but the program was aborted by the Civil Aviation Administration of China (CAAC) in 1985. After 15 years of development only three aircraft were produced, and the technology was mostly outdated. The program largely failed because Chinese aerospace technology lagged the West and China's aerospace industry was inexperienced as a systems integrator.

In the 1980s, McDonnell Douglas, which is now part of Boeing, began manufacturing its MD-82 aircraft in China. The MD-82 aircraft is in the same class as the B737 and the A320. In 1985 a historic agreement was signed between McDonnell Douglas and CAAC. The agreement was the first ever between a U.S. aerospace company and China. The McDonnell Douglas aircraft subassemblies were produced in the United States and the MD-82 aircraft were assembled under license by the Shanghai Aviation Industrial Corporation (SAIC). The first MD-82 aircraft were built in Shanghai by SAIC in 1987.[4] Another aircraft, the MD-90, was also made in China, but the program became difficult to manage for McDonnell Douglas and eventually fizzled in the 1990s. In total, about 30 MD-82 and a couple of MD-90 aircraft were assembled in China.[5]

A NEW CHINESE STRATEGY

In the 1990s China began to pursue a new strategy for producing large aircraft. The Chinese realized that a phased approach would be necessary to produce a large commercial aircraft in China. The Chinese learned a valuable lesson with the failure of the Y-10 in the 1980s. It was not possible for China to start a completely indigenous large aircraft program on its own. The Chinese aviation industry was too far behind the West to catch up without a different approach. Chinese aviation would first need to build its knowledge by manufacturing modern aircraft components and then pursue its ultimate goal to become a systems integrator for large aircraft.

As a step in this direction, Airbus opened a final assembly line in Tianjin on September 28, 2008. Airbus, the Tianjin Free Trade Zone, and China Aviation Industry Corporation (AVIC) established this manufacturing

SOURCE: This case was written by Eric Johnson and Ilkka Ronkainen.

facility as a joint venture. On May 18, 2009, the first A320 from the Chinese assembly line made its maiden flight. As of August 2010, the Tianjin plant had delivered twenty A320s and five A319s.[6]

Boeing depends on China for portions of its aircraft production. On October 24, 2006, Boeing, Shanghai Airport (Group) Co. Ltd., and Shanghai Airlines Co. Ltd. started construction on a maintenance, repair, and overhaul facility. A new entity Pudong International Airport was created to manage the facility, Boeing Shanghai Aviation Services.[7] Currently, Boeing buys parts from a multitude of Chinese suppliers for its 737, 747, 767, and 787 aircraft.

China has become a valued outsource manufacturer for both of the world's large aircraft companies: Boeing and Airbus. This outsource manufacturing has allowed China to build important technical and manufacturing knowledge. Manufacturing aircraft components and assembling aircraft has also allowed China to develop world-class manufacturing and assembly facilities.

Exhibit 1 shows China's progression in the aircraft industry. China has pursued the parallel approaches of final assembly, coproduction, manufacturing as part of aircraft offset programs, and in-country design. In-country design is the most advanced effort and allows China to gain experience as a systems integrator.

The Chinese systems integrator strategy is to use joint ventures with Western firms to fill key knowledge gaps. China selects its joint venture partners based on their expertise in key areas, which allows China to fill these key knowledge gaps. These Western partners are the leaders in their technology areas and respected globally. China solicits help in development and production of their aircraft from its experienced joint venture partners.

Having partners also reduces China's risk. The new aircraft that China produces need to obtain airworthiness certifications from governments around the world. China's partners are based out of many of the same countries as the regulatory agencies that issue the certifications and understand the processes by which the certifications are obtained. China will also need to market its aircraft in other countries, and partners are expected to provide marketing and enhance global sales channels.

ADVANCED REGIONAL JET FOR THE TWENTY-FIRST CENTURY: ARJ21

The first aircraft produced as a result of China's aggressive strategy is the ARJ21. While important for patriotic reasons, the development of the ARJ21 is also important to China's goal to produce aircraft indigenously. In order to produce the ARJ21, China exercised its plan to utilize Western partners and suppliers. After announcing the ARJ21 project, China conducted an evaluation process that allowed Western companies to compete for the opportunity to partner with the Commercial Aircraft Corporation of China (COMAC) to produce the new aircraft.

The ARJ21 regional jet was developed by the COMAC (formerly ACAC), based in Shanghai. Formed in 2002, six companies and aerospace research institutes make up the COMAC consortium: the Shanghai Aircraft Research Institute, the Xian Aircraft Design and Research Institute, Chengdu Aircraft Industry Group, Shanghai Aircraft Company, Shenyang Aircraft Corporation, and Xian Aircraft Company. The consortium is charged with developing and manufacturing the ARJ21. Chengdu Aircraft Industry Group will construct the nose of the aircraft, and Shenyang Aircraft Corporation will manufacture the complete tail unit. Xian Aircraft Company is manufacturing the aircraft wings and fuselage, while Shanghai Aircraft Company is responsible for

EXHIBIT 1 Chinese Aircraft Industry Progression

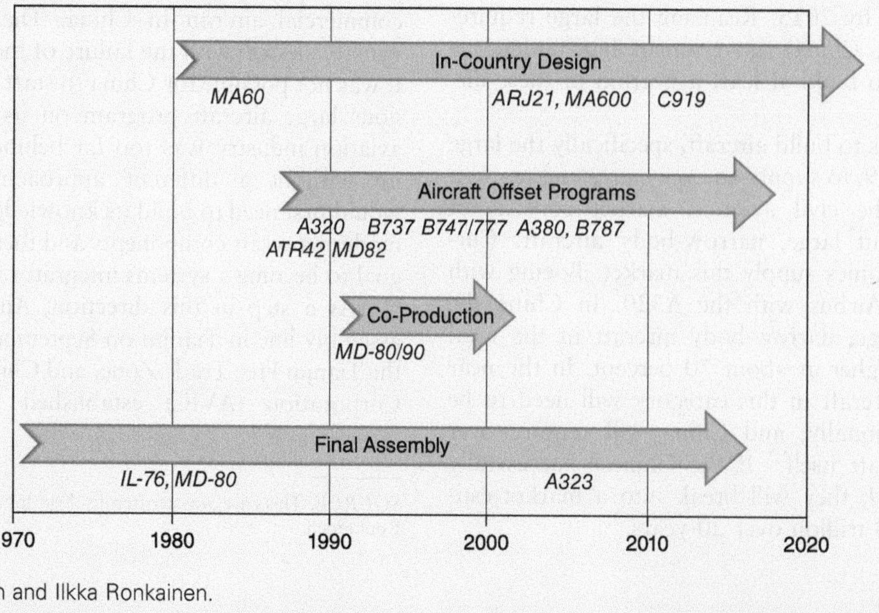

SOURCE: Eric Johnson and Ilkka Ronkainen.

EXHIBIT 2 **ARJ 21 Suppliers**

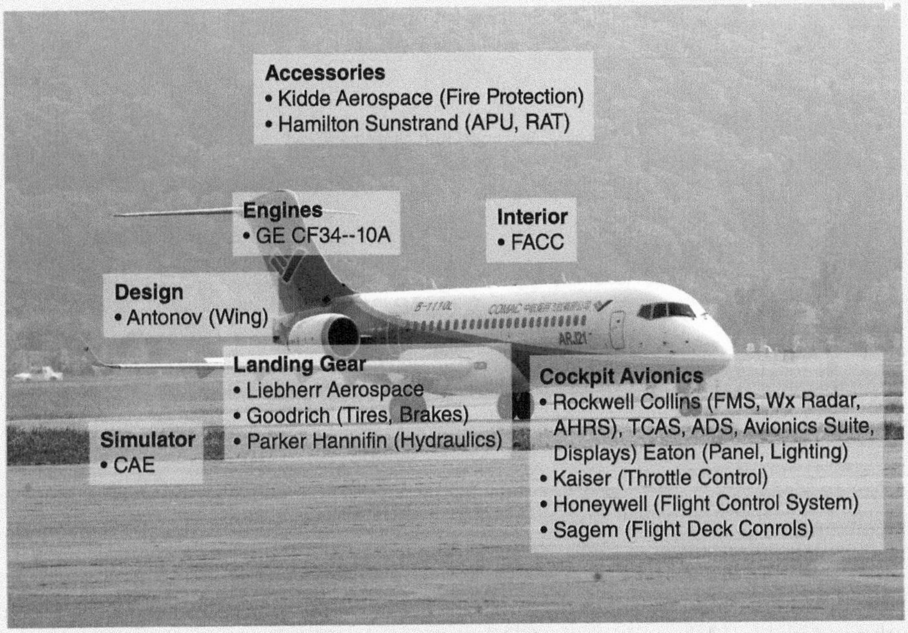

SOURCE: Image © Nelson Ching/Bloomberg via Getty Images.

final assembly.[8] The ARJ-21 consists of approximately 40 percent foreign content from 19 different foreign suppliers. While many non-Chinese companies contributed to the development and design of the ARJ21, two firms stand out for their contributions. General Electric (GE) was an important Western partner in the development of the ARJ21. In 2002, ACAC chose GE's CF34-10 engine for the ARJ21 regional jet.[9] GE has been an investment partner in the ARJ21 project, and GE Commercial Aviation Services (GECAS) ordered 25 of the first ARJ21s.[10] Antonov Design Bureau from the Ukraine designed a completely new wing for the aircraft that will increase aerodynamic performance and fuel efficiency.

The importance of the ARJ21 program is that it places COMAC in the role of systems integrator. This is arguably the first time that a Chinese entity has taken on the role of systems integrator for a modern commercial aircraft that is in most ways comparable to its Western analogs. The price of the ARJ21 is about US $30 million; it will seat 70 to 90 passengers and offer a range of up to 2,000 nautical miles, which covers 80 percent of domestic routes.

The ARJ21 program has certainly had its challenges. The aircraft was originally slated to perform its first test flight in 2005 but did not make its maiden flight until November 28, 2008, after multiple delays. Although the ARJ21 has been delayed, it is scheduled to go into production in 2011. This still places the aircraft three years ahead of one of the regional competitors, the Mitsubishi Regional Jet (MRJ), which is not scheduled for production until 2014.

When China first attempted to produce commercial aircraft indigenously with the Y-10, it lacked technological sophistication and experience as a systems integrator. Through the ARJ21 program, China has corrected these deficiencies. The Chinese aerospace industry now has the capabilities necessary to pursue its ultimate goal to produce large commercial aircraft and compete directly with Boeing and Airbus in this category.

C919: SINGLE-AISLE PASSENGER PLANE

In 2007, the Chinese government decided to launch the indigenously produced C919, the first all-new, large, narrow-body commercial aircraft in about 30 years.[11] The C919 grew out of the large aircraft program and further advances China's goal to compete directly with Boeing and Airbus. The name, C919, has special meaning: C represents China as well as COMAC, the first 9 implies "forever" in Chinese culture, and 19 means the large aircraft will have up to 190 seats.[12] The C919 single-aisle large aircraft is equivalent in size to Boeing's 737 and Airbus's A320, which places the C919 right in the sweet spot for Chinese demand.

The C919 is a big step for Chinese aerospace. COMAC utilized a similar supplier partnership approach to the ARJ21 for the C919 program. China is coupling the manufacturing skills learned from supplying components and subassemblies to Boeing and Airbus with the systems integrator skills acquired during the ARJ-21 project.

On November 16, 2010, COMAC signed order agreements for the first C919 large passenger aircraft.

EXHIBIT 3 **Chinese Aerospace Progression**

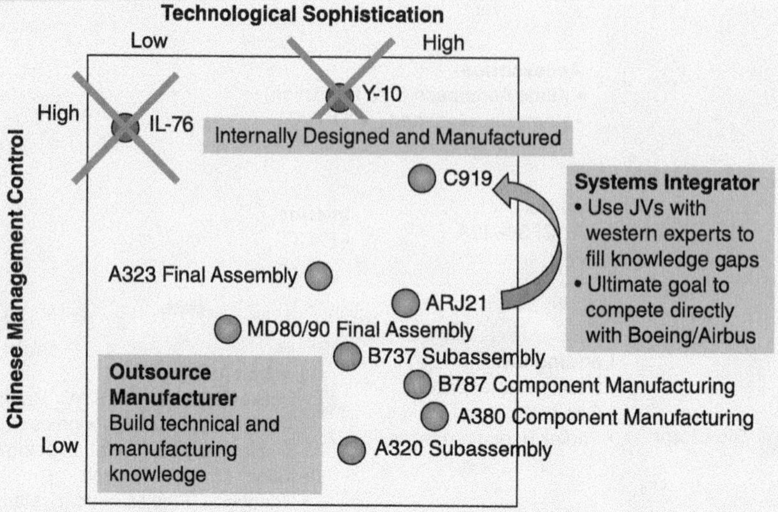

SOURCE: Eric Johnson and Ilkka Ronkainen.

The orders were placed by Air China, China Eastern Airlines, China Southern Airlines, Hainan Airlines, CDB Leasing, and GECAS.[13] While the exact number of planes ordered is up for debate, the number ranges between 50 and 100. The Chinese planned to complete the C919's preliminary designs in 2010 with detailed designs in 2012. The maiden flight is scheduled for 2014, and the goal is to acquire the airworthiness certificate in 2016 and put the C919 on the market the same year. The Chinese have stated that they plan to sell more than 2,500 C919s over 20 years.[14]

COMAC has gained the necessary systems integrator skills, and the next step is to gain the remaining technical expertise to produce an entire aircraft. Like the ARJ21, much of the high-tech equipment for the C919 is made by Western companies. The engine is one of the key aircraft components that China has had to acquire for both the ARJ21 and the C919. The C919 will initially be made using a version of the LEAP-X engine, the LEAP-X1C, supplied by CFM International, a 50-50 joint venture between GE and France's Snecma.[15] CFM International and COMAC signed the master contract for the LEAP-X engine at the Paris Air Show opening ceremony on June 20, 2011. Wang Zhilin, general manager of COMAC, said a domestic-made engine for the C919 is scheduled to be delivered by 2020.[16] If COMAC is successful in developing the next engine for the C919, China will be one step closer to producing a completely indigenous large-body aircraft.

The C919 will compete in the top aircraft category. The equivalent aircraft, the Boeing 737 and Airbus 320, have 4,500 and 3,400 aircraft in service, respectively. The Boeing 737 holds the title of the top-selling aircraft in history. While both Bombardier and Embraer have considered building similar-sized aircraft, the C919 has a head start in the top category. The C919 will also feature several advanced technologies, including the latest engine technology, supposedly superior to the Boeing 737. In addition, the Chinese have plans to increase economic performance, reduce emissions, and enhance comfort. These features could enable the C919 to sell not only because of demand but also thrive as a real competitor in the market.

In a recent major development, Ryanair, a European discount airline, reported that they will explore an agreement with COMAC to help design the C919. COMAC and Ryanair are expected to sign an agreement at the Paris Air Show on June 21, 2011. If the two companies move forward with this arrangement, Chinese aerospace will make a historic move forward with this strategic development. A partnership with a European airline will further legitimize the C919 program and potentially open up a major Western market in Europe. Ryanair's assistance could be instrumental in helping COMAC receive certification from the European Aviation Safety Agency and eventually the United States Federal Aviation Administration (FAA).

SUMMARY

While many questions remain for the Chinese aerospace program, COMAC has made huge steps forward with the ARJ21 and now the C919. Even with significant delays the ARJ21 is still on track for production in 2011. The C919 may also experience timeline adjustments, but more importantly the C919 program is still moving forward and seems to be gaining in legitimacy. After several attempts in past decades, Chinese commercial aerospace appears to have entered a new era. An offering is on the way in the largest commercial aircraft category, and China is not looking back. The Chinese have already announced the nomenclature for the next two aircraft after the C919, the C929 and C939. On the way to the ultimate goal, China has overcome major technology and experience hurdles. The remaining challenges for the large aircraft program are maintaining the schedule and

EXHIBIT 4 Chinese Aircraft Programs

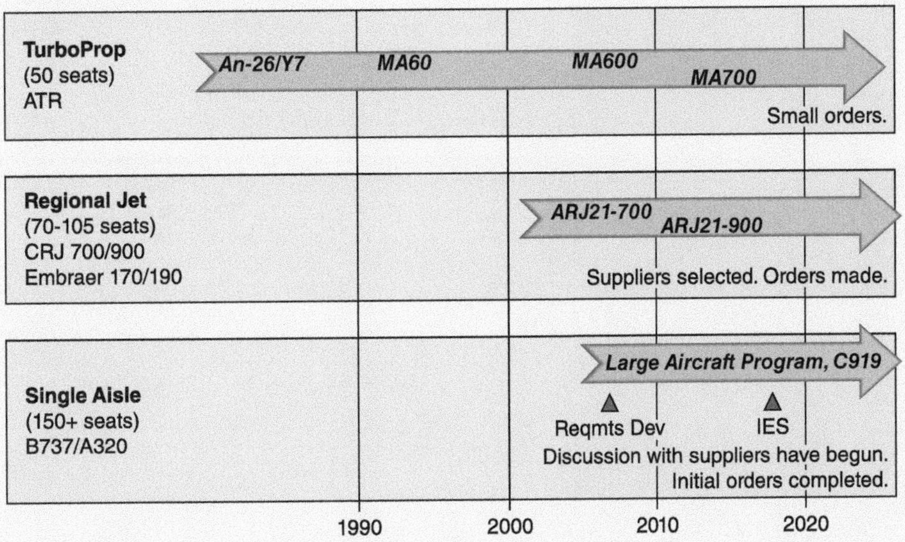

SOURCE: Eric Johnson and Ilkka Ronkainen.

marketing the C919. If China is successful in cracking the Boeing and Airbus duopoly, they will take a giant step forward not only in aviation but also in international business at large.

QUESTIONS FOR DISCUSSION

1. The Chinese systems integrator strategy is to use joint ventures with Western firms to fill key knowledge gaps. What challenges can Chinese firms encounter when depending on other sources?
2. General Electric is an important Western partner. What problems could this cause for General Electric?
3. What other partnerships may further legitimize the C919?

ENDNOTES

1. www.chinamilitary.net/china-made-regional-aircraft-arj21-700-received-240-orders.html, accessed April 9, 2011.
2. http://2jjj.com/?p=2846, accessed April 9, 2011.
3. Wing-Gar Cheng, "Comac Sees First C919 Order as China Challenges Airbus, Boeing," *Bloomberg*, November 8, 2010, www.bloomberg.com/news/2010-11-09/comac-sees-first-c919-order-as-china-challenges-airbus-boeing.html.
4. Arthur Pearcy. *McDonnell Douglas MD-80 & MD-90.* 1999, Motorbooks International.
5. "China Continues Its Long, Slow Climb to the Skies," www.global50discoveries.com/Library/ArticleView/tabid/559/ArticleId/70/China-Continues-Its-Long-Slow-Climb-to-the-Skies.aspx, accessed April 9, 2011.
6. Airbus in China, www.airbus.com/company/worldwide-presence/airbus-in-china, accessed April 9, 2011.
7. Boeing Logbook: 2–5-2006, www.boeing.com/history/chronology/chron18.html, accessed April 9, 2011.
8. ARJ21-700 Regional Jet, www.jrlucariny.com/Site2008/arj700/arj700.html, accessed April 9, 2011.
9. GE, the history of aircraft engines, www.geae.com/aboutgeae/history.html, accessed April 9, 2011.
10. K. K. Chadha, "ARJ21 first flight marks China's return to jet set," AIN online, December 30, 2008, www.ainonline.com/ain-and-ainalerts/aviation-international-news/single-publication-story/browse/0/article/arj21-first-flight-marks-chinas-return-to-jet-set-19363/?no_cache=1&tx_ttnews%5Bstory_pointer%5D=7&tx_ttnews%5Bmode%5D=1.
11. Ray Kwong, "China's First Homegrown Jet—And Why It Matters," *Forbes*, August 24, 2010, www.forbes.com/sites/china/2010/08/24/chinas-first-homegrown-jet-and-why-it-matters.
12. "China Commercial Aircraft Corp," *Live Trading News*, October 21, 2010, www.livetradingnews.com/china-commercial-aircraft-corp-25448.htm.
13. "100 initial orders placed for China's C919 large passenger aircraft," *People's Daily Online*, November 17, 2010, http://english.peopledaily.com.cn/90001/90778/90860/7202261.html.
14. Kwong, "China's First Homegrown Jet—And Why It Matters."
15. "China's first home-grown large passenger jet unveiled," *Gizmag*, November 16, 2010, www.gizmag.com/chinese-c919-passenger-jet/16961, accessed April 9, 2011.
16. Xu Tianran, "Aviation firms enter engine market," *Global Times*, April 13, 2011, www.globaltimes.cn/NEWS/tabid/99/articleType/ArticleView/articleId/661460/Aviation-firms-enter-engine-market.aspx.

GLOSSARY

absorption A pricing approach in which foreign currency appreciation/depreciation is not reflected (either entirely or partially) in the target market price.

accidental exporter Firms which become international due to unsolicited orders, such as those placed via a website, requiring export; unplanned participation in the international market.

acculturation Adjusting and adapting to a specific culture other than one's own.

adaptation A process where a firm, usually an experienced exporter, adjusts its activities and overall strategy to incorporate factors such as changing exchange rates, tariffs, and other variables.

agent An intermediary for the distribution of goods who earns a commission on sales. See also *distributor*.

ambush marketing The unauthorized use of an event without the permission of the event owner; for example, an advertising campaign that suggests a sponsorship relationship.

antidumping law Laws prohibiting below-cost sales of products.

area structure An approach to organization based on geographical areas.

area studies Programs providing factual preparation for a manager to operate in, or work with people from, a particular country.

arm's-length price A basis for intracompany transfer pricing: The price that unrelated parties would have arrived at for the same transaction.

augmented feature Elements added to a core product or service that serve to distinguish it from competing products or services.

awareness One of the key corporate export stages in which the firm becomes aware of the international opportunities as unsolicited export orders or other international stimuli continue over time.

back-translation The translating of a foreign language version back to the original language by a different person from the one who made the first translation.

bailout A situation in which a business, individual or government offers money to a failing business in order to prevent the consequences that arise from a business's downfall. Bailouts can take the form of loans, bonds, stocks, or cash.

banker's acceptance A method of payment for exported goods: When a time draft, with a specified term of maturity, is drawn on and accepted by a bank, it becomes a banker's acceptance, which is sold in the short-term money market. See also *documentary collection; discounting*.

barrier to entry Obstacles to trade created by governments and market conditions.

barter Exchange of goods for other goods of equal value.

best practice An idea which has saved money or time, or a process that is more efficient than existing ones; best practices are usually established by councils appointed by a company.

bilateral negotiation Trade agreements carried out mainly between two nations.

black hole A situation that the international marketer has to work its way out of; a company may be in a "black hole" because it has read the market incorrectly or because government may restrict its activities.

blog A website on which individuals make regular entries of commentary or descriptions of events.

born global A newly founded firm that is established as an international business from inception.

boycott Refusing to purchase from or trade with a company because of political or ideological differences.

brain drain Foreign direct investors attracting the best and brightest employees from a domestic firm; said to be depriving domestic firms of talent.

brand Name, term, symbol, sign, or design used by a firm to differentiate its offerings from those of its competitors.

Buddhism A religion which is an offspring of Hinduism but without caste system, with an emphasis on spiritual achievement rather than worldly goods.

budget Short-term financial guidelines in such areas as investment, cash, and personnel.

built environment Modifications made to the natural environment by the people living in it; for example, the structures created by human activities in most cities.

bureaucratic control A limited and explicit set of regulations and rules that outline desired levels of performance.

buyback A form of countertrade: A compensation arrangement whereby one party agrees to supply technology or equipment that enables the other party to produce goods with which the price of the supplied technology or equipment is repaid.

cash in advance A method of payment for exported goods: The most favorable term to the exporter; not widely used, except for smaller, custom orders, or first-time transactions, or situations in which the exporter has reason to doubt the importer's ability to pay.

cause-related marketing Marketing that links a company or brand with a cause, such as environmental protection or children's health.

center of excellence An organizational unit that incorporates a set of capabilities that have been identified as an important source of value creation with the explicit intention that these capabilities be leveraged by and disseminated to other parts of the firm.

centralization When a firm maintains tight controls and strategic decision making is concentrated at headquarters.

change agent An international business entity that introduces new products or ideas and practices and causes changes in culture.

chill effect A sharp reduction in demand for both consumer and industrial goods due to buyer uncertainty about the state of their nation's economy.

Christianity A religion, based on the life and teachings of Jesus Christ, made up of two major groups: Catholicism and Protestantism.

clearing arrangement A more refined form of barter, aimed at reducing the effect of the immediacy of the transaction.

climate A natural feature that has profound impact on economic activity within a place.

cocooning A cultural trend toward staying at home and turning away from the world and anything new.

code law A comprehensive set of written statutes; countries with code law try to spell out all possible legal rules explicitly; based on Roman law and found in a majority of nations.

commercial risk Refers primarily to an overseas buyer suspected of insolvency or protracted payment default.

common law A legal perspective which is based on tradition and depends less on written statutes and codes than on precedent and custom.

complementary strengths The differing strengths of partners that help in building a profitable joint venture, for example, often the partners have different product, geographic, or functional strengths, which the alliance can build on in order to achieve success with a new strategy or in a new market. They can then either operate jointly as equals or have one partner piggyback by making use of the other's strengths.

computer-aided design (CAD) A combination of hardware and software that allows for the design of products.

concentration A market expansion policy characterized by focusing on and developing a small number of markets. See also *diversification*.

confiscation Transfer of ownership from a foreign firm to the host country without compensation to the owner.

Confucianism A code of conduct rather than a religion, the teachings of which stress loyalty and relationships and have been broadly adopted by followers throughout Asia, especially among the Chinese.

consignment selling A method of payment that allows the importer to defer payment until the imported goods are actually sold.

consumer ethnocentrism The tendency to view domestically produced goods as superior to those produced in other countries.

consumer-generated media (CGM) Online bulletin boards, blogs, podcasts, and other websites at which consumers can post product complaints and compliments.

contender A local company whose assets are transferable, allowing it to compete head-on with established global players worldwide.

content analysis A research technique investigating the content of communication in a society; for example, counting the number of times preselected words, themes, symbols, or pictures appear in a given medium.

contributor A role of a country organization; a subsidiary with a distinctive competence, such as product development or regional expertise.

controlled market test A research method that allow companies to assess an item's sales potential in a real-world environment with real consumers making real purchases.

coordinated decentralization Overall corporate strategy is provided from headquarters (centralized decision making) but subsidiaries are free to implement it within the range established in consultation between headquarters and the subsidiaries.

core product Product or service in its simplest, generic state; other tangible and augmented features may be added to distinguish a core product or service from its competitors.

corporate citizenship A company's involvement in supporting their local and national communities through a variety of roles, including support for nonprofit organizations vital to a community's social development.

corporate governance The relationships among stakeholders used to determine and control the strategic direction and performance of an organization.

corporate image advertising An umbrella marketing communications plan to make the company itself be correctly understood or perceived more positively.

corporate philanthropy The act of corporations donating some of their profits, or their resources, to nonprofit organizations.

corporate social responsibility (CSR) Commitment displayed by the corporate employers towards employees, community, and environment. Generally this commitment is expected to give prime importance to treating and paying employees well.

corruption The misuse of one's influence, capabilities, or funds in order to provide or obtain preferential treatment.

cost-plus method A pricing strategy based on the true cost of a product (inclusive of domestic and foreign marketing costs).

counterpurchase A form of countertrade that is a parallel barter agreement: The participating parties sign two separate contracts that specify goods and services to be exchanged (some cash may be exchanged to compensate for differences in value).

countertrade Transactions in which purchases are tied to sales and sales to purchases.

country of origin (COO) The nation where a product is produced or branded.

cross-border transaction A transaction which means that people, information, and money cross national borders during the exchange process.

cross-subsidization The use of resources accumulated in one part of the world to compete for market share in another part of the world.

crowdsourcing The act of mining a group of customers for new product ideas, improvements in marketing methods, and other useful outcomes.

cultural assimilator A program in which trainees must respond to scenarios of specific situations in a particular country.

cultural clashes Conflicts arising due to differences in cultures, especially differences in religion.

cultural control Informal rules and regulations that are the result of shared beliefs and expectations among the members of an organization.

cultural convergence The growing similarity of attitudes and behaviors across cultures.

cultural imperialism Threat to cultural heritage due to the disinclination of international marketers to make culture-specific adaptations.

cultural knowledge Knowledge of a culture acquired through factual and experiential information.

cultural universals Generalizations that may apply to all cultures.

culture An integrated system of learned behavior patterns that are distinguishing characteristics of members of any given society.

curative international marketing A kind of marketing that restores and develops international economic health and may be the next step up for marketing.

customer involvement The degree of participation of the recipient in the production of a service.

customer relationship management (CRM) The collecting, storing, and analyzing of customer data to develop and maintain two-way relations between the firm and key customers aiming at maximizing value to the firm's most important customers so they remain customers indefinitely.

customer structure An approach to organization that is based on the customer groups that are served are dramatically different; for example, consumers versus businesses versus governments.

data equivalence A consideration that ensures comparative structure in survey questions by taking into account cultural variations.

database marketing A form of direct marketing in which database information (developed through direct mail or the Internet) allows the creation of an individual relationship with each customer or prospect.

death of distance A phrase coined by Frances Cairncross, which suggests that distance may no longer be a limiting factor in people's ability to communicate and interact.

decentralization When a firm grants its subsidiaries a high degree of autonomy; controls are relatively loose and simple.

decoding The process by which the receiver of a message transforms an "encoded" message from symbols into thought.

defender A local company that has assets that give it a competitive advantage only in its home market.

demographic divide The measure of the inequality in the population and its age distribution between rich and poor countries.

deregulation Reduction of governmental involvement in the marketplace.

derived demand Business opportunities resulting from the move abroad by established customers and suppliers.

direct question A question in a survey questionnaire which is very direct, formal, does not have an introductory phrase, and is less polite. The degree of societal sensitivity must be taken into account when determining the directness or indirectness of questions.

discounting When a time draft, a method of payment for exported goods with a specified term of maturity, is drawn on and accepted by a bank, it may be converted into cash by the exporter by discounting; the draft is sold to a bank at a discount from face value. See also *banker's acceptance.*

discretionary product adaptation Ensuring a product or service to meet prevailing legal and regulatory, social, economic, and climatic conditions in the market. Motivation for such adaptations does not have to be government fiat, but can also be a sense of corporate social responsibility.

discriminatory regulations Regulations that impose larger operating costs on foreign service providers than on local competitors, provide subsidiaries to local firms only, or deny competitive advantages to foreign suppliers.

distribution culture Existing channel structures and philosophies for distribution of goods.

distributor An intermediary that purchases goods for resale through its own channels. See also *agent.*

diversification A market expansion policy characterized by growth in a relatively large number of markets. See also *concentration.*

documentary collection A method of payment for exported goods: The seller ships the goods and the shipping documents and the draft demanding payment are presented to the importer through a bank acting as the seller's agent; the draft, also known as the bill of exchange, may be a sight draft or a time draft.

dodger A local company that sells out to a global player or becomes part of an alliance.

domestication Gaining control over the assets of a foreign firm by demanding partial transfer of ownership and management responsibility to the host country.

downstream change As a good flows from a commodity to becoming a specific product, changes in composition, sophistication and value can take place which help its competitiveness.

draft A method of payment for exported goods: Similar to a personal check; an order by one party to pay another; documentary drafts must be accompanied by specified shipping documents; clean drafts do not require documentation; also known as the "bill of exchange." See also *documentary collection.*

dual pricing Differentiation between domestic and export prices.

dual-use item Goods that are useful to both military and civilian purposes.

duty drawbacks A refund of up to 99 percent of duties paid on imports when they are re-exported or incorporated into articles that are subsequently exported within five years of the importation.

e-commerce The business practice of offering goods and services over the web.

economic bloc A measure designed to encourage trade between countries, whereby agreements are formed by groups of nations to deal with common issues, ultimately aiming at the free movement of capital, services, and people across national borders, and the joint development of common international policies.

economic crisis A situation in which the economy of a country experiences a sudden downturn often brought on by a financial crisis. An economy facing an economic crisis will most likely experience a falling GDP, a drying up of liquidity and rising/falling prices due to inflation/deflation.

economies of scale A measure aimed at encouraging trade between countries, whereby groups of nations arrive at various agreements to deal with common issues. Free movement of capital, services, and people across national borders, and common international policies are some outcomes of this measure.

efficiency seeker Firms that attempt to obtain the most economic sources of production in their foreign direct investment strategy.

ehrbarer Kaufmann A concept, which emerged in the sixteenth century, that focuses on maintaining long-term successful international trade efforts with distant and often unfamiliar people. Key requirements are a good understanding of other cultures, dedicated research and planning for opportunities, and scrupulous honesty.

electronic word of mouth Computer mediated communication where consumers can share their opinion.

embargo Governmental actions that terminate the free flow of trade in goods, services, or ideas, imposed for adversarial and political purposes.

encoding The process by which a sender converts a message into a symbolic form that will be properly understood by the receiver.

Environmental Superfund A fund to cover the costs of domestic safety regulations and made up from fees imposed on U.S. chemical manufacturers, based upon volume of production.

ethnocentrism The belief that one's own culture is superior to others.

evaluation One of the key corporate export stages in which the firms conduct an assessment of their export efforts; based on this assessment, they arrive at a decision on whether or not to continue these efforts.

experiential knowledge Knowledge that can be acquired only by being involved in a culture other than one's own.

export consortia An alliance of domestic firms, that work together in a manner similar to Japanese sogoshoshas, to overcome trade barriers through cooperative efforts.

export control system Governmental policy designed to deny or at least delay the acquisition of strategically important goods by adversaries.

export license Written authorization to send a product abroad.

export trading company (ETC) A company formed under a legislation designed to improve the export performance of small- and medium-sized firms in the United States.

expropriation Seizure of foreign assets by a government with payment of compensation to the owners.

extender A company that is able to exploit its success at home as a platform for expansion elsewhere; this calls for markets or segments that are similar in terms of customer preferences.

facilitating payment Small fees paid to expedite paperwork through customs; also called "grease"; not considered in violation of the Foreign Corrupt Practices Act or OECD guidelines.

factoring A trade financing method; companies known as factoring houses may purchase an exporter's receivables for a discounted price; factors also provide the exporter with a complete financial package combining credit protection, accounts receivable bookkeeping, and collection services.

factual information Objective knowledge of a culture obtained from others through communication, research, and education.

feedback Responses to communications that seek to generate awareness, evoke a positive attitude, or increase purchases; collection and analysis of feedback is necessary to analyze the success of communication efforts.

field experience Placing a trainee in a different cultural environment for a limited time.

financial incentive Special funding by the government for the investor by providing land or buildings, loans, loan guarantees, or wage subsidies.

financial transactions tax A tax placed on a specific type of financial transaction for a specific purpose.

fiscal incentive Special funding legislated by government to attract foreign investments.

focus group A group consisting of 8 to 12 consumers, representative of the proposed target audience, put together for the purpose of fine-tuning research studies.

foreign affiliate A U.S. firm in which at least 10 percent is owned by foreign entities.

foreign availability High-technology products that are available worldwide, from many sources.

foreign direct investment (FDI) Capital funds flow from abroad; company is held by noncitizens; foreign ownership is typically undertaken for longer-term participation in an economic activity.

foreign-market opportunity analysis Basic information needed to identify and compare key alternatives when a firm plans to launch international activities.

forfaiting A trade financing technique; the importer pays the exporter with bills of exchange or promissory notes guaranteed by a leading bank in the importer's country; the exporter can sell them to a third party at a discount from their face value for immediate cash.

forum A site where people hold conversations about a product, a brand or some other specific topic, in the form of posted messages.

forward market exchange A method used to counter challenges in currency movements; the exporter enters into an agreement for a rate at which it will buy the foreign currency at a future date; the rate is expressed as either a premium or a discount on the current spot rate.

franchising A business model in which a parent company (the franchiser) grants another, independent entity (the franchisee) the right to do business in a specified manner. This right can take the form of selling the franchiser's products or using its name, production, preparation, and marketing techniques, or its business approach.

functional lubrication Bribes that are not imposed by individual greed, but that serve to "grease the wheels" of bureaucratic processes; amounts tend to be small, the "express fee" is standardized, and the money is passed along to the party in charge of processing a document.

functional structure An approach to organization that emphasizes the basic tasks of the firm; for example, manufacturing, sales, and research and development.

future A method used to counter problems of currency movements; in the currency futures market; for example, a buyer agrees to buy futures on the British pound sterling, which implies an obligation to buy in the future at a prespecified price.

Generalized System of Preferences (GSP) A program designed to promote economic growth in the developing world by providing preferential duty-free entry for up to 5,000 products when imported from one of 128 designated beneficiary countries and territories.

geologic characteristic The characteristic of a place relating to its natural attributes.

global account management Account programs extended across countries, typically for the most important customers, to build relationships.

global brand A brand/product that has worldwide recognition.

global consumer Individuals or organizational buyers that exhibit similar needs and tastes worldwide.

global market segment A group of customers who share common characteristics across numerous national markets.

global media Media vehicles that have target audiences on at least three continents.

glocalization An approach of building in organizational flexibility to allow for local/regional adjustments in global strategic planning and implementation; uniformity is sought in strategic elements such as positioning of a product; care is taken to localize tactical elements, such as distribution.

gray market Distribution channels uncontrolled by producers; goods may enter the marketplace in ways not desired by their manufacturers.

Group of Five Five major industrialized nations regarded as economic superpowers: The United States, Britain, France, Germany, and Japan.

Group of Seven Seven major industrialized nations: The United States, Britain, France, Germany, Japan, Italy, and Canada.

Group of Ten Ten major industrialized nations: The United States, Britain, France, Germany, Japan, Italy, Canada, the Netherlands, Belgium, and Sweden.

Group of Twenty Countries in the Group of Seven plus Argentina, Australia, Brazil, China, India, Indonesia, Mexico, Russia, Saudi Arabia, South Africa, South Korea, and Turkey, as well as the European Union.

high-context culture Cultures in which the speaker and the listener rely on a common understanding of the context, which is at least as important as what is actually said.

Hinduism A religion, and also a way of life predicated on the caste, or class, to which one is born.

household All the persons, both related and unrelated, who occupy a housing unit.

hydrology The impact of rivers, lakes, and other bodies of water on the kinds of economic activities that occur in a place.

implementer Country organizations that provide the opportunity to capture economies of scale and scope that are the basis of a global strategy.

Incoterms Internationally accepted standard definitions for terms of sale, covering variable methods of transportation and delivery between country of origin and country of destination, and set by the International Chamber of Commerce (ICC) since 1936.

in-depth study A market research tool that is used for gathering detailed data after studying consumer needs across markets.

indirect question A question in a survey questionnaire that is open-ended, informal, has an introductory phrase, and is very polite. The degree of societal sensitivity must be taken into account when determining the directness or indirectness of questions.

infant industry Relatively new firms that are sometimes seen as deserving of protection, which allows the industry to "grow up" before having to compete with "adult" global industries.

inflation The increase in the level prices in an economy, over a period of time.

infrastructure Economic, social, financial, and marketing support systems, such as housing, banking systems, communications networks, etc.

infrastructure services A provision model in which an organization outsources the equipment used to support operations, and are comprised of telecommunications, insurance, banking, and logistics.

innate exporter Start-up exporters; exporting firms who commence their export activities within two years of establishment.

innovation The generation of new ideas (or) adaptation of new ideas towards the provision of higher quality goods and services, sustained growth, and new knowledge.

intangibility The quality of not being seen, touched, or held. A key difference between goods and service.

intellectual property (IP) A legal entitlement of exclusive rights to use an idea, piece of knowledge or invention.

intellectual property rights Safeguarding rights by providing the originators of an idea or process with a proprietary compensation, at least, in order to encourage quick dissemination of innovations.

interactive digital media A digital media platform that enables customers to be directly connected to the brand and the development process.

interest The second stage in the key corporate export stages where the awareness about the international opportunities causes the management to gradually become interested in international activities.

intermediary Independent distributors of goods, operating primarily at a local level. See also *distributor; agent.*

international comparative research Research carried out between nations, particularly those with similar environments, where the impact of uncontrollable macrovariables is limited.

international logistics The design and management of a system that controls the flow of materials into, through, and out of the international corporation. It encompasses the total movement concept by covering the entire range of operations concerned with goods movement, including both exports and imports.

interpretive knowledge Knowledge that requires comprehensive fact finding and preparation, and an ability to appreciate the nuances of different cultural traits and patterns.

intranet A company network that integrates a company's information assets into a single and accessible system using Internet-based technologies such as e-mail, newsgroups, and the World Wide Web.

inventory carrying cost The expense of maintaining inventories.

Islam A monotheistic religion, guiding its followers, Muslims, with the help of the *shari'ah* (law of Islam).

joint venture Collaborations of two or more organizations for more than a transitory period, in which the partners share assets, risks, and profits.

Kyoto Protocol An international agreement, signed in 1997, that calls for reductions in the emissions of carbon dioxide and five other greenhouse gases.

lead user Companies, organizations, or individuals who are ahead of trends or have needs that go beyond what is available at the present time.

letter of credit A method of payment for exported goods: An instrument issued by a bank at the request of a buyer; the bank promises to pay a specified amount of money on presentation of documents stipulated in the letter of credit, usually the bill of lading, consular invoice, and a description of the goods.

licensing An agreement in which one firm (the licensor) permits another firm (the licensee) to use its intellectual property in exchange for compensation designated as a royalty.

lobbyist Well-connected individuals and firms that help companies influence the governmental decision-making process by providing access to policymakers and legislators.

low-context culture Culture in which most information is contained explicitly in words.

management contract An agreement where the supplier brings together a package of skills that will provide for the ongoing operation of the client's facilities.

mandatory product adaptation Ensuring a product or service to meet prevailing legal and regulatory, social, economic, and climatic conditions in the market. Motivation for such adaptations does not have to be government fiat, but can also be a sense of corporate social responsibility.

maquiladoras Mexican plants that make goods and parts or process food for export to the United States.

marginal cost method A pricing strategy that considers only the direct cost of producing and selling products for export as the floor beneath which prices cannot be set; overhead costs are disregarded, allowing an exporter to lower prices to be competitive in markets that otherwise might not be accessed.

market pricing Determining the initial price of a product by comparison to competitors' prices.

market seeker Firms that search for better opportunities for entry and expansion in their foreign direct investment strategy.

market transparency Clarity of the offering made to the customer; transparency in service delivery is often difficult to ensure, because services may be customized to individual needs.

market-differentiated pricing Export pricing based on the dynamic, changing conditions of each marketplace.

marketing dilemma The ethical concern of the company about the demand of the customer and the expediency of what is marketed, in relation to the individual and the society.

master franchising system A system wherein foreign partners are selected and awarded the franchising rights to territory in which they, in turn, can subfranchise.

materials management The timely movement of raw materials, parts, and supplies into and through a firm.

matrix structure An approach to organization based on the coordination of product and geographic dimensions of planning and implementing strategy.

m-commerce The exchange of goods and services via the use of smart mobile handheld devices that allow web browsing.

metanational innovator Company that innovates across borders and across companies.

microfinance Programs in developing markets that allow consumers with no property as collateral, to borrow sums averaging $100 to make purchases, and to have access to retail banking services.

mini-national Born globals—newer companies with sales between $200 million and $1 billion.

mixed aid credit Loans composed partially of commercial interest rates and partially of highly subsidized developmental aid interest rates, for the purpose of meeting foreign export-financing conditions.

mixed structure An approach to organization that combines one or more possible structures; also called a hybrid structure.

modes of transportation Choices among airfreight and ocean freight, pipeline, rail, and trucking.

multilateral negotiation Trade agreements carried out among a number of nations

national security Protecting the welfare—economic, cultural, or military—of a nation's people; tariffs, barriers to entry, and other obstacles to trade often are established to ensure such protection.

noise Extraneous and distracting stimuli that interfere with the communication of a message.

nondiscriminatory regulations Regulations that offer less opportunity for international criticism; may be inconvenient and may hamper business operations.

nonfinancial incentive Incentives that include guaranteed government purchases, special protection from competition through tariffs, import quotas, and local content requirements, and investments in infrastructure facilities.

nontariff barrier Trade barriers that restrict imports by measures, other than tariff, such as preferential treatment of domestic bidders over foreign bidders, or the establishment of standards that are not common to foreign goods or services.

norms Explicit or implicit rules for accepted behaviors within a society or group.

not-invented-here (NIH) syndrome Local resistance or decline in morale caused by the perception that headquarters is not sensitive to local needs.

offset A form of countertrade: Industrial compensation mandated by governments when purchasing defense-related goods and services in order to equalize the effect of the purchase on the balance of payments.

open account A method of payment, also known as open terms; exporter selling on open account removes both real and psychological barrier to importing; however, no written evidence of the debt exists and there is no guarantee of payment.

open innovation The use of purposive inflows and outflows of knowledge to accelerate innovation.

operating risk Exposing ongoing operations of a firm to political risk in another nation.

opportunity cost Costs resulting from the foreclosure of other sources of profit, such as exports or direct investment; for example, when licensing eliminates options.

option A method used to counter challenges in currency movements; gives the holder the right to buy or sell foreign currency at a prespecified price on or up to a prespecified date.

outcome The results of meeting objectives that seek to generate awareness, evoke a positive attitude, or increase purchases.

overinvest Tendency in the initial acquisition process to buy more land, space, and equipment than is needed immediately to accommodate future growth.

ownership risk Exposing property and life to political risk in another nation.

parallel importation Gray markets referring to authentic and legitimately manufactured trademark items that are produced and purchased abroad but imported or diverted to the market by bypassing designated channels.

pass-through A pricing approach in which foreign currency appreciation/depreciation is reflected in a commensurate amount in the target market price.

Pax Romana "The Roman Peace"; an approach by the Romans who built, maintained, and protected communication networks with the aim to encourage international business activities.

penetration pricing Introducing a product at an initial low price to generate sales volume and achieve high market share.

perishability The rapidity with which a service or good loses value or becomes worthless; for example, unused capacity in the form of an empty seat on an airplane quickly becomes nonsaleable.

physical distribution The movement of a firm's finished product to its customers.

Physical Quality of Life Index (PQLI) A composite measure of the level of welfare in a country, based on social indicators such as life expectancy, infant mortality, and adult literacy rates.

piggyback In a joint venture, one partner can piggyback by making use of the other's strengths.

plan Formalized long-range financial programs with more than a one year horizon.

podcast Pre-formatted audio or video files that can be downloaded, often used by companies to reach employees or consumers.

political instability Conditions which lead to frequent and major changes in the government and its rules within a country.

political risk The risk of loss when investing in a given country caused by changes in a country's political structure or policies, such as tax laws, tariffs, expropriation of assets, or restriction in repatriation of profits.

population The mass of humans occupying a place.

portfolio investment An international investment flow that focuses on the purchase of stocks and bonds.

portfolio model An organization's plan of action for distribution of resources between different countries and segments.

positioning The presentation of a product or service to evoke a positive and differentiated mental image in the consumers' perception.

price controls Government regulations that set maximum or minimum prices; governmental imposition of limits on price changes.

price elasticity of consumer demand Adjusting prices to current conditions; for example, a status-conscious market that insists on products with established reputations will be inelastic, allowing for more pricing freedom than a price-conscious market.

price escalation The higher cost of a product resulting from the costs of exporting and marketing in a foreign country.

price manipulation Adjusting prices of exported goods to compensate for changing currency rates.

pricing-to-market Destination specific adjustment of mark-ups in response to exchange-rate changes.

process structure An approach to organization that uses processes as a basis for structure; common in the energy and mining industries, where one entity may be in charge of exploration worldwide and another may be responsible for the actual mining operation.

product placement Creating brand awareness by arranging to have a product shown or used in visual media such as movies, television, games, or websites

product structure An approach to organization that gives worldwide responsibility to strategic business units for the marketing of their product lines.

profit repatriation The transfer of profits made by doing business or investing in a foreign country, back to the country of origin.

protectionistic legislation A law created by a government to protect local businesses and widely used as a bargaining tool in international negotiations.

proxy variable A substitute for a variable that one cannot directly measure.

psychological distance Perceived distance between a firm and a foreign market, caused by cultural variables, legal factors, and other societal norms; a foreign market may be geographically close but psychologically distant.

purchasing power parities (PPP) A measure of how many units of currency are needed in one country to buy the amount of goods and services that one unit of currency will buy in another country.

qualitative data Data gathered to better understand situations, behavioral patterns, and underlying dimensions.

quality perception The evaluative impression that customers develop of a service, largely determined by the behavior of the employees that they contact.

quantitative data Data amassed to assess statistical significance; surveys are appropriate research instruments.

quota system Control of imports through quantitative restraints.

R&D consortium Companies that collaborate in long-term research and development projects to create technologies without the threat of antitrust suits.

R&D cost Costs resulting from the research and development of licensed technology.

realism check A step in the analysis of data in which the researcher determines what facts may have inadvertently skewed the responses; for example, if Italian responders report that very little spaghetti is consumed in Italy, the researcher may find that the responders were distinguishing between store-bought and homemade spaghetti.

reference group A social group that provides values and attitudes that become influential in shaping one's behavior.

regulatory practice The primary source of barriers to services destined for the U.S. market; fields such as banking, insurance, and accounting are regulated at both federal and state levels, often posing formidable barriers to entrants from abroad.

relationship marketing The building of long-term relationships with key customers, supply chain partners, collaborative venture partners and other key connections in the firm's value chains worldwide; most typically achieved by emphasizing activities that ensure consistent customer satisfaction.

research consortia An association or a combination of financial institutions, or investors, for the purpose of engaging in a joint venture in order to combat the high costs and risks of research and development.

research specification In the centralized approach to coordinating international marketing, specifications such as focus, thrust, and design are directed by the home office to the local country operations for implementation.

resource seeker Firms that search for either natural resources or human resources in their foreign direct investment strategy.

reverse innovation The strategy of innovating in emerging (or developing) markets and then distributing/marketing these innovations in developed markets.

safety-valve activity The use of overseas sales as a way to balance inventories or compensate for overproduction in the short term.

Sarbanes-Oxley Act Law enacted in the United States in 2002, in the wake of major corporate corruption scandals (such as Enron and WorldCom), intended to protect investors by improving the accuracy and reliability of corporate disclosures.

scenario analysis Evaluating corporate plans under different conditions, such as variations in economic growth rates, import penetration, population growth, and political stability over medium to long-term periods.

self-reference criterion The unconscious reference to one's own cultural values when faced with values of other cultures.

sensitivity training A training focused on enhancing a manager's flexibility in situations that are different from those he faces at home; based on the assumption that understanding and accepting oneself is critical to understanding a person from another culture.

service capacity The ability to supply service on demand, including the planning of backup during peak periods; similar to an inventory of goods.

service consistency Uniformity or standardization in the offering of a service; unlike products, services are often subject to individual influences and the need to customize to satisfy unique customer interactions.

shared value Policies and operating practices that enhance the competitiveness of a company while simultaneously advancing the economic and social conditions in the communities in which it operates.

simulated test market A research method that offer simulation under realistic conditions from a 360° marketing vantage point.

skimming Offering a product at an initial high price to achieve the highest possible sales contribution in a short time period; as more market segments are identified, the price is gradually lowered.

social community Social network that converges around shared interests, goals, values, or attitudes, and fosters a common identity among its members.

social contagion The extent to which people are exposed to, and influenced by, the knowledge, attitude, or behavior of others, particularly those in their peer group.

social desirability A guidepost or motivation or activity which makes an entity acceptable or even in demand in social or interpersonal relations. It is related to social acceptance, social approval, popularity, social status, leadership qualities, or any quality making him a socially desirable companion.

social media The use of communications technology, such as the Internet and mobile telephones, to facilitate meaningful interaction among individuals and organizations.

social network A communal structure consisting of individuals or organizations connected with each other through friendship, common interest, commercial transactions, information exchange, or other types of relationship.

social networking service An online service, platform, or site that focuses on building and reflecting social networks that share interests or activities.

social stratification The division of a particular population into classes.

soft power The capability of attracting and influencing all stakeholders, whether through energetic brands, heroic missions, distinctive talent development, or an inspirational corporate culture.

sogoshosha Large general trading companies of Japan playing a unique role in world commerce.

soil Variations in the soils found in different geographic regions (and their interactions with climate) have a profound impact on agricultural production.

standard worldwide price A pricesetting strategy in which a product is offered at the same price regardless of the geography of the buyer.

stateless corporation A corporate organization which does not have an established nationality and/or headquarters and is transnational in nature.

strategic alliance A special form of joint ventures, consisting of arrangements between two or more companies with a common business objective; they are more than the traditional customer–vendor relationship, but less than an outright acquisition.

strategic leader A role of a country organization; a highly competent national subsidiary located in a strategically critical market.

structured question In a survey questionnaire, structured questions typically allow the respondent only limited option in reply.

supply chain management An integration of the three major concepts of the logistics in which a series of value-adding activities connect a company's supply side with its demand side. See also *systems concept; total cost concept*; *trade-off concept*.

sustainability As given in the Brundtland Report (WCED 1987), sustainability or sustainable development is an activity that meets present needs without compromising the ability of future generations to meet their needs.

switch-trading Credits in a clearing account (established for countertrading) can be sold or transferred to a third party.

systems concept One of three major concepts of the logistics of international management, based on the notion that materials-flow activities within and outside of the firm are so extensive and complex that they can be considered only in the context of their interaction. See also *total cost concept*; *trade-off concept*.

tariffs Import control mechanisms that raise prices through placement of a tax.

terminology Specific designations or definitions of terms, used by trade bodies (such as the WTO) or in trade agreements; these terms can often have unintended or distorted applications in political discourse.

terrain The geology of a place expressed in terms of its regional characteristics.

terrorism The systematic use (or threat) of violence aimed at attaining a political goal and conveying a political message.

theocracy A legal perspective that holds faith and belief as its key focus and is a mix of societal, legal, and spiritual guidelines.

trade deficit Measure of a country's economic balance where imports of products exceed exports.

trade promotion authority (TPA) The U.S. negotiating authority that negotiates international trade agreements which can be approved or disapproved but not amended by the Congress.

trade sanctions Governmental actions that inhibit the free flow of trade in goods, services, or ideas, imposed for adversarial and political purposes.

trade surplus Trade conditions under which exports exceed imports.

trademark licensing The ownership of the name or logo of a designer, literary character, sports team, or movie star, for example, which can be used on merchandise.

transfer cost The costs incurred in negotiating licensing agreements; all variable costs resulting from transfer of a technology to a licensee, and all ongoing costs of maintaining the agreement.

transfer risk Exposing the transfer of funds to political risk across international borders.

translation–retranslation approach The practice of reducing problems in the wording of questions by translating the question into a foreign language and having a second translator return the foreign text to the researcher's native language.

transnational structure A structural designs that goes beyond national boundaries.

triad The megamarkets of North American, Europe, and Asia-Pacific.

trial An exploratory stage where the firm begins to export systematically though its management is not yet committed to international marketing activities.

T-shaped organization An organization that follows the T-shaped management approach wherein there is less corporate hierarchy and knowledge is shared freely across the organization (horizontal part of T), yet staying committed to the individual business unit performace (vertical part of T).

unstructured question In a survey questionnaire, unstructured (or open-ended) questions permit the capture of more in-depth information, but they also increase the potential for interviewer bias.

urbanization The growth and concentration of population in an urban area.

value-added tax (VAT) A tax on the value added to goods and services charged as a percentage of price at each stage in the production and distribution chain.

viral marketing The technique that facilitates and encourages people to pass along a marketing message to other users or sites, leading to potentially exponential growth of communications.

virtual team A group of individuals who work across time zones and regions through electronic communication.

vitality lab A research method that provides a directional gauge of the initiative's potential in a real-world environment, with real consumers making real purchases.

voluntary restraint agreement Nontariff import control mechanisms consisting of self-imposed restrictions and cutbacks aimed at avoiding punitive trade actions from a host.

web-based research Surveys and other data collection techniques administered using the resources of the Internet.

webcast A transmission of live audio/video broadcast in digital format via the Internet.

wiki A website developed and maintained by a community of users who add informative content on a variety of topics.

world mindedness A consumer's interest in, and openness to, acquiring goods from other countries.

NAME INDEX

COMPANY INDEX

SUBJECT INDEX

A

B

C

D

E

F

J

K

N

O

P

Q

R

T

U

V

W

Y

Z